CW00833213

Disobedience and Conspiracy in the German Army, 1918–1945

Disobedience and Conspiracy in the German Army, 1918–1945

by ROBERT B. KANE

with a foreword by
PETER LOEWENBERG

McFarland & Company, Inc., Publishers
Jefferson, North Carolina, and London

Library of Congress Cataloguing-in-Publication Data

Kane, Robert B., 1951–
Disobedience and conspiracy in the German Army, 1918–1945 /
by Robert B. Kane ; with a foreword by Peter Loewenberg.
p. cm.
Includes bibliographical references and index.
ISBN 0-7864-1104-X (illustrated case binding : 50# alkaline paper) ∞
1. Germany. Heer — Officers — History — 20th century.
2. Loyalty oaths — Germany — History — 20th century.
3. Allegiance — Germany — History — 20th century.
4. Conspiracy — Germany — History — 20th century. 5. World War, 1914–1918 — Germany. 6. World War, 1939–1945 — Germany.
I. Title.
UB415.G4K35 2002
355'.00943'0904 — dc21 2001054437

British Library cataloguing data are available

Manufactured in the United States of America

Cover photograph ©2001 Corbis Images

McFarland & Company, Inc., Publishers
Box 611, Jefferson, North Carolina 28640
www.mcfarlandpub.com

In memory of Madison Leigh McFarland,
who provided an all too brief moment of joy
to her parents, Jeff and Stefani McFarland

Acknowledgments

I dedicate this book to the few brave officers of the German Army who, after much thought and psychological struggle, finally realized their true soldierly duty to Germany and the people of Europe. On July 20, 1944, they tried to rid Germany and the world of Adolf Hitler before he completely destroyed their nation and — when their coup failed — paid with their lives for their belated recognition of his evil rule and their true duties as professional soldiers.

I would like to thank my deceased parents, Murray and Virginia Kane, who, early in life, gave me a love for education and an ethic to work hard, qualities that made this book possible; and my adoptive parents, Homer and Agnes Corley, whose love, kindness, affection and constant encouragement over many, many years helped me keep going after my parents' deaths.

I must also thank my wife Anita, children Virginia and David, and mother-in-law Ms. Lamberta van Deursen, who "suffered" beside me over the years throughout my doctoral program and the additional time spent to produce this book.

In addition, I wish to thank the many people who contributed in their own ways to this book. First, there is my doctoral committee, Dr. David Myers, Dr. Deborah Larson, and especially Dr. Peter Loewenberg, my committee chair, who provided many years of patient instruction and guidance during my doctoral studies. I especially thank Dr. Loewenberg for his continuing encouragement as I worked to turn my doctoral dissertation into this book. I owe special thanks to the staff of the Graduate History Department of UCLA, particularly Ms. Barbara Kelley, who graciously accepted my application for the doctoral program in December 1983, and Ms. Barbara Bernstein, who provided invaluable advice and assistance from 1984 through 1997 during my years at UCLA.

This book would not have been possible without the invaluable assistance of the information, circulation, and interlibrary loan staffs of the Graduate Research Library, UCLA. I also thank the circulation and interlibrary loan staff of the Fairchild Library, Air University, Maxwell Air Force Base, Alabama, particularly Mses. Judy Voight, Edith Williams, Betty Weaver, and Rebecca Howze. I also must thank the Veterans Administration and United States Air Force, most particularly the Education Services Office, Los Angeles Air Force Base, California, which provided the tuition assistance funds that allowed me to pursue my doctoral studies. I must also thank past supervisors—Colonel John Porter, Colonel Wayne Jones, Colonel Juri Randmaa, Colonel Rosemary Denton, Lieutenant Colonel Sharon Branch, Mr. William Maikisch, and Mr. Leslie Bordelon—for their inestimable support and understanding over many years.

Finally, I also gratefully acknowledge the following publishers for their permission to use assorted excerpts from their works:

Reprinted by permission of Madison Books. *The German Army 1933–1945*, by Matthew Cooper. Copyright 1978 by Cooper and Lucas Ltd.

Reprinted by permission of the University of Minnesota. *Hitler and His Generals—The Hidden Crisis, January–June 1938* by Harold C. Deutsch. Copyright 1974 by the University of Minnesota.

Reprinted by permission of Bolchazy-Carducci Publisher. *Hitler: Speeches and Proclamations*, volumes 1 and 2. Copyright 1990 and 1992 by Wolfgang Domarus.

Reprinted by permission of Dutton, Penguin, a division of Putnam, Inc. *Panzer Leader* by Heinz Guderian, translated by Constantine FitzGibbon. Copyright 1952 by Heinz Guderian.

Reprinted by permission of the University of California, Berkeley. *The Reichswehr and Politics 1918–1933* by F. L. Carsten. Copyright 1974 by F. L. Carsten.

Reprinted by permission of Simon & Schuster. *The Rise and Fall of the Third Reich* by William Shirer. Copyright 1959, 1960, 1987, 1988 by William L. Shirer.

Reprinted by permission of Dr. John Risher, co-executor of the estate of Lady Wheeler-Bennett. *The Nemesis of Power* by John Wheeler-Bennett. Copyright 1956 by Macmillan and Co., Ltd.

Contents

Figures and Tables

Figures

Tables

German Terms and English Equivalents

Abwehr	OKW Counterintelligence department 1935–44
Allegemeine Heeresamt	General Army Office
Allegemeines Wehrmachstamt	Armed Forces General Office
Alterkämpfer	Old fighter — early member of Nazi Party
Anschluss	(Political) Union (with Austria)
Arbeitskommandos	Work groups
Bürgerwehr	Citizen's militia (1848)
Bund Deutscher Offiziere	German Officer's League
Bundesfeldherr	Federal commander-in-chief
Chef der Heeresleitung	Chief of the Army Command 1919–34
Chef des Truppenamt	Chief of the Troop Office 1919–34
Deutsche Volkspartei	German People's Party
Dolchstoss	"Stab in the back"
Dulag	German transient POW camps
Einsatzgruppen (-stab)	Special Groups (Staff)
Ersatzheer	Replacement, or Home, army
Feldherr	Warlord
Freikorps	Free Corps
Femegericht (Feme)	Secret Court
Frontsoldaten	Front soldiers
Führer	Leader
Führerarmee	Army of leaders
Führerprinzip	Leadership principle
Geheime Staatspolizei	State Secret Police
Gleichshaltung	Coordination (nazification) of society
Hitler Jugend	Hitler Youth
Kriegsakademie	War Academy
Kreigsherr	Warlord
Kristallnacht	"Night of Broken Glass"

Landesherr	Head of State
Landser	German enlisted soldier
Landsknechte	Renaissance German mercenary
Landspolizei	State police
Landtag	State parliament
Landwehr	Militia
Lebensraum	"Living space"
Machtergreifung	Nazi seizure of power January 1933
Mein Kampf	*My Struggle*
Ministeramt	Ministry office of the Reichswehr — forerunner of OKW
"Nacht und Nebel"	"Night and Fog"
Nationalkommittee Freies Deutschland	National Committee for a Free Germany
Nationalsozialist Deutsche-arbeitspartei	National Socialist German Workers'(Nazi) Party
Nationalsozialist Führerstab	National Socialist Leadership Staff
Nationalsozialistisches Kraftfahrer Korps	National Socialist Motorized Corps
National Verbände	National organizations
Oberkommando des Heeres	Army High Command 1935–45
Oberkommando der Luftwaffe	Air Force High Command 1935–45
Oberkommando Wehrmacht	Armed Forces High Command 1935–45
Oberstbefehlshaber Ost	High Command East
Oberstbefehlshaber West	High Command West
Oberste Heersleitung	Supreme High Command 1914–18
Ostministerium	East Ministry
Putsch	Literally "hit," coup d'état
Rassanschande	Race crime
Reicharbeitsdienst	Reich Labor Service
Reichsbanner	Social Democratic
Reichsicherheitshauptamt	Reich Security Main Officer
Reichsmarks	German monetary units
Reichstag	German parliament 1919–45
Reichswehr	Technically, German armed forces 1919–34 — army only, in many uses
Reichswehrminister	Weimar "minister of war"
Schutzstaffel	Protection Detachments
Sicherheitsdienst	Party Security Service
SS Allgemeine	General (Staff)
SS Leibstandarte Adolf Hitler	Hitler's personal bodyguard
SS Totenkopf	SS Death's Head units — concentration camp guards
SS Verfügungstruppe	SS General Service Troops — forerunner of Waffen SS
Stahlhelm	Steel Helmet — World War I veterans' organization
Stalag	German permanent POW camps
Stürmarbeitlungen	Stormtroopers
Überparteilichkeit	"Above politics," unpolitical
Vaterland	Fatherland
Vereinigung Graf Schlieffen	Graf Schlieffen Society
Vertrauensleute, -männer	Trusted men

Volk/Völkische	People or People's/"Folkish"
Völkischer Beobachter	*People's Observer*—Nazi Party paper
Volksgericht	People's Court during Third Reich
Waffen SS	Armed SS
Wehrkreis	Military district
Wehrmacht	Technically, German armed forces 1935–45—army only, in many uses
Wehrmachtsamt	Successor to Ministeramt after 1935
Weltanschauung	Worldview
Westwall	Western defensive fortifications
Wolfschanze	"Wolf's Lair"—Hitler's East Prussian headquarters

Abbreviations

Allegemeines Wehrmachtsamt	AWA
Arbeitskommandos	AK
Bund Deutscher Offiziere	BDO
Deutsche Volkspartei	DVP
Hitler Jugend	HJ
Nationalkommittee Freies Deutschland	NKFD
Nationalsozialist Deutsche-arbeitspartei	NSDAP
Nationalsozialist Führerstab	NSF
Nationalsozialistisches Kraftfahrer Korps	NSKK
Oberkommando des Heeres	OKH
Oberkommando der Luftwaffe	OKL
Oberkommando Wehrmacht	OKW
Oberstbefehlshaber Ost	Obost
Oberstbefehlshaber West	Obwest
Oberste Heereleitung	OHL
Reicharbeitsdienst	RAD
Reichsmarks	RMs
Reichsicherheitshauptamt	RSHA
Schutzstaffel	SS
Sicherheitsdienst	SD
SS Verfügungstruppe	SS-VT
Stürmarbeitlungen	SA

German Army Officer Ranks and American Army Officer Equivalents

German Title	*American Army Equivalent*
Leutnant	Second Lieutenant
Oberleutnant	First Lieutenant
Hauptmann	Captain
Major	Major
Oberst Leutnant	Lieutenant Colonel
Oberst	Colonel
Generalmajor	Brigadier General (one-star)
Generalleutnant	Major General (two-star)
General (des _____)*	Lieutenant General (three-star)
Generaloberst (Colonel General)	General (four-star)
Generalfeldmarschall (Field Marshal)	General (of the Army) (five-star)

*Infantrie (Infantry), Kavallerie (Cavalry), Artillerie (Artillery), Panzertruppen (Panzer Troops)

Note: I have used the American equivalents throughout this book except for generaloberst (colonel general) and generalfeldmarschall (field marshal)

Foreword

Lieutenant Colonel Robert B. Kane has written much more than a military history of the Wehrmacht in the Nazi period and also more than just the story of the small heroic group of German officers who defied their personal oath to Hitler by conspiring to assassinate him. The author's personal experience as an officer on active service in the United States Air Force has made him particularly sensitive to the conflicts of professional soldiers in tension between their moral conscience and perception of a higher national good, on the one hand, and their oath of military obedience, on the other.

Arnold J. Toynbee referred to historical situations "in which a relatively small minority of the participants in a society, constituting a more or less strictly closed social circle, control between them one or more of their society's more important institutions, or even the society's whole life." By focusing on the social upbringing of the military conspirators, their interlocking family networks, religious beliefs, schooling, travel abroad, emotional experiences, shared value systems and world-views, Kane has clearly identified, closely examined and biographically analyzed the small group of deviant Prussian Junker elite who were the heart of the anti–Hitler conspiracy.

The author has discovered a secure subculture of shared thought styles an ideological assumptions — much older than National Socialism — in a safe social area where political doubts, critical views and anxieties about the course of the war and the post war configuration of Germany could be uttered without betrayal to the Gestapo. It is a remarkable fact, which itself indicates a shared subculture of honor, that in all the years of conspiratorial planning prior to July 20, 1944, during which many of the military elite were approached and turned away from the conspirators, the anti–Hitler conspiracy was never betrayed, even by those such as generals Halder, Manstein and Bock, who chose not to participate. Kane has discovered the common emotional affinities and styles of the conspirators and established their shared cultural assumptions and motivations. His book is an important contribution not only to German and Third Reich military history but also to the comprehension of small group collective thought and action in a time of crisis.

Peter Loewenberg, Ph.D.
Professor Emeritus
University of California, Los Angeles

Introduction

By 1943, many officers of the German Army had come to realize that Germany was in the midst of a war of attrition she could not win. Commanded by a megalomaniac who knew little about the strategic needs or tactical conduct of modern war, most of the German army officers still gave their complete obedience to Adolf Hitler. Even though most of them cursed Hitler under their breath and had seen him humiliate many of their best leaders, they continued to obey his orders, despite the ultimate futility of doing so. Only a handful ever came to the conclusion that to prevent Hitler's amateurish leadership from bringing Germany to further destruction and disaster, he had to be assassinated. This decision did not come easy to those professional military officers who came to conspire against Hitler, the person to whom they had sworn their personal loyalty. This book will show why a few well-meaning officers chose disobedience and conspiracy over blind obedience while the majority chose obedience in Germany's most desperate hours.

In 1952, General Dwight D. Eisenhower, former Supreme Allied Commander Europe during World War II, asked General Adolf Heusinger, the German Army Chief of Operations during the same war and then military adviser to the West German Ministry of Defense, "How is it that you never succeeded in getting rid of Hitler?" "He came to power quite legally," Heusinger replied. "If I asked you to get rid of Truman, would you do it?"[1] Eisenhower's inquiry prompts a more general question: why did most members of the German officer corps, particularly the generals, of the late war not revolt and overthrow Hitler, despite his many affronts to their sense of military professionalism and their traditional code of honor, the virtually complete destruction of German society brought on by the war he had caused, and the horrific war crimes and atrocities committed in his name and made possible by the military genius of the officers themselves? Heusinger's reply hints at the traditional duty of loyalty and obedience owed by a nation's military forces to its head of state that is embodied in the oath of loyalty sworn by soldiers throughout history.

The answer to this problem can be found in a study of the origins, consequences, and significance of the personal oath of loyalty that the German armed forces swore to Adolf Hitler, *Führer* (leader) of the Nazi party and Chancellor of the Weimar Republic, in the afternoon of August 2,

1934. Earlier that morning, Paul von Hindenburg, the second and last president of the Weimar Republic, had died at the age of 87 at his East Prussian estate of Neudeck. His death cleared away the last obstacle to Hitler's assumption of full and complete power in Germany as head of state and commander in chief of the German armed forces. All members of the armed forces took the following oath of loyalty, probably composed by the pro–Nazi head of the War Minister's Office, Generalfeldmarschall Walter von Reichenau[2]:

> I swear by God this sacred oath that I shall render unconditional obedience to Adolf Hitler, the Führer of the German Reich, supreme commander of the armed forces, and that I shall at all times be prepared, as a brave soldier, to give my life for this oath.

At the time, only a few German officers, particularly in the senior ranks, realized the significance of their action in taking this oath to Hitler *personally*. As O'Neill wrote, "There is little evidence to show the dangers of this situation had been appreciated by the Army leaders."[3] The Army Chief of Staff General Ludwig Beck was one of only a few officers who had a sense of foreboding after the oath taking.[4] Only later, after Hitler had led Germany into a world war and then into a series of military setbacks and defeats after 1942, did others finally realize just how significant that the Hitlerian oath had become.

Even then, most of the soldiers obeyed their oath to Hitler and supported the Nazi regime to the very end of the "Thousand Year" Third Reich. The majority felt bound by honor to obey the orders of their supreme commander and the officers over them without question. After Germany's surrender on May 7, 1945, they would use the oath of loyalty to rationalize their acquiescence to Hitler and his regime's criminal activities, to excuse their commitment of barbaric atrocities in a catastrophic world war in which an estimated 30 to 40 million people perished in Europe, and to remove themselves from personal responsibility for these acts. As Shirer wrote, "[B]y honoring their oath they dishonored themselves as human beings and trod in the mud the moral code of their corps."[5]

Only a few officers put forward any serious opposition to the regime. They had also initially felt honor-bound to obey Hitler despite a long list of his attacks and insults on the army: (a) the murder of army generals Kurt von Bredow and Kurt von Schleicher in the Blood Purge of June 30, 1934 with little criticism from the other generals; (b) his support to Heinrich Himmler's Schutzstaffel (SS) (Protection Detachments) in raising a rival army, the Waffen (Armed) SS; (c) the Blomberg-Fritsch Crisis of 1938; (d) the creation and the extension of the power and authority of the Oberkommando Wehrmacht (OKW) (Armed Forces High Command), at the expense of the Oberkommando des Heeres (OKH) (Army High Command); and (e) Hitler's self-appointment as the Chief, OKH in 1942. Despite these attacks and insults, the few officers who became conspirators still found it extremely difficult to escape the psychological trap posed by the oath of loyalty.

For years, these well-meaning officers struggled with this professional dilemma, and their struggle was compounded by Hitler's growing popularity and seeming infallibility. They offered little opposition to Hitler's plans to reoccupy the Rhineland in 1936, to his dismissal of Blomberg and General Werner von Fritsch, Commander-in-Chief of the OKH, in early 1938, or to his plans to invade Czechoslovakia in September 1938 if negotiations failed to obtain the Sudetenland for Germany. After the Munich Conference settled this crisis peaceably in Hitler's favor, only General Beck, the Army Chief of Staff, resigned in protest at Hitler's war-threatening policies—before the Wehrmacht was ready — and joined the small but growing opposition. After the war began in September 1939, other disenchanted officers would join the military opposition, but action against Hitler became increasingly more difficult until after the defeat and capture of the German Sixth Army at Stalingrad in January 1943. Only after this debacle did others begin to question Hitler's infallibility.

During this period, as some officers struggled with their duty to obey Hitler, to whom they had so willingly sworn by the Hitlerian oath, and their responsibilities to humanity, the members of the military opposition planned and carried out about a dozen unsuccessful attempts to assassinate the Führer. Their last attempt was made on July 20, 1944, at Hitler's East Prussian headquarters at a time when the continued existence of Germany and the German nation was seriously threatened by utter destruction after the breakout of American and British forces from the Normandy beachhead, the entry of Soviet forces into eastern Poland, and the constant Allied air bombardment of Germany itself. Following this last attempt, Hitler and Himmler relentlessly rounded up virtually all of the members of the opposition, humiliated the ones who did not initially escape by suicide, in the infamous People's Courts, and ultimately executed most of them, many in a most brutal manner. However, for all their heroism in opposing Hitler, the dangers of their opposition, and the ultimate sacrifice most of these officers made in the aftermath of their last attempt, their primary motivation was derived from a belated recognition of their duties to the German state and people — not to stop the regime's atrocities per se.

This book proposes that most army officers generally followed their oath to Hitler throughout the Third Reich because people were generally taught to obey authority figures, as demonstrated by the research of Dr. Stephen Milgram in the early 1960s. For the older officers obedience to Hitler was strengthened by their narrow military training, their conception of obedience and loyalty to a "warlord," a carryover from their service in the Imperial Army, and their general dislike of the Weimar Republic. For the younger officers this general teaching was bolstered by the Hitlerian oath, Nazi education and participation in the Hitler Youth and Reich Labor Service during the 1930s, and Hitler's foreign policies successes through late 1939. The few officers who eventually saw the "moral crisis" of blind obedience to Hitler had experienced a nurturing family life, liberal education, and strong belief in an ethical and moral value system (spiritual Christianity). These early life experiences, combined with interlocking familial and collegial relationships, provided a safe "playspace" to discuss opposition to Hitler, to conspire against him, and eventually to plot his assassination. Thus, for different groups of officers the oath had significance but for different reasons and with different consequences.

The origins and consequences of the Hitlerian oath lie ultimately in the nature of German militarism, the subject of an extensive historiography. The history of the Nazi regime — biographies of its leaders, such as Himmler, Göring, Heydrich, Goebbels and Hitler himself; its more famous generals, including Rommel, von Rundstedt, and Kesselring; and histories of the Nazi party and its organizations, such as the SS and Gestapo, alone — would fill a library. The works on World War II in Europe, many of which are solely or primarily concerned with the military operations, tactics, and weapons of the armies of both sides, are also quite extensive. Another important genre of German military historiography is the apologies — the official histories of the Wehrmacht and its subordinate units, the memoirs of former German generals, and other secondary works — which seek to excuse the actions of the army and its leaders for their role in supporting Hitler in his rise to power, his actions in bringing about the Second World War, and the conduct of that war. While they may accurately describe German military operations, they generally ignore, omit, or minimize the army's acquiescence in the criminal activities of the regime or its roles in these activities.

Within the historiography of the Nazi era, there are also the more scholarly works on the relationship of the senior army leaders to Hitler, their role in Hitler's accession to and continuance in power, the gradual loss of their own power position in the regime, and their failure to resist Hitler even after his "true nature" became known after the 1938 Blomberg-Fritsch Crisis. Some of the more important works include Gordon Craig's *The Politics of the Prussian Army 1640–1945* (1955), Walter Görlitz' *History of the German General Staff* (1953), and John Wheeler-Bennett's *The Nemesis of Power: The German Army in Politics 1918–1945* (1953). More recent accounts include Robert O'Neill's *The German Army and the Nazi Party 1933–39* (1968), Harold Deutsch's *Hitler and His Generals* (1974), and Matthew Cooper's *The German Army 1933–1945* (1974). All these works discuss these general issues to some degree, and the impression one gets from them is that the "aristocratic," apolitical general officers were little prepared for Hitler's ruthlessness, were either hoodwinked or overcome by his superior abilities, and had essentially become by 1942 the mere executioners of his military policy.

Although these works do address the legal and moral issues involved, the responsibility of the military commanders to civil authority and to their troops, and the soldier's right to resist, they generally make only passing reference to the significance of the Hitlerian oath of loyalty. For example, as Wheeler-Bennett writes, the oath

> was unequivocal and did not permit of ambiguity. At that moment when the Army believed that all opportunities lay open to them, they had made a capitulation infinitely more complete than their surrender to the allies in [1918]. Henceforth such opposition as the Army wished to offer to the Nazi regime was no longer in the nature of a struggle with an unscrupulous partner, but of a conspiracy against legitimate and constituted authority, a fact which was to sow the seeds of a harvest of doubt and moral conflict at all levels of the military hierarchy.[6]

Craig makes only a passing reference to the oath toward the end of his history of the German army in society: "...when Hitler's ambitions had brought the nation to the brink of disaster, the careless commitment of 2 August 1934 was to make effective preventive action by the army impossible."[7] Görlitz makes even less of a reference to the oath in his *History of the German General Staff*.[8]

Deutsch assesses the events of August 2, 1934, in these words:

> In form and reality [Hitler's] exploitation of the death of the old President on August 2 can be labeled a dual *coup d'état.* However artfully it was camouflaged by official verbiage and the provision of a plebiscite, the absorption of the presidential functions and prerogatives by the "Führer and Chancellor" was subversive of the Reich Constitution. And in his usurpation Hitler not only appropriated a chief of state's command over the armed forces but transformed the bond between commander and soldier into a personal one by requiring an oath of slavish obedience to himself.[9]

Deutsch then describes the origins of the new oath of loyalty within the War Ministry: its authorship by Reichenau, its proclamation on the "dubious authority" of the War Minister Generaldfeldmarschall Walther von Blomberg, the only other pro-Nazi general officer in 1934, and the oath taking throughout Germany by all members of the German armed forces. However, that is the extent of Deutsch's examination of the oath. He himself states,

> The compass of this study does not permit a thorough analysis of the longer range effects of the oath of personal allegiance to Hitler. Unquestionably it had vital consequences at every stage of Opposition actively involving military figures. [10]

Demeter entitled one chapter of *The German Officer-Corps in Society and State* "The Oath to Hitler's Person and Its Consequences." He states that the vast majority of the German officers obeyed Hitler because of their tradition of unquestioning obedience to their superior that had developed during the monarchy and continued under Seeckt and Hindenburg. This tradition allowed almost no room for questions, conscience, or legal or moral justifications of an order. The Hitlerian oath was "a turning-point" for the relationship between the officer corps and the Nazi regime: "From that day onwards, every innovation, moral or immoral, with which the corps of officers was reproached, went back to the oath of allegiance, sworn 'before God.'"[11] However, he provides little additional analysis of why the majority followed Hitler and only a small minority chose to oppose him, citing only that the motives of the latter group were religious, patriotic, ethical, metaphysical — "and no doubt much else besides."[12]

O'Neill offers more explanation about the oath than the others. He briefly examines the British, American and pre–1990 Soviet oaths, and states that the main differences between them and the Hitlerian oath "seem to be formal." To O'Neill, the Hitlerian oath replaced the impreciseness of the Weimar oath sworn by the members of the armed forces to a republic and a constitution they had little understanding of and liking for.[13] Most importantly, the German soldier placed more importance on the oath than soldiers of the British and Commonwealth armies. The latter took their oath in the privacy of an adjutant's office, received little training in its meaning and relevance, and took for "granted" fighting for their monarch over the centuries with little additional thought. On the other hand, the turbulent history of Germany had led the German soldier to attach greater significance to the oath of allegiance in order to know for whom one fought. He received training on the oath's meaning and its moral and legal significance. The oath taking itself was performed in a solemn public ceremony in the presence of family and the whole regiment "on the most sacred of military objects, the colours." Finally, given the German penchant for written rules and regulations, "...many Germans regarded their oath as the positive embodiment of the essence of their honour."[14]

Cooper offers an even more extensive view of the significance of the oath of loyalty. Concentrating on the relationship between Hitler and the senior generals and the strategic development of the Army, he concludes that the Army was a prisoner of its political and military heritage of unconditional obedience to and identification with the autocratic head of state. This situation, coupled with a self-imposed isolation from the politics, particularly the politically confusing realities of the 20th century, led the generals to underestimate National Socialism. In a sense, they were largely innocent of the blame often laid on them; at the same time, however, they had inexcusably and knowingly allowed an ungifted amateur to gain operational control of the Army, pervert its strategy, and lead it to disaster. In the end, the generals had neither reason nor the opportunity to mount politically inspired opposition. In summary, they

> had failed to distinguish between their political duty to Hitler as Head of State, which demanded obedience, and their military duties as soldiers, which did not. The reasons for the German generals' abnegation

> of their military duty, and the betrayal of their tradition are many. Certainly, the oath of loyalty sworn to Hitler held great significance for them....[15]

In his interpretation, Cooper reverses the charges that others have made against the German generals. In reality, they had a *military* duty to obey Hitler, a duty to which they had sworn on August 2, 1934, by the oath of *personal* allegiance to him. The Prusso-German military tradition allowed little room for subordinates to disobey the legal orders of their superiors. Prussian and German soldiers were trained to follow orders on *what to do* and only allowed latitude on *how to do* it; the emphasis was on training subordinate leaders and soldiers to carry out *tactical* missions independently, once they had received an order, not to determine what those missions were.[16] At the same time, however, the German officers, like all soldiers, had a civic responsibility to act as moral persons and to disobey orders contrary to the humane conduct of war. Obviously, each one must weigh the ethical considerations of disobeying an order and, therefore, must be willing to suffer the consequences of such a choice. During the Third Reich, the officer corps and especially its senior leaders — except the few of the military opposition — failed to follow the higher calling to humanity. Instead, the majority of the officers chose to follow a supreme commander who had turned the rules of normative society upside down by making criminal activities legal. As a group, the German officer corps is, in fact, guilty of the blame that many historians have laid on it.

Even the literature of the German resistance movement fails to adequately examine the origins, consequences, and significance of the Hitlerian oath of loyalty. They generally provide a fair to outstanding narrative of the heroic but tragic and desperate story of the anti–Hitler resistance as its members, both military and civilian, tried to muster the moral courage and physical resources to create an opposition movement and then to carry out the assassination of Hitler and the overthrow of the Nazi regime. As in the more general works on the Nazi regime, Hitler and his generals, and World War II cited earlier, these works generally go no further than stating that the oath of loyalty posed a major psychological block for most German officers to take any significant action against Hitler and that those who ultimately lost confidence did so because of Hitler's recklessness in bringing about a two-front war which Germany could not win, the monstrous war crimes and atrocities committed in his name, and the increasing level of destruction and deaths as the war progressed.[17] Again, discussion of the 1934 oath of loyalty, despite its stated impact on the formation of the anti–Hitler resistance, is only a minor theme within the greater work.

Two examples will suffice. Hans Rothfels, one of the earliest German historians after 1945 who told the story of the German resistance, wrote in 1948 that the army was "tricked" into taking the personal oath to Hitler which "...constituted a moral bond, however, immoral in content, and an obstacle which, in accordance with all traditional standards, could not easily be overcome." Later Rothfels accurately summarizes the dilemma faced by the army officers:

> It required very strong convictions and a realization of a threat to the highest human values to break through the code of duty and patriotism [that is, violate their oath of loyalty to Hitler] to the point where one was prepared to revolt in the midst of an all engulfing struggle, or eventually not only to wish and pray but also to work for the defeat of one's own country.[18]

Almost 50 years later, Joachim Fest, another German historian, wrote,

> The consequences of this fateful step [the August 2, 1934, oath taking] would

> continue to make history after the illusions of those days had been dashed.
>
> ...Once aroused, these doubts would eventually lead some of them to distance themselves from the regime and a few to resist it, despite the numerous obstacles in their way — not the least of which was the oath of personal loyalty they had sworn to the Führer.[19]

In reviewing the extensive historiography of the German Army, German militarism, and the Third Reich, I have found no complete study of the origins, consequences, or significance of the Hitlerian oath of loyalty. Only Cooper and O'Neill have provided anything more than a couple of paragraphs on this vital issue; yet, even their remarks are subsumed within the larger work.[20] Historians of Nazi Germany, the German Army, and the anti–Hitler resistance give varying significance to the Hitlerian oath of loyalty in the initial acquiescence of the officer corps, particularly the German generals, to Hitler and his policies and ultimately to their acceptance and even participation in the criminal activities of the regime during World War II. Additionally, they acknowledge that the oath did contribute to the inability of the generals to form any significant opposition to Hitler even after it became evident that he, as supreme commander and commander in chief of the Army, was leading Germany to military disaster. They also agree that the oath served as a serious obstacle to those few officers who joined the military opposition, participated in the failed July 20, 1944, bomb plot, and ultimately paid with their lives the price of their failure. Despite these general comments, there is no in-depth examination of this significant problem: why the oath of loyalty was a major psychological stumbling block to "professional" military officers who followed Hitler along his road to disaster and even participated in the atrocities of the Nazi regime, and why only a handful developed into an opposition that plotted to assassinate him.[21]

Chapter 1 provides a theoretical and historical perspective of the oath of loyalty and its meaning to the military professional, particularly officers as the leaders of a military force. I first examine the oath's structure and the wording by comparing current military oaths to the Hitlerian oath and then demonstrate the ideal meaning of the oath in terms of professionalism and ethical behavior — the "Duty, Honor, Country" ideals of General Douglas MacArthur's famous 1962 West Point retirement speech.[22] I also present the forms of dissent officers may use to express disagreement with a superior's orders or government policies, and propose some psychological basis for why some people demonstrate dissent, disagreement, or opposition. I then briefly cover the origins and development of the military oath from prehistoric societies through the Renaissance, then its specific development in Prussia-Germany from 1660 to 1918 and the importance of obedience of the officers to their military superior, the Prussian king, and, after 1871, the kaiser.

Chapter 2 covers the creation and the development of the new German Army, the Reichswehr, under the Weimar government from 1918 until 1930. I first cover the impact of Germany's military defeat and surrender in November 1918 on the officer corps. I then review the influence of Hans von Seeckt on the new army, the Reichswehr, and its composition, which, after 1920, was largely composed of former members of the Freikorps, the rightist, freebooting groups, who had fought the Poles and the Red Army in eastern Prussia and the Baltic states and who had put down the various leftist revolutions of 1919 in the immediate aftermath of the war's end. These former Freikorps members would provide fertile ground for the growth of National Socialism within the army in the late 1920s and 1930s. We shall see that the republican government failed to produce an army, especially an officer corps, that would be loyal to it in spirit, not just legally through the oath taking.

Chapter 3 covers the relationship between Hitler, the Nazi movement, and the army from the rise of the NSDAP in the late 1920s to Hindenburg's death in August 1934 and the subsequent oath-giving ceremony. I especially cover the "love-hate" relationship between the Nazi leader, his Stormtroopers, the senior Army leaders, and the young officers as Hitler courted the army for its support while maneuvering for power. After Hitler's appointment as Chancellor, we see the generals and Hitler grow closer together as the former, afraid that Hitler would accede to Röhm's demand to combine the Army with the SA, looked to the new Chancellor to curtail the SA's excesses and prevent such an occurrence. At the same time, Hitler, needing the conservative Army's support for now to rebuild Germany's armed forces to support his aggressive foreign policy, eventually sacrificed his SA friends and comrades in the Blood Purge of June 30, 1934. This phase ended with the infamous oath-giving ceremony on August 2, 1934.

Chapter 4 covers the period 1934–39 when the army grew closer to Hitler in certain respects as he rebuilt the economy and rearmed Germany in preparation for a second world war. This period is characterized by the subtle steps of the new War Minister Blomberg to bring the army and the Nazi party closer together. Each step, while small and delicate in itself, represented a growing acceptance, or, at least, toleration, of Nazism by the army leadership. The army also accepted the creation of the OKW and the increase in its authority, which diminished the relative influence of the Army in military affairs, and the SS-VT, the forerunner of the Waffen SS, as a rival party army. The chapter ends with Germany and Europe on the eve of the Second World War.

Chapter 5 covers the formation of the military opposition from its first seeds in the generals' objection to the remilitarization of the Rhineland in 1936 through late August 1939. I discuss the initial reasons why Beck, Witzleben, and others decided to first protest then oppose Hitler's adventuresome foreign policies that risked war before the rearmament program was complete. I also discuss the events surrounding the odious Blomberg-Fritsch crisis of January 1938. We see how and why Hitler ousted Blomberg, his Army commander in chief Generaloberst Freiherr Werner von Fritsch, and other conservative generals. Following this action, Hitler assumed the title of War Minister himself and selected a weakling, then Generaloberst Walther von Brauchitsch, as the new Army commander in chief. Finally, we see the impact of the Munich crisis of late summer 1938 in preventing a coup by the military opposition and the futile attempts to stop Germany's plunge into war.

Chapter 6 covers the German Army during the Second World War and emphasizes the effects of the prewar nazification efforts and conscription on the army. Although less "nazified" than the other services, particularly the officer corps, the army certainly was affected by the strong support for the Nazi regime among the military-age population. Those who turned 21 years of age in 1940 had been born in 1919, had lived through the economic and political chaos of the Weimar period, and had subconsciously felt the effects of the complete destruction of their parents' life savings by the superinflation of 1923. Many had also been members of the Hitler Jugend (Hitler Youth) or the Reicharbeitsdienst (Reich Labor Service) before joining or being conscripted into the army in the late 1930s. Some historians have discounted these issues as reasons for the general support that Hitler had and retained even to the last days of the regime and the commission of atrocities during the war. Only a few, such as O'Neill and Omer Bartov, have considered them as major factors in the "nazification" of the army.[23] The point here is to demonstrate why most German soldiers, officers and enlisted, generally followed orders — even those that resulted in gross violations of the laws of war and horrific atrocities in occupied Europe.

Chapter 7 covers the development of the military opposition from September 1939 to its tragically heroic end after the abortive July 20, 1944, bomb plot. I will look at the attempts — and ultimate inability — of the few members of the Military Opposition to recruit additional conspirators, particularly from among the commanders of combat troops who consistently fell back on the 1934 oath as the basis for their inaction. The narrative keys in on the efforts of the more significant members, such as the retired army chief of staff Ludwig Beck and later Claus Graf Schenk von Stauffenberg, to convince others to join the anti–Hitler conspiracy. The failure on July 20, 1944, condemned the members of the opposition as traitors and, for those who did not commit suicide, public humiliation in the People's Courts, excruciating torture, and ultimately a barbaric execution in the depths of various prisons.

The last chapter demonstrates why these few senior officers came to oppose Hitler while the vast majority remained as followers or nonconspirators. Of special interest will be how the early childhood experiences of these senior officers led only a handful to conspiracy while most either remained blindly loyal to Hitler or "straddled the fence." An additional interesting and significant characteristic of the conspirators was their interlocking familial and collegial relationships that formed a safe "play space" for them to discuss and plot conspiracy against Hitler. In the end it appears that the early childhood experiences of all groups — conspirators, nonconspirators, and followers — framed their initial moral development; it also played the most significant role in framing their view of the 1934 oath of loyalty to Hitler and, therefore, their degree of loyalty to him. The events from November 1918 forward were seen through the lens of these early experiences.

Notes

1. Heusinger quoted in Pierre Galante, *Operation Valkyrie: The German Generals' Plot against Hitler* (New York: Harper & Row, 1981), p. ix. In 1957, Heusinger was appointed Inspector General of the Bundeswehr (Army of the Federal Republic of Germany (West Germany) and served as president of the Military Committee of NATO, 1960–64.

2. Robert J. O'Neill states unequivocally that Reichenau, because he disliked the old Weimar oath, composed the new oath on his own without any suggestion from Hitler, in anticipation of Hindenburg's death and Hitler's assumption of the positions of head of state and supreme commander. *The German Army and the Nazi Party, 1933–1939* (London: Cassell & Company Ltd., 1968), p. 54. Harold Deutsch is equally sure that Reichenau originated the idea of a new oath and dictated its wording to a subordinate on August 1, 1934, the day before Hindenburg's death. *Hitler and His Generals, The Hidden Crisis January–June 1938* (Minneapolis, MN: University of Minnesota Press, 1974), pp. 19–20. See also Matthew Cooper, *The German Army 1933–1945* (New York: Bonanza Books, 1968), p. 30; Barry Leach, *German General Staff* (New York: Ballantine Books, Inc., 1973), p. 43; and Martin Kitchen, *A Military History of Germany from the Eighteenth Century to the Present Day* (Secaucus, NJ: The Citadel Press, 1976), p. 292. Gordon A. Craig, however, assigns "probable" authorship of the new oath to Generalfeldmarschall Werner von Blomberg, the new War Minister. *The Politics of the Prussian Army 1640–1945* (London: Oxford University Press, 1968), p. 480. Albert Seaton argues that the "real" author of the new oath was Hitler himself since such a significant change to the oath could not have occurred without Hitler's and Blomberg's knowledge and prior agreement, and he cites Hitler's propensity to use plebiscites and other people to ratify or carry out his own actions. *The German Army 1933–45* (New York: New American Library, 1982), pp. 51–52. This oath replaced the military oath, promulgated in December 1933, that officially replaced the Weimar oath. The 1933 oath read: "I swear by God this sacred oath that I will serve my people and fatherland at all times faithfully and honestly and, as a brave and obedient soldier, will be prepared at all

times to stake my life for this oath." Ordinance of December 2, 1933, in Ernst Forsthoff, ed., *Deutsche Geschichte von 1918 bis 1938 in Dokumenten* (Stuttgart: Alfred Kroener, 1938), p. 384.

3. O'Neill, p. 55. See also John W. Wheeler-Bennett, *The Nemesis of Power: The German Army in Politics 1918–1945* (London: Macmillan & Co. Ltd, 1956), pp. 338–4; and Craig, pp. 480–81.

4. Deutsch reports (p. 21), from a 1970 interview with Beck's former secretary Fräulein Luise von Brenda, that Beck returned from the Great Hall of the War Ministry, where Blomberg had proclaimed the new oath, "shaking his head gloomily." Apparently commenting on the *manner* by which the oath had been proclaimed, Beck said, "One cannot do things in this way." Later that evening at home, Beck "described the day to a comrade as the darkest of his life. He felt he had been taken unawares and never rid himself of the thought that he should have refused then and there to take the oath." Beck tried to tender his resignation in protest, but Blomberg, after great difficulty, talked his chief of staff out of it.

5. William L. Shirer, *The Rise and Fall of the Third Reich* (Greenwich, CT: Fawcett Publications, 1960), p. 315.

6. Wheeler-Bennett, p. 340.

7. Craig, pp. 479–81.

8. Walter Görlitz, *History of the German General Staff 1657–1945* (New York: Frederick A. Praeger, 1953), p. 290.

9. Deutsch, p. 19.

10. Deutsch, pp. 20–22.

11. Karl Demeter, *The German Officer-Corps in Society and State 1650–1945* (London: Weidenfeld and Nicolson, 1965), p. 207.

12. Demeter, p. 213.

13. The Weimar Oath: "I swear loyalty to the Reich Constitution and vow that I will protect the German nation and its lawful establishment as a brave soldier at any time, and will obey the President and my superiors." Ordinance about the Oath-Taking of Public Officials, August 14, 1919, in Bernhard Schwertfeger, "*Hindenburgs Tod und der Eid auf den 'Führer,'*" *Die Wandlung*, VI (October 1948), p. 569.

14. O'Neill, pp. 54–58.

15. Cooper, p. 553.

16. See Martin van Creveld, *Fighting Power: German and U.S. Army Performance 1939–1945* (Westport, CT: Greenwood Press, 1982), pp. 35–41, for a more detailed discussion of German army command principles and their comparison with those of the American army.

17. See, for example, Constantine FitzGibbon, *20 July* (New York: Berkley Publishing Corporation, 1968), pp. 87–88; Peter Hoffman, *The History of the German Resistance 1933–1945* (Cambridge, MA: The MIT Press, 1977), pp. 27–28; James P. Duffy and Vincent L. Ricci, *Target Hitler: The Plots to Kill Adolf Hitler* (Westport, CT: Praeger, 1992), pp. 1–27; Herbert Molloy Mason, Jr., *To Kill the Devil: The Attempts on the Life of Adolf Hitler* (New York: W. W. Norton & Company, Inc., 1978), p. 35; Galante, pp. 34–35; Anton Gill, *An Honorable Defeat: A History of German Resistance to Hitler, 1933–1945* (New York: Henry Holt and Company, 1994), pp. 36–37; Eberhard Zeller, *The Flame of Freedom: The German Struggle against Hitler* (Boulder, CO: Westview Press, 1994), pp. 12–13; Joachim Fest, *Plotting Hitler's Death: The Story of the German Resistance* (New York: Henry Holt and Company, 1996), pp. 55–56; and Theodore S. Hamerow, *On the Road to the Wolf's Lair: German Resistance to Hitler* (Cambridge, MA: The Belknap Press of Harvard University Press, 1997), p. 106. Most of these works do not provide any reference to the 1934 oath other than those cited here with the exception of Hoffman. Hoffman mentions the oath at many other places within his extensive narrative of the German resistance movement but does not provide any extensive discussion of the oath's importance, impact, or significance.

18. Hans Rothfels, *The German Opposition to Hitler* (Hinsdale, IL: Henry Regnery Company, 1948), pp. 67–68, 74–75.

19. Fest, pp. 55–56.

20. In fact, there is very little literature that deals explicitly with the Hitler oath of loyalty specifically or even the military oath of loyalty in general. I did find two journal articles in German that I used. For a brief historical review and legal analysis of the American military oath of loyalty, especially on why many U.S. military officers left the Union to fight for the Confederacy while others stayed with the Union at the beginning of the American Civil War, see "An Officer's Oath," *Military Review*, Vol. 44 (January 1964), pp. 24–31; "An Officer's Oath," *Military Law Review* (Department of the Army Pamphlet 27-100-25) (July 1964), pp. 1–41; and "The Oath of Allegiance," *U.S. Naval Institute Proceedings*, Vol. 91 (September 1965), pp. 52–63 — all written by Lieutenant Colonel Thomas H. Reese. Also, Edward M. Coffman, "The Army Officer and the Constitution," *Parameters*, Vol. 17 (September 1987), pp. 2–12.

21. This book concentrates on the German Army, especially its officers. Throughout the Third Reich the Luftwaffe (Air Force) and the Kriegsmarine (navy) were more or less steadfast supporters of the regime. The Air Force, banned by the Versailles Treaty, owed its creation to the Nazi regime and Hermann Göring, one of its leading personalities, an ex–fighter pilot of World War I, and an early member of the Nazi Party. The Navy, more divided, felt compelled to support Hitler to overcome the dishonor of the 1918 Navy mutinies.

Hitler himself recognized this situation, once stating, "I have a Prussian Army, an Imperial Navy and a National Socialist Air Force." Hitler quoted, no date, in Shirer, *Third Reich*, p. 209.

22. See Douglas MacArthur, *Reminiscences* (New York: McGraw Hill Book Company, 1964), pp. 423–26.

23. Omer Bartov develops this thesis more fully in his *The Eastern Front 1941–45: German Troops and the Barbarization of Warfare* (London: Macmillan, 1985) and *Hitler's Army: Soldiers, Nazis and War in the Third Reich* (New York: Oxford University Press, 1992).

1

The Military Oath of Loyalty: Theoretical and Historical Background

Before looking at the Hitlerian Oath of Loyalty itself, I first want to examine the concept and historical development of the military oath of loyalty. This discussion will provide the background for a full understanding of the meaning that the oath of loyalty (or allegiance) has for soldiers in general and of its historical development. In this way we can properly evaluate why, after 1934, most German officers obeyed their oath and followed Hitler and why it become a psychological obstacle to all but a handful of German officers. The first part of this chapter will delve into the meaning of the military oath of loyalty to the soldiers who take it and to the government or head of state who gives it. I will also examine its structure, particularly the wording and finally the expected code of conduct, or military ethics, that flows from the oath with some emphasis on the concept of obedience in the military context. I will then review the ways by which an officer may display his disagreement with superior orders and policies, and, more importantly, when and why they protest or disobey some orders. Lastly, I will briefly review how the oath of loyalty developed historically in some Western societies from prehistory to the 1600s and then specifically in Prussia-Germany from the mid–1600s through 1918.

The Military Oath of Loyalty, Obedience, and Disobedience

The military oath of loyalty has great significance both to the members of the military forces who receive (and occasionally reaffirm) it and to the government or head of state who gives it (usually by delegation rather than in person)—the oath is not "mere" words. The term itself can mean "(1) the invocation of God to witness the truth of what one says and (2) that which one pledges to do."[1] The invocation of God and the use of sacred language gives the oath a transcendent meaning, directing attention beyond the receiver or witnesses to the oath. It conveys to the receiver (in our case, the soldier) the special moral commitment that he is taking upon himself and invests him with special authority, trust and confidence. At the same time, the oath gives the receiver some degree of professional independence, not subservience, as the latter "would destroy the transcendent focus of the oath."[2] For the government or ruler, it is the initial way used to obtain the loyalty of its soldiers, to bind them to its norms, to obtain legitimate obedience to its orders transmitted down through the soldiers' superiors, and to demand from them the ultimate sacrifice of their lives when they are required to do so. The oath is, in essence, the seal to a legal and binding contract between the government and the soldier.

In the oath, the receiver generally swears to defend his country's form of government or way of life, to uphold the country's constitution, if there is one, and its laws, and to obey the orders of his commander in chief and other superior officers. In most Western countries before 1945, the new soldier would swear the oath to God, like the oath of fealty sworn by medieval knights to their liege lord or king. However, with increasing secularization, some countries either have a separate oath for those who wish to *affirm* their allegiance or have eliminated the phrase "so help me God" or "by God" altogether. In most contemporary military oaths, the receiver swears (or affirms) allegiance to the government and its laws and obedience to the commander in chief as a designated position at the apex of the military hierarchy, not to the individual currently in that position *personally*. Only a few oaths, such as the one in the United Kingdom, have the military member swear allegiance to the reigning monarch by name and, even then, such personal allegiance to the monarch is largely symbolic. Several others had the receiver swear to give his life in defense of his country. These latter two types are analogous to parts of the Hitlerian oath of loyalty.[3] The Hitlerian oath is in a small minority of oaths, but it is not unique in its swearing to a *person* as the commander in chief or in asking the soldier to sacrifice his life, if required to do so.

Most countries with a military oath have some sort of formal induction, or oath-taking ceremony. Some are performed in semiprivacy, but most are formally conducted in public view of family members, friends, organized military units, or other new military members. The oath-taking ceremony is not just another administrative formality but a momentous, quasi-religious ritual that marks the passage of an "ordinary" member of society into one of "a community of disciplined discourse [in our case, the military brotherhood], aimed at discovering, renewing, adapting, and applying the fundamental principles that support our public order."[4] Stephen Westman, called into the Kaiser's army in April 1914, described his oath-taking ceremony:

> In front of the battalion, drawn up in a square, we had to take the oath of loyalty to the Kaiser. The regimental colours were ceremoniously unfurled and about ten of us, I amongst them, had to step forward. We had to hold up our right hands, had to touch with our left the richly embroidered silken flag and repeat the words of the oath spoken by the adjutant.[5]

The military fraternity, unlike other public administration agencies, imposes upon the new member a special obligation — defense of their government and nation literally at the risk of their life — and a commitment between the soldier and his commander in chief, both as a position and to the occupant of the position personally. This latter concept is crucial to a government whose head of state and commander in chief is a civilian, and whose civilian control of the military is a basic feature of its constitution, such as in the United States.[6]

After the oath is given, the new military members go through the training processes that will inculcate in them the military's values of professionalism, create conformity to its norms, and develop a sense of group cohesion that allows the soldiers to endure the impact of battle. These processes also bolster the socialization of the new members into the military fraternity that began with the oath-taking ceremony.[7] They learn to keep faith with their fellow soldiers, to remain loyal to their country and its form of government, to uphold the constitution and laws of their nation, and to follow the orders of their superiors. These requirements are part of the code of conduct, or ethics, both formal and informal, that military professionals, particularly the officer corps as the leadership unit of the armed forces, are expected to follow.[8] The officers are also guided by customs, traditions, and "the continuing spirit of the profession" that give them, more so than the enlisted members, a special responsibility to society and the state, like other professionals.[9]

However, this special responsibility of military members to society and state also places them in a dilemma that other professionals do not face to the same degree, because they are managers of violence. On one hand, they have an obligation to obey the orders of their superiors — an obligation considered to be nearly unquestionable in peacetime and particularly imperative during times of war. Without an unquestioning attitude towards obeying orders, the successful conduct of military operations, the success of a military campaign, and even the survival of a nation would be seriously threatened. Yet, the soldier, and especially the officer, also has a legal obligation to disobey orders that violate the constitution or the law, and has a moral and ethical obligation to disobey orders that are contrary to societal norms. Thus, the soldier's requirement to obey orders is not open-ended, and the oath of loyalty is not an excuse for blind patriotism or blind obedience to orders, the infamous "I was only following orders" defense.

Even within the German military tradition, such a defense is not legally permissible, despite its use by the defendants at the Nuremberg war crimes trials (as well as at other war crimes trials). Article 47 of the 1872 German Military Penal Code, still legally *in force*, if not *enforced*, down to 1945, stated:

> If execution of an order given in line of duty violates a statute of the penal code, the superior giving the order is alone responsible. However, the subordinate obeying the order is liable to punishment as an accomplice if ... he knew that the order involved an act the commission of which constituted a civil or military crime or offense.[10]

Ironically, even Josef Goebbels, the Nazi Minister of Propaganda, reiterated the essence of Article 47 and refuted the "I was only following orders" defense in a May 28, 1944, article in the German newspaper *Deutsche Allegemeine*.[11] As we shall see later, there is precedence within the Prusso-German military tradition for disobedience to orders.

The oath is not an excuse which the soldier can use to justify immoral acts after the fact, as we saw it used by numerous former German military officers during the various war crimes trials that followed World War II or by the defendants in the My Lai Massacre trial in 1971.[12] Military legal experts generally agree that such a defense is not legitimate for a finding of "not guilty" for the commission of a war crime itself. However, soldiers, especially those in the lower ranks, may use the "I was following orders" defense to mitigate the punishment. At those times when soldiers are ordered to commit illegal or immoral acts, they must find the "moral courage" to disobey those orders: "When the laws of war are clear, honor insists that they be obeyed."[13]

Yet, there is a greater tendency among soldiers to obey orders, even when such obedience is contrary to accepted ethical behavior. First, soldiers, like all people, are subject from birth to the authority of their parents who require a certain conformity to societal norms. Later in life we all encounter analogous structures in schools and then jobs that channel our behavior to obey the authority figures of these institutions. As a result, people learn to obey recognized authorities, a propensity which significantly impedes their ability to disobey these authorities.[14] In turn, these authorities and the bureaucracies that they represent have developed structures that penalize those who "rock the boat" and especially those who exhibit overt disobedience.[15] Disobedience to orders, especially under combat conditions, can result in severe penalties, including execution. As a result, for anyone, but especially for a soldier, to disobey orders, they must find the moral courage to face the consequences of disobedience and know absolutely what they are doing is "right" and "moral." They must be willing to accept the penalties that will result from their act of disobedience. "People who have no difficulty identifying when someone else should disobey forget that reasons for obedience are far more compelling than they appear from the perspective of those not caught up in the immediacy of a situation."[16]

Despite the high esteem that the soldier places on obedience and the penalties they may incur for disobedience, soldiers throughout history have disobeyed orders. Why, then, do certain soldiers disobey orders but most do not, and at what point do they make that decision? If the soldier generally obeys orders because they place value on obedience and hold the superiors who give or transmit the orders to them in some degree of awe or legitimacy, then disobedience must occur when the soldier no longer values obedience or no longer recognizes the legitimacy of the authorities giving and/or transmitting the order. In doing so, the soldier justifies his disobedience by redefining the situation as illegitimate or unjust and then resorting to an alternative authority.[17] The great mutinies in the French Army in 1917 and in the German Navy in October 1918 demonstrate how these fighting forces over the long years of the war — the French *poilus*, fighting in the terrible conditions in the trenches of northern France, and the German sailors "rotting" away in port and subjected to leftist propaganda — gradually lost confidence in their superiors and no longer valued the cause for which they had been fighting. They then disregarded their oath to obey orders and mutinied.

Most cases of disagreement or disobedience, unlike mass mutinies, such as these two cases, involve individuals or small groups who have perceived that a "moral crisis" has occurred. In this situation the soldier has become dissatisfied or has lost confidence in the leader or government to whom he once had sworn to defend. A question that must be asked — and answered — is why do only a few out of the group see the moral crisis and act upon it but most either do not see it or ignore it. Since the members of a group share the same "historical" experiences, individuals of small groups apparently see the moral crisis because they are more morally developed than others. Research into the development of moral judgment in humans offers important insights into this subject.[18]

I will only review the basics of what are probably the two most significant modern theories of moral development: the psychoanalytical and cognitive-development theories. Sigmund Freud (1856–1939) laid the basis of psychoanalytical theory in his basic proposal that humans are driven by affective, irrational, and egoistic impulses that are frustrated by parental constraints, resulting in hostility and resentment toward the parents. Altruistic motives and behaviors are expressions of anxiety, fear, hostility, sexual desire, jealousy, and guilt. At about the age of five or six, children repress their own aggressive and erotic drives out of fear of punishment, identify with the attitudes and behavior of their parents, and internalize their moral standards. More recently, some psychologists of this tradition de-emphasize instinctual drives and early parent-child relations and view moral development as a long-term process connected to growth in personality, intelligence, and self-understanding. They appeal to experience and psychological changes during late childhood, adolescence, and early adulthood and see other groups, besides parents, as influencing children as they develop moral judgment and behavior. The adherents of the psychoanalytic approach essentially believe that people act morally by following their conscience in order to avoid guilt.[19]

On the other hand, cognitive developmentalists, most notably Jean Piaget before World War II and Lawrence Kohlberg in the 1950s, reject the psychoanalytic theories of moral development. According to them, moral development is a process in which children develop moral judgment by interacting with their peers and environment. They adjudicate conflicting claims, using universally recognized moral principles, through a sequence of stages over time. Children, adolescents, and young adults progressively move from lower to higher stages as they meet difficulties and inconsistencies and construct a new framework to resolve them. To the cognitive developmentalists, peers are more important in promoting moral development, but parents, as one of the groups who interact with children, can influence their moral development by encouraging them to think, to analyze situations, and to come to their own conclusions.[20]

As mentioned earlier, the cognitive developmentalists believe that moral development occurs in stages over time. Piaget conceptualized two stages:

> Constraint: present from about ages four to eight years; based upon unilateral respect by the child for the parent whom the child sees as superior; accepts the parents' rules as unchangeable. Moral responsibility is based on conformity to the rules, not the intention of the agent. Child does not understand the basis for justification but recognizes what the rules allow or forbid.
>
> Cooperation: develops at ages eight to ten; based upon mutual respect between child and peers who are seen essentially as equals; sees moral rules as mutually beneficial products of reciprocal understanding; rules are created and modified by mutual agreement, not as externally or coercively imposed, or fixed and unchangeable.

Kolhberg's six-stage model is essentially a more graduated analysis of Piaget's model:

Preconventional Level

Stage 1. Heteronomous Morality: right is avoiding breaking rules; and obedience is for its own sake and to avoid physical damage to property and people.

Stage 2. Individualism, Instrumental Purpose and Exchange: right is following rules because it is in the child's own interest. Right is what is fair, equitable.

The Conventional Level

Stage 3. Mutual Interpersonal Expectations, relationships and Interpersonal Conformity: right is living up to what people close to someone expect, particularly in the role that the person has (father, son, brother, friend, so on) within a group. "Being good" means having good motives, showing concern for others, keeping mutual relationships.

Stage 4. Social System and Conscience: right is fulfilling duties which a person has agreed to fulfill. That person upholds laws except in extreme cases where they conflict with other social duties.

The Postconventional Level:

Stage 5. Social Contract or Utility and Individual Rights: right is being aware that people have a variety of values and opinions, that values and rules are relative to a person's group, and a person should usually uphold these relative rules. However, a person must uphold some nonrelative rights, such as life and liberty, regardless of majority opinion.

Stage 6. Universal Ethical Principles: right is following self-chosen ethical principles, which are universal principles of justice. When laws violate these principles, a person must act according to the principles.[21]

I will be referring back to Kohlberg's model in particular in the last chapter to demonstrate why some German officers became anti–Hitler conspirators, some, the nonconspirators, flirted with conspiracy but did not join the resistance, and most remained followers.

Some of the follow-on research by Kohlbeg and others on his theories, especially his six-stage model of moral judgment, is especially relevant to this study. First, people in formal education, as opposed to people who cease their formal education, appear to improve their ability to demonstrate moral judgment over time. The type of education also appears to be significant as moral philosophers and political scientists as a group have the highest scores in psychological testing for moral judgment, indicating that humanistic, liberal education would further moral development over narrower, more technical education.[22] Also, children who are more socially active and popular, who assume leadership positions, and who are reared in more democratic (that is, authoritative, not *authoritarian* or *permissive*) families also score higher on moral judgment.[23]

Kohlberg also distinguishes morality from personal and religious values or "right" from "good." To him, what is "right" or moral is obligatory, but what is "good" is left to individual choice as long as it harmonizes with what is "right." As a result, moral education in schools should stimulate moral reflection and criticism among students and encourage them to explain and justify their views and to understand those of others. In this respect, Kohlberg essentially separates the moral or ethical teachings of religion from the specific rituals and spiritual teachings of particular religious ideologies.[24] As a result, he fails to appropriately consider the reliance by many people on their religious beliefs to resolve moral conflicts in real life. In other words, for *some* people, their moral framework is inseparable from their religious belief system and goes beyond the mere forms of religious activity (attendance, religious rites, so on), especially as they mature from children who participate in religious activities to adults who deeply internalize their religious belief system. In fact, some people may even accept the moral and ethical tenets of their religion more than its rituals and rites.[25]

Moral judgment thus appears early in a person's life and is most developed and nurtured within a "loving" family and circle of like-minded friends. A liberal, broad-based education and a deep adherence to a system of ethical moral values, such as spiritual Christianity, further reaffirms normal moral judgment during adolescence and the teen years. As I will show later, none of these factors alone are determinative in producing a "moral" person who will act morally. These influences, working together, however, seem to produce within the individual a broader view of life. As a result, this type of individual can more readily "move up" Kohlberg's hierarchy than other "less developed" individuals, should more readily recognize the moral crisis, and can, thus, formulate a variety of alternatives to resolve the crisis, which can include disagreement, disobedience, and even conspiracy.

Returning to the subject of disobedience by soldiers, their disagreement with and disobedience to orders, their superior officers, or the government can take several forms. At the low end, soldiers can register an oral or written protest through the chain of command. Depending on the situation and the level of moral conscience involved, most soldiers will ultimately obey the order or agree with the policy. If the soldier persists and refuses to execute an order, they will normally be removed from their position and subjected to disciplinary action, which can range from a verbal or written reprimand to court-martial with a penalty that includes execution, particularly during wartime. An officer who feels sufficiently strongly about disobeying an order can also publicly resign his commission or retire if he has sufficient active service time. A group of soldiers can mutiny when their conditions of service have seriously deteriorated. Finally, a group of officers can threaten to take over a government or to withhold their support in order to get it to conform to their views, or they can attempt to overthrow the government in a coup d'état. However, the latter options are undertaken only in the most extreme conditions: to cope with serious threats to the public order, to become the real force behind a civilian facade, to alter or prevent change in the balance of political forces, or to establish their own government.[26] Figure 1.1 shows these relationships of obedience, disobedience, and blind obedience that the oath exemplifies.

The oath of loyalty, then, is a powerful means to obtain and maintain the soldier's loyalty and obedience to the state and to their commander-in-chief. However, we must not overestimate its power to hold the soldier's obedience or ignore other means used to bolster their loyalty and obedience. These other factors include adequate and regular pay, adequate housing, reasonable food, competent and interested commanders, fair recognition methods, a fair disciplinary system, opportunity for leave, and acceptable conditions under combat. Also, the military must feel that its position in society is not threatened by the political system, especially an unstable government. All of these factors work together with the oath to ensure a soldier's loyalty and obedience throughout his professional military career. Obviously, problems with any one or two of these factors may produce disgruntlement but not disobedience among a group of soldiers. However, serious degradation of several of these factors can result in overriding the soldier's propensity to follow his oath because the soldier no longer views his government or commanders as legitimate authorities, worthy of his loyalty.

Historical Background: Prehistory to the 1660s

Having reviewed the concept of the oath of loyalty and its meaning to soldiers and their government in terms of obedience, I will now provide a brief review of the development of the oath of loyalty in Western society from prehistory to the mid–1600s. In prehistoric societies man was organized into nomadic tribes. When these tribes needed a force of armed men to hunt, seek vengeance, or raid other tribes, they formed warrior bands and chose a war chief— sometimes the legal chief of the tribe but not always — to lead the band. Generally this war chief was a warrior who had already proven himself through bravery and physical courage on previous hunting or raiding parties. In either case, he would be given authority to recruit warriors, to lead the band, and, most importantly, to give orders with the expectation he would be obeyed. In return, he would receive the "loyalty" of those warriors who comprised the armed force.

Figure 1.1. Relationship of Obedience to Disobedience and Blind Obedience

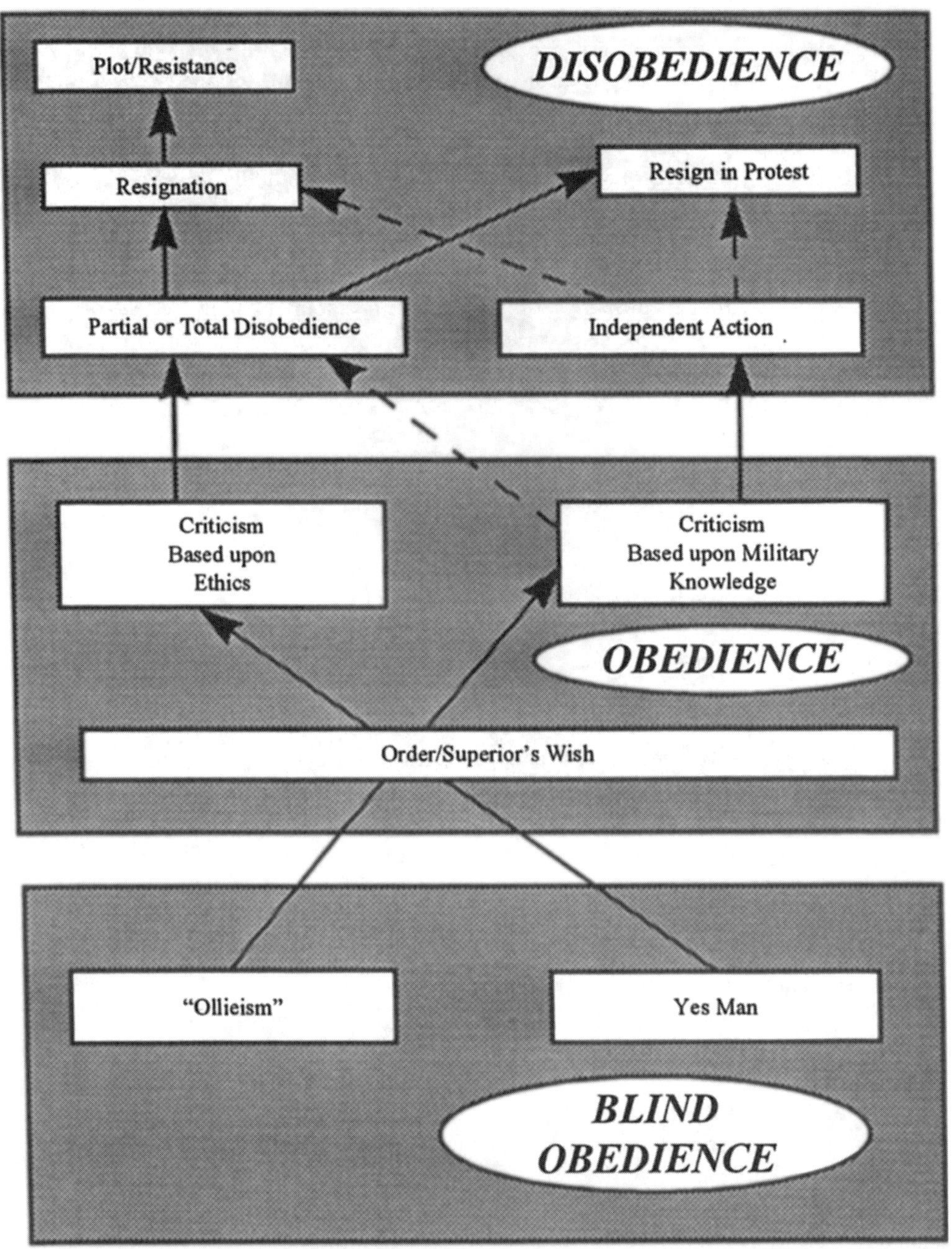

Note: Dotted line means less frequent outcome.

Obedience is the normal case. Orders or wishes of superiors are followed as long as they are legal or moral. However, criticism of orders can occur, based upon ethical or military knowledge, in a thought process that may only take a few moments. Verbal disagreement is part of this process. Only the action determines a person's obedience or disobedience. *continued*

Possibly the formation of the warrior band and the selection of the war chief would be accompanied by some sort of religious ceremony to invoke the authority of the gods and confer success on the chief and his warriors before they marched off. In these prehistoric societies, kinship formed the greatest thread binding the war chief and the warriors together.[27]

Around 6000–5000 B.C., human society began changing from groups of nomadic tribes, dependent on hunting and gathering, to more sedentary, urbanized societies, based on agriculture and eventually trade. Hierarchies and bureaucracies developed to rule and administer these growing societies, and excess hunters developed into a specialized warrior class that would become the first standing armies. As the numbers of human beings in these urban societies grew, the ties of kinship between the ruler and the warriors became increasingly distant, producing an apparent need to create a substitute—a religious oath of loyalty—to bind the warriors to the ruler and the state.[28] For example, new recruits for the Assyrian armies (c. 1367 B.C.–c. 626 B.C.) had to swear a loyalty oath to their deity and to the king and his household.[29] These kings also usually maintained a personal bodyguard of elite troops who owed a closer degree of loyalty and obedience to their sovereign than the regular soldiers. In the armies of ancient Greece, loyalty between soldier and leader and obedience to orders derived from the relationship of the soldiers as citizens of the city-state to which they belonged and to its ruler. Military functions appear to have been concentrated at the top of the social hierarchy by an aristocracy, ruled by a king, which also controlled political and economic affairs. Claiming descent from the gods, the king was the chief priest, chief judge, and supreme war lord. He, however, was guided by a council of chiefs, and his decisions required ratification by the assembly of citizens. Conflicts were conducted as private wars between kings, using fluctuating bands of "companions," bound by personal dependence or by a common objective, as armies. Kings and princes earned the loyalty and obedience of their subordinates through divine right, kinship and personal courage in battle. The king was expected to lead his band of companions into battle and seek individual combat with the opposing leader in full view of his troops.[30] The Greek warrior fought for the love of glory and fame, and war was a contest of champions in the pursuit of virtue—"to die fearlessly with one's sword in hand."[31]

By the sixth century B.C., the tyrants and aristocracies had generally given way to democracies, and military service, the mark of citizenship, was gradually extended to the members of other classes. The ability to bear

Disobedience, when it occurs, is based upon ethical or military knowledge. Resignation, resignation in protest, and resistance occurs more commonly for ethical, rather than purely military, reasons.

Blind obedience can be subdivided into "Ollieism" and the "yes man." The former derives from U.S. Marine Lieutenant Colonel Oliver "Ollie" North who secretly sold arms to Iran, violating a congressional arms embargo on Iran, to obtain illegal funds for the "Contra," anti–Communist guerrillas fighting the Communist government of Nicaragua in the 1980s. North decided to do so because President Reagan wanted to continue American military assistance to the Contras after Congress cut off funding. An "Ollieist" is a subordinate acting illegally and unethically to get a job done to please his boss. A "yes man" is someone, like Keitel and Jodl, who will do whatever their superiors want, without further questioning.

Source: Major Dr. Ulrich F. Zwygart, "How Much Obedience Does an Officer Need? Beck, Tresckow, and Stauffenberg—Examples of Integrity and Moral Courage for Today's Officer," Combat Studies Institute, U.S. Army Command and General Staff College, Fort Leavenworth, KS, 1994, pp. 29–30.

arms (that is, to be sufficiently wealthy to purchase and maintain weapons and armor) became an essential condition to becoming a full citizen and participating in the political life of his city-state. Each citizen owed allegiance only to his city-state and had an important stake in defending the state since he had a greater say in its political life, especially in relation to the members of other contemporary societies.[32] Each young man between the ages of 18 and 20 began his first year of military service with a tour of the religious sanctuaries where possibly he took the following oath:

> I will not dishonor the sacred arms; I will not abandon my comrades in battle; I will defend both the sacred and the secular (rules of the community) and I will hand on to my juniors a fatherland in no way diminished, but larger, and more powerful so far as it is within my power and with the aid of all. I will obey the magistrates, the established laws and those which may be introduced; if any man seeks to overthrow them I will oppose him with all my strength and with the aid of all. I will venerate the cults of my ancestors. I take as witnesses to this oath the gods, Aglauros, Hestia, Enyo, Enyalios, Ares, Athena, Areia, Zeus, Thallo, Auxo, Hegemore, Heracles, the boundary-stones of the country, the wheat, the barley, the wines, the olive-trees, the fig-trees. [33]

Other religious rites relating to military service included armed processions and ritual battle, both of which were part of the new recruit's induction.[34] For most Greek city-states, war was a temporary interruption to normal daily life, and the army was called up to meet crises as they occurred. In Sparta, the army was the state, but even there officers did not necessarily give blind obedience to their ruler.[35]

The Macedonians, led first by Phillip II and then by Alexander the Great, now swept into history. Taking advantage of the chaos following the Pelopennesian War (431 B.C.–405 B.C.), Phillip II of Macedon conquered the Greek peninsula by 338 B.C. His son Alexander then invaded Asia Minor and, within ten years (334 B.C.–323 B.C.), had swept all opponents from his path all the way to the Indus River. The Macedonian king was the hereditary chief of the army and derived his authority as supreme war lord from his position as their religious leader in a state that had no professional priesthood. He was so recognized by an assembly of its members in which the soldiers acknowledged his "election" by brandishing their shields and swords. Only men under arms could possess full citizenship, indicated by the title "Macedon," and participate in this ceremony. As king, Phillip and Alexander exercised total command of the army and demanded total obedience. Like the Greek heroes, the king was expected to lead his troops into battle and fight like one of them, seeking out the opposing king. Assisting him were his friends and companions, selected close male relatives and nobles of the royal household. Bound to each other religiously and socially, they formed a royal personal bodyguard, expected to protect the king at all times, especially in combat.[36] The armies of the Greek city-states contrasted with the Macedonian armies in that they saw respect for the laws as the basis for military discipline while the latter saw this basis as loyalty to the leader.

The soldiers of the Roman armies from city-state to the end of the empire went through approximately the same induction rituals for acceptance into military service. The potential recruit had to pass a medical examination and present references of good character. He entered an initial training period; then, upon completion of all proficiency tests, would be placed on the unit rolls and take an oath of allegiance to the laws, the "sacrementum."[37] This oath was possibly inspired by Samnite customs, "which consecrated the soldiers in a magico-legal sense to the service of the state, and an oath of mutual solidarity (*iusiurandum*) to reinforce the personal relationship within the army."[38] In the induction ceremony one soldier would recite the complete oath, and the remaining recruits would step forward and recite, "The same in my case." All soldiers renewed the oath at least once a year.[39] The new recruit, to complete induction, also received a cord necklace with a piece of inscribed lead, the "signaculum," similar to today's dog tag. By the fourth century A.D., he received an indelible mark on his hand, either by branding or tattooing, apparently to make desertion more difficult.[40]

Throughout the history of Rome, as the form of government changed so did the object to which the Roman soldier swore his oath. According to the oath, the Roman soldier bound himself to be loyal to the consul or magistrate appointed to command his unit and to obey his orders. He also swore not to leave military service without the consul's instructions and not to desert in battle. When commanders changed, the soldiers would reswear the oath.[41] Livy reports an incident in which some soldiers threatened to assassinate their consuls, an act that would have freed them from their oath to them. They decided not to when someone warned them that such an act would be criminal and would not release them from their sacred obligations.[42] In 216 B.C., a supplementary oath of loyalty to the magistrates commanding the armies replaced the *iusiurandum*. In the early first century, following the reforms of Marius, the soldiers swore the oath to the republic. Marius also allowed individual commanders to enroll soldiers so that, over time, soldiers increasingly gave their loyalty to them, instead of the republic. This situation contributed to the start of the civil wars, such as the one between Julius Caesar and Pompey (49 B.C.–48 B.C.), that ended the republic and established the empire.[43]

After the battle of Actium (31 B.C.) and the establishment of the empire, the object of the oath became the emperor. In addition to the annual swearing-in, the Roman soldier also swore the oath to the new emperor upon the death of his predecessor, emphasizing the personal bond between the soldier and his emperor. To further secure the army's loyalty, the first emperor Augustus took the first steps to dedicate a portion of the state's budget to pay the army regularly. Emperors also spoke to the troops directly (the *adlocutio*) or circulated texts of their speeches to legions in the provinces. Other methods of bolstering loyalty and obedience initiated by the oath included the use of unit designations and the eagle standard, imperial triumphs and military ceremonies, discharge bonuses, and the payment of donatives (irregular distributions of cash usually to celebrate a special event).[44] However, the use of the latter to mollify the troops soon became abused, and, on numerous occasions, soldiers, particularly of the Praetorian Guard, dethroned emperors who failed to provide sufficient donatives. Additionally, other reasons—service conditions, irregular pay, and excessive immoral behavior—contributed to the removal and, sometimes, murder of the reigning emperor.[45]

The intervention of the Roman legions and the Praetorian Guard in the empire's political life was one of many reasons for its eventual demise. Between the third and seventh centuries A.D., imperial authority and control completely broke down, and the empire splintered into smaller states, controlled by local nobles and princes. Small landowners increasingly sought protection from invaders and local bandits by giving their plots of land to larger landowners in return for security. In the Frankish lands, the Merovingian kings and great landowners, in turn, would redistribute portions of the land as benefices, called fiefs, to lesser nobles and certain public officials, in lieu of money which was in short supply. These lesser nobles and officials now became vassals to the landowner, the liege lord, and were required to perform homage and swear an oath of fealty to him. The act of homage and the oath of fealty originated in the commendation, or "comendatio," by which two men bound each other to specified obligations. When one man "commended" himself to another, he did so by placing his hands between the hands of his future lord — the act of homage. With his hands on the scriptures or a casket of relics, the vassal would swear the oath of fealty by which he agreed to fulfill faithfully and loyally whatever obligations he and his new lord had made. Probably the most important obligation was to rally to his lord's call for military service and bring additional men-at-arms if the vassal had so agreed to do. In return, the lord agreed to faithfully and loyally support his vassal. The completion of these two acts created a legal bond between the vassal and his lord.[46]

By the early 700s A.D., public office, landholding, and vassalage had become intertwined, forming the basis of feudalism that would dominate military, social, and economic life in western Europe for the next 500 years.[47] About A.D. 730, during the administration of Charles Martel, benefice holders were required to pay their lord with military service. At the same time, the group of trusted followers, similar to the Germanic "comitatus,"[48] surrounding the kings and many of the great landowners and bound by an oath of allegiance to them, was developing into the Frankish aristocracy. These men-at-arms probably rode to battle but dismounted to fight, but, with the introduction of the stirrup, soon developed into mounted knights with body armor. After Charlemagne's death, his successors made land ownership and its associated military service hereditary, accelerating the growth of great feudal estates. Feudal lords could now put additional mounted knights into the field, usually under their own direct command — not the king's. The king became, in essence, only one lord among many, commanding only his own vassals; and the feudal army, in actuality, was groups of men with conflicting loyalties and obligations. Charles the Bald, king of the West Franks (840–877), also decreed that every man who had a horse should come mounted to the call to arms. These developments, by the 11th century, led to the evolution of a class of aristocratic, mounted knights, each one bound to a lord by specified obligations.[49]

In the early Middle Ages, knights could elevate almost anyone to knighthood, and, by the 12th century, the institution became hereditary. To become a knight, a young man at about the age of 20 would go through the "dubbing" ceremony, the medieval equivalent of the commissioning ceremony, which originated in the maturity rites of ancient Germanic tribes.[50] In the ceremony, the prospective knight's lord would perform one or more symbolic acts, such as fastening the knight's helmet or spurs and belting his sword. Later ceremonies added the accolade — the touching of the knight's shoulders with his sword — and concluded with an oath by the knight to his lord. In some regions the prospective knight spent the night before his dubbing, praying over his weapons in the local church, a ritual called the vigil, followed by a ritual cleansing bath. The dubbing ceremony, which usually took place in the lord's castle but could occur on the battlefield, signaled not only the fitness of the feudal noble to carry the knight's weapons but also his legal coming of age.[51]

By 1300, knighthood had become a way of life, sanctified and civilized by the church. Theoretically, the code of chivalry guided knights in all aspects of their life. Although the code contained clerical and romantic ideals and Christian virtues, it was essentially a military code with values, such as honor, pride, and fealty, of which honor was the most important. Honor governed the knight's conduct in battle as we can read today in medieval chronicles and the French chansons de geste — death in battle was far more noble than survival through cowardice. Knighthood was seen as an ennobling experience for the elite aristocratic class, not the masses. As such, knights of different nationalities, like officers of later ages, believed they had more in common with each other than with men of other classes of the same nationality. By the 1500s, the code of chivalry had evolved into a social code, governing speech and manners and represented by elaborate romantic tournaments and jousts. However, many elements of the chivalric code did survive until the devastating total wars of the 20th century.[52]

By the mid–1300s, mercenaries were increasingly becoming the major source of military power, particularly in the Italian peninsula and central Europe. Although armies throughout history had used mercenaries to supplement native forces, their use was generally limited since rulers had limited resources to pay them and could secure their loyalty only with regular pay. Some rulers bolstered the loyalties of the mercenaries by awarding them honors and, in some cases, citizenship. Feudal lords and kings used mercenaries, mainly as infantry (and later as gunners with the invention and use of artillery), but they were considered social inferiors by the mounted knights. The use of mercenaries increased as the cost of armor, weapons, and specially bred horses for the knights rose, and as several battles of the Hundred Years Wars (1337–1453) demonstrated the vulnerability of the French knights to English crossbowmen. Also, the rise in trade and the resulting increase in hard money allowed rulers to hire soldiers, and those who owed military service to a lord, to convert their obligation to a money payment.[53] Finally, the end of the Crusades and the temporary peace settlements between campaigns of the Anglo-French conflict provided thousands of unemployed soldiers for the mercenary companies. These factors joined with the need for soldiers in the rivalries between the Holy Roman Emperor and the Pope over the investiture issue, resulting in the increased use of mercenaries, particularly on the Italian peninsula.[54]

Typically, a contractor, or military entrepreneur, would gather together a number of out-of-work knights who brought along their attendants, arms, and horses, or attracted a number of small bands of such men. The entrepreneur then made a contract with a ruler that specified the size of the force to be provided, types of equipment, the length of service, and the amount of payment. However, the mercenary system became plagued with numerous problems. The soldiers gave their "real" loyalty only to the captain who commanded them and led them into battle, not to the state that hired them. Often, mercenaries would desert the state which had originally hired them to work for its rival, drawn by the lure of more money or the promise of booty—sometimes they would switch sides in the middle of battle. Also, the military entrepreneurs soon began limiting the brutalities of actual combat, producing relatively "bloodless" campaigns, to protect their investments in their soldiers. Finally, the system became abused by shady contractors who inflated the rolls without actually providing the agreed-upon numbers of soldiers. These are the types of abuses that caused Machiavelli to decry so much the mercenary system of his times.[55] However, not all mercenaries were bad; the English mercenary captain Sir John Hawkwood was particularly known for his extraordinary loyalty and service to Florence.[56]

In the late Renaissance, another type of mercenary, the "Landsknechte," appeared in the western portions of the Holy Roman Empire. Between 1482 and 1486, the Archduke Maximilian of the Hapsburgs, the future Holy Roman Emperor, authorized a colonel, essentially a military entrepreneur, by imperial patent to recruit men from the

Rhineland and the lower Rhine as soldiers. These mercenaries would take an oath to their own constitution, the "Artikelbrief," or letters of articles, the contractual obligations between the "Landsknechtes" and whoever paid them. They agreed to obey all orders they received while the emperor swore to be faithful to them and pay them according to the agreement. They had their own induction ceremony for the new recruits. The latter entered the mustering-in area through a makeshift entrance way of two halberds, crossed by a pike. They were formally enrolled into the regiment's books, read the disciplinary code, and then swore to the code by raising a hand with two fingers extended upward. During the late 1400s and early 1500s, the "Landsknechtes" were a formidable fighting force in central Europe, but they tended to be more loyal to their captains than the emperor, given the latter's problems in paying them regularly.[57]

The use of mercenaries dominated European warfare from the 15th century into the opening decades of the 17th. The first battles of the Thirty Years War (1618–48) were fought by mercenary armies, but that war also saw the beginnings of national armies with uniforms and regularized logistical support, such as those of Gustavus Adolphus of Sweden and Wallenstein of the Holy Roman Empire. The devastation to central Europe during these three decades by roving bands of mercenaries and the effectiveness of the new armies over mercenaries led the budding nation-states of Europe to continue this line of development. These nations were consolidating their power and felt the need for more permanent military forces than the mercenaries of the previous two centuries. These new national armies would be composed of long-term "volunteers" from the lower classes of society who joined by a mixture of bribery and coercion and were led by officers drawn from the declining feudal nobility. By 1700, European armies were becoming professional military forces with officers who increasingly saw themselves as servants of the state, not as members of a warrior caste or as military entrepreneurs. The Prussian army would come to be considered by many to be the epitome of these developing professional armies.

Historical Development: Prussia-Germany, 1660s–1918

The foundations of the modern Prussian army were laid by Frederick William (1640–88), known as the Great Elector, after the end of the Thirty Years War.[58] At that time, his army was composed of a few thousand "Landsknechtes," incapable of any major military operations. He purged these forces of the undesirables, the unfit, and the rebellious, which left him a tiny force of only 2,500 men which he organized into regiments. Their colonels, who provided a specified number of men, were united only through their oath to Frederick William. He established the position of general field marshal to bring various military functions under direct royal control, especially the rights to commission company grade officers and to veto commissions made by the colonels. He also obtained the right to levy a direct tax in exchange for exempting the nobility from the tax, transformed their estates from feudal fiefs into absolute ownership, and confirmed rights and privileges granted to them by his predecessors. Throughout his reign, the Great Elector worked to increase the size and fitness of the army and, at his death in 1688, left an army of an estimated strength of 30,000 men.[59] His son and successor Frederick III of Brandenburg (1688–1713) gradually increased the size of the army to 40,000 men.[60]

Frederick's son and successor Frederick William I (1713–40) continued this line of development, ultimately achieving an army of 83,000 men, the fourth-largest in

Europe although Prussia was only tenth in territorial size and 13th in population.[61] He established the canton system as the basis for recruitment in which all young males at age ten were placed on their respective regimental lists and would take the oath after confirmation in the church so, in the king's words, "they would not profane the oath."[62] He also forbade the Prussian nobility to serve in foreign armies, personally selected the young noble sons for attendance at the cadet school in Berlin, and ultimately commissioned them as officers. Unlike many of his fellow monarchs, Frederick William I wore the same uniform—the king's coat—as his officers and granted direct interviews to any officer, down to the lowest subaltern, to strengthen the class solidarity between him and his officers.[63] By the time of his death in 1740, the Prussian nobility had come to view the officer corps as its own special domain, its natural profession.

Under these conditions, the Prussian officer came to see himself as the servant of the monarch who, in turn, became the personification of the state. The oath of loyalty that the noble officer swore directly linked him personally to Frederick William and his successors. As Görlitz writes, "Indeed, this conception of personal loyalty was the real moral foundation of the Army and was the thing that shaped the highly distinctive mental attitudes of the Prussian and later the German Officer corps as a whole."[64] In exchange for raising the nobility to this special status, Frederick William demanded complete obedience to his commands. For instance, a portion of the regulations of 1726 states: "When one takes the oath to the flag one renounces oneself and surrenders entirely, even one's life and all, to the monarch, in order to fulfill the Lord's will; and through this blind obedience one receives the grace and the confirmation of the title of soldier."[65]

Under Frederick II the Great (1740–86), the nobility came to dominate the Prussian officer corps almost completely with only a few officers of bourgeois origins, mostly in the artillery and engineering branches. Frederick believed that only men of aristocratic origins could possess those qualities needed by his officers, such as loyalty, courage, obedience, discipline, and honor, and that the bourgeoisie were driven by materialistic motives, rendering them unable to obtain these virtues. For example, during the Seven Years War (1756–63), because of severe losses among the aristocratic officers, Frederick commissioned officers from the middle class (as well as recruited aristocratic officers from other states). However, he purged them out of the army after the end of the war.[66] To confirm the bond with his officers, Frederick wore the plain blue Prussian officer's coat with red collar and cuffs, pitched his tent along with his officers during campaigns, and actually led his troops into battle: he had no commanders, staff, or ministers between him and his troop commanders and only a handful of special assistants to advise him.[67] As Rosinski wrote, "[The] intense cult of 'honor' among the officers of Frederick's army served the common bond of uniting them amongst themselves and with their King and State and also as a compensation for the many hardships of their profession."[68]

Of the military virtues that Frederick valued, obedience perhaps was the one he held in the highest esteem. He wrote in *The History of My Own Times*,

> [The] men still are worth nothing if they are undisciplined. An army, if one wishes to accomplish, anything with it, must obey and be in good discipline, which in turn rest upon obedience and punctuality. Discipline begins with the generals and works down to the drummer boys. Its foundation is subordination: no subordinate has the right to contradict orders. If the commander orders, the other must obey. If the officers do not do their duty, then still less the common solider be expected to perform his: it is a chain in which no link can be missing.[69]

Although most of Frederick's officers obeyed his orders explicitly, as in all armies and despite the myth of total obedience surrounding the Prussian army, there were officers — even senior officers — who occasionally disobeyed the king's orders. For example, Colonel Frederick August von der Marwitz disobeyed the king's order to sack a chateau in 1760, and General F. C. von Saldern refused Frederick's order to ransack the hunting lodge of the elector Augustus of Saxony at Hubertsberg in 1761.[70] Undoubtedly, there are other such incidents, both recorded and unrecorded; they demonstrate that while orders were generally obeyed, obedience was not absolute — even in Frederick the Great's army.

Unfortunately for Prussia, Frederick's army would deteriorate under the next two kings, Frederick William II (1786–97) and Frederick William III (1797–1840). As a result, the Prussian army was no match for the revolutionary armies of Napoleon Bonaparte and lost two disastrous battles, Jena and Auerstedt, in 1806. These defeats forced the Prussian King to sign the humiliating peace treaty of Tilsit.[71] The King and his court left Berlin for Potsdam with the French army at their heels. General Gebhardt Leberecht von Blücher, who later led the Prussian cavalry at Waterloo in 1814, bemoaned, "All is lost and honour too."[72] Within a year, the remaining Prussian forces and fortresses, after only a handful of successes, surrendered to the French forces who were warmly greeted by magistrates and merchants throughout Germany. When, in 1809, the French army routed the Austrians at Wagram and the Prussian King ignored the Austrian pleas for help, scores of Prussian officers resigned in disgust, and, this time, Blücher threatened to resign.[73] One of the outraged officers, Major Karl von Grolman, first joined the Austrian army and then fought with the British in the Peninsular Campaign. These military disasters severely shook the confidence of these officers in their sovereign and led to significant military and political reforms by General Hermann von Boyen, General Count August Neidhardt von Gneisenau, General Gerhard von Scharnhorst, and Baron Karl von Stein.

The reformers instituted a number of important military reforms from 1807 through 1814. First, they replaced the multitude of military agencies with a single war department, the Kriegsdepartment, whose chief, the war minister, would report directly to the King. However, the King insisted that the General Staff remain outside of this department and that the chiefs of the war department's two main divisions report directly to him. Boyen, Prussia's first war minister, would later eliminate the two division chiefs and incorporate the General Staff into the war department: in essence, he became both the army's operational commander and its chief administrator. During the 1800s, however, conservative elements within the army with their sovereign's support would erode the authority of the war minister as the single chief in military matters while the King maintained the fiction that he led the army directly and every officer had direct access to him as their liege lord.[74] Stein also wanted to change the objects of the military oath from the King as "Kriegsherr" (war lord) alone to "Landesherr" (head of state) and the "Vaterland" (nation) to emphasize that military service was a function of the relationship between citizens and the state. He was successful in replacing the term "Kriegsherr" with the term "Landesherr" but not in adding the term "Vaterland."[75]

A third major reform was the creation of the "Landwehr," or militia, by royal order in March 1813. Remembering the warm welcome that many Prussians had given the French troops in 1807, the reformers believed that, to drive the French from Prussian territory and ultimately defeat Napoleon, they had to arouse the "national" will of the people to fight for the Prussian state, not just its ruler. To imbue the people with this national spirit, they wanted to create a national militia to fight alongside the regular army. To broaden support for the army, the reformers also wanted to open the officer corps to members of the middle class and make educational qualifications a decisive factor in obtaining a commission. Additionally, the reformers argued that to gain the support of the masses the King would also have to grant social and political reforms, such as the abolition of serfdom. Although the King granted these reforms, he was influenced and advised by the conservative elements at the Berlin court and did not really want a popular army or other changes that might threaten the existing social order for some time in the future. After the French were driven from German territories and Napoleon was safely exiled after Waterloo, the conservatives worked tirelessly to water down and even reverse these reforms. For the rest of the 19th century, the liberals and the conservatives continuously fought each other as these issues were revisited.[76]

Frederick William's continued cooperation with the French generated additional protests from his officers. His signature on an 1811 treaty with Napoleon produced a second wave of resignations. About 30 Prussian officers, including Karl von Clausewitz, joined the Russian army. Scharnhorst also resigned but, unwilling to serve under foreign colors, retired to Silesia until he was recalled to duty in early 1813 at the start of the Wars of Liberation that drove the French from Prussian territory. In February 1812, Frederick William negotiated another agreement with Napoleon to provide 20,000 troops to the French "Grand Armee" for the upcoming invasion of Russia, free passage for the French troops to Russian territory, and provisions for both soldiers and horses. This agreement sparked increasing pressure to liberate the German states from the French.

In late 1812, General Hans David Yorck von Wartenburg, the commander of the Prussian division that was designated to participate with the French in the invasion of Russia, managed to limit his unit's participation in the invasion. Then, in December, contacts between Yorck and the Russians over prisoner exchanges led to Yorck's convention at Tauroggen by which he neutralized his forces for two months — without any instructions from the King — and allowed Russian forces to occupy territory between Memel and Königsberg. On January 13, 1813, Yorck wrote his king, "With bleeding heart I burst the bond of obedience and wage war on my own account. The army wants war with France, the people want war with France, and so does the King, but the King has no free will. The army must make his will free." Six days later, indignant at Yorck's disobedience, Frederick William repudiated Yorck's convention, leading temporarily to an open break between the two. In early February, Stein summoned the East Prussian estates to Königsberg and opened Prussian harbors to the Russians and Swedes. Frederick William now rejected the French treaty of February 1812 and signed a treaty of alliance with Russia on February 28, 1813. The Wars of Liberation would officially begin two and a half weeks later on March 17.[77]

During the decades after 1815, the conservatives in Prussia were increasingly successful in ousting the reformers and diluting their reforms or rendering them ineffective. They continued to view the king as "warlord" which demanded the total obedience of the troops, particularly the officers. In 1832, Prince Wilhelm, the future Prussian King and Kaiser of the Second German Reich, wrote in his defense of a three-year service term for the regular army that discipline and blind obedience were important to properly indoctrinate the army as the throne's defense against the current liberalism.[78] K. G. von Rudloff in the *Handbuch des preussischen Militärrecchts* (1826) wrote that an individual surrendered certain civil rights when he took the oath of loyalty and entered the military profession. Furthermore,

> [t]he entire inner workings of the army depend on unconditional subordination. All independent judgment by lower echelons on the morality, efficiency, and legality of orders is excluded, except for certain unusual and borderline cases affecting only higher officers. Absolute loyalty to the king and absolute obedience to his orders, whether issued directly or through others, are the heart of the soldier's duties....[79]

This continuing emphasis on absolute loyalty and obedience to the king, derived from his need to assert supreme command over his army, was not a particularly Prussian phenomenon: when the Electorate of Hesse had its troops swear allegiance to its new constitution in 1831, the results were "painful conflicts of conscience among the officers" and disputes between its sovereign and parliament.[80]

During the Revolution of 1848, the issue of the oath of allegiance rose again. On March 19, revolutionary agitation forced Frederick William IV (1840–61) to order the withdrawal of the army from Berlin and create a "Bürgerwehr" (citizen's militia) to assume protection of the capital. Three days later, the King told a group of Assembly delegates that the army would have to swear an oath of allegiance to a proposed constitution, once it was written. These events deepened the feelings of humiliation among army officers who had sworn allegiance only to the King but now felt that he was abandoning them. From May to October, the members of Prussia's National Assembly endlessly debated the provisions for a constitution, one of which would have required the soldiers to swear an oath to that document. However, when the first draft was ready in October, the King bitterly criticized the inclusion of the oath: "This oath would cost me all my officers and is therefore impossible." By early November, the National Assembly had lost popular support, and the King suspended it and brought loyal troops back into Berlin. On December 5, he formally dissolved the Assembly by royal decree.[81]

On the same day, Frederick William promulgated Prussia's first constitution but without a provision for an oath by the army to the constitution.[82] Although the King had publicly intimated that it would include such an oath, the requirement was apparently deleted from the draft at the last minute. The new constitution did, however, require the war minister to swear an oath to the constitution, the only officer to do so throughout the remaining history of Prussia and later the German empire. He had to countersign all legislative acts dealing with the military and to defend them in the Prussian Landtag (parliament). The revised constitution of 1850 officially rejected an oath to it but reaffirmed the king's command over the army and his right to appoint officers.[83] Theoretically, the legislature could increase its control over the military through its prerogatives over the budget and the responsibilities of the war minister to it.

However, reality would turn out to be quite different. The constitution had placed the war minister — all of them until 1918, a general because a Hohenzollern would never allow a civilian to come between him and his officers — in the untenable situation of owing allegiance to both the king (and later the emperor) and the constitution. From 1850 until 1918, they generally placed their allegiance to their sovereign above their allegiance to the constitution. For example, Albrecht von Roon, appointed war minister in 1859, "expressly declared that as a general he was pledged to unconditional obedience to the king as commander-in-chief of the army."[84] During that time they allowed and even assisted in the transfer of virtually every important military function out of their hands, placing them beyond effective legislative control: operational planning in peacetime and operational control during war fell to the chief of the General Staff; and officer selection, assignments, and promotions went to the chief of the Military Cabinet. By 1890, the war minister could sign only totally administrative measures. He had essentially become the sovereign's "whipping boy" in the Reichstag, required to argue the military budget before its delegates yet had no authority over its formulation or expenditure.[85] As Craig states, "[T]o all intents and purposes, the army was left outside the constitution, subject only to the king's control and serving to protect his authority against legislative encroachment."[86]

That army, under the leadership of General Helmuth von Moltke (the Younger), conducted three victorious wars (Denmark, 1864; Austria, 1865–66; and France, 1870–71) that produced the Second Reich and greatly increased the popularity of the army. The wars strengthened the bond between the Prussian officers and their sovereign. In 1867, Wilhelm I (Regent, 1858–61; King of Prussia, 1861–71; Kaiser of the German Empire, 1871–88) was named "Bundesfeldherr" (commander in chief of the federal German Armies) under the constitution of the North German Confederation with complete command authority over the armies of the member states. Later, in 1871, he received direct command of the armies of all German states, except for Bavaria.[87] The military structure that evolved by 1890 gave the war minister, each troop commander, and the chiefs of the Great General Staff and the Military Cabinet direct access to the kaiser as supreme war lord.[88]

Additionally, wealthy bourgeois fathers now eagerly sought reserve officer commissions for their sons as a sign of social prestige as the demand for more officers outran the ability of the "pure" nobility to provide them. Wilhelm II opened the doors to the upper middle class by royal order, March 29, 1890: "As I see it, the future of My Army lies in the hands not only of the offspring of the noble families and of the sons of My worthy officers and civil servants, whom ancient tradition has made the chief pillars of the corps of officers, but also in the hands of sons in whom respectable bourgeois families have planted and cultivated a love for their King and Country, a warm feeling towards the profession of arms and a sense of Christian morality."[89] In other words, he would allow into the army as reserve officers those men who possessed the "aristocratic" temperament in order to maintain the officer corps as a bulwark against the rising tide of liberalism and social democracy in turn-of-the-century Germany. As the Kaiser hoped, the middle-class officers adopted the traditions of the aristocratic officers.[90] The end result was an officer corps unconditionally pledged to the Kaiser by a personal oath sworn in a quasi-religious ceremony as the world moved towards World War I.

At the outbreak of the war, Wilhelm II (1888–1918) assumed personal control of military operations as the "Oberste Heeresleitung" (OHL) (Supreme High Commander). However, he was an amateur strategist, not a professional soldier in contrast to his grandfather. Consequently, he increasingly surrendered his authority as Kriegsherr to the professional soldiers. With stalemate on the Western Front and the disastrous German casualties at Verdun, Wilhelm, in August 1916, appointed Field Marshal Paul von Hindenburg and General Erich Ludendorff as War Minister and First Quartermaster General, respectively. Over the next two years, these two senior officers, especially Ludendorff, came to overshadow their emperor by threatening to resign unless he supported their actions, and Wilhelm lacked the will to prevent it. By October 1918, they had essentially established a military dictatorship and issued commands in the Kaiser's name, directed military operations, made economic and foreign policy, and removed and selected ministers — prerogatives rightfully belonging to Wilhelm.[91] As Rosinski writes, Hindenburg and Ludendorff had reduced their war lord to "impotence. It made the dictator's protestations of respectful obedience sound like hollow mockery."[92] Craig further stated, "It is ironical that the blow [to the monarchy] should have been delivered by the army, which had so steadfastly opposed political and social reform precisely because it might weaken the power of the Crown."[93]

The two officers who directed the Imperial German Army and the German empire in the last two years of the war exemplified the dichotomous composition of the army during the war. Rosinski called Hindenburg a typical Prussian officer of the old type: he had few convictions but they were deeply held; he was monarchist and devoutly Christian; and he was moved more by duty than ambition. On the other hand, Ludendorff was the product of the new age: ambitious, with a thin outer veneer of traditional Prussianism but without any real feeling for its aristocratic spirit.[94] By 1914, the majority of the officers came from the middle class but had only a thin overlay of the aristocratic tradition (see Table 1.1).[95]

During the war, their numbers would significantly increase from a total of 29,000 in 1914 to 226,000 by November 1918 as the demand for officers outran the ability of the nobility to replace the casualties of modern total war. Table 1.2 illuminates the impact of the First World War on the German Army officer corps that significantly changed its composition and character. Also, the brutality of the war by 1916 was producing a new type of soldier — the "frontsoldat," or front soldier, "the man to whom war had become daily, bloody, hard work stripped of all the gay trappings that formally used to conceal its worst horrors and of all its pseudo-heroics."[96] These two conditions destroyed the social uniformity of the officer corps and contributed to the dissolution of the Imperial Army in November 1918.

Table 1.1
Composition of the Prussian Officer Corps, All Ranks

Year	*Noble*	*Middle Class*
1860	86%	14%
1900	61%	39%
1913	52%	48%

Source: Demeter, pp. 28–29.

Summary

The military oath of loyalty was — and is — an important means of binding the soldier to the government they served. It means that a soldier is legally bound to defend their government, their nation, and their way of life and that they must generally obey the orders from their commander in chief and from their superior officers. The oath is not, however, a justification to commit war crimes although it, in the "I

Table 1.2
Status of German Army Officers, 1914–18

Active-Duty Officers in August 1914	22,112
Reserve Officers in August 1914	29,230
Combat deaths among the active-duty officers	11,357 (over half)
One-year volunteers (*Einjährig-Freiwilliger*)	Over 200,000
Officers of all groups in November 1918	Over 270,000

Source: Waite, pp. 45–47.

was only following orders" defense, has repeatedly been used to justify immoral actions in war. Dr. Milgram provides a convincing psychological explanation for a general obedience to authority which includes the commission of crimes that people believe they normally would not commit. His explanation also provides the reasons why people disobey orders and why it is so difficult for them to do so. My discussion of moral development provides additional insight into why some people take the road to disobedience but most do not. Finally, I reviewed the general history of the military oath of loyalty from prehistory to the 1660s and its specific development in Prussia-Germany from the 1660s until 1918 as a prelude to the origins of the Hitlerian oath of loyalty. For the German officer the oath of loyalty had great significance for his perception of his duties to his ruler and his concept of honor as these flowed from the oath.

Perhaps the German officer, to a greater degree than officers in more democratic societies, had a greater sense of obedience to his commander in chief because of the historical and social circumstances that surrounded the development of the Prussian-German Army. However, that sense of obedience was not absolute as the disobedience of Saldern and Marwitz under Frederick the Great, numerous officers, such as Clausewitz, Blücher, Scharnhorst, and Yorck, under Frederick William IV, the sailors at Kiel in 1918, and others whose acts have gone unrecorded have demonstrated. These decisions were made because each individual chose—and it was a decision that only they as individuals could make—to take the action they did. Given this background, we will now see how the circumstances of 1918–19, and the relationship of the Weimar Republic and the army, provided a specific historical background for the tolerance that developed between the army and Hitler by 1933, and how this tolerance affected the rise of National Socialism and the demise of democracy in Germany.

Notes

1. Note 49, John A. Rohr, *To Run a Constitution—The Legitimacy of the Administrative State* (Lawrence, KS: University of Kansas Press, 1986), p. 263. In his book Rohr's focus is the oath of office required of public administrators. His discussion concerning the oath of office, however, is pertinent to this discussion of the military oath of loyalty.

2. Rohr, pp. 187–92.

3. I requested English translations of the military oaths of loyalty from the embassies of 145 countries. Of the 145, 36 responded with copies of their oaths from which I derived this analysis. Panama, Costa Rica, Iceland and the Bahamas reported they have no military forces so they have no oaths. Denmark reported that it has not required a military oath of allegiance since the 1850s. However, Danish military officers must declare they will faithfully follow the Danish Constitution upon entry into the military. The oaths varied in length from two typed lines to several paragraphs.

4. Rohr, 192.

5. Stephen Westman, *Surgeon with the Kaiser's Army* (London: William Kimber, 1968), p. 29. The Austrian Embassy sent me a photostatic copy of a photograph depicting an induction ceremony similar to the one described here, along with a copy of their military oath of loyalty. As an active duty member of the US Air Force, I had similar feelings when I first took my initial commissioning oath in May 1973 and on those occasions when I have reaffirmed that oath since then.

6. Morris Janowitz, *The Professional Soldier—A Social and Political Portrait* (New York: The Free Press, 1971), p. 220. See also Malham M. Wakins, "The Ethics of Leadership I" in Wakins, ed., *War, Morality, and the Military* (Boulder, CO: Westview Press, 1986), p. 185; and Armed Forces Information Service (AFIS), Department of Defense, *The Armed Forces Officer* (Washington, DC: US Government Printing Office, 1975), p. 1.

7. Uniforms, emblems, badges, and awards and decorations for distinction for combat and noncombatant deeds also contribute to bolstering the soldier's conformity to the military fraternity. See note 14.

8. For example, the American Military Code of Conduct, first adopted in 1955 and revised in 1988. Its essence "is that the American fighter will hold his honor high, however he be assailed. He

will not quit the fight, he will never say or do that which might hurt the United States or demean its uniform. In captivity, he will join with other loyal Americans to help them and himself. In sum, come hell or high water, he will acquit himself as a man." AFIS, p. 18.

9. Samuel P. Huntington, *The Soldier and the State—The Theory and Politics of Civil-Military Relations* (New York: Vintage Books, 1957), pp. 15–16.

10. Quoted in Telford Taylor, *Nuremberg and Vietnam: An American Tragedy* (New York: Bantam Books, 1971), p. 47. The 1926 official German government law bulletin, the *Reichsgesetzblatt*, reported that the Reichstag reconfirmed the 1872 penal code. Opening Address for the United States, *Nazi Conspiracy and Aggression* (hereafter *NCA*) (Washington, DC: United States Government Printing Office, 1946), I, p. 168.

11. Quoted in Telford Taylor, p. 48.

12. See Hannah Arendt, *Eichmann in Jerusalem —A Report on the Banality of Evil* (New York: The Viking Press, 1963) for a critique of one such SS officer's use of this defense to absolve himself psychologically of any guilt and to transfer personal responsibility to his superiors for sending millions of Jews and other peoples to their deaths. Dr. Stephen Milgram, a professor of psychology at Yale University, called this phenomenon the "agentic state." He derived this phenomenon after a series of experiments on obedience, that eventually involved several hundred "ordinary" people, during the period 1960–63. He had these people, designated as "teachers," to administer a test of paired words to a "learner," who was actually an actor. When the learner responded incorrectly to a word, the teacher "gave" him a small electrical shock that "increased" in intensity with successive incorrect answers. Many of his "teachers" continued to raise the "voltage" in response to incorrect answers, despite apparent cries of pain from the "student" and at the continued urging of the experimenter that the experiment "demanded" the teacher continue. Even those "teachers" who experienced apparent distress at raising the voltage continued the experiment. *Obedience to Authority—An Experimental View* (Harper & Row, 1969), pp. 132–34.

13. Sidney Axinn, *A Moral Military* (Philadelphia, PA: Temple University Press, 1989), p.60. I also consulted Richard A. Gabriel, *To Serve with Honor—A Treatise on Military Ethics and the Way of the Soldier* (Westport, CT: Greenwood Press, 1982), pp. 31–34, 157–74; Sir John Hackett, *The Profession of Arms* (New York: Macmillan Publishing Company, 1983), p. 174; Philip M. Flammer, "Conflicting Loyalties and the American Military Ethic," pp. 157–70, Michael O. Wheeler, "Loyalty, Honor, and the Modern Military," pp. 171–79, Malham M. Wakin, "The Ethics of Leadership I," pp. 181–99, and "The Ethics of Leadership II," pp. 200–16, in Wakin; and Huntington, pp. 73–77.

14. Milgram, pp. 135–43. During Milgram's experiments the "experimenter" wore a lab coat, the "uniform" of members of the scientific community. In effect, it bolstered his authority as a scientist who knows what he is doing when he tells the "teacher" to increase the voltage for each wrong answer — even when the "subject" is crying out in pain or has ceased to say anything. Milgram, p. 139. See also Herbert C. Kelman and V. Lee Hamilton, *Crimes of Obedience Toward a Social Psychology of Authority and Responsibility* (New Haven, CT: Yale University Press, 1989), p. 53–57.

15. Gabriel, p. 12. Sir John Winthrop Hackett, "The Military in the Service of the State," in Wakin, p. 116. Huntington, pp. 75–78. See also Kelman and Hamilton, p. 144.

16. Don Mixon, *Obedience and Civilization Authorized Crime and the Normality of Evil* (London: Pluto Press, 1989), pp. 3–4. Mixon (p. xii) criticizes Milgram, particularly the construction of the latter's experiments and his concept of the agentic state, but not his general conclusions. If anything, Dr. Mixon believes that people in general — including Americans — "are indeed far more obedient than they think they are" and, in actuality, less "autonomous and independent."

17. Kelman and Hamilton, pp. 137–39.

18. See Kohlberg, "Chapter 7. The Development of Moral Judgment and Moral Action," in Kohlberg, et al., *Child Psychology and Childhood Education—A Cognitive-Developmental View* (New York: Longman, 1987), pp. 259–328; Kohlberg, *Essays on Moral Development*, Vol. I, *The Philosophy of Moral Development* (Cambridge, MA: Harper & Row, 1981); James L. Carroll and James R. Rest, "Moral Development," in Benjamin B. Wolman, et al., eds; *Handbook of Developmental Psychology* (Englewood Cliffs, NJ: Prentice-Hall, Inc., 1982), pp. 434–451; F. Clark Power, "Moral Development," in V. S. Ramachandran, editor, *Encyclopedia of Human Behavior* (San Diego: Academic Press, 1994), vol. 3, pp. 203–12; and Ernest Alleva and Gareth B. Matthews, "Moral Development," in Lawrence C. Becker and Charlotte B. Becker, editors, *Encyclopedia of Ethics* (New York: Garland Publishing, 1992), vol. II, pp. 828–35. Samuel P. Oliner and Pearl M. Oliner, *The Altruistic—Personality Rescuers of Jews in Nazi Europe* (New York: The Free Press, 1988), especially Chapters 1, 7, and 10, examines an analogous problem: why only a few people chose to risk their lives and those of their families to rescue Jews from the Nazis during World War II. In this case, many people chose this dangerous mission, despite the conformity of millions of their fellow compatriots to the Nazis' extermination policies, for reasons similar to

those why only a handful of German officers chose disobedience and opposition to Hitler.

19. Alleva and Matthews, pp. 830–31. Power, p. 204.

20. Alleva and Matthews, pp. 831–32. Power, p. 204.

21. Alleva and Matthews, pp. 832–33.

22.

23. Power, pp. 211–12. Carroll and Rest, pp. 440, 442

24. Alleva and Matthews, p. 833. Power, p. 207.

25. Lawrence J. Walker, Russel C. Pitts, Karl H. Henning, and M. Kyle Matsuba, "Reasoning about Morality and Real-Life Moral Problems," in Melanie Killen and Daniel Hart, eds., *Morality in Everyday Life Developmental Perspectives* (Cambridge, UK: Cambridge University Press, 1995), p. 383. For a more extended discussion of religion and moral development, see Arthur T. Jersild, *Child Psychology* (Englewood Cliffs, NJ: Prentice-Hall, Inc., 1968), pp. 519–24; and Lester D. Crow and Alice Crow, *Child Development and Adjustment—A Study of Child Psychology* (New York: The Macmillan Company, 1962), pp. 409–21.

26. Between 1945 and 1970, there were some 274 cases of direct military intervention in 59 states with an increasing number since then. Martin Edmonds, *Armed Services and Society* (Leicester, UK: Leicester University Press, 1988), p. 111. In the last 20 years, numerous works on civil-military relations have written about the *coup d'état.* Many are case studies of coups in specific countries, mainly in Latin America, Africa, Asia, and the Middle East. Of these, I consulted Lang, pp. 121–29; Amos Perlmutter and Valerie Plave Bennett, *The Political Influence of the Military—A Comparative Reader* (New Haven, CT: Yale University Press, 1980); Bruce W. Farcau, *The Coup Tactics in the Seizure of Power* (Westport, CT: Praeger Publishers, 1994); and Edward Luttwak, *Coup D'état A Practical Handbook* (Cambridge, MA: Harvard University Press, 1979).

27. Very little evidence exists on warfare in prehistoric societies. Much of the evidence that does exist consists of cave drawings, showing small orderly groups of men advancing in rudimentary tactical formations. General Sir John Hackett, "Introduction," p. 7, and Trevor Watkins, "The Beginnings of Warfare," pp. 15–16, in Hackett, ed., *Warfare in the Ancient World*, (London: Sidgwick & Jackson Limited, 1989). See also Arthur Ferrill, *The Origins of War* (London: Thames and Hudson, Ltd., 1985), pp. 18–22. I have assumed that societal structures of prehistoric societies were analogous to those of modern-day preindustrial societies and used these studies by modern-day anthropologists to derive this analysis: Ronald Cohen, "Warfare and State Formation: Wars Make States and States Make Wars," in R. Brian Ferguson, ed., *Warfare, Culture, and Environment* (Orlando, FL: Academic Press, Inc., 1984), pp. 339–42; Christian Feist, *The Art of War* (London: Thomas and Hudson, 1980), pp. 16–20; and Harry Holbert Turney-High, *Primitive War—Its Practice and Concepts* (Columbia, SC: University of South Carolina Press, 1949), pp. 61–90.

28. Richard A. Gabriel, *The Culture of War—Invention and Early Development* (New York: Greenwood Press, 1990), pp. 25–37.

29. D. J. Wisen, "The Assyrians," in Hackett, p. 41.

30. Yvon Garlan, *War in the Ancient World—A Social History* (London: Chatto & Windus, 1975), pp. 82–85; Gabriel, *Culture of War*, pp. 84–85.

31. Gabriel, *Culture of War*, p. 86. Homer' s *The Illiad* provides an excellent description of classical Greek warfare, especially the cult of the "heroic" warrior and the importance of individual glory and courage.

32. Gabriel, pp. 88, 100.

33. This oath was inscribed on a stele, found in the Attridene of Acharnae. Garlan, p. 175.

34. Garlan, p., 173

35. J. F. Lazenby, *The Spartan Army* (Warminister, UK: Aris & Phillips Ltd., 1985), p. 44.

36. John Frederick Charles Fuller, *The Generalship of Alexander the Great* (New Brunswick, NJ: Rutgers University Press, 1960), pp. 49, 302. N. G. L. Hammond, *Alexander the Great King Commander and Statesman* (London: Chatto & Windus, 1981), pp. 15–18, 24–25. For classical histories of Alexander's campaigns and the Macedonian way of war, see Arrian, *The Campaigns of Alexander* (Hammondsworth, UK: Penguin Books Ltd, 1971) and Quintas Curtius Rufus, *The History of Alexander* (London: Penguin Books Ltd, 1984).

37. Roy W. Davies, *Service in the Roman Army* (Edinburgh, UK: Edinburgh University Press 1989), pp. 3–18. G. R. Watson, *The Roman Soldier* (Ithaca, NY: Cornell University Press, 1985), pp. 31–44.

38. Garlan, pp. 178–79. In the fourth century AD, Vegetius wrote, "[The Roman soldiers] swear by God, by Christ, and by the Holy Spirit; and by the Majesty of the Emperor, which, after God, should be the chief object of the love and veneration of mankind… . The soldiers, therefore, swear they will obey the Emperor willingly and implicitly in all his commands, that they will never desert and will always be ready to sacrifice their lives for the Roman Empire." Flavius Vegetius Renatus, *The Military Institutions of the Romans* (Westport CT: Greenwood Press, 1985) p. 40. We can assume that the sacrementum in its original form was similar in words, minus the references to Christ and the Holy Spirit, and referencing instead the gods of Rome. The form of government or person to which the oath was sworn would also change, depending on

the time period. Watson (p. 49) reports variations in wording, referenced in the works of Dionysis of Halicarnassus, Servius, and Isadore of Seville and written at different times during Rome's history. The sacrementum was the military oath. The iusiurundum signified the religious and legal obligations imposed by the military oath. J. B. Campbell, *The Emperor and the Roman Army 31 BC–AD 235* (Oxford, UK: Calendon Press, 1984), p. 19.

39. Watson, pp. 44–49. Polybius, *The Rise of the Roman Empire* (Harmondsworth, UK: Penguin Books, Ltd, 1979), p. 319.

40. Davies, p. 14. Vegetius, pp. 17–18. Watson, p. 50–51.

41. Campbell, pp. 19–20.

42. Livy, *The Early History of Rome* (Harmondsworth, UK: Penguin Books, Inc., 1960), pp. 140–41.

43. H. M. D. Parker, *The Roman Legions* (Cambridge, UK: W. Heffer & Sons Ltd., 1971), pp. 24–26, 54–70. Campbell, pp. 20–21, 31–32.

44. Campbell, pp. 25–32, 70–101, 165–203. See also Tacitus, "The Annals," pp. 125, and "The Histories," p. 190, 204, and 285 in *Tacitus* (Chicago, IL: Encyclopedia Britannica, Inc., 1952), and Plutarch, *The Lives of the Noble Grecians and Romans* (Chicago, IL: Encyclopedia Britannica, Inc., 1953) pp. 859–66 for examples from contemporary historians.

45. During the history of the western Roman Empire, the Praetorian Guard helped enthrone ten emperors and dethroned 12. Robert F. Evans, *Soldiers of Rome—Praetorians and Legionaires* (Cabin John, MD: Seven Locks Press, 1986), p. 132.

46. F. L. Ganshof, *Feudalism* (New York: Harper Torchbooks, 1964), pp. 5–9, 26–28, 87–88, 94–95. Ganshof (p. 30) also had this Carolingian oath of fealty used in AD 802 as the model for the oath of fealty Charlemagne imposed upon all his subjects: "By this oath I promise to be faithful to the lord Charles, the most pious emperor, son of King Pepin and Bertha, as a vassal should rightfully be to his lord, for the preservation of his kingdom and of his rights. And I will keep and hope to keep this oath which I have sworn as I know it and understand it, from this day henceforward, with the help of God, the creator of heaven and earth, and of these sacred relics." Ganshof described (p. 71) the act of homage and the oath of fealty of the vassals of the murdered Count of Flanders to the new count William Clito in 1127, from the record of Galbert of Bruges. Other views of these acts can be found in Geoffrey de Villehardouin, "The Conquest of Constantinople," in Jean de Joinville and Geoffrey de Villehardouin, *Chronicles of the Crusades* (Harmondsworth, UK: Penguin Books, Ltd, 1963), p. 97; Jean Froissart, *Chronicles* (Harmondsworth, UK: Penguin Books, Ltd, 1968), p. 55; and *The Song of Roland* (Baltimore, MD: Penguin Books, 1963), pp. 59, 78.

47. John Beeler, *Warfare in Feudal Europe 730–1200* (Ithaca, NY: Cornell University Press, 1972), pp. 2–15. Ganshof, pp. 15–19.

48. The commitatus was a group of Germanic warriors who freely gave their personal service to a war chief and fought with him and on his behalf. They sealed their dependence on the war chief with a ceremonial oath of allegiance. Ganshof, p. 4. Beeler, p. 2.

49. Beeler, pp. 9–18, 36–37. H. W. Koch, *Medieval Warfare* (Greenwich, CT: Bison Books Corp., 1985), pp. 38–40, 69–70.

50. The word *dub*, from Middle English, has four meanings: (1) to create a knight; (2) to give the accolade with the sword; (3) to give the accolade with hand or fist; and (4) to invest with the sword. Note 6, Robert W. Ackerman, "The Knightly Ceremonies in the Middle English Romance," *Speculum*, XIX (July 1944), p. 286. Koch, p. 66.

51. Ackerman, pp. 285–89. A. V. B. Norman, *The Medieval Soldier* (New York: Thomas Y. Crowell Company, 1971), pp. 150–51.

52. John Barnie, *War in Medieval—Society Social Values and the Hundred Years War 1337–99* (London: Weidenfeld and Nicolson, 1974), pp. 58, 70–72, 81–82. Norman, pp. 1, 14, 20, 27, 143–45. Ackerman, p. 290. For examples, see Froissart, pp. 63, 90, 109–10, 144; *The Song of Roland*, pp. 80, 92–95; Villehardouin, pp. 55–56, 69, and 121; and Jean de Joinville, p. 224, in *Chronicles of the Crusades*.

53. "Scutage" was the term used to designate the conversion of service obligations to money payments. Beeler, p. 41.

54. On the Italian peninsula, where warfare involving mercenaries became the norm during the Renaissance, mercenaries were called "condottiere" from the "condotta," or contract between the entrepreneur and the government that employed them. Geoffrey Trease, *The Condottieri—Soldiers of Fortune* (London: Thames and London, 1970), p 17. See also E. R. Chamberlain, "The 'English' Mercenary Captains," *History*, VI (May 1956), pp. 334–43; and J. R. Hale, *War and Society in Renaissance Europe 1450–1620* (Leicester, UK: Leicester University Press, 1985), 69–71, 148–49.

55. Niccolo Machiavelli, *The Art of War* (Indianapolis, IN: The Bobbs-Merrill Company, Inc., 1965), p. 16, and *The Prince and Selected Discourses* (New York: Bantam Books, 1966), pp. 46–50. About the virtues of mercenaries vs. one's own army, he concluded "that no state, unless it have its own arms, is secure. Indeed, it is a hostage to fortune, having no trustworthy power to defend it in adversity.... By one's own forces I mean those composed of subjects, citizens, or dependents." *The Prince*, p. 53.

56. Trease, pp. 55–154.

57. Koch, pp. 192–97. Hale, pp. 150–51.

58. Frederick William, the head of the Hohenzollern family, ascended to the throne of Brandenburg in 1640, a small duchy in central Europe with a few other smaller states, scattered across the region. As the heir to the Brandenburg throne, he was one of the ten electors who "elected" a new Holy Roman Emperor upon the death of the current incumbent. Following the battle of Fehrbellin in 1674 against the Swedish army, Frederick William became known as the Great Elector.

59. Robert Ergang, *The Potsdam Führer Frederick William I, Father of Prussian Militarism* (New York: Columbia University Press, 1941), p. 65. Craig, pp. 3–6.

60. Craig, p. 7. In January 1701, the Holy Roman Emperor allowed Frederick, without any protests from the other powers, to become Frederick I, King *in* Prussia, recognizing his sovereignty over his non-imperial possessions and his continued subservience to the emperor on imperial matters.

61. Craig, p. 8.

62. The canton system divided Prussia into a series of recruiting districts, to provide conscripts for the army to fill the gap between the number of men required and the number of men volunteering for duty. Ergang, pp. 75–76. Frederick William I's quote is found on p. 77. The officers and men took separate oaths of loyalty to their king. The enlisted men would recite their oath on the annual publication of the Articles of War. William O. Shanahan, *Prussian Military Reforms 1786–1813* (New York: Columbia University Press, 1945), p. 25, 138. The Swiss poet Ulrich Braeker recounts in his memoirs *Der arme Mann im Tockenburg* (1852) his induction ceremony during Frederick the Great's reign. From Christopher Duffy, *The Army of Frederick the Great* (New York: Hippocrene Books, Inc., 1974), p. 57.

63. Duffy, *Army of Frederick*, p. 24. Craig, pp. 9–11.

64. Görlitz, p. 4.

65. Quoted in Görlitz, p. 68.

66. From Frederick II, *The History of Our Times*, in Jay Luvaas, ed., *Frederick the Great The Art of War* (New York: The Free Press, 1966), p. 89, 91–92. By 1786, only ten percent of 7,000 officers were from the middle class. Of these, there were only 22 bourgeois officers out of 712 in the rank of major and above. Christopher Duffy, *Army of Frederick*, p. 27. See also Craig, pp. 16–17, 23, 25.

67. Duffy, *Army of Frederick*, pp. 21–22, 161–63. Herbert Rosinski, *The German Army* (New York: Frederick A. Praeger, Inc., 1966), pp. 36–37.

68. Rosinski, p. 39.

69. Quoted in Luvaas, p. 77.

70. Marwitz was forced into retirement, never to return to Frederick's favor. His tomb was inscribed: "He witnessed Fredrick's heroic age and fought with him in all his wars, chose disgrace where obedience brought disfavor." Saldern told his king, "Your Majesty may send me to attack the enemy batteries, and I will readily obey. But to act contrary to my honour, oath, and duty is something my will and conscience do not permit me to do." More fortunate than Marwitz, Saldern resumed a successful military career after a long period in disfavor. Christopher Duffy, *Frederick the Great—A Military Life* (London: Routledge, 1988), pp. 110, 334. Peter Paret, *Yorck and the Era of Prussian Reform 1807–1815* (Princeton, NJ: Princeton University Press, 1966), p. 33.

71. According to the treaty's terms, Prussia ceded to France its territories west of the Elbe River, the portion of the Polish provinces acquired in 1793, and part of west Prussia, and had to pay a large indemnity, unspecified at the time of signing, before French troops would evacuate Prussian territory east of the Elbe River. In time, the indemnity steadily increased from 73 million francs to 154 million francs, then to 200 million francs. Even then, Napoleon demanded an additional 140,000 francs with no sign of French troops leaving Prussian territory. Roger Parkinson, *The HussarGeneral—The Life of Blücher, Man of Waterloo* (London: Peter Davies, 1975), pp. 77–78, 80.

72. Quoted in Parkinson, p. 93.

73. Blücher wrote Frederick William, "I ask Your Majesty to hand me my discharge without pension even if I am poor and have to look for my daily bread in the service of strangers. I would leave the service with the greatest sorry...." Quoted in Parkinson, p. 87.

74. Gerhard Ritter, *The Sword and the Sceptor*, vol. I, *The Prussian Tradition 1740–1890* (Coral Gables, FL: University of Miami Press, 1964), pp. 167–71.

75. Demeter (p. 160) states that Stein was successful in changing the term Kriegsherr to "King and Fatherland," Shanahan (n. 40, p. 139) states that the term Landesherr did replace Kriegsherr in the oath but the word Vaterland was not included in the new oath. Ritter quotes Stein's comments on Gneisenau's draft of new articles of war: "The notion of a warlord is the counterpart of that of a mercenary. When war service is seen to flow from the citizen's relation to the state, the king appears as head of state rather than as warlord, and it is to the head of state and to his country that the soldier swears fealty... . I would omit the term warlord from the oath and replace it with king and country, etc." However, Ritter doesn't clarify whether or not Vaterland was included in the new oath. Ritter, vol. I, p. 166. Manfred Messerschimidt, "*Die preussische Armee*," in Militärgeschichtliches Forschungsamt, *Handbuch zur deutschen Militärgeschicte 1648–*

1939, vol. IV, *Militärgeschicte im 19. Jahrhunderts* (Munich: Bernard & Graefe Verlag, 1979), p. 141. This oath underwent only minor changes until 1918. See Appendix A for wording.

76. See Craig, pp. 59–62; Ritter, Vol. 1, pp. 94–108; Demeter, pp. 8–19; and Shanahan, pp. 193–212.

77. Rosinski, p. 73. Parkinson, pp. 93. Paret, pp. 191–92. Wheeler-Bennett, n. 3, p. 7. Yorck quoted in Parkinson, p. 99. Although a board of inquiry exonerated Yorck for his unilateral action, he continued to suffer minor adverse comments and injustices from the King who found it difficult to forgive Yorck's insult to his authority. Paret, p. 195.

78. Ritter, vol. I, p. 110.

79. Rudloff quoted in Ritter, p, 113.

80. Ritter, p. 111. An 1860 essay, "The Origins and Development of the Spirit of the Prussian Officer, Its Manifestations and Its Effects," written by Prince Frederick Charles presents a somewhat different point of view. In this essay, the prince stated that Prussian officers had a great deal of independence, especially in tactical operational matters. He used the resignations of the Prussian officers between 1807 and 1812 and Yorck's convention of Tauroggen as examples of how honor demanded disobedience and disloyalty. Appendix 1, Demeter, pp. 258–60.

81. Craig, pp., 106–7, 110–11, 118–21. Frederick William's quote is found on p. 118.

82. In March 1848, the officers of the Bavarian, Saxon, and Württemberger armies swore a new oath to the new constitutions of their respective states. The Bavarian officers favored this action. Most of the Saxon officers thought it was "a needless formality," and some die-hards resisted taking it. The new Württemberg oath was abolished in 1851. Demeter, pp. 160–61.

83. Craig, p. 123.

84. Ritter, vol. I., p. 177.

85. Rosinski, p. 242. Ritter, vol. I, pp. 173–75, 180–81. Craig, pp. 217–54.

86. Craig, pp. 123.

87. The constitution of the Second Reich combined the armies of all member states, except for those of Bavaria, Saxony and Württemberg, with the Prussian army. The Bavarian king retained command of his army during peacetime, and the other two states kept their own general staffs. The use of General Staff officers from the Prussian (now called Great) General Staff to the general staffs of each of these armies provided consistency in training and tactics and linkages for operational planning and deployments. The expanded Prussian army and the armies of Bavaria, Saxony, and Württemberg formed the Imperial Army. Article 64 of the constitution required all German troops to obey unconditionally the orders of the kaiser, an obligation to be incorporated into the military oath. The kaiser also had authority to appoint the commanding officers of all contingent armies and fortresses and to approve all other general officers. Document 83, the Constitution of the German Reich of April 16, 1871, in Johannes Hohlfeld, ed., *Dokumente der Deutschen Politik und Geschicte von 1848 bis zur Gegenwart*, vol. I, *Die Reichsgruendung und das Zeitalter Bismarcks 1848–1890* (Berlin: Dr. Herbert Wendler & Co. KG, 1952), p. 222–23.

88. With the creation of the German High Seas Fleet after 1890, the naval command structure mirrored the army's arrangement: each fleet commander and the chief of the Naval Cabinet all had direct access to Wilhelm II.

89. Quoted in Demeter, p. 25.

90. On the reserve officers, see "The Genesis of the Royal Prussian Reserve Officer," in Eckert Kehr, *Economic Interest, Militarism, and Foreign Policy—Essay on German History* (Berkeley, CA: University of California Press, 1977), pp. 97–108; Demeter; pp. 20–32; Craig, pp. 236–37; Ritter, vol. II, *The European Powers and the Wilhelmine Empire, 1890–1914* (Coral Gables, FL: University of Miami Press, 1970) pp. 93–104; and Martin Kitchen, *The German Officer Corps 1890–1914* (Oxford, UK: Clarendon Press, 1968), pp. 115–23. The naval officers, although they were mostly of middle-class origins, underwent a similar process of adopting the aristocratic tradition. See Holger H. Herwig, *The German Naval Officer Corps—A Social and Political History 1890–1918* (Oxford, UK: Clarendon Press, 1973).

91. Rosinski, p. 143.

92. See especially Ritter, *The Sword and the Scepter*, vol. III, *The Tragedy of Statesmanship—Bethmann Hollweg as War Chancellor* (1972) and vol. IV, *The Reign of German Militarism and the Disaster of 1918* (1973); and Martin Kitchen, *The Silent Dictatorship* (New York: Holmes & Meier Publishers, Inc., 1976). For the military's role in setting Germany's war aims in the West, see Hans Gatzke, *Germany's Drive to the West* (Baltimore, MD: The Johns Hopkins Press, 1950). On Germany's war aims in the East, see Wheeler-Bennett, *Brest-Litovsk: The Forgotten Peace, March 1918* (London: Macmillan, 1938).

93. Craig, p. 328.

94. Rosinski, pp. 139–40.

95. The bourgeois composition of the officer corps was even more pronounced in the company grade ranks. In 1913, they were only 27 percent noble and 73 percent bourgeois because the aristocratic officers had become concentrated in the higher ranks. There were also definitely higher concentrations of noble officers in certain "elite" infantry and cavalry regiments and of middle-class officers in artillery and engineer units. The General Staff experienced a similar embourgeoisement;

in 1906, it contained 60 percent noble officers and 40 percent middle-class officers, but, by 1913, it was essentially fifty-fifty. Rosinski (pp. 97–98) reports different figures for the officer corps as a whole — 65 percent/35 percent for nobles/middle class in 1860 and 30 percent/70 percent in 1913. However, the general trend remains the same. Demeter provides additional statistics (pp. 33–46) to show that the armies of Bavaria, Saxony, and Württemberg were significantly less influenced by the aristocratic tradition than the Prussian army.

96. Rosinski, pp. 146–48. Overwhelmingly, officer replacements came from the one-year volunteers, males of 17 or 18 years of age who spent a brief time at the front, were then hastily trained in officer candidate schools, and were finally commissioned as second lieutenants. They were disparagingly called "ninety day wonders" by the enlisted soldiers, and "civilian officers" by the regular officers. During the war a few NCOs were promoted to officer rank and commissioned as second lieutenants. They were viewed by the regular officers as social inferiors. The nonregular officers tended to ape the mannerisms and attitudes of the regular officers and would prove unwilling to give up their officer status after the war's end. Robert G. L. Waite, *Vanguard of Nazism—The Free Corps Movement in Postwar Germany 1918–1923*, (Cambridge, MA: Harvard University Press, 1952), pp. 45–47.

2

The Army and the Weimar Republic, 1918–1930

On November 11, 1918, World War I ended and, with it, the Hohenzollern monarchy when Kaiser Wilhelm II abdicated and fled to Holland two days earlier. Despite the resumption of unrestricted submarine warfare in April 1917, the military successes in Russia, Italy, and the Balkans, and the initial success of Ludendorff's March 1918 campaign, Germany could not sustain its military offensives. Additionally, the Allied blockade was causing severe economic hardships inside Germany. After the collapse of the German forces in France within a month of the Allies' September 1918 push, many German leaders realized that their nation could no longer continue the war. This defeat irrevocably swept away the foundations of the Prusso-German military system and broke the bonds, exemplified by the oath, between the soldier and his sovereign. This issue would consistently be demonstrated in the development of the military forces of the new republic and the internal military crises it would face.

In this chapter, I will focus only on those events that directly relate to the loyalty — and disloyalty — of the soldiers, particularly the officers, of the new German Army towards the new regime. We will see how they consistently failed to support the civilian leaders of the republic as they attempted to create a viable democracy in postwar Germany. Furthermore, although the soldiers had taken an oath of loyalty to the Weimar constitution, they never really came to terms with that government. Only a handful of soldiers made any attempt to accept the reality of Weimar Germany. In the end, the policy of General Hans von Seeckt, the most important military person of the Weimar era, to keep the army above politics prevented the officers from forming any ties to the budding democracy that would give them any reason to preserve it and from forming the ability to discern the threat of National Socialism to their own existence.

Defeat and Revolution

The Allied offensive of September 1918 marked the beginning of the end of the war. After the initial push over 40,000 German soldiers voluntarily surrendered, large numbers of soldiers deserted, and many on leave refused to return to the front.[1] By October, many German leaders had realized that Germany could not defeat the Allied armies in France, and Ludendorff, particularly shaken by these events, begged the new chancellor Prince Max von Baden to sue for peace. On October 26, Lieutenant General Wilhelm Groener replaced Ludendorff as First Quartermaster-General. Hindenburg, however, remained as War Minister until OHL ceased to operate as supreme headquarters in June 1919. While Matthias Erzberger, a member of the Catholic Center Party and the secretary of state, negotiated armistice terms with the Allies, German sailors at Kiel mutinied on November 4, and revolution spread like wildfire throughout the country. Groener now recommended, with Hindenberg's reluctant agreement, that the Kaiser abdicate.[2] After making his goodbyes, Wilhelm II stepped down and fled Germany for exile in Holland. On November 9, demonstrators in Berlin swept away the remains of the monarchy, and the Majority Socialists, led by Philip Schiedemann, established a republic. Two days later, representatives of the civilian government signed the armistice, ending the war. A number of officers, including Hindenburg for a short time, believed that the German Army should continue fighting for the sake of its honor. However, Groener recognized that to do so would be hopeless because such action would probably result in the extension of the fighting into Germany itself and the destruction of the officer corps.

This ignoble end to the empire would haunt the new republic throughout its existence and left a psychological void in the minds of many officers. For example, Heinz Guderian, future tank leader, wrote his wife, "Bismarck's work lies in ruins. Villains have torn everything down to the ground.... All comprehension of justice and order, duty and decency, seems to have been destroyed."[3] Then Major Ludwig Beck, at the end of November, wrote "I know of no revolution in history that was carried out in such a cowardly fashion, a revolution that—and this is actually much worse—has aggravated beyond any doubt the difficult situation in which we have been for a long time now leading perhaps to complete ruin." In a November 29, 1919, letter to his sister, he wrote of the recent events: "I had until then considered such an abyss of vileness, cowardice, and unscrupulousness impossible. In a few hours five hundred years of history have been destroyed." Hans Oster, another future anti–Hitler conspirator, was a convinced monarchist and conservative and was also shocked by the November Revolution.[4] However, both officers, as well as many others, would serve the new Weimar Republic through service to the German nation.

By the end of November, the German Army, numbering over six million men, no longer constituted a viable fighting force. The vast majority of those in the field army just wanted to return home, and most did so, either as individuals or in their units by the end of the year. Once reaching the German frontier, they simply melted away without waiting for official demobilization orders. The soldiers of the home army, heavily infected with leftist propaganda, were in worse condition as, even before the armistice, many of them had joined revolutionary groups, led by Soviet-style soldiers' and sailors' councils. These councils advocated the dismissal of Hindenburg, the dissolution of the cadet schools, the transfer of supreme command of the armed forces to the Control Committee of the Councils, the elimination of rank insignia, the election of officers by the troops, the transfer of control over conduct and discipline to the soldiers' councils, and the replacement of the regular army by a civil guard.[5] Ebert opposed the resolution but ultimately lost to a substantial majority of Independent Socialists and Spartacists.[6] Most of the army leaders also opposed the curtailment of their authority over their troops by the soldiers' and sailors' councils. However, Gustav Noske, the new Reichswehrminister (Minster of Defense), and General Walter Reinhardt, the new Chef der Heeresleitung (Chief of the Army Command), supported the resolution. Hindenburg also opposed the resolution, vowed never to give up his epaulettes or sword, and called upon the government to "'carry out its promise to preserve the Army.'"[7] Groener and Hindenburg now proposed the creation of "Vertrauensleute" (trusted men), elected by the men in each unit to hear complaints on nonmilitary matters. This proposal was intended to lessen the resolution's impact and allow the military authorities to retain firm control of the troops.[8]

Groener also recognized that the spreading leftist demonstrations posed a threat to the continued existence of the officer corps and the Reich. On the evening of November 9, Groener made his famous telephone call to President Friedrich Ebert through the secret line to the Chancellery, now surrounded by demonstrators. Groener guaranteed that the officer corps would support Ebert's government of Majority Socialists if the government would maintain order and discipline in the army and fight Bolshevism. Ebert agreed to these terms as there was no other military force that could control the increasing revolutionary activity. Most officers grudgingly agreed to support the new government — despite their personal monarchism and dislike for Socialists (unlike Groener they did not or could not distinguish the differences among the various Socialist factions) and the indignities imposed upon them by the soldiers' and sailors' councils — in order to reestablish order and save Germany from complete anarchy. This momentous decision gave the military a secure and dominant position in the Weimar Republic from its very beginning.

The "hero's welcome" that many of the soldiers received upon their return to Germany further increased their stature and added to the *Dolchstoss* ("stab-in-the-back") myth.[9] The preface to the Prussian War Ministry's instructions on preparing for the soldiers' welcome home read in part: "Our field-grey heroes return to the Heimat [homeland] undefeated, after having protected the native soil from the horrors of war for four years." The government and OHL praised the soldiers who had "stood their ground undefeated up to the last minute."[10] On December 11, 1918, some of the returning units proudly marched through Berlin where Ebert addressed them: "I salute you who return unvanquished from the field of battle."[11] Such incidents contributed to the inability of the many soldiers to accept the fact that the army had been defeated on the battlefield and led them to project the cause of the defeat onto the civilian leaders. As a result, the fledgling democracy would carry a damaging political legacy during the postwar years.

Meanwhile, antigovernment forces from both the left and the right were increasing the level of unrest in the capital. Again, Ebert, on December 6, 1918, asked OHL for help to deal with the increasing violence in Berlin. Two days later, Hindenburg reaffirmed to Ebert the army's and his personal support for the present government "without reservation."[12] Army units under General Arnold Lequis entered the capital on December 12, despite opposition from the Socialists. Five days later, the few remaining loyal soldiers pledged to serve the new government until the National Assembly could ratify a new constitution.[13] Mutinous sailors of the People's Marine Division besieged Ebert and his cabinet in the Chancellery on December 23, but, on Christmas Eve, withdrew to the stables of the former royal palace. When Lequis's troops failed to dislodge the leftists from their quarters, most of them deserted, leaving the government with only about 150 loyal troops in Berlin, not including officers.

With almost no loyal and reliable men, the government adopted Major Kurt von Schleicher's suggestion to organize the "Freikorps," volunteer corps from officers and men of the former Imperial Army. In short time, a multitude of units, composed of displaced and dissatisfied former soldiers and a large number of university students, sprang up all over Germany. Each Freikorps, although varying in size, normally had its own infantry, artillery, and cavalry sections, and was usually organized and led by a company grade officer; in many cases, a former Frontsoldat. So many men of all ranks flocked to the Freikorps recruiting stations that even former generals would serve under former captains and NCOs. One of the more famous Freikorps leaders, Lieutenant Gerhard Rossbach, described these footless groups of men, reminiscent of the Renaissance Landsknechte,

> as the beautiful old freebooter class of war and postwar time ... organizing masses then losing them just as quickly; tossed this way and that way just for the sake of our daily bread; gathering men about us and playing soldiers with them; brawling and drinking, roaring and smashing windows—destroying and shattering what needs to be destroyed. Ruthless and inexorably hard. The abscess of the sick body of the nation must be cut open and squeezed until clear red blood flows. And the blood must be left to flow for a good long time till the body is purified.[14]

The nature of the loyalty between the leaders and their men was personal, like that of the Renaissance Landsknechte. Therefore, most Freikorps units were generally extremely ill-disciplined and resistant to any centralizing authority.

Most of the Freikorps rose, flourished, and disappeared between November 1918 and March 1920. They first struck at the leftists in Bremen and then put down the Spartacist revolt in Berlin in January 1919. By the end of April, Freikorps units, led by Colonel Franz Ritter von Epp, had ended the brief reign of the Red Guards in Munich. Everywhere, they bloodily eliminated the leftist forces in battles in which both sides committed atrocities, including the murders of the Spartacist leaders, Rosa Luxemburg and Karl Liebknecht, in Berlin in January 1919. By June, the Freikorps, now numbering some 400,000, had ended the temporary leftist governments in Germany.[15] Other Freikorps units, the "Baltikumer," commanded by Major General Count Walther von der Goltz, went to the Baltic states with the partial sanction of the Allies, halted the advancing Red Army, and captured Riga in May 1919.

The Latvian government now began to pressure the Allies to force the German Freikorps to withdraw from their territories as some of the Freikorps leaders were dabbling in local politics with the leaders of the Baltic German minority. Instead, the Baltikumer revolted against their Latvian superiors and defied Berlin's orders to return to Germany; even their commander sided with the rebels. Feeling rejected by the republic, they joined the White Russians to fight the Red Army but eventually returned to Germany after a series of defeats. Several senior army officers resented the government for giving into the Allies. General von der Goltz later wrote General Hans von Seeckt, newly selected Chef des Truppenamt (Chief of the Troop Office):

> I cannot accept the point of view that one has to carry out the orders of a government which one serves without condition and without will.... You have the duty to stick to your opposite point of view to the last consequence.... If I may make a personal point, I request you to remember that the whole officer corps puts its hopes in your politically clear-sighted and independent thoughts and action, ... On this too depends whether the Reichswehr remains, as it has always been, a national and independent instrument under its leaders, standing above party, for the

> entire fatherland, or whether it deteriorates to the position of a soulless mercenary force in the hands of changing governments, in which no honourable man will be willing to serve. Believe me, innumerable officers think as I do.[16]

The Baltic Freikorps were dissolved, and some of their members joined existing units.

To give the Freikorps a legal foundation, the government promulgated the Law of the Provisional Reichswehr on March 6, 1919. The law authorized the president to dissolve the Imperial Army and create a provisional army, based on the Freikorps, in its place. It provided for voluntary enlistments of six or more years, the promotion of enlisted men to officer rank, election of a soldiers' council by each unit that replaced the "Vertrauensraete," the creation of special military schools, and the soldier's right to vote. The implementing decree of the same day invested the president with the office of the supreme commander of the armed forces, authority which Ebert delegated to the defense minister. The defense minister had full authority over senior officers, except for generals who were selected, promoted, and, if need be, dismissed by the president. Commanding generals retained authority over all their officers below the grade of generals, including the right to recruit new soldiers and select company grade officers.[17]

The most difficult task was how to reduce the 400,000 men in the many Freikorps down to a more manageable 200,000, organized into 20 brigades and distributed among seven "Wehrkreise," or military districts. To accomplish this formidable task, Seeckt dissolved those units which had a poor combat record or were insubordinate. He also joined two or three units to form a provisional unit and discharged the excess men. As a result, the new Provisional Reichswehr came to be composed of the Imperial Army units which had kept together during the revolutionary period, those Freikorps which had shown a reasonable ability to accept discipline and a willingness to support the republic, and individuals, such as former General Staff officers, who had a recognized ability or had belonged to a specialized arm or service.[18] Some Freikorps units refused to enter the provisional army or to dissolve themselves, and the government was powerless to force them to do so.

All of the men who became part of the new army had to take an oath to the republic.[19] Those who refused were dismissed. Of those who agreed to serve in the new army, most held little enthusiasm for the republic, despite their oath. The feeling of Captain Ernst Röhm, destined to lead Hitler's SA (Stürmabteilungen, or Stormtroopers), was typical of many: "The oath to the constitution, that is to a *thing*, is something unnatural. An oath is something that can be given only from one man to another — not to an impersonal *thing*."[20] The officers generally still held to their monarchical loyalties and conservative social norms. Furthermore, since the Provisional Reichswehr law allowed regimental commanders to retain the right to select new junior officers, they usually selected officer cadets with the "right" background and political views. Over the life of the republic, this provision effectively kept out those with more democratic views. Furthermore, the first group of the rank-and-file soldiers, the former members of the Freikorps, resented the republic they served and were contemptuous of its leaders.[21] Both groups would be centers of discontent towards the republic during its lifetime.

As the republican government put down the leftist revolution and struggled to form a new army from the Freikorps, delegates of the victorious Allies — but notably no Germans — had been meeting at Versailles to write the peace treaty with Germany. When they were done, they told the German government to send its delegates to Versailles. The German delegates — none from the army—expected to participate in the negotiations and were shocked when the Allies presented them with the treaty on May 7 for signature. They were even more shocked when they read the provisions of the treaty, especially the clause on the extradition of war criminals, the military clauses, the reparations clause with the final amount still not fixed, and the war guilt clause.[22] The first delegation refused to sign and returned to Germany. The Allies gave the German government one week to discuss the treaty and then sign it or face a resumption of hostilities.[23]

The reaction among the officer corps was especially severe.[24] Shocked and outraged, some advocated a war against Poland while others favored a last-ditch offensive against the Allies for honor's sake. Still others, like General Märcker, most of his officers, and the commander of Infantry Regiment 39, stated that they could no longer serve a government that willingly accepted sole guilt for the war and which had agreed to surrender their former leaders to the enemy. Later, the general and Noske's chief of staff, Major Erich von Gilsa, appealed to the minister to defend the German state and the nation's honor. Furthermore, if he would declare a military dictatorship, they would guarantee that the army and the officer corps would stand behind him.[25] In late June, to express his anger, General Otto von Below, the commander of XVII Army Corps, attempted a putsch with his Freikorps units but failed. Both Hindenburg and Groener realized that Germany had no forces to resist an Allied attack, but again Hindenburg left Groener with the task of so informing the government.

On June 24, 1919, Hindenburg told Groener "You know as well as I do that armed resistance is impossible." After a moment Groener slowly said, "You realize all that this decision means?" Hindenburg temporarily left Groener alone; Groener now telephoned Ebert over the secret line and told the president that resistance was impossible. Hindenburg then returned to the room and said to Groener, "The burden which you have undertaken is a terrible one." This action further increased the officer corps' dislike of Groener.[26] For the second time in less then a year, Groener had acted courageously and realistically to deal with a major crisis. At the same time, Hindenburg had again avoided responsibility for an adverse but necessary action and the taint that would go with it, a characteristic of much of Hindenburg's decision making later during his term as president of the Weimar republic. Recognizing that he had lost the confidence and popularity of the officer corps, Groener now resigned as First Quartermaster-General.

After the civilian government reluctantly signed the Versailles Treaty, relations between it and the newly forming army worsened. Added to the continuing existence of some Freikorps units, the discontent among the officers from the government's signing of the peace treaty, and the general contempt of the rank-and-file for the republic, was the increasing fear among the soldiers of dismissal from the army as the government pared it down to the treaty limits. Seeckt was in the enviable position of selecting one out of four active duty officers for his new army. He also could pick and choose the best NCOs, using highly stringent criteria in the selection process.[27] The soldiers were also concerned about the low level of material comfort (pay, clothing, and housing) and the lack of promotion opportunity. Finally, the soldiers resented the failure of the government to curtail the verbal attacks upon the army by the leftist parties and delegates of the Reichstag.[28] These events, all occurring at about the same time, created a situation like a cauldron, waiting to boil over.

Symptomatic of the wide gap between the government and its "defenders" was the serious, almost violent, reaction of the soldiers to the change in the national colors. The new constitution changed the colors from the imperial black, white, and red to the republican black, gold, and red of the revolutionaries of 1848.[29] The commander of Regiment 29 declared he and his men would only take the oath if they were allowed to continue wearing the imperial cockades. Colonel Wilhelm Reinhard, commander of Infantry Brigade 15, wrote that he would never wear the new colors. Both Major-General Arnold Ritter von Moehl, commander of the Bavarian regiment, and Colonel Ritter von Epp, now the commander of Bavarian Infantry Brigade 21, reported that their troops disliked the new colors and wanted the imperial colors retained.[30] Social Democratic deputy Quarck later complained on November 16, 1919, and again in February 1920, that an army unit at Frankfurt still wore the old insignia. Noske offered only excuses as to why the soldiers were still wearing the imperial colors, rather than forcing the soldiers to change to the new colors.[31] Additionally, many army barracks displayed the imperial flag and pictures of the former Kaiser.[32] As late as 1927, the defense minister still had to remind the officers and men of the colors which they must wear and show.[33]

By the beginning of 1920, the relationships among the civilian leadership of the government, the army leadership, many of the troops, and the remaining Freikorps had become increasingly more tense. The senior army leaders had decided to disband the remaining Freikorps and end their irregular activities. The ill-disciplined Freikorps, resistant to the centralizing authority of the army, had served their purpose, and both General Walther Reinhardt and Seeckt now saw them as a danger to the republic. In a 1927 article, the latter wrote that he had realized

> it was impossible to take [the Freikorps] over into the Reichswehr wholesale and in formations, under their leaders.... In the new Reichswehr there had to be a very strict discipline, not resting on the individual alone; the free corps were partly not willing and partly not capable, of submitting unconditionally to such discipline.[34]

Some of their leaders, including Captain Waldeman Papst, had created a rightist political organization, the Nationale Vereinigung, to plan the overthrow the government.[35] From within the army, former Freikorps leaders, such as Colonel von Epp and his chief of staff Röhm, illegally recruited men for and channeled army funds and equipment into antirepublican military and paramilitary formations, despite their oath to defend the republic.[36] This growing antagonism would come to a head by March 1920.

The Kapp Putsch

General Walther Freiherr von Lüttwitz, the commander of Group Command I, headquartered in Berlin, and Dr. Wolfgang Kapp, a high official of the East Prussian administration, provided the leadership for the growing antigovernment forces. General Lüttwitz had initially rejected plans for a *coup d'état* when he was approached by high-level political figures before June 1919. However, after the signing of the Versailles Treaty, he became the spokesman of the antigovernment soldiers, and at two conferences on June 24 he advocated to Noske the establishment of a military dictatorship. On both occasions Noske told the general it was not the business of the soldiers to dictate policy to the government. During the summer and into the fall, Lüttwitz grew closer to the Kappists and began contacting other military figures for their support for a coup.[37] Seeckt learned of these treasonable activities and warned the General Staff officers "against the acceptance of such overtures not merely in the interest of the Officer

Corps itself, but, far more, in that of the Fatherland."[38] (Notice he did not counsel them to reject these overtures because of their duty to the republic!) Seeckt also informed Noske and Reinhardt of his suspicions about Lüttwitz's antigovernment activities. Rather than dismiss the treasonous general, Reinhardt hoped to persuade him against a putsch.[39]

The antigovernment sentiment coalesced in late February 1920 when the government ordered the dissolution of the 5,000-man Ehrhardt Brigade, a primary base of Lüttwitz support, as part of the treaty reductions. Lüttwitz promised the members of the brigade he would not accede to the government's demand, but several officers attempted to dissuade their commander from such action. Two officers, General von Oldershausen and Major Kurt Freiherr von Hammerstein-Equord, refused to take part in a mutiny even if they were ordered to do so. On March 10, Lüttwitz demanded that the government agree to his demands, which included maintaining the army at it present level and replacing Reinhardt with General Ernst von Wrisberg. Ebert and Noske rejected his demands and told Lüttwitz that no general had a right to present such demands to the government. When the general failed to resign as they had expected, Noske took action to relieve him of his command, place him on leave, and force him to resign. To encourage Lüttwitz to resign, Noske offered to promote him to generaloberst upon discharge. The general and his cohorts, instead, finalized plans for a putsch.[40]

On March 12, 1920, the Ehrhardt Brigade marched on Berlin and occupied the government buildings without any opposition from the army or the police. Lüttwitz met the mutineers and gave Ehrhardt control of the police. The government only had about 3,000 soldiers in Berlin, mostly of Reichswehr Regiment 29, which had formerly been the Reinhardt Freikorps, and many soldiers were still disgruntled over the dismissal of their former commander. Noske called a council of war with Generals Reinhardt, Seeckt, and others and demanded that the officers lead the Berlin garrison out to stop the mutineers. Only Reinhardt and Gilsa favored such action. Gravely concerned that this would lead to the total breakdown of discipline and camaraderie among the soldiers, Seeckt, speaking for the others, stated, "Troops do not fire upon troops!" Seeckt returned to his home for the next four days to wait out events since his refusal to carry out the legal orders of his civilian superiors constituted disobedience and insubordination.[41] Critical of the officer corps for their lack of support, Noske and the cabinet left Berlin for Dresden, leaving only a few civilians to represent the government. Noske bitterly told them, "My faith in the Officer Corps is shattered. You have all deserted me. There is nothing left but suicide."[42]

Army commanders throughout the country flooded the Reichswehr Ministry with telephone calls, wondering which of the two governments to follow.[43] Seeckt called for the officer corps to "help and collaborate" with the government in this "critical hour," to exhibit its "old spirit of silent self-effacing devotion in the service of the army...."[44] Colonel von Thaysen, the commander of Regiment 6, guarding the government quarter, prepared to carry out his duty. Colonel Hans von Feldman, the chief of the Equipment Office, reminded his officers of their duty to the government as a result of their sworn oath to protect it. Failure to do so "... will deprive [the officer corps] of the last remnant of respect in which it is held by the people." General Hans von Hahnke, the commander of Regiment 104, also realized the dilemma that the mutiny had placed the officer corps in because of its sworn duty to the constitution and the republic.[45] In general, army commanders and their units in the west and south remained loyal to the republic, and most officers at the Reichswehr Ministry remained at their posts, carrying out their routine duties and ignoring the orders of the Kappists. Fortunately, only a few garrisons, such as the one at Potsdam, showed any enthusiasm for the Kappists; most wavered between the two sides, hoping for negotiations to end the crisis.

For three days, Kapp and Lüttwitz tried to consolidate control, but quickly demonstrated their inability to govern even Berlin. Furthermore, a general strike, called by the government, and the lack of any significant support from the army at large doomed the putsch. By March 16, Kapp had lost his nerve, and some of the troop commanders who had initially supported the coup deserted the rebel regime. Kapp handed his "government" over to Lüttwitz and fled to Sweden. The remaining troops now threatened to mutiny unless Lüttwitz resigned, and he reluctantly called an end to the putsch. Seeckt then returned to the Reichswehr Ministry to preside over the orderly withdrawal, disarmament, and disbandment of the Ehrhardt Brigade. When a friend later asked Seeckt why he remained true to the republic, the general — who had refused a lawful order to use the army against the mutineers — answered, "A general does not break his oath."[46] With the threat from the right temporarily over, the government was now faced with violent leftist uprisings throughout Germany, particularly in the Ruhr, spawned by the general strike it had called. As the army was recovering from the disarray and low morale of the Kapp Putsch, Seeckt ironically called upon the same rebellious, antirepublican Freikorps to put down the leftist violence.

Following the abortive coup, the Reichswehr underwent a major cleansing. On March 24, Noske was forced to resign by his own party, and Reinhardt followed suit the next day. He wrote in his letter of resignation:

> Starting from entirely different political attitudes, we were united in the convictions that a competently led armed force, divorced from party politics and high in morale but undeviatingly faithful to the Constitution, is a vital necessity for the German people, because without such a force neither can order be preserved at home, nor our sovereign rights be protected nor our borders defended.[47]

In their places, Ebert appointed Otto Gessler as Reichswehr Minister and Seeckt as Chief of the Army Command. Again ironically, one of the few military supporters of the republic during this crisis resigned after the attempted coup while the general who refused a legal order from his superiors became the republic's senior military personage.

To investigate the conduct of the soldiers themselves during the coup, Ebert appointed a special civilian commission. However, Seeckt, believing that the committee would undermine discipline, punish innocent officers, and interfere in the army's internal affairs, convinced Ebert to prohibit the civilian commission from dismissing any officer and took those actions himself. Ultimately Seeckt dismissed 12 generals (including Lüttwitz), four colonels, one lieutenant colonel, seven majors, and a number of company grade officers — a total of 172 officers — for either participating directly in the coup or disobeying his orders to stay aloof from the coup. Others were removed from their current positions and reassigned to lesser positions.[48] Seeckt wanted to make it clear that

> Political quarrels within the Reichswehr are incompatible with both the spirit of comradeship and with discipline and can only be harmful to military training. We do not ask the individual for his political creed, but we must assume that everyone who serves in the Reichswehr from now on will take this oath seriously.[49]

Ebert granted a general amnesty to the rest of the conspirators, mainly company grade officers and enlisted men who had only followed the orders of their superior officers. However, the Kapp Putsch had again demonstrated the relative weakness of the republic, its relative dependence on the army, and the contempt in which many officers held that government. They waited for the day when "a savior" would appear to end Germany's shame and weakness and restore its and the army's greatness.[50]

Organization and Development of the Reichswehr

At this point, I am going to backtrack a bit to describe the organization of the army of the Weimar Republic in greater detail. Earlier I mentioned the applicable provisions of the Weimar Constitution, the Law of the Provisional Reichswehr, and the military clauses of the Versailles Treaty as part of my discussion of the army's role in the republic's first two years. The constitution designated the president of the republic as the supreme commander of the armed forces with authority to appoint and dismiss all officers. In actuality, President Ebert delegated authority to appoint and dismiss field and company grade officers to the regimental commanders but retained this authority over general officers.[51] The separate armies of Prussia, Württemburg, Saxony, and Bavaria were dissolved. In deference to Bavarian particularism and against the wishes of both Groener and Seeckt, the Military Law of 1921 allowed the Bavarian state government to select a state commandant who also served as the commander of Reichswehr Regiment 7 (also called the Bavarian Reichswehr). The Reich president could veto the nominee but had no choice in his selection.[52] The Law of the Provisional Reichswehr created an army of two groups, consisting of seven infantry divisions and three cavalry divisions and divided them among seven military districts. This new army incorporated the remaining parts of the Imperial Army and the best of the Freikorps into the new army. It also created a Reichswehr Ministry, headed by a minister, and an army, headed by the chief of the Army Command, and a navy, headed by the chief of the Naval Command. The office of the chief of the Army Command had four major offices of which the Truppenamt, essentially the successor to the outlawed General Staff, was the most important. The Military Law of 1920 reconfirmed these provisions.

The military clauses of the Versailles Treaty, combined with the singular personality of the first chief of the Truppenamt, General Seeckt, made the Reichswehr a truly professional army. Recognizing that a 100,000-man army was not even sufficient for defense from an attack by any one of Germany's neighbors, he strove to develop the Reichswehr into a "Führerheer," or an army of leaders. Every member was required to serve long terms and was expected to study their profession as if it were a calling. Seeckt strove to foster a strong sense of dedication, similar to that of a religious order. Every man was prepared and trained to assume higher posts whenever Germany would be able to expand its army: field graders to assume general officer positions; company grade officers, field grade positions; senior NCOs, company grade officer positions; and lower ranking enlisted, NCO and senior NCO positions. Since the treaty had abolished the prewar military schools, the Reichswehr became one large military training organization. The army was allowed one officer training school for each service branch (infantry, cavalry, artillery, and engineers) to prepare officer candidates for commissioning. Officers received advanced training in special courses. NCO training occurred within the normal activities of the troop units. The effectiveness of the Führerheer would be well demonstrated by Germany's rapid rearmament and military expansion in the 1930s and its string of victories in the first years of World War II.

The army's initial cadres, as previously mentioned, came from those Imperial Army units which did not fall apart upon their return to Germany and the better disciplined Freikorps. In selecting his officer corps, Seeckt gave preference to former General Staff officers over the Frontsoldaten, who were favored by the Personnel Office and General Reinhardt. Seeckt's personnel policy made the officer corps essentially uniform mentally and politically. It also stifled the ability of the soldiers to move up, a situation made even worse by the treaty limitations. During the Weimar period, company grade officers averaged about 3,400, out of a total of 4,000–4,200. On the other hand, there were only about 45–50 general officers. The remaining 450–560 were field graders.

Promotion was almost exclusively by seniority although some officers were preferentially promoted. The army leadership planned to discharge a certain number of officers every year to make room for new "blood" and increase the extremely limited number of promotion opportunities, but there obviously were not sufficient promotions to satisfy the large numbers of lower grade officers. For example, in early 1928, Colonel Freiherr von dem Bussche Ippenburg, stated that recruiting was unnecessary since the ratio of applications and acceptance was 15 to 1, and, in 1929, there were 1,600 applicants vying for 196 vacancies, a ratio of over 8 to 1.[53] Hans von Luck reports that, in 1929, he "was one of the lucky few" selected from over a thousand applicants for about 150 officer positions.[54] Not only were positions scarce but time between promotions was long. F. W. Mellenthin, another future tank commander, stated that he waited four years from officer cadet to commissioning.[55] Hans Speidel, future chief of staff to Generalfeldmarschall Erwin Rommel, spent ten years as a second lieutenant, and Helmuth Stieff, a future anti–Hitler conspirator, served five years as a second lieutenant and seven as a first lieutenant until his promotion to captain in 1934.[56] This situation would contribute significantly to the spread of National Socialist views among the company grade officers after 1923.

Since regimental commanders selected new enlisted recruits and officer candidates, men who held republican or socialist political views were virtually excluded from becoming soldiers, even those few who desired to do so. Additionally, it became easier for commanders to identify and ultimately root out "those kind" of men if they did somehow enter the army. On May 30, 1920, the Undersecretary of State in the Reichswehr Ministry, Bernard Rausch, resigned because of this seemingly deliberate policy of dismissing soldiers with republican views, despite their loyalty to the constitution (or because of it), after the Kapp Putsch.[57] As a another example of the antirepublican attitude of most army offices, future army chief of staff Beck reflected to his wartime commander General Konrad Ernst von Gossler on the fifth anniversary of the armistice,

> Social Democracy has mismanaged everything; the democratic blessings are no longer effective. We need iron leadership that can reestablish authority, force people to work, and provide bread for the industrious. [If no one could be found to provide such leadership, Germany would] soon have famine and civil war everywhere, and France will have her ultimate success.[58]

The Social Democrats founded the Führerbund to implant "a republican and democratic spirit" in the German Army as a counter to its political conservatism. This organization was to consist of those officers and NCOs truly committed to the republic, but it failed as the large majority of the officers found its aims unacceptable.[59] The army continued to be conservative politically, despite efforts to create a central recruiting office that would remove this power from the local commanders and allow the government to recruit from all social classes, eventually liberalizing the army as a whole.[60]

At best, the officers of the Reichswehr were neutral towards the republic, serving in its army faithfully and generally obeying their oath but without any real liking for the form of government. The feeling of General Oskar Munzel was typical:

> We did not value the Republic very highly, [and] would have preferred a constitutional monarchy (like England's). We supported it, however, true to our pledged loyalty because it was chosen by the majority of the people and because the maintenance of the Fatherland traditionally was more important to us than any personal wishes.... [61]

General Friedrich von Lossberg wrote,

> The officers were convinced monarchists. In 1918 they were released from their oath by the Kaiser. In the Republic they continued to serve Germany, and swore their oath now to the Republic without relinquishing their conviction that monarchy was a preferable form of government for Germany.... [62]

In other words, the officers made the best of a bad situation, but they did not give their complete loyalty to the republic. Not only was the Kaiser, the officers' personal warlord, gone, perhaps forever, but the new oath had eliminated references to God, leaving little for the officers to anchor their loyalty to. The officer corps now turned its allegiance to the abstract concept of the German state and looked at Seeckt as their surrogate Kaiser.

To inculcate the traditional imperial values into the new army, Seeckt established the system of the "tradition companies." Each infantry company, cavalry troop, and artillery battery of the new Reichswehr represented a regiment or part of a regiment of the Imperial Army. The new unit received the standards, history, and customs of its designated regiment to keep alive its memories and foster esprit de corps. In this manner, the 21 infantry regiments of the Reichswehr carried on the proud traditions of the 217 infantry regiments of the old army.[63] Since the German officer gave his basic loyalty to the regiment into which he had been originally commissioned, no matter how many subsequent units he may have been assigned to, this procedure further bolstered the officers' loyalty to the conservative traditions of the Imperial Army, rather than creating a new loyalty to the republic.

The termination of the Kapp Putsch signaled the triumph of Seeckt as the most important figure in the development of the German army during the first half of the Weimar Republic. During its first years, Seeckt had already placed his stamp on the Provisional Reichswehr. He had recognized that the Freikorps were essential on several occasions to save Germany from leftist revolution but were generally too ill-disciplined for regular military service. Once they had served their—and his—purpose, they were either incorporated into the regular army or forced to disband to ensure that the army was the only authorized bearer of arms in the German state.[64] His predilections were also exemplified in his preference to retain former General Staff officers in the 100,000-man army, rather than the Frontsoldaten, to the dismay of thousands of men like Röhm, Rossbach, and Ehrhardt. As Chief of the Truppenamt (1919–20) and Chief of the Army Leadership (1920–26), Seeckt would be the republic's leading military figure, in his own eyes as well as those of his officers, heir to the Kaiser as the soldiers' object of obedience, and would indelibly stamp the Reichswehr with his own ideas.[65]

It is, therefore, crucial to understand Seeckt's ideas and beliefs about the relationship of the army to the state. A confirmed monarchist, he believed that "[i]t was monstrous for a higher authority" to come between the regimental commander and the selection of his subordinate officers. As a result, commanders were free to select new officers who held the same conservative views as their own. To Seeckt, the army was more than just a "state within a state"; it "should become the purest image of the state." In other words, "[t]he army serves the state and the state alone, for it *is* the state." To reconcile his personal distaste for parliamentary government with his Prussian sense of devotion to duty and confirmed monarchism, he conceptualized "Government," based on any principle—absolutist, constitutional, or parliamentary—as a separate entity from the "state," the German Reich. Governments were temporary institutions while the state was permanent, transcending all current forms of government.[66] In essence, the army would give its support and loyalty to the current government, in whatever form, of the German Reich and protect it as long as that government met the needs of the army. The army's permanent loyalty, however, was to the state, and the officers' duty was "unconditional obedience," a virtue that would make the army "the most powerful factor in the state."[67]

Key to Seeckt's concept of the relationship of the army to the state was his belief that the army must remain above party politics, a policy called "Überparteilichkeit." To him, the Reichswehr would suffer if it had to deal with political problems. Furthermore, he saw the radicals on both the left *and* the right as threats that would engulf Germany with civil war.[68] He had punished the officers involved in the Kapp Putsch because they had not remained "above politics." In March 1922, several officers and men were punished for their part in a forbidden meeting held by the former Lieutenant Rossbach near Berlin.[69] Later that summer, unrest—stemming from the mass dismissals the Provisional Reichswehr was making in order to reach the Versailles Treaty's limits—grew among the soldiers and led to a mutiny among the garrisons of Loetzen and Langwitz. Seeckt promptly had the mutiny suppressed and its ringleaders dismissed.

The government and Seeckt went to great lengths to prevent party politics from eroding the discipline of his soldiers. Until his resignation in 1926, he forbade military bands to play during elections. Soldiers could not take active parts in political activities, join political organizations, or attend celebrations where political speeches might be given. Soldiers also could not attend celebrations of certain Imperial Army regiments and had to obtain higher headquarters permission to attend veterans' celebrations. He banned violently political publications of both the radical left and the radical right from army installations and newspapers, and prohibited political parties from politicizing among the troops.[70] Most of the officers believed, like he did, that party politics must be kept out of the Reichswehr to maintain internal discipline and cohesion.[71] For example, Major A. D. Riecker complained about the radical rightist attitude of some of the officers of Wehrkreis I (East Prussia). He believed that this attitude would impede the work of the Wehrkreis Command. It was "irreconcilable" for officials and officers of the republic to hold office and yet call it the "Jewish Republic" and a "crappy state court of justice."[72]

Despite the official ban on political activities and a general dislike for party politics, many soldiers did establish and maintain contacts with political groups, all on the political right—even those that advocated the overthrow of the government. Along the eastern frontier, the army, with Seeckt's knowledge, gave paramilitary groups, many of whose men were former Freikorps members, arms to fight Polish insurgents. After the end of the fighting, these groups hid their weapons and became "Arbeitskommandos" (AK) (work groups), attached to the local military districts. Called the Black Reichswehr, these units would be a political "sore spot" between Seeckt and the Social Democrats in the Reichstag.[73] Many former soldiers had also joined various right-wing and "völkische" groups, including the National Socialist German Workers' Party (NSDAP), and maintained contacts with their active duty comrades.[74] However, only some officers, mostly of the 7 Reichswehr (Bavarian) Division, were outspokenly racist and ultraconservative. In this situation, the senior officers, Generals von Moehl and Otto Hermann von Lossow, not only failed to discipline them but also protected them from dismissal.[75] Contacts between Wehrkreise commanders and members of these groups continued, despite Gessler's February 22, 1923, decree prohibiting such contacts.[76]

At the same time Seeckt as the senior military leader did not exempt himself from making his own "political" statements. His refusal to order the army to fire on the Ehrhardt Brigade as it advanced on Berlin was itself a political statement. Both as Chief of the Truppenamt and Chief of the Army Command, he essentially ran the army, despite his legal subordination to the civilians, President Ebert and Reichswehrministers Noske and Gessler, as if the army was his own personal province. Seeckt always managed to find convenient excuses to avoid being present with President Ebert at official functions and did his best to discourage Ebert from official visits to the troops and attendance at parades. Seeckt never appeared in the Reichstag (leaving the Reichswehrminister as the official representative of the armed forces to defend the activities of the Reichswehr before the hostile delegates) and never attended the official ceremonies on Constitution Day. He did his best to exclude the civilian authorities from interfering in the purely military affairs of the army, such as its secret activities in Soviet Russia, despite the obvious foreign policy implications of these activities.[77] Seeckt wanted to maintain the internal independence of the army and keep it from direct parliamentary control, goals reminiscent of pre–1918 German and Prussian leaders.

Seeckt, however, was sufficiently astute to recognize that he could not turn back the clock and accepted the present conditions, albeit as temporary ones. He recognized the constitutional position of the president as commander in chief, his obligation to obey the president as such, and the reality of the situation in postwar Germany.[78] In general, they worked well together because of Ebert's tendency to give Seeckt the freedom to act as his senior military advisor and commander. In return, Seeckt expected all members of the Reichswehr "to protect the fatherland" and be "willing to sacrifice his life, loyal to his oath and in the fulfillment of his duty."[79] Interestingly, Seeckt did not say "protection of the republic" and "loyalty to the constitution." His soldiers were expected to demonstrate the same self-effacing sacrifice and devotion to duty that exemplified pre–1918 Imperial General Staff officers: "Silent, self-less work, devotion to the whole, which always places the cause above the person — those are the virtues, which have made the General Staff what it was, is, and will remain...."[80] Seeckt's policy of accommodating the present regime significantly strengthened the Reichswehr's position within the Weimar Republic and enhanced the dependence of the civilian leadership on the army.[81]

Yet, neither Seeckt nor most of the officers viewed Ebert or the civilian Reichswehrministers as *military* personages per se and, therefore, as their *military* superiors. He had written that his oath did not extend to the person — Ebert — who held the position of president.[82] The officers looked upon the Reichswehrminister in much the same way as the imperial officer corps had viewed the Prussian war minister — their representative and defender in the Reichstag, not as the appointed director and trainer of the armed forces, since he was a civilian. As a result, it was necessary to place a general at the head of the army.[83] General Munzel wrote later, with some hindsight:

> Gessler and Noske were initially regarded with caution. Later they won [us] by their unobjectionable personalities. As the liaison between army and parliament they scarcely came into contact with us. For us, Seeckt was the man who would take care of us.[84]

Seeckt's answer to a question about the army's reliability in 1922 exemplifies this relationship: "I don't know whether it is reliable, but it obeys me." On another occasion, he told Ebert, "The Reichswehr stands behind me."[85] Seeing himself as the chief military assistant to the Reichswehrminister, Seeckt, however, worked closely with Noske since he, like the president, also gave Seeckt a great deal of latitude in purely military matters.

However, Seeckt did not get along well with General Reinhardt, the first Chief of the Army Command and Seeckt's nominal military superior before the Kapp Putsch. Reinhardt was willing to subordinate the army to its new civilian authorities and to accept some civilian interference in its affairs. He demonstrated a willingness to work with the new republic's political leaders, which made an excellent impression on them. His liberal views, lack of seniority to Seeckt (by date of rank), and his non–Prussian origins (he was, like Groener, a Württemburger), unfortunately, lessened his popularity among many officers and contributed to Seeckt's own personal dislike of his superior. Additionally, many officers considered Seeckt to be the more able officer. As a result, since his authority drew mainly from his personal relationship with Noske, Reinhardt felt compelled to resign, following Noske's resignation after the Kapp Putsch.[86]

Although Seeckt followed his own agenda in the development of the new army, he did have a genuine interest in improving the living conditions of his soldiers to minimize or eliminate those conditions that would further foster bad morale or ill discipline. He tried unsuccessfully to increase the officers' pay above the general wage increases of 1924 and 1926. As a result, most officers were forced to have private incomes to maintain themselves. The retiring soldier did receive a certificate which made him eligible for a position in the national, state, or municipal civil service. (It, however, did not guarantee him a position.) If he actually entered civil service, his military service, including twice his war service, was used to calculate his retirement pension. An officer after four years of service could receive a separation pay equal to that of an enlisted person after completion of his full term. If he separated for military reasons, he would receive a full pension for life. The money due him could be paid as a lump sum to invest or establish his own business. He could also receive service-connected disability compensation.[87]

The Hitler Putsch

As Seeckt worked to develop the Reichswehr into a professional military force, dissident forces of the radical right were gathering in Bavaria. Many discontented former Freikorps members and, after 1920, some of Kapp's followers, found homes in Bavaria, especially Munich. The Bavarian capital had become a center for radical rightists and their secret societies, plotting to undermine and, if possible, overthrow the republic. The rightist leaders found sympathy for their opposition to the republic among many members of Reichswehr 7 Division, headquartered in Munich. The Bavarians, who comprised most of its members, deplored the loss of their general staff and the predominance of Prussians in the senior army leadership. Against Seeckt's policy of Überparteilichkeit, the Bavarian Reichswehr maintained informal relations with local right-wing paramilitary groups and Freikorps. The military commander of Munich, General Ritter von Epp, the "liberator" of Munich in 1919, and his chief of staff Ernst Röhm, who had access to the army's arms and munitions depots in Bavaria, were both members of the NSDAP. Recognizing the particularism and political activism of the Bavarian officers, the army leadership, for its part, had attempted to bring them under greater central control by reassigning or discharging the more radical among them.

Then in late 1922, another crisis struck Germany. Because of the rapidly falling mark and resulting economic crisis, Germany defaulted on its reparation payments, and French and Belgian troops occupied the Ruhr industrial area in early 1923. The invasion and occupation of German territory produced a huge upsurge in patriotism and national passion, but both the government and Seeckt realized that the army could do nothing about the foreign occupation. The government called for passive resistance in the Ruhr, and a number of underground groups formed to carry out acts of sabotage against the invaders. Seeckt decided to create an illegal reserve army from post–Freikorps "labor associations," "sports societies," and other semilegal paramilitary groups and to begin preparations to enlist and train temporary volunteers. Although many of the former Freikorps members were unwilling to serve Seeckt unconditionally, those who were willing to serve him to some degree joined these reserve units, which were disguised as "labor troops," or Arbeitskommandos (AK). The members of this so-called Black Reichswehr, led by Lieutenant Colonel von Bock, were billeted in army barracks, wore uniforms, carried arms, trained as soldiers, and were expected to supplement the active-duty Reichswehr.[88]

The more radical rightists, fuming against the government, called for stronger measures against the invaders. The leader of the NSDAP, Adolf Hitler, ranted against the traitors in Berlin and the "November criminals." In late January 1923, he ordered five thousand stormtroopers into Munich, but the city mayor prohibited the Nazi parade. When Hitler ranted at the police president to permit the SA, the city official not only refused to do so but also prohibited Hitler's scheduled public speeches. Faced with a possible Nazi putsch, General von Lossow, the commander of the Bavarian Division, asked his officers for their opinions. Epp fumed at the government's treatment of the Nazis, and Röhm accused the ministers of treason and refused to fire on his "comrades." A number of captains and majors surprisingly disagreed with these sentiments, asking Röhm, "How can you combine your attitude with your oath to the flag?" Lossow dismissed his officers; for now, the army would not object to the government's actions.[89] Then, in the spring of 1923, Hitler demanded that the army issue rifles to the SA on the pretext of a leftist putsch on May Day, but Lossow refused. After the SA obtained rifles through a ruse, the army cordoned them off until they surrendered the weapons.[90] Apparently, Seeckt's policies were taking hold among many officers, even some Bavarians.

During the spring and into the summer of 1923, the economic crisis worsened. The government's passive resistance policy appeared to be harming the Germans more than the foreign occupiers. The value of the mark plummeted as the government printed more and more paper money.[91] Food was becoming increasingly scarce, and the general strike sparked increased violence by leftists in Thuringia and Saxony. Under these circumstances, Chancellor Wilhelm Cuno resigned on August 12, and Gustav

Stresemann, the leader of the Deutsche Volkspartei (German Peoples' Party), became the new chancellor and foreign minister.[92] Before and immediately after his appointment, Stresemann tried to assuage any fears of the military about him as chancellor through several meetings with Seeckt and even by his agreement to continue the army's secret activities in Russia. However, the officer corps still believed that Stresemann's policies would weaken German will to resist the French and Poles and he would try to curtail the army's rearmament projects. Furthermore, some officers believed the new chancellor would replace Seeckt as their military leader and hoped Seeckt would himself establish a military dictatorship. He would disappoint them by remaining loyal to the Reich.[93]

On September 25, 1923, the government ended its passive resistance policy, and the nationalists howled at the unpatriotic gesture of the government. Lieutenant Colonel Joachim Stülpnagel wrote that the end of passive resistance was a "new lost war" and that his fellow officers had to carry out two duties, the "protection of the constitution, of a diseased system, and preparation of the war of liberation, which is prevented by the system...."[94] On October 1, Major Ernst Buchrucker, a former officer expelled from the army for his part in the Kapp Putsch but now the leader of some Arbeitstruppen of Wehrkreis III, led two hundred of his men, many of whom were veterans of the Baltic and Upper Silesian Freikorps, to seize the government quarter in Berlin.[95] They occupied the fortress at Kuestrin while other dissident units occupied the citadel at Spandau. Military and police forces quickly ended the putsch, dispersed the rebels, and arrested the ringleaders. On October 25, Buchrucker was tried for high treason by a special court, sentenced to ten years of honorable imprisonment, and fined ten gold Reichsmarks. This incident justified to Seeckt his distrust of the radical right and the unreliability of the Black Reichswehr, and he used it as the reason to disband this unofficial army.[96]

The increasing leftist violence and dissatisfaction with the central government led the Bavarian state government on September 26, 1923, to call in Gustav Ritter von Kahr as General State Commissioner and give him broad dictatorial powers. After declaring a state of emergency, Kahr recruited radical rightists, including Ehrhardt, for an emergency police force and received the support of General von Lossow. In response, Berlin declared a state of emergency throughout Germany and gave Reichswehrminister Gessler emergency powers. Seeckt authorized the Wehrkreis commanders to oversee the state civil authorities and maintain order. Hitler now joined forces with Kahr to oppose the central government. When the newspaper of the NSDAP, the *Völkische Beobachter*, viciously attacked Seeckt, claiming he was close to the Jewish newspaper, the *Berliner Tageblatt*, and his wife was Jewish, Gessler, in turn, officially suppressed the Nazi paper and ordered Lossow to prohibit its printing and sale. Lossow refused to do so and turned the order over to Kahr who, in turn, also refused to enforce the order. Negotiations over the next several weeks failed to resolve the issues.[97]

For Seeckt, the situation was primarily one of a subordinate officer failing to obey a lawfully issued order to suppress the Nazi paper. For this breach of military discipline and deliberate disobedience, he sharply reprimanded Lossow and also suggested he should resign since he had lost confidence in his ability or willingness to command the local Reichswehr forces against possible local opposition.[98] Lossow gave the reprimand to Kahr who informed Berlin that Lossow, as plenipotentiary for the Bavarian state of emergency, was a civil official, not a military personage, and, therefore, not subject Seeckt's orders. On October 19, 1923, Gessler officially dismissed

Lossow and appointed General Friedrich Freiherr Kress von Kressenstein as his successor until the Bavarian government appointed a new state commandant. Kahr publicly refused to accept Lossow's dismissal and called upon all Bavarians to stand behind him.

To emphasize his position, on October 23, Kahr ordered the men of 7 Division to swear allegiance to the Bavarian government. On November 4, Seeckt issued a counter order to the men of 7 Division:

> Whoever responds to the action of the Bavarian government breaks his oath to the Reich and makes himself guilty of military disobedience. I solemnly enjoin the 7. (Bavarian) Division of the Reichswehr to remain true to its oath to the Reich and to submit unconditionally to the orders of its highest military commander. I regard the loyalty of all other parts of the army to the Reich as assured now and always.[99]

Again, Seeckt used the soldiers' loyalty to the Reich, not to the constitution, although they had originally taken their oath to the constitution. To him, the main issue at stake was not the survival of a constitutional government, run by Social Democrats, which was contrary to his political thinking.[100] Seeckt's most important issue was the maintenance of unity and discipline within the Reichswehr, "the strongest factor in the state."[101]

Many Bavarian officers and the cadets at the Infantry School in Munich followed the men of Regiment 7 and took the loyalty oath to the Bavarian government. They had been taken by the oratory and vision of a new Germany of the former Freikorps leader Rossbach, now in Munich to recruit men for the coming revolt, and the still quite extensive prestige of retired General Ludendorff. On October 30, Hitler himself addressed the cadets and was enthusiastically applauded after denouncing their oath to the republic: "The first obligation of your oath, gentlemen, is to break it!"[102] None of the officers present took any steps against Hitler's invitation to perjury. The efforts of the school commandant, Major General Hans Tieschowitz von Tieschowa, to maintain order and discipline proved quite ineffectual, and discipline and morale among the school's men were lost. As a result, he gave them a leave of absence.

The non–Bavarians at the Infantry School generally remained loyal to the army command as did most of the rest of the Reichswehr who saw the rebels as Bavarian particularists. For example, there was Lieutenant Hansjochen Leist:

> From the outset I had strongly upheld the view that for us the only thing that mattered was the question of discipline or indiscipline in the army, and that the prestige of the officer corps would be at stake if we lightheartedly disregarded our oath to the Reich government.... In my opinion the *völkische* movement which alone can save the Reich if it proceeds reasonably must be fought absolutely if it is linked with mutiny and perjury. I consider myself in honour bound to defend a government by all means, the policy and the members of which I desire to go to hell.[103]

Like the mutineers, many of these officers supported the *völkische* movement and detested the republican government. However, they remained loyal because they saw the issue not as the conflict between Bavaria and the republic, but as a matter of honor and loyalty as professional soldiers or dishonor and disloyalty to their sworn oath.

Tension in Bavaria escalated as Hitler called in members of various nationalist and racist paramilitary groups, such as the Bund Oberland and the Reichskriegflagge. Most of them had been former soldiers dismissed from the army because of the treaty reductions and were looking for an opportunity to march on Berlin and overthrow the current government. However, neither Kahr nor Lossow were anxious to unleash a civil war. Seeckt was satisfied, for the time being, to prohibit contact by the Recishwehr with 7 Division and to suspend promotion consideration for Bavarian officers. Seeckt also wanted to dissolve the infantry school, to return the Bavarian Guard Company in Berlin to Munich, and to dismiss all Bavarian officers assigned to the Reichswehrministry. When the Chancellor and the Cabinet forced Seeckt to cancel these orders, he resented the civil interference in what he saw as a purely military issue, but he obeyed their orders.[104] Seeckt apparently even considered seizing power himself, but such action became unnecessary when Ebert gave him emergency powers to rule through the Wehrkreise commanders.[105]

By early November, Germany was poised on the edge of another civil war. On November 3 and again five days later, Ebert and Gessler ordered Seeckt to use the army to suppress the Bavarian revolt. However, Seeckt refused to obey their order and, along with General Otto Haase, convinced the civilian leaders that such action was too hasty and might give France an opportunity to destroy Germany. As a precaution, however, units of 5 Division were sent to the northern frontier of Bavaria, where they freely fraternized with Bavarian nationalists. Seeckt also warned the State Police Commandant Hans von Seisser and Kahr that the army would fire on the rebels if need be. Possibly the general's warning caused Kahr, Lossow, and Seisser to lose enthusiasm for an armed clash with the Reich, and they began to waver. Also, Major General Ritter van Danne, General von Kressenstein, and Major General Adolf Ritter von Ruith stayed loyal to the government and kept most of 7 Division from joining the revolt although some did. Most units remained neutral, at least technically siding with neither side. One such unit was the garrison at the fortress of Ingolstadt whose commandant refused an order to send his men to Munich. He was allowed to retire in 1925. The fourth company of Infantry Regiment 19 disbanded, rather than shoot their comrades. Others supported the revolt to some degree; for example, some units gladly removed the republican red, gold, and black cockades from their caps, signifying their support for the putschists.[106]

However, Hitler and his followers were not to be denied a putsch. On the night of November 8, he pushed the wavering Kahr, Lossow, and Seisser into open rebellion at the Bürgerbräukeller. Röhm, who had resigned from the army but was still on active duty, gathered his paramilitary forces, including active-duty soldiers who belonged to these groups illegally and veterans of the Baltic and Upper Silesian Freikorps, and marched on the Wehrkreise headquarters in Munich. The official sentries allowed Röhm's men to take up positions next to them. Meanwhile, Rossbach went to the infantry school, obtained 79 of the 80 cadets present, and arrested the school's loyal commandant. The next morning, the cadets swore an oath of loyalty to Ludendorff. As antiputsch forces gathered to oppose the revolt, Kahr, Seisser, and Lossow, seeing the handwriting on the wall, now publicly rejected the growing movement. On the morning of November 9, Hitler and Ludendorff marched on the center of Munich to join Röhm. On their way, they met policemen — not soldiers — who began firing. Very quickly the putschists dispersed, and Ludendorff was arrested. He later persuaded Röhm, ensconced in the military headquarters building, to surrender. Hitler fled the scene but was soon arrested, and the attempted rebellion died.[107]

In the aftermath of the Beer Hall Putsch, Seeckt took action to cleanse the Reichswehr — again. He ended the special considerations given to the Bavarian Division under the Military Law of 1921. However, neither Kahr, Seisser, nor Lossow were indicted for treason. Seeckt allowed Lossow, having changed sides during the coup, to retain temporary command of 7 Division and then to retire quietly from the army. Other army officers who had participated in the putsch were dismissed, and there were no Bavarian officers on the promotion list published in December 1923. (Bavarian officers who had remained loyal to the army command, on the other hand, were rewarded with promotions and good assignments.) Seeckt also discharged the loyal General von Tieschowitz, whom he saw as too weak, and moved the Infantry School to Dresden. Ironically, however, he took no action against the rebellious cadets other than "chewing them out" for their undisciplined conduct and ordering additional training for them. Seeckt blamed their actions on their superiors, the active duty officers at the school, whom he did dismiss from the army, for leading the cadets astray.[108] On March 7, 1924, Ebert finally lifted the state of emergency as no longer required.

In the meantime, on February 26, 1924, the trial of Adolf Hitler for treason opened in Munich. He used the trial to show his contempt for the convening authorities and to condemn Kahr, Lossow and Seisser for betraying the national revolution. He tried to show that his movement was not against the army but in concert with its goals and ideals. To excuse his own actions, Lossow told a crowd at the trial:

> We had realized that there was a healthy kernel in the Hitler movement, ... we saw a healthy kernel in the fact that the movement possessed the power to make converts among the workers for the cause of nationalism.[109]

The Nazi leader concluded his defense with this prophecy:

> When I learned that it was the "Green Police" which had fired, I had the happy feeling that at least it was not the *Reichswehr* which had besmirched itself. The *Reichswehr* remains as untarnished as before. One day the hour will come when the *Reichswehr* will stand at our side, officers and men.[110]

Hitler was sentenced to ten years imprisonment in Landsberg Prison. He completed only ten months and was then released.

The Reichswehr After Seeckt

With Hitler safely in prison (at least, temporarily) and many of the conspirators dismissed from the army, Seeckt appeared to be at his highest point of power to continue the development of the Reichswehr along his lines. By this time, he had established virtually complete control over the officer corps and, thus, the Reichswehr. Although he was not particularly popular or even liked by most officers, they did recognize him as their leader and the "First Soldier" of the Reich. His successful leadership of the army through numerous crises had won him unquestioned obedience from the officer corps. Furthermore, he had successfully turned his position as the Chief of the Army Command into that of a pseudo–supreme commander, especially since the civilian leadership generally deferred most military decisions to him. Kurt Ulrich von Gesdorff, a junior officer in the early 1920s, succinctly put it this way—Seeckt had become "a substitute monarch" who filled the void left by the Kaiser's abdication in 1918.[111] This role suited Seeckt as long as he had no serious opposition from the civilian leadership.

However, after September 1923, he now had to work with Stresemann, whom he and the generals disliked.[112] In fact, during the Munich coup, Seeckt had intrigued against Stresemann, telling President Ebert that the Chancellor did not "enjoy [the army's] confidence." Later, the general told the Chancellor the same thing to his face.[113] Ebert, however, supported Stresemann, and Seeckt and the generals had to tolerate Stresemann as the chancellor. Although the Reichswehr supported such measures as the creation of a "Grenzschutz" (border guard) force along the eastern frontier, the acceptance of the Dawes plan, which restructured Germany's reparations payments, and the Russo-German Friendship Treaty of April 26, 1926. It opposed Germany's entry into the League of Nations and the Locarno policy of rapprochement with France. The fact that Seeckt was unable to unseat Stresemann marked an important, although probably unnoticed at the time, diminution of the army's power in the republic.

Seeckt would have only a few years left on active duty after the Hitler putsch. On February 28, 1925, Friedrich Ebert suddenly died. After the ensuing elections, retired Generalfeldmarschall von Hindenburg was elected president. Although he himself was no friend of the Weimar Republic, the old field marshal did view himself as the protector of the German nation and government. Furthermore, he possessed the one attribute that Ebert never could — as a retired field marshal of the Imperial German Army, he could be supreme commander in fact as well as in name, particularly in the eyes of the officers, who had been either benignly neutral or intensely belligerent to the civilian Ebert. Some of the officers, in fact, came to see Hindenburg as a regent for the monarchy. Hindenburg took his position as supreme commander of the armed forces more seriously than Ebert and the civilian defense ministers had — perhaps more seriously than his position as Reich president. He insisted on personally deciding all military questions and resisted all attempts by the civilians to impose on his prerogatives as supreme commander. Hindenburg was equally opposed to any independent actions by his military officials.[114] The old field marshal, as both the most senior civilian *and* military authority of the state, could more truly be the surrogate Kaiser than Seeckt ever could. It would not be long before the two would have a parting of the ways.

Relations between the two started off quietly enough. Hindenburg accepted Seeckt's secret activities in Soviet Russia and made no real attempt to change any of his policies. Soon, however, it became increasingly evident that Hindenburg would consult Seeckt only on purely military matters whereas Ebert had consulted Seeckt on political matters as well. Additionally, Seeckt could never push his disagreement over an issue to the point of insubordination with Hindenburg as he would — and did — with Ebert. As the president began to involve himself in military matters and exercise his prerogatives as supreme commander, the officers began to shift their undying loyalty from Seeckt to Hindenburg, a process which Seeckt could not very well prevent or protest against. Ultimately, Seeckt was forced to resign on October 8, 1926, after a press campaign against him, following the appearance of the Crown Prince at the maneuvers of Infantry Regiment 9 four months earlier.[115] His replacement as the Chief of the Army Command was General Wilhelm Heye, a more docile man than Seeckt, more willing to accept the superior position of the civilian authorities.

During Heye's tenure, some, more forward-thinking officers tried to move the army to a closer relationship with the republican government. In late 1926 and early 1927, Heye and Schleicher attempted to cooperate with the Social Democratic government of Prussia on border defense along the eastern frontier. In May 1927, Dr. Gessler, Heye and General Werner von Blomberg, the new Chief of the Truppenamt, informed Stresemann of the extent of the army's illegal activities in Soviet Russia. The Chancellor agreed to continue most of the projects and, in doing so, acquired a measure of control over the army's independent policy in the east. The military authorities took steps to obtain additional public funds for border defense and to inform the civil government about its secret arms caches, giving up additional independence of action.[116] Lieutenant Helmuth Steiff expressed the general opinion of the majority of army officers on these attempts:

> That we cannot organize a frontier defense force together with the *Reichsbanner*, because these scoundrels would betray everything, must be obvious to you. We alone are too weak and must have the support of circles with military leanings.[117]

There was also some discussion about changing the method of recruiting for the army. Colonel von Bonin of the Truppenamt recommended that the Reichswehr recruit men from the republican parties and organizations to democratize the army and make it more representative of the nation as a whole. Although Schleicher, among others, supported Bonin, he was recalled from East Prussia in early 1927 and resigned soon after. He was replaced by Colonel Ritter von Mittelberger, a soldier from the "old school" who absolutely disliked Heye's idea of inviting the parliamentary deputies of all political parties, except the Communists, to social gatherings with army officers.[118] In an October 21, 1926, article for the *Breslauer Volkswacht*, Paul Loebe, president of the Reichstag, wrote that various rightist organizations had significant influence on the selection of recruits for the army. He continued, "This state of affairs is untenable if the republic does not want the Reichswehr to lead it by the nose." Dr. Gessler and most of the military leaders rejected Loebe's plan to change the recruitment process and defended the existing system. Some of them, like Kress von Kressenstein and Reinhardt, however, wondered if the army should continue to oppose the republic.[119] In general, though, the army remained unwilling to take in "republicans" and continued to recruit the few men it could from the politically rightist, nationalist, and veteran groups.[120]

Exacerbating the poor relations between the army and the republican government were the attacks on the Reichswehr by the more liberal Social Democrats and leftists in the Reichstag. With Seeckt now gone, they more frequently and openly complained about the army's violations of the disarmament clauses, its secret activities in the Soviet Union, its connections with the rightist political groups and secret organizations, and its secret arms caches. These open attacks worsened the relations between the military and the politicians and produced disappointment among many of the more moderate officers who were trying to come to terms with the government. As a result, cooperation between the two, according to General Reinhardt was "difficult, if not impossible."[121]

Summary

I end Chapter Two at about 1930, just before the trial at Leipzig of three army officers accused of spreading Nazi propaganda in their units, an episode that was part of the spread of National Socialist influence within the army. In this chapter, I have discussed the birth of the Reichswehr out of the ashes of defeat and revolution and its relationship with the government of the Weimar Republic from 1919 to 1930. I have also discussed the role of Hans von Seeckt in molding the new army into a Führerheer. From this discussion we can discern four important factors that made the men of the Reichswehr ripe for Nazi propaganda and, therefore, so willing both to accept the Nazi regime and to take a new oath of allegiance to Hitler personally on August 2, 1934.

First, the Reichswehr never developed an honest relationship with the Weimar Republic. Although the soldiers took an oath of allegiance to defend the constitution, most never internalized that commitment. When opportunities presented themselves to overthrow the government, there were always some, including senior officers, who joined the conspirators and many more who followed those who became active in the conspiracy. Most of the soldiers, who came primarily either from the old Imperial Army or from the Freikorps, viewed the republican government at best with suspicion and at the worst with fanatical hatred, as Beck commented to General Gossler in November 1923.

The significant controversy over wearing the republican colors was indicative of the dislike of the vast majority of the soldiers for the new government, especially, as we shall see later, when compared to the generally uncontested acceptance by the soldiers of the new Wehrmacht and Nazi emblems on their uniforms. Many secretly sympathized with the right-wing political parties and paramilitary groups, and some, despite the legal ban, joined these organizations. Only a few, like Reinhardt, Groener, and Heye, made any attempt to come to terms with the republic.

Second, a major reason for the failure of the Reichswehr to truly accept the democratic government was the extraordinary influence of Hans von Seeckt. His view that "governments" were only temporary meant that the army could — and did — withhold its true allegiance from the Weimar government. His policy of Überparteilichkeit, furthermore, gave the soldiers more reason to remain aloof from the government, especially during times of crisis. During both the Kapp Putsch and the Hitler Putsch, the majority of the army remained more neutral, awaiting the outcome, than actually supporting the government. The Reichswehr, as a whole, took its cue from Seeckt — if he had ordered the Reichswehr to support the putschists in either attempt to overthrow the government, it would have undoubtedly done so to rid itself of the hated democratic government. Additionally, Seeckt personally disliked the parliamentary system and made no outward demonstrations of support for Weimar, a position which other officers undoubtedly picked up on and openly displayed themselves.

Third, the Weimar government must share some of the blame for the failure of the army to accept the new regime. From the beginning, the government demonstrated first a need then a willingness to embrace the new army as was. Certainly, the instability and civil unrest of 1918–19 left the government with few choices in how to protect itself; so the initial compromise with the old officer corps and the use of the Freikorps is understandable. However, once the situation had stabilized, the government could have been more aggressive in its attempts to democratize the army. Instead, it left the recruitment of new officers and men in the hands of the regimental commanders, officers who had no love for the government. The government let loyal officers resign (Reinhardt) or be dismissed (Tieschowitz) while it promoted to the republic's highest military post the man who had disobeyed lawful orders during a time of crisis. It condoned his secret activities with a foreign government that directly impinged on its own prerogatives to conduct foreign policy. The Weimar Republic could not — or would not — ensure that the Reichswehr maintained its sole role as the nation's bearer of arms.

Finally, the military clauses of the Versailles Treaty — not to mention the soldiers' general hatred of the treaty itself— significantly limited the ability of the Weimar Republic to develop a truly democratic army that would be loyal to the constitution. The 100,000-man cap on the army's strength allowed Seeckt to choose the men he wanted for his army, and he generally chose former General Staff officers or members of the more reliable Freikorps, men who had little stake in maintaining or defending a democratic regime. Furthermore, this cap, combined with the treaty's long service terms, made recruitment virtually unnecessary and promotion opportunities almost totally nonexistent. For the Reichswehr, and especially the up-and-coming company grade officers, this situation made them particularly ripe for any movement that promised them rearmament and the greater opportunities for promotion that would result from an expanding army. I have already touched on the acceptability of National Socialism among the cadets at the infantry school and the company grade officers in general. In the next chapter, we will see how these factors combined to produce an army ripe for ideological subversion from within by the special appeal of National Socialism.

Notes

1. Harold J. Gordon, *The Reichswehr and the German Republic 1919–1926* (Princeton, NJ: Princeton University Press, 1957), p. 3.

2. About Groener's courageous actions on November 9, 1918, King William of Württemburg wrote in his diary, "Groener [a Württemburger,] was right, but he should have said to the Marshal [Hindenburg]: 'Find a Prussian to say these things.'" Quoted in Note 1, Wheeler-Bennett, p. 22. Although a Court of Honor in 1922 declared that Groener had acted with the highest motives, the Prussian officers never forgave him for this incident.

3. Letter to wife, November 14, 1918, in Kenneth Macksey, *Guderian: Creator of the Blitzkrieg* (New York: Stein and Day, 1975), pp. 43–44.

4. Beck letters and Oster quoted in Hamerow, p. 21.

5. Resolution of First Soviet Congress of Germany, December 18, 1918, in Wheeler-Bennett, p. 32.

6. The German Socialists were divided into three major groups. The Majority Socialists were the most moderate. Further to the left were the Independent Socialists. To the far left were the Spartacists, members of the Spartacist League, named after the leader of the Roman slave revolt, led by Rosa Luxemburg and Karl Liebknecht. Both of them would be killed in January 1919 during the leftist uprising in Berlin. The Spartacist League was the forerunner of the German Communist Party (KDP).

7. Hindenburg to Groener in Wheeler-Bennett, p. 33. At a December 20 meeting of representatives of the military and the People's Commissars of the Sailors' and Soldiers' Councils, the OHL delegates, Groener and Schleicher, flatly told Ebert that unless he rejected the resolution the supreme command "could not be responsible for the existence of the government." Quoted in Waite, p. 9. See also Groener Letter to Ebert, January 27, 1919, in F. L. Carsten, *The Reichswehr and Politics 1918 to 1933* (Berkeley, CA: University of California Press, 1973), p. 27.

8. Groener Report to the Government, December 14, 1918, in Carsten, p. 16. Document 1, Hindenburg Telegram to All Army Groups, November 10, 1918; and Document 7, Hindenburg Letter to Ebert, December 8, 1918, in Otto-Ernst Schueddkopf, ed., *Das Heer und die Republic: Quellen zur Politk der Reichswehrfüherung* (Hanover: Norddeutsche Verlagsanstalt O. Goedel, 1955), pp. 19–20 and pp. 35–36, respectively.

9. According to the myth, the civilian leaders, not the military leaders, through their pacifism and defeatism, had caused the defeat of the German army and the surrender to the Allies. After the war, Germans conveniently forgot that it was the military leaders who had asked to end the fighting. They only remembered the civilian leaders who negotiated the armistice terms. Later, it was the military leaders who told the civilian leaders they had to sign the Versailles Treaty because Germany could not defend itself in case the Allies invaded the country if Germany did not sign the treaty. The Allies further contributed to the myth by their insistence that military representatives be excluded from the German delegation sent to Paris to sign the treaty. Conveniently forgetting his own role in the surrender proceedings, Hindenburg coined the catchy phrase during his testimony to a parliamentary committee established in November 1919 to inquire into the responsibility for the outbreak and length of the war and to preclude Allied extradition of "war criminals" as demanded in the peace treaty. The civilian leaders who acted so courageously to the reality of the situation in 1918–19 would quickly be branded by the growing rightist, nationalist groups as the "November criminals." See, for example, Ludwig Beck's letter to his sister-in-law, November 28, 1918, in Nicholas Reynolds, *Treason Was No Crime: Ludwig Beck* (London: William Kimber, 1976), pp. 29–30.

10. Quoted in Richard Bessel, *Germany After the First World War* (Oxford, UK: Clarendon Press, 1993), p. 85.

11. Ebert quoted in Wheeler-Bennett, p. 31.

12. Document 7, Hindenburg Letter to Ebert, December 8, 1918, in Schüddekopf, pp. 34–36.

13. Karl Freiherr von Aretin Otmar, "*Die Eid auf Hitler*," *Politische Studien*, VII (January 1956), p. 2. See Appendix A for text of this temporary pledge.

14. Rossbach quoted in Konrad Heiden, *Der*

Führer Hitler's Rise to Power (Boston: Houghton Mifflin Company, 1944), p. 145. In Chapters 1 and 2 of his book, Waite provides an excellent description of the psychology of the men who joined the Freikorps. As we will see later, Hitler's National Socialism would find fertile ground among many former Freikorps members. One of the few well disciplined and professional Freikorps was the Jägerkorps of General Ludwig Märcker. On January 4, 1919, his assembled troops passed in review at Zossen for Ebert and Noske, the first time in the history of the Prussian army that a Prussian military unit had paraded for civilians. As they left the field, Noske told Ebert, "You can relax now. Everything will be all right." Noske quoted in Waite, p. 16.

15. Rosinski, p. 156–57. Gordon (pp. 59–66) describes 146 Freikorps for which records exist in detail. He lists over 400 Freikorps units in Appendix I, Part 1, pp. 431–36. The list is not all inclusive as the exact number cannot be determined since many rose, fought, and disappeared with little trace. For the same reason, historians cannot determine the exact number of men who served in the Freikorps.

16. Von der Goltz, letter to Seeckt, November 2, 1919, in Carsten, p. 65.

17. Rosinski, p. 157. Carsten, pp. 32–33.

18. Gordon (p. 73) estimates that at least 80 of the 146 Freikorps units that he identified can be traced to successor Reichswehr units. Large portions of an additional 13 appear to have also entered the new army, while only 18 were specifically excluded. Finally, portions of other Freikorps whose fate is unknown also probably entered the Provisional Reichswehr, either completely or partially.

19. Article 176, Constitution of the German Reich of August 11, 1919, in Hohlfeld, Vol. III, *Die Weimarer Republik 1919–1933*, p. 92. The Reich President was given the authority to determine the specific wording. See Introduction, Note 12, p. 7, and Appendix A for wording. Note that there is no references to God. Those who took the oath would receive a certificate to that effect, which they had to keep. Ordinance of August 14, 1919, in Schwertfeger, p. 569.

20. Röhm quoted in Note 13, Waite, p. 187. When fellow Freikorps members reproached him for taking the Weimar oath, he justified his actions through his belief that "... service in the Army [is], and will remain for all time, the most beautiful profession ... [and he] could not bring [himself] to leave the service." In other words, he loved military service for its own sake, especially the camaraderie with other military professionals who had shared the Frontsoldaten experience of World War I.

21. Craig, p. 363. Görlitz, p. 211.

22. The military clauses of the treaty outlawed conscription; the General Staff; submarines, tanks, airplanes, and other offensive weapons; and the war academy and cadet schools. They also reduced the army to 100,000 men (4,000 officers serving for 25 years and 96,000 men serving for 15 years) and the navy with ships no more than 10,000 tons. The High Seas Fleet was to be surrendered to the British at Scapa Flow; but its ships were scuttled before the British could take possession. The Rhineland was to remain occupied until Germany fulfilled these provisions and was to be demilitarized thereafter. Finally, the Kaiser and other war leaders were to be turned over to the Allies and tried as war criminals. The Allies appointed an Inter-Allied Military Control Commission to monitor the German government's compliance with the military clauses. The commission could travel throughout the country and inspect all German military installations and arms factories with all expenses paid by the German government.

23. The nationalist and rightist propagandists called the Treaty of Versailles the "infamous" Diktat. The men who signed it joined the November criminals who signed the armistice and were condemned as traitors. The leader of the German delegation, Matthias Erzberger, would be assassinated by members of a right-wing terror group, called the Feme, in 1923. For more on the Feme, see note 73, page 95.

24. See, for example, Guderian Letter to his Wife, July 12, 1919, in Macksey, pp. 49–50.

25. Telegram of Reichswehr Regiment 39 to Noske, July 26, 1919, in Carsten, p. 62. Wheeler-Bennett, pp. 56–57.

26. Conversation quoted in Wheeler-Bennett, p. 58.

27. The government had reduced its army to 325,000 by June 1919, and pared off another 35,000 by February 1920. By April, the army numbered 231,000 with 9,000 officers. The treaty had set March 31, 1920, as the original date to achieve the 100,000-man cap. The Allies agreed to extend the reduction schedule to October 1, 1920, the cap to 150,000, and the treaty limit to January 1, 1921. Gordon, pp. 78–81, 150.

28. Gordon, pp. 82–87.

29. Document 10, The Constitution of the German Reich of August 11, 1919, Article 3, in Hohlfeld, Vol. III, p. 60. To dampen the soldiers' resentment, the government created a special war flag for the Reichswehr: black, white, and red with a small black, gold, and red inset in the upper corner near the flag staff. Carsten, p. 125.

30. Lieutenant Colonel von dem Hagen, Colonel Reinhardt, Major General von Moehle, and Colonel von Epp quoted in Carsten, pp. 58–60. See also Moehl letters to Seeckt, March 3, 1920, and August 9, 1920, in Carsten, pp. 124–25.

31. Quarck in Carsten, pp. 62–63.

32. Quarck in Carsten, pp. 126–29.

33. Reichswehr Minister Decrees of April 1, 1925, and August 15, 1927, in Carsten, p. 219 and p. 262, respectively. Another symbolic issue for the officers was the prohibition on wearing their epaulettes, one result of the seven-point resolution of the soldiers' and sailors' councils during the early part of the revolution. At this time, the government had replaced the epaulettes—"the symbol of all that [the officer] is and represents ... the belt and spurs of a modern knight"—with rank insignia. Gordon, pp. 83–84. This issue was resolved in favor of the officers when the government ended "the shame of November 9, 1918" by reintroducing the epaulettes in February 1920. Carsten, p. 75.

34. Seeckt quoted in Carsten, p. 75.

35. Papst had formerly been the chief of staff of the Garde-Kavallerie-Schuetzen Division. In July 1919, he was dismissed from the army for attempting his own putsch. After his dismissal, he spread antigovernment propaganda among like-minded military leaders, soldiers, and angry Freikorps units.

36. Waite, p. 187.

37. Gordon, pp. 95–101.

38. Seeckt Order to the General Staff Officers, October 18, 1919, quoted in Gordon, pp. 102–3.

39. Gordon, pp. 102–3.

40. Gordon, pp. 105–11. Interestingly, Hammerstein-Equord was married to Lüttwitz' daughter. He was destined to become Chief of the Army Leadership from 1930 to 1934 and a longtime opponent of Hitler.

41. Gordon, pp. 112–16. Seeckt quote found on p. 114. General von Oldershausen, at the 1921 Jagow trial, echoed Seeckt's belief that Reichswehr troops would not fire on their comrades "[a]lthough the majority of the officers would doubtless carry out their duty to the utmost...." Quoted in Carsten, p. 79.

42. Noske quoted in Wheeler-Bennett, p. 77.

43. Rear-Admiral von Trotha, Chief of the Naval Leadership, and virtually the entire navy, including a young Lieutenant Walther Werner Canaris, declared themselves in full support of the Kappists.

44. Seeckt at March 13, 1920, meeting, quoted in Rosinski, p. 165.

45. Feldman Address, March 13, 1920; and Hahnke to Seeckt, March 25, 1920, in Carsten, p. 81 and p. 87, respectively.

46. Seeckt quoted in Gordon, p. 132.

47. Reinhardt quoted in Gordon, pp. 222–23.

48. Carsten, pp. 93–97. Gordon, 128–29. Four naval officers, including Rear Admiral von Trotha, were discharged, 18 relieved of their duties, and 40 sent on leave. The mutinous naval brigades of Ehrhardt and Löwenfeld were incorporated into the active navy. Löwenfeld himself was promoted twice and became the chief of the Flottenabeitlung (Naval Construction) in the Naval Command in Berlin. Carsten, pp. 95, 98–99. Major von Gilsa, Noske's chief of staff, resigned soon afterwards, fearful of retribution. Fifteen months after the end of the coup, on May 21, 1921, the Reich Ministry of Justice officially announced that the state had charged 705 men with high treason: 412 were amnestied although the law specifically excluded putchists from amnesty; 108 were dismissed because of death or other reasons; 11 were yet to be reviewed; and only one, the former police president of Berlin, von Jagow, was punished with five years of honorary confinement. In comparison, the republic sentenced the Bavarian leftists (number not provided) to a total of 615 years, two months in prison. Waite, p. 162.

49. Seeckt quoted in Craig, pp. 385–86. Seeckt was severely criticized by both sides of the political spectrum for his actions. From the right came criticisms, such as that from General von Plessen who wrote in his diary after the coup, "At the head of the general staff an officer of the Alexander regiment [, one of the most elite units of the old Imperial Army,] pays allegiance to democracy." Plessen quoted in Rosinski, p. 165. From the left came criticisms that Seeckt was using this opportunity to remove officers with republican or democratic sympathies. Carsten, p. 97.

50. Guderian quote, April 8, 1920, in Macksey, p. 55. Beck would have similar feelings after the abortive November 1923 Hitler Putsch. Beck Letter to Gossler, November 11, 1923, Reynolds, p. 34.

51. Articles 46 and 47, Constitution of the German Reich of August 11, 1919, in Hohlfeld, Vol. III, p. 69.

52. Gordon, p. 286.

53. Gordon, pp. 194–97. Carsten, p. 264.

54. Hans, Luck, *Panzer Commander: The Memoirs of Colonel Hans von Luck* (New York: Dell Publishing, 1989), p. 12.

55. F. W. Mellenthin, *Panzer Battles: A Study of the Employment of Armor in the Second World War* (New York: Ballantine Books, 1971), pp. Xi–xii. See also Görlitz, p. 227.

56. General Ulrich de Maiziere, "An Impressive Personality: A Notable Soldier," in *To Remain Ready for Action* (Cologne: Markus Verlagsgesellschaft, 1967), p. 31. Hamerow, p. 110.

57. Document 51, Schüddekopf, p. 114. Document 47, "On the Inner Attitude of the Troops," reports additional incidents. Schueddekopf, pp. 110–11.

58. Beck quoted in Hamerow, p. 28.

59. Document 34, "The Aims of the Republican *Führerbund*," in Schüddekopf, p. 97.

60. A sample of 1,100 army officers of the

mid- to late 1920s revealed that about one-third were sons of officers or military officials, another third were sons of civilian officials of one type or another, about 16 percent came from the free professions, and most of the remaining 16 percent came from the families of businessmen, industrialists, farmers, and landowners. Throughout the 1920s, about 20 percent of the officers came from noble families and were concentrated in the higher grades (in 1925, 23 generals out of 42 were nobles) and in the "tradition" units of the old imperial guard and cavalry units. As a result, the officer corps fairly represented the middle and upper classes of German society — those that were generally politically conservative. Gordon, pp. 199, 201–2.

61. Munzel Letter to Gordon, date not provided, Gordon, p. 319.

62. Lossberg Letter to Gordon, date not provided, Gordon, p. 315. See also Major Joachim von Stülpnagel Letter to Seeckt, June 28, 1919, in Carsten, p. 30.

63. Gordon, p. 174.

64. General (Hans) von Seeckt, *Thoughts of a Soldier* (London: Ernest Benn Limited, 1930), p. 86.

65. In these positions, Seeckt was the senior military person in the Weimar government. Ultimately promoted to Lieutenant General, he also became the most senior in rank, although not in time in service, to hold the latter position. He used this position to eliminate rivals and replace them with his own protégés.

66. Seeckt, *Thoughts.*, pp. 77, 80, 90. See also Seeckt's *The Future of the German Empire: Criticisms and Postulates* (New York: E. P. Dutton & Co., 1930), pp. 122–23, 138–40.

67. Seeckt General Order of the Day, November 4, 1923, in Charles R. Allan, Jr., *Heusinger of the Fourth Reich* (New York: Marzsani & Munsell, Inc., 1963), p. 33. See also Seeckt Circular on the Principles of Training, January 1, 1921, Appendix 28, Demeter, p. 349.

68. Document 83, Entry in Seeckt's Memoirs, August 12, 1924, in Schüddekopf, p. 201.

69. Gordon, pp.280–81.

70. Military Law of March 23, 1921, in Forsthoff, p. 218.

71. Gordon, pp. 278–80.

72. Document 87, Schüddekopf, p. 208. See also Lieutenant Colonel Erich Marcks, quoted in Carsten, p. 218.

73. Carsten, pp. 148–52, 271–72. The members of the Black Reichswehr were particularly upset when Reichswehrminster Gessler officially denied their existence to the Reichstag, and Reichswehr officials publicly denied their existence. Waite, pp. 243–45. The Reichswehr, through the Black Reichswehr, may also have had contacts with the Femegerichte (Secret Courts) (Feme for short), reminiscent of late medieval German criminal law. During the early years of the republic, members of the Feme assassinated informants and government officials, including Matthias Erzberger and Walther Rathenau, Weimar's Jewish foreign minister. During the trials of the assassins, the Black Reichswehr's existence became known. In a letter to the President of the Supreme Court of Berlin, though, Seeckt not only admitted the existence of the illegal army but also defended the Feme's actions as a necessity to combat treason since "normal and ordinary means ... could not be applied." Wheeler-Bennett, pp. 94–5. See Appendix B for a more detailed look at political justice during the Weimar Republic.

74. The NSDAP originated from the very small German Workers' Party (DAP), founded by a railway mechanic, Anton Drexler, in the early days of postwar Munich. After the war had ended, Hitler, now a corporal recently released from a military hospital, worked for the Army to spy on the many radical movements and political parties, including the DAP, spawned in those tumultuous days. After attending several meetings, Hitler quickly became enthralled with its program and soon joined as member number 20. He separated from the Army to devote himself full time to developing the party along his lines and quickly transformed the DAP into the NSDAP. Gordon estimates that about 162 members of the NSDAP in 1923 were former officers: perhaps 20 were regular officers, 39, reservists, and the remaining 103, unknown. By rank there were five cadets, 67 second lieutenants, 35 first lieutenants, 36 captains, 16 majors, and three lieutenant colonels. Gordon, Harold J., Jr., *Hitler and the Beer Hall Putsch* (Princeton, NJ: Princeton University Press, 1972), p. 83. In November 1923, he estimates the Bund Bayern und Reich had ten generals, 65 field-grade officers, and 71 company-grade officers among a possible 60,000 members. Gordon, pp. 109–11.

75. Gordon, *The Reichswehr and the German Republic*, p. 414.

76. Carsten, p. 162. In addition to maintaining contact with the radical right, Reichswehr officials participated in a number of illegal actions to supplement its official funding: "voluntary contributions" from industry, trade, finance, and agriculture, and, after Seeckt's resignation in 1926, the diversion of budgeted funds from other ministries into secret accounts. Carsten, pp. 224–25, pp. 274–75.

77. In early 1920, Seeckt appointed a group (Sondergruppe R) of select army officers to open secret military negotiations with Soviet diplomats. Their objective was to establish German industrial enterprises in Soviet Russia to manufacture airplanes, tanks, artillery and shells, and poison gas — weapons expressly prohibited by the Versailles Treaty. In exchange, Reichswehr officers, dressed

as civilians, would train the Red Army in various aspects of modern warfare at special military installations in Russia. The Chancellor Joseph Wirth knew about the arrangements since he, as finance minister, had to approve the funds for these activities. Seeckt expressly stated, "In all these enterprises, which to a large extent are only beginning, the participation and even the official knowledge of the German government must be entirely excluded. The details of the negotiations must remain in the hands of the military authorities." Apparently, President Ebert was not fully informed of these activities until he read a memorandum in mid–September 1922 from the German ambassador to Soviet Russia, Count Ulrich Brockdorff-Rantzau, about the army's enterprises. He agreed with the military's secret activities: "a different opinion would be madness." Later, Stresemann, Wirth's successor as Chancellor, also allowed the army to continue these secret activities. They continued until the end of the Weimar Republic and beyond—even after the Manchester *Guardian* publicly revealed the extent of the army's secret enterprises on December 2, 1926, and the Social Democratic Reichstag deputy Phillip Scheidemann launched a major attack on the army and its flaunting of the civilian government's prerogatives to conduct foreign policy. Ebert's quote from Carsten, p. 142. Seeckt quote from Seeckt Memorandum, September 11, 1922, in Carsten, p. 141.

78. Seeckt Letters to his wife, February 6 and February 12,1919, in Carsten, p. 31.

79. Seeckt, Heeres-Verordungsblatt, no. 79, quoted in Carsten, p. 114.

80. Seeckt Order of July 1919, in Gordon, p. 272.

81. Selchow (Seeckt's adjutant) diary entry, November 27, 1923, in Carsten, p. 189. During the Kapp Putsch, some officers approached Seeckt to stage his own coup. He refused, not out of love for the republic but because of the probability such action would draw his beloved army into the political disorder. Karl Dietrich Bracher, *The German Dictatorship: The Origins, Structure, and Effects of National Socialism* (New York: Praeger Publishers, 1970), p. 106.

82. Schwertfeger, p. 570.

83. Seeckt Letter to Noske, January 16, 1920, in Gordon, *Reichswehr*, p. 326.

84. Munzel Letter to Gordon, date not provided, in Gordon, *Reichswehr*, p. 326.

85. Seeckt quoted in Gordon, *Reichswehr*, p. 229 and p. 279, respectively.

86. Seeckt quoted in Gordon, *Reichswehr*, pp. 220–21, 276, 325–26.

87. Seeckt quoted in Gordon, *Reichswehr*, p. 212.

88. Gordon, *Reichswehr*, pp. 257–58. Waite, pp. 239–40, 242–46. Schleicher, Hammerstein, and Eugen Ott formed the liaison unit in the Reichswehrministry between the Reichswehr and the AK.

89. Heiden, pp. 164–65.

90. Footnote 1, Wheeler-Bennett, p. 167.

91. During the superinflation of this period, the German mark declined in value from 8.9 marks per American dollar in early 1919 to 4,200,000,000 marks per dollar by November 1923. By this time, over 300 paper mills and 2,000 printing firms worked 24-hour shifts to supply the Reichsbank with the required bank notes. Life savings were literally wiped out overnight. Wheelbarrows of money were needed to carry a day's wages and to purchase a few items from the store. The psychological damage to the urban middle classes permanently marked their members. Koppel S. Pinson, *Modern Germany: Its History and Civilization* (New York: The Macmillan Company, 1966), pp. 446–47.

92. The Deutsche Volkspartei (DVP) was the successor party to the National Liberals after World War I. It was a right-of-center bourgeois party that supported universal secret suffrage for men and women, liberal free enterprise policies in economics, and nationalist domestic and foreign policies. The party, however, carefully avoided committing itself totally to the ideal of republican government.

93. Carsten, pp. 163–64. Werner von Fritsch, future army commander in chief, wrote to Joachim von Stülpnagel, on August 24, 1924, of a possible leftist plot to undermine Seeckt. Carsten, p. 201. Later, in November, the same Fritsch, hoping Seeckt would establish a military dictatorship, criticized him and Schleicher for compromising with the President and Stresemann. Fritsch summarized, "For in the last resort Ebert, pacifists, Jews, democrats, red and gold, and the French are all the same thing, namely the people who want to destroy Germany." Fritsch to Stülpnagel, November 16, 1924, in Carsten, p. 201. See also note from Kress von Kressenstein to Seeckt, December 2, 1924, in Carsten, p. 204. Carsten called Fritsch "one of the bitterest enemies of the republic among the senior officers." Carsten, p. 248.

94. Stülpnagel quoted in Carsten, p. 164.

95. Upper Silesia was a mixed German-Polish region along the southeast frontier with Poland. After a League of Nations plebiscite on March 20, 1921, the voters (707,122 to 433,514) favored overwhelmingly staying with Germany. Polish officials in the region initiated internal violence, supported by the Polish government and favored by the French plebiscite troops. When France strongly forbade Germany from using its army troops to end the violence, Seeckt authorized the Freikorps to protect the German areas of Upper Silesia. Ultimately, Poland received the southern half, includ-

ing most of the coal mines. Gordon, *Reichswehr*, pp. 226–27. Many soldiers lost confidence in the central government, believing "it a shame that defence organizations have to defend the soil of Upper Silesia, while it is not permitted to employ Reichswehr soldiers, whose vocation it is in the first place to defend the German homeland." Commanding Officer, Infantry Regiment 19, 7. Division, Munich, June 21, 1921, in Carsten, pp. 130–31.

96. Gordon, *Reichswehr*, pp. 233–34. Carsten, pp. 168–69. Wheeler-Bennett, p. 112.

97. Gordon, *Reichswehr*, 235–37. Carsten, p. 173.

98. Seeckt to Lossow, October 9, 1923, in Carsten, pp. 173–74.

99. Seeckt in Gordon, *Reichswehr*, p. 239.

100. Document 79, Seeckt Letter to Kahr, November 5, 1923, in Schüddekopf, pp. 187–88.

101. Document 78, Seeckt Proclamation to the Reichswehr, November 4, 1923, in Schüddekopf pp. 185–86. Seeckt first met Hitler on March 11, 1923, in Munich and noted, "We were one in our aim; only our paths were different." Quoted in Allan, p. 37.

102. Hitler, quoted in Carsten, pp. 79–80.

103. Leist Letter to Lieutenant Colonel von Hammerstein, October 22, 1923, in Carsten, pp. 175–76.

104. Gordon, *Reichswehr*, pp. 239–40.

105. Craig, pp. 418–19. Wheeler-Bennett, p. 110.

106. Gordon, *Reichswehr*, pp. 244, 352–53. Carsten, pp. 180–83.

107. Gordon, *Reichswehr*, pp. 244–47. Carsten, pp. 183–84

108. Gordon, *Reichswehr*, p. 248–51. Carsten, p. 184.

109. Lossow quoted in Wheeler-Bennett, p. 157.

110. Hitler's Closing Statement at 1924 Trial, in Norman H. Baynes, ed., *The Speeches of Adolf Hitler* (New York: Howard Fertig, 1969), vol. I, *April 1922–August 1939*, p. 86.

111. Gersdorff in Carsten, p. 107

112. Seeckt Letters to his Wife, June 26, 1925, and July 2, 1925; to his Wife and Sister, October 4, 1925; and to his Sister, April 4, 1926, in Carsten, pp. 207–8.

113. Carsten, pp. 170–71.

114. Wheeler-Bennett, p. 151.

115. Gordon, *Reichswehr*, pp. 323–24. Rosinski, pp. 170.

116. Gordon, *Reichswehr*, pp. 313–14. Carsten, pp. 266-67, 277–78. As a side note, in January 1928, Dr. Gessler resigned as Reichswehrminister when news broke about the illegal financial activities of a naval officer, Captain Lohmann, the head of the Sea Transport Division of the Naval Command. For most of 1926, Lohmann had invested appropriated funds in the German film industry and other ventures to obtain additional funds for defense spending. Gessler's successor was Wilhelm Groener who then terminated these illegal activities. Lohmann had cost the government 26 million marks. Carsten, pp. 285–88.

117. Steiff to fiancée, October 11, 1930, in Carsten, pp. 271–72. The Reichsbanner Schwarz Rot Gold was the paramilitary group organized by the Social Democrats as a counterweight to the paramilitary groups on the right. Major Koestring, a subordinate of Seeckt's in Turkey during the war, wrote his mentor, "now they want to convert us finally and energetically to the republic. I fear that this will not work so quickly, for we officers of medium rank and younger officers have been educated in the German way and do not bother about parties...." Koestring to Seeckt, November 30, 1926, in Carsten, p. 259.

118. Carsten, pp. 261–62, 271.

119. Carsten, pp. 256-60.

120. Carsten, p. 264.

121. Document 93, Conference in the Foreign Ministry, December 1926, pp. 214–17, and Document 100, Reinhardt to deputy Dr. Haas, January 25, 1917, p. 228, in Schüddekopf.

3

The Army and National Socialism, 1930–1934

By 1930, the senior military positions of the Weimar army were held by moderates. Groener had replaced Gessler as Reichswehrminister, Heye had become Chief of the Army Command, and Hammerstein-Equord had replaced Blomberg as Chief of the Truppenamt. Schleicher, as Chief of the Ministeramt, intrigued behind the scenes in the troubled republic for himself and for the army.[1] At the republic's helm stood the stolid Hindenburg. Although not a supporter of democratic government himself, he did see his duties to protect the Fatherland and to steady its course through the deteriorating economic conditions after the Great Crash of 1929. The British Military Attaché to Germany, Colonel J. H. Marshall-Cornwall, commented in September 1930, "The Army Command is now passing into the control of a group of the younger and more pushful generals who tolerate the Weimar Constitution and all that it stands for only so long as the field-marshal remains as the representative Head of State."[2] The new army, surviving three major and numerous lesser military crises since 1918, would seemingly ensure the continued existence of the Weimar Republic, at least as long as Hindenburg lived.

However, a significant portion of the Reichswehr had not given its loyalty to the republic and its constitution although every member had sworn an oath to defend the constitution. The same limitations that had enabled it to reach high levels of proficiency and professionalism also had virtually eliminated any chance for promotion and career development and had reduced military life to a monotonous existence in peacetime garrisons, broken only by occasional maneuvers and field exercises. Inside the army, many company-grade officers seethed for the opportunity to launch a "war of liberation" that would eliminate the Versailles constraints and re-establish Germany's position as a European power. Many senior officers also strained at the Versailles "leash" for the chance to re-exert themselves and restore the status they had had during the days of the Imperial Army. Only a few, such as Groener and Heye, made any attempts to come to terms with the republic.

The antirepublican feelings of many Reichswehr officers struck sympathetic chords in the program of Hitler's NSDAP and ultimately led to that fateful day of August 2, 1934, when the entire Reichswehr took the oath of loyalty to Hitler with virtually no thoughts as to the consequences of this action.

To see how the Reichswehr reached that event, I will examine in this chapter how the army came to support Hitler's coming to power in January 1933 and then how it acquiesced in taking a new oath of loyalty, one that would have such cataclysmic consequences for the officer corps as a whole. I will first examine the extent of the sympathy within the officer corps for the National Socialist movement. Of particular interest is the October 1930 trial for high treason of three army officers, two on active duty and one retired, in Leipzig. I will then review the relationship of the Reichswehr to Hitler and the Nazi party during his rise to power in January 1933. I will follow this discussion with a review of Hitler's relationship with the army after the "Machtergreifung," Hitler's accession of power on January 30, 1933, until the Röhm Purge, especially Blomberg's activities to "nazify" the army. The last section of this chapter will cover the death of Hindenburg and the fateful oath-taking ceremony itself.

The Leipzig Trial

After his trial, Hitler spent eight months of a five-year sentence in Landsberg Prison. During this time, he reflected on the attempted coup, wrote his memoirs *Mein Kampf*, and came to two conclusions: first, never again to attempt to seize power by force but obtain it legally; and, second, to obtain the benevolent neutrality of the Reichswehr, if not its support, in any attempt to gain control of the government. During this time, the party declined in strength and influence. Upon his release in early 1925, Hitler began rebuilding the party organization and membership with the help of such men as Gregor Strasser and Heinrich Himmler. Gradually, the party began to regain its former strength through the creation and spread of a national grassroots organization. However, despite all of the organizational activity, the Nazis gained only 2.6 percent of the vote for 12 Reichstag delegates in the 1928 national elections. After analyzing the voting results, Hitler changed the party's orientation to target the fractious middle classes and the agrarian class, and turned Germany's deteriorating economy after the crash of 1929 and the debates over the Young Plan into a cause célèbre. These efforts paid off in the September 1930 elections when the NSDAP garnered 18.3 percent of the votes for 107 delegates.[3] Hitler had now become a force in the politics of the Weimar Republic.

As the NSDAP gained increasing political strength and popular support, Hitler also gained increasing influence among the disenchanted younger officers of the Reichswehr through his continuous condemnations of the Weimar Republic and the Versailles Treaty. In *Mein Kampf*, Hitler called the men who had signed the armistice (an act which he called "a monstrous event") "[m]iserable and degenerate criminals" who had forgotten the sacrifices of multitudes of Germans during the war.[4] He ranted against the November criminals who had betrayed the Fatherland and "stabbed the army in the back" by signing the Versailles Treaty—"the most dishonorable and the basest crime of all times"—and promised to call them to account for their betrayal of German honor.[5] Hitler called the Versailles Treaty an "instrument of boundless extortion and abject humiliation" with "sadistic cruelties," unbounded "oppression," and shameless demands.[6] He railed against the "lazy and decayed State" and "the muddle and pestilence of party politics" of the republican government, a "Jewish-Democratic Reich ... a true curse for the German nation." He also accused the government of willingly giving away German territory and yielding to the demands of the foreign powers who enslaved the German people.[7] Hitler consistently propagated these themes to the Germans during the 1920s.

Many of his ideas about war and the military also struck sympathetic chords among the restless soldiers. Hitler promised to cut the shackles of Versailles, restore Germany's greatness, obtain Lebensraum (living space) in the east, and restore the army's former status. From the party's beginnings, he especially concentrated on the need to abolish the "mercenary army" of Weimar and Versailles and create from it an expanded "people's army," based on compulsory military service. Echoing the thoughts of many young officers, Hitler condemned the Reichswehr as a police force used to maintain internal order that had departed from its tradition of glory and from the national spirit; it was not the means to defend the Fatherland from external enemies, to fight "victorious wars to the end."[8] To Hitler, the old Imperial Army was the means to train the people in discipline, manliness, efficiency, courage, aggressiveness, and honor — "the mightiest school of the German nation ... and the bastion of our national freedom against the power of the stock exchange."[9] Hitler foresaw the need for a mass army, dedicated to the ideal of National Socialism and loyal to him, to fight a future war against the Jews and the Slavic races of the East and to obtain living space for Germans.

Many Reichswehr officers saw in Hitler's mass army, opportunities for career development and promotion denied to them in the small Reichswehr. The army leadership had taken a dim view of National Socialism after the 1923 abortive putsch but also realized its appeal to their subordinates, particularly newer members who had come from the rightist paramilitary organizations. Also, most of the older officers disliked the movement's revolutionary methods, crude propaganda, and its former Frontsoldaten and Freikorps members and the "Bohemian lance-corporal" who led it. Yet, many secretly sympathized with some Nazi ideas — the restoration of the army's position in German society, the elimination of the Versailles restrictions, and future military expansion. The younger officers were particularly susceptible to Nazi entreaties: They "in the gray dullness of their uncompromising service" saw in Hitler and his pledge of a larger army the promise of fast promotion.

> For these officers were not only desperate patriots, but also poor devils in need of money. A large section of them came from the class that had lost its fortune in the inflation [of 1923]; they led somewhat threadbare private lives on monthly salaries of two hundred marks and upward, and complained bitterly that the German officer was no longer the social lion he had been. It was a new society, plutocratic but bourgeois and unfeudal; it set new social types, famous artists and writers, for instance, higher than members of that armed class which, after all, had lost the war.[10]

They also appreciated the cooperation of the SA with the Grenschutz (Border Guards) along the German-Polish frontiers. In the late 1920s, Hitler purposefully courted the members of the Reichswehr through articles in the *Völkische Beobachter*, edited by a former Imperial Army officer Wilhelm Weiss, and in the party's military periodical, the *Deutsche Wehrgeist*. These articles attacked the Reichswehr leaders for their nonpolitical stance and support of the Social Democratic republic, and the leaders of the republic for their pacifism, and openly called on the officers to repudiate their oath to the republic.[11]

Several army commanders, including the Reichswehrminister and the future Chief of Staff Beck, reported significant support for the Nazi movement among their younger officers.[12] Heinz Guderian later wrote that he, like many other officers, was disenchanted with the frequent governments of the Weimar Republic and had no enthusiasm for its ideals; however, they "were quickly roused to enthusiasm by the patriotic ideas which the [NSDAP] held out to them."[13] Heye's son, a naval officer, wrote Schleicher that the officers were pro–Nazi, not because of the Nazi program, but because the Nazis were "a force which fights the decline of the Reich,..."[14] Colonel Kuehlenthal of the Truppenamt told Colonel Marshall-Cornwall that Nazism offered many young officers an escape from Germany's financial and political ills. Young officers of Cavalry Regiment 4 at Potsdam declared Hitler to be Germany's sole savior. Following the September 1930 elections, some officers declared to the British military attaché, "[The Nazi movement] is the *Jugendbewegung* (youth movement); it can't be stopped."[15]

Perhaps we can best see just how much National Socialism had penetrated the army by looking at a young lieutenant, Henning von Tresckow, who would become one of the driving leaders of the future anti–Hitler conspiracy. Hans Bernd Gisevius, one of the few survivors of the anti–Hitler conspiracy, later described Tresckow in the 1920s as an officer like many others who saw only "the side of National Socialism attractive to a soldier: the assertion of discipline, the reestablishment of military primacy, and the revision of the Versailles Treaty."[16] In the 1920s, he lectured in the officers' mess of Infantry Regiment 9 on "breaking the chains of usury"—a popular Nazi slogan—and influenced other members of his regiment toward the Nazi movement.[17] As the economic and political crisis caused by the Great Depression deepened in Germany after 1930, he recommended to a friend that he vote for Alfred Hugenberg, the conservative leader of the German Nationalist Party—or even better, for Hitler.[18] Other future opponents to Hitler, such as Beck, Stieff, and Oster, would harbor pro–Nazi sentiments (that is, criticism of the current parliamentary government, need for strong presidential leadership, and the reestablishment of the army's pre–1918 position) during the early 1930s.[19]

To combat the penetration of the Reichswehr by Nazi propaganda, the Army Command reminded the troops about its principle of Überparteilichkeit.[20] In the July 21, 1929 issue of a Magdeburg newspaper, Hammestein stated that the army officer's loyal service was to the permanent identity of the state, symbolized by the Reichspresident standing above temporary ministries and incoherent government agencies. In the autumn, Schleicher stressed the nonpolitical attitude of the Reichswehr, particularly the officers and the officer cadets, and the need to oppose the propaganda of all extremist parties.[21] In January 1930, Groener, recognizing the danger of the Nazis, decried their attempts to woo the troops for their own purposes and called upon the soldiers to refrain from politics and to serve the state above politics. On April 3, Heye reminded the officers and cadets at the Infantry School of their oath of allegiance and the need to support the constitution or quit.[22] Later, on May 9, he reiterated the "above politics" principle in a speech to his troops.[23] However, the trial of three army officers for treason in Leipzig in September 1930 would reveal their failure to turn the younger officers away from National Socialism, vividly demonstrating how much Nazi ideas had penetrated the Reichswehr.

In the spring of 1930, two lieutenants of Artillery Regiment 5, Hans Ludin and Richard Scheringer, and retired First Lieutenant Hans Friedrich Wendt were arrested by military authorities for spreading Nazi doctrines in the army, attempting to form Nazi cells within the army, and trying to convince their fellow officers not to fire on rebels in case of a Nazi revolt. Earlier, after reading the Nazi newspaper and journal, they became convinced that only the Nazis could save Germany and contacted the Nazi party leader in Ulm, offering to act as contacts between the party and the army. On November 1, 1929, Ludin and Scheringer visited the Brown House, NSDAP headquarters in Munich, and met with Captain Weiss, the editor of the *Völksiche Beobachter*; Captain Franz Pfeffer von Salamon, the Chief Leader of the SA, and Captain Otto Wagnener, the SA Chief of Staff. They freely discussed obtaining the support or, at least, the neutrality of the army's officer corps in case of a Nazi revolt.[24] During that meeting, Ludin told the SA leaders present, "We are determined to revolutionize the officer corps in so far as it is not yet senile, even if we are sent to prison...."[25] The two officers returned to Ulm and began to proselytize among their fellow officers. They succeeded in converting First Lieutenant Wendt, who joined them for five months, traveling about Germany, spreading the Nazi message among other officers, and distributing a nationalist pamphlet they had written.[26]

By the end of 1929, the military authorities had gotten wind of their activities. Heye, the newly appointed Chief of the Army Command, spoke to their commander Colonel Ludwig Beck about the activities of his lieutenants. Beck, in turn, reviewed the documents from Heye's investigation and decided that Scheringer had only disobeyed an order to stay quiet about the investigation, and had not committed treason. In January, 1930, Beck confined the young officer to quarters and warned him about Captain Pfeffer von Salamon. In the following weeks Ludin and Scheringer ended their contacts with the Nazis, and the army investigation petered out. However, new evidence against the lieutenants came to light, and they were arrested on March 6, 1930, in their Ulm barracks. Beck offered to resign at this point to demonstrate his support for the arrested officers, but his divisional commander persuaded him to withdraw his resignation. Beck may have even asked the president's son Oskar von Hindenburg to have his father intercede on the lieutenants' behalf. The three officers, including Wendt, however, were arraigned before the Supreme Court of the Reich at Leipzig and charged with high treason.[27]

The trial lasted from September 23 through October 4 during which the three defendants spoke out in "heated tirades" against "the pacifism, the spinelessness of the German government and all its works."[28] Their testimonies revealed the causes of their dissatisfaction: the restrictive measures of the government under the pressure of the Versailles Treaty, the forced retirement of Seeckt in 1926 as the result of newspaper demands and political intrigues, and the attitude of the Reichswehrministry during the Black Reichswehr trials. These grievances over the years led them to approach "the patriotic associations," which Scheringer defined as those "which worked for the liberation of the Fatherland," to maintain the fighting spirit of the Reichswehr. After their visit to the Brown House, they intended to contact "like-minded" officers for the purpose of forming a "political-military patriotic union."[29] Scheringer testified, "An officer must be nationally minded. His slogan must be 'All for the people; all for the Fatherland.' The Reichswehr must be fanatic." Furthermore, he essentially declared to the judge that the Reichswehr would not be bound to support a government with which it disagreed politically: "And if we have a pacifist or Communist Government, should the Reichswehr follow suit? I have lost faith in the older generation if that is its opinion." Ludin echoed Scheringer:

> [W]e can not have faith in a government which continually acts against our convictions. Every theatre is filled with plays

> against officers, against war. The newspapers unceasingly attack officers. Why does not the government take measures against the newspapers that assail us?[30]

The state prosecutor discovered the extent to which Nazi ideas had penetrated the Reichswehr after a number of officers whom the defendants had contacted testified about their discussions with them. The testimony of Lieutenant Ernst Fuersen indicated that "a conflict of conscience" existed among the troops. He stated that the troops should "be properly educated so they would be nationalistic and would thoroughly realize at whom they were required to shoot." Fuersen stated he would give an order to shoot rightist rebels but the troops should know who their opponents were: "A soldier is allowed to think. He is not a machine."[31] Lieutenant Lohr confirmed the severity of the confidence gap between significant numbers of officers and the government in case of a Nazi revolt.[32] The state also discovered that these officers were more reluctant to be as open in court as they had been in giving their pretrial depositions, stating they didn't remember their exact words. Apparently they essentially believed in the cause for which Ludin, Scheringer, and Wendt were on trial and did not want to risk incriminating their fellow officers.[33] Lieutenant Helmuth Stieff wrote his fiancée that the younger officers "unfortunately" agreed with the accused and "[p]erhaps the good side of the affair is that the eyes of the fellows on top will be opened to the colossal dissatisfaction in the officer corps...."[34]

Scheringer's commander Colonel Beck then testified on behalf of his subordinate. He told the assembled court that the young officers loved their country and their profession, that the questions they had were the same ones that troubled other officers. Beck talked about their ideals. He continued that the Reichswehr was a "Führerarmee" as a basis for an expanded army, sometime in the future. The problem with Ludin and Scheringer, according to Beck, was how to maintain the "martial spirit" of the present army until it was possible for Germany to create that expanded army. His testimony confirmed the sympathy he, along with many other officers, had for the concerns of the defendants but without condoning or defending their illegal actions.[35]

On September 25, the Reichswehr authorities announced their intentions of also indicting Hitler for treason, a threat with which they did not carry out.[36] The next day, the Nazi leader showed up at the trial as a defense witness to discredit the senior military leaders without alienating the soldiers. He spoke for hours, confirming—under oath—that the NSDAP had no intentions of subverting or replacing the Reichswehr or of overthrowing the present government: "I have always held the view that any attempt to replace the Army was madness. None of us have any interest in replacing the Army." Instead, he vowed, he would work to regenerate the German nation morally and ultimately use constitutional means to obtain power legally. Once in power, however, he would try and execute the leaders of the 1918 revolution, scrap the Versailles Treaty, and "see to it ... that out of the present Reichswehr a great Army of the German people shall arise."[37] Wheeler-Bennett called Hitler's performance "a masterpiece of intellectual dishonesty; a *tour de force* in the reconciliation of 'legality' with 'illegality.'"[38]

Hitler's declarations under oath greatly impressed the officer corps, especially many previously skeptical senior officers. They felt reassured that Hitler had no intentions of undermining the discipline of the Reichswehr although they still viewed the movement itself with some amazement and apprehension. For instance, Beck felt that National Socialism was in tune with his own politics. He saw that the movement promised to re-establish Germany's greatness and to return some of the glory of Imperial

Germany, especially that of the Imperial Army.[39] Schleicher recognized the effects of Nazi ideas on the soldiers but believed that they would not turn their minds and lead them to accept the ideology of the movement.[40] Hitler's statements helped the army leaders to rationalize their unwillingness to act against the movement and convinced them of possible cooperation with the Nazis. His statement also helped preclude a ban on the NSDAP in 1930, despite its wild excesses.[41] Additionally, they caused many officers to conclude that the Nazi movement could not be stopped. We now can see the dangers of Seeckt's Überparteilichkeit policy: the soldiers only saw the promises of the Nazi movement for the army's expansion, their career and promotion opportunities such an expansion offered, and the reestablishment of its previous position; few, if any, saw its dangers.

On October 3, the 12-day trial ended with the closing statements of the state prosecutor and the three defendants. The latter reiterated that they had had no desire to subvert the army, only to prepare it for the war of liberation.[42] They were found guilty of treason and sentenced to 18 months of fortress imprisonment (to include the six months and three weeks of their arrest) and dismissal from the army. The judge stated that their actions were definitely treasonable under current law and they had failed to utilize "proper channels" to protest their complaints to their superiors. Furthermore,

> [t]hey are not mature men, as their observations in court repeatedly showed. Lastly, their motives unquestionably were pure, if misguided.
>
> When active officers of our army go behind the backs of their superiors and carry on political propaganda for any party whatsoever, it represents a serious blow against military discipline, a serious breach of soldierly duty.

The judge, however, left open the question of whether or not the actions of the Nazis were also treasonable.[43] Eight days later, President Hindenburg rejected a defense appeal to pardon the officers, citing "the necessity, especially in times of political unrest, to maintain unimpaired discipline and subordination in the Reichswehr,...."[44]

After the trial, the military leaders, particularly Groener, faced numerous protests and severe criticism over the verdict. Dr. Kumbacher, a former first lieutenant, wrote a stinging article that recounted the "crimes" of the republic — the "stab in the back," the Versailles Treaty, the War Guilt Clause, the 1918–19 revolution — of which the Leipzig trial was just the latest example of attempts to mentally disarm the German nation.[45] Seeckt accused Groener of weakening the camaraderie and solidarity of the officer corps. He defended himself to Seeckt by pointing out the absolute necessity for the army to maintain its neutral position above party politics and his determination to suppress all political action by all parties, Nazi or Communist, in the military. Groener then cited the dismissal of a bombardier after a civil court acquitted him of charges of spreading Nazi propaganda.[46] Groener publicly responded to Major General Graf von der Goltz,

> It must not be party programmes or resounding slogans drawn from them that determine the manner in which the Reichswehr serves the fatherland, but the will of the *Reichspraesident* and those higher leaders appointed by him.[47]

Groener answered the criticism of Elard von Oldenburg, a veteran Prussian Junker, by repeating his belief in the need for absolute obedience from his soldiers and his determination to maintain that standard.[48] Chancellor Brüning defended Groener in the Reichstag in his response to a Nationalist deputy, Captain Otto Schimdt, who had earlier remarked that it was shameful for Reichswehr recruits to swear allegiance to "such a doubtful creation as the Weimar Constitution."[49]

The senior Reichswehr leaders attempted to further control the penetration of the officer corps by Nazi ideas. In a message to all officers, Groener recounted the results of the trial, severely criticized the convicted officers for their actions, whatever their motives might have been, and clearly readmonished the officers to remain "above party politics." He discounted the postwar belief among many young officers that they were free to criticize their superiors' decisions and to demand that the senior officers explain every order to them. Groener further explained the necessity for absolute obedience of every soldier: "Soldiers who want to see whether an order suits their own ideas before they carry it out are absolutely worthless." Such officers were not fit for continued service, and Groener expected "any officer with a sense of honor and the courage of his convictions to resign from the Reichswehr at once...."[50] He reiterated similar thoughts in a special message to the senior commanders, urging them to "re-train" their subordinates along these lines.[51] Schleicher directed senior army officers to deliver lectures to their subordinates on their proper conduct as officers. However, the younger offices did not receive either Groener's circulars or Schleicher's lectures very well.[52]

These measures had little effect in turning the younger officers away from National Socialism. From his confinement Scheringer severely criticized Groener in an open letter for ordering Reichswehr members to participate in the military delegation to the civil clubs, such as the Reichsbanner, as a way of demonstrating the gap between the "Front" and the "Office."[53] Lieutenant Stieff of Artillery Regiment 5 wrote his fiancée,

> The trial has proved beyond a doubt that the ministry of defence, with its General von Schleicher... has caused a severe crisis of confidence.... Without a doubt the accused have acted wrongly and have violated the rules of military discipline. But are not their troubles ours? All of this I have told you often enough, and at least 90 percent of the officer corps think the same way.... If we did not hope that this whole clique of Schleicher and Co., for whom we are mere pawns in their own advancement, will be swept away one day by the true national movement which nobody can stop, we should resign our commissions right away.[54]

Captain Lindemann, commander of a battery of Artillery Regiment 6 in Silesia, had similar thoughts.[55] As Julius Leber, the Social Democrat's parliamentary expert on the Reichswehr, noted six months after the trial, National Socialism found support in the army because "it had been intelligent enough to offer the young men substitutes for the things the Republic has not been able to offer...."[56]

The Army and Hitler, 1930–1933

While the Leipzig trial gave Hitler a great propaganda victory in his drive to obtain power legally, it also gave the senior army leaders a false sense of confidence in their ability to control the Nazis. Hitler had already banned SA and SS members from joining the Reichswehr.[57] In 1930–31, he replaced some of the more radical SA leaders, such as Walter Stennes and Pfeffer von Salamon who were disgruntled over this prohibition, with more moderate men.[58] At a May trial of four Nazis, Hitler declared, "I have never allowed anyone to doubt that I demand from the SA absolute observance of the legal way, and when this veto on violence has in any case not been observed I have brought to book the leaders or subleaders concerned."[59] Closer relations developed between the SA and the army as local SA units augmented the army's border forces in East Prussia, the army provided the SA with some military training, and

Schleicher had a 1929 law revoked that prohibited defense plants from hiring NSDAP members.[60] In 1931, Röhm met with Schleicher on several occasions and convinced the army general of the legality of the NSDAP's aims.[61] By now, other army leaders had become impressed with the SA's ability to mobilize German youth, who were unable to join the army, and had come to view the SA, along with the Stahlhelm, as an unofficial army reserve.

The SA had originally been formed in 1921 to protect NSDAP meetings from rival political parties, especially the Communists, and to battle the party's enemies on the streets of Germany. After 1926 under the leadership of Pfeffer von Salamon, it had fast become an important quasi-military organization. It had its own flags, uniforms, insignia, badges, and pageantry. Prospective Stormtroopers had to be members of the NSDAP and swear a personal oath to Hitler upon joining.[62] Under Röhm as the new SA Chief of Staff, the SA quickly grew in size from 250,000 to 400,000 men.[63] The more radical Stormtroopers wanted to make the SA the nucleus of a new mass people's army after the Nazis took control of the government. Although Hitler had espoused this idea in the party's 1920 20-point program, he was not ready to openly advocate such an idea because it would cause ill-feeling with the Reichswehr; it did, however, cause ill-feeling between the SA rank and file and Hitler.[64] Röhm wanted to destroy the traditional military hierarchy and replace it with men of the Frontsoldaten experience, but he temporarily agreed to Hitler's wishes to keep the SA a strictly political army.

Apparently Schleicher, other generals, and even Groener, to some extent, believed Hitler was sincere in his promise to keep the SA a totally political army and not develop it into a mass army that would swamp the Reichswehr. They also believed they could use Hitler and his growing broad-based support for their own purposes as they both wanted the same thing.[65] Schleicher now began to set in motion a plan to create a conservative government ruled through the emergency powers of the president (Article 48 of the Weimar constitution); he was influenced in this decision by his position in the Reichswehrministry and his relationship with the president through his son. He wanted to build a general front of younger politicians, supported by President Hindenburg, with a common ground and inspiration that would weather the current economic and political crises. Obviously, any viable government needed the active support of the army, and Groener even openly proclaimed at the 1930 autumn maneuvers, "In the political structure of Germany, no stone may be moved without the Reichswehr casting the decisive vote."[66] From 1931 to December 1932, Schleicher schemed to create and then demolish presidential cabinets, composed of "picked" men, mostly conservatives, but he was unsuccessful in providing governmental stability. The failure to create a stable cabinet demonstrated the government's inability to cope with the economic crisis, wearying many Germans.

The political stability of Weimar Germany was further tested by continual street battles between Stormtroopers and Communists that had become a part of Germany's everyday life. Although Groener had expressed some belief in Hitler's sincerity about using legal methods only, now also Minister of the Interior, he recognized the growing menace of the SA to Germany's political stability and the danger of the SA as a military rival to the Reichswehr. In early 1932, expressing his disapproval of the SA, Groener warned Hitler not to depart from legal political methods and to keep away from any activities to subordinate the army to his own militia. He especially reemphasized that "[t]he Wehrmacht [was] the highest institution in the state."[67] Hitler maintained that the SA was only "an association of men with a political purpose ... not an ethical institution for the education of gentlewomen," thereby excusing their excesses (many, including Röhm were known homosexuals). The Stormtroopers took Hitler's comments as a charter to continue their lawless actions, despite his pledges of legality.[68] In the end, their violent acts would serve their purpose — to create a broad-based demand for a Nazi-controlled government that would provide greatly desired stability.

Meanwhile, with the presidential elections scheduled for April 10, 1932, Groener, on April 8, informed the military chiefs of his decision to ban the SA because of its lawlessness and to prevent separate action by the state governments. Admiral Erich Raeder, Chief of the Naval Command, asked if the ban should extend to the Reichsbanner, the paramilitary formation of the Social Democratic Party, to avoid making a bad impression on the Reichswehr," but Schleicher was against including the Reichsbanner in the ban. Over the objections of Hammerstein and General von Bock, the commander of the Second Division at Stettin, Hindenburg hesitatingly signed the ban that dissolved the SA, including the smaller, elite SS, on April 12. Even before Groener promulgated the ban, Schleicher, however, began to undermine Groener's authority by confidentially informing the Wehrkreise commanders that the army opposed the ban. Furthermore, he collected information against the Reichsbanner with which he intended to discredit Groener in Hindenburg's eyes by having the president question its exclusion from the ban. This smear campaign against Groener created a cabinet crisis which resulted in Groener losing the confidence of the president and the army.[69] On May 10, Groener, whom Telford Taylor called "a most steadfast and incorruptible servant of the Reich," resigned after furious attacks from the extreme right in the Reichstag.[70] Brüning resigned on May 30, and Hindenburg appointed Franz von Papen as his successor and Schleicher as Reichswehrminister in the last non–Nazi cabinet of Weimar Germany. One of Papen's first acts was to recall the ban on the SA.

From June to the end of the year, events moved quickly to allow Hitler to become Chancellor and, from there, obtain complete control of Germany. Once the government lifted the ban on the SA, its members renewed their street brawls with Communists and Social Democrats. The violence reached its peak on July 15 when 15 people were killed and 50 injured in Altona. Between June 16 and July 20, there were nearly 500 clashes in Prussia alone, causing 99 dead and 1,125 wounded.[71] Papen used the increasing violence to get the president to appoint him Reich Commissioner of Prussia on July 20. Papen used this position to dismiss the Social Democrats of the Prussian State Ministry, and declared a state of emergency in Prussia to justify using troops of Wehrkreis III, commanded by Lieutenant General Gerd von Rundstedt, to forcibly unseat the state's senior officials. By July 26, Papen lifted the state of emergency in Prussia, but his actions had removed the last effective barrier to an eventual Nazi assumption of power.

The increasing instability and the ineffectiveness of the republican government drew the attention of a number of army officers who held mixed views of the political situation. For example, Lieutenant Stieff wrote to his wife that summer,

> [T]he government must be freed from the chains of parliamentarianism so that it can work independently, supported by the confidence of the president and the power of the army." Only the president and the army could provide "the only basis for a government of the sort we need now.[72]

Others saw that only a government led by Hitler and the NSDAP could provide the desperately desired stability. General Alexander von Falkenhausen, then commander of the Infantry School at Dresden, reported that Beck, "an old friend of [his]," was in Dresden in 1931 and told him that he "wholeheartedly [favored] National Socialism and would not admit the validity of [Falkenhausen's] profound doubts" of such a government (quoted in Reynolds, p. 43). Many officers believed that the current political instability could not continue, and it served only to reinforce their dislike of parliamentarian government.

When the general elections of July 31 gave the Nazis 14 million votes, increasing the NSDAP's Reichstag delegation from 107 to 230 members, the NSDAP became the largest party in the legislature — but not the majority party. As a result of this major shift of power in the Reichstag, Hindenburg should have called Hitler to form a coalition government. However, the old President resisted the idea of a cabinet led by the "Austrian corporal" and dominated by Nazis. On August 13, Papen invited Hitler to speak with Hindenburg to clarify the current situation. Believing he would be offered the chancellor's office, Hitler first met with Schleicher who told the Nazi leader of the President's qualms to include him in a new cabinet as Chancellor. Sensing he would not get the position he so coveted, Hitler turned now on both Papen and Schleicher.[73] Hitler's hatred of Schleicher increased after the minister attempted to convince Gregor Strasser and his followers to leave the NSDAP. Hitler discovered Schleicher's scheme and quickly put an end to it. Both men paid with their lives in the June 30, 1934, massacre for crossing Hitler. Papen, protected by Göring, would barely escape Schleicher's and Strasser's fate.

Feeling duped, Hitler could now barely be persuaded to see Hindenburg. At this meeting the President completed the Nazi leader's feeling of humiliation by asking him, with military curtness, if was he willing to join the cabinet. When Hitler refused, Hindenburg told him that he could not conscientiously turn the government over to a single party and warned Hitler to conduct his opposition policies in a knightly manner. Otherwise, he, as president, would severely counter the SA's acts of violence. Hitler left in a fit of rage and pledged himself to seek revenge on Schleicher for placing him in such an embarrassing position. Falkenahusen now warned Schleicher to take advantage of the NSDAP's current financial and political weakness to dissolve it or at least the SA, but Schleicher refused.[74] Well into autumn, Hindenburg resisted all entreaties to bring the "Austrian corporal" into the cabinet.[75] Hitler publicly railed against the "little group of old Junkers," the "few run-down aristocracy," and his "great adversary" Hindenburg who had denied him the chancellorship despite his great electoral victory.[76] Yet, Hitler, despite this humiliation, felt Hindenburg would have to call him sometime soon to create his own cabinet.

Hitler also contended with the restlessness of the more radical SA men who were demanding that he seize power by force. Because of his seeming inaction, some party members left, and the influx of new members slowed down. During that fateful summer, tensions between the Reichswehr and the SA also grew as the Stormtroopers demanded that the soldiers salute them.[77] The rising tide of SA–initiated violence raised the specter of a Nazi revolt. Some senior officers reported that, despite the significant Nazi sentiment in the army, they believed their troops would fire on the Stormtroopers if they attempted to seize the government.[78] The army leadership also became more critical of the Nazi leader as the Nazi rank and file spread the worst defamations about the Reich President. Interestingly, Seeckt in retirement, at the same time, advocated Hitler's election as president.[79] Hitler realized that an attempted coup so close to success would risk a violent confrontation with the police and, more importantly, with the Reichswehr.[80] Despite his humiliation before Hindenburg in August and his own private thoughts about the president and the general, Hitler continued to publicly claim he would adhere to legal means to achieve power.[81]

The specter of a civil war in which the army would have to fight both Nazis and Communists caused grave concern among some army officers. Giving some credence to this concern was the transport workers strike in Berlin, supported by both extremist groups, following the November 3 elections. Schleicher was especially worried that the army and police would be unable to cope with such large-scale violence, especially in case of an unlikely attack by the Poles at the same time.[82] To validate his concerns, he called a war game whose final report, given to the cabinet by Lieutenant Colonel Eugen Ott, confirmed in his mind his worst nightmare — especially since it had used the worst-case scenario.[83] Schleicher, in turn, used the report's conclusions to pass on to Papen, now Chancellor, the blame for a possible civil war in order to discredit him in the eyes of the army leaders.[84] The scheming of the Reichswehrminister ultimately brought about Papen's resignation as Chancellor after which Hindenburg now selected Schleicher for this position. By the end of 1932, Schleicher had obtained the highest political post in the republic, below the president, a position he would hold for only six weeks, the shortest term for a chancellor in the turbulent political life of the Weimar Republic.

Schleicher's scheming, however, had lost him the support of many in the government. He had already lost the confidence of many senior officers, the younger officers, and the enlisted men and had little support in the Reichstag. His lack of support outside his own military entourage caused Hindenburg to force Schleicher to resign in mid–January. Despite many entreaties, the President had told the army generals, even as late as January 26, 1933, they surely did not believe he would make Hitler chancellor.[85] However, Papen, who had been secretly talking to Hitler, now convinced the old generalfeldmarschall that with him as vice chancellor and other conservatives in the cabinet, he could control Hitler if Hindenburg would call the Nazi leader to form a government. The aging president, weary of the political instability, finally agreed. As for the new Reichswehrminister, Hindenburg and Papen finally settled on Generaloberst Werner von Blomberg, former Chief of the Truppenamt and now the German military delegate to the Geneva Disarmament Conference. The new cabinet became effective on January 30, 1933. Hitler had finally obtained power legally. The senior army leaders, believing they could still control Hitler, offered no resistance to his accession as the new Chancellor. Craig later wrote, "Of all the mistakes made by the political generals in the long history of the Prussian Army, this was the greatest and, for the nation, the most tragic."[86]

The Army and Hitler: The First 18 Months

Upon becoming chancellor, Hitler knew he needed the support of the army, particularly of the officer corps, the real power in Germany, and generally left the army's internal affairs alone until 1938. For now, the army could sustain him in power — or could overthrow him. He also realized he would need the army's support to consolidate his power in the coming months and to attain complete power when the aging Hindenburg died. For this reason, he did not interfere in promotions, which were based on professional competence rather than political outlook, change the sentences of courts-martial, or get involved in operational planning. In time Hitler would make the army completely obedient to him in order for him to carry out his war of revenge against France in the west and his war against the Slavs for "living space" in the east. Helping him in gaining the army's complete loyalty was the soldiers' view of his appointment as Chancellor as "a return of the typical German values of order and discipline."[87] These traditional Prussian values and Seeckt's policy of Überparteilichkeit helped Hitler win the acceptance and ultimately the loyalty of the officers, tired of Schleicher's political intrigues.

From the beginning, Hitler worked to bolster the loyalty of the officers, particularly that of the more senior officers.[88] He purposefully appealed to their sense of tradition, repeatedly reiterating the army's role as the defender of the German nation and the party's role as the propagator of the Nazi *Weltanschauung* (world-view) as two separate functions, and promising them a greatly expanded army. On January 31, four hours after his appointment and in an unprecedented move, he went to the barracks of the Berlin garrison and spoke to the troops of the future of a National Socialist Germany. Three days later, he talked for two hours to the senior army and navy leaders in Hammerstein's Berlin apartment. He promised to ensure the continuance of the army as the nation's sole bearer of arms and to keep the party formations separate from the army to counter any stories from Röhm and the SA that the Stormtroopers would soon supersede the army. He reiterated that he would work to repeal the Versailles Treaty and its restrictions of Germany's military forces and would greatly increase military spending. Apparently, Hitler's speech was well received by the assembled officers.[89] He would repeat these themes to both the army and the SA down to the Röhm Purge.[90]

Hitler was particularly adept at using the symbols of the army's past glory to gain its affection. On March 10, he restored the imperial black, white, and red flag as the official army banner and obtained Hindenburg's "permission" to give the NSDAP swastika flag equal status.[91] Four days later, Hindenburg replaced the black, gold, and red uniform insignia of the republic with the imperial black, white, and red insignia.[92] Hitler's greatest "coup" occurred on March 21 at the opening of the Reichstag at the Potsdam Garrison Church, the burial place of Frederick William I and Frederick the Great.[93] After his speech—in which he praised Hindenburg's long military career—Hitler, in civilian attire, crossed the platform and, in front of the assembled guests, who included the Reichstag delegates (except the Social Democrats), Crown Prince Wilhelm, and retired Generalfeldmarschall von Mackensen and General von Seeckt, grasped the hand of the aged generalfeldmarschall and President, in full military uniform, in a respectful symbolic humbling of the "New Order" to the "Old Order." Mackensen commented afterwards,

> We German officers used to be called representatives of reaction, whereas we were really bearers of tradition. It is in the sense of that tradition that Hitler spoke to us, so wonderfully and so directly from the heart, at Potsdam.[94]

Hindenburg then laid a wreath on the sarcophagi of the dead kings and, for several hours, watched Reichswehr, SA, SS, and Stahlhelm formations parade past his platform. Hitler's performance that day probably also increased his standing among the officer corps.

Aiding Hitler in the subtle nazification of the army was the new Reichswehrminister Blomberg, who was completely enthralled by the Führer. Before his selection for this position, he was the Chief of the Truppenamt from 1927 to 1929. During that time he visited the secret German military training activities in Soviet Russia, where he had been strongly influenced by the Red Army's close links to the masses. In 1929, he was replaced by Hammerstein-Equord and reassigned as the commanding general of Wehrkreis I (East Prussia). There he accepted the unofficial cooperation of the East Prussian SA to bolster the Reichswehr's defences against a possible Polish attack. In 1930, his military chaplain Ludwig Müller — and future Reichsbishop under Hitler — convinced Blomberg to attend a mass meeting in Königsberg where he first heard Hitler speak. In 1932, at the behest of Hindenburg and Schleicher, he had also worked out plans to use the SA as a militia. The local army–SA cooperation, his contact with the Red Army, and the influence of chaplain Müller and his chief of staff Colonel Walter von Reichenau contributed to Blomberg's acceptance of National Socialism by January 1933. Blomberg was probably the only general officer both Hitler and Hindenburg could agree on to occupy this vital military position.

The following quotes from Blomberg illustrate his own belief in the new ideology and regime:

> The year 1933 brought to me an experience altogether and certainly undeserved, since I was allowed to become an assistant to the Führer and to be in his immediate entourage.... Things I never expected to find after 1919 fell into my lap overnight: at first, faith, veneration for a man, and complete adherence to an idea; later on, a field of activities holding great possibilities for the future.... I pledged myself to National Socialism in 1933 because I considered its ideas promising for the future. I found that in the core of this movement everything was right.[95]

He described Hitler's appointment as Chancellor:

> It was the Army, removed from the political conflict, which laid the foundations on which a God-sent architect could build. Then this man [Hitler] came; the man, who, with his strength of will and spiritual power, prepared for our dissensions the end that they deserved, and made all good where a whole generation had failed.[96]

Because of his obvious subservience to his Führer, his fellow officers nicknamed him "Hitler Youth Quex" after a character in a 1933 propaganda film based on a novel, first published in the *Völkische Beobachter*, or "Gummi-Loewe" ("Rubber Lion").[97] O'Neill called Blomberg "impetuous, intense, and over-simplifying," spontaneous to the point of impulsiveness, and easy to dominate.[98]

Because of his acceptance of National Socialism, Blomberg encouraged the senior army commanders to set aside Seeckt's policy of Überparteilichkeit and embrace the new movement "with complete devotion."[99] On May 15, he directed all members of the Reischwehr to salute the members of the Nationale Verbände, and their flags and colors when carried by formed units at public rallies and parades, and to join in singing Nazi songs — these were actions that placed the Nazi organizations on the same level as the armed forces.[100] The army law of July 20 terminated the jurisdiction of the civil courts over the military, the Vertrauensmänner, the military and naval chambers, and the last remnants of state control over local armed forces.[101] In September, he directed military members to use the party salute in certain situations.[102] On the tenth anniversary of the Munich Beer Hall Putsch, Blomberg and other senior army offices participated in the memorial ceremony at the Feldherrnhalle, the end place of the attempted 1923 coup, along with Hitler and other party officials.[103] The total effect of Blomberg's actions were to bring the army and the Nazi movement closer together.

In 1934, Blomberg continued to cement the relationship of the army to the Nazi movement. In February, he directed that the "Aryan clause" of the Civil Service Law of April 1933 be applied to the armed forces and that non–Aryans be expelled from the military services. Although very few individuals were affected by the decree (five officers, two officer cadets, one medical officer cadet, and 31 NCOs and men from the army; and two officers, four officer cadets, and five NCOs and men from the navy), the action gave de facto recognition to the regime's discriminatory doctrines and engendered only a few complaints from the officer corps.[104] He also directed that the party insignia, the eagle clutching a swastika, be placed on all military uniforms. On March 10, Blomberg suspended the old regulations prohibiting soldiers from joining political organizations.[105] In April, he included Nazi political indoctrination in the military's regular training program.[106] On April 21, he issued an appeal to the armed forces for them, in their public conduct, to stress that:

1. The Wehrmacht was the only bearer of the arms of the nation.
2. The Wehrmacht was completely loyal to the National-Socialist regime.
3. The Wehrmacht had been systematically educated in National-Socialist thought.[107]

On May 25, Blomberg issued an eight-point statement, "The Duties of the German Soldier," written in *völkische* style. The statement read, in part, that the protection of "the Reich, the people (*Volk*) now united in National Socialism, and its living space was the first duty of the army." The statement, probably written by General Werner von Fritsch, the new Chief of the Army Command, was published under both the President's and the Reichswehrminister's signatures. It was given to every new recruit upon enlistment. On June 1, 1934, Blomberg directed that this statement be read to the new recruits before they took the oath of allegiance, that every soldier memorize it, and that it be posted in every barracks.[108] These actions produced only a few protests — in contrast to the earlier extended debates over the republican insignia and flag.

In addition to taking steps to draw the army and the NSDAP closer together, Blomberg also replaced Schleicher's men with his own to assist him and Hitler in rebuilding the German Army. Colonel Walter von Reichenau, his Chief of Staff in East Prussia and also a Nazi sympathizer, became chief of the Ministeramt in the spring of 1933. Wheeler-Bennett characterized Reichenau differently from Blomberg. The former was more of a political realist than the emotional idealist Blomberg was. He saw cooperation with the new regime as an opportunity to bring him personal and professional advancement, and the army advantages as well. Reichenau appreciated the idea of a "people's army" as he already fraternized with his troops to a much greater extent than other, more traditional officers.[109] Cooper states that although Reichenau was characterized as a "party general," he was not a blind follower of Hitler, like Blomberg. He liked the revolutionary aspects of National Socialism that promised to throw off the "dead weight of the past" and substitute "in its place effective action beneficial to both the Army and the nation." However, Reichenau disliked the cruder aspects of the Nazi philosophy and its leaders and, in the future, became disillusioned with Hitler and National Socialism. He wanted to bring the army and the people together spiritually and saw the National Socialist movement as having the capability of doing that.[110] Both Blomberg and Hitler wanted to appoint Reichenau as Chief of the Army Command when Hammerstein was forced to retire in January 1934.

Because Hindenburg and other senior officers disliked Reichenau for his blatant opportunism, lack of command experience, and unorthodox views on fraternization with the troops, the President instead chose Generaloberst Werner von Fritsch. A strict Protestant with only two loves — his work and horses — a Prussian of the old school, and an outstanding officer, he was well suited to the task of rebuilding the army. Through the years, Fritsch had gained a reputation of high personal morality, popularity, and authority throughout the army. However, he had little political consciousness:

> I have made it my guiding rule to limit myself to the military field alone, and to keep myself apart from any political activity. I lack everything necessary for politics. Furthermore, I am convinced that the less I speak in public, the more speedily can I fulfill my military task.[111]

During his tenure as Chief of the Army Command (later Commander in Chief of the Army) until 1938, Fritsch had very little contact with Hitler personally. He had no right of direct of access to the Führer, and Blomberg was always present with Fritsch and Hitler. At the beginning, Hitler told him, "Create an army of the greatest possible strength, inner resolution and unity, on the best imaginable foundation of training." As a professional Prussian soldier, Fritsch took this task to heart. Only occasionally and then sarcastically did he criticize the regime for which he worked. Although Fritsch disliked the crudeness of the Nazi regime, he was impressed by its achievements and the popularity of its leader and would complete his duties enthusiastically and efficiently with little thought to their political ramifications.[112]

As Chief of the Truppenamt, Blomberg selected Ludwig Beck — the same Beck who had testified on Lieutenant Scheringer's behalf at the Leipzig trial — another soldier of the Prussian tradition. Like Fritsch, Beck had a reputation throughout the army as an outstanding soldier with great moral courage and integrity but, like his superior, he lacked political astuteness in dealing with the Nazis.[113] A comment to his predecessor, General Wilhelm Adam, is revealing: "Events might turn out differently. Perhaps the propagandist and demagogue Hitler, who showed such great skill in building up his power, will ... develop into a real statesman...."[114] Like other senior officers, he disliked the Weimar Republic and saw advantages for the army in a National Socialist regime: "I have wished for years for the political revolution and now my wishes have come true. It is the first ray of hope since 1918."[115] In his new position, he immersed himself in the details of Germany's rearmament program and the army's expansion, and limited his opposition to the practical details of the Nazis' plans, not their moral aspects.

The Röhm Purge and Its Aftermath

Meanwhile, Röhm and the more radical SA leaders continued to agitate for greater control of the army. He continuously pressed Hitler to introduce a militia system, based on the SA, with him as the militia's commander in chief. With Hitler at the head of the government, Röhm wanted the SA to take over the army while they still had the tempo and spirit of the "revolution"— they had not achieved "absolute victory."[116] While the Nazis proceeded to systematically "nazify" other sectors of German society, a process called "Gleichschaltung," the Führer consistently resisted Röhm's demand to give him control of the army because of the generals' strong opposition. Hermann Rauschning, the Nazi commissioner of Danzig, reports a conversation in spring 1933 in which Röhm reproached the generals for their reactionary views and Hitler (whom Röhm called a "swine") for associating with them.[117] Throughout 1933, Hitler reiterated that the Reichswehr was the sole bearer of arms of the German nation.[118] For the generals, "Rearmament," as General Walther von Brauchitsch remarked later, "was too serious and difficult a business to permit the participation of peculators, drunkards, and homosexuals."[119] Once the Stormtroopers had helped him to power, Hitler realized he needed the army now more than he needed the SA.

Hitler did take several actions in an attempt to mollify Röhm. Stormtroopers were allowed to join the army as individuals. In May 1933, the Reichswehr reached an agreement with the SA that placed the SA, the SS, and the Stahlhelm under army control in military matters. In early July, Reichenau further agreed to allow the army to train certain SA leaders and men in short courses and prepare 250,000 SA men as reserves, and, in August, the Reichswehr established the Nationale Verbände as the army's main source of recruits. In October, another order increased army-SA cooperation, and by a February 13, 1934, agreement, the army agreed to provide limited premilitary training to SA males between the ages of 18 and 26 and allow the SA to augment the border forces. Röhm privately called the February 1934 agreement a new "Versailles Diktat" and Hitler an "ignorant corporal of the World War."[120] Both Fritsch and Beck believed that the army was wasting its valuable and limited resources to train the Stormtroopers, men who they believed would destroy the army's moral and ethical foundations and discipline.[121] In December, Hitler allowed Röhm into the Reich Cabinet as a minister without portfolio. These actions, however, failed to satisfy the SA radicals and actually increased tensions with the army.

As 1934 progressed, there were increasing signs that Röhm and other SA radicals were still not satisfied. Within the SA, now numbering 2,500,000 men, he had formed special aviation, motor, engineer, intelligence, and medical units and had established an SA Ministeramt and press bureau.[122] In February, Röhm sent Reichenau a telegram in which he declared that the defense of Germany was the sole domain of the SA.[123] Later that month, the SA leader proposed that the armed forces, the paramilitary organizations, and the veterans' organizations be placed under one ministry with the implication that he would be its chief.[124] From the spring, Röhm organized large-scale parades of uniformed SA to demonstrate its strength and vigor, obtained quantities of arms, and stepped up the SA's military training.[125] Papen reports that Röhm demanded Hitler force the President to accept 500 SA leaders as army officers and 2,000 SA men as NCOs.[126] In every case, Hindenburg, the army generals, and Hitler firmly rejected Röhm's claims and proposals, and incidents between Stormtroopers and soldiers, ranging from verbal insults to physical blows, increased. Hitler would ultimately create his mass army, loyal to him, but not with Röhm as its head and not in 1934.[127]

Complicating the growing antagonism between the army and the SA was the broadening battle for control of the police and security forces. By the spring of 1933, over 25,000 SA and 15,000 SS men had become police chiefs, officers, or auxiliary police under the control of Hermann Göring, the Minister of the Interior for Germany and for Prussia.[128] Röhm, however, maintained that he had control of the police forces through their membership in the SA. Göring denied Röhm's claim and, in May, forbade his police chiefs to belong to the Nationale Verbände. Three months later, he let the SA and SS who were auxiliary police go, sending Röhm into a rage.[129] Furthermore, Himmler, the appointed leader of the SS but technically subordinate to Röhm, wanted to control the security forces and achieve independence for his elitist SS. In April 1934, Göring allowed Himmler to become the chief of the Gestapo, and Himmler, with the assistance of an ex–naval officer, Reinhard Heydrich, began moving selected SS men into the police organizations. The three began conspiring to remove Röhm and the SA as a threat to their own schemes for power, and also began to draw the army into their plans.

By spring of 1934, the senior army leaders were becoming concerned about a successor for Hindenburg whose health had begun to deteriorate. From April 11 to April 15, Hitler took a trip aboard the pocket battleship *Deutschland* with Blomberg, Admiral Raeder, and other senior military leaders. During that voyage, they probably discussed the Reichswehr's future, the reintroduction of conscription, and the succession issue. Wheeler-Bennett reports that military leaders made a pact to support Hitler as Hindenburg's successor in exchange for his support to end Röhm's claims on the army and to assure the army's primacy in military affairs.[130] Later, on May 16, some of them met at Bad Nauheim to discuss the succession issue and unanimously confirmed their support for Hitler over other possible candidates, such as General von Epp and the Crown Prince. In May, there were also rumors, possibly started by the SS, that Schleicher and his assistant General von Bredow were intriguing with Röhm and French agents.[131]

By mid–June, there were other rumors, again probably spread by the SS, of a possible SA revolt.[132] As the rumors multiplied, the army leadership took steps to counter a SA revolt if it occurred. Reichenau now collaborated with Himmler to curtail the danger, and Blomberg threatened to have the President declare martial law and use the army to restore order unless Hitler took action to do so. Around June 20, Himmler ordered the SS to negotiate with the army at the local level for arms. On June 25, the Abwehr, the counterintelligence department of the Reichswehrministry, received an alleged secret order from Röhm calling his Stormtroopers to arms. That same day, General Ewald von Kleist received information that the SA were feverishly preparing for some activity. General Wilhelm Kleist, the Area Commander for Silesia, flew to Berlin to report directly to Fritsch and Beck his suspicions about Himmler's role in the escalating tensions. When Kleist repeated his report to Reichenau, the latter retorted, "That may well be right, but it is too late now."[133] The SA leaders were going on a four-week leave to Bad Wiessee, and the conspirators took this opportunity to get rid of them and other opponents.

No one knows for sure how many people were murdered during the June 30 purge, but we know that the army gave support to the SS executioners.[134] On June 25, Blomberg placed the Reichswehr on alert, canceled leave, and confined the troops to their barracks. Army headquarters in Berlin issued specific instructions to all Wehrkreise staffs of the threat of an SA putsch.[135] Three days later, Röhm was formally expelled from the German Officers League and other veterans organizations. Also that day, Blomberg proclaimed in a *Völksiche Beobachter* article the military's full support for Hitler, essentially giving Hitler a free hand.[136] Army units of Wehrkreis VII issued 12,000 rounds of ammunition and 1,000 rifles to local SS. Army installations were ordered to give refuge to SS units or provide trucks to transport the killing squads. Other army units were used to disarm SA units or act as guards.[137] Papen, when he learned of the SS actions, went to the Reichswehrministry and asked Fritsch why the army was not interceding to stop the violence. The senior army commander said that he had no explicit orders from Blomberg or Hindenburg upon which he could act.[138] In these ways, the army became a coconspirator of the SS butchers.

When the killing ended, the army deepened its complicity with the SS. On July 1, Blomberg congratulated the Führer in a statement for his "soldierly decision and exemplary courage [in crushing] the traitors and murderers.... The army, as the bearer of arms of the entire people ... will show its gratitude through devotion and loyalty."[139]

Two days later, the Reichswehrminister issued a decree that legalized the actions of the SS, made necessary it said in the defense of the state.[140] From his East Prussian estate, the dying Hindenburg, surrounded by pro-Nazi advisors, issued a telegram, congratulating Hitler and Göring for their handling of the "conspiracy."[141] As the French military attaché to Germany wrote Paris, the German military generally approved of Hitler's actions completely—"they were fully satisfied with the triumph of the Reichswehr."[142]

Far worse, the majority of army leaders said or did nothing to counter Reichenau's and Hitler's accusations of Schleicher's and Bredow's involvement in Röhm's "plot" and with "foreign powers."[143] Blomberg forbade all military members to discuss the generals' deaths or to attend their funerals. The German Officers' League, which had earlier terminated Röhm's membership, now drew away from the murdered Schleicher because he "had forfeited by his everlasting intrigues the confidence of all decent officers."[144] In August, Reichenau even told a reporter for the *Petit Journal* that "[t]he death of Schleicher, our former chief, caused us pain, but we are of the opinion that he long ago ceased being a soldier."[145]

A few did protest, albeit in a limited way, the brutal execution of the two generals. Of the army's senior leadership, only Hammerstein attended Schleicher's funeral in full uniform and with the murdered general's decorations. Generals Gerd von Rundstedt and Erwin von Witzleben, and Colonel Erich von Manstein called for a court of inquiry to investigate the actions of the two generals, but Blomberg and Reichenau remained silent.[146] After Hitler's July 13 Reichstag speech, Fritsch protested to Hindenburg but took no further action when the President did not respond. As Fritsch told a high-level army officer, "We can not change politics [only] do our duty." Fritsch and Beck requested an investigation into these deaths from Blomberg, but he refused. The two generals went no further in their protest.[147] Hans Oster, a young office in the Abwehr, the Wehrmacht's counter-intelligence division, condemned the assassinations and recognized that the army's collective failure to protest would mean a weakening of the army vis-à-vis National Socialism. Erwin Rommel told a friend, "Now would be the time to get rid of Hitler and his entire gang."[148] However, there was no real effort to actually carry out Rommel's proposal.

Generalfeldmarschall von Mackensen and Hammerstein went the furthest to obtain rehabilitation for the murdered generals. They sent the ailing President a letter (which he probably did not see), dated July 18, demanding that those responsible for the generals' death be punished, and they continued to agitate for rehabilitation throughout 1934. Blomberg and Fritsch apparently counseled Hitler to issue some sort of statement to placate the growing number of officers who realized the falsities of the charges against the dead generals. On January 3, 1935, at the Kroll Opera House, Hitler added an "off the record" comment to his speech to the senior army officers that the two generals had been killed in error, that his subsequent statements had been based on incorrect information, and that their names would be returned to the honor rolls of their regiments.[149] On February 28, Mackensen stated before the Vereinigung Graf Schlieffen, that, in effect, the "personal honor" of the dead generals had not been affected by their political activities. He added, "Our fallen comrades, the Generals von Schleicher and von Bredow, died in all honour and have fallen on the field of honour."[150] Mackenson's statement produced a counterstatement from Blomberg on April 2, that his statement had not, in effect, resulted in rehabilitating the two generals: "No alteration of the standpoint of the Government and of the view held up until now by the officer corps on this question has taken place, and, furthermore, this is impossible."[151] There was no further discussion of this issue.

As for Hitler, he immediately confirmed his part of the "deal" in eliminating the SA leaders. He replaced the executed Röhm with a less forcible figure, Victor Lutze, as the Chief of the SA, and the SA ceased to be a threat to the army. In his July 1 order of the day to Lutze, Hitler stressed that "...above all, each SA officer must conduct himself toward the Army in a spirit of perfect honesty, loyalty, and fidelity." The army also received the large stores of arms that the SA had obtained.[152] While the generals had gotten their wish, they, in their shortsightedness, failed to see the new threat posed by the SS. Made independent of the SA on July 26, the SS, with Himmler as its head directly under Hitler, would develop into the armed force of the Nazi revolution, the true rival to the Wehrmacht. Finally, the army's participation in the June 30 slaughter and its acquiescence in the murder of two of its comrades would corrupt it sufficiently so it, too, would soon pose no real threat to Hitler.

Meanwhile, early on August 2, Hindenburg suddenly died at his East Prussian estate, an event that gave Hitler the opportunity to assume complete power. The day before, Hitler had gotten the cabinet to promulgate a law that would combine the office of president with the office of chancellor in his person upon Hindenburg's death.[153] This act clearly violated the Weimar Constitution and the Enabling Act of March 24, 1933. A month before Hitler's appointment as Chancellor, the Reichstag had amended the constitution to give the president of the High Court of Justice the authority to act as president until the holding of new elections.[154] Furthermore, the Enabling Act specifically forbade the chancellor from interfering with the presidency.[155] However, not one to allow such "legal" issues to stand in his way, Hitler held a plebiscite on August 19 to "confirm" his actions and complete his attainment of total executive power, including control of the armed forces as supreme commander.[156]

Hindenburg's death changed the Reichswehrministry's plans to hold parades that day to commemorate the 20th anniversary of the start of German mobilization in 1914. Instead, Blomberg, on his authority as the Reichswehrminister, ordered all military personnel to take the new oath of allegiance "in a solemn ceremony" to Hitler. His order also directed that a cheer be raised to the new commander in chief and both national anthems be played. Those on leave would take the new oath upon their return.[157] Apparently, Reichenau dictated the text of the new oath to a subordinate, Major Foertsch, on August 1. When Foertsch questioned Reichenau about the inclusion of the words "God" and "sacred oath," given the general's pro–Nazi views, Reichenau stated that an oath without a reference to God was not an oath.[158] At 3:00 P.M. on August 2, the Berlin Watch Regiment became the first unit to take the oath, and Hitler received the oath personally from Blomberg, Fritsch, and Raeder as the senior military leaders.[159] From Berlin, the oath-taking ceremonies spread throughout the country to every military installation. Later that day, Blomberg sent Hitler a telegram that every officer and man of the armed forces had sworn their loyalty to him as Führer and Chancellor.[160]

Not only was there no requirement for a new oath, but also the new one was, strictly speaking, illegal and unconstitutional. A new oath, created by law on December 1, 1933, had already changed the original Weimar oath by adding the phrase "I swear to God," thus, reviving the religious tone familiar to many officers who had taken their original commissioning oath before November 1918. This oath was sufficient for new recruits to declare their loyalty to the Nazi regime. Furthermore, since the new oath was promulgated on Blomberg's authority, not by a change in the law as had been the case with previous oaths, the order was not published in the *Reichsgesetzblatt*, the official government record, but in a military publication, the *Heeresverordnungsblatt*. Unlike previous oaths, all military personnel had to take the oath, not just the new recruits. Furthermore, Blomberg issued the order without the signature of Hitler or the Minister of Interior. Finally, the new oath was sworn to Hitler as President and commander in chief, not to the constitution, as the 1919 Weimar Constitution required. Apparently these were the difficulties with which Beck and a few other officers mentally grappled, not the oath taking per se.[161] Although neither Blomberg nor Hitler were obviously concerned with its legality or constitutionality, the oath was legalized on August 30, 1934.[162]

In the month following Hindenburg's death, Hitler paid lip service to the traditions of the military. He announced that Hindenburg would be buried at the Tannenberg Monument that commemorated the field marshal's major victory over the Russians in 1914.[163] At the funeral, Hindenburg's coffin was borne between two rows of uniformed men — one from the army and the other from the SA and SS. (During the funeral, Blomberg suddenly offered to Hitler that the members of the armed forces now address him as "Mein Führer," rather than "Herr Hitler," as warranted by his "civilian" position as Chancellor.[164]) For the time being, Hitler would pay homage to the dead field marshal.[165] On August 17, he recognized the distinction between the "political sphere," supported by the National Socialist movement and the "military sphere," supported by the military. The military would "be the sole bearer of arms."[166] On August 20, Hitler in a congratulatory letter thanked Blomberg for the military's "pledge of allegiance" and pledging himself "to support the existence and inviolability of the Wehrmacht" and "to establish the Army as the nation's sole bearer of arms."[167]

Summary

From the 1930 Leipzig trial to the August 2, 1934 oath-taking ceremony, there were significant changes in the political attitudes of the officers, most whom no longer believed in Seeckt's "above politics" policy. The younger officers saw opportunities for promotion and career development in Hitler's destruction of the Versailles Treaty and the resulting expansion of the army. The senior officers detested the crudeness of the Nazi movement and its "low class" leader, but many of them disliked the Weimar Republic more. To them, Hitler would be the means to re-establish the army's position in a rearmed Germany. Unfortunately, they believed that they could control Hitler once he came to power legally — a most serious error caused by Seeckt's Überparteilichkeit policy.

Furthermore, some historians, like Wheeler-Bennett and Craig, condemn the Army leadership for its acquiescence in Hitler's attainment of power in January 1933. However, this judgment appears to derive from hindsight, looking at the destruction and atrocities of the regime during its 12 years of existence, not at Germany in 1933–34. Hitler and his movement had a great deal of support among the German population in general and within the army in particular. In 1933, the officers saw no reason to prevent Hitler from coming to power and not to support his policies during those first years of the regime. For them to intervene in the domestic politics of the time would have meant going against their tradition and may even have resulted in civil war. Furthermore, many officers favored the rearmament and the resulting promotions, the re-establishment of the army's former position in German society, and a limited war of revenge against Poland that Hitler promised. However, certainly in 1933 and 1934, no one, especially the politically neutral and naïve senior officers, could foresee that their support in rebuilding Germany's military would lead to world war in 1939 and the attendant atrocities.

As a result, the few questions at the time appear to have been over the manner in which the oath was promulgated, not the wording of the oath itself. The more senior officers were more familiar with an oath to a person than one to an inanimate constitution, and especially one to a government that they, at best, tolerated if not outright detested. They generally viewed the new oath as a revival of the oath they had taken to the kaiser before 1918. Furthermore, first to Seeckt, then even more to Hindenburg, and finally Hitler, they had a "person" upon which they could project their loyalties, rather than a constitution or a republic. Many, like Guderian, did apparently understand the meaning of the oath, if not its long-range consequences or Hitler's ultimate abuse of it: "Pray God that both sides may abide by it equally for the welfare of Germany. The army is accustomed to keep its oaths. May the army be able, in honor, to do so this time."[168]

For the first years of his regime, Hitler courted the senior officers, even agreeing to eliminate Röhm — the only person he ever referred to in the familiar German *du*— and his radical SA followers. Furthermore, the younger officers were already enthralled with the Nazi movement and Hitler's promises to expand the army and to undo the humiliations of the Versailles Treaty. The testimony of many officers at the 1930 Leipzig trial revealed the degree to which Nazi sentiment — but not the *völkische* ideology — had permeated the younger officers. Blomberg's gradual introduction of National Socialism into the army caused no heated reactions among the officers like the violent disagreements over the republic's flag and uniform insignia between 1919 and 1927. By June 1934, apparently none of them had any qualms about taking a personal oath of loyalty to the man whom they perceived would lead them back to greatness — restoration of the officer corps' status in German society and of Germany's place among the European powers.

The following two statements express the sentiment of many of the army officers, both junior and senior, toward Hitler and his programs in August 1934. Stieff wrote to his wife soon after Hindenburg's death,

> But *le roi est mort, vive le roi*! We soldiers must not remain standing still. And as we become bound by a new oath to our new commander in chief, we can best express our thanks to our great model by fulfilling our duties to our new leader as we filled it toward Hindenburg, firmly trusting in God and believing in the future of our fatherland. And the more closely we are committed to the Führer, the more he will depend on us for success of further developments. I am firmly convinced of this in view of the Führer's pure character, and that gives me strength again to look to the future with new hope in spite of all the blows of fate.[169]

Hans Oster, shortly before his execution after the abortive July 20, 1944, assassination attempt, testified to his initial support for Hitler: "The return to a strong national policy, rearmament, and the introduction of conscription signified, for the officer [corps] a return to earlier traditions."[170] Other future anti-Hitler conspirators, including Stauffenberg, Tresckow, and Canaris, expressed similar pro-Hitler sentiments in the regime's early years.[171] The next chapter will show how Hitler further courted the officers through his rearmament program and foreign policy — short of war — so that when it was time to get rid of those senior officers who opposed war, he could do so with little fear of a coup.

Notes

1. The Ministeramt was a new department created in early 1929, combining various offices of the Reichswehrministry — legal, intelligence, public relations, Reichstag relations — into one under the Reichswehrminister. Its chief, with the title of under-secretary, had more political than military duties. Interestingly, Schleicher knew Oskar von Hindenburg, the President's son, through their ties to their old imperial regiment, the Third Foot Guards. When the field marshal was elected President, his son Oskar became his chief personal advisor. During the remaining years of the republic, Schleicher would exploit this relationship to gain access to the aging President for his own uses but, in many respects, to the detriment of the government and the army.

2. Marshall-Cornwall quoted in Carsten, p. 303.

3. See Thomas Childers, *The Nazi Voter: The Social Foundations of Fascism in Germany, 1919–1933* (Chapel Hill, NC: The University of North Carolina Press, 1983), pp. 119–91, for details of this transformation.

4. Adolf Hitler, *Mein Kampf* (Boston: Houghton Mifflin Company, 1943), p. 205.

5. Hitler Speech, Munich September 18, 1922, pp. 45–46; and Hitler speech, Munich, April 13, 1923, p. 55, in Raoul de Roussy de Sales, ed., *My New Order* (Selected Speeches of Adolf Hitler) (New York: Reynal & Hitchcock, 1941). Adolf Hitler, *Hitler's Secret Book* (New York: Bramhall House, 1986), pp. 89–90, 123. Hitler apparently dictated at least part of this work in May 1928. For various reasons, given in the Introduction by Telford Taylor, Hitler directed that the book not be published. In 1945, an American officer found the manuscript, but it remained hidden among other captured German documents until 1958. It was published in Germany in 1961 as *Hitlers Zweites Buch*.

6. Hitler, *Mein Kampf*, p. 632.

7. Document 5, Hitler Speech, October 26, 1920, in J. Noakes and G. Pridham, *Nazism 1919–1945: A History in Documents and Eyewitness Accounts*, vol. I, *The Nazi Party, State and Society 1919–1939* (New York: Shocken Books, 1983–84), p. 17. Hitler Speech, April 17, 1923, in Baynes, I, pp. 56–57. Hitler Speech, March 15, 1929, quoted in Wheeler-Bennett, pp. 210–11. Hitler, *Mein Kampf*, pp. 425, 574.

8. Document 3, NSDAP Program, February 24, 1920, in Noakes and Pridham, I, pp. 14–5. Hitler Speech, April 24, 1923, pp. 66–7; and Testimony at Beer Hall Putsch Trial, p. 109; Hitler Open Letter to Brüning, October 14, 1931, pp. 552–53; in Baynes, I. Hitler Speech, Munich, August 1, 1923, in de Roussy, p. 65. Hitler, *Secret Book*, pp. 80, 83–5.

9. Hitler, *Secret Book*, pp. 26–7. Hitler, *Mein Kampf*, pp. 279–81.

10. Heiden, p. 397.

11. Document 112, Hitler Speech on Relationship of National Socialism to the Reichswehr, March 15, 1929, in Schüddekopf, p. 285. Carsten, pp. 309–10. Craig, p. 434.

12. Decree of the Defense Minister, November 19, 1929, in Carsten, p. 317. Beck reportedly celebrated the Nazis' electoral success of September 1930 in the officers' mess. Carsten, p. 310.

13. Guderian quoted in Macksey, p. 76.

14. *Kapitänleutnant* Heye Letter to Schleicher, January 17, 1930, in Carsten, p. 312.

15. Carsten, pp. 310–11.

16. Gisevius quoted in Hamerow, pp. 10–11.

17. Hamerow.

18. Hamerow, p. 31.

19. General Alexander von Falkenhausen, "Von Falkenhausen 1922–1945," MS #B-289, December 21, 1950, p. 3, in Donald S. Detwiler, Charles B. Burdick, and Jürgen Rohwer, *World War II German Military Studies* (New York: Garland Publishing, Inc., 1979), Vol. 24. Note: The page numbers in the footnotes citing Detwiler, et al., refer to page numbers within each manuscript as the volume itself is not numbered consecutively from beginning to end. Hamerow, pp. 32, 47.

20. The Reichswehr also actively combated Communist propaganda activities within the army and navy, particularly the distribution of Communist literature in military barracks and the formation of Communist cells within military formations. For such activities, a number of Reichswehr members were convicted for carrying on political activities and were discharged from the service. "German Communist Activity," (London) *Times*, January 31, 1930, p. 13.

21. Notes from Schleicher Speech, Autumn 1929, in Carsten, p. 305.

22. "Asks Loyalty to Republic," *New York Times*, April 4, 1930, p. 9.

23. Wheeler-Bennett, p. 200.

24. Wheeler-Bennett, pp. 213–15.

25. Ludin, quoted in Carsten, p. 316.

26. Carsten, pp. 315–16.

27. Reynolds, pp. 36–38, 41.

28. "Indictment of Hitler for Treason Sought as Three Officers Are Tried," *New York Times*, September 24, 1930, pp. 1, 9. See also Document 109, Army Officer writing in the *Deutsche Allgemeine*

Zeitung, February 9, 1930, in Schüddekopf, pp. 263–4.

29. "Security in Germany," (London) *Times*, September 24, 1930, p. 12.

30. "Indictment of Hitler Sought...," *New York Times*, September 24, 1930, pp. 1, 9. For example, many of the younger, nationally minded officers resented Groener's attempts to establish social contacts with the Social Democrats whom they regarded as defeatists and pacifists. Also, some of the senior officers still remembered Groener's actions in the last days of the war and the early days of the republic — although the 1922 Court of Honor had cleared him of any wrongdoing. Wheeler-Bennett, p. 195. Carsten, pp. 295–6. Interestingly, Scheringer repeated his antigovernment beliefs in an article he wrote while in detention during the trial. This article was smuggled out of his cell and subsequently printed in the *Völkische Beobachter*. Extract quoted in Wheeler-Bennett, p. 216.

31. "Show Fascism Rife in the Reichswehr," *New York Times*, September 30, 1930, p. 20.

32. "The Leipzig Trial," (London) *Times*, September 30, 1930, p. 12.

33. "Show Fascism...," *New York Times*, September 30, 1930, p. 20. See also Document 116, Extracts from the Testimony of Some Officers at the Reichswehr Trial at Leipzig in October 1930, Schüddekopf, pp. 289–90.

34. Stieff letter, September 25, 1930, in Carsten, p. 319.

35. Reynolds, p. 41.

36. "Indictment of Hitler for Treason...," *New York Times*, September 24, 1930, p. 1. "Leipzig Trial," (London) *Times*, September 27, 1930, p. 10.

37. Hitler Testimony at Leipzig Trial, September 26, 1930, quoted in Shirer, p. 198. Document 63, Extract of Hitler Testimony at Leipzig Trial, September 26, 1930, in Noakes and Pridham, p. 90. "Hitler Would Scrap Versailles Treaty and Use Guillotine," *New York Times*, September 26, 1930, pp. 1, 11.

38. Wheeler-Bennett, p. 218.

39. Reynolds, p. 42.

40. Document 125, Schleicher Speech on the Morale of the Reichswehr, October 25, 1930, in Schüddekopf, p. 320.

41. Noakes and Pridham, I, p. 90. As late as 1932, Schleicher told Hitler, "If you come into power legally, that will be all right with me: if not, I shall shoot." Quoted in Demeter, p. 197.

42. "The Leipzig Trial," (London) *Times*, October 30, 1930, p. 11.

43. "German Officers Guilty of Treason," *New York Times* , October 5, 1930, p. 14. Fortress imprisonment was considered an "honorable" punishment, involving no loss of prestige. The prisoners would have considerable freedom to walk about some old fortress and to have food and drink sent in.

44. "Leipzig Sentences," (London) *Times*, October 11, 1930, p. 11. Scheringer became a Communist while in prison. Wendt joined Otto Strasser's revolutionary Nazis. Ludin remained loyal to Hitler, later becoming a high-ranking SA leader and German ambassador to Slovakia. Carsten, p. 319.

45. Document 121, Letter of Dr. jur. Kumbacher, in Schüddekopf, pp. 298–9. The letter was originally printed in the October 17, 1930, issue of the *Völksiche Beobachter*. See also Document 122, Letter from some Reichswehr Lieutenants, in Schüddekopf, p. 301.

46. "The Leipzig Sentences," (London) *Times*, October 30, 1930, p. 13.

47. Groener Letter to von der Goltz, October 6, 1930, quoted in Craig, p. 435.

48. "Brüning Is Victor in Reichstag Voting; Disorders Continue," *New York Times*, October 19, 1930, p. 14.

49. "Von Seeckt Calls on Germany to Arm," *New York Times*, October 22, 1930, p. 13.

50. Appendix 30, Groener Circular to all Reichswehr Officers, October 6, 1930, in Demeter, pp. 356–7.

51. Appendix 31, Groener Special Circular to Senior and Regimental Commanders, October 1930, in Demeter, pp. 358–9.

52. Demeter, p. 194. Carsten, pp. 313–4.

53. Document 123, Scheringer Open Letter to Groener, October 28, 1930, in Schüddekopf, pp. 302–3.

54. Lieutenant Steiff to his fiancée, October 7, 1930, in Carsten, pp. 319–20.

55. Lindemann Letter to Schleicher, April 7, 1931, in Carsten, pp. 312–3.

56. Leber quoted in Demeter, pp. 195–6.

57. Document 111, NSDAP Directive, December 5, 1928, in Schüddekopf, p. 280.

58. Pfeffer von Salamon had been chief of the SA since Röhm's resignation in April 1925. He had wanted more freedom to propagandize among the soldiers and to train the SA as the core of a new German army. However, Hitler at this time did not want to antagonize the army leaders by encouraging active subversion against the army. As a result, Pfeffer resigned as chief of the SA in September 1930, and Hitler recalled Röhm, who had been training the Bolivian army since 1928, to Germany. Dietrich Orlow, *The History of the Nazi Party: 1919–1933* (Pittsburgh, PA: University of Pennsylvania Press, 1969), pp. 211–12.

59. Hitler Testimony at May 8, 1931 Trial, in Baynes, I, p. 178.

60. Document 130, Schleicher Notice, January 2, 1931, in Schüddekopf, p. 326. Bracher, p. 189.

61. Wheeler-Bennett, p. 227. Document 133, Schleicher Letter to Röhm, November 4, 1931, in Schüddekopf, pp. 328.

62. The SA Oath: "As a member of the storm troops of the NSDAP, I pledge myself by its storm flag [Sturmfahne]; to be always ready to stake life and limb in the struggle for the aims of the movement; to give absolute military obedience to my military superiors; to bear myself honorably in and out of service; to be always companionable to my other comrades." Document 12, Noakes and Pridham, I, p. 24.

63. Footnote 1, Craig, p. 440. Conan Fischer reports SA strength at about 30,000 in August 1929; about 60,000 in November; 100,000 in January 1931; 290,00 in January 1932; 445,000 in August 1932; 425,000 in January 1933; and over 2 million in March 1933. *Stormtroopers: A Social, Economic, and Ideological Analysis, 1929–35* (London: George Allen & Unwin, 1983), pp. 5–6. Röhm had organized the SA along military lines: Gruppen (groups), Standarten (regiments), and Stürme (companies). The SA also had its own motorized units and air squadrons.

64. SA Inspector General report, December 1931, Fisher, p. 85. For example, in 1931, the gap between the "politicians" of the party and the more militant, military-minded Stormtroopers in the northern and eastern Germany, led by Stennes, resulted to a series of brawls between the two groups. Hitler called these "rebels" "[f]reebooters ... clique of mutinous officers ... traitors without honor ... rabble ... men without character...." Heiden, p. 372.

65. For example, Hammerstein after a four-hour meeting with Hitler at a private apartment in September 1931. Carsten, p. 333. Schleicher and Groener Speech to Division and Corps Commanders, January 11, 1932, in Carsten, p. 334. Document 132, About Meeting between Schleicher and Hitler, October 1931, pp. 327–8; and Document 134, Groener's Opinion on Hitler, December 1931, pp. 328–9, in Schüddekopf. Schleicher went as far to say again and again "that the NSDAP was developing fealty to the state and under Hitler's influence could be made into a party capable of governance." Bracher, p. 189.

66. Groener quoted in Rosinski, p. 174.

67. Document 134, Groener Speech at Military Commander's Conference, January 11, 1932, in Schüddekopf, p. 329.

68. Joachim Fest, *Hitler* (New York: Harcourt Brace Jovanvich, 1973), p. 307.

69. For details, see Carsten, pp. 339–47. Shirer, pp. 225–6. In 1923, before the Beer Hall Putsch, Hitler created the Stosstrupp as an elitist group of SA members to serve as shock troops who swore loyalty to him personally. After his release from prison in 1925, Hitler recreated his elitist troops as the Schutzstaffel (Defense Corps) (SS). They wore black uniforms, similar to Mussolini's Fascisti who had marched on Rome in 1922, with Hitler's own motto, "My honor is loyalty," engraved on their belt buckles. Although Hitler expanded the SS as a counterweight to Röhm's SA and gave it increasing independence under a former chicken farmer, Heinrich Himmler, the SS still numbered only 280 men by 1929. See Appendix A for the SS oath.

70. Telford Taylor, *Sword and Swastika: Generals and Nazis in the Third Reich* (Chicago: Quadrangle Books, 1969), p. 61. Two days before Groener resigned, he prophetically wrote, "It will be up to the generals to see that the Army does not in the end kiss Herr Schickelgruber's hands like hysterical women." Quoted in Cooper, p. 3.

71. Fest, *Hitler*, p 353. Craig, p. 456.

72. Stieff quoted in Hamerow, p. 32.

73. Carsten, pp. 370–3.

74. Falkenhausen, MS #B-289, p. 3, in Detwiler, et al.

75. Falkenhausen, MS #B-289, p. 3, in Detwiler, et al.

76. Heiden, p. 488.

77. Wilhelm Keitel Letter to Father, Summer 1932, quoted in Demeter, p. 201. Notes of Colonel Hahn on Commander's Speech, August 20, 1932, in Carsten, p. 374.

78. Lieutenant General Liebmann, Commander of Fifth Division; Hammerstein to Under Secretary of State Planck, August 15, 1932; Lieutenant Steiff Letter to his Wife, August 21, 1932; and Report of General Freiherr Geyr von Schweppenburg (1956), in Carsten, pp. 374–5. Carsten (p. 375) writes that, given these declarations, the Reichswehr would, in fact, have fired on Nazi rioters in the summer of 1932 if the SA had attempted a putsch, despite the widespread Nazi sentiment among the troops. Perhaps many of the army troops would have obeyed orders to shoot rioting Nazi Stormtroopers if such an order had the firm backing of the president. However, such an order would certainly have split the army wide open. The testimony of the young officers at the Leipzig trial indicated a serious confidence gap between the senior leadership and the troops, similar to, if not as great in an extent as, that between the French High Command and the *poilus* in the trenches in 1917. To order them to fire on a group of people whom they held in greater esteem than the army's senior leadership, might have been sufficient to cause a serious breach in discipline and the mutiny of a significant number of the troops during that summer.

79. Taylor, *Sword and Swastika*, p. 67. Carsten, pp. 336–7.

80. Document 81, Hitler Reply to Gregor Strasser Speech, December 8, 1932, in Noakes and Pridham, I, p. 113.

81. Hitler Speech in Munich, September 7, 1932, in Max Domarus, *Hitler Speeches and Proclamations 1932–1945* (Wauconda, IL: Bolchazy-Carducci Publishers, 1990), vol. I, *The Years 1932 to 1934*, p. 163.

82. This perceived, almost paranoiac, threat originated in the Versailles Treaty in which the reconstituted Poland received most of Pomerania and a corridor to the Free City of Danzig to give Poland a port on the Baltic Sea, an action that severed East Prussia from the rest of Germany. This region contained a mixed Polish-German population with about two million Germans. There was also the dispute over Silesia discussed earlier in Chapter 2. Throughout the 1920s and early 1930s, the army feared, however improbable it was, a major Polish attack from the east that would overrun East Prussia and threaten Germany's eastern frontier — this constituted a major scenario in Weimar military planning. This planning also envisioned difficult and dangerous operations to ferry troops to East Prussia across the Baltic Sea. The Reichswehr's leaders knew that Germany could not withstand a simultaneous offensive from France and Poland without additional forces. From this fear came the army's illicit cooperation with the Black Reichswehr and then the SA and the construction of defensive fortifications and antitank ditches along the eastern and East Prussia frontiers. Future general Johannes Blaskowitz believed that "the question of the Polish Corridor ... would have to be settled by force of arms.... [Such a] war was regarded as a sacred though a sad necessity. " Richard John Giziowski, *The Moral Dilemma of Leadership: The Case of German General Johannes Blaskowitz* (Ann Arbor, MI: UMI Dissertation Services, 1991), pp. 100, 140–42. See also Gaines Post, Jr., *The Civil-Military Fabric of Weimar Foreign Policy* (Princeton, NJ: Princeton University Press 1973), pp. 98–108, 295–98. Luck (p. 13) called the existence of the Polish Corridor "a plundering of German territory." In late August 1939 he (p. 26) did not believe Goebbels' propaganda that the Poles were about to attack Germany, but he did write that "we [the Germans] wanted the corridor and Danzig returned to Germany."

83. See Franz von Papen, *Memoirs* (London: Andre Deutsch, 1952), pp. 220–22, for the Ott report.

84. Schleicher Address to Divisional and Corps Commanders, mid–December 1932; and Notes by Under-Secretary of State Meissner, December 2, 1932, in Carsten, pp. 381–3.

85. Noakes and Pridham, I, p. 121.

86. Craig, p. 467.

87. Görlitz, p. 273.

88. Heusinger wrote in his autobiography that Hitler at first did not have the respect of the professional officers of the General Staff. Many of the aristocratic officers contemptuously referred to Hitler as "the Bohemian corporal." They saw him, according to Allan, "as an uneducated crude and vulgar clod who knew nothing of the mysteries of military strategy and tactics." Allen, p. 43.

89. Summary of Hitler's Speech by Lieutenant General Liebmann, February 3, 1933, in Allen, pp. 239–40. Wheeler-Bennett, p. 291.

90. For example, Hitler Statement in the Reichstag on the Presentation of the Enabling Act, March 23, 1933, p. 282; and Hitler Speech to the Reichstag, May 17, 1933, pp. 330–4, in Domarus, I. Hitler Speech at Bad Reichenhall to SA Leaders, July 1, 1933, p. 554; and Hitler Speech on September 23, 1933, pp. 555–6, in Baynes, I.

91. Hitler Order to the Party on the Day of National Mourning, March 10, 1933, in Domarus, I, p. 264. Papen wrote in his *Memoirs* (p. 287) that he was appalled at Hitler's request but was even more shocked when the President gave into Hitler's and Blomberg's pressure.

92. Footnote 129, Domarus, I, p. 585.

93. The original Reichstag building had been gutted by a fire on February 28, supposedly started by a retarded Dutch Communist, Marius van der Lubbe. Hitler used the fire as an excuse to obtain the Enabling Act, passed by 444 votes to the 94 votes of the Social Democrats. This act gave him dictatorial powers to rule Germany in a state of emergency for four years. See Document 108 in Noakes and Pridham, I, pp. 161–2. Through extensions of the act in 1937, 1941, and 1943, Hitler "legally" ruled Germany until his death in April 1945. The Weimar Constitution was never "officially" rescinded, revoked, or replaced.

94. Mackensen quoted on Craig. p. 470.

95. Blomberg quoted in Taylor, *Sword and Swastika*, p. 80.

96. Blomberg quoted in Allen, p. 38.

97. Domarus, Vol. II, *The Years 1935–1938*, p. 1000.

98. O'Neill, pp. 16–17.

99. For example, Blomberg Address to Divisional and Corps Commanders, June 1, 1933, in Carsten, p. 397; and Blomberg Speech to Officers of the Sixth Division, September 15, 1933, in O'Neill, p. 64. Blomberg ordered that copies of this speech be printed and sent to all army and navy units.

100. O'Neill, p. 33. The National Verbände (National Organizations) were the Stahlhelm, the SA, the SS, the Nationalsozialistisches Kraftfahrer Korps (National Socialist Motorized Corps) (NSKK), and the Hitler Jugend (HJ) (Hitler Youth).

101. Craig, p. 471.

102. O'Neill, p. 37.

103. Domarus, I, pp. 389–91. Hitler made this ceremony an important annual event for the party. Starting with the 1933 ceremony, new recruits for the SS Leibstandarte, the first SS armed unit, and the SS Adolf Hitler, his personal bodyguard, would pledge their loyalty to Hitler unto death before the memorial to the Nazi dead of November 9, 1923. Hitler recited the following: "I demand of you that

you lay down your lives just as the sixteen men who were killed at this very spot. Your lives must have no other purpose but loyalty. These dead are your examples, and you shall be the unattainable (!) examples to the others." Hitler would then recite the SS oath for the recruits to repeat. Domarus, p. 392.

104. Cooper, p. 29. Footnote, O'Neill, p. 39.

105. O'Neill, pp. 38, 44.

106. Blomberg Important Political Instruction, April 4, 1934, in O'Neill, p. 70.

107. O'Neill, p. 44.

108. Demeter, pp. 363–4.

109. Wheeler-Bennett, p. 298.

110. Cooper, pp. 22–23. Heiden, pp. 528–9. Reichenau Article, "The Reichsheer, Shoulder to Shoulder with the New Chancellor," February 6, 1934, in Taylor, *Sword and Swastika*, p. 80.

111. Fritsch Letter, May 17, 1937, in O'Neill, p. 28.

112. O'Neill, pp. 28–30. Cooper, pp. 23–24.

113. For example, in response to a comment made by a friend in the summer of 1934 about the expulsion of Jews from the veterans' organizations, Beck believed that they should voluntarily leave these associations to avoid unpleasantness for everyone. Reynolds, p. 54.

114. Adam from his memoirs in Reynolds, p. 46.

115. Beck Letter to Fraulein Gossler, March 17, 1933, in Reynolds, p. 44.

116. Document 115, Röhm, Newspaper Article, June 1933, in Noakes and Pridham, I, pp. 167–8.

117. Hermann Rauschning, *Hitler Speaks* (London: Thornton Butterworth Ltd, 1939), pp. 153–6.

118. Hitler Speeches to SA Leaders at Kiel, May 7, 1933; in the Reichstag, May 17, 1933; to the SA at Bad Reichenhall, July 1, 1933; to the SA at Bad Godesburg, August 19, 1933; and on the Radio, October 14, 1933, in O'Neill, p. 265. Hitler Letter to Röhm, December 31, 1933, p. 401, and Hitler Speech to Reichstag, January 30, 1934, pp. 422–3, in Domarus, I.

119. Brauchitsch quoted in Wheeler-Bennett, p. 310. Brauchitsch would become Army Commander in Chief in 1938 and ultimately be promoted to generalfeldmarschall.

120. O'Neill, pp. 33–35, 42. Röhm quote in O'Neill, p. 42.

121. Demeter, p. 202.

122. Noakes and Pridham, I, p. 173.

123. Max Gallo, *The Night of the Long Knives* (New York: Warner Paperback Library, 1973), pp. 88–9.

124. Wheeler-Bennett, p. 309.

125. Fest, *Hitler*, p. 474.

126. Papen, p. 313.

127. Rauschning, pp. 157–9.

128. Gallo, p. 36. In the latter position, Göring created the Geheime Staatspolizei (State Secret Police) (Gestapo), which would soon spread its web of evil and torture throughout Germany and ultimately occupied Europe after 1939.

129. Heiden, p. 724.

130. Wheeler-Bennett, pp. 311–2. Domarus, I, p. 447. Some historians dispute the so-called *Deutschland* Pact since no historical record of what Hitler and the military leaders actually said has yet to be found. However, it is certainly probable that Hitler and the senior military leaders did, in fact, discuss such issues and may have, in fact, made such a "pact."

131. Gallo, pp. 109–10.

132. Gallo, p. 106.

133. Fest, *Hitler*, p. 479.

134. O'Neill (p. 50) states the purge claimed nearly 50 top SA leaders and other victims. Bracher (p. 239) states the official number was 77 but estimates the actual number to be between 150 and 200. The victims included Röhm and most of the senior and more radical SA leaders who maintained their loyalty to the Führer up to the last minute; Ritter von Kahr from the 1923 coup; Schleicher (and his wife) and Bredow; and even a music critic, mistaken for a Nazi opponent. Two of Papen's aides were also murdered, but the former Chancellor himself barely escaped execution through the protection of Göring.

135. Gallo, p. 216.

136. Wheeler-Bennett, pp. 321–2. Heiden, p. 754. Blomberg Article in *Völkische Beobachter*, June 28, 1934, in Domarus, I, p. 467.

137. O'Neill, p. 50. Gallo, p. 282.

138. Papen, pp. 318–9.

139. Blomberg Address to the Army, July 1, 1934, in Baynes, I, p. 332.

140. Wheeler-Bennett, p. 326.

141. Gallo, p. 300. The telegram was issued with Hindenburg's signature affixed, but it is possible that it had been actually written and issued by his son Oskar.

142. Gallo, p. 311.

143. Reichenau News Conference, June 30, 1934, Gallo, pp. 281–2. Hitler Press Release, June 30, 1934, in Domarus, I, pp.478–9. Hitler Speech to the Reichstag, July 13, 1934, in Baynes, I, pp. 290–338.

144. Görlitz, p. 289.

145. Footnote 143, Domarus, I, p. 602.

146. Görlitz, p. 289.

147. O'Neill, pp. 50–51. Fritsch quote from Bracher, p. 237. Reynolds, p. 54.

148. Rommel quoted in Hamerow, p. 112.

149. Wheeler-Bennett, pp. 335–7. O'Neill, pp. 51–52.

150. Mackensen quoted in O'Neill, p. 52. The Vereinigung Graf Schlieffen was a society of former General Staff officers dedicated to the memory of General Alfred Graf von Schlieffen, former Chief

of the Great General Staff and author of the Schlieffen Plan.

151. Blomberg Order, April 12, 1935, in O'Neill, p. 53.

152. Gallo, p. 290.

153. Law of the Head of State of the German Reich, August 1, 1934, in Domarus, I, pp. 508–9.

154. Document 152, Law about the Change in the Constitution, December 17, 1932, in Hohlfeld, III, p. 455.

155. Document 108, Enabling Act, March 24, 1933, in Noakes and Pridham, I, p. 161.

156. The plebiscite gave him a large approval for his actions although it was not unanimous. Only 89.9 percent of the eligible voters voted for Hitler; more than five million Germans voted against him or submitted invalid ballots. Domarus, I, p. 525.

157. *Heeresverordnungsblatt* 21, August 2, 1934, in Schwertfeger, p. 572.

158. Otmar, p. 15.

159. Wheeler-Bennett, p. 332.

160. Gallo, p. 314.

161. See footnote 3, Introduction, p. 2. General P. Mahlmann, in 1955, stated, "I have also asked myself [why I took the oath]. However, it had deliberately come from above...." General Stieve also expressed internal misgivings about the oath-taking. Major Foertsch, in 1951, called the Hitlerian oath "an abnormal alteration of the old oath." Otmar, pp. 17–18.

162. Document 133, Law of August 30, 1934, in Noakes and Pridham, I, p. 185. This law also required civil servants to take a personal oath of loyalty to Hitler as Führer and Chancellor.

163. Domarus, I, p. 509.

164. O'Neill, p. 58.

165. See Hitler's Memorial Address, Berlin, August 6, 1934, pp. 513–4; Hitler's Speech at Hindenburg's Funeral, August 7, 1934, p. 516; and Hitler's Speech on the Plebiscite of August 19, August 19, 1934, pp. 520–4; in Domarus, I.

166. Baynes, I, p. 494.

167. Hitler Letter to Blomberg, August 20, 1934, in Domarus, I, p. 525.

168. Letter to Wife, August 2, 1934, in Guderian, p. 23.

169. Stieff quoted in Hamerow, p. 113.

170. Oster quoted in Hamerow, p. 47.

171. See Hamerow, pp. 92–93, 108, 109.

4

The Army and the Nazi Regime, 1934–1939

During the five years from the oath-taking ceremony to the outbreak of the Second World War, Hitler successfully courted the officer corps through continuing nazification, extensive rearmament, and aggressive and highly successful foreign policy. The effects of these programs would greatly raise the esteem in which the members of the growing Wehrmacht, particularly the officers, held Hitler, and bolster the importance of their personal oath of loyalty to him.[1] Through these efforts Hitler would again make Germany a first-class, modern European military power, provide opportunities for the officers of the old Reichswehr to advance into the higher ranks of the new army and the newly created Oberkommando Wehrmacht (OKW), and create numerous places for many young men in the lower-ranking officer positions. His foreign policy successes would wipe out the disgrace of Versailles, humiliate the Western democracies, and significantly increase the size of the Reich by 1939 without war. Hitler's success in winning over the officer corps was seen in early 1938 by his dismissal of the military's two top generals in a bloodless "coup" with hardly a whimper from the rest (the details of which I will cover in the next chapter).

Totally involved in the army's growth and keeping with their Überparteilichkeit (above politics) training, the senior officers usually suppressed their personal thoughts of the regime's repressive activities — the Gestapo's suppression of civil liberties, creation of concentration camps, and the systematic elimination of Jews from German political, economic, and social life — although they were aware of them. They kept their doubts to themselves or discussed them privately. Their criticism was directed mostly at the radicals among the Nazi leaders and rarely at Hitler himself. What protests occurred were usually intermittent and weak and concerned the growing power of the SS, the creation of the Waffen SS as a second army despite Hitler's own promise to maintain the army as the sole bearer of arms, and the creation of OKW. Furthermore, by the time of the Blomberg-Fritsch crisis in January 1938, the army was fast becoming Hitler's army, as new and younger officers who had undergone partial nazification in the Hitler Youth and the Reich Labor Service became mesmerized by Hitler's foreign policy successes. These factors severely weakened the influence of the conservative, "Prussian" senior army leaders and commensurately increased Hitler's influence over and control of the army.

In this chapter, I will examine the development of the Reichswehr of 1934 into Hitler's army by 1939. I will first review the growth of the army under the direction of Blomberg as Minister of War and Fritsch as army commander in chief, emphasizing the continuing nazification process, the impact of rearmament on the army as a whole and the officer corps in particular, and the development of a German joint military command organization, the OKW. I will then examine the beginnings of the Waffen SS as a second army, created at the insistence of Himmler, a truly revolutionary army loyal only to the Führer. As a result, by September 1939, the army was well on its way to becoming Hitler's army about which Omer Bartov wrote.[2]

Continuation of the Nazification Process

From 1934 until their dismissals in early 1938, Blomberg and Fritsch led the German army through a tremendous modernization and growth program that would establish it again as the foremost army in Europe. The officers, trained to leave politics to the politicians, contentedly—and falsely—believed that Hitler was only interested in furthering their interests and in creating an adequate military force to defend Germany. The destruction of the SA, the personal oath to the Führer, and the presence of the senior military leaders, alongside members of the party organizations at the annual party congresses and on Wehrmacht Day, seemed a reasonably modest price to pay in exchange for his pledge to maintain the army as the sole bearer of arms and to rearm Germany. In recognition of this seeming ascendancy of the army, Alfred Vagts wrote in September 1935, "[T]he National Socialist Party has ceased to be a formidable rival of the Army ... the reign of the Party is over."[3] Like Vagts, many army leaders, including Blomberg and Fritsch, believed that the army was in control and that they could trust Hitler to ensure their mastery over the military. Unfortunately they all failed to recognize the growing impact of Nazi propaganda and Hitler's own influence on the hundreds of thousands of new soldiers who would soon be entering the army.

Even those officers destined to become anti–Hitler conspirators within a few years, first held the Nazi regime in some degree of awe. Like most other officers, Stauffenburg, Tresckow and Oster initially sympathized with many of the aims of the regime and accepted the government's repression as the price of national regeneration and an end of the Versailles Treaty. Rear Admiral Max Bastian, a former superior of then Captain Canaris, reported in Novemeber 1934 that Canaris "served as a model" of support for the Nazi regime, lecturing his crew "on the ideas of the national movement and the principle of the political structure of the new Reich." Even Beck supported the regime's military and foreign policy goals although not necessarily the means, as indicated by his comment on the back of an April 11, 1935, army report: "What is so bad is not what we are doing but how we are doing it."[4]

Hitler continued to pay lip service to the status of the army as the sole bearer of arms and one of the two pillars, along with the NSDAP, upon which the new German Reich stood. In speeches to the German nation, assembled army leaders, and loyal party followers, the Führer reiterated this position. At one meeting on January 3, 1935, he contended that he would ignore any adverse information about the army's loyalty to him, and he gave the army credit for his success. Publicly, his "faith in the Armed Forces was unshakable."[5] During the November 1936 ceremony, honoring the anniversary of the 1923 Putsch, Hitler reminded his audience of his prediction made at his 1924 trial, that the army would stand with the party as one, a prediction that now had become fact.[6]

Although Hitler took strides to maintain this coequal but separate status of the army and the party until he could more completely "coordinate" the army as the party had done with other government agencies, he also made it clear that he considered the army to be the "school of the nation." He had made the creation of a *Volksheer* (people's army) one of the party's Twenty-Five Points and had discussed this concept in *Mein Kampf* (as I mentioned earlier in Chapter 2). Faced with rebuilding the armed forces with conservative, "Prussian" senior officers in 1934, he realized that he could not *yet* carry out these plans to the fullest. Until he would no longer need the "Becks" or the "Fritsches," Hitler contented himself with making speeches on the closeness of the army with the German *Volk*. For example, at the 1936 Wehrmacht Day in Nuremberg, he referred to the assembled troops as "my soldiers" and "my comrades." To him, "[w]ith the Volk, the Party and the Army, we make up an indissoluble sworn community."[7] He flattered them as the inheritors of the great pre–1918 Imperial Army and the Freikorps of 1918–19, "the protectors of the honor, the strength, and the magnificence of the German nation."[8] Hitler particularly liked to remind the German people and the soldiers of the new army that he, at one time, had also worn the field gray uniform of the German army.[9]

To further the closeness of the army with the party and parade his growing military might, Hitler established three annual major events: Heroes' Remembrance Day in March; Wehrmacht Day, in conjunction with the annual party congress, in September; and the anniversary of the 1923 putsch in November. These events became opportunities to stage large-scale spectacles during which mass formations from the military services and the party organizations marched together with thousands of flags, military standards, and, at night, torches and searchlights. On the Wehrmacht Days after 1934, Hitler personally addressed the assembled soldiers and accepted a marching salute from the senior army generals — whom he had ordered to participate as a sign of solidarity with the party.[10] In his speeches, he exhorted the soldiers to sacrifice their freedom and "exhibit obedience and subordination, ... toughness, endurance and, above all, an utmost sense of duty."[11] Siegfried Knappe expressed the exhilaration at participating at the September 1936 party rally that others must have felt:

> ...[W]e all knew that Chancellor Hitler, Generalfeldmarschall Göring, and all the important government figures were there watching us. That knowledge induced a peculiar tingle of excitement in us. We felt ten feet tall and indestructible! This was pageantry of the highest order, and it inspired enormous national pride in us. It was a jubilant extravaganza with the unmistakable message that Germany was being reborn. I felt extremely proud.[12]

To complete the appearance of the army's solidarity with the party, the senior military leaders, on November 9, 1936, joined Hitler, Göring, and members of the Blood Order to commemorate the march from the Bürgerbräukeller to the Feldherrnhalle in Munich.[13]

Further bolstering the closeness of the military and the party was the passage of the Reich Flag Act on September 10, 1935. Red, white, and black became the Reich's official colors; and the party flag (red field with a white circle and a black swastika in the middle), the national flag of Germany.[14] Göring remarked, "The victory of the swastika gave us back our pride and gave us back our might. The Wehrmacht yearns for the insignia under which it was resurrected."[15] Soon afterwards, the swastika replaced the imperial eagle on the naval ensign. Hitler introduced the new flags at the swearing-in ceremony for the first group of conscripts on November 7, 1935. To the troops at Giebelstadt on September 17, 1935, Hitler stated that these new flags signified

> the spirit of the new German uprising and the German resurrection. Your flags wave in the colors and symbols of the new Reich, of a Reich of the *Volksgemeinschaft* [community of the people] whose sons you are; your parents have sent you here to serve the German nation.
>
> It is on behalf of this new Reich that I present to you these flags and standards. You shall be loyal to them just as the regiments and battalions of the old army were loyal to their banners. As sons of our Volk, as soldiers of the National Socialist Third Reich, as the guard of the new Germany shall you march behind these banners.[16]

Just as when Blomberg had the party insignia placed on the military uniforms in 1934, there was no dissension when Hitler made the party flag the official military standard.[17]

Additionally, Blomberg continued his efforts to increase the closeness of the army and the party. Like Hitler, he saw the army as the "great school of national education" whose purpose was "the successful education of the youth in the spirit of National-Socialism, according to the will of the Supreme Commander."[18] While the Defense Law of 1935 prohibited soldiers from undertaking any political activity, including membership in political organizations, it allowed them to participate in National Socialist welfare organizations and to pay party dues, and it permitted party members to wear their military uniforms to party functions, but not publicly speak in uniform.[19] He later relaxed the prohibition on party membership by the military, prohibited soldiers from shopping in Jewish stores, and extended National Socialist indoctrination to reserve officers. Blomberg directed commanders to report politically unreliable soldiers to the Gestapo and increased the authority of the party courts (concerned with violations of party regulations) over military members to include incarceration in concentration camps. Blomberg also increased cooperation with the National Socialist Industrial Organization and the National Socialist Motor Corps (NSKK).[20]

In addition to eroding the ban on National Socialist activities, Blomberg also introduced the systematic indoctrination of military members in National Socialist principles through various means. In April 1934, he issued semimonthly bulletins that were essentially condensations of Nazi propaganda. In mid–1935, he established a special chain of officers to control army publicity from the Defense Ministry to the local military units as a way of bypassing Fritsch's censorship. Military units were given state funds to purchase the party newspaper, and the Propaganda Ministry provided Nazi books and pamphlets for unit reading rooms, either for free or at low cost.

National Socialism was also taught directly to officers and soldiers in training. After the Kriegsakademie (War Academy) secretly reopened in August 1934, Beck ordered the teaching of "racial hygiene" and "racial biology." In 1935, Fritsch suggested, and Beck agreed, to invite senior party officials to the Kriegsakademie to give lectures on the history of National Socialism, the fight for the German race (the Jewish question), and related topics.[21] Finally, in early 1936, Blomberg ordered the introduction of special political instruction for all officers at officer training schools, the staff colleges, and the Wehrmacht Academy. He established special courses, taught by party specialists, to train officers selected to give this instruction. Blomberg liked these courses so well that he had similar courses established down to the Wehrkreis headquarters and local units.[22]

Blomberg also allowed the party to intrude into the private lives of military members. The government could impose the "Block and Cell" administration on the families of military members as long as the soldiers themselves were not bothered.[23] Blomberg also encouraged the soldiers to participate in the party's charities, especially Winterhilfe, and its welfare organization, Kraft durch Freude, and in news items on these activities. He also urged officers to lecture at party schools to publicize the unity of army and party. He agreed to allow the party to contact married soldiers on strictly personal matters and to obtain information on their political views and knowledge of National Socialist thought. Army officers had to invite party leaders to social functions, and military barracks were named after party martyrs.[24]

Perhaps more damaging to the moral underpinning of the German soldiers was Blomberg's decrees that eroded the influence of Christianity within the army. In mid-1935, he made attendance at church parades, the mandatory attendance of church services by entire units, voluntary, and commanders were expressly forbidden to force their troops to attend. In December, he forbade chaplains to force soldiers to attend religious services. In February 1936, Blomberg permitted only the official unit chaplain to provide spiritual services and forbade the distribution of religious materials within the Wehrmacht. In April 1937, he made attendance at "barracks evening hours," mandatory religious instruction conducted by chaplains, voluntary for both active-duty and reserve soldiers.[25]

A 1937 speech to the Catholic chaplains of Wehrkreis IX by General of the Artillery Friedrich Dollman, who was not particularly known as a strong admirer of Nazism, indicates the impact of Nazi indoctrination within the officer corps:

> You may not introduce any political strife into the Wehrmacht. You may attend only to those soldiers who approach you voluntarily.
>
> The soldier must never be placed in a dilemma internally by the fulfillment of voluntarily religious duties. The Oath which he has taken to the Führer and Supreme Commander of the Wehrmacht binds him unto the sacrifice of his own life to National Socialism, the concept of the new Reich. It follows then, that no doubts may be permitted to arise out of your attitudes towards National Socialism. The Wehrmacht, as one of the bearers of the National Socialist state, demands of you as chaplains at all times a clear and unreserved acknowledgment of the Führer, State, and People."[26]

In other words, obedience to the Führer and service to the state should override adherence to personal values.

In the regime's first years, these attempts to bring the army and the party together produced numerous areas of friction between the army and the SS and continuing protests from Fritsch. Many soldiers continued to shop in Jewish stores, despite the party's ban, and SS men regularly refused to salute army officers. Such incidents led individual soldiers and SS men to call each other names, throw insults, and, all too often, brawl in public. These incidents were recorded in the War Ministry, the Army High Command, and the Wehrkreise headquarters.[27] Numerous military members ignored the changes on mandatory church attendance and flocked to services, particularly those of the Confessing Church.[28] The army leadership, with the exception of Fritsch, did little to protest the changes, and even his protests had little effect.[29] Perhaps Fritsch felt that once he made his protests, he had satisfied his professional conscience and could continue his duties to rebuild the army. Other generals, seeing no effects from their commander's own protests, saw no reason to enter the political fight and continued to perform their soldierly duties.

For his efforts in rebuilding the army and closing the gap with the party, Blomberg received the somewhat exaggerated personal gratitude of his Führer.

> Field Marshal von Blomberg had contributed greatly both to the rebirth of the Wehrmacht and to the consolidation of the old Army with the young Party. The Reich Minister of War deserves to be lauded for his merger of the two organizations, and especially for his avoidance of friction between the two parties. He has brought this about in precisely the manner the Führer desired.
>
> An army cannot exist devoid of an ideological base from which it can derive its mission. It is the unrivaled accomplishment of the Reich Minister of War that the National Socialist Weltanschauung was able to provide this moral foundation. In this effort, the Reich Minister was aided by his capacity for facile comprehension and his unerring loyalty.[30]

To be sure, the party paper overstated the "coordination" of the army with the party at this time and ignored the numerous incidents between soldiers and the SS. Yet, it did capture, to a great extent, Blomberg's impact on nazifying the army.

Rearmament and Its Effects

Adding to Blomberg's continued nazification efforts was German rearmament that increased the 100,000-man Reichswehr of 1934 to over one million men by 1939.[31] In December 1933, the army secretly decided to increase the active strength to 300,000 men in 21 divisions and hinted at general conscription in the near future.[32] On April 1, 1934, between 50,000 and 60,000 new recruits, assigned to special training battalions, entered the army. That summer, the army leadership began to plan for a new army, introduced on October 1, 1934, of 21 infantry divisions, three cavalry divisions, and enlargement of the Wehrkreise headquarters to the size of a corps headquarters. The army also received 70,000 more recruits, bringing its size to 240,000.[33]

Table 4.1. Strength of the German Army, 1918–41
Progress of German Rearmament

Date	*Active Divisions*	*Tanks*	*Men (Active)*	*Air Squadrons*	*Aircraft*
Nov 1918	?	2	2,000,000+	306	306
Jan 1919	(24 brigades)		400,000	?	?
Apr 1920	?		200,000	3	
Jul 1920	9?		100,000	0	
1930	?		100,000	3	
Jan 1933	10		102,500		
1934	10		240,000	16	
Aug 1934	10		c. 350,000	48	c. 502
1937	37		500,000	213	1,230
Sep 1938	42		550,000	243	1,230
Jan 1939		2,241			
Jun 1939	51		730,000		
Sep 1939	117		1,400,000	266	
May 1940	157	2,574	2,400,000		2,500
Jun 1941	180		3,200,000		

Source: Table 7, Whaley, p. 69.

Table 4.2. Army Growth in the Late 1930s

	1937–38	*1939–40*
Field Army Total*	2,104,355	2,750,064
Replacement Army Total**	1,239,121	996,040
Combined Total	3,343,476	3,754,104

*Field army was the peacetime active and reserve forces.
**Replacement army consisted of trained replacement units for the Field Army and first-wave reserve units committed to combat.

Source: O'Neill, p. 91.

Table 4.3. Manpower Requirements in the Late 1930s

(Trained men need to meet establishment totals in Table 2)

	1937–38	*1939–40*
Men on Active Duty	550,000	730,000
Reservists I	200,000	500,000
Reservists II	250,000	600,000
Total	1,000,000	1,830,000

Source: O'Neill, p. 92

Table 4.4. Organizational Growth, 1933–39

UNIT	*1933*	*1934*	*1935*	*1936*	*1937*	*1938*	*Peace 1939*	*War 1939*
Army Group HQ	2	2	3	3	4	6	6	11
Corps HQ	10	10	12	13	19	22	26	
Division HQ	10	24	29	39	51	51	51	102
Battalions								
Infantry	84	166	287	334	352	476	476	906
Artillery	24	95	116	148	187	228	228	482
Panzer	6	12	16	24	34	34	34	

Source: O'Neill, p. 91

Table 4.5. German Army (Total Available) in September 1939

Officers	105,394	Field Army	2,321,206
NCOs	481,009	Replacement Army	958,040
Enlisted	3,090,206	Reich Labor Service*	426,798
Officials	29,495		
Total	3,706,104	Total	3,706,104

*Construction troops

Source: Cooper, pp. 164–65.

Hitler gave the army's growth additional impetus. In March 1935, using a new French law that increased the term of service for French recruits from 18 to 24 months as a pretext, he officially re-established general conscription and decreed a target size of the army of 12 corps, divided into 36 divisions and numbering 550,000.[34] Two months later, he officially renamed the Reichswehr the Wehrmacht, with himself as supreme commander, and the Truppenamt the General Staff, signifying an end to the Versailles military restrictions. Under him, he established the Reich Ministry of War and made the minister of war the commander in chief of the Wehrmacht over the service commanders in chief.[35] In August 1935, Hitler decreased the period of military service to one year to create large numbers of trained reserves.[36]

Hitler's original goal was an army of 300,000 men by the end of October 1934. However, the army leaders had planned to reach that level by 1938 through a much more gradual increase. Although they managed to have that target date postponed to the end of 1935, the army had already reached 280,000 by the end of February 1935. In March 1936, the army again changed its peacetime target from 21 divisions to 30 to 36 divisions, numbering nearly 800,000 men on active duty, and a 63-division field army, by October 1939.[37] By November 1936, the German army had only 28 infantry divisions with a few more in early stages of development, and three armored divisions, all assigned to 12 Wehrkreise, an increase of five Wehrkreise, and the first conscripts had begun to appear.[38] Ultimately, the Germans planned for a full-strength army of 72 infantry divisions, three of which would be armored, three light, and 21 reserve; and seven armored and one cavalry division, and two mountain brigades. This expanded army, including reserves, was expected to total 3,612,673 men by the year 1940-41.[39]

Some senior leaders, such as Fritsch, Beck, and Joachim von Stülpnagel, were alarmed at the great increase in such a short time. This increase, according to Beck in 1934, was "...not a building up of a peacetime army, but a mobilization." His major concern was the speed by which the army grew and, along with Blomberg, how Britain and France would react to these provocative actions, not rearmament per se.[40] For instance, in mid–1934, Beck favored the reintroduction of conscription, the current program of a 31 division army, and the remilitarization of the Rhineland.[41] He wanted to end Germany's present defenseless state and create a peacetime army, capable of fighting "a defensive war on many fronts with a good chance of success," as soon as possible. However, the creation of such an army must be "on a sound basis and with provision for reserves."[42] Beck especially feared that the quick pace would reduce the quality of the officer corps.[43] By November 1936, some of Beck's concerns were showing themselves in the form of shortages of supplies and equipment and numerous logistical and tactical problems.[44] Fritsch also was less than enthusiastic about the fast pace of the rearmament program. His was more methodical and economical than the pace Hitler demanded. Fritsch also used more traditional methods, preferring infantry over the armored units and air force in which Hitler was far more interested.[45] However, when those favoring a slower pace for the army's expansion protested to Blomberg, he repeatedly replied, "The Führer is cleverer than we are, he will plan and do everything correctly."[46]

Although Beck and Blomberg did not have to worry about the British and French responses to rearmament, Beck was correct to show concern over its impact on the officer corps. To achieve the planned force structure, the army leaders dispersed most of the 100,000 professionals of the Reichswehr as initial cadres to train the incoming conscripts assigned to them. As each company and battalion reached a certain level of training and efficiency, it was divided (and redivided again) to create more cadres to train new units for the army of 1939. To lead these new units, the General Staff estimated it would need almost 34,000 active duty officers by 1941 (the army would actually have about 20,000), starting from an available 3,000 of the Reichswehr in 1934.[47]

The army leadership was now faced with a most serious problem — obtaining drastically more officers. Initially, they commissioned 1,500 NCOs, transferred 2,500 officers from the Landespolizei (state police forces) to the army, recalled about 800 former Imperial Army officers, and took in an unknown number of former SA leaders who had served in World War I. Some 300 legal officers came from excess employees of the Ministry of Justice. (After the Anschluss in 1938, the German army obtained about 1,600 officers from the Austrian army.)[48] To make up the gap, the army, by 1937, had created four officer candidate schools (Munich, Hannover, Dresden, and Potsdam), each of which could accommodate about a thousand students for a nine-month long training program.[49] The army also created the grade of Ergänzungs-offiziere (officer on the supplementary list) for older former officers recalled to active duty to supply a specific experience or specialty. A significant result of this drastic increase in the numbers of officers was that only one sixth of them were fully trained professionals by September 1939. Adding to problems with the falling quality of officers and their percentage to men in the expanding German Army were the shortages of trained reserves, problems in training, shortages in qualified instructors, lack of vehicles, and low quality of many weapons (rifles, pistols, artillery, and tanks).[50]

In essence, the needs of the expanding army meant that "quality gave way to quantity." In 1934, the proportion of officers was 7 percent; within two years it had fallen to 1.6 percent (2.6 percent with the E-officers).[51] The meticulous standards (social background, political background, educational qualifications) of the old army were relaxed to obtain the numbers of officers now required. (Under the expansion, the SS also managed to sneak in some of its men to spy on the army.) These new officers came from every socioeconomic class while the senior officers had generally come from the old imperial military class. Also, between 1930 and 1936, the average age of majors decreased from 41 to 35.5 years; of lieutenant colonels, from 47.5 to 39 years; and of colonels, 52.25 to 43 years.[52] The influx of officers broke down the artificial barriers that had characterized both the Imperial Army and the Reichswehr. Hans Bernd Gisevius, a leading member of the infant anti–Hitler opposition, recognized, "That the officers' corps had been so greatly expanded that it was utterly heterogeneous."[53] The expansion also meant the promotion of many officers to higher ranks and positions — many beyond their capabilities. The net effect was the virtual destruction of the social homogeneity of the officer corps and an officer corps increasingly loyal to Adolf Hitler — the man who had provided these opportunities for promotion and career advancement.

The expansion of the army also meant more senior officers. The Reichswehr in 1932 had 44 major generals or higher. By October 1938, there were 275, not including 22 medical and eight veterinary officers with general's rank.[54] From 1932 to 1936, the number of colonels would also rise from 105 to 325.[55] During this growth period — and into the war — Hitler freely granted promotions and distributed decorations and money. One result of this wielding of special favors, as Domarus writes, was the creation "among the Generals of devoted paladins who were even willing to tolerate patiently the former corporal's unjust accusations, rude insults, and schoolmasterly reprimands without a word of contradiction."[56] Hassell writes about them also: "The majority are out to make careers in the lowest sense. Gifts and field marshals' batons are more important to them than the great historical issues and moral values at stake."[57]

How did Germany as a whole and its soldiers in particular receive these events — and view Hitler in light of them? Perhaps Guderian's opinions were indicative of those of many soldiers. He greeted these changes as the re-establishment of Germany's "right to military self-determination.... Every soldier greeted this news, which meant the canceling of a humiliating portion of the Versailles Treaty, with delight."[58] He and other soldiers welcomed the increased activity with enthusiasm after the "day-to-day monotony" of life in the Reichswehr.[59] William Shirer's diary entry for March 16, 1935, is also informative:

> And the Junkers who are running the army will forget a lot — and — swallow a lot — now that Hitler has given them what they want.... Today's creation of a conscript army in open defiance of Versailles will greatly enhance his domestic position, for there are few Germans, regardless of how much they hate the Nazis, who will not support it wholeheartedly. The great majority will like the way he has thumbed his nose at Versailles, which they all resented, and, being militarists at heart, they welcome the rebirth of the army."[60]

The fact that Hitler had also "unilaterally broken" the Versailles Treaty coincided with the feelings of most Germans, particularly among the officer corps.

Even the conservative senior leaders credited Hitler for re-establishing the army's "rightful" position in Germany. On April 9, 1935, Beck praised the reassertion of "the heroic spirit [of the German people] to respect its history under the strong leadership of Adolf Hitler."[61] At the 1936 Heroes' Remembrance Day, he called Hitler in his presence "a God-sent architect" and extolled the National Socialist revolution for recreating the army, not destroying it as other revolutions had. Beck continued, "The National Socialist state places at our disposal its entire economic strength, its people, its entire male youth." Blomberg prophetically concluded, "An enormous responsibility rests upon our shoulders. It is all the more heavy because *we may be placed before new tasks.*"[62]

The Impact of Nazi Education, the Hitler Jugend, and the Reich Labor Service

After 1935, young Germans increasingly began entering military service as a result of the general conscription law. By 1939, the army would comprise over three million active-duty and reserve soldiers, many of whom had attended schools using Nazi curricula and had served in the Hitler Jugend (Hitler Youth) (HJ) and later the Reicharbeitsdienst (Reich Labor Service) (RAD).[63] While it is very difficult to determine just *how much* impact that attendance at the nazified schools and service in the HJ and the RAD had on the young officers and soldiers of 1939, this education and service must had have some impact that bolstered their obedience to the Führer, given in the personal oath of loyalty and furthered by his prewar foreign and domestic policy successes.

After the Machtergreifung, the Nazis sought to control every aspect of the daily lives of all Germans, especially education and the media. Even before 1933, *völkische* ideas of the Nazis had found their way into the German educational system. After 1933, the Reich Ministry of Popular Enlightenment and Propaganda, led by Dr. Joseph Goebbels, sought to control the minds of the German people, especially the young people, and influence intellectual life for the National Socialist revolution.[64] Educational syllabi were changed to stress subjects relating to racial, national, and political ideas, and by 1938, there were new official texts that introduced these subjects more systematically. Non-Aryans were ousted from the teaching profession, and those who were left came under the control of the National Socialist Teacher's League, comprising 97 percent of the teachers. After May 1936, all teachers had to complete a series of one- to two-week political indoctrination courses. The intent was to inculcate the regime's nationalist spirit and racial principles into the school-age population, bolstering the work of the HJ.[65]

Hitler viewed the HJ (and the RAD, the SA and the SS, and the army) as "all national and social melting-furnaces in which gradually a new German man will be formed."[66] In December 1936, the regime encouraged membership in the HJ for all German young people, ages 14 to 18, to educate them "physically, intellectually, and morally in the spirit of National Socialism to serve the nation and the community."[67] Younger German boys, ages ten to 14 years, entered the Jungvolk, after a quasi-military induction ceremony.[68] After the HJ, at age 18, they would go into the RAD for 18 to 24 months (or the SS, SA, NSKK, or other party organizations). After six or seven months, many young men would then enter military service for two years.[69] Joining the HJ was theoretically voluntary until 1939, when the new directives made membership compulsory, but most youths and parents recognized the advantages of joining — and the disadvantages of not joining.[70]

After 1933, the HJ instructed German youth in the spirit and ideals of National Socialism for the benefit of the state. Political education consisted of instruction in racial theories, notions of German supremacy, the Nazi version of history, and the National Socialist movement. Innocent activities, such as camping and hiking, became Nazi political forums. The HJ also had its own newspapers, theater productions, films, and radio shows.[71] After December 1936, Reichenau, now commander of Wehrkreis VII, provided the local HJ with training in shooting, instruction of HJ leaders, small unit maneuvers, visits to military installations, and social gatherings. On April 29, 1937, Keitel designated the HJ a government body to preclude violating the prohibition on the army from engaging in political activities. During 1938 and 1939, OKW and OKH authorized additional training to HJ leaders and increased HJ use of army resources and facilities, producing excellent HJ-army cooperation.[72] The overall program inculcated Nazi ideals, including emphasis on paramilitary training, into German youth.

Following completion of the HJ, the German teenager entered the RAD, which was intended to educate German workers in Nazi ideology and acquire a proper respect for manual labor, according to the Reich Labor Service Law of June 26, 1935. A decree of September 6, 1935, established the six months compulsory service for all males, ages 18 to 25.[73] During their service in the RAD, German males underwent rigid discipline and close-order drills in camps, commanded by officers, that essentially freed the army from conducting basic military training. Thousands of RAD members also participated in select annual party rallies at Nuremberg, along with the SS, SA, HJ, and the army.[74] Upon completion of his RAD service, a young German male would either enter the army, the SS, the SA, or another party organization before release to civilian life.

By 1939, obviously many of the younger soldiers and the new company-grade officers had been members of the HJ and the RAD. Tables 4.6 and 4.7 indicate that after 1934 many of the German teenagers — Germans born after 1912 and who became 10 to 18 years old during the period 1932–38 — and in increasing numbers must have gone through the HJ and, in some cases in the later 1930s, on into the RAD. By 1939, many had undoubtedly absorbed at least part of the Nazi ideology. Unfortunately, there are no figures that further break down the HJ membership data more precisely. However, by comparing this data with the data in Tables 4.2, 4.3, and 4.5, we can see that an increasing number of young men who entered military service must have served some time in the HJ and the RAD; interestingly, though, only a small number of them became die-hard Nazis. Also, HJ training, about which many complained, may have impeded the inculcation of Nazi ideas. However, the HJ and the RAD did propagate and reinforce the Nazi ideology which was, in turn, reinforced by the regime's use of coercion and terror to obtain at least silence, if not obedience.[75] Excerpts from the diaries and letters of German soldiers during the war will attest to at least a superficial acceptance of Nazi ideas, as we shall see later.

The Development of the Oberkommando Wehrmacht (OKW)

A third factor that diminished the influence of the traditional senior army leaders was the creation and development

Table 4.6: Birth Data, 1913–30

Year	*Age*	*Number Born in 1939*	*Year*	*Age*	*Number Born in 1939*
1913	26	1,393,577	1922	16	1,359,135
1914	25	1,356,508	1923	15	1,296,151
1915	24	1,053,319	1924	14	1,289,605
1916	23	787,353	1925	13	1,304,997
1917	22	709,429	1926	12	1,240,932
1918	21	736,307	1927	11	1,188,415
1919	20	1,112,897	1928	10	1,212,684
1920	19	1,469,075	1930	8	1,180,079
1921	18	1,445,486			

Source: Section I, Table 8, *Die Bevölkerung nach Geburtsjahren und Familienstand am 17. Mai 1939, Statisches Jahrbuch für das Deutsches Reich 1939–40*. Berlin: Statisches Reichsamt, 1940.

Table 4.7: Membership Data for HJ, 1932–38

End of Year	*HJ Boys (14–18)*	*JF Boys (10–14)*	*BDM Girls (10–14)*	*JM Girls (10–14)*
1932	55,365	28,691	19,244	4,656
1933	568,288	1,130,521	243,750	349,482
1934	786,000	1,457,304	471,944	862,317
1935	829,361	1,498,209	569,599	1,046,134
1936	1,168,734	1,785,424	873,127	1,610,316
1937	1,237,078	1,884,883	1,035,804	1,722,190
1938	1,663,305	2,064,538	1,448,264	1,855,119

Source: Document 301, Noakes and Pridham, I, p. 421.

of the OKW. As part of the overall rearmament program and in acknowledgment of the changing nature of modern warfare, Blomberg and Reichenau, chief of the Ministeramt, wanted to expand the latter's agency into a Wehrmacht general staff, ultimately to become the OKW. Blomberg saw increased roles for the navy and the air force in any future war and wanted to exert more control over the army's operational planning. He wanted to increase his authority as Reichswehrminister (later War Minister) over the commanders in chief of the individual services through joint planning by his own general staff, independently of the army General Staff. To this end, in 1935, Blomberg added a small operations staff to the Wehrmachtsamt to serve as a "roof" over the high commands of the three services (it became the Wehrmacht General Staff), and established the Wehrmacht Academy to train officers for this new joint staff.[76]

Beck opposed Blomberg and Reichenau in these efforts. He realized that the creation and effective operation of an OKW would diminish the army's authority and control over its forces. He argued that the army was Germany's senior and most important military service, given Germany's traditional position as a continental power. Beck proposed that in case of war the army commander in chief would become the deputy war minister to recognize the army's senior position, the army General Staff would plan its major operations, and the chief of the General Staff would directly command the army's forces in the field, which was reminiscent of the arrangement of the Imperial General Staff. The Reichswehrminister would only provide overall direction and coordination of military operations.[77] Beck's objective was to return the General Staff to its pre–1919 dominant position in German military affairs, not limit the influence of National Socialism.

Both Blomberg and Fritsch opposed Beck's position, albeit for different reasons. While Fritsch also opposed the creation of an OKW, he opposed that part of Beck's proposals that limited his authority as the army commander in chief to overall coordination of the army's forces in wartime and gave the chief of the General Staff command of the army's field forces. In April 1934, the two came to an agreement so that they could defend the army's interests against Blomberg throughout the remainder of 1934 and 1935. As the organizational dispute continued, a wedge developed between Blomberg and Beck as the latter attempted to protect the army against the encroachments of the Wehrmachtsamt. Fritsch supported Beck in his efforts by forbidding the army's section chiefs to deal directly with Blomberg.[78] However, Beck lost the battle with the enactment of the Army Law of May 21, 1935, by which the War Minister received responsibility to coordinate the direction of the organization, intelligence, war propaganda, economic warfare, and operations of all three services.[79]

The dispute intensified with the replacement of Reichenau by Wilhelm Keitel, "an embarrassing frank advocate of the Führersprinzip [leadership principle of infallible belief in Hitler]," in October 1935.[80] Deutsch called Keitel "the epitome of an easy subordinate, a receiver of orders rather than a producer of ideas."[81] Keitel himself once declared, "I am no Field Marshal." His subservience to Hitler quickly earned him the nicknames "Lakaitel" (Lackey) and "Nodding Ass." Albert Speer recounted that Hitler himself characterized Keitel as "loyal as a dog."[82] Ulrich von Hassell, German Ambassador to Italy, who was fired after the Blomberg-Fritsch crisis in January 1938 and had joined the anti–Hitler Opposition, told "W—" (perhaps Walther Warlimont, who became Jodl's deputy on the OKW staff) that "Keitel was simply too stupid to understand [political actions]." Later, he called Keitel a "stooge."[83] Beck countered by assigning Colonel Alfred Jodl to the Wehrmachtsamt to monitor its activities. However, Jodl soon defected to Keitel, and, with Keitel's support, proceeded to create a true operations department within the War Ministry with authority over the operations staffs of the three services.[84] As Müller writes, men like these, unlike Beck, saw the military as a mere instrument of power in the hands of the political leader, subject to his orders and obedient to his will. To them, men like Beck and the General Staff were "a bastion of outmoded tradition."[85] Beck's opposition to Keitel's and Jodl's plans increased, and both Raeder, now designated as the chief of the kreigsmarine (navy), and Göring added their opposition, in order to maintain the independence of their respective services.

Together Keitel and Jodl developed war games, studies, exercises, and the only joint maneuvers ever (those of 1937) to test the joint command organization. The results produced additional criticism and "well-nigh open rebellion [from the other services]—a most unmilitary state of affairs."[86] Both Fritsch and Beck, clinging to more traditional views of the army's position in the German military structure, rejected joint command of the army. In a long memorandum in August 1937, Fritsch strongly protected the army's prerogatives as the senior service and argued that the senior army commander should be the Führer's chief military advisor in all military matters, including naval and aerial warfare.[87] Over Fritsch's and Beck's objections, Hitler, however, would confirm OKW's organization in an announcement on February 4, 1938, with Keitel as its head.[88]

Although Hitler sanctioned OKW, it did not gain operational control of the armed services. In fact, Hitler soon afterwards effectively reduced OKW to his own personal military staff and worked directly with the separate service commanders through the service adjutants (two from the army and one each from the air force and navy). The service commanders continued to make their own decisions on individual service budgets, training, weapons acquisition, and operations. Göring, as an *Alterkämpfer* (old fighter) and as Hitler's Plenipotentiary for the Four-Year Plan, particularly had better access to the Führer than either Fritsch (and later Brauchitsch) or Raeder. The net effect of this situation was to reduce the influence of the army General Staff in relation to that of OKW and then OKW's influence and prestige in relation to the new adjutants.[89]

However, throughout the OKW disputes before the war, Hitler apparently personally directed little, if any, of the effort to create a joint military command organization. Blomberg and Reichenau and later Keitel were the main forces in the push for an OKW. When war broke out on September 1, 1939, there was still no central headquarters for controlling Germany's military operations and no one man—except Hitler himself—directing the war effort. As Germany prepared for war in the autumn of 1939, each service established its own separate war headquarters, and Hitler refused all proposals to create a centralized OKW HQ. The army located its war headquarters at Zossen, some 25 to 30 miles south of Berlin.[90] However, Hitler apparently saw—and used—the OKW organizational dispute as a way to break up the solidarity of the senior officer corps by providing career opportunities to ambitious men, like Keitel and Jodl, outside the old military caste. Hitler would staff its senior positions with men who would unquestioningly carry out his orders, men whom Keitel would later call "impotent tools unable to inhibit [Hitler]" in carrying out his plans.[91] Even after September 1939, Hitler continued the practice of divided military command so he could more effectively control—and interfere in—military operations.[92]

The Creation of the Waffen SS

The period 1934–39 also saw the creation and development of the Waffen SS as a military rival to the regular army and the true revolutionary arm of the National Socialist revolution. This development directly violated Hitler's own repeated promise to the army leadership to maintain the army as the sole bearer of arms, made after the Röhm Purge. In early July 1934, Himmler received Hitler's — and Blomberg's — approval to increase the size of the SS Leibstandarte (then numbering a mere 120 men) to regimental size, to add two additional regiments, and to form them into the SS Verfügungstruppe (SS-VT) (SS General Service Troops).[93] On July 4, 1934, Blomberg over Fritsch's protest informed a group of generals that parts of the SS would receive weapons and be expanded to a full division. In September, he announced the creation of the SS-VT which would be under Himmler as Reichsführer SS during peacetime and under the War Ministry during wartime.[94] Blomberg agreed to the creation of the SS-VT as an armed force for purely internal police duties, Himmler's ostensible reason for its creation and a role the army did not wish to play. Individual members could then be called for the army when needed.[95]

The creation of the SS-VT gave the army leadership another sore point with Hitler and Blomberg. To illustrate the anti-SS bias of Fritsch, Shirer relates an incident at Saarbrücken in which Fritsch "kept up a running fire of very sarcastic remarks — about the S.S., the party, and various party leaders as they appeared. He was full of contempt for them all."[96] The army had to provide the training and the weapons to the new SS-VT (for which the SS paid the army), but at a time when the professional army was already being strained by its own training and rearmament programs. Despite his own misgivings, Beck began preparing guidelines to carry out this cooperation with the SS. Himmler met with Beck on October 10, 1934, to allay any fears that the new SS force would become a rival of the army. He assured Beck that the SS would be developed as an elitist party organization, "a kind of ethical and racial knighthood." He specifically denied any ambitions for the SS to compete with the army in its military role. Believing that the SS-VT would be "almost exclusively political," Beck ignored the implications of creating and arming another military force within the Reich.[97]

Even as the army reluctantly began training the members of the SS-VT, trouble between the army and the SS was brewing. First, not satisfied with light weapons, the SS in East Prussia wanted artillery. Hitler, for now, supported the army in prohibiting the SS-VT from increasing its firepower and got the SS to agree to allow the army to inspect its units in training.[98] There were also several incidents between soldiers and SS men, the most serious one occurring at the Altegrabow training grounds. Fritsch submitted a report of the incident and demanded the dissolution of the Leibstandarte, first to Blomberg and then directly to Himmler and Hitler, but Hitler, of course, did not accede to Fritsch's demand.[99] Also, the SS had apparently started rumors that Fritsch and Beck were planning a coup. On January 3, 1935, Hitler, personally interceding in the disputes, publicly reiterated his confidence in the army leadership and his position on the army as the nation's sole bearer of arms. Also, Fritsch and Beck apparently received an apology from Himmler.[100]

As Himmler turned to consolidating his position as head of the Reich's police forces during 1936–37, the SS went on harassing soldiers, despite Himmler's apparent concessions to the army. Incidents continued at the local level and steadily grew in numbers and seriousness, causing Blomberg to issue a special memorandum on January 25,

1938, the eve of his dismissal, on how to handle the increasing incidents. General Walther von Brauchitsch, Blomberg's successor, however, amended the original order by applying it only in cases of infringements of military discipline, not military law, thus robbing it of much of its intended power.[101]

More importantly, Himmler attempted to discredit Fritsch before Hitler with information that purportedly made the senior army commander appear to be a homosexual. For now, Hitler brushed aside the dossier and ordered its contents destroyed. SS general, Karl Wolff, reported, "Himmler came away from this parley in a downcast mood because Hitler had said that though Fritsch was doubtless one of the strongest and most important opponents of National Socialism, he could not be dealt with in this fashion."[102] Hitler knew that he still needed Fritsch and his reputation among the other army officers to complete the army's growth since his absence would harm the rearmament program and his dismissal on such a falsified charge could result in a large outcry from other senior officers, a reaction Hitler could not afford in mid–1936.

The source of the incidents between the SS men and the soldiers was the attitude of the newcomers to the SS-VT who saw themselves as the core of a new National Socialist revolutionary army to replace the tradition-bound army. These new recruits brought with them "a certain dynamism and the arrogance of the elite Imperial Guard, the blind fervor of the Hitler Youth generation combined with the reforming zeal of ex-officer heretics to produce a sense of mission and superiority."[103] To enhance this feeling, Himmler decreed that the members of the SS must prove their Aryan ancestry as far back as 1750, which sent them into lengthy searches through genealogical documents to ensure they had no "hidden" Jews in their family tree. He also developed a program to indoctrinate the members of the SS in order to create an elite racial and military force, to replace all traces of middle class Christian morality in them, and to instill in them an unwavering loyalty to the German nation and to Hitler personally. To complete the process, Himmler developed a series of paganlike rites and ceremonies to imbue into the new SS cadet a sense of belonging to an exclusive brotherhood and a fanatic religious sect.[104]

Despite Himmler's original declared limitations for the SS-VT, it continued to grow in size and independence. In May 1935, it numbered 8,459 and, by March 1936, it had two officer training schools and its own inspectorate.[105] In March 1936, units of the SS-VT accompanied the German army into the Rhineland. In early 1937, Himmler pressed Fritsch and Blomberg to create an SS border guard, but the army leaders firmly rejected his request. In 1938, units of the SS-VT also accompanied the German army into Austria and the Sudetenland. On August 17, 1938, Hitler formally removed the SS-VT from the army's jurisdiction and made it "an armed troop exclusively at [his] disposal." He gave the Reichsführer SS the responsibility for recruitment and education and made service in the SS-VT equivalent to military service as required by the conscription law.[106]

By the summer of 1939, the SS-VT numbered 18,000 men, the size of a full army division, and these men were assigned to four regiments: the Leibstandarte Adolf Hitler (Berlin), the Deutschland (Munich), the Germania (Hamburg), and the Das Führer, which had been formed with Austrian recruits after the Anschluss, and completed its initial expansion. Himmler, in November 1937, had already confidently declared that the SS-VT was prepared for war according to the army's present standards.[107] Beck had noted,

> [I]t was interesting to observe that an organization, which Hitler had categorically stated would never bear arms in military operations, was now taking part in every

> coup the Führer pulled off. Not only were they taking part, but they were, by 1938, wearing Army uniforms instead of their own, except on ceremonial occasions.[108]

Fritsch noted on February 1, 1938, "[A]ll sources agree that the attitude of the SS Verfügungstruppe towards the Army is frigid if not hostile. One cannot avoid the impression that this hostile attitude is deliberately cultivated."[109] Again, Hitler had reneged on a promise to the army leaders, again the generals had meekly protested, and again, having salved their professional consciences, they went about their soldierly business.

Summary

By September 1939, Hitler and the army generals had made great strides in again making the German army the best in Europe. It was now 18 times the size of the Reichswehr that Hitler had inherited in 1933. This new army was armed with formidable modern weapons, especially tanks, and had an effective offensive doctrine to go with them. The results of Hitler's, Fritsch's, and Beck's efforts of 1934–1938 would be seen in the successful Blitzkrieg campaigns against Poland, the Low Countries and France, and the Balkans, and the initial phase of the invasion of the Soviet Union that would give Hitler control over most of Europe by the end of 1941. We can also see their efforts in the more or less orderly retreat of the German armies without any rout or massive disorder in front of overwhelmingly larger armies in the last 12 months of the Third Reich. O'Neill rightly praised this situation as "an unparalleled achievement."[110]

To create this army, Hitler initially accommodated its conservative leaders and then, when he was done with them got rid of the most recalcitrant senior officers and co-opted most of the remainder. The officers generally accepted this ever increasing pace of expansion with minimal protest as it satisfied their own personal agendas for promotion, career opportunities, and increased social status. There were a few protests about the accelerating pace of the army's expansion, especially the effects it was having on the quality of the officers; there were a few others about the creation of an OKW that could potentially control the army's operations and planning, and about the creation and development of a rival armed force, the SS-VT. Hitler used these changes in the army to further diminish his dependence on it and its conservative officer corps, while making both more dependent on him.

At the same time that Fritsch, Beck, and others rebuilt the German Army into a mighty war machine, they generally ignored the increasing elimination of civil liberties among the general population and the worsening persecution of the Jews. When some officers had doubts about specific policies or actions, they generally complained about them privately or directed their criticisms at the radicals around Hitler — Göring, Himmler, and the like — not at Hitler specifically, even as late as 1938. When a few genuinely protested the regime's repressive measures against the church and the Jews to Blomberg, he generally did not pass these protests upward, believing that these matters were the concerns of other ministers, not his as War Minister.[111] Here again we can see how the long-term effects of Seeckt's Überparteilichkeit policies of the 1920s affected the "neutral" political attitudes of the former Reichswehr officers in the late 1930s.

Perhaps more important were the political attitudes of the new officers and men, who entered military service after 1934. They had grown up during the worst days of the Weimar Republic and had been further indoctrinated in National Socialism and Hitler's role in its development and in the development of the HJ and the RAD.

They had seen how Hitler had eliminated unemployment, returned glory to a once prostrate Germany, restored "German" territory to the Fatherland, and humiliated the Western democracies in doing so. They did not need to be "nazified" to see Hitler as their Führer. For them, taking the Hitlerian oath after 1934 would not cause the pangs of conscience that a few, like Beck, in August 1934 had suffered.

Perhaps Hermann Rauschning, the Nazi President of the Danzig Senate (1932–36) and later a critic of Hitler, best summarized the great transformation of the army by 1939:

> The army leaders are overburdened with professional duties; the older generation among them are undecided and divided in opinion. But the younger ones are filled with the utmost confidence and energy, and are equally critical of the past methods of the Third Reich and of the old traditions of the Prussian officers' corps. The army leaders will be compelled before long to make up their minds: the spirit of the new movement has much in common with their own traditions, but they find everything that is utterly repulsive to every soldier in the un-Prussian, unmilitary, hazy, rhetorical emotionalism and dilettantism of the present regime of declasses.[112]

In 1938, Halder, thinking about his five sons-in-law serving as army captains and believing their attitudes were "fairly representative of the temper of the corps of officers," remarked to Gisevius, "The attitude of the generals was irrelevant; the decisive factor in any projected coup d'etat would be the attitude of the lower officers, because they had the closest contact with the bulk of the soldiery and, therefore, with the broad masses of the people."[113] The German army of September 1939 was, in many respects, already Hitler's army as the attitudes of Halder's sons-in-law confirmed. We shall see in the next chapter how these attitudes limited the development of the military opposition and the number of officers who would become a part of it.

Notes

1. Before the induction or commissioning ceremony in which he took the Hitlerian oath of allegiance, the German military member would receive instruction, usually conducted by the prospective soldier's commander, on the oath's meaning. During his active duty he would receive short briefings on such topics as orders and obedience and the Hague Convention on Land Warfare of 1899. Alexander Stahlberg, *Bounden Duty: The Memoirs of a German Officer 1932–45* (London: Brassey's UK, 1990), pp. 66–68. See Stahlberg, p. 67, and Henry Metalman, *Through Hell for Hitler* (Wellingborough, UK: Patrick Stephens Limited, 1990), pp. 20–21, for descriptions of the induction ceremony.

2. See footnote 19, Introduction, p. 13.

3. Vagts, "The Reichswehr over Europe," *Harper's Magazine*, September 1935, quoted in Taylor, *Sword and Swastika*, p. 121.

4. See Hamerow, pp. 10–11, 32, 47. Beck quoted in Hamerow, p. 107. Bastian quoted in Hamerow, p. 108.

5. Hitler quoted in Cooper, p. 17. Hitler Speech at Hamburg, August 17, 1934; Hitler Speech at Nuremberg, September 10, 1934, p. 557; Hitler Speech at Stettin, June 12, 1938; Hitler Speech in Nuremberg, September 22, 1938, p. 564 in Baynes, I, p. 556. Hitler Speech to the Reichstag, February 20, 1938, in Baynes, II, pp. 451–52. Hitler Speech at Party Congress, September 16, 1935, in Domarus, II, *The Years 1934–1938*, p. 711.

6. Hitler Speech at the Bürgerbräukeller, Munich, November 8, 1936, in Domarus, II, p. 849. Hitler instituted this annual ceremony to celebrate his victory over the Weimar Republic and to honor those killed during the abortive November 1923 coup as martyrs of the Nazi revolution. Also at this ceremony, Hitler would initiate new members of the SS and have them swear a personal loyalty to him unto death.

7. Hitler Speech at Nuremberg, September 14, 1936, in Domarus, II, p. 837.

8. Hitler Address to Fifth Army Corps, Giebelstadt, September 17, 1936, in Domarus, II, p. 842. See also Hitler Speech to Army Representatives, September 15, 1935, in Baynes, I, pp. 559–62; and Hitler Commemoration Speech, November 8, 1936, in Baynes, II, p. 158.

9. Hitler Speech on Wehrmacht Day, Nuremberg, September 16, 1935, p. 709; and Hitler Speech at the Bürgerbräukeller, Munich, November 8, 1936, p. 849, in Domarus, II. Hitler Speech, Munich, November 8, 1935, p. 127; Hitler Speech

to Reichstag, January 30, 1937, p. 215; and Hitler Proclamation at Party Congress, Nuremberg, September 6, 1938; in Baynes, I. Hitler Proclamation at Party Convention, September 9, 1936, p. 397; and Hitler Speech, September 26, 1938, p. 519, in de Roussey.

10. Domarus, II, p. 710.

11. Hitler speech on Wehrmacht Day, Nuremberg, September 16, 1935, in Domarus, II, p. 708.

12. Sigfried Knappe and Ted Brusow, *Soldat: Reflections of a German Soldier* (New York: Orion Books, 1992), p. 86. See also letters to parents, August 22, 1937, Karl Fuchs, *Sieg Heil! War Letters of Tank Gunner Karl Fuchs 1937–1941* (Hamden, CT: Archon Books, 1987), pp. 29–30.

13. In March 1934, Hitler created the Blood Order that awarded a silver medal to those who had taken part in the 1923 attempted coup.

14. Reich Flag Act, September 10, 1935, in Domarus, II, p. 689.

15. Göring's Remarks, Nuremberg, September 15, 1935, in Domarus, II, p. 707.

16. Hitler Speech, Giebelstadt, September 17, 1936, in Domarus, II, p. 842.

17. Stahlberg, a young officer in the German army, reported in his memoirs (pp. 27–28) that while the military had no love for the black, red, and gold of the Weimar Republic "we found it unthinkable that a party flag should now become our national flag...." Even if this sentiment had been widely held within the German officer corps, there were no vocal demonstrations or debates, similar to the ones that accompanied the adoption of the republican black, gold, and red after 1918.

18. Blomberg Decree, April 16, 1935, in O'Neill, p. 66.

19. Document 483, Defense Law of May 21, 1935, in Noakes and Pridham, II, *Foreign Policy, War and Racial Extermination*, p. 643. Keitel Order, December 15, 1937, in O'Neill, p. 69.

20. O'Neill, pp. 72–73. Between 1933 and 1939, the NSKK would provide about 187,000 tank and truck drivers for Guderian's growing armored and motorized units. Macksey, p. 83.

21. Reynolds, p. 74. The War Academy prepared General Staff officers for senior staff positions by emphasizing practical operational tactics with few courses on philosophical subjects. As Beck wrote, "The academy must remain free of academic drudgery. The goal is not to produce 'polymaths' but competent commanders. The ... military principles must be rooted in technical skill and leadership ability." His own lack of political astuteness is visible in this extract from his October 10, 1935 speech, given on the 125th anniversary of the War Academy: "Today the Führer and his superior officers look with confidence to the *Kriegsakademie*.... I close with the hope that the *Kriegsakademie* will justify the confidence placed in it.... I hope that the officers who pass through the *Kriegsakademie* will always remain conscious of its proud traditions and their debt to the man who renewed and increased the *Wehrmacht* and finally broke the chains of Versailles. They must not forget their responsibility to the new state which provides us with a united people [who will support the *Wehrmacht*] in case we again have no choice but to sound the call to arms." Beck quoted in Reynolds, pp. 73–75. Fritsch echoed these thoughts in his own speech. O'Neill, p. 91. The history of the German officer corps through the 1930s and the war would demonstrate their great military technical abilities and a continuing lack of political astuteness.

22. O'Neill, pp. 71–72.

23. The NSDAP had divided all of Germany into groups of 40 to 60 households, formed into "Blocks," and six to eight Blocks into "Cells." The Block and Cell directors were charged with spreading National Socialism, recruiting for party organizations, soliciting donations for party charities and funds, and handling general questions, investigations, and complaints. O'Neill, pp. 78–79.

24. O'Neill, pp. 78–80.

25. Blomberg Important Political Instructions, May 29, 1935; December 9, 1935; February 14, 1936; and April 1937, in O'Neill, p. 74.

26. Dollman quoted in O'Neill, p. 75.

27. O'Neill, p. 182.

28. Hans Rothfels, *German Opposition*, p. 65. The Confessing Church grew out of opposition to the party's "coordination" of the Protestant Church. The NSDAP tried to impose a "German Christian" church, based on German nationalism and opposition to Marxism, Jews and Free Masonry, under the leadership of Reich Bishop Ludwig Müller, Blomberg's former chaplain in 1930 in East Prussia. This effort failed in its efforts although the great majority of the Protestant clergy did maintain political obedience to the Nazi rulers. Individual Protestant Christians as well as Protestant churches in Nazi Germany struggled to reconcile their traditional beliefs of obedience and German nationalism with the outrages and criminal activities of the Nazi regime — just as the army officers did. A small group of pastors, led by Martin Niemöller, a former World War I U-boat commander, Dietriech Bonhoeffer, and Hans Christian Asmussen, resisted the Nazi pressures and formed a separate Confessing Church. Many of its leaders were persecuted, imprisoned in concentration camps, and died or were executed before the war's end. See Victoria Barnett, *For the Soul of the People: Protestant Protest Against Hitler* (New York: Oxford University Press, 1992) for a well-balanced presentation on this subject.

29. Fritsch recognized that the basis of the army was National Socialist but wanted to keep out

"party-political influences ... [that could] lead only to fragmentation and dissolution." Document 487, Fritsch Notes, February 1, 1938, in Noakes and Pridham, II, p. 645. Although he opposed the measures to "nazify" the army, he issued a decree, dated December 21, 1934, that instructed officers to seek wives from among the "Aryan groups of the nation." On January 15, 1936, Fritsch issued an order for officers to refrain from speculating on the non–Aryan origins of any officer's wife, a decree reinforced by Hitler on May 13, 1936, that forbade the marriage of a professional soldier to a non–Aryan woman. O'Neill, pp. 76–77. Fritsch's first order is probably not indicative of any *racial* anti–Semitism held by him but reflects his traditional Prussian social anti–Semitism. The second order, on the surface contradictory, was probably aimed at keeping the SS and SD out of what Fritsch saw as the proper business of the officer corps, similar to the army's attempts to protect the few Jewish officers who were on active duty in 1934 when Blomberg applied the Aryan paragraph to the armed forces.

30. Hitler speech, March 13, 1937, in Domarus, II p. 883.

31. See Tables 4.1 through 4.5 for details of the army's expansion from 1934 to 1939. I do not intend to cover the weapons acquisition and modernization programs, begun secretly during the Weimar Republic and then openly by Hitler after he pulled Germany out of the Disarmament Conference in Geneva, Switzerland, in October 1933. For a discussion of these programs, see Wilhelm Diest, *The Wehrmacht and German Disarmament* (Toronto: University of Toronto Press, 1981) and Barton Whalen, *Covert German Rearmament, 1919–1939: Deception and Misperception* (Frederick, MD: University Publications of America, Inc., 1984).

32. Document 473, Memorandum of Meetings at Defense Ministry, 20–21 December 1933, in Noakes and Pridham, II, pp. 632–33.

33. O'Neill, p. 86.

34. Law on the Establishment of the Wehrmacht, March 16, 1935, in Domarus, II, p. 656. Whaley, p. 55. As a commentary on how Hitler ran the government of the Third Reich, most local commanders first heard about these increases on the radio, not through the chain of command. O'Neill, p. 88. Also, at the beginning of March, Germany created the Luftwaffe under Göring's command in defiance of the Versailles Treaty. Initially, several thousand men were transferred from the army to man the new air force. Some army generals, who desired an air arm subordinate to the army command, chastised Blomberg for allowing the creation of a separate service. However, given Göring's personal relationship with Hitler, there was very little the War Minister could have done, even if he had wanted to.

35. German Military Service Act, May 21, 1935, in Domarus, II, p. 666.

36. Hitler Decree on Military Service, August 24, 1936, in Domarus, II, p. 824.

37. This expanded army would consist of 25 infantry divisions, four motorized divisions, three armored divisions, three light divisions, one mountain division, and one cavalry brigade. The field army would number 4,626,000 men. Noakes and Pridham, II p. 678.

38. Wheeler-Bennett, p. 349. Noakes and Pridham, II, pp. 663, 676. Taylor, *Sword and Swastika*, pp. 107–9.

39. Walter Warlimont, *Inside Hitler's Headquarters 1939–45* (Novato, CA: Presido Press, 1964), p. 45.

40. Cooper, p. 50. Beck Notes on Conference with State Secretary Bernhard von Buelow, July 30, 1934, in Klaus-Jürgen Müller, *The Army, Politics, and Society in Germany, 1933–45: Studies in the Army's Relation to Nazism* (New York: St. Martin's Press, 1987), pp. 82–84.

41. Müller, p. 83.

42. Beck, "Creation of the Future Peacetime Army," December 14, 1933, in Reynolds, p. 86.

43. Beck, "Against the Formation of the 300,000-Man Army," in Reynolds, pp. 94–95.

44. Wheeler-Bennett, p. 349.

45. Craig, pp. 484–85.

46. Blomberg quoted in O'Neill, pp. 94–95.

47. Deist, p. 46. Of the 4,000 active officers in 1933, 450 were medical and veterinary officers, and some 500 went to the newly created Luftwaffe. Cooper, pp. 159–60.

48. Cooper, pp. 159–60. Demeter, p. 58.

49. Knappe, pp. 103, 108. Prior to 1934, the annual intake of officer candidates was limited to only about 120–180.

50. See Cooper, pp. 160–64, for details on these problems.

51. Müller, p. 83. Deist, p. 46.

52. Taylor, *Sword and Swastika*, p. 94.

53. Hans Bernd Gisevius, *To the Bitter End* (Westport, CT: Greenwood Press, 1975), p. 313.

54. Hoffmann, *German Resistance*, p. 40. By May 1943, the army would have over a thousand general officers. By the end of the war, the army would have 2,530 generals, the air force, 418, and the navy, 235 admirals. Footnote 327, Domarus, II, pp. 1349–50. On April 20, 1936, Hitler promoted Blomberg to the rank of generalfeldmarschall, the first since World War I. He would promote an additional 27 officers to the ranks of generalfeldmarschall and grand admiral by 1945. Footnote 107, Domarus, II, p. 1309.

55. Taylor, *Sword and Swastika*, p. 94.

56. Domarus, II, p. 240.

57. Ulrich Von Hassell, *The Von Hassell Diaries 1938–1944* (Garden City, NY: Doubleday & Company, 1947), p. 393.

58. Guderian, p. 23.

59. Guderian, p. 14.

60. William L. Shirer, *Berlin Diary: The Journal of a Foreign Correspondent 1934–1941* (New York: Popular Library, 1961), p. 27.

61. Beck Radio Broadcast, "The War Lord Ludendorff," in Reynolds, p. 71.

62. Blomberg Speech in Berlin, March 8, 1936, quoted in Shirer, *Diary*, p. 47. Blomberg quoted in Wheeler-Bennett, p. 338.

63. Baldur von Schirach was the leader of the HJ from July 1928 and became Reich Youth Leader on June 17, 1933. The HJ had originated in March 1922 as the Jugendbund der NSDAP to instruct "Aryan" German teenagers in the *völkische* idea. Every member swore allegiance to the Führer and were taught the party's 11 statutes and its political program (see appendix A for the HJ oath). In the last years of the republic, the HJ had attracted thousands of German teenagers from a generation that increasingly abhorred the despair, hopelessness, and insecurity of parliamentary democracy. The members of the HJ became embroiled in the political brawls in the streets of Germany, where they came to regard themselves as young soldiers fighting for the aims of the NSDAP. Peter D. Stachura, *Nazi Youth in the Weimar Republic* (Santa Barbara, CA: Clio Books, 1975), pp. 8, 44–46.

64. Document 266, Goebbels Press Conference, March 15, 1933; Document 267, Goebbels Speech to Radio Officials, March 25, 1933; and Document 268, Supplementary Regulation, June 30, 1933, Noakes and Pridham, I, pp. 380–82.

65. Noakes and Pridham, I, pp. 430–32, 436–37. Bracher, pp. 260–64.

66. Document 241, Hitler Speech, May 1, 1934, in Noakes and Pridham, I, p. 354.

67. Document 299, Law on the Hitler Youth, December 1, 1936, in Noakes and Pridham, I, p. 419.

68. Before taking an oath to the Führer, an HJ leader would instruct the children: "Today for the first time you swear allegiance to the Führer which will bind you to him for all time.... And the Führer demands of you and of us all that we train ourselves to a life of service and duty of loyalty and comradeship." Document 302, Induction Instructions for the Deutsches Jungvolk, Trier HJ, April 1940, in Noakes and Pridham, I, p. 421. See Document 303, in Noakes and Pridham, I, p. 303, for HJ Vow.

69. Document 297, Hitler Speech at Reichenburg, December 4, 1938, in Noakes and Pridham, I, p. 417. Girls had their analogous organizations: the Bund Deutscher Mädel (Union of German Maidens), the Jung Mädel (Young Maidens), and the *Glaube und Schönheit* (Faith and Beauty).

70. Stachura, p. 201.

71. Stachura, pp. 200–1.

72. O'Neill, pp. 178–79.

73. Documents 242 and 243 in Noakes and Pridham, II, p. 355–56.

74. Knappe, pp. 82, 84.

75. For a favorable picture of life in the HJ, see Metalman, pp. 14–16. For a favorable picture of life in the RAD, see Letters to Parents, April 11, 1937 and August 11, 1937, pp. 24, 28–29, respectively. Document 3751-PS, Excerpt from Diary of German Minister of Justice, NCA, VI, p. 638, is a song HJ members sang at the 1934 party rally that extols Hitler and the atheism of National Socialism. See Documents 306, 307, and 308, Noakes and Pridham, I, pp. 427–29, for contemporary criticism of the ideological and paramilitary activities of the HJ.

76. Reynolds, pp. 90–92. The Wehrmacht Academy lasted only two years because of fierce opposition from the three services. O'Neill, p. 108. Fierce opposition from the service chiefs also killed Blomberg's proposal in early 1937 to replace the army Wehrkriese commands with Wehrmacht (joint) Wehrkreise commands. Warlimont, p. 9.

77. Reynolds, pp. 90–92.

78. Reynolds, pp. 91–93.

79. Cooper, pp. 84–85.

80. The *Führerprinzip* essentially meant that all should unquestioningly bow to Hitler's authority as party leader (Führer), political leader (Chancellor), head of state (President), and military leader (supreme commander). His "legal" authority was based on the Weimar Constitution (which was never revoked), the Enabling Act of March 1933, and subsequent renewals. In the Third Reich the law was seen as the expression of the people as interpreted by the Führer and carried out by party organs, governmental agencies, and personalities. His decrees and laws put into effect the unwritten principles of *völkische* communal law and, therefore, represented the highest form of law. The conduct of the police (and the army) was legal as long as it carried out the will of the government (that is, the Führer), and only fate could appropriately judge his actions, not any existing morality. Document 343, Statement of Hans Frank; Document 345, Statement of Ernst Rudolf Huber; and Document 389, Statement of Dr. Werner Best, in Noakes and Pridham, I, pp. 474, 476, and 519, respectively. In essence, as Göring proudly proclaimed on July 12, 1934, "the law and the will of the Führer are one." Shirer, *Third Reich*, p. 370. This was reiterated by others throughout the existence of the Third Reich, including Jodl, who stated on November 3, 1942, "[F]or us the Führer's will is the supreme law of the land." Warlimont, p. 269. See NCA, I, pp. 191–96, for a fuller explanation of the Führerprinzip.

81. Deutsch, *Hitler and Generals*, p. 35.

82. Keitel and Speer quoted in Cooper, p. 88.

83. September 4, 1938 and October 24, 1938 entries, Hassell, pp. 3, 13, respectively.

84. Reynolds, pp. 93–94. Even Hitler recognized Keitel's subservience to his whim. During Operation Citadel in June 1943, Hitler at his East Prussian headquarters told his adjutant Schmundt, "Keitel's as faithful as a spaniel, he does whatever I tell him to, but he doesn't count for much with the others." Galante, p. 195.

85. Müller, pp. 67–68.

86. Warlimont, pp. 9–10.

87. Cooper, p. 85.

88. Cooper, pp. 86–87. In this announcement Hitler also confirmed himself as War Minister, succeeding the discredited Blomberg, a suggestion made by Blomberg himself as we shall see in the next chapter.

89. Deist, pp. 91–95. Görlitz, pp. 322–23. For an insider's view, see Warlimont, pp. 17–25.

90. Warlimont, pp. 27–28.

91. Cooper, pp. 86–87. Such organizational "messiness" characterized the Nazi regime. Hitler apparently deliberately created multiple levels or many centers of responsibility for many high-level tasks. For example, both the army engineers and the Todt Organization, which had built the autobahn system, held responsibility for constructing Germany's Westwall, the defense system along the Franco-German frontier. Both the Foreign Office and Joachim von Ribbentrop, the Nazi ideologue, had separate responsibilities for the conduct of foreign policy until his appointment as Foreign Minister in February 1938.

92. For example, Galante (p. 105) records a discussion on October 28, 1940, at OKH headquarters at Fontainebleau. Several officers were reviewing the situation maps on what Germany should do next. General Adolf Heusinger, Army Chief of Operations, observed, "Then our three supreme commanders [Brauchitsch, Raeder, and Göring] would have a joint operation to work on, which is as it should be. The three branches of the Wehrmacht must stop working in isolation, with no liaison and no coordination of policy and outlook." "Unfortunately," the naval officer who was present began, "the Führer wants to hold all the reins himself— he distrusts the idea of his generals' working together."

93. In 1928, the entire SS numbered a mere 280 men. By 1934, it consisted of three parts: the Allgemeine SS, or General SS, the purely party organization; the SS Leibstandarte Adolf Hitler, Hitler's personal bodyguard; and the Totenkopf (Death Head) units, the concentration camp (and later the extermination camp) guard units. It numbered about 50,000. Heinz Höhne, *The Order of the Death's Head: The Story of Hitler's SS* (New York: Ballantine Books, Inc., 1971), pp. 30, 86. After the Röhm Putsch, Himmler made the SS more stylish and "acceptable" by opening its ranks to upper-class Germans, especially those from the old aristocracy. They, in turn, wanted to join as a way of finding favor and career opportunities in the new regime. The SS became known as the Schwarze Korps (Black Corps) because of the stylish, crisp black uniforms the SS men wore. The SS insignia was done in embroidered silver thread, especially the "SS" shaped as Teutonic runes on the uniform's collar lapels. The members of the Totenkopf units also wore a silver death's head on the front of the garrison cap.

94. Reynolds, pp. 56–57. The expanded SS-VT division would consist of three infantry regiments, one reconnaissance battalion, one engineer battalion, and some organic artillery. The SS also established its own officer training school at Brunswick. O'Neill, p. 102.

95. Noakes and Pridham, II, p. 644. Hitler, like Blomberg, also wished to maintain the army solely for national defense and not allow it to be in a position to possibly fire on its compatriots as the Reichswehr had been during the Weimar Republic. Furthermore, he wanted an internal security force "...which has within its ranks men of the best German blood and which identifies itself unreservedly with the ideology at the base of the Greater German Reich...." Hitler Statement, Spring 1941, quoted in Taylor, *Sword and Swastika*, pp. 133–34.

96. March 1, 1934 entry, Shirer, *Berlin Diary*, p. 24.

97. Reynolds, pp. 57–58.

98. Görlitz, p. 290.

99. Deutsch, p. 31.

100. Reynolds, pp. 62–66.

101. O'Neill, pp. 99–101.

102. Wolff quoted in Deutsch, p. 31. Although Hitler ordered the destruction of the dossier, Heydrich, Himmler's deputy in the Security Service, apparently was looking toward the future when he secretly retained copies of its contents before destroying the original material.

103. Hoehne, *Death's Head*, p. 502.

104. Hoehne, pp. 162, 169.

105. O'Neill, pp. 102–3.

106. Hitler Decree, August 17, 1938, in Domarus, II, pp. 1131–32.

107. Cooper, p. 43. By September 1939, Himmler also had authority from Hitler to call up 50,000 members of the Allgemeine SS and parts of the Totenkopf units to reinforce the SS-VT. At the outbreak of the war, the SS-VT numbered 23,000 men, formed into four motorized infantry regiments, an artillery regiment, a signals, pioneer, reconnaissance, antiaircraft machine gun, and antitank battalion for each regiment, and their own supply and replacement units. In March 1940, the SS-VT was renamed the Waffen SS (Armed SS) at which time it numbered over 100,000 men. It would continue to grow, recruiting suitable men from among the conquered and allied nations of Europe — Norway, Denmark, the Netherlands,

Belgium, France, Italy, Occupied Russia, Bohemia and Moravia, Hungary, Rumania, Croatia, and Bosnia. By the end of the war, the Waffen SS had formed 40 divisions and numbered over 900,000, including 310,000 *Volkdeutsche* (ethnic Germans living outside of Germany). Most of the Waffen SS units fought in the Soviet Union. The German SS divisions did so with great fanaticism, resulting in grievous losses and the commission of untold suffering on their Soviet opponents, both military and civilian. The foreign divisions, totaling about 125,000 West Europeans and more than 200,000 from other ethnic groups and nationalities, varied in quality from good to virtually useless. Cooper, p. 165. Höhne, *Death's Head*, pp. 515–20. Samuel W. Mitcham, Jr., *Hitler's Legions: The German Army Order of Battle, World War II* (New York: Dorset Press, 1985), pp. 24, 439–71.

108. Beck quoted in Cooper, p. 43.

109. Fritsch quoted in Hoehne, *Death's Head*, p. 506.

110. O'Neill, p. 92.

111. For example, Knappe (p. 122) writes that he and his fellow soldiers did not talk about [Kristallnacht, the Night of Broken Glass, November 8-9, 1938, when the SA and SS rampaged through Germany, destroying Jewish-owned businesses and synagogues] ... because we were ashamed that our government would permit such a thing to happen.... We all felt that Hitler had been very good for Germany,... but there was a coarseness about him that we *silently* abhorred." (My italics.) On the other hand, Karl Fuchs apparently participated in and approved of the pogrom: "I can tell you that the authorities didn't miss one of those pig Jews." He had apparently absorbed at least part of the anti–Semitic message of the HJ and the RAD. Letter to Parents, November 23, 1938, pp. 36–37.

112. Hermann Rauschning, *The Revolution of Nihilism: Warning to the West* (New York: Alliance Book Corporation, 1939), pp. 66–67. Rauschning fled to Switzerland in 1936. See also Guderian quoted in Macksey, p. 76; Stahlberg, p. 88; and Knappe, pp. 74, 124–25.

113. Halder quoted in Gisevius, p. 293.

5

The Beginnings of the Military Opposition, 1936–1939

In the mid–1930s, the officer corps generally agreed with Hitler's plans to wipe out the stain of the Versailles Treaty by restoring the army's greatness through a major rearmament program and an aggressive foreign policy. The major concern of the senior army leaders was not the army's expansion program itself but its accelerating pace, with consequent adverse effects on the quality of the officer corps and possible adverse reactions from Britain and France that might trigger an untimely major war, one they believed Germany could not win at this time. For example, after Austrian Nazis assassinated the Austrian Chancellor Dr. Engelbert Dollfuss on June 30, 1934, Beck stated, "Our entire international position is hopeless. Everything is in danger. All that has been achieved in that respect is lost. All the Powers that matter are against us."[1] Nine months later, he wrote on the back of an April 11, 1935, army report, "What is so bad is not what we are doing but how we are doing it."[2] The senior army leaders had also protested the creation of and army assistance to the SS-VT and the formation of the OKW. Yet, they continued to develop Hitler's army even after the Führer pushed aside or ignored their protests, believing they had done their duty, once they had protested, and now their duty was to obey and continue building and training the new army.

However, as rearmament continued and Hitler increasingly advocated a more aggressive foreign policy to completely unravel the Versailles Treaty, the concern of the army leaders gave way to alarm. At the same time, the weak responses of the Western democracies to the steady progress of the rearmament program further emboldened Hitler to redress the wrongs of that treaty. In early November 1937, when Hitler secretly unveiled his plans of aggression to his most senior leaders, some, like Blomberg and Fritsch, became truly frightened at the prospect of another European war. At the same time, the Führer realized that he needed more obedient and aggressive leaders to carry out his plans. The crisis that resulted from Blomberg's unfortunate marriage in January 1938 gave Hitler the opportunity to rid himself of these "weaklings" and "cowards" and replace them with more aggressive (i.e., more ambitious, obedient, and loyal) men willing to carry out his plans. In the wake of the Blomberg-Fritsch crisis in January 1938, the military opposition solidified from these concerns, protests, and disagreements.

In this chapter, I will examine the specific events that caused some officers to lose confidence in Hitler, question their sworn loyalty to the Führer, and ultimately form the military opposition. They were daring and honorable — but tragic — men who now had some realization of Hitler intentions and decided to oppose him.[3] I will first look at the events surrounding Hitler's remilitarization of the Rhineland, the secret November 1937 conference and the reaction of some of the more senior army leaders to these events. I will then review the Blomberg-Fritsch crisis of January 1938 and its impact on the military opposition, the Czechoslovakian crisis from September 1938 to March 1939, Beck's subsequent resignation, and the final events leading to war in September 1939. Finally, I will briefly review the army's response to the regime's repressive internal policies. We will see that the military opposition formed primarily because of the loss of faith in the Führer by a small group of officers who rightly feared that Hitler was leading Germany into another world war before her armed forces were sufficiently prepared to fight and win such a war — not over the regime's repressive internal policies, such as the increasing persecution of Germany's Jews and the Gestapo's use of terror and torture against the regime's political enemies.

The First Signs of Opposition

Perhaps the embryo of the anti–Hitler Military Opposition can be found in the sporadic protests by some officers to the murders of Generals Schleicher and Bredow on June 30, 1934. In the previous chapter I briefly discussed the weak protests of a number of senior officers to these murders. However, of these, only Hammerstein and especially Hans Oster — who had served under Bredow when the latter had been chief of the Abwehr prior to January 1933 and developed a "furious hatred for everything Nazi" after the Night of the Long Knives — would seriously oppose the Nazi regime prior to 1938. From that time forward Oster with the help of Gisevius in the Gestapo collected information on the criminal actions of the SS and the SD for possible use in the future.[4]

However, the first significant signs of protest by a few senior army officers came over the accelerating pace of the rearmament program with its deleterious impact on the quality of the army, especially the officer corps, and possible repercussions from France. For example, in May 1935, Beck, as Chief of the Truppenamt, refused Fritsch's request to develop a detailed study of a surprise attack on a state southeast of Germany (Czechoslovakia?). Beck requested to "...be relieved of [his] position ... if the intent to begin actual preparations lies behind the Minister's directive. [He felt unable] to bear responsibility for such preparations."[5] Beck's threat to resign was probably driven more by the current state of the army's unpreparedness for war with France than any inhibitions about invading that country itself.

A greater crisis occurred in early 1936, less than two years into the army's expansion program, when Hitler tested the will of the Western democracies by the remilitarization of the Rhineland. Hitler used the ratification of the French-Soviet friendship treaty on February 27, 1936, as an excuse to reoccupy this key region which had been demilitarized since 1919, believing he could do so without Western retaliation. Even though the army had secretly made plans before March 1936 to remilitarize this area, Blomberg and Fritsch were still shocked by Hitler's intentions, announced in February, to send troops into the Rhineland. The army leaders felt there was insufficient time to conduct staff studies of this operation and feared strong French resistance to the move. Furthermore, because of the dispersal of trained men as cadres for the expanding army, the army had only four brigades at full combat strength.[6] As it was, Beck only found out about Hitler's intentions on March 6 — the day before the action.[7]

The senior army leaders flooded Hitler with protests at his orders to send German troops into the Rhineland. He brushed aside all suggestions for less provocative action although the army leaders did convince him to send only small units into the Rhineland and to withdraw them at any sign of serious French opposition.[8] At dawn March 7, advance units of the small German occupation forces entered the demilitarized zone for the first since 1918, followed by three battalions later that day. Later, Hitler formally repudiated the Locarno Treaty. In response, the French mobilized and deployed 13 divisions to positions in the Maginot Line. Hitler, Blomberg, and Fritsch prepared to withdraw their troops at the slightest movement towards war while they waited France's next move. Fortunately, for Hitler and the army, France made no further response. However, Shirer reported meeting Blomberg in Berlin's Tiergarten later in the day of March 7, 1936, and noticed the general's face "was still white, his cheeks twitching."[9] Hitler also recognized the danger of a serious French response to his risky venture. "A retreat on our part," he admitted later, would have spelled collapse."[10]

Hitler's success in bringing this gamble off without a war with France had two major effects. First, it fostered a growing sense of infallibility within Hitler's mind and among many Germans, a myth that would ultimately have dire consequences for Germany and the army. Hitler told his entourage on the trip back to Berlin from Cologne, "Am I glad! Good Lord, am I glad it's gone smoothly. Sure enough, the world belongs to the brave man. He's the one God helps."[11] A referendum, held on March 29, confirmed Hitler's bold and risky action: 99 percent of Germany's 45,453,691 registered voters voted, and 98.8 percent favored his move.[12] The second effect was the increasing deterioration of the relationship between Hitler and Blomberg, Fritsch, and Beck. He called them cowards and weaklings, causing them to question their own professional judgment in regard to their opposition to his abilities. Hitler's future foreign policy successes — the Anschluss and the annexation of the Sudetenland — would serve only to further this infallibility myth, cause him to discount his generals' professional military advice and warnings, and lead to his miscalculation of the Western response to his invasion of Poland in 1939.[13]

Soon after the occupation of the Rhineland, the Spanish Civil War began with the revolt of the anti–Republican, nationalist Francisco Franco against the legally elected government of Spain. Hitler saw another opportunity to humiliate the Western democracies by supporting Franco. He first dispatched aircraft to transport Franco's forces from Spanish Morocco to Spain at the start of the revolt. During the war, he sent up to 20,000 Germans, mostly civilian technicians and military advisors assigned to 11 Luftwaffe squadrons — the Condor Legion. Other German military advisors trained Franco's armored units. Beck protested the decision to send military aid to Spain, given the state of Germany's military forces in 1936. Initially, Blomberg supported the army in protesting Hitler's orders, but he soon acquiesced to the Führer, widening the gap between the Wehrmacht leadership and the army leadership.[14] Hitler ended the movement of German soldiers to Spain after

January 1937 but continued to dispatch military supplies to Franco.[15] Fed by optimistic reports of German exploits in Spain, Hitler privately fumed at the cautious warnings of the generals, calling them "medieval knights."[16]

These and other risky actions by Hitler, such as the withdrawal from the League of Nations and the termination of the Locarno Treaty, produced rising concern among some officers throughout the military, who would ultimately coalesce into the military opposition. They included the former chief of the Truppenamt and now retired General von Hammerstein, Colonel Hans Oster and Admiral Wilhelm Canaris of the Abwehr and Colonel Franz Halder, a section chief of the General Staff in 1936 and future Chief of the General Staff. They sought to bring Beck closer into the infant opposition, but, for now, he stayed true to his nonpolitical heritage and did not respond to their entreaties.[17] He reportedly told a confidant of Hjalmar Schacht, the Minister of Economics, "that to change the regime was a civilian affair, but if the civilian opposition took the initiative, the army would not fail them."[18] Fabian von Schlabrendorff, a prominent member of the anti–Hitler opposition who, following the July 20, 1944, bomb plot, survived the Gestapo's tortures, imprisonment, and the war relates in his memoirs that the civilian members needed the top military leaders for any resistance to the Nazi regime to be successful.[19] So here was the dilemma: to overthrow Hitler required the support and participation of the military; yet, many of the military leaders, like Beck, would not act until the civilians did.

Others included General Erwin von Witzleben, commander of Wehrkreis III, and Major General Count Erich von Brockdorff-Ahlefeld, commander of the Potsdam division and a subordinate of Witzleben. According to the wife of General Hermann von Witzleben, the cousin of Erwin von Witzleben, the latter believed that Hitler's relentless drive toward war was "criminal." Witzleben recognized "the burden" that he and "his friends" must assume. Knowing that they would need help in any anti–Hitler conspiracy, they considered both General Rundstedt, commander of the Berlin Army Group, and General Erich Fromm, chief of the Allgemeine Heeresamt (General Army Office) in charge of training units. However, Witzleben rejected both as "unsuitable."[20] In the autumn of 1937, General Brockdorff was also considering an anti–Hitler plot and discussed with August Wining and Count Fritz-Dietlof von Schulenburg a number of likely recruits from among the general officers, such as General Erwin von Kleist, commander of the Breslau Wehrkreis, General Erich Hoepner, future commander of a panzer division, and the two generals Joachim and Karl Heinrich von Stülpnagel.[21]

By 1937, there were already a number of military leaders and civilians who were concerned about the direction in which the Nazi regime was going. The civilian members of the infant opposition, unofficially led by the former Lord Mayor of Leipzig, Dr. Carl Goerdeler, were more concerned about the regime's internal suppression of civil liberties and "criminal" activities of the Gestapo and the SS. He hoped to stir the military to action by providing its senior leaders with numerous reports from Oster in the Abwehr, but Blomberg simply took no official notice of this material.[22] On the other hand, the officers were more concerned that Hitler's risky foreign policy would provoke a war with France and Britain before Germany was adequately prepared to defend itself— and defend any territorial gains it had made. The only common characteristic of these men was their general opposition to the Nazi regime. As a result, the anti–Nazi opposition would suffer from the lack of a tightly organized apparatus, common goals and objectives, and an agreed-upon plan of action — other than to somehow get rid of Hitler and his cronies.

On November 5, 1937, Hitler revealed his aggressive plans at a secret "war" conference at the Reich Chancellery in Berlin. Blomberg, Fritsch, Raeder, Göring, Constantin Freiherr von Neurath, Hitler's Foreign Minister, and Colonel Friedrich Hossbach, Hitler's military adjutant since 1934, attended, among others. Hitler outlined his reasons to obtain Lebensraum, possible courses of action, and an estimated timetable that would mean war in Europe.[23] Blomberg, Fritsch, and Neurath, believing France was stronger than Hitler thought, favored caution and moderation. After Beck heard about the conference, he now had reason to criticize Hitler's foreign policy directly (not just his means), Blomberg, and his subordinates.[24] Hitler, already showing less consideration for the army's concerns, became even more suspicious and critical of the cautiousness of some of the army's senior leaders.

The Hossbach conference was a major turning point in Hitler's relationship with the army's more conservative leaders. Hossbach, in his memoirs, wrote that the discussion between Blomberg, Fritsch, and Neurath who favored moderation and restraint, and Göring who supported the Führer, became "quite heated" as Hitler watched the disputing parties quietly and did not say anything. However, the arguments, wrote Hossbach, apparently made

> an impression on Hitler as I could see from the expression on his face. In view of his attitude, the behaviour of Blomberg and Fritsch must have made it clear to the Führer that his political ideas had simply produced sober and objective counter-argument instead of applause and approval. And he knew very well that the two generals rejected any involvement in a war provided by us."[25]

Deeply disappointed with his two senior generals, Hitler no longer referred to them as "my dear Field Marshal" and "my dear Colonel General" and realized he could no longer depend on them to implement his future plans.[26] Despite temporary reassurances to the contrary, he knew now that he would soon have to get rid of them somehow.

The Blomberg-Fritsch Crisis

Fate gave Hitler that opportunity after Blomberg married Erna Gruhn, a secretary in one of the ministries, in December 1937. Prior to the marriage ceremony, the War Minister had sought advice from the Wehrmacht legal department whose director told him that the officer corps would be against him marrying someone "beneath their social class"— not to mention she was already several months pregnant. Blomberg also sought the advice of Göring and the approval of Hitler, and they both approved of the marriage as a way to end the social bias of the officer corps. Göring even arranged the reassignment of a younger officer — and rival for Ms. Gruhn's hand — in the War Ministry to give Blomberg a "clear path." On January 12, 1938, Blomberg married his secretary at a ceremony with only Hitler, Göring, a personal friend of Blomberg, and the bride's mother present. Except for Reader and Fritsch hardly anyone else in the Wehrmacht knew about the marriage. When the marriage became more widely known in the army, "[t]he shock of the news reverberated through military quarters in Berlin and in the Wehrkreis commands."[27]

During the Blombergs' honeymoon, the chief of the criminal police, Wolf Heinrich Graf von Helldorf, discovered that the new Mrs. Blomberg had a shady past. At an earlier age, she had posed for pornographic pictures and may have been arrested for prostitution. On January 20, 1938, he took the police dossier to Keitel who, in turn, gave it to Göring. Although he had "stood" with Blomberg at his wedding, Göring also coveted the position of war minister and, therefore, took the file to Hitler after a conference with Himmler and Heydrich. In considering what to do, Hitler may have realized that Blomberg's actions over the last four years had distanced him from his fellow general officers. Furthermore, although Hitler himself probably had no problem having a war minister with a commoner as a wife, the other senior generals would certainly have problems with one of their own who had married not only a woman beneath them but also one with such a sordid past.[28] Beck expressed the problem this way: "One cannot permit the highest-ranking soldier to marry a whore; he should be forced to divorce the woman or else be taken off the list of officers; he could no longer be the commander of even a regiment."[29] Anyway, this situation provided Hitler with a perfect excuse to dismiss Blomberg on January 24, not only without arousing the suspicions of the other generals to his true purpose but with their apparent blessings.[30]

With Blomberg's impending dismissal, the Führer now had to decide who would replace Blomberg as war minister. On January 26, Hitler asked Blomberg this question, and he offered several suggestions. Fritsch was the most obvious and eligible candidate as army commander, next in the "line of succession." However, Hitler had mentally rejected Fritsch as the type of Prussian officer whom he particularly disliked. Fritsch had also protested the speed of the rearmament program, the formation of the SS-VT, the remilitarization of the Rhineland, and, most recently, along with Blomberg, the plan of aggression outlined at the Hossbach conference. Hitler declared to Blomberg that he could not appoint Fritsch to this positon because of the impending charges of homosexuality. Blomberg then suggested Göring, but Hitler knew the other generals would not accept the corpulent and lazy air force chief as their war minister. He also did not want to increase Göring's power by giving him control of the Wehrmacht.[31]

When Fritsch first came up as a possible successor to Blomberg, Himmler reminded Hitler about the 1936 dossier that purportedly provided proof that Fritsch had committed a homosexual act. An unsavory character Otto Schmidt had supposedly witnessed Fritsch at a Berlin train station in 1933 where he had a liaison with a known homosexual. In actuality, Schmidt had been blackmailing a retired Captain Achim von *Frisch* for a total of 3,000 marks. In 1936, Schmidt was convicted of extortion and sentenced to seven years in prison. Possibly to obtain early release or better treatment, the convicted blackmailer later gave the police several hundred names, including Frisch's. Frisch became von Fritsch, then General von Fritsch. The SS chief conveniently resurrected the dossier, supposedly destroyed in 1936, with additional "evidence" from Heydrich of Fritsch's guilt.[32] With this evidence, Hitler could not only reject Fritsch as the next war minister, but also indefinitely suspend him from his post, which he did on January 26.

On the surface, such action may seem contradictory, since Hitler had previously rejected the original charge and had also tolerated homosexuals among leading party leaders. However, the dossier first appeared in 1935 when Hitler needed Fritsch's expertise, professionalism, and reputation among the officer corps to rebuild the army; by January 1938, he no longer needed him. Intending to dismiss Fritsch soon (although officially he was only suspended), Hitler and Keitel now discussed who would succeed Fritsch as the army commander in chief. Such action was highly irregular since a suspended officer normally received an opportunity to present his case and then, if he was acquitted, resumed his position, but obviously Hitler did not want Fritsch returning to OKH. He first suggested his favorite Reichenau as the new army commander in chief, but Keitel, knowing that the other generals would not accept him, talked Hitler out of that. Keitel then suggested General Brauchitsch, the commander of Army Group 4 at Leipzig, recommended personally by Blomberg and highly regarded by other senior officers.[33]

Hitler selected Brauchitsch after the reluctant and weak general had accepted three conditions. The prospective army chief would have to move the army closer to the state and Nazi ideology, bring in a more amenable chief of staff, an obvious reference to replacing Beck, and endorse the new Wehrmacht command structure. After some thought (particularly on the third condition), a threat from Hitler to appoint Reichenau, and the Führer's and Göring reassurance that they would help him with a certain personal problem, Brauchitsch agreed, essentially selling his professional soul to Hitler.[34] At a January 30 meeting with Hitler, Brauchitsch reaffirmed his allegiance to National Socialism and agreed to transfer a number of senior officers whom Hitler disliked.[35] Hitler's *fait accompli* effectively forestalled any possible action by the other generals against him.

Brauchitsch, like Blomberg, also had woman troubles. He had been separated from his legal wife for five years and was "in love" with another woman. However, he did not have the large sum of money his wife was demanding for a divorce settlement. By August 1938, Brauchitsch had received 80,000 Reichsmarks (RMs), probably from Hitler's funds, and he divorced his wife and married his "love" on September 23, 1938. His second wife, a "die-hard" Nazi, would never let Brauchitsch forget how much they owed their Führer. As Brauchitsch once confessed to Halder, "Please do not hold it against me. I know you are dissatisfied with me. When I confront this man, I feel as if someone was choking me and I cannot find another word."[36] Deutsch scathingly criticizes Brauchitsch's conduct:

> "[T]o all intents and purposes [he] had sold out his fellows when he sold himself. However much he may have salved his conscience by telling himself that he had, after all, 'saved the Army from Reichenau,' he henceforth carried a burden from which, even after he left office four years later, there could be no complete escape."[37]

After deciding to dismiss Fritsch and appoint Brauchitsch as his successor, Hitler now faced the irate indignation — but not revolt — of those who did not believe the charges. They knew Fritsch to be an honorable soldier who had no known vices except a passion to ride horses and would not allow Fritsch to be treated as offhandedly as Blomberg had been. General Wilhelm Adam had once told Hans Frank, the Reich Minister without Portfolio, that Blomberg was "not our Field-Marshal but yours."[38] After Hitler told Beck about Blomberg's and Fritsch's ouster, Beck told the Führer that while Blomberg "had excluded himself from the Army by his outrageous conduct" Fritsch's situation "demanded an exhaustive investigation by the military judicial authorities."[39] Hossbach also realized the apparent justification for dismissing Blomberg but thought the charges against Fritsch as "wholly incredible[,] ... a pretext of Hitler's to rid himself of the inconvenient general. The adjutant now realized what he was up against."[40] In fact, Hossbach disobeyed Hitler twice, first by telling Fritsch, on January 25, about the trumped-up charges and then by discussing them with Beck on January 26 and 27. As a result, Hitler dismissed Hossbach to prevent him from interceding with the expected string of generals coming to the Reich Chancellery to protest the charges against their commander.[41]

In early February, Hitler made his final decisions about changes in the senior military leadership. On February 3, he asked Fritsch to resign; he did so immediately and without a fight. On the next day, Hitler formally announced to an assembly of senior officers Blomberg's dismissal as War Minister and early retirement and Fritsch's resignation. The Führer also announced that he would become his own war minister — at Blomberg's own suggestion — and that the Wehrmachtsamt would become OKW with Keitel as its first chief. OKW took over the functions of the War Ministry, and its chief, as the Führer's deputy, received the authority and functions of the former War Minister.[42]

Hitler assumed only the title and authority of the war minister to directly command the armed forces. He realized that he could not take care of all the required *staff* duties and would need a qualified assistant for this purpose. When Hitler asked Blomberg for a recommendation, the disgraced War Minister provided Keitel, calling him "no more than *my chef de bureau.*" Hitler responded positively to the recommendation: "That is exactly the kind of man I want."[43] Keitel's fellow generals referred to him as "Bürogeneral" ("office, or desk general") and "Witzblattgeneral" ("funny paper general"). They remembered that he had gone through all of World War I as a captain, one of the very few officers who did not receive a promotion or citation for distinguished service. During the interwar years he was a "bureaucratic nobody" until he replaced Reichenau at the Wehrmachtsamt.[44]

Brauchitsch, now promoted to Generaloberst, became the new army commander in chief. Finally, 16 generals were relieved, without any protests, of their posts and retired, and another 44 were transferred to lesser posts, apparently because of their aristocratic background or anti–Nazi leanings.[45] Hitler remarked: "After such sorrowful experiences I must consider anyone capable of anything. The 100,000-man Army had failed to produce any great leaders. From now on I shall concern myself with personnel matters and make the right appointments."[46] In a bloodless coup Hitler had rid himself of potential opponents, opened a number of senior posts for officers like Keitel, Jodl, and Brauchitsch, and obtained direct command of the armed forces.

Meanwhile, during the short interregnum between Fritsch's suspension on January 26 and the announcements of February 4, Beck, as Chief of the General Staff, was technically the "acting" army commander. Given his stature, official position, and personal prestige, he probably could have moved the other generals to stand by Fritsch or possibly to take action against the regime. Even Hitler recognized Beck as a threat, telling Franz Guertner, the Minster of Justice, "I want to tell you something. The only one I fear is Beck. That man is capable of something."[47] Although Beck did demand and obtain a military tribunal for Fritsch to formally defend himself against the charges, Beck did nothing to rally the other generals to support Fritsch — or something more drastic, such as take action against the Gestapo and SS as Halder and Carl Goerdeler had pressed him to do.[48]

Throughout all of these machinations, Fritsch adamantly and categorically denied the charges. Although he pressed to obtain a court-martial trial as the forum to clear his name, he failed to take more forceful action. The essence of the problem was his continuing belief in a conspiracy by Himmler and Göring against him personally, and his failure to comprehend the attack on the general officer corps by Hitler. For example, Fritsch did not call on the other army generals to support him, fearing such action would bring about a civil war and split the army, a possibility that immobilized most generals who may have wanted to help.[49] Deutsch wrote that Fritsch's failure to ask for solid support from the other generals "sealed not only his fate but that of the Army and, in some measure, of Germany."[50] Hitler did reluctantly concede to a court-martial for Fritsch, mainly to assuage the fears of the generals that their commander would not be railroaded on trumped-up charges. By this time, Hitler knew that the outcome of the trial was now immaterial — Brauchitsch was already the army commander in chief.

Hitler and Göring now tried to set up a Gestapo-dominated special court to try Fritsch. However, on January 28, Dr. Heinrich Rosenberger, head of the Wehrmacht legal department, told Keitel that, according to military law, Fritsch could only be tried by a military tribunal, composed of a senior judge and general officers, appointed by the head of state.[51] Although Hitler was not one to particularly follow the law, he did so in this case. Göring, Himmler, and Heydrich now worked to delay the court-martial as long as possible and used blackmail, bribery, forgery, and even death threats to build their case against Fritsch. Hitler also stacked the court-martial panel against Fritsch by appointing Göring, the only field marshal on active duty, as the president, with Brauchitsch and Raeder, along with Dr. Carl Sack, the Judge Advocate-General of the Army, and another senior member of the Judge Advocate-General's office. Among rumors of a military coup in Berlin, Hitler set March 11 as the date to open the trial.[52]

On his side, the wronged general had Dr. Sack, and Ruediger Graf von der Golz, the son of the old general, and the assistance of Oster and Hans von Dohnanyi from the Ministry of Justice. Their investigation turned up increasing evidence of the sordid tricks of the SS and Gestapo. Then, on March 1 or 2, they discovered the retired Captain von Frisch, the evidence Beck and members of the opposition needed to prove an SS–Gestapo conspiracy against Fritsch. With this evidence Fritsch's friends attempted to persuade Brauchitsch that a trial was not needed, that all *he* needed to do was present the evidence of the Gestapo's conspiracy against his former chief to Hitler. However, Brauchitsch was not a man for such direct action and counseled the defense team to let the trial take its course. If the evidence presented caused a serious enough "explosion" to destroy the Hitler myth before the German people and the world, then he would take action.[53]

However, fate again intervened to Hitler's benefit when the Austrian Chancellor Karl Schuschnigg suddenly announced a plebiscite on the question of union with Germany (Anschluss) for March 13, 1938. Since the abortive coup of July 1934, agitation by Austrian Nazis for the Anschluss had grown, resulting in Schuschnigg's announcement. Unwilling to risk unfavorable results, Hitler decided to force the Anschluss. He put the court-martial on temporary hold to discuss the Austrian situation with Göring, Reichenau, and two other generals — but not with OKW or OKH. On March 10, he discussed military options against Austria with Keitel, Jodl, Beck, and Manstein, none of whom offered any moral objections to an invasion. Beck only objected on the grounds that the plans would have to be improvised, but reluctantly complied when Hitler threatened to use the SA and the SS, instead of the army, for the impending operation. Beck now worked feverishly during the next hours to draw up the plans.[54]

On March 13, the day scheduled for the plebiscite, German troops entered Austria without any opposition. They only met jubilant, cheering crowds on the road to Linz, Hitler's boyhood home, and then Vienna. Austria became a province of the Third Reich, the Ostmark. Hitler had his unilateral action confirmed by a Nazi plebiscite in April. Guderian greeted the orders to march into Austria: "I felt that for both countries it was an occasion of rejoicing."[55] Beck was likewise pleased at the success of his plans, particularly since his worries of French and/or British intervention proved needless: "We [all] want to fulfill our duty to the *Führer* and the great German (*grossdeutsches*) National Socialist Fatherland in a spirit of unity."[56]

Fritsch's court-martial reconvened on March 17 and ended after two days. Göring, the president of the court, did everything he could to direct the trial in favor of the conspirators and to stymie the defense, ably presented by von der Goltz. For example, General Count Hans von Sponneck tried to denounce the "powers who had set themselves above the state" (the SS[?]) and had conspired against Fritsch and the army, but Göring declared his comments to be irrelevant. Göring had also apparently intimidated both Raeder and Brauchitsch who said hardly a word during the entire trial.[57] Then the prosecution put their star witness Schimdt on the stand, and, despite Göring's interruptions, the defense team finally wrangled the truth from the hapless blackmailer — Captain von Frisch was the real culprit, not General von Fritsch. Fritsch was acquitted.[58]

Unfortunately for the army and Fritsch, his vindication was lost among the general excitement resulting from the Anschluss. The bloodless and unopposed union with Austria only added to Hitler's myth of infallibility. Furthermore, with Brauchitsch in place, Fritsch could not resume his old position, and Hitler could well afford a simple letter of congratulations on his acquittal without apologizing for his mistreatment of Fritsch. The official news agency reported that Hitler had only congratulated Fritsch on his recovery of health. Additionally, there was no trial of Göring, Himmler, and Heydrich or public exposure of their perfidious actions throughout the entire affair. Gisevius tried to push Brauchitsch into action, but he was not the man to do anything so politically damaging to the Führer or the party. Meanwhile, Canaris and Hossbach worked on Beck to expose the Gestapo's role in the crisis but to no avail.[59]

The opposition was also hampered by insufficient or uneven knowledge at the lower levels of the army of exactly what was going on "at the top." Many officers outside of OKW and OKH had very little, if any, inkling about the affair. For example, Guderian learned about the dismissal of the senior officers, including Blomberg and Fritsch, from a newspaper on the morning of February 4, 1938, and was caught off guard:

> We were flabbergasted. These serious allegations against our most senior officers, whom we know to be men of spotless honor, cut us to the quick. They were quite incredible, and yet our immediate reaction was that the first magistrate of the German State [Hitler] could not simply have invented these stories out of thin air.[60]

Without knowledge of the true situation, he wrote his wife, "The Führer has acted, as usual, with the finest human decency. It is to be hoped that he will be approved by his colleagues."[61] Other officers, having heard rumors about a possible SS coup, received accurate information quite soon. Exhibiting respect for their commander in chief, some believed they would have fired on the SS — if they had received orders to do so.[62] Guderian wrote a postmortem on the army's senior leadership: "[B]lame can be apportioned only to the few individuals at the top [because for] the majority [of the officers], the true state of affairs remained obscure."[63]

With the trial now over, Fritsch entered a bitter forced retirement. He noted, "No nation ever allowed the Commander-in-Chief of its Army to be subjected to such disgraceful treatment.... Such treatment is not only undignified for me, at the same time it dishonors the whole Army." Furthermore, Fritsch recounted, "Yet if I had known wholly this man is without scruple and how he gambles with the fate of the German people, I should have acted differently and taken myself the odium of having acted through egotistic motives."[64] He finally had some idea of the kind of man Adolf Hitler was and that the conspiracy against him, Fritsch, was more against the army as a whole and the general officer corps in particular than against him personally. On April 7, Fritsch replied to Hitler's "congratulatory" letter, berating the Führer for the bad treatment he had given him, on the accusation of a criminal and without a proper investigation. He requested Hitler to call to account the conspirators and to restore his honor before the court and the nation. However, Hitler took no action.[65]

With Fritsch's vindication by the trial, many senior officers, especially Beck, deluged Brauchitsch with requests to rehabilitate their ex-commander. The weak army commander took their requests but did nothing initially although he probably realized that their support for him depended upon his action to press their requests.[66] The protests continued, but no one saw a coup as a possibility; Beck, thinking back to the troubled days of 1918–19, told Halder, "Mutiny and revolution are words which will not be found in a German soldier's dictionary."[67] Then, in May 1938, General Guenther von Kluge told his chief of staff that the 12 Wehrkreise commanders had agreed to threaten collective resignation unless Hitler took action to rehabilitate Fritsch. On June 13, Brauchitsch told an assembly of senior army leaders at Barth, with Hitler present, that he firmly intended to resign as a sign of support for Fritsch. However, one must question Brauchitsch's sincerity since he knew about the growing crisis with Czechoslovakia.[68]

The consummate politician that he was, Hitler now realized that his generals were in earnest about rehabilitating Fritsch. At Barth, he formally announced Fritsch's rehabilitation by appointing him an honorary colonel of Artillery Regiment 12. Speaking about the growing crisis over Czechoslovakia, he then "pleaded" with the generals "not to abandon the flag at so critical a time.... He placed his entire trust in the Wehrmacht and begged it to bestow a similar confidence on him."[69] Given an impending international crisis, neither Brauchistch nor the generals could, within their conscience and by their obligation to their oath, resign. Furthermore, Fritsch accepted the honorary appointment, and all reasons for any possible resistance evaporated.[70] The general officers had lost another opportunity to use current tension to overthrow Hitler if they had wanted to. As Captain Gerhard Engel, Hossbach's replacement as Hitler's army adjutant, wrote,

> We, in the Army, have missed out in everything it was imperative to do. In February 1938 I was with the troops. The fury of the officers was tremendous. At that time the troops would have still obeyed us. Now, it is all over, for the successes [of Hitler] have been too great.[71]

The relative obscurity of the actual events surrounding Fritsch's ouster played into Hitler's hands in another respect. Keitel wrote that he believed that the situation "should be left to take its time; it was hard for Hitler to admit that he himself had been the victim of deceit or even of an intrigue."[72] Many senior officers similarly believed that the entire crisis was an SS and Gestapo plot of which Hitler had no knowledge until the trial brought out the false evidence from Schmidt. Most historians believe that Hitler had sufficient knowledge of Fritsch's innocence but supported the conspiracy as a way of getting Fritsch out of the way. The appointment of Brauchitsch as Fritsch's replacement — not as temporary army commander during the investigation and court-martial — supports this conclusion as this action made it impossible for Fritsch to return to his old position without Hitler suffering total humiliation.

Although no one in the army leadership seriously contemplated an anti–Hitler coup, Hitler's slanderous treatment of Fritsch further outraged a few dissident officers. For example, the affair served as a turning point for a few officers such as Georg Thomas, Wilhelm Adam, Erich Hoepner, Karl-Heinrich Stülpnagel, Erwin von Witzleben, Wilehlm Canaris, Dohnanyi, and Tresckow. The latter even contemplated resignation in protest. Oster, already involved in antiregime activities, helped Beck obtain the facts surrounding the former commander in chief's case. In fact, following the affair, Oster and Beck, both passionate horsemen, spent time horseback riding in the Gruenwald where they had peace, quiet, and solitude to discuss resistance matters.[73] In this respect the Abwehr officer probably had a profound impact upon Beck's growing opposition to Hitler and his ultimate resignation as chief of staff later that year over Hitler's risky foreign policies.

The Military Opposition and the Road to War

Although the Blomberg-Fritsch crisis did not bring about a general officer revolt as some had hoped, it did act as a catalyst to bring together disparate parts of the civilian opposition and the military opposition. The civilian opposition, influenced by Gisevius, now hoped to move the army to action against the SS and the Gestapo for its criminal — not political — activities. They believed that the army would surely take action against such practices as murder, deprivation of liberty, extortion, and corruption, and, once his criminal leaders were imprisoned, then Hitler could not continue his reign of terror.[74] Although the civilian opposition had misplaced its confidence in the generals' willingness to act against Hitler for his criminal *domestic* policies, its leaders did begin discussions with the growing number of dissident officers — such as Canaris, Witzleben, Brockdorff-Ahlefeld, Hoepner, Helmut Groscurth, and Oster — over the summer of 1938.

The Fritsch Crisis also became the final "straw" that broke Beck's allegiance to the Führer. Beck had initially remained at OKH, hoping to positively affect foreign and military policies. He became an indefatigable proponent for Fritsch's rehabilitation, and his constant stream of memoranda to Brauchitsch only served to irritate the new army commander. Then, in late April 1938, Hitler announced his intention to attack Czechoslovakia and annex the , and, on May 28, directed OKW — not the army General Staff— to prepare a plan for Operation Green without any army inputs. Beck responded with several memoranda to Brauchitsch and Hitler, averring that such an attack was militarily unsound. Hitler rejected Beck's objections, and Brauchitsch became so irritated at Beck that he began to bypass him and work directly with the new army chief of operations, Franz Halder.[75] Hitler now recognized Beck as "too much old-fashioned" and realized "he could not have a Chief of Staff who did not share his faith." He concluded that Beck would have to be replaced soon.[76]

As the summer progressed, Beck's situation worsened. In late June, Lieutenant Colonel Rudolph Schmundt, Hossbach's replacement as Hitler's senior adjutant, viewed him as a man "who does not understand the dynamism of the new regime.... If it were up to Beck, we would still sit begging at the conference tables of Geneva." An air force officer commented, "More than thirty days to overrun these ridiculous Hussites! As if we had no air force! ... For Beck our squadrons are merely auxiliaries for the infantry."[77] More interested in pleasing Hitler and Keitel, Brauchitsch wearied of Beck's memoranda and concerns. By mid–July, Beck had ordered the OKH staff not to speak to its counterparts on the

OKW staff although the coming crisis over Czechoslovakia depended upon open communications between the two.[78] When Beck tried to pin Hitler down on his near-term plans over the , Hitler told his chief of staff, "The army is an instrument of politics. I shall assign the army its task when the moment arrives, and the army will have to carry out this task without arguing whether it is right or wrong." Beck made it known he would not be responsible for orders which he could not approve of.[79]

The situation climaxed in mid–July after Beck wrote a memo to Brauchitsch in which he argued that the generals should resign their positions to protest Hitler's aggressive moves:

> All upright and serious Germans in positions of high responsibility must feel themselves bound to make every conceivable effort ... to prevent a war against Czechoslovakia which would, of necessity, lead to a world war which would spell *Finis Germanie.*
>
> The leaders of the *Wehrmacht* are especially suited and called to fulfill this responsibility, for the *Wehrmacht* is the instrument of state power that carries out orders in war.
>
> The future well-being of the nation is being risked. History will burden the leaders of the *Wehrmacht* with blood-guilt if they do not make use of their expert knowledge and act according to the dictates of their consciences. There is a limit to soldierly obedience. It is reached ... when the soldiers' sense of responsibility forbids them to carry out an order.[80]

Beck captured the essence of the soldier's, especially the officer's, duty to his people and nation that transcends his absolute obedience to orders that the oath of loyalty implies. However, he failed to consider the criminal activities of the regime as others would fail to react to future Nazi atrocities. Unfortunately, no one followed his lead in 1938, and only a handful would ultimately find the moral courage to act against Hitler and his regime in the future—and, then, only when Germany and much of Europe was being devastated.

Beck now tried and failed to obtain the support of Brauchitsch and the other generals for a mass protest against Hitler's foreign policies. Brauchitsch, possessing neither the political strength nor the character to do much, later wrote, "Why, in heaven's name, should I, of all men in the world, have taken action against Hitler? The German people had elected him, and the workers, like all other Germans, were perfectly satisfied with successful policy."[81] On August 4, with Brauchitsch present, Beck presented his case to the senior commanders. Although the generals generally agreed with Beck's reasoning, none, with the exception of Adam, came to his side; and none were willing to take any action. General Ernst Busch, promoted with the February 4 shake-up, could only speak about obedience and the oath of loyalty.[82]

Reichenau "tattled" to Hitler about Beck's attempt to obtain the collective support of the generals against the projected attack on Czechoslovakia. At first, the dictator wanted to fire Beck, but Brauchitsch talked him out of it. Instead, Hitler ordered Brauchitsch to ensure Beck sent him no more letters and began a campaign to discredit Beck among his colleagues, particularly the younger ones. On August 15, Hitler met with the generals to put out any sparks of opposition. The next day, Hitler, through Brauchitsch, ordered the army to cease interfering in political affairs and demanded "unconditional obedience" from all commanding generals and the chief of the General Staff. Beck refused and demanded that Brauchitsch follow suit. The army commander refused, saying, "I am a soldier; it is my duty to obey."[83]

Realizing he had completely lost the confidence of Hitler and Brauchitsch and no longer able to support Hitler's plans for aggression, Beck resigned as Chief of the General Staff on August 18. Later he would often say, "Brauchitsch angrily left me in a lurch." The resignation became effective on August 27 when Halder took over his duties, but Beck inexplicably agreed to Hitler's request to remain silent about the resignation and "officially" retired at the end of October.[84] Keitel wrote about Beck's resignation:

> I wept no tears over Beck in view of the shameless way he had treated me; I was always the first to recognize his great virtues; and I would never [have] thought him capable of selling his soul to treasonable intriguers as early as 1938, or being their spiritual leader from that point on. One can seek his motives only in his injured vanity and his abysmal hatred of Hitler; that was why this formerly impeccable officer made common cause with our enemies and stiffened their resolve while awaiting our overthrow, something Beck was impotent to bring about himself.[85]

The delay in announcing Beck's resignation minimized its impact and robbed the opposition of an opportunity to publicize its cause to the German people and the world.

Halder, like Beck, had undergone a transformation from an admirer of Hitler to an opponent since the exhilarating first years of the Third Reich. In August 1934, he believed that the other Nazis unduly influenced Hitler: "The Chancellor's intentions are pure and inspired by idealism; but they are being abused and sometimes actually reversed in practice by swarms of utterly incompetent — often downright useless — Party organizations ... the Führer [wanted] to build on existing values...."[86] In March 1938, Halder turned 180 degrees against Hitler, calling him a "criminal [who] is deliberately dragging us into war, no doubt in order to gratify his pathological sexual impulses and his blood lust."[87] In September 1938, meeting with Gisevius, Halder called Hitler "a bloodsucker and a criminal ... and should be done away with."[88] Despite these outbursts and future disagreements with Hitler over military policy, Halder would go no further than sympathy with the aims of the military opposition and never became a "full-fledged" member.[89]

As a pretext for overthrowing the Nazi regime and eliminating Hitler and the Nazi criminals, Halder wanted a foreign policy setback as opposed to a demonstration of the criminal nature of the Nazi internal policies. In the summer of 1938, he saw Hitler's drive to annex the Sudetenland at the risk of war with France as the opportunity to show the German people that Hitler would ultimately engulf Germany in a major European conflict. Only in this way could the opposition, Halder believed, obtain the necessary support among the German people and within the army for a successful coup. He also desperately wanted to minimize the potential for civil war so that the soldiers would be seen as saviors, not traitors. Because of this position, Halder did not support the plan of Gisevius to seize the government buildings in Berlin with the help of the Berlin police.[90]

As Hitler relentlessly pushed Germany to the brink of war over the Sudetenland, many army generals, including Rundstedt and Reichenau, who were charged with developing the plan for the attack, were noticeably reluctant to attack Czechoslovakia. Fearing a general European war, they were counseling caution and restraint. Jodl noticed that there was still a "strong current of resistance to Hitler's intentions and plans," despite Beck's departure. After the September Nuremberg Party rally, he noted in his diary,

> ...[T]he Führer is aware that the Commander-in-Chief of the Army asked his commanders to support him in his attempt to make the Führer see sense on the subject of the adventure onto which he seems determined to plunge. The Commander-in-Chief himself, so he said, unfortunately had no influence with the Führer. The atmosphere in Nuremberg was consequently cool and frosty. It is tragic that the Führer should have the

> whole nation behind him with the single exception of the Army generals.[91]

Keitel passionately declared that he would not tolerate criticism or defeatism by the OKH and accused the generals of jealousy; to them, Hitler was "the Corporal of the World War, not the greatest politician since Bismarck."[92] However, despite their "inner" opposition to Hitler's plans, most held their thoughts to themselves and dutifully complied with their orders to prepare for the inevitable invasion.

Further vexing the Führer was what he viewed as the slow pace of construction of the Westwall, Germany's system of fortifications along the border with France. Throughout the spring and summer, General Adam, as commander of the army group at Kassel, had continually and vocally presented his professional opinion that the fortification line would not hold back a French offensive. Hitler retorted, "The man who does not hold these fortifications is a scoundrel." After reviewing a report conducted by Göring in May 1938 on the status of the project, Hitler became bitterly disappointed at what he saw as incompetence by the army engineers and transferred responsibility for the project to Major General Fritz Todt, the Inspector General of Road Building, who had built the autobahn system. Hitler ordered Todt to accelerate the pace of construction and even made suggestions on types of fortifications to include.[93]

As Germany approached war over Czechoslovakia, General Erwin von Witzleben was one of the few who was willing to act. Uninterested in politics but realizing it was time to end the Nazi regime, he and Gisevius developed a plan to occupy key points and government buildings in Berlin with the help of the Berlin police president, Helldorf, and his police force, and to arrest Hitler. Troops under Brockdorff-Ahlfeld and Major General Paul von Hase, who had also turned against Hitler after the Fritsch affair, would march on Berlin and an armored division, stationed in Thuringia and commanded by General Hoepner, would block any movement of the SS Leibstandarte, stationed in Munich. Aware of Halder's caution and of Brauchitsch's poor performance, Witzleben was willing to act with or without Halder's approval and direct control of the coup.[94]

Halder, aware of Witzleben's plans, wanted not only to give the signal when the troops were to move but also to know what the conspirators would do with Hitler if the coup was successful. Some wanted to try Hitler by exposing files of documents that Doynanhi had collected on the regime's criminal activities to the German public. Others wanted to put Hitler into a psychiatric hospital. There was some discussion of possible execution. Many of the conspirators had no idea of what to do after they seized control of the government. Halder was concerned that the army would be accused of acting "illegally" or that civil war would ensue in which the army, or, at least, a part of it would be pitted against the SS. He also feared that the army, especially the younger officers, would split on whether to obey their immediate commanders supporting the coup or follow their oath to support "unto death" their supreme commander.[95]

Gisevius could not understand Halder's reticence in committing to the coup:

> I was extremely disconcerted. This method of gauging the temper of the times by noting the viewpoint of the lower officers was something entirely new for me. I remarked and my comment was taken very graciously—that as a rule the generals counted a good more than did the young officers, and that in my opinion the latter undoubtedly obey the orders of their superiors. If there was any doubt of that, then obviously the army's sense of discipline and confidence in leadership had seriously deteriorated, and, if that were true, I said, it was all the more reason to act as quickly as possible.... All my persuasion was in vain. I could not overcome Halder's

> fears. He no longer had confidence in his troops and wanted to have his "setback" before he took action.[96]

Apparently Gisevius did not remember or know about the split in the Reichswehr during the 1920 Kapp Putsch, the army's fear of civil war, or the degree of support for Hitler within the army, particularly among the younger officers.

In early September, Keitel and Jodl developed a timetable for the invasion of Czechoslovakia by September 30 that pleased Hitler. Meanwhile, the British Prime Minister, Neville Chamberlain, and the French Premier, Edouard Daladier, frantically sought a diplomatic solution to meet Hitler's ultimatum and avoid war, but Hitler rejected their concessions. From 1937 through the summer of 1938, civilian members of the opposition had been urging the British government to stand firm against the German dictator, but their efforts produced little from the British.[97] By mid–September, the situation appeared hopeful that France and Britain would remain steadfast against Hitler — the conspirators needed the threat of war to obtain popular support for a coup. On September 26, Halder told Hammerstein (who doubted Halder's resolution to act despite his declaration), "There will now be action unless Hitler abandons his plans."[98] As late as September 28, Brauchitsch, despite Halder's urgings, could not make up his mind on which way to go.

As September 30 approached, the diplomatic negotiations intensified as Chamberlain attempted to head off a war that it appeared only Hitler — and the German opposition — wanted. For example, as units of the German Army in full battle dress marched through the streets of Berlin, they were met by an uneasy silence from the crowds and not the jubilation that had accompanied the soldiers going to war in August 1914 or, more recently, into the Rhineland and Austria.[99] General Hans von Kluge, then the commander of Wehrkreis VI, believed that a war at that point would have resulted in popular uprisings and mutinies among the troops.[100] By this time, even the vacillating Brauchitsch appeared to support a coup if Hitler ordered the attack on Czechoslovakia. Halder, as Chief of the General Staff, was trying to get Hitler to commit to giving him a three- or four-day mobilization notice so Halder could signal Witzleben to begin preparations for the coup at the right moment. On September 29, the latter went to his headquarters to vainly wait for the signal to start the coup.[101]

On September 29, Mussolini intervened by proposing a conference in Munich to attempt a negotiated settlement. To Hitler's surprise, Chamberlain, and Daladier, prodded by the British Prime Minister, agreed to allow Germany to annex the Sudetenland — without even consulting with the Czech president Eduard Benes. Gisevius bemoaned, "Our revolt was done for."[102] Goerdeler wrote to an American friend,

> ...A magnificent opportunity has been missed. The German people did not want war; the army was ready to do everything to prevent it. Only Hitler, Himmler, and Ribbentrop were for war.... [T]hey insisted to the army that England and France were neither willing nor able to protect Czechoslovakia. No one in Germany would believe them, but they were right.... The world had been warned and informed in time. If these warnings had been heeded, and if one had acted accordingly Germany would be free of her dictator today.[103]

Goerdeler prophetically concluded, "...By refusing to take a risk, Chamberlain now has made war inevitable...."[104] Stahlberg realized that the jubilant German crowds that cheered his unit at Stettin did so because war had been averted as much as they did over the annexation of the former Czech territory.[105] After the conference, only the Western democracies were satisfied with Chamberlain's "Peace in our time." Both Hitler and the conspirators had been denied the war they desperately needed — for different reasons.

Yet, Hitler still reaped tremendous benefits from his diplomatic triumph at Munich. This achievement further augmented his infallibility myth among the Germans. Halder in a moment of dejection supposedly cried on September 28, "What can we do? He succeeds in everything he does."[106] Guderian wrote to his wife that Hitler was a

> ...very great man. To achieve such a victory without a stroke of the sword is perhaps unprecedented in history. It was of course only possible because of the new sharp sword in our hands and with the will to use it had peaceable means not been possible. Both these determinations were evident from this courageous man.[107]

Jodl wrote in his diary,

> The genius of the *Führer* and his determination not to shun even a world war have again achieved victory without the use of force. One hopes that the incredulous, the weak and the doubters [the other generals ?] have been converted, and will remain so.[108]

Echoing the thoughts of most Germans, Knappe believed that Hitler "had righted a wrong that had been done to [Germany] by the Versailles Treaty."[109]

Hitler's triumph also increased his lack of respect for his cautious and skeptical generals. After Munich he commented, "What kind of generals are these whom I as the Head of State may have to propel into war? By rights, I should be the one seeking to ward off the generals' eagerness for war...." From then on, he declared, "I do not ask my generals to understand my orders but only to carry them out." In January 1939, at a meeting of senior officers, Hitler condemned their spirit of faintheartedness, declaring, "I want no more warning memoranda from anybody." He also directed Brauchitsch to give the officer corps a new purpose and select only officers who believed in the Führer.[110] It was now perfectly clear that Hitler would not tolerate any disaffected senior officers and effectively silenced most officers except those inexorably opposed to him.

Hitler used his success from Munich to make several important personnel changes. He retired Rundstedt and the doubting Adam on November 17. Most importantly for the opposition, Witzleben was transferred to command Group Headquarters No. 2 at Frankfurt am Main — he no longer directly commanded combat troops. He and Major General Georg von Sodenstern, his new chief of staff, agreed that Hitler's policies would ultimately lead to war and concluded that they had reached the limit of military obedience to him. Unwilling to resign, they decided that the various opposition groups must be consolidated and develop a long-range plan of action although they had lost significant ability to do so.[111] Ulrich von Hassell, former Ambassador to Italy and now a member of the opposition, recognized that the army, although it still had power, had "suffered enormous losses politically" with the retirements of Beck and Adam.[112]

For the army leadership, the year from the Munich Conference to the invasion of Poland was a frantic race to what would assuredly now be war. After promoting Halder to Generaloberst, Hitler ordered OKW to prepare plans for the occupation of the rest of Czechoslovakia. Goerdeler and Beck urged Halder to act against Hitler but, heavily influenced by the success at Munich, Halder decided not to act until the British and French actually intervened — which they did not. Later that winter, Hitler stripped operational planning away from the General Staff and made it responsible only for the army's training and organization.[113] In March 1939, the German army marched into Prague and reorganized "rump" Czechoslovakia into the semiautonomous protectorates of Bohemia and Moravia.

Prime Minister Chamberlain declared that Britain and France would stand solidly behind Poland if attacked by Germany.

On April 3, 1939, Hitler directed OKW to prepare an operational plan for an attack on Poland. Keitel, Brauchitsch, and other generals believed that such an attack would mean a general European war, and they knew that Germany was not prepared for a long war and that it could not win a two-front war.[114] During the summer, they merely warned Hitler of the consequences of his aggressive moves — their duty, as Keitel recorded, was "to leave Hitler in no doubt that both the General Staff and his leading generals shared the gravest anxiety about the possibility that a war might break out;..."[115] However, only Beck felt compelled to resign to protest Hitler's actions — no one else followed his lead — and all but one of those fired in February 1938 would soon return to duty.[116]

On May 23, Hitler called together his senior military leaders to unveil his plans for the attack on Poland and Western Europe if Britain and France intervened. At the conference, attended by all the senior service chiefs, among others, Hitler defined the tasks of the armed forces and expounded on the consequences of these tasks. He gave them an inkling about what would become the Nazi-Soviet Nonaggression Pact, signed in late August 1939. He also foreshadowed the forced deportation of slave laborers to Germany and German exploitation of the conquered areas to the east. Hitler had decided on his war and would not be robbed as he felt he had been at Munich: "We must burn our boats, and it is no longer a question of justice or injustice, but of life or death for 80 million human beings."[117] No one walked out, and no one protested later.

Just like the previous summer, Chamberlain in the summer of 1939 frantically attempted to negotiate a settlement to the "Polish question" while maintaining a solid stand against appeasing Hitler again. The German dictator remained intransigent to anything less than his demand for the Polish Corridor and Danzig. To demonstrate British resolve, Chamberlain even opened negotiations with Stalin for a collective security agreement against further German expansion. However, after Chamberlain refused to pay such a high price for an agreement with Stalin at the expense of the Poles, the Soviet dictator signed the Nonaggression Pact with Germany on August 23.[118] When the High Command received news of the treaty with Germany's supposedly ideological enemy, many probably greeted it favorably as a resurrection of Seeckt's pro–Russian, anti–Polish policies and an opportunity to conduct a quick war against Poland before Britain and France could intervene. Therefore, these officers saw no reason to overthrow Hitler if he achieved a quick and decisive victory against Poland. Only a few, like General Thomas, accurately foretold that the attack on Poland would lead to a more general war of attrition for which Germany lacked the required raw materials and food supplies.[119]

On August 22, after saying goodbye to Ribbentrop who was going to Moscow to sign the Nonaggression Pact, Hitler flew to the Berghof in Bavaria to address his senior military commanders. Full of confidence and optimism, he declared, "War must come in my lifetime." Hitler reminded them that the pact with the Soviet Union should minimize the intervention of the Western powers on Poland's behalf, and that many generals only a year before had doubted him — it was as if he wanted to remind them of his infallible political-military judgments of the last several years. Perhaps as an overstated boast of his intentions in the East, Hitler then told them that his Death Head units in army uniforms would accompany the army into Poland "with orders to kill without pity or mercy all men, women, and children of [the] Polish race or language."[120] As a result of this meeting and the one on May 23, none of the senior army leaders could plead ignorance of what Hitler had in mind after unleashing his war. Again none protested, apparently satisfied as long it was not the army but the SS and SD who committed these atrocities.

During the last months before the invasion of Poland, the anti–Hitler opposition tried to prevent a war that they believed would ultimately be disastrous for Germany. In late March 1939, Beck and Oster sent a warning to Britain through Ian Colvin, the Berlin correspondent of the *News Chronicle*, hoping that such a message would encourage the British to take stronger measures against Hitler that would prevent further aggression. The Western leaders did issue a strong but unheeded ultimatum to Hitler. Opposition emissaries, such as Goerdeler and Schlabrendorf, visited Winston Churchill, the leader of the parliamentary opposition, in Britain and asked him to urge his government to stand fast against Hitler. Sir Robert Vansittart, a career diplomat in the British Foreign Office and critic of National Socialism, commented on the stream of opposition visitors to Britain: "We have no need of a Secret Service in Germany, for these fellows are bringing us all we want to know."[121] Later Beck gave the Associated Press and the American and British embassies in Berlin minutes of the August 22 meeting. The opposition also tried to press for a military coup to keep Hitler from going to war but had no success in rallying the generals, many of whom saw a war against the Poles as natural.[122] Some also apparently believed that Hitler would "make everything right" as he had in the past. As Erich von Manstein wrote, "Why, we asked ourselves, should it be different this time?"[123] In neither case did the opposition receive any encouragement to proceed beyond planning for a coup, and its members resigned themselves to an inevitable war.

As in September 1938, the German people grimly greeted the oncoming war that no one except Hitler wanted or could stop. Beck wrote Brauchitsch about the impending threat, but the weak commander in chief did not even respond to his concerns.[124] Major General F. W. Mellenthin recalls the last days of August as his units went through Berlin on the way to the Polish frontier:

> Everyone was quiet and serious; we all realized that for good or ill Germany was crossing the Rubicon. There was no trace of the jubilant crowds whom I had seen in 1914 as a boy of ten. Civilians or soldiers — nobody felt any elation or enthusiasm. But determined to do his duty to the very last, the German soldier marched on.[125]

Shirer reported similar feelings in Berlin when the government announced food rationing in preparation for the approaching war: "...I was amazed to see less than 500 people out of a population of 5,000,000 turned out in front of the Chancellery. These few stood grim and silent. Almost a defeatism discernible in the people."[126] Thus, Germany went to war for the second time in 25 years almost to the day, despite a large degree of reticence in the army for such a conflict. Unfortunately, that reticence had not translated into sufficient opposition to Hitler to prevent the war, much less overthrow the government.

The Military Opposition and Hitler's Domestic Policies

To this point, I have concentrated on the responses of the army, especially its officer corps, to Hitler's foreign policies because it was primarily these adventuresome and risky policies, rather than the repressive domestic policies of Himmler's police state, that caused some officers to form the military opposition. Of course, most of the officers disliked the repressive measures that had ended all political life except that of the NSDAP. Most officers had disliked the butchery of June 30, 1934, that resulted in the deaths of two of their own, although they did not particularly dislike the main result of that night — the curtailment of the SA's power. They also detested the crude terror methods of the Gestapo and the infamous concentration camps of the SS for opponents of the Nazi regime. As I have previously mentioned, some officers, like Oster, had even used their positions to collect evidence of these crimes for use in some future trial against Himmler, Göring, and possibly even Hitler. However, those officers who ultimately came to oppose the regime did not do so primarily because of the oppression of the Nazi regime or its domestic crimes. In other words, the internal policies of the regime were sufficient to cause some of the officers who would become resistors to mentally doubt their continuing loyalty to the regime and Hitler, but they were *not* sufficient alone to cause them to oppose the Führer and ultimately conspire against him.

A few examples will suffice to see how the officer corps reacted to the regime's internal policies of repression. After January 1933, there were only limited protests to the law that eliminated Jews from the armed services and the civil service. The senior army leaders did seek relief for the few Jewish war veterans in the civil service and the few Jews on active duty, primarily because they saw these laws as encroachments on the prerogatives of the military to deal with its own people, not because of any particular liking for the Jews or as a protest against the elimination of civil rights in Germany. In general, the senior army leaders were more concerned about the crude methods of the SS than with the incarceration of German Communists and Socialists or the persecution of the Jews. As we saw earlier, the army detested the leftist parties for their "defeatism" and pacifism. Before all Jews had been eliminated from the German economy, the continuing patronage of Jewish-owned shops by German soldiers was more of a protest against the SA and the SS than one of support for the increasingly oppressed Jews. These factors, plus the enduring legacy of the Überparteilichkeit policies of the Seeckt era and the fast-paced rearmament program, precluded any real action and interest by the army leaders in Hitler's domestic policies.

The reactions of some army officers to the anti–Jewish riots of November 9, 1938, Kristallnacht ("Night of Broken Glass") vividly illustrate these points. Kristallnacht, like other seminal events, such as the risky march into the Rhineland and the brinkmanship over the Sudetenland, probably did cause future resisters to search their souls and deepen their mental questioning of their loyalty and obedience to such a regime. For example, Helmuth Groscurth wrote in his diary in the fall of 1938, "In November major activities against the Jews. The orders issued for the 'spontaneous' activities are kept separately. One has to feel ashamed of still being a German."[127] A fellow officer Werner Reerink, who knew Stauffenberg, commented after the war that the future resister "savagely" condemned the pogrom and afterwards more severely criticized the distasteful Nazi leaders.[128] A former commander, Friedrich Wilhelm Freiherr von Loepner, after the war went further, stating that Stuffenberg's anti–Nazi opposition came "primarily" from the persecution of the Jews and Catholics.[129] However, while shame and criticism of the regime's domestic policy may have awakened doubts among future conspirators, they were a long way from actual conspiracy and treason — it would take military defeats, unspeakable atrocities, and the threat of total destruction of Germany to force them finally to act.

The reactions of two other officers to

Kristallnacht is also illustrative. Knappe reports in his memoirs,

> We did not talk about it in the barracks, because we were ashamed that our government would permit such a thing to happen. We did not want to admit it to ourselves, much less to each other, so we did not talk about it. Strong anti-Semitism has always been just beneath the surface in the German population, but no one I knew supported this kind of excess. We all felt Hitler had been very good for Germany ... but there was a coarseness about him that we silently abhorred. His hatred of the Jews made no sense to any of us, and we just wanted to distance ourselves from the ugly side of his character.[130]

Young Second Lieutenant Alexander Stahlberg, on November 10, discovered the burned-out remains of the Jewish synagogue and the shattered windows of Jewish businesses in Stettin, his home city. At first, he thought that an arsonist had caused the destruction until he saw the SA men in front of the remains and realized who in reality had caused the damage. He wrote, "Everything was quiet, so everything was fine. I was ashamed of my city." After pondering the end of what Frederick the Great had called "[o]ne of the grandest achievements of 18th century enlightenment"— freedom of worship — Stahlberg wrote, "What had we come to now?"[131]

As in the past, the army officers, including those who formed or would form the anti-Hitler opposition, generally detested the violence and destruction of Kristallnacht. However, their dislike of the violence did not originate from its anti-Semitic nature per se but from its "outburst of mob violence, its display of raw mass brutality." Its "undisciplined, ... lawless and chaotic" nature went against their sense of orderliness and legality. Jews, they believed, were very different from Germans, and the two nationalities should be separated but by "legal, deliberate, and, if possible, humane" means. One could expect pogroms from the Russians or Ukrainians, but not Germans.[132] The fact that Germans had committed these atrocities apparently concerned them more than the fact that they had occurred against the Jews. Reerink wrote that he noticed a change in Stauffenberg, who was "...always particularly insistent upon justice, decency, and morality" after November 10, 1938.[133] Was that change because of what the Nazis had now openly done to the remainder of Germany's Jewish community? Or was that change because Stauffenberg, and others like him, now realized what his fellow Germans were capable of?

Summary

In this chapter we saw how a small group of officers by September 1939 had become opponents to Hitler, primarily over his aggressive foreign policy that threatened to cause a two-front war before Germany's armed forces were ready to fight and win such a war, although they were concerned about the regime's domestic repressive policies. The formation of this group illustrates the phases of opposition presented in Chapter 1. First, only a handful of officers had come to see Hitler's risky foreign policy moves as Germany rearmed — its most vulnerable period — as a deep moral crisis for them. They first registered verbal and then written protests through the chain of command. When these increasingly sharp protests failed to moderate Hitler's policies, some officers, such as Halder, decided to "fence sit," and see how the events "played out." Others continued to serve the Nazi regime, hoping to moderate Hitler's aggressive policies in some way. Still others committed acts of treason by informing the British government of their leader's intentions. A few, like Witzleben progressed to planning for a coup d'etat against Hitler, at the right moment. Only one man — Ludwig Beck — saw his moral crisis as so severe that he could no longer serve the Nazi regime and resigned his post.

The main reason that only a handful of officers, despite Hitler's humiliation and emasculation of the officer corps, developed into the military opposition was that only a few truly experienced the moral crisis required for them to lose sufficient confidence in Hitler as their commander and oppose him. As we saw in Chapter 4, in five short years Hitler had turned the officer corps from a potential source of powerful opposition to an almost totally subservient instrument to carry out his aggressive plans in Europe. The great expansion of the officer corps during the rearmament program had destroyed its homogeneity, and, by September 1939, it was divided into four major but somewhat overlapping groups of which the military opposition was one of the two smallest.

At the other end of the spectrum were the few officers who were or became diehard Nazis — the "true believers." They came mainly from the younger and newer men — although there were several senior officers — and had become heavily indoctrinated in the nazified schools, the HJ, and the RAD prior to military service and by Blomberg's nazification programs during their military service. They were also heavily influenced by Hitler's rearmament program and foreign policy successes that nullified the Versailles Treaty and humiliated the Western democracies. These factors bolstered their sense of loyalty and obedience to Hitler, required by the oath first sworn in August 1934 and then repeated by successive groups of new officers. Many had come to believe in Hitler's infallibility in political-military affairs and would do anything for their Führer.

Between the two were the majority of the officers, divided into two groups, who saw no crisis of a sufficiently moral nature to lead them to open protests or opposition. One group of these officers were the "careerists" who saw in rearmament and the increasing possibility of war personal career advancement and greater promotion opportunities; these were exemplified by army officers like Keitel and Jodl at OKW. Others, such as Guderian, saw opportunities in Hitler's army for them to develop new equipment and test new doctrinal and tactical ideas that were stifled by the old-fashioned, more traditional leadership. These officers superficially adhered to the Nazi ideology and obeyed Hitler because it was in their best self-interests to do so.

The last and probably the largest group was the "silent majority." Also adhering to the "party line" more than believing it, these officers obeyed because they did not want to suffer the penalties of disobedience. They also appreciated what Hitler had done in rearming Germany, restoring their social status, and giving them opportunities to advance. Many of them, potentially members of the military opposition, were silenced by Hitler's callous dismissal of Blomberg, Fritsch, and other senior officers in February 1938. Given a "natural" tendency to obey for the "right" reasons," they followed their oath, never saw the moral crisis as outweighing the penalties for disobedience, and silently did want Hitler told them to do. As a result, the majority of the German officers followed Hitler into the Second World War.

Henry V. Dicks reports the results of a wartime study of German POWs which revealed some connection between character structure and political ideology. For this study, about 1,000 unselected German POWs were surveyed and interviewed to determine what percentage of all POWs would fall into each of five categories of political attitudes, empirically developed before the surveys and interviews were given. The results were as follows:

1. Fanatical, "hard core" Nazis, 11 percent.

2. Believers with reservations, "near Nazis," 25 percent.
3. Unpolitical, men with private motives, 40 percent.
4. "The divided," passive anti–Nazis," 15 percent.
5. Active convinced anti–Nazis, 9 percent.[134]

In general, these categories correspond roughly to those that I empirically developed independently for this study. German officer and enlisted POWs captured during the last 12 months of fighting made up Dicks' sample groups while my groups are exclusively of officers at the beginning of the war. Furthermore, I cannot corroborate the specific percentages for my group although I believe that they conform to those for his groups. Yet the two sets of groups do have a general correlation in relative size and political and ideological beliefs.

These divisions within the German army of 1939 did not go unnoticed by a number of contemporaries. A certain Major Woeffler, attached to the General Staff, told fellow officers on the evening of September 27, 1938, the day Hitler sent his troops through Berlin to an unenthusiastic greeting by it its citizens:

> The real crisis won't be long in coming now. A great rift is opening up with a handful of officers of the old Reischwehr on one side and a vast horde of newcomers on the other. There are some good fellows among them, and some pretty unsavory types as well—the Party boys, the careerists who're looking out strictly for themselves, and the ne'er-do-wells who've messed up everything else in their lives. It will take years before you'll get all the lumps out of the batter, and I only hope they give you enough time to get the job done.[135]

Shortly after the war, General Thomas, Chief of the OKW Economics and Supply Section, alluded to these circumstances in his comment that the late 1938 planned coup did not occur because of Witzleben's fear that "...the young officers did not prove to be reliable for a political action of this sort."[136]

For all groups of German officers in 1939, the oath of loyalty sworn to Hitler, either on that fateful day in August 1934 or at later commissioning ceremonies, had great psychological significance. To any soldier, the oath of loyalty is a binding contract by which they give obedience to their superiors up to the supreme commander or head of state as Brauchitsch, Keitel, or Hossbach so stated.

However, they forgot that they, as soldiers, also had duties to the German nation and to humanity that transcended their personal loyalty. At the same time, a soldier's superiors also make a binding contract not to ask the soldier to commit unlawful or illegal acts. In Nazi Germany by 1939, Hitler had successfully turned upside down what was right and what was wrong through his policies. He had capitalized on the lack of political astuteness among the senior army officers (a detrimental legacy of Seeckt), and on the desire among the younger officers for a rebirth of Germany's position in Europe.

As we saw earlier, the opposition had a number of opportunities, especially the Blomberg-Fritsch and Sudeten crises, to stage a coup d'etat that could have had some degree of success. Given the conditions at *that* time, the conspirators might have secured sufficient support among the troops and the German people for success. However, the military conspirators had struggled with their oath of loyalty to a Führer in whom they were increasingly losing confidence. Many were haunted by memories of the disorder and mutinies that followed Germany's defeat in 1918, and the Kapp and Hitler coups of the early 1920s that threatened to bring about a civil war and divide the army. As Fest writes, many generals

> ...feared [Hitler's] gambler's instincts and the recklessness with which he risked war, even with Great Britain. Most remained paralyzed, however, from taking serious action, partly by the personal oath of allegiance they had sworn to the Führer and partly by their ingrained belief in such ideals as loyalty and obedience.

Only a few like "Oster and his friends realized that even though Hitler had already demolished any basis for such loyalty, it persisted and could only be uprooted through threat of a major foe."[137]

As we did in 1934 when the army took the personal oath of loyalty, we must again consider the situation that these fine but tragic men faced in 1938-39, and we should not automatically condemn from hindsight. These men believed they had no tradition of revolt. Caught up in the initial glory of the Nazi regime and only remembering the events of 1918-19, they failed to remember they had precedence for protests and even revolt — Blücher, Clausewitz, and Yorck von Wartenburg during the Napoleonic Wars. Those that did had to overcome a great psychological struggle between loyalty and obedience to Hitler, epitomized by the personal oath, and the greater call to the German nation and humanity. Even then, only a few in the summer of 1939, such as Tresckow in a comment to Schlabrendorff, saw that "both duty and honor demand from us that we would do our best to bring about the downfall of Hitler and National Socialism in order to save Germany and Europe from barbarism."[138] In the next chapters, we shall see how their sense of obedience led many of them to participate in the atrocities of war while only a few actively conspired against Hitler.

Notes

1. Beck quoted in Wheeler-Bennett, p. 392.
2. Beck quoted in Hamerow, p. 107.
3. I do not intend to provide a complete history of the anti-Hitler opposition or even the military opposition. That task has been done in the works by Rothfels, Hoffmann, Fest, and Hamerow that I have used and in other more complete works. I will bring in only that basic information needed for my discussion to show the changing views of loyalty (for example, the loss of confidence in Hitler as commander in chief by some of the senior officers, the vacillation of others as they struggled with their oath of obedience, and so on) and their impact and significance in relation to the oath of loyalty.
4. Gill, p. 40. Mason, p. 34. Heinz Hoehne, *Canaris* (Garden City, NY: Doubleday & Company, Inc., 1979), pp. 261–63.
5. Beck quoted in Reynolds, p. 99.
6. Whaley, p. 58.
7. Görlitz, p. 305.
8. Reynolds, pp. 107–8. Wheeler-Bennett, p. 352.
9. Entry of March 7, 1936, Shirer, *Berlin Diary*, pp. 44.
10. Hitler quoted in Shirer, *Third Reich*, p. 403.
11. Hitler quoted in Fest, *Hitler*, p. 519.
12. Footnote, Shirer, *Third Reich*, p. 405.
13. Wheeler-Bennett wrote (p. 289) that since January 1933 Hitler "had a pronounced complex against Generals. From the earliest days of the National Socialist movement every successive attempt to achieve power had been prevented by a General; at the end of every avenue there had appeared a bemonacled figure in field grey, and claret-coloured trouser stripes, with uplifted hand crying 'Halt!'" While there is a great deal of truth in his statement, since Hitler did have Bredow and Schleicher murdered during the Röhm Purge, it also reflects Wheeler-Bennett's own particular bias against the aristocratic "Prussian" officers. By the end of the war with the Third Reich on its death kneel, Hitler would carry his phobia against the generals to the extreme. Rather than blaming his failure and inadequacy as a military commander on himself, Hitler reportedly told his pilot in April 1945, "It should be written on my gravestone, 'He was the victim of his generals.'" Hitler quoted in footnote 4, Domarus. I, p. 595.
14. Reynolds, pp. 110–11. Görlitz, p. 302.
15. Taylor, *Sword and Swastika*, p. 136–38.
16. Hitler in Taylor, *Sword and Swastika*, p. 124.
17. Reynolds, pp. 81–82.
18. Rothfels, p. 57.
19. Fabian von Schlabrendorff, *The Secret War Against Hitler* (New York: Pitman Publishing Corporation, 1965), p. 72.
20. Interview with Ursula von Witzleben, February 10, 1970, in Deutsch, p. 45. Deutsch (p. 44) gives Witzleben "a special place of honor among the generals who at one time or another formed part of the military Opposition. He was the first to unreservedly commit himself and never swerved or

faltered in his dedication.... He is perhaps best described with a good fund of common sense. To his downright nature answers came simply: Nazism was a criminal abomination, the military oath a swindle, Hitler's chosen path the road of national disaster. Others agonized and procrastinated where he was prepared to act." Hjalmar Schacht, president of the Reichsbank, called Witzleben "the first and ... most determined general to recognize the necessity for Hitler's removal and to tackle this task wholeheartedly." Quoted in Klaus-Jürgen Müller, "Witzleben, Stülpnagel, and Speidel," in Barnett, p. 51.

21. Klaus-Jürgen Müller, "Witzleben, Stülpnagel, and Speidel," in Barnett, 46–47.

22. Gisevius, p. 186.

23. Document 503, Hossbach Memorandum, November 10, 1937, in Noakes and Pridham, II, pp. 680–87. Colonel Hossbach took notes of the conference and prepared the memorandum ten days after the conference. It became a major document at the Nuremberg War Trials after the war to prove that Hitler had planned the war in Europe. Historians have generally considered the memorandum, along with Hitler's discussion on Lebensraum in *Mein Kampf*, as proof of a definite plan by Hitler to conduct a major war to dominate Europe and obtain territory in the East. The major exception is the British historian A. J. P. Taylor who, in 1961, wrote a major revisionist history *The Origins of the Second World War*. In this work Taylor maintains that Hitler blundered into war as a result of miscalculations and errors by outsiders, especially Neville Chamberlain, the British Prime Minister (1937–40), not as a result of planned aggression. Taylor believed that Hitler used the Hossbach conference to confuse his opponents.

24. Reynolds, p. 117.

25. Document 504, Hossbach, in Noakes and Pridham, II, p. 688.

26. Domarus, II, p. 972.

27. Deutsch, pp. 92–93, 96.

28. Gisevius, pp. 219–25.

29. Beck to Keitel, Jodl's Diary, January 28, 1938, in Taylor, *Sword and Swastika*, p. 149.

30. Blomberg and Hitler met for the last time on January 26, 1938, and the Führer promised Blomberg, "When Germany's hour strikes, I will see you at my side and the whole past will be regarded as wiped out." Hitler quoted in Fest, p. 564. Following the crisis, Blomberg and his wife left for Italy and the Dutch East Indies, a trip presumably paid for from Hitler's personal account, to let the affair blow over. When the war started, Hitler did not recall Blomberg to active service. He lived through the war in a small Bavarian village and died in 1946. Deutsch, p. 121. Taylor, *Sword and Swastika*, pp. 151–52.

31. Deutsch, pp. 116–21.

32. Höhne, *Death's Head*, pp. 266–67. Deutsch, pp. 134–47.

33. Deutsch, pp. 221–22, 226–27.

34. Deutsch, pp. 222–23.

35. Reynolds, p. 133.

36. Brauchitsch quoted in Cooper, p. 81.

37. Deutsch, pp. 226–27.

38. Adam quoted in Wheeler-Bennett, p. 366.

39. Beck in Deutsch, p. 168.

40. Deutsch, pp. 110–11.

41. Deutsch, pp. 171–72. Hossbach returned to the General Staff at the beginning of the war, was ultimately promoted to general of the infantry, and was again dismissed on January 30, 1945, for disobedience in withdrawing his troops in defiance of Hitler's orders to fight to the last man.

42. Decree about the Leadership of the Wehrmacht, February 4, 1938, in Domarus, II, p. 1007.

43. Reynolds, p. 128.

44. "Eastern Theater Second Wind, Third Week," *Time*, 38 (July 14, 1941), p. 19.

45. Cooper, pp. 77–78. Of these 16 generals, all, except for Kressenstein, returned to active duty after the start of the war and were eventually promoted to generalfeldmarschall. In addition to these changes, Hitler dismissed Neurath, who was replaced by Ribbentrop as the Foreign Minister; Ulrich von Hassell, Ambassador to Italy; and Hjalmar Schacht, Minster of Economics.

46. Hitler quoted in Cooper, p. 104. The lack of protests to his actions led Hitler later to declare to some of his old SA comrades that the generals were either fools or cowards. Görlitz, p. 319.

47. Deutsch, pp. 196–97.

48. Reynolds, pp. 135–36.

49. Deutsch, pp. 212–14.

50. Deutsch, p. 170.

51. Deutsch, pp. 184–89.

52. Wheeler-Bennett, pp. 376–77.

53. Wheeler-Bennett, pp. 376–77.

54. Warlimont, pp. 14–15. O'Neill, p. 151. Reynolds, pp. 143–45.

55. Guderian, p. 31. Guderian's wife Gretel wrote her mother, "One can as yet hardly believe that Austria has become German. One Reich, one people, one Führer. He who does not understand that Hitler is a very great man and leader cannot be helped. I am deeply moved and cried for sheer joy...." Letter of Guderian's Wife, March 12/13, 1938, in Macksey, p. 94.

56. Beck quoted in Reynolds, p. 144.

57. Deutsch, pp. 347–49. In 1942, Sponneck was convicted of disobeying an order in South Russia by not fighting to the last man as Hitler had ordered and was sentenced to six years in prison. He was murdered in prison on July 23, 1944, after the failed bomb plot.

58. After the trial, the Gestapo continued to

hold Schimdt. Ultimately, he was moved to Sachsenhausen concentration camp where the SS executed him on July 29, 1942. Hoffmann, *German Resistance*, p. 39.

59. Hitler Letter to Fritsch, March 30, 1938, in Deutsch, p. 396. Reynolds, pp. 145–46. Gisevius, pp. 257–61.

60. Guderian, p. 28.

61. Guderian Letter to His Wife, February 7, 1938, in Macksey, p. 94. Despite his great concern over these events, he probably found them at least partially welcome. That same morning, he also learned about his appointment as the commander of XVI Army Corps and may have felt that the new army leadership would assist him in obtaining an independent armored force.

62. Deutsch, pp. 244–52.

63. Guderian, p. 30.

64. Fritsch quoted in Cooper, pp. 64, 66.

65. Deutsch, pp. 397–98.

66. Görlitz, ed., p. 55.

67. Beck quoted in Gerhard Ritter, *The German Resistance: Carl Goerdeler's Struggle Against Tyranny* (New York: Frederick A. Praeger, 1958), p. 78.

68. The "crisis" was over the Sudetenland, the mountainous region of northern Czechoslovakia, inhabited primarily by ethnic Germans. It also contained the Czechs' fortress line, known as the "Little Maginot Line." The Nazis wanted to annex this region and had created numerous "incidents" with the aid of the Sudenten Nazi party as pretexts for German interference in the region.

69. Deutsch, pp. 401–5. Cooper, pp. 74–75.

70. At the official appointment ceremony, Brauchitsch declared that the army was sad over Fritsch's departure. Fritsch then respectfully thanked Hitler, the man who had disgraced him in such a dishonorable fashion, and called for "his" men to offer a salute to the Führer. Later, when Halder asked Fritsch if he would lead a coup against Hitler, Fritsch refused. Until September 1939, he grew more despondent and fatalistic. With the German invasion of Poland, Fritsch joined "his" regiment although he had no legal obligation to do so. On September 22, he was killed by Polish gunners in the outskirts of Warsaw. Hitler gave Fritsch a state military funeral with full honors and sent Göring — the president of Fritsch's court-martial — to represent him. Görlitz, p. 335. Wheeler-Bennett, pp. 380–82.

71. July 5, 1939, entry, Engel Diary in Deutsch, p. 250.

72. Keitel, p. 55.

73. Fest, *Hitler's Death*, p. 68. Gill, p. 41. Annedore Leber, *Conscience in Revolt: Sixty-four Stories of Resistance in Germany 1933–45* (Westport, CT: Associated Booksellers, 1957), p. 174.

74. Gisevius, p. 290.

75. O'Neill, pp. 152–56.

76. May 20, 1938, Entry, Diary of Colonel Gerhard Engel, in Reynolds, p. 150.

77. Quoted in Reynolds, p. 155.

78. Reynolds, p. 155.

79. Hitler quoted in Schlabrendorff, *Secret War*, p. 80.

80. Beck Note to Brauchitsch, June 16, 1938, in Erich Zimmermann and Hans-Adolf Jacobsen, eds., *Germans Against Hitler July 20, 1944* (Berlin: BERTO-Verlag, 1960), pp. 20–21.

81. Brauchitsch quoted in Cooper, p. 97.

82. Taylor, *Sword and Swastika*, pp. 198–99.

83. Cooper, p. 98. Reynolds, pp. 164–67. Interestingly, Hossbach had made a similar remark in early 1935 to Hitler's personal adjutant Captain Wiedmann: "We are soldiers. We do not want to have anything to do with and understand nothing about politics. We occupy ourselves only with military affairs." Hossbach quoted in Deutsch, p. 276.

84. Beck quoted in Hoffmann, *German Resistance*, p. 79.

85. Görlitz, ed., p. 66.

86. Halder quoted in Cooper, p. 27.

87. Halder quoted in Galante, p. 69.

88. Halder quoted in Hoffmann, *German Resistance*, p. 82–83.

89. Gisevius characterized Halder: "What Halder lacked was not intelligence or awareness of his position or patriotism. He lacked will." Quoted in Hamerow, p. 257.

90. Ritter, *German Resistance*, pp. 101–3.

91. Jodl quoted in Cooper, p. 101.

92. Keitel from Jodl's Diary, September 13, 1938, in Wheeler-Bennett, p. 419.

93. Taylor, *Sword and Swastika*, p. 204. Görlitz, ed., pp. 64–69.

94. Ritter, *German Resistance*, pp. 102–3. Duffy and Ricci, pp. 66–67.

95. Duffy and Ricci, pp. 66–67. Gisevius, pp. 292–94.

96. Gisevius, p. 294.

97. Rothfels, pp. 60–61.

98. Halder quoted in Hoffmann, *German Resistance*, p. 95.

99. September 27, 1938, Entry, Shirer, *Diary*, p. 110. Shirer also reported Hitler's reaction to the silence of the Berliners to his troops marching to a possible war: "Hitler reported furious.... [He] looked grim, then angry, and went inside [the Reich Chancellery], leaving his troops to parade by unreviewed. What I've seen tonight almost rekindles a little faith in the German people. They are dead set against war."

100. Gisevius, p. 303.

101. Schlabrendorff, *Secret War*, pp. 102–3.

102. Gisevius, p. 326.

103. Goerdeler Letter to American Friend, October 11, 1938, in Rothfels, p. 61, and Gisevius, p. 327.

104. Goerdeler Letter to American friend, October 11, 1938, in Schlabrendorff, *Secret War*, p. 103.

105. Stahlberg, p. 93.

106. Halder quoted in Görlitz, p. 338.

107. Guderian Letter to Wife, October 5, 1938, in Macksey, pp. 97–98.

108. Jodl Diary, September 29, 1938, in Wheeler-Bennett, p. 425. The German generals would be even more grateful for the peaceful annexation of the Sudetenland after they toured the formidable Czech fortifications in the region. They realized that to have attempted to take them by force would have indeed been costly in terms of German casualties.

109. Knappe, p. 120.

110. Hitler quoted in Cooper, p. 105.

111. Hoffmann, *German Resistance*, p. 101. See Sodenstern's specific view of his loyalty and obedience to Hitler and that of his friend and superior officer Witzleben in his postwar report "Events Leading Up to the 20 July 44 [Plot]," MS-#B-499, March 1947, pp. 29–31, in Detweiler, et al.

112. November 27, 1938, entry, Hassell, p. 16.

113. Görlitz, p. 342. Wheeler-Bennett, pp. 433–34.

114. An April 15, 1939, OKH note reported that some units had no arms and equipment, that 34 of the infantry divisions had only some of their required weapons and equipment, that the reserve force had only 10 percent of their required small arms, and that the overall munitions supply was adequate for only 15 days of combat. The occupation of the rest of Czechoslovakia in March 1939 provided sufficient arms and equipment to complete the equipage for 15 infantry and three armored divisions. Deist, pp. 88–89.

115. Görlitz, ed., p. 86.

116. The situation with the German generals in summer 1939 is analogous to that of American generals during the Vietnam conflict, particularly the period 1965–72. Despite personal misgivings by many about increased American intervention and conduct of that conflict, none resigned to protest those policies.

117. Schmundt's Minutes of Meeting with Hitler and Senior Military Leaders, May 23, 1939, in Taylor, *Sword and Swastika*, pp. 264–67.

118. The published treaty provided that neither country would attack the other and that one country would remain neutral in case the other country was attacked by a third country. In a secret military protocol, Hitler and Stalin agreed to divide Poland after a successful German invasion and allow Stalin to occupy the three Baltic states, Estonia, Latvia, and Lithuania.

119. Shirer, *Third Reich*, pp. 690–91.

120. Document L-3, Hitler Speech to Keitel and Generals, August 22, 1939, NCA, VII, p. 753. See also August 22, 1939, entry, Franz Halder, *The Halder War Diary 1939–1942* (Novato, CA: Presidio Press, 1988), p. 31. Schlabrendorff (p. 111–12) wrote that several years after the invasion of Poland by then Generalfeldmarschall Fedor von Bock confirmed that he had also been present at that conference and that Hitler had spoken about exterminating the Polish race. However, in his war diary Bock only acknowledged that Hitler had spoken about the forthcoming invasion but did not mention the Führer's plans for the Poles. August 22, 1939, entry, *Generalfeldmarschall Fedor von Bock: The War Diary 1939–1945* (Atglen, PA: Schiffer Military History, 1996), p. 34–35.

121. Mason, pp. 64–66. Vansittart quote in Mason, p. 65. Gill, pp. 97–98.

122. Reynolds, pp. 182–84. For German attitudes about war against Poland, see footnote 83, p. 147.

123. Field Marshal Erich von Manstein, *Lost Victories* (Novato, CA: Presido Press, 1994), p. 24.

124. Hamerow, pp. 14–16.

125. Mellenthin, p. xix.

126. August 29, 1939, entry, Shirer, *Diary*, p. 144. See also August 31, 1939, entry, p. 145, and September 3, 1939, entry, p. 150–51.

127. Groscurth quoted in Hamerow, p. 225.

128. Reerink, June 1963 report, in Joachim Kramarz, *Stauffenberg: The Architect of the Famous July 20th Conspiracy to Assassinate Hitler* (New York: The Macmillan Company, 1967), p. 71.

129. Loepner report, June 1963, in Kramarz, p. 71.

130. Knappe, p. 122.

131. Stahlberg, p. 96.

132. Hamerow, pp. 226–27.

133. Reerink quoted in Kramarz, p. 71.

134. Henry V. Dicks, "German Personality Traits and National Socialist Ideology," in Daniel Lerner, ed., *Propaganda in War and Crisis Material for American Policy* (New York: George W. Stewart Publisher, Inc., 1951), p. 112. This article was originally published in *Human Relations*, Vol. III, June 1950.

135. Woeffler quoted in Galante, p. 76.

136. Thomas quoted in Hamerow, p. 243.

137. Fest, *Hitler's Death*, p. 71.

138. Hoffmann, *German Resistance*, p. 265.

6

The Army at War, 1939–1945

From the invasion of Poland on September 1, 1939, until Germany's unconditional surrender on May 7, 1945, war raged in Europe from Britain in the west to the gates of Moscow in the east, from Norway to North Africa. Before the fighting was over, much of continental Europe would lie in complete devastation, between 30 and40 million men, women, and children — soldiers and civilians — would be dead, and countless others would be wounded, injured, sick, or homeless. Millions of these casualties from the world's costliest war did not result from direct military operations but from a Nazi racial war against Jews, Slavs, and Gypsies or in reprisal for the deaths of German soldiers and occupation officials. This almost incomprehensible level of destruction, death, and misery resulted from the victories of a nazified German army, led by officers who demonstrated an almost unparalleled military genius for war but very little understanding of the consequences of their actions. Their victories not only made possible the large-scale atrocities of the SS but resulted also in atrocities and war crimes of their own.

During World War II, the Germany army, officers and enlisted men, generally followed Hitler's orders, first from victory to victory and then from defeat to disaster. The first period, September 1939 to November 1942, was marked by a series of great victories for the German army that resulted in the occupation of almost all of continental Europe and North Africa, with the exception of the neutrals, Spain, Portugal, Switzerland, and Sweden. During this period the army suffered only one major setback — the failure to capture Moscow by December 1941. The second period, November 1942 to February 1943, from the defeat of the Afrika Korps at El Alamein through the Anglo-American landings in North Africa to the surrender of the German Sixth Army at Stalingrad, was a transition period that marked the limits of Germany's military success. The third and last period, February 1943 to April 1945, saw the steady retreat of the German army on all fronts to a devastated Berlin, and the inglorious end of the Third Reich. Throughout the war the army's loyalty to Hitler generally did not waver, despite temporary doubts, additional outrages against it, and its involvement in the regime's heinous occupation policies.

This chapter will review the relationship of Hitler to his senior army generals and to the lower-ranking officers and enlisted personnel, and the army's participation in war crimes throughout occupied Europe, emphasizing the "purely" military aspects of these relationships. We will see why German soldiers at all levels generally followed their oath to Hitler to the end of the war and obeyed orders to commit war crimes that resulted in the death of millions of civilians and the plundering of Europe even as defeat became increasingly inevitable as the war progressed. I will first look at the general obedience of the senior officers even as Hitler took control of military operations from them. I will then briefly review why the lower-ranking officers and the enlisted force also generally followed orders and why the German army after 1942 did not mutiny or fall apart during its retreat towards Germany. Finally, I will look at the army's reaction and general obedience to orders to commit numerous war crimes in which millions of Europeans were killed. We will see that the German army as a whole generally obeyed orders and remained loyal to their Führer and that a significant part of the opposition to Hitler's policies originated from disagreements on his *military* conduct of the war.[1]

The Senior Officers and Hitler

At least until late 1942, the army and its officer corps had little reason to oppose Hitler as the early campaigns redressed the territorial humiliation of the Versailles Treaty, humiliated the hated French and British, and took the war to the ideological enemy, the Soviet Union. What opposition that did come from the generals was more directly related to Hitler's strategic and tactical conduct of the war, not especially war crimes. The attitudes of the senior officers are especially important since most of them were not "true believers," like generalfeldmarschalls Reichenau, Ferdinand Schoerner, and Walther Model.[2] Furthermore, the generals' criticisms of the regime's atrocities usually demonstrated more concern for their effects on the morale and discipline of the soldiers than *specifically* on *moral* grounds.

After the Polish campaign many generals, remembering the trench warfare of the first World War, strongly opposed Hitler's September 1939 proposal to invade the Low Countries and France that autumn and favored a negotiated peace or at least a long defensive period in the West. Even his favorite Reichenau voiced his opinion directly to Hitler that the proposed violation of Belgian and Dutch neutrality was a criminal act.[3] Bolstered by this opposition and support of other generals, even the weak-willed Brauchitsch, on November 5, 1939, defended postponing a western offensive. He argued that an attack in the West was not possible for sometime because of, among other things, the army's poor performance and lax discipline toward the end of the Polish campaign. This comment enraged Hitler who then ranted about the "spirit of Zossen"— defeatism and cowardice within the OKH headquarters staff— and forced Brauchitsch to back down. Hitler repeated his dressing-down of the senior officers on November 23 when he prophetically told them, "I shall shrink from nothing and shall destroy whoever is against me." Fortunately, the weather in western Europe turned bad, resulting in postponing the offensive until spring 1940.[4]

However, by April 1940, the attitudes of the generals in the west had changed. Intoxicated by the victory over Norway, Leeb, Rundstedt, Erich von Manstein, and even Sodenstern — who had plotted with Witzleben to overthrow Hitler in 1938 — listened politely to a plea by General Georg Thomas to refuse orders to invade the Low

Countries, but they were now no longer interested in peace and did nothing.[5] Interestingly, Tresckow used his personal friendship with Hitler's adjutant Schmundt, an old regimental comrade, to have Manstein's plan for the western offensive — the one that recommended sending the German tanks through the supposedly impassable Ardennes — presented to Hitler.[6] Even Generaloberst Fritz Fromm, commander of the Ersatzheer (Replacement or Home Army) whom Hassell called "something of a stuffed shirt," predicted a quick German victory against France contrary to the skepticism of the other generals and Beck.[7] The blitzkrieg victory over the Low Countries and France in May-June 1940 only served to further the generals' adulation of Hitler. Even the lukewarm Halder was taken by the overwhelming success of German arms. To his wife, he wrote, "My operations are rolling like a well edited film.... I push pieces across the chess board in accordance with my conception of how they should come into play ... [and] after two or three days ... there they stand, all ready for action in the right place."[8] Lieutenant Colonel Helmuth Groscurth, an early conspirator who participated in the invasion of France, commented after its outstanding success, "I am happy that I was able to lead troops in battle and that won satisfying victories. That makes a soldier proud."[9]

Gradually OKW (that is, Keitel and Jodl) became increasingly involved in operational planning at OKH's expense, except for Operation Barbarossa and the ensuing extended campaign in the Soviet Union. For example, in early 1940, Hitler wanted to occupy Norway to preclude a British occupation of the country that would shut off Germany's shipments of Swedish high-grade iron ore, but OKH absolutely refused to plan the operation because of the risks involved. With Hitler's guidance, OKW took over the planning and conduct of this combined operation, and its success, despite initial losses in naval vessels and nerve, gave Hitler and OKW additional encouragement to interfere in military operations.[10] When Hitler became the army commander in chief in December 1941 after firing Brauchitsch, he gave OKW control of military operations and occupation policies in all theaters of war except the Eastern Front — the center of his ideological war against the Jews and the Bolsheviks — where the army and, therefore, he himself retained overall control.[11] Giving OKW authority over military operations in the West at the expense of OKH reflected his general policy of "divide and conquer" within the power centers of the Nazi regime and enabled him to laud his own amateur "military expertise" over the professional soldiers.

With the army's initial military successes Hitler now increasingly and more directly interfered in the army's operational planning and tactical operations. Using his limited combat experience from the First World War, he regularly and increasingly gave his military leaders directions on the war's strategic, operational and tactical conduct. He felt "at home" with directing the ground war, which was expressed by his wearing some form of military uniform after the war began. He often said that he was a better judge of troops than were the "Prussian" generals. For example, on August 24, 1942, during a very stormy session between Hitler and Halder over the "no retreat" orders, Hitler angrily told Halder,

> Colonel-General Halder, how dare you use language like that to me. Do you think you can teach me what the man at the front is thinking? What do you know about what goes on at the front? Where were you in the First World War? And you try to pretend to me that I don't understand what it's like at the front. I won't stand that! It's outrageous![12]

Hitler's increasingly direct control of the army represented his way of overcoming his perceived inferiority vis-à-vis the generals and competing with their military expertise.

Additionally, Hitler could demonstrate his general hatred for the old "Prussian" senior officers. One OKH officer in May 1940 remarked that Hitler was "[m]ean-spirited. The Old Prussian ruling class is anathema to him — he even thinks they're dangerous. That's part of the reason why he doesn't get along with Brauchitsch and Manstein."[13] During the French campaign Hitler called Brauchitsch a "monocled old Junker [who] had never ceased to plead the cause of weakness, and ... set himself against all my ideas." Hitler continued this diatribe by heaping additional abuse on the generals in general —

> those old fossils, those idiots; I denounce them for their total lack of imagination, for their refusal to accept National Socialist ideology, for their contempt of the Party and its leaders... . I can't expect them to understand me but I can force them to obey me![14]

In early 1941, he raged at the vacillation and weakness of the General Staff:

> Before I became Chancellor, I believed that the General Staff was somewhat like a butcher's dog, whom you had to hold tight by the collar to prevent its attacking all other people. After I became Chancellor, however, I realized that the General Staff is anything but a ferocious dog. The General Staff, in fact, has constantly impeded every action I deemed necessary. It objected to rearmament; to the occupation of the Rhineland; to the march into Austria; the occupation of Czechoslovakia; and finally, even the campaign against Poland. The General Staff warned me against an offensive in France, and counseled against war with Russia. It is I who at all times had to goad this "ferocious dog."[15]

In December 1941, Hitler remarked to his aides, "General Staff officers do too much thinking for me. They make everything too complicated. That goes even for Halder."[16] These angry outbursts well illustrate Hitler's passionate dislike for the General Staff and the "Prussian" generals as a group whom he tolerated only as long as he needed them.[17]

As the OKH fell into increasing disfavor with Hitler, Keitel and Jodl, to augment their own power and authority over the Wehrmacht, soon replaced the generals at Hitler's two daily situation conferences. At these conferences Hitler received briefings from his senior service commanders, asked detailed questions about current operations even down to the tactical level, and made specific suggestions on the conduct of these operations. Theater commanders only briefed on their own specific current operations if they happened to be at Hitler's headquarters of the day. Hitler also used these conferences to heap verbal abuse upon the "defeatist" army in general and upon specific commanders, depending on the current military situation. Hitler increasingly stamped his own amateur mark on daily military operations that ultimately became fatal as the war progressed. After the conferences, the OKW leaders would turn Hitler's comments and orders into operational orders and directives for implementation by the respective services. As a result, OKW became little more than Hitler's military secretariat with scant direct command authority over the armed forces or control over their daily operations.[18]

As Hitler and the OKW increased its control over daily military operations, the army commensurately lost its independence, especially after he fired Brauchitsch in December 1941 and assumed the position of army commander in chief. Like Brauchitsch — and other generals who chose to oppose the Führer on operational matters — Halder increasingly became the butt of Hitler's abuse because of the Chief of Staff's disagreements with Hitler's decisions. Other staff officers would agree with Halder only when the Führer agreed with him. "Otherwise — at best — they [would] keep silent, to take sides with the Führer." Jodl would sometimes side with Halder, but Keitel generally did nothing: "[B]ut we will say nothing of Keitel, except that he is careful not to get his whiskers singed."[19] The effect of such outbursts was staff officers who more readily agreed with Hitler, despite their best professional military judgment, to avoid such scenes. The entry in Halder's diary for September 24, 1942 — the day he was fired as Chief of Staff — is revealing: "(…Necessity for educating the General Staff in fanatical faith in The Idea. [Hitler] is determined to enforce his will also into the army.)"[20] After July 20, 1944, Hitler declared an officer's sole military duty was to blindly obey his orders and essentially wanted to personally know and approve every action taken at division and higher levels.[21] What Hitler wanted and got from all but the most recalcitrant — and "thinking" — officers was "unquestioned authority downwards."[22]

At the same time, Hitler feted the generals by liberally bestowing them with medals, promotions, and other "honoraria" to further bend their will to his. After the six-week French campaign, Hitler, on July 19, 1940, promoted Brauchitsch, Keitel, Rundstedt, Fedor von Bock, Wilhelm Ritter von Leeb, Wilhelm von List, Guenther Hans von Kluge, Witzleben, and Reichenau to the rank of generalfeldmarschall (they all received personal hand-crafted batons); Halder, Fromm, Ewald von Kleist, Guderian, and five others to generaloberst; and Jodl and six others to general officer. The promotions of Brauchitsch, Halder, Keitel, and Jodl were especially noteworthy since they were for staff work, not direct combat service. Hitler throughout the war awarded decorations, including the "coveted" Knight's Cross, generous gifts of money from his personal account (in addition to their annual field marshal pay of 36,600 RMs), and estates, to many of them. For example, in October 1942, Kluge received a check for 250,000 RMs (about $100,000 at the official 1943 rate), and Guderian received an estate of 2,600 acres in the Warthgau, worth over 1.25 million RMs. These payments — "a breach of the code of honor of the German officer" — for "services rendered," plus the military victories, turned the heads of many generals, despite previous protests and opposition, and "bound" them to Hitler "with a chain of gold."[23]

Kluge's acceptance of the donative from Hitler was particularly onerous to a number of the conspirators, perhaps because they were trying to obtain his support for an anti–Hitler coup. For example, Hassell has especially uncomplimentary comments about Kluge.[24] Hitler had written a personal note on the back of Kluge's check: "For your birthday, my dear Field Marshal; 125,000 you may use to build on your estate — Reichsminister [Albert] Speer has orders." Speer, Hitler's personal architect and Minster of Armaments and War Production in 1942, among other things, controlled public construction during the war, and Kluge needed Speer's permission to build on his estate, permission that the Führer had apparently told Speer to grant.[25] Schlabrendorff and Tresckow spoke directly to Kluge: "He could … only justify the acceptance of the check if he were able to show before history that he had accepted it in order not to be sacked and to maintain himself in a position in which he could undertake action against Hitler."[26] Captain Kaiser was also very critical of Kluge's acceptance of the money: "Imagine Scharnhorst or Gneisenau, or Clausewitz and you see the difference in the officer of today!"[27]

In addition, many officers were taken by Hitler's personal magnetism, a charisma to which thousands of Germans of those times attest. After June 1940, the once skeptical Quartermaster-General Eduard Wagner, affected by the military victories and Hitler's charisma, commented: "And wherein lies the secret of victory? Indeed, in the enormous dynamism of the Führer ... without his will it would never have come to pass."[28] Prior to the disaster at Stalingrad, Hassell attempted to recruit General Fromm, commander of the Ersatzheer, which the conspirators would need for a successful coup. Fromm, in adulation of Hitler because of the new strings of victories, responded, "Yes, but our Führer has more strategical ability in his little finger than all the generals together."[29] Keitel, Jodl, and Schmundt, Hitler' senior adjutant, idolized their Führer and reproached other generals for thinking otherwise.[30] In early 1943, Lieutenant General Hermann Balck, recipient of the Oak Leaf Cluster on the Knight's Cross, spoke to a group at Rheinbaben about "the greatness and brilliant generalship of the 'Führer,' who alone had saved the military situation, the Army, and Germany this winter [in Russia]."[31] Hitler had his detractors, like General Frido von Senger und Etterlin, especially after military disasters had replaced the early victories. Senger wrote about his June 22, 1943, meeting with Hitler at his Bavarian retreat, the Obersalzberg, to personally receive a medal from the Führer: "The personal sway that Hitler was alleged to hold over so many people made absolutely no impression on me. It could hardly be otherwise, since I detested him for all the misfortunes he had brought upon my country."[32] However, many, especially among the younger officers, would idolize Hitler to the very end.

The relationship between Hitler and his generals received its greatest test in the campaigns in the Soviet Union, especially once the initial offensive of Operation Barbarossa had petered out at the very gates of Moscow by December 1941.[33] From its beginning, Hitler and the generals had serious differences about the campaign. Some officers, for instance, Tresckow, now chief of staff to Bock, commander of Army Group Center, criticized the decision to invade Germany's ally as "an irreparable mistake."[34] Others wanted to use their initial superiority in tanks and tactics and the element of surprise for great strategic thrusting movements, while Hitler wanted to use small encircling actions on a tactical level to defeat the Soviets bit by bit. The generals also wanted to concentrate on Moscow, the Soviet "center of gravity," while Hitler wanted to capture Leningrad, Stalingrad, and certain economic objectives.[35] As a result, for 18 months the army dissipated its initial surprise and armored strength without capturing and holding any strategic objective, and it was ultimately forced onto the defensive. Meanwhile, the Balkan and North African campaigns continually drew off troops, supplies, and equipment badly needed for the Eastern front.[36]

In the first phase, June 22 through mid–August 1941, German panzer units covered great distances, occupied huge areas of territory, and captured hundreds of thousands of Soviet soldiers. In August, Hitler then halted Army Group Center, advancing toward Moscow, and reassigned its armor to the German thrusts toward Leningrad in the north and Stalingrad and the Donets Basin in the south, a decision some officers severely criticized.[37] Then, in October, Hitler permitted Army Group Center to renew its offensive toward Moscow, and Kluge fought his way to the very gates of Moscow by mid–December. Fighting in bitter cold for which they were unprepared, the Germans, 20 miles from the Kremlin, were repulsed by the Soviet army and the city's workers. They were without reserves, supplies, clothing and lubricating oil required to fight in the subzero winter weather, and Hitler reluctantly authorized an orderly 200-mile retreat.

Before he did so, however, several commanders, once they realized the futility of continued fighting in the severe weather without adequate clothing or reserves against a numerically superior enemy, had requested permission for orderly retreats to a more defensive line to the west of Moscow. Hitler had adamantly refused to approve any such retreats, partially because of a fear that a well-meaning retreat would turn into a rout.[38] While Hitler's decision to stand fast may have precluded a rout, such stubbornness in the face of military realities also demonstrated his belief in the power of the human "will," the same will that had produced his bloodless successes of the late 1930s and the early victories of the war, despite the advice of his generals.[39] Only when he *believed* that the military situation mandated a strategic retreat did Hitler authorize one.

Numerous senior officers became "casualties" of the disastrous winter campaign and retreat from Moscow. Hitler fired Rundstedt and his favorite Guderian for ordering retreats against his personal orders to stand fast, or for significantly disagreeing on the conduct of the Soviet offensive. The Führer also "allowed" Brauchitsch, by now a mere messenger boy and suffering from poor physical and mental health from Hitler's continual browbeating, to retire because of the army's failure in the Soviet Union, and he himself assumed direct command of the army in December 1941.[40] In January 1942, Leeb, unable to take the strain, asked to be relieved of duty, and Bock went by the wayside in June. In addition to these generals fired or relieved of duty, Hitler relieved some 35 corps and divisional commanders of their duties. By the end of the war, he had fired ten of the 17 generalfeldmarschalls and 18 of 36 generalobersts, some several times.[41] Hitler replaced these men with officers who would be more malleable to his will or, at least, be fearful of the consequences of disagreeing with him. In addition, younger officers were moving into the general officer ranks, especially at the division and corps levels. They had "a faith in the regime, [and were] ever optimistic, enthusiastic and free of political cares" and replaced those of the "school of Beck."[42]

The case of General Hoepner, the same officer who offered to support a military coup in 1938 prior to Munich, exemplifies Hitler's treatment of his senior officers when military operations went against Germany and, more importantly, against Hitler's obsession for blind obedience. On January 8, 1942, Hoepner ordered his XX Corps (Army Group Center) to retreat, against Hitler's direct orders, to avoid their total destruction. When Halder informed the Führer of Hoepner's tactically sound movement, Hitler went into a rage: "This is a criminal betrayal of the men under his command! I'll show this fellow what it means to defy one of my strict orders... ." He continued,

> This retreat is a filthy business, and I have no intention of putting up with it. The generals are obliged to obey me, just as much as the rank-and-file soldiers, and this general's idiotic decision will be on his head. What a sham! I'm the one who's in command, and all others are supposed to carry out my orders without questioning them. Where would we be if all our officers behaved like that? It's cowardice in the face of the enemy, and I'll make an example of this fellow so that he won't ever feel like doing this sort of thing again.

Hitler then angrily ordered Keitel to relieve Hoepner of his duties, effective immediately, and to discharge him from the army for cowardice. The humiliated Hoepner returned to Germany in disgrace and was refused permission to even wear his uniform and decorations in public, a traditional custom, or receive a pension.[43] Before departing, he told his troops,

> I'm relieved as Commander of the 4th Tank Army because I disobeyed an order of the Führer. Since my youth I have felt bound to the Army and the German soldier. My decisions [nonetheless] were always based on the feeling of being responsible to a higher God.[44]

The disgraced officer now became an active member of the military opposition, would be arrested and tried after the July 1944 plot, and executed on August 8, 1944.[45]

The Germans began their 1942 eastern offensive with new objectives — Stalingrad on the Volga River and the oilfields of the Caucasus.[46] Although great armored movements again achieved stunning successes against the Soviets, they were becoming more and more reactions to Soviet maneuverings and less the result of German initiatives as Hitler's micromanagement caused German commanders to become less willing to take chances and, thereby, incur Hitler's wrath and probable firing.[47] Major Alfred Count von Waldersee, who had been flown out of Stalingrad before the surrender, told Hassell about the "insane ... commands from the top, how high generals behaved like subalterns in their abject obedience."[48] Others began to see the "complete loss of confidence between the higher commanding officers and the highest leaders."[49] Signaling the end of the General Staff of Moltke the Elder and Schlieffen, Hitler finally fired Halder in September 1942 as Chief of Staff because he had become, as Hitler called him, "a prophet of doom ... infecting the commanders," and he replaced him with a sycophant, General Kurt Zeitzler.[50] Tresckow told Stahlberg that all Hitler now wanted of the General Staff were "subservient debt collectors." "Debt collectors for a capital offender!" He cried and repeated the words.[51]

During the second, transition, phase, German forces had reached Stalingrad and were fighting in the Caucasus by November 1942. The 300,000-strong Sixth Army of Generaloberst Friedrich von Paulus finally captured the city of Stalin in bitter fighting. The Soviets now counterattacked, shattering the Rumanian and Hungarian armies on Paulus's flanks and trapping the Sixth Army. Stahlberg later called the decision that led to this disaster "an irresponsible, criminal strategic error, a senseless sacrifice."[52] Hitler prohibited Paulus, cutoff from reinforcements and supplies, to break out or surrender, despite his own request and one from now Generalfeldmarschall Manstein, commander of Army Group Don; no one was willing to incur Hitler's wrath by disobeying his orders. In January 1943, Hitler promoted Paulus to generalfeldmarschall, perhaps to induce him to "fight to the last man" and then commit suicide to satisfy honor.[53] As he remarked to Jodl, "There is no record in military of history of a German Field Marshal being taken prisoner."[54] Contrary to Hitler's expectations, Paulus surrendered himself and the remnants of the Sixth Army in early February, once food, ammunition, and hope were gone. Upon hearing that Paulus had surrendered rather than fighting to the last man and then committing suicide, Hitler went into another rage:

> I can't understand how a man like Paulus wouldn't rather die. The heroism of so many tens of thousands of men, officers, and generals is canceled out by a man like this who hasn't got the character when the moment comes, to do what a weakling of a woman can do.

Later, Hitler said, "What hurts me the most personally is that I went on and promoted him [to] field marshal.... That's the last field marshal I promote in this war."[55]

A last group of letters from the entrapped soldiers generally reflected their resignation to a cold death or a harsh incarceration as POWs and a loss of faith in the High Command and Hitler (66.2 percent of the letters reflected doubtful or worse attitudes). For example, one soldier wrote:

> No one can tell me any longer that the men died with the words "Deutschland" or "Heil Hitler" on their lips. There is plenty of dying, no question of that; but the last word is "mother" or the name of someone dear, or just a cry for help. I have seen hundreds fall and die already, and many belonged to the Hitler Youth as I did, but all of them, if they still could speak, called for help or shouted a name which could not help them anyway.

> The Führer made a firm promise to bail us out of here; they read it to us and we believed in it firmly. Even now I still believe it, because I have to believe in something.... It is terrible how they doubt here, and shameful to listen to what they say without being able to reply, because they have the facts on their side.

Only a few of the soldiers inside Stalingrad retained their faith in and loyalty to their Führer (2.1 percent of the letters were positive toward the higher leadership, Hitler and the senior officers).[56]

This defeat signaled the beginning of the third and final phase of military operations, the steady westward retreat of the German army in front of the advancing Red Army all the way to Berlin in April 1945. It had significant impact on the German officer corps. Although the German army in the East had suffered small defeats before, after Stalingrad, it became readily evident to many, such as Knappe, that Germany had lost the initiative in the East and probably the war.[57] Numerous officers thought Hitler's orders to never retreat were senseless because they resulted in increasing numbers of losses, including POWs, especially since he was forced to approve retreats anyway to prevent more losses. Yet, the generals, many cowed by Hitler's maniacal rages against them, did nothing to stop the impending military disaster and the ultimate loss of the war. For example, after a long debate at a mid–June 1943 over Hitler's strategic blunders, all that the assembled generals could conclude was that the Führer needed to appoint a commander in chief for the eastern front and form a genuine war cabinet.[58] Additionally, to the numerous and constantly changing weak generalfeldmarschalls and generaloberststs, Hitler "added an inflationary number of generals, of which a certain number, at any rate, were blind followers of Hitler."[59]

At the same time during this period, a new group of officers appeared, younger offices who, like Lieutenant Colonel Claus Schenk von Stauffenberg, despaired at the present military situation and recognized the weakening authority of many senior offices. In June 1942, he complained to General Paulus about the difficulty of keeping

> up one's enthusiasm when one saw the troops "staking their all ... while the commanders, who should set an example, squabble about prestige and are unable to pluck up the courage to put forward their views or indeed their convictions even though thousands of lives may depend on them."[60]

At least by mid–1943 Stauffenberg had probably become a full member of the anti–Hitler conspiracy. A little over two years later, only weeks before the abortive assassination attempt, Stauffenberg told another conspirator Eberhard Finckh, "We have no real field marshals any more. They all shake in their shoes and stand to attention when the Fuherer gives an order. They are not assertive enough with their views regarding the seriousness of the situation."[61]

The Stalingrad disaster and the argumentative generals led Hitler to institute a number of programs to reinforce the generals' obedience to him and to further Nazi indoctrination in the army. The OKW already had a liaison officer at the Propaganda Ministry, primarily to keep Goebbels informed about "defeatism"—talk against the regime—among the officer corps. In December 1943, Hitler instituted the NS-Führerstab (NSF) (National Socialist Leadership Staff), the Nazi version of Communists' political commissars, to indoctrinate the regular army in Nazi ideology and instill fanaticism into the fighting will of the soldiers. The NSF program was first under the chief of the OKW General Administration Office, General Reinecke, who assigned NSF officers (reserve officers, since regular officers could not conduct political activities) to all military staffs down to divisional level. To emphasize their importance and role, Hitler normally closed each NSF course himself. After the July 20, 1944, plot, Deputy Führer Martin Bormann further expanded the system and had the NSF officers report directly to him. The NSF officers essentially became spies for any further "treason" among the senior staffs, reporting directly to the party's highest level.[62] Although it is impossible to accurately measure the actual influence of the NSF program on the soldiers, the increasingly desperate appeal to loyalty and obedience "seems to indicate that ideological training as a means to instill fanaticism was by and large a failure." The greatest significance for this program seems to be that it had to be implemented in the first place.[63]

Hitler also wanted personal reassurance of his senior officers' continuing loyalty and obedience, possibly in reaction to the news about the formation in July 1943 of the Nationalkomitee Freies Deutschland (NKFD) (National Committee for a Free Germany) by German officers captured at Stalingrad, including General Walther von Seydlitz-Kurzbach, a descendant of General Friedrich von Seydlitz of Frederick the Great's army and a Major von Seydlitz at Tauroggen. Other officers, including Paulus, founded the Bund Deutscher Offiziere (BDO) (German Officers' League) on September 11, 1943. After the BDO voted to join the NDFD, Seydlitz-Kurzbach referred to the current day as a "new Tauroggen." The members of the NDFD and the BDO issued proclamations, for example, that stated that the war was lost and that Germans should overthrow the Hitler regime, and they worked in the POW camps to recruit other anti-Hitler sympathizers.[64] At the end of January 1944, with a number of the headquarters officers present, Hitler said that he expected his generals to demonstrate greater loyalty because of the worsening military situation. Stahlberg, now Manstein's aide-de-camp, wrote that Hitler had spoken to the generals as if they "were totally oblivious to obedience and loyalty, and as if he had forgotten that we had all sworn an oath to him." When Hitler was done, Manstein sarcastically interjected, "That is how it will be, *mein Führer*."[65] On March 19, 1944, Hitler called all of his generalfeldmarschalls to Berchtesgaden where they swore their personal oath of allegiance to him anew; the words were read by Rundstedt, the army's most senior general.[66]

Despite these measures, the personal relationships between Hitler and many of his generals continued to deteriorate as the military situation worsened on both fronts. Hitler's reactions to the Allied landings at Normandy are familiar to most, particularly his continuing belief that these landings were only a feint and that the "real" landings would come at the Pas de Calais, the narrowest point between France and England, in early July. When he finally realized that the Normandy landings were the main thrust of the Allies onto *Festung Europa* (Fortress Europe), it was too late to push them back into the sea. Effectively illustrating this deteriorating relationship is the story that began with a telephone conversation from Keitel at the OKW to Generalfeldmarschall Rundstedt on June 30, 1944. After Keitel asked about the current military situation, and Rundstedt responded, "What shall you do? You should put an end to the war, you idiots!" Because of this remark, Keitel fired Rundstedt, who declared at his farewell on July 4 that he would never again assume a command. Kluge arrived in France as his replacement. When Kluge demanded Rommel's unconditional obedience, the panzer commander "blew up." Kluge apologized to Rommel after the former visited the front lines, explaining that he had been deceived by Keitel and Hitler, "who exists by wishful thinking, and when the dreams fade he looks for scapegoats."[67] Despite this severe dislike for Hitler and his minions and the continuing defeats and losses on the battlefield, none of the field commanders, as we shall see later, joined the anti–Hitler opposition in the last planning stages of the Führer's assassination.

The army's losses incurred on the eastern and western fronts proved to be nearly irreplaceable as the war of attrition in the Soviet Union continued and the Allies advanced through France. (See Table 6.1 for status in October 1943.) To provide combat troops for the east, the German army was forced to adopt a number of "band-aid" solutions: use of younger and older year groups ahead of schedule for combat duty as Germany ran out of first-line soldiers in the prime age groups, and the formation of "special" combat groups from decimated units. Only the skillful leadership of the senior officers and the diligence of the fighting troops in the field, now fighting to save the Fatherland and their families from the "Asiatic hordes," prevented an uncontrollable rout in the field; instead, they produced a slow but steady retreat back to Germany.

The general attitudes of the senior officers towards Hitler and his treatment of them waxed and waned with the vicissitudes of victory and defeat. First, he liberally bestowed upon them promotions, decorations, and rewards when they were victorious. Then, when the tide began to turn against Germany, he heaped scorn upon them for their failure to overcome the growing Allied armies and their mounting logistical support. As Hassell wrote, "[Hitler] again fumed like a maniac, for when things go wrong it is not 'the most brilliant military leader of all time who commands,' but 'the generals.'"[68] Furthermore, Hitler brushed aside their sound strategic, operational, and tactical suggestions (based on years of professional military education and experience) to limit further losses. He instead called them cowards and defeatists, possessed with "the spirit of Zossen," unable to carry out his "will." Yet, despite this treatment, the generals for the main could not (or would not) honorably contemplate a coup and generally continued to serve him. For example, when Hitler fired Rundstedt for the second time in early July 1944, he declared at his command post that he would never accept another command.[69] Yet, when Hitler recalled Rundstedt in December, the old Prussian said, "My Führer, whatever you order, I shall do to my last breath."[70] I shall return to the reasons why in the next chapter on the evolution of the military opposition during the war.

Table 6.1. German Strength in 1943

Available Army Manpower in 1943		
Year Classes	***Age in 1943***	***Available Recruits***
1894–1899	44–49	18,000
1900–1922	21–43	6,000
1923	20	1,000
1924	19	3,000
1925	18	45,000
1926	17	468,000

German Military Strength on October 1, 1943	
Component	***Strength***
Field Army	***4,555,000***
Replacement army	2,185,000
Waffen SS	402,000
Navy	2,007,000
Air Force	711,000
Total	9,860,000

Source: Document 172, Warlimont Lecture to Reich and Gau (Party District) Leaders, November 7, 1943, NCA, VII, p. 967.

The Lower-Ranking Officers and Enlisted Personnel, and Hitler

Having looked at the senior officers and their problems with Hitler over military matters, we now need to briefly review the attitudes of the lower-ranking officers and the enlisted soldiers, the *Landsers*, who formed the bulk of the army. Since most of the senior officers continued to follow their oath and obey Hitler's orders, it is not surprising that the lower-ranking men also followed their oath and obeyed the orders from above. First and probably foremost, most lower-ranking soldiers in all armies generally follow orders, despite the most grievous circumstances, unless they have reason to believe that the orders are illegal. The questions now become: when does a soldier, trained to follow orders, know when an order is illegal? Then, if he does realize an order is illegal, does he disobey that order, knowing there are penalties for disobedience? Penalties are even more severe for disobedience in combat. These questions were valid even for the German soldiers, caught up in the war of attrition in Russia.

One important factor is that the more junior officers and the enlisted soldiers increasingly came from the younger, more indoctrinated groups of German males. They believed in Hitler's ideological message as many had been members of the HJ or the RAD or both before 1939. Their service in the HJ had not only allowed them to complete basic training sooner but also prepared them ideologically to fight for the Fatherland and their Führer.[71] During the Russian campaign, when Knappe stopped one of his senior NCOs who was shouting at a Polish Jew and slapping him, the NCO responded, "But he is a Jew." Knappe attributed the NCO's actions to the Nazis' anti-Semitic propaganda.[72] As more replacements were needed with the increasing numbers of casualties, the army called up younger year groups, those increasingly indoctrinated with the Nazi ideology.[73]

Furthermore, the Nazis made significant efforts to reinforce the National Socialist ideology among the troops through radio broadcasts, propaganda films, newspapers, military newssheets, leaflets, and political lectures.[74] Also, the higher political leadership wanted to further limit the church's influence by replacing Christian reading material with National Socialist literature, and ensuring that attendance at church services was truly voluntary and would not interfere with military duties.[75] The lectures on National Socialism by the NS-Leadership Officers also had some, although limited, impact on the troops. This continual barrage of Nazi propaganda must have had some influence on the morale, esprit de corps, and ideological conviction of the younger soldiers.

We get some idea from their postwar memoirs and letters written to friends and relatives during the Russian campaign. For example, their letters describe the living conditions of the Russian peasants as "dirty, filthy" and the people without "a trace of culture." Soviet soldiers looked "emaciated" with a "wild, half-crazed look in their eyes [that made] them appear like imbeciles, ... led by Jews and criminals,..." They were "sub-humans ... drunken Russian criminals ... scoundrels, the mere scum of the earth."[76] To Henry Metalman, the Russians "were Slavs of a lower racial order" because he and his fellow soldiers had frequently been told that at school, in the HJ, in newspapers, and on the radio.[77] Prueller expresses similar feelings about the Russians.[78]

Additionally, the younger soldiers also became as enthralled with Hitler and the first victories as the officers. These victories and Hitler's prewar achievements created a Hitler myth among many Germans. Soon after the Polish campaign, Prueller noted:

> In all the towns of the Reich, the flags of our nation adorn the windows: the visible sign that the war with Poland has been brought to a victorious end. It is victory of right. It is a victory of sacred belief in our eternal Germany, a victory of National Socialism, and thus a personal victory of Hitler.
>
> For it was Adolf Hitler who canceled the shameful debt of Versailles for all of us, canceled it in a way which at the beginning no one believed possible.[79]

In 1942, somewhere in Russia, he recorded the idolizing reactions of his comrades and himself to one of Hitler's radio broadcasts.[80] Many soldiers believed Hitler would prevent "these subhumans, led by Jews" from polluting Europe.[81] Commanders and chaplains bolstered this sense of crusade by proclaiming the campaign to be a spiritual mission against the godless Bolsheviks: "... [O]ur task in Russia was a holy one and ... we had God on our side."[82] The German Army prayer even included a request that God bless the Wehrmacht, strengthen its members "to make the supreme sacrifice for Führer, Volk, and Fatherland" and "bless Hitler in all the tasks laid upon him."[83] Some commanders credited the soldiers' ardent fighting spirit to their confidence in Hitler.[84]

The military victories also created a growing sense of the invincibility of Nazi Germany's military forces and the rightness of its cause. Prueller saw the fear of France and Britain during the western campaign in the spring of 1940 and enjoyed the cheers that greeted the German soldiers in Rumania.[85] Karl Fuchs wrote, "Our children should be raised with the belief in our Fatherland! That too is a religion and the good Lord surely won't condemn that. It is the same whether we are Protestant or Catholic."[86] After a victory in autumn 1941, Fuchs wrote his father, "God, were we overjoyed. I guess the strength of the German soldier is unique and it seems that he is invincible."[87] Prueller wrote the fiancée of a comrade killed in battle, "[His] death was not, it shall not be in vain! ... The survival of our great Fatherland, our imperishable people, and the victory over our accursed enemies shall have been accomplished partly through his death."[88] Stahlberg wrote about a new panzer commander, who, in June 1941, excitedly talked about Germany's future in the East and the Germans as the "chosen people."[89] The early victories of 1939–41 confirmed to many German soldiers the righteousness of their cause and their invincibility, especially in the fight against the Slavs and Bolsheviks in the East.

Starting in the harsh winter of 1941-42, we begin to sense a change in their adulation for Hitler, an increasing sense of despondency and despair. These feelings would worsen as combat conditions did, especially after the fall of Stalingrad.[90] The retreating soldiers complained about the subzero weather, the lack of adequate clothing and proper medical care for the wounded, and their inability to stop the Russians. Many would remember the heady days of the first quick victories and the promises of more. For some there were growing doubts about the righteousness of their cause.[91] These feelings were certainly not uniform throughout the army in Russia, much less in the German forces in other parts of Europe. However, they do represent a growing discontent within the army as defeats replaced victories, as more and more soldiers began to realize that neither their sheer fighting abilities nor the promises of victory from their leaders would defeat the Soviet Army (and later, other Allied armies).[92]

Despite this poignant but tragic story of the German soldier caught in a desperate war of attrition against the numerically superior Red Army in horrendous combat conditions, the army conducted a steady and relatively orderly retreat between mid–1943 through April 1945. The German soldiers in Italy and France also generally fought well and retreated steadily but orderly back towards Germany, overcome more by the numbers and weight of Allied logistics than by a great loss of faith in their cause or fighting abilities. In fact, the American army in France would feel the last gasp of German fighting abilities in the Battle of the Bulge that came close to tactical victory during the winter of 1944-45. The retreat along all fronts did not turn into a rout, truly an outstanding military achievement that speaks greatly about the leadership qualities of the company-grade officers and the tenacity and fighting will of the *Landsers*.

From their memoirs and letters, we can discern a continuing general belief in their cause, despite terrible combat conditions (for example, in the USSR, the subzero weather would literally freeze skin to their weapons), the lack of adequate equipment and supplies, numerically superior enemy forces, and no real hope of defeating them. Further strengthening their fighting will was knowledge of the Allied bombing campaign that placed their families in jeopardy of serious injury or death, their love of the Fatherland, and the soldiers' own inbred sense of survival that went beyond their loyalty to Hitler or the Nazi regime. Furthermore, criticism of the regime or Hitler, cowardice in combat, desertions, and self-inflicted wounds to avoid combat were all severely punished, including by firing squads.[93] Despite a growing realization that their world, built on the early quick victories, was just as quickly unraveling, the *Landsers* fought on, motivated as much by Nazi ideology as by patriotism to defend Germany, love to protect their families, and their own need to survive under these desperate combat conditions.

I found two divergent theories that attempt to explain the orderly retreat of the German Army from the Soviet Union for the better part of two years, why there was no rout or general debacle in combat, despite the primitive conditions in which it fought. Shils and Janowitz in 1948 theorized that the German Army in the East did not fall apart because of the cohesiveness of the primary combat group and the identification of the individual soldiers with this group; to them, Nazi ideology was not a significant factor. Bartov, however, refutes their theory, stating that by 1943 the war in the USSR had destroyed the original primary groups, and combat units were increasingly composed of the remnants of decimated larger units and hastily trained recruits. To him, Nazi ideology played an increasingly important role in unifying these disparate units and in maintaining discipline as the German army retreated back toward Germany.[94] Their role as the defenders of Germany — their homes and families — from the Asiatic hordes and their innate sense of survival bolstered their oath of loyalty to Hitler and kept the rank-and-file soldiers focused on fighting during the long but orderly retreat to Germany.

The Army and War Crimes

While the preceding two sections examined the military consequences of the general obedience to superior orders and loyalty to Hitler by both the officer corps and the enlisted force of the German army during World War II, this section will review the criminal consequences of the obedience that followed from the oath of loyalty. In no other war in modern history had the professional army of a state perpetrated such violations of the laws of war and humanity as did the German army of 1939–45. These crimes directly contravened the various pre–1939 conventions that tried to "regulate" the increasing brutality of modern warfare, conventions that Germany had signed and that the Nazi regime did not officially abrogate. I obviously cannot retell the complete story of such heinous crimes that took the lives of millions of civilians and POWs. This discussion will show how the army besmirched its professional reputation by obediently following criminal orders and, thus, became part of the Nazi regime's criminality.[95]

In the first six months the army tried to protest atrocities, at least symbolically, committed by troops, particularly the SS, under its control. During the Polish campaign, Reichenau ordered an investigation of the murder of several hundred Polish Jews in the town of Radom by SS units under his command, and General Bock court-martialed several members of an SS artillery company for the massacre of 50 Jews in a Polish synagogue. However, General Georg von Kuechler, commanding the German Third Army, refused to confirm the sentences because they were too lenient — only one year in prison.[96] Brauchitsch annulled the sentences after Himmler intervened. Hitler then issued special orders that removed the SS, SD, and Gestapo from the army's legal jurisdiction and amnestied any SS or German soldier who committed acts of violence against Polish Jews. Brauchitsch issued a supplementary order by which the army could prosecute soldiers for such crimes, but it is doubtful that many commanders overrode Hitler's higher authority. General Wilhelm List, commander of the 14th Army, in a September 18 order also prohibited looting, rape, burning of synagogues, and the shooting of Jews, but it applied only to the soldiers.[97]

Noting that the OKH had made no provision for a civil government for occupied Poland, Himmler took action to move into this void.[98] Additionally, he obtained an agreement with Keitel to allow five SS Einsatzgruppen (Special Groups) to pursue a deliberate campaign to rid Poland of the more "undesirable" segments of society (clergy, intellectuals, nobles, socialists, Communists, and Jews), fulfillment of Hitler's prewar pledge. Canaris learned about the agreement in mid–September and vainly protested to Keitel that the army's reputation would be "indelibly sullied" and prophetically told the OKW chief, "The day will come when the world will hold the Wehrmacht under whose eyes these events occurred responsible for such measures."[99] General Helmuth Steiff, now chief of the Organization Department of the OKH, spoke out against the SS atrocities in Poland: "I am ashamed to be a German! This minority has defiled the name of Germany with their murder, looting, and arson. They will be the doom of the entire German nation unless we manage to stop them."[100] The army leadership, however, gave into the SS plans to carry out its so-called "political tasks" without further protest and carefully and precisely defined the responsibilities of the SS and the army's occupation forces to prevent *the latter* from participating in such crimes.[101]

The army leadership ceased its protests, but the commander of the German occupation forces in Poland, Generaloberst Johannes Blaskowitz, did not.[102] Between November 1939 and February 1940, he forwarded several memoranda to higher headquarters, detailing SS atrocities in Poland, their effects on the soldiers, and the insolent attitude of the SS toward the army.[103] However, his protests not only produced no condemnation of the atrocities but also earned him the undying dislike of Frank, Heydrich, Himmler, and Hitler himself. After reading his first memo, Hitler "once again starts making serious criticisms of the 'childish attitudes' among the Army leadership; one can't fight a war with Salvation Army methods."[104] Adding to Hitler's dislike of Blaskowitz was the revelation to the world of the SS atrocities, particularly those against the Catholic clergy, in Poland *with* specific mention of the general's opposition to the SS activities. Hitler and Himmler who had tried to keep the SS atrocities against the Poles secret must have been further angered at Blaskowitz.[105] Despite his personal promise of a command in the western campaign,

Hitler fired Blaskowitz as commander of Obost on May 29, 1940, and placed him on the reserve list, ending any chance of a generalfeldmarschall's baton.[106]

Blaskowitz's memoranda generally produced some level of outrage from those who became aware of the atrocities in Poland. After seeing the December 1939 memo, Helmuth Groscurth at the OKH wondered, "Why does nobody interfere with these ongoing conditions?"[107] Although he did not participate in the Polish campaign, Senger was disgusted with the atrocities but advised his friends only to keep silent and perform their duty honorably.[108] After June 1940, Stahlberg became aware of the extent of SS crimes in Poland: "...[D]id this mean we were in the hands of a criminal state? Were we risking our necks for such a regime?"[109] However, despite this level of outrage from some officers, others were only concerned if *army* troops were involved.

Upon reading Blaskowitz's report, Brauchitsch issued an order in which he expected all members of the army in Poland "to respond with high integrity and straightforward moral behavior" and with force, if necessary, to restore order in Poland and the "respect of the German nation abroad."[110] Apparently, nothing came of this order. By the summer of 1940, the situation was different as General Kuechler, commander of 18th Army, issued an order which prohibited the occupation troops from criticizing the activities of the "Party units" engaged in the "final solution of this ethnic struggle, which has been raging for centuries along our eastern frontier,...."[111] Perhaps, General Wagner, the OKW officer who had negotiated the initial agreement to allow the Einsaztgruppen to operate in Poland, best summarized official policy: "We have no intention of rebuilding Poland.... *Polish intelligentsia must be prevented from establishing itself as a governing class.*"[112]

The conduct and the aftermath of the western campaign in the spring and early summer of 1940 would be quite different from the Polish campaign and Operation Barbarossa — there would be no racial war against western Europeans, with the exception of Jews and Gypsies.[113] For example, Witzleben, the commander of the First Army in the West, originally prompted by Lieutenant General Theodor Groppe, commander of the 214 Infantry Divison on the Westwall, ordered all units under his command to prevent violence against the Jews by party units, by force if necessary.[114] At the start of the western campaign, the soldiers received explicit orders

> Looting or other excesses [would be] severely punished ... as soon as they became known.... I myself clearly recall how the Commander-in Chief of the Army had a major of the Reserve shot under martial law during the Western campaign because he had laid hands on French property. The sentence and its execution were made generally known while the fighting was still going on....

He also reports that a lieutenant colonel and several soldiers received ten years' imprisonment and "long prison terms," respectively, for looting during the French campaign. [115] Furthermore, German soldiers could not mistreat French POWs and, in fact, they received food and transportation to the POW camps.[116] The Germans did show great animosity toward the French colonial troops serving with the French army, but, in general, the soldiers conducted themselves well.[117] Military occupation policies in western Europe, except for those dealing with the Jews and guerrillas, were somewhat less brutal than those in eastern Europe and the Soviet Union because of Nazi views on "race."[118]

However, the proposed invasion of the Soviet Union would result in a completely different way of conducting military operations. In preparation for this offensive, first scheduled for April, Hitler assembled his senior commanders in March 1941. At two conferences, March 17 and 30, he unveiled his intentions to conduct an ideological war of extermination against the Bolsheviks. According to Hitler, Bolshevism was a sociological crime that, as a result, made political commissars automatically criminals, not soldiers. He clearly stated that the war in the USSR "was no place for soldierly chivalry or 'out-of-date notions' of military comradeship. This was a struggle in which not only must the Red Army be beaten in the field but Communism must be exterminated for all time." The army could shoot all political commissars on the spot and turn over those who were found among POWs to SD field units for "special treatment"—what became the Commissar Order.[119] Furthermore, Hitler exempted all soldiers from court-martial who summarily executed "noncombatants" who threatened them—the Jurisdiction Order.[120] He concluded the March 30 meeting: "I do not expect my generals to understand me; but I shall expect them to obey my orders."[121] In June, Hitler further justified these extreme measures because of the army's "leniency" in the growing guerrilla war in the Balkans.[122]

Although the generals were horrified by Hitler's comments, they protested little at the conferences. Warlimont reported on the March 30 meeting:

> Many have subsequently expressed the view that Hitler's fulminations should have led some of those present to give vent to some protest or adverse reaction after he departed. There is nothing to show that anything of the short happened; I was myself present.... It may therefore be taken as certain that none of those present availed themselves of the opportunity even to mention the demands made by Hitler during the morning. It was generally realized of course, that, as had frequently been proved before, open opposition generally did more harm than good.[123]

Afterwards, many expressed their objections to Brauchitsch although they should have known that he would do little. As events happened, the Army Commander's opposition was weak and ineffective.[124] In fact, Brauchitsch had *draft* orders prepared for review by both the OKH and OKW, which he and Keitel, despite the latter's "private" misgivings, eventually signed.[125] Görlitz aptly commented: "So they passed the buck to one another, instead of openly admitting that when it was a question of moral weakness, in fact, none of them had any right to reproach anybody."[126] Hassell also recognized the impact of the criminal orders on the honor of the army:

> We came to the conclusion that nothing was to be hoped for now. Brauchitsch and Halder have already agreed to Hitler's tactics. Thus the Army must assume the onus of the murders and burnings which up to now have been confined to the SS. They have assumed the responsibility, and delude themselves and others by reasoning that does not alter the essence of the problem—the necessity for maintaining discipline, etc. Hopeless sergeant majors![127]

Right before Barbarossa began, the OKW, the OKH, and army group commanders passed the Commissar Order and the Jurisdiction Orders down to the lower-ranking officers. Many of them also had extreme misgivings about their meaning and impact. Tresckow remarked to Rudolf von Gersdorff, Bock's intelligence officer,

> ...[R]ember this moment. If we cannot persuade the Field Marshals to do everything to rescind these orders, then Germany will have finally lost her honor. The efforts will be felt for centuries, and not only Hitler will bear the guilt. Everyone will be guilty, you and me, your wife and my wife, your children and my children, that woman crossing the street, and those children over there playing ball.[128]

On June 21, Stahlberg called the order "murder" upon learning about it from Tresckow, who added, "And for that reason we are not allowed to give it to the troops in writing, but you will receive it by word of mouth to the companies."[129] Tresckow decided to ignore the order as well as treat Russian POWs "decently."[130] Gersdorff "conspired" with his counterparts at Army Group North and Army Group South to ignore the Commissar Order and rendered false reports to higher headquarters on alleged shootings of political commissars.[131] Because of this lower-level opposition, the Commissar Order was haphazardly implemented.

Many commanders, fearful of the effects on the maintenance of discipline among the troops, did their best to avoid carrying out the orders.[132] For example, Leeb did not transmit the Commissar Order to the rank and file, and Tresckow persuaded Bock, commander of Army Group Center, to submit an official protest to the OKH. However, when Tresckow presented Bock with the order, the generalfeldmarschall expressed ("feigned") surprise, repeatedly exclaiming "Unbelievable!" and "Horrible!" I say "feigned" because Bock had been present at the March 30, 1941, meeting where Hitler spoke about his intentions for an ideological war against the Soviet Union. After Gersdorff returned from Berlin without obtaining higher headquarters support for further protest or withdrawal of the order, he related to Bock and Tresckow what had transpired. The generalfeldmarschall self-righteously lauded himself for his protest—"Let it be noted, gentlemen, that Field Marshal Bock protested"—but he protested no further![133] Bock did, however, obtain verbal agreement from other corps commanders, including Kluge, Weichs, and Guderian, to ignore the Commissar and Jurisdiction orders.[134] Although Manstein held strong anti–Bolshevik, almost Nazi, views, he also refused to implement the order because, again, of its impact on the soldiers' discipline. According to him, his troops duly executed the majority of their captured political commissars as partisans after a trial according to military law.[135] However, Hitler discovered that the majority of the political commissars were in the transit and POW camps and ordered the Wehrmacht POW Service to open the camps to the SD who seized them, along with Communists and Jews, for summary execution.[136]

The protests of some senior officers and the general refusal to implement the Commissar Order eventually had some impact. In May 1942, Hitler temporarily suspended the order after Kluge's personal intercession.[137] Kluge's intercession was not made primarily out of humanitarian reasons. He, like other generals, was more concerned about the impact of the Commissar Order on the "good order and morale" of the German soldiers in general. Furthermore, the indiscriminate killing and execution of the political commissars in the POW camps and the brutal treatment of Soviet POWs served only to stiffen the will to fight among Soviet soldiers and to reduce the number of deserters. After hearing the reports of German inhumanity toward POWs, Soviet soldiers figured they might as well fight to the death for Mother Russia as be summarily executed or treated so inhumanely by the Germans.[138]

Although many senior commanders protested these criminal orders and took steps to ameliorate their effects, others carried them out. Some, like Hitler, saw the coming campaign against the Bolsheviks as a war between good and evil. For example, Generaloberst Hoepner, whom Hitler would cashier in December 1941, approved a directive about the forthcoming operations that read in part:

> The war against Russia is an essential part of the struggle for existence of the German nation. It is the old struggle of the Germanic peoples against Slavdom, the defense of European culture against the Muscovite Asiatic flood.... Bolshevism is the mortal enemy of the National Socialist German nation. Germany's struggle is

> directed against this destructive ideology and its supporters.

He reminded his troops that one objective of the campaign was to defend "against Jewish Bolshevism" and that the campaign would require "ruthless and forceful action against Bolshevist agitators, guerrillas, saboteurs, and Jews, and the total suppression of all active and passive resistance."[139] A July 10, 1941, report recorded that Hoepner's men executed at least 101 political commissars. [140] Future conspirator Helmuth Steiff wrote similar thoughts in a letter to his sister in late August 1941.[141]

During the campaigns in the Soviet Union, the German army captured an estimated 6.7 million Soviet soldiers. By April 1945, some 3.7 million of them had died from the worst treatment — or lack of treatment — of any group of POWs in modern warfare and of any belligerent of this war, with the possible exception of those held by the Japanese. Because that treatment demonstrates the degree to which the German Army had embraced the Nazi ideology, bolstering its general obedience to Hitler, I describe that treatment in greater detail in Appendix B where I contrast the German treatment of Russian POWs during the First World War and their treatment of western POWs during the Second World War with the brutal treatment of Soviet POWs to clearly show the differences; I provide only a summary here. By early 1942, the Nazis began to change their policy toward Soviet POWs — the maltreated, sick, and dying POWs represented a huge economic and military drain. By January 1945, some 600,000 Soviet POWs (Table 6.2) (an unknown number had died as slave laborers) were working in Germany under terrible conditions, and many ex–POWs had joined Vlassov's anti–Stalin army.

Before the start of Operation Barbarossa, the OKW and the SS made two important formal agreements which received the approval of Brauchitsch. First, the army would provide logistical support — billeting, supplies, and so on — for the four Einsatzgruppen, charged with the execution of political commissars, Communist officials, Gypsies, and Jews, in the rear areas of the three army groups.[142] Second, the army agreed to a formal demarcation of its jurisdiction in the operational zones immediately behind the front lines and that of the SS–controlled civil administration in the occupied territories.[143] Several Einsatzgruppen commanders reported that the army provided excellent support, and, in some cases, the participation of soldiers in their killing operations.[144] SS General Franz Walter Stahlecker, commander of Einsatzgruppe A, pointed out the exemplary close cooperation of General Hoepner's Tank Group 4.[145] In effect, the SS had successfully co-opted the army into its grim killing operations and repressive occupation policies and obtained the army's formal recognition for its extermination of "undesirables."

In response to the growing guerrilla war against German forces in the Soviet Union and Balkans, the OKW ordered the execution of 50 to 100 civilian hostages — men, women, and children — for every German soldier killed by guerrillas. German forces also executed "suspected" partisans and took "collective action" against the nearest village for guerrilla activity.[146] Even the future conspirator General Karl-Heinrich von Stülpnagel directed reprisals against Soviet youth organizations for guerrilla attacks against German soldiers in a July 30, 1941, order.[147] In some areas, German soldiers seized and executed Jews, rather than local civilians — a regular practice of the army in the Balkans. It complied with OKW's order to execute local civilians for the death of German soldiers and with Hitler's Final Solution for the Jews, without further antagonizing the local populace.[148] The execution of local civilians became standard throughout occupied Europe in a vain effort to stem the growing resistance movements — terror begot terror which begot more terror in an increasingly downward spiral.[149] Various *army* commanders issued supplementary directives and orders that implemented or reiterated the OKW's antipartisan directives.[150] German soldiers mercilessly executed hundreds of thousands of Europeans, a policy which produced, in effect, new recruits for the growing resistance movements.[151]

The initial fears of the senior commanders, expressed at the beginning of Barbarossa, were soon realized as the eastern campaign progressed and unconscionable conduct there spread to other parts of occupied Europe. Some local field commanders, such as Bock, Rundstedt and Kleist, issued orders prohibiting *their* soldiers from participating in the SS executions of Jews or excesses against the civilian population, leaving such tasks to the "political units." Others, like Paulus, prohibited the execution of suspected partisans without a proper court-martial, but their motivation was primarily to limit the effects of this "legal" killing on the troops' morale and discipline, not to prevent the carrying out of criminal orders.[152] These commanders wanted to restrict the brutality of the Soviet campaign to "organized barbarism" strictly according to official orders.[153] Some, such as Senger, refused to implement such orders because of their basic illegality as well as the probable effect on the troops.[154]

The army also played a significant part, along with the SS and other "political" organizations, in the Holocaust. In imitation of Hitler, Keitel also equated the fight in the East with Bolshevism as a war with the Jews, "the main carriers of Bolshevism."[155] Many field commanders took a "hands-off" view, like Generaloberst Ernst Busch, commander of Sixteenth Army of Army Group North when he heard about the shooting of the Jews of Kovno in the autumn of 1941: "Well, I can't do anything about it; these are political matters which don't interest us [the army?], or rather they interest us but we shouldn't do anything. These things don't concern us."[156] Military governors of the occupied territories in the west implemented various anti-Semitic measures (wearing of the Yellow Star, forced ghettoization, and deportation) with no apparent opposition to them.[157] In addition to executing Jews as suspected partisans, the army through the Military Transportation Command controlled the trains which took Jews to the extermination camps. The army's opposition to this task was driven by the need for the trains to transport supplies and reinforcements to the various fronts, not to prevent the deportation of Jews to the death camps per se, and it usually lost to Himmler's demands for more trains for this purpose over more urgent military needs.[158] The army (like the SS) also used Jewish labor in war-related industries in Poland; in this respect, the army tried to protect their Jewish workers for purely economic reasons.[159]

The army participated in other war crimes that many have normally associated with only the SS and the Gestapo. Army commanders carried out higher headquarters orders to shoot captured enemy commandos — even if clothed in a proper military uniform.[160] The army throughout Europe assisted in the roundup and deportation of men, women, and children to Germany as slave labor (Table 6.2, p. 167) to relieve an increasing shortage of men who were being drafted into military service.[161] Keitel signed and army commanders carried out the "Nacht und Nebel" ("Night and Fog") order that directed the transfer of certain people, such as captured resistance members, to Germany where they would vanish without a trace, and that forbade the authorities to divulge any information on their whereabouts.[162] The army also participated in the looting and transportation of art treasures from all over Europe to satisfy

Table 6.2. Numbers of Foreign Workers in Germany (January 1945)

	Workers	*Pows*	*Politicals*	*Total*
Russians	1,900,000	600,000	11,000	2,500,000
Other Groups	2,895,000	1,273,000	12,200	4,191,000
Totals	4,795,000	1,873,000	23,200	6,691,000

Source: NCA, I, p. 894.

the desires of high Nazi Officials, especially Reichsmarschall Göring.[163] The documents speak loudly about the army's direct participation in the Nazi regime's crimes, negating the claims of those, such as German generals, that the army remained free of its taints.

After the war, Major General Erwin Lahousen testified that Himmler and Heydrich wanted to deliberately and directly involve the army so that it would "no longer 'wear a white vest without spots' so to speak, and leave the execution of these orders to the SS and the SD, ... which it did in fact."[164] Descriptions of the army's direct participation in the Third Reich's war crimes amply demonstrate that Himmler and Heydrich had succeeded. The army murdered Jews, plundered the continent's art treasures, almost routinely executed civilians and destroyed their homes and villages, deported hundreds of thousands of Europeans to Germany as slave labor, and caused the deaths of millions of POWs. The fact that a number of the army generals — in addition to Keitel and Jodl — were convicted of war crimes testifies to the complicity of the army, along with the SS, SD, and Gestapo, in Nazi war crimes. These crimes of the army were committed in compliance with an oath that Hitler himself had violated and then used to bend the army to his will.

Summary

During the war, millions of German soldiers of all ranks dutifully followed their oath to Hitler, obeyed orders, and caused untold death, destruction, and misery. Part of this obedience to orders by the lower-ranking officers and the enlisted men can be partially explained by the general propensity of soldiers to obey orders with little questioning as they always have in all armies and across the centuries. In such situations, the lower-ranking soldiers had to weigh their actions against the severe penalties for disobedience in combat, which usually meant execution.[165] Furthermore, the youths who became soldiers during the war had become indoctrinated with National Socialism, evidenced by the National Socialist verbiage and idioms in their letters, diaries, and memoirs, especially in those of the troops who served on the Russian front. While most did not become ardent Nazis, this Nazi indoctrination allowed them to rationalize their war crimes against Jews, Bolsheviks, Slavs, partisans, and all other "enemy" groups. Finally, these younger soldiers owed much to Hitler and the early victories — pride, status, position, and promotion. Understanding why the "average" soldier followed their oath and carried out such orders, despite the suffering that doing so caused, becomes *almost* comprehensible.

What is much less than comprehensible was the obedience of most of the senior officers to their oath. The senior officers as a group generally continued to obey, to follow their oath, despite serious disagreements with Hitler over both purely military matters — the strategic and tactical conduct of the war — and over the army's participation in large-scale war crimes. They also did nothing when Hitler assumed direct command of the army despite their own general lack of confidence in him as a war leader and strategist. Furthermore, they continued to obey even after Hitler heaped additional scorn and abuse upon them for military failures that derived from his *own* failure as a war leader, strategist, and tactician. Few directly protested his firing of many of Germany's best field commanders for failure to avoid defeats against overwhelming enemy forces. Finally, with few exceptions such as Blaskowitz, the senior officers did not strongly or directly oppose the criminal orders, only weakly protested them to assuage their sense of military professionalism, and resorted to local subterfuges to avoid implementing them with minimal effect on the large-scale atrocities committed by the army.

Most of the senior officers were not ardent Nazis, like Reichenau, Schoerner, and Model. Most of them had been commissioned before or during the First World War when a military officer was seen as a professional with a certain code of honor and conduct. They abhorred the careerism of the Keitels and Jodls and the politicization of the Reichenaus and Schoerners. Yet, they did not prevent the war, the atrocities of that war, or the army's involvement in those atrocities based on their inherent illegality or inhumanity. Their sole concern was to limit the army's participation in order to maintain the morale and discipline of the troops. The generals, despite the good intentions of some to circumvent the criminal orders, quickly discovered that their actions were insufficient — the execution of partisans without penalties led to the indiscriminate killing of innocent men, women, and children and wholesale destruction of villages and towns all over Europe.

Additionally, the generals as a group failed to redress Hitler's humiliation of them as military professionals. On one hand, he feted individuals with decorations, promotions, generalfeldmarschall's batons, estates, and special donations, while he regularly heaped scorn and abuse upon them as a group. He fired many who had led the army to its first victories but were unable to provide the same victories in the vastness of the Soviet Union against a numerically superior enemy. Hitler's frequent abusive rages on the "spirit of Zossen," coupled with the firing of those who disagreed with his decisions, had several significant effects. First, Hitler got rid of the more recalcitrant generals and replaced them with more malleable senior officers willing to do his bidding. They also served as warnings to others of what to expect if they too thought about opposing his will; the less strong-willed would, therefore, fall in line. The net effect was the appearance of numerous senior officers who were either committed and loyal to Hitler or who were so sufficiently cowed that they no longer offered opposition.

Two other subgroups of generals require discussion — those who were fired yet maintained a continuing willingness to serve, such as Rundstedt, and those who were part of the military opposition, such as Tresckow. The first subgroup continued to serve Hitler, despite his abuse and humiliation of their fellow officers, because of their narrow view of their professional calling, originating in their original pre–1914 concept of military service and continuing in Seeckt's concept of the unpolitical officer. These generals served the Nazi regime as long as that government served the needs of the "state" and the "nation," and they concerned themselves strictly with the defense of the state and related military matters. Unfortunately, such attitudes prevented these officers from determining when the "government" no longer served the legitimate needs of the state or the nation and blinded them to Hitler's ruthlessness.

Could strong, concerted opposition by the majority of senior officers during the Second World War have made any difference?

The united determination of most of the senior officers in Russia prevented the effective institution of the Commissar Order as originally planned. The senior army officers were also able to obtain the revocation of the October 29, 1939, directive from Himmler that encouraged his SS men and police to have sexual relations with the wives of the soldiers at the front to produce more children. Lieutenant General Groppe was so incensed over this order that he sent a copy to his commander and obtained the support of Witzleben and Leeb among the senior commanders, and even Brauchitsch worked up enough courage to oppose the SS "free love" order based upon the adverse effect it would have on the fighting soldiers. Eventually Himmler was forced to withdraw the order in the face of their strong opposition.[166]

Fest provides this accurate characterization of the general officer corps as a whole during this devastating war:

> It is true, of course, that opposition would have had little more than a delaying effect. This is no excuse, however, for either Brauchitsch or the other commanders. They failed to see that the restoration of the long-lost moral integrity of the army was at stake. Their failure to act seems even more egregious in the light of the unanimous sense of outrage expressed by the officers, of which so much was made following the war. It illustrates not only the widespread awareness of criminal activity but also the broad support that a determined commander who refused to carry out orders would have enjoyed. It is difficult to comprehend why three or more commanding generals could not agree to protest the orders as a body. It has repeatedly been argued that such a gesture would have been pointless, but it must be said that it was never really tried.[167]

Only the few members of the military opposition ever reached the point of trying.

Notes

1. Since my focus is on the attitudes of the German officers and men, I will limit discussion of strategy and military operations to that specifically needed to place the discussion in proper historical context. Furthermore, I will overwhelmingly refer to the war in the Soviet Union after June 1941 since this theater was the major scene of military operations for most of the war — Scandinavia and France were under relatively peaceful occupation except for the anti–Nazi resistance movements and the fighting after June 6, 1944. North Africa was a secondary front from early 1941 through April 1943 when the Afrika Korps surrendered to the Allies, and the German army did not become significantly involved in combat operations in Italy until June 1943 with the Sicily landings, followed by General Bodoglio's overthrow of Mussolini. In Yugoslavia after April 1941, the German army carried on a desperate campaign against both Communist and non–Communist guerrillas that, in many ways, resembled the war in the USSR.

2. Knappe (p. 263) called Schoerner, the commander of Army Group Center in 1945, "a political general and a 'yes man' to Hitler. He was a rarity a high-ranking German officer who was also a Nazi." Model was Hitler's "fireman" in the last two years of the war in Russia, demonstrating an uncanny ability to organize last-minute tactical defenses that slowed Soviet advances sufficiently to allow numerous German units to escape total decimation. Model condemned Paulus's surrender at Stalingrad: "A field-marshal does not become a prisoner. Such a thing is just not possible." At the war's end, he commanded the German forces in the Ruhr pocket and, after giving subordinate commanders authority to surrender their forces at their discretion, he committed suicide, rather than surrender himself and betray his oath to Hitler. Carlo D'Este, "Model," in Barnett, pp. 324–30.

3. Duffy and Ricci, p. 259.

4. General Seigfried Westphal, *The German Army in the West* (London: Cassell and Company, Ltd., 1951), p. 76. Cooper, pp. 184, 187. Ritter, pp. 145, 149. November 5, 1939 and November 23, 1939 entries, Halder, pp. 78, 80, respectively. Hitler quote in Ritter, *German Resistance*, p. 154. Klaus Jürgen-Müller, "Witzleben, et al.," in Barnett, pp. 52–53. Hitler's outbursts of November 5 and 23, 1939, had a secondary effect on Brauchitsch and Halder. They thought that Hitler knew about a planned military coup to overthrow the regime at this time. The supposed plotters would be using the proposed attack on the west as the excuse for the coup, and as support for its opposition from many generals to such an attack. Brauchitsch and Halder hastened to have all documents relating to the prospective plot destroyed, and completely severed

their support from the military opposition. See the next chapter for more. Ritter, *German Resistance,* p. 149.

5. Allen Welsh Dulles, *Germany's Underground* (New York: The Macmillan Company, 1947), p. 60.

6. Fest, *Hitler's Death,* p. 174.

7. April 29, 1940, entry, Hassell, p. 137.

8. Barry A. Leach, "Halder," in Barnett, p. 111. In the intoxicating fervor of victory over the traditional enemy, Halder conveniently forgot that Hitler had rejected the OKH's original plan for the attack on the west and approved Manstein's plan.

9. Groscurth quoted in Reynolds, p. 211. Groscurth would become one of the 90,000 German soldiers taken prisoner after the surrender of Stalingrad in February 1943; he died two months later of typhus in a Soviet POW camp.

10. Brian Bond, "Brauchitsch" in Barnett, pp. 84–85. Hitler personally chose Generaloberst Nikolaus von Falkenhorst to command the invasion force, and he remained in Norway throughout the war as military commander. In the summer of 1946, Falkenhorst was tried by a mixed British-Norwegian court-martial for turning captured British commandos over to the SS for execution. On August 2, 1946, he was found guilty of war crimes and sentenced to death, a sentence that was commuted to life imprisonment. Footnote 1, Wheeler-Bennett, p. 494.

11. Leach, "Halder" in Barnett, p. 120.

12. Warlimont, pp. 49, 244, 252. See also Hitler Speech, November 8, 1935; Hitler Speech to Reichstag, January 30, 1937; and Hitler Proclamation at Party Congress at Nuremberg, September 6, 1938, in Baynes, I, pp. 127, 215, 490–92, respectively; Hitler Speech, Linz, Austria, April 6, 1938, in Domarus, II, p. 1086; and Manstein, pp. 280–81.

13. Hitler quoted in Galante, p. 99. Furthermore, because of his close relationship with Göring and the specialized nature of aerial warfare, Hitler generally allowed his fellow Nazi and *Altekämpfer* to direct air force operations with little overt direction until Göring began showing signs of his inability to do so. Raeder and, later, Admiral Karl Dönitz generally had unhampered control and direction of the Kriegsmarine (navy) since it was very small and Hitler understood little about naval warfare. Guderian (pp. 66–67) relates that in November 1939 he and other generals attended a series of lectures, given by party leaders, including Goebbels and Göring, in Berlin in which they held up the loyalty of the air force and navy but denigrated that of the army, especially the generals. Taking offense at the accusations — although none of the other generals present made any comment — Guderian visited Rundstedt and even Hitler to discuss the problem, and Hitler related his past problems with the generals.

14. Hitler quoted in Galante, p. 97.

15. Hitler quoted in Schlabrendorff, *Secret War,* p. 127. See also similar quotes from Hitler about his generals in Galante, pp. 97, 155–56, and 195.

16. Hitler quoted in Warlimont, pp. 216–17.

17. Others noted Hitler's growing dislike of the army generals; for example, Goebbels: "He is absolutely sick of the generals. He can't imagine anything better than having nothing to do with them. His opinion of them is devastating.... All generals lie, he says; all generals are disloyal; all generals are opposed to National Socialism; all generals are reactionaries...." May 9, 1943, entry, Goebbels' diary, quoted in Warlimont, p. 313.

18. Görlitz, ed., pp. 107–10. Keitel Statement III, "The Origins of the Directive of the Supreme Commander of the Armed Forces," September 15, 1945; and Keitel Statement IV, "The Position and Powers of the Chief of OKW," October 9, 1945; NCA, VIII, pp. 669–72, 672, respectively. See Halder and Warlimont to see how this procedure worked in practice.

19. Heusinger quoted in Galante, p. 144.

20. Halder, p. 670.

21. Hitler Directive, January 21, 1945, in Cooper, p. 541.

22. Warlimont, p. 57. See also Galante, pp. 129, 155–56, 195, for further views of Hitler on the "Prussian" generals and General Staff.

23. Cooper, p. 243. Richard Lamb, "Kluge," in Barnett, p. 404. Peter Hoffman, *Stauffenberg: A Family History. 1905–1944* (New York: Cambridge University Press, 1995), p. 185. Fabian von Schlabrendorff, *They Almost Killed Hitler* (New York: The Macmillan Company, 1947), p. 40. May 9, 1943, entry, Diary of Captain Hermann Kaiser, Ludwig Kaiser, "The Goerdeler Movement 1942–1944," MS #B-285, December 20, 1950, p. 40, in MS # B-285, et al. In September 1939, Hitler revived the Iron Cross for bravery and created a new grade, the Ritterkreuz (Knight's Cross) with three ascending grades to bridge the gap between the Iron Cross (First Class) and the Grand Cross as Germany's highest military decoration. The decoration was originally awarded for combat bravery of the highest order, but "[by spring 1944 the award] ceremony had lost any personal significance now that hundreds of people wore the decoration." Louis L. Snyder, *Encyclopedia of the Third Reich* (New York: Paragon House, 1989), p. 297. Quote from General Frido von Senger und Etterlin, *Neither Fear nor Hope* (New York: E. P. Dutton & Co., Inc., 1964), p. 241.

24. March 6, 1943, entry, Hassell, p. 286.

25. Schlabrendorff, *Secret War,* pp. 146-47.

26. Schlarendorff, *Killed Hitler,* p. 40.

27. April 6, 1943, entry, Kaiser, MS # B-285, p. 37, in Detwiler, et al.

28. Wagner quoted in Cooper, p. 245.

29. Fromm quoted, November 13, 1942, entry, Hassell, p. 276.

30. Görlitz, ed., pp. 167–68. Warlimont, p. 48.

31. April 20, 1943, entry, Hassell, p. 298.

32. Senger, p. 126.

33. For Barbarossa, Hitler committed virtually all of his ground forces: 3,050,000 men divided into 153 divisions (17 of 21 panzer divisions with 3,350 tanks, all 13 motorized divisions, and almost all of the artillery with 7,146 guns). Until the 1922 year group was called up in November 1941, the German Army had only 385,000 troops in reserve. Between June 22, 1941, and April 30, 1942, the army suffered 1,167, 835 killed or wounded. Noakes and Pridham, II, p. 817.

34. Tresckow, June 21, 1941, quoted in Stahlberg, p. 157. See also Knappe, pp. 186–87. War games in the autumn of 1940 had highlighted the extreme logistical problems of a major offensive in the vastness of western Russia. The initial front of 1,300 miles would quickly expand, like a funnel, to 2,500 miles. The invasion force required 500,000 horses — proof of the inadequate motorization and mechanization of the German Army in 1940–41. Furthermore, the Soviet Union had few paved roads, and many of the unpaved roads they had would quickly turn to mud in the spring and autumn rains. Finally, the Soviet Union had a different gauge railroad that required the unloading of supplies at the border and then their reloading onto eastbound trains. Bond, "Brauchitsch," in Barnett, p. 87.

35. July 26, 1941, entry, Halder, p. 487. Bock told Keitel that he completely disagreed with this strategy. July 25 and July 26, 1941, entries, Bock, pp. 262–63.

36. The German Army had unfortunately become involved in these secondary campaigns just prior to Operation Barbarossa. In February 1941, Hitler had made treaties with the pro–Nazi regimes in Hungary, Rumania, and Yugoslavia to secure his southern flank. An anti–German, royalist faction in Belgrade overthrew the pro–Nazi regent and established a young King Peter on the throne. Enraged, Hitler ordered the army to crush the Yugoslav revolt, crucially delaying the attack on the USSR from April until June and creating a vicious guerrilla war in the Balkans. Meanwhile, earlier in February, Hitler had sent one of his best panzer generals Erwin Rommel and the Afrika Korps to North Africa to assist the Italian army which had suffered a series of defeats by the British Eighth Army. For 18 months, Rommel's forces, undermanned, undersupplied, and underequipped, matched wits with the numerically superior but poorly led British forces in a seesaw tank war between Libya and Egypt until placed on the defensive by a new British general, Bernard Montgomery, at El Alamein in November 1942.

37. Halder, p. 515. Stahlberg, p. 172.

38. Document 594, Hitler Order to Army Group Center, December 16, 1941, in Noakes and Pridham, II, pp. 827–28. December 20, 1941, December 21, 1941, and January 2, 1942, entries, Halder, pp. 593, 594, and 598, respectively. Görlitz, ed., p. 166. Wheeler-Bennett, pp. 520–23. After the British breakthrough at El Alamein in November 1942, Rommel also faced a "no retreat" order from Hitler, and, at first, obeyed it, despite the entreaties of General Wilhelm Ritter von Thoma. Wanting to save his troops, Thoma stated, "Hitler's order is a piece of unparalleled madness. I can't go along with this any longer," and, soon afterwards, surrendered to Montgomery. Rommel wrote in his diary, "I finally compelled myself to take this decision because I myself have always demanded unconditional obedience from my soldiers and I therefore wished to accept this principle for myself." However, he quickly reversed himself and ordered the retreat. Hitler reluctantly confirmed Rommel's action. Shirer, *Third Reich*, p. 1203.

39. Manstein, pp. 276, 279.

40. December 19, 1941, entry, Halder, pp. 592–93. Hitler commented, "Anyone can do the little job of directing operations in war. The task of the Commander-in-Chief is to educate the Army to be National-Socialist. I do not know any Army generals [who] can do this as I want it done. I have therefore decided to take over command of the Army myself." Quoted from Halder's memoirs in Warlimont, p. 214. Three generalfeldmarschalls and five generalobersts were executed or committed suicide as a result of the failed July 20, 1944, plot. One generalfeldmarschall was taken prisoner, and three were killed or died during the war. Additionally, of the remaining generalobersts, five died in combat. Of the general officers listed in 1944, about 500 did not return from the war: most were killed or recorded as missing in action, and about 20 were executed. Only one generalfeldmarschall and three generalobersts made it through the war in their positions. Footnote, Shirer, *Third Reich*, p. 1180. Westphal, pp. 63–64.

41. Warlimont, pp. 222–23. Görlitz, ed., pp. 162, 166–67. Shirer, *Third Reich*, pp. 1132–34. While Leeb remained in permanent retirement for the rest of the war, Rundstedt was recalled and fired twice more before the war's end. Guderian was recalled to duty as Inspector General of Panzer Troops and later replaced Zeitzler as Army Chief of Staff on July 21, 1944. Bock had been a staunch supporter of Hitler and often closed his orders with "Long live the Führer!" He closed a farewell order to his troops with "you have done your duty and I am certain that you will gladly fulfill all further tasks which the *Führer* gives you." Before Hitler fired Bock, the general tried to assure his Führer that his concern about disobedience and disloyalty

among the senior officers was unfounded. August 5, 1941, entry, pp. 273–74; October 2,1939, entry, p. 68; and June 25, 1942, entry, p. 506, respectively; in Bock.

42. Senger, p. 60.

43. Hitler quoted in Galante, pp. 133–34.

44. Hoepner quoted in Zwygart, pp. 16–17.

45. Footnote, Shirer, *Third Reich*, p. 1180.

46. By February 1942, German casualties in the USSR numbered 1,005,636 men — 31 percent of the original Barbarossa forces: 202,251 killed; 725,643 wounded, including 112,627 from frostbite; and 46,511 missing, not including Rumanian, Hungarian, or Italian losses. Shirer, *Third Reich*, p. 1138.

47. Stahlberg, p. 188. Galante, p. 129.

48. December 20, 1942, entry, Hassell, p. 277.

49. Letter from son (Major) Hans Dieter, February 15, 1942, in March 3, 1942, entry, Hassell, p. 244.

50. Görlitz, ed., p. 183. Hitler also assumed control of the army's Personnel Branch through his army adjutant, enabling him to directly influence all senior officer assignments. Previously, Halder's authority over this function had enabled him to place anti-Hitler generals into important positions where they might be helpful if and when a coup did occur. Halder went into retirement and was arrested after the July 20, 1944, plot. He and numerous other well-known internees were moved through a number of concentration camps until they were liberated by American soldiers at Dachau in late April 1945. Shirer characterized Zeitzler "as little more than the Führer's office boy until [he too was fired on July 20, 1944]." *Third Reich*, p. 1200. The editors of *The Halder War Diary* (p. 671) described Zeitzler as "an officer known for his ambition and dedication. Zeitzler had a reputation for brutality toward subordinates and subservience to superiors. He was a useful representative of the new order." Galante (p. 157) wrote that Zeitzler "was not so much an anti–Nazi as a non–Nazi — a political [and] not particularly [an] intellectual.... He was a plain-spoken but essentially dutiful officer." While on Rundstedt's staff, he would end memoranda to army commanders with the phrase, "Heil, Hitler!" Footnote 1, Galante, p. 157. Following his appointment, Zeitzler, on September 24, 1942, issued an order to require "...every staff officer ... [to] believe in the Führer and his method of command. He must on every occasion radiate this confidence to his subordinates and those around him." Zeitzler quoted in Warlimont, p. 260.

51. Stahlberg, p. 202.

52. Stahlberg, p. 220. See also Knappe, p. 225, for similar comments.

53. Of the original 300,000 soldiers, about 140,000 wounded were flown out before the Soviets captured the airfields. About 90,000 officers and men were captured, including 22 German and two Rumanian generals, which meant about 70,000 Germans died during the siege. By July 1943, only 15,000, POWs, were left alive because of the rampant progress of disease among them. Of those remaining, only 6,000, including Paulus, were eventually returned to Germany in 1950. Uli Haller, ed., *Lieutenant General Karl Strecker: The Life and Thought of a German Military Man* (Westport, CT: Praeger Publishers, 1994), p. 54. The German army suffered a similar defeat in North Africa. Pushed on both flanks, Rommel's Afrika Korps retreated to Tunisia. Although it inflicted a stunning tactical defeat on the American forces at Kasserine Pass, Generaloberst Hans Jürgen von Arnim (Hitler had recalled Rommel back to Europe) surrendered 250,000 Axis troops to the Allies in May 1943 because Hitler refused to evacuate them and ordered Arnim to fight to the last man. Snyder, p. 4.

54. Hitler quoted in Shirer, *Third Reich*, p. 1216.

55. Hitler quoted in Warlimont, pp. 305–6.

56. Excerpt from letter #12, *Last Letters from Stalingrad* (New York: William Morrow and Company, 1962), pp. 50–51. Goebbels originally intended to publish the letters, found in a pouch on the last airplane out of the besieged city, for propaganda purposes but hid them after their contents were analyzed (p. 16). We read similar feelings in Senger, pp. 74–76. He had commanded a unit in the German column that attempted to reach the beleaguered Sixth Army in Stalingrad. It came within 40 miles of breaching the Soviet lines before it was forced to retreat, exhausted from constant fighting, severe losses in men and equipment, and the subzero temperatures.

57. Knappe, p. 226.

58. Galante, p. 193.

59. Falkenhausen, MS # B-289, p. 33, in Detwiler, et al.

60. Stauffenberg Letter to Paulus, June 12, 1942, in Kramarz, p. 108.

61. Stauffenberg, quoted in Kramarz, p. 173.

62. Warlimont, p. 420. Clark, p. 399. Bartov, *Eastern Front*, p. 75. Knappe, pp. 255–56.

63. Helmut J. Schmeller, *Hitler and Keitel: An Investigation of the Influence of Party Ideology on the High Command of the Armed Forces in Germany Between 1938 and 1945* (Hays, KS: Fort Hays Kansas State College, 1970), pp. 42–45.

64. Seydlitz was sentenced to death in absentia, and his wife was forced to divorce him. Haller, pp. 63–69. Gill, pp. 222–23.

65. Stahlberg, p. 326.

66. Stahlberg, pp. 330–31. Interestingly, Manstein does not mention this incident in his memoirs.

67. Rundstedt quoted in Mason, pp. 148–49.

68. November 26, 1942, entry, Hassell, p. 273.

69. General Hans Speidel, "Background for 20 Jul 44 Ideas and Preparations for Genfldm Rommel

for an Independent Termination of the War in the West and for Plotting an End to Nazi Despotism," MS # B-721, p. 12, in Detwiler, et al.

70. Earl F. Ziemke, "Rundstedt," in Barnett, p. 201.

71. Metalman, p. 19.

72. Knappe, pp. 183–84.

73. For example, the German army had 89,075 officers in active units at the beginning of the war. The officer corps reached a peak level of 246,543 on September 1, 1943. From September 1, 1939, through January 31, 1945, the German army suffered 203,886 officer casualties. Bartov, *Eastern Front*, p. 41.

74. Bartov, *Eastern Front*, pp. 69–74.

75. Document 101-PS, Bormann Letter to Rosenberg, January 17, 1942, p. 161; and Document 117-PS, Bormann Letter to Keitel, January 28, 1939, pp. 171–72, in *NCA*, III.

76. Letters to wife and parents, August 3, 1941, pp. 122–23; and letters to wife, August 15, 1941, pp. 125–26, Fuchs.

77. Conversation with German officer, Autumn 1943, Metalman, p. 113.

78. July 16, 1941, entry, p. 83; July 21, 1941, entry, pp. 84–85; October 13, 1941, entry, p. 114; October 15, 1941, entry, p. 115, Wilhelm Prueller, *Diary of a German Soldier* (New York: Coward-McAnn, Inc., 1963).

79. October 8, 1939, entry, Prueller, pp. 46–47. See also entries for December 19, 1939, pp. 49–50; and April 9, 1940, p. 50. See also letter to wife, November 9, 1940, Fuchs, p. 80; and Mellenthin, pp. 349–51.

80. "The Führer Speaks," December 1942, Prueller, p. 160.

81. Letter to father, August 4, 1941, Fuchs, p. 124. See also "Thoughts About Our Battle," September 1943, Prueller, pp. 163–67.

82. Commander's speech, Christmas Eve, 1941, p. 37; and Chaplain's service, 1942, pp. 71–72, Metalman.

83. Metalman, p. 206.

84. Lieutenant General Edgar Roehricht and Lieutenant General Siegfried Heinrici in B[asil] H. Liddell-Hart, *The German Generals Talk* (New York: William Morrow & Co., 1948), p. 257.

85. May 16, 1940, and March 2, 1941, entries, Prueller, pp. 51, 58, respectively.

86. Letter to mother, February 28, 1940, Fuchs, p. 53.

87. Letter to father, September 3, 1941, Fuchs, p. 133.

88. Letter to Mitzi Trunka, February 23, 1942, Prueller, p. 144.

89. Stahlberg, pp. 161–62.

90. These "feelings" begin to appear in the entries, starting about October 25, 1941. Prueller, p. 116. See October 15, 1941, entry, Bock, p. 333.

91. Metalman, p. 151.

92. For details, see Bartov *The Eastern Front* and *Hitler's Army*; Metalman; and Guy Sajer, *The Forgotten Soldier: The Classic WWII Autobiography* (Washington, DC: Brassey's [US], Inc., 1990).

93. Bartov, *Eastern Front*, pp. 27–35. Metalman, p. 110.

94. Edward A. Shils and Morris Janowitz, "Cohesion and Disintegration in the Wehrmacht," in Lerner, pp. 367–415. Originally published in *Public Opinion Quarterly* (Summer 1948). See also Bartov, *Eastern Front* and *Hitler's Army*; and Stephen G. Fritz, Frontsoldaten*: The German Soldier in World War II* (Lexington, KY: The University of Kentucky Press, 1995).

95. As I mentioned in the Introduction, most of the vast number of works on the German army in World War II — memoirs, unit and official histories, and secondary works — deal with overall military strategy, operations, tactics, and weaponry with virtually no mention of the army's perpetration of war crimes. One interesting feature of several of the primary sources that I used is that they readily described "war crimes" committed by enemy forces against German soldiers. Prueller relates atrocities against German soldiers in Poland, France, and the Soviet Union (September 12, 1939, entry, p. 25; September 19, 1939, p. 31; June 10, 1940, entry, p. 53; and July 1, 1941, p. 69). Stahlberg (p. 179) wrote that during the late fall 1941 fighting the Russians did not respect the red crosses on German ambulances. Manstein (pp. 180–81, 186) and June 30, 1941, entry, Bock (p. 233) also reported that in the first months of Barbarossa, Soviet soldiers mutilated the bodies of German wounded and would pretend to be wounded and then fire on German troops after they had passed. Shirer relates the story of O.W. (perhaps a German soldier back from the front) who reported "he'd seen some of the horribly mutilated bodies of Germans killed by Poles." September 9, 1939, entry, *Berlin Diary*, p. 155.

96. September 10, 1939, entry, Halder, pp. 52–53. Duffy and Ricci, p. 93. Stahlberg (pp. 121–25) also reported an incident in which SS guards had shot "many" Polish POWs and detained civilians, "trying to escape," and had done nothing to help the sick. Although Stahlberg reported the incident, apparently nothing was done to the SS guards for their actions. Shirer relates that O.W. described the summary court-martial and execution of Polish civilians — men, women, and boys — as *franc-tireurs* by German soldiers. He did not (perhaps could not) specify whether or not the "soldiers" were regular army or SS. September 9, 1939, entry, *Berlin Diary*, p. 155. *Franc-tireurs* is the term given to French guerrillas who harassed the invading German army during the Franco-Prussian War, 1870–71, and during World War I.

97. Giziowski, pp. 183–85; footnote 50, p. 219.

98. The portion of Poland allotted to Germany by the German-Soviet Nonaggression Pact was further divided into two sections. The western section of mixed German-Polish inhabitants was formally annexed to Germany: its Polish inhabitants were forcibly removed to the eastern section, and the General Government and ethnic Germans were resettled in the evacuated areas. The army's concern about the misery caused by this mass evacuation was limited to the difficulty of taking an accurate census. This census problem precluded the systematic use of Jewish labor which presented an immediate danger of upheavals to the economy. "The War Economy of Poland, 1939–40" in Nora Levin, *The Holocaust: The Destruction of European Jewry 1933–1945* (New York: Schocken Books, 1973), p. 160. Hans Frank headed the civil administration of the General Government, and a senior army officer directed the military administration, Oberstbefehlshaber Ost (Obost) (High Command East), with authority over only purely military matters and the small number of occupation troops. After the war Frank was tried, found guilty of war crimes, and executed.

99. Affidavit A, Maj. Gen. Erwin Lahousen (Chief, Abwehr Section 2), Jan 21, 1946, *NCA*, VIII, p. 590. Canaris quoted in Wheeler-Bennett, pp. 461–62.

100. Stieff quoted in Schlabrendorff, *Secret War*, pp. 184–85.

101. Levin, pp. 155–56. Halder noted in his dairy (September 19, 1939, entry, p. 57), "Army insists that 'housecleaning' be deferred until army has withdrawn and the country has been turned over to civil administration."

102. Blaskowitz was a deeply religious man but also, like other German officers, recognized Hitler's positive achievements. He had commanded the troops that occupied "rump" Czechoslovakia in March 1939 and served as the first Reichs Protector for three weeks. He tried to rule with an even hand to the point of calling a court-martial to review atrocities committed by an SS regiment. In the Polish campaign Blaskowitz directed the siege and bombardment of Warsaw that resulted in its capitulation. He also put together the victory celebration that Hitler attended after the capture of the city, but received severe criticism from Hitler because Hitler wanted a simple lunch with the troops, instead of the elaborate meal Blaskowitz had prepared. During the war Blaskowitz was recalled to active duty several times for relatively short periods of time. After the war he was indicted as a minor war criminal. However, hours before his trial on February 5, 1948, he either committed suicide or was murdered by SS prisoners kept in the same prison. Giziowski, pp. 1–2, 103, 132, 152–66.

103. December 25, 1939, entry, Hassell, p. 100. Document 655, Memorandum from Blaskowitz to Brauchitsch, February 6, 1940, in Pridham and Noakes, II, pp. 938–39. Blaskowitz's February 1940 memo included a report of an SS officer living with a Jewish actress in Warsaw — a clear case of *Rassenschande* (race crime) that surely, if reported, would result in the expulsion of the officer from the SS — as a minimum. By including this incident in the report, Blaskowitz may have also intended to disgrace the SS in Poland as well as to expose their atrocities. Raul Hilberg, *The Destruction of the European Jews* (New York: Harper Torchbooks, 1961), p. 127.

104. Document 656, November 18, 1939, entry, Diary of Major Engel, in Noakes and Pridham, II, pp. 940–41.

105. The January 30, 1940, issue of the *New York Times*, p. 1, has the subheadline "Even Gen. Blaskowitz Balks at Tactics Held Aimed at Virtual 'Racial Extermination'...." under the headline "Nazis Admit 'Firm' Polish Policy; Cardinal Sees National 'Disaster.'" See also Otto D. Tolischer, "Polish Row Ended by Nazis and Army," December 20, 1939, p. 12; and "Poland Protests German 'Horrors,'" January 30, 1940; *New York Times*, pp. 8–9.

106. Giziowski, pp. 267–68.

107. Groscurth quoted in Giziowski, p. 162.

108. Letter to Cecile von Keudell, December 18, 1939, Ferdinand von Senger und Etterlin and Stefan von Senger und Etterlin, "Senger," in Barnett, p. 381.

109. Stahlberg, pp. 148–49.

110. Brauchitsch order, December 21, 1939, Giziowski, p. 213.

111. Document 657, Kuechler Order, August 20, 1940, in Noakes and Pridham, II, p. 941.

112. Wagner quote (italics in original), October 18, 1939, entry, Halder, p. 73.

113. Stahlberg, p. 131.

114. Groppe, "Events, as Experienced by an Old Soldier during the Nazi Period 1933–1945," MS # B-397, November 9, 1945, pp. 5–6, in Detwiler, et al.

115. Westphal, p. 85.

116. Bartov, *Eastern Front*, p. 110.

117. The French had used Black troops from their African colonies on the Western Front during World War I also and, most humiliatingly for the Germans, during the 1923 occupation of the Ruhr. Manstein (p. 135) commented about the French army fighting at the Somme in early June 1940: "The enemy fought bravely — the negroes with their characteristic bloodthirstiness and contempt for human life,...."

118. Liddell-Hart (p. 22) gives Blomberg the credit for the more civilized conduct of the German army in World War II compared to World War I, at least in the west, despite the addition of "Nazism" or "Prussianism," in contrast to the behavior

of the Gestapo and the SS. Since his focus is on purely *military* aspects, Liddell-Hart apparently chose to ignore the commitment of numerous atrocities by the German occupation forces in Belgium, France, and The Netherlands, such as shooting civilian hostages, plundering art treasures, and deporting their citizens as slave laborers and Jews to the death camps.

119. For text of the Commissar Order, see Document NO-3414, Extract from Operational Order No. 8, July 17, 1941, *Trial of War Criminals Before the Nuernberg Military Tribunals Under Control Council Law No. 10, October 1946–April 1949* (Washington, DC: US Government Printing Office, 1949–53), IV, pp. 123–32.

120. Warlimont, p. 161. Halder, pp. 339, 345–46. See Document C-50, Court-Martial Order, May 13, 1941, *NCA*, VI, pp. 873–74. These orders were formally published by OKW on June 6 and May 13, respectively.

121. Görlitz, ed., p. 136. May 6, 1941, entry, Halder, p. 384.

122. Görlitz, ed., p. 144.

123. Warlimont, p. 162. Interestingly, Bock's brief entry for March 30, 1941 (pp. 206–7), does not mention Hitler's directions on the treatment of political commissars.

124. Wheeler-Bennett, p. 513.

125. Görlitz, ed., pp. 136–37.

126. Görlitz, p. 252.

127. June 16, 1941, entry, Hassell, p. 199.

128. Tresckow quoted in Robert Weldon Whalen, *Assassinating Hitler: Ethics and Resistance in Nazi Germany* (London: Associated University Press, Inc., 1993), p. 96.

129. Stahlberg, p. 159.

130. Schlabrendorff, *Secret War*, p. 137.

131. Hoffman, *German Resistance*, pp. 267–68.

132. Stahlberg, pp. 159–60. Guderian, p. 126. Warlimont, pp. 167, 170–71; footnote 47, p. 609. Haller, ed., pp. 42–43. July 13, 1941, entry, Hassell, p. 202. To ameliorate the effect of the Commissar Order, the army field commanders used an order Brauchitsch promulgated on May 24, 1941, which directed them to maintain discipline of the troops to ensure a German victory. Footnote 45, Warlimont, p. 609.

133. Alexander Dallin, *German Rule in Russia 1941–1945: A Study in Occupation Policies* (Boulder, CO: Westview Press, 1981), pp. 32–34; footnote 1, p. 3. Bock quoted in Fest, *Hitler's Death*, pp. 175, 177.

134. Hoffman, *German Resistance*, pp. 167–68.

135. Manstein, pp. 179–80, 255. In 1949, Manstein was tried by a British court-martial for war crimes. Although he was acquitted of any direct breaches of the Geneva Convention and other laws of war, he was found guilty of a number of other "minor offenses." Field Marshal Lord Carver, "Manstein," in Barnett, p. 231. The Jurisdiction Order received a similar reception among many senior officers. Senger, p. 99.

136. Warlimont, pp. 170–71. A December 21, 1941, report from Heinrich "Gestapo" Müller to General Edward Wagner, Army Quartermaster General, gave a figure of 22,000 Soviet soldiers, Jews and non–Jews who had been so selected; about 16,000 of them had been executed by then. Later figures are not available. Hilberg, pp. 219–24. See Appendix B on German treatment of Soviet POWs.

137. Warlimont, pp. 170–71; footnote 557, p. 608. Manstein, p. 180. I present more about the impact of German occupation policies throughout this section and in Appendix B.

138. I present more about the impact of German occupation policies throughout this section as well as in Appendix B.

139. Hoepner quoted in Hamerow, pp. 282–83.

140. Matthew Cooper, *The Nazi War Against Soviet Partisans 1941–1944* (New York: Stein and Day, 1979), p. 21. See also Müller, "Stülpnagel, et al.," in Barnett, pp. 57–58.

141. Hamerow, p. 283.

142. Document 502-PS, Directives for the Commander of the Security Police and of the Security Service, July 17, 1941, *NCA*, III, pp. 422–24.

143. Warlimont, pp. 150–60. OKW Directive for Special Areas, Case Barbarossa, March 13, 1941, Appendix 1, Cooper, *Nazi War*, pp. 163–65. In occupied Russia, overall authority was divided among the OKH (area from the front lines to a depth of 100 miles westward), the Ostministerium (East Ministry) under Nazi ideologue Alfred Rosenberg (civil government and general occupation policies), and the SS and SD (overall police and security duties outside the OKH area, including antipartisan operations). However, the OKH retained military jurisdiction over the Waffen SS units fighting as part of the three operational army groups and security forces within the operational areas. Cooper, *Nazi War*, pp. 39–40.

144. Document 3257-PS, Letter to General Thomas, December 2, 1941, *NCA*, V, p. 995. Document L-180, Report of Action-Group A to October 15, 1941, October 31, 1941, *NCA*, VII, pp. 984, 993. Document 818, Report from *Einsatzgruppe C* (Ukraine), November 3, 1941, Noakes and Pridham, II, pp. 1095–96. Allen, p. 97. Testimony of Erich Heidborn, Ernst Klee, Willi Dressen, and Volker Ries, *"The Good Old Days": The Holocaust as Seen by Its Perpetrators and Bystanders* (New York: The Free Press, 1988), pp. 118, 127. Klee, et al. (pp. 26, 30), has a number of photographs, taken by German soldiers, that show other soldiers watching as Lithuanians beat Jews to death in a "spontaneous action" in Kovno (Kaunas). Soldiers also wrote home about the shootings and beatings of Jews in the east. Levin, pp. 260–61.

145. Report of Franz Walter Stahlecker, October 15, 1941, Hilberg, p. 196.

146. OKH Directive, "Handling of War Enemy Civilians and Russian Prisoners of War," July 25, 1941, Dallin, p. 75. Conversation between Hitler and Jodl, December 1, 1942, Warlimont, pp. 288–92. "Collective action" meant hanging or shooting innocent civilians and destroying their village, which turned the local populations against the German occupation forces throughout Europe. In occupied Russia, they were particularly detrimental because many of the indigenous nationalities were anti–Stalinist in 1941. They initially welcomed the advancing German army, and turned against it only when German occupation policies, driven by Nazi ideology, turned the occupation into a nightmare of terror. Ironically, Mellenthin blamed the German civil authorities of the Ostministerium for turning the local populations against the Germans. Mellanthin, pp. 255–57, Knappe, p. 195, and Guderian, p. 156. During the Nazi occupation of the western USSR, the German army destroyed or severely damaged 1,710 cities, more than 70,000 villages and hamlets, and 6,000,000 buildings, and made about 25,000,000 persons homeless. International Military Tribunal (IMT) Indictment, *NCA*, I, p. 46. Alexander Werth described the devastated condition of several Soviet towns and cities which the German army, not the security forces, had essentially destroyed and depopulated through terror, executions, and mass deportations of thousands of people, including women and children, for slave labor in Germany. *Russia at War 1941–1945* (New York: Avon Books, 1965), pp. 200, 556–59, 579, 631–32. In addition, the German army recruited some 800,000 non–Russians from the peoples of the Caucasus, the Cossacks, Uzbeks, and anti–Soviet POWs into an Army of National Liberation, nominally commanded by ex–Soviet General Alexander Vlassov. Most of these men were killed in fighting the Red Army, or, on Stalin's orders, including Vlassov, after they were abandoned by the Germans at the war's end and forcibly repatriated to the USSR. Wheeler-Bennett, p. 613.

147. Hamerow, p. 298.

148. Order of Army Group South Rear Area/Section VII, August 16, 1941, Levin, p. 258. See Christopher Browning, "Wehrmacht Reprisal Policy and the Murder of the Male Jews in Serbia," in Browning, *Fateful Months Essays on the Emergence of the Final Solution* (New York: Holes & Meier, 1991), pp. 39–101, for an excellent essay on the development of this policy in Serbia. The antipartisan war in Yugoslavia was just as brutal as, if not more brutal than, that in western Russia. See Paul N. Hehn, *The German Struggle Against Yugoslav Guerrillas in World War II* (Boulder, CO: East European Quarterly, 1979) for a brief treatment of this struggle. According to Hehn (p. 3), many German soldiers preferred duty in Russia to Yugoslavia. After the war, General Wilhelm List, commander of the Balkans from June to October 1941, was tried and convicted of war crimes in Yugoslavia and sentenced to life imprisonment but was later pardoned and released in December 1952.

149. SS Obergruppenführer and General of the Waffen SS, Erich von dem Bach-Zelewski, commander of German antipartisan forces in occupied Russia, testified at Nuremberg, "Today it is clear to me that anti–Partisan warfare gradually became an excuse for the systematic annihilation of Jewry and Slavism." Heusinger reiterated Zelewski's statement. Quoted in Allen, pp. 100–2. After Marshal Pietro Bodoglio overthrew Mussolini in July 1943, Italy joined the anti–Nazi coalition, and Hitler extended the "collective action" practices to Italian partisans. Document UK-66, Kesselring Directive, "Combating of Partisans," July 14, 1944; and Area Headquarters Covolo (Italy) Directive, July 11, 1944, *NCA*, VIII, pp. 576–78, 582, respectively. The eight volumes of *NCA* contain additional documents — too many to list here — that verify the brutal and criminal policies of the army toward partisans and local inhabitants for helping them. See Allen, p. 94, for an eyewitness account of one such execution in occupied Russia.

150. Rundstedt Speech to Commanders, December 8, 1941; 11th Army Order from General von Manstein, November 20, 1941, and Reichenau Order, October 10, 1941, Cooper, *Nazi War*, pp. 77, 171–72, respectively. (Karl Heinrich) Stülpnagel Order, August 21, 1941, Müller, "Witzleben, et al.," in Barnett, pp. 57–58. Hitler liked Reichenau's order so much he had the OKH reissue it to all army commands in the east.

151. For example, by the end of 1941, Soviet partisan forces numbered only about 30,000 active irregulars over a territory of 850,000 square miles. By the end of 1942, that number had increased to 130,000 partisans in European Russia: 57,000 in Belorussia; 44,000 in central Russia; and 30,000 dispersed throughout the Baltic states, the Ukraine, the Crimea, and the Caucasus. This drastic increase resulted from mounting control and logistical support of the partisan movement from the central government in Moscow and from the Germans' brutal and inhumane treatment of the indigenous populations who provided the increasing numbers of recruits. Cooper, *Nazi War*, pp. 18, 59.

152. Metalman, p. 67. Schlabrendorff, *Secret War*, pp. 175–76. Rundstedt Order, Combating Anti-Reich Elements, September 24, 1941, Klee, et al., p. 116.

153. Bartov, *Eastern Front*, p. 115. Bartov (pp. 27–35) also examined the somewhat incomplete legal records of the units he discusses. They revealed that German soldiers in the Soviet Union

were normally punished for such crimes as desertion, cowardice in the face of the enemy, and self-inflicted wounds to avoid combat but not for plundering, looting, rape, or shooting of civilians, crimes for which they *were* generally punished in the west.

154. Senger, pp. 346–47.

155. Document 878-PS, Keitel Memorandum, "Jews in the Newly Occupied Eastern Territories," September 12, 1941, *NCA*, III, p. 636.

156. Busch quoted in Hoffman, *German Resistance*, p. 269.

157. Belgium and northern France: General Alexander von Falkenhausen: active anti–Hitler conspirator, arrested by the Gestapo after July 20, 1944; subsequently freed, then rearrested by the Allies for war crimes in western Europe; sentenced to 12 years' imprisonment for executing hostages and deporting Jews but soon released. Occupied France: General Otto von Stülpnagel, October 1940–February 1942: had French hostages executed, and deported French Jews to the east; General Karl Heinrich von Stülpnagel, February 1942–July 1944: active anti–Hitler conspirator, also had hostages executed and Jews deported. He tried to kill himself on the way to Berlin on July 21, 1944. He failed and was tried by the People's Court and hanged in Berlin on August 30, 1944. Stülpnagel may have inadvertently implicated Rommel in the plot while recovering from his self-inflicted wounds. Levin, p. 441. Snyder, pp. 89, 338–39.

158. Affidavit C, Dieter Wisliceny, November 29, 1945, *NCA*, VIII, pp. 612–13. Document 2194-PS, Reich Defense Law, September 4, 1938, *NCA*, IV, p. 847. Military Commander Ostland to Reich Commissioner Ostland, November 20, 1941, Hilberg, pp. 233, 314, 446.

159. Hilberg, pp. 237, 332–45.

160. Document 498-PS, Führer "Commando" Order, October 18, 1942, pp. 416–17; Document 508-PS, Teletype "Commando Raid" in Norway, November 21, 1942, pp. 432–33; Document 531-PS, "Treatment of Commando Men" (a reinforcement of the original order), June 23, 1944, pp. 435–37; *NCA*, III. General Anton Dostler was tried, convicted and executed in October 1945 for the execution of 15 Allied commandos in northern Italy in March 1944. Senger, pp. 343–45. Document 2610-PS, Deposition of Major Frederick W. Roche, US Army, *NCA*, IV, pp. 330–32.

161. Rosenberg Memorandum, June 12, 1944, Shirer, *Third Reich*, p. 1235. Document 031-PS, "Evacuation of Youths from Territory of Army Group Center," June 12, 1944, *NCA*, III, p. 71. Document 1162-PS, Order of Army Occupation Forces in the Netherlands, no date, *NCA*, III, p. 817. Document 580-PS, "Recruiting of Civilian Workers from the Occupied Eastern Territories," March 6, 1942, *NCA*, Supplement A, p. 349. Other documents in *NCA* report the roundup of civilians by the army in the occupied territories and their deportation to Germany as slave laborers.

162. Shirer, *Third Reich*, p. 1248. Görlitz, ed., p. 153.

163. The Nazi regime created Einsatzstab (Special Staff) Rosenberg for this purpose and enlisted the help of the army to seize, protect, and transport art treasures from occupied territories to Germany. For example, Document 035-PS, October 26, 1943, pp. 76–77; Document 041-PS, October 3, 1942, pp. 80–82; Document 149-PS, April 7, 1942, p. 191; and Document 1107-PS, May 7, 1944, pp. 789–90, *NCA*, III.

164. Affidavit A, Major General Erwin Lahousen, January 21, 1946, *NCA*, VIII, p. 593.

165. For example, see August 18, 1941, entry, Hassell, p. 207; and Metalman, p. 168.

166. Groppe, pp. 9–14, MS # B-397, in Detwiler, et al. The order is reprinted on pages 7–9 of this manuscript. Neither Keitel nor Himmler forgot Groppe's affront to the Reichsführer SS. In January 1940, Keitel tried to summarily discharge Groppe from the army, but Leeb directly intervened to prevent such drastic action at this time. However, Keitel did formally discharge Groppe from active service by a letter, dated May 3, 1942, and prohibited him from wearing his uniform. After July 20, 1944, Groppe was arrested by the Gestapo on Himmler's personal orders and imprisoned in various prisons until he was liberated by American troops, along with relatives of Stülpnagel, Fellgeibel, Kluge, Hoepner, and Hassell, and with Hans Speidel.

167. Fest, *Hitler's Death*, p. 178.

7

The Military Opposition During the War, 1939–1945

In the previous chapter I reviewed how the German soldiers, officers and enlisted, generally followed their oath to Hitler and obeyed orders that produced massive devastation and death throughout continental Europe for 5½ years. The vast majority of them did so despite Hitler's humiliation of the officer corps and his military blunders that produced defeat and large-scale, often unnecessary casualties. Even most of the general officers, many of whom severely criticized Hitler for his conduct of the war and his criminal orders, still honored their personal oath to him through general obedience to his orders. Most intriguingly, they did so even though Hitler heaped abuse and scorn upon them as a group and as individuals and summarily dismissed many of them. Finally, in general, the limited opposition they posed to him was primarily on military matters, and even their opposition to his criminal orders was generally, although not exclusively, based on military, rather than humanitarian, concerns.

While most officers blindly followed their oath and obeyed orders, a few courageous but tragic officers chose to oppose and then conspire to assassinate Hitler. From the summer of 1940 through the summer of 1944, various military officers made at least 12 attempts to kill Hitler. This chapter will not discuss these attempts in depth, as other works have done so. This chapter instead will review the evolution of the military opposition during the war and *how* and *why* these officers decided to disavow their oath and choose conspiracy and disobedience, rather than acquiescence and obedience. To accomplish this task, I will first review how the members of the military opposition evolved in light of the military conduct of the war and the criminal acts of the Nazi regime, and their attempts to recruit field commanders who could provide the troops to oppose a probable countercoup from loyal elements. I will then review the events of July 20, 1944, to see how various officers acted and reacted to the abortive coup and its aftermath. There are several underlying questions that require answers: why were the conspirators willing to commit treason during a desperate but losing struggle while most of the field commanders were not? What role did the oath of loyalty play in the psychological struggle of both the conspirators and those who refused to participate? We will see that the oath of loyalty, taken so lightly so many years before, was significant, and that for all of them it was not just "mere words."

The Evolution of the Military Opposition, 1939–1943

Like so many others, the members of the military opposition had become resigned to the inevitability of war over Poland, having failing to act decisively before September 1939. By that time Beck had become its recognized leader. Although the major leaders of the civilian opposition — Goerdeler, Schacht, and Hassell — often acted without consulting Beck, they did meet frequently with him and informally recognized his overall leadership. They also began to develop a program for a civilian government, and the civilians agreed to designate Beck as head of state in a future government. The question of what to do with Hitler especially bothered the conspirators. Beck had concluded that he must be disposed of to release the officers from their oath. Halder and Thomas were afraid that the General Staff's involvement in assassination would destroy the army's "moral and political authority." Hammerstein, commanding the troops working on the Westwall, had no problems — he would lure Hitler to his location and assassinate him there. Unfortunately, Hitler did not visit the west until after the Polish campaign and Hammerstein's retirement.[1]

Soon after the successful campaign over Poland, members of the opposition came to learn about the SS atrocities in Poland, recounted briefly in the previous chapter. After a visit to Warsaw in November 1939, Stieff was outraged by the atrocities perpetrated by the SS against Poles and Jews alike and passionately denounced the Nazi regime which perpetrated them. Stating that they would even make "a Genghis Khan green with envy,"[2] he realized that Germany would eventually be held accountable for these war crimes unless someone stopped them. Failure to do so would mean that "this rabble [the SS] [would] one day do the same things to us decent people and terrorize their own nation with their pathological passions."[3] How ironic, given that Himmler's police state had been terrorizing "decent" Germans for years.

Beck with Oster and Dohnanyi had developed plans for a military coup when Hitler ordered the attack on France. "Loyal soldiers" would seize the government quarter in Berlin and arrest Nazi leaders from Hitler down to Kreis party leaders, and Beck would become head of state and impose martial law. He would then tell the German people that he seized power because Hitler had ordered an attack on the west against the advice of his generals and that he was "ill," temporarily unable to carry out his duties. Beck would tell the Germans that other Nazi leaders had been arrested for various crimes, proof of which he would soon publish. The Wehrmacht would also take an oath of allegiance to the new government. The plan needed a general with troops to carry out the coup and then protect the new government from a countercoup. As Reynolds writes, the plan demonstrated the naiveté of the conspirators in the context of the political realities of 1939: six years of terror and indoctrination, and a personal oath of loyalty by the armed forces and the SS that few would break just because Beck gave his coup an appearance of legality.[4]

Meanwhile, the conspirators tried to obtain support for the coup from officers at the OKH. Beck and others circulated "anonymous" memoranda among the officers at the

OKH, but no one came forward. Many found his "frequent appeals to their intellects and their consciences tiresome and embarrassing." General Tippelskirch, the General Staff's chief of intelligence, wrote on one of the memos, "Is this the work of an Englishman or a German? In the latter case he is over-ripe for a concentration camp."[5] Halder had shown some interest in a coup, and Goerdeler believed Brauchitsch might follow his lead or, at least, "tolerate" a coup. Unfortunately, Halder's support ran "hot and cold" as he came close to a nervous breakdown by October 16.[6]

Hitler's announcement of an impending offensive against France spurred Halder to authorize Stülpnagel to visit the generals on the Western Front to obtain their opinions on the prospects for an attack and a revolt. During the first six months of the war, General Falkenhausen had several conversations with Beck, Olbricht, and Oster of the military opposition and Schacht, Popitz, Goerdeler, and Dr. Adam Trott zu Solz of the civilian opposition. Falkenhausen later wrote that they had realized that the time to overthrow the regime was before the start of the western offensive.[7] However, only Leeb offered his support in a direct letter to Brauchitsch as the other commanders feared a civil war or lack of support from the troops.[8] Hassell could partially understand why some of the younger officers would not rebel in the face of the enemy "[b]ut if the generals are united and give out the right orders the people and the Army will obey."[9] Like Gisevius in 1938, he obviously did not have the same memories of 1919, 1920, 1923, or 1930 as the generals who feared a civil war that would split the army.

While some officers plotted, an anti-Hitler group in the Foreign Office in late October had prepared a memorandum for use in letting the German people know about the threat from Hitler. The document prophesied that an offensive against France would produce a stalemate and economic misery for Germany. The writers demanded an end to Hitler's tyranny and implored the military to act. "The oath of allegiance to Hitler had lost its meaning since he was ready to sacrifice Germany to his mad designs. Rather it was 'the supreme national duty to be true to the Fatherland against this criminal.' The memory of Yorck and von der Marwitz was conjured up. Now was the time to act."[10] Ironically, it was resistors in the Foreign Office who had realized that Hitler had invalidated the oath of allegiance and there was precedence in the "disobedience" of Yorck and von der Marwitz for disobedience to the present tyrant. Only a small group of officers would ever come to that conclusion before Germany was completely devastated.

In any event, the plans for a coup based on the impending western offensive soon fizzled. Halder, afraid that Hitler knew about a prospective coup, withdrew his support, following Brauchitsch's November 6 browbeating from Hitler.[11] On November 23, when Hitler tried again to convince the generals of the need for an offensive against France, Brauchitsch offered his resignation, but Hitler refused it. Halder tried to persuade his superior to join the revolt, but the weak and frightened Brauchitsch declined, fearful of another Kapp Putsch.[12] General Fromm also refused to join the conspiracy, believing that most of the troops would not obey an order to turn against the regime "because they had too much trust in Hitler."[13] As recounted earlier, both Halder and Brauchitsch now withdrew what little support and encouragement they had given to the military opposition for fear that Hitler knew about the conspiracy. Their reluctance to more forcibly oppose Hitler's planned offensive and use it as an excuse for a coup turned Beck against them.

The conspirators now tried other approaches, such as giving the Dutch military attaché to Berlin, Colonel Gijsbertus Jacobus Sas, the plans for the western offensive and sending out peace feelers to the British through the Vatican. Oster had known Sas since the early 1930s, and they had become close friends after the 1936 Munich Olympic Games. On October 8, 1939, Oster had told his Dutch friend about the impending invasion of Holland and Belgium. Sas duly informed his government about Hitler's plans, but the western governments were reluctant to believe Sas, especially when the invasion was postponed. Over the next several months Oster kept his friend informed of each new invasion date, but new postponements only served to increase the doubts of the concerned governments. These plans all came to nothing when bad weather over western Europe postponed the offensive against France until spring 1940.[14]

Oster did not take his "treason" lightly. After leaving Sas's apartment on October 8, 1939, he told his driver Franz Liedig,

> It is far easier to take a pistol and kill someone, it is far easier to charge into a hail of machine-gun fire when you believe in the cause, than it is to do what I have done. If things should ever come to this pass, then please be the friend even after my death who knows how it was and what moved me to do things that others might never understand or undertake themselves.[15]

From this confession we can see the mental anguish that Oster must have been going through as he "betrayed" military secrets to a prospective enemy. On one hand, he was "honor bound" to obey an oath to a maniacal dictator in whom he no longer saw as a legitimate authority. Yet, on the other hand, he clearly saw a greater duty that "required" him to inform a foreign government about his own government's secret plans for war. Finally, he also understood that others would consider him — and others like him — as traitors, not as brave men attempting to stop a criminal. Similar thoughts must have haunted other anti–Hitler conspirators as the world progressed to disaster.

During the unusually severe winter of 1939-40, the conspirators planned and waited. Colonel Hans Groscurth visited the headquarters of Leeb, Witzleben, Rundstedt, and Bock with revelations of the SS atrocities in Poland, but, again, only Leeb took any real action by sending a letter to Halder, complaining about the SS.[16] In January 1940, Oster again warned Colonel Sas about the rescheduled French offensive and, in April, he warned Sas and the Norwegian ambassador about the upcoming invasion of Norway and Denmark.[17] At the time, Oster remarked, "There are those who will say that I am a traitor, but I am truly not. I consider myself a better German than all those who run after Hitler. My plan and my duty is to free Germany, and with it the world, of this pestilence."[18] Meanwhile, Brauchitsch immersed himself in the details of operational plans for the OKH, but Halder maintained some noncommittal contacts with the conspirators. For example, in April 1940, he passed to Brauchitsch a document from the Vatican which outlined terms on which the British would negotiate peace with a post–Hitler government. Brauchitsch called it "national treason" and wanted to arrest the person who had given it to Halder.[19] Without any sign of support from the two top army leaders, the conspirators broke off their negotiations with the Pope — three days before the invasion of the Low Countries.[20]

Although the feelings of invincibility produced by the successful invasion and occupation of western Europe worked against the conspirators, Hitler's military blunders and the barbarities on the eastern front gave the anti–Hitler opposition renewed impetus that would ultimately lead it to the Wolfschantze (Wolf's Lair, Hitler's headquarters near Rastenburg, East Prussia) on July 20, 1944. Still, forward movement was imperceptibly slow. After June 1941, Beck and Hammerstein slowly began rebuilding their network of contacts, and Hassell visited

Falkenhausen, the military governor of Belgium and the Netherlands since mid–May 1940, and his immediate superior in Paris, Witzleben, commander of Obwest. Both generals found his proposals for a coup at this time unrealistic and were unwilling to help.

The conspiracy found more fertile ground in the headquarters staff of Army Group Center, commanded by Generalfeldmarschall Fedor von Bock, on the eastern front. Supporters for an anti–Hitler coup included the group's chief of staff— Bock's nephew — Henning von Tresckow, his aide-de-camp Fabian von Schlabrendorff, Gersdorff, and others. The growing groups of conspirators even included Bock's own aides Graf Hans von Hardenburg and Graf Heinrich von Lehndorff. Tresckow had used his influence with Hitler's army adjutant Schmundt to have like-minded officers assigned to Bock's headquarters. Wheeler-Bennett called the group of conspirators a "nest of intrigue and treason." Fest described Tresckow's circle as "the largest and most tightly knit resistance group of these years."[21] These officers began conferring with Beck as early as December 1941.[22]

From June 1941 through July 1942, Tresckow worked hard to convince Bock to join their cause. He discussed the serious military situation with Bock, placing the blame squarely on Hitler. However, Bock, though he opposed Hitler's military direction of the war and National Socialism, was not a conspirator and on one occasion stormed out, shouting, "I shall not tolerate any attack upon the Führer. I shall stand before the Führer and defend him against anyone who dares to attack him."[23] He called the entire conspiracy "absolute rubbish!"[24] After June 1942, Tresckow and his aide worked equally hard to convert Bock's replacement Kluge. Through Schlabrendorff, Goerdeler visited Kluge at Smolensk shortly after he assumed command. From their discussions, the conspirators thought that they had "bagged" the new commander. However, as soon as Goerdeler left, the generalfeldmarschall began to waver. In a letter to Beck, Kluge criticized the "surprise-assault" of Goerdeler's visit and wished to avoid possible "misunderstanding." Even Tresckow's attempt to use Kluge's acceptance of the 250,000 RMs from Hitler to blackmail or embarrass the generalfeldmarschall failed to confirm his support.[25]

The opportunities for a successful coup at this time were indeed dim. The winter of 1941-42 produced rumors of a putsch after the failure of the winter offensive in Russia, the retreat from Moscow, and the forced retirement of Brauchitsch. The eastern commanders would refuse to obey Hitler's orders while the army remained in place, and Falkenhausen and Witzleben in the west would march on Berlin, depose Hitler and his followers, and prepare the way for the civilian opposition to establish a new government. However, Witzleben had only a few like-minded officers and poorly trained Landwehr at his disposal as his best troops had been used to replace the losses in Russia. Halder's dismissal in late 1942 severed the conspirators' direct link with the OKH. Oster was able, however, to recruit General Friedrich Olbricht, chief of the Allegemeine Heeresamt (General Army Office) and Fromm's deputy, to the military opposition. From this position, he could direct the troops of the Replacement Army and transfer reserve units to support an anti–Hitler coup under the guise of a loyalist counter-coup, codenamed Operation Valkyrie (more later).[26]

By now, the conspirators had learned about the brutal combat conditions and the atrocities in the east. In late autumn 1941, Groscurth wrote "graphic and passionate" letters to Beck about the lack of food, rest, and equipment for his soldiers, and their "superhuman efforts" that achieved some successes. He severely criticized the senior commanders for their lack of knowledge of the conditions at the front and concluded that the best that an officer could do was to "lead his troops well, fight bravely, and hope for the best."[27] The conspirators also knew of Hitler's orders to execute political commissars, Jews, and Gypsies and of the activities of the Einsatzgruppen. Beck, however, had difficulty in believing the existence and activities of the mass extermination camps, but Gisevius did finally convince him of it. In July 1942, Hossbach, Hitler's ex-adjutant, returned from Russia and discussed his experiences with Beck. According to Reynolds, Beck lost control at the "thought of defeat and needless bloodshed" and cried "out in rage, … 'What has this swine Hitler done to our beautiful country?'"[28] Incensed at the atrocities but moved more by the lack of action by the generals, Beck by 1943 was now convinced Hitler had to be assassinated to sever the bond between him and the army. Although Goerdeler initially wanted Hitler publicly tried for his crimes, even he now had come around to accepting the necessity of Hitler's death.

Stauffenberg and the Military Opposition, January 1943–June 1944

As Germany's military fortunes worsened by early 1943, the conspirators hoped to use the military disasters in the east, especially Stalingard, to reinvigorate their cause. The dislike of General Hans Speidel for the Nazi regime's corruption, violence, and terror and the brutalizing fighting in the east now blossomed into conspiracy (which would later have importance to the anti–Hitler resistance). Stülpnagel, who had spoken with Speidel in December 1942, also re-established contact with the military opposition in Berlin through Falkenhausen during the summer of 1943.[29] Hassell noted in his diary that, after Stalingard, Zeitzler "summoned up courage to resist idiotic orders"; Kluge and Manstein "managed to get more freedom of movement. And Herr Fromm, this weather vane, now trumpets brave opinions. But in spite of all efforts, what is still lacking is a spark plug."[30]

Lieutenant Colonel Klaus Schenk Graf von Stauffenberg would become that spark plug. Born into an aristocratic family with a long tradition of military service to Prussia-Germany, he counted Gneisenau and Yorck in his extended family tree. As a child, he was reared in a cultural and intellectual atmosphere and educated at a private grammar school and later a Gymnasium, the German equivalent to the American high school, rather than a cadet corps. Later at the Infantry School, Stauffenberg learned Russian, often played his cello, and read Homer's *Odyssey* and *Iliad*— in Greek.[31] Stauffenberg also had a passion for the poetry of Stefan Georg (1868–1933), a German humanistic poet of the late 19th and early 20th centuries; his favorite poem became Georg's "Anti-Christ," a good description of his real-life Anti-Christ — Hitler.[32] During the war, Stauffenberg, during his assignment to the 10th Panzer Division in North Africa, would often discuss philosophy, literature — as well as Hitler's removal — with his commander Brigadier General Friedrich Baron von Broich.[33] Certainly Stauffenberg was not, by any means, the stereotypical Prussian army officer.

Stauffenberg, however, was also a nationalist as well as an intellectual. Like other officers, he disliked the Versailles Treaty and Germany's humiliation by the French and British. Also, like other officers during the 1930s, he had supported many of the Nazi aims, but, by 1938, he, like Beck, came to disapprove of Hitler's reckless foreign policies.[34] After the war, Halder also reported that discussions with the future conspirator, assigned to the General Staff from May 1940 to early 1943, revealed that Stauffenberg was dissatisfied with Hitler and the military situation.[35] He probably first met Tresckow and Schlabrendorff during a trip to the east in July 1941. By mid–1942, he became convinced of the need to do away with Hitler as the only way to save Germany. When one general, who apparently still believed Germany's military defeats came from the Nazi cronies and not Hitler himself, announced, "We must tell the Führer the truth!" Stauffenberg openly retorted, "It's not a question of telling him the truth but of killing him, and I'm ready to do it myself."[36] Like other conspirators, the convoluted command structure, the barbaric war in Russia, the atrocities against Jews, Soviet civilians, and POWs, and the unattainability of ultimate victory turned Stauffenberg against Hitler, and he now began to develop a resistance cell of like-minded officers within the OKW.

Meanwhile, Tresckow, now commanding an infantry regiment assigned to Army Group South under Manstein, began to "work on" his new commander in southern Russia through Manstein's deputy chief of staff, Colonel Ebehard Finckh.[37] However, Manstein would not participate in a coup and wrote Beck in early 1943, "After all a war is not lost until one gives it up for lost."[38] On January 26, 1943, Stauffenberg visited the generalfeldmarschall to discuss several subjects, including the bad leadership at the top and the military command structure. Manstein was willing to discuss the command structure but not "illegal activities." When Stauffenberg mentioned "Tauroggen," referring to Yorck's convention with the Russians in January 1813, the general took it to mean that he should make an agreement with the Soviets. Stauffenberg was probably trying to convey the limits of loyalty and obedience, and the conversation ended after it became "impassioned [and] ... louder."[39] Later, in early February 1943, Tresckow tried again to obtain Manstein's support for an anti–Hitler coup, but the generalfeldmarschall again refused him "once and for all ... [because] Tresckow's ideas were quite simply appalling."[40] Manstein remained steadfast in his loyalty to Hitler, despite his dislike for the "messy" command relationships for the eastern front and Hitler's military blundering, even into retirement after March 1944.[41]

Failing to obtain Manstein's support, the conspirators once again tried to "nail down" the ever slippery Kluge, commanding Army Group Center. Lieutenant Colonel Rudolf-Christian Freiherr von Gersdorff, who had also tried to convert Manstein to the conspiracy, using Tauroggen as precedence, now tried to convert Kluge.[42] In July 1943, Goerdeler made another plea to the elusive Kluge for him to join the conspiracy. In the letter he emphasized his belief that Germany could negotiate a favorable peace if they could rid Germany of the "insane leadership that despises divine and human laws." In July at Obersalzberg, Kluge and Rommel also mutually pledged to serve under Manstein if the latter joined the opposition. When Kluge finally answered Goerdeler in November, he now agreed with him.[43] Kluge's belated response to Goerdeler, along with a candid secret meeting with Beck in Berlin at the end of August, apparently confirmed his own beliefs and gave at least the impression of his support for a coup.

Despite the addition of Stauffenberg to the military opposition and Kluge's seeming support, the anti–Hitler conspiracy generally had a bad year in 1943. The conspirators hoped that Paulus, inside Stalingrad, would join them, but, in late January 1943, he accepted his promotion to generalfeldmarschall and then allowed himself to become a POW; only later did he join the anti–Fascist officers in Soviet captivity. General Huesinger on the OKW operations staff also turned the conspirators down, citing his oath and military duty to obey.[44] Without the support of a major field commander, the conspirators could not use Witzleben's January 1942 plan for a coup in early 1943, and another plan to overthrow Hitler died in conception.[45] An assassination attempt after Hitler's March visit to Smolensk failed when the bomb, placed on his personal aircraft, failed to explode. On another occasion, Kluge, waiting for a "more favorable" opportunity, did not approve another attempt by members of his staff during another visit.[46] However, when Kluge heard that Gersdorff had tried to kill the Führer earlier, he was shocked: "Gersdorff, what did you do? How could you do something like that?" Gersdorff unequivocally replied, "Because, *Herr Feldmarschall*, we take the position that is the only way to save the German nation from complete ruin."[47] Despite his knowledge of the conspiracy and the attempts on Hitler's life and his own aloofness from these activities, the generalfeldmarschall would not oppose — and, more interestingly, turn in — the conspirators.[48]

The resistance also suffered irreparable harm after a chance arrest led to the exposure of an Abwehr program to help Jews. Dietrich Bonhoeffer and Dohnanyi had been helping some Jews escape extermination by recruiting them, ostensibly for undercover work outside of Germany, and then providing them with false identity papers and currency to help them escape to Switzerland. A chance arrest of one such Jew soon led to the exposure of the Abwehr scheme, and, in April, 1943, the Gestapo arrested Bonhoeffer and Dohnanyi ironically because of these illegal financial transactions, not political intrigue. Although the Gestapo later released Dohnanyi, it placed Canaris under close surveillance and later forced Oster to retire in December. Following the Anzio landings, a number of Abwehr agents defected to the Allies, and, on February 18, 1944, Hitler dissolved the Abwehr and distributed its parts to various sections of the Reichssicherheitshauptamt (RHSA).[49]

Other events furthered stifled resistance work in 1943. Beck underwent surgery in the spring for intestinal cancer and took the summer to recover during which time the resistance drifted. In the autumn Kluge was injured in an automobile accident and was replaced by the pro–Nazi Generalfeldmarschall Ernst Busch, the same Busch who had stood with Reichenau in support of Hitler and against the other generals at the August 4, 1938, commander's meeting. On October 12, Tresckow himself was seriously injured in a car accident and, after his recovery, became the chief of staff of the Second Army under Busch's overall command.[50] The conspirator had wanted to become Manstein's chief of staff, but Manstein refused to accept him because of his "negative attitude toward National Socialism."[51] The postwar comment of Stauffenberg's commander in Africa accurately captures the attitude of the German field commanders in 1943: "They all told [Stauffenberg] that they entirely agreed that things could not go on as they were and that something must happen. But no one showed himself ready to act or take the lead."[52]

Another more significant setback — at least, initially — occurred in the spring of 1943. On April 7, Stauffenberg, assigned to the 120th Panzer Division in North Africa, was gravely injured when a British aircraft strafed his staff car. He lost his left eye, his right hand, and two fingers on his left hand. Additionally, he received severe injuries to his left ear and knee and barely survived these wounds. But survive he did and even managed to be returned to active duty. During his recovery, he told his wife, "I feel I must do something now to save Germany. We General Staff officers must all accept our share of the responsibility."[53] To his uncle Count von Uxkuell, Stauffenberg, he said, "Since the generals haven't accomplished anything, then it's up to the colonels now."[54] His uncle also helped Stauffenberg find a position on the staff of a friend of his and Beck's — General Olbricht, deputy to the commander of the Ersatzheer, General Fromm. When Stauffenberg reported for duty at the end of August 1943, he and his new boss discussed the recovered officer's capabilities to participate in the anti–Hitler coup, instead of his new duties as one would have expected.[55]

Despite the setbacks, the conspirators continued to plan for Hitler's assassination and a follow-on coup. With Lieutenant General Olbricht's help, they secretly reworked an existing plan, Operation Valkyrie, for their own uses. Ironically, Olbricht and Canaris had originally developed the plan in 1941–42 to counter large-scale sabotage, raids by airborne troops, or a possible revolt by the millions of foreign workers and enemy POWs inside Germany, using the Ersatzheer — troops in training, troops on convalescent leave, and overage garrison troops. In the revised plan, the uncommitted Fromm would direct units of the Replacement Army to seize key areas of Berlin after Hitler's assassination and protect them against a countercoup. If he wavered, Hoepner would replace Fromm and *he* would order its units into position.[56] The plan had drawbacks: the replacement army was not homogeneous in composition, was not trained, equipped, or organized as a fighting force, and its "units" were scattered all over Germany. In reality, the Ersatzheer was less a "real" army than a collection of recruits in training that were "fed" to the field army as replacements, and various overage garrison troops who performed guard duty in Greater Germany. However, it did provide a command network outside of the control of the party and government and might be able to seize some population centers long enough for an anti–Hitler coup to succeed.[57]

The key for a successful coup continued to be a field commander who would support their coup with combat soldiers. The conspirators approached Rundstedt and Guderian but failed to win either one to their cause. The former would not participate in a coup but would not object to one. The latter rebuffed the "offer," stating he was bound by his oath of allegiance to Hitler and later informed Goerdeler that he could not find any other general who would join because of the oath.[58] The conspirators had become increasingly convinced that the field commanders would not directly participate in any attempt to overthrow Hitler. However, they also believed that most detested Hitler and the Nazi regime and many would probably throw their support to a new government once Hitler was out of the way. The military opposition now had several key people — Olbricht and Stauffenberg, in particular — in positions to plan and launch another attempt on Hitler's life. The conspirators, at least, knew that they would have to try soon as time was running out for Germany.

The July 20, 1944, Assassination Plot and Aftermath

As the military situation worsened for Germany into 1944, the conspirators finalized their plans for Valkyrie and confirmed the participation of key players in the prospective coup. Yet, they still had not obtained the support of any field commander with sizable forces. Then, in April 1944, fate provided them with a glimmer of hope. Since January, Generalfeldmarschall Erwin Rommel, who had lost a degree of confidence in Hitler since the debacle in North Africa, had commanded Army Group B in France and Holland, which was tasked to prepare German defenses for an expected Allied cross-channel invasion. He had learned about the anti–Hitler resistance through Stülpnagel and Falkenhausen but initially disagreed with their assessment of the situation. On April 15, 1944, Hans Speidel was reassigned from Russia at Rommel's request to be his chief of staff, and for the next several months, took every opportunity to convince his new commander to join the conspiracy. Colonel Finckh, now Rommel's deputy chief of staff, urged on by Stauffenberg, and Luftwaffe Lieutenant Colonel Caesar von Hofacker, Stauffenberg's cousin and the aide to General Stülpnagel, tried to convince the generalfeldmarschall to join with them.[59] Unfortunately, while he gave a dismal assessment of the present military situation, he expressed his distaste for the assassination plot and a military coup and apparently never fully converted to the conspiracy before July 1944.[60]

As the time to launch Valkyrie approached, the conspirators received two significant boosts. On July 1, 1944, Stauffenberg was promoted to colonel and appointed Fromm's chief of staff. This position gave him direct access to Hitler as the latter demanded more and more replacements for Germany's increasing losses. Stauffenberg could also issue orders in Fromm's name, meaning he could "legally" authorize Operation Valkyrie.[61] Interestingly, upon meeting General Fromm, the conspirator made it known to his superior just how he felt about Hitler. While Fromm acknowledged Stauffenberg's treasonable comments, he made no offer to support, join, or oppose the plot. He did comment, "For God's sake don't forget that fellow Keitel when you make your putsch."[62] Again, we have another situation when a nonconspirator had sufficient knowledge of what the conspirators were planning but did not turn them into the Gestapo, a phenomenon examined in greater detail in the next chapter.

In addition to Stauffenberg's appointment to Fromm's staff, the anti–Hitler conspirators received another boost. As mentioned in the previous chapter, Kluge replaced Rundstedt as military commander in France in June 1944 after the Allied landings at Normandy. In this position, bolstered by the conspirators in the west, he might be more willing to support an anti–Hitler coup when they launched it, despite his reputation of blowing "hot and cold." Although Hitler specifically courted Kluge's favor as Germany's savior when the Allied invasion came, Kluge soon had his doubts after touring German defenses in France and seemed to agree, albeit hesitantly, with Falkenhausen's assessment after a July 9 meeting at Tourcoring, France.[63] Apparently, both he and Rommel had agreed to support the impending coup if Hitler failed to correctly respond to the deteriorating military situation in France, and a Beck-Goerdeler government once Hitler was dead. Yet, in another instance of weakening, Kluge held back a July 15 message from Rommel until after Rommel had been wounded and the assassination attempt had failed. In the message, Rommel chastised Hitler for the inadequate equipment and men and, in essence, gave Hitler an ultimatum.[64]

The Allied invasion of France and new Soviet offensives in the east made it imperative that the conspirators make another attempt to kill Hitler. Sometime in May, Tresckow told Stahlberg that the coup d'état was ready although he was very pessimistic about its success. During a visit to Berchtesgaden, General Erich Fellgiebel, OKW chief of communications and a conspirator, confirmed the plot's timing to Stahlberg: "Manstein will be free of his oath at any moment."[65] By mid–July, Kluge had agreed to allow the western Allies through his lines after Hitler's death although he was unsure if his soldiers would obey such orders.[66] Also, Falkenhausen had just been relieved of his position as military governor of Belgium because he had refused an order to deport Belgians, born in 1925, to Germany as slave laborers.[67] On July 18, First Lieutenant K. von Barsevisch, Guderian's Luftwaffe liaison in Russia and now a conspirator, tried to persuade the tank commander to join them since Rommel had been seriously wounded in France, but Guderian again invoked his oath to Hitler as the reason he could not.[68] The conspirators had decided to try again to assassinate Hitler, this time at his East Prussian headquarters, the Wolfschanze (Wolf's Lair), on July 20, 1944: Stauffenberg was going to brief Hitler on the status of replacements on that day.

On July 20, 1944, Stauffenberg left Berlin by air for Rastenburg and, after landing, was driven to the heavily guarded Wolfschanze. After entering the compound but before entering the briefing hut, he set the timing mechanism on the bomb and then proceeded to the hut. Stauffenberg undoubtedly practiced this meticulous procedure several times before that fateful day because of the debilitating injuries he had received in North Africa. Stauffenberg placed the briefcase near Hitler, made an excuse, and left the hut. He managed to get out of the highly guarded compound just after the bomb exploded and made it to the airfield for the three-hour flight to Berlin. Unfortunately, the bomb did not kill Hitler—the "soft" construction of the hut had absorbed part of the explosion's force and someone apparently had moved the briefcase with the bomb behind one of the heavy timber legs of the briefing table away from Hitler. Keitel led a badly shaking and disheveled Führer, suffering from minor burns and some ear damage, out of the ruined hut and began a "telephone war" with Stauffenberg, now in Berlin, to notify the various military commanders that Hitler was still alive. General Fellgiebel had failed to cut the communications lines between the Wolfschanze and the outside world, the second critical reason for the plot's failure.[69]

Prior to leaving the headquarters compound, Stauffenberg made a telephone call to Berlin to inform the conspirators, gathering at the War Ministry, that Hitler was dead. Based on this word, Olbricht, at 4:00 P.M., Berlin time, issued orders to direct Valkyrie into operation, but Fromm wanted specific assurance that Hitler was dead before he would act. While Olbricht proceeded, Fromm was placed under arrest in another part of the War Ministry. Beck, as the "acting" head of government, now called the OKH at Zossen to inform General Josef Wagner that Hitler was dead and he was taking over, but the general wanted further evidence before he would act. Beck also appointed the retired Witzleben as the new army commander in chief, and Witzleben went to Zossen but returned home to await further events. The officers at the OKH refused to obey either Beck or Witzleben because of the conflicting stories about Hitler's death.[70]

As Stauffenberg carried out his part of the assassination plot in East Prussia, in Paris Stülpnagel (who on July 17 had declared his complete support for the revolt even if Kluge had not) and his coconspirators completed their preparations for the coup.[71] After receiving word of Hitler's "assassination," he had the SS and Gestapo leaders in Paris arrested and also looked for Kluge to get his support for the coup. Unfortunately, Kluge was in Normandy; upon his return to Paris, he heard about the coup but wanted verification that Hitler was, in fact, dead. When he heard in a message from Keitel that the Führer was still alive, Kluge lost his nerve again, despite Stülpnagel's prodding and a teletype from Witzleben, and ordered the release of the SS and Gestapo leaders.[72] Even Beck's plea to Kluge that "the fate of Germany is at stake," failed to dislodge Kluge from his fence. In the end he refused to support the attempted coup in Berlin or even in Paris.[73] Within weeks Hitler would recall Kluge to Berlin and replace him with Rundstedt as the commander in the west, the third time the latter was recalled to duty.

Back in Berlin, the conspirators turned their attention to protecting the coup. Beck appealed to General Joachim von Kortzfleisch, commander of the Berlin military district, for his support, but the general refused, citing, like others, his oath to Hitler. Beck countered, to no avail, with Hitler's numerous violations of his oath to the constitution and his neglect of his responsibilities to the German people. Stauffenberg, now back in Berlin, spent the late afternoon and early evening diligently handling telephone calls from the Wehrkreise commanders. He implored, pleaded, and even threatened them to carry out their orders under Valkyrie, but none did.[74] The conspirators now made their third critical mistake of the day by ordering a Major Otto-Ernst Remer, the commander of the guard battalion Gross Deutschland, to surround the immediate area against a countercoup until "loyal" troops could move into Berlin and arrest Goebbels. When Remer contacted Goebbels, the young major told the Propaganda Minsiter, "I am with the Führer 100 percent" and promised "as an honest National Socialist officer to perform my duty under any circumstances, true to my oath of loyalty to the Führer."[75] Goebbels then called Hitler, still in East Prussia, who then spoke directly with Remer. Ordered to crush the revolt (and promoted to colonel on the spot), Remer did so, and the coup was over by 10:15 P.M.[76]

Aftermath of the July 20, 1944, Coup

Almost immediately, the Nazi regime began exacting its price for the coup's failure, a task that did not end until the war did. Fromm offered Beck the opportunity to commit suicide, rather than face the Nazis. However, he only managed to gravely wound himself, and a soldier had to finish off the former chief of staff. Fromm then had Olbricht, Stauffenberg, and several others summarily executed in the courtyard of the War Ministry after a quick court-martial. Supposedly Stauffenberg shouted "Long live holy Germany" shortly before he was shot. On the evening of July 20, shortly before being shot, Olbricht told his son-in-law Friedrich Georgi:

> I don't know how posterity will later judge our deed or how it will judge me personally. But I know with certainty that all of us acted free of any sort of personal motives and that we dared attempt the ultimate only in a situation which was already desperate, in order to protect Germany against total destruction. I am convinced that posterity will some day recognize and understand that.[77]

Fromm's "prompt" actions that night, however, ultimately did not win favor with the Führer as we shall see later.[78] The next day, Tresckow heard that the plot had failed. He told his aide Schlabrendorff,

> Everybody will now turn upon us and cover us with abuse. But my conviction remains unshaken — we have done the right thing. Hitler is not only the archenemy of Germany: he is the archenemy of the world. In a few hours I shall stand before God, answering for my actions and for my omissions. I think I shall be able to uphold with a clear conscience all that I have done in the fight against Hitler....
>
> Whoever joined the resistance movement put on the shirt of Nessus. The worth of a man is certain only if he is prepared to sacrifice his life for his conviction.[79]

He then drove close to the front lines and killed himself with a hand grenade.

Recovering from the explosion in the Wolfschanze, Hitler called for swift justice for those involved in the conspiracy: "There will be no mercy. No long speeches from the defendants. The People's Courts will act with lightning speed. And two hours after sentencing. It will be carried out. By hanging — without mercy."[80] He now called a halt to the summary executions so the Gestapo could determine the full extent of the conspiracy and he could exact his full vengeance on the conspirators. The widespread conspiracy that the ensuing investigation revealed even amazed the Gestapo. Hitler ordered Guderian, who had replaced Zeitzler on July 21 as army chief of staff, to convene a military court of honor and expel the army conspirators from the service so they could be tried in a civilian court. Rundstedt served as president with Guderian and three other generals as members, and they proceeded to do Hitler's bidding. Forbidden to resign, Guderian absented himself from as many of the sittings of the court of honor as he could. When he was present, he did what he could to save the marginally implicated, and at least kept Speidel from a trial and execution. The court of honor expelled 55 officers, including one generalfeldmarschall (Witzleben), 11 general officers and 17 general staff officers.[81] In August, eight of the conspirators, including Witzleben, Fellgiebel, Peter Yorck von Wartenburg, descendant of the Yorck of Tauroggen, and Hoepner, were tried before the People's Court and sentenced to death by hanging.[82]

Other senior officers followed them by one way or another. On July 21, Stülpnagel, ordered to Berlin, tried to kill himself near Verdun. He was hanged on August 30 but not before he apparently implicated Rommel in the abortive plot during his recovery.[83] Germany's most popular general, Rommel, was still recovering from his own wounds, and was given the choice of public humiliation and trial — which would include his family — or suicide. He chose the latter and took poison at a military hospital on October 14 after which Hitler gave him a funeral with full military honors. In early August, Kluge was again contemplating an "arrangement" with the western Allies to surrender his forces but again apparently lost his nerve, and on August 17 was replaced by Model. Ordered to Berlin by Hitler, Kluge, suspecting his arrest upon arrival, committed suicide on the roadside during the way to Berlin. Curiously, before killing himself, Kluge wrote in a farewell letter Hitler,

> When you receive these lines I shall be no more.... Life has no more meaning for me.... Both Rommel and I ... foresaw the present development [the military debacle in Normandy]. We were not listened to.... I have always admired your greatness.... If fate is stronger than your will and your genius, it is Providence.... Show yourself now also great enough to put an end to a hopeless struggle when necessary....[84]

Fromm also fell victim to the Nazi executioners — his actions on the night of July 20 did not save him from Hitler's revenge. Soon after the abortive plot, he was arrested, court-martialed for cowardice and for failure to inform higher headquarters about his knowledge of the conspiracy, and was shot on March 19, 1945.

For the next several months Himmler and his Gestapo conducted an intensive investigation into the various threads of the anti–Hitler movement which revealed a network so extensive that it astonished even the Reichsführer, although he did have some general idea that an anti–Hitler opposition existed. The failed plot gave Himmler the opportunity to clean out the conspirators and arrest anyone even remotely connected to them. The number of men and women arrested and executed by hanging, garroting, gassing, shooting, or beheading, following the abortive coup, will probably never be exactly known. Official Gestapo records estimated 7,000 people were arrested; Rothfels reports some 4,980 people were executed, including about 700 Wehrmacht officers.[85] Among them were Helmuth von Moltke, direct descendant of the famous chief of staff; Dr. Justus Delbrueck, son of the historian Hans Delbrueck; Erwin Planck, son of the physicist Max Planck; and Dr. Georg Albrecht Haushofer, son of the geopolitician Karl Haushofer. Many, like Schlabrendorff, were horribly tortured before their trials in the infamous *Volksgerichthof* (People's Court), presided over by the even more infamous Roland Freisler.[86] Initially Hitler also wanted to execute the "kith and kin" of the conspirators, but saner people talked him out of such a drastic measure because of the probable impact on the fighting morale of the officer corps. However, many of their wives, children, and relatives were sent to concentration camps and were probably saved from eventual execution only by the Allied victory.[87]

Hitler, with the complicity of the new chief of staff, completed the humiliation of the German officer corps. Keitel and Jodl forced the army to use the Nazi salute on all occasions as a sign that the Nazi Party was in charge, and Hitler agreed.[88] On July 23, Guderian, feeling compelled to do so, made a radio broadcast to the German people, stating in part

> A few officers, some on the retired list, have lost courage and by an act of cowardice and weakness preferred the road to disgrace to that of duty and honour.... The people and the Army stand closely behind the Führer.... I guarantee the Führer and the German people the unity of the generals of the officer corps and of the men in the Army in the single aim of fighting for and achieving victory under the motto created by the venerable *Generalfeldmarschall* von Hindenburg, "Loyalty is the essence of honour."[89]

On July 29, he issued his first order of the day which declared,

> Every General Staff Officer must be a Nationalist Socialist officer-leader, this is not only by his knowledge of tactics and strategy, but also by his attitude to political questions and by actively co-operating in the political indoctrination of the younger commanders in accordance with the tenets of the Führer....[90]

Hitler also appointed Himmler head of the Replacement Army to replace the disgraced Fromm and made the Waffen SS a separate and coequal military service.[91]

How did other officers react to the abortive coup? Despite his own dislike for Hitler, Warlimont wrote he could never have considered assassinating him.[92] Knappe wrote that he would have been glad if the coup had succeeded because success might have provided better terms to end the war other than the Allies' terms of unconditional surrender.[93] Senger ignored the questioning looks of his soldiers about the meaning of the abortive plot, rather than risk lowering their morale, and questioned whether Hitler's assassination would have had any real impact, considering that the other Nazis remained.[94] Mellenthin, near Lvov at the time, was "dumbfounded" and "disgusted by the attempt on Hitler's life. "[T]he fighting soldier did his duty to the bitter end."[95] In Normandy, Luck had "mixed feelings" but "the younger ones were angry." It is a stab in the back to us here at the front."[96] Prueller echoed similar sentiments in a letter to his wife.[97] Bock wrote, "They wish to change the course of history with such means? Apart from everything else [the issue of loyalty and honor?], it is of benefit only to the enemy."[98]

Summary

The failure of the July 20 coup was the death knell of the anti–Hitler resistance and the Prussian officer corps. The very few resistors, who were not arrested, tortured, and eventually executed, were cowed into silence and could only wait patiently and silently for the eventual Allied victory to save what was left of Germany. Yet, for the remaining months of the war, the German army continued to oppose the ever-growing and advancing Allied armies. The introduction of new weapons — guided bombs (the V-1), ballistic missiles (the V-2), and jet fighters (the Me 262) — were too little and too late to stem the Allied advances. The limited advances of Germany's remaining armored reserves during the Battle of the Bulge lasted no longer than the bad weather that kept British and American airplanes grounded and only prolonged Germany's agony a few more weeks. Despite the fighting tenacity of the German soldier, the mobilization of young boys of 14 and old men of 80, and Hitler's maniacal will, total defeat was inevitable. Yet, the loyalty of most officers to their Führer remained intact to the end although it is virtually impossible to determine which part of their fighting will could be attributed to loyalty and which part to patriotism and defense of the Fatherland, home, and family.

On August 9, 1944, the *New York Times* reported the story of the August 8 "show trial" that condemned eight of the leading conspirators to death by hanging. The paper also provided an editorial, quoted here in part:

> In point of fact, the details of the plot suggest more the atmosphere of a gangsters' lurid underworld than the normal atmosphere one would expect within an officers' corps and a civilized Government. For there were some of the highest officers of the German army ... plotting for a year to kidnap or kill the head of the German state and Commander in Chief of its army; postponing the execution of the plot repeatedly in order to kill his high executioner as well; and finally carrying it out by means of a bomb, the typical weapon of the underworld.
>
> All of this is so contrary to all the tenets of the "Code of Potsdam" that the world is till skeptical as to whether it is all true. Yet there is no reason to doubt the essential truth of the plot itself. And that truth is merely evidence that the underworld mentality and methods which the Nazis brought from their gutters and enthroned on the highest levels of German life have begun to pervade the officers' corps as well, and were, in fact, considered to be the only effective weapons against the Nazis themselves. For, knowing that many of their number had already fallen victim to Nazi terror, the dissident officers obviously came to the conclusion that this terror could only be met with counter-terror as the necessary preliminary to their contemplated coup d'etat. Their tragedy was that while they were willing to stoop to Nazi methods they lacked the Nazi cunning to make effective use of them. And so they were hanged.[99]

While the editor provided some elements of truth in his assessment, he missed the psychological struggle that had to take place before these officers could even act. His comparison of the attempted coup to the American gangster underworld is most certainly an injustice to these tragic men who finally "came to their senses" to end Hitler's crimes.

This chapter presented the tragic story of a handful of brave men who tried to write a different end to the Third Reich. The members of the military opposition struggled during the war years to obtain support for an anti–Hitler coup from their friends and comrades and to devise a plan that would succeed in ridding Germany of a criminal. We also saw how most of their friends, fellow classmates, and colleagues turned a blind eye to the terrible things that the army was doing in the name of Hitler and National Socialism. They cited that their honor as officers demanded that they obey their personal oath to Hitler, despite the fact that Hitler had heaped scorn and abuse upon them. The nonconspirators and the Nazi followers never saw the moral crisis that Hitler and the Nazi regime had brought onto the German soldier, particularly the officers. Ironically, those who chose to follow their oath did so believing that they were right and that the conspirators were traitors to Germany, while the conspirators felt that their cause was the righteous one and that honor demanded that they attempt to rid Germany of Hitler.

The following quotes express the diametrically opposite views of honor, loyalty, and obedience of German officers. When asked in late June 1944 if the opposition should carry out the coup, Tresckow replied,

> The assassination must be attempted at any cost. Even should it fail, the attempt to seize power in the capital must be undertaken. We must prove to the world and to future generations that the men of the German Resistance Movement dared to take the decisive step and to hazard their lives upon it. Compared with this object, nothing else matters.[100]

Guderian had these thoughts about a successful coup:

> The odium thus created by [Hitler's] death would have been attached primarily to the corps of officers, the generals, and the general staff, and would have lasted not only during but also after the war. The people's hatred and contempt would have turned against the soldiers who, in the midst of a national struggle for existence, had broken their oath, murdered the head of government, and left the stormracked ship of state without a captain at the helm.[101]

Yet, this chapter presents only the historical evolution of the military opposition to Hitler. While I have particularly emphasized the role of the Hitlerian oath of loyalty so easily given ten years before the fateful July 20, 1944, plot, the presentation is essentially no more than a shortened version of what virtually all the major works on the anti–Hitler opposition provide. Like those works, this chapter still leaves many questions unanswered about why these specific officers — Beck, Tresckow, Stauffenberg, Hofacker, and their compatriots — became conspirators while most of the their fellow officers, even those who disliked Hitler as much as the conspirators did, did not. As I thought about these questions, especially in light of Dr. Milgram's obedience experiments and the research of psychoanalysts and cognitive psychologists on moral development, I came to realize that there had to be more to obedience and disobedience, to followership and conspiracy, than the historical events. There had to be a psychological dimension from the backgrounds of the conspirators, the nonconspirators, and the followers into which traditional historians have not yet looked. In the next and final chapter, I will, by looking into this psychological dimension, offer some insight into why those officers who chose conspiracy did so and why the majority did not.

Notes

1. Reynolds. p. 190. Wheeler-Bennett, p. 459. See Reynolds, pp. 192–94, for details of the government planned by the Opposition.

2. Stieff letter, September 5, 1941, quoted in Hamerow, pp. 291–92.

3. Stieff letter, quoted in Zeller, p. 216.

4. Reynolds, p. 191.

5. Reynolds, p. 194.

6. October 30, 1939, entry, Hassell, p. 83. Reynolds, pp. 194–95.

7. Falkenhausen, MS # B-289, pp. 20–21, in Detwiler, et al.

8. Müller, "Witzleben, et al.," in Barnett, pp. 53–54. October 31, 1939, entry, Gisevius, p. 384.

9. December 5, 1939, entry, Hassell, p. 93. See also conversation with General Vogl, December 23, 1939, entry, Hassell, p. 99.

10. Ritter, *German Resistance*, pp. 146–47.

11. Müller, "Witzleben, et al.," in Barnett, p. 54. Gisevius, pp. 387–89. Reynolds, p. 196.

12. Ritter, *German Resistance*, p. 154.

13. General Roehricht, Chief of the Training Department of the General Staff, in Liddell-Hart, p. 110.

14. Dulles, pp. 58–59. Reynolds, pp. 199–205. See J. G. de Beus, Tomorrow at Dawn (New York: W. W. Norton & Company, 1980) for the full story of Oster's "treason." DeBeus was a member of the Dutch Legation in Berlin in 1939–40 and knew then Major Sas personally. In the 1970s the author was appointed as Dutch Ambassador to the Federal Republic of Germany.

15. Oster quoted in Fest, *Hitler's Death*, p. 139.

16. Leeb quoted in Giziowski, p. 210. In February 1940, Beck received the same reaction from Halder and Brauchitsch through Generalfeldmarschall von Mackensen when he informed them about the SS atrocities. Reynolds, pp. 198–99. February 15, 1940, entry, Hassell, pp. 114–15.

17. Dulles, pp. 58–59.

18. Oster quoted in Schlabrendorff, *Secret War*, p. 114.

19. Bond, "Brauchitsch," in Barnett, pp. 83–84. See Hoffmann, *German Resistance*, pp. 158–61, for details.

20. Reynolds, p. 206.

21. Fest, *Hitler's Death*, p. 175.

22. Oberstbefehlshaber West (High Command West), abbreviated Obwest. Reynolds, p. 215. Wheeler-Bennett, pp. 514–15. Zwygart, p. 175.

23. Bock quoted in Schlabrendorff, *Secret War*, p. 136. Wheeler-Bennett (pp. 515–16) is not too kind to Bock: "Though he despised National Socialism and found repellent its increasing bloodlust, he was consumed with vanity and egotism, and the insignificance of his character prevented him from lifting a finger to overthrow a system for which he felt nothing but contempt."

24. Report of a Staff Lieutenant Colonel, February 4, 1942, entry, Bock, p. 198.

25. Dulles p. 63. Reynolds, p. 215. Gisevius, p. 463. During a September 1943 visit to Berlin, Kluge talked with Beck and Goerdeler and supported Beck in the latter's argument for assassinating Hitler. Yet, once away from the conspiracy's center, he still wavered in completely supporting a future coup. Ritter, *German Resistance*, pp. 246–47.

26. Ritter, *German Resistance*, p. 231. Müller, "Witzleben, et al.," in Barnett, p. 55. Gisevius, p. 464.

27. Reynolds, pp. 212–13.

28. Reynolds, pp. 213–14. Artur Nebe, the chief of the Reich Criminal Police Office in September 1939, was also a conspirator. Just prior to Barbarossa, Himmler selected him to command Einsatzgruppen B behind Army Group Center in the east. Nebe had initially decided to refuse the appointment but reluctantly accepted it to avoid any suspicions by Himmler. Additionally, Nebe's position would allow him to continue to receive information on what was going on within the SS and the Gestapo. Here is an excellent example of the dilemma in which conspirators within a government often find themselves: plotting to overthrow the leader and his regime while participating in its activities to prevent suspicions falling on them or retaining a position to obtain intelligence and warnings. After July 20, 1944, Nebe was arrested and ultimately hanged on March 12, 1945, for his participation in the anti-Hitler conspiracy. Hoffmann, *German Resistance*, pp. 268, 528. Reynolds, p. 214.

29. Müller, "Witzleben, et al.," in Barnett, pp. 56–57.

30. February 14, 1943, entry, Hassell, pp. 284–85. Captain Hermann Kaiser similarly characterized Fromm: "Fromm is always looking for his advantage, honor, glory, ambition; he sacrifices everything to it.... Fromm deprived [Olbricht] of everything, tries to always outbid him with the Führer with the words 'I do more.' " Kaiser, MS # B-285, p. 28, in Detwiler, et al.

31. Hoffmann, *Stauffenberg*, pp. 1–6, 49.

32. Hoffmann, *Stauffenberg*, pp. 18–25. The last three verses of the "Anti-Christ" can be found in Wheeler-Bennett, p. 582.

33. Gisevius, p. 484. Hoffmann, *Stauffenberg*, pp. 139, 150–54.

34. Hoffmann, *Stauffenberg*, pp. 104–5, 111.

35. Halder letter to Kramarz, March 23, 1962, in Kramarz, p. 81.

36. Conversation quoted in Galante, p. 186.

37. Colonel Finckh was later reassigned as Senior Quartermaster West under Stülpnagel, would take an important role in the arrest of SS and Gestapo leaders in Paris on July 20, 1944, and was executed as a result. Stahlberg, pp. 310–15. Stahlberg, Manstein's aide-de-camp, was also Tresckow's nephew.

38. Manstein quoted in Gisevius, p. 469.

39. Stahlberg, p. 246. Manstein's memoirs do not mention this incident at all. Manstein did confirm to Kramarz in two letters (August 20, 1962, and November 15, 1962) that Stauffenberg had privately spoken to Manstein during a visit to his headquarters in western Russia but said nothing about a coup d'état. Kramarz, pp. 108–9. Given Manstein's loyalty to Hitler during the war and the general operational orientation of the memoirs, I would expect him to omit this crucial detail.

40. Stahlberg, p. 257.

41. See Manstein, p. 74–75, for his views of Hitler's military leadership.

42. Hoffmann, *German Resistance*, p. 290.

43. Gisevius, pp. 471–72. Reynolds, p. 225. Stahlberg, pp. 309–10.

44. Whalen, p. 97.

45. Dulles, pp. 64–65. Reynolds, p. 219.

46. Alan Clark, *Barbarossa: The Russian-German Conflict 1941–45* (New York: Quill, 1985), p. 308. Reynolds, pp. 220–21. Wheeler-Bennett, p. 561. Schlabrendorff, *Secret War*, pp. 229–39.

47. Conversation quoted in Hamerow, pp. 312–13.

48. January 21, 1943, entry, p. 29; April 6, 1943, entry, pp. 37–38; April ?, 1943, p. 39; April 11, 1943, p. 39; and January 9, 1943, p. 49; Kaiser's Diary, Kaiser, MS # B-285, in Detwiler, et al.

49. The Reichssicherheitshauptamt (RHSA), or Reich Central Security Office, was the main security department of the Nazi regime. Established in 1939, it combined all existing police forces, including the Gestapo and the SD, into one "super" organization. A subbranch of the RHSA, Amt VI, headed by SS Colonel Adolph Eichmann, directed the roundup of Jews from all over occupied Europe and their deportation to the extermination camps in the east.

50. Ritter, *German Resistance*, pp. 236–37, 248.

51. Duffy and Ricci, p. 138.

52. Broich Letter to Kramarz, June 20, 1962, Kramarz, p. 107.

53. Shirer, *Third Reich*, p. 1336. See also

Stauffenberg quotes in Galante, p. 187, for his growing sense of duty to *save* Germany from Hitler's madness.

54. Stauffenberg quoted in Galante, p. 187.

55. Galante, p. 187.

56. Shirer, *Third Reich*, pp. 1343–44. New Version of Draft for Operation "Valkyrie" of July 31, 1943, with Regulation of February 11, 1944, Zimmermann and Jacobsen, eds., pp. 73–80.

57. Hoffmann, *German Resistance*, pp. 301–4. FitzGibbon, p. 74. Mason, p. 144.

58. Hoffmann, *Stauffenberg*, p. 186. Guderian, pp. 239–40.

59. Mason, pp. 148–50.

60. Wheeler-Bennett, pp. 604–7. Müller, "Witzleben. et al.," in Barnett, pp. 60–62. Martin Bluemenson, "Rommel," in Barnett, p. 314. Most of what is known about Rommel's limited involvement in the anti–Hitler conspiracy comes from Speidel. The manuscript that Speidel wrote for the US Army after the war provides some details about various meetings, involving Rommel and anti–Hitler conspirators, in which the possibility of an armistice with the Allied forces in the west was discussed. See Speidel, MS # B-721, June 16, 1947, in Detwiler, et al. There is still little evidence to support any conclusion that Rommel was an active member of the military opposition and supported Hitler's assassination. At most, like the majority of other field commanders, Rommel probably condemned the Nazi regime's excesses and lawlessness and Hitler's military blundering, but would not participate in an attempt on Hitler's life. Yet, he would not oppose such an attempt either, would support an anti–Nazi government that would follow any coup, and would not report the conspiratorial activities to the OKH, OKW, or the Gestapo beforehand.

61. Shirer, *Third Reich*, p. 1356.

62. Mason, p. 145.

63. Falkenhausen, MS # B-289, p. 41, in Detwiler, et al.

64. Müller, "Witzleben, et al.," in Barnett, p. 63. Richard Lamb, "Kluge," in Barnett, pp. 405–7. Mason, pp. 152–53. In the message, Rommel wrote, "I must ask you to draw the conclusion from this situation without delay." See also Speidel, MS # B-721, pp. 15–16, in Detwiler, et al., for additional details. Text of Rommel's ultimatum to Hitler, July 15, 1944, in Zimmermann and Jacobsen, eds., pp. 93–94.

65. Stahlberg, p. 349. Fellgeibel quoted in Stahlberg, p. 356.

66. Ritter, *German Resistance*, pp. 279–80.

67. On July 30, 1944, Falkenhausen returned to Berlin where he was arrested by the Gestapo. From that time to early December, he was moved to various prisons and finally questioned. Although the Gestapo got no information about the failed plot from Falkenhausen, the secret police kept him in their custody until the end of the war. Falkenhausen was incarcerated with other illustrious persons, such as Schacht, Halder, Niemoller, and others, from December 1944 until their liberation by American troops on May 5, 1945.

68. Macksey, p. 216.

69. Görlitz, "Keitel, Jodl, and Warlimont" in Barnett, p. 153.

70. Reynolds, pp. 257–59.

71. Müller, "Witzleben, et al.," in Barnett, pp. 62–63.

72. Müller, "Witzleben, et al.," in Barnett, p. 63.

73. Conversation quoted in Mason, p. 271.

74. Reynolds, pp. 263, 265.

75. Mason, pp. 176–81.

76. Mason, pp. 267–30. Shirer, *Third Reich*, pp. 1378–80. Hitler decorated Remer for his actions in crushing the July 20 coup. At the award ceremony Remer declared, "Today we are political soldiers. Our political mission is: Safeguarding of the space which we need to live in defense of our national socialistic ideal. And we are going to carry out this political mission come what may, until our final victory." He was promoted to major general by the end of the war and cocreated the neo–Nazi Socialist Reich Party in 1950. In this party's platform was a new *Dolschtoss* myth — the July 20, 1944, coup had stabbed the German army in the back and resulted in Germany's ultimate defeat. On March 15, 1952, the German High Court at Braunschweig sentenced Remer to three months in prison for slandering the participants of the July 20, 1944, plot as traitors. On September 12, 1952, the Constitutional Court of the Federal Republic declared Remer's party unconstitutional. In November, the party was formally dissolved, and Remer disappeared into obscurity just as fast as he had risen into historical prominence. Remer quote from Document 3054-PS, Script of a documentary film of representative individuals and scenes, 1921–45, prepared as evidence for the Nuremburg Trial, *NCA*, IV, p. 852. Wheeler-Bennett, pp. 700–1. Snyder, p. 294.

77. Olbricht quoted in Hamerow, p. 345.

78. Stauffenberg quoted in Hoffmann, *Stauffenberg*, p. 277. Schlabrendorff, *Secret War*, p. 392.

79. Shirer, *Third Reich*, p. 1395. Tresckow was referring to incident in the story of Hercules from Greek mythology. After completing his 12 labors, he shot the centaur Nessus with a poisoned arrow for trying to violate his new wife. The dying Nessus told the wife to preserve his blood in a garment which, when worn, would cause the wearer to love her forever. Several years later, Hercules fell in love with another woman, and his jealous wife sent him a garment smeared with Nessus's blood, apparently to ensure Hercules would love only her. Instead, the

blood turned out to be poison, and Hercules died when he put on the garment.

80. Hitler quoted, Allen, p. 144.

81. Earl F. Ziemke, "Rundstedt," in Barnett, p. 201. Macksey, p. 221. See List of Officers expelled from the army by the Court of Honor, from Microfilm, July 20, 1944, Institut fuer Zeitgeschicte, in Zimmermann and Jacobsen, eds., pp. 176–78.

82. The condemned men were taken to the basement of Plozensee Prison, stripped naked, and placed on chairs. The executioners then placed piano wire nooses attached to meat hooks around the necks of the men and then kicked away the chairs. The conspirators died in a long, torturous manner. The executions were filmed, and the film was processed immediately and brought to Hitler for his viewing that night. Goebbels then had the film shown at a Berlin Cadet School as a demonstration of how the regime treated traitors. The "test" audience was so horrified by what they saw that Goebbels ordered all copies destroyed, and apparently all were as none have ever been found. Wheeler-Bennett, pp. 680–84. See descriptions of the condemned conspirators by some of the cameramen who filmed the hangings, "The Spectacle of Horror," in Zimmermann and Jacobsen, eds., pp. 189–91.

83. Hofacker, after his capture following the failed plot, also apparently implicated Rommel in the plan to end the war in the west once Hitler was dead. These pieces of testimony were apparently sufficient for Hitler to confirm Rommel's knowledge, if not complicity, in the conspiracy and to provide sufficient cause to obtain the suicide of the generalfeldmarschall in October 1944.

84. Quoted in Shirer, *Third Reich*, p. 1398.

85. Rothfels, pp. 9–10; footnote 1, p. 10. Wheeler-Bennett lists 161 names in Appendix D, pp. 744–52. Knappe (pp. 254–55) relates "[E]ven some junior officers were arrested because they had been on an implicated general's staff for some time and had become confidants of the general.... Everybody knew somebody who had been arrested."

86. Shirer (*Third Reich*, p. 1328) called Freisler "...perhaps the most sinister and blood-thirsty Nazi in the Third Reich after Heydrich...." Schlabrendorff was arrested and tortured by the Gestapo and stood before the People's Court and Justice Freisler on February 3, 1945. An American bomb fell on the court building, killing, among others, the infamous justice, and caused a fire that destroyed the folder of evidence against Schlabrendorff. He languished in Gestapo hands for the rest of the war and was ultimately freed by the Allies, one of the very few of the major conspirators to have survived the Gestapo and the war.

87. Wheeler-Bennett, pp. 676–77. Some, like Stauffenberg's widow, had their children taken from them and placed into "good Nazi" homes. She was able to find them after the end of the war. Not all of those arrested, were executed; for example, Halder spent the remainder of the war forced to move from one concentration camp to another until he, along with other dignitaries, was finally liberated by Allied troops. Others, like Canaris, were not so lucky; they were executed by the SS in Berlin as the battle for the capital of the "Thousand-Year Reich" began, 12 years after its inception.

88. Knappe, p. 255.

89. Guderian quoted in Macksey, pp. 221–22. See Kaiser, MS # B-285, pp. 2–3, in Detwiler, et al., for texts of similar speeches by Göring and Admiral Karl Doenitz — Raeder's successor as Commander in Chief of the German Navy — to their respective services.

90. Quoted in Allen, p. 153.

91. Wheeler-Bennett, p. 678.

92. Warlimont, p. 441.

93. Knappe, p. 255.

94. Senger, pp. 274–75. Senger and Senger, "Senger," in Barnett, p. 387.

95. Mellenthin, p. 435.

96. Luck, pp. 201–2.

97. July 21, 1944, entry, Prueller, p. 174.

98. Bock, p. 545.

99. "Hitler Hangs His Generals," *New York Times*, August 9, 1944, p. 16.

100. Tresckow quoted in Shirer, p. 1353.

101. Guderian, p. 276.

8

Conspirators, Nonconspirators, and Followers

This final chapter will look at various characteristics of the "conspirators," the "nonconspirators," and the "followers" to discover why the members of these groups acted as they did. Since the end of the war, many people have tried to fathom why "good, rational" professional military officers would support and then blindly follow a man whom they believed to be a "madman" or at least a criminal, a man who had regularly heaped abuse and scorn upon them and who had fired many of them — some more than once; why they would continue to serve Hitler with complete loyalty. In the previous chapters I have mainly used a historical approach to get to the answer to that question, and certainly the reactions of the members of all three groups to the historical events of the period 1918–44 are important. However, their responses to the historical events do not provide the complete answer. I began to realize that there had to be more than just the historical events underlying why a few chose conspiracy but the majority chose acquiescence or blind obedience. Despite the historical information that I have presented in the previous chapters, I still had the feeling that there were great questions which still needed answers.

The most significant question seemed to be: why did the resisters conclude that conspiracy and assassination were morally correct during this time of war, requiring them to violate their oath to Hitler, but the vast majority of their contemporaries did not? From this basic questions, others followed. In what ways were the conspirators different from the nonconspirators and the followers? Was there something in the backgrounds of the conspirators that enabled them to eventually see the moral crisis that Hitler and National Socialism had precipitated within the German army, something to which the majority of the general officers were blinded? These questions consistently floated in the back of my mind as I set about presenting the historical background through the last chapter.

As I discussed earlier, the conspirators came to doubt their continued loyalty to Hitler and then reject their oath for a variety of reasons. The first signs of doubt and protest came after the murder of Generals Schleicher and Bredow during the 1934 Röhm Purge, followed by the increasing pace of rearmament in the mid–1930s. These initial protests blossomed into opposition to Hitler's aggressive foreign-policy moves and his humiliation of Fritsch in 1938. Once the war began and the exhilaration of the early victories diminished as the conflict degenerated into one of desperate attrition in the Soviet Union, others turned against Hitler. The increasing casualties and destruction of Germany that resulted from Hitler's disastrous strategic and tactical decisions and the immorality of the atrocities committed by both the party organizations, the SS and the Gestapo, and by the army at war, caused others to turn from obedience to disobedience and conspiracy.

These reasons combined inside the minds of the conspirators to first produce a loss of confidence in Hitler as their leader and then a moral crisis upon which they felt obliged to act. At the same time, I wanted to know why these same outrages produced only protest opposition to Hitler but not conspiracy among the nonconspirators. It reasonably seemed that the answers to the questions lay within the process of how people develop moral judgment. Therefore, using the psychoanalytical and cognitive development theories of moral development presented in Chapter 1, I will examine the careers and family backgrounds and significant familial and collegial relationships of a number of German generals to validate this hypothesis. We will see that the familial and educational experiences of the conspirators appear to have produced a higher level of moral discernment in them than in other officers while the second issue, familial and collegial relationships allowed the conspirators to plot against Hitler with minimal fear of the conspiracy being revealed to the Gestapo.

Comparison of Conspirators, Nonconspirators, and Followers

In Table 8.1, Military Careers of Selected General Officers, we see that they all entered the army before 1915 and, therefore, had sworn a personal oath to the Kaiser. They went through World War I and the Weimar period, and the restoration of German greatness and the early victories under Hitler. Also, we see a slight acceleration in promotion rates during the 1930s, but all of the officers in this sample were already generals by 1939. Therefore, careerism may have been important during the prewar years, but had minimal, if any, effect on their susceptibility to resistance, especially after 1939. Finally, the fact that all shared the same historical events and experiences nullifies the impact of these experiences on any given officer in determining whether or not he would become a conspirator.

Yet, if these were the only factors that impacted or affected the loyalty and obedience of the senior officers to Hitler, there would have been no — or very, very few — conspirators among them. Since there were conspirators among them, other factors must have been at work, factors from the officer's family background and early childhood. An analysis of Table 8.2, Family Backgrounds of Selected General Officers — which presents a variety of such factors for selected general officers — provides several important indicators. First, social class (parents' background) alone did not impact an officer's susceptibility or nonsusceptibility to conspiracy — conspirators, nonconspirators, and followers came from both the middle class and nobility. Second, state, especially military, service by the father (or ancestors) does appear to have significance, especially for the nonconspirators and followers. Third, of the listed generals, except for Witzleben, those who went through the

Table 8.1. Careers of Selected German General Officers

RANK	*Fritsch*	*Beck*	*Witz-Leben*	*Stülp-nagel*	*Brau-chitsch*	*Halder*	*Rund-stedt*	*Bock*
2LT	1900	1899	1901	1906	1900	1904	1893	1899
1LT	1909	1909	1916		1909	1912	1902	1908
CPT	1913	1913	1919	1924	1913	1915	1907	1912
MAJ	1917	1918	1923	1925	1918	1924	1914	1916
LTC	1923	1923	1929	1930	1925	1929	1920	1920
COL	1927	1929	1931	1932	1928	1931	1923	1925
MJG	1930	1931	1934	1935	1930	1934	1927	1929
LTG	1932	1932	1934	1937	1933	1936	1929	1931
GEN		1934	1935	1939	1936	1938	1932	1935
GO		1936	1938		1938	1940	1938	1938
GFM			1940	1940	1940		1940	
FINAL STATUS	Dismissed 1938; KIA 1939 1944	Resigned 1938; suicide	Executed 1944	Executed 1944	Dismissed 1941, POW 1945	Dismissed 1942, POW 1945	Dismissed 3 times, 1941–45, POW 1945	Dismissed 1942

RANK	*Manstein*	*Kleist*	*Rommel*	*Model*	*Arnim*	*Senger*	*Gude-rian*	*Blasko-witz*
2LT	1907	1901	1912	1910	1909	1914	1908	1902
1LT	1914	1910	1915	1915	1915	1918	1914	1912
CPT	1915	1914	1918	1918	1917	1927	1915	1914
MAJ	1927	1922	1932	1929	1928	1934	1927	1922
LTC	1929	1926	1933	1932	1932	1936	1931	1926
COL	1933	1929	1937	1934			1938	1933
MJG	1936	1932	1939	1938	1938	1942	1936	1932
LTG	1939	1933	1941	1940	1939	1943	1938	1938
GEN	1940	1936	1941	1941	1941	1944	1939	
CGN	1942	1940	1942	1942				
FM	1942	1943	1942	1944				
FINAL STATUS	Dismissed 1944	POW 1945	Suicide 1944	Suicide 1945	POW 1943	POW 1945	POW 1945	Dismissed 1940; POW 1945

Sources: Barnett; Guderian; Bock; Senger; Giziowski; Reynolds

cadet corps, which prepared teenage boys for military service as officers, were either nonconspirators or followers. Attendance at a liberal gymnasium, however, is not determinative since members of all three groups attended the gymnasium. In summary, the combination of a family history of military service and education in a cadet corps appears to produce in the officer a greater belief in "blind obedience" and, thus, a view of the oath of loyalty as an unbreakable sacred bond.

Influence of Education and Family Background

In this section I will review the influence of education and family background on the early development of the selected officers to demonstrate how many conspirators differed from the nonconspirators. To do this, I will briefly discuss the liberal education program of the German gymnasium that many of the senior German officers of the 1940s attended in the late 1800s and

Table 8.2. Backgrounds of Selected German General Officers

General	*Father's Background*	*Mother's Background*	*Birth Year*	*Education*
Witzleben	Military, Nobility	Nobility	1881	Cadet Corps, 1891
Brauchitsch	Military, Nobility	Nobility	1881	Corps of Pages
Halder	Military		1884	Gymnasium
Blomberg	Military, Nobility	Nobility	1874	Cadet Corps
Keitel	Upper Middle Class	Upper Middle Class	1883	Private Tutor
Jodl	Military		1890	Grammar School, Cadet Corps
Warlimont	Middle Class	Middle Class	1894	Gymnasium
Rundstedt	Military, Nobility	Nobility	1875	Cadet Corps
Reichenau	Military	Middle Class	1884	Cadet Corps
Manstein	Military, Nobility	Nobility	1887	Lycee, Cadet Corps
Rommel	Middle Class	Nobility	1891	Gymnasium
Model	Middle Class	Middle Class	1891	Gymnasium
Paulus	Middle Class	Middle Class	1890	Gymnasium
Senger	Middle Class	Middle Class	1891	Gymnasium, University
Kluge	Military, Nobility		1882	Cadet Corps
Guderian	Military	Middle Class	1888	Cadet Corps
Beck	Middle Class	Middle Class	1880	Gymnasium
Fritsch	Middle Class	Middle Class	1880	?
Bock	Military, Nobility	Nobility	1880	Cadet Corps

Sources: Barnett; Guderian; Senger; Giziowski

early 1900s. I will also discuss the education program of those who went through the cadet corps prior to commissioning, and the officer commissioning program, to see how the two compare to get an idea of how the educational background of these officers during early childhood and adolescence could impact their moral development. I will also review early family life of some of those who became senior officers of the 1930s and early 1940s. The end purpose is to provide some empirical and anecdotal evidence to support my contention that a firm but not authoritarian family life and the more liberal education of the gymnasium gave the conspirators as a group the ability to discern the moral crisis that at some point led them to disobey their oath and conspire against Hitler and the Nazi regime.

The basic education of many senior officers of the Nazi period, as we can see from Table 8.2, occurred in the Gymnasium. The Gymnasium, dating back to the Middle Ages, was the equivalent of the American high school. While the grammar schools provided a somewhat superficial general education, the secondary schools concentrated on the classics. The Gymnasium curriculum consisted of courses in religion, German, history, civics, science, geography, and, of course, classical literature and the classical anguages, Greek and Latin. In the early 1860s, the Realgymnasium was created alongside the Gymnasium with a more modern curriculum: the number of study hours for classical studies was reduced, French and English replaced Greek and Latin, and modern science and mathematics received additional study hours. Males entered the Gymnasium at nine years old for the next nine years and graduated at age 18 or 19 with the scholastic achievement of an American student in the second year of an American college. According to Friedrich Paulsen,

> The ideal of the new education is a human being whose faculties enable him to form a clear and definite conception of the actual world; who, by virtue of his will, is

> able to recognize and follow his original bent, whose imagination and fine emotions are trained to the perception of the beautiful and the heroic. This is a man in the full sense of the word: this true humanistic culture.[1]

The education of the German secondary schools was intended to provide a general—as opposed to an especially technical or vocational—preparation of males for positions in the learned professions (law, theology, and medicine) and the higher positions of the civil service and the military. A secondary aim was to transmit German culture, especially after the establishment of the empire in 1871. The Kaiser even took an interest in educational reform as he saw the educational system as a means to bring the German states closer together.[2] Although the curricula of the Gymnasium and the Realgymnasium were generally similar, graduates of the latter schools could attend only technical schools and were barred from the learned professions and certain positions in the civil service. As Russell wrote, "[P]opular prejudice [was] so strong that only graduates of the *Gymnasien* [*sic*] [were] regarded as cultural."[3]

Although the secondary education system leaned toward liberal humanistic development, there were problems with the curriculum and teaching methodology that hampered complete intellectual development of the students. Much of the teaching was accomplished through repetition and memorization. Most teachers were not of the highest quality and were not trained to encourage their students to think independently. The church also had significant influence over education, particularly in the primary schools, so both the state and church combined to suppress liberalism in education. Furthermore, many of the teachers were reserve officers, and the pervasive German nationalism following the wars of liberation spilled over into the schools. By the 1890s, curricula and textbooks had become more heavily imbued with contemporary German nationalism while they generally denigrated socialism and liberalism. Russell provides this characterization: "Germany is nothing if not military. The school system is pervaded by the marital spirit."[4] Friedrich Nietzsche, Paul de Lagarde, and Julius Langbehn were just a few of the many critics of the stultified German education system who favored better-trained teachers, more individualism and creativity, and less burden on the students.[5]

The other method of secondary education for the Nazi-era senior officers was the cadet corps. With the "right" social position and "connections," parents could get a son as young as ten admitted to one of about a dozen junior cadet corps scattered throughout Germany. The curriculum concentrated on the military sciences: strategy, tactics, close order drill, weapons training, and tactical exercises. There were also courses in world history, languages, and literature. During their final two years, equivalent to the last two years of the Gymnasium, the cadets would attended a military academy to complete their military education and training—the Gross Lichterfelde in Berlin was the pre-eminent of these. Following graduation from the academy, each cadet applied to a regiment and, if accepted, served as a cadet officer (*Portepee Faehnrich*). The cadet officer also attended the Kriegschule for six months and served additional probationary time with his regiment before receiving a commission as a second lieutenant. A graduate of the Gymnasium or the Realgymnasium could obtain his commission by applying directly to a regiment to become an aspirant officer (*Faehnrich*), served in the enlisted ranks for six months, and attended the Kriegschule to receive six months of officer training. If he passed the final exams, he returned to his regiment as an officer cadet for an additional probation before receiving his commission.[6] The cadet officer who came through the cadet corps had a slightly higher status than the officer cadet who did not.

This initial military training was further bolstered for those fortunate few first lieutenants who were selected to attend the Kriegsakademie (War Academy). Attendance at the academy was required for an appointment as a General Staff officer and essential for promotion to the higher grades. The pre–1914 War Academy course was three years long, and the institution had a student body officially set at 400. However, it usually had fewer in attendance, divided into three classes. Of the 130 or so admitted each year, only about 20 percent would complete the full three years. Military topics included military history, military cartography, fortifications and siege warfare, and tactics. Nonmilitary courses, taught by civilian professors, included world history and literature. The first two years consisted of lectures, oral and written work with an examination in each June which, along with regular reports, was used to determine which students would return the next year. The academic program concluded with a staff ride (field exercise) so the officer students could demonstrate what they had learned to the academy's faculty and the army's senior officers.[7]

As we can see, the German Army's professional military education system furthered a very narrow emphasis on military subjects to the neglect of intellectual subjects. Messenger writes, "The drawback of this long training, the backbone of which was the traditional strict Prussian discipline, was that it tended to produce officers with a narrow and rigid outlook." General von Beseler, a famous siege specialist and later Rundstedt's superior, remarked once to British General Sir James Edmonds that this system was "numbing" and produced officers who were "faithful to duty, but stupid."[8] Giziowski calls it "in fact a very narrow education."[9] Tresckow, as a lieutenant colonel, once told Halder's secretary, "We are trained to be machines and must adapt our opinions. Little value is placed on our development as individuals."[10] Senger also recognized the danger of this problem:

> We, the higher German commanders, suffered excessively from a narrow tutelage. This subservience found its nadir in the sheltering behind the directives of Hitler who was regarded as the real cause of degeneration in the so-called "promulgation of executive orders for a task."[11]

Schalbrendorff held similar beliefs about the German officers.[12] Even Keitel, perhaps belatedly to justify his actions during the war, recognized the one-sidedness and limitations of the professional military education of a German officer.[13]

To see the significance of education and father's service to the state, let's look at comments from historians about several of these generals. Ziemke wrote about Rundstedt, "Childhood in an officer's household and military schooling from the age of twelve on had aroused in him an exceptionally strong sense of duty and had as well confined his outlook to military matters [with the exception of] reading adventure and detective stories,..."[14] Lord Carver similarly characterized Manstein: "Both at home and in the army, he was brought up in the traditions and general ethos of the old Prussian military caste, reinforced by that of his Lutheran puritanism: what he described as the army's traditional notions of simplicity and chivalry and its soldierly conception of honour."[15] Captain Kaiser characterized Manstein as an officer with "only military and operative abilities and not understanding of politics; he is a man without a *thorough* [author's italics] education."[16] He also reported that Schlabrendorff called Guderian an "unrestrained opportunist.... He is the incarnation of characterlessness."[17] We see similar tendencies to some degree in other followers and nonconspirators.

Let's take a closer look at Generalfeldmarschall Fedor von Bock. Bock was born in 1880 in Küstrin of a Prussian Protestant aristocratic family with a military heritage dating back to the army of Frederick the Great. His father General Moritz von Bock had been an officer during the Franco-Prussian War and "was a stern advocate of austerity and discipline as the cardinal virtues of Prussianism. [F]rom the age of ten his young son lived the life of a soldier,..."[18] At the military academy at Potsdam and at the Gross Lichterfelde, Bock "followed the strict, disciplined routine of a Prussian military cadet" and also became quite adept at modern languages, mathematics, and history. Instead of partying with the other cadets, Bock would visit the tomb of Frederick the Great or wander the streets of Potsdam. He soon became known as the "The Holy Fire of Kustrin." He would diligently follow the Prussian tradition of the profession of arms as a man's highest calling.[19] As Turney wrote,

> From an early age, under his father's tutelage, he became imbued with the concept of unquestioning loyalty to the state and dedication to the military profession.... Bock was taught that it was his life's obligation, as a professional military officer, to serve Prussia-Germany's further glorification. These early teachings were to remain with Bock throughout his life. They were to close his mind to every consideration except the most immediate consequences of his status as a soldier in the service of the Fatherland. [20]

Thus, we can now account for his reactions to the Commissar Order and to Tresckow and Gersdorff when they tried to solicit his full support to have the order rescinded, for his criticism of Hitler's military blundering in Russia, and for his refusal to join the anti–Hitler conspiracy.

Gerd von Rundstedt is another example of the "Prussian" Junker whose sense of duty led to blind obedience, even after Hitler had fired him three times. Rundstedt could trace his ancestry back to the year 1109. His male ancestors had served in the armies of various German states and various countries as mercenaries, in addition to Prussia. His father was a serving army officer when Rundstedt was born in 1875. He first attended a Gymnasium for two years and then went to the junior cadet college at Oranienstein in 1888.[21] His biographer characterized Rundstedt as follows:

> ...[c]oming as he did from a family with many generations of soldiers, the [Prussian] Code of Honour would have been imbued in him virtually from birth and was to exert a deep influence on him throughout his life.[22]

Let's now compare these two with two conspirators who attended a Gymnasium, Beck and Stauffenberg. Reynolds writes that Beck was raised "in [an] atmosphere of disciplined humanitarianism in stark contrast to the empty pomposity and cultural despair of Wilhemine Germany." His education gave him "a good grounding in history and literature" that complemented his father's readings from classical German drama, the Bible, and Shakespeare. Like his father, he "enjoyed intellectual pursuits of a relatively abstract nature and he seems to have acquired his political outlook along with the attendant shortsightedness." Beck's "breadth of education ... [distinguished] him from his comrades who came from a long line of soldiers and never learned to appreciate anything but the military art."[23] Beck, in November 1939, was elected to Groener's seat on the Mittwochgesellschaft, a social and nonpolitical society for scientific discussion established in the 19th century and composed of 14 prominent authorities in their own fields.[24] Professor Werner Karl Heisenberg, a respected German physicist and member of the society, also noted Beck's scholarly and philosophical interests beyond those of most soldiers.[25]

Schlabrendorff gives us two characterizations of Beck. In *They Almost Killed Hitler*, he wrote,

> Beck ... did not look like a career officer. He made one think rather of a sage or a philosopher. Every word, every gesture, betrayed the even poise of his mind and temperament, and he had a singular talent for imparting the finest shade of meaning to anything he deemed right to say.[26]

In his other work, *The Secret War Against Hitler*, he wrote that Beck was

> a man of wide-ranging cultural interests, a somewhat introverted intellectual whose main characteristic was that he thoroughly studied any matter before attempting to pass judgment on it. The fact that he was a General Staff officer was not immediately apparent; he gave the impression rather of being a profound philosopher.[27]

We can see a similar intellectualism, discussed briefly in Chapter 7, in Stauffenberg that influenced his views on military service. As I mentioned earlier, he grew up in a home which encouraged intellectual development—his mother Caroline Gräfin von Stauffenberg, a great-granddaughter of Gneisenau, had a strong interest in Goethe, Shakespeare, and contemporary poets. He attended a humanistic Gymnasium in Stuttgart and developed a special interest in the classics, including translating from the original languages, an interest he retained after entering the army. When he left school, he considered a career as an architect or a musician—he was an accomplished cellist and often accompanied his brothers Berthold on the piano and Alexander on the violin. Stauffenberg retained his intellectual interests on active duty, attended lectures and concerts, and often engaged his fellow officers in such discussions.[28] Apparently, some of his fellow officers did not understand him as they, according to Hoffman, "had other interests; they were simpler characters and at times were sickened by his continuous political talk which they found pretentious and tiresome...."[29] Schlabrendorff made this assessment of Stauffenberg: "[he] had been interested in matters of the mind and spirit, in poetry and literature,..."[30] The sculptor Ludwig Thormaelen provided this impression of Stauffenberg at age 17:

> Young though he was, his radiant energy, which he was ready to turn to everything around him, produced an impression of absolute reliability. He would intervene in a manner which showed his intelligence—frank and honest in opposition, good humored in criticism, but equally vigorous in agreement or in support of any justified demands by others.[31]

Besides his mother, the German humanistic poet Stefan Georg also exerted a great influence on the future conspirator. Stauffenbeg met the poet in 1923 and was soon accepted into his circle. More than a poet, Georg was also a teacher and philosopher who wanted to build his students into a new elite. He spoke of new obligations to readily and selflessly serve, a capacity for devotion, and self-sacrifice. Georg did not spell out the specific duties but believed his students would perceive what these duties were and fulfill them.[32] Stauffenberg once told his wife that Georg was the greatest poet of the age. According to Thormaelen, Georg did not have to instill his beliefs into Stauffenberg but merely to confirm those that already existed in the future conspirator.[33] Later in life he, in turn, passed on Georg's philosophy onto others that he met, including fellow conspirators. According to Margarete Gräfin von Hardenberg, Stauffenberg's fellow resisters "found their aims clarified and their actions justified through the medium of Georg's poems; one of these poems was the foundation of the friendship between Henning von Tresckow and Stauffenberg."[34] Georg's beliefs in self-sacrifice, selfless devotion to duty, and responsibility would extend beyond Stauffenberg to the circle of conspirators.

We can see the future conspirator's views on service and obedience in his response to the essay "The Essence of Being a

Soldier," written by Major General Georg von Sodenstern, Chief of Staff of Army Group 2 at Frankfurt am Main, over the winter of 1937-38. The general's essay extolled the idea that soldiers were a community ready to fight and die for the nation. Their highest ideals were devotion to the commander in chief and death in battle. Officers and men must implicitly trust their leaders and eliminate conflicts between orders and their views.[35] Stauffenberg wrote in a letter to the general that he generally appreciated his essay but then qualified the general's concept of blind obedience: "We cannot afford to withdraw into the purely military, meaning a purely professional environment, although the best of us are particularly inclined to do so in view of the situation...."[36] In other words, while he generally believed in the soldier's duty to the state, Stauffenberg, even in 1939, felt that the soldier could not completely remain unconcerned about its political actions.

Let's look briefly at three other conspirators—Fellgiebel, Oster, and Tresckow. Fellgiebel was born in 1886 and grew up on his father's estate in Posen. He attended the Johannes Gymnasium in Breslau, where he developed a great gift for exact natural sciences and acquired a broadly based education that included reading the ancient Greek philosophers and Immanuel Kant. Hoffman wrote that Fellgiebel was well regarded by his fellow officers "as a highly-educated, sensitive soldier, upright and human, well versed in the natural sciences with a bent for philosophy...."[37] Oster, born in 1887, was the son of a Saxon parson in Dresden. Gill writes, "The family had a liberal, humanistic outlook and Oster was devoted to his cultivated mother, who died when he was seventeen. Oster became a keen horseman and a good cellist."[38] Tresckow, born into a family with a long military tradition, received his education in the Realgymnaisum in Goslar. After World War I, he went into banking, became a broker on the stock exchange, went on a world tour in 1924, and spent six months in South America. He would often invite subordinate officers for evening discussions of nonmilitary subjects, historical figures, ethnology, and other intellectual subjects.[39] In other words, these officers had experiences beyond their strict military calling and demonstrated a quest for intellectual development that went beyond purely military subjects.[40]

In addition to mode of education, religious upbringing also appears to significantly influence an officer's susceptibility to conspiracy. Earlier I mentioned that Manstein's Lutheran puritanism contributed to his undying loyalty to Hitler, and so it was with other nonconspirators and followers, a trend found among many Germans. Those with a Lutheran background felt that their religious beliefs demanded absolute obedience to the political authority—after all, Luther's beliefs had flourished under the alliance between the Lutheran church and German princes of the 16th and 17th centuries. Furthermore, these beliefs enabled them to separate public morality from private or personal morality, as Luther had taught. While they disliked the Nazis and their criminal activities, their reaction was to compartmentalize their thoughts, keep them to themselves, and confine themselves even more to their military duties.[41] On the other hand, the religiosity of many followers and nonconspirators, like that of many nominal believers of any religious belief system, probably did not go much beyond the forms of Christianity with little true acceptance of its spiritual values.

There were, however, a number of "spiritual Christians," like Neimöller and Bonhoeffer, in the anti–Hitler opposition. Niemoeller served as pastor of the evangelical parish of St. Ann's, Dahlem, a Berlin suburb, where both Oster and Hammerstein attended church. After learning about the regime's atrocities first hand, Oster wrote that Hitler was a "mad criminal who is engaged in destroying everything that is sacred to me as an officer, as a human being, as a Christian, and as a German."[42] Many of his colleagues called him "a man after God's heart," without personal ambition.[43] Zeller writes, "Those who worked with [Oster] knew his driving patriotism and his deep devotion to the religion and ethical code of his youth."[44] Gersdorff, who also extolled Statuffenberg's moral and religious principles, stated that Stauffenberg found "a similar type of man in Tresckow."[45] Bernd von Kleist reported that "Tresckow grew up to be a God-fearing man with a strong sense of duty and a great respect for tradition."[46] Canaris was seen as "a pronounced intellectual of strong religious convictions and a certain tendency towards the world of the abstract."[47] Schlabrendorff called General Obricht "a deeply religious man by conviction, opposed to National Socialism,..."[48] Although General Groppe, the officer who had opposed the SS "free love" order, was not an active conspirator, he stated that he was opposed to the Nazis, like many of the conspirators, because of his love of Germany and because of his Catholic beliefs. According to him, this hostile attitude to the Nazi movement resulted in the animosity of and censure by local Nazi functionaries.[49]

In addition to his intellectual pursuits, Stauffenberg was also known as a deeply devout Catholic. As Schlabrendorff wrote:

> Thus Stauffenberg's objection to Hitler was fundamentally a spiritual one and in no way based on a fear of impending military defeat or any other material considerations. Moral conviction and the acknowledgment of Christian truths turned Stauffenberg into an uncompromising fighter against the German dictator.[50]

Gisevius wrote, "His deep religious feeling also marked him as many notches above the average of his colleagues."[51] After the war Stauffenberg's former commander in North Africa, General von Broich, reported, "The decision to use force he found particularly difficult and serious being a confirmed Christian and Catholic."[52] Galante tempers these views of Stauffenberg as a devout Catholic by pointing out that he had not been to confession since his first communion. He became a regular churchgoer as a sign of protest when the Nazis began persecuting the clergy and became even more steadfast in his religious observance when Hitler advised the military officers not to attend church in uniform.[53] However, one can adhere to the ethical and moral values of spiritual Christianity, or any belief system, without participating in its formal rituals.

For some of the conspirators, their spiritual beliefs created in them a growing sense that they must do penance for the crimes of their country and their army. As the assassination plans developed, many came to feel that the plot would ultimately fail yet they must continue to conspire and must attempt to assassinate their "Anti-Christ" as if Hitler's assassination would somehow exorcise their own souls as well as the collective soul of the German nation. In Chapter 7, as part of the narrative, I mentioned several conspirators who had this feeling and provide some additional comments here. Steiff in early 1942 wrote,

> All of us have brought so much guilt upon ourselves — for we are after all *co-responsible*; I see in the judgment falling upon us no more than a just atonement for all the crimes we Germans have committed or permitted in the last years. Actually, it satisfies me to see that there is, after all, retaliating justice in this world! Even if I myself should be its victim, I am tired of this horror without end.[54]

Oster, while apparently awaiting his execution, wrote his son:

> We shall all remain to our last breath the decent fellows we were brought up to be as children and as soldiers. Let come what will. The only fear we have is that of the anger of God, when we are not upright and decent and fail to do our duty.[55]

Olbricht on the evening of July 20, 1944, expressed similar feelings to his son-in-law Friedrich Georgi — that Hitler's assassination was necessary to save Germany from destruction and that posterity would certainly recognize and understand the pure motives for their actions.[56] The young Lieutenant Peter Yorck wrote in the farewell letter to his wife:

> I hope my death will be accepted as an atonement for all my sins, as an expiatory sacrifice.... By this sacrifice, our time's distance from God may be shortened by small measure.... We want to kindle the torch of life; a sea of flames surrounds us.[57]

Beck also expressed a high probability of failure but felt a moral duty to try.[58]

Stauffenberg felt a particular spiritual duty to rid Germany of its "Anti-Christ." In mid–1944, he commented to Jakob Kaiser, "We have put ourselves to the test before God and before our conscience; it [the assassination] must be done, for this man [Hitler] is evil incarnate."[59] A few days before the July attempt on Hitler, Stauffenberg commented to the wife of Bernd von Pezold: "It is time now that something was done. But he who has the courage to do something must do so in the knowledge that he will go down in German history as a traitor. If he does not do it, however, then he will be a traitor to his own conscience."[60] Finally, Stauffenberg told a friend, Urban Thiersch, on July 1, 1944: "To yield passively to infamy and paralyzing force is worse than failure. Only action is capable of gaining freedom *inwardly* [author's emphasis] as well as outwardly."[61]

So it appears that many conspirators opposed Hitler because their moral and ethical values of spiritual Christianity, inculcated in them earlier in their lives, ran counter to the gross immorality and criminality of the Hitler regime. Although most of the conspirators had initially agreed with Hitler's goals and policies, they, over time, came to first disagree with his means to obtain them and then with the atrocities that had occurred in the wake of the military victories that they had provided. At some point—1934, 1938, or 1943, depending on individual circumstances — they rejected Hitler's legitimacy. The combination of a liberal, humanistic education, a familial environment that encouraged wide-ranging intellectual development, and a spiritual Christianity allowed these officers to see the growing moral gulf between them and the criminal Nazi regime that other officers either failed to see or ignored — a blindness which prevented them from acting against Hitler. As Whalen writes,

> Generations of Tresckows, Stauffenbergs, Moltkes, Yorcks, Kleists, and others had molded values and standards that the conspirators inherited, felt themselves bound by, and responsible for transmitting to yet another generation. Violating this tradition was quite literally unthinkable.[62]

Effects of Familial and Collegial Relationships

A most significant characteristic of anti–Hitler opposition was the close familial and collegial relationships of many of the conspirators. As Whalen wrote,

> The conspirators' families were bewildering tribes of parents and grandparents, siblings, cousins, in-laws, and friends who had become honorary family members. Their families provided them with their values and moral bearings; they served as places of refuge, conspiratorial lairs, and spaces where one could freely talk and plan to act.[63]

For example, there were two General von Witzlebens, Erwin and Job, in the conspiracy, and one of the few surviving conspirators Schlabrendorff was not only Tresckow's aide and fellow conspirator but also his nephew. A more in-depth look at the extended families of Dietrich Bonhoeffer and Stauffenberg proves enlightening.

First, let's more closely examine the extended Bonhoeffer and Stauffenburg "families" to really see how these familial relationships aided the conspirators. Two of the Abwehr conspirators, Dietrich Bonhoeffer and Hans Dohnanyi, were distant cousins to by blood. Additionally, the two were double brothers-in-law: Hans was married to Dietrich's sister Christina, and Hans's sister Grete was married to Dietrich's older brother Karl-Friedrich. Bonhoeffer's uncle on his mother's side was General Paul von Hase, City Commandant of Berlin in 1944, executed for his support of the July 20 plot. Peter Yorck von Wartenburg, descendant of the Yorck of Tauroggen and a member of the Kriesau Circle,[64] was also related to Bonhoeffer, who was also related to Peter's famous ancestor through another line of marriage. One of Peter Yorck's sisters had married into the Gersdorff family, one of whose members, Rudolf, was a conspirator. Yorck was also a distant cousin of Stauffenberg whose mother was related to the Yorcks as well as to another hero of the Napoleonic era, Gneisenau. Fritz-Diertlof von der Schulenberg of the civilian opposition was a classmate of Yorck and Hofacker.[65]

The extended Stauffenberg family and group of friends also produced a number of active conspirators. Klaus's older twin brothers Berthold and Alexander were deeply involved in the anti-Hitler conspiracy. Their uncle Nicholas Graf von Uxkuell and several cousins, including Ceaser von Hofacker, were conspirators. The von Häften brothers, Werner and Hans-Bernd, joined the conspiracy. Interestingly, Brauchitsch was their uncle, they grew up in the same area as Bonhoeffer, and Niemoeller was their pastor. Werner served as Stauffenberg's aide and died at his side on July 20, 1944. Hans-Bernd worked in the Foreign Office, served as Stauffenberg's contact to Adam von Trott zu Solz, another member of the Civilian Opposition, and was executed several months later.[66]

In addition to and, in many ways, complementing the familial relationships, were the collegial relationships among many conspirators and nonconspirators. Most had known each other for decades through the cadet corps, the prewar Imperial Army, the military schools, and the Reichswehr's numerically small officer corps (4,000 total).[67] As a result, many of the senior officers of the late 1930s and the war had served with or under each other between 1919 and 1939. For example, Oster, as a young officer, had served under both Halder and Fritsch and with Canaris. Hossbach, Hitler's adjutant, also knew Oster. When he turned against the regime because of the murder of Bredow and later Hitler's treatment of Fritsch, Oster turned to former army friends, like Olbricht, Witzleben, and Georg Thomas, to form his opposition network.[68] Blaskowitz's fellow cadets at the Gross Lichterfelde cadet school included Brauchitsch, Bock, Busch, Kluge, Witzleben, Falkenhorst, and Hammerstein.[69]

Other examples abound among the nonconspirators and conspirators. As previously mentioned, Sodernstern, the Chief of Staff of Army Group W at Frankfurt am Main in December 1938, had General Erwin von Witzleben as his commanding officer, whom he had already known from previous assignments. For the first four months of the Second World War, he served as the Chief of Staff of Army Group C, commanded by General Ritter von Leeb, with whom he had served before 1918 in the Bavarian Army.[70] On October 1, 1920, when Rundstedt was promoted to lieutenant colonel — along with Blomberg, Bock, Hammerstein-Equord, and Leeb. Rundstedt served with Heinz Guderian in the Second Infantry Division in Pomerania in March 1923. In February 1932, when Rundstedt took over command of Wehrkreis III, he handed over command of the Second Cavalry Division to General Ewald von Kleist. Later in the year, he commanded the "Blue" forces in the autumn maneuvers, and Bock commanded the opposing "Red forces."[71]

There were other collegial relationships to serve as examples. When Stauffenberg entered his Staff College course in October 1936, Mertz von Quierheim and Eberhard Finckh, also future conspirators, were among the 99 other officers there.[72] In 1938, Stauffenberg was assigned to Hoepner's First Light Division at Wuppertal.[73] Rommel and Stülpnagel had known each when they had both been instructors at the Dresden Officer Candidate School in the early 1930s. Speidel himself had known Rommel since the First World War—they had both fought in the Argonne Forest and served together in the 13th Infantry Regiment (Württemburg) of the Reichswehr.[74] Speidel had also served on the General Staff and was well acquainted with Beck.[75] Colonel G. Schultze-Buettiger, executed on July 20, 1944, had been Beck's adjutant for many years.[76] Before the war Beck had visited Speidel at the latter's home, and Speidel had accompanied Beck on an official army visit to France.[77] Heusinger had served with Paulus in 1927, and Tresckow had served as one of Heusinger's staff officers before 1939.[78]

In essence, these familial and collegial relationships allowed the conspirators to create a "playspace" free of Gestapo spying, as Whalen first presented.[79] Johan Huizinga described "play" as

> a free activity standing quite consciously outside "ordinary" life as being "not serious," but at the same time absorbing the player intensely and utterly. It is an activity connected with no material interest, and no profit can be gained by it. It proceeds within its own proper boundaries of time and space according to fixed rules and in an orderly manner. It promotes the formation of social groupings which tend to surround themselves with secrecy and to stress their difference from the common world by disguise or other means.[80]

The "playspace" or playground is the area "marked off beforehand either materially or ideally, deliberately or as a matter of course" where play occurs. It is the "temporary world [*sic*] within the ordinary world, dedicated to the performance of an act apart."[81]

The anti–Hitler conspirators used their familial and collegial relationships to form a creative group, a conspiratorial "playspace," free of Gestapo spies. Admittance was based on personal knowledge of each individual, through either family ties or long-term military service with each other in the Imperial Army or the Reichswehr. Within this group, the conspirators could freely share ideas and thoughts about plans to assassinate Hitler. In a totalitarian society like Nazi Germany, carving out a secret "space" to discuss something as dangerous as disloyalty, conspiracy, and eventually assassination, was vital to maintaining secrecy and providing any possibility of success. Perhaps, more importantly, the conspirators could find moral justification—and support—from like-minded men so they could overcome their general tendency to obey and ultimately disavow their oath of loyalty given to the "madman" and "criminal" who, by 1943, was obviously taking Germany to destruction. They could also rediscover their true selves as decent and honorable men, parts of their lives that they had lost during the heady years of the 1930s and the early victories of the war.[82]

To visualize the conspiratorial "playspace" as it looked in mid–1944, I have diagrammed representative familial and collegial relationships in Figure 8.1. The center of the diagram represents the active core of the conspiracy, centered on the extended families of Bonhoeffer, Stauffenberg, and Tresckow. The concentric circles surrounding the core represent the collegial conspirators and nonconspirators. The outermost circle represents the followers, the "Nazi" senior officers, separated from the others to demonstrate their distance and separation

Figure 8.1. The Anti-Hitler Conspiracy "Playspace," 1944

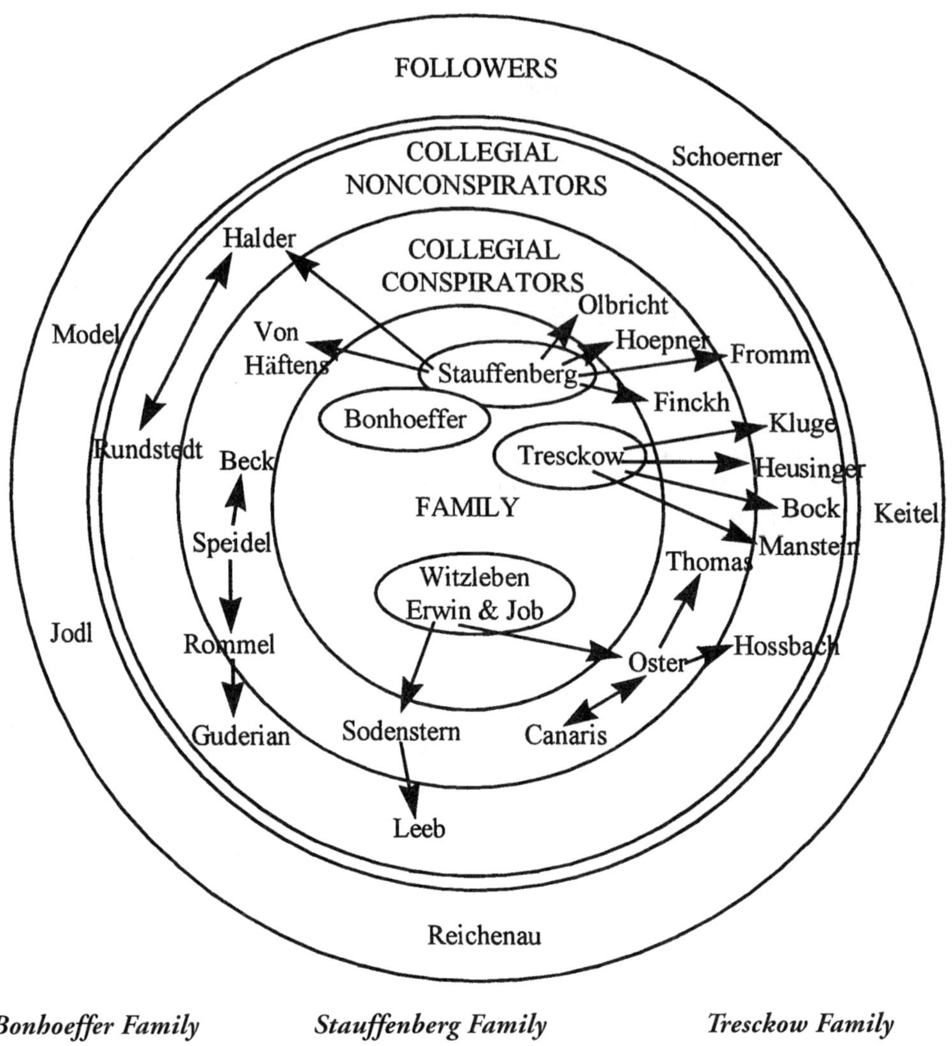

Bonhoeffer Family
Dietrich Bonhoeffer
Hans Dohnanyi
Paul von Hase
Peter Yorck
Rudolf Gersdorff

Stauffenberg Family
Klaus von Stauffenberg
Berthold von Stauffenberg
Alexander von Stauffenberg
Nicholas Graf von Uxkuell
Ceasar von Hofacker
Mertz von Quierheim

Tresckow Family
Henning von Tresckow
Fabian von Schlabrendorff

from the conspiracy. The arrows show representative "professional" relationships between various officers who at one time or the other had served together. The relationships presented in the figure are obviously not all those that existed but merely serve to demonstrate the relationships among conspirators, nonconspirators, and followers.

These special relationships allowed the conspirators to recruit others who might be susceptible to conspiracy and to discuss their anti-Hitler plots among those who were not conspirators but would not turn them into the Gestapo. These relationships also allowed the conspirators to avoid those who would most likely be pro–Nazis, like Model and Schoerner. In other words, they knew who to include and who to exclude in their conspiratorial "play." For example, Stauffenberg would first ascertain an officer's susceptibility to conspiracy by determining whether he was a relative of an opposition member, a known opponent to Hitler or the Nazi regime, or an officer who had voiced objections to the regime. He would then invite the officer to Berlin on some official pretext to talk to him. Stauffenberg would open with a review of the current military situation and the inability of Germany to replace losses, and then lead him into the logical political consequences. If the officer made objections, based on the oath of loyalty sworn to Hitler, as Freiherr von Leonrod did in late 1943, Stauffenberg would argue that the oath was no longer valid under the current conditions. Stauffenberg might even base his argument to conspire against their Führer on asking the prospective conspirator to search his conscience and think about his religious upbringing.[83] Undoubtedly, this general pattern was used by other conspirators to recruit new members to the growing military opposition.

As stated earlier, the Gestapo was amazed at the extent of the anti–Hitler conspiracy, following its investigation after the July 20, 1944, coup. Many army officers "freely" discussed Hitler's mismanagement of the war effort, the criminal orders, and the atrocities of the SS and the Gestapo among themselves. Senger wrote, "I had long been aware of the plan for the conspiracy."[84] Bock, Manstein, and Kluge were well aware of the anti–Hitler conspiracy but, despite their distaste for conspiracy and their loyalty to Hitler, none of them informed on the conspirators to their superiors or the Gestapo. Apparently, while Bock and Manstein would not reject their oath and join the conspiracy, they understood the views of Tresckow and Stauffenberg and would not turn their fellow officers over to the Gestapo. Guderian, Rundstedt, and Heusinger repeated this behavior in their responses to entreaties to join the resistance. Unable psychologically to join the conspiracy, they, nonetheless, would protect fellow officers from outsiders like the Gestapo, the SS, and the pro–Nazi officers. The "freedom" to discuss conspiracy and assassination of the head of state provided by this playspace is particularly significant in Nazi Germany, a totalitarian state in which children were taught to spy on their parents and report anyone suspected of expressing ideas against the state and its leader.

Summary

I do not want to overestimate the impact of a nurturing childhood, spiritual Christian home life, and humanistic education on the small sample of general officers that I examined, or use that impact to draw sweeping conclusions. None of these factors individually can explain why some officers chose conspiracy and others did not. However, these three factors, working together and complementing each other, appear to have produced a moral and ethical value system and a "thinking mind" within those officers. At "the right moment" these men saw a "moral crisis" that led them to consider conspiracy against Hitler: as early as 1938 for some; as late as 1943 for others. Further research is needed to examine in more detail the childhoods of a far greater number of German generals to determine if these tendencies have greater validity. However, the evidence I do present certainly seems to indicate that these early experiences provided the conspirators with the psychological means to realize the moral crisis that led them to disavow their oath of loyalty and resulted in conspire to assassinate

Hitler; the lack of those same experiences, it could be argued, explains the refusal of the followers and nonconspirators to join the conspiracy to end the Hitler "madness." In other words, the early life experiences of conspirators, followers, and nonconspirators allowed the first group to move to the higher levels of Kohlbeg's stages of moral development — and prevented the latter two groups from doing so.

Since most of the World War II generals had experienced the same set of traumas and victories, the historical events of the period 1918–1944 could only partially explain why some officers became conspirators but most did not. Ultimately, the value systems of their childhood and families brought many to the point that they parted company with Hitler over his risky foreign policy in the late 1930s, the mass deaths of innocent civilians and POWs, and the threat to Germany's very existence; the values of others, the majority, prevented them from following the same course. Questioning their loyalty and obedience to Hitler, the conspirators came to believe in their "heart of hearts" that it was more honorable to abrogate their oath to Hitler and conspire to assassinate him than to allow the continuance of atrocities and destruction. In describing the political and military situation in late 1943, early 1944 to his fellow officer Leonrod, Stauffenberg told his friend that if he was a "believing Catholic" he "owed it to his conscience" to act against his oath to the Führer.[85] It is truly tragic that the conspirators did not decide to do so earlier, that they were unable to convince many others to support them, and that they failed in their task when they ultimately chose to act.

Notes

1. Thomas Alexander and Beryl Parker, *The New Education in the German Republic* (New York: The John Day company, 1929), pp. 269, 272–73, 295. R. H. Samuel and R. Hinton Thomas, *Education and Society in Modern Germany* (London: Routledge & Kegan Paul Unlimited, 1949), pp. 41–46. James E. Russell, *German Higher Education: The History, Organization and Methods of Secondary Education in Germany* (New York: Longmans, Green and Co., 1916), p. 125. Paulsen quoted in Russell, p. 122.

2. Samuel and Thomas, pp. 42–45, 71–72.

3. Russell, pp. 124, 127.

4. Samuel and Thomas, p. 60. Russell, p. 121.

5. See Chapter 5 in Fritz Stern, *The Politics of Cultural Despair: A Study in the Rise of Germanic Ideology* (Berkeley, CA: University of California Press, 1974), pp. 71–81, for a critique of the German educational system.

6. Charles Messenger, *The Last Prussian A Biography of Field Marshal Gerd von Rundstedt 1875–1953* (London: Brassey's [UK], 1991), pp. 4–5. Haller, ed., p. 5. "Portepee" is the term for the officer's sword knot.

7. Messenger, pp. 10–13. Guderian essay on the 1913 Kriegsakademie curriculum, Reynolds, pp. 22–23. See also Martin van Creveld, *The Training of Officers from Military Professionalism to Irrelevance* (New York: The Free Press, 1990), pp. 24–34, for a discussion of the Kriegsakademie curriculum.

8. Messenger, p. 5.

9. Giziowski, p. 28.

10. Tresckow quoted in Barry A. Leach, "Halder," in Barnett, p. 116.

11. Senger, pp. 219–20.

12. Schlabrendorff, *Killed Hitler* (New York: The Macmillan Company, 1947), p. 65.

13. Keitel's Comments to Defense Counsel, 1946, Görlitz, ed., p. 243.

14. Ziemke, "Rundstedt," in Barnett, p. 176.

15. Field Marshal Lord Carver, "Manstein," in Barnett, p. 222.

16. Kaiser, MS #B-285, p. 37, in Detwiler, et al.

17. Kaiser, MS #B-285, pp. 49–50, in Detwiler et al.

18. Küstrin was a small garrison town, "a grim citadel of Prussianism in the midst of the wasteland and scrub pines of the Mark Brandenburg." In the early 1700s, Frederick William I had imprisoned his son, the future Frederick II, the Great, there when the latter tried to escape to England to get away from the harsh military discipline of his father. William Bayles, "Generals Rommel and Von Bock," *The American Mercury*, Vol. 55 (August 1942), p. 187.

19. Alfred W. Turney, *Disaster at Moscow: Von Bock's Campaigns 1941–1942* (Albuquerque, NM: University of New Mexico Press, 1970), pp. 3–4. Bayles, p. 187.

20. Turney, p. 4.

21. Messenger, p. 9.

22. Messenger, pp. 1–5.

23. Reynolds, pp. 17–20. Gill, p. 42.
24. Reynolds, pp. 232–38.
25. FitzGibbon, p. 135.
26. Schlabrendorff, *Killed Hitler*, p. 44.
27. Schlabrendorff, *Secret War*, p. 149.
28. Kramarz, pp. 23–24, 38, 116.
29. Hoffman, *German Resistance*, p. 316.
30. Schlabrendorff, *Secret War*, p. 245. Kramarz (pp. 39–41, 54–56) reports similar views by others who knew Stauffenberg.
31. Thormaelen quoted in Kramarz, pp. 32–33.
32. Kramarz, p. 32.
33. Kramarz, p. 34.
34. Hardenberg interview with Kramarz, February 3, 1963, Kramarz, p. 29.
35. Hoffman, *Stauffenberg*, p. 108.
36. Letter to General Sodernstern, March 13, 1939, in Hoffman, *Stauffenberg*, p. 289.
37. Zeller, p. 218. Hoffman, *German Resistance*, p. 337.
38. Gill, p. 38.
39. Zeller, pp. 147–48.
40. Certainly, there were others. Hans Speidel, for example, was the son of a professor at the University of Tuebingen. After completing his studies in a well-established Gymnasium, he entered the army. Between 1919 and 1925, Speidel studied history and political economy at the universities of Berlin and Tuebingen and the Stuttgart Technical College. In early 1925, he received a doctoral degree in history, entitling his dissertation "1813–1924: A Military-Politico Investigation." Between 1933 and 1939, Speidel served in the German embassies in London, Rome, Prague, Bern, Madrid, and Lisbon, which helped him broaden his political experiences and knowledge during the prewar years. He also wrote articles for several German newspapers and a military history journal. Hans Rothfels, "The Life and Career of a German General," pp. 29, 32; and General Ulrich Maiziere, "An Impressive Personality, A Notable Soldier, pp. 10–12, in *To Remain Ready for Action* (Cologne: Markus Verlagsgesellschaft, 1967). Colonel Truman Smith, US Army, who knew Speidel from 1935 to 1939, wrote in the introduction to Speidel's account of the allied invasion of France in June 1944, "...Speidel acquired in his youth at the home hearth unusually broad intellectual interests which later were to prove invaluable, when his military career took forms which compelled him to grapple with political and diplomatic problems." Hans Speidel, *Invasion 1944: Rommel and the Normandy Campaign* (Chicago: Henry Regnery Company, 1950), pp. ix–x.
41. See Neumann, *Behomoth*, pp. 85–92, for a fuller explanation of the impact of Lutheranism on obedience to state authority.
42. Oster quoted, date not provided, in Giziowski, p. 186. Gill, p. 45.
43. Snyder, p. 263. While we extol the ethical and Christian values of Oster the conspirator, we also need to remember that Oster, in his early military career, had quite a reputation as a lady's man. In fact, he had been forced to resign from the army on December 31, 1932, because of an illicit love affair with the wife of a reserve officer. In May 1933, he managed to return to the War Ministry and was assigned to the Abwehr that September. At the time General von Bredow was its chief— the same Bredow the Nazis murdered on June 30, 1934. While at the Abwehr, Oster met Dr. Hans Bernd Gisevius.
44. Zeller, p. 21. Other testimonials of Oster's Christian character can be found in Gill, p. 107, Duffy and Ricci, p. 41, de Beus, p. 170, Hoene, *Canaris*, p. 259, and Schlabrendorff, *Killed Hitler*, p. 15.
45. Maj. Gen. Rudolph-Christoph Freiherr von Gersdorff, "History of the Attempt on Hitler's Life (20 July 1944)," MS #A-855, p. 19, in Detwiler, et al.
46. Leber, ed., p. 178.
47. Affidavit A, Maj. Gen. Erwin Lahousen, January 21, 1946, *NCA*, VIII, pp. 588–89.
48. Schlabrendorff, *Killed Hitler*, p. 47.
49. Groppe, MS #B-397, pp. 1–2, in Detwiler, et al.
50. Groppe, MS #B-397, pp. 1–2, in Detwiler, et al. Gisevius (July 12, 1944, entry, pp. 510–512) presents a different, more opportunistic picture of Stauffenberg as a "disillusioned military man" who switched sides only after the defeat at Stalingrad.
51. July 13, 1944, entry, Gisevius, p. 515. Wheeler-Bennett, p. 581.
52. Broich letter to Kramarz, June 14, 1962, in Kramarz, p. 119. See also Halder's comments in Kramarz, pp. 27, 81; and Colonel Meichssner's deposition to SD Chief Ernst Kaltenbrunner in Kramarz, p. 147.
53. Galante, p. 185.
54. Stieff quoted in Zeller, p. 217.
55. Oster quoted in Zeller, pp. 21–22.
56. Hamerow, p. 345.
57. Yorck quoted in Roger Manvell, *The Conspirators: 20th July 1944* (New York: Ballantine Books, Inc., 1971), p. 159.
58. Hamerow, p. 350.
59. Stauffenberg quoted in Leber, p. 260.
60. Bernd Pezold interview with Kramarz, May 17, 1963, in Kramarz, p. 185.
61. Stauffenberg quoted in Hamerow, p. 345.
62. Whalen, p. 63.
63. Whalen, p. 64.
64. The Kriesau Circle, formed in 1933, was an important group of opponents to Hitler who met regularly at the country estate of Helmuth James Graf von Moltke, the great-grandnephew of Helmuth von Moltke (the Elder). Moltke the Elder was

the Chief of the Prussian General Staff during the Prussian-Danish War (1864), the Prusso-Austrian War (1866), and the Franco-Prussian War (1870–71), and Kaiser Wilhelm II had granted the Kriesau estate to Moltke for his leadership of the German armies that produced the victories leading to the Second German Reich. This circle of civilians was more a semiorganized opposition to Hitler and his criminal regime than an organized resistance group plotting a coup d'etat. However, they did produce some specific ideas for a post–Hitler government. Most of its members were rounded up after July 20, 1944, and ultimately executed.

65. Whalen, pp. 64–68.

66. Whalen, pp. 66–69.

67. As an officer of the US Air Force for a quarter century, I have been part of an officer corps that has numbered about 35,000 to 40,000 on active duty per year during that time. I have held ten permanent assignments and numerous temporary assignments during that time at locations stretching from Europe to the Far East. Over the years I have met numerous officers and enlisted members whom I had known at previous assignments. If my own experiences are any kind of indicator of the closeness of serving officers, then the officers of the Imperial Army who went on to serve in the extremely small officer corps of the Reichswehr and later of Hitler's army must have been very close indeed.

68. Whalen, p. 68. Hoehne, *Canaris*, p. 259

69. Giziowski, pp. 23–24.

70. General of Infantry Georg von Sondenstern, "Events Leading Up to 20 July 44," MS #B-499, March 1947, pp. 29, 34–35, in Detwiler, et al.

71. Messenger, pp. 44, 46, 48, 53, 57.

72. Kramarz, p. 52.

73. Gill, p. 230.

74. Speidel, MS #B-721, pp. 1–2, in Detwiler, et al.

75. Hans Rothfels, "The Life and Career of a German General," in *To Remain Ready*, p. 11.

76. Gersdorff, MS #A-855, p. 8 in Detwiler, et al.

77. De Maiziere, *To Remain Ready*, pp. 33–34.

78. Galante, pp. 171, 245.

79. See Whalen, pp. 70–77.

80. J[ohan] Huizinga, *Homo Ludens: A Study of the Play-Element in Culture* (London: Routledge & Kegan Paul Limited, 1949), p. 13.

81. Huizinga, p. 10.

82. This discussion comes from a review of D. W. Winnivott, *Playing and Reality* (New York: Basic Books, 1971), pp. 47, 53–55, 96–100. I am grateful to Dr. Peter Loewenberg for leading me to this book.

83. Kramarz, pp. 148, 153.

84. Senger, p. 271.

85. Kaltenbrunner Report in Kramarz, p. 148.

Summary

At the Nuremberg trials after the Second World War had ended, ex–Army Chief of Staff Franz Halder provided the following personal testimony that captures the essence of the psychological dilemma which the German army officers faced under the Hitler regime:

> May I make a personal remark? I am the last masculine member of a family who for three hundred years were soldiers. What the duty of a soldier is I know. I know too that in the dictionary of a German soldier the terms "treason" and "plot against the state" do not exist. I was in the awful dilemma of one who had the duty of a soldier and also a duty which I considered higher. I chose the solution for the duties I esteem higher. The majority of my comrades esteemed the duty to the flag higher and more essential. You may be assured that this is the worst dilemma that a soldier may be faced with. That is what I wanted to explain.[1]

The dilemma of which Halder speaks was not (and is not) unique to the army officers of the Third Reich. Military officers of other countries in the course of history have faced similar situations in *principle*, if not in the same *degree*, to the crimes of the Nazi regime; they too faced dilemmas over what authority they owed their obedience and loyalty to. The study that I have presented examines this general problem of how much obedience is enough, by focusing on the 1934 oath of loyalty to Hitler and the agonizing over it by of the German army officers of the Third Reich. It offers, I believe, a different perspective than those of previous studies of this problem.

When the officers of the German army took the personal oath of allegiance to Hitler on August 2, 1934, none of them foresaw the catastrophes that lay ahead for them, the army, Germany, or Europe which resulted from following that oath. At the time, only Ludwig Beck offered any criticism of this event, criticism which centered more on the way it occurred than the oath itself. This failure to act, to have reacted differently, would haunt him until his death.[2] Within four years, he had resigned from the army, no longer able to follow Hitler. By then, Witzleben and a few other officers, like Beck, had also lost sufficient confidence in Hitler to form the core of the budding military opposition that ultimately attempted a coup in violation of that oath. From 1938 to 1944, the opposition attracted only a few more officers to its cause, while others, though increasingly disgusted with Hitler, only flirted with conspiracy. The majority of their comrades religiously followed their oath of allegiance, despite the abuse and scorn Hitler heaped upon many of them, his militarily unsound strategic and tactical decisions, and the widespread devastation and atrocities his army caused during World War II. Yet, despite the differing views of their oath to Hitler, for the officers, be they followers, conspirators, or nonconspirators, their oath to Hitler was not "mere words." As Bracher wrote (as have others), "[T]he oath continued to tie the Army to Hitler, a one-sided arrangement with dire consequences that continued to the very last day of the Third Reich."[3]

To discover the fundamental reasons for this general obedience to Hitler and compliance with his criminal orders, I applied Milgram's propositions from *Obedience to Authority* to the German officer corps after World War I. According to Milgram, people are generally socialized to obey authority figures. These authority figures use various means to bolster that general obedience, such as training, awards, decorations, penalties for disobedience, and loyalty oaths. From the theoretical and historical background of the military oath, we saw that the use of the oath is an important means of bolstering obedience and loyalty and that it has general significance for the officer corps of the military forces of any country in any era. The brief review of the military oath in Prussian-German military history, furthermore, showed its importance to the German officer corps as a group and how it established the conditions for the trauma of defeat and the Kaiser's abdication in 1918. We also saw how the specific conditions of these traumatic events and of the Weimar Republic established the conditions for the officers' obedience to Hitler and the resulting massive devastation and mass atrocities of World War II.

However, not everyone continually obeys the authority. At some point a few people, such as the members of the military opposition, encounter a "moral crisis" of sufficient significance that overrides their general socialization to obedience, causing them to reject their authority figure. These people now "silently" and openly criticize their authority, may actively protest the authority by resignation, and even conspire to overthrow the authority. Since most members of the group have generally shared the same "historical" experiences, these "conspirators" must have had some influences that differentiate them from conformers. These influences — a nurturing family life, "liberal" education, and a strong foundation in an ethical system, like spiritual Christianity — occur early in life and allow the conspirators not only to see the moral crisis but also to act on it. Research on the process of moral development in people, as I presented in Chapter 1, generally supports these conclusions.

Unlike the conspirators, most people, such as the group I called the nonconspirators in this study, only recognize the existence of a moral crisis but do (or can) not translate that recognition into action. To satisfy their conscience and offer an explanation to others, they will rationalize their inaction in some way. Again, because of *their* particular background, they might come to disagree — and do so severely — with their authority figure, but they can not muster sufficient psychological courage to overcome their general obedience to authority or their fear of the penalties for opposition. For the military officer in particular, this inability to move from recognition of a moral crisis to acting on it was usually rationalized by falling back on their sense of soldierly honor and duty, embodied in the oath of loyalty. As Heusinger stated, "I had taken an oath of allegiance. To be sure the man [i.e., Hitler] had misused it. To be sure. But did this exonerate the officer from his oath? *That oath was more than a gesture! It had been taken before God!*"[4] (Italics are Heusinger's.)

Heusinger's comment provides a more specific problem within this general problem of obedience: whether or not obedience is unconditional—that is, "blind obedience"—or conditional/limited. Most of the nonconspirators saw obedience to Hitler as unconditional. In addition to the previous comment from Heusinger, another example from mid–1944 illustrates the dilemma in which the nonconspirators believed themselves to be. On D-Day, June 6, 1944, Heusinger told General Fellgiebel, the OKW Chief of Communications and a conspirator, that Germany "must end the war before all of this crumbles into nothing." Fellgiebel reminded Heusinger about their oath of allegiance to Hitler. "The future of our people transcends every other consideration," replied Heusinger. "I've wrestled with my conscience far too long." Yet, when it came time to act, Fellgiebel moved forward and paid for his actions with his life, and Heusinger remained on the fence. Although he was interrogated by the Gestapo after the July 20 plot, he lived to serve Germany again after the war. The nonconspirators believed they had to follow Hitler—even when he violated his obligations to them through his risky foreign policies, disastrous military decisions, the degradation of the general officers, and the issuance of illegal orders—because the oath was a sacred bond, made before God, which they could not break.

The followers also saw obedience to Hitler as unconditional but took their oath even further. To them, Hitler was infallible, and they followed him because of their firm belief in him and their sense of military honor. Two comments from Jodl well illustrate the followers' view of obedience and loyalty to their authority. After a meeting of senior army commanders at the Wolfschanze in mid–June 1943, Heusinger told Jodl, "Something must be done to stop this headlong progress toward disaster." Jodl responded, "I agree entirely—we're simply hastening to meet our doom, but the man who is leading us is our destiny, and one does not escape one's destiny."[5] Later, on May 13, 1945, Jodl said, "As a soldier I obeyed and I believed my honour required me to maintain the obedience I had sworn."[6] Jodl was executed for this sense of honor and duty to Hitler. For both the nonconspirators and the followers only Hitler's death—or theirs—could release them from their oath to him.

On the other hand, the conspirators came to view obedience as conditional/limited and the oath as more of a contract between them and Hitler than a sacred vow. They followed Hitler as long as he lived up to his part of the contract—August 1934 to summer 1938 or later. They generally approved of the 1934 purge of the radical SA leaders, the rearmament program, and his bloodless acquisition of territory through 1938. Their belief in Hitler began to falter when his foreign policies threatened to involve Germany in another world war and dissolved when that war occurred. Others continued to believe in him until the war produced extensive atrocities, military defeats, and numerous casualties, and threatened Germany's very existence. This group now came to believe that Hitler had failed to protect the German nation and state and felt relieved of the personal allegiance to him. These men could, with good conscience, plot his overthrow and, if necessary, assassination. As Blomberg so aptly put it after the war, "[Before 1939, t]here was no need to oppose Hitler since he produced the results which they desired. After that time some generals began to condemn his methods and lost confidence in the power of his judgment."[7] Again, to make this recognition, an officer had to "see" beyond his immediate military calling, and the followers and nonconspirators could not psychologically do so.

Although some historians have seen some connection between the increasing numbers of middle class (nonnoble) army officers and the army's general obedience to Hitler, I have shown that general obedience to Hitler went much deeper than social origins alone. Certainly Hitler drew significant support from the middle class in general, and army officers, especially with the army's expansion after 1934, came increasingly from this class. Also, the officer corps of the late 1930s represents a transitional stage between the aristocratic officer corps (by birth and by temperament) of the early 1900s and the increasingly nonnoble officer corps of the war years. Finally, the aristocratic officers still dominated the senior general officer and generalfeldmarschall positions from which they could have directed troops to protect an anti–Hitler coup if they had chosen to do so. Yet, even among the most senior officers, we find men, like Rundstedt, Manstein, and Bock, who remained loyal to Hitler and refused to join the anti-Hitler conspiracy, despite all that he had done and ordered. As I have shown in Chapter 8, family life during early childhood, type of education, and degree of belief in some system of ethics and moral values appear to be of more importance than socioeconomic origins alone. The research done on moral development in people by Piaget, Kohlberg, and others generally support these conclusions.

Origins

The 1934 oath and, therefore, the general obedience of the army officers to Hitler originated in the "psychological trauma" of the German army, particularly the officer corps, from the army's defeat in the First World War and its humiliation under the Versailles Treaty. Because of this trauma, most German officers did not come to terms with the Weimar Republic, and many, particularly among the younger officers, responded favorably to the rising Nazi movement. Furthermore, Seeckt's policies to make the Reichswehr "unpolitical" during its formative years degraded the officers' abilities to recognize the evil nature of Nazism. Instead of accepting the republic, the army stood "above politics," which meant, in practice, that it did not exhibit "true" allegiance to the Weimar government, despite its oath to do so. This lack of support for Weimar is well demonstrated by the army's failure to defend the republic during the Kapp Putsch and the Hitler Putsch, and to stop the widespread support for the Nazi movement within the army (as revealed in the Leipzig trial) and the ongoing protests against the republican colors in the flag. As Guderian stated,

> The [Reischwehr officers] had to relinquish many privileges and forego many traditions, and they did so to save their Fatherland from inundation by the flood of Asiatic Bolshevism then already threatening. The Weimar Republic did not succeed in turning this marriage of convenience into a love match. No genuine attachment evolved between the officer corps and the new State.[8]

The psychological trauma of the army officers is also exemplified by their search for a personal supreme commander. When Kaiser Wilhelm II abdicated and went into exile in 1918, the army officers lost their personal *Feldherr* (warlord) to whom they had sworn to serve and obey. They reluctantly swore allegiance to the Weimar constitution but believed they could not "truly" serve a "thing." The officers also did not give true allegiance to President Ebert, a civilian supreme commander, as they had to the Kaiser. Instead, they found surrogate warlords in Seeckt until his dismissal in 1926 and then Hindenburg, who could more truly be their *Feldherr*, more so than either Ebert or Seeckt. By August 1934, the officers, both those of the pre–1918 army and the Reichswehr, were psychologically willing to accept Hitler as *Feldherr*; he had promised to tear up the humiliating Versailles Treaty, restore Germany's greatness, and re-establish the army's position in this new Germany.

Apparently, Reichenau or Blomberg or both now decided to prepare a new oath to link the officers personally to Hitler as the new head of state. Although the military oath of December 1933 was still legally sufficient, they wanted to re-establish that personal link between the military and the head of state, broken by the Kaiser's abdication and exile, probably in exchange for some quid pro quo from Hitler. To the pre–1918 officers, such a personal oath was more "natural," and the younger officers certainly would not question swearing a personal oath to the man who would tear up the Versailles Treaty, humiliate the western democracies, and restore Germany's great power and the army's internal status. The minimal adverse feeling about the oath and the oath-taking ceremony in August 1934 centered more on Blomberg's unilateral and extralegal introduction of the new oath, rather than its promulgation per se.

Consequences

As I mentioned in the Introduction, Deutsch characterized the oath-taking ceremony as a coup. Hoffman reiterates this theme in the following:

> For soldiers, therefore, loyalty to the constitution or the country no longer existed; there was only loyalty to the "*Führer*." Henceforth, the only valid order or channel of command was that approved by the "Führer"; this was now the law. The new legislation met with no opposition of any significance, and Hitler had succeeded in releasing the *Reichswehr* from all previous traditional obligations and in attaching it to himself personally.
>
> This new hurriedly organized oath-taking process was more than a mere *coup d'état*, designed to take the *Reichswehr* by surprise as in the Fritsch crisis of 1938; it was also intended as a powerful obstacle to any form of resistance to the deified "command."[9]

While I certainly agree with Hoffmann in most respects, I am not so sure that Hitler, Blomberg, or Reichenau, as the principals involved in the new oath, originally saw the new oath as a means to prevent *future* resistance. Not until 1938 was there any substantial resistance within the army to Hitler's policies.

Still, the personal oath of allegiance had serious consequences for the officer corps, Germany, and Europe, especially after September 1, 1939, as we have seen. It gave the followers complete and unquestioned license to obey Hitler's orders, passed down and implemented by senior commanders. They did so even when those orders transgressed the laws of war found in prewar conventions signed by Germany, endorsed by Germany's military legal code, and still legally binding on Germany since Hitler had not formally abrogated these agreements. Yet, when Germany went to war against Poland and later the Soviet Union, Hitler essentially suspended the application of those laws to conduct a racial war against the Bolsheviks, the Slavic *Untermenschen*, the Jews, and other "undesirables" of Europe. As a result, the nazified army committed war crimes against enemy soldiers, POWs, and noncombatants that almost rivaled those of the SS and the Gestapo, with little and ineffective questioning of these criminal orders by senior commanders.

The blind compliance of the followers meant that all of Hitler's orders, including the ones that sanctioned what were "normally" criminal actions, had to be obeyed. This group can be broken down into three subgroups — the "true believers," those who idolized Hitler as their "destiny," and the careerists — although the boundaries between them is blurred. We do not find very many true beleivers among the senior officers. Perhaps Blomberg and Reichenau were the only truly nazified "true believers" among them. Most of the true believers can be found among the lower-ranking officers, increasing in number by rank from lieutenant colonel down to second lieutenant, and the enlisted men. These were the men most affected, as children and teenagers, by the hyperinflation of 1923 and the unsettling years of parliamentary government. They were the ones subjected to Nazi ideology in the nazified schools, the HJ, and the RAD. When war came to Europe, they became willing participants in the cleansing of Europe proclaimed in Nazi ideology and reinforced through various media over the years. In essence, their moral development was framed by the new morality of Nazi Germany, a society in which Hitler had turned the norms of "Western society" upside down.

The second and third subgroups of the followers — the idolizers and the careerists — are closely related since it would be nearly impossible to find one who idolized Hitler completely because of who he was and what he did as distinct from another who followed Hitler for purely career enhancement.[10] Most within the two subgroups followed Hitler for varying mixtures of these two reasons. Within them we would find a number of senior officers, like Keitel, Jodl, Reichenau, and Model. The idolizers specifically followed Hitler and complied with his orders because, as Jodl so aptly stated, one does not "mess" with one's destiny. Entranced by Hitler's personal charisma and the developing myth of his infallibility, they came to believe that their Führer could do no wrong. When military operations went badly, then, to them, someone else was at fault and somehow Hitler would make things right again. The careerists followed Hitler willingly because it was in their best personal interest to do so, especially through the first three years of the war. In both cases, these men came to stake Germany's and Europe's destiny on Hitler. In the end, with much of Europe totally devastated and Germany days from total capitulation, at least one, Model, chose suicide, rather than disgrace his Führer and his oath. Others, like Keitel and Jodl, chose to surrender and were eventually executed, the final consequence of their obedience to their oath and to their undying belief in Hitler.

In some respects, the oath had even greater consequences for the nonconspirators than the followers. As early as 1938, some of the nonconspirators, like Halder, had realized that Hitler's adventuresome foreign policies risked another two-front war which they correctly believed would mean defeat for Germany. Their fears came true after the June 1941 invasion of the Soviet Union and the entry into the war of the United States that December. However, the elation from Hitler's "bloodless" diplomatic victories of 1935–39 and the seemingly endless military victories, except for the failure to capture Moscow, through late 1942 gave them a false sense of Hitler's political and military genius. After 1942, the nonconspirators came to realize Germany's hopeless situation as the Soviet and American military forces grew in strength and the tempo and destruction of the strategic bombing offensive increased. Many also began to realize the significance of the army's commission of atrocities and war crimes throughout occupied Europe. The nonconspirators belatedly recognized the dangers of Hitler to the German nation and people, but they felt unable to support the opposition because of their sworn oath to Hitler.

Why then were the nonconspirators unable to become conspirators and, as self-exculpation, fell back on their oath? Although generals, like Halder and Kluge, flirted with conspiracy, they always at the last moment backed away from such action, repeatedly citing their oath to Hitler as the roadblock to full support of the conspiracy. In discussions with Hassell and Goerdeler,

Beck complained that only by assassinating Hitler could the link between the dictator and his generals be severed, which was *de facto* recognition of the power of the oath. The nonconspirators could not become active conspirators, despite recognition of Hitler's criminal actions, because of their narrow view of military honor. This view developed from a family life in which duty and loyalty to the state were paramount virtues and the oath a sacred vow, and from a narrow military education that stressed obedience, strategy, and tactics, instead of independent thinking. An early 1935 remark of Hossbach to Hitler's personal adjutant Captain Fritz Wiedemann captures the essence of the nonconspirators' view: "We are soldiers. We do not want to have anything to do with and understand nothing about politics. We occupy ourselves only with military affairs."[11] As a result, the nonconspirators could not psychologically break their oath to Hitler as long as he was alive, despite increasing and indisputable evidence that he had failed to protect the German nation and people.

The conspirators, on the other hand, viewed the oath as more of a contract between them and Hitler than as a one-sided sacred vow to him. Given their predisposition for a personal link with their supreme commander and the desire to restore that link after 1918, those officers who became conspirators initially had no problems with swearing allegiance to their new *Feldherr* on August 2, 1934, and initially supported him for the same reasons as the followers and nonsconspirators did. Hitler's testimony at the 1930 Leipzig trial, his purge of the radical SA leaders, and his initial "hands off" policy after the Machtergreifung furthered their favorable impressions of him in the first years of the Nazi regime. At the same time, they were concerned about Hitler's support for the creation of the OKW and the SS-VT and Blomberg's efforts to nazify the new army. Yet, in general, the faith of the army leaders in Hitler by 1938, including those who would soon become conspirators, and their misperception of his ultimate intentions was such that he could cashier the highly respected Fritsch with virtually no opposition from within the officer corps.

The conspirators only began to lose confidence in Hitler when his risky foreign policies threatened to involve Germany in a war before the rearmament program was completed and later in a two-front conflict that they prophetically believed would destroy Germany as the previous war had nearly done. The first inklings of this divergence occurred with the remilitarization of the Rhineland and the Munich crisis. However, it became increasingly more difficult for them to act as Hitler's popularity and infallibility myth grew after the bloodless annexations of Austria, the Sudentenland, and "rump" Czechoslovakia and then the quick military victories through September 1941. Once the war began, the conspirators became concerned that they would be labeled traitors and feared a possible civil war or the creation of a new *Dolchstoss* myth. Yet, unlike the other two groups, they saw the "moral" crisis of continued adherence to the Hitlerian oath and the conflict of that adherence with their own concept of honor and obedience. For them, the problem them became one of transforming recognition into effective action. For them, not to act against Hitler was dishonorable.

Essentially what had happened was that over time the conspirators in their minds had lost respect for Hitler as their higher authority. This loss was caused by the entry into another major war, the military defeats after late 1942, and the atrocities and war crimes of Hitler's army. These significant occurrences produced within the minds of the conspirators a growing sense that Hitler could no longer adequately defend the German nation, the true duty of the soldier. Stieff, for example, commented in August 1941, "Every day that passes here [at Führer Headquarters] strengthens one's dislike of this proletarian megalomaniac.... At any rate my respect for certain people has sunk very low ... the whole thing is simply disgusting and disgraceful!"[12] Stauffenberg, several years later, reiterated similar feelings about Hitler:

> [A] defeat and the destruction of the material and human resources [of Germany] are inevitable, if we continue on the present course.... [T]he fate threatening us can be averted only through the removal of the present leadership, [which] was unable to avoid a two-front war. The current regime has no right to drag down the entire German nation in its own collapse.[13]

De Beus wrote that Oster committed treason — informing the Dutch government of the impending German invasion — because he "...was convinced that there are crucial moments in ... history ... when higher standards may render disobedience — even betrayal of secrets — a moral obligation"[14] Finally, Sondenstern wrote that he and Witzleben had become aware by 1939 "that limits of the soldierly duty to obey [had become] visible ... and that he who feared the transgression [of these limits] also had to bear the responsibility for the further development. Lawful methods to cope with these matters did not exist."[15]

Yet, while the conspirators were deeply distressed about the atrocities and war crimes of the regime, this distress was not the primary motivation for them to conspire against Hitler and the Nazi regime. During the first years of the Third Reich, they were generally not that concerned about the regime's treatment of the Jews and expressed only general distress at the application of the Aryan provisions of the racial laws to army recruitment and at the anti–Jewish riots of Kristallnacht.[16] Several conspirators, like Oster, did collect files that documented "political crimes," such as the extralegal imprisonment of undesirables and political opponents and torture by the Gestapo, for use against the Nazi leaders after a successful coup. Yet, the officers showed more concern about the arrest of Pastor Martin Niemoller, an anti–Nazi activist, in 1937 than Kristallnacht, probably because he was a retired naval officer, "one of them." During the war, the conspirators' concerns about war crimes committed by the army were generally centered more on their impact on the morale and discipline of the soldiers and the adverse effects on the army's honor than on the inhumanity of such crimes per se. To be sure, Stieff, Stauffenberg, and others expressed "outrage" at the mass murder of Jews and others and came to believe that the army and the German nation would have to "pay" for these crimes in the future.[17] However, their distress and outrage over these crimes were insufficient of *themselves* to produce resistance to Hitler but probably, as the minimum, did serve as some justification for their "treason."

Unlike the followers and the nonconspirators, most conspirators had experienced significant influences — a nurturing family life, a broader liberal education, and a deeply held system of ethical and moral beliefs (spiritual Christianity) — in their early life that gave them a broader view of the world than the other two groups had. These influences produced a certain intellectualism and a wider perspective of their military service, one beyond mere obedience to orders. They saw the oath as more of a contract between themselves and Hitler by which they "agreed" to defend the German nation and state, in exchange for a larger, rearmed, modern army and the end of the Versailles Treaty. During the war, many also realized the serious effects of the criminal orders and war crimes on the morale and discipline of the soldiers, although some ordered the commission of various war crimes themselves. This same wider perspective of military service allowed them to see, at a specific point in time for each conspirator, that unless they tried to overthrow the regime they would have failed not only in their duty to properly protect the German nation and people, but also in their duty to themselves and their own personal sense of honor.

Treason, conspiracy, and assassination did not come easy to the conspirators. Even after they decided that they must get rid of Hitler, they still commanded his soldiers in combat, and some of the conspirators did even commit war crimes as I have documented earlier. Above all, they, as well as the nonconspirators, held their military duties to be paramount. After all, they were still entrusted with the lives of German soldiers in, by mid–1944, desperate combat for the very existence of Germany and their own families against Germany's enemies, especially the hated Bolsheviks in the East. For example, Sondenstern an early Hitler opponent, felt unable to join the assassination conspiracy because he, in the summer of 1942, commanded German troops in combat in Russia.[18] Additionally, for some, their military duties provided effective cover for their resistance activities. For example, Tresckow could easily shuttle to and from the eastern front and Berlin to keep in contact with the resistance there as much as to report on military operations, and this study has shown that such a double life presented a dilemma for people like Artur Nebe. Others, like Groppe, believed that they could oppose the Nazi regime best from within the "system."[19] Finally, many conspirators continued to have pride in carrying out their military duties and in receiving recognition (awards and decorations) and increased responsibility and pay that came with a "job well done." Thus, for various reasons, the conspirators continued to perform their military duties as they actively plotted against Hitler.

Significance

In the final analysis, the Hitlerian oath of loyalty had great significance for all groups of officers — followers, nonconspirators, and conspirators — and for the history of the world. Because of the oath, the followers maintained a blind obedience to Hitler that resulted in war crimes committed by the army that approached those of the SS and the Gestapo during the Second World War. Because of the oath, the nonconspirators struggled psychologically with whether or not to support the small anti–Hitler opposition which ultimately tried to rid Germany of its psychopathic tyrant. In the end, however, they fell back on their oath and remained neutral in this struggle, dooming the July 20, 1944, coup to failure and its participants, to public humiliation, unspeakable torture and a horrendous execution. Because of the oath, the military opposition attracted only a few officers who finally saw the dangers of the Nazi regime to Germany and the world and tried to do something about that. Unfortunately, they controlled few combat soldiers who might have been able to protect the coup from a Nazi countercoup. Again, Bracher seems to summarize the problem:

> As it became evident, the German military tradition in the last analysis did not constitute a real foundation for political resistance. Opposition remained confined to the personal initiative of intellectually and morally independent officers. Its basis was not the tradition of the Army but the conscience of individuals whose eyes were opened by the reality of the new regime, who grew aware of the problem inherent in unquestioning military obedience, and finally, who were ready [and psychologically willing — my addition] to step out of the narrow framework of military thinking and make contact with the civilian resistance.[20]

Of the three groups, the greatest impact of the personal oath to Hitler was probably on the nonconspirators. The followers were the "true believers" with a virtually unshakable faith in and loyalty to Hitler. While their number had grown significantly since 1933, a result of the drastic increases in the army's size, the followers were still a relative minority among the officers in 1944. The military opposition was also numerically small, consisting mainly of staff officers at the OKH and a few from the OKW. Noticeably absent from both groups were senior field commanders who could have provided soldiers to protect the coup in Berlin from an SS–Gestapo countercoup and then ensure an orderly transfer of power once "the smoke had cleared." We find most among the nonconspirators. Some had flirted with conspiracy but, because of the risk and their oath, they refrained from action when it was needed, taking a "wait and see" attitude: if the coup succeeded, they would be glad that Hitler and his Nazi cronies were gone; if the coup failed (as it did), then they would not be at risk. Schlabrendorff "saw in the non–Nazis among the generals the greatest obstacle to action [and he complained] 'their lack of backbone caused us more trouble than the wanton brutality of the Nazis.'"[21]

Also, only the nonconspirators had to really struggle with their oath to Hitler during the entire Third Reich. For the followers, the problem never occurred; they remained clear and firm in their belief in Hitler even as the Soviet Army besieged Berlin in April 1945. For the conspirators, the oath produced a psychological struggle on just how far they should go in their loyalty to Hitler, but, once they had crossed over to opposition, the oath became more of a nuisance than a stumbling block. However, the oath did remain a psychological stumbling block or an excuse, depending on the individual nonconspirator, that prevented many important "fence straddlers" from joining the opposition. Even the conspirators recognized the problem, after first wondering why the generals could not "see" the terrible things that were occurring around them or the responsibility they bore for them.[22] The firm weight of men like Kluge, Rommel, and Halder at the critical times might have ensured the success of the military opposition but they, and other important nonconspirators, did not act because they had failed to understand that as soldiers they still had an ethical duty beyond the strictly military, that they were still ethical people, as Francis Lieber wrote in the 1863 American army regulations: "Men who take up arms against one another in public war do not cease on this account to be moral beings, responsible to one another and to God."[23]

Perhaps two quotations can best summarize the conflict over the oath. Ironically the first one is from Hitler himself. In contemplating the problems of parliamentary government, Hitler asked several rhetorical questions, including some that might have caused the Kluges and Halders to join the military opposition:

> In such a case, doesn't a man of true character find himself in a hopeless conflict between knowledge and decency, or rather honest conviction?
>
> Where is the dividing line between his duty toward the general public and his duty toward his personal honor?
>
> Mustn't every true leader refuse to be this degraded to the level of a political gangster?[24]

The second is from the post–World War II civil-military conflict between President Harry Truman and General Douglas MacArthur. The latter stated,

> ...I find in existence a new and heretofore unknown and dangerous concept that the members of our armed forces owe primary allegiance and loyalty to those who temporarily exercise the authority of the executive branch of the government, rather than to the country and its Constitution which they are sworn to defend. No proposition could be more dangerous.

> None could cast greater doubt upon the integrity of the armed forces.
>
> For its application would at once convert them from their traditional and constitutional role as the instrument of defense of the Republic into something partaking of the nature of a pretorian [*sic*] guard, owing sole allegiance to the political master of the house.[25]

The struggle over the limits of obedience, imposed by the oath of loyalty, continues even in the American armed forces with a different constitutional tradition than that of Germany. No American general openly protested or resigned over the conduct of the war in Southeast Asia, despite widespread discontent in the armed forces. The army first covered up the March 16, 1968, massacre of over 500 South Vietnamese civilians at My Lai and then court-martialed only Lieutenant William Calley for that atrocity. At his court-martial Calley stated he was only carrying out orders. In early 1995, the army court-martialed Captain Lawrence Rockwood for disobeying orders because he visited a prison in Haiti after his superiors had ordered him not to. In his defense, the captain argued that "international human rights standards and his own military oath of office compelled him to act."[26] Finally, in late 1996, air force major Tim McIlhenny stated, "Our job is to train to do our mission. We sign up to serve, and that's what we do.... It's not our job to critique or agree or disagree with General Butler. Our job is to go out and fight."[27] So the psychological conflict over obedience and disobedience and the oath of allegiance is as relevant to today's military forces as it was to those of Nazi Germany.

The Bible offers some "advice" that should have helped more of the German officer corps—and others—with the moral dilemma in which they found themselves. The Pharisees attempted to entrap Jesus by either having him antagonize the Jews or commit treason in the eyes of the Roman government. When they asked him if the Jews should pay taxes to Rome, Jesus asked for a Roman coin. He then asked the Pharisees whose head was engraved on the coin. After they responded that Caesar's was, Jesus said to them, "Then render to Caesar the things that are Caesar's; and to God the things that are God's" (Matthew 22:21, New American Standard). In other words, the Jews owed Imperial Rome their temporal loyalty since Rome currently governed Judea, but they owed their spiritual allegiance to God. Peter later reinforced this principle with the apostles when the Jewish Sanhedrin (religious court) ordered them to stop preaching; he told the apostles, "We must obey God rather than men" (Acts 5:29). Finally, Jesus warned his disciples about the cost of following Satan so that they might temporarily prosper: "For what will a man be profited, if he gains the whole world, and forfeits his soul? Or what will a man give in exchange for his soul?" (Matthew 16: 26). The German officer corps after 1918 learned too late the wisdom found in these scriptures. Those who today serve in the armed forces of their countries should also remember the essence of these verses as they carry out their military duties—soldiers do not become less ethical merely by their military service.

Notes

1. Halder quoted in FitzGibbon, p. 88.
2. Gisevius, p. 79.
3. Bracher, p. 243.
4. Heusinger quoted in Allen, p. 42.
5. Conversation quoted in Galante, p. 193.
6. Jodl quoted in Demeter, p. 152.
7. Document 3704-PS, Blomberg Statement, *NCA*, VI, p. 414.
8. Guderian quoted in Macksey, p. 56. See also Haller, ed., p. 30, for Strecker's views and Allen, p. 27, for Heusinger's views of the Weimar Republic and their favorable reaction to Hitler and the growing Nazi movement, respectively.
9. Hoffmann, *German Resistance*, p. 28.
10. Carlo D'Este reports that Model demonstrated characteristics and actions of both the "true

believer" and the careerist. See "Model," in Barnett, pp. 322–23.

11. Hossbach quoted in Deutsch, p. 276.

12. Stieff Letter, August 23, 1941, quoted in Zeller, p. 216.

13. Stauffenberg quoted in Hamerow, p. 318.

14. De Beus, p. 172.

15. Sondenstern, MS #499, p. 30, in Detwiler, et al.

16. For example, Strecker was ashamed of the destruction on Kristallnacht and was angered by other anti-Semitic actions. These actions, however, "...did not lead him [or other Germans] to active resistance." Haller, ed., p. 40.

17. See for example, Hamerow, pp. 316.

18. Sondenstern MS # B-499, p. 39, in Detwiler, et al.

19. Groppe, MS # B-397, p. 1, in Detwiler, et al.

20. Bracher, p. 392.

21. Schlabrendorff quoted in Rothfels, p. 27.

22. September 22, 1940, entry, Hassell, pp. 150–51.

23. Excerpt from 1863 US Army Regulations, by Francis Lieber, quoted in Taylor, *Nuremberg and Vietnam*, p. 41.

24. Hitler, *Mein Kampf*, p. 80.

25. MacArthur Speech, Massachusetts State Legislature, July 25, 1951, in Richard Halworth Rovere, *General MacArthur and President Truman: The Struggle for Control of American Foreign Policy* (New Brunswick, NJ: Transaction Publishers, 1992), p. 318.

26. Correspondence Report, May 3, 1995, at http://www.intac.co,/PubService/human-rights/newstand/1995/may95/3may/HAITI—COURT-MARTIAL. Stephen Wrage, "A Question of Duty," *Newsweek* (November 22, 1999), pp. 52, 54.

27. Mark Potok, "Air Base Doesn't Echo General's Anti-Nuke Opinion," *USA Today*, December 6, 1996, p. 3A. The major's comments were in response to remarks made by former Commander-in-Chief Strategic Air Command and now retired U.S. Air Force general, Lee Butler, in a speech against nuclear weapons.

APPENDIX A

Prussian-German Military Oaths

Prussian Oath, 1808

I (name) swear to the Omniscient and Omnipotent God, a physical oath to His Majesty the king of Prussia Friedrich Wilhelm III, my most gracious sovereign, that I will be resolute in all and every occurrence on land and on water and serve faithfully and honestly in war and peace. I will read aloud the Articles of War, completely obey and conduct myself in the performance of my duties, always as one who loves honor as a fearless, qualified, and proper soldier. So help me God."

Note: This oath underwent only slight changes after 1815 as the German states formed the North German Confederation in 1866 and federal empire after 1871. The name of the king, then the kaiser, changed when a new one succeeded one who died. The officers exchanged "military and service regulations" for "Articles of War" when they took the oath. Before 1914, the last sentence was changed to read "So help me God through Jesus Christ and His sacred gospel. Militärgeschichtliches Forschungsamt, p. 141. Schwertfeger, p. 568.

Preliminary Pledge(Oath) to Weimar Government, December 17, 1918

I vow by my own signature that I will loyally support the temporary government of the Reichs Chancellor Ebert until the National Assembly has decided upon a new Reich constitution.

I submit to the military laws that were valid until November 1, 1918, except those obligations to the person of the Kaiser and the *Kontingentsherren* (quota men).

I vow, as a brave German soldier to fulfill my duty faithfully and conscientiously and not to leave my unit without timely termination.

Original Weimar Oath, August 14, 1919

I swear loyalty to the Reich Constitution and vow that I will protect the German nation and its lawful establishment as a brave soldier at any time, and will obey the President and my superiors.

Revised Weimar Oath, December 2, 1933

I swear by God this sacred oath that I will serve my people and fatherland at all times faithfully and honestly and, as a brave and obedient soldier, will be prepared at all times to stake my life for this oath.

Hitler Oath, August 2, 1934

I swear by God this sacred oath that I shall render unconditional obedience to Adolf Hitler, the Fürher of the German Reich, supreme commander of the armed forces, and that I shall at all times be prepared, as a brave soldier, to give my life for this oath.

The HJ Oath

In the presence of this blood banner, which represents our Fürher, I swear to devote all my energies and my strength to the savior of our country, Adolf Hitler. I am willing and ready to give up my life for him, so help me God.

The SA Oath

As a member of the storm troops of the NSDAP, I pledge myself by its storm flag [*Sturmfahne*]; to be always ready to stake life and limb in the struggle for the aims of the movement; to give absolute military obedience to my military superiors; to bear myself honorably in and out of service; to be always companionable to my other comrades.

The SS Oath

I swear to you, Adolf Hitler, as Leader and Chancellor of the German Reich, loyalty and bravery. I pledge to you and to the officers appointed by you obedience unto death. So help me God!

APPENDIX B

Political Justice in Weimar Germany

In Chapters 2 and 3, I discussed several political crimes during the Weimar Republic: the murders of many leftist leaders of the 1918–19 revolutions and of several Weimar leaders, such as Matthias Erzberger and Walter Rathenau; the 1920 Kapp Putsch; the 1923 Hitler Putsch; and the incidents leading up to the 1930 Leipzig trial. In each of these cases the perpetrators were from the right-wing elements of the Weimar political spectrum. In each of these cases the accused received relatively light sentences in relation to the crimes (political assassination and treason) they committed. Because of the importance of these incidents to the general discussion of this book and to the political development of Weimar Germany, I have included this brief discussion of political justice during these turbulent times as an indicator of the difficulty that reformers in Weimar faced in their attempts to truly democratize the institutions of government, like the legislature, the court system, and the army.

As I discussed earlier, Weimar Germany was born from the leftist revolutions of 1918–19 during which many revolutionary leaders were summarily executed when captured by rightist forces. For example, during the Spartacist Revolt of January 1919 in Berlin, Karl Liebknecht was shot while "trying to escape," and Rosa Luxemburg was brutally beaten to death and her body thrown into a canal from which it was recovered on May 31. The troops that put down the Communist revolt indiscriminately brutalized, terrorized, and shot leftist prisoners. In a second leftist revolt in March 1919, President Ebert declared martial law which allowed the Defense Minister Noske to issue orders to shoot on sight anyone found with weapons and fighting against the government. The Freikorps used this order to take revenge on captured leftists. In all, about 1,200 people, mostly leftists, were killed; many in reprisal for the brutal treatment of rightist prisoners.[1]

Similar savagery characterized the civil war in Bavaria from late February through early May 1919. The leftist leader Kurt Eisner was assassinated on February 21, 1919, and Gustav Landauer, like Luxemburg, was beaten to death. These murders sparked a leftist revolt that set up a revolutionary government in Munich. Both sides, leftist rebels and rightist Freikorps, sent by the republic to re-establish order, treated hostages and civilians brutally, indiscriminately shooting many, and summarily executing others. A total of 557 people were killed during the

Munich revolt. Ebert, Noske, and the Majority Socialists, horrified by the "excesses" of the counterrevolution, publicly denounced these incidents as "acts of lynch justice which disgrace the German people." Yet, they still allowed military rather than civil courts to try the murderers of Luxemburg, Liebknecht, and others, who, as a result, received light sentences and then were "allowed" to escape from prison.[2]

In the early years of the Weimar Republic, German courts handled hundreds of cases involving political crimes. After the 1918–19 revolts, they tried 2,210 people, mostly leftists, and sentenced one to death, 65 to imprisonment at hard labor, 1,737 to imprisonment, and 407 to fortress imprisonment. The prison terms totaled 6,080 years of which 4,400 were actually served.[3] From 1918 to 1921, the courts imposed eight death sentences and 177 years of imprisonment on leftists implicated in 13 political murders. During the same period the courts imposed no death sentences, one life sentence, and only 31 years of imprisonment on right-wing nationalists implicated in 314 murders.[4] During the period 1922–23, Feme (Secret Court) assassins committed 17 murders; the courts discharged or did not prosecute eight of these cases; sentenced three people to prison with hard labor in relation to them; imprisoned another five; and the outcome of one case was not stated at all. The courts used the penal code provision that covered treason to the country (betrayal of military or other secrets to foreign agents) to prosecute liberals, pacifists, socialists, and Communists who denounced the illegal Black Reichswehr in the press.[5]

Several examples will suffice to demonstrate the general leniency of Weimar courts toward right-wing nationalists. After the Kapp Putsch, the Reich Minster of Justice examined 705 charges of high treason: 412 of the cases were amnestied under the amnesty law of August 14, 1920, although it specifically excluded putsch leaders from its provisions; 108 became obsolete because of death or other reasons; 174 were not pressed; and 11 were still pending on May 21, 1921. Of the latter, only ex–Police President von Jagow was convicted, and he received five years honorary confinement. Dr. Kapp died before he could be tried, and the other major leaders either were allowed to escape, such as Lüttwitz and Papst, or were not tried, such as Generals Ludendorff and Lettow-Vörbeck. After the 1923 Hitler Putsch, Hitler and three others received five years' imprisonment each, and Röhm and three others, one year and three years each. Ludendorff again was not prosecuted. Furthermore, the government did not deport Hitler, technically still an Austrian citizen, in accordance with the Law for the Protection of the Republic, which clearly directed such action for aliens convicted of high treason.[6]

Political murder and deaths from violent political activity also ranked high as major political crimes during the republic. The police counted 376 political assassinations between 1919 and 1922, 95 percent committed by right-wing nationalists, and another 3,000 cases of political violence by members of rival political parties from 1919 to 1930. Most of the latter occurred after 1927 as Nazis battled Communists and socialists throughout Germany.[7] Among the political murders were the assassinations of two of Weimar's most prominent statesmen, Matthias Erzberger and Walter Rathenau.

As a signer of the Versailles Treaty, Erzberger had received a number of death threats. One night, several soldiers went looking for "Erzberger, the swine." In January 1920, he sued Karl Helfferich, former Imperial Secretary of the Interior and now a German Nationalist in the Reichstag, for writing several accusatory and slanderous articles. On March 12, the court found in Erzberger's favor but imposed a fine of only three hundred marks on Helfferich. A 20 year old, Oltwig von Hirschfeld, fired two shots at Erzberger, wounding him, but he received only 18 months' imprisonment. On August 16, 1921, two men, Heinrich Schultz and Heinrich Tilleson, murdered Erzberger in Bad Griesbach. The two assassins escaped to Hungary through Bavaria, helped by army lieutenant, Manfred von Killinger. Hungary refused to extradite the assassins, and Killinger, tried for aiding and abetting the murderers, was acquitted for lack of evidence.[8]

Like Erzberger, Walter Rathenau, former Economic Minister of Imperial Germany and Foreign Minister for the Weimar Republic, was also vehemently hated by the right-wing nationalists. He advocated that Germany fulfill the terms of the peace treaty and other commitments as the way to reassume its position as a great power. Worse still, Rathenau was also an assimilated Jew. On June 24, 1922, a group of assassins stopped his car on the way to the Foreign Ministry and shot him to death. One of the assassins was shot as he left the scene, and another committed suicide. The driver of the assassins' car received 15 years in prison but was pardoned after serving only seven years of the sentence. Ten others received lighter sentences. After Hitler's accession of power in 1933, the bodies of the two dead assassins were placed in a special tomb.[9]

During the trials of political criminals, the courts regularly gave credence to the character of the defendant and the motivations for his their actions. For example, at the trial of Jagow, the only person actually prosecuted for the Kapp Putsch, the government prosecutor emphasized the defendant's "undoubtedly noble motives," and the judgment itself emphasized the defendant's "selfless love for the fatherland." Jagow was pardoned after serving three years in prison and successfully appealed to have his government pension restored. Lüttwitz not only had his pension restored, but it was granted retroactively to the time of the putsch itself. In stark contrast, 97 percent of the leftists sentenced to prison in Munich "were found to have dishonorable motives," which translated into longer and stiffer sentences. In general, rightists had "honorable motives" for committing treason against the Weimar Republic; leftists and republicans did not.[10]

These following tables on political justice in the Weimar Republic illustrate the high level of political crime during these times, the generally more lenient treatment of right-wing nationalist political criminals than leftist political criminals, and, vice versa, the harsher treatment given to leftists arrested and prosecuted for political crimes. The Weimar courts and judges overwhelmingly favored right-wing political criminals over leftists (republicans and socialists as well as avowed Communists) in terms of convictions and severity of sentences. The Nazi regime easily "coordinated" the Weimar legal system after Hitler's accession to power in 1933.

Table A.1. Political Murders, 1918–22

	Committed By		
	Leftist Groups	*Rightist Groups*	*Total*
	22	354	376
Not expiated	4	326	330
Partially expiated	1	27	28
Expiated	17	1	18
Number of judgments against	38	24	
Discharged despite guilty plea	0	23	
Promoted despite guilty plea	0	3	

	Committed By		
	Leftist Groups	*Rightist Groups*	*Total*
Incarceration for murder (average time per person)	15 years	4 months	
Number executed	10		

Table A.2. Number of Political Murders, 1924–31

1924	3	1928	6
1925	3	1930	20
1926	4	1931	18
1927	5	(Jan-Jun)	

Table A.3. Persons Convicted of High Treason and Treason to the Country, 1895–1925

1895	18	1923	137
1900	6	1924	516
1913	35	1925	561
1921	111		

Table A.4. Cases of Treason to the Country Pursued Through the Press, 1924–1927 (incomplete)

Information advanced against	360
Not prosecuted	45
Prosecuted	315
Unwilling to pursue	252
Pending	63
Sentenced	3

Data for Table A.4 compiled from 1928 sources;

Source: Data for all tables taken from Footnote 31, Neumann, p. 479.

Notes

1. Pinson, pp. 382–86.
2. Arnold Brecht, *The Political Education of Arnold Brecht—An Autobiography 1884–1970* (Princeton, NJ: Princeton University Press, 1970), p. 152. Pinson, pp. 386, 388–91.
3. Franz Neumann—*Behomoth The Structure and Practice of National Socialism 1933–1944* (New York: Harper & Row, 1966), pp. 21–22. Ingo Mueller, *Hitler's Justice—The Courts of the Third Reich* (London: I. B. Tauris & Co Ltd, 1991), p. 12.
4. Richard Grunberger, *The 12-Year Reich—A Social History of Nazi Germany 1933–1945* (New York: Ballantine Books, 1972), p. 128.
5. Neumann, p. 22; footnote 31, p. 479.
6. Neumann, pp. 21–22.
7. Haller, ed., pp. 29–30.
8. Brecht, pp. 170, 177–78, 218–19.
9. Brecht, pp. 231–32.
10. Ingo Mueller, pp. 13–14.

APPENDIX C

German Treatment of Soviet POWs in World War II

As developed in Chapter 6, the Germans captured between five and six million Soviet POWs during World War, and about 3.3 million of them — two-thirds — died in captivity. Nearly two million died on the way to the transit or permanent camps or in the camps themselves, and another 1.3 million escaped, died as slave laborers, died in transit, were executed, or otherwise are unaccounted for. Only a little over one million of the Soviet POWs survived the war. Of the five million, the vast majority were captured in the first 18 months of the eastern campaign, and only 746,000 in the last 21/2 years of the war.[1] The brutal treatment — or lack of treatment — by the Germans can best be explained by the ideological context of the war against the Soviet Union, created by Hitler before the campaign started and fostered by the nazified German soldiers during that campaign.[2] To demonstrate this proposition, I will first discuss that treatment in some detail, followed by a brief discussion of the general treatment of Western POWs with emphasis on American POWs, especially Jewish and black Americans, during World War II and the general treatment of Russian POWs by Germany during World War I. I have a special interest in the German treatment of Jewish-American POWs since my father, who was Jewish, landed with the American forces at Normandy, June 6, 1944.

The Treatment of Soviet POWs

Theoretically, POWs were to be treated in accordance with the Prisoner of War Code of the Geneva Convention, signed by 42 nations, including Germany, before the war. In general, POWs were to live in sanitary camps and to receive food and medical treatment commensurate with those of their captors. They could receive mail and small parcels and were entitled to religious freedom and legal counsel before signing any documents. Enlisted men could work at nonmilitary and nonhazardous duties, NCOs had to supervise such work but could volunteer to perform menial labor, and officers were not required to work but could volunteer to do so. If they worked, POWs were supposed to receive wages for their labor. To ensure that POWs were treated according to these agreements, representatives of the protecting power (the neutral country that represented—"protected"—the interests of a country or countries at war with another. For example, during World War II Switzerland represented the interests of the United States and Britain to Germany and sent representatives to visit the POW camps in Germany.[3]

At the beginning of the war, the OKW through its Allegemeines Wehrmachtsamt (AWA) (Armed Forces General Office), headed by Generaloberst Hermann Reinecke, had overall responsibility for POW affairs. The AWA, in turn, allowed each service to take care of POWs from the same enemy service: the Luftwaffe had responsibility for captured enemy airmen; the army, captured soldiers; and the Kriegsmarine (navy) for captured seamen (of which there were few). In reality, the OKH controlled the army POW camps, usually temporary holding camps located within the army's operational areas, while those outside came under greater OKW control. The Luftwaffe camps (Luft Stalags) operated virtually independently of the AWA because of Göring's status and influence within the Nazi hierarchy. In fact, the Oberkommando Luftwaffe (OHL) (Air Force High Command) fought vehemently with Himmler and the SS over control of their camps but ultimately lost to the SS after the July 20, 1944, abortive coup.[4]

Before the start of Barbarossa, Hitler had already compromised any humane treatment of Soviet POWs. He had told his generals that since the USSR had not signed the Hague Convention it would not abide by its provisions to properly treat German POWs; therefore, German soldiers would not treat Soviet POWs according to those provisions.[5] Secondly, he had also declared that uniformed political commissars, Communists, and Jews would not be considered POWs and would be executed on the spot. If they were later found in POW camps, they would be subject to "special treatment" by the SS; that is, executed. The result of Hitler's precampaign statements and the general unpreparedness of the German army to take care of such great numbers of Soviet POWs was the extremely inhumane treatment of Soviet POWs.

Because of this deliberate maltreatment, great numbers of Soviet POWs died in the early months of Barbarossa, mainly in the transit camps, *dulags*, or on the way to the permanent camps. They were forced to march, sometimes for hundred of miles, to temporary transit camps, which the army had set up in its rear areas. Since the OKW had authorized the use of "ruthless and energetic action" against any sign of resistance by Soviet POWs, German soldiers regularly beat and abused them and provided them with little water and food on the way to the camps. Many POWs fell by the wayside, too exhausted to continue, and died, or were shot without warning if they tried to escape.[6] The *dulags* themselves were usually huge "open air" enclosures where the POWs were exposed to the hot summer sun, torrential autumn rains, and subzero winter temperatures. Hundreds of thousands died from starvation, exposure, and rampant disease, and there were reports of cannibalism among them. Because of these horrendous conditions, German guards periodically entered the camps only to "clean them out," dead and dying together, with flamethrowers. The only medical treatment these Soviet POWs received came from Soviet doctors if there were any among them.[7]

From the transit camps Soviet POWs usually had to march additional long distances to the nearest railhead for transportation in freight cars to the permanent camps. Often, these trains had to wait—during the hot, sweltering summer or the subzero winter—on sidings while other trains passed on the main lines. Again, many died along the way from thirst, disease, and exposure. During the winter thousands froze to death in the unheated freight cars as German soldiers, without proper winter clothing, had stolen their greatcoats.[8] A memorandum of the chief of the security police (SIPO) noted that the commandant of the permanent camps *complained* that 5 to 10 percent of the Soviet POWs selected for execution were arriving dead or nearly so. Many, on the way to the camp itself, would collapse from exhaustion, were dead or half dead, and had to be picked up by trucks.[9] German guards were "not only authorized but [were] obliged by duty" to use force as required to secure obedience from the POWs.[10]

Although German field commanders had orders to shoot political commissars on the spot, apparently many did not do so, fearful of the effects that such action would have on the morale and discipline of the troops. Also, as I mentioned earlier, since Hitler discovered there were many commissars in the POW camps, it appears most of them had simply melted into the larger groups of POWs, hoping to escape detection. To remedy this "problem," Hitler ordered the army to allow special SS detachments to comb the POW camps for these "undesirable" elements. At first, the SS would set up a "mini" interrogation and execution center within the camp itself but, at the urgings of army commanders, later moved the executions away from the main camps. In addition to commissars and Jews, the SS executed thousands of non–Communists, because other Soviet POWs denounced them as Communists, and non–Jews, because they looked "Jewish," including many anti–Stalinist POWs of Asiatic or Moslem origins.[11]

Various commanders objected to this inhumane treatment but not on strictly or primarily humanitarian grounds. At a summer 1941 conference on the treatment of Soviet POWs, General Reinecke remarked that the campaign in the Soviet Union was a war to the death between National Socialism and Bolshevism. In such a war, Soviet POWs could not expect to receive the same treatment as western POWs. Colonel Lahousen objected to these remarks for military reasons: the executions in front of the troops caused morale problems, the army found it more difficult to recruit agents, and the Soviet soldiers would fight more fiercely, rather than surrender, increasing German casualties.[12] To a note on a directive for the treatment of Soviet POWs, Canaris added that this inhumane treatment would require large numbers of German soldiers as guards, provide material for anti–German propaganda, alienate many prospective collaborators, and increase resistance among Soviet soldiers.[13] Few were as stalwart as the commander of Lieutenant Alexander Stahlberg who, at a June 21, 1941, briefing, insisted that his officers treat Soviet POWs and wounded according to the Hague Convention and warned he would court-martial anyone who abused POWs.[14] Despite such objections and warnings, "the senseless shooting of both POWs and civilians" continued.[15]

Some army commanders also opposed the execution of selected Soviet POWs within the boundaries of the POW camps. For example, Bock opposed permitting the SS inside POW camps under army control to separate and execute "undesirables." Therefore, he proposed in a telegram to Brauchitsch that the SS separate the POWs they wanted for "political reasons" and transfer them to "civilian" camps where they could "be dealt with as the political necessities and the security of the Reich demand."[16] In other words, since the army had full responsibility for the security of the inmates in the POW camps, allowing the SS executions within the camps infringed upon that responsibility. Once the "undesirable" POWs were removed from the camps — that is, from army responsibility and control — the SS could do what it wanted with them.

German policies toward Soviet deserters, further complicated by Stalin's policies toward them, had significant effects on the combat capabilities of the Soviet soldiers. Since initial German policy was to treat all Soviet deserters—even if avowedly anti-Communist—as POWs, and since Soviet soldiers were learning about the brutal treatment of their captured comrades, they soon saw no point in deserting. Keitel only changed in this policy in April 1943.[17] To further reduce desertion and increase resistance by his soldiers, many of whom detested the Stalinist regime, Stalin declared that captured Soviet POWs (and the tens of thousands of Soviet soldiers bypassed by the great strategic movements of the Germans) were considered to be traitors. Those that managed to return to Soviet lines were treated as suspects by the state, and many were placed in punitive battalions or sent to labor camps.[18] Between the brutal policies of both Hitler and Stalin, many "average" Soviet soldiers probably decided that they were better off fighting to the death in battle for Mother Russia against the German invaders, rather than languishing in either a German POW camp or a Soviet labor camp.

By early 1942, the Germans finally realized that the large number of Soviet POWs (as well as POWs in general) represented an untapped, cheap-to-maintain labor supply for German industry which was then starting to suffer from a shortage of males. With the agreement of the OKH, Franz Sauckel, Plenipotentiary for Labor Allocation (that is, chief of the slave labor program that deported hundreds of thousands of foreigners from the occupied countries—with the help of the army), obtained over 750,000 Soviet POWs between mid-1942 and mid-1944 (see Table C.1 for overall usage of POWs in Germany's war economy). They usually worked in various armaments industries and on German farms.[19] The army also used Soviet POWs in construction units in the occupied eastern territories to construct defensive fortifications, and in the OKH's own war industries.[20]

In general, Soviet POWs working for army construction units, war industries, or farmers fared better than their comrades left in the POW camps, but barely. One document stated, "All the men must be fed, sheltered and treated in such a way as to exploit them to the highest possible extent at the lowest conceivable degree of expenditure."[21] A report on POWs at a factory of the great Krupp industrial firm stated that they lived in "ash bins, dog kennels, old baking ovens and in self-made huts." As "racial inferiors," they barely received sufficient food, medical care was virtually nonexistent, and they were regularly brutalized by guards.[22] Furthermore, Germans were prohibited from showing any kind of sympathy for Soviet POWs—considered "defeatists," they could be prosecuted for "subversion of the armed forces."[23] Although relationships, other than

Table C.1. POWs Working in German War Economy (in thousands)

Sector of Economy	*1939*	*1940*	*1941*	*1942*	*1943*	*1944*
Agriculture		249	642	759	609	635
Non-agriculture		99	674	730	954	1,196
Total Economy		348	1,316	1,489	1,623	1,831

Country of Origin by Autumn 1943

France	739	Belgium	53
USSR	496	Serbia	94
Poland	29	Others	54

Source: Document 638, Noakes and Pridham, II, p. 908.

necessary for work, between Soviet POWs and German civilians were strictly prohibited, there were cases of *Rassenschande* (racial crime)—sexual relations between POWs and German women—mostly in rural areas. The civilians were severely fined, and the POWs, executed. Interestingly, the Germans used 30,000 Soviet POWs to man antiaircraft guns against the British and American strategic bombers.[24]

Finally, the Germans used Soviet POWs for "medical" and "scientific" experiments. For example, the SS gassed Soviet POWs at Auschwitz during initial testing of Zyklon-B (the German trade name for hydrogen cyanide or prussic acid, a pesticide), the gas that became the standard substance to exterminate millions of Jews and others during the war.[25] Soviet POWs were used in a series of "experiments," called Aktion Kugel (Operation Shooting), to observe the effects of shooting on humans. The SS also used Soviet POWs in vivisection operations to "examine" the effects of various diseases on human tissue, in decompression chamber experiments to "observe" the effects of high-altitude flying on humans, and in "freezing" experiments to "observe" the effects of freezing on human flesh.[26]

The Treatment of Western POWs

In general, military members of the Western European countries and the United States were treated much better than those from the east. To be sure, POWs captured in the 1940 campaign had to march hundreds of miles to POW camps inside Germany with minimal food, and many died from exhaustion or hunger or were shot as stragglers. At the camps, guards would often beat prisoners, stab them with bayonets, or whip them for minor infractions of camp rules or failure to work. Sick or exhausted POWs were sometimes murdered.[27] The Germans also segregated French Jews from the POWs taken in 1940, but they did not wear any special markings. However, German Jews serving with the French army were usually shot before the remaining POWs were transferred to permanent camps. Otherwise, French POWs were treated relatively "the same."[28] For most of the war, Germany "generally" observed the Geneva Convention for western POWs; Britain, and later, American, POWs had Switzerland as their Protecting Power.[29] In general, Germany provided for these POWs as well as it could, although this became harder and harder to do, especially when food shortages began to appear in the latter years of the war.

Although there were no *systematic* policies that caused the mass deaths of western POWs, there were many scattered instances of brutality and several deliberate practices aimed mainly at captured Allied commandos. As I mentioned in Chapter 6, several German commanders executed captured commandos and special agents in uniform, or turned them over to the SS for execution under the Commando and the "Night and Fog" orders. After September 1943 Hitler also had Italian POWs segregated because he considered them to be traitors. The Gestapo, in the spring of 1944, executed 50 British flyers who had escaped from a maximum security POW camp and had been recaptured, and an SS panzer unit during the Battle of the Bulge massacred 71 American POWs near Malmédy, Belgium.[30] By mid–1944, the German leadership also permitted the execution or lynching by German civilians of downed Allied airmen if they had attacked passenger or hospital trains, hospitals, schools, or civilians.[31] Keitel also authorized turning over escaped POWs who had been recaptured—except British and Americans—to the Gestapo and the SD which, in turn, transported them to Mauthausen concentration camp, where many were worked to death. Captured Allied commandos were also sent to various concentration camps where many were either executed or worked to death.[32] Finally, in the spring of 1945, many POWs died or were shot on forced marches westward to prevent them from falling into the hands of the advancing Red Army.[33]

To illustrate the different way they treated Soviet POWs, I will now discuss the way the Germans treated American POWs in general and black and Jewish American POWs in particular.[34] During the war Germany captured nearly 93,000 Americans (32,730 airmen and 60,235 soldiers), starting with the first airmen in April 1942.[35] Although available evidence about the German treatment of black and Jewish American POWs is ambiguous, two general conclusions are discernible: (1) despite Nazi racial ideology, the Germans *generally* did not treat them much differently than the general POW population; and (2) that treatment, however, differed from camp to camp. In some camps, Jews were allowed to receive Red Cross packages and even hold religious services. In others, camp guards tried to incite other POWs, usually those already prejudiced, against Jewish and black POWs. However, these attempts in most camps failed, and POWs usually—but not always—stood by their comrades.[36]

The Jews among the American forces in Europe reacted in a variety of ways after entering combat with its risk of capture by the Germans. The US Army had placed a religious designator on the soldiers' identification or dog tags; for Jews, it was an "H" for Hebrew. (British tags did not have any designation for religious affiliation.) Some soldiers did nothing and continued to wear their dog tags. Others made some effort to hide them in case they were captured. Still others threw them away. My father, a Jewish soldier from New York, served as an infantryman from the Normandy landings until after the liberation of Paris when he was wounded. He related to me that after he had landed at Normandy on June 6, 1944, he threw away his "dog tags" for fear of what the Germans would do to him if he were captured.[37] Most Jewish-American soldiers probably kept them and generally did not suffer, at least as a group, for doing so.

In the last months of the war, there was a noticeable change in the treatment of Jewish American POWs. During the Battle of the Bulge, the SS reviewed the identification tags of captured American soldiers, looking for the "H." Some Americans threw them away, others hid them, and non–Jewish soldiers did what they could to protect their Jewish comrades. Sometimes, according to unverified accounts, some "zealous" German soldier would shoot a Jewish-American POW.[38] In January 1945, some camp commanders segregated Jews from non–Jews and moved them into another part of the camp, but the other POWs generally turned out to protest this segregation. The Germans also transported 350 "Jewish" POWs from the Bad Orb POW camp to the Berga work camp, part of the Buchenwald concentration camp complex. There, four of them were executed for trying to escape and about 250 died from disease and starvation, victims of the general inhumane treatment of the regular inmates. The Americans liberated only a hundred of these POWs after the SS had evacuated the camp in early April.[39]

The movement of the Bad Orb Jewish POWs was one of several incidents in which the Germans incarcerated Jewish and non–Jewish POWs at concentration camps. For nine weeks, 82 American fliers, along with 86 other Allied fliers, who had been shot down over France, spent nine weeks at Buchenwald. Of these POWs, two (one British and one American) died, and the others were maltreated and were exposed to diseases before they were removed to regular POW camps in October 1944. From autumn

1944 to the end of the war, other small groups of American and British airmen were sent to various concentration camps (Dachau, Sachsenhausen, and Flossenburg) where they were executed. Still other small groups of American POWs were sent to Mauthausen camp where they received similar bad treatment, and many died.[40]

Postwar document searches have not produced a specific order from Hitler or Himmler to dispatch these groups of POWs to concentration camps. Given their sporadic nature, it is doubtful that either one issued a *written* order. The incidents, involving Allied airmen, may have been a "test program" to specifically punish airmen for their "cowardly acts of terror" in line with the previously cited directives on the treatment of Allied "terror flyers" over Germany. Similarly, the isolated dispatching of Jewish American POWs to concentration camps may have been a preliminary "test program" of the SS on the feasibility of executing Jewish POWs, along with European Jews, since these transports came after Himmler gained official control of the POW camps and had time to consolidate that control. Both operations were just as quickly terminated in early 1945. At about this time, Himmler had also terminated the extermination of the Jews and begun evacuating the most eastward camps (and destroying evidence of these crimes) before the Red Army could overrun them.

The Treatment of Russian POWs during World War I

I will now briefly review the German treatment of Russian POWs during World War I as a contrast to the previous discussion of the German treatment of Soviet POWs in World War II. In the First World War, Russia suffered about 9,300,000 military casualties (1,600,000–1,850,00 deaths from all causes, 4,950,000 wounded, and 2,500,000 POWs/missing in action).[41] Since Germany held about 1,500,000 Russian POWs in November 1918, Russia suffered about 1,000,000 POW deaths and missing in action (MIAs), producing a casualty rate of about 60 percent. If we could somehow separate out the MIAs, the actual death rate of Russian POWs would probably be much, much lower, certainly much lower than the World War II death rate of 66.7 percent.[42] Since the war between Germany and the tsarist empire was not ideologically motivated, German treatment of Russian POWs was not ideologically motivated either. Instead, the deaths of Russian POWs resulted from Germany's general unpreparedness — like the other warring powers' — to deal with such numbers, compounded by the increasingly adverse effects of the Allied blockade on Germany.

World War I introduced numerous new problems to warfare which none of the warring powers had anticipated, nor did they learn to effectively deal with many of them. Any history of the war would point out several of the major problems: the inability to control the mobilization process once it had started, the use of massed infantry attacks against trenches defended by machine guns, and new weapons, such as airplanes, tanks, and submarines. The problem of providing for masses of POWs was another problem of this total war of mass armies. Within six months, the warring nations of Europe collectively held between 1,300,000 and 1,400,000 POWs. Of these Germany alone held 625,000 POWs and, by the end of the war, would have 2,500,000 living POWs. Each belligerent had to "scramble" to develop a system that could secure and care for so many men. None did a perfect job in complying with Article 7 of the Hague Convention on Land Warfare of 1907 (which provided for the general treatment of POWs and was signed by most belligerents, including Germany and Russia), but all tried.[43]

The German treatment of Russian POWs was generally no different from that of all POWs. German POW camps mixed POWs of various nationalities, rather than segregating them into ethnic or cultural groups. As a result, POWs of all countries, held by Germany, received essentially the same level of treatment. The major differences were in the application of procedures from camp to camp, and some were better than others. Most camps suffered, to some degree, from overcrowding, inadequate barracks, lack of proper or sufficient food, lack of adequate medical care, short-lived epidemics of various diseases, or a combination in varying degrees of all these problems. POWs of all nationalities died of disease, and some, from maltreatment. Yet, these problems were more the result of a general inability to deal with the overwhelming nature of the total POW problem rather than a deliberate policy to maltreat POWs of any specific nationality, much less the Russians. Furthermore, as the war progressed and the Allied blockade of Germany tightened, the POWs came to feel the adverse effects as much as, if not worse than, the Germans in general. American camp inspectors — in accordance with the responsibility of the United States as the protecting power for the European belligerents until April 1917 — wrote 629 detailed reports that attested to these general conditions in the camps.[44]

In contrast, Russia during World War I had a far worse record than Germany; roughly 25 percent of its 2 to 2.4 million POWs (Germans, Austro-Hungarians, Bulgarians, and Turks) died in captivity, primarily because of "incompetence, not malice." Referring to the more than 300,000 POWs Russia took in the first six months of the war, Speed concluded, "It was simply incapable of organizing care for so many prisoners on such short notice while fighting a major war."[45] Russia's ability to fight the war stretched its capacity to the limit even without having to run an elaborate system of POW camps. With the onset of revolution and then civil war, the Russian army lost all ability to care for enemy POWs in its care. Adding to this situation, Russia generally sent most of its German POWs to camps in the cold vastness of Siberia while spreading the remaining POWs, mostly Slavs, among camps closer to the front, to exploit the ethnic differences of the Slavs in the Austro-Hungarian and the Bulgarian armies. Finally, there was no formal system to inspect the Russian camps as in the case of the German camps, and Russians looked suspiciously on the inspection procedures that did eventually come into existence. Under these adverse conditions, somewhere around 400,000 to 600,000 POWs — about 20 to 30 percent held — perished in Russian hands.[46]

On the German treatment of Russian POWs during World War I,

> ...it is clear that the German government intended to care for the prisoners it captured in a humane and appropriate manner. It is also clear that its prison camps were rigorous but not overly harsh places of confinement. Although many prisoners died in German custody, it is notable that deaths constituted fewer than 5 percent of the total.... In short, German policy during the First World War was radically different than it was during the Second World War. During the earlier conflict, Germany, like its Western opponents, made a serious if sometimes faltering effort to conform to the tenets of the liberal tradition in the administration of its prison camp system. Consequently, it is difficult to conclude that German prisoner of war policy during the Great War foreshadowed subsequent Nazi policy.[47]

Given the low overall death rate of POWs in German hands during World War I, the Russians POWs must have formed a very high percentage of those who died in captivity, as other nationalities had an extremely low death rate. A partial answer may be the generally poorer health and clothing of Russians soldiers than those of western POWs when they were captured. Also, Russian POWs (or POWs from Italy and the Balkan states who also suffered relatively high death rates) did not receive food packages from relief agencies, unlike British and American POWs. As a result, the Russians became more susceptible to disease in the camps and had a significantly higher death rate than that of other nationalities, despite German attempts to provide reasonable medical care to all POWs.[48]

Summary

As we have seen, the German treatment of western European and American POWs in World War II was relatively free of deliberate policies that resulted in mass deaths. The policies toward these groups of POWs lacked the ideological basis that colored German policies toward the fighting against the USSR in general and the treatment of Soviet POWs in particular. There were occasional incidents of atrocities against Western POWs at large, such as sporadic brutality on marches to POW camps, for much of the war's duration. Also, Hitler targeted Allied commandos, who usually wore uniforms during their raids into Nazi occupied territory and were, therefore, entitled to protection as POWs. However, it was only in the last year or so of the war when Germany was clearly losing that we see the appearance of deliberate policies to single out special groups of Western POWs, and even then they were only temporary or sporadic. For example, the Gestapo executed 50 British flyers in 1943 as an object lesson to other POWs to prevent escapes, and the more zealous, less scrupulous Waffen SS massacred American POWs at Malmédy in December 1944.

In stark contrast, during World War II, Germany carried out deliberate and horrifying policies of ideological war against captured Soviet soldiers. For years, German soldiers, as young teenagers, had been told that the Slavs were racially inferior and that Bolshevism was a plague threatening Western civilization. Part of Hitler's plans to invade the USSR and free Europe from the "Asiatic hordes" included the removal of all normal restraints against punishing his soldiers for brutalities against the Soviet people and soldiers, brutalities that earned German soldiers court-martials when committed in France. The memoirs and letters of these young German soldiers, sampled in Chapter 6, testify to the extent to which they were prepared to carry out Hitler's ideological war against the USSR that produced large-scale death for the Soviet peoples in general and Soviet POWs in particular. Compared with the German treatment of Polish POWs and the guerrilla war in Yugoslavia, it is apparent that the brutal and inhumane treatment of Soviet POWs was ideologically motivated and contrasts greatly with the treatment of even Jewish and black American POWs in World War II and the German treatment of Russian POWs in World War I.

Notes

1. Annex: The Fate of Soviet Prisoners of War (as of May 1, 1944), Dallin, p. 427. As mentioned in Chapter 6, the Germans released an additional 800,000 who joined Vlassov's anti–Stalin army. According to German records, the breakdown by year for a total of 5,754,000 is as follows:

1941	3,355,000	1944	147,000
1942	1,653,000	1945	34,000
1943	565,000		

2. The German treatment of Polish POWs was not any better. Most of the 787,000 (including 240,000 taken by the Soviets) POWs languished in POW camps, and most were eventually liquidated, used in various "medical" and "scientific" experiments of the SS, or were sent to Germany as slave laborers under the most primitive conditions. After the Polish campaign, Germany turned over 10,000 to 20,000 Polish officers to the Soviets who probably executed them in the Katyn forest. Stalin first

said that the Germans had executed them, but an independent Red Cross investigation in 1943 assigned responsibility for the atrocity to the Soviet secret police sometime in early 1940. Clark, p. 386. Snyder, pp. 191–92.

3. Document 3737-PS, (Hague) Convention Respecting the Laws and Customs of War on Land, October 18, 1907, pp. 590–93; and Document 3738-PS, Geneva Convention of July 27, 1929 (treatment of POWs), pp. 599–620, *NCA*, III.

4. David A. Foy, *For You the War Is Over: American Prisoners of War in Nazi Germany* (New York: Stein and Day, 1984), pp. 17–18. Clark, p. 206. Document 058-PS, Bormann Circular Letter, "Reorganization of the Concerns of Prisoners of War," September 30, 1944, *NCA*, III, pp. 103–4.

5. Document EC-338, Abwehr Notes of Speech, "Directives for the Treatment of Soviet POWs," September 15, 1941, *NCA*, VII, pp. 411–14.

6. OKW Directive, "Prisoners of War in Operation Barbarossa," June 16, 1941, in Dallin, p. 410. Also July 1941 OKH Instructions, Clark, p. 206. See October 20, 1941, entry, Bock, p. 337.

7. Bartov, *Eastern Front*, pp. 112–13. Clark, p. 207. Cooper, *Nazi War*, pp. 21–22. Luck, p. 71. See short descriptions from Benno Zieser, *The Road to Stalingrad*, and memoirs of a Hungarian officer, quoted in Werth, pp. 643–44. General Nagel, chief of the OKW's economic branch, declared in September 1941: "In contrast to the feeding of other captives [e.g., British and Americans] we are not bound by any obligation to feed Bolshevik prisoners. Their rations must therefore be determined solely on the basis of their labour performance for us." Quoted in Clark, p. 207.

8. Bartov, *Eastern Front*, pp. 110–11.

9. Document 1165-PS, Chief of SIPO Memorandum, "Transportation of the Russian PWs,..." November 29, 1941, *NCA*, III, p. 823.

10. Document 656-PS, OKW Order, "Self-Defense against Prisoners of War," January 29, 1943, *NCA*, III pp. 471–72.

11. Document 078-PS, Directives for the Chief of Security Police and Secret Service Teams Assigned to PW Camps, June 28, 1941, *NCA*, III, pp. 123–24. Metalman, pp. 77–79. Bartov, *Eastern Front*, p. 109. Dallin, p. 418. Bond, "Brauchitsch," in Barnett, pp. 91–92. Werth, pp. 212–13.

12. Hilberg, pp. 222–23. See also Rosenberg Letter to Keitel, February 28, 1942, in Dallin, p. 417.

13. Document EC-338, Abwehr Notes of Speech, "Directives for the Treatment of Soviet POWs," *NCA*, VII, September 15, 1941, pp. 413–14.

14. Stahlberg, p. 160. Stalhberg was Tresckow's nephew and would become Manstein's aide-de-camp.

15. Order of General Lemelson, June 25, 1941, in Bartov, *Eastern Front*, p. 117.

16. Bock, p. 353.

17. Document 081-PS, "Prisoners of War," February 28, 1942, *NCA*, III, pp. 126–30. Bartov, *Eastern Front*, pp. 118–19. Dallin, pp. 422–23.

18. Werth. P. 395.

19. Dallin, pp. 423–25.

20. Document EC-194, OKW Directive, "Use of Prisoners of War in War Industries," October 31, 1941, *NCA*, VII, pp. 336–37.

21. Document 016-PS, "The Labor-Mobilization Program," April 20, 9142, *NCA*, III, p. 57.

22. Document D-339, Special Medical Report by Dr. Jaeger, September 2, 1944; and Document D-354, Sworn Statement by Six Germans, Krupp Sheet Metal Shop, Essen, *NCA*, VII, p. 28 and p. 35, respectively. To further exemplify the German attitude toward Soviet POWs, on July 20, 1942, Keitel proposed that they be branded with an indelible mark that would make it even more difficult for them to escape. The order was never promulgated, however. Footnote, Shirer, *Third Reich*, p. 1243.

23. OKW/AWA Directive, "Handling of Prisoners of War," October 26, 1943, Dallin, pp. 424–25.

24. Werth, p. 646.

25. Robert Jay Lifton, *The Nazi Doctors: Medical Killing—and the Psychology of Genocide* (New York: Basic Books, Inc., 1986), p. 160.

26. Werth, p. 647.

27. IMT Indictment, *NCA*, I, pp. 41–42.

28. Hilberg, pp. 400–1.

29. Western POWs have noted in memoirs that German POW camp officials ensured that they received their regular Red Cross parcels, mail, blankets, and somewhat reasonable food—especially right before the regular visit of representatives from the International Red Cross and the protecting power.

30. Document L-51, Affidavit of Adolf Zutter, August 2, 1945, *NCA*, VII, pp. 798–99. Shirer, *Third Reich*, p. 1244.

31. Documents 730-PS, 731-PS, 732-PS, 735-PS, 737-PS, 740-PS, 741-PS, 744-PS, dated between June 4 and June 30, 1944, "Treatment of Enemy Terror Aviators," *NCA*, III, pp. 526–38, 543–44.

32. Document 1650-PS, Gestapo Memorandum, "Measures to be Taken against Captured Prisoners of War," March 4, 1944, *NCA*, IV, pp. 158–59.

33. Mario Garbin in Tom Bird, *American POWs of World War II: Forgotten Men Tell Their Stories* (Westport, CT: Praeger, 1992), pp. 61–62.

34. Even the American POWs noticed the difference between their treatment and that of the Russians. Mario Garbin noted that his camp held POWs of different nationalities: Serbs, Belgians, Frenchmen, British, New Zealanders, "you name

it." The Germans, however, kept the Italians and the Russians in separate areas—"the Italians because they were traitors...." and the Russians "because the Germans believed them to be animals and because they didn't subscribe to the Red Cross;...." Mario Garbin in Bird p. 57.

35. The Military Intelligence Service of the US War Department provided these figures. In 1980, the Veterans Administration calculated that 95,532 Americans became POWs of the Germans. Foy, pp. 12–13. Charles A. Spenger reports that Germany either captured or interned 93,941 Americans of whom 1,121 died in captivity; that is, 1.19 percent. Bird, p. 141.

36. Peter Neft in Bird, p. 90. Foy, pp. 128–31.

37. Personal communication with the author, date unknown.

38. Mitchell G. Bard, *Forgotten Victims: The Abandonment of Americans in Hitler's Camps* (Boulder, CO: Westview Press, 1994), pp. 37–40.

39. Bernie Melnick and Ray Weiss, in Bird, pp. 97–101 and pp. 121–22, respectively. Bard, pp. 71–103. I used Jewish in quotes as the camp commandant could not find 350 Jews in his camp and made up the difference with "Jewish" looking POWs.

40. Bard, pp. 42–43, 52–53, 57–69.

41. Table "Allied Military Effort and Losses 1914–18," Randal Gray, *Chronicles of the First World War* (Oxford, UK: Facts on File, 1991), II, p. 288. Civilian dead numbered about 2,000,000, including about 500,000 Poles and Lithuanians. Table "Civilian Dead 1914–18," Gray, p. 292.

42. Richard B. Speed III, *Prisoners, Diplomats, and the Great War: A Study in the Diplomacy of Captivity* (New York: Greenwood Press, 1990), p. 76.

43. Speed, p. 6–7.

44. Speed, pp. 19–30, 63–79.

45. Speed, p. 7.

46. Speed, pp. 107–22.

47. Speed, p. 79.

48. Speed, pp. 73–77.

Bibliography

A. Published Primary Sources, Memoirs, Etc.

Baynes, Norman H., editor. *The Speeches of Adolf Hitler*. New York: Howard Fertig, 1969. Two volumes. First published in 1942.

Bock, Fedor von. *Generalfeldmarschall Fedor von Boc: The War Diary 1939–1945*. Atglen,PA: Schiffer Military History, 1996. Edited by Klaus Gerbet. Translated from the German by David Johnston.

Brecht, Arnold. *The Political Education of Arnold Brecht: An Autobiography 1884–1970*. Princeton, NJ: Princeton University Press, 1970. Originally published in German in 1966–67 in two volumes.

Caesar, Julius. *Ceasar's Gallic War*. Woodbury, NY: Barron's Educational Series, Inc., 1962. Translated by Joseph Pearl.

De Joinville, Jean, and Geoffrey de Villehardouin. *Chronicles of the Crusades*. Harmondsworth, UK: Penguin Books, Ltd., 1963. Translated by Margaret R. Shawl.

De Roussey de Sales, Raoul, editor. *My New Order*. New York: Reynal & Hitchcock, 1941.

Domarus, Max, editor. *Hitler Speeches and Proclamations 1932–1945*. Wauconda, IL: Bolchazy-Carducci Publishers, 1990–94. Four Volumes. Translated from the German by Mary Fran Gilbert. Originally published in Germany in 1962, 1963, 1973, and 1987.

Forsthoff, Ernst, editor. *Deutsche Geschichte von 1918 bis 1938 in Dokumenten*. Stuttgart: Alfred Kroener Verlag, 1943.

Froissart, Jean. *Chronicles*. Harmondsworth, UK: Penguin Books, Ltd., 1968. Translated and edited by Geoffrey Brereton.

Fuchs, Karl. *Sieg Heil! War Letters of Tank Gunner Karl Fuchs 1937–1941*. Hamden, CT: Archon Books, 1987. Edited and translated by Horst Fuchs Richardson.

Gisevius, Hans Bernd. *To the Bitter End*. Westport, CT: Greenwood Press, 1975. Translated from the German by Richard and Clara Winston. First published in Germany in 1946.

Görlitz, Walter, editor. *In the Service of the Reich*. New York: Stein and Day, 1979. Originally published in Germany in 1961. Translated by David Irving.

Guderian, Heinz. *Panzer Leader*. New York: Ballantine Books, 1952. Translated from the German by Constantine FitzGibbon.

Halder, Franz. *The Halder War Diary 1939–1942*. Novato, CA: Presidio Press, 1988. Edited by Charles Burdick and Hans Adolf Jacobsen.

Haller, Uli, editor. *Lieutenant General Karl Strecker: The Life and Thoughts of a German Military Man*. Westport, CT: Praeger Publishers, 1994.

Hassell, Ulrich von. *The Von Hassell Diaries 1938–1944*. Garden City, NY: Doubleday & Company, Inc., 1947.

Hitler, Adolf. *Hitler's Secret Book*. New York: Bramhall House, 1986. Translated from the German by Salvatore Attanasio. First published in Germany in 1961.

_____. *Mein Kampf*. Boston: Houghton Mifflin Company, 1943. Translated from the German by Ralph Manheim.

Hohlfeld, Johannes, editor. *Dokumenten der Deutschen Politik und Geschichte von 1848 bis zur Gegenwart*. Berlin: Dokumenten-Verlag Dr. Herbert Wendler & Co., 1952. Four volumes.

Klee, Ernst, Willi Dressen and Volker Riess, editors. *"The Good Old Days": The Holocaust as Seen by Its Perpetrators and Bystanders.* New York: The Free Press, 1988. Translated by Deborah Burnstone.

Knappe, Siegfried, and Ted Brusow. *Soldat: Reflections of a German Soldier.* New York: Orion Books, 1992.

Last Letters from Stalingrad. New York: William Morrow and Company, 1962. Translated by Franz Schneider and Charles Gullans. Originally published in German in 1954.

Luck, Hans von. *Panzer Commander: The Memoirs of Colonel Hans von Luck.* New York: Dell Publishing, 1989.

Luvaas, Jay, editor. *Frederick the Great on the Art of War.* New York: The Free Press, 1966.

MacArthur, Douglas. *Reminiscences.* New York: McGraw Hill Book Company, 1964.

Machiavelli, Niccolò. *The Art of War.* Indianapolis, IN: The Bobbs-Merrill Company, Inc., 1965.

_____. *The Prince and Selected Discourses.* New York: Bantam Books, 1966. Translated and edited by Daniel Donno.

Manstein, Erich von, Field Marshal. *Lost Victories.* Novato, CA: Presidio Press, 1994. Originally published in German in 1955. Edited and translated by Anthony G. Powell.

Mellenthin, F. W. von. *Panzer Battles: Study of the Employment of Armor in the Second World War.* New York: Ballantine Books, 1971. Originally published in 1956. Translated by H. Belzer.

Metalman, Henry. *Through Hell for Hitler.* Wellingborough, UK: Patrick Stephens Limited, 1990.

Nazi Conspiracy and Aggression. Washington, DC: United States Government Printing Office, 1946. Ten Volumes.

Noakes, J., and G. Pridham, editors. *Nazism 1919–1945: A History in Documents and Eyewitness Accounts.* New York: Shocken Books, 1983–84. Two volumes.

Papen, Franz von. *Memoirs.* London: Andre Deutsch, 1952.

Prueller, William. *Diary of a German Soldier.* New York: Coward-McCann, Inc., 1963. Translated by H. C. Robbins Landon and Sebastian Leitner.

Rauschning, Hermann. *Hitler Speaks.* London: Thornton Butterworth Ltd, 1939.

Sajer, Guy. *The Forgotten Soldier: The Classic WWII Autobiography.* Washington, DC: Brassey's (US), Inc., 1990. Originally published in France in 1967.

Schlabrendorff, Fabian von. *The Secret War against Hitler.* New York: Pitman Publishing Corporation, 1965. Translated by Gilda Simon.

_____. *They Almost Killed Hitler.* New York: Macmillan, 1947.

Schüddekopf, Otto-Ernst, editor. *Das Heer und die Republik Quellen zur Politik der Reichswehrführung.* Hannover: NorddeutscheVerlagsanstalt O. Goedel, 1955.

Seeckt, General (Hans von). *The Future of the German Empire: Criticisms and Postulates.* New York: E. P. Dutton & Co. Inc. 1930. Translated from the German by Oakley Williams.

_____. *Thoughts of a Soldier.* London: Ernest Benn Limited, 1930. Translated from the German by Gilbert Waterhouse.

Senger und Etterlin, General Frido von. *Neither Fear nor Hope.* New York: E. P. Dutton & Co., Inc., 1964. Originally published in Germany in 1960. Translated by George Malcolm.

Shirer, William L. *Berlin Diary: The Journal of a Foreign Correspondent 1934–1941.* New York: Popular Library, 1961. Originally published in 1941.

Speidel, Hans. *Invasion 1944! Rommel and the Normandy Campaign.* Chicago: Henry Regnery Company, 1950.

Stahlberg, Alexander. *Bounden Duty: The Memoirs of a German Officer 1932–45.* London: Brassey's UK, 1990. Originally published in German in 1987. Translated by Patricia Crampton.

Trial of War Criminals before the Nürnberg Military Tribunals under Control Council Law No. 10: October 1946–April 1949. Washington, DC: US Government Printing Office, 1949–53. 15 volumes.

Warlimont, Walter. *Inside Hitler's Headquarters 1939–45.* Novato, CA: Presidio Press, 1964. First published in Germany in 1962. Translated by R. H. Barry.

Westman, Stephen. *Surgeon with the Kaiser's Army.* London: William Kimber, 1968.

Westphal, General Siegfried. *The German Army in the West.* London: Cassel and Company Ltd., 1951. Originally published in Germany in 1950.

Zimmermann, Erich, and Hans-Adolf Jacobsen, editors. *Germans against Hitler July 20, 1944.* Berlin: BERTO-Verlag, 1960. Translated by Allan and Lieselotte Yahraes.

B. Secondary Sources

Adcock, F. E. *The Greek and Macedonian Art of War.* Oxford, UK: Clarendon Press, 1993.

Allan, Charles R., Jr. *Heusinger of the Fourth Reich.* New York: Marzani & Munsell, Inc., 1963.

Arendt, Hannah. *Eichmann in Jerusalem: A Re-*

port on the Banality of Evil. New York: The Viking Press, 1963.

Armed Forces Information Service, Department of Defense. *The Armed Forces Officer.* Washington, DC: US Government Printing Office, 1975.

Axinn, Stephen. *A Moral Military.* Phildelphia, PA: Temple University Press, 1989.

Bard, Mitchell G. *Forgotten Victims: The Abandonment of Americans in Hitler's Camps.* Boulder, CO: Westview Press, 1994.

Barnett, Corelli, editor. *Hitler's Generals.* New York: Quill/William Morrow, 1989.

Barnett, Victoria. *For the Soul of the People: Protestant Protest against Hitler.* New York: Oxford University Press, 1992.

Barnie, John. *War and Medieval Society Social Values and the Hundred Years War 1337–99.* London: Weidenfeld and Nicolson, 1974.

Bartov, Omer. *The Eastern Front 1941–45: German Troops and the Barbarization of Warfare.* New York: St. Martin's Press, Inc., 1986.

_____. *Hitler's War: Soldiers, Nazis, and War in the Third Reich.* New York: Oxford University Press, 1992. First published in 1991.

Beeler, John. *Warfare in Feudal Europe 730–1200.* Ithaca, NY: Cornell University Press, 1972.

Bessel, Richard. *Germany after the First World War.* Oxford, UK: Clarendon Press, 1993.

Bird, Tom. *American POWs of World War II: Forgotten Men Tell Their Stories.* Westport, CT: Praeger, 1992.

Bracher, Karl Dietrich. *The German Dictatorship: The Origins, Structure, and Effects of National Socialism.* New York: Praeger Publishers, 1979. Translated from the German by Jean Steinberg.

Browning, Christopher. *Fateful Months: Essay on the Emergence of the Final Solution.* New York: Holes & Meier, 1991.

Campbell, Brian. *The Roman Army 31 BC–AD 337: A Sourcebook.* London: Routledge, 1994.

Campbell, J. B. *The Emperor and the Roman Army 31 BC–AD 235.* Oxford, UK: Clarendon Press, 1984.

Carsten, F. L. *The Reichswher and Politics 1918 to 1933.* Berkeley, CA: University of California Press, 1973. First published in Germany in 1963.

Childers, Thomas. *The Nazi Voter: The Social Foundations of Fascism in Germany 1919–1933.* Chapel Hill, NC: The University of North Carolina Press, 1983.

Clark, Alan. *Barbarossa: The Russian-German Conflict 1941–45.* New York: Quill, 1985. Originally published in 1965.

Cooper, Matthew. *The German Army 1933–1945: Its Political and Military Failure.* New York: Bonanza Books, 1978.

_____. *The Nazi War against Soviet Partisans 1941–1944.* New York: Stein and Day, 1979.

Craig, Gordon A. *The Politics of the Prussian Army 1640–1945.* London: Oxford University Press, 1968. First published in 1955.

Dallin, Alexander. *German Rule in Russia 1941–45: A Study in Occupation Policies.* Boulder, CO: Westview Press, 1981. Second Revised Edition.

Davies, Roy W. *Service in the Roman Army.* Edinburgh, UK: Edinburgh University Press, 1989. Edited by Bavid Breeze and Valerie A. Maxwell.

Deist, Wilhelm. *The Wehrmacht and German Rearmament.* Toronto: University of Toronto, 1981.

Demeter, Karl. *The German Officer Corps in Society and State 1650–1945.* London: Weidenfeld and Nicolson, 1965. Translated from the German by Angus Malcolm. First published in 1962.

Deutsch, Harold C. *Hitler and His Generals: The Hidden Crisis January-June 1938.* Minneapolis, MN: University of Minnesota Press, 1974.

Duffy, Christopher. *The Army of Frederick the Great.* New York: Hippocrene Books, Inc., 1974.

_____. *Frederick the Great: A Military Life.* London: Routledge, 1988. First published in 1985.

Dulles, Allen Welsh. *Germany's Underground.* New York: The Macmillan Company, 1947.

Ergang, Robert. *The Potsdam Fuehrer Frederick William I: Father of Prussian Militarism.* New York: Columbia University Press, 1941.

Evans, Robert F. *Soldiers of Rome: Praetorians and Legionnaires.* Cabin John, MD: Seven Locks Press, 1986.

Farcau, Bruce W. *The Coup: Tactics in the Seizure of Power.* Westport, CT: Praeger Publications, 1994.

Feist, Christian. *The Art of War.* London: Thomas and Hudson, 1980.

Ferguson, R. Brian, editor. *Warfare, Culture, and Environment.* Orlando, FL: Academic Press, Inc., 1984.

Fest, Joachim C. *Hitler.* New York: Harcourt Brace Jovanovich Inc., 1973. First published in Germany in 1973. Translated from the German by Richard and Clara Winston.

Fischer, Conan. *Stormtroopers: A Social, Economic and Ideological Analysis 1929–35.* London: George Allen & Unwin, 1983.

Foy, David A. *For You the War Is Over: American Prisoners of War in Nazi Germany.* New York: Stein and Day, 1984.

Fritz, Stephen G. *Frontsoldaten The German Soldier in World War II.* Lexington, KY: The University of Kentucky Press, 1995.

Fuller, John Frederick Charles. *The Generalship*

of Alexander the Great. New Brunswick, NJ: Rutgers University Press, 1960.
Gabriel, Richard A. *The Culture of War: Invention and Early Development.* New York: Greenwood Press, 1990.
_____. *To Serve with Honor: A Treatise in Military Ethics and the Way of the Soldier.* Westport, CT: Greenwood Press, 1982.
Gallo, Max. *The Night of Long Knives.* New York: Warner Paperback Library, 1973. Translated from the French by Lily Emmet.
Ganshof, F. L. *Feudalism.* New York: Harper Torchbooks, 1964. Translated by Philip Grierson. First published in Belgium in 1944.
Garlan, Yvon. *War in the Ancient World: A Social History.* London: Chatto & Windus, 1975. Translated from the French by Janet Lloyd.
Giziowski, Richard John. *The Moral Dilemmas of Leadership: The Case of German General Johannes Blaskowitz.* Ann Arbor, MI: UMI Dissertation Services, 1991. DA Dissertation Illinois State University.
Görlitz, Walter G. *History of the German General Staff 1657–1945.* New York: Frederick A. Praeger,1963. First published in 1952. Translated from the German by Brian Battershaw.
Gordon, Harold J., Jr. *Hitler and the Beer Hall Putsch.* Princeton, NJ: Princeton University Press, 1972.
_____. *The Reichswehr and the German Republic 1919–1926.* Princeton, NJ: Princeton University Press, 1957.
Grunberger, Richard. *The 12-Year Reich: A Social History of Nazi Germany 1933–1945.* New York: Ballantine Books, 1972. Originally published in 1971.
Hackett, Sir John. *The Profession of Arms.* New York: Macmillan Publishing Company, 1983.
_____, editor. *Warfare in the Ancient World.* London: Sedgwick & Jackson Limited, 1989.
Hale, J. R. *War and Society in Renaissance Europe 1450–1620.* Leicester, UK: Leicester University Press, 1985.
Hamerow, Theodore S. *On the Road to the Wolf's Lair: German Resistance to Hitler.* Cambridge, MA: The Belknap Press of Harvard University Press, 1997.
Hammond N. G. L. *Alexander the Great: King Commander and Statesman.* London: Chatto & Windus, 1981.
Heiden, Konrad. *Der Führer: Hitler's Rise to Power.* Boston: Houghton Mifflin Company, 1944. Translated from the German by Ralph Manheim.
Heln, Paul N. *The German Struggle against Yugoslav Guerrillas In World War II: German Counter-Insurgency in Yugoslavia 1941–1943.* Boulder, CO: East European Quarterly, 1979. East European Monograph No. 57.
Hilberg, Raul. *The Destruction of the European Jews.* New York: Harper Torchbooks, 1961.
Höhne, Heinz. *The Order of the Death Head: The Story of Hitler's SS.* New York: Ballantine Books, Inc., 1971. Originally published in Germany in 1966. Translated by Richard Barry.
Hoffmann, Peter. *The History of the German Resistance 1933–1945.* Cambridge, MA: The MIT Press, 1977. Originally published in Germany in 1969. Translated by Richard Barry.
_____. *Stauffenberg: A Family History 1905–1944.* New York: Cambridge University Press, 1995. Originally published in Germany in 1992.
Huntington, Samuel P. *The Soldier and State: The Theory and Politics of Civil-Military Relations.* New York: Vintage Books, 1957.
Janowitz, Morris. *The Professional Soldier: A Social and Political Portrait.* New York: The Free Press, 1971. First published in 1960.
Kehr, Eckert. *Economic Interest, Militarism, and Foreign Policy.* Berkeley, CA: University of California Press, 1977. Edited by Gordon A. Craig.
Kelman, Herbert C., and V. Lee Hamilton. *Crimes of Obedience: Toward a Social Psychology of Authority and Responsibility.* New Haven, CT: Yale University Press, 1989.
Kitchen, Martin. *A Military History of Germany from the Eighteenth Century to the Present Day.* Seacaucus, NJ: The Citadel Press, 1976.
_____. *The German Officer Corps 1890–1914.* Oxford, UK: The Clarendon Press, 1968.
Koch, W. W. *Medieval Warfare.* Greenwich, CT: Bison Books Corp., 1985.
Kohlberg, Lawrence. *Essays on Moral Development.* Cambridge, MA: Harper & Row, 1981.
_____, *Child Psychology and Childhood Education: A Cognitive-Developmental View.* New York: Longman, 1987.
Lang, Kurt. *Military Institutions and the Sociology of War.* Beverly Hills, CA: Sage Publications, 1972.
Lazenby, J. F. *The Spartan Army.* Warminister, UK: Aris & Phillips Ltd., 1985.
Leach, Barry. *German General Staff.* New York: Ballantine Books, Inc., 1973.
Lerner, Daniel, editor. *Propaganda in War and Crisis Materials for American Policy.* New York: George W. Stewart, Publisher, Inc., 1951.
Levin, Nora. *The Holocaust: The Destruction of European Jewry 1933–1945.* New York: Schocken Books, 1973.
Liddell-Hart B(asil) H. *The German Generals Talk.* New York: William Morrow & Co., 1948.
Lifton, Robert Jay. *The Nazi Doctors: Medical*

Killing and the Psychology of Genocide. New York: Basic Books, Inc., 1986.

Livy. *The Early History of Rome.* Harmondsworth, UK: Penguin Books, Inc., 1960. Translated by Aubrey de Selincourt.

Luedtle, Alf. *Eigen-Sinn und Fabrikalltag, Arbeitsfahrungen und Politik von Kaiserreich Bis in den Faschimus.* Hamburg, 1993.

Luttwak, Edward. *Coup d'État: A Practical Handbook.* Cambridge, MA: Harvard University Press, 1979. First published in 1968.

Macksey, Kenneth. *Guderian: Creator of the Blitzkrieg.* New York: Stein and Day, 1975.

Milgram, Stephen. *Obedience to Authority: An Experimental View.* New York: Harper & Row, 1974.

Militärgeschichtliches Forschungsamt. Handbuch zur deutschen Militärgeschicte 1648–1939. Munich: Bernard & GräfeVerlag, 1979. Ten volumes.

Mitcham, Samuel, Jr. *Hitler's Legions: The German Army Order of Battle World War II.* New York: Dorset Press, 1985.

Mixon, Don. *Obedience and Civilization: Authorized Crime and the Normality of Evil.* London: Pluto Press, 1989.

Müller, Ingo. *Hitler's Justice: The Courts of the Third Reich.* London: I. B. Tauris & Co Ltd, 1991.

Müller, Klaus-Jürgen. *The Army, Politics, and Society in Germany, 1933–45: Studies in the Army's Relation to Nazism.* New York: St. Martin's Press, 1987. Originally published in Germany.

Neumann, Franz. *Behemoth: The Structure and Practice of National Socialism 1933–1944.* New York: Harper & Row, 1966. Originally published in 1942.

Norman, A. V. B. *The Medieval Soldier.* New York: Thomas Y. Crowell Company, 1971.

Oliner, Samuel P., and Pearl M. Oliner. *The Altruistic Personality: Rescuers of Jews in Nazi Europe.* New York: The Free Press, 1988.

O'Neill, Robert J. *The German Army and the Nazi Party, 1933–1939.* London: Cassel & Company Ltd., 1966.

Orlow, Dietrich. *The History of the Nazi Party 1919–1945.* Pittsburgh, PA: University of Pittsburgh Press, 1969. Two volumes.

Paret, Peter. *Yorck and the Era of Prussian Reform 1807–1815.* Princeton, NJ: Princeton University Press, 1966.

Parker, H. M. D. *The Roman Legions.* Cambridge, UK: W. Hefter & Sons Ltd. 1971. First published in 1928.

Parkinson, Roger. *The Hussar General: The Life of Blücher Man of Waterloo.* London: Peter Davies, 1975.

Perlmutter, Amos, and Valerie Plave Bennett. *The Political Influence of the Military: A Comparative Reader.* New Haven, CT: Yale University Press, 1980.

Pinson, Koppel S. *Modern Germany: Its History and Civilization.* New York: The Macmillan Company, 1966.

Plutarch. *The Lives of the Noble Grecians and Romans.* Chicago: Encyclopedia Britannica, Inc., 1952. Great Books of the Western World, Vol. 14.

Polybius. *The Rise of the Roman Empire.* Harmondsworth, UK: Penguin Books Ltd., 1979. Translated by Ian Scott-Kalvert.

Post, Gaines, Jr. *The Civil-Military Fabric of Weimar Foreign Policy.* Princeton, NJ: Princeton University Press, 1973.

Rauschning, Hermann. *The Revolution of Nihilism: Warning to the West.* New York: Alliance Books Corporation, 1939.

Reiche, Eric G. *The Development of the SA in Nürnberg, 1922–1934.* Cambridge, MA: Cambridge University, 1986.

Reynolds, Nicholas. *Treason Was No Crime: Ludwig Beck.* London: William Kimber, 1976.

Ritter, Gerhard. *The German Resistance: Carl Goerdeler's Struggle against Tyranny.* New York: Frederick A. Praeger, 1958. Translated by R. T. Clark.

_____. *The Sword and the Scepter: The Problem of Militarism in Germany.* Coral Gables, FL: University of Miami Press, 1969–73. Four volumes. First published in German in 1954–68. Translated by Heinz Norden.

Rohr, John A. *To Run a Constitution: The Legitimacy of the Administrative State.* Lawrence, KS: University of Kansas, 1986.

Rosinski, Herbert. *The German Army.* New York: Frederick A. Praeger, Inc., 1966. Edited by Gordon A. Craig. First published in 1940.

Rothels, Hans. *The German Opposition to Hitler.* Hinsdale, IL: Henry Regnery Company, 1948.

Rovere, Richard Halworth. *General MacArthur and President Truman: The Struggle for Control of American Foreign Policy.* New Brunswick, NJ: Transaction Publishers, 1992.

Schmeller, Helmut J. *Hitler and Keitel: An Investigation of the Influence of Party Ideology on the High Command of the Armed Forces in Germany between 1938 and 1945.* Hays, KS: Fort Hays Kansas State College, 1970. New Series History Series, No. 7, June 1970.

Seaton, Albert. *The German Army 1933–45.* New York: New American Library, 1982.

Shanahan, William O. *Prussian Military Reforms 1786–1813.* New York: Columbia University Press, 1945. Studies in History, Economics and Public Law, No. 520.

Shirer, William L. *The Rise and Fall of the Third Reich: A History of Nazi Germany.* Greenwich, CT: Fawcett Publications, Inc., 1960.

Snyder, Louis. *Encyclopedia of the Third Reich.* New York: Paragon House, 1989. Originally published in 1976.

The Song of Roland. Baltimore, MD: Penguin Books, 1963. Translated by Dorothy L. Sayers.

Stachura, Peter D. *Nazi Youth in the Weimar Republic.* Santa Barbara, CA: Clio Books, 1975.

Stern, Fritz. *The Politics of Cultural Despair: A Study in the Rise of the Germanic Ideology.* Berkeley, CA: University of California Press, 1974. First Published in 1961.

Tacitus. Chicago: Encyclopaedia Britannica, Inc., 1952. Great Books of the Western World, Vol. 15.

Taylor, Telford. *Nuremberg and Vietnam: An American Tragedy.* New York: Bantam Books, 1971. Originally published in 1970.

_____. *Sword and Swastika: Generals and Nazis in the Third Reich.* Chicago: Quadrangle Books, 1969. First published in 1952.

Trease, Geoffrey. *The Condottiere: Soldiers of Fortune.* London: Thames and London, 1970.

Turney-High, Harry Holbert. *Primitive War: Its Practice and Concepts.* Columbia, SC: University of South Carolina Press, 1949.

Van Creveld, Martin. *Fighting Power and U. S. Army Performance 1939–1945.* Westport, CT: Greenwood Press, 1982.

_____. *The Training of Officers from Military Professionalism to Irrelevance* New York: The Free Press, 1990.

Vegetius, Renatus Flavius. *The Military Institutions of the Romans.* Westport, CT: Greenwood Press, 1985. Translated by Lieutenant John Clark. Edited by Brigadier General Thomas R. Phillips.

Waite, Robert G. L. *Vanguard of Nazism: The Free Corps Movement in Postwar Germany 1918–1923.* Cambridge, MA: Harvard University Press, 1952. Reissued in 1970.

Watkin, Malham M., editor. *War, Morality, and the Military.* Boulder, CO: Westview Press, 1986. Second revised edition.

Watson, G. R. *The Roman Soldier.* Ithaca, NY: Cornell University Press, 1985. First published in 1969.

Werth, Alexander. *Russia at War 1941–1945.* New York: Avon Books, 1965. First published in 1964.

Whalen, Robert Weldon. *Assassinating Hitler: Ethics and Resistance in Nazi Germany.* London: Associated University Press, Inc., 1993.

Whaley, Barton. *Covert German Rearmament, 1919–1939 Deception* and *Misperception.* Frederick, MD: University Publications of America, Inc., 1984

Wheeler-Bennett, John W. *The Nemesis of Power: The German Army in Politics 1918– 1945.* London: Macmillan & Co Ltd. 1956. First published in 1953.

Winnicott, D. W. *Playing and Reality.* New York: Basic Books, 1971.

Wise, Terence. *Medieval Warfare.* New York: Hastings House, 1976.

Wolman, Benjamin B., editors. *Handbook of Developmental Psychology.* Englewood Cliffs, NJ: Prentice-Hall, Inc., 1982.

C. Periodical and Electronic Articles

Ackerman, Robert W., "The Knightly Ceremonies in the Middle English Romance," *Speculum*, XIX (July 1944), 285–313.

Bayles, William, "Generals Rommel and Von Bock," *The American Mercury*, Vol. 55 (August 1942), 183–90.

Chamberlain, E. R., "The 'English' Mercenary Captains," *History Today*, VI (May 1956), 334–43.

Correspondence Report, May 3, 1995, at http://www.intac.com/PubService/humanrights/newstand/1995/may95/03may/HAITI-COURT-MARTIAL

"Eastern Theater Second Wind, Third Week," *Time*, 38 (July 14, 1941), 19.

Otmar, Freiherr von Aretin, Karl, "*Der Eid auf Hitler*," *Politische Studien*, VIII (January 1956), 1–19.

Schwertfeger, Berhard, *"Hindenburgs Tod und der Eid auf den 'Führer,'" Die Wandlung*, VI (October 1948), 563–78.

Wrage, Stephen, "A Question of Duty," *Newsweek* (November 22, 1999), 52, 54.

D. Newspapers

(London) Times
New York Times
USA Today

Index

BY

STEPHANIE HUDSON

The Quarter Moon
The Afterlife Saga #4

Published by Hudson Indie Ink
www.hudsonindieink.com

The Quarter Moon/Stephanie Hudson – 2nd ed.
ISBN-13 - 978-1-913769-21-5

I would like to dedicate this book to the 52 people who lost their lives in the 7 July 2005 London bombing and the families, friends and rescuers this terrible day affected.
I will never forget the emotional feelings on my birthday to hear that so many innocent people had lost their lives and would never again celebrate their own birthday. I am happy that I finally get to dedicate a book to you all and your everlasting memory.

We all

For once you hope the train will never come,
Standing, waiting shocked at the world and all it's done,
Creating monsters that think to change with tools of death,
But the only tool needed is blind madness with each breath,

You want revenge for the wrongs not yet made right,
To strip yourself of your working armour and join in the fight,
Hunting those long dead who remain responsible,
Our feelings are raging, furious and unstoppable.

They thought to change the world by killing innocent people,
Hiding behind actions not condoned in any Mosque, temple or steeple,
But still 52 people were unjustly taken from us,
Bringing Hell to London by Underground Train and bus.

We did not engage you in battle or wage your war,
We were not soldiers holding our weapons at your door,
We were but living out our peaceful lives,
On the way to work or meeting our wives,

We were parents, students and more,
Not battleships invading your shore,
We were not the fighters in the sky,
We weren't the ones invading your homes shouting 'die'.

You lived among us and gained our trust,
Then you used and buried us into dust,
But we will be the ones to live on,
As greater people in name although we're gone,

We say learn this lesson world and not fight,
For things better than ourselves we do right,
Holding on to the memories we love,
We send you this important message from above,

All humans are equal no matter your faith,
So put an end to the destruction and do so with haste,
Say goodbye to the hate and revenge in your sorrow,
For the sun will rise on a happier tomorrow.

WARNING

This book contains explicit sexual content, some graphic language and a highly addictive Alpha Male.

This book has been written by a UK Author with a mad sense of humour. Which means the following story contains a mixture of Northern English slang, dialect, regional colloquialisms and other quirky spellings that have been intentionally included to make the story and dialogue more realistic for modern-day characters.

Please note that for your convenience language translations have been added to optimise the readers enjoyment throughout the story.

Also meaning…

No Googling is required ;)

Also, please remember that this part of a 12 book saga, which means you are in for a long and rocky ride. So, put the kettle on, brew a cup, grab a stash of snacks and enjoy!

Thanks for reading x

PROLOGUE

"He's dead, Keira."

"NOOOOOO!" I screamed out at the impossible words as my knees impacted the ground and the next thing I knew darkness surrounded my soul.

After that, time didn't make any sense to me. It was as if it was lost… pieces of a cosmic puzzle breaking away and leaving massive black holes in its wake. I could see my body freefalling down into a pit of space, where ink coloured arms would stretch out and try to rip pieces of my soul from my body as I fell. I screamed…at least I think I screamed, as I felt my mouth open but heard no sounds escaping.

Then I heard it…was that what my name was?

Was that what it sounded like?

"Keira!" A voice was trying to pull me back and whoever it belonged to was putting the fear of God into the Beings that were trying to drag my soul down into their underworld.

Who was that?

"Keira! Come on girl! Bring yourself back!" I closed my eyes and tried to control my weightless arms to wrap around myself. I was letting go, despite the voice I heard and the urgency I felt in my name being called out it didn't make me want to hold on any longer.

It wasn't the right voice I needed to pull me back, so what was the point? These Beings could take my soul. Hell, they could tear it to shreds and scatter it like confetti if they wanted, as there was only one man that would ever own it and his was the one voice I would never hear again.

"KEIRA!" The voice boomed and the shockwaves hit the edges of the tunnel to Hell I travelled. Then, I felt the thunder crack before I heard it…pain. Pain erupted across a face and when my eyes flashed open, I was looking into the piercing eyes of a scarred bear. I had to blink a few times before the image disappeared and what was left was the tear-stained face of Leivic.

I looked around and saw the familiar clear sky I had woken up to that morning. The hard gravel floor started to dig into my back where I lay and I turned my head to the side to see the creaky front steps leading up to a door that someone I loved would never walk through again. It was only then that I realised my body was shaking uncontrollably and my vision was like opening your eyes underwater.

"I am so sorry Keira…so, so sorry." He spoke to me in hushed tones that had blurred into meaningless words of a truth that I would never be able to understand.

I would never want to understand.

I was being held by strong arms that would never be strong enough and being softly spoken to by a voice that would never be soft enough. The wrong breath in my ear, wrong fingers curled around my arm and the wrong heart pounded wildly in the wrong chest.

It was all wrong.

And Draven was really gone from this world and had left behind a shell of a girl, who was now not only missing half her soul, but also…

The whole of her heart.

CHAPTER ONE

HEART OF THE ABYSS

I woke to the sound of my alarm going off and it might as well have been screaming "no life, no life, no life", instead of its annoying beeping sequence. I hit it with a little too much force and the pain was welcomed. These days it was the only feeling that let me know I was still alive.

The week that followed the worst day of my life was like walking in the dark and having to feel my way around blindly with my hands. To say that I felt numb was not exactly true. Oh, don't get me wrong, I felt plenty numb but only when I had to be around other people. But it was times like now, the times I was alone and the only emotion and physical feeling was the same and that was pure, unfiltered pain. A pain which cut so deep, that with every movement my body made I felt like screaming in agony.

Some days I found I couldn't actually get out of bed. I was too exhausted and mentally drained, yet at night I couldn't even close my eyes for fear of dreaming. See, it wasn't nightmares that haunted my nights but wonderful dreams of Draven that were like ripping open an old wound every morning I woke. So, I tried the technique of not sleeping. It was like a blissful torture, one that would break the little left of my soul. I would cry for hours, until that was all my body knew what to do. It was a complete lie when people said that your tears ran dry, that you could cry so much that you had nothing left, because a week later and it was still all my body knew what to do.

I would love to have said that after that day things got easier, but I would be lying. The only changes were the different responses I took to the news. The first day my body seemed to shut down. Even after Leivic had carried me through the empty house and carefully placed me on the bed, my eyes wouldn't focus, my lips refused to form words and my body began to sink further into the hole it was being sucked into. It was as though my mind had no say in the fact that my body had given up and was ready to die along with the other half of me.

I think if Leivic hadn't stayed there with me that day to keep pulling me back, I would have died. It was only after a full twenty odd hours that it was finally safe enough to leave me. That's when the tears and screaming started.

Libby had come back to find me in such a state that she could get little from me but from the way I kept repeating,

"He left me, he left me..." She made her own conclusion that Draven had broken up with me. And still, to this day, I had not found it in me to correct her. Because she was right in a sense, Draven had left me, but unlike living with even the smallest possibility that he would come back, no, I was living in the shadows of what his body left behind.

The second day had me waking to even more tears as my cruel brain had spent the night replaying every touch, smell and loving word he had bestowed on me. Libby had tried to talk to me again that day but still couldn't get anything from me. I couldn't eat. I could barely keep down liquids before having to run to the toilet to exercise my stomach muscles.

The third day however, my mind took on another approach. It was the day that my brain finally kicked into living gear and started to try and form a plan. It was only then that I started to realise that no one and I mean no one had been in contact with me! I mean, not even a phone call or a message from either Vincent or Sophia. It was only then that I realised even Ragnar, my bodyguard, had disappeared. It was as if time had been rewritten and I had gone back in time to when I first arrived.

I had grabbed my phone and started ringing every number on there to try and get answers, but every number came back with a dead dial tone as if that phone was no longer in use. I had even driven to Afterlife, just to sit in my car for three hours, to stare out at a lifeless club that had been my second home. It had been shut up tight and even when I finally got my cramped legs out of the car, I found there was little point.

All I found was a notice on the door,

Afterlife will be closed until further notice,
Thank you

This had started a whole load more crying but added to this was also a whole load of fist banging that ended with a couple of bruised hands and cut up knuckles. I walked away with some sick hope that my blood on the notice would be seen by those who had caused my pain. Because it wasn't just Draven that had caused my heartache, it was also those that I had considered family, the ones who had abandoned me. A brother and a sister, a Viking bodyguard whose life I had saved, a Vampire king who I had taken a knife in my heart for and an Imp who I had let into that heart. But no one was there, no one had come and I was very much alone.

This was what led me into day four, which I would rightly call 'Anger Day'. This was the first day that I cried not tears of pain and heartbreak, but pure rage. I had walked back to the cabin which was still in pieces in the forest clearing and it was the first time I had been back to the scene that changed my past forever. The night that had killed my demons once and for all and at that moment I was so angry that I wished Morgan had been there waiting for me.

I wasn't the same person I was back then and the shaking in my arms from clenching my hands so hard was the proof. I wanted to see him. I wanted to smash his face into my fist and watch him crumble at my feet. I wanted him to suffer as I had done, like I was doing now. I wanted someone who deserved to feel my pain and when I punched my fist through one of the only pieces of wood left standing, I knew I had lost it.

Anger Day ended with a trip to the hospital and a fracture at the neck of the fourth metacarpal bone, or so the doctor informed me. He asked me what I had hit and I told him not to worry and not to expect to see someone coming in with a broken face…not surprisingly, he didn't respond.

I left the hospital with a splint that extended from my mid-forearm to the fingers, leaving my fingertips exposed and a shit load of Ibuprofen. He told me to put ice on it to help with the swelling and take the painkillers as needed. With the price of an X-ray, two thoughts entered my mind in the back of the taxi, one I was glad I had taken out health insurance and two, how I missed the National Health Service in England.

I returned home and managed to form enough words to lie to Libby by saying I had fallen on my hand awkwardly when out walking. I knew I wasn't being fair to my sister, but it was hard to explain things I didn't even yet understand myself. For one, I couldn't tell her that Draven had died because where was his funeral? Where was his goodbye to the world and where did his body rest? These were the soul destroying questions my 'supposed' family could have answered for me but no, they had left me just like Draven had, as though he hadn't been the only one to die that day.

It all added to the reasons that we're best to just let Libby and Frank believe he'd finished things with me. I hated that they thought badly of Draven and hearing Frank one night saying how he would kick his ass if ever he saw him again, had me crying once more. I loved my sister and Frank but the very last thing I wanted during her last weeks of pregnancy, was to add any stress, which was why things changed on the fifth day.

Day five brought back an old friend of mine and I woke up to see the fake Keira back in business. I got up, decided to finally use the bathroom for more than the toilet and endless rolls of tissue paper to dry tears, to have a much needed shower. I dressed in something other than pyjamas and pulled a pair of gloves on over my splint. It looked as if I had stuffed a tennis ball on the top of my hand but the pain of it I welcomed. It was like a sick release on my overwhelming emotions and it helped in finally talking to Libby. Every time Draven's named was mentioned I would flex my hand and the shooting pain had me biting my lip at the sweet agony. Every time I would think, well at least there is one pain in my life that I could control!

The conversation with Libby was just as hard as doing anything else in the day. Getting up, washing, eating… Christ, even breathing was a chore, but one that I would no doubt continue doing. I think at one stage of my first week, I even tried pretending he wasn't dead and that any day now he would be coming back to me and knocking on my door. This ended in me sat in the corner of my room fisting my necklace and holding myself into a protective ball, saying over and over,

"It's a mistake, it's a mistake," until my voice didn't feel like working any longer. Holding on to the necklace that Draven had given me was another coping mechanism I used, one that only brought me slight comfort, as without Draven around it felt colder against my skin as though some part of it was lost as well.

My week pretty much continued the same way, only with the added no sleeping rule. I would get up…or force myself up on most days and start the day with a new depressing thought to drag me down into a pit of misery that I would walk through like a bloody zombie. A zombie that even having Stephen Hawking's big brain to suck on wouldn't satisfy!

I was lucky those days if I made it downstairs without pathetic tears emerging or squeezing my broken hand for my pain rush. I let out a sigh of relief when I saw the kitchen empty and a quick call out told me I was in the house alone. I treasured those moments and would find myself sat at the table, with an abandoned cup of tea waiting for me to take notice, just staring at the window. I think in the cruel subconscious of my mind I was just waiting, or more like praying, to see one of Draven's lavish and ultra-expensive cars pull up on my driveway. I think by the end of an hour I was imagining things as a car's engine was the only thing I would hear. Of course, it would never be a car and I could not even blame my craziness on Libby or Frank coming home.

But no one ever came at these times.

I got up and discarded the cold tan coloured liquid down the sink and grabbed a bag of crisps from the cupboard, as it was the only thing I could even think of to eat right then. I thought at some point I would reach for the tubs of ice cream and my body weight in chocolate phase but until then I was reduced to putting little effort, or care for that matter, as to what I fuelled my body with.

I had the bag open and was stuffing four crisps in my mouth at once when I walked out of the kitchen. I crunched down as I turned after something caught my eye. It was a single envelope, which was odd for two reasons. One being that these days whenever the mail came it was always full of baby related leaflets as I think Libby had joined every bloody baby group in the state! Oh and big reason number two, there had definitely been no mail when I came down earlier and after looking through the window for the entire time, I was pretty damn positive I had not seen any mailman!

I walked to the door, but as I got closer the bag of crisps dropped from my hand and rained salty snacks to the hardwood floor. I gasped and my shaking hands flew to my mouth. Because there, on the crisp white envelope, was a red wax seal that was glued to the paper like large drops of my own blood.

I don't know how long I stood dumbstruck like a daft blonde character out of the movies we all mock, but I finally came out of it and literally scrambled for the door and ended up on my knees to grab the small rectangle to my chest like it was 'My Precious'. I gripped it to the heart of me, as though it would be the very thing to save my life, the very cure to all my pain and the very thing that could bring Draven back to me.

By the time I ran up the stairs I had orchestrated this whole scenario that Draven had come back and was sending me instructions on where to find him… maybe he needed my help or maybe it was from Vincent who knew a way for us to get him back. It pretty much went on like this until I reached the secret lair that had become a messy version of my room.

I jumped on the bed and placed the letter in my lap all the while shaking, which was no doubt going to hurt my hand later but right then no other sensation could penetrate my small bubble of hope. I turned it around and saw that it must have been delivered by hand as it had no stamp or postal mark. I traced my finger around the wax seal and over the indents of the Draven family crest. It was the same crest that was carved into the doors of Afterlife and that of the chair in which he'd sat on in the VIP. That thought tore through me like a jagged piece of metal that made up some of the artwork in the club.

The last time I had seen that chair, Draven's body had filled it. I bit down on my lip remembering how sometimes he would reach out and pluck me from my own chair to rest me on his lap, like a pet he could stroke. Most of the time that happened he would simply ignore everyone around him and spend the night just focused on smoothing his hand down my hair and whispering endearments in my ear that had me blushing like a nun in a BDSM club!

I swallowed down a sob and finally took a big enough breath to enable me to rip into the letter and somehow breaking the seal felt wrong. But I ignored the pang of pain and pulled out the thick paper that had been folded neatly twice. I opened it up and gasped as I automatically saw who it was from…

It was a letter from the grave, a letter from…

My Dominic Draven.

CHAPTER TWO

MY MR GOODBYE

I looked down at the elegant handwriting of my lost soul mate and I had to concentrate on how to breathe. I felt the momentum of shakes travel through my body and I closed my eyes, squeezing out the tears that had already formed. I needed to control myself enough to at least read what were no doubt, Draven's very last words to me.

Over the days since all my nightmares came to a head, I had read and re-read every text message from not only Draven but anyone that I once called family, just to try and make any sense of what was happening to me now. But nothing ever made any sense. In fact, there was not one shred of evidence to suggest this was even coming.

No, 'It's getting dangerous' or 'It's worse than I thought'… nothing like that. If anything it had been the opposite, with messages that suggested he would be seeing me soon and couldn't wait to hold me again. There wasn't one single thread of worry in my mind thanks to these texts from him, so the blow of things to come was like an A-bomb given to me to hold tightly to my chest by the grim reaper himself.

And looking down at the black inked calligraphy of more words for me to take in was going to be like setting a match to any body parts I had left.

So what did I do?
I lit the flame.

Dear Keira,

I fear that this letter will ever reach you for I know what it must mean. I sit here now, as I have never done before, to write a letter to the only love of my very long life, one that at this time, has no doubt come to an end. I wish for nothing more than to hold you my darling. To keep you so close that I can literally burn the memory of your soul to mine for all time but the troubles and truth I have encountered today means that my time by your side is at an end.

I know with absolute certainty that without you, Heaven will never be enough.

It pains me to say the words I know I need to say in letting you go, words I never thought I would have to say, but the fact remains, my Love, that this is my Goodbye.

With my last orders as the King I once was, I have ordered for all ties to my life, this supernatural life that had been thrust upon you, to be severed. Please do not be angry with those on my side whom you love, for they are only following my orders. Vincent and Sophia will always love you and were less than pleased with my decision, but it is mine to make. I never wanted this pain for you and I know that there is no way to go back, so if this is the last final good thing I can do for you, then I will.

My wish for you, dearest Keira, is for you to live.

To live in your world as you once did, without the stains that Heaven and Hell could blemish the world's most beautiful of minds, for yours was my saviour in all ways possible and even having you in my life for a short time showed me the greatest happiness I have ever known. So here they are, my last words to you my Love,

Live for me, live a full life, with that laughter I love so much, use that mighty heart of yours that has become fused to my very own and live in the knowledge that I will be watching you from my very own Heaven, that just witnessing your life has created for me.

So live Keira, live for me, live for your wonderful family and those you care deeply for but most importantly, live because,

I Love You.

Know that I am thinking of you,
Wherever I am in this world or the next.

Always Your
Dominic Draven.

As I read the very last words, my tears joined those already stained in parts from eyes I would never see again. Draven had shed his tears just as I did now and that very thought broke me. But even in my devastation I knew I couldn't do damage to the most precious thing I would ever own, so I lay my letter down and gathered my sobbing self from the bed to run from the room.

I flew down the stairs with tears streaming from my eyes and ran from the house, just as Libby was coming through the door.

"Whoa, where's the fire? Keira? Keira, what is it… what's happened?" Libby asked me in a panic and I just had enough mental strength in me to turn and take a deep shuddering breath to say,

"Dra…Draven… wrote…wrote me a…a letter," I said with more tears overflowing the confines of my stormy eyes. Upon hearing this Libby's face relaxed into a sadder version of the look she already gave me, but now with the worry gone from her beautiful eyes. I continued to run back out of the front door and across the gravel drive.

"Keira! Keira, please wait!" She shouted.

"I'm sorry…Just…please, just give me some time…just some time… *just some time…just…time.*" I whispered out a strangled cry when I realised I was far from the house and had repeated the same words over and over. I ran from my home, from the brutal reality and from the letter that was like the last nail in the coffin that buried my heart.

I just kept going, running until I couldn't breathe and even then, I would just fold my body over until my breath returned and then I would do the same thing again. The same, until it hurt. It seemed that the pain was all I understood. It was all I controlled and when I finally ran until my legs gave out, I hit the ground with an angry scream,

"WHY! WHY, WHY, WHY? IT'S NOT FAIR! GODDAMN YOU! IT'S NOT FAIR! *It's not... fair...it's... it's...*" I finally lost all my steam, as my head followed my weak limbs and hit the ground. I sobbed the last of my emotions out into the earth, hoping in some way they would not only be heard by the Gods, but felt as well. Damn them and their rules and damn them for their fates. Fates that had ripped Draven away from me and for reasons I didn't know. Would I ever know? Would anyone ever be able to tell me what happened or was what Draven told me going to remain so forever?

He spoke of his orders, orders I didn't agree with in the slightest, but yet I had to live with them! It wasn't fair. Hell, it was so beyond fair it was convoluted and torturous. These people had become my family and now, along with Draven, I had lost them. What had Draven been thinking? Did he really believe this was the best thing for me? To just turn my back on all that had happened and continue my life like some good little mortal?

NO! I couldn't do it and more importantly, I wouldn't do it! It was like walking away from my own body while watching it burn. I sat up as my inner battle raged on and the two sides of me continued the struggle between what I wanted and what Draven wanted. He had asked this of me and ordered it from everyone else. Could I really follow through with his last wishes upon this earth, the very last thing he asked of me, which just so happened to be one of the hardest? How did he ever think that being torn from this world I had followed him into would be better for me? It was insanity!

I don't know how long I sat there, but by the time I tried to move I had to shake my legs out to try and get rid of the pins and needles. I also needed to get some ice on my hand at some point because it was throbbing so much it brought tears to my eyes. I looked down at it and yelped when I tried to move my fingers. I decided not to do that again for a while.

It was only when I was picking myself off the ground and patting myself free from dry mud and dead leaves that I heard a noise. My head snapped up and around in a heartbeat, but as my eyes scanned the forest they found nothing.

"Who's there?" I said feeling as foolish saying it as it sounded. I mean really, did anyone ever just pipe up and say, 'Oh I'm sorry it was me, did I frighten you, I am awfully sorry'.

"Stupid. Jesus, Keira what's next, running topless in the wrong direction screaming? Dumb ass…" I was still grumbling when I heard it again, only this time it sounded like a short grunt of laughter.

"Shit!" I said whipping around until coming full circle, but still not finding anything. Ok, now I was definitely freaked!

"I know you're there!" I shouted, putting on my bravest voice and hoping it wasn't being affected by the hours of raw crying I had put it through. I flinched as I heard another deep grunt and decided I had outstayed my welcome. I started walking backwards but being surrounded by a vast forest with too many hiding spots to think about, I didn't know where to look for danger.

"Man, what I wouldn't give for a big Ragnar right about now," I whispered to myself, but received a heavier grunt of laughter in return. This time I spun too quickly in response and caught my foot in a creeping arched root, acting like a very effective Keira trap. I was about to go down when strong hands grabbed me from behind, making me scream.

"Hush now." A deep voice said in my ear and it was a voice I didn't recognise. I could feel a very tall presence behind me and when I tried to turn, long fingers bit into my shoulders preventing me from doing so.

"Let go of me!" I shouted looking down for a foot to stamp on. My eyes found two heavy booted feet that looked a bit like you would expect to see from the military. I let out a frustrated sigh on seeing that they were steel toe-capped for sure and I just knew my size four Nike trainers weren't going to cut it.

"What do you want?!" I demanded trying to wriggle my way free to face the guy.

"Time to go home, *lille øjesten*" Said one of the deepest voices I had ever heard. At that, fingers left me and I turned quickly ready to face him but he was gone.

"What the Hell?" I looked around in a mad panic thinking

any minute he would take me off guard and then I would find myself at an even greater disadvantage.

"Where did you go?!" I shouted in frustration, which even in my heated state sounded lame.

"Run home, lille øjesten, run home *now*." The voice purred in my ear and I screamed at it being so close yet nowhere to be seen.

"STOP DOING THAT!" I screamed walking backwards and alternating my eyes ahead, where the voice had been and down on the ground so that I wouldn't fall again. Then it happened. The wind picked up and rolled towards me as though it was being controlled. I could even see it forcing its way through the trees like an invisible wave before it crashed into me. The sound that echoed told me it hadn't been wind at all; it had been a shouted order consisting of only one word,

"GO!" I fell backwards and scrambled back like a frightened little crab until I turned and found the same black boots. I was just looking up at black leather covered legs that reminded me of the most solid tree trunks before I was picked up like I was a quivering leaf in the midst of a storm. I tried to see what was happening and follow the actions that were spinning me around but all I caught was a blurred black shadow.

"He said that you were stubborn! Go home, run now and you will be in time!" He said again, only this time the depth of the voice had a new rippled edge of power.

"Who did?! Who are you, who sent you?!" I fired out the questions quickly and I moaned when his hold shook me.

"Time lille øjesten, time is what she doesn't have, neither of them…run home, fast as you can now and don't stop. I will do what I can to guide you, but you must be quick…your sister calls for you." On hearing this I froze in utter terror.

"What do you mean, what has happened to Libby?! Tell me!" I heard him groan in frustration and he said one last thing before I took off running like the blazes of Hell were on my heels,

"A new life comes forth this day and Death is watching in wait to take them both."

"NO!" I screamed as I ran like I had never run before and I

did as the voice told me, I didn't look back. It was amazing to watch as the forest opened up for me like I was a poisonous force touching the earth and everything around me retreated in fear of being infected. Tree branches folded back just before I would have hit into them, snapping the bark off in chunks and roots dug further underground to hear my pounding feet overhead. Not one branch, not even one rock stood in my way, nothing touched me… even the wind seemed to spur me on faster than I would have ever been able to move.

I had only one focus in my life right then and that was keeping the two heartbeats on this earth, one whom I loved with every fibre of my being and the other whom I would soon be welcoming to this world with the very same love. They were all I had left. Nothing meant more to me at that moment than getting home and doing everything in my power to save them both.

As soon as I got closer, the sound of my sister screaming seeped into my bones like liquid ice. My smooth skin was no more and was covered in bumps that spoke of only the chilling sound of a loved one in serious pain.

"LIBBY! HOLD ON, I'M COMING!" I screamed and devoured the remaining space between me and the open door with a new energy. It was an impossible speed and I knew, without anyone explaining it to me, what I was doing. I was using up the very last power Draven's body passed on to me as supernatural fuel. I could literally feel the last remains of his essence leave my body as if it was leaking out of every pore. The more I was driven forward, the more of Draven I was saying goodbye to, but for the only time in my life…

I didn't care.

I leapt up the steps with the last power surge and came to a halting stop when I first took in the scene.

"Libby!" I shouted and her crying eyes whipped round to me. Her skin was almost the colour of her hair and she was sat sprawled up the stairs with her legs open and panting.

"Oh, thank you God! The baby! The baby is coming, oh shit…oh shit, here it comes again…oh…ARRRRHH!" She screamed through what I could only assume was a contraction.

The baby was coming and there was no time, the guy in the woods had been right about that. Only when I looked away from Libby, I saw that wasn't the only thing he had been right about, for there in the corner stood…

Death.

CHAPTER THREE

NOT A GREAT TIME FOR A REUNION

"Carrick!" I shouted at the very man responsible for my kidnapping and one scary mother at that!

"One and the very same my dear." He responded with a respectful head nod.

"GET OUT!" I screamed making both him and my panting sister jump.

"Kaz, who the Hell are you talking to?" Libby asked me with rising panic. I nodded over to the corner, but from where she was positioned she couldn't see…well, that or he had shielded himself from her.

"Now that is hardly a greeting." He said actually having the audacity to look hurt.

"Well, that's the only one you are gonna get 'cause if you think you are going anywhere near those I love, then you will have to take me along as well, kicking, screaming and trying to rip you to pieces!" I said feeling the rage build and build until the pressure of it was starting to pound inside me like a pneumatic drill.

"Then you will be pleased to know that I think you made it in time." He reached into his suit jacket, which was once again beige and pulled out a little book the size of his palm. As he flipped it open I saw in disgust that the book's binding was made from sewn human skin held together like a crude jigsaw by thick black cord. He ran his finger down a few lines and then made a humming noise like he was looking for something.

"Jesus, Keira who are you talking too? Don't just stand there for God…Oh Ahh, here comes another one…AHHHHH… AHH!" Libby started screaming again and I rushed to the bottom of the stairs she was leaning against and did the only thing I knew to do.

"Just breathe through it, just breathe…come on Libs…that's it, just breathe…deep breaths." I repeated over and over trying to get her twisted face of pain to cooperate.

"I am BREATHING!" She screamed just as the pain hit harder. Meanwhile Carrick was still checking his book, as though there wasn't a screaming woman in the room trying to push a person out! Finally, his humming stopped and he snapped the book closed.

"Exactly as I thought, the names are back in the assessment stage, but they are not out of the dark yet, so I will wait and see I think." He said calmly, about to take a seat.

"The Hell you will, get your bony ass over here!" I shouted at him and he scoffed at my insult.

"NOW!" I screamed this time making him change his mind. He came over to us both and raised an eyebrow at the scene in front of him.

"Have you lost it? You gotta be kidding me Kaz, at a time like this for fuc…"

"Libby, calm down, I can explain." I said interrupting her.

"I doubt that," Carrick said under his breath making me snap my cutting gaze to his.

"Get down here and help! Oh and while you're at it make her see you!" I demanded and was utterly amazed to see him do as I ordered. He folded himself gracefully to the floor by my side and he touched Libby's knee gently. I was about to stop him from touching her, but it was too late and soon Libby was freaked.

"AH! Who… the Hell…are you?!" She shouted between puffs.

"Calm down Libby…this is…umm…the doctor." I said

weakly shooting a look of disbelief to Carrick and receiving the same one back.

"Oh Hell no." He whispered sideways to me.

"OH, thank God!" Libby said visibly relaxing a little after her contraction.

"Oh, now that's fitting," Carrick responded dryly.

"Just roll with it and help me through this!" I snapped through gritted teeth.

"Fine! But you do realise this is kind of the opposite to what I do, don't you?" I looked sideways and said,

"Yeah, thanks, I got the memo. Now help me with this. What do I do?" I was close to grabbing him by his suit lapels and shaking the shit out of him. I was sure with my bubbling rage that I would hear his bones rattle with little effort.

He let out a big and exaggerated sigh before turning to face Libby.

"Right my dear, as you no doubt know your baby is coming and your contractions are too close together to get you to the hospital, we are going to have to deliver the baby here but don't fret, you are in good hands." I snorted at this and he gave me a look as if to say, 'do you mind?'

"We need to get her lower half bare." He said, taking off his jacket and folding it neatly over the bannister. I looked down at the soaked jeans my sister was still wearing in a daze and jolted when fingers snapped in front of me.

"Do you fancy catching the baby through her pant leg? No, I didn't think so. Keira, you are going to have to focus now, first undress her, then go and fetch as many towels, sheets or cloths to soak up the blood and dry the baby. GO!" He shouted, and I jumped before I got to work.

I yanked down her jeans and knickers off together throwing them over my shoulder and running to the hamper my sister had left situated by the door to the basement. I grabbed the towels and washing I had brought down with me this morning. As I was running back to the bottom of the stairs, I noticed a pair of my dirty knickers stuck to the pile so threw them over my shoulder, slipped to the side as I rounded the corner with an armful of material going flying.

"Shitty, shit shit!" I cursed as I scrabbled along the floor, arms wide open scooping back up everything I'd dropped.

"Will this be enough?" I asked breathless from panic as I made it back to them on another skid.

"That will be fine." He responded so calmly it made me thankful I wasn't doing this alone. Well, that was until I asked him my next question,

"You have done this before…right?" I whispered through Libby's screaming.

"I have seen it done once…." Then he looked thoughtful for a moment and continued,

"…but the cow died." Then he started to lift Libby down until she was sat up against the last step with a cushion he placed behind her head.

"A COW!" I shouted, and he shot me a look, one eyebrow raised.

"I'm sorry, would you prefer to see my résumé before I aid you in saving your sister and her child's life or would you just like to crack on?" He nodded back to the point where my sister was clearly pushing out her baby.

"Oh shit! Ok, yeah, you're right, sorry… Come on Libby! You're doing great!" I said moving up to her and taking her hand in mine, which she was soon trying break. Thankfully I'd given her the one that wasn't already broken.

"AHHHH!" She screamed once more and then started breathing in great puffs and blows. She was bright red and I pushed her wet hair back from her sweat covered face.

"Oh God! The baby, it's coming, I need…I need… AHHHH!" She took a deep breath and pushed her chin to her chest to push down.

"That's it Libs, you're doing great, you're doing it!" I felt the tears running down my cheeks and I looked to Carrick whose face was serious and frowning.

"What is it?" I asked, and his answer chilled my blood.

"The baby's heart rate is dropping."

"NO!" I shouted and then moved to closer to Carrick.

"Do something!" He frowned at me and then turned back to Libby.

"You need to push harder!" He said sternly to Libby but she just let out a strangled sob and kept shaking her head.

"I can't, I can't…I…" My heart broke at seeing my sister in so much pain.

"You must or your baby will die." He said, and I hit him on the arm.

"Don't tell her that!" I said seeing my sister burst into body shaking, harder sobs that weren't helping her in pushing.

"What can I do, tell me! I need to help her!" I demanded grabbing him by his rolled-up sleeves.

"You need to help her push, I suggest trying anger."

"WHAT?"

"Anger will help in this case trust me, make your sister angry, in fact, make that *very* angry." I frowned at him and was about to tell him I needed a more practical answer, when Libby screamed as another contraction hit.

"Right, Olivia, you need to push and push hard!" I said as sternly as I could muster with what I was seeing.

"I can't! AHHHH!"

"Yes you can, you must! If you don't, I will tell mum!" I said thinking that always did it in the past, but then again, she wasn't trying to fit something the size of a melon from a place that… well you get the picture!

"I CAN'T!!!" She screamed, and I could see her trying to find the energy to push harder but it just wasn't enough.

"Try harder." Carrick said opening her legs wider.

"She is trying." I said in Libby's defence, but he shook his head in small motions.

"Not her, you! Anger her Keira, I am sure you have it in you for pissing people off." He shot me a look that told me I could indeed.

"Right Libby, listen up, if you don't push and I mean push like your life depends on it, then I will tell Frank about the time you kissed those two brothers in college and then got drunk and played strip poker!" I shouted at her, feeling like the worst sister in the world. She gave me a look of utter disbelief and then scowled,

"You wouldn't!"

"Oh yes I would, NOW PUSH GODDAMN IT!"

"I am going to…AAHHHHHH…kill you!" She screamed at me, but I just held her hand and screamed with her,

"AHHHHH, YES, THAT'S IT!" We then both took deep breaths together.

"COME ON! PUSH!" I shouted at her again.

"I am PUSHING FOR CHRIST'S SAKE!" She said, half in rage half in pain but Carrick was right, it was working.

"I see the head, now one big push and the baby will be here." Carrick said just as calmly as if he was ordering a Big Mac from the drive-thru!

Just then Frank burst through the open door, out of breath and in a mad panic.

"LIBBY!" He shouted and then took in the scene quickly.

"Oh SHIT!" He added.

"Oh, thank you, thank you." Libby said looking up to the Heavens and I blinked back the onslaught of tears.

"Frank, the baby…the baby, it's coming, it's coming!" He rushed over to take my place, skidded landing on his thigh and Carrick grabbed my hand to drag me to where the baby would come.

"Oh baby, you're ok, you're ok sweetheart," Frank said holding on to her.

"The baby isn't coming… the baby is here! Now push!" Carrick ordered her and I looked down to see the baby's head emerge. It was by far the most beautiful, yet at the same time the most nauseating thing I had ever witnessed in my life.

"I see the head, Libs! I see it!" I said looking up at Libby gripping on to her husband with force enough to rip his shirt. Then Carrick grabbed my hands.

"You must see the baby into this world, I cannot bring new life forth into this plane, but you can." Carrick positioned my hands ready.

"Now Libby, you are doing really well, but this last contraction I want you to push gently and the baby will slip out nicely… are you ready?" He said soothingly, and I was touched at the knowledge that even Death himself could be so sweet.

Libby nodded quickly and Frank held her tighter.

"This is it babe, you're doing so good, oh baby I love you." He said making the tears come even harder than before.

"Oh…now, now! Coming now!" She said and then took one last breath before pushing her baby into the beautiful world we live in.

"Yes Libby, you're doing it…I can see, Oh my God, I can see!" I said and then a baby literally slipped out and into my waiting hands.

We all cried out and I tried to control my shaking as I held the tiny person in my hands. Carrick handed me a towel and told me to clean the blood off her.

"Her?" I asked and then looked down over the slightly blue baby who was getting a pink colour rising up through her little limbs.

"Yes Keira, congratulations, it is a little girl." He said beaming at me and I turned to Libby and held up her baby.

"Libby! It's a girl!" I shouted, and she lifted her green eyes from her husband's chest and the look of pure love touched her daughter for the first time, mother to baby.

I picked the first thing I could from the pile on the floor and wrapped my niece up in it.

"Rub her back Keira, to get her crying." Carrick said and then nodded. I did as I was told and before long she let out the best sound in the world.

The sound of new life.

I looked down at her once more and was grinning like a fool when I saw what I had wrapped her in was my dad's old college sweater. I couldn't think of anything more fitting at that moment and I quietly told her I loved her before handing the baby to her mum and dad. The afterbirth came shortly after that and even with the cord still attached it wasn't a problem as they took their daughter in their arms for the very first time.

Frank was crying along with Libby and then he grabbed her by the head and pulled her to him to kiss her deeply. He pulled back and looked from mother to baby and said,

"I am so, so unbelievably proud of you! Both of you, both my girls! I love you so much! Thank you, God! Christ, I love you baby, I love you… You did it...! Jesus, Libby we did it!" He said and Libby looked down and kissed her baby on the head.

"Yes, we did. I love you too, both of you." Libby said and the heart melting moment was perfect.

"So, we were a bit late then?" A paramedic said from the doorway, smiling at the sight. I quickly moved out of their way to let them get to work on helping my sister and when I stood up, I knew that this was one of those rare times in life that I was witnessing pure greatness. I don't think for as long as I lived that I would ever forget this moment in time, this sight right now that had me realising just how precious life really was. Of course, one look to the man on my right had me backing up that statement with a shudder.

Carrick walked over to reclaim his jacket and bent down to retrieve the black case that never seemed to leave his side. That's when I added a deep shiver to the shudder, as I remembered in detail at just what powers lay within that innocent-looking case. He came back over to me and nodded to the door and I followed him out.

His hair shone like silver thread in the sunlight and I saw him lift his head to the fresh air to inhale deeply.

"Nope, still prefer the smell of death I am afraid." He said looking back at me smiling and I wrinkled my nose.

"Uhh, gross Carrick!" He laughed and the sound of it actually had me smiling. He was a really nice guy if you could overlook the whole 'Soul collecting' thing.

"So, don't fancy a career change then?" I asked only half joking. He gave me a dazzling smile and for an older gentleman he certainly didn't lack in the looks department. His steel coloured eyes that matched the silver in his hair gleamed at me.

"I think not. Besides, most deaths aren't half as messy." I laughed in disbelief and he raised an arched eyebrow at me. He then looked me up and down and I followed his eyes to find my top soaked in blood.

"But all births are without a doubt… bloody affairs." He added and I took in his crisp beige suit wondering if he owned any other colour, but thankfully I stopped myself from asking.

"I can't believe I am going to say this Carrick, but I am

actually glad you were here." I said and then offered him my hand. He looked taken aback for a moment and there was no hiding the emotion my gesture put in his eyes. He transformed his cool features into a breath-taking grin and took my hand in his. He started to shake it and I was so overcome by the moment that I said out loud,

"Oh, bugger it, come here!" And I pulled his hand to me as I stepped in to wrap my arms around him. If someone had told me five months ago that I would be hugging Death himself in thanks, I would have been asking who supplied their crazy pills!

He stiffened in my hold at first and then decided to just roll with it. He patted me on the back softly before I let him go. When I pulled back I had tears running down my face. He reached up and took away one of my tears, holding it in his closed palm before lifting it to his mouth. I gasped when I saw him lick it from his skin and then close his eyes. Once again, he was looking up to the sky as if listening to someone.

"Such an unpolluted soul and rare…*very* rare indeed." He said to himself before looking back at me.

"And of course, still as feisty as ever, which I am most pleased about. There are not many people that would be so bold as to threaten Death itself Keira, but I must say, you do so very nicely. Until next time, Chosen One." He said, nodded and then he turned to walk away.

"I hope not Carrick, but no offence!" I shouted back and without even turning his head he responded,

"Oh, but we will Electus, you can be sure of that. Oh and Keira…" I didn't say what I wanted to but instead just waited for him to finish.

"…take care of that niece of yours…she is special that one and…most important to him." He said and without a look, he simply swung his briefcase over his head as a way of goodbye. He left me stood there feeling baffled by his cryptic parting comment, but I was soon brought back to the now when Libby was being lifted into the ambulance I had only just noticed waiting there.

I ran over to my sister and gave her a teary kiss and told her I loved her. I touched the baby's head, who was now resting her little eyes in sleep on her mother's chest and was touched to see her still snuggled peacefully in my dad's old sweater.

Libby was still so emotional and Frank had to pry her curled fingers from my top to let me go so that they could both go and get checked out at the hospital. After a mammoth bear hug from Frank, I told him that I would stay at the house and clean up, ready for when they got home. He thanked me again, only this time there was a single tear running down his cheek.

He leant down and whispered in a thick emotional voice,

"I could never thank you enough for saving them both, you did it…you saved my family and…man…Jesus kid, I love you!" He said, and I felt more tears hit my neck before he turned his face away and jumped in the back of the ambulance, wiping his cheeks as he went. Once they were out of sight I fell to the ground and cried, but for the first time since Draven had left leaving my chest feeling empty, I felt it full and the tears I shed were finally ones of utter happiness.

The rest of that day I spent cleaning up, which I am ashamed to say also made me a little sick. I didn't know how all these great people that became nurses and doctors did it, but they had my deepest respect even more, that was for sure.

I got a phone call from Frank later, telling me they were keeping them overnight just to be sure, but for me not to worry. Libby was doing great and the baby was sleeping and feeding like a trooper, Frank's words not mine. He also told me quite a few times how damn beautiful his baby girl was and I knew by the added 'F' word that Libby wasn't in hearing distance.

It was this amazing feeling that had me on this sort of cloud the rest of the day and for the first time in a week I couldn't wait for people to come home. I just kept seeing my little niece's face looking up at me and my heart seemed to swell. It was only when I was washing up humming 'You'll be in my Heart' by Phil Collins to myself, that I looked up and saw a shadow of a man in the forest that surrounded the driveway.

I squinted my eyes as the sun was going down, but I could still make out the giant of a man who stood staring at the house. I still couldn't make out any features, only that he wore black, was extremely tall and had a heavy frame to match. It wasn't a wild guess to know that it was the same man I had met in the woods, the one who had helped me get to Libby in time.

So, what did I do...? The only thing I could think of, I clicked the kettle on.

I was soon walking out to the forest that now looked even darker than from the kitchen window and with both hands I held on to the steaming mug.

"*Hello*...Hello?" I said a bit louder, but I didn't get any response or see anyone through the thickness of the trees. But something in my gut told me he was still there waiting, so I did what I came to do.

"I umm…I wanted to say thank you… for my sister and the baby, what you did…well, I will be forever in your debt…I wish I could say this to your face, but something tells me that isn't going to happen, so this was the only way I could think to thank you." I placed down my Homer Simpson mug and then dug out the mini packet of Oreo cookies from my coat pocket to place next to them.

"I made this for a friend of mine once and he seemed to enjoy it. It's hot chocolate and some biscuits. If you need anything else or want anything else to drink, just let me know." I said feeling like a right dork talking to the trees. I started to walk back until I whizzed back round, thinking of something else.

"Unless, that is, you're a Vampire! 'Cause trust me, I have seen enough blood for one day and that didn't go so well for me…oh God, now I am babbling! What I mean is…if you fancy a beer or soda or something but NOT blood! No blood for you…Ok well… I guess bye then and thanks." I said hurrying back to the safety of my house after freaking myself out.

He wouldn't really be a Vamp would he? I mean, being behind my neck like that he would have had a taster, wouldn't he? No, he wasn't a vamp but that still raised the important question…

Who was this guy?

CHAPTER FOUR

DRAVEN'S LEGAL MIND

The next week came and went in a baby blur. It was filled with sterilizing bottles, changing nappies, feeding, bathing, changing the tiniest baby clothes and playing host to a stream of people, all desperate to see the new baby. It was a heart-warming time, the second Libby and Frank came home with the new family addition.

And the very first thing they did was ask me to name her. I was so touched I just sat there dumbstruck for the entire time it took for Frank to make me a cuppa.

"So, what do you think?" Libby said finally, bringing me from my shock.

"I…Lib's, you can't…I mean…really?" Not my brightest literary moment, but what do you say to something like that?

"Absolutely!" Frank joined in, handing me a steaming LFC mug.

"Guys, I am touched but come on, you really want me to name your child?" I just couldn't get my head around it. I mean, it was a massive responsibility even for a parent but for an Aunt, this could literally be a make or break situation…what if she hated it while growing up?!

"I know what you're doing Kaz, but please don't. There is no need to try and talk us out of this, we have talked about it and we couldn't think of anything more fitting than having the very person who brought her into the world name her." Libby said wiping a stray tear from her eye and Frank was nodding like a little dog on a dashboard with a massive grin, next to her.

Of course, I soon realised that Carrick had left them both with a void in their mind as to his role in her birth, which had left me looking both crazy when asking them about it and also looking like the heroine of this baby miracle. Next time I saw Carrick, if ever, I would be giving him an earful for the lack of a heads up, that was for sure.

"Yeah and can you imagine if a doctor named Donald had delivered her, I mean how do you change that into a girl's name?! Poor kid would get crucified in school, that's for sure." Frank said making light of the situation and we all laughed.

"Are you guys really sure about this?"

"Yes!" They both said at the same time, so I gave in, getting up to hug them both.

Later that day I had thought about the baby and must have run through every name I had ever heard but nothing seemed right. It was only when stirring a big pot of chilli that night that I thought about something that was significant to the whole situation we all went through when bringing my niece into this world. So at dinner I explained myself.

"I've thought of a name," I said causing both Libby and Frank to drop their forks at the same time. They looked up at me and Libby took Frank's hand in hers as they waited for the sound of their baby girl's name to be said for the first time.

"I umm, well ok, I guess I'd better just come out and say it. I was thinking about Carrie Ella but like me, using her second name Ella for most of the time…what do you think?" I asked, biting my lip waiting for the name to sink in. They just turned to each other and my sister tested the name, saying out loud,

"Carrie Ella…Ella, Umm…baby Ella, I like it…no, no…in fact I love it! Oh Keira, it's perfect!" She said and jumped up and threw her arms around Frank who laughed heartily with his wife. He looked to me over Libby's shoulder and winked.

I went to bed that night smiling.

The naming of baby Carrie Ella was a big hit with everyone

and soon everyone took Libby's lead and started calling her just Ella. She asked me that night where I had got it from and I shrugged and told her 'it just came to me'. I mean it wasn't like I could tell her that it was the only female version of my buddy Death Carrick or the fact that Ella came from the 'Helluva' time we had delivering her into this world, of course I just knocked off the H U and the V to make Ella.

That was over a week ago and I was now sat in the house alone, trying to catch up on end of the college year coursework that I had missed due to the depression I'd had thrust upon me. I can't say that life was ever going to be what it was for me, but Ella's arrival had at least given me an even greater purpose to life. I found every time things got too much for me all I needed to do was look at my perfect niece lay sleeping, to feel better.

I still went about my life and instead of finding the time to cry, I would use it helping Libby with the baby or cramming in last minute studies. This was enough to put off the inevitable questions about Draven, where my friends were concerned but I knew it wouldn't be long.

The only other question that was never answered was that of the mystery man in my life, who hadn't shown himself again since that day. I had, however, found a Homer mug waiting for me one morning and I smiled down at it for a few minutes before picking it off the porch. I examined it to find it had been cleaned and I even sniffed at it to find it smelled like it had been washed in the stream not far from the house, one I often passed on my walks.

He may not have shown himself, but I still felt myself being watched sometimes. And in a strange way I was comforted by the fact, however annoying it was that I still didn't know who he was.

I was just getting up after a three-hour round with one of Reed's history assignments, when my need for tea dragged me downstairs. I had just clicked on the kettle when I heard the knock at the door. I was alone, which was unusual these days and I didn't like being without Ella in the house. Libby and Frank had gone to Frank's parents to stay the night, so that the rest of his family got a look in with the babe. Of course, they had invited me, but having the amount of work I had to finish, I knew I couldn't say yes.

So now I was answering the door to a suit who drove a silver Mercedes.

"Can I help you?" I asked cautiously knowing, one, I had never seen this dude before and two, I was in the house alone.

"Miss Williams?" This instantly put me on guard considering very few people actually knew my real last name. I knew, now that Morgan had died, that there was little point still keeping up the charade, but it just never came up to the point of changing it. And besides, most people still thought that Morgan was still out there somewhere, so it was just easier letting them carry on believing the crazy bastard had probably killed himself and at some point the authorities would be discovering a body. Well, even if they did start searching the bottom of a ravine that was extremely difficult to get to, by that time I doubted there would be much left to discover or so Draven had told me, I thought with a shiver.

"Yes." I finally answered, coming back from darker pasts.

"I have much to discuss, may I come in?" I arched my eyebrow in question before I asked,

"And you are?" His answer blew me away.

"I am Mr Jenkins, Mr Draven's attorney."

I soon found myself sat opposite a softly spoken English man, dressed in an impeccable crisp navy suit, white shirt and startling red tie. He was handsome in an unconventional way, with sharp features and soft blue eyes. He must have been in his late forties and took his tea with lemon instead of milk. I decided when he told me this, to give him the posh stuff we had gathering dust at the back of the cupboard.

"So, Mr Jenkins, is it too soon to ask what you are doing here?" I said after he had just taken the tea and smiled at me.

"Ah, direct and to the point… a much preferred personality trait in my line of business." He said nodding after he took a sip of the tea. I gathered I was on to a winner with the posh stuff.

"Which is?" I prompted.

"Well, unfortunately right now, dealing with Mr Draven's Estate." He said placing the cup down and lifting his briefcase.

The word 'Estate' had me slopping my own tea on my jeans. I closed my eyes for a few painful seconds to try and barricade the torrent of emotions that singular word brought me.

"And why does that include me?" I forced the words out, still keeping my eyes shut.

"And why wouldn't it? After all, the information I had from the man himself suggests you weren't far from being his bride. Of course, as you no doubt know, he was a man who liked to take care of his business in *all* aspects." I shook my head on hearing this and rubbed a spot on my forehead as I processed his words.

"I am…was… his girlfriend, *not* a business deal. I think I know why you are here, and I don't mean to be rude, but I think you will find it has been a wasted trip."

"How so, Miss Williams?" He asked me, being genuinely shocked.

"Well knowing Draven as I do…did…" I swallowed hard at the slip ups I kept making and carried on,

"…you are no doubt here to give me some ridiculous amount of money he left me, or something even crazier like a car, house… Christ, I don't know, maybe even a horse, but I am telling you now, I don't want any of it!" I said getting up making him do the same. However, he didn't take the hint and instead of following me to the door, he just stayed where he was and started laughing. The look I sent him was deadly.

"Sorry, I umm…I guess I can see now why Mr Draven did things in this manner." I frowned at him and held up a hand.

"Stop right there and rewind…what do you mean, 'in this manner'?" This got a little smirk from him which kept me frowning.

"I am afraid that if you wish for me to say anything else on the matter you will have to sign this paperwork." He said getting a cream folder out of his case.

"Oh no, I have seen this movie, this is where I get screwed over for something and find I'm legally bound to running some bloody hillbilly ranch in the wilderness! I am not signing anything without first reading it!" I said folding my arms across my chest.

"Certainly, but I must inform you, I doubt you will be able to make much sense out of it." I rolled my eyes and shook my head.

"I may not be a hotshot lawyer, but I can read." I responded coldly.

"Persian?" He said handing me the paperwork, which was indeed written in a language Draven knew that in no way would I be able to make sense of.

"Ok, so Draven expected me to sign something I can't read so that I am forced to receive some of his money that he knew I wouldn't want. Nice try Love…" I said looking up to the Heavens and then handing the paperwork back to him saying,

"…but no dice. I thank you for coming but I will not, nor will I ever be signing that."

"He thought that would be the case, so he added something that would interest you. If you sign the paperwork, at any point, you will then receive this letter from the man himself, which is only addressed to you, but only to be yours with this little condition of course." He added smugly when he saw my eyes light up at the sight of more words from Draven.

He held it up for me to see like bait to a fish, but the question was, would I survive the hook? It took me all of a nanosecond to decide as I snatched the paperwork back off him and took the pen he had offered me. I signed on the line at the bottom and an emotional shiver rippled along my body when I saw it was next to Draven's own signature. I had to sign three more times but got to keep one copy. I asked what the point was, but he just shrugged and said he'd had his orders.

He placed the other copies back in the folder and into the safety of his briefcase. He held out a hand to me and I shook it, doing close to anything he wanted just to get my hands on that letter. He gave a little laugh at my eagerness when I took the letter from him and held it to my chest. I at least had the mental ability to walk him to the door, remembering my upbringing well even under the circumstances.

"It was an experience doing business with you, Miss Williams," he said kindly and I smiled.

"Likewise, Mr Jenkins…oh and please call me Keira." I said

thinking this was a bit late but saying so anyway. He nodded and then shook my hand once again.

"Only if you call me Daniel, as I am sure I'll be meeting you again, in the future of course." He said giving me a wink before getting into the back of the expensive car thanks to the driver who held open the door for him. I was left wondering what on earth that had meant and why would he need to be seeing me again? But none of these were the reasons I was running to the car window, tapping on the side.

The blacked out glass slid down and I could see he wasn't alone but being hidden with a full black hood, I couldn't tell who the other passenger was.

"Yes, Miss Will…Keira?" He said correcting himself.

"You never explained to me what I actually signed…what did I get myself into?" I asked feeling slightly embarrassed asking this in front of someone else, someone I was trying desperately to make out.

"I left you the paperwork, Keira. I think you will find by the time I have gone you might be able to make more sense of it." He said with a smile.

"But how…I…" He nodded at me, stopping me mid question.

"Have trust in my Master." He said before sliding the window back up and I followed the motion of it trying to see who else was in there with him.

"But…?" I said weakly as the car drove off. Something told me the other person in the car, I not only knew who they were, but they also watched me until I went out of sight.

I did the same.

So now I was once again sat on my bed with another letter in my lap with the added legal paperwork I couldn't yet read.

"Just what are you playing at, Draven?" I asked out loud and then unable to resist any longer, I pulled up the seal…

Dear Keira,

I wrote you this letter directly after the first, but I knew you needed time to process all that has happened. I know it must not have been easy adjusting back to 'normality' and I know my decision no doubt made you angry and upset, for this I am sorry but I still believe it was the right thing to do on my part. By now I wonder if a new being has made it into the world and if so, I do hope she is healthy and I can imagine her to have her mother's beauty, it is after all, in the family.

I did know it was a girl and never told you as I knew the surprise would light up your face the way I always loved to see. That was the face only the baby deserved to see first-hand of her beautiful Aunt. I think now what I wouldn't give to see a baby in your arms and I can't tell you of the utter bliss it would have given me to see such a sight.

But, back to the reason at hand for this particular letter and also the part that, if I know you, will be making you angry very soon, as by the time you finish reading this letter the paperwork you signed will be understandable to you. I knew this was the only way to get my stubborn girl to sign the terms of my Will. However, I do find myself smiling at the thought of being able to get one over on you and not being there for you to battle it out with me, which must be most frustrating to my Little Vixen, but please know you make me most happy in doing so, therefore it is not in vain My Love.

I will now say my last Goodbye to you My Keira, but it is out of necessity rather than wanting, please be sure of that.
My Everlasting Love

Your
Draven X

It was no surprise that I had tears streaking my cheeks by the time I had read it and re-read it, but I didn't feel the utter emptiness I had with the first letter. However, it did make me miss him just as much, if not more as I did that day and every day since. It was getting harder to ignore the fact that he wasn't coming back, but now I understood that feeling sorry for myself wouldn't ever be bringing him back…planning would.

I don't know when exactly it had happened, but I firmly believed that somehow, someone should be out there to help guide me on how to do this. I mean, if there was one man in the supernatural world that could come back from Heaven or Hell, then that man would surely be Draven. Wasn't it? I mean… he just had to…right?

I always ignore the internal battle at this point, the one trying to tell me that if he could, then why wasn't he already here. But then I would argue that he just needed my help to do it and that he just didn't want to put me in danger…well screw that! I didn't care whether or not I had to go to Hell and back again to drag him out myself, as long as there was a chance I would be doing it! And if I died in the process, then I would just meet him on the other side, but I wasn't giving up without a fight that I was certain about.

I folded the letter back up carefully and put it under my pillow to join the other one. Corny place to keep a love letter, but in the middle of the night, when I would wake in a blind panic and it would take me heart wrenching seconds to come to terms with the cruel reality, then I would reach out for his written words. As my fingers touched the smooth paper, which always seemed to stay cool to the touch, I would find my tears would dry and my shaking would stop. I would instantly calm and find then that my sleep would take me to a more peaceful place.

Once I did this, I then remembered the reason I had possession of this letter in the first place and the reason Draven knew I would be angry.

"Well, better get it over with, but if you left me your Ferrari collection I will freak out mister!" I said looking up as if he could somehow hear me. I unfolded the thick bound paperwork and looked down at it with new eyes. The whole document was now in English and it didn't take me long before I came to the part that turned my roots red.

"Oh Hell, No!" I shouted thinking the Ferrari idea didn't look so bad compared to the words that spelt out the truth I was facing…

I was now a bloody Millionaire!

CHAPTER FIVE

POOREST MILLIONAIRE AND THE BIG BAD WOLF

I was still in shock and I had to stop myself from tearing up the paperwork in anger. Ha, frustration Draven had said, well yeah that combined with about 'sixteen million' other emotions!

The paperwork stated that every month I would receive a cool million dollars in my bank account, with the exception of every birthday, when I would then receive five million! It was absurd and completely irrational! I never wanted a penny of Draven's money and the very idea that I had no choice in the matter was making me see red.

It took a lot of stomping around and swearing to eventually calm down. I mean, I knew that Draven wanted to take care of me, but I was a bit sensitive to the money fact and had this crazy idea of earning my own money in life.

By the time I had eaten my lunch, even chewing angrily, I decided what the first thing I would be spending my money on. I got up, fetched my laptop and was checking my online account to find, that yep, I was now a million dollars better off…fine, if that was the way things were to be played, then oh, I would play alright.

I started looking through a list of charities that didn't ever receive much support and decided on one. I then checked the website and clicked on the link to send money directly to them, anonymously of course. The first charity I chose was to make a statement as to how ridiculous it was in sending me all that money. The rest were Cancer and Children's charities that got the majority of the money but 'The Badger Rescue Trust' in England was going to get a surprise when they found someone nicknamed Badger Bee Boo had just given them $200, 000.

This was what I decided to do every month and I found I soon had a big grin when I'd finished, with my account having just my original savings in it. Of course, I had the usual phone call from the bank thinking some nutter had decided to play charity roulette with my account, but after assuring them with my security details that I was in fact sane, they could do little with my decision other than to proceed with the donations. When I then informed them that this would be a regular thing every month, the guy nearly wept on the phone. He even suggested a really good hotel in the Caribbean that he and his wife went to on their honeymoon. He said I sounded like I could do with a holiday to you know, think things through. I asked for his details and sent him enough money to go on another holiday with his wife and kids…this time in a five star resort. At this point he did weep on the phone.

I felt quite good after my little spending spree and I had to giggle, hoping Draven could see me now. I was in the bath shaving my legs that looked as though they belonged on a Yeti, when I had looked up, as if I could see him above me and said,

"Don't mess with me matey, you think you can get one over on me…Ha! Not this Vixen!" It would have been a cool statement if my leg hadn't slipped off the rim of the bath and I hadn't just taken a thin slice from my ankle. Man, that smarted!

I got out of the bath and started to get ready as I had promised to see the gang tonight. It was times like this I was glad Afterlife wasn't open, as I didn't think I would have been able to cope with that just yet. Seeing that place and knowing that Draven wasn't up there looking down at me, would have been a first-class ticket to Misery City with a stopover at Homicidal Central.

Thankfully, we had decided on a pizza place before going to

the movies. I was still trying to dress when I heard the beep of Jack's truck. I dragged the top over my head and went over to wave out of one of the bedroom windows to hold up my hand to indicate five minutes. In that time, I dried off the rest of my hair while stuffing my feet into my Doc M's. I was still putting on my gloves when I reached the front door.

Everyone asked me about baby Ella and I held the conversation until Jack was parking the car outside Pizza Pie Palace or known as the 3P's to everyone around here. Once we were seated in one of their biggest booths, one Chaz and Drew had waiting for us, we started chatting about what we were doing for summer.

"Yeah Kaz, are you still going travelling with Draven?" RJ asked me, before taking a bite of a slice of pizza that I swear was bigger than her head. I, of course, snorted in my coke.

"You ok Kaz?" Jack said patting me on the back while I wheezed, coughed and tried to find my breath that eluded me.

"Yeah…just…went…down…wrong way." I said hoping RJ still wasn't waiting for an answer. Of course, one look squashed that hope like a bug on a windscreen.

"Well?"

"Umm…" I looked around and now every one had stopped and was looking at me, waiting. I closed my eyes briefly and took a deep breath. I knew I couldn't have held this off forever, but it still felt far too raw to be talking about this and even Libby hadn't asked me the details.

"Me and Dra…Dominic… broke up." I said and in that moment all hope of my friends being tactful was lost. Lanie dropped her pizza, Drew's glasses slipped down his nose, Chaz stopped drinking with his straw still caught against his lip and RJ…well RJ actually shouted,

"WHAT THE FUCK!?" There only seemed to be Jack that I could depend on for even a normal response.

"Yeah, well it kind of just happened and as you can imagine, I really don't want to talk about it." I added hoping like Hell RJ would get the hint.

"Who finished with who?" Well Hell really was never going to be on my side now was it, I thought dryly.

"Ok, if you must know, he finished with me." I said knowing there was no other way I could play this card. I mean come on, no one in their right mind would have believed that I finished things with him!

"Why?" She asked and I rolled my eyes thinking just how blind, deaf and dumb could one person be at this moment. What part of I didn't want to talk about it did she not get exactly?

"Come on sis, what part of 'she doesn't want to talk about it' don't you get?!" Jack said as if reading my mind. Did I just project that or what? Either way it worked and even though she rolled her eyes, she still saw the insensitivity in her question.

"Sorry…I guess I am just shocked is all." She said but I shrugged my shoulders before responding,

"No more than me, I can assure you."

"Is that the reason the club is closed?" She asked, and Jack groaned.

"What! I can ask that can't I?"

"It's fine, Jack. Look, I don't really know all the ins and outs about the club or why it closed, but I do know that the Dravens won't be back for a long time." I said taking a sip of my drink to mask the emotion in my voice.

"Oh, that's a shame." Lanie said quietly. I didn't even have it in me to smile at her cute little comment.

"So, what movie we gonna see? 'Cause, I am thinking horror." Jack said steering the conversation away from me and I nudged his leg under the table and mouthed a 'Thank you' when no one was looking. He winked at me and continued with the tactic the rest of the afternoon.

It was only later that evening when he dropped me off last, after Lanie, that he turned the engine off outside my house.

"Do you want to talk about it?" He asked me, shifting in his seat to face me.

"Do you want to come in?" I asked thinking that, no, I didn't want to talk about it but on the other hand, I really didn't want to walk in the house on my own.

"Sure."

He locked his door and followed me into the house. Once

inside, I made us both hot drinks and we sat down in the living room.

"Do you wanna watch something?" I asked him getting up, but he stopped me with a hand on my arm, one I wasn't used to being touched by human hands.

"Keira, stop." I gave up on pretending and slumped down in the seat next to him.

"I am no expert Keira, but I have had my fair share of heartbreak and know what it feels like to go through the emotions being left behind can bring. I am not asking you to tell me all the details honey, but I am going to ask that you consider me as a friend to talk to when you're ready, despite my devilish good looks, there is a good listener in here as well." He said making me laugh at this last part.

"I know you are." At me saying this he did a dramatic head flip and pushed all his floppy hair back with both hands while saying,

"Thanks sugar, no face for radio in this house, nope, not us!" He said breaking into a laugh when I elbowed him in the ribs.

"Hey, watch the merchandise, gotta take this hunka burning love all the way to Hollywood someday."

"Hunka burning love…really?" I said sarcastically and we both burst out laughing.

Jack stayed to watch a movie and it was nice not being alone in the house. We chatted like we used to do and Draven didn't come into the conversation again. He explained that his plans for the summer were travelling and most of the gang were going along, if I was interested in getting away for a few weeks. I was just telling him I would think about it when he checked his phone.

"Whoa, I didn't realise the time." He said standing up and stretching his tall frame. I could just see the strip of tanned stomach under today's rock T-Shirt that was a faded Metallica logo in grey with a coiled snake underneath.

"You working tomorrow?" I asked following him to the front door.

"Yeah, although I was supposed to be taking some tourists

up for a hike, only the sheriff put a stop to that. Hope it's not for long though."

"Why, what's wrong?" this piqued my interest.

"Haven't you heard? Man Kaz, you really need to start reading the papers, the damn world could be ending tomorrow and you wouldn't even know it." He said and I shuddered thinking he really had no clue how close that statement came to being true last December.

"Well, that is what I've got my buddy Jack for, to bring me all this happy, feel good news that just makes me all warm and fuzzy inside." I said making him arch an eyebrow before he ruffled my hair like a child.

"Sure do and don't you forget it! Ok, here's the heads up. Some weird stuff has been happening in the National Park, so do us a favour…don't go walking in the woods alone…K?" He said becoming more serious as he put on his khaki combat jacket.

"Why?" I asked having a very bad feeling about this.

"Because some hikers didn't fare so well the other week and from what I heard, it took a large crew to collect all the scattered body parts." I hit him on the arm to tell him to stop joking with me but then I saw his look and knew there was no messing around in the story he just told me.

"Please tell me you have exaggerated that 'body part' bit?" He shot a look to the woods before coming back to my worried eyes.

"Hey don't worry, it was probably just some wild animals or something."

"You mean they don't know that for sure?!" I asked not being able to keep the high-pitched squeak from the question.

"Well, from what I heard, they have had loads of trackers and wildlife experts up there, but so far none of them can say with certainty what animal they are dealing with, but you wanna know the weird part?"

"There's a weirder part to that story?" I responded in disbelief.

"Sure is and the whole thing kind of gave me the heebie jeebies, 'cause when they did their search of the campground they found some strange stuff." He said pulling his jacket together and zipping it all the way up.

"Like what?"

"Prints around the bodies that suggested someone else was involved, someone who wouldn't exactly go hiking in biker boots but the weirdest part was, it was as if someone had been looking over one of the bodies." The mention of biker boots had me almost breaking out in a cold sweat. I remembered boots that looked as if they belonged on a biker, but it wasn't just this part that had me close to freaking out, it was the answer to my next question.

"How would they know that someone was looking over the bodies?"

"Because of what they found lying on top of the remains, as though it had fallen from someone's pocket..." He pushed his hair back and I noticed the little shiver he did before carrying on,

"An Oreo cookie packet."

That night I didn't sleep too well and dreamt of tall men in biker boots chasing me through the forest. I even woke up, still in my dream, and saw a shadow stood at the bottom of my bed. I screamed again and then woke for real, to find I was alone but there was no going back to sleep after that.

I just kept playing it over and over in my head. I had even dug yesterday's old newspaper out of the bin to look at. Jack hadn't been exaggerating at all, even though the authorities were still holding out for it to be a wild bear or pack of wolves, as the extent of the damage done to the bodies was too extreme for a single person to do. They even found claw marks to back up their theory, but I knew differently. I knew first-hand what the other side could become, let alone do to a human body with ease.

Jack knew about the things the press had kept out of the paper thanks to a cousin he had on the force and with this type of thing rarely happening in Evergreen Falls, it was being talked about everywhere. Of course, RJ hadn't thought it bigger news than the Dravens doing a disappearing act on the town, which was probably why I was only hearing about it now.

I found, for once I was bypassing the kettle and going for the hard stuff. I grabbed the first bottle I could see and poured myself enough to down in one. It burned all the way and made me cough but it still felt good. I tried not to think about it but the two elements put together were too much of a coincidence in my world. Could he have done this…my mystery guy? I wanted to say no way 'cause he had helped me but what if he had been told not to attack me but anyone else was fair game? What if I had been right and he was a Vampire? It must get pretty hungry up in those woods.

"Stop it, Keira!" I said out loud, pouring myself another shot. I mean a lot of people like Oreo cookies…I mean for Christ's sake they were like the Nations biscuit of choice, probably having them in most homes. Like rich tea or digestives in England I thought as I swigged another back, this time wiping my chin from the over slurp of what I now knew was Vodka.

I went on like this until I could remember that I hated Vodka neat, but by that time I was far too wobbly to move. I woke the next day with the feeling something had crawled in my mouth and died, possibly a rodent, and a head that felt like someone had used it to go bowling! I was also still in the kitchen and had to peel my cheek from the table. That's when I decided drinking alone was never a good idea or in trying to solve a murder by reading the paper. Nancy Drew would not have approved, nor would she have passed out on the kitchen table drooling over her face, making the newspaper soggy, which happened to be my only source of information.

It wasn't any better when I finally dragged myself to the toilet and looked in the mirror.

"Well at least I didn't lose *all* of the article." I said rolling my eyes on seeing a large section of the print ink had transferred to my face where I had slept on it. I was glad when Frank and Libby brought the baby back so that I could find some normality again to my days.

I tried not to follow the story after that and last I heard it had been declared an animal attack by the coroner and the investigation was dropped. This didn't put me at ease in the slightest or make me want to go on any forest walking days out anytime soon. Even after weeks later and still no sightings of the biker booted man, it wasn't enough to get me into those woods.

So, with that, I spent my time locked away most days in the house when not at college and kind of became a hermit version of myself. It wasn't that I had lost my backbone all of a sudden but considering all my supernatural chums had up and left me to handle things on my own, I wasn't sure how I would have done this when faced with another supernatural threat.

The other downside to this was that the longer I went without seeing any of my old life, the more withdrawn I became. I would try and think of plans in my quest to rescue Draven, but I kept falling back to a point where all ideas fell back to one question…where to start?

I woke weeks later to the sight of the same old hollow eyes that looked back at me every morning. It was as if you could actually see the missing pieces of me that left only the shell to function… And function I had to. So with that in mind I did as I usually did and got ready for a day I couldn't wait to see the back of.

"Morning." I said to Libby and she looked at me with tired bloodshot eyes.

"Is it morning? I can no longer tell." She said in a hopeless tone I tried not to match.

"Don't worry, I will take the next night shift, so you guys can get some sleep." At this she found the energy to get up and hug me, putting some much needed hope in her eyes.

The new love of my life wasn't big on sleeping through the nights but that was just fine by me as I didn't sleep well myself these days. Ever since I was left alone I wouldn't do so well and having little baby Ella with me soothed the ache in my soul like no other could. She was the reason I kept myself going, the reason I didn't fake my smiles when I looked down at her precious face and the only reason I was still living in a place that reminded me of the only man I could ever love at every turn.

I got up after clicking the kettle on ready for my daily fix of Tetley, when I heard a knock on the door.

"Who would it be at this time in the morning?" Libby snapped in her obviously deprived sleep mode. I smiled at her, giving her an 'I understand' pat on her shoulder as I passed to find who exactly it was.

"Coming." I said after nearly tripping up on a bag of nappies that was now half spread across the floor thanks to my foot.

I finally made it and was still trying to push the knotted hairs that had escaped my plait back from my face as I opened the door. I was taken back by the sight of a messenger all dressed in black and complete with flat cap to match. What the other startling thing was, that the boy must have been no more than twelve and was sat on a very old fashioned bike that should have been in an antique store.

I frowned before I managed to smile at the lad.

"Umm…hello." I said wondering why the kid was just staring at me.

"You've only just got up…I can tell 'cause your hair's a mess." He said with a slight accent I couldn't place. Ok, so now I was frowning again.

"Umm…yeah, cheers for that." I replied sarcastically.

"I'm just saying, 'cause the misses said you'd be pretty and all but I'm a guessin' shit hasn't been that shiny lately." He said and I think at this point my mouth actually dropped open with a 'pop' sound. Was this kid for real?!

"Is it ever?" Was the only thing I knew to say, that or to scold him for swearing at his age.

"Hey I guess not, so look I need you to sign this before I can give you what's in my bag." He said pulling out a little black book! Oh God, this was just getting weirder and weirder…I mean, was this actually happening or was I still asleep?

"Ok, do you have a pen?" I asked but then I was made to feel stupid by a twelve-year-old riding something that looked older than my Nan! The look he gave me nearly had me feeling the top of my head to check that I hadn't in fact grown a twin from the side of my neck.

"You're not very savvy to these things are you…? Look Blondie, just place your finger here and think of Snow White's mother." I placed my finger on the pad just as I said,

"Uh?" Which was quickly followed by,

"Ouch! Hey, it pricked my finger!"

"Yep it sure did, just like Snow White's mother and look what happened to her, kid with bloody coloured lips, husband off with a witch and dead as a doornail! Some people have no luck…here you go." The lad said, making not a lick of sense and handing me a vanilla coloured envelope. I then watched as he snapped his little book shut, but not before I saw my full name along with my bloodied fingerprint underneath it.

"Aren't you a little young to be out here delivering on your own?" I said feeling that I had to at least ask before letting him go riding off.

"Oh well, aren't you a sweet one but don't worry Blondie, I am older than I look…well I'd better be on my way…you do something with that hair now." He shouted before running alongside his bike and then flinging a leg over to wobble down the gravel drive.

I closed the door shaking my head and made my dazed way back into the kitchen.

"Who was it?" Libby asked, having just made my tea.

"Just some delivery lad." I said lifting up the envelope for her to see. I then took my Homer mug from her and sat down to open the letter.

Dear Chosen,

(Electus, Catherine, Keira, Kazzy, Vixen, My little Keira girl or whatever other name I have not included)

You don't know me but I know a great deal about you and I think it is time we should meet, in fact I know it is time we should meet, that's why I wrote this letter.

Ok, so I have established we should meet, but now here comes the tricky part.

See the thing is, I am not allowed to write down where I am in the world or tell anyone, so this is where the fun begins. I do hope you like puzzles, well I know actually you don't because like I said, I know you, but that's just tough shit as this is the only way to play the game.

So, my first puzzle lies with Leivic at the warehouse. I know you have been there before and that didn't end well. This time it will be different, I know this because I know this and when I say that, it is because I know I mean it. So first come to the warehouse and pick up what I left there for you and then you will need to book a flight to Europe but my letter will tell you the destination.

Your code name will be: Tricks

And the name to get into the warehouse will be: Treats

P.S Be there this Monday no later than 4am and bring a large bottle of water with you. You will also need to bring fifty dollars, a jacket with a hood and a long umbrella with a hooked handle. Oh and to make things easier, wear red, hair down and dark lipstick.

Follow my instructions, Chosen One and I will help you discover the biggest secret of all…

How to take back what the Gods took from you.

See you soon

P

"Anything interesting?" Libby asked once I had read it four times and was still in a state of shock. Was it true, could it really be possible or was I running away with myself? The only thing the Gods had ever taken from me was the one man I had ever loved, surely everyone in the Supernatural world knew this!

I actually felt myself shaking and then smile for the first time in weeks. Could this person be on to something or was I walking into a trap!? I don't think I cared if that could be a possibility as nothing in the world could have stopped me from being at the warehouse and following those instruction to the letter.

I felt my blood begin to thaw after all this time and I felt like jumping up and down and screaming, just to release the other half of me that I had locked away ever since that heart-breaking day I said goodbye to Dominic Draven.

"Not really, just college stuff." I said realising I hadn't answered my sister and I think if she hadn't been so tired then she would have noticed the first big grin I'd had on my face for a long while.

"So, summer break is coming up, have you thought of any

plans yet?" She asked over her mug and I picked up my own, took a long drink and answered her question.

"I think I might do some travelling." I said then got up eager to get upstairs and start planning. I got to the door and turned back to Libby's question,

"Sorry, what did you say?"

"I asked where to…you know…travelling?" She repeated and my smile widened as I said with utter certainty…

"Europe."

CHAPTER SIX

IT'S ALL IN THE PLANNING

That very day I started getting things ready but soon realised I would have to go shopping to get most of the stuff I was instructed to bring. It didn't take a genius to guess that the letter had been written to me by Pythia the Oracle. That was the only explanation for it, but this just led to more questions, like for starters…wasn't she supposed to be missing?

This was just the tip of the question iceberg that was boggling my mind and I found on my drive to the shopping mall more than once my hands would grip the steering wheel in frustration. However, by the time I pulled into the car park I knew one thing for certain, there was only one person who could answer all my questions and that person was one I vowed to find…*Pythia.*

The Mall was quiet but it was a weekday and I was thankful for it. First stop was the easiest item to get as I knew just where I would find one. So I walked straight up to the counter at the expensive men's store that specialised in suits and business wear. I remembered seeing one of the faceless fancy metal mannequins dressed in a pinstriped suit and holding an umbrella on top of a suitcase. I only remembered it because I was laughing with Libby, as someone had gone to the trouble of making it out like he was hailing a taxi or Cab, as they say here. We laughed at the idea of anyone doing that in a place like Evergreen.

However, it all became clear when I walked up to a snotty nosed assistant who looked at me as though I came in shaking an empty can for spare change at her.

"Hi, there's an umbrella in the window I would like to buy." I said as nicely as possible, given the look she gave me. She looked thoughtfully at her manicured nail before finally taking me on.

"It's one hundred and fifty dollars, so may I suggest Wal-Mart where you can get one for about ten bucks, that would suit you much better I think." She wrinkled her nose up at me which, added to her behaviour, reminded me of a little pug dog. At that point I took a moment to ask myself if it was worth biting back, but then when she flicked her hand motioning me to leave, I decided 'oh Hell yeah' it was worth it.

"It's a shame you don't have one more expensive, but I am sure my boyfriend will understand… I will take it." I said with a fake smile. At this she dropped her relaxed pose and stood up a bit straighter, only to cock her hip out to one side.

"Oh yeah and who's your boyfriend then?" She said one hand on that bony assed hip of hers.

"Ah Miss Johnson what a lovely surprise, how are you my dear?" The owner of the store came from the back and Miss Attitude lost her Pug bitch face like it fell off her in seconds.

"Hey Mr Stanton, how are you today?" I said remembering the same guy who had served Draven and me once when I dragged him in here shopping. I had wanted to buy him something and settled on a tie that matched his eyes when his other side came through. I felt a pinch to my chest when I remembered what the first thing he'd done with that tie when we got home…I had been right, it was a perfect match to the purple that flashed in his eyes as he found his release. I had to swallow the memory down like a lead weight wrapped in sandpaper.

"Oh please, please, call me Thomas. So, what can we help you with today? I hope Mandy is taking good care of you?" He said and for a second I saw a flicker of worry in her make-up caked eyes. Good, I thought, serves her right.

"Oh Mandy has been just dandy and was just about to show me your selection of umbrellas." I said shooting her a look as if to say, you're a lucky cow that I am not vindictive like you! I saw her release a held breath and then say in her nicest tone,

"This way Miss Johnson." I followed her to the section where men's accessories were displayed and with her boss still watching us we both kept up the charade of being friendly.

"Who the Hell is your boyfriend?" She whispered to me and I laughed without answering her. I looked at the umbrella while she gave me all the sales spiel and halfway through her, 'Luxury Microfibre and hi-tech fibreglass ribs' I interrupted her and said,

"I will take it." She blushed and nodded, taking it over to the counter to ring it through the till. I didn't really give two hoots about what it was made from, all I cared about was that it had a curved old-fashioned handle, like I had been told to bring. I still had no clue what this list meant, but I wasn't about to doubt the fates on something like this. Hell, if she had told me to turn up in a bikini, shaking my behind with half a fruit stall on my head, singing 'Copacabana' by Barry Manilow I would have!

"Would you like it gift wrapped?" She asked when prompted by her boss and I felt a little evil as I enjoyed seeing her uncomfortable expression whilst trying to be nice.

"That won't be necessary, thank you." I said smiling but, once I paid for my purchase and said my goodbye to the owner, I leaned over the counter.

"Some advice for next time… never judge a book by its cover 'cause sometimes that cover is going to judge you back." I said as I left the store, leaving the snotty attendant asking her boss who my boyfriend was. I had to smile at hearing her little gasp when he told her.

The rest of the shopping went more smoothly until it came to buying something red and I knew that unless I was going to turn up in workman's overalls in maroon, I was going to have to buy a dress. As expected it was going to take time…

Three hours later I was on my way home.

Once I had everything ready I was itching to get going but I had two whole days to wait. For that time I was as edgy as Hell and the only time I would calm was when I was looking after Ella. I don't know what it was about her, but as soon as someone placed that cute little bundle in my arms, it was like being injected with 'happy' liquid mixed with a sprinkle of 'serene'.

Of course, after trying to stay awake and survive on a few hours sleep each night, it finally caught up with me. I went to bed to read, under the pretence of going to sleep like everyone else did, but I knew I would have to leave the house at about 3am if I was going to make it on time to the warehouse, because tomorrow was the big day. I was just turning the page when I felt a shift in the air that had the hairs on the back of my neck prickling.

I set the book down and looked around my room, but it was just as it always had been. No shadows stood in the corner or at the bottom of my bed and my windows displayed only the darkness the night brought. Then I jumped as my bedside lamp started to flicker before a pop sounded, plunging the room and my vision into a black void. My heart was pounding as I was still for seconds wondering if the power had blown. I really didn't fancy getting up and fumbling around in the dark.

"Close your eyes." I would have screamed at the sound of a voice in my ear, but a hand clamped over my mouth to prevent it from ever being heard. I started shaking my head in the dark as blind panic set in but then a hand came up to my face and smoothed back my hair before turning to brush the back of a hand down my cheek.

"Ssshh and calm… *my Vixen*" That name! I instantly went still as if a deep freeze had taken over my body and allowed only my mind to spin out of control. How?!

"That's it, calm for me." That voice! I soaked it up like a sponge that would keep me alive from its liquid. I needed it to breathe.

"Come now, close those eyes for me." This must have been a trick! It had to be I thought, even as I did as the voice told me to. Was there ever going to be a point in my life where that voice couldn't pull at me like a Master with strings attached to his hand?

"Good girl. I need light to play." He hummed and as soon as I inhaled I felt my frozen limbs melt deeper into the bed I lay on. The sound, the smell and then the touch. This was the last element to confirm one of Heaven's sons now sat at my side.

"Draven?" I whispered so quietly, too afraid that this bliss would leave me too soon. His fingers grazed down my neck as softly as if I had been made from petals and I took in another lung full of his delicious scent. I sensed the glow of soft light through my closed lids and had to use all of my willpower not to open my eyes.

"How?" I asked as his hand continued lower and I heard the hum of pleasure in his growl.

"No questions my Love…don't think, just…*feel.*" He said against my skin before he tasted my neck. I moaned and arched up to him knowing this was crazy, but that I would have been even crazier not to accept this feeling. To say that I had missed it was just not enough. It was like dying in a drought and suddenly finding yourself swimming. And at this point, I didn't care if I drowned.

When his lips touched mine and his hand found the core of me, I was released from the spell and I woke from my invisible bonds. I reached up, buried my hands in his hair and took his lips at greater need. My eyes opened to find Draven as I always remembered him, in the only place he should ever be…in my arms.

It was perfect, stunning and soul consuming all at the same time. It was my Heaven and I had died with him.

He kissed me to a fever pitch and took my orgasm with him when he finished. I came screaming in his mouth as his fingers played me into a fine tune that all nine circles of Hell could have heard. I gripped onto his granite shoulders, just for something to anchor myself to as I floated into my euphoric bliss. It was like saying hello to an old friend and with every wave that crashed into me, it was like another hug to my soul. Of course I hugged back.

"I take it you miss me?" Draven said on a laugh before

kissing my forehead too gently for my liking. Hell, I wanted him to mark himself no me so hard, I wanted to feel crushed, to feel imprinted against every last inch of his skin. I think if I could have crawled inside of him I would have.

"You left me." I said in a small voice that was close to breaking. He laid his forehead to mine and whispered,

"I know."

"But why, why did this happen?" I asked him and his eyes seemed to melt at my question.

"Because there are other ways on the path to take, ones that may take us in opposite directions, but there is always purpose in the destination." I shook my head, not understanding.

"Then take me with you." I said over his lips, but he pulled back.

"I can't"

"Why?" The pain was clear in my question and I saw him wince at it.

"Because you don't belong where I am, you belong in your own world, Keira." He stated softly.

"No!" I said as he started to get up from me. I reached out to him but he moved quickly and before long he was stood over me at the side of the bed.

"Yes Keira. I am sorry for this but it must be done. You must be made to watch me go and know that you can't follow." He looked so lost saying these things as if he was forcing the words from his lips in a painful process.

"No Draven…don't do this…" I said feeling the tears roll down like little rivers of pain.

"I have no choice and my time is at an end. I am being summoned back. This is for your closure, Keira and my chance at seeing you one last time and to tell you I am sorry. I never meant for it to be this way, Keira but the fates have left me with no other choice. Please understand, everything I have ever done is because I love you and that will remain so until my soul is nothing more than mere black desert sand. *I will always love you…*" He said moving away from me back into the shadows and I shot out of bed after him.

"NO! Draven, no!" I shouted and followed him into the

darkness. I ran and I ran but my room had become an endless corridor of space. As though someone had taken my walls and pulled them back like a slingshot in time. I kept running as I saw him being pulled backwards by invisible hands of light.

"Draven! I am coming with you!" I shouted as I started to gain distance. I then saw a light at the end behind where he was headed and just as my mind told me it was Heaven, the closer I got I realised the cruellest fact of all. Draven wasn't going back to Heaven at all. He was going back to Hell!

"NO, NO, NO!" I screamed!

The flames licked out at the shadows as though they were feeding from them and soon the hands that I saw on Draven became black and charred around his arms. They burnt through his skin where they touched him and I reached out to him one last time even through the burn. He was just being pulled back into the breasts of Hell's keepers when I lunged for him.

I flew at him only to fall straight through him as his body disintegrated into nothing but the black desert sand he spoke of. I landed on the floor in a heap and was frantically waving and kicking my limbs out as if I was burning up in the pits of Hell.

I finally came to as I opened my eyes to see not only my lamp still lighting the room but my book was open and next to my head. It took me a minute to focus but when I did, I found the first words on the page closest to my head,

"God pardon me!" he subjoined ere long; "and man meddle not with me: I have her and will hold her."

I picked up the copy of Jane Eyre and hurled it at the window on a screamed cry.

"NO!" I felt like my damned heart had broken all over again and my anger was coming out in a mangled stream of pain and suffering. As the book hit the window I looked on, I then cried out again at what I saw behind the glass.

"AVA!" I screamed out her name and ran to the window, but she had already taken off. I struggled with my window and cursed this life, just as it opened. I reached out into the night that Draven's bird seemed to own but it was too late…she was gone.

After that I didn't know what to think but I certainly knew what to feel and that was close to desperation. Did it all mean what I thought it did? Had I been lied to and Draven wasn't in Heaven after all? The thought of him living in Hell was too much to bear, but the one thing it did do was force my plan into action.

It didn't take me long to get ready as I had laid out my clothes yesterday and put any other items I needed in my truck ready. All I needed to do was brush my hair, leaving it down and get dressed into my designated clothes bought for the occasion. I decided as it was cold to wear jeans under the dress, so that I could slip out of them if need be and I wore thick black boots, good for running and even better for kicking. I decided it was time to be practical in the world I lived in and whatever the morning brought me, I had a feeling it wasn't going to be like taking a walk to the post office and picking up a letter!

I grabbed my old faithful jacket with a massive floppy hood and just as I closed my door, I unfolded the letter I'd written to Libby. It just said that I couldn't sleep and decided to take an early morning drive. I used my bedroom door handle to punch through the paper so that it would stay there and she would see it if she decided to check on me when she woke up.

I soon found myself in my truck driving along the twisted dark back road out of town. It wasn't the best time to be alone after what I had just dreamt and every time my mind touched on what had happened, I would then find myself wiping away my tears along my jacket sleeve in an angry one handed swipe. This was why I hated sleeping, but this time it had been worse. It hadn't just been a bombardment of past memories of my time with Draven, no this time he had actually come back from the dead and I couldn't think of anything crueller!

I shook my head and hated what I saw every time I would catch my reflection in the rear-view mirror. My eyes looked like two hollow points, connected with how my soul felt…empty and cold. Was this what an empty glass felt like to an alcoholic? Or more like the last breath to a dying man? I had no answers, but only one thing I was certain of…I didn't like what I saw in the mirror anymore, not without the other half of my soul and whole of my heart back in place.

I didn't know how far away I was, as I was just going from memory and trying to ignore all the beautiful parts of that journey that included looking to my side and finding Draven sat there with me. The clock on the dash said it was only 3:27 when something started to go wrong. The engine started to splutter and nothing I was doing was helping the dying truck to carry on. It quickly gave up on me and I had to cruise to a stop by the side of the road.

I hit the steering wheel with the palms of my hands and even though it had been weeks since my broken hand it still hurt like an SOB when I did this.

"Bitches and ball bags!" I swore at my truck, flinging my arms up in the air before trying to find my calm place. Problem was, these days I didn't bloody have one!

After sitting there for five minutes and then another ten minutes trying to start it, I gave up and got out to have a look at something I knew I would have no clue at what to do. It was cold and the ground was covered in an eerie morning mist that was like walking in a fallen cloud.

"But of course, being out here all alone was going to be as creepy as being in some horror, with a side of teen slasher movie. What's next, a family of zombie hillbillies to come moaning from the woods?" I muttered as I circled the truck. I even kicked the wheel as I passed. I touched the bonnet and swore out as it burned my fingers.

"Shit me, that's hot!" I said somehow feeling better talking to myself. I saw the steam coming from the grill and knew I was in deep doo-doo. What now? I had my mobile on me, but if I called Frank then I doubted he would take me all the way to where I needed to be and then he would be asking too many questions, ones I had no way of answering.

I was just in the middle of considering calling a taxi, when a noise had me spinning around. The road was a long strip of dark grey and floating mist, with the looming forest on either side. I hadn't seen any cars and the air was thick with morning dew, where just breathing hard made your skin feel damp. It was so still I knew it must have been an animal or something and just as the thought entered my head, I saw it.

A deer crossing the road just before the bend, had stopped to watch me. I wondered if it thought, 'Daft Cow' before continuing with a little run to the other side and disappearing into the darker forest.

"Better you than me mate." I said thinking there was nothing that could get me to go that way… when I heard it again, only this time it sounded like twigs snapping under a heavy pair of boots. I froze just like the deer had, only I was too afraid to turn and look at what made the noise.

That news article came rushing back to me in a jumble of words, like 'mauled to death' and 'ripped apart' and then even Jack's voice jumped in there and added 'body bags' and 'claws'. When I heard it again only this time closer to where I stood, I knew the time had come to be brave. I took a deep breath and turned, only to expel it just as quickly. As the gasp left my body I could see it in the cold air almost like a cartoon voice bubble. For there, in the woods, stood the same tall shadow I had seen that day, only now he wasn't staying back, hidden and watching…

No, now he was walking forward in long strides to where I stood and my horror movie reference was about to come true.

As obviously…

My killer had just arrived.

CHAPTER SEVEN

OLD HAUNTS FROM HELL

I screwed up my eyes to try and make out more of the dark figure coming towards me, but his features remained hidden. It was extraordinary the way he used the shadows around him. I was actually watching him move them with a little flick of his wrist, although his hand remained by his side. I could even hear the strain on his leather gloved hand as one finger came out and made a turning motion. Then the shadow wrapped tighter around his body, shielding himself before travelling up his body like a massive ink coloured eel. It floated, using the air like water as it circled him like a pet to its owner.

The further up it went the more it slowly revealed. I couldn't help my sharp intake of air at the sight of those thick heavy boots, but more importantly, they were continuing to take slow steps towards me. Leather encased legs showed thighs thicker than my waist and I felt my back bump into my truck as I had been allowing my body's natural flight reflex to take over. The bottom of a long black jacket moved at the back of his knees as the shadows played with his body and just as I was getting to his waist, high beam lights from a car coming around the bend lit the scene.

The high-pitched cry hurt my ears and I looked back to see the shadow had formed ahead on the end nearest to his face and was crying out at the invasion of light. It wasn't quite the head of a snake but that of a thinner dragon, only made from black smoke. It hissed once and just as the headlights were coming closer, it vibrated until its body grew and grew. The man's hands whipped out and the shadowed beast obeyed his silent command. The shadow spun around then erupted into a fine mist and unbelievably, took the man's body with him.

The car was just pulling to a stop in front of mine when one last look told me that there was nothing left of my shadowed stalker.

"You alright, need a hand?" A man's voice asked, and I stiffened, being on my guard. Who was I kidding? My back was as straight as a ramrod since the first sighting of the biker man. I tried to speak but had to cough first just to clear my throat.

"Umm, yeah, I broke down." I said being very tempted to add on a 'durr', to myself. I mean, I think he gathered as much and doubted he encountered a lot of girls out here at near four in the morning for a quiet drive.

"Ok, let's pop the hood and see what we got." He said coming closer. He was a big guy and my skin prickled, but when his face came into the light I let out a breath. He actually looked like a jolly Ginger Father Christmas, with a lovely smile and kind brown eyes. Half his face was covered in a copper coloured beard and the same colour hair could be seen under his woollen hat which looked as if it had been knitted by someone losing their sight. The trim around the edges started as a zigzag and then joined the other side in a wobbly wave as if someone had given up halfway through.

There was just something about this beer bellied man that said kind-hearted and when the hood opened and steam bellowed up, he let out a gut jiggling laugh.

"Whoa! Now we're smoking girly!" He said still laughing after I had released the bonnet for him to open.

"I guess I won't be going anywhere in a hurry eh?" I said laughing with him, just because his was an infectious sound. The situation still sucked the big one!

"Ah, now don't ya worry. Let big J take a look, I will just go and fetch my tools and flashlight." As he walked away I couldn't help my eyes from trailing to the forest. I just knew the guy was still out there watching me, but if he was this 'Hikers' Killer' then why was the sight of this harmless logger enough to get him to back off? I shook my head lightly as Big J came back.

It was amazing what you could learn about a person in the space of fifteen minutes. Take Jimmy here, aka big J. His wife was named Betty but he calls her Rubble Bubble 'cause he thinks she looks like Betty from the Flintstones. Her mother was the one who knitted him the 'damn hat' as he put it, but he didn't have the heart not to wear it, as she was slowly losing her sight and lived in a nursing home that he and his wife visited every three days. Jimmy was definitely a talker, but I found it eased my nerves just listening to him and nodding with a smile.

I think I knew what his technique was because he was trying to put a young girl, stranded in the middle of nowhere on a dark road, at ease. Well Jimmy had this down to a T, as it was working like a charm…Hell by the end of it I couldn't stop myself from giving him a hug in thanks. He smelled like chopped wood and rolling tobacco.

I was soon able to be on my way after he had discovered a slow leak in my radiator. When he asked me if I had any water, he must have wondered at my beaming grin. I had almost tripped over myself getting to the gallon bottle I had in the back.

"Well that was bloomin' handy, Girly." He said scratching his head and then rearranging his hat. He showed me how to fill it and said,

"She'll get ya where ya headed, if where ya headed isn't too far." He chuckled making his plaid covered belly wobble. He also told me not to let 'her' overheat as I could warp the metal and blow a gasket. I had nodded all the while not really understanding any of it.

He waved me on as I drove past and I just hoped stopping to help me hadn't put him in harm's way. I had tried to convince him all was good for him to get back to his 'Rubble Bubble' but he was adamant to see me on my way. I watched him in my rearview mirror and with a big sigh of relief saw he was safely in his own truck.

So the Oracle had foreseen my car breaking down and told me to bring water, which had me wondering why she didn't just tell me to forget the truck and get the bus or something? Or better still, warn me about my busted radiator so I could have had it fixed beforehand. As I made it all the way to the outskirts of the city, I thought of another million other ways she could have played this 'Little Clue Game' of hers. I nearly missed the turning.

"Shit!" I said as I had to slam on my brakes and reverse to catch the service road. I remembered passing the sports complex and since then it was fairly easy to find the rest of the way. Big J had told me not to go too fast but I was close to running late and I needed to be there by four, so I hadn't strictly followed that rule.

I only had to drive down the road for a few minutes until my next obstacle lay ahead in the form of an armed guard, heavy barrier and electric fencing. I very much doubted I was going to get away with doing an action movie stunt with this one, so I slowed down.

"ID!" The guy ordered in a gruff manner. I was quickly transported through time and all the little details of that first ride came back to me.

"Tony?" I said remembering the guard's name, who Draven had wanted to rip a new one for being rude. Well, given the way he asked me for my ID just now, I was guessing he hadn't learnt his lesson.

He dipped his head and that was the new detail I never got last time. He was in his early thirties, shaved head, thick neck and he acted like he was a cop or an army man. My guess was that he failed the exams and ended up a security guard instead. Well, I wasn't one to judge but I was just hoping this made him easier to bribe, as I was quickly gathering he wasn't in need of an umbrella or about to compliment me on my loose hair! I just hoped fifty dollars was enough.

"You know me?" He looked shocked and I decided to play it cool.

"You don't remember me, huh? I was in the Aston Martin

that day, when Mr Draven came through here." I said and his eyes grew wide.

"Oh yeah, my first week on the job. I've seen him coming through here a few times since." He said and my eyes widened at the information he was giving me.

"When was the last time?" I asked trying to reign in the heavy dose of desperation that came with that question. He frowned and looked as if he wasn't going to answer me at first but then shrugged his shoulders like it didn't matter either way.

"Back in May I think." This was the point where my heart started to pound. May? But he wasn't around in May…maybe it was someone driving his car, like Vincent or someone…it couldn't have been Draven…could it?

"Do you remember if it was Mr Draven driving?" I asked heart pounding and then he really started to get wary.

"Look lady, I don't know what your game is but no more questions, I ain't his damn secretary!" Whoa, ok Rent a Rude Cop! I didn't say this, as I had enough restraint to know this wouldn't have got me anywhere so I smiled instead.

"I'm sorry, a strong looking officer like you, doesn't need me bugging him. I must be taking up too much of your time as it is." I said in an admittedly pathetic attempt at flirting, so I was surprised when his eyes softened.

"Well now, don't you go being sorry at me being rude to a pretty lady like yourself. But if you're looking for Mr Draven, then he hasn't been around for a while." I tried not to show my shock at cracking his rude shell and gave him another smile, hoping it didn't look as awkward as it felt.

"Actually, I have to meet someone but it's a bit of a surprise, do you think you could help me out?" At this he took a step back as if he was thinking about radioing it in.

"I wouldn't normally ask, but I have travelled quite a way for her birthday and would be gutted if she found out now… you understand I'm sure and in thanks I would love to compensate you for your time." I said holding up the fifty, thinking this guy was no way going to accept so little, but I was left surprised again when he plucked it out of my hand and waved me on without a word.

"Wow, maybe I should notch up the sex appeal in this spy game more often." I said out loud as I drove on to the warehouses. I passed a darkened version of the place I remembered and as soon as I approached, I found a nervous sweat had broken out. It was as if I could even hear Draven's voice in my head telling me I shouldn't be here and looking back to what happened the last time I was, then it was the reason I couldn't get out of the truck.

I saw myself being pushed into the van and the memory flashed in front of my eyes, like an out of body experience. I was seeing it being ripped open by a scarred bear that had been to Hell and back and had his King drag him out again. I saw Draven destroying the vehicle to get to me and once free, had it flipping to the side like a toy car at the hands of a small boy.

I saw the demon he sent back in a puddle of holy water and the prayer he said after the act. All I saw was a man protecting his own and what had the Gods done in thanks…taken his life!

I knew I needed to get out of the car and in the end only one memory did it. It was before all the worst part of that day reared its ugly head. It was the sight of Draven playfully pulling up my hood and calling me cute at the sight. And, as if that memory alone contained the magic I felt that day, it took away the vision of being kidnapped. It just flew away at the sight of two lovers in the middle of the madness around them. The two memories were playing alongside each other and the destructive force became a faded shadow in the sight of true love. It just flew away like the rolling fog on the empty road that had led me here.

With that last sight in my mind I got out of the truck feeling stronger than before. I shimmied out of my jeans after removing my boots, only to put them back on again. They didn't exactly match my dress but I wasn't here for a bloody catwalk, so I didn't care too much on accessorizing.

The dress was a deep red that was cut straight across the neckline to my bare shoulders. It was plain and simple, cut to my waist where a thin black belt was tied. The skirt flared out to just above my knees and it was one of those dresses that could have been worn to the office with the right jacket and shoes or could have been worn on a night out with some heels. I, however, was attending neither, so I didn't think anything of my added woollen gloves that reached the top of my arms and were knitted to allow my fingers and thumbs free rein.

I smoothed down my hair, applied the dark red lipstick and took out the remaining items on my list. I folded the jacket over my arm and hooked the umbrella under it, so it swung down thanks to the hooked handle. I checked myself one last time and with a deep breath walked to the right door.

It was a small access door to one of the warehouses nestled further back in between two larger buildings. Nicely tucked away for hiding what lay behind those doors I thought as I reached up to the metal door. I knocked and when I heard nothing I knocked again, only this time with a little more force.

"Piss off!" Ah, that was more like it I thought, remembering the same welcoming reception from last time.

"Open up please." I said using my sternest tone, even though I had added the please.

"You got the wrong door little girl, nothing but big bad wolves behind this one, now piss off…please." He added the 'please' as a sarcastic afterthought and I banged the door harder.

"The password is Treat…. Now open the bloody door!" I shouted hoping to at least shock him into opening the door or to at least take me more serious, which thankfully worked.

"You got some balls, I will give ya that!" He shouted through the door and I heard the heavy locks slide back before the door swung open to reveal a four hundred-pound Samoan. He filled the entire door space and that was without his head! He wasn't short of seven feet and it actually hurt my neck to look up at him. From the looks of his gut alone, it looked like it could playhouse to someone my size with ease. I think if he hadn't been so damn intimidating then the massive gulp I did would have been a comedy moment.

"It's you!" He said with the clear look of being stunned, changing his honey coloured eyes to a glowing amber. He looked pretty much the same as last time, long shorts resting under his impressive sized gut, a massive black vest I didn't think they made in his size and Jesus sandals.

"Umm… yeah." Wasn't the smartest thing to say, but I was lost for words and even more so when I saw him lower to his knees in front of me. I stepped back, giving him more space and looked around in case someone important had just entered.

"Electus Unus." He murmured as his knees cracked when putting all that weight on them.

"What are you…?"

"My name is Ira and I serve the balance, my Heaven's Light." 'O…kay' was my only thought.

"But you told me to piss off?" I don't know why this was the first thing I asked, let alone said it at all.

"And my most sincere apologises, Light Bringer." He said still looking at my feet, making me more uncomfortable by the second.

"Umm, please…you don't have to kneel or anything…but can I ask, what do you mean by Light Bringer?" I asked as he heaved himself off the ground with one beefy hand.

"You are the 7th light, the Chosen One by the Gods." He said this as if I should have known this already. I felt like telling him that I must have skipped that class!

"I don't really know what you're on about with the whole 'light bringer' bit, but I do know that I must get into this club, so can I pass?" I said shifting round to get closer to the door. As soon as he frowned I knew I had pushed my luck and was waiting for the big 'Hell no' and given his size, I didn't think there was anyone better at delivering it.

"You wish to pass?" He asked wide eyed and suddenly shifting his large bare feet. I mean what did he think…that I had popped in for a visit to introduce myself? The sound of his sandals on the hardwood floor was the only noise as he studied me.

"If you mean do I want to go in there again, then the answer is yes," I said firmly. His big hand smoothed back his plaited Mohawk and I could have sworn I saw the tattoos on his face move around like the cogs in his mind.

"If you would take the advice of a mere servant I would

suggest before you do, you cover yourself. Here, give me your umbrella and I will give it back to you when you leave." He held out his hand and I did as I was told because I hadn't had any other instructions to do otherwise. So, doing as he suggested, I put my jacket on and when he nodded to the hood, I covered my face. I just hoped what I was doing was right because there was no going back now.

"Come, I will walk you in, I gather you are here to see Leivic." He said motioning the way with his big outstretched arm. The loose skin I would have called a bingo wing looked more like the wing on a small aircraft! It swayed as he moved like a waving flag of skin and I gave him a crooked smile as I passed.

The club was a lot different than when I had last been here and it wasn't only due to the serious lack of people. For one thing, I could now see more than just my feet, even if my hood was covering a lot of my face. I easily followed my new big Samoan friend, Ira by his shuffling alone. The place reminded me of somewhere someone would pound metal for a living. It was a steel worker's wet dream. The place had open iron girders covering the ceilings and the walls were metal plates riveted to concrete pillars to create different spaces. Glass bricks were also used as room separators and the same theme made up the bar area in one corner.

As I followed on, I soon realised that the hardcore clubbers didn't require a more comfortable space, as that had been saved for the VIP section we were now headed to. A crimson wall of material was the barrier between the two vast differences in interior decorating. It shimmered with its own magic and the grittier other side could be seen, as though looking through rippling water.

Now this I remembered, as it was like stepping through a portal to a different land. The walls were covered in booths of rich, deep reds, pinks, sunset oranges and yellows. But, unlike before, this time there was only one booth not empty.

Leivic was sat in the middle of the centre booth, on a raised platform covered in large flat pillows with smaller ones scattered between the other female bodies that accompanied him. He was smoking a large pipe the length of his arm. As soon as he saw us coming he sat up and the lounging half-naked beauties startled. It looked like chicks dug scars on big handsome warriors, I thought with a hidden smile. His silver blue eyes grew wide with both shock…and was that… fear?

"Leave us!" He snapped making me jump and after a few pouts the five females left quietly. I found my eyes following them, everyone strutting their beauty like peacocks being dismissed unhappily. He placed his pipe down on a small table and stood up to greet me, but his smile didn't meet his eyes. This instantly made me wary.

"Keira, what an unexpected but lovely surprise!" He said in that easy-going manner I now knew was being put on for my sake. I folded my hood back and smoothed my loose hair back from my face.

"Well, that isn't completely true now is it?" I said deciding to put a stop to the bullshit before it clouded my reasons for being here. For only a moment he looked taken back but with a quick flick of his wrist, he dismissed Ira and held out his hand for me.

"Keira, please join me." I took his large hand and let him lead me to the same booth. I had to walk up a few steps to get there and once in, the only thing I could do with my legs was to sit as if I was about to start meditating. When I saw him sit the same way I did a mental shoulder shrug and waited for him to say the first thing. After all, I didn't really have a plan here and was just going with the rocky flow.

Leivic picked back up his pipe and from here I could see the tiny and intercut carvings along the thin, twig like pipe that got thicker towards the end. A little copper cup sat at the end and I gathered this was where the tobacco was put for smoking. He puffed on the flattened end and he gave me a sideways glance as if still trying to comprehend that I was actually here and more importantly, how he was going to deal with that very fact. He then sucked in a lung full and like before, he let out a smoking Dragon he knew I liked watching from last time. For a second he seemed pleased with my wide eyed reaction. Then his voice cut through the smoky creature and with its end came the end of the silence as well.

"Why are you here, Keira?" His voice brought me back to that very day when I learnt words could nearly kill you. *"Draven is dead!"* Those words would not only haunt me to the end of time here, but in the next life as well. I closed my eyes momentarily as I tried to breathe through the pain. For a few seconds the memory hit me so hard I had to fight the run reflex my brain was screaming at me. It just wanted me to get as far away from that voice as I could, just to spare me the agony demons that would come collecting soon after.

But I stayed.

"What happened to him, Leivic?" I asked the one question I had been regretting not asking him that day. It was the same question that had troubled my every thought and the amount of times was long ago lost in the masses. I heard his reaction through the pipe he was sucking, and I knew my question was like a sucker punch to the gut.

"Keira…I…can't." He said with trouble and that was when I finally looked at him. His usually pale scar was now an angry red through his flustered skin and at that moment, I couldn't help what happened next. I reached out to him and placed my hand on his scarred face. He flinched but didn't move away.

The feeling I got was an overwhelming comfort. My hand grew warm and my body tingled. It was as though my cells were crying out for the supernatural side that I had been denied and now they finally had contact, it was like they were singing.

"Please, my friend." I said and he closed his eyes. I thought I had lost my only chance and was about to move my hand away, when his covered mine and held it to his cheek.

"It's been a long time since I felt a touch like this." He whispered as if to himself and me hearing him was like an afterthought. I smoothed my thumb along the part of his scar that cut across his nose and I heard a rumble as if his inner bear was enjoying being petted.

"You are such a good clean soul, Keira and do not deserve the pain my friend inflicted on you." He turned his face to fit more firmly in my palm that neither he, nor I wanted to move at that point.

"Then help me understand, Leivic. Help me heal. I need to

know what happened to him or I will never move on." I said knowing this wasn't entirely true. See, something about him told me not to disclose the real reason I was here, as soon as I saw Leivic's reactions to me. He obviously had no clue and if he didn't, then that was because the Oracle didn't want him to. And at this point, I was terrified of anything that could jeopardise my plans.

"I am so sorry Keira, I wish I could…I really do, but it is utterly forbidden. I should not be talking to you as it is, but to explain details to you would surely get me a one-way ticket to a place I vowed never to visit again." He said shaking his head free of the memory.

"What! But why? Surely it is not as severe as that, is it?" I asked in utter disbelief.

"What, you doubt a King's order to be heard and to be obeyed? I can most certainly say it is as severe as that! Anyone who breaks his orders is only going to end up in one place Keira, his words and his rules." He said in all seriousness.

"But how...? He's… he's dead Leivic, how can he rule still?" At this his head hung down and he shook it in a quiet little motion that looked so sad.

"Please Keira, I will beg of you if that is what you require, but please…don't put me in this situation. That day my vow was paid, don't make it in vain." I felt a single tear of frustration fall before I nodded.

"Alright, I will give up on knowing…for now. But trust me in this Leivic, I will one day know what happened and make no mistake when I say I will never stop trying, that is the truth! NEVER!" I got up at that, scooting to the edge as I knew there was nothing more I would get from this single-minded meeting. He'd had his orders and I had my own quest to follow.

I was just leaving when I thought of one last thing, one I will always regret asking.

"At least answer me this, for I think it is owed to me." I turned to find him slumped over resting his face on his open palms, his knees holding his elbows. He looked so young and lost. I almost gave him a break and left… Almost.

He lifted hurt eyes to mine and just nodded.

"Is Draven in Hell?" I waited and when I saw his head lower and his eyes slam shut, I didn't really need to hear his answer but I got it anyway,

"I have no doubt…that yes…

"He is living in Hell, Keira."

CHAPTER EIGHT

RING 'A' ROUND THE WAREHOUSES

I walked away from Leivic feeling as if the walls of my world had been torn down. I now knew without the shadow of a doubt that Draven now lived out his time, not watching me from above like he suggested, but from down below. The thought nearly brought me to my knees. I hiccupped a cry back and hurried out of the club, just so that I could breathe. It was as if the whole room was clouded in a dark looming presence that was making my skin itch. By the time I made it back to Ira, my scars were burning and I was nearly desperate to rip off my gloves.

Ira didn't look surprised to see me and when I saw him put a finger to his temple and say,

"She is here." I knew he was communicating with Leivic. I think he must have been making sure I was leaving, as it seemed to me that he couldn't see the back of me quick enough. In my mind I wanted to say something like, 'don't worry tough guy, I am leaving' but in the end, the sight of the giant of a man kneeling once again stopped me. Being rude wasn't going to get me anywhere and if anything, it would have just made me feel even shittier all the way home.

"Electus," he said in respect, lowering his head.

"By the way, it's Keira...*just Keira.*" I whispered the last part after I took my umbrella from him and walked through the door. Once it slammed shut behind me I didn't even flinch, I just felt numb. It was only when I felt little rivulets of rain running down my forehead that I realised I was just frozen in the pouring rain. At this point I lost it completely and burst out into a humourless laugh that didn't sound as if it belonged to me.

"An umbrella for the rain, great…just great!" I shouted lifting it up.

"Like I give a shit if I get wet at a time like this! Good one on predicting the weather!" I shouted looking up as if the Oracle could hear me, from where I didn't know. I bitterly pressed the bottom releasing the black material in a whoosh. I lifted it over my head in one motion and just saw a sheet of paper fluttering down. I caught it just in time before the puddles ruined it for me.

I ran for my truck to get out of the rain and once inside I opened the letter with shaky hands. Little droplets ran down from my wet hair and dropped on to the paper making some of the ink run. I read it quickly and tried to make sense of it.

Dear Tricks,

I know if you are reading this right now, then no doubt your mind is a whirlwind of questions, it is always the way of you Chosen Ones but the key is trust and with this next clue, you will need it. For it is time to introduce Little Red to Big Ugly.

On the back of this note I have included some rather useful information for you about Big Ugly which you WILL NEED TO READ. After all, my game can't work if there are no pieces left on the board to play with…if you catch my drift. And with the King gone there is now only the Queen, so take the hint and don't get eaten! Try really hard about that last part as even the fates can't prevent stupidity.

Given that, you should be fine if you follow my instructions.

Number 1: Place – There is a warehouse three buildings down from the one you are sat opposite right now. Go there, for my next clue waits for you inside. Beware, he takes being grouchy to a whole new level!

Number 2: Tools: Your umbrella is not just for keeping you dry. It is a shield and a hook…use them both.
Number 3: Entrance: The ladder is your friend. It is good for escaping when escaping isn't needed and for breaking and entering when breaking isn't needed.
Number 4: Red is the colour of blood, blood comes from flesh, flesh in a pound becomes a payment…NEVER pay Tricks.

One last thing
Remember, the shadows may be where people lie, but a liar is easily hidden in the shadows.
P.t.o

I turned over the page and read the last short paragraph,

'Pishachas Demons enjoy the feast of flesh and prefer the solitude of dark places, only coming out to feed. Their eyesight is near blind with the exception to red, this being blood, the colour to feed on, it is what gives them strength to see when needed.
They are known to possess human beings and alter their thoughts, before sucking the madness they inflict dry and taking with them what is left of your conscious soul. Pay this demon with your flesh and they will leave the fruits of your mind intact'

So shields up my dear and trust in your ability as I do.
The King needs you!
P :o)

Reading this made me nearly throw the damn letter from the window and hightail it out of there but like a magic word, the Oracle's last sentence had me hook line and sinker. I knew this wasn't ever going to be as easy as just walking up to Leivic, getting some answers, along with a happy note and some plane tickets to where I would find the Oracle. Nope, not me!

The letter was a mind twister if ever there was one and left me with more questions than answers. I wasn't certain that by the end of this little 'game' of hers that when finally meeting her, I wouldn't be tempted to shake her by the neck instead of the hand!

I drove closer to the warehouse she'd written about, just in case I needed a quick getaway. Christ, I was starting to feel like Jackie Brown being dragged into all this. What was next…a gun for my birthday? Well, after reading that description it was looking like a better idea by the minute!

As Little Red I got out of Big Blue, umbrella in hand and walked over to the metal door. I tried the handle but had a feeling it wouldn't have been that easy, when I found it locked. I debated whether or not to knock for a moment, but I decided to trust my gut and hold back. I lowered my fisted hand back from the door and decided to look around. Thinking this, now I was really feeling the part. Forget about just the gun, now I was thinking about adding a long beige trench coat.

"Female version of Columbo, that's me! Just short of a good head rub, one cigar and I have cracked it." I muttered as I rounded the corner. I don't know what I was looking for but I thought back to the letter and knew I was most likely supposed to find a ladder.

"Bingo!" I shouted when I saw the alleyway. There was a metal fire escape on the side and although I had never used one, I remembered there being one in almost all American movies that had alleyways in them. I walked closer and looked up at the series of ladders and metal balconies they were attached to.

"I hate heights." I muttered looking around for something to stand on. The first ladder up needed to be pulled down and it was only when I couldn't find anything that my mind went back to the clues the Oracle had left me.

"Haha!" I said in triumph as my mind clicked in gear. I lifted the end of the umbrella and hooked the last spindle on the ladder to then pull it down with a groan. It was stiff but once it moved the first bit it started to play ball. It came down with a rush and I fell backwards landing with a thump on my behind.

"Smooth Columbo…real smooth!" I picked myself up and patted my coat free from wet dirt. I bent back down to pick up my umbrella and started to climb to the next level. I tried not to look down but of course I did, without anyone saying the standard movie line 'Don't look down'. I seriously needed to get a grip…preferably one that wouldn't let go at the wrong moment. I also need to stop watching movies!

When I made it to the top I saw a window that was half open and all I needed to do was push it all the way up and I was in. I unfolded myself and soon found I was in a messy looking office. The desk that was near the window was piled high full of paperwork that had long ago become beyond organised. I moved the worn chair out of my path and made my way to the only door. Once out of the office, which smelled like someone had a mouldy cheese fetish, I took in a deep breath and looked around the massive open space.

It was a fairly large warehouse with a metal balcony all the way around the top that only seemed to lead to a few doors and I gathered these to be more offices. Looking down, I could see pallets of boxes piled high and all wrapped together with clear plastic. There was also a forklift and a few handheld devices for moving heavy items. But that was it, not a soul was in the building…or at least not one I could see.

I had to walk around the edge to get to the staircase at the other end and the sound of my booted feet on metal grating was the only noise to be heard… and it wasn't a comforting sound.

I did a quick check of the other rooms, the one with 'Manager' on the door was locked and the others empty, so I continued down the staircase. The main part of the warehouse was a bit like a shiny maze of clear plastic towers and a chill crept up my spine when I realised just how many shadows in this place could be filled with these 'Pishachas Demons'.

"This is insane." I whispered out loud as I made my way around them and gingerly checked every dark corner, although I needn't have bothered. As I soon heard a cackling laugh that sounded like a combination of wood burning and a child's high-pitched giggle, I knew I had been found.

"I love the smell of chilled flesh in the morning…like coffee to you humans." A strained voice said from further away. I wrinkled my nose at the thought of getting anywhere near someone who I smelled like breakfast too, but at this point, did I really have a choice?

I zigzagged through the piles of boxes until it opened up into what looked to be a loading dock. I could see the big rolling doors and some sort of conveyor belt. But it was the two red glowing orbs in the dark that had me stopping fast enough to tip back on to my heels.

"Lose the jacket, Tricks!" He snapped and I was sure I could hear the clicking and grinding of teeth at the order. I couldn't yet see him as he remained hidden in his favourite place, using the shadows to his advantage. I did as I was told knowing now the reasons behind my dress…I just hoped it wasn't like dressing the Salmon before the buffet opened!

As I peeled the jacket back I heard a sharp intake of breath and I purposely hid my umbrella behind my back as I moved my coat. I tucked the handle into my belt at the back, so it hung out of sight. I had a feeling it was going to come in handy pretty soon.

"Throw it away, up on that crate," he ground out, all the while still gnawing those teeth. What was he doing back there, filing them into sharper points?! Did I look that chewy?

I did as he said with a frown, as I really liked that jacket and doubted I would be given the time, when running for my life, to have the chance to grab it.

"Ah, now that is better, come closer," he said and now, instead of the grinding teeth, there was more of a slurping sound, like he was sucking back up the saliva that was dripping down his chin, if he even had a chin.

"Umm…I think not, no in fact, I think I am good right here." I said in my firmest tone. He started laughing again and the sound made bile want to rise up. There was something so disgusting in the sounds he made that even without seeing him, I was repulsed.

"Silly, silly, silly…if you don't come closer, then how are you to retrieve this?" He said and I saw a shadowed arm come out from the darkness holding an envelope. I fisted my hands at the sight, wishing I knew how I was going to get that letter with every pound on my body still intact. I mean, most girls liked the idea of losing a few pounds but the Hannibal Lecter diet wasn't one I wanted to try any time soon!

"Let's cut the spooky shadows crap and cryptic messages that are really just giving me a damn headache now…what do you want for that letter?" I said losing my patience and letting my frustration take control of the situation.

"They say that you are f…"

"Feisty, yes I know." I interrupted dryly.

"Fresh." He corrected back and I shivered.

"The price is a penny for your thoughts or a pound for your flesh…which do you value more?" Nice saying I thought but doubted it would make it as a bumper sticker!

"My thoughts are the payment I choose, but first the letter." I said knowing with the shield I had in place, if Lucius couldn't have cracked them then this lower Demon would have no chance, so let him try as I walked away. Well this was the plan, I thought with hope.

"I accept, although I must say what a shame it is that I wouldn't be tasting the marrow from your bones…that colour suits your skin." It was one thing being told 'nice dress', but saying that how pretty I would look bleeding to death was quite another and even in the supernatural world I wasn't about to take that as a compliment!

"Jeez, thanks. Now can we get this over with." I snapped and as soon as I said this I heard the envelope skidding along the floor. It stopped right at my foot. I picked it up quickly and stuffed it into the top of my boot until it was flush against my leg. As soon as I straightened I felt it. It was like someone was pulling at the edges of my brain with one of those tiny metal hooks the dentist uses to scrape plaque from your teeth. It nicked and scratched away at the seams but it couldn't get in. Then it tried something bigger and replaced the hook with claws. It was painful in a strange way but after a few minutes of concentration, the pain receded and soon its clawing gradually seeped away until it was nothing but a murmuring around the edges.

"Impossible! Impossible for a human! Give it to me!" The voice grew into a growl and I took a step back.

"I said GIVE IT TO ME!" It screamed, and the sound cracked the windows, making one give out and smash to the floor behind me. I jumped and held up my hands.

"Hey, it's not my fault you can't feed from me, we made our deal." I said playing dumb.

"Then your flesh will just taste all the sweeter!" It said before I finally got my first glimpse of the creature itself.

It stepped from the shadows and I screamed at the sight. The first light to hit the Demon sizzled like it was being burnt but the further it came forth, I soon realised it wasn't its own skin that cooked it was the skirt it wore that was human skin sewn together like a horrific patchwork quilt. Soon the room started to fill with the smell of charred skin and burning hair. Some pieces of his demonic uniform even had tattoos from the pieces of flesh he had taken from humans. As he stepped closer the skinsuit was made like a coat that had thick straps criss-crossing all his torso and it reminded me of a straight jacket made in Hell.

One arm looked broken and twisted back to lie flush against his back while the other, a long and thin black bone, had several joints as though it belonged to a spider. It had a pincer on the end that clicked as it snapped out and back in on itself. The claw type bone looked as if it had been carved out of flesh as it bled from the tip and it alone was the size of my hand.

When the last of him came into view, it was the face of a man with long, grey hair, centre parted and it hung down his torso in two strands straight as a board. His eye sockets were impossibly deep and the two eyes staring at me with a mixture of hate and feeding lust were bleeding tears. Like two pools overflowing from the source, they flickered as something in him started to ripple from his smoking chest.

The nauseating smell was making me keep swallowing my own bile back down, but when he took the last step and I saw what his face was doing, I could no longer keep it back. The rippling had travelled up his chest to his neck and then started to literally rip his face apart. The split started at his chin and spread up his face, spraying blood out in a fine mist.

Once the blood cleared the air, it left me staring at a face cut in two, only now with tiny rows of teeth running vertical up the sides of the hanging flesh. His face had now become one massive sideways mouth and his eyes were the only things spared from the change, as even his nose had become two nostrils inches apart.

I turned my head and heaved up my vomit, finishing just in time to move out of the way. His one arm had swung out to grab me and missed by so little, I had felt the whoosh of air from the action on my face. As I was taking steps further back something in my mind clicked and one word flashed like a neon sign.

'Shield'.

In one swift movement I brought the umbrella I had back round from the hook of my belt and pressed the button. It flew out and I held it out in front of me hiding myself behind it. It covered my dress perfectly and when I heard the roar in frustration, I knew he couldn't see me. I heard the movement of a frantic arm looking for prey as it blindly whipped this way and that. I took little steps back, not knowing how well it relied on its hearing but not willing to take any chances. As soon as I thought I was far enough away I stopped to look around for an exit. To get back to the stairs I would have had to have passed 'Big Ugly' and I now realised why that name was picked for him, as it was oh so very fitting.

I saw on the other side an exit door and I made my way towards it making sure to keep myself from view the whole time. It was slow going walking backwards but I soon made it. I let out a sigh of relief when I pushed on the bar in front and it opened near where my truck was parked. I fumbled with my umbrella while running for the door and it was only when I was safely inside my vehicle that I could breathe.

I didn't feel like waiting around here while I studied the letter, so I turned Big Blue around and squealed the truck down the road back to the guard who let me through with a wave. I only just managed to make it out of sight before I cut the engine, threw myself out the car to throw up again on the side of the road. When nothing was left, I spit a few times to get the taste out of my mouth and got back in the truck.

It wasn't what you would have called my finest hour, that was for sure, but at least I had done what needed to be done. I tried to tell myself this over and over but it didn't help when trying to open the envelope with shaking hands. I pulled the letter out feeling something weighty in the corner of the envelope but left that for later.

I unfolded the page and thought my eyes were deceiving me for a minute but no, I read it over and over again and then said the first thing that came to mind,

"Son of a Bitch!"

CHAPTER NINE

PAID FOR MY WASTED HOPES

I just couldn't believe that all I had gone through was for a piece of paper that said what, another damn riddle!

'If Alice is sick of Wonderland then pull an ET, But if she wishes to meet the Royalty down the Rabbit hole, then wait ten minutes for one to show up'

And that was it! I screamed out in frustration and fisted my hands. How that was any help to me at all I didn't know, but one thing I did know, was that I was being led on a merry dance! Question was how did I know what the bloody steps were without any music? All this cryptic crap was getting me no closer to Draven and I was close to jacking it all in. I mean I had just nearly become a main course for a Demon to chow down on and for what...? A letter and a...

I tipped the envelope, just remembering there was something else in there and something weighty fell into my gloved palm.

"A coin?" I said looking down. It was a misshapen silver coin which looked like it belonged in a museum. It was so old it could barely even be classed as being round in shape. On one side had the head of a person, man or woman I couldn't tell, but they had their mouth open and their tongue hanging down. Tiny round circles surrounded the head that could have been curls or snakeheads, I couldn't tell. I turned it over and the other side looked like an anchor with three symbols around it at different points.

I don't know how long I stared at it but when another car passed me it brought me back from my trance. I put the coin back in the envelope along with the pointless letter and started the truck. All the way home my mind kept going back to that coin and what I was supposed to do with it. Of course, it was at this point my truck decided to give up for the second time and I cursed like a sailor as I pulled it over.

Old tricks came back and I hit the steering wheel in hopes the truck would know yet again how pissed off I was with it! I got out, dragged my hands through my hair and tried to calm down. This was turning out to be one Hell of a day and it wasn't even past morning yet.

"I doubt I will get another chance at seeing Big J," I said finding that my own comfort in this situation was to talk to myself like a crazy lady that lived with a shopping trolley, collecting cans. I once again saw the smoke coming from the grill on the front and I wasn't about to burn my hand twice in one day doing the same stupid thing, like touching the bonnet.

Well, it looked like I only had one choice. I got back in the truck and fished my handbag from under the seat where I had stuffed it and rummaged for my mobile.

"Time to phone…*home.*" I said slowly and then dropped my phone along with the penny in my mind.

"Phone home! That's it!" I shouted reaching for the letter I had stuffed angrily back in the glove box. I read the letter again and groaned out loud.

"I don't know what you're playing at Pythia, but I am starting to see you've got one pain in the ass sense of humour. Ok, so I will keep playing…ET indeed." I said shaking my head at the last part. So she was saying if I was to call Frank, game over but if I waited here, for only she knew what to show up, then I was still a piece on the board. So that is what I did, I waited.

It was almost the longest ten minutes of my life as I

painstakingly waited for each number to change and when spot on ten minutes hit, I saw help coming my way. I got out to meet the tow truck as it pulled up in front of me. I watched as a stocky guy got out of the truck and approached. He was about five foot ten but was square in the shoulders and had a shaved head that he rubbed on his way over. When he lifted his gaze to me, he looked uncomfortable for a moment and when he looked me up and down, I realised why.

I was still wearing my dress and with the combination of gloves and heavy black boots, I didn't exactly fit the expected profile of someone broken down at this time in the morning. I bit on my lower lip and when I still felt the remains of lipstick there, I winced. I really hoped he didn't think I was a working girl.

"Are you Keira?" He asked in a deeper voice and I frowned at him.

"How do you know that?"

"A guy came into my garage as I was opening up. He told me that a girl called Keira in a hot…umm…red dress was in need of a tow." He said rubbing his head again and it looked to be a nervous habit. When his gaze finally found mine, I was surprised to see light green eyes and a rough but handsome face. He had week old stubble on a strong jaw, a flat nose that added to his roguish charm and a pair of full lips. And I hadn't missed the blush his little 'hot' slip up had caused him. Although I really didn't see why, as I felt like a swamp critter at the moment, with wet hair and no doubt a red nose due to the cold the early morning brought. I missed my jacket already.

"Well, I appreciate it." I said not knowing what else to say.

"Hey, you're British!" He said and then looked as if he instantly regretted it. He walked past me to my truck to hide another blush.

"Sure am." I said in a higher pitch than was needed, but the smile he flashed me to the side told me that he was thankful for my light-hearted response.

"Let's see what we got here then, can you pop the hood?" It was amazing how many times you could hear the same sentence in the space of a few hours, from two very different guys.

"I will do but I can tell you now what's wrong." I said and he straightened from the bonnet and folded his arms. He had a playful glint in his eyes as he said,

"Oh really?" I smiled back when he raised an eyebrow.

"Yes, Mr oh really..." At this he gave me a beaming smile and I knew if I wasn't already in love with the world's most handsome man, then this smile would have made me melt. I went to my door to pull the latch for the bonnet. By the time I closed the door he was still waiting for me to elaborate.

"There is a small leak in one of the pipes from the radiator. I know I should have been watching my temperature gauge so it didn't overheat but I...well, I had more important things on my mind at the time... anyway, I think I might have warped the metal and blown an overhead gasket." I finished, and he now looked stunned. He actually had to clear his throat and I laughed a little when he turned from me.

"Let's take a look, should we?" He said, his voice dropping an octave. I tried not to notice when he covertly adjusted his jeans slightly. He looked at my steaming engine and started nodding his head.

"Well sugar, you know your stuff, I will give ya that." I laughed making him look my way.

"Not really...I kind of...well I broke down earlier this morning and some guy helped me then. I just remembered what he told me and reeled off the same stuff to you." I confessed, and this granted me another beaming grin.

"I can see I am gonna have to watch myself around you." He laughed out a husky sound and rubbed his head again.

"Ok sugar, I am gonna have to get her hooked up and tow her back to my shop, can I drop you off somewhere on the way?" I giving him my address and he nodded. I stood back to let him work and he told me to wait in the cab as it was warmer in there. At first he had tried to give me his jacket but I convinced him I was fine. Just before he was about to strap my poor truck up, I remembered something vital.

"Wait!" I shouted and ran to my truck door.

"Sorry, I forgot my bag and stuff." I said making him shrug his shoulders and motion for me to go ahead. I reached in, grabbed the most important thing which was the frustrating envelope and my bag.

"Thanks." I said letting him get back to it.

We were soon on the move and after a few silent minutes he startled me by reaching across me while driving and offered me his hand.

"I'm Edison Tucker but my friends call me Eddie or Tuck." He said as I shook his hand.

"ET!" I blurted out and he raised his eyebrows.

"Sorry, I just mean…your initials, are ET right?" I said, now being the one to blush.

"I guess, hey…you're not comparing me to a short, wrinkly alien are you, 'cause man, I will tell ya, that will hurt any guy's ego?" He said joking, making me laugh and shake my head at the same time.

"Sorry, I have this bad habit of speaking without thinking… I think I need a new brain filter or something." I said hoping that letting him know I was a little mental would help. He let out a mighty laugh that shook his large frame.

"I think your brain is just fine…*damn fine*." Did I hear that last part right? I chose to ignore his whispered compliment, but I couldn't hide the damn blush that went with it.

"So, was that guy your boyfriend?" The question caught me off guard.

"Sorry?"

"I mean…sorry it's none of my business." He looked uncomfortable now and I put my hand on his arm before I could stop myself.

"Which guy?" I asked feeling my pulse quicken at just the thought…why wasn't I even thinking straight. I mean someone had walked into this guy's workplace and told him where I would be. Did the Oracle have someone working for her on this little game or could it have been someone I knew?

"He never told me his name, but he paid me for the tow and more than enough to fix what's wrong with your truck, I just guessed he must have been your boyfriend is all."

"This guy paid for the work?!" I said a bit dumbfounded.

"Yeah and I am guessing with that tone, you don't know

who he is?" I just shook my head at him and gave him a blank look of pure confusion.

"Apart from paying for the job, what else did he say?"

"Well it was weird 'cause he told me not to hurry with fixin' your truck, 'cause you won't be needing it straight away…and I am taking by that cute wide eyed look of yours that this is not the case?"

"Umm, that would be a big Hell no! Why would anyone say that?" This last part I asked myself out loud. He shrugged his shoulders and then jumped a little as if remembering something.

"I almost forgot. He also gave me something to give you when he paid."

"What was it?" I shouted eagerly grabbing his arm again. Man wasn't I the touchy feely one today, I thought letting go of the poor guy.

"Sorry, I guess my social skills need working on today." I mumbled.

"Hey, don't go saying sorry for touching me…I mean…oh shit, I didn't mean that sexually or anything…shit! Now look who is the one that needs to find their social skills." He said rubbing his large palm over his shaved head. I laughed thinking this had been one Hell of a morning.

"Let's start over, my name is Keira, I have a broken truck, that hopefully you will be able to fix, because I have a real soft spot for that hunk of junk, and the guy you met wasn't my boyfriend." I said shaking his hand again, making him grin at me. That look had me regretting all this as I now thought he got the wrong impression that this was flirty…was this flirting?

"Eddie, the idiot that keeps putting his foot in it and will, without a doubt, thanks to my mad skills as a mechanic be able to fix your hunk of junk." I laughed and slapped him lightly on the arm.

"Hey, less of the junk bit!"

"Hey yourself sugar, you said it first and besides…she isn't that bad." He added with a sideways smirk.

The rest of the journey to my house continued on in this playful conversation and I found I liked Eddie and his easy, blushing smile. That was until he pulled up to my house and asked me his next question,

"So Keira, I…umm, well I wanted to ask you if you fancied going for a drink sometime…or maybe, I don't know, like dinner?" Right at this point my mind got slammed with a vision so strong I couldn't breathe. I don't know how it happened or where it came from, but it put me on a crossroads with two paths to choose. To the left was a sign that said 'Blooming Orchard Drive' and when I closed my eyes that path filled my mind with an onslaught of images.

It started with chatty dates, evenings filled with laughter thanks to Eddie's playful manner. Then nights sat kissing on his battered couch in the flat above his shop. Teasing nicknames like 'ET' for him and 'Hot Red' for me. Introductions to friends and family. Him holding little Ella and shaking hands with Frank after having a beer from out of our fridge. BBQ's, birthdays, Christmases all merged into one. Then a simple wedding flashed up and a beautiful man in a Tux who had shaved for the occasion.

Then there it was, a sign we drove past that said 'Blooming Orchard Drive' where a little quaint house that needed painting and a new fence sat. What came with it was a montage of snippets of our time there. Chasing each other with paintbrushes, that ended in a tangle of limbs on the floor in one of the rooms. I swallowed hard when I saw us making love and me calling out a different name.

The visions only stopped on the cruellest of all. I was being wheeled into the hospital by an anxious Eddie at my side and my breathing was laboured in pain. My hands were protectively on my pregnant belly, as I was ready to give birth to our first child.

Then time dragged itself back at such a speed it was like the sight one would see in a blur going too fast for our eyes to keep up. It snapped me back to that same crossroads and had me facing my one other path. This one was named,

'7 Breaths to make, to 7 Steps to take, to 7th Heaven you will wake'

One step in this direction took me to one vision and one alone…the only one needed.

I was back in Draven's arms looking up at him. He raised his hands to frame my face and he placed his forehead to mine. I saw his lips move but I didn't need to hear the words to know what he said, it was as clear as the sky we stood under, as beautiful as the summer sun which shone down on us. We stood on his balcony and Ava landed next to us but we didn't look her way, we couldn't move and stand the thought of turning away from each other, I couldn't, not as he told me,

He loved me.

I was suddenly slammed back to the now and turned to see Eddie waiting for my answer. I felt my heart pinch in my chest as I looked into the eyes of the man who could no doubt bring me a life filled with happiness. But it just wasn't enough. It would never be enough. I knew that without the help of any vision. I knew that, thanks to this heart that beat inside of me for the only one person that would ever own it.

The other half of a beating muscle that kept my blood still pumping around an empty vessel. Empty, until I could step back into those arms and feel him as he gave me back my soul…

Dominic Draven, my soul's keeper.

"I'm sorry Eddie, I would love to say yes and would… if … well…if I wasn't already in love with someone else." I said biting my lip and feeling like I had just sealed a fate with a locked door, one as thick as a bank vault. He gave me a little head nod but the disappointment was clear.

"I figured a beauty and funny sweetheart like you wouldn't be single. He's a lucky guy, whoever he is." He said lifting my hand and giving the back a little kiss. I was so touched, I couldn't stop myself from giving him a hug and I felt him breathe me in, making a shudder vibrate through his chest.

"Thank you for asking Eddie, and someday I have no doubt you will make someone a great catch. You take care of yourself…oh and my truck of course." I finished with a wink and he laughed. I opened the door and was just getting out when he stopped me.

"I almost forgot to give you this." He said pulling out an envelope from his jacket and handing it to me.

"Thanks ET," I said making him chuckle. We may not ever have a life together, but no one was ever gonna get to call him that nickname but me.

"You're welcome, Hot Red." He said smirking and I burst out laughing. I left his truck on a massive high and in the complete opposite mood to when I had left this morning.

I waved to him and watched him until he went out of sight. I then rushed into the house to find a letter left back on top of mine in the kitchen. It was from Libby saying they had gone shopping and were going to grab pizzas for tonight.

Normally finding no one here would have me feeling low within seconds but with this new letter in my hands and everything that had happened this morning, I was in need of the solitude.

I rushed up the stairs, whipped the dress over my head, dumping it in my wash basket and tied up my hair. I changed into some comfy clothes and sat on my bed, ready to read the next part. I opened it up and when I pulled out the thick wad I noticed the first part was in the form of plane tickets. I looked at the destination and like last time, one comment came to mind,

"Son of a Bitch!"

CHAPTER TEN

ROYAL PAIN IN THE CRYPTIC ASS

I looked down in my hands that not only held my ticket out of here but more importantly, my first real footstep in the direction to bringing Draven back.

"London." I said the destination out loud and flopped back on my pillows as I blew all the air out through my cheeks. It took me a moment to absorb it all and I had to shake my head to carry on with the letter. I picked it up and confusion hit me big time. It was an A4 sized piece of paper with only one sentence in the centre,

'Didn't fancy pulling ET?'

"WHAT!?" I shouted out loud reading it again and again. Was this it?! Was this all I was going to get? This was unbelievable and just confirmed two things, the first being that this Pythia was truly and completely nuts! The second was that, when I finally met this nutter, I was going to strangle her!

"No, I didn't bloody pull ET! What is wrong with you people, just talk normal!" I shouted at the ceiling whilst slamming the pathetic excuse for a letter down.

"Arrrggghhhh!" It was only when I was panting through my little rage episode that I looked down to see that the piece of paper had started to mist over. I could see little ink veins travel from the underneath around the top and they came together growing into thicker branches.

"What the Hell!" I whispered as all the branches joined together and swirled around until they suddenly splattered outwards making me jump back. It was as if someone had a water balloon full of ink and had just thrown it at the page. Then I watched on as the ink seeped into the page leaving only words behind. The first line made my mouth drop open.

There is no need to shout, I was only asking!
But as I now have your answer, it is time to proceed.
Good choice by the way!

I then couldn't believe it as I read on and it began like any other letter....

Dear Tricks,

Well that was exciting now wasn't it? Ok, so now it is time to crack on and flip the coin. The next steps will take you further into a place you have never known but have faith young traveller, as it won't be your only friend on this journey.
First you must go back to where it all began and take steps into the past that put you at the King's level. Only in his footsteps will the answers come into the light.
A coin is just a payment for the ferryman but when kissed by Angelic Royalty it becomes a key into the palace. Take this key to the Hellfire gates and the mouth will drop at the sight of the depths Charon will go. Cross over to the other side with aid from which payment is granted and walk the path your lover's fate will take you.

There you will find your King and with it your answers,
Now is the time to put pen to page for the riddle it dances,
To find the Ahoy and your deck,
Place your true name in order of its peck.

The last letter in your name is where you will begin,

Then jump to the start, find 3 A's, put two in the bin.
To see the next 3 we'll leave your name behind,
And look back to my words where the same 3 you will find.
The same letter you will see in my madness of double 3,
Never have over a traveller's level lover for tea.
But then look back to what you find in half a ship's greeting,
Before continuing on to find where we will be meeting.

So back we jump to your name once again,
Time to jot down the doubles and leave out the N,
But the L we won't need until the last in the word,
Have faith in your King for this next letter to be heard.
For there is one who you love, this much is true,
But take him away and the answer left is in the do.
For with 4 in this Journey is Key to Royalty,
Here you will use 1 and then the A you find in loyalty.

The last word comes out on the page as a whole,
With the last step in my game for reaching your goal,
For a whistle and flute is the name of the place,
He pays at the end and leaves with his case.

Oh, and Keira…have fun!
P x

"Oh, you gotta be kiddin' me!" I shouted shaking the letter. This was unbelievable! Not only was I crap with riddles but this one looked like the Holy Grail, Mother of all that is Crazy and New York Times crossword level of difficult! Well, there went my good mood I thought as I dropped the letter. I don't know how long I sat there giving the paper my death ray look with my arms folded but sometime later my stomach rumbled at me. I got up, determined to leave the paper where it was, but it was suddenly as though it had become a bloody puppy, whiney about being left.

"Fine!" I snapped as I picked it back up and went downstairs with it in my hand. I slapped it down onto the kitchen table making it shake under the force.

"I haven't finished with you buster!" I said to it thinking that by the time I finally did meet this Pythia I was going to be as crazy as she was! I mean here I was talking to a piece of paper and all I wanted to do with it was ram it down the loo!

"Tea…I need tea!" I said turning away from the table and clicking on the kettle. I made myself a sandwich and was chewing angrily, thinking this was doing nothing for my poor molars. All the time I couldn't take my eyes from that damn letter. It was as if it had some sort of spell. Like a magical pull that wouldn't let me go until I knew its meaning. I rolled my eyes and wiped the crumbs from my mouth with the back of my hand.

"Fine, let's do this." I said and plonked myself down to start the unlikely task of decrypting this mad code. Five seconds later I was swearing at it. None of it made any sense and forget about needing a degree, this thing needed a technologically advanced little green man with a PHD!

"Holy shit Pythia, why didn't you just send me a bloody Rubik cube! It would have been faster…or here's an idea, why not just do it the normal way and write down a bloody address! Oh no, couldn't do that for me now, and while we're at it try stepping into the modern day and emailing me! Hell, I wouldn't say no to a homing pigeon as long as it didn't come with a quiz up the stairs…letter in hand of course.

I deflated into my desk chair and stared at the letter until the words started to blur and then slam, the first answer came to me.

"No way!" I shouted as I wrenched open the drawer so hard I nearly pulled it from its runners. I grabbed a piece of paper and a pencil. I ignored the first three lines until it got to the part about my 'true name'. At first I wrote down Catherine but then it didn't make any sense so I added the rest,

Catherine Keiran Williams

Then I followed the rules. The last letter in my name was S so I wrote that down. Then I found the next one was A so added that. The next part about 'madness of double 3' which I gathered meant 6 but that was all I could get from the next part, so I moved on. I had no clue to the 'Traveller's level lover' so passed on that as well.

So I went back to my name as it told me to and looked for the double letters in my name. Ok so there were two N's, L's and R's but after reading on I could eliminate N and L so wrote down R on my paper. Didn't get the next bit but saw the A, I would 'find in Loyalty' so added it to the page. So now I had SA letters missing and then R and A. I quickly scanned the next part and think it meant O. Yes because if you took away the one I love, which was Dom, and the answer was in the 'Do' then that would leave O, also meaning 1-1 =0, so I added that to the list.

"Ok so what next, I have the S.A….3 letters missing and then R.O. Letter missing and then A." I bit my lips as I read on hoping I was on the right track so far. I read the other part more slowly and asked myself what 4 had to do with 'This Journey is Key to Royalty'…when I saw it…that sentence had 4 Y's and it asked me to only use one and then an A!

So, after a quick scan of the rest I saw a bit that said 'But the L we won't need until the last in the word' so when I added that too it spelt out,

'S.A…R.O.Y.A.L'

After reading the last part it came to me quicker this time as the only thing 'Whistle and Flute' could be is Suit in cockney slang. And then the 'Pays at the end and leaves with his case' meant hotel so these two put together could only mean 'Suite'.

"I got it!" I shouted going back to the top and reading 'You find in half a ship's greeting' which she mentioned at the beginning in the 'To find the Ahoy and your deck'.

I wrote down the place she was going to finally meet me and couldn't help but make a 'whoop whoop' shout out. It might have taken me a few hours to figure it out but I finally made up the place name with the last letters…

'SAVOY ROYAL SUITE'

I knew it was one of the most famous hotels in London, so this could be the only place she meant. I felt so great after I finally figured it out and it was only when in the shower later that it occurred to me why she did things in this way. All of the letters so far only made sense after the next piece of the puzzle. So, if anyone was to get their hands on one of the letters then they wouldn't be able to make out where she was, or even what they meant. She told me in the beginning she couldn't just write down where she was and in this last letter, without the right name you wouldn't have figured it out.

It was crazy madness and frustrating as Hell, but you couldn't deny the genius in her ways. The one part I still didn't get was why hand over the coin and letter to someone that wanted to eat a piece of me? That one I think would have to be explained by the lady herself.

After I got out of the shower, changed, and dried my hair, I was starting to feel more human again. I picked up the tickets and the rest of the letters and hid them all in my top drawer apart from the last letter. I sat down on my bed cleaning the water from my ears with an earbud while I scanned the first part of the letter. It just felt like there was something I was missing, something I needed to do and soon.

It was a strange feeling, like some invisible hand was pulling at my fingers until I got it right. I mean everything so far she'd predicted. That was until the one choice I was given. Eddie was like the ultimate test to where my loyalties lay. It was like handing me my one and only chance at a normal life. Like the Gods had given me a way out of being the Chosen One. But why...was this my very own version of 'free will', the same chance at it that everyone else got?

At this point there was only one person with any answers for me but first I needed to figure this part out. I knew the key was in these words but it was like trying to make sense of a small child that can't quite talk yet. They knew what they were saying but as adults we already had the correct way of saying things drummed into us, so the key was thinking like a child. Was it the same with this? If I ever wanted to make sense of it I needed to think like her. Like someone who was trying to give me orders in a way only I would understand.

'First you must go back to where it all began and take steps into the past that put you at the King's level' Well, surely the only thing meant by this was 'Afterlife', as that was after all where this all began and to put me at Draven's level was in the VIP. The next part I didn't understand yet but I knew one thing, I would have to get back into Afterlife before I went anywhere. And it had something to do with this coin. So, with that in mind, I rooted out that envelope and placed the coin in my pocket, feeling comfort instantly on feeling its tiny weight in my jeans, so I continued to keep it there.

After a few days I had it all planned out in my head. The tickets said I was to travel on the fifth of July, two days before my birthday, which gave me enough time to put my plans into action. But there was one thing I knew I needed to do to make sure my plan worked and for that I needed Jack, which was why I was scrolling down to his number and calling him right now.

"Hey stranger, what's up?" His easy going voice helped calm the buzzing I felt in my head from being ready to burst with excess energy. All this cracking codes and planning a rescue mission had had me pumped and ready to go for days.

"Umm, nothing really, just kinda need to ask you something but don't want to do it over the phone…do you fancy meeting up?"

We arranged for him to come round after his shift the next day and this gave me time to talk to Libby. I didn't know how Libby would take to the idea that I was going to go on a mission on my own, to try and find Draven, so this is where I had to do the hard part…lie. I hated the thought of doing it but I hated the idea of her worrying even more. I knew after all this time that she thought Draven had broken up with me and she would have thought I was crazy travelling the world to find a man who clearly didn't want me, but what else could I have told her?

'Well see Lib's, Draven is actually in Hell, so me and an Oracle are trying to come up with a way to bust him out' … umm I didn't think so! So, as I found her nursing little Ella in the living room, I sat down near her.

"Hey, you ok?" She said shifting the baby, getting ready to wind her.

"Yeah, but I wanted to speak to you." I said dreading the next part that was until she interrupted me.

"Yeah, I kind of wanted to speak to you too." She said so I decided to see what she had to say first.

"Well, you know Frank's mum and Dad have that cabin they vacation at?" I nodded for her to continue.

"They asked if all of us wanted to go and spend two weeks with them, they invited you as well of course and I know that college has wrapped up for you, so I wanted to know what you thought?" She must have seen my face because she frowned.

"What is it?"

"Well, I was just about to tell you about my plans for travelling, I was asked to go with the rest of the gang and well, I really want to go." I was surprised when I saw her smiling.

"I think that's great Kazzy, I mean you could do with some fun, ever since that ass…"

"Libby don't." I warned just like I did every time someone tried to turn Draven into the bad guy.

"Why do you bother defending him…? You do remember what he did to you? I mean you should have seen what you were like…I…"

"Trust me, I remember Libs, but it's over now and I don't want to hear his name being dragged through the mud just for not wanting me." She looked as if she was about to argue her point further but something in my face stopped her.

"Fair enough. I am glad you're having some fun though and Jack's going, right?" She waggled her eyebrows at me and I groaned while rolling my eyes.

"Not this again." I muttered making her laugh, one that jiggled Ella. Not that she minded much as she had fallen asleep slumped over my sister's arm. We both laughed, and she cradled her. I had been hearing from my sister nonstop lately on her thoughts about how she thought Jack and I should date and every time I would stop her mid flow.

"So, when are you going, 'cause I hate to spring this on you but you know how Frank's folks leave everything to the last minute…?"

"Why, when are you going?" I asked hoping for sooner as it would make my plans much easier.

"Tomorrow." She winced as she said it but I smiled.

"That's fine Lib's, I won't be here long before I go either."

"But I will miss your birthday."

"Libby it's fine, it's not like it's an important one or anything and I won't be on my own, I will no doubt be celebrating it in some bar somewhere, having one too many and then being carried back to my room by…

"Jack." She giggled when I groaned.

"So, you guys go tomorrow for a couple of weeks, and I fly on the 5th, but I think we will be gone for most of the summer." She already knew this from when I first started talking about going to Europe travelling and this was where Jack would come into my plans.

"I can't believe I won't see you for ages." She complained and I gave her a little grin.

"I know but hey, we did it before, remember when you turned to the other side and married a Yank." I joked and she gave me a beaming grin which I copied.

"You will too, one day." I walked away smiling and whispered under my breath,

"I have a thing for old Persian Kings," as I took the stairs two at a time.

The next day consisted of me running around helping Libby get ready for their trip and as we brought stuff downstairs, Frank loaded it into their car.

"Remember the days when we could just pack one bag and drive off?" Frank complained light heartedly.

"What happened to those days?" He asked me, and I patted him on the arm as I handed him another bag loaded with baby stuff.

"You had a baby, Frank." He looked down at me with a massive grin and then looked over to where Libby was feeding Ella. He beamed at them both and then said,

"Yes, yes I did." Then he walked out of the door whistling.

When they were all loaded up and after an emotional goodbye from both sides, I was soon waving them off. I hated the thought of not seeing my niece for so long but I knew that what I needed to do next was one quest in life I had to take alone.

I was just getting out of the shower later when I heard my phone ringing. I made a mad dash dripping water all the way downstairs to get the phone. I picked it up and when I heard the dial tone I replaced the phone down with extra force. I hated it when that happened and was just about to go stomping up the stairs, when I heard something being pushed through the letter-box. I spun around and saw the letter emerge and I ran over to the door, but by the time I opened it, whoever had delivered it had gone.

I closed the door after searching for a good few minutes and when I was sure no one was going to jump out at me and say, 'yep it was me' I closed the door. I grabbed the letter and followed a familiar pattern by going to my room to read it. I wrapped the towel around me tighter and took off the one I had wrapped around my hair like a turban. I sat on the bed and opened the letter with shaking hands.

The emotions that would come barrelling my way whenever I would get another letter were heart pounding and breath stealing. It was like every piece of paper was another step taken towards Draven and this was my driving force.

'Those with eyes can easily see the changes one makes for the journey ahead, but no matter what the looking glass holds, it is our souls that don't ever change colour'

It was a tiny scrap of paper that held these words and I re-read them over and over until as usual, it clicked. She wanted me to change my appearance before I went anywhere.

"Ok, I get it." I said out loud and as soon as I did this, the words blurred and changed into something else,

'A Lion can't smell the other Lioness when she turns into a moth, even one burnt by the flame'

And then suddenly it started to burn in my hand from the inside outwards.

"Shit!" I said shaking it free before it burnt me. It floated in the air as the paper turned into tiny black pieces and then disappeared. So, what she said this time, she didn't want anyone knowing about. Well that was fine, but if I was going to change anything then there was first one place I needed to go and that was back to the beginning....

Back to Afterlife.

CHAPTER ELEVEN

BREAKING AFTERLIFE LAW

When I heard Jack's truck pull up outside, I was pumped and ready to go. I was even wearing all black for my mission. I had everything I needed in my bag and I could feel the coin in my pocket where it always was.

I walked out of the house, locked the door and ran over to Jack. He was such a gentleman, he even leaned over and opened the door for me.

"Hey you," he said and I smiled at him as I climbed in.

"Hi Jack, how are you?" I asked with a grin.

"I'm all the better now for seeing you." He said winking at me and I laughed. I don't think there was ever a point where Jack didn't flirt with me, so it would have been weird if he ever started acting any different. It was just one of those relationships we had and had never thought to change. It caused no harm and even the very few times he had seen Draven, he had been nothing but respectful around him. Jack was a good friend and this was the reason I had asked for his help.

"Hey, I like your hair that way, never seen it like that before but it suits you." He complimented, making me blush. I had never worn it like this out of the house before but tonight was different. I had tied it into a low ponytail and then plaited it, tying it at the end with one of the purple ribbons I got from Draven that he used to tie around a rose left on my pillow. It had grown longer since then and the end of my hair swung past my waist to my behind.

"Thanks and hey, new T-shirt?" I asked looking at his 'Black Sabbath' T-shirt that had some sort of brown helmet with a gas mask on the front which also had 'U.S TOUR '78' underneath the picture.

"Yeah RJ got me it, it's the one Tony Stark wears in the Avengers movie." I knew he was a big comic book fan and his favourite was Ironman.

We were just chatting about everyday stuff when he pulled into our dingy diner that had become a quick favourite, thanks to the laugh we had in there every time when doing our 'people watching'.

Once inside and as comfy as you were ever going to get in one of those hard booths, Jack put his menu down and said,

"Ok Kaz, what's up?" I took a deep breath and placed my menu down ready to explain my crazy plan.

"Jack, this is going to sound insane, but I need your help with something." His eyes widened for a second and he nodded for me to continue.

"You can't tell anyone though, not even RJ. You cool with that?" I asked first and he laughed.

"Well that's a given, tell that girl anything and then wait five minutes for it circle the town's ear for it to get back to you. Gotta love Facebook!" He said shaking his head smiling.

"Yeah, but we love her." I said before ordering a coke from the less than happy waitress.

"Ok, so we have established me not telling anyone but question still stands...are you gonna ask me...you know like some time before I need a walking stick?" I rolled my eyes and threw my menu at him.

"Ok, but please don't judge me." At this he held up his hands and said,

"I am never one to judge, you know that Keira."

"I know but this...well... you're gonna think I am crazy."

"I already do if that helps." I laughed with his teasing and we went silent as 'happiness' brought over our drinks.

"So what is it, you're not joining the circus are you, 'cause you know you need a bit more stubble for the next bearded lady?" I laughed and this time flicked my ice at him.

"You would know…didn't you date her last week?" I hit back at him making us both crack up.

"Ok, serious time…I…"

"Just spit it out, I mean jeez, it can't be that bad." He said so I did just that.

"I am going to London to find Draven, but no one knows." I blurted out and his face dropped.

"Why?" Was the only thing he said after minutes of stunned silence.

"Let's just say we have unfinished business." I said and shrugged my shoulders.

"I don't think that's a good idea, Kaz." His face got serious and I felt even worse for including him in this.

"It's been decided, and my flight has already been booked." I wanted him to know how serious I was about this, but I hated seeing the spark in his eyes die out, knowing I had done this.

"On your own?" I simply nodded at his question.

"And he has no idea?" Well this part I didn't need to lie about.

"No one does but you and the friend I am meeting there." He seemed to relax a bit on hearing this.

"So you won't be completely on your own?" He asked as it was clear he was worried about me.

"I guess not, but now for the part where I need your help."

"What do you need me to do?" He said not having to even think about it.

"I hate this, but I have no choice and I know it isn't fair…I wish there was another way…"

"Keira, look at me…I am your friend and I know anything you have to do is because you are most likely trying to spare the feelings of others." His words touched me and I reached across the sticky table and said,

"Thank you, Jack, that means a lot to me."

After the dinner I asked Jack not to drop me off at home as there was something I needed to do. He raised his eyebrow at me but didn't comment. We had just pulled up outside and a deep sigh released from me.

"It looks so barren, so empty." I said looking out to a building that had become a part of me and seeing it this way hurt something deep inside me, making me feel as empty as the place now looked.

"That's because it is, Keira." Jack said in a quiet voice that was full of meaning.

"Why are you doing this to yourself?" His question took me off guard. I knew he only asked because he cared, so I turned to him fully, shifting in my seat.

"Because if I didn't try then I would always have regret and I couldn't live like that. Just like you tried everything in your power to find Celina, I have to do the same before I reach that point where I know I have done everything and still I walk away with the same answers I started with. Only then I know it won't have been in vain…do you understand?" I asked softly.

"I think I do. But Keira, can I give you some advice?" I nodded for him to continue.

"Don't lose who you are in the answers. Sometimes, no matter the outcome and how much we tell ourselves it will just be better once we know, sometimes it doesn't work out like that. Sometimes…things are better left without an ending, that way it is easier to make a new one, one that makes us smile…sometimes…" He looked as though he was about to get choked up so he turned to stare out of the window, not looking at me but his next words cut deep, without him even knowing it,

"…things are better left…dead."

After I said my goodbyes to Jack, his words kept repeating round in my head as I walked up to the front entrance of Afterlife. I had told Jack that I would call Frank for a lift back as I hadn't told him that they had left already. I didn't need another person worrying about me and I had told him too much already. But I knew someone in the world needed to know the truth in case something happened to me. I wanted my family to at least have closure and I knew that Jack was the key.

I asked him, if the occasion ever arose, to back up the lies I had told my family. I needed them to believe I was travelling with them to Europe, when in actual fact they were taking a road trip to the Grand Canyon, Las Vegas and then on to California. I told him what to say in case anyone ever called him and we made up our different excuses together. I said I would call him and keep checking in with him at least twice a week.

By doing this I was trying to cover all bases. I had even found out the address for 'Transfusion' in Germany, being surprised they actually had a website. I had written down all the addresses, email, website and town, telling him if he didn't hear from me in over a week to get in contact with someone called Judas and tell him that Toots was in trouble, to then tell him everything he knew and that would help. Jack had been dying to ask questions about it, but when I started shaking my head, he got the hint. The one thing I did tell him was,

"Let's hope it doesn't come to that, but if something ever does go wrong, then know that is the one guy who will definitely be able to help." After telling him this, he didn't look relieved but more worried. It was at that point that I hugged him goodbye and told him not to worry about me, I had all bases covered. I just hoped I was right.

I walked up to the front door, but it was all locked up tight as it was last time. But the one thing I noticed that was missing was the note that I had hit with my fist, smearing my blood on it. It had me wondering who'd taken it down.

I decided to play at detective once again and take a look around. I decided my best bet was trying the access door on the side of the building close to the bins. This was one door that led straight through the back and then into the bar area. I walked up the few metal steps and entered the code I knew from memory. When the thing beeped at me I tried again.

"Oh come on!" I shouted as I realised someone had changed the code. Well, what was I going to do now, that was my only idea at getting inside? I stood back and looked up to the balcony higher up, which I knew was the one attached to the VIP area. Now, if I could just get up there somehow. I went through the most obvious options that came to mind at a time like this and the first being the quickest to cross off the list. Even if I had a ladder at home, I didn't have the truck to get it here. Big blue was still with Eddie and because I chickened out talking to him, I had Frank ring up and ask about it.

He was told that there were a few more things to fix than he first thought, and it would take a little longer, as he'd had to order a part. As it turned out I wasn't going to need my truck for a while anyway. Now a ladder was another thing, I thought as I moved back a few more steps.

I looked around and then a crazy idea formed in my head. Could it really be done? I stood to the side of the bins and saw that the thicker part of the ivy was within reach if I stood on them. I knew this was more than a little risky, but it wasn't like I could just call someone to let me in. I knew from bumping into Mike one day while out with the rest of the guys that everyone, including Jerry and Gary the twins who managed Afterlife, had been given the summer off and been paid well for the time. He told me how he couldn't complain about having a paid holiday, but what was weird was that Jerry had to hand over his keys, something he had never been asked to do before.

Of course, I knew why, but I faked my confusion to Mike the best way I could. So knowing this, it left me little option than the crazy one I was considering right now. So, I did the unthinkable as a person scared of heights. I put my bag over my head across my body, climbed onto the massive bin, using the metal on the sides as a foothold. Once I was up, I heard it groan in protest.

"Oh shut up, I'm not that heavy!" I said as I reached up and grabbed one of the thicker bits of ivy. I pulled at it to test my weight, but it was so thick and old that it was almost as though it was welded to the building. I looked down and saw there was a perfect part for my first foot and I took three deep breaths, told myself I was crazy, and heaved myself up.

I had closed my eyes as if waiting to fall backwards with the ivy coming with me, but when it didn't I let out a breath. I opened my eyes, saw a wall of green, lush leaves and took in the scent of earth into my lungs before reaching up for the next piece. If anything, it was easier than I thought it would be, as it was just like climbing a netted rope wall. I just had to keep my eye on that balcony ledge and I knew I would be fine, just fine. It was only when I reached out for the next bit that the pain I sometimes got in my hand had me slipping. I gripped on tighter with my other hand so I wouldn't fall but it took me a minute of panicking to get over the pain and near drop to my death, to carry on.

By the time I could reach out and touch the stone balustrades my hand was causing me a lot of pain, enough for tears to spring up. I just kept telling myself, not far now, just a little bit further, which was the only thought moving me forward. Finally, I was high enough to haul my leg over the side and I kind of collapsed onto the balcony in a heap. I pulled my sore hand to my chest and when I moved my fingers I cried out. I knew the first thing I would be doing when I got home was downing some pain killers and raiding the freezer for a bag of peas.

I got up and looked over the edge to see how far I had come. I couldn't believe I'd managed it but then given my situation, there was nothing more motivating than a vision of Draven in Hell. I looked down at my hands that were scratched and grazed from the rough treatment I had just put them through, but I didn't care, I just rubbed them down my black jeans.

Now came the tricky part, I didn't know what I was going to do if this door wouldn't open because I didn't know if I could manage to climb back down. Looking up to your goal and the skies was one thing but looking down to the earth and possible death was quite another.

I walked over to the double glass doors that prevented any view of the room beyond thanks to the ice like frosting and I held my breath as my hand raised. Well this was it, no going back now. I closed my eyes and reached out until I felt the cool glass beneath my palm. When I heard the whoosh and felt the air of them opening hit my face, I smiled. When opening my eyes I was welcomed with a lightning bolt of emotions.

"I'm home." I said as I walked through the open doorway. The sight and smell of the place filled every pore in my body and I felt my body start to hum inside. It was the same feeling I had when touching Leivic. It was as if my body was craving all things supernatural and being here now was the most comforted I had felt in a long time. I even felt the pain fade in my hand and I tested my fingers but there was nothing. I didn't know how it was possible but the building itself was healing me and I thought that if I hadn't had a job to do, I would have moved in here and never left.

I walked further into the room and heard the door close behind me. It looked so strange knowing no one had been here and as I walked around I looked right at the bar without its barman. I could never get used to the fact that Karmun wasn't here anymore. One of the other waitresses had taken over the duty until a replacement could be found, but I would feel a little pinch in my chest whenever I saw it. But as I moved past it that was nothing compared to the feeling that stabbed me at seeing the top table.

I felt like I was walking in thick mud with every difficult step I took towards my past. I came to stand opposite to where Draven sat and I was hit with the memory of last Halloween when I stood here challenging Draven with my bravery. That was the night I met Malphas and then only a few months later he tried to kill me. How my life had changed since that night and the thought brought tears to my eyes.

The room was mostly hidden in the empty shadows and it felt like the ghosts of those who once used to spend their nights here were all that were left. Seats lay waiting for their usual customers to come back. Metalworks of art that were once considered beautiful were left to hang like forgotten cars at a scrapyard. It had left the mysterious lure behind and had been replaced by something sad and depressing. The room was once a haven of supernatural energy that seeped from every stone in the building, now all that was left was an empty shell where life once blossomed. It felt like this room was a mirror image of myself and the empathy I felt was enough to have me shaking.

I walked around running my hand along the back of the seats as I went, until I came to the only one that mattered. I pulled the heavy weight back and I looked down at the space where the man himself used to sit. There, with my eyes adjusting to the light, I caught sight of something and just as I was about to pick it up and take a seat, a voice from behind me made me stop.

"What do you think you are doing?!" I jumped at the sound and whipped round to face the trouble I was in. After all, I had just broken into a locked building. I was just getting ready to explain myself when the figure stepped from these forgotten shadows.

My mouth dropped open but no words came out. I mean what could I say…was I dreaming? Did I have to climb that damn ivy again!? This could not be happening… could it?

"Keira?" He said my name and it pulled me from the dream and dipped me straight back to this reality and what I found there was both unbelievable and beautiful. That perfect voice, that strong frame and that Angelic face. I said the only thing I could manage through the fog of emotions,

"Vincent?"

CHAPTER TWELVE

THE KEY IS IN THE MISSING KISS

"Keira!" Vincent said my name and that's when I let all emotion take over. I ran over to him and flung myself into his arms. He caught me and for the first time since that dreadful day all was taken from me, I could truly breathe.

"Oh, Keira." He said as he held me to him and I soaked up the contact like a starved woman. He cradled my head to his chest using the full length of his forearm. His elbow was by my shoulder blade and his palm secured me, as his other arm held my back, as though he never wanted to let go. It was only when he started making soothing sounds as he looked down at me and making small comforting circles with his hand at my back, that I realised I was sobbing.

I had wrapped my arms around his waist as if I would never let go and I don't know how long we stood locked together, but he only eased his hold of me when my tears ceased. He allowed me to pull back and look up at him. His eyes held too many deep thoughts to catch just one, but when he smiled down at me, it was nearly my undoing. He gently used both his thumbs to wipe the remains of my tears away and I stuttered for breath.

"Do you feel better?" He asked me and I blushed at how I had behaved.

"Well, this is a better colour on you, that's for sure." He said brushing a single fingertip down the length of my rose-tinted cheeks.

"Vincent…I…"

"Hush now, I know you have questions Keira, but let us first sit, you look exhausted…come." He said as he took my hand in his and strong pale fingers tapped against my hand for me to look up at him. Once I did, I saw a flash of pain in his crystal blue eyes that turned them darker for a second. I wanted to ask him what was wrong, but he just smiled at me before he pulled me along. It surprised me when we didn't sit up in the VIP and it hurt me when we didn't go to the back through the doors to what was still his home. It was as though I wasn't welcome in that part of his life anymore.

Instead he led me down the main staircase into the lower part of the club, where I had only seen him twice before. The first was all that time ago when the Dravens first entered my life that night. The next was when he came to pry me from scratching my cousin's eyes out, but I never thought it was to be again in this situation. It was as if he was almost getting ready to escort me out of Afterlife for good.

I let myself be led down the stairs and closer to the entrance. When I saw those heavy carved doors, I pulled back on his hand and gave him my plea,

"Please don't…don't make me go…please." I said as he turned to me and I saw that same pain flicker through his pale blue eyes like a navy coloured lightning bolt. I had never seen Vincent's eyes do this before and worst of all I didn't know what it meant. He didn't reply but just held his arm out to a small seating area. There were four red velvet chairs against black lacquered painted wood, with a heavy iron round table in the centre. He positioned me at one of the chairs and pushed gently at my shoulders until I complied and sat. He towered over me as he took every inch of me in, before he turned to take the seat opposite me.

"I know I should be walking you out of that door Keira, but I will be condemning myself to a world of hurt if I do, so be damned the consequences." He said spitting out the words like they tasted foul.

"Oh no, not you too." I said knowing all too well what those words meant. When he raised a perfectly shaped eyebrow at me I elaborated.

"Before he died, he ordered you not to speak to me...didn't he?" I said in a voice close to cracking at the idea. That same pain sliced through him and I realised just how much his brother's death affected him. Just the words had him grinding his teeth and the colour in eyes swirling like the storm was coming in.

"Dominic's death was not anything you were ever supposed to go through Keira, but it has been decided by those more powerful than I. If I could have changed things, then I would have given my own soul to do so. I want you to know I never wanted this, not for you or for my brother, but the..." He looked as though he couldn't continue, as if he was first trying to swallow the lead before his next words could emerge, so I finished it off for him.

"The fates had other ideas." I said softly and Vincent's response surprised me. He stood quickly and threw the iron table out of the way. It flipped too many times for my eyes to catch but it travelled the width of the room before crashing into the stage area. I jumped at the sound and looked at Vincent as he lost his temper for the very first time in my company.

"Damn the fates, Keira! Damn them for involving you and damn them for taking my brother to the place he is! He is dead alright and in a place I cannot reach him, even as I have tried to swim through the madness of his cell, even he himself has thrown away the key and given up on ever being with the one he loves. So I say Fuck the fates and their very reason for this death! They took him from me just as they have taken him from you and even if I could deny my brother's wishes, how can I deny my King's?!" He shouted and his voice boomed around the room in the echoed anger I felt. It was the first time Vincent really scared me and I watched as his bare arms started to glow with the power he was keeping locked down. Thick corded muscles tensed and I saw the blue glow race through his veins as the Angel in him screamed out at the injustice.

At that point I knew how he felt, the pain that lanced through him and what was left of my heart broke for him. I sucked in a staggered breath that seemed to break through his anger. I watched as his chest rose and fell through his tight faded Harley Davidson T-shirt as he tried to calm himself further. He sighed as he looked down at me and closed his eyes before taking a few deep breaths. He then ran a frustrated hand through his tight curls that were cut short and then stormed back over to me to once again taking his seat opposite me.

"I apologise." He said in a voice that had not completely turned back to the softly spoken Vincent that I was used to.

"Keira, look at me."

"I am so sorry, Vincent…so…sorry…" I said not being able to give him what he asked for as I knew as soon as I looked into those eyes of his, I would crumble at the pain I found there, one that was so foreign to see.

Then I saw his hand snatch out to grip the centre of my chair in between my legs and I watched as the muscles on his forearm twitched as he pulled me to him. The sound of the chair's legs scraping along the slate floor bounced around the room like a charged current. I couldn't look up but saw his legs spread wide as I came closer to him and he only stopped pulling me once I was seated in between his legs. He must have been able to hear my heavy swallow.

"Look. At. Me. Keira." His voice was now nothing short of commanding and this was a completely different Vincent who now faced me, one that had me close to whimpering at his feet. I felt him grip my chin, first lightly and then more firmly as he lifted my face to his. There I met icy blue eyes ringed with navy and almost glowing with their intensity. He looked for a moment like he wanted to devour me whole and I couldn't have been sure that I would have been able to say no.

"You need to listen to me now. I want you to move on with your life. You deserve so much more and now you have a real chance at finding a happiness that was destined for you. The Gods want you Keira, but even they cannot make you do something you do not wish to do. Even our Chosen One gets a chance at free will, and this it seems, is your chance and my advice for you…take it Keira. By the Gods take it!" I stared at him in disbelief.

"How can you say that…how…?"

"Because it is your only choice. Embrace this chance and regret nothing because I will warn you Keira, regret is not your friend and will do nothing to your soul but grind it down." His eyes held me and I tried to pull back from his words. I didn't need this and he could take his advice back to the heavenly place from which he was born! As he took in my actions I saw his grip tighten on my armrests. He looked so desperate for me to hear his plea that he was slowly losing his grip of anger.

"And you know this?" Again, the colour in his eyes lashed out like an angry sea at my words.

"Yes Keira, I know this and this is not something I want for someone I care for." At this I bit my lip, a motion he followed with his heated stare.

"Someone you care for?" I dared to ask.

"Deeply," was his only reply but the purr behind every letter pronounced caused a tingled wave to wrack my body.

"I don't see what you are trying to protect me from Vincent, your brother is gone and you said it yourself that not even you can bring him back…what are you expecting me to do, just forget him and join lonely hearts online, post an ad in the paper and start dating again… 'cause you know I can't do that!" I snapped feeling hurt that he could even think I ever could. However, his eyes softened back to clearer blue skies and he cupped my cheek with his palm.

"No, I don't expect that of you Keira, but at some point I would like to know someone is taking care of something so precious. But more to the point, why are you here and why would you ever put yourself in danger by doing so?" He said taking my hands in his and turning them over as if seeing the healed scratches that were there but minutes ago. This had me blushing and pulling my hands from his, which he allowed me to do.

"I needed comfort and this place…well it became a part of

me too." I said not enjoying the feeling explaining myself invoked.

"You don't understand!" I said getting up and pushing him away when he tried to stop me.

"No, now you will listen to me!" I snapped as I walked away before turning on my heel abruptly and staring at him.

"You think it is as easy to walk away from this, as easy as just giving up and carrying on?! I mean Christ Vincent, it was easier getting bloody kidnapped, tortured and having some whack job think I was possessed by demons!" I saw him flinch at this but I couldn't stop what came next.

"It was easier taking a mirrored shard to my own skin and slicing my life further away with every swipe, than living this life after Draven. The only reason I even take a breath every morning is for the lives I would hurt if I didn't. Every damn day I think about joining him, I am that miserable walking this earth without him! I know he is your brother, Vincent and I know you are hurting, but telling me to just move on is like asking you to do the very same!" Once I had finished tears streaked from my eyes but not in sadness, but in pain and anger. I was panting and my actions had become stomped feet and fisted hands.

"I under…"

"Oh no, don't you dare say you understand! How the Hell could you, Vincent?! You still live in a world where you can at least draw comfort from those around you. You still wake to a world surrounded by those comforts! Me...well, I was ripped from those comforts and why, because Draven had some warped idea that it would be better for me…well you know what, screw him and you *and* most of all your sick, warped ideas of me living a better life because I am living in Hell just like he is!"

"I wake in my own version of it every damn day and every damn day I know it's because he put me there! So, what do you say now Vincent, still think I should meet a nice guy and settle down?!" I know I was blaming others but I couldn't help the pent up bitterness that had just been released. I had no other person that I could even talk to about this and now I had finally found one, I just wanted to erupt! And bless his Angelic heart, he just sat there and took it.

Once he knew I had finished, he stood and I burst into another pitiless sob and ran to him. He caught me and held me to him as I mumbled my sorry into his chest, one still wet from my earlier tears.

"Ssshh, it's alright, I have you…I have you now." He said smoothing back my hair and rubbing my back. After I really didn't have anything left this time I looked up at him.

"I'm so sorry, I didn't mean…"

"Yes you did and you had every right. Dom's reasons for sending you out in the world were not so you could feel alone, but to give you a new start, foolishly he could not be convinced otherwise. I thought…well…I thought this might happen but not as severely as it has. I didn't realise…I" He paused and tore his gaze from me as if seeing the answers there.

"What?" He locked his emotions with me then, with just one look and if his arms hadn't been holding me up I would have buckled to the ground. I knew his next words would be confirmation to how I had felt since that day.

"I didn't realise your soul had become so entwined, so locked in to the beings we are that you would not make it out in the world alone. I should have known, but none of us expected this outcome to be true. We thought the longer without Draven's essence, the easier it would become, not harder…I feel like we failed you." He said lowering his forehead to mine and the zing of energy it gave me just confirmed his words to be even more powerful.

"The fates failed me, no other. I cannot blame Draven for dying as much as I can blame you for going along with wanting the best for me, I just wish that this changed things, but I know you'll still have to leave me…don't…y…you?" My last word broke with just the thought and he couldn't answer me with anything but a nod.

"Then you now know why I can never move on Vincent, not while there is breath in my body and blood pumping in my veins. I cannot and *will not* ever move on from Draven, what is left of my heart won't let me. I thought he would have known this." I said looking down, as seeing the pain in his eyes grow with every word heard from me was just mirrored pain.

"I agree, he should have known and handled things very differently and I wish…"

"What? What do you wish, Vincent?" I asked knowing his answer would only be driving the spear further through my heart.

"Never mind, come, there is no place to hold you here anymore and no need to add to your torment, I will take you home." He said taking my hand and pulling me in the direction of the bar. I really wanted to know what he was going to say, but his next move halted me. He turned to face the stage and with his outstretched arm he moved the table he threw. It lifted and shot back into place with a simple flick of his wrist. The upturned chairs its destructive path had caused righted themselves and soon the place looked as untouched as when we had entered it.

I saw him swipe up a leather jacket from the bar where he had left it and he led me out through the very doors I had first tried. He pushed the door open and held it for me. Then he turned to the door and instead of moving away, I watched as he reprogrammed the code on the door in front of me. I smiled when I saw it was my birthday. I don't know why he did this, knowing I would no doubt use it to get in if ever I came back but when he looked over his shoulder at me he winked.

"Let's have no more climbing up the side of buildings, Keira." He said as he came down the steps to my level and he gently brushed a loose strand of hair from my face. I gave him a cheeky little grin and said,

"You know Spiderman is my favourite superhero?" This was the first beaming grin he gave me and it transformed his entire face into such beauty it was almost blinding. He grabbed my chin and shook it slightly, almost playfully and replied,

"I thought as much." He said then leaned down so close to my face that his next words were said over my lips,

"But let's leave the heroics to the professionals and the breaking and entering to the bad guys…yes?" I smiled at him and just shrugged my shoulders before walking past him laughing at my response. I could feel him following close behind and as we walked around the corner I could just see a lone motorcycle waiting there. I say motorcycle but what I really should have said was a black metal panther waiting like a predator for someone to ride on its back at death speeds.

I must have stopped dead as I was staring at it because he passed me, walking right up to it like meeting an old friend, or in this case a new one as it looked like it had just been driven straight out of the factory. He had also put on his jacket when behind me and the sight of a tight grey denim ass and fitted leather encasing his upper body was nothing short of mouth-watering. It wasn't right for me to admit it or to even think it, but a girl was only human!

He looked back at me and the grin he gave me was pure bad boy, one not expected on an Angel like Vincent.

"Is there a problem, Keira?" He asked doing a lousy job at trying to hide the humour he found at the expression on my face.

"Umm, no, no, not a problem, I will just wait for Frank to pick me up, that's all." I said thinking…actually scrap that… knowing, there was no way in Hell I was getting on that thing!

"Then we both know you will be waiting a while, when are they back…in two weeks?" He said surprising me and when he saw my stunned face he walked back up to me and his expression turned serious for a moment.

"Don't ever lie to me again...we understood?" I bit my lip at the new tone from Vincent and I wondered in that minute if he had taken his brother's shoes in the control department. He sounded very much the royalty that was in his blood in this moment.

"How did you know?"

"How and why is not important but your safety is, so don't ever lie to me about it again and we will be just fine. Now come on, time to get you home." He said taking my hand and leading me numbly towards the mass of black steel and chrome.

"Wait!" I shouted pulling back and I heard a sigh whisper from his lips.

"It's just…I don't want to go home." When he raised an eyebrow at me I quickly carried on.

"I need to do something first and I need your help." This

time he crossed his arms across his chest making the leather of his jacket groan. That's when I noticed he now also wore black leather gloves and a naughty image flashed into my mind of him running them down my bare skin. Jesus, what was wrong with me, I mean this was Draven's brother for God's sake! I just blamed it on my fragile, comforted and sexually starved brain. Yep, that was it!

"Keira" He said my name and I blushed as I realised I had been eyeing him up like a candy stick, one I was almost panting to lick! Now this was embarrassing!

"Umm…sorry, where was I?" He at least had the decency to laugh about my weak moment and if anything he looked quite pleased about the way my eyes wandered.

"You need me to do something?" He purred and the way he lingered on that one word made me gulp. Oh I needed something alright, it was just a shame I would never let any other man give it to me but Draven…wait not a Draven, I mean Dominic…yeah that was better.

"Yeah, sorry, I was going to ask if you could take me somewhere…you know…to say goodbye." I added softly. He unfolded his arms and simply nodded.

"Alright Keira. Come on then, your chariot awaits." He motioned towards the beast with two wheels and I shivered.

"Don't you have a car around here somewhere?" He laughed.

"Didn't you hear…I am more of a biker than a petrol head." Now I laughed as a thought popped in my head and I made the next comment without activating that handy little filter that was supposed to stop these things from happening.

"Next you will tell me you are a lover not a fighter." My cheeks nearly melted when I saw his heated look.

"Now we both know you have been witness to both and I think it is easy to say which I prefer…given the right partner of course."

"Or partners?" I said letting it slip out again when I could have kicked myself. Where was the bloody filter anyway, on holiday?! Of course, I was referring to the time I had opened the door to find Vincent being kept company by two beauties in his bed…very, very close company…as in naked company.

I was glad when he laughed and was about to laugh with him until he quickly grabbed me around the waist and pulled me to him. My hands flattened on his chest and I shook as he continued to let out a rumbled laugh.

"Flirting will not save you from a ride on my bike Keira, if anything it will only get you on there sooner, so stop stalling." He pulled me over towards his 'ride' and I nearly bit through my lip at the thought of getting on that thing! I let him pull me to the bike that looked far too heavy to sit in between someone's thighs and that thought wasn't ever going to help with my red face that gave me away like a fire alarm.

I felt him come up behind me so if I decided to back out of taking this ride, then he would be there blocking my only exit.

"Umm…it's a nice bike." I said not knowing what else to say about something I could die on. I knew I was being a bit dramatic but for someone as cautious on the roads as I was, bikes I didn't understand. I liked to feel nice and safe when travelling killing speeds…boring… yes, but to be boring you had to be alive.

"This one I have been waiting for. She's a Moto Guzzi California1400, custom of course." He said with pride and I smiled at hearing the passion in his voice.

"Of course," I said playfully and I felt him poke at my side for my cocky comment. Then he leant down to softly speak in my ear like a lover's whisper,

"She is a handmade beauty, every single component a perfect combination of power and sleek grace and with 96 horsepower she is a forceful touring bike. That said I will take her gently as a beauty should be for her first ride with an Angel." As I sucked in a quick breath at his sexual words I could feel him smile at my neck. I didn't realise I even closed my eyes until his next words snapped me from his promised words.

"Time for something cute." He said with a cockiness that was new on Vincent. I looked to see him lifting a black helmet to my head and I ducked out of the way.

"Umm, actually I think I will pass on this, maybe I could just get a taxi or something?" At this he laughed.

"You're not scared are you, Keira?" He said making me frown. I knew his game and I didn't like it, so I crossed my arms to show him so. Of course, he just laughed.

"I didn't think so, not the brave beauty I know so well." His complement momentarily distracted me and before I knew it, he had the helmet over my head.

"Hey!" I moaned.

"Hey yourself, now hold still while I adjust the strap." He said first holding down my arms from trying to take it off and then his hands came back up to rest on my neck. My pulse pounded and it wasn't just down to the ride he wanted me to take.

"We don't want this pretty little head of yours to get hurt now do we?" He said as his fingers first tapped against my pulse point before going to tighten the strap under my chin. He smiled as he felt my heavy swallow of doubt.

"And is there much chance of that happening?" I asked unsurely.

"Not a single one." He said with a level of certainty that burnt away my fears.

"Leg over, sweetheart." He said and before I could have blinked he was on the bike and patting the space behind him. I looked down at the Emblem of an Eagle pressed into the saddle and just hoped that these weren't the only wings that would keep me safe.

I took a deep breath, took the last few steps towards the bike and did as I was told. I felt awkward mounting the bike as if ready for it to start bucking or something but the knowledge of its heavenly rider was the only thing forcing me to sit down. Once there, Vincent looked over his shoulder at me. The way the back part of the seat was raised put me at the same level as him.

"Hold on to me and put your feet here." He pointed to the footrest further back from his own and that's when I noticed his booted feet. I couldn't help but shiver as I noted the heavy biker boots with steel caps. He must have taken this for worry about the ride, which could have easily been a factor.

"Keira, don't worry if you get scared or want me to slow down just tap my stomach and I will pull over…ok?" I nodded when he looked around and then when he seemed satisfied, he flipped my visor down and he kicked the stand back with one foot before taking the weight of the bike. I gripped on tighter and heard him chuckle.

"So, where are we headed sweetheart?" He asked me before firing up the beast.

There was only one answer to give and only one place I wanted to be for this next part, so I didn't hesitate,

"Draven's cave."

CHAPTER THIRTEEN

CUTTING OFF THE REASONS

He didn't say a word about the choice of destination I had in mind and instead of a comment, he just put the key in the ignition and started the brute of steel that thundered beneath us. It was my first experience on a bike and I couldn't help but grip onto Vincent like my life depended on it. I held on until my fingers ached and we hadn't even moved yet. I didn't want to be a wuss and tried to convince myself it was just a bike…just a bike. Yeah right! I mean the fact that it was one mean looking bike was one thing but the fact I was sat on a bloody engine was quite another. I was just about to tell Vincent that I couldn't do this when the bike started to move and I was left with only the urge not to die.

I tightened every muscle in my body to grip on with great force to the steel between my legs and the Angel in front as we started to pick up speed. I couldn't help what came next as I found myself tapping madly on his stomach but when I felt it vibrating I just knew he was laughing at me…Not surprising, he didn't stop.

After about ten minutes of trying to convince myself I wasn't going to die and I had in fact faced worse things than this in my life, I finally started to relax. I watched the world whiz by and soon I felt a type of liberation. It was as if my fear was being replaced by pure adrenaline and it was almost like getting drunk on fun. I couldn't believe I was actually enjoying this, even though the first corner we went round had me shrieking out in my helmet. But the way he controlled the bike was nothing short of beautiful…and oh, so goddamn sexy.

The time fell into a supercharged hole that shot us right to our destination in what seemed like only minutes. When I saw we were at the top of the mountain track, I actually felt disappointment that it had come to an end. It was only when I felt Vincent's hand on mine and tap a few times that I knew that was my cue to release him. He had already cut the engine and once I let him go, he got off first. He didn't say a word as he undid my helmet and lifted it off me.

"Well, look at you smiling."

"Wow, that was…just wow!" I said knowing I was beaming up at him. His grin made my heart stammer but I tried pass it off as I told myself it was just from the ride nothing more.

"Umm…Another biker in the making I think." He said and when I wrinkled up my nose he laughed.

"Maybe not."

"I loved it, but I don't think I would ever be brave enough to ride one myself." At this he smoothed back some hair that had come loose from my plait and sweetly planted a kiss on my forehead. I didn't know what prompted it and I didn't ask.

"Be careful when getting off, you might be a bit unsteady." He said giving me more room to swing my leg round. I felt tiny on this massive machine and even more so with Vincent, who was at least six foot two. He wasn't as bulky as his brother but he was still made from pure muscle on a sleeker level. His body was made for stealthier actions, his fighting skills more of a graceful dance that were the steps to a deadly song. Even his Angelic looks could be turned into a weapon with just one stare. He was like his brother in the way of the essence of leadership that just poured from him and it was easy to see the warrior commander beneath the cool countenance his eyes usually held.

As soon as my feet touched the ground I did the pathetic girly thing and nearly toppled over. He caught me as if he had been ready and pulled me to him for the second time.

"Easy." He hummed and I wondered if he was aware that his arms had tensed around me. It was only when I placed my hands on his chest that he let me go.

"Thanks." I muttered shyly, still filled with the lush scent of male musk and leather.

I brought my bag round to the side, happy that it had survived the journey and glad I had brought one with me that had a long strap that crossed over my body. There were things inside that I was going to need.

"So, how did you know about this place?" I asked Vincent as I thought that no one but Draven and I were supposed to know about it. When I first told him my destination I had been surprised when he didn't ask me where, not that I would have explained in full detail but getting to this point on the mountain was as close as a human like me would ever get to it. But Vincent hadn't asked for directions or questioned why, he had just told me to hold on and off we went.

"Dom told me about this place when he thought you might have been in danger." He answered as he walked to the edge to look over at the sheer drop.

"Why would he think that?"

"Because Keira, he may be King, but even Kings have enemies." He said, again without looking at me.

"He *was* King but now…?" I let the horrible question linger and it was only then that Vincent turned to me and the pain there was understandable.

"Now…well that danger is over at least." At this I shook my head making him raise an eyebrow at me but I didn't comment. No, instead my mind just went back to that day in the warehouse and I wondered just how many more times on this journey were going to be filled with dangers just like that one.

"So when was that?" I asked getting back to the subject.

"Just before we left to look for the Oracle." He said and he shrugged his shoulders as if it wasn't a big deal. So, I pushed further.

"Did you at least find her?"

"No." Was the only answer I got and one I knew with absolute certainty was a lie. In a way the fact that it came from an

Angel just made it all the worse and it was hard to hide the fact from my face. But nothing more was said and I walked past him further to the cliff's edge.

"This will be fine." I said kneeling down and opening my bag but I jumped when I felt myself being picked up.

"Hey! What are you doing?!" I said as I was being adjusted so that he had me in a more secure hold. He had taken his jacket and gloves off and I saw the way his biceps bunched when he had one arm under my knees and the other holding my back.

"Hold on to me, put your arms around my neck." He said ignoring my surprise at suddenly being picked up.

"W…why?"

"Because this isn't the cave, Keira" He stated calmly as he walked us both to the very edge.

"Vincent?" This time I was rewarded with an Angelic smile that was underlined with crazy intent.

"Oh God, not again!" I said grabbing him around the neck and burying my head there.

"Don't worry sweetheart, I fly my wings better than I drive my bike." Once he said this I looked up to see a pair of massive pure white wings erupt just as he took that last death step off the cliff. I screamed at our free fall and my plait fluttered past my head along with my stomach.

"Vincent!!!!!" I shouted and I could feel him laughing as the air tunnelled around us as we plummeted to the bottom. Then I felt a great whoosh and his heavenly wings opened and took us straight up like a deploying parachute.

"Come on, open those eyes for me, it's beautiful up here and it would be a shame to miss it." He spoke into my hair and I was surprised he could even manage words with the way I held on to his neck. Hell, it was a miracle he could still breathe!

"I think I am good like this." I said into his neck and being this close to him, the natural scent I inhaled was near intoxicating. He chuckled and I felt him tickle my back.

"Ahhh! What are you doing! Don't you dare do that again, you got me?" I said sternly and this time he laughed harder.

"Oh, I wouldn't dare me, not from up here…now come on,

just open your eyes and take one peek and I promise not to tickle you again…or I could…"

"Don't you dare...! Ok, ok, I will look for heaven's sake!" I snapped, not that he was bothered by it but at least it stopped him tickling my side.

I lifted my head from the little nook I preferred to stay in and opened my eyes for longer than a few seconds. Once I did this I found he was hovering at the same level for me to see the sunset over the mountains. It cast the skies out like fire and the National Park was the perfect shadowed frame to such beauty. The clouds created patterns on the landscape and beams shone down in the distance. It was one of the most beautiful sights I had ever seen this earth create and if I wasn't being held over the deepest ridge so many feet in the air, then I would have loved nothing more than to paint its splendour and magnificence.

"See, I told you it was worth a look and as if I would ever drop you." I looked up at him and he winked at me before we started to move again. I looked at the next beautiful sight behind us as his wings manipulated the air around them. They were so graceful and pure I wanted to smack him about lying to me earlier, knowing that nothing this heavenly should be allowed to sin.

He looked ahead and we changed directions slightly making me slam my eyes shut again. Like this I was being held more directly over the immense drop and I was happy when I felt Vincent's muscles pull me closer against him.

"Keira, we are here." He said after a minute and I peeled my eyes open to find the dark cave. He let my legs slide down him and he held me steady until he knew I wouldn't wobble all over the place like last time.

"It…it looks so cold." I said wrapping my arms around myself and feeling the familiar tugging at my heart. Vincent didn't say anything but just turned from me, lit one of the torches on the wall and walked back to the edge.

"I will give you the time you need." He said in an emotionless tone and I watched as he launched himself up in the air with a little bend of his knees. I ran to the rock wall to grip on as I saw him fly off to where his bike was sat on the top of the mountain.

"Oh Vincent." I whispered as the whiplash of his playful mood disappearing stung. I knew he was hurting just as I was but there was something else I couldn't place, almost as though he had felt betrayed by someone. Of course, he knew how Draven had died so maybe that was it. Was that the reason he cursed the fates, had he felt betrayed? 'Cause if that was the case then didn't we all? Or did it have something to do with the Oracle? Could she have betrayed them and if so, what were her plans for me…was this journey, I was so blindly throwing myself into, safe?

There were just too many questions and never enough answers for someone like me. I was now out of the loop and that fact hurt a lot more than what I wanted to fully admit, but the main question was…should I be telling Vincent about my plans? Every gut instinct in me told me no, but what if all this was a trap? Oh God, this was just hopeless!

I pushed away from the rock once I saw Vincent as a tiny speck walking over to his bike on the far side and he sat down as if to wait for me. Well I sure hope so, 'cause otherwise the next people to find this cave would be in for a shock finding 'cave dweller' Keira's remains curled up on a massive bed.

I looked around the space and became consumed with the image of Draven and me. His hands holding me down as he found home inside my body. The endless kiss that had rooted his soul to mine every second that connection lasted. Every word uttered in that blissful sense of peace just being together created. Everything hit my chest like a tsunami of memories that made my knees give out. I landed on the bed and once again my body was overtaken with the depth of my loss. The very level of it was enough to render my body useless as the only thing it wanted to do now was weep, sob and cry out at the cruelty my life's path had been thrown down.

I couldn't understand why. Why lay my body down for only one person to take, someone I was supposedly made for, my one true soul mate if such things exist, why then let us join together in a love so strong it could withstand all we had been through and still they decided to take him from me…? It just didn't make sense!

"I just want him back! Please…please…oh Gods hear me now…I am on my knees begging! BEGGING! Pl…ple… please." At this point I lost it and fell forward into the bed and gripped the covers so tight I could hear them start to tear. I sobbed all I had left out into the one place I knew was so special to Draven and it just so happened to be the place I gave a dark Angel my virginity.

But where was my dark Angel now?!

After all the tears had broken the dam and all memories had seeped from my veins, I finally sat up. I took one last look around our special place and knew that there were only two possibilities that were going to happen. I was either going to be back here one day with Draven or if everything else failed, then I would never see this place again. Either option meant there was only one thing left for me to do.

"Time to say goodbye."

I pulled my bag around and took out the two things I needed. One was a letter I had written to Draven and the other was a large pair of scissors.

"I know there is no way for me to bury you or even attend a proper funeral, so this is the only way I know how to tell you one last time that I love you and that I will never stop believing that one day we will be together again. Whether in this life or the next, I will see you again but until then, I wanted you to have a part of my body along with that part of my soul you own. And well, I know how much you love this part so, now it can be yours forever. I love you Dominic Draven." I said and then I held the blades to where I needed to cut and closed my eyes as I felt them cut through every strand of hair.

I felt the weight lifted from my head and it felt strange without something I had carried around with me every day for years. But now it was done and I shook my now short hair around my face and looked down at the plait that lay by my side. I had cut all my hair off for Draven to have and I just hoped that one day he would know what I had given him.

I picked it up and placed it on top of the letter before

covering both with the pillows. I didn't want the weather getting to them, if it even could from this far in but just in case, I kept them hidden. I got up from the bed, stared down at it for what could be the last time before turning around to find an Angel stood watching me. With the sun now set, all that I could see was the shadow of a man with wings and my heart hammered in my chest for a second as I thought it was Draven. But then a voice cut through the illusion and I sucked in a breath.

"Keira…what…what have you done?" Vincent asked as he stepped forward into the light. His eyes were framed by a frown, but his voice was a soft lure.

"I buried him and I said goodbye the only way I knew how." I said walking past and the strange sensation of the ends of my hair brushing against my neck had me touching the tips with both hands. I looked out to the night and the moon that had graced the land with its full glow.

"You didn't need to do this…you…"

"It is done Vincent, now please take me home." I said knowing that by home I meant Afterlife, but also knowing that the place he took me would be far from there. I felt him come up behind me and he placed his hands on my shoulders then down my arms.

"I wish…" He started to say something but then stopped and after a moment of hoping he would continue, he just cleared his throat and I could feel him shaking his head behind me.

"It matters not what I wish and it is like you said, it is done now. Come, I will take you home." Then he hoisted me up into his arms once again and this time I couldn't help but hold him to me tighter than before. The comfort having him so close gave me, was something I needed right now and I was not in the right mindset to hold back the deep currents of my emotions.

So, I clung onto him like I never wanted him to leave me and when I felt the kiss planted to my temple, I knew he knew it too. He held me tight and we took off into the night.

I didn't know how he knew where he was going but soon we were descending, and the moon could be seen glinting off the chrome on his bike. He set me down, put back on his jacket and gloves and lastly my helmet. All was done in silence, as there were no words for either of us to find after the great sadness that had infected us once more.

We rode home but this time I didn't get the same thrill from the ride as I did earlier. I knew why, it was easy to gauge, as the bike took me closer to the time that we would have to part ways and the thought that I might never see Vincent again was too much to stand.

I even tensed as my house came into view and Vincent knew it because he covered my hand with one of his and gave me a little squeeze.

"It will be ok." He said once he cut the engine, getting off his bike and turning back to face me. I really didn't know who he was trying to convince with this statement because it wasn't ever going to be me. However, I didn't respond, instead I just nodded my helmeted head before fumbling with it to try and get it off.

"Here, let me." He said pulling my hands back down and going to the strap. He pulled it off me and then looked down at me all wide eyed. I bit my lower lip and he smiled. He reached out and rubbed a strand of my cut hair in between his leather covered thumb and forefinger.

"You know it suits you, although it makes you look even more innocent and cute, something I never thought would be possible." He started doing the same with his other hand and soon he was smoothing the hair behind my ears. His leather hands remained on either side of my face for the longest time but no words were said. There was one moment when it looked as though he was going to even kiss me, but abruptly he shook his head, as if to clear his mind.

I was left feeling breathless but once again he helped me off the bike to keep me steady. He even walked me to my door as if this had been a date. The thought made me blush.

"Would you like to come in?" I asked and for a second I saw his eyes flash lighter before a darker shade overtook them too quickly.

"You know I can't, Keira." He said quietly and I nodded in

shame. Yes, I had known that, but a girl could only hope couldn't she.

"I know, but since we were already breaking the rules I thought that by you staying a little longer wouldn't hurt." I said trying to justify something his look said I didn't need to.

"But it will hurt Keira, it will hurt both of us and even now, this should not have happened but…"

"But?" I couldn't keep the hope out of my voice.

"I could not have turned you away for all the Gods' commands, let alone my brother's." He closed his eyes for a second and his long dark lashes created shadows on his high cheekbones.

"Thank you, Vincent."

"For what, Keira?" His eyes snapped open and he took a step closer to me.

"For helping me today and for not turning me away like you should have." At this his eyes seemed heavy lidded by my words.

"You are welcome, my sweetheart." His voice turned to warm honey and I felt myself take a step closer to him. Soon we were so close together you couldn't have got anything between us, but we were just staring at each other like we were trying to take every single piece in, to store in our precious memory bank.

"I should go." He finally spoke but it was far from breaking the spell as despite his words, he didn't take a step from me.

"Me too." I uttered but again it didn't change things. My heart was pounding and he must have been able to hear it. I didn't know what was happening between us, but it not only felt electrically charged but also magically. What I wanted and what was right was being merged into something else and the need for him to place his lips to mine was confusing. I had never wanted anyone to kiss me as badly since Draven and that thought was sobering.

Then another factor came into play as I felt a tiny vibration of the coin in my pocket. 'A kiss by a Royal Angel'. This was what it wanted but could I really take that step, could I do that to Vincent?

While I was thinking about this I watched Vincent as he raised one hand to my cheek and then he frowned.

"Not enough." He said and before I could ask him what he meant he raised one of his fingers to his mouth and he gripped the leather between his teeth. I gulped at how sexy a simple action could be but the sight of Vincent gripping his leather gloves in his teeth as he pulled them off was definitely a hard swallowing moment.

Once he had both gloves off his hands he threw them to the ground and went back to running his fingers down my cheeks and neck.

"You are so beautiful, so perfect… it pains me to know I won't be able to see you like this again." I could have cried on hearing this but instead, I reached out and grabbed onto his jacket.

"I wish you didn't have to leave me." I whispered and this time he ran the pad of his thumb over my lips that had started to tremble.

"And I too wish I didn't have to leave you, but I have no right to you, Keira…no right at all." He said leaning his forehead to mine and I took a shuddering breath.

"I…I wish…"

"Please don't finish that sentence Keira, or nothing will hold me back and we would both regret the aftermath greatly." He was right and I forced my body to pull back on hearing it. He let me and the coin vibrated harder in my pocket. I took another step back and I watched as he did the same. I knew part of my quest required this kiss, but I couldn't do it. I couldn't take that from Vincent, even if it wasn't for the wrong reasons. I didn't want Vincent to feel any guilt at all and I knew that if we would have taken that step then it would have hurt both of us. So I would just have to take my journey without the coin but keeping my heart intact in the process.

"Goodbye, Keira." He said and it was as if I could hear another crack split its way down to my fragile heart.

"Goodbye… Vincent." I said and felt the single tear drop down as my eyes overflowed on a blink. He took in the motion and looked like he was going to reach out again but then held himself back. Then he nodded and turned around to walk back to his bike. I painfully did the same and made my way back to the house, this time letting the tears flow more freely without him looking. I was waiting for the sound of his motorbike to fill the silence and at least then it would mask the sounds of my pain.

"Oh, fuck the aftermath!" I heard Vincent shout and when I turned back his way, he was storming his way back to me. Before I could fully take in what was happening he gripped the sides of my head, slanted my face and took possession of my lips.

And I finally got my wish…

Kissed again by an Angel.

CHAPTER FOURTEEN

FLIP SIDE OF A COIN

I couldn't believe what was happening, but just because I couldn't believe it, it didn't mean I could have stopped it. It was fast becoming an unbreakable force and one certainly to be reckoned with.

My gasp was an open invitation for his tongue to sweep in and taste me, which managed to light up every nerve in my body. If I thought just being around the supernatural had my cells singing, well this had them all screaming out the chorus!

He took things deeper and fisted a hand in my shorter hair that he then gripped and turned my face to enable him to delve even deeper. If I thought a kiss by an Angel was going to be a gentle and soft affair, then how wrong I was. It was all mind consuming, heart stopping and blood racing to jump into a red ring of fire!

His other arm anchored my body to his as if I was never going anywhere again and at that moment, I didn't want to. It was a kiss I would never be able to forget and one that would be imprinting itself onto my very skull, it would be that deeply embedded in my memory.

I don't know how long it lasted, as time seemed to belong to us and do with it what we wanted, and right now we wanted it to last a lifetime. I don't know when it clicked for Vincent that forever wasn't ever going to be in our cards, but it didn't make him just drop me and let me go. No, instead he pulled back slightly making his kisses softer until he trailed them to my neck and back up again until he hovered over my lips.

"That is how I've always wanted to kiss you and it scares me at how something so wrong, felt so right. But I promise never to touch you in such a way again, as much as it pains me to say so, it is the only way it could ever be." Even as he said this he still held me to him and dipped his lips to mine one last time. He lingered there, tasting the seam with one last swipe of his tongue and I looked up to find him smiling. I couldn't help but do the same.

"Thank you," I said and he winked at me.

"If you're thanking me for attacking your sweet lips, then I must be better a kisser than I thought." He joked and I poked him in the side for being cocky.

"Oi!" But he just laughed harder before pulling me in for a full-bodied hug. I wrapped my arms around him and I felt him breathe me in deeply at the neck before letting me go for a final time.

"Thank you for your greatest gift, Keira, I will forever treasure the memory." He said taking my hand and kissing the back of it. I then watched him walk back to his bike and this time, he didn't look sad but more…liberated.

"Wait! Just tell me, what did you mean…what gift?" I shouted to him, staying closer to the house, afraid if I went over there I would never let him go. He looked up at me and I could see his eyes flash for a second before he answered me.

"The brief encounter in giving me the gift of your heart." He said and then put the helmet on his head and before I could blink, he had skidded the bike around and rode off out of sight. I turned back to my front door, took the coin out of its hiding place and kissed it on each side before replacing it. It even hummed in pleasure.

I was sat back in this lonely house that for once didn't get to me. It was like that kiss had given me a kind of hope and filled me with peace. I couldn't find one single emotion that even touched on guilt or regret. Vincent had given me a gift also and I wasn't sure he knew it or not. The heart I thought broken was healing and doing so in the knowledge that one day soon, I might be seeing not only him again, but also his brother. It was as though in that one kiss I felt the power of the coin come to life and with that my hope bloomed.

Now I was sat in the kitchen, where I had stayed since coming in and was picking at the sandwich I had made whilst on autopilot. I thought the sight of Vincent leaving me behind would mean a night of needing a vodka bottle just to get by, but it wasn't the case. Every time I touched my lips it took me back to the way he heated my body and it was nice to know it was still working right.

It was only when I felt my neck as I was burning up that I realised something. I dropped my crust and bolted from the chair.

"Shit!" I said as I ran up the stairs to the main bathroom. I still hadn't even taken off my jacket or my bag, I realised as it flapped around me when I bounded up each step.

I came to the main bathroom and practically skidded to the mirror to check out the butcher's job I had done on my hair.

"Double shit!" I cursed as I took in the straight cut of my hair that now hung longer at the front from where I had cut it in a hairband. I moved my hair back and forth and knew I would need to cut it into more of a style, so I took out the scissors and started snipping away.

By the time I had finished it didn't look that bad. I had first levelled it out as much as I could and then trimmed little layers into it as I had once done for my friend in high school. I feathered the shorter parts round my face into a side fringe that flopped into one eye. It took me longer than I thought but after using a handheld mirror behind me, so I could see the back, I managed to get it into something that didn't look like I had cut it with my teeth.

I mean, I wasn't about to win any hairdressing awards, but I was just happy I didn't look like someone had put a bowl on my head and cut around it…I didn't think I would suit the monk look! Of course, the next part was harder to do. I walked back in my room and got out a plastic bag that I had kept the hair dye in, away from Libby. I knew I had no choice and there would be a few surprised looks when I got back from this 'Mission' but the most important thing was that I'd done as the letter had told me to and changed my appearance.

I didn't know how much of the supernatural world knew about me or whether they even knew what I looked like, but the less chance of me sticking out like the 'Lucky dip human Godchild' the better. Nevertheless, my hands still shook as I looked down at the colour.

I got changed into some old clothes Libby had given me that I wore to help her paint Ella's room, so that I wouldn't get hair dye on any of my clothes. I then went into the bathroom to do the deed and didn't come out again until a different Keira was looking back at me in the mirror.

One with black hair.

Hours later I found myself sat in my room, once again going over all the letters and that's when I decided to take a closer look at the coin. I fished it out of my pocket and my first thought was a panicked, 'it had been swapped'. But then I held it under my lamp and saw that the symbols had changed since the kiss and something told me this was all part of the plan.

The side that once held the head now had the Draven's family crest engraved there but the other side was even stranger. It was a large circle with a smaller circle inside but around the edge had the letters A.S.M.O.D.A.Y and then an intricate symbol in the middle. It started with a vertical line in the centre with a devils tail to one side. The other side had a U shape on its side with smaller circles attached and in the centre was a number two in roman numerals on its side. The last part had a tiny cross inside the design that would be easy to miss and it reminded me of the same cross a solider would have received for bravery.

By the time I had finished examining the coin my eyes stung from squinting to see all the minute details and I had to turn off my lamp.

I had no clue what any of it meant but the very fact that the coin had changed told me the deed was done. It had received the kiss and was now ready for the next part of my mission.

But was I?

Later that night I was just drifting in and out of sleep when I was transported back in time. I heard the same scratching at my window I'd heard on my second night in this house and the very same reasons for it went through my mind. Was it a cat, no we didn't have one, was it a tree, no there wasn't any close enough. This was when one name slammed through my system and I bolted upright.

"Ava!" I looked to the window and saw her sat on the ledge on a window that was now wide open. But how? I was just about to get up to go to her when I noticed Ava hadn't come alone.

There was a massive shadow of a man stood watching me from the corner and I froze.

"Don't be afraid." That voice! Could it be?

"Draven?" I whispered, too afraid it would disappear, and this living fantasy would go back to the confines of my life's most perfect memories.

"I shouldn't be here." He said this time stepping closer but remaining in the shadows and the second time hearing his voice, the beautiful reality was confirmed, it was Draven.

"You told me that once before." I said softly as he approached the bed. I couldn't move but I wished I'd had the courage to. I was more than stunned as this didn't feel like a dream but more and more like living, breathing, certainty that this was really happening and more importantly, it was happening now.

"How?" I asked and I wished I could have taken it back as soon as I saw Draven halt his footsteps. He didn't answer me and I hated the distance between us but more importantly, I didn't understand it.

"Draven?" I said after he just seemed frozen to the spot. I still couldn't see his face but from his voice alone I knew it was him.

"This is wrong, I should not be doing this." He said but it sounded more directed at himself than at me.

"What's wrong, why is your being here wrong…I…don't understand?" I said trying not to feel the massive weight crushing me down every time he spoke.

"I can't control it…I need to control it… I didn't mean to come here." He said but again I didn't know if it was meant for me to hear.

"Why are you saying these things?" I almost crumbled and broke down.

"I am sorry…so sorry, this should not be happening… but…" His voice sounded so strained, like someone speaking whilst lifting weights.

"But what? Tell me!" I shouted feeling more and more hurt by the second.

"But I can't help myself, it's not just my body that is drawn to you, but it is my very soul and it seems even Hell itself can't keep me away." He said and at this point I couldn't stand it a moment longer. I jumped off the bed, into the shadows and flung myself into his arms. He tried to move back at first but as soon as I reached up and pulled his face to mine, all resistance fled him.

He descended on me like a starved man and his kiss broke every rule. But I didn't care, he was here now and that was all that mattered. As soon as our lips connected, so did our souls reunite. It wasn't gentle and it wasn't soft, but it was undiluted raw lust and love combined. His mouth took possession of mine and claimed it with every move and every taste.

His hands gripped onto me like someone would soon be dragging me away and it was the point just before pain. Again I didn't care. If anything I wanted it harder, rougher just so that I could feel every hard inch of him. I was close to crawling up him like a cat and it was only when my hands went for his hair that something clicked. Draven's hair was shorter, cut close to his head and it didn't feel like the usual straight, thick strands that I remembered entwining with my fingers.

"Draven?" I said his name but then he lost all willpower that was holding him back, because the next thing I knew he had hoisted me up around his waist and was pushing my back into the wall, taking the kiss further.

I was panting and quickly getting lost in the feel of what I once had every day of my life, but all the while that niggling little feeling something wasn't quite right kept scratching at my brain. It was as if there was a miniature version of myself pounding on the window of my mind, screaming something was wrong. But I couldn't hear her words.

"Just…need…you." Draven's voice filled my mind and started to cloud out that same window. His touch, his smell, his taste all told me this was him, really him. The man I needed in my life and now here he was. He was really back.

"Draven." I said before he took my lips once again. I could feel him trying to tear my clothes from me to get to the skin underneath. I felt dizzy and lightheaded by the drug that Draven was injecting into me with every grip his fingers made. Of course, this tripled when his fingers dipped down and found my core. They ran down the centre and flicked at the bundle of nerves there sending my head back and a cry of pleasure to escape.

"Yes…yes." I said and he growled.

"Come, I need you to come for me." He said, his voice turning into that demonic creature that at this point couldn't be contained. It commanded my pleasure like it needed it to breathe. He drummed at the entrance, drawing it closer and closer until,

"Come!" He growled as he plunged deep with two fingers and this was my undoing. I screamed out my orgasm and he pulled at the waves as if feeding his addiction.

"Draven!" I shouted as he continued his sexual demands, trying to draw another out for his feast. He took my plea and pulled from my sensitive flesh that had now coated his hand with the evidence of my release. He raised it up to his mouth and sucked every drop from his fingers, all the while in shadow.

"I want to see you." I said but I saw him shake his head to indicate no, then he spoke,

"I want you." And then he carried me to the bed and I landed with Draven's massive frame caging me in. His large palms ran the length of my arms until he shackled my wrists and then drew them up over my head. He imprisoned me there and I saw the darkness as if he was pulling the night closer in around him.

"I need you…need to…" He sounded pained and I tried to pull against him to reach out for his face but he wouldn't let me. His hold on me intensified and he looked like he was shaking, trying to control something.

"They are… trying to take me back, I can't…No!" He shouted and I shifted my legs to grip around his waist.

"They can't have you." I said holding on tight but then his back bowed as if in pain but there was no bellow to indicate his suffering.

"Draven?"

"I…what is this…? Dominic no...! By the Gods you can't do this!" There was another voice in the room then and with utter horror, I realised it came from above me.

"What's going on?!" I said getting more and more panicked.

"No! Leave us, I need her…I need…" Draven said on a growl but then he was once again someone else.

"Not like this…don't do this!" The other familiar voice argued but Draven's hands wouldn't let go.

"No…she's mine…MINE!" The demon screamed and I flinched in his hold.

"Dominic, come back…don't do this…not to her, don't do this to her…*to us.*" And then it came with a flash of lightning, the horrifying reality that could never be taken back. And the next words just confirmed what the blaze of light had shown me.

"I need her, can't go back there, not yet…not yet…need her…Keira…" His voice was so full of pain, however that pain was far away from the figure of the man that lay above me.

"Now, brother! LEAVE NOW!" Vincent shouted and I screamed as the body above me flew backwards, all the darkness evaporating from him and then he landed on his back in the corner of my room.

I shot up and as soon as I saw Vincent getting up from the floor that was when I found my limit and the last thing I saw before darkness was an Angel running forward to catch me.

"I am so sorry…so…sorry…*oh…Keira.*"

CHAPTER FIFTEEN

IMPOSSIBLE DREAMS AND CLASHING NIGHTMARES

I woke up in a twisted mess on the floor screaming. I tore off the covers and got up trying to make sense of what had just happened. I didn't know whether I had just had a blissful dream or a disastrous nightmare but somewhere along the line, the two had merged into one, just like the Draven brothers.

I didn't know where my warped brain was at, but that dream had seriously thrown me. I deflated back onto the bed and I dragged the covers from the floor back around me, as if they would somehow make me feel safer. I wanted to know where the Hell my head was at dreaming craziness like that, but then I only had myself to blame. I mean really, what type of person was I, kissing Vincent like that…? I felt my mind screaming at me from inside, 'he was Draven's brother for Christ sake!'

I sat there shaking, feeling horrified with myself and the lengths I went to, to feel comforted. I should never have done that and now this was my penalty. A dream that quickly spun out of control and ultimately became a punishing memory I would have to hold with me forever.

After beating myself up some more, I finally dragged myself

up and tried to scrub the dream from my body in the shower. I felt both sick and ashamed, but the guilt wasn't just for Draven, but also for Vincent. There was no denying that the kiss we shared meant something deep for both of us and I didn't want to ever wish it had never happened, so I didn't really know what to do with it…that was ultimately my biggest problem.

After my shower I got dressed, went downstairs and forced some breakfast into my stomach. It was strange getting ready and not having a mane of hair to deal with, but what was weirder and harder to get used to was every time I caught my reflection I saw someone so different looking back at me. One of these times I had to take a minute to figure out some stranger wasn't outside the window peering in at me.

It was only when pouring my second cup of tea that something twigged in my head. Something that once I was in the same room with any Draven, flew straight out of my head and stayed there until now. I got up and rummaged in one of the kitchen drawers until I found a small taxi card that looked like it had spent most of its life in a man's wallet as it was still ass cheek shaped. I then called a 'Cab' and raced upstairs to get my stuff together before it arrived.

Fifteen minutes later I found myself sat in the back of 'Catch a Cab', leaning forward and telling a cool looking rock chick, my destination,

"Afterlife."

As we pulled up outside the massive building that looked more like a perfect setting for an English period drama rather than being a Goth nightclub, I felt the twinge in my chest. Even the building was like another person in my life that had been ripped away from me and seeing it this way, all closed up tight and not welcoming with life, it was hard to take in.

"Right Chicky, here you go." Said the cool looking taxi lady, who could have entered a Daisy Duke contest and come away with first prize. I looked to the meter and fished out the cash, including a tip.

"Just a quick question." She said slapping her glossy lips together a minute to judge my reaction. I nodded for her to continue.

"Why are you here anyhow? I mean, the joint don't exactly look like its rocking any time soon." She said as she scanned the closed doors and deserted car park.

"Someone's waiting for me." I told her in a voice that screamed 'emotional' and after a frown she handed me a card and told me to ring the number if I needed another cab and told me to ask for 'Jax'. I thanked her then watched her until she was out of sight.

Then I just stood there and took in the building as though it was the last time I would ever see it. I followed the green lines of the thick ivy that was closer to taking over than the first time I had seen its beauty. I flashed back to that first day and I found I was still overwhelmed by its imposing structure.

This was Afterlife and inside, I had found that in the literal sense in more ways than one. It both contained the elements of dreams and nightmares, Heaven and Hell's creatures and the living Gods of a world most people would run screaming from if they only knew the truth. But me…well I was running screaming into the arms of that world and praying with every step that it would take me back. So, with that in mind, I did what I had come here to do. I entered my Afterlife.

I now at least knew why Vincent had let me see the new code he'd programmed into the panel at the door. One look up at what I had climbed yesterday and I shuddered at the thought of doing that again. I think he knew right off the bat that my craziness knew no limits and at least this way he was ensuring that craziness didn't lead to a broken neck.

I entered the date of my birthday, one that would be with me in three days time and let myself into the club. The place was stark and eerie in its silence, but more so when I knew that not one soul but mine was contained within its walls. The bar area had been stripped of all bottles and the glasses had been covered in thick clear plastic. All signs pointed to a place that would be locked up tight and closed for the long haul. It was sad to see a place I loved become so forgotten and lost to me. With that in mind, I quickly walked through that large open space until I was stood looking up at the next heartbreak.

The last time I was here didn't give me long enough to

process the emotions that seeing this place again did to me. I could easily put this down to one big playing factor and his name was Vincent. As soon as I took one look his way, I think I even forgot where I was. But now…now there was no time for forgetting, there was only time for hurting.

I walked numbly to the focal point in the vast open space that was the main part of the club. I wondered what it was like for all those who came here and had those double staircases taunting them like that. What went through their heads when that one time each year they saw the Dravens descend on their little town and up those steps like royalty they could never touch? And then there was me, the only one to infiltrate that dream and find soul shattering love on the other side.

I walked up the steps shaking my head asking myself how I had even survived it all, when the final bullet to the heart was that damn chair coming into view! There it stood waiting for its master, one that wouldn't be coming home any time soon and one that made me run to its core like an anchor in the devastating twister that was my feelings.

There I found what I had dropped and left forgotten for the arms of an Angel. I picked up what I knew was another letter from the Oracle, but I couldn't open it yet. What I did do was what I would have done if Vincent hadn't found me and that was to crawl onto Draven's chair, curl up tight and let myself go. I allowed my tears to fall freely as I thought back to all the things I had lost and I told myself this was the very last time I was going to cry about this situation the fates had thrown me into.

I shook like a sobbing child and started to claw at the high back as if searching there for Draven's scent. I pressed my face deep into the padding and continued to take deep breaths, filling my lungs with what I thought was the last remnants of Draven's Godly fragrance and felt my body go tight, so tight everywhere just ached and I froze when I couldn't get any tighter. For then I knew each breath might be the last. I wanted to scream again in an anger that always came booting its way back to my gut and kicking me there until I was out of that precious breath. The need to have Draven back in my life wasn't just consuming but it was lifesaving. It was as though I was drowning in my own ocean of misery and I was kicking and twisting my whole body, trying to stay afloat.

This was when I saw it. This was the precise moment I saw myself that very night. I couldn't believe my eyes, just as I couldn't all that time ago. It was after the night with Justin and Draven had taught him what he thought was a very valuable lesson, one that meant not ever coming on to his woman. I say this because this was what he had told me days later.

But now I was looking back at myself, one with long blonde hair and a confused look that said my other self couldn't understand what she was seeing, just as I couldn't. I remembered that night, the one crazy moment I had witnessed this horrible space in time that was now confirmed to be my future. It was just before I walked into Sophia's playroom and found Draven dripping in beauties, all to teach me a cruel lesson.

I watched the moment my breath caught, and my step became staggered in the past. I wanted to scream out at her, to tell her to run from the hurt she was about to endure, but would that have stopped me? I mean, would I have really run a mile and hitched my way back to England, if I knew the outcome? The thought of all that time with Draven, even if it was going to get ripped away from me at some point, would I have really turned my back on that? I knew the answer to that one and it went a bit like 'not bloody likely'!

The image of my other self faded away like thick smoke being wafted by someone's hand. At this point I pulled myself together and forced my fingers to uncurl the letter I had subconsciously held to my chest. Then I got up and just because I needed to know, I walked over to the large carved doors at the back that led into the Draven fortress. I don't know why, but when they didn't open, it still caused that crater that was in my chest to erode further. I mean, I was expecting it, but that just went to prove the point that even the greatest expectations hurt like the Hell they put us through. Expecting the worst can always get worse and expecting the best can always get better. The lesson learnt in this still made me do daft shit and trying to open this door was one of them.

I just ended up walking away feeling even worse than before and these days it was surprising that could even happen. So, I walked over to the balcony, placed my hand on the glass and sucked in the fresh air in the hopes of cleansing the pain. Once there I used the light of day to read my next letter.

Kissing Angels is the price you pay getting into Hell,
For the time you spend there will be as quick as ringing the Bell,

As to what you find, then the choice will be yours,
I am only the map but you are the key to those doors,

So take heed of my warning, for it will be your last,
The quest you take will drag you under, hard and fast,

So learn how to swim my dear and make that current your own,
Ride the wave of doubt to your destination that will bring you home,

Being that of course…
'Roses in a Dome'

With that all said enjoy your flight Tricks,
And don't forget to add a drink to the mix!

P x

I stared at this for a few minutes and then noticed a few lines on their own written on the back, so I turned it over and read the rest.

P.S
In five minutes you will find, many black circles all entwined,
Suffice to say this booted man, will easily bring down this angry clan,
So rest assured and hold on tight, for Mr Handsome to take flight.

I re-read this part about three times before I heard the evidence of what the Oracle was trying to tell me. I turned and walked back into the VIP but as soon as I did, I froze. Voices were making their way up to where I stood and I looked down in horror as there were now five men dressed in what looked like black combat gear spreading out searching the bottom part of the club.

I held myself as still as possible but then realised from many nights of experience when I first started working here, that you could barely see up here. So, with that in mind, I stuffed the letter in my pocket, feeling the coin I always kept there and got down on all fours. I started to crawl closer to the balcony, making sure I kept in the shadows. From here I was close enough to hear what they were saying.

"I know she is here…Find her!" A crackled voice spread out like prickly thorns along my skin and I shuddered. These men were looking for me, but why? Ok, so forget the why, more like how the Hell was I going to get out of here?!

I looked around and only saw two exits, one meant climbing the ivy and possibly falling to my death or the other was a door I hadn't yet tried and one that might possibly be locked. The door I usually used to get into the VIP so I wouldn't ever have to use the stairs, was sitting there like a calling beacon, so after weighing up my options one sentence from the thugs made my decision,

"Find her, knock her out and drag her ass back to the boss." This came from the obvious leader and kicked in my flight mode and the mental shotgun sounded in my head…RUN!

And I did just that. I scrambled up and ran towards the door I had used too many times to count. I weaved in and out of tables and chairs as I ran for the door, praying that this one would be open and then my access into the depths of Draven's home would be available for me to hide in. There were only two places to go and one of those took me straight down to the main part of the club, somewhere right now I really didn't want to be. But there were two parts of this plan that I didn't figure happening, one would be that the commotion I was causing with my running into furniture and the fact the men clearly now knew where I was and the other was having to skid to a halt when the door swung open and a dark figure emerged.

I took one look at the massive hooded giant coming towards

me and turned to bolt in the other direction. If I could just make it back to the balcony, then maybe I would have a slim chance at getting away from this new nightmare. My heart was pounding with the surge of adrenaline pumping through my system and I thanked God for it, for without it, it would be times like this that I would have just curled into a frightened ball and shook. But no, not thanks to this natural drug that was a driving force.

I circled around and just before I came close to the railings of the staircase I was grabbed from behind. An arm that felt like it could have belonged to the Terminator snaked around my waist and slammed me back into a wall of chest. Another hand quickly grabbed my throat and his hand was so large it spanned the entire column of my neck. He held me still and when I tried to break free he applied a little pressure as a warning. I then felt slight movement behind me as he lowered his head, closer to my ear.

"Ssshh, lille øjesten." That incredibly deep voice vibrated through me once again and as I shivered I felt his thumb create little soothing circles along my skin.

"Down!" He ordered then he moved quickly and I found myself being pushed down to the floor by heavy hands at my shoulders. He pushed so hard that if I hadn't bent my knees my legs would have snapped. This being the case he also gripped my jacket so that my knees didn't bang too hard on impact as he lowered me until I was tucked below his leg.

My last thought before the sounds of destruction erupted around us was…

Thick black boots were back.

CHAPTER SIXTEEN

BLACK INK

I looked up to find myself in between the legs of giant, one who was clearly getting ready to kick some ass! He widened his stance and I saw him start to shrug one arm out of his long dark grey jacket. It came down to the back of his knees and its heavy hood remained hiding his face. I wondered how he even saw anything with only his square chin being exposed.

Underneath this massive cloak-like jacket, I could see black leather trousers, black t-shirt and some kind of leather straps across his huge chest. Every single thing about this guy screamed dangerous and colossal and this was coming from someone who knew a Ragnar!

He was so tall I could have easily lived in between his legs and still had room to spare…of course not in a rude way. That thought alone terrified me, one hug and you would be crushed, let alone what a night with a man like this could do. One thing was for sure, he would roll over and you would lose weight pretty quickly!

Once he had freed his arm, I sucked in a quick breath when I saw it was practically covered in tattoos. Only these were unlike any I had ever seen before, as it wasn't like a sleeve tattoo as there were spaces in between each one. They were thick black bands, each one different in design and they all got thicker the further up his arm they went. I noticed one as he brought his arm to the railing by my head and it was then I noticed they were all snakes ringed around strong muscle eating their own tails.

The commotion downstairs was getting louder and three of the men had started to come up the staircase at us. I sank down lower and gave a startled little moan when I saw that the snakes had all started to move, each one circling round his arm in opposite directions.

The very last one was the smallest on his middle finger, about an inch thick and just past the first joint closer to the tip, this moved clockwise. The next was a banded snake that had little spikes and was slightly thicker running across the back of his hand and palm, this one moved anti-clockwise. This was the theme running up until I couldn't see past the sleeve of his t-shirt.

The closer the men got, the faster they all spun and soon I watched wide-eyed as they started to move down and join together creating an entire arm of black ink. Then I gave a surprised cry as the ink shot from his arm like black tar and ran down the length of the bannister towards all three men. It was like thick glue and I couldn't hold in the scream when it reached the men and whipped out like elasticated webbing and latched onto their necks. Once there, it became hard, setting like cooling lava rock and all three branches that had necks in their grasp, all twisted at the same time and the sound of bone snapping echoed in the vast space.

After seeing the life leave the eyes of three men, the branches uncurled like a sticky vine and all bodies dropped to the steps, two of which rolled backwards down until they finally came to rest at the club's floor. The other two men watched this, as it all happened in seconds and then after a quick nod to each other, they pulled two guns each from behind their backs. That's when I got my first encounter with flying bullets.

I thought I would see the flash or something coming from the end of a gun, but the only sensory encounter was sound, because before I knew it the world around us had gone black.

The man above me had literally sucked the rooms shadows tight to our bodies and then I felt myself being hauled up into solid arms and carried off to only he knew where.

The shadows followed us and the sound of shots still filled in the gaps as to what was happening. Added to this was the sound of something whipping out like a tension wire had snapped, which was quickly followed by a scream. Then I felt the man carrying me rear back a bit before it felt as though he kicked forward. Glass exploded in front of us, this I could barely see in the dark grey cloud, but the shards got so far and then dropped to the ground before they could touch us.

I saw the shadows around us disperse with one step and it didn't take a genius to guess why. The blinding sun was beaming down at us and I had to blink over and over to try and gather that sense back into working. As soon as I got my bearings I saw we were now on the balcony and the last man left was just coming through the space where sliding glass doors used to be. He held the gun up and pointed at us both.

"Give me the girl, Sigurd and I won't put a bullet through your Snake Eye." It was the leader who was left, as I recognised the crackled voice that was making me shudder. He was wearing all black like the rest and he had a thick belt with some serious weaponry attached all the way around. His face was like mahogany, red with thick scarred skin that looked like someone had taken a searing hot blade to leather. His hair slicked back into a ponytail and two small eyes pierced me with a sneer that also made his thin lips curve up on one side.

"That bullet won't kill me." The man holding me stated and I felt the vibrations of that deep voice all the way through my jacket. The combat thug shrugged his shoulders before cocking the hammer and raising the barrel higher.

"That maybe so, but it will slow you down enough to get the girl and deliver her to my boss." He said and without fail my skin crawled. He sounded like he had been kicked in the larynx recently after being made to swallow nails.

"Gastian." Mr Deep Voice at my back snarled the name and surprise flashed for a second on the thug.

"This is for my men." He said before pulling on his trigger

finger. Now, if this had happened in slow motion I might have seen a flash or spark simultaneously as I saw the smoke, considering I was staring down the barrel of a gun. But the only thing I did see was the man behind me when his hand shot up and black ink moved as though it was oil underwater from his palm. It caught the bullet before it hit, in a fist of three black fingered claws and held it up for the guy behind me to see.

"My turn." He thundered and then the ink hand threw it up in the air and when it caught it again, it had formed the spiked shape of a crude hellish gun and fired the bullet right back at the thug's head.

It hit him dead centre in the forehead and the man dropped with a frozen look of shock on his weathered face.

"That was for me, dickhead!" He snapped back at the dead body and I had to hold in the vomit at seeing a man on the ground with a hole in his head and a pool of blood quickly forming. I think I at least screamed at all this or at least my mouth was still open ready for it.

In my utter disbelief, I was still in stunned mode when he pulled me tighter to his chest, which I could imagine was very similar to being held against a brick wall. He turned calmly to face the balustrades and he ran a few steps before jumping up onto the ledge. This was when I finally found my nerve to speak…heights will do that to you!

"Put me down!" I shouted and when he led me over the edge I fisted my hands in his jacket.

"I doubt you really want me to do that right now." He said as he leaned forward slightly to emphasise his point. When my grip got tighter, I heard the grunt of a short laugh escape.

"Who are you?" I asked for the first time, looking up and seeing him in the light of day. All I got was a square chin covered in dark stubble and full lips that curved on one side as my answer…then he jumped.

"AAARRRHHH!" I screamed and by the time I had to inhale he had landed us both on his heavy booted feet and was walking round to the front of a building.

"I really wish people would stop doing shit like that while holding me." I muttered and thought I heard the light rumbling of his deep laughter, only I couldn't be sure considering my ears were still ringing from my own scream.

We got to the car park and I saw a large black van with blackout windows, and it didn't take a whole lot of guessing to know that this was the vehicle the bad guys had turned up in. Well, one thing I was certain about and that was me being grateful that I wouldn't be seeing inside it, thanks to my mystery giant.

He carried me closer and when we were around the other side of it he let my legs swing down from his arm under my knees. Then he walked away from me and closer to the van.

"Are you gonna check for ID or something?" I said thinking back to my Columbo days and all I got in answer was a shake of his hooded head. He went to the fuel cap and pulled it out with little effort even though it was locked. Out here I could finally see the full size of him and it made me do a comedy gulp.

This guy was friggin' huge and trust me when I say that up until recently, I was used to being around massive guys, Draven being one of them. But this guy was at least six foot six and had shoulders that wouldn't have fit inside a doorway without turning side on. If anything, I think I had just found a contender for Ragnar, but with this guy having a bit more stealth reactions rather than the man bull that Ragnar was.

I didn't really know what to say, so I decided that he obviously knew what he was doing and didn't need little nagging Keira asking stupid questions…like the ID one. So instead, I watched as he held his middle finger over the hole to the tank until it turned black, the same as his entire arm had done inside. It dripped down like crude oil from his fingertip and after four drops it sucked back up his hand, leaving the tattoo around his finger.

He turned back to me after dropping the cap over his shoulder and walked past me, snagging my arm in the process. He pulled me over to a motorbike I had only just noticed, and this was when I heard other voices coming from the side of Afterlife.

"There's more of them?!" I said in a panic.

"Yeah, so get on the Harley." He responded, while looking

their way and not really sounding concerned or even looking surprised. I did as I was told and ran the remaining steps over to the bike, after I saw six more men around the side of the building where we came from and once they saw us, they started running.

"Oh shit!" I said and just before I could mount the bike, I felt a steel band wrap around my torso and he lifted me with one arm. I found, due to his height, he could actually lift me quite high up and with my legs kicking out in surprise he lowered us down into the seat.

"Umm… shouldn't I…like… get behind you?" I stammered as I was positioned in front of him.

"Why, are you bulletproof?" He asked dryly and then reached around me and started the bike until a deep rumble vibrated beneath me. I jumped when his hand rested in front of me, but then I shrieked when that same black stuff started to ooze from his hand. It travelled up and over the top of my thighs and half way up my waist.

"What are you doing?!" I screeched out as the ink started to harden which ended up forming a secure seat that anchored me to the bike. It even ran down the bike and attached itself to my feet to keep me more firmly in place. Then we roared off just as shots were once again being fired.

"Jesus!" I shouted as he skidded the bike round causing a dirt cloud and bringing us low to one side. He pulled the bike around again, kicking up a ring of dust that hid us from view and thankfully from the raining bullets. Then he righted the bike up and steered us onto the road, leaving the bad guys running for the van.

I didn't think it would be possible to ride a bike with a person in front of you but the handlebars were higher than the ones on Vincent's, so he just kept me caged in his arms, while he rode us the Hell outta there. Unlike my first ride on a bike with a sweeter Angel, this one was a badass ride that sped off at a speed I didn't want to think about and had me hanging on to a lump of black rock in front of me like my life depended on the tight use of my fingers. At least I now knew why he had gone to the lengths of securing me to the seat like some lava ass shaped saddle.

We just cut through the tunnelled greenery the forest created when I heard it. An almighty boom exploded behind us and I would have looked but the immense body behind me hid everything from that we'd left behind.

"Was that you?" I asked…or more like shouted over the roar of the engine.

"Yeah, that was me." This was his only answer and also the last time he spoke to me until we pulled up in front of my house.

Halfway home, he had slowed down somewhat, which told me the danger was now over or at least I hoped so, considering he'd blown up a van load of bad guys. After seeing all that had happened in the last hour, I was actually surprised I was still coping without girly hysterics and lip biting. If anything, on the way home, I had somehow felt the urge to relax into the body at my back and I had to say…man I felt safer doing so!

It was, however, when we pulled up in front of my house that the lip biting started. My mind started to speed up and I was racking my brain as to what to say. I mean, what was the standard procedure for times like this… 'Thanks for finding me, snapping necks, dodging bullets, blowing ugly dude's brains out and then blowing up a van full of thugs before taking me on a death ride home'…? Umm…I didn't think so.

He cut the engine after leaning closer into me and then the solid black substance around me started to liquefy and left me, flowing back to its master. I think my mouth dropped open at seeing it happen this close up. It was nothing like watching it when it came out of him, which just looked like he had a hidden tube under his palm or something but this…this was something else.

The black substance up close looked like it was made from thousands of tiny strands of black wired thread that all entwined together to become sticky like the silicone gel I had once seen my dad using in the bathroom on tiles. This altogether folded over itself to travel back into the hand that mastered it and it soaked into his skin as if every pore was a gateway.

When the last drop found home, he moved his hand away from the front of me and I felt him kick up the stand ready to lean his bike to one side. He got off and his whole hand circled the top of my arm, with plenty of length still left on his large fingers. He pulled me up and I had nowhere else to go but up and off the saddle.

I found myself looking up at him and my neck strained, it tipped that far back. He still had his hood hiding his face and his lips looked tight when he saw I was trying to discover who was under there.

"Who sent you?" I asked frowning and tilting my head to one side.

"That is not your concern." He said and whenever I heard the deepest level of his voice, I would feel my heart kick up a notch. I listened and tried to detect an accent but the way he spoke he didn't really have one. It was stern and it was precisely firm, only ever saying what he needed to, that was unless he was shooting back at a guy that had tried to put a hole in his… 'Snake Eye', whatever that was supposed to mean.

"Righteven" I muttered as I started to walk past him towards my door.

"So what, you're just going to keep showing up and saving my ass?" I asked not hiding the sarcasm, despite the fact that he had in fact saved me, my sister and my niece. I decided to put it down to being shot at for the first time.

"Whatever it takes to get the job done." His voice hummed in my ear and I jumped at how close a man his size was able to sneak up on me without making not one bloody sound!

"What does that mean?" I asked on a whisper. I felt the weight of his hand rest on my shoulder first, before running gently up my neck and then brushing my new shorter hair off to one side. In doing so he exposed my neck for his next set of cryptic words.

"Of course, it would be easier if you didn't keep getting yourself into trouble, lille øjesten." He called me that again and I still didn't know what it meant, but whenever he said it was the only time his voice changed and a hint of an accent could be heard. It was just a shame I wasn't the best at detecting where people came from, so I was still left in the dark as to where the biker dude was from.

"What did those men want with me anyway?" I asked, still with him locked to my back and his hand still planted firmly at my neck.

"Gastian never forgives or forgets and from what I heard, you pissed him off big time, øjesten." He replied only to make my head spin even more.

"I don't even know this Gastian! And why do you keep calling me o-ost-een?" I said trying to say it like he did, only given his grunted laugh I didn't quite get it right.

"Maybe one day I will tell you, but right now is not the time, lille *øjesten*." He said the name slower this time, ran a single finger down my neck and then…

He was gone.

After my mystery biker had disappeared yet again, I had walked back into the house and made myself some lunch consisting of two boiled eggs (runny) and toast soldiers, which I considered comfort food. It was the first thing my mum made me when I didn't get picked for a team sport at school, when I fell over the handlebars on my new bike on New Year's Day, and when Bobby Carlson told me we would be better off just staying as friends. But the most meaningful time was when it was the first thing my mum made me when I got back from the hospital after the whole kidnapping incident.

So here I was again, dipping make-believe soldiers into runny yolk and remembering the first time when my mum told me the soldiers were there for me and would turn the hurt and disappointment into yummy bites. Of course, I doubt she ever intended they would solve the issue of getting shot at, but I couldn't say that it wasn't working.

After I had finished eating and amazingly keeping it down, I rang the 'Catch a Cab' number and booked a taxi to take me to the airport, after asking for my new friend Jax. It was then that I started packing and getting things ready for my flight to London. I had no idea what I was going to need, let alone how long I was going to be travelling, but the only thing I did know was that I was supposed to be in disguise.

So with this in mind, and with how my hair had turned out, I decided to play little Goth chick. I was now thankful for the two shopping bags of the last of season's line store clothes RJ had given me from the Goth store she worked at, ones she had bought for next to nothing and ones she said would have been a crime to leave, even on sale. What she hadn't factored into it was that she had next to no bust and most of the stuff was far too baggy considering she liked her clothes tight…as in skintight.

I never had the heart to say no and I was thankful she didn't ever ask me if I wore any of it. The answer would have been no, but now, they would be coming in handy. Although most of the clothes made me start biting my lip at the thought of wearing, I knew I needed to play the part, so I sucked it up and filled my big duffle bag with black, black and even more black.

I was lucky with my footwear at least, seeing as my Doc Martins would suit most of the outfits, but just in case I packed the pair of Libby's knee-high black boots that I had worn at Halloween. I knew she wouldn't mind as they were in the part of her wardrobe of things that she never wore but couldn't yet give up.

After I had packed most of my stuff, I then went downstairs to ring Libby and have my last chat with her before I went 'travelling'. Once I had finished and received my early birthday wishes, I did the same with my mum and dad. After being told to be careful about fifty times and to make sure I wore one of those hidden pouches around my waist with my money in, I finally said goodbye.

Now, I was stood in the kitchen waiting for the kettle to boil and looking out onto our driveway as the sun was going down over the national park. It cast beautiful shadows and stunning colours, causing me to take a moment to absorb the idea that this could be the last time I saw this. I didn't mean I could die or anything equally as morbid, although I didn't think it would be a walk in Central Park. No, I just had made the decision that if this didn't work, I didn't think I could live in this town anymore.

Just the thought of spending the rest of my life living in the memory of what I once had, wasn't ever going to be the right life for me to live.

So, even though I didn't know where I would end up, at least I knew the reminders weren't going to be there to haunt me for the rest of my days. So this was why I stood there and watched the sunset over a place I both loved and unfortunately…feared.

I held onto my Homer mug and felt its warmth seep into my fingers as I sipped my personal nectar, when my eyes scanned the dark woods ahead. Once there I almost dropped my mug at what I saw. There were now two dark figures that looked close to the same size, that size being gargantuan and being obvious that at least one of the men was my mystery biker, but then that led to the most important question…

Who was the other guy?

CHAPTER SEVENTEEN

FLYING WITH A CLUELESS MIND

I think I was still in shock and I was sure I would still be this way until I landed. From the moment I walked up to the check-in desk in Chicago O'Hare International Airport after a short internal flight to get there, I was stunned speechless. It all started when a smart looking lady in a blue tailored suit took my ticket and sent me off to the first-class lounge. At first, I thought she had made a mistake and when I asked again, she simply looked back at her computer screen and said,

"No, no, it's right here, you were upgraded, Miss Williams." This was when the surprises started. After entering a whole new world into a luxury dimension that made me feel like a fraud, mutton dressed as lamb, wolf in sheep's clothing, a fish out of water…ok, now I was hungry and quickly losing my point. But lucky for me, being in this new dimension meant being surrounded by the most luscious and mouth-watering food. So there was no thinking about it when I chose the fish starter and the lamb main for dinner.

Of course, after being sat in the private lounge, where you could get a pre-flight dinner, a facial and champagne handed to you by your own private concierge all before take-off, was enough to keep my mouth hanging open before even stepping on board. But once there and being shown to my own little flight hub that was complete with a chair I would have been happy to die in it was that comfortable, I finally had a minute to process the magical whirlwind that was first class.

So here I was, sipping another glass of champagne, above the clouds watching the sunset on another day feeling guilty that I was enjoying the experience, while the man I loved was literally living in Hell. After that thought I gulped back the golden liquid, refused any more and ate my exquisite meal like it was acid infused cardboard feeling guilty for every bite I took.

I shouldn't be here and I definitely should not be enjoying any part of this journey. I scolded myself repeatedly, trying to ease the ache I felt in my heart when thinking about Draven. I knew right then that the only reason I wasn't drowning in my misery and despair at being without him was that with each mile consumed by this plane, I was a mile closer to bringing him back to me. Failure in this plan was not an option. I just wouldn't let myself think it and this was backed up with the idea that if the Oracle herself thought this was worth a shot, then there was a shot!

"Miss?" I shook myself out of my thoughts as a beautiful stewardess stood next to my little space.

"Sorry, I didn't catch that," I said shrugging my shoulders as it was obvious she was waiting for an answer about something. She smiled sweetly down at me and motioned with her head at my half empty tray.

"Would you like me to take that for you?" I nodded and moved slightly back as she reached across to get it and before she left me back to my mindful turmoil, she asked if there was anything else I needed. I was tempted to ask if she was a demon and could sneak me backstage in Hell but refrained. After all, there was no need to freak out the people that provided the alcohol.

"Just a rum and coke please," I said doubting they did tequila shots! She smiled at me and turned with the tray in hand only to start scowling at the entrance to first class.

"Oh wow, look at this place… Hey, are there any famous people in here?" I heard a lively voice ask and I arched my head round to see who was speaking.

"Excuse me miss, you can't be back here, this is first class." The stewardess said in an authoritative tone which you could tell she used often.

"No shit, it's first class, I mean look at this…you guys get actual plates and stuff…and look at this…real glass…fancy." The newcomer said waggling her eyebrows at me and I found I had to stifle a laugh. She was a big English woman with a cute face and massive brown eyes that sparkled as she took in the living myth that was the luxury of First Class. I couldn't say I blamed her as I was exactly the same when I first saw it… minus the faded Mickey Mouse T-shirt, peach lipstick that was smeared and tight curly hair that was held back with a flowery scrunchy hairband.

"I am sorry Miss, but you really can't be here." The flustered stewardess repeated.

"Miss? Ah Hell, I ain't been a Miss for over thirty years Lovey and I have had my share of hunks to prove that fact…" She said and then stepped closer making the poor stewardess wince before she continued with something that made me choke on a swallow.

"…think, throwing a stick down an alleyway, I swear I am lucky I don't whistle as I walk!" She said nudging her and I couldn't hold it back any longer, I burst out laughing, while the stewardess stepped back horrified and looked as though she would catch something if she got too close.

"See, she found it funny, didn't ya Lovey?" She said nodding to me and I winked back at her when the stewardess wasn't looking, feeling like a naughty child laughing at the school joker.

"You have to leave…NOW!" She said more firmly to the newcomer, but the bigger lady just smiled.

"Alright, alright…don't twist your ironed pantyhose and untwist those knick knackers while you're at it, I am here to give someone a letter…Keira Johnson…anyone of you fine folks called Keira whatsit face?" This sobered my humoured smile and I raised my hand before saying,

"That would be me." She smiled down at me and then said,

"Of course, it is, only one of you lot with any sense of humour for this old fart…alright, I'm a'leaving, just wanted to give the little cutie pie a letter is all." She said while pulling it out of her 'fanny pack' as the Americans called it. She passed me the letter with a wink and then let herself be escorted out of First Class by another stewardess who soon got in on the authority act.

"Peace out, Richies!" She shouted before the manhandling could start. Meanwhile, I just turned my head from the commotion in dumb silence as I looked down at the newest letter on my lap.

"I am very sorry about that, Miss." My head snapped up at the stewardess who was apologising for completely the wrong thing. If anything, I was very close to getting up and hugging the cuddly Brit who had brought me what I could only class as a gift from the Heavens! It did bring forth the question of how the Hell did she even get her hands on it, which was why I found myself getting up from my seat and waving off any apology before asking where it was the lady was sat.

"I...umm, did you know that lady?"

"No, but I do want to know how she knew me." I said to the confused looking stewardess as I gripped my letter tighter to my side.

"She was... sat in Economy," she said pausing and whispering the words like they were dirty. I smirked at her and gave her a comical wink for no good reason other than finding the situation funny. I left a stunned looking stewardess in a navy suit in my wake as I made my way back through the plane.

I looked like a crazy person as I scanned each and every passenger I went past, looking for Mickey Mouse that had seen better and brighter days... pre a million spins in the washing machine. Of course, I heard her before I saw her.

"I tell ya, these seats don't half pinch my denim fillers, my cheeks will have armrest marks in them for a week!" I stifled a giggle at her comment and smiled when her cute round face came into view. She was shifting this way and that, trying to get comfortable and the man sat next to her looked disgusted with her blatant disregard for where her elbows jabbed at him. Again, I had to swallow my amusement.

"Umm…excuse me," I said clearing my throat getting her attention.

"Well hello again. What are your little rich britches doing back here, slumming it?" She asked without malice. I smiled at her before answering,

"I am actually a waitress and had this flight paid for me." I shrugged my shoulders when she gave me a surprised look.

"Well, I hope you're gonna marry him, anyone that doesn't want to put your shiny butt through this torture for eight hours is a keeper!" She said squirming.

"Here, please sit down, it is a comfy seat for some… but I need a drink and to… *escape*." The man next to her said standing, whispering the last part as he passed me.

"Thanks," I said but this was drowned out by my new friend.

"I heard that!" She shouted at him and I cringed at the scowls she received from other passengers.

"I don't know how anyone can be comfy with a parker pen shoved so far up their ass they must blow ink when they sneeze…do you?" I burst out laughing and failed trying to hide it.

"So, what can I do ya for skinny Minnie, what's her face?" She asked cracking open her tiny Coke can before taking a large swig.

"I just wanted to know who gave you this letter." I asked holding it up to her, which wasn't needed but done out of impulse. This, however, created a response that I wasn't expecting.

"Holy shit!" I said leaning back away from her when I saw her eyes start to glow. The toothy grin she gave me was sheer mischief and then she nodded which was contradicting my shaking head.

"You're…you're a… bloody demon?" I whispered the last part, looking round to make sure no one could hear my crazy statement.

"Of course, who else would you trust with something like that?!" She said minus the 'Well Durr'.

"Of course, it still doesn't help with me ending up with piles after a long flight." She winked at me as I snorted a laugh.

"Who are you?" I asked feeling my eyebrows lower as the distrust seeped in.

"Merry Weather Jones at your service." She said wiping a plump hand down her jeans leg a few times before offering it to me.

"Merry Weather?" I couldn't help but ask as I took her hot and sticky hand that dwarfed my own.

"Yeah, the bitch that was my possession officer had a twisted sense of humour alright, plus she just loved the fat fairy from Sleeping Beauty and those, my dear skinny friend, are the reasons you will never get my awesome big booty in a blue dress…man what a bitch!" She said again before swigging the rest of her Coke back.

"So where were we?"

"You were about to tell me who gave you this letter?"

"Ah, well now I would gladly want to ruin the surprise being it's in my nature and all, but I am afraid I don't know." She said offering me a peach coloured smile.

"I doubt that…I mean how can you not know?" I said raising a sceptical eyebrow, one she ignored. She simply raised her empty Coke can at a passing stewardess and shook it until the poor girl got the hint.

"Easy, it's above my pay grade and definitely my ranking, but I will tell ya one thing, the pay was worth every hour my ass is going to be numb for! So thank you for that part." She said lifting her empty coke my way and this time showing a bit of fang with her coy grin.

"So you can't tell me anything?" I said feeling deflated and pulling my letter closer to my chest as my own comfort.

"Only this…whoever gave me that letter put some badass voodoo on it as the only soul that can open it is you and trust me when I say that shit right there is the real thing…power like that…well it makes my Merry Weather ass look like bird shit hitching a lift off a Ferrari! And I ain't 'bout to claim myself as being that Ferrari if you catch my wheels 'a drift-ing!" I nodded even though her unique code had me suppressing the need to scrunch up my face and tell her she was crazy.

So instead of pointing out the obvious screw loose she had going on, I got up and nodded my thanks before letting the stewardess through with another shot of caffeine…that, if you asked me, was the last thing that Demon needed.

I made my way back to First Class even more confused than before and instead of tearing into the letter as I usually wanted to do, something about this one now felt different. Of course, when I was back in my private pod chair, feeling like a Bond villain, I found out just how warranted my feelings were…

You think this is a wise decision, to trust in the fates when they abandoned you?
You think you are capable of playing with the Gods and bring forth the Dead?
You think that by travelling this path will lead you to righteous arms in Hell?

You think wrong human!

Now it is time for what I think,

I think that the death of a King will not bring you peace but the death of a girl will bring peace to a King.
I think that the Dead will rise and with him revenge, redemption and retaliation will be found in your End.
I think the time is coming for those who have been chosen by the Gods and the mistakes found in those souls.

I think it is time for you to
Die right along with your King!

By the time I finished reading it for the third time my face ached from frowning and I had to uncurl my fingers from fisting the parchment that hard. Who the Hell had written this?! And how dare they try and stop me from doing what needed to be done! I slammed the paper words face down on the little table in front of me, making a few of the other VIP's around me jump from my outburst.

My anger bubbled and coiled around me like something waiting to find the right victim to strike! I curled my top lip in disgust at the words of obvious hate on my part. So, someone out there knew what I was doing and was trying to use me, this 'Mistake of the Gods', to flee running scared with my tail between my legs. Well at least one thing was clear…they obviously didn't know me!

After giving the offending sheet my best death ray stare for about an hour I finally folded it back up, still tasting the acid of anger inside, as I shoved it back into the plain envelope.

After that the rest of the flight was a blur as my mind crashed along the shore of doubt with a stormy vengeance. I hated that I was letting the words get to me in any way, but it was so hard not to. What did they know? Who were they and what if they spoke even a tiny element of the truth? Had the Gods made a mistake in picking me or now without Draven here what did that mean…was my Heavenly contract being the Electus now void?

My mind continued like this for the remainder of the flight and even when I was handed my jacket, I was still asking myself questions and using my zombie responses when thanking the stewardess. I hated what the letter had done to my courage and confidence in my plan and I found myself now stood in the bathroom at Gatwick airport staring myself down. Palms flat on the counter, I hung my head as my doubtful eyes finally got to me.

I couldn't do this now! Hell, I couldn't do this ever! This was not going to get me anywhere and besides, why should I be listening to the words of someone who obviously wanted me dead! For Christ's sake, it could have come from Layla for all I knew, someone who was still high on the wanted list and had gone into hiding her hellish bimbo self to get out of the death sentence that clearly awaited her.

With my mind made up, I slammed my hands down on the counter shouting,

"Fuck it!" Scaring an old lady in the process, who walked out muttering about young ones today and having no respect.

"Sorry!" I shouted back, getting a slammed door as my answer. I looked back at my reflection to see the dark doubt leave my eyes, only to be replaced with a fierce determination that looked so much better on my grey blue eyes.

"I can do this…I can do this!" I said, the last time with more of a bite to my bark. I stormed from the bathroom as though I could hear my very own badass theme song pounding a heavy baseline through my veins. My Doc Martins sounded out my purpose with every step as I made my way out of the arrivals gate and I almost missed the guy stood there with my name typed out on an iPad he was holding. So much for the cardboard days I thought as I stopped in front of him.

"Keira Williams?" He asked and on hearing my real name being voiced I didn't know whether this was a good sign or a bad one. In the end I just nodded and followed him when he told me he had a car waiting. He waited by the open door of a black Mercedes for me to catch up. He looked like any other chauffeur, dressed in a black suit and hat worn low to his eyebrows. Black sunglasses that reminded me of Blade wrapped around his eyes and hid most of his features from my studying.

"Where to?" He asked abruptly as I approached.

"The Savoy Hotel please." I said and with a nod, he closed the door after me and didn't say much all the way there. I tried to ask him a few times during the drive, who sent him but I never really got an answer. I did however hear briefly about 'Where the boss wants him, he goes' oh and 'Bloody London Traffic' was another he thought to tell me.

So now here I was, pulling up to one of the most lavish hotels I was to stay in, knowing two things for certain. One was a bubble over my head as to how much one night was going to set me back and dip into my savings and two…how on earth was I going to be able to sneak into the Royal Suite?!

The Savoy was situated further back from the main street and as we drove down the hotel's driveway, we passed a huge topiary cat on either side. The outside had an art deco feel with its black cut marble lines along its multiple pillars. Its driveway circled a Mackintosh style glass water feature and its covered roof was lit up in square panels giving the posh exterior a warm orange glow. The front entrance was framed either side with two tall palm trees, which would have looked odd in England but for some reason it fit the theme nicely.

A Bellboy was stood there ready to open my door and another was loading luggage from a fancy metal lift. Then my door was opened and I looked up to see a cheeky smiley face welcome me. He was wearing a black top hat, a long black jacket that had a thick gold trim and two rows of high shine buttons.

"Welcome to the Savoy, Miss." He said standing back so I could exit the vehicle. The driver was already pulling my bag from the boot and handing it to the Bellboy. Instantly, without Draven by my side, it was moments like this that I felt completely out of my depth as though any minute someone would be walking up to me and asking me to leave.

I knew it was my insecurities that were making me feel this way, as the staff were nothing short of pleasant and polite. But this, I was to find, was kicked up a notch when I was shown to the reception area. After walking through one of the sets of revolving doors, I stepped back in time into a treasure trove of antique furniture, grand oil paintings and solid wood panelled walls. The ceilings were a masterpiece in their own right. Cut into sections of squares from the free-standing pillars that were topped with gold gilded leaves that arched out. The theme continued onto a wide border that spanned the top of the room, displaying beautiful mouldings of white figures against a light mint colour.

I gulped down an anxious lump as I walked over to the desk.

"Welcome to the Savoy Miss, may I help you?" A smartly dressed gentleman asked and I first had to clear my throat before I answered him. I mean, what was I going to say, 'I probably can't afford to stay here without my boyfriend, (who's stuck in Hell by the way) but I was just wondering if I could take a peek at your Royal Suite'. No, I didn't think that was going to fly with the posh folk now looking at me.

"Umm…well I…" I started in a quiet voice not really having planned this far ahead.

"May I take your name, Miss?" He said obviously thinking he was helping me out.

"Keira Williams, but I don't…" I was cut off when I saw his eyes grow wide and he stood up abruptly.

"But of course, Miss Williams, it is a pleasure to meet you. Please allow me to show you to the Savoy's Royal suite." After he said this I just hoped that my mouth wasn't hanging open, as one thing struck me…

Man, that was easy.

CHAPTER EIGHTEEN

'SUPERNATURAL' ROOM SERVICE

Ok, so if I thought that the front entrance was intimidating in its extravagance, then this right here was something else. I now felt like I had sneaked into a royal palace! I kept expecting Prince Charles to come walking through the door and ordering tea to be served promptly in the sitting room.

The staff had quickly taken my numb state as a cue to leave me to it, especially after I almost screamed when I found one maid unpacking my bag and hanging up each Goth item as though she was handling ballroom gowns made by Gucci. I tried to explain that this really wasn't necessary as I thought a huge mistake had been made, but I was quickly informed that I was the one making the mistake. I think it was the choking sound that garbled from my throat that had them convinced they now had a rich mental case staying in their hotel.

These fears of theirs were more than warranted even when I first stepped off the elevator and here's why. The Royal Suite was certainly a well-earned name as that was exactly what it was fit for…royalty! The suite spread over the front of the entire 5th floor which boasted stunning views of the River Thames. The other eight, yes eight, windows also held the magnificent London vista from Canary Wharf to the Houses of Parliament.

The suite's private butler introduced himself, but to be honest my mental capability wouldn't have been able to register his name, even if he had introduced himself as Little Bo Peep. This was because I had been shown through the suite's marble foyer into a guided tour of what real money could buy you for the night. A private wood panelled office, a dining room big enough to seat eight people and a beautiful sitting room that had you thinking about English gardens. And most staggering of all, the whole suite was complete with Magic Mirrors! Yes, that's right, I said magic mirrors, as in mirrors that with the flick of a switch turned into high definition flat screens. So, I could now even watch TV in the bath!

I would have expected, from my time with Draven, that I would have been used to the level of luxury and in some ways, I was. But not having Draven by my side in this had me feeling like a kid's goldfish that had lived in a bowl and just taken a nosedive into a tropical aquarium. Well, I guess I just had to hope it was a Piranha free zone but considering the last letter I'd just received I very much doubted it.

"Time to swim Keira, not sink," I said to myself as I took in the spacious en-suite, complete with his & hers bathroom, deep soak tub and steam shower. I shook my head as I walked back through the walk-in dressing room lined with cedar wardrobes that now held a few dark clothes.

At the time I had been in shock on hearing that the suite had been booked for me and already paid up for the week. I didn't even manage to ask by whom as I played guppy on the entire elevator ride, with the poor concierge trying to keep a straight face.

"So now what?" I asked myself after checking the massive suite for clues. I did the obvious looking first, drawers, desk and anything else that opened among the antique furniture. But then I started to get creative and soon was even looking through the fresh flower arrangement, DVD player, sewing kit, newspapers, bathrobe pockets and shamefully even behind the pictures, like some Pink Panther thief. In the end, I just huffed down exhausted, sinking into a yellow couch that felt so comfortable it actually felt like the furniture was hugging me.

I must have only closed my eyes for a few frustrated seconds when I heard a knock on the door. I wrestled with the couch that had taken me prisoner and ended up half slumped on the floor before I got up to answer the door. I had my hand on the fancy handle but stopped myself before I opened the double doors.

"Who is it?" I asked, using my wits and past experience of deception.

"Room service." A musical voice said and before I could think about it I opened the door. It was as if my hand was being taken over, not by another force but more like an emotional urge. It felt like being in a large theatre alone and then hearing a heart-wrenching song being sung by a singer with tears falling down her face. The response was a shudder, a cold chill that touched my skin leaving a bumpy trail and my view misted with emotions too thick to keep buried. And all that just from two plain words spoken through a door.

In walked the only woman I would have given that magical voice to and the expression, fallen straight from Heaven, became reality. She was stunning to a point it nearly hurt to look at her. Even though she wore a serving uniform, it in no way at all detracted from her ethereal perfection that was now pushing a trolley into the sitting room with the grace of an Angel.

Fair white blonde hair looked like each strand was spun from the silkworm and twisted majestically at the back of her head. High cheekbones that held a natural rose blush upon ivory satin skin. Her large almond-shaped eyes were a kaleidoscope of colours that shone like permanent tears caressed her soul. Little heart-shaped lips were naturally puckered and only lost their unique shape when she smiled down at me. Long legs and slight curves of a tall hourglass made a body worthy of the Gods to feast upon and with such grace it was highly likely she held that position above.

I closed the door as she passed me and for the countless time today, I had my mouth hanging open as she wheeled the covered table into the centre of the room. And there was no doubt that finally I was now staring into the face of the Oracle.

"Pythia?" I asked gobsmacked that finally after all this time waiting and cracking codes I would at last find my answers.

"No, sorry" Okay, maybe not!

"But I am." A spunky voice said and I gasped as a little black girl unfolded herself from under the white tablecloth. She stood up and patted herself down, which was a denim tutu skirt and a woollen striped roll neck jumper that was a rainbow of colours. She shook out her thick black hair that was a mass of corkscrew curls that remained around her head like a crash helmet.

"You're a child!" I shouted tactlessly and she put one hand on her hip and cocked her pint-sized frame to one side.

"So?" Well I didn't really know what I could say about that one, but if I was to think of an all-powerful Oracle who held the weight of the fates on her shoulders, then the cutest seven year old with the biggest brown puppy eyes was probably the last image my brain would have found.

"I'm…uh…sorry." I said lamely.

"Don't sweat it Electus, we are never what people expect." She said fluffing up her skirt, showing the spotty tights underneath.

"We?"

"Yeah, us Chosen Ones." She said like it was obvious, and she was in fact the one speaking to a child.

"Anyway, I brought cream tea, and Armi bakes a wicked scone, don't you Armi?" She looked to the Heavenly knockout after jumping on the couch like…well like a child.

"One can only hope others think so." She replied once again in that musical voice that could have brought Hell's Demons to their knees in harmonic beauty. She winked at me and I nearly proposed marriage as she pulled the trolley closer to Pythia. Soon all the items were unloaded onto the table in front of the couch, including a three-tiered cake stand.

"So, are you gonna come sit down or stare at me like a Gorgon Leech?" She said patting the space next to her.

"You know I have seen a few Gorgon leeches." I said as I moved to sit down next to her.

"I know you have."

"Of course, you do," I commented a little too dryly than I intended, but I was glad when I heard her laugh.

"Nasty little beasts, but I feel sorry for them all the same." She shrugged her shoulders when I looked at her like she was crazy. I remembered these creatures when seeing them in the hundreds and the last emotion I would have had when seeing them trying to attack Draven was sympathy. I don't think I could ever forget that night as long as I lived, as it was the first time I'd seen that amount of demons in one place, not in my dreams.

It was when Draven was battling it out with Sammael and I watched on as with one roar from him the cliff face transformed into a swarm and breeding ground for some of the creatures of Hell. I shuddered as the sight came back to me of so many broken bodies that had learned to walk with twisted limbs that were cracked at the seams. Bleeding holes where eyes should have been, attached to faces full of gnashing teeth.

And most of all, the memory of their screams as Draven set each one alight and released Hell back on them in the form of ruptured earth. The lava hands grabbing the flesh full and dragging each one back to what I imagined was their final resting place...only just how much rest you could get in Hell was a doubtful amount.

"I know that look and of course what you're thinking..." She commented tapping on the side of her head before she continued,

"You see the Greeks, who took their mythology very seriously, knew how to tell the best stories. But unfortunately this time they got a few things wrong with these naughty little critters. Ok, so Medusa 101, you know she had snakes for hair and one look turned men to stone...yeah?"

"Yeah, that's what I heard." I said thinking how surreal this conversation was right now and if I ever thought I would be here speaking for the first time with the Oracle, who held all my answers, the last thing I wanted to be talking about was bloody Gorgon Leeches!

"Ok, so Gorgon was the name given to the three daughters of the Gods, Ceto and Phorcy. These fine lasses were more than envied for their breath-taking beauty and one of the very reasons their curse included 'breath taking' of sorts." She shifted in her seat and leaned over her folded legs to pour the tea, while the one called Armi sat opposite us like a delicate flower, listening and nodding petals in the gentle wind.

"I remember this bit, the sister Medusa was seduced by Poseidon in a Temple and then someone got upset and cursed her," I said trying to remember back to my days in my Grandparents' library, reading the massive books about Mythology on a worn Indian rug.

"Yeah, Athene, she was always such a jealous bitch and if that was my man that was taking advantage of some young beauty with more than a slap and tickle, then his balls would be the one slapping, as in on the ground when I chopped them off!" She said nodding at Armi before taking a gentle sip of her tea and I couldn't help but feel shocked at hearing this kind of speech coming from a seven year old! It felt a bit like the same reaction to hearing if Yoda ever told Luke to just F off one day during his training.

"Well anyway, that is an even longer story and that fruit is too juicy to drink right now, if you catch my meaning. But the point is that after that happened it meant all three sisters had to ride the ugly train and even after Medusa lost her head, her sisters Eurale and Stheno continued the curse."

"But that's not fair!" I shouted making them both smile.

"Ah, but this is where things get confused, you see people think that they just turned men to stone with one look, but this isn't the end of it. I think they were quite clever as they twisted their curse to their advantage, turning each victim into a creature they could use to build an army, one for hire…I mean a girl's gotta eat right and money is money in any dimension, plane, realm…whatever you want to call it." I frowned at her as the cogs turned and with a slight shake of my head she decided to elaborate.

"They became 'The Gorgons' Leeches'…The sisters' private leeches or army and I will tell ya, they were mighty pissed at Draven that he killed a load of them off, but he's hot, so they soon forgave him and what woman wouldn't do a bit of forgiving for that grade of eye candy." She said winking at me and my frown deepened.

"Right, well getting back to more important things like *my* eye candy, what the Hell happened!?" I said forgetting all about the stupid leeches that yes, I now felt a bit sorrier for but it was time to get down to why I was here.

"Now don't get upset young one and drink your tea, it will soothe you." On hearing this I found myself having to close my eyes in frustration. I mean, it was one thing being called 'young one' by someone that came barely above my waistline, but to then be told to drink tea at a time like this, even for me that was the last thing on my mind! But nevertheless, I picked up my fine china teacup and did as I was told.

"Ahh, I love a cup of tea in this country. Right, so you have questions, I understand this, as trust me, I get it a lot…my entire being actually, so please let me explain the rules."

"Rules?" I repeated, having a bad feeling that finally meeting with the Oracle wasn't going to live up to the hype.

"What, you didn't think that you could just go ahead and have me answer all your questions did you? I mean for one, knowing you I would be in my teens again before you even took a breath." I made a noise as I started to argue with that statement but one reprimanding look had me shutting up.

"I know you, remember and besides, my King has told me plenty." This shocked me and made me blush…what exactly had Draven being saying about me.

"So, before we go off track again, this is the low down on taking tea with the fates." She placed her cup and saucer down and held out one tiny finger as she was getting ready to count off the rules.

"One, you can ask questions but those I won't be able to answer, so what's the point right…?"

"What!" I shouted which she ignored and continued.

"Please understand, I am the only one who knows the truth behind our fates, and although it gives me a bloody massive headache, it also means that I cannot speak of it, as imagine this…" She turned to face me and I knew that even the cutest eyes could shut me up with their seriousness.

"…a man comes to me and asks 'When will I die and how will it happen?' So I tell him, 'You will be hit by a bus tomorrow at twelve.' Said man then decides to take the car to work the next day and the reason he felt like taking the bus in the first place he ignores. On the way in his car, he suffers a massive heart attack causing a pile up and ends up killing that entire busload of people and still getting hit by a bus at twelve."

"But you said he would be killed by the bus?" I said not being able to help myself, making her smile.

"Did I? I merely told him what I saw, he died because of the heart attack and that was the reason the bus hit him. This way only he died because he loved too much cheese and smoked his body weight in cigarettes. But now we have forty dead and the King will never meet his Chosen One."

"Why?"

"Because *you* were on that bus on the way to school, Keira." She said now grabbing a scone from the plate and just dipping it first into the clotted cream followed by the jam. She took as much as her little mouth could take and groaned.

I was still speechless by her story…could it be true? Was that the amount of power the fates had?

"Ok so I get it, what's the next rule?" I said as things started to fit into place.

"Rule two, you lean across and eat one of these righteous scones, by the Gods, Armi, these are to die for…no pun intended." I rolled my eyes before just doing as I was told and grabbing one. Of course, one bite and I couldn't prevent the same groan of pleasure as my taste buds exploded.

"Mm....umm…these are…sooo…good!" I said with my mouth full and she smiled sweetly at me before bowing her head.

"Right ok, I know this rule is a ball ache even for someone without them, but there is a way around it…like the…"

"Letters?" I said without thinking, just knowing.

"Well, would you look at our little Chosen One Armi, she's all grown up, I am so proud." She mocked in jest.

"Ha, ha, so I am right then?"

"Hell Yeah, see I am allowed to hand you a map but you are

the one who chooses where on that map to go, if to even use that map at all…I mean it might be raining and you want to keep your hair dry with it…the point is, it won't be you making that decision because you know it was going to rain that day."

"So that is why all the letters, at any point I could have got it wrong and that would have been my personal fate to do so?" She nodded as she couldn't speak with her second scone in her mouth.

"I think I get it but that still doesn't really help me in getting Draven back…I still don't know what to do." I said feeling even more deflated than before my first letter. Pythia cleared her throat after swallowing.

"Not necessarily, there is a wormhole to seek comfort in. I can continue my masked guidance but the decision will always be yours if you choose to pull The King back from where he has gotten himself into."

"You mean Hell and from what I was told, he didn't exactly put himself there now did he?! He came looking for you when you went missing, thinking you had been taken and then the next thing I knew was that he was dead and no one will tell me how…now it's your turn." I demanded sternly.

She eyed me from the side and it was only the briefest of flickers of doubt or surprise that shone in her features. That was when it hit me and I almost screamed,

"That isn't what happened?!"

"Keira…calm down…I…"

"NO! I can't believe this, I was lied to, wasn't I?" I said getting up and storming away until storming right back to face big brown eyes. I couldn't even find myself feeling guilty looking down at the face of a child and shouting out at them.

"That is something you will have to choose to find for yourself, but this is not that time, now is the time to bring your lover back from where he has been imprisoned." This knocked the wind from my sails.

"He's in prison?!" I almost crumpled to the floor at this point.

"Some decisions the King makes are the decisions not yet recognised by the Gods. Thus an intervention is required and this brings me to this point. But more importantly, you to yours." She didn't make much sense but the whole decision part had me asking the next and possibly the most important, heart-breaking question of all.

"This decision…did it have to do with me?" I asked in a voice close to cracking and fading completely away.

"Yes." And with that my world ended and was replaced with my own Hellish prison. I cracked, I broke and I just now prayed to fade away. I had done this, I had been the cause. She said it herself, I was the reason…and that combined with her statement about the Gods not yet recognising some of his decisions, it took me back to a place in the past, one where he told me loving a mortal was against the rules.

And Draven had fallen for a mortal.

So all this time, when I thought the Gods had chosen me as the Electus, it was actually Draven that had chosen me. And now he was just waiting for the Gods to catch up and get the memo. But instead of that happening he had been punished, sent to Hell and now was rotting away in a prison…all because of me!

I must at some point have passed out or something. I definitely felt like I had closed down and retreated back into the same black abyss I travelled down that very day Leivic had told me of Draven's death. Well now it felt like that day all over again, only now with the added person to blame.

I now had someone to hate for taking away the other half of my soul and killing the one who brought my world into colour. Well now I was plunged into the darkness and it was the only place I deserved to be. This needed to be my prison for the way I felt, I needed to take control and more importantly take his place. There was now my new purpose, to seek revenge on the one who had taken Draven from this plane and get him out of Hell's prison. And the only way to do this… the only way to seek justice against the person that had killed him,

Was for that person to take his place and go to Hell, after all…

I had killed Draven.

CHAPTER NINETEEN

ROSY BIRTHDAYS

"Wakey wakey, eggs and bacey." I felt the poking in my cheek before the words floated under the closed door I had shut on my mind. But no matter how strong I made those mental locks, the sound of the Oracle obliterated them with the combination of crazy words and the smell of cooked bacon!

"Ah, see Armi, I told you crispy bacon was the key. Now she finally wakes." I opened my eyes and winced as the bright sun shone through the windows, blinding me. My head ached like the mother of bad words and I groaned like I had drunk my way through a bottle of Jack.

"Happy Birthday!" Pythia shouted and I felt her little feet jumping on the bed in excitement. I sat up and rubbed the crusted sleep from my eyes before trying to focus on the two faces smiling at me. Then it all hit me and knocked me backwards, as though someone had decided to see how much a body could break from a sledgehammer to the heart.

"Oh shit!" A sweet voice said and then two tiny hands were on me shaking my head in a panicked 'No' action.

"Keira, listen to me, don't go back there! Stay with us and listen to my voice…You did nothing wrong, all that has happened, all that is happening now, is through the choices you had no say in…Stay with us!" I heard her words, but it felt like I was listening to them as I fell backwards from a plane's open door. The air rushed around me and I felt weightless, not like I was falling at all. Only then I felt a mighty slap and my head whipped to the side before plunging me back on that plane.

My eyes snapped open and I saw the face of an Angel child with the biggest brown eyes, stunning smooth skin the colour of melting chocolate and a mass of corkscrew curls that stuck out from the cutest little girl I ever saw…But man, did that kid pack a punch!

"Oww!" I said rubbing the stinging sensation that heated my left cheek.

"Yeah, sorry about that, but snap out of it would ya! Now get your ass out of bed, eat your bacon and eggs and then shower your birthday suit, we have work to do!" She said with her arms folded the whole time, while sat on my lower stomach. I frowned at her before a mischievous side of me showed in the form of a sneaky grin. Then before she could act I shoved my feet into the bed for leverage before flinging her little frame into the air and onto the bed beside me, thanks to firing my hips upwards.

I fell backwards and we were both now lay next to each other, staring up at the elaborate ceiling and I could hear Armi laughing sweetly from the chair close by.

"Does this make us even?" She asked me and after a deep sigh I nodded my answer.

"Good, 'cause you smell and like…really need a shower, Birthday girl."

After an amazing shower, one that seemed to blast open every pore on my body, I felt a miniscule better. After yesterday's bombshell exploded, I passed out and spent the rest of the night in a war, mind against body. Pythia had said it was lucky she had been here to 'keep my soul safe', whatever that meant. The point was that my body refused to let go, while my mind seemed to have gone on lockdown. And even now I couldn't let myself think about Draven. It was just too painful. Which brought me back to what I was doing now, which was unbelievable.

"Aren't you going to blow them out?" Pythia said looking over the huge three-tiered cake that looked too much like it should be cut by a bride and groom. I shut down the urge to moan as this was the very last thing I wanted to be doing. I didn't give two dog turds that it was my birthday, as any happiness was not likely to be found on this day. If I was honest, it was one of the days I had been dreading since Draven…well since Draven left. I raised my hand to touch the necklace he had given me at Christmas and that's when it started to hit me.

So with that thought, even though I knew it was too painful, I decided to torture myself. I remembered that day so well and it made everything hurt even thinking back to it. It was Valentine's Day and I woke to the feel of something tickling my skin. I think I must have grunted or something even less sexy, as it was the sound of a deep laugh that had me waking up fully. I opened my eyes to see Draven propped up on his side looking down at me with amused eyes.

"It's nice to know at least one of us is a morning person." I said in a croaky sleepy voice. He laughed again and it sent shivers through me as he shook next to me. Seeing Draven this way always caused my body to react, as Draven naked was a sinful sight for anyone with a pulse.

"Then let me give you a reason to be a morning person." He hummed seductively in my ear causing heat to flare in my belly and spread out to other places. He kissed me there before pulling back and giving me a wicked grin that spoke volumes at what his intentions were this fine morning. I cleared my throat and his smile widened as my cheeks blushed for him.

"What's that?" I asked referring to the one hand he kept hidden behind his back, an action that caused his biceps to bulge. I almost said sod what's behind his back and grab him by his powerful arms to pull him closer to me. But then, with a wink and bad boy smirk, he produced a perfect dark red rose that had opened fully. I smiled at the sight of a purple ribbon that wound all the way up the stem and tied into a simple knot under the head.

"Happy Valentine's," he said softly and then ran the petals just as softly along my bare arm. I soon recognised it as being the same feeling that tickled me from sleep. He had obviously been having fun with it before I woke.

"It's beautiful… and thornless I see." I added with a cheeky smile.

"As it should be, you really think that I would allow something sharp near that heavenly skin of yours, no matter how beautiful it appears? Sometimes beauty can hold the most deadly of stings, Keira." He said seriously and I nodded silently. Just looking at the man himself proved that statement true enough. Here in his bed, looking like a living God and even gracing me with an easy going smile, I still knew what the supernatural power underneath could do. But I would never have told him that, nor would it have ever been a danger to me. If anything, the very thought of the power he held had me wanting to claw it to the surface like a cat and scream for him and it to take me as one.

"Well, I am lucky then I have you to protect me from this mighty enemy, you are after all my hero." I said in an overdramatic girly voice and then flung the back of my hand to my forehead making him burst out laughing.

"Your acting skills are adorably dreadful Keira, but if you wanted me to ravish you then you only need ask, my dear one." He said before discarding the rose and taking me into his arms. There we made love until both our releases were spent, calling out each other's name in rapture. Mine was screamed against the skin by his neck and his, with his body bowed and head thrown to the Gods above. The hands that had kept me gripped tightly to the bed unshackled my wrists and slid down my arms as we floated down from our addictive high.

"Y…you know…I think…you finally did it," I said still panting into his delicious skin. He cradled the back of my head to keep me there, obviously not wanting to break our closeness.

"What's that, my love?" He asked as he shifted enough to keep his bulky weight from crushing me.

"I think I finally became a morning person." I said and then felt the vibrations of deep laugher radiate across my body which was securely held under him. The laughter continued and he could feel my massive grin against his neck before it turned into little kisses I peppered up his jaw. Soon his laughing turned to a lustful groan.

He turned us both quickly, causing a 'whoosh' sound to escape my mouth, as I was now looking down at his amused face. We were still firmly connected and I felt him strengthen inside me as I shifted, extracting another moan from us both.

I planted my palms on his chest and leaned down to lick the seam of his lips before pulling back quickly avoiding the kiss he wanted to take deeper.

"Uh oh, not yet, not until I have had my Valentine's fun." I said leaning across to pick up the rose which thanks to our activities had now lost a few petals. I picked those up as well and scattered them on his chest, marvelling at the contrast of colours. It looked like little pools of blood dripped on honey and as ever morbid that thought was, it was still startlingly beautiful to behold.

"I have never seen a red rose so deep in colour," I said reaching out to trace a line around each petal, causing him to close his eyes at one point.

"I picked the rose not just for its beauty but also for its meaning, Keira." He said still keeping his eyes closed. My hand stilled and I stopped tormenting him. I leaned down close to his face and whispered above his lips,

"Tell me." He took a deep breath and I smiled to myself at the little shudder I just caused him.

"Dark red roses represent unconscious beauty. They symbolise the deepest and boldest expressions of love, Keira and most of all, they leave nothing unsaid. One speaks of desire, but more than one speaks of a person's commitment to not just that desire, but to the united love that means that desire will never falter. This is the level of my commitment to you, Keira." He said opening his eyes suddenly and then the curtains around his bed opened fully on their own. They let through the rest of the day's light in and soon the room was almost glowing red from the sea of deep red roses that graced every surface of the room.

"Oh…my" I whispered as I took in the room that had been transformed into a dreamlike rose garden.

"I love you, Keira." He said sitting up and holding me to

him with his arms up my back. His hands entwined in my hair as he gently pulled my face round to look at him. My expression was dumbfounded. He laughed and then took the lip that was hanging open in shock into his mouth to suck on.

"Do you like it?" He asked after he played with my lip, letting it fall back into place. I nodded my head like a dog on a dashboard.

"Words, Keira." He ordered softly, like he had a million times before.

"I don't know if there are any words Draven, other than, I love it! Thank you." I said blushing when I saw the purple flash in his eyes that drank me in.

"You're very welcome, my love."

"I wish now I had bought you something different." I said thinking how embarrassed I was going be when it was time to give him his gift.

"Oh Keira, don't you know by now, my gift is the reaction I receive when your eyes take in anything I do, that is the best gift in touching my heart and with that in mind, I can't wait until your birthday." Now I was the one smirking at him.

"My Birthday? Draven, that isn't for months." I said still getting excited about the thought.

"That may be true but the idea that I have will need about that much time in planning." He tried to keep his mouth straight but one light smack from me saying, 'Oi, that's not fair' had him breaking out into a full blown grin.

"So, what did you get me?" He asked emphasizing his excitement with a hug and a little shake to my body that still sat snugly on top of him.

"Candy nipple tassels, do you want to wear them now or save them for later?" I said and now I was the one laughing at the sight of his face dropping.

"Right, that's it! Now you're in trouble, little Miss!" He said lifting his hips slightly, so he could slap my bottom.

"Hey!" I shouted playfully but he just flipped me again, until I was lay under him, caged in his straight arms holding himself above me. Once there he started tickling me into a snorting mess but soon the actions has us transformed from giggling idiots into moaning each other's names once again.

The glorious morning ended with the only words that truly mattered being heard from my well used lips…

"I love you, Dominic!" I shouted as I came apart under my man, my love…My heart's only owner.

"Snap out of it!" Pythia said which brought me back to the now and a load of half melted candles.

"Come on, just make your birthday wish already, you never know…it might come true." She said winking at me and I had to blink a few times to halt the tears that started to form there from falling. I stared at the cake until it blurred and I shook off the image of a room full of roses. Then I closed my eyes, letting two tears to slip down past the dam and made my wish…

"I wish for one day to live the birthday that Draven had planned for me."

I took a deep breath, blew all over the cake and had to smile when not one flame flickered back at me. Pythia and Armi both clapped, cheered and handed me a knife to cut the cake.

"Right, time for your present." She said getting up and sifting through a rainbow coloured fluffy bag that Pip would have loved.

"Ok, so it's not conventional and it's not that sparkly dagger I wanted to get you…do you remember that one Armi, wasn't it pretty?" Pythia said to a nodding Armi.

"Stunning." She agreed making my chest ache with just the divine sound of one word. I wondered if she just had a trail of people weeping at her feet as she nipped out for a newspaper at the local corner shop. I had no doubt that a few words from Armi could have brought down a barracks full of SAS soldiers and Navy Seals to blubbering babies, she was that heavenly.

I looked down at the square parcel which was wrapped up in parchment that looked like Egyptian papyrus paper with red ink symbols blotted into it. It was tied with brown string that had little wooden beads at the end. I looked up to see that

Pythia actually looked excited and I wondered if she had already seen my reaction and if so, why would she even get excited?

"Because it is the start of a new beginning, four points to an arrow leading the way to The Quarter Moon." She said as I opened the parcel. She had heard the question in my head along with all my other ones no doubt, but this Quarter Moon business had me more than a little confused.

"Yes, I did and trust me when I say, this will help with that." She nodded to my lap as I pulled back the sides to reveal a smaller square of tissue paper on top of a leather bound book. I decided to open the smaller gift on top of the book first. I tore away the thin cream paper and soon was looking down at a very unusual piece of jewellery.

It was a bracelet of thick black cord with four round stones situated at 12, 3, 6 and 9 o'clock. Each stone had silver wire wound round in such a way it looked like a Quarter Moon on one side of each smooth surface.

"It goes this way." Pythia said handing it to Armi, which had me raising an eyebrow. Armi came to sit next to me on the sunny coloured couch and motioned for my wrist.

"Armi is the only one who can open it for its new owner…*for now anyway*…" She whispered this last part and it fell into the quickly filling category of 'I had no clue' part of my brain.

"…But once the stones have connected with your inner Chakras then you will be the only one who can wear or remove it." Pythia explained before nodding for Armi to proceed. I was just about to ask a question as to why I would need such a thing, when a bright blue light grew from Armi's delicate fingers. Even her fingernails looked to be made from pearls as they glistened in what looked like a piece of the sky she now held in her hands.

Suddenly the black cord snapped open from one of the stones and quicker than I could see it was clasped onto my wrist. I jumped at the feel of heated tingles that shimmied up and down my arm, paying special attention to my scars. I hadn't bothered with gloves when getting out the shower, as I thought there was little point to it in front of a girl who knew everything that had happened in my life. The very reason I ever did in the first place was that I hated it when strangers would jump on the suicide train and ride it all the way to pity central.

I looked down at my wrist, now kind of liking the feeling it created just under my skin and it was something similar to the necklace Draven had given me. In fact the more time I gave it, the stronger the pull they had to each other and I had the strangest feeling that they were communicating in some way to each other, using my veins as a motorway in between.

"Each stone will help you on this journey Keira, in ways you wouldn't have thought possible." Pythia said to me and I dragged my eyes away from the four beautiful stones that were still humming against my skin.

"What do you mean, will help me?" I asked.

"The four stones all represent a stage of your journey, four Quarter Moons will pass until you reach your goal and each stone holds the power to help the emotional strength you will need for each cycle." I tried not to gulp at the sound of even a glimpse of what was to come. But four Quarter moons…how much time was that?

"The first Quarter Moon is tonight and therefore the beginning." This time it was Armi who spoke and Pythia just nodded once before leaning across to touch my knee.

"Never let fear of the unknown cloud over the truth you know lies deep within your heart…remember that and you will rise above all obstacles." I took in her treacle eyes that swam in the depths of knowledge and lowered my head before saying,

"I understand and….and I am ready. Where do I begin?"

"Right, well…" She said after clapping her hands, making me jump at the loud noise such tiny hands could deliver.

"First, back to the rules. As you already know, I cannot outright tell you where to go or what to do once you get there, but you're a smart girl, you will figure it out…and your next gift will help with that part also." I looked down at my last 'gift' and my eyes grew large as I ran my fingertips around the symbol that was embossed in leather. It took me a moment to realise where I had seen that symbol before and when it finally hit me, I stood quickly and the book fell from my lap.

"AHH!" I screamed as I shot away from the book, as though the snake on its front would lash out and attack me.

"Now, now Keira, does the symbol of someone who has saved your life really scare you so?" Pythia asked tilting her head to one side in that adorable way children do when they don't understand something.

"You know!?" I screeched.

"Well…durr! Oracle remember?" She said this time a little less…umm…Oracley.

"There is truly nothing to fear." She added but I just shook my head. They hadn't seen the power behind those symbols as I had and considering the last time I had seen that massive tattooed biker, he hadn't been alone when watching me, well… let's just say it didn't scream knight in shining armour!

Pythia once again was tapping the side of her head, like I was always missing something, which in this instance I guess I was. Of course, she had seen that day at Afterlife. She had seen as I had, the way the tattooed serpents had swirled around his muscles in a never-ending attempt at trying to consume themselves.

"They are called Ouroboros and your lovely Knight just so happens to be the Master of them."

"What! This…he…I…Ok let me start over…what!?" I said looking down at the rich red leather that was tied together with a simple knotted thong in darker leather.

"Look Electus…"

"Please don't call me that anymore." I said cutting her off with the strained sound of pain that name now caused me. She frowned at me and looked as though she wanted to comment about it, but instead I was happy when she just shrugged her little shoulders before continuing on.

"Fair enough Keira, I see that time needs to heal some wounds and that is to be expected, it really is, but right now the only thing that you need to focus on is simple…"

"Which is?"

"Suck it up! This is some serious shit and not that you need the added pressure here, but if you don't keep that pretty little mind on the job at hand and fight for it, then it really won't matter what we call you." This was said with the tutu she still wore cocked to one side thanks to cocking her hip out and now she looked like a small antsy teenager. But it was when what she said started to playback in my head that something snapped into place.

"You messed up...! Didn't you? That's why I am here in the first place and why you're even getting involved…But of course, man, I am such a shmuck!" I smacked myself on the side of the head before carrying on with my rant,

"I mean, Draven was the one who told me that you don't get involved and only…you only meet on the…" I trailed off as even more puzzle pieces fitted together.

"…7th day. Yes I do and yes I did. I messed this up and now it is not only me that needs your help in fixing this…"

"How…?"

"Did I mess up? Keira, you know that I can't tell you that and even if I did, it would not change things. No…now we must use what we have in getting the fates back on track, where they belong." She said standing up to face me…or more to like face my stomach.

"And these fates, they include Draven and me…right?" I asked the first part to the most important information of my life and I nearly crumbled to the floor in relief when she simply nodded.

"Oh thank God! Thank you!"

"Keira, there's more…" I closed my eyes momentarily, blocking the rest of the world from my mind. I knew there was more…I mean Christ there was always more but right now, right this very second, the only thing that mattered was that the fates needed me and Draven to be in it together. For the first time in a cold age my heart soared. That was until Pythia finished her 'more'.

"I am sorry Keira, but you don't understand the reasons."

"And those are?" I asked not even bothering to open my eyes as I knew as soon as she spoke the words, that they would just slam shut anyway.

"The Prophecy Keira, the one story that remains untold until…" She paused finally making me look down at her and I was surprised to find tears swimming so close to the surface, but with her last breath taken she released them with one sentence…

"…Judgement Day."

CHAPTER TWENTY

PULLING ON INVISIBLE STRINGS

"Whoa…now back up! What did you say?" I even stumbled back when she spoke about both the Prophecy and Judgement day in the same sentence. Now my eyes were open, like wide friggin' open!

"Keira, please try and understand…." She started but my hand flew up to put a stop to her patronising tone. I mean, it wasn't even the fact that it was coming from a child, it really wasn't, but more the fact that after everything I had been through, all that I had seen, well I think that gave me an equal footing, alright!

"Oh I think I understand alright, I think I have been royally screwed over is what! That Prophecy, that Judgement Day you're speaking of, well that day came and went Pythia, remember…some crazy dude named Malphas… 'cause trust me, I do! Of course, a memory like that would stick, considering when getting stabbed to death by the guy!" I shouted stomping round the suite and throwing my hands around to emphasise my point.

"That *wasn't* the Prophecy, Keira." She said softly but this just sent me over the edge.

"Bullshit! That was my Judgement Day, Oracle and the only one I will ever live through again! I died that day for what I believed in and now you people want me to what, do it again?! What am I now, a damn cat?" I felt like tearing my hair out listening to all this.

"Calm down, Keira."

"What the Hell is wrong with you people? Calm down… calm down…really?! You just told me that all that shit I went through wasn't even the bloody Prophecy that you have all been harping on about since the day I came along!"

"Keira, CALM DOWN!" Suddenly there was a huge flash of light that blinded out any other colour in the room, like a sun bomb had just gone off with her screaming words. It knocked me for six and I stumbled backwards until my ass fell into a convenient chair. Then magically the light got sucked back into Pythia's chest like a vacuum and left us both staring at each other panting.

"Shit!" Was all I could say.

"Are we good now?" She asked once she had reined in her outburst, that made mine look like a RJ's VW playing chicken with a tank!

"I would say so, yes." I squeaked out.

"Good, now let me explain, as much as I can anyway." She took a deep breath and sat back down, placing her elbows on her tutu covered knees.

"What happened with Malphas was not the Prophecy, Keira it was more like someone trying to create their own. See the Prophecy speaks of a day of judgement that the Gods have no part in. In other words, they are useless in this coming fight. They are allowed no part in it and as you know that day you had help, thanks to someone's mother." I nodded remembering it well. Not exactly how I would have expected to have met one of the in-laws.

"This time, you will have none and it is through your choices alone that will determine all our fates, but first we need to get the fates back in play before that day arrives, which brings us to now and the now is what needs fixing." She placed her hands on her knees and pushed herself up like she was a grown adult.

"So now comes the most important question there is Keira,

the question that hangs all the world's fate in your hands, the one that only you can choose as the Gods decided it should be." She walked over to me and held out her hand to me.

"Ask me." I said looking up slowly.

"Are you ready to walk the steps of your destiny?" And that was it. That was what every single thing I did came down to. So, after a deep breath and a couple of squeezes of my fists, I answered her with the only answer there ever would be.

"Yes, I am Pythia." I slapped my hand into hers and wasn't surprised at the strength such a tiny frame possessed as she pulled me up.

"Good…now let's eat cake."

I had to smile.

After everything I had learned this day, I thought my mind would have been on some sort of supernatural overload and gone into lockdown mode, which was what usually happened. So I was somewhat surprised to find that instead of spending the rest of the day in my pyjamas, curled up in bed making good use out of the 24hour room service, I was now leaving the hotel taking my first steps in this journey.

I had learnt everything from Pythia that I could and the most important part was the book she had left me. At first I hadn't believed her, that was until she and Armi had left the suite and I found my proof. Pythia had told me that the book was the best way to communicate from now on and I snorted when she referred to it as better than a mobile phone or email. A baby could have detected the doubt on my face on hearing that one. Of course, then she opened the middle of the book, slashed her palm open with her tiny teeth and slapped a bloody handprint on the two pages…suffice it to say I stopped laughing pretty quickly.

I was left to watch, with my mouth agape as the blood soaked deep within the pages and travelled like blood ink into the centre of the book. I didn't really understand what was happening, but if I could have guessed, it looked like Pythia was marking the book with her essence. It was only when she spoke next that I snapped out of my amazement.

"Your turn."

"Uhh…I think I will pass, but you can have a pinkie promise if that helps." I said holding up my little finger in hopes this would be a doable option. I knew when she laughed it was doubtful, but it really became a no brainer when she produced a small dagger. Then quicker than my eyes could follow she slashed out at my little finger I was still holding up.

"Ok…Oww!" I said making her roll her eyes before she slapped my hand down on the same page. There she held onto my little finger and milked the blood from it making me feel like some freaky ass cow!

This whole process she explained was so the connection between us both could be formed and the Ouroboros on the front of the book could protect the messages within. I couldn't help myself when I pointed out that all the pages were in fact blank, but once again she rolled her eyes. At that moment I thought that for an Oracle, she wasn't a very patient one and when I received the cutest little death stare, I knew she had heard me.

Another very important thing she explained was the reasons behind all the cryptic letters and this was simply because nothing she told me could ever end up in the wrong hands or read by the wrong eyes. I gathered because she had already messed up once, she was a little paranoid now and for good reason. If I had the power to tell people their future, not only would I hate keeping something like that to myself, but also on the other end of the scale, I would hate being the one that could tip those scales the wrong way by telling them that future.

The one last part of the puzzle I really didn't understand was about the warehouse. Why had she sent me to my near death to retrieve a coin, one that still remained firmly in my pocket. Her answer however was surprisingly basic. It was simply because the Pishachas Demon is sort of a treasurer of Hell and the only one that can bring with it the coins of the underworld, a coin that in the not so distant future I would apparently be needing.

After all bases were covered, she gracefully rose from where she was sat crossed legged on the floor and took Armi by the hand. She passed me, patted me on the shoulder where I was sat and wished me luck. Her last glance wasn't on me to see if I was listening to that wished luck, but strangely it was on the bracelet I now wore.

After they left I took the Oracle's place and sat by the coffee table to take a closer look at the book. I shook my head as I flicked through its empty pages and when I got to the middle, I saw that no trace of our blood remained. Getting frustrated I dropped my head to the table, resting my forehead on the thick pages beneath me before banging it gently.

"So what now genius?" I said out loud in a frustrated hiss after spending the last twenty-seven minutes examining it and staring at it hopelessly. It was only when I felt the little vibrations underneath me did I react. I lifted my head and saw the little china plate my cake slice had been on started clinking on the glass top. I watched the leftover crumbs jump and dance as the whole table moved.

"What the…?" I said and then I touched the book realising that was where it was coming from. I flipped the book closed and yelped when I saw why. The snake on the front was spinning round and round, never making any headway in eating itself further but all the while trying faster and faster until finally…it just… stopped.

I tentatively reached out to touch it and I soon snatched my hand back to my chest as it flipped open suddenly, shocking me. The first page started to produce words written in fancy script and I felt like gagging slightly when I saw it wasn't in black ink, oh no, not this book, this book was soaking up the words written in blood. I really tried not to think about it too much but my mind was already disobeying me by coming up with the possibility it could be our blood combined.

Soon my senses went wild, first with the mixed smell of brushed leather, the unique musk smell of old paper and the coppery scent of blood. My ears blocked out all surrounding sound and just seemed to home in on the soft blow of the wind that couldn't possibly have been there. Finally, my eyes drank in every word like they could be my last.

Here be the rules of the Ouroboros blood bound book:

Once a blood bond has been accepted then the only way to break this bond is to kill the serpent by starving the source of its power.

Anyone not blood bound may not view its contents and if an attempt is made then the accused will feel the venom of the serpent's sting.

The blood bound carrier is now responsible for all secrets enclosed within its pages and entrusted with the power of all words read.

Each page will fade in time as will the words, indicating that time passes, so if your eyes still see, then time will still play a part in your future.

If there is something you wish to know then grow a patient mind for it will take you seven skips to skip a seventh step and find your mind stepping forward seven to the seventh time, then your question will be answered.

A hand raised in anger and a deed corrupted by hateful actions cannot take effect, for ashes still remain and so do the blood bound of the same.

Communication of the bound cannot converse in a parallel time but speaking what needs to be said will find a time unparalleled.

Heed all rules and your blood will remain in safe hands.

I let all that sink in and understood most of it, apart from the skipping seven thing, that was just way too confusing. As I read each word the red lettering turned to a normal and safer looking black ink before soaking away only to re-appear on the leather flap of the cover. But the closer I looked the more it seemed as though each sentence had been burned into the skin than stained by a quill's point. This was obviously something that never went away and I guess for good reason. I, for one, would be the last person ever wanting to break its rules, as even reading them sent cold shivers up and down my spine.

After that I spent almost every minute for a full hour plus, asking it questions, just in the hopes of cracking the skipping seven code and it was only when looking at the clock and seeing ink for the first time on the seventy seventh minute at 6:53 did the writing start to appear once again. So that was the key to asking my questions, to wait exactly 77 minutes before seven minutes to seven and I would then get my answer. So after using my not so mathematical brain, I figured at 5:36 every day was my only chance at asking the book anything. Man, my head hurt!

I wondered later on what was with the number seven anyway, what part did it play in all this, was it only connected to the Oracle or was it connected with me as well? Of course, this question was going to have to wait for another day, as finally after waiting what seemed like ages, I finally had my first answer.

The Ouroboros:
This is an ancient symbol depicting a serpent or dragon eating its own tail. The name originates from the Greek language; (oura) meaning "tail" and (boros) meaning "eating", thus "he who eats the tail". The symbol is known to many ancient cultures as representing the eternal cycle of the renewal of life and infinity, the ultimate concept of eternity and the eternal return of life, death and rebirth, leading in the end to the path of immortality.

'My end is my beginning.'

But however, in the Demon realm it is known as the symbol for Mastering Chaos and rightly so as the idea of the human race ever gaining the knowledge for such immortality will ultimately bring forth the end of all realms. Heaven, Hell and all in between will fall and the serpent will no longer circle life as it does death. For take one away and the balance will crumble in on itself, destroying Man once and for all.

This is known as the Day of Judgement for all.

After reading this and understanding its value I knew it was something not to be taken lightly. If I was honest, it kind of scared the living bejesus out of me. I was in way over my head, so much so I could almost see my shadow from above! But however much it scared me, I couldn't help also drawing comfort from the fact that I now had a means to gain the answers I needed.

After reading it quite a few times and eating a delicious steak sandwich at the same time, I finally closed the book. I heard the antique grandfather clock chime and when I looked up I saw that it was now Eight pm. I got up and walked over to the massive windows that showed a stunning sight of London not yet lit up thanks to the long summer nights and I looked up from the hundreds of years old architecture. I could feel the hum of what I couldn't yet see and it travelled from my wrist all the way up to my necklace, like it had a little time ago.

The Quarter Moon couldn't yet be seen but already I was starting to feel it there. I raised my hand to the glass as if trying to reach out and touch it, even though it remained hidden from me but the humming pulse started to beat faster. So, when I heard the vibrating, at first I thought it was the beat of my own heart pounding. I turned and saw that the book was once again communicating something.

I actually laughed as it was just like Pythia had said it would be, which was a mobile phone vibrating to tell me it had received a text message. My fingertips slipped down the cool glass, leaving the comforting sight of the moon behind as I walked away.

"Time to get to work." I said breaking the silence that had left the suite feeling cold and eerie. As soon as that thought entered my head I found myself humming the theme tune to 'Mission Impossible' just to break the tension of seriousness to what I was about to do.

I sat down on the couch, dragged the table closer and waited for the snake to stop spinning. I even found myself biting my fingertips as the seconds ran into everlasting minutes. Finally the book settled down and I opened it to find the blood ink had already started to appear on the second page. I smiled as I read the first line.

To my dear Tricks,
I hope this next letter finds you sane and well,
As now I must give you seven clues,
On where to find Hell.

Seven is the number of words you must find,
Then put them in order that best fit in your mind.
The clues are all there open in broad daylight,
Use the Savoy's entrance and start on your right.

An English Rose sits proudly on the plaque
At the bottom of the words of nobles in black.
This is the point at where you should start
And remember that marrying off girls isn't always from the heart.
The first letter before ladies of the word not behind
That's also the letter in the number that's the third in your find.

Now jump a side step and find the crown jewels,
Read on about building the palace to find the right tools,
Take the first 2 letters of the king you see
And add on the LL'S you don't find in Army.

Making sure to keep on the same side
See at the bottom what you find on any bride.
When the Duke of Lancaster was given a home
What is the right word both written and rhymed in chrome.
It begins with the O you find there in who's who
And the first name of Gaunt is the last letter on view.

Now you must ride on the wings of an eagle
Where on the 3rd of September a marriage became legal
So find out the time words were said by the priest,
Add a B to the mix and find your man for the feast.

Cross the road and you will see
It is the A you're looking for not the B
So forget about the R MR

Or you won't get very far.
Right now you're here
The 14 should soon appear
So start at the Top
Keep counting and don't stop.

3 Feathers are waiting
And anticipating
As you connect the dots in your mind
As you look for a place
Not fallen from grace
Look closely at the plaque and you will find
Take the names into account
But find the S and I you need left out
Use the second name to begin
And see the Pressure within.

A sign of the Gods and a king of the second
Is also the number of 8 that is reckoned
The last word on the plaque is where this refers
After this letter figured take the first 2 from Hers
Reuse the E and S that you also find in Bees
Then you have the place where you must say please.

Which brings me back to the now. I was outside the Savoy hotel looking along the building to my right and just as a London taxi came around the corner it flashed its headlight, and I caught a glimpse of the polished plaques that the cryptic poem spoke of. I must confess this wasn't something I ever thought I would be doing on my birthday, looking for clues for a way into Hell but hey ho, there you go.

I even groaned aloud when my mind locked onto the rhyming shit and even now was doing the same with my own thoughts. I hated trying to solve puzzles and was next to useless doing so but this seemed to be the way the Oracle wanted to play things. To be honest, I wasn't entirely convinced at her reasoning either. I mean if no one but me could read the book, then why not just give me the bloody answer right from the start?

It was too frustrating to even think about and right now I was going to need all the brainpower I had if I was ever going to crack this code…

Sometimes, it just sucked to be me!

CHAPTER TWENTY-ONE

DO YOU WANT CHEESE WITH THAT?

"Impossible!" I shouted for like the hundredth time tonight. I was currently sat on the floor of the sitting room with seven sheets of paper spread out in an arch above the cryptic message that was mocking me in the book. It hadn't taken me long to realise that standing in front of each plaque outside, looking like a right plebe, wasn't going to help in solving the mother of all puzzles. So I quickly snapped a picture of each one with my phone and returned to the comfort of the Royal suite.

Of course, the Royal suite had its own office, complete with laptop, wireless printer and a desk big enough for two people to sleep on. So after first figuring out the top notch technology, I managed to print out the pictures so that I could easily read the words…not that this was currently helping much!

So this brought me back to the now and the now sucked big time! It was easy to say that each plaque was a word and unfortunately there were seven of the buggers. The only progress I had made in two hours was to use the clues and match them with the pictures that were at the bottom of every plaque. The order they read in went as such, the Rose, the Crown, Flowers, the Eagle, the initials AR-MR, Feathers and at last a Cross with the Royal mark for Charles the second. This had me back and forth and crossing the road looking like a headless chicken. Needless to say, about the funny looks I had received from the Bellboy when walking back into the Savoy.

"Ah ha, Hell! That one must be Hell!" I shouted as the first word came to me. The second plaque, which was the Crown, told me to take the first two letters of the King I find, which was Henry the third. So I took the H.E and added the LL'S that it asked, getting my second word of HELL'S which I have to say wasn't reassuring in the least.

"Beast! Oh beast, beast!" I said repeating over and over until I wrote it down on my scrap paper, which was the fourth word. This was only because I took a moment to go through the list of words that rhymed with Feast and Priest, but stupidly coming up with East and Least before saying the one that was needed with the actual B in it, like it asked.

Ok so now I had…

Blank. Hell's. Blank. Beast. Blank. Blank. And another bloody Blank!

"Arrrhhh!" I shouted slapping my open palms to the rest of the papers. This was just too damn hard and getting me nowhere fast. I had been at this for over two hours now and only got two stinking words and about 50 headaches! This was the very last thing I ever wanted to be doing on my Birthday and in my little frustrated rage, I almost punched the cake that still sat there with only a few slices missing.

"Ok, so think Keira, I need to find the Hell's something Beast…didn't that just sound like a jolly outing…ok so where on this Earth am I ever going to find that!?" I finished on a groan but then something about saying that out load must have snapped into place.

"Wait a minute…Find…that's it, that's the first word!" I shouted as I grabbed the book to read it again.

"Son of a bitch!" I said as it was right there the whole time. It was the last word!

"Oh for God's sake…right if that is how you are playing this Pythia, then let's do this shit!" I said not even caring about what was happening to my mental health if I wasn't even batting an eyelid at talking to myself.

So before I knew it, I had another two words, after playing the rhyming game once more and getting the word OWN that rhymed with Chrome. Then I finally got the word CHEESE from not only rhyming with BEES but also from counting that the plaque held 8 C's and taking the H.E from HERS like it told me to. At first, I thought I must have been wrong, as how random is putting the word CHEESE with HELL'S BEAST, but no matter how I looked at it, the more it made me sure of its place.

After writing this down it then clicked that the word after BEAST must be the word AT as the only letter that appeared 14 times was T and it already told me to use the letter A. Of course, when I wrote it down it made more sense. Now I had most of the sentence minus one word that I just couldn't get but I was hoping it would be enough…

FIND. HELL'S. OWN. BEAST. AT. BLANK.CHEESE.

"Well, it's a good enough start as any." I said aloud before unfolding my numb legs from the floor and trying to shake off the pins and needles that assaulted me. I looked at the clock and saw that it was 11:17 at night but I knew the late hour wouldn't stop me. So, before I could talk myself out of it, I walked into the bedroom and grabbed my long black hooded jacket. I quickly stuffed the book under the mattress and then thought better of it in case maid service was going to come in and turn down the bed. Instead I stuffed it under the sofa, hidden from view. I then hooked my bag over my body and left the suite.

I fidgeted with the thumb holes on my top and debated with going back into the suite to grab the book or not. This continued right until I got to the main Lobby, where I finally decided that if I carried it on me and anything were to happen, then it would be better safe and hidden. I nodded to myself and walked through the revolving doors to find it pouring down with rain.

"Of course." I whispered to myself, but the Bellboy raised his eyebrows.

"Typical English summer you'll find." He said smiling and I grinned back.

"Yeah, can't say I missed it." He smiled again and then asked,

"Can I call you a taxi, Miss?" I nodded at a smiley face that was complete with warm eyes and dimpled cheeks. He lifted a long whistle to his lips and called one of the taxis waiting along the drive to come forward. He then opened the door and tipped the rim of his top hat in parting. It made me feel like a Jane Austin character.

"Where to sugar?" Now this was the part of my plan I was kind of dreading…the embarrassing part. The guy in front turned around and the first thing I noticed was the reddish tattoo that swirled up the left side of his face in an unusual design. It looked almost like the tail part of something bigger as it forked at the end near his eye. He looked to be in his late forties and was big framed. His small grey eyes scanned me over momentarily before he cleared his throat. He was obviously waiting for me to answer.

"Um…I know this is going to sound a bit strange, but you don't happen to know a place around here with the name Cheese in it, do you?" I asked waiting any minute for either a confused look or one of those short laughs that says, 'you're joking right?' so imagine my surprise when I didn't receive either.

"That will be the Cheshire Cheese pub then." He said seriously as he pulled the car around the fountain and down towards the main road. My mind quickly flashed back to the clues that I had practically memorised and put the word 'Cheshire' as the possible answer.

"Cheshire! Of course." I said and when the taxi driver turned around and said, 'excuse me?' I knew I had shouted it out loud and now he must think he'd picked up a loon. The ride there really didn't take that long and I could have walked it in less than 20 minutes.

He pulled up alongside a street filled with shops and a popular coffee chain all closed up for the night. Thankfully, the rain had eased into light spitting droplets.

"See that alleyway there, well just down that you will find the pub." He said taking my money. I nodded and thanked him as I got out.

"Now what?" I said looking down at the alleyway called 'Wine Office Court'. It was dark, looming and didn't exactly scream inviting. But I knew there was obviously a good reason for me being here. So with that in mind, I pulled my hood up, hitched up my strap before my bag slipped off my shoulder and walked forward. I looked to the sides trying to make out the signs written in old script, but it was just too dark as the lights above flickered as I passed. It was as if my presence was causing an electrical interference or something because they sprang back to life once I had passed.

I was starting to feel as if I was on some sort of bad horror movie. Any minute I would see a dark figure step from the shadows that would then come racing at me wearing a long cape. Then my mind started to think about Jack the Ripper and the last thing I would scream as he raised his butcher's knife… that being 'I'm not a prostitute, so don't hurt me!'

After shaking the stupid thoughts from my overactive imagination and a quick wonder if Jack the Ripper wasn't in fact a Demon, I was soon stood outside a very quiet looking pub. The alleyway had opened up into a corridor of tall buildings either side but at least I could now see the sky. I shivered as I saw the Quarter Moon playing centrepiece to this gloomy situation and I felt the tingling sensation at my wrist. One I tried to ignore.

I looked up at the round wrought iron sign that stated,

'Ye Olde
Cheshire Cheese
Rebuilt 1667'

"Well, this must be the place." I said looking left and right not finding a soul, or more importantly a shadow. The sign wasn't even lit up and everything from outside looked like it was closed for the night. This was then confirmed when I saw the opening times and that it closed at 11pm.

"Shit!" I said clenching my fists. If I hadn't spent so bloody long trying to decrypt something with the same level of intellect needed for cracking codes for MI5, I would have been here in time. Now what was I supposed to do? I didn't know but I wasn't about to give up that easily. I took my still clenched fist and knocked on the door, hoping someone was still inside. It felt like I waited forever, when someone finally decided the knocking idiot just wasn't going to go away.

"We're closed!" I got shouted at through the door first before I heard the locks grind.

"Yes I know, I'm sorry but I think…" I wasn't given time to finish as I saw a hand come out first with a palm flat out as if waiting for something to be placed there. The slither of a moon had become brighter thanks to the passing clouds and it now shone on the hand in front of me. It cast an eerie glow to reflect back from the palest skin. I could even make out the blue veins that bulged underneath the skin like thin tissue paper over electrical wires.

"Umm…oh…oh ok, alright, money…I see," I mumbled as I fished out my purse and took out a twenty. I folded it and placed it in the hand and then jumped back when it curled up and shot from sight.

"What the Hell is this!? Sod off and stop wasting my time!" A gruff voice shouted and threw the twenty back at my face, all the time keeping their face clear from the door.

"But wait! What do you want if… not money?" I said in a rush, but it ended up trailing off into a whisper when the door slammed in my face. Then I found my anger at the rude reply and instead of knocking, I used my palm to bang louder on the door. I was actually surprised when it opened again and even more so when I saw why. The same hand flashed out, gave me the middle finger and said,

"Piss off human and come back when you have earned the right for an invite!" This time when the door slammed shut I heard the locks to make it final.

"Well at least that confirms I have the right place…YOU ASSHOLE!" I shouted at the door before storming off down the alleyway where I had come. I had no clue what I was going to do now, but I knew one thing for sure and that was, I was pissed... oh man was I pissed! In fact, I was so angry I decided that I needed to work off some of the steam I was sure was coming from beneath my top. I started walking in the right direction back to my hotel and all the while my mind was reeling. I had no more clues to go on and had no idea what was meant by 'Earning the right to an invite'. So in plain English...I was so screwed!

And in true Keira style, this last statement became ever more true when I felt myself being grabbed from behind. A sweaty hand clamped around my mouth, while an arm banded my waist to pull me backwards. I started struggling as soon as the situation hit me and I heard the 'Umff!' sound when I connected with a leg behind me.

"Keep hold of her and drag that bitch back here so I can get this shit injected!" Another voice said from further behind us. I looked frantically for another soul who had seen me getting dragged into a shadowed alleyway, but there was no such luck. The old-fashioned lamp attached to the side of the building flickered like the one near the Cheshire Cheese and I saw a sign saying 'Cliffords Inn Passage'.

"I am trying but she's strong for a short little shit." Said the voice of the brute who was currently manhandling me backwards.

"Just hurry up would you, those wards won't hold forever and we can't risk being seen...fucking human lemmings." I felt the guy turn to the guy speaking and I used this to my advantage as his hand loosened. I quickly brought my head forward and then flipped it backwards as hard as I could, cracking the back of my head into the guys throat and then bit down quickly on the hand over my mouth.

Numerous things happened at once, the first being the screaming bellow that came from my actions, the blood that I tasted in my mouth and the arm that left my waist making me drop suddenly to the ground. I fell hard on my knees but cursed through the pain and scrambled to my feet. It was amazing how much the F word can actually help in situations like this, I thought at the most inappropriate moment. I even spat out the blood to the side as I ran for the road that was still in view ahead.

I was just starting to make headway with my escape when I felt my hair being grabbed and then I was spun around and thrown back deeper into the alleyway. I fell for the second time, only this time I felt my jeans rip along with my skin below my knee. I looked up and actually hissed at the looming shadow blocking my only exit. Well, I'd been practically begging for something like this to happen, what with all that Jack the Ripper crap swimming around my brain earlier, I thought bitterly.

"Now that wasn't nice, sugar." That voice suddenly had me squinting my eyes and remembering someone else that called me that not long ago.

"You were the taxi driver!" I snarled, but all I got in return was a dark laugh.

"And first prize for the most 'obvious dumb little bitch' goes to little shit." The voice said behind me and I jumped at it coming from too close to my ear.

"Hi bitch, I think I owe you a knuckle kiss don't you?" Before I could answer or deflect what was coming, I felt the side of my face explode from the downward punch he delivered. The burn broke out across my skin and I felt like I must have bitten through my lip as I felt blood trickling down my chin and the coppery taste mixed with the saliva I had to swallow. Ok, so now I was really pissed!

The taxi driver walked past me and joined his friend. I watched as he reached down to a darker shadow on the floor that was near a massive door at the end of the alleyway. I could just make out the old stone words that were carved from sandstone.

'Clifford's Inn'

I got up and they both laughed when I staggered a bit, which I was counting on as I let the rage I didn't know I could find engulf me. It was as if another person was possessing my body and it was actually true when people say they just see red. My vision actually blurred and my fingers started to tingle, so much so, I shook from it, but before they could see what was happening, I charged them both. I don't know where it came from but I just ran and threw myself into the middle of the one that hit me. The power I didn't know I still had inside impacted with his waist and I took him off his feet in an unconscious rugby tackle. I heard the 'umf' that came from us both but as soon as I was on the floor, I started attacking his face like a wild animal.

"Get this bitch off me!" He screamed as he tried to protect his face from the nails I was raking down his skin, taking away with me sick bloody skin curls. I cried out briefly as I felt a piercing pain inflict my shoulder, making me twist out my arms, hitting someone behind me. Then I quickly went back to my mission and the asshole underneath me.

I was just pounding at any part of him with the sides of my fists as I was still sprawled on top of him, but I quickly found myself being ripped away. It didn't quite register at first when I struggled in the hold of gentle hands that gripped me.

"LET ME GO!" I screamed trying to get back to the one who had hit me, and it felt like my outer shell couldn't contain the fire being pumped around my body. My lungs burned from breathing so hard and I was cutting into my own palm with my nails being fisted in the solid bends of my fingers.

"Calm, øjesten!" The same deep voice that I was getting used to hearing when in need of rescuing, ordered me. In my mind I was so utterly thankful that I was now safe, but the furious part of me wasn't yet done with tearing these guys a new place for bathroom use. I was a wild cat in the arms of someone about to dunk them in the river and I fought stupidly every second I was caught in his arms.

He made a grunting sound that sounded like it stemmed from frustration. I was so far gone in my frenzy, that I didn't realise I was being lifted higher and walked over to the right of the door in the corner. I was then quickly dumped over the high iron gate and landed on the other side with a thud. I got up and ran back to the gate to watch what was happening.

My massive shadowed saviour stood in front of the door ready and it was only now that my brain could process the pouring rain that drenched every scrap of clothing I wore. His large hood still covered his face but now the rain dripped down the front point in streaming rivulets. He looked up at the two men that were approaching him from both sides and that was when my mind started to get foggy.

My vision was starting to blur and I kept blinking rapidly trying in vain to clear it. My grip started to loosen on the rusting iron spindles that locked me in like a cage. The flaking black paint broke off in places as I tried to hold on tighter. I shook my head, seeing the world spinning around like I was driving past it at a hundred miles an hour.

"Look man, just give up the girl and we won't kill you, just walk away." I heard the taxi driver's voice stretch out like it had become an instrument someone was playing. Then I heard a grunted laugh that was starting to become familiar. I was sure that I then saw my shadowed hero crack his neck to one side.

"You two are already dead for touching the girl, so time to die…and *quickly,*" he said before he spun into action. I saw the glint of something being drawn from his back and I swear I could even hear the tapping of heavy water droplets dancing on steel. Then my world started to come to an end.

"Wh…at…'s…happ…ing?" I slurred my words as finally my hands released their hold. I fell down as my legs crumpled underneath me and I tried to will my eyes to stay open. I caught the sight of a massive shadow moving at impossible speeds and then I heard a death cry before the echo of snapping bone and slicing flesh. Rain battered my body and I rolled over to my back with the last of my strength. The water came down at me in long lines as I looked up to the night sky and my last thought was of the first Quarter Moon and how the tingling in my wrist had finally stopped…

Why had it stopped?

CHAPTER TWENTY-TWO

SNOW WHITE NEEDS MORE THAN A KISS

I didn't know what was happening, but it felt like I had drunk my body weight in Absinthe. I wasn't so much asleep as I was numb and paralysed with an unexplainable drunken fog. I kept having the past and present mixing up in my head. One minute I was on the ground pummelling into a face I hated and then I was being held upright against what felt like a worktop counter. It was too hard to figure out what was happening and it hurt too much to open my eyes right now.

That was until I felt my clothes being removed. I fought through the sting and peeled my eyes open, only to slam them closed at the bright spotlights that flooded my retinas with pain. Even without my sight, just the feel of someone touching my skin had me trying to fight. What if I had been wrong and the sound of death had in fact come from my protector, not from the two men that tried to take me.

This thought thankfully didn't last long as I felt the immense bulk of a muscle clad body loom closer and a soft baritone spoke in my ear.

"Hush my lille øjesten, calm now for me as you are safe… I've got you now." I instantly relaxed in his hold and my head drooped forward onto his chest. I then felt a large hand run up my neck and hold the back of my head to him. His fingertips did this slight gripping motion in my hair and I groaned at how nice and soothing it felt. It was definitely having its desired effect as I started to relax enough for him to continue whatever it was that he was doing before I reacted.

It was as if I was being lulled into a false sense of security, until I felt his other hand slide down my side and then across my belly. I felt calloused fingers graze the skin there and then I felt him grip the bottom of my top before he started dragging it upwards. He shifted back from me so that he had room to manoeuvre his hand between our bodies. It was only when I felt the cold air hit my bare flesh just under my breasts that I woke clearly to the fear of what was happening.

"No…plea…se." I stammered as I tried to twist out of his hold.

"Ssshh, calm now. Your body is shaking from cold and it will go into shutdown if I don't get you warm. Your clothing is wet and is keeping your temperature too low, so I must first remove it…don't fight me on this, øjesten." I tried to process his words and in the end, I found myself just giving in. I was too exhausted to fight even if I had wanted to. He waited until I relaxed once again before I felt the material being peeled off my skin like a thick film of glue. I grunted as my arms were forced up with the motion. The top's neck quickly pinged off my head and hit the floor next to us with a slap, proving just how wet it was.

I knew he said I was shaking with cold, but I was so numb I just couldn't feel it. I did, however, hear a clicking noise my teeth were making as they rattled away as audible evidence. With my forehead still resting against the rock wall that stood as Biker dude's chest, I felt him moving next to me. His actions seemed to get more urgent as I felt the sharp tug at my waistband and then I heard what sounded like the metal button from my jeans hitting the tiles.

"Can you hold on behind you?" He asked as his hands stilled on my hips. I nodded my head that still rested on him and moved my arms behind me. There I felt for the counter's edge and held on but as he started to pull down my jeans I was given more of my own weight to hold. I shamefully crumpled and would have hit the floor if massive hands hadn't shot up and grabbed my waist.

"Easy now." He hummed softly.

"Let's try another way. No panicking now, I will not hurt you, lille øjesten." The sincerity in his voice spoke volumes to the promise said in my ear. I nodded and then I was spun around quickly making me nearly lose my footing altogether. Instead of falling, I found the top part of my body being pushed forward until I had nowhere to go but over the counter. The hefty hand splayed out against my back was unyielding until I was fully over. I knew at this point that I must have been frozen half to death, as I couldn't even feel the heat from an automatic blush that needed the spare blood to blossom in my cheeks.

Soon my legs were rid of the soaked denim as they were quickly ripped away. I tried not to think about what this must look like, me bent over the bathroom counter, quivering in my underwear with a giant of a man at my back. In fact, I wasn't given much time to think about it, as I felt the man in question taking my limp form in his arms.

My head flopped backwards like a puppet missing the hand that brought them life. His bicep became an inflexible pillow beneath me and I found myself praying to feel the softness of a mattress soon. However, what I felt was far from that wish. I heard a door being opened and then a bellow of heat hit me. I groaned as the obvious steam worked its magic and then pressured water added to the sensations. He had walked us both into the shower.

"This should help raise your temperature, hold onto me if you can, I am going to set you down." His voice could barely be heard over the sounds of powerful jets coming at me from various angles.

"I am going to adjust the heat slowly, so you don't go into shock." He said as he let my feet find the wet base of the shower. I suddenly had a feeling I was going to fall as there was no way I could hold myself up. I reached out and grabbed handfuls of his wet T-shirt but I needn't have bothered thanks to the iron girder that belted around my waist, securing my chest to his. His muscles flexed as his arm shifted me closer and then he bent forward to reach for something.

The water grew warmer ever so slightly and he pushed me backwards so that all my body was under the biggest spray above. I felt his free arm reach up and gently start running his fingers into my hair, massaging my scalp.

"You have some blood on you...no, no… don't fret now, I am going to wash it from you, so don't startle when I start to touch you…understand?" He waited for something and when I murmured against his T-shirt, he took that for the 'alright' it was meant to be. It took only seconds before his hands began their journey along my skin. When he started by my neck, I was thankful he had left my underwear on as my nipples felt like rock pebbles rubbing against his rippled abs. I felt tiny in his hold and even more so when one of his hands engulfed my entire shoulder.

I don't know how long it took him to get me clean as I think I passed out a few times. My mind was finding it too damn hard to keep my body responsive, even when I felt his hand washing me, coming closer to each tender area. I didn't know what was wrong with me, but I found myself more than thankful at being looked after, even if it was utterly embarrassing.

I was vaguely aware when I was being carried out of the shower and dried off with a soft towel. At one point, I kind of felt sorry for the big guy as he struggled in getting my body into the Savoy's bathrobe. I gathered he was more used to getting women out of clothes rather than in them, much like any man. Lastly, I was hoisted up and heaved over his colossal shoulder in a fireman's lift and taken into what I presumed was the bedroom.

I felt myself being lowered down and as soon as the mattress I had earlier prayed for made contact, this time there was no stopping my mind from bailing out on me. Darkness followed.

"It's like I said before, they were waiting for her." I heard the deep voice penetrate my senses through the shadows my mind had given itself to. I turned my head so that both ears were free in the hope that I would hear the one sided conversation.

"What do you think I did, you sent me here to do a job and

I am seeing it through, that included the death of the two low ranking Warlocks that were given the girl as a mark." Hearing this made me shudder and I wondered why the strength in my body hadn't yet returned.

"And I said that she was fine, old man! I got there in time… barely in the end but not before she took on some damage." His accent was coming out thicker as his emotions rose to the surface and it was easy to hear he was getting pissed. He was, however, still trying to control the level of his voice.

"Do not take that tone with me Elder, I know what you told me, and it didn't include her being marked and hunted. It also didn't include her running off halfway around the damn planet!" He hissed into the phone I couldn't see.

"She got hit, that much is obvious, but I finally found her near The Devil's Ring…Yeah well, no shit Elder, I would like to know the very same thing." I really wanted to hear what was being said on the other side of this conversation and more importantly, who on earth was Elder?

"I have no choice but to do just that. If it was only for the bruises, I would let it go, but one of the bastards must have injected her with something." I finally had the strength to open my eyes into little slits and I just caught the shadowed figure of a frustrated male. His free hand raked through his hair and it was almost painful to watch, knowing Draven did the exact same thing.

"The Hell if I know, but I can feel it swimming around in her system and I know only one way to get it out of her." This time he growled low and when he spun round to check I was still asleep, worried no doubt that he had awakened me with his outburst, I shut my eyes. He must have been satisfied because he continued his rant.

"By Odin, you think I don't know that, old man! But by all means feel free to explain why the Chosen One can barely move, when your shit hits the fan! I am ruler of my own world Elder, thanks to the choices *you* made, but that does not mean I will bow down like you do to your frightened fates!" I watched on in amazement as he seemed to suck the shadows in the room, pulling them to his form until they cloaked him in writhing swirls of darkness.

"I still have a job to do, so I suggest you let me get it done and quit wasting my time with your Royal ramblings. I care little for the ramifications of your actions, I only care for the debt of life you hold. Now, if you will retire your tongue and trust in my abilities, I will be getting back to the small task of keeping the small human alive. Contact me only when the situation unfolds and I will do the same." He waited and listened to something on the other end before shaking his head.

"Viðara." He said sharply and then ended the call. He growled low before throwing the phone onto a chair, where I noticed his long black jacket was resting over the back. This was the first time I had seen this much of him and how much did it suck that it was a bloody time where I could barely focus!

Even my eyelids didn't have any strength and felt like they were holding up mini bricks. I managed to catch a glimpse of him turning around before they fell again. The next time I managed to get them all the way open I would have jumped if I had the energy, as now his masterful shadow was next to me on the bed. I think I at least managed a groan.

"Hush now and save that strength, for you will need it soon enough." His voice was so different now as opposed to the conversation he was having not long ago. It was still impossibly deep but also soothing when whispered gently in my ear. This he must have known as I started to relax almost instantly. What was it about this guy that had me so trusting when around him?

"Wh…at happ…?" My voice broke as it had done in the bathroom.

"You were injected with something and it is making you…" He hesitated and it felt like I was waiting for my lottery numbers to come up. In the end I tried to clear my throat which thankfully he got the hint and I got my numbers, although they weren't the winning ones.

"…more compliant." He must have seen the look of inner pain as he carried on,

"I only mean in the physical sense, lille øjesten. The drug will continue to run throughout your system until an antidote is administered and as you can gather, I am without these means." On hearing this I closed my eyes and willed the tears to stay away. There must be a way of stopping this! I utterly refused to stay trapped in this numb and weak state when Draven needed me.

"I can see the pain you are trying to hide and there is no need. Have no fear of my words, I am not without my means, it was only meant to explain the reason as to what I must do next." I couldn't help my internal shudder at his words. In this crazy supernatural life I was living, his idea of 'fixing' me could be anything from chewing on my toenails to pulling rabbits from his ass to feed me!

"Just try and relax." He said and I was happy when I managed a grunt of humourless laughter.

"Yo…u're…kid…ding…right?" I stammered through shaky lips. The sound of his deep laughter echoing around me actually helped in relaxing me, mentally anyway, as I don't think my limbs could get any more relaxed. Hell, it felt like that bastard had injected me with a concoction of jelly and antifreeze!

The huge body shifted his bulk into lying down next to me and I tried to will my eyes to focus on details of his face, but all it came back with was a shadowed haze and I wondered if it was down to my inability to see or his doing in controlling the darkness of the room. Either way, I still couldn't make out anything about the man, other than the sheer size of him, which was nothing short of gigantic.

I was brought out of my massive man musings as he came to lie flush with my body and his arm snaked out, no pun intended, around my waist. His front was as close to my side as he could get and his arm felt like it weighed the same as a small person. With him on his side and me on my back, I could feel him looking down at me and the silent minutes were near unbearable. What was he waiting for? But more importantly, what would he do when the timer ran out on his waiting?

"Now, I want you to listen to me, lille øjesten, as I promise not to hurt you in any way, but what I am about to do will feel…" He cleared his throat and it was as if he was about to talk about sex to his grandma or something.

"…odd and well…ah shit, how do I say this?" I was sure my fuzzy vision could make out the frustrated actions of him raking his hand through his hair and letting out a deep breath.

"J…Ju…st…say." I managed.

"It will make you come." He blurted out and at first, I didn't think my stunned brain heard him right. In fact, if it wasn't so difficult to speak I know I would have said, 'Come again' shortly followed by 'What the F word'!

"This feeling can't be helped and trust me if there was another way, then I wouldn't be putting it off. I tried torturing the Warlock that injected you, but he was just a lackey taking orders and didn't know shit. Plus, he kind of died quicker than I intended, so here we are." He sounded like he was nervously rambling, while my mind was still trying to cast out the word 'torture' and 'died' before it could create an image.

"This will start to feel strange, so try not to fight my darkness when it touches you." He whispered gently and when I flinched I felt a soothing touch at my cheek, where the back of thick knuckles caressed my chilled skin.

"Dddark…ness?" I couldn't help but feel frightened by his words.

"Remember øjesten, don't fight us." He repeated, choosing to ignore my fears. I just knew that if I had the inner strength I would have been panting like a cornered animal in the sights of a beast. So with this in mind, I had to wonder where he thought I was going to find the strength to fight. That would be like Snow White getting up just before Prince Charming kisses her and breaking his nose before pepper spraying his ass for sexual assault!

And suddenly that's exactly what it felt like. Some dark but modern Gothic version of Snow White and I now even had the hair to match that image as I lay motionless in waiting. And wait I did. It felt like he was powering up next to me for something. Every time I pried my lids back all I could make out was the swirling of black serpents that swam around his stretched-out frame. I was about to try and say something but then it started.

I watched as long as I could as his body bent backwards and bowed in what looked like extreme strain on his muscles. He let out a howling groan before jackknifing forwards which ended in him curling his body around me. I felt like he was turning his body into a Boa Constrictor and I was about to feed his appetite.

Once his body seemed to come under some sort of control, his movement slowed down from the vibrations that had shortly racked his body into convulsing tension. However, this didn't prove to be a good thing, well not for me anyway. No, this new control he found only meant whatever he had planned was about to come to light and it started with him crawling over on top of me. He held, what I imagined was an immense weight, all above me and caged me in.

"Just breathe, lille øjesten…just…breathe." He whispered the last words resting his forehead to mine and I once again pulled my eyes open long enough to get my first glimpse of his eyes.

"Ah!" A startled yelp escaped before I sucked in a quivering breath. This was in response to the flaming flash I had seen encircling one eye, like someone had taken a glowing hot branding iron to his iris. I slammed them closed but I could see the moving lava spinning around his eye in the shape of a snake. It was like when someone takes a picture of you and you can still see the flash long after your image was captured.

"Plleeassse" I moaned as fear was overriding any other emotion there should have been. I mean, I knew deep down that he wouldn't hurt me, but this fear seemed to be stemmed from a deeper root. Apart from in my dreams, this was the first time I'd had a man's body so close to me since Draven and I felt trapped, both in body and mind.

"Ssshh now and be brave small one, for it is coming." He hummed from above me like there was now an electrical current transforming his voice. His masterful tone wasn't asking for me to try and be brave, no, it was demanding it, for there was no stopping what was coming and soon, I would be joining it.

Then it hit me with the force of a Freight train. It touched me like a sexually charged blanket that covered me from top to bottom. At this I no longer had to try and keep my eyes closed, as strength started to seep into my body. I looked up to see that the shadowed snakes I had seen him rule and master were now swimming all over me. They came from the home of his body like thick black ink tentacles that connected us together, like being bound by the hands of darkness. They kept hold and with every stroke they made the sensations they invoked doubled. The pleasured trail they left was leaving my chest heaving and my thighs damp with need.

I felt like the need was going to burn right through me and leave me with nothing but ashes instead of flesh. I needed to find release like I needed my next breath. I looked up to the figure above me that seemed to be having his own trouble keeping control as this other part of him explored every inch of my body, inside and out. I felt the pressure of the shadows as though they were made by the flesh of a man and each touch was a scorching caress. It seemed to touch parts of me that had long been left untouched and I cried out as it connected with each sensitive nerve.

At one point I even lost my mind and reached out to the man above me. I would have begged his own hands to take the place of supernatural fingers but as if he knew this, he quickly snapped out and restrained my wrists in an unbreakable hold. Almost bruising were his fingers as they curled into the tightest shackles, but I didn't care. I was too lost in my need to care other than at least he made contact, no matter how brief.

The controlled darkness seemed to latch on to the connection like a live feed as its strength seemed to amplify. I cried out into the night in what seemed like a wishful howl and I heard it being mirrored back at me from above.

"Please…oh God please…I need…I…" I begged without even letting the shame of it to register. I just didn't care. I just needed to feel myself shatter beneath him. It was like having a room full of hands on your body all at one time and I felt like each one was vibrating along my hypersensitive skin.

"I know…and…Uhh…Ahh…you will!" He shouted in between obviously seeking the points of his own pleasure. I felt the bed beneath me shaking and I followed its source, that being the body of muscle above. He was trying to hold onto something and I had an idea what. So, just as I felt that ultimate climb to a never ending and all-consuming pleasure cliff I knew I would soon jump from, I arched my head up as far as it would go and spoke my wishes,

"Let go and come with me." I whispered breaking both of our controls like high tension wire.

"AHHH…OH, OH YES…ARHHH!" We both screamed out only in different ways. Mine was a scream whereas the body above me still shook from howling a roar that made the fixtures in the room shake with the force of it. I clenched my muscles that I could once again feel working and rode out the blissful waves until the tsunami destroyed all coherent thoughts.

Shortly after came the part of floating down to earth on a weightless cloud of euphoria. The feeling that power had flowed back into my being, only to be taken away by the power of such an orgasm. Oh, he had healed me alright and in the most shameful way imaginable but right now I couldn't find the spare energy to care. No, all I could find now was the extra senses it took to notice two things, one was the man above me was trying to get his breath and the most important…Was that wet patch on my skin mine or his…

Or both?

CHAPTER TWENTY-THREE

MASTER OF THE OUROBOROS

The next morning I woke after one of the deepest sleeps I could remember in a long time and the reasons made me blush. It wasn't hard to understand why my body had felt it necessary to shut down to such a degree. When was the last time I had such a firecracker of an orgasm…? Wait… that really wasn't a memory I wanted to explore in the pits of my mind. If anything, those memories I kept well hidden behind a solid and impenetrable vault door, one labelled 'My Heart'.

It was too deep for me to swim in and it made me vulnerable in its depths. No, I was going to put a stop to any of that immediately and focus on the now, not the past and unless I had a bottle of something I could shoot to get me through it, then that wasn't about to change. So, back to the other reason I had slept so well and was also one of the most confusing facts. It was the first time since pre orgasm that I was also held in bed until I fell asleep in the arms of another. I don't know whether he knew I was aware of this fact, as when I woke his warm body was no longer wrapped protectively around me. But nevertheless, it didn't change what I already knew.

After last night's risky and turbulent events transpired, the aftermath of coming apart under the hands of darkness had left me wiped…but I wasn't the only one this affected. My shadowed saviour, whose face I still hadn't seen and whose name I still didn't know, had only had enough energy to roll to one side and pull my shaking body closer to him. We didn't speak another word after that and once I heard his breathing mellow into an even rhythm, it didn't take me long to follow suit. This didn't mean that I wasn't aware of his movements in the dead of night, one he seemed to command entirely.

I didn't know what time it was, but at some point his protective bulk left me and I heard water running. I had never been more tempted to get up and perv at someone in the shower before. The reasons weren't just to get myself a shot of colossal eye candy soaping down a naked body, no matter how much I knew the amount of muscle I would find. Hell, I could easily feel that this dude had muscle on top of muscle when he had pressed himself against me in bed, but this had nothing to do with wanting to haul myself up from the comfy bed. It was solely for the reason to find out who this guy really was. And unless he showered in the dark, I was fairly certain I would get a good glimpse of him this time.

This plan in theory was a sound one, so what kept me from following through? Easy, it was plain and simple… fear. I still didn't know who had sent him other than a guy named Elder and the fact that he owned a soul debt. These are the things that I got from his own mouth when talking on the phone, but they still left me confused as to their full meaning.

So, I had waited until I heard the water turn off and kept my breathing as even as possible, faking sleep. I did so well at this I didn't even jump when I felt the covers being slowly pulled from my body. I don't know if frozen was the right word to describe how I felt at that moment, as the blood pounding its way through my veins felt anything but cold. My skin felt on fire just whenever he came near me and I had a feeling this had something to do with the aftereffects of what he did to heal me.

After the safety of the covers left me I then felt fingers lightly trace up my bare leg and the urge to bite my bottom lip was torturous. At first I didn't know what he was planning on doing to me but then his actions left me stunned. He was cleaning me?! I could barely believe it when I felt a warm wet washcloth start to clean the evidence of what happened between us earlier. He used slow and careful movements, no doubt in an attempt to try not to wake me. I decided it was better for both of us for me to still pretend to be sleeping as I didn't know who would be more mortified when he realised I knew what he was doing. And now that I knew there was nothing sexual in his actions, I decided what was the harm in a little aftercare?

That was, of course, until he travelled further up and I couldn't help the little jolt it caused. He stopped his movement suddenly and waited. Once he was obviously happy I wasn't going to fully wake he continued to wipe down my most private place until he was satisfied. It didn't take that long before his job was done and he rose from kneeling on the bed. Once he had rid himself of the damp cloth and towel he had used to dry me gently, he once again resumed his place by my side. This time instead of tugging me closer to him, he inched closer slowly until he was flush against me.

Then his last move of the night once again astonished me. He gently lifted my head while he shifted his full arm underneath me, before rolling me to my side. I found my back curled slightly to the wall of his front and tucked securely in the cradle of his big body. My head found a comfortable nook on his arm to snuggle into and I could have sworn I heard a deep inhale of breath at the gesture. Finally, once the covers were pulled back over us both, his arms wrapped around my torso holding me in place for the night. I slept soundly that moment onwards thanks to the comfort of safety I found in his hold.

It was strange to say, considering what had passed between us, but it felt like being held protectively by a friend or a brotherly figure more than a lover, one would have expected after the night we had together. But this brought me back to the now and how different that felt once I opened my eyes. As now, my soft and gentle protector was back in full shadowed biker mode and his hooded face gave nothing away.

He sat next to the bed after bringing closer the chair that had held the jacket he now had covering him. He was leaning forward with his forearms resting on the top his thighs and his hood fell forward as he regarded the floor. I took a moment while this deep contemplation occupied his attention, to take in as many details about him as I could.

The long leather jacket he wore was draped at the legs over each side of the chair, thanks to the slit up the back, made for easier movement. It was the first time I had noticed that the hood was made from a different material and looked as if it was a separate piece of clothing under all that leather. The thick dark grey wool had specks of lighter grey and it was big enough to cover his eyes completely. In fact, the only thing that I knew I would see when he lifted his head was dark stubble on a square chin with full lips above.

This thought brought me a flashback to last night when I saw what looked like a flaming serpent swimming in one of the eyes that looked down at me through the controlled darkness. Did he even realise what he had revealed, or had it been a result of what was happening at the time to my overwhelmed brain… was I once again seeing things?

I didn't have much time to look deeper into the reasons as a head on square set shoulders snapped up. And yep, stubble chin and full lips were all I was rewarded with. I mean jeez, you would have thought after last night we would have at least been on a first name basis, let alone faces being seen.

"You're awake." He said and his deep voice sounded grated and strained. I found I could only nod, which he took for a different reason.

"There is no need to fear me little one, my hands will remain right here." He said looking briefly at the hands he held firmly at his knees. I shook my head slightly, trying to think of the best way to say what clearly needed to be said.

"I…" I had to first clear my throat, which prompted him into passing me a bottle of water. I had a moment of craziness, hoping that it wasn't from the mini bar in the suite, as God only knows how much that would set me back! I took the water and my eyes took note of the black snake that circled his middle finger at about an inch thick. The contrast of the deeply engraved ink was startling against his pale rough skin. The weathered and thin scars on strong hands told me that once upon a time he was no stranger to hard labour outdoors, only in a cold country at least.

"Thank you." I said after taking a strong gulp. He lowered his head slowly in acknowledgement.

"And what I was going to say was that I am not afraid. I think I know by now that you do not mean me any harm." I think this must have shocked him as his head came up quicker and this time I could just see the end of his nose.

"This is good as I think it is time you and I had a little chat about the way of things…" I was about to speak but his hand shot up to stop me in my tracks.

"But first, I think your body would benefit the effects of a hot shower." I smirked at him and narrowed my eyes in a playful mocking before saying,

"Hey, if you think I smell bad, all you needed to do was say, Caveman." His reaction was priceless. He stood quickly and stammered to speak. He didn't know I was joking. I laughed and after wrapping the robe tighter under the covers, I swung my legs around and walked up to him.

"Relax Caveman, I was joking with you." I said patting his chest, which I noticed was without the strange leather straps that he had across his chest when at Afterlife. He grunted and I smirked again as he proved my new nickname for him. I started to walk away when he grabbed my hand suddenly, shocking me. He yanked me back to him and my hands found his chest as the only way to steady the quick flight.

I looked up at him and one of his hands held me to him with his palm plastered to the small of my back. I felt embarrassed and had to look away but he made a tutting sound. He raised his fist to my face and his knuckles skimmed the apple of my cheek. However, this proved not enough to get me to look back at him, so he moved down my neck and then journeyed back under my chin. He raised my head up with his fingers still curled into a fist and I had nowhere to go other than to look up at his hidden face. There was something disconcerting about someone that could see your every emotion being played out on centre stage in an opera, while their face remained hidden in the wings. Just when I thought he wasn't going to speak as the silence had started to make me squirm like a fish in a sushi bar, he killed the tension.

"My name is not Caveman, lille øjesten."

"And my name is not lil…le ogestin." He smirked at the way I had said it wrong and I noticed a slight dimple to one side dip before disappearing.

"To me it is, Keira. Now go shower…" He said and then leaned down to me to say the rest,

"Because you are starting to smell a bit." I laughed as I smacked him on the chest, little good it did me but it made him laugh with me all the same.

"Yeah, well you don't smell so hot yourself Cavemen, what'd you do last night, sneak out to go mud wrestling?" I shot back and this time it got me a full blown grin, one I would have loved to have seen the effect it had on a pair of eyes.

"Very good little human and no, it wasn't mud I was wrestling in last night, but in an alleyway saving your little behind, now go shower before room service arrives as I don't think it will go down well if I answer the door, do you?" He said with humour lacing his every word. But of course, his words did beg the question, how exactly did he get me back up here last night without anyone seeing?

I laughed once and then left him standing there watching me go. I was just about to walk into the bathroom when the sound of my name being called stopped me. I looked back over my shoulder at him and raised my eyebrows in question.

"My name is Sigurd, I live in a loft apartment in New York, not a cave and I am hungry little human, so hurry up and don't make me wait." I shot him a smile and a little wink with my next statement,

"It's nice to finally know you, Sigurd."

My shower was a quick one and not just because I was told to by one big ass biker dude in a hood. I found myself excited that he was finally here and that I might actually get some answers out of him this time. I mean there was nothing like a near death experience followed by a shared orgasm to bring a friendship together, right? So with this in mind I was in and out of the shower in no time and I was finding with my new hair…or lack of, that it was a lot quicker than I was used to.

I didn't know why I felt so comfortable around him but it felt as though I had known him for years. Like someone close to me had introduced him once and that alone stood the weight of any suspicions. Besides the fact that he had saved me from being taken or even killed, it was also the fact that he had saved those closest to me. Which was surely something he hadn't needed to do, so that begged the question…Why did he?

I decided to put all these overwhelming feelings down to what had happened last night. I mean, being connected in such a way was bound to have its consequences and I knew from extensive experience what the effects of a 'healing' can do. So that was most likely it and now I could find myself having a deep connection to the big guy…what was his name…Sigurd. Was that Dutch or something?

Once dressed in a comfy pair of stonewash jeans and a stretchy long sleeved, maroon coloured top with those trusty thumb holes I loved so much, I walked back into the sitting room hoping to see the delicious sight of freshly baked goods.

"So what's on…the…menu…" I trailed off quietly as I processed the situation in front of me.

"Hey! What the Hell do you think you are doing?!" I shouted just as I saw the man dressed from head to toe in black bending on one knee by the yellow couch. I caught him just in time to see his hand resting flat on the plush carpet right by where I had stashed my book. He tapped his fingers in a certain rhythm and I jumped as the book shot out to his waiting hand. It almost looked like a pet of his that he had been trying to lure out of hiding.

As soon as he had the book in his hand his head snapped up in my direction, but still his face was hidden in those mastered shadows. He simply rose from his bent knee in an alarmingly graceful way considering his size.

"I could ask you the same thing, øjesten." He said calmly and I needed a minute to gather my courage. It wasn't long ago that I was looking for the reasons why I felt so safe with him and now, with that predatory stance, I was feeling a little naive. I mean what did I really know about this guy? For all I knew he could have been sent by someone who wanted me for themselves and that is why the previous 'Capture Keira' attempts had failed.

"Give that back to me!" I demanded in my strongest, I take no shit voice, one that wasn't reinforced by a brick wall body like he had to back up that unspoken threat. He straightened to his full height and crossed his arms across his chest like a black granite statue.

"I think not little human. Not until you explain to me in full exactly how you got your hands on *my* book." He said with his voice dropping to an almost demonic growl. I gulped in a way that would have been comical if I didn't have a considerable threat stood in my hotel suite.

"Wait a minute…*your* book?" I asked picking up on the important part of that demand. He nodded his head gently, but I could hear the crack of his knuckles from his fisted hands echo in the room. There was nothing gentle about that noise, I can tell you.

"But I…I…it's mine." I finished in a weak little voice that even I detested hearing. But it must have had its desired effect on the big guy Sigurd as his fists uncurled and his arms came back to his sides. He exhaled a big sigh and I could tell he wanted to run a frustrated hand through his hair.

"Come øjesten, come and sit with me." He moved to the side and motioned a place on the couch for me to park myself. I nodded and followed his instructions. What choice did I have? It wasn't like I could call security and tell them someone that looked like a professional wrestler stole my book!

I sat down and waited for him to do the same. I think I actually felt sorry for the battering the cushions took when taking his weight. We both sat in silence for a moment and I noticed I looked like a child does when sitting next to an adult. His legs looked like they belonged to a forest with a mass of leaves attached.

"Now tell me, who gave you this book, Keira?" Somehow I knew by him calling me by my name this was serious business. But what should I tell him? Was I even allowed to tell him anything? Oh God this was too much! What was I supposed to do?

"You can tell me, have no fear, as no harm will come to you in doing so." He sounded calmer now and almost soothing to my tense nerves.

"I am not sure I am allowed though." I said truthfully.

"Then trust in me and look deep down into what you know is right. When I tell you that it is my birthright to know whatever happens with this book, I speak no lies. Feel the truth in my words, Keira." He said engulfing my hand in his. I closed my eyes and replayed his words over and over. But then he spoke them for real once more and I found myself stunned to know with utter certainty that he was telling me the truth. I found myself nodding at him before opening my mouth.

"The Oracle gave me the book, Sigurd." His hand tightened on mine for a moment but thankfully he released my bones before he broke them. It was obvious this had not been good news. He took a moment to struggle through the reason I gave him and then I silently screamed out in a caught breath as he grabbed my hand once more and placed it over the snake on the cover of the book.

"What are you doing?!"

"Ssshh." Was all he said before he placed his tattooed hand over mine. I then watched in dark fascination as the black snake on his finger began to spin and shortly the one across his palm started to do the same. However, this time they all travelled in the same direction, unlike before when he was fighting the guys at Afterlife. I didn't know what this meant but I was praying for it to mean that he was dealing with a friendly…as in friendly fire in shooting games…although I wasn't quite sure what was friendly about firing any type of weapon, especially one that got you killed. Ok, focus here Keira and forget about Frank playing Call of Duty.

Soon, just like before, his whole hand went black like he had just dipped it into a bucket of treacle and I watched as the substance started to flow over onto the small helpless hand underneath…my hand. I felt the tingling flicker of constant cooling and then a flare of heat continue until every fingertip was covered and when I felt the vibrations start I tried to pull away.

"Just wait for it, human!" He said sternly and I found myself obeying. The vibrations turned to spinning under my palm and although I couldn't see the snake, I knew it was moving and getting ready for something. I heard a deep growl coming from the chest next to me and it sounded as if he was changing into some sort of furious animal. I started to panic inside and my heart was pounding to the point of near pain. I was breathing heavy and felt the thin sheen of sweat start to damp my clothes.

I closed my eyes and that was when the nightmare began.

I felt locked in a cage without bars. A cage of darkness that was creeping into my soul and keeping that precious part of me open for probing. My horrific past secured deeply in the abyss I had created for my murderous captor was bubbling up. My secured vault door that held my secret memories of Draven popped open and came spilling out. And a nightmare of a flaming version of myself running through a river of blood, fed by the deep slashes cut into my veins by my own hands. It was now all playing out in a flickered film of black and white. Surrounded by a derelict Victorian theatre, where plush velvet seats were filled by every supernatural form I had ever seen in my now 24 years. And of course the front row held those that were dearest to me.

I ran down the centre of the aisle screaming 'No, turn it off!' But it was too late. Everyone was already watching my nightmare, both real, past and feared future, premiering on the crumbling screen. The closer I got the harder it became to run. All the faces of Demons and Angels in their true form were laughing in chorus, some choking on their spitefulness and hellish glee. But the closer I got, all the heads of those I cared for turned at the same time, all but one.

Libby, Frank, Justin, Jack, RJ, Sophia, Vincent, Pip, Adam, Lucius and many more were all at the front row now staring my way as the piece of glass in my hand dug deeper into my flesh on screen.

"Dead, dead, dead, little Keira girl! Dead, dead, dead little Keira girl!

We will get you and we will kill you!
They are coming back for you, wolf in a suit's silk will walk by your side while you cry and when your back is turned and knife plunged in deep, that will make you die!"

They all chanted cruelly and I staggered in my steps.

"No, no, no! This isn't real…YOU ARE NOT REAL!" I shouted before my knees hit the mouldy floor that was covered in rotting wood and pieces of once red carpet. My long blonde hair fell forward and touched the floor to cover my crying face. I reached out and touched the golden strands that I knew were still tucked safely away on Draven's hidden bed. Then I heard the laughter.

"Is that what you think, you pathetic human?" No it couldn't be! There was no way my mind would conjure up something so cruel. But no matter, in my disbelief I had to look, I had to prove how wrong it was. I raised my head and took in the cruellest beauty of all, the one of betrayed love…Draven.

His face was now the singular one in the room and I looked in horror as all others had now decayed into skeletal corpses. Their grey bones becoming one with the perished theatre that started to peel and fade upwards like floating ash. But none of this mattered to me as the one face remained.

"Why?" I whispered and I flinched at the cruel sound of his laughter.

"Why? WHY?! You know why Keira! You! You killed me and sent me to this place, it is because of my stupidity that I am now to live the rest of my days in chains!" He lifted his arms and that's when I first noticed the metal entwined around every inch of him but his face. They started to glow red like they had only just been forged and I started to howl from the pain the sight caused me to see them branding his skin.

"But…but I didn't know! I will help you! I will…will come for you!" I shouted as the chains started to get tighter around him and I saw him gasp for breath.

"You can't! Leave me! RUN! RUN NOW BEFORE…" The glowing links started to cut into his skin and then he was being dragged backwards towards the screen, towards the mistakes I had made still being played out on a torturous loop.

"Before what?!" I shouted and then I saw with one outstretched hand the entire screen melt into burning film. Behind it was Hell itself and Draven was now getting dragged back to it.

"DRAVEN!" I screamed running towards him until his last words stopped me dead and I stared at the truth he believed in every word come through his purple eyes.

"...BEFORE I KILL YOU!"

CHAPTER TWENTY-FOUR

BOUND TO ASK

"You are blood bound?!" Sigurd shouted bolting from the chair just after I yanked my hand free and fell to the floor. I looked up still in a state of shock at what his darkness had shown me. I held my hand protectively to my chest while still kicking my legs to put greater length between us. I moved like a wounded crab and only came to a stop when my back bumped into one of the horseshoe shaped chairs that were covered in thick olive green velvet.

"What…what did you do to me?!" I shouted back, having little care for the giant presence now looming over me. He leaned forward and trapped me in with his hands holding his weight on the arms of the chair.

"Answer my question, NOW!" He growled that last command and I flinched back like he had lashed out with the back of his hand.

"I…she…we…ok look, I don't know why she did any of this, all I know is that she took some of my blood and then told me the book was connected with me in some way and that's it! So do me a favour and back OFF!" I shouted finally replacing fear with anger. He didn't seem too concerned with me screaming at him, but he did at least push his weight off the chair to give me space. I closed my eyes briefly and took a deep breath in relief.

"FUCK!" He snarled with his back to me and if I were to take a guess, I would say it looked like he was trying real hard not to pummel his fist into something. Well, as long as it wasn't someone then that was fine with me!

"What on this earth's realm was that crazy bitch thinking of?!" He snapped and I got myself off the floor silently. I straightened down my jeans from where they had ridden up in my haste and that's when I heard a sharp,

"Well?"

"Oh…you were actually asking me a question? Well…I…" I shook my head and then anger sparked again,

"…I mean how the Hell am I supposed to know? Good God, what is it with you people?" I threw up my hands dramatically before carrying on with my rant.

"You think I know why or how or any bloody details as to why anyone does what they do in the supernatural world? I mean for Christ's sake, I have a big ass biker guardian stood in my hotel suite and I don't even know who sent you, so why you think for one minute I know why the Oracle is using me as a pawn, I can't figure! All I know is what she tells me and what I can figure out with all this riddle shit that now comes from that book, instead of weird kids on antique bikes, creepy warehouse guys that get the munchies for human flesh…I mean what the holy shit…? Eat a cheeseburger for God's sake!…and then there was that weirdo on the plane, Miss pop drinking Merryweather…although that one wasn't from the Oracle but more likely from this Gastian person, who for some reason hates me and wants revenge but there's the problem...I don't even know this guy!" I shouted as my rant that had me storming all around the sitting room was much too slowly running out of steam.

"I mean what was next…what did I miss this time?! Huh? Come on, tell me handsome, 'cause I don't know! What's next, because at this point it wouldn't surprise me if a canary flew from my ass and sang me the next riddle in Swahili!" I said finally coming down from my anger mountain and deflating in the same chair I had backed up into.

I seemed to have stunned the man in black, as he didn't move. He just stood in front of the couch with that bloody hood covering every revealing feature on his face. Thinking back I wasn't even sure why I had called him handsome, I mean it's not like I had even seen most of his face. He could look like good old Quasimodo for all I knew.

"Have you finished?" He said folding his arms making the leather groan around his impressive biceps.

"Yes!" I said with plenty of attitude.

"Good, now we will eat and you can answer my questions." I was about to reply with some witty response about the food not even being here yet, but the sound of knocking shut me up…how did they do that?

"Good hearing." He answered my unspoken question and motioned me to get the door with an outstretched hand. I rolled my eyes and got the door, muttering about how chivalry was clearly dead and buried.

We both ate in silence… well he ate while I, on the other hand, just picked crumbs off a sweet pastry and nibbled like a mouse. I guess that analogy worked better than any other, given it felt like I was eating breakfast with a frustrated panther.

"Soo…" I started to break the tension while brushing the flakes of buttery goodness from my hands and lap.

"So?" He mocked after swallowing what looked like a whole piece of bacon.

"So, are you going to tell me what is going on and what it was you did to me with that damn book?!" I snapped.

"Watch your mouth, human. That 'Damn' book holds a piece of my 'damned' soul, one you are now bound to…you get it now, sweetheart?" He said in a growl, twisting the endearment into something sour.

"Yeah well this 'Sweetheart' didn't exactly buy what you were selling now did she...? Hey wait a minute…let's rewind here… what do you mean bound to?" I forgot about the insulting tone he had now switched to and homed in on the words he used.

"What part are you finding difficult?" He asked not dropping the attitude for a second.

"Hello! Human here, remember? I don't exactly have a supernatural degree in all this, so let's play a game should we, let's play the 'I am obviously talking to a human who doesn't know shit about that book and need to use layman's terms' game…is that cool with you, big guy?!" I was losing my rag quickly and it wasn't helping knowing I was only going to get my answers from Mr Clueless Human communicator over there!

He growled in response and that was when my last thread of patience snapped. I stood up and walked over to him to point in his hidden face.

"Now that's not exactly going to help us now is it? So here's what you're going to do, you're going to man up, put down the bacon butties and explain to me, in detail just what the Hell that book has to do with this!" I motioned between us with my hand but didn't get very far as he grabbed my wrist to shackle. Even sat down with me stood up, he was large enough to put us at the same height. "Butties?" He said cocking his head to the side and I huffed out my frustration when pulling from his hold.

"God, what is wrong with you people? All this time on the Earth and you don't even know Northern slang for a sandwich. It's hopeless!" I said going to sit back down in my chair and it was nice to hear his laughter for a change, rather than him growling at me.

"Ok, so I know this isn't easy for you and I am not helping as I am clearly overestimating your knowledge on this."

"Gee, you think?" I said and I just knew that if his hood had been back, he would have been raising an eyebrow at my sarcasm.

"Look, let's start over shall we?" He nodded his head slowly at my suggestion and then rubbed his stubbled chin with his hefty hand.

"Explain…"

"Tell me…"

We both spoke at the same time and it became very apparent that we both had more than our fair share of questions for each other.

"Ladies first." He motioned and I smiled as I realised that chivalry had just been resurrected.

"Tell me about the book and why you think the Oracle gave it to me…I mean if it belongs to you or your soul or whatever, then how did she even get it in the first place, did you just leave it hanging about on the coffee table or something, 'cause I gotta tell ya, if it held a piece of my soul it would be in nothing short of a Bank Safe and…" He cleared his throat to stop me and I blushed when I realised I had been a runaway train with my thoughts.

"He told me you were always so full of questions, I thought it was just a human thing…how wrong I was." He muttered looking to the side as if trying to weigh up the best way of dealing with me.

"Who told you that?"

"That's five questions in total, so tell me lille øjesten, which one would you like me to answer first?" Ok, so I had to give him that, I had already been told it was an annoying trait of mine. One that given circumstances like this, it was near to impossible to control. When I finally kept my mouth shut I think he took this as his cue to start talking.

"To your last question, that you will never know, so stop asking me about my employer as it is none of your concern… understood?" The only answer he would get from me about that was an eye roll and a little shake of my head. If he thought for one minute that I would let something like that go then he was hugely mistaken.

"Good enough. Now for the Ouroboros, Book of the Blood Bound. The book was given to me as a tool of information that I would need to do my job. This is something I will not be going into detail about as you wouldn't likely understand, even if I did." I was about to call him on that but he held up one hand to silence me.

"Just know that I have a job to do as my place among my people and to do this job I need certain guidelines from higher powers, that book gives me them. I have been bound to that book from my rebirth and a piece of my soul resides within its bindings…now along with a piece of yours." I was calm until he said this last bit.

"What!" I said standing once again.

"Keira, sit down." He ordered softly and I only complied because of his gentle tone.

"I believe this was the Oracle's plan, as it seems my employer isn't the only one trying to keep you safe, although with you that is becoming a full-time job in itself." He commented dryly.

"But we will get back to that shortly, won't we my bound one?" I could only nod as I knew I also had some explaining to do.

"The book was taken from me while I was watching over you and I gather the Oracle not only foresaw my involvement, but also made walking away from protecting you impossible"

"You what? But you said…" I asked, utterly shocked that he was planning on walking away.

"Try and understand, after last night, after what was needed to heal you…well, it became too much for both of us and this was one situation…umm…person… I didn't think wise to continue to grow attached to, am I making myself clear?" I frowned at him in confusion. No, he wasn't making sense and one look at my face was all it took for him to continue.

"Keira, I take it for a fact that knowing the trouble you find, that you are more than familiar with being healed, am I correct?"

"So?" I questioned his point.

"Then you will know that a part of my essence has found home in your veins and although it will fade in time, for the moment I will be drawn to that part of you, the darker side of you." He whispered the last part like it was shameful to him.

"And that's why I saw those nightmares when your…your black stuff touched me?" He nodded and then held the lower part of his face with his hand.

"That is why I was going to leave and trust me when I say it, I did not make this decision lightly, when I give my word, I give it with my life, but after the new circumstances I would do you more harm than good, as no one wants to relive their nightmares daily." My mouth dropped slightly with the thought of being attacked by that vision every day.

"But I am afraid that option no longer is available for me, as now we are bound by the book and until that bond is broken, then I must remain by your side. This is why the Oracle has intervened, it seems it is in both of our destinies to see this through, which brings us back to what it is I am facing…what are you doing here, Keira?" Now this was the part that I was dreading. How was I ever going to explain this crazy quest to someone who obviously wanted me to make their job easier and stay tucked up safely in a small town like Evergreen?

I remained silent and tight lipped as I gathered my thoughts. And that in itself was the main problem. With the people I dealt with being immortal, then time wasn't a massive issue for someone who grew patience like other people grew tomatoes! This was proven after ten minutes of silence and him obviously still waiting for an answer.

"I take it you would not believe me if I told you I was just taking a vacation for my birthday?" I said in a quiet voice.

"I am afraid not, øjesten, but what if I started by telling you what I do know."

"I…" He rose from his chair and plucked a lush apple from the breakfast fruit bowl, stopping my excuses as he flipped the fruit along the top of his arm. Seeing this move reminded me of some orphaned, cocky street kid in years gone by, surviving by pickpocketing and stealing from market vendors.

"Here's what I know." He started, catching the bouncing apple with his free hand before taking a crunching bite of its flesh, talking with his mouth full.

"The King goes underground and goes to extreme lengths in trying to keep you safe by giving you a life free from our existence, so what do you do…? Go looking for it anyway!" He snapped at me taking another vicious bite to chew.

"But I…"

"I haven't finished. So, after your little expedition to the warehouse, which thankfully Leivic was around to keep you out of trouble as I am forbidden to go there, I find you about to get kidnapped at Afterlife."

"Why were you forbidden to go to the warehouse?" I asked and was surprised when I got his humourless grunted laughter.

"Of course, *that* would be the part you focus on." He laughed again and turned around before wiping a hand down his hooded head and over his face. I gathered it would have gone through his hair if his hood hadn't been concealing it.

"Why do you still hide your face from me?"

"No! No, no, no…" He started spinning round to face me (well sort of).

"No?"

"Yes no! As in NO more questions!" He shouted and then took another bite of the apple that had been forgotten during his little outburst.

"So where was I…oh yeah, but of course, you being kidnapped. But was this a clue for you to stay safe, oh no…not my blood bound little human, pain in my ass…no, you just hop on a plane to London and I find you just in time after trying to get into the Devil's Ring…"

"But I don't…" He quickly showed me his palm to stop me in my tracks.

"And of course, when you obviously weren't admitted, you were then pursued by two Warlock lackeys and dragged into an alleyway." He shook his head as he obviously played out the scene in his head but then he smiled before saying,

"Well, at least you're not afraid of fighting dirty, lille øjesten, I will give ya that."

"Well that's something that comes from dating a badass, over-protective half Angel/Demon King like Draven. He kind of rubs off on you." I said without thinking about the pain saying something like that would bring me. And one look at my face told Sigurd all about that pain.

"Keira…I…"

"Just forget about it, big guy." I waved off his concern and reburied the memory of me and Draven down in his training room with him throwing me down on the mats, showing me some self-defence moves. Of course, it turned into a different kind of work-out pretty quickly after Draven tossed me to the floor gently and commented on how good I looked down there.

I felt the tears mist up and that little burn you get in your nose when you try to hold them off, reminded me about trying to stay strong.

"I know about the pain there, øjesten and I am sorry for it, but maybe it is time to just go home and try to live a normal life." He said softly and I found I couldn't conjure up my anger as I wanted to with hearing that idea being voiced.

"But that's just the thing Sigurd, I never had a normal life and wouldn't know how to start living one even if I had the damn handbook. Besides, that life you talk about just doesn't exist for me without Draven. So you want to know my plan, here it is, I am going to Hell and I am not coming back again without bringing Draven back with me." I stated standing up and folding my arms over my chest.

I saw him take a staggered step back as the truth of my mission came to light. His lips got tight and he looked so taken aback that it stunned him to silence.

"So there you have it and before you do something pointless and stupid like trying to talk me out of this plan, I will just remind you that the Oracle not only knows about the reasons I am here, but she is also the one backing up this plan. She gave me the book to communicate the steps I must take in reaching my goal and neither you nor every bloody supernatural being is going to stop me!" I tried to storm past him to get myself to a place I could freely cry without him seeing me, as I clearly wasn't as strong as I made out. However, this didn't happen the way I wanted, as a solid arm snaked out and pulled my body back to his.

He held my back firmly to his chest and whispered for me to stop struggling against him.

"Just think Keira, just…just take a minute to think about what you're saying. You want to try to get into Hell for a man who has made it clear he wants you to get on with your life. Why would you darken the memory of him by going against his last wish for you?" He asked this question in hushed tones by my ear and I could almost hear the crack in my armoured resolve his words caused.

"Because I know if it was the other way around, he would

stop at nothing in trying to get me back, no matter what I asked of him." I counteracted and I felt him stiffen behind me. Then he took a deep breath and delivered the final blow,

"Yes, but what if he *doesn't* want to be rescued, Keira?" I let the tears roll down as I slammed my eyes shut at what that sentence did to me.

"That's...that is not true, he...my Drav...he wouldn't feel like that...I..." I stammered out my argument but even coming from my lips it sounded like a far cry from what I truly believed. I mean how could I be sure? What if he was right, what if Draven just wanted me to move on and forget him in his new resting place? I mean, what was Hell like for him anyway, was he down there partying with the big red boss man?

"NO! That's not true, get off me!" I shouted twisting out of his hold, killing all thoughts like that. No, Draven just wanted me to be safe and that was the only reason he wanted me to move on. No other thought was worth the wasted time thinking about.

I whirled around and faced the mask of material, but I could swear I could see a flash of something looking up into the shadows, where his eyes should be.

"Now you listen to me and listen good. I don't care if you have to protect me or if you walk out that door right now, but nothing you say will stop this from happening, do you understand me? I am going to find a way into Hell, one way or...or the dead way...you get me?! Now you can either help me or get the Hell out of my way, either of those choices I won't lose sleep over, no matter what type of darkness you say will inflict my mind, because Sigurd, if there is one thing this 'Little Human' is used to, it's living with seeing the worst type of nightmares...so trust me, anything you show me will just be a walk in the damn park when it comes to the demons in *my* dreams." I said walking away from him.

"Wait...where are you going?" He said in a gruff tone that was clearly affected by my little speech.

"I have to go and get ready." I stopped on the way through the sitting room after looking at the clock, to notice the afternoon had come and gone. I looked at him one more time, pausing at the door wondering if this wasn't the last time that I would see him. I mean I wouldn't have blamed him after what I had just said, but I needed him to be on my side. If not, then there was just no point having someone around who kept on trying to stop me all the time. After all, I had a job to do, just as he had his. So with this in mind I said the one thing that would seal his decision, which was the truth and a sure glimpse of things to come.

"I've got a pub to go to and a Devil's Ring to find."

CHAPTER TWENTY-FIVE

BANDS OF BONE

I spent a long time getting ready and must have changed my outfit choice ten different times. It was just too tempting to go with jeans and a dark top, clearly ignoring all the revealing clothes RJ had given me. But then I knew the mistake I would be making as I remembered the Oracle's words about having to disguise myself. And after a night playing victim in an alleyway, I could now see her point.

It was obvious the new hair was not enough, so it was time to play little Goth girl to the fullest. I ended up grabbing a mixture of stuff, having no idea if it went together or not. But I didn't really care what people thought, just as long as they didn't think, 'Oh look, there goes the Chosen One'.

I stood in front of the ornate mirror for a long time staring at the Keira that was no longer there, as in my place was the girl I had to become to get the job done. So, I took in the multiple holes in black rose pattern tights, the short black combat skirt that had straps hanging lower than the hem. I tucked the long sleeved dark red top in so that the thick belt buckle was showing and to prevent the brushed copper skull cross bone from digging in my belly.

The front of the top had a faded grey skull that looked half decayed. The sleeves not only had thumb holes but also crude stitch work in thick black cord that crisscrossed up the arm. This continued along the neck, pulling it in different angles that gave it a plunging neckline. I decided that I didn't think it wise to show my necklace as I wasn't sure if people would use it as a tool to recognise who I was or not.

But this wasn't the only reason I grabbed the little jacket that zipped up to a high neck that passed my chin. It was also because I didn't think it a good idea to draw any unwanted attention to myself and having the puppies on display the way the low neckline promised, wasn't a good idea in my book.

The little jacket had cute puffy little capped sleeves that cut off at the top of my arm. The material was black canvas cut into sharp lines and a pointed bottom half. The top part was soft velvet that met the stiff canvas in a V shape in between my breasts. And the side zip was reinforced with three large leather buckles that were fiddly to get through the copper squares. The last one was the easiest to deal with as it was across my covered neck and once secure, the weight made the neck flop to show my painted black lips.

By the time I had finished with smoky eyes, thick mascara, and lots of black liner, I looked like a different person altogether. I had towel dried my hair and layered on the hairspray to give it more volume in a messy style at the back.

And little Goth girl was ready to play in the big leagues.

It did occur to me that this wasn't going to be like a night at Afterlife. That was if I even got in there in the first place. Which reminded me, just how much I really wanted to see Sigurd still waiting in the sitting room when I finally plucked up the courage to walk back in there. After what I said to him, I wouldn't have blamed him if he had walked away without looking back, but it was an unfortunate test he needed to pass. I just knew I couldn't continue this quest with him holding me back at every turn.

So, with this in mind, I took a deep breath, as much as the tight clothes would allow, grabbed my knee high boots, courtesy of Libby and walked back into the sitting room, head held high. I was so sure I was going to be embarrassed facing Sigurd again, especially dressed like this, which is why when I walked into the sitting room I almost stumbled to a stop.

He wasn't there.

He had left me.

"Crap, crap, crappy, crap, crap and double crapola!" I shouted storming into the centre of the room.

"That's a lot of shit, even for a troublesome lille øjesten like yourself." The deep gravelly voice from behind me had me dropping my boots. I spun round to see Sigurd leaning against the door frame like some biker version of Robin Hood.

"You're back!"

"I never left, sweetheart." He pushed off the frame and came closer to where I stood until I had to look up at him.

"Besides, without that book I would have been forced to take a vacation and I don't fancy Florida this time of year..." He leaned down closer to my ear and whispered,

"It's the damn humidity...its pisses off my darkness."

"And here I was thinking you were going to tell me you hate having frizzy hair." I said causing him to throw his head back where a deep laugh erupted. I thought this might have been my chance to see him but that damn hood stayed in place all the same. I did notice he had a thick corded neck though, which wasn't a shocker considering how gigantic and muscular my dark guardian was.

"Well I think I can safely say that this job won't be boring, not with you around." He said taking a slow and predatory intake of my body. The way that lip raised higher on one side told me he didn't mind what he saw. That thought made me blush, which I tried to hide with humour.

"That's the spirit." I said patting him on the chest and bending to pick up my discarded boots. I turned to walk over to the yellow couch to put them on when a hand circled the top of my arm.

"Why are you dressed like that?" He asked all traces of good humour worn away. I looked down at myself and then shrugged my shoulders like it was nothing, feeling the heat in my cheeks start to betray my actions.

"Why do you think?"

"Well, unless you tell me you are off to a Goth style Pyjama party, you are not stepping one foot out of that door dressed like that." His stern voice sent shivers down my spine and prickled my skin.

"Is that a fact?" I said looking him up and down, outrage clear as day twisting my tone.

"Oh sweetheart, that is a FACT. 'Cause if I find you as delicious as I do, then trust me, others will see you as just as sweet, and I don't mean to look at." He whispered seductively causing a deep shiver to scurry along my spine. I knew he was just saying this to try and scare me, but I couldn't let fear prevent me from going through with this, no matter how crazy it sounded.

"You know, that last time I checked, you weren't the name on my birth certificate on the line under Daddy!" I snapped making him growl.

"And would you stop that, I am not a damn cat!" I yanked my arm from his grip after my little jab. My God, what was wrong with us, it was like our friendship would take one step forward and then a car journey backwards.

"Look øjesten..."

"No, you look big guy, if you think for one minute I am just going to sit here and wait for stuff to happen, you are mistaken. I am walking out that door and I AM going to find this place, with or without you... like I said, your choice." I said after huffing down on the sofa and jamming my foot into the boot with enough force to hurt my toes.

"Are you always this stubborn?" He snarled crossing his arms across his chest in what I was coming to recognise as his macho 'me man, you weak woman' stance.

"Yes, so either get used to it or cut me loose, your ch..."

"My choice, yes, yes, you said that. Fine! But I am telling you now, you'd better listen to me once we are inside or this little crusade of yours won't end with a slap on the wrist, but more like a good mauling of the flesh and the last I heard, humans die from shit like that!"

"Fine!" I snapped.

"Fine!" He growled.

And that was pretty much the ground rules laid out for me ready to break.

The rest of the daylight hours were spent with me and Sigurd sharing yet another room service selection while talking shop. I first had to explain from the beginning how this plan came to unfold and brought me to this point. Most of the way through this conversation I could tell he wanted to express his feelings and it was clear which direction those feelings were headed. I was thankful that he had it in him to refrain from commenting, as this was a good sign for things to come. Especially when he started to explain exactly what it was I was getting myself into.

The Devil's Ring was a fight club where the supernatural could come and bet on just about anything. Humans were forbidden unless they were 'owned' which was highly illegal in its own right. But according to Sigurd bringing an owned one to fight night was like bring a snack to eat between rounds. I didn't take this piece of news well.

This then, of course, brought on a heated discussion as to why anyone, let alone the Oracle, would think it a good idea to send me to the wolf's lair.

"Exactly my thoughts, lille øjesten, which is why I think it's safer to just forget this kamikaze mission. It's time to go home." He said which had me shaking my head even before he had finished. I slammed my plate down on the coffee table and then gripped the armrests in frustration.

"No! That is not an option so get that out of your head now. There must be a reason the Oracle wants to send me there." I said tilting my head to one side and scratching my eyebrow.

"Well, I can't think of a reason, other than getting you killed and unless you broke all ten commandments in your spare time that you're not telling me about, then I would say there is no reason, as you don't exactly have a one way ticket to Hell." He stated and that's when I saw it.

"Wait…say that again."

"You don't have a one-way ticket to Hell." He repeated cautiously.

"No, no, not that, the first bit." I demanded and this time I watched him more closely.

"Well, I can't think of a reason?" The way he said it was definitely questioning my sanity but none of that mattered as I now had my proof.

"You lied!" I shouted getting up.

"What!"

"Don't try and deny it, you're a shitty liar and I may not be a poker player but trust me when I say I know when I see a 'tell' like that one! My father can't lie for toffee, which is probably who I get it from." I muttered this last bit turning around to face the window to gather my thoughts. He just lied about not knowing why the Oracle would send me there, which meant he knew a lot more about this place than he was willing to tell me.

"How did you know?" He asked me quietly and I was at least happy he wasn't trying to deny it.

"Whenever my father had to lie to my mother about stuff, he would rub his chin like he was relaxed but his body would be as stiff as a board, you know, shoulders tense like yours were and the way your free hand had the side of the couch in a death grip…you hate lying, don't you?" His growl was all the answer I needed, and I knew it wasn't helpful, but I couldn't keep in the knowing smile.

"So what if I do, Human?" He barked and again I couldn't suppress the grin.

"My father was the same, that's why he hated buying my mother gifts on her birthday, he can't keep a secret to save his life and yours won't save mine." At this he grunted.

"Can't blame me for trying, it would, after all, make my job a lot easier."

"You don't strike me as the type to take the easy way out of things, so 'fess up matey, why does the Oracle want me to go there?" And we were once again back to me crossing my arms over my chest being about as intimidating as a snail is to a booted foot. I waited and waited and then…I waited some more.

"Oh, for Christ sake Sigurd, just tell me!"

"Fine! She…well the only reason she would send you there

is to meet Jared Cerberus." It was made quite apparent that this was information he didn't want to tell me and the way the name was uttered at the end made my skin bump after a shudder.

"Yeah, that's the right reaction you got there, lille øjesten." He remarked darkly.

"So…so who is he?" I was almost scared to ask. Sigurd shook his head down as though thinking a silent plea for me to just drop it.

"He not only owns the Devil's Ring…if only it were that easy…no, he lille øjesten, was the guardian into Hell itself and the very thing where your myths about werewolves come from."

"What?" I shouted. NO way! Could this life of mine get any weirder?

"Wait, Demons, Angels, Vampires, even Warlocks but now you're expecting me to believe in Werewolves too…please tell me you're kidding, right…this is just a ploy to scare the shit out of me…right?" He started laughing, although there was obviously no real humour behind it.

"Hell, if I thought I could get you to give up this insane plan of yours by scaring you shitless, then I would be happy to tie you down until you have heard everything there is to know about what's truly frightening in this world." He said then his lips got tight before he carried on,

"But I doubt even then that would stop you. So here it is øjesten, Jared Cerberus is not merely a wolf in his other form, as none are. No, the myth started with a beast and fairy tales took that horror and twisted it into something cute and fluffy but trust me sweetheart, there is nothing cute and fluffy about Jared Cerberus." I bit my lip as I waited for him to continue, suddenly not feeling quite as brave about going to this place.

"This guy…I mean Jesus… this guy even gives me nightmares and I deal with guys like this for a living, you get me?" I nodded bringing my knees up under my chin in a defensive manoeuvre.

"He is still known for being Master of the Gates and that is why she is sending you to him. You say you want into Hell to bring back lover boy, then this is the only flawed way."

"Flawed?"

"Oh yeah øjesten, most definitely flawed as it's damned near impossible." I took a deep breath and then let it out in a hiss as something from my love of mythology hit me. Hell, it didn't just hit, it near knocked my bloody teeth out!

"Wait! No, it can't be…it can't be possible but…his last name, that's not anything to do with…?" It couldn't be, could it?

"He's one and the same. Cerberus is the Alpha Hellhound and before the bastard was forced to retire on earth, he used to guard the gates of the Underworld to prevent those who are stupid enough to cross the River Styx trying to escape." Well yeah, that just confirmed it!

"Oh shit!"

"Oh shit is right." He confirmed.

"So what, he looks like a man but is in fact a three headed vicious dog?!" This was not good…so not good!

"Oh no sweetheart, he doesn't have three heads."

"Oh well that's something." I said sarcastically.

"No, when the beast takes hold and transforms his body, the Hounds of Hell will play and they play pretty damn fast. His head can move so quickly that it seems as though he has as many heads as your eyes can see but *dog* he is not." All the air left me.

"And this is someone that the Oracle thinks can help me...? She really is crazy isn't she?"

"Yep, 'fraid so." I lifted my arms up in a defeated motion.

"Well then, I have no choice, do I?" I said getting up and smoothing my skirt down.

"About bloody time, lille øjesten, you're making the right decision." Oh yeah, he was jumping the gun.

"I'm glad you think so. Let's go." I swear if I could have seen his eyes they would be framed by slashed eyebrows frowning.

"But you just said…" he trailed off and then exhaled a big sigh when he realised what this meant.

"Right, of course… but what was I thinking? I tell you how we have to ask Hell's Alpha for an escort into the Underworld and you are what...? Ready to go? I swear only you sweetheart."

His deep voice took on that masterful tone as he rose to his full height, adding to the intimidation that still affected me.

"So, you in?" I asked and added in secret the 'Oh please say yes, oh please, oh please.'

"Ah shit! Yeah I'm in, but if you get me killed I swear to you then I will be coming back to drag your ass to Hell myself!" He walked over to me and before he passed, I stopped him with a hand on his jacket.

"Umm, wouldn't it just be easier to…you know…" I made a slitting throat action with my hand and tried not to laugh as his lips made a tense line.

"Don't even say it little girl, as you wouldn't want to see what I look like in Hell!" He growled and I released my hold on him.

"Kidding! Just kidding big guy! Hey, you need to chill out a bit, maybe when this is all over that vacation to Florida might not be such a bad idea." I joked as he walked to the door.

"Shut it, Shorty!" He said trying to keep the smirk from his covered face.

"No, I'm serious, you could hang with Mickey and his missus, go watch killer whales jump over crazy people, a roller-coaster or two, then dinner and a show." I said trying to keep a straight face.

"I think I would rather death." He commented dryly making me laugh.

"Well that should be relaxing, although definitely not as much fun."

"Oh, I think any death you bring sweetheart, would definitely not be of the boring kind."

"Ha ha, well this is your last chance tough guy. Florida or demonic fight clubs run by Hell's beasts?"

"And there's a difference? Get your bag, øjesten."

"Yes Sir!" I said, happy he had chosen to stick with me in this. I got my bag and wrapped the long strap across my torso.

"You know I think you should call me that from now on." He said closing the door behind me.

"Not a chance, sugar plum." I smiled when I heard him groan behind me. Well this was a good start, I thought as I took in the night through a passing window. London was lit up in all its beauty reflecting an orange glow across the river and I just had one thing in mind... I hoped that the same city would be holding more for us than just pretty lights.

So here I was once again, back staring at the same door I did the night before. The only difference this time was the comforting muscle I had at my back. Getting out of the hotel had been an experience in itself, so this was going to be a blast I thought sarcastically.

When walking down into the lobby I quickly realised no one could see Sigurd walking by my side. Which was a very good thing considering he kind of looked like death, minus a trusty scythe tapping next to him. Of course, the fact that Death actually wore a beige suit and carried a briefcase didn't exactly scream 'Horror' which made me wonder where that misconception actually came from.

The reason that no one was able to see Sigurd was down to his talent with shadows, which had me hoping it didn't look like I was walking with a black cloud next to me. Thankfully though, my fears were unwarranted as no one batted an eyelid as us that was until the concierge stopped us. He just wanted to ask if I needed anything but the growling sound that came from thin air had him nearly tripping up over his own feet to get away from me. The last look he gave me before backing away told me he not only thought of me as strange looking but now he could add to that, growling crazily.

"Yeah, thanks for that Sigurd." I commented through gritted teeth, one he ignored.

So now here we were, stood outside the Cheshire Cheese pub and once again it was closed up tight for the night. Only at least this time I had reinforcements, I thought with a little mental 'Boo yeah' on the end. I knocked on the door and waited but nothing.

"Allow me." Sigurd's deep voice rumbled behind me. One long arm came forward over me and pounded on the door until the old wood rattled on its hinges.

"Do this often by any chance?" I remarked mockingly just before we heard a familiar,

"Piss off, we're closed!" From behind the dark door.

"Obviously not often enough, as I think I am losing my touch." He replied light heartedly. Then he let rip.

"Open the fucking door, NOW!" His tone broke no messing with as the locks on the other side could be heard turning. I looked up and slightly behind me to find the big guy grinning close to my shoulder.

"Guess I still got it." He whispered then turned his attention back to the slight crack the door had opened. Then it was like déjà vu all over again as a sickly looking hand snapped out like it had a mean bite. Bony fingers covered with translucent skin uncurled requesting payment. I was waiting for Sigurd to place something in its hand, like an old coin or maybe some kind of ancient relic. But when the time came I couldn't suppress the scream his actions caused.

And just like the spider that attacks the fly, he sprang into action. The same hand that had knocked to request entrance was now a deadly predator over my shoulder. He grabbed the outstretched hand, yanked hard and then sunk his teeth into the papery skin and powdery flesh. This all happened with me wedged in between them, too stunned to move.

A great howl came from behind the door where the owner to the savaged hand was still hiding behind. I then watched as Sigurd retracted a set of fangs I hadn't seen before, but he didn't let his prisoner go. No, instead he let the shadows that ruled half his body flow over his hand down to his fingertips. The darkness seeped from every pore and overflowed onto the palest hand, creating a living Yin and Yang of the flesh.

I was so close to both their hands I was seeing every detail lit only by the faint moonlight and the flickering of the old round sign above us. The black liquid oozed into the deep gash his teeth marks had made and when one single black drop was solely consumed, Sigurd finally released his victim.

The hand snatched back through the door with a slam and I was about to turn to unleash my anger on the big oaf when we both heard the door swing open fully.

"Well that was subtle."

"No sweetheart, that was payment and proof. Now, after you" He countered.

We both walked through the door and I looked around to try and finally see who the hand belonged to. The pub didn't open up into a large room like I would have thought, more like a hallway you would find in an old house. The walls were lit with candles which added to the eerie gloom and I looked to my left to see a door. Above it an old sign said, 'Chop Room' and above that was a painted portrait. It was a picture of an elderly woman with her arms folded as though even she disapproved of me being here. She even looked like a strict headmistress, with her grey hair, regal demeanour and three strings of beads hung around her neck.

That doorway had one opposite it, so I turned to see what lay hidden there but doing so nearly stopped my heart dead from ever beating again. Now I could see who the hand belonged to and it was one action I wished I could have taken back!

The creature stood in the doorway and no amount of mental fortress my mind had built could get the image to fall back. A tall thin figure was like a hellish bone snowman against the background of a night sky. Its body was made from a twisted set of endless bones all entwined with no reasoning behind them. It reminded me of a body made from hundreds of white elastic bone bands but wrapped around and around bigger bones of its long limbs.

Its head was similar to its body, only more elongated at the back of its skull. Again, this was covered in the same bands of bone and an opening for its mouth was its only facial feature. Other than that it appeared blind.

I took a step back and was comforted by the hard chest my back found. When an arm secured me tighter to him I felt my body instantly relax into the hold.

"Lead on!" Sigurd commanded the large albino stick man.

"Very well you bastards, this way." The thick London accent didn't really match the picture I was seeing. Then he started to move and when I looked down I realised the humanoid figure was tapping away on the floor with bone stumps as he was missing his feet. I had to make a conscious effort to hold down the bile.

I little nudge from behind me told me that it was time to move and I had to force my grateful feet to follow the white ghostly form in front of us. As I passed both doorways I noticed another sign on the left. It had different names like 'Court Bar' and 'Johnson Bar' on the wooden board and underneath, written in chalk whether or not the places were open. I didn't take a genius to gather this place must be a honeycomb of different rooms, if they needed a sign by the front door.

"Keep going, sweetheart." Sigurd told me gently as I stopped to look up at the sign. I nodded and walked past but as the flames flickered with my movement I saw something twist in the words painted on the wood. 'Cellar Bar' was there one minute in yellow paint and with my next blink it had been replaced with 'Hell's Bar'. It looked as though some small child had finger painted the words with blood. A chalked arrow pointed down and I shuddered when I saw the tangled bone man disappear down the small staircase.

I think Sigurd heard the frightened lump I swallowed as I received a reassuring squeeze on the arm. I looked down at my feet that only half willingly moved towards the stairs and I noticed a strange type of sawdust on the floor. It was almost like the creature in front was leaving a trail of tissue or skin like breadcrumbs for Hansel and Gretel to follow. But somehow, I doubted I would be finding a cute little gingerbread house at the end of this road.

I turned fully back on myself to climb down the narrow staircase and noticed another sign painted on one of the steps above. This one, like the others, once again morphed the words, so instead of saying 'Mind Your Head' as I passed it said, 'Mind Your Soul'.

"Careful!" Sigurd said behind me as I nearly slipped on a narrow step because of it. I looked back and saw that to get down the steps he had to almost bend in two it was that tight a space. I saw the snow figure waiting for us at the bottom. It was a small square room with a dark stone slab floor and four shut doors all close together. To my right there was an open doorway which is the way I thought we would go.

There were two doors straight in front of me with only enough space for a fire extinguisher in between. Then to left there were two more doors, one Ladies, the other Gentlemen… neither of which I was expecting to find where I was going. When I saw the grotesque figure stop by the two doors in front, I thought this is where we were to continue on alone. Well, a girl could only hope.

"No øjesten, just wait for it." My large protector said after stopping me from walking through the open doorway. So I did as he asked and waited for something to happen. I didn't have to wait long. The bone stick man moved closer to where there was a wall mounted strip light and it flickered madly the closer he drew. Then he raised his hand to the plastic casing and pushed against the light. The beam of yellow turned crimson and then the two doors ahead of us swung open with such force I jumped back. Sigurd's arms locked around me to hold me steady.

The two doors now touched each other as their hinges had been together in the middle. I looked into the red glow and where I expected to see a tunnel leading to doom, what I saw made me speak.

"A cleaning cupboard...! Really?" I heard a chuckle behind me and then a hiss from the creature in front.

"Just watch, lille øjesten."

I did as I was told and soon found myself gasping. The Demon in front pushed the light until it disappeared all the way into the painted brick wall and then the red light started to come from inside the cupboards. The doors started to shake as the glow got brighter and then before I knew what was happening, the parts that were hinged switched sides. Now as the doors slid shut they had become a set of double doors instead of two separate ones. The fire extinguisher in the middle of them started to melt just as the doors were closing and it puddled on the floor causing me to step back.

The new substance spread out in a line as though forming some sort of demonic red carpet. It stopped an inch before my booted toes. I whipped my head up in shock and saw the white figure holding out one painfully thin arm. Did this guy even have flesh?

"After you, Bitches." He said and I cringed in place of a smile. The doors now held a pair of knobs that looked like stone skulls in the shape of rabbit's heads. I took one step forward on the remains of the fire extinguisher and then nearly jumped a mile when the doors started to reopen.

"I'm not sure she wants to go down there, Hunter." The demon all but sniggered and I heard the usual growl vibrate from behind me.

"Go ahead øjesten, I'll take care of you." He whispered sweetly in my ear, emphasizing his words with a little squeeze of my shoulders. So I took a deep breath and tried to ignore the dread lying in the pit of my stomach like a block of dry ice. I walked forward and thought sarcastically, well I wanted to know where the dark tunnel to doom was, now I'd found it! Of course, now it looked like I was about to walk down a staircase straight to Hell and the red lighting that seemed to come from nowhere was helping with that fear.

My one constant strength in all this was the feeling of Sigurd at my back and every now and again I would draw comfort from his touch. The further we went down the harder it became to breathe, as though the air was being sucked out through the rough cut stone that belonged to deep earth. You could actually see the tool marks that had chipped away at the stone no doubt through years of hard labour.

A few times I almost slipped and it would have been a painful time for my back landing on stone steps, if it hadn't been for my guardian. I was happy though that the sides of the tunnel travelled up into a high peak and this wasn't only to help with the claustrophobia, but more down to my large friend being able to descend the steps in comfort.

I don't know how long it took us but it felt like we had made our way down thousands of steps and I wondered if this actually wasn't the route to Hell itself. Surely we were deep enough? I was just about to start voicing these opinions aloud when finally the bottom could be seen. My relief was let out in a grateful sigh and Sigurd grunted his laughter by my neck.

"Now for the tricky part." I nodded my understanding but just as we came to the bottom he spun me round to look at his covered face. His lips were in a grim line and I soon found out why with his next words.

"No, you don't understand. I know how well your mind blocks out my kind, but down here, so close to the forces that breed us, those walls you built will crumble to dust the second you step through that door." I turned to see the door he spoke of but his grip tugged my attention back to him.

"You will be defenceless in this Keira, if they want you to see them you will have no choice…you think you're ready for that? And if the time is forced upon us…ready for me?" Was this what he was really worried about, that I would see his other side? That I would freak out and run from him? I may not be able to see this fear in his eyes, but I knew anxiety when I felt it.

"Please don't worry about me Sigurd, I know what I am getting myself into." I said trying to smooth his fears but when I turned around to face the entrance that held my own fears, his words made my breath hitch.

"I sure do hope so, lille øjesten, because…" He walked past me and stood near the door ready to open it and release a world that I really wasn't ready to become a part of.

"…the Beast knows we're here."

CHAPTER TWENTY-SIX

FREAKIN' SHOW ME THE HOST

The door opened and instead of the sound of flesh hitting flesh and grunts of pain, my ears filled with the musical chimes of…fairground music? It was an eerie, disturbing sound that didn't remind me of happy childhood memories, that was for sure. It was a darker version with its tap tapping and dings on triangles with an undercurrent of haunting cries, humming to a deadly tune.

I couldn't help the shudder, quickly followed by goosebumps adorning my flesh.

"Sigurd, what…what is this place?" I asked on a whisper and grabbed his jacket from behind. He turned his head down and around looking at me over his shoulder before stating softly,

"This is a Demon's playground."

I followed his movement closely as we walked into a curtained area, where the music grew louder, along with my anxiety. Swathes of material in dirty yellows, oranges and reds swept down from the ceiling where they were gathered and pulled back to create an entranceway. A box that came up to my waist stood to one side and this was made from worn looking crates that some time ago had been painted in white and red strips. Sigurd stopped at the box and thumped down a sideways fist, making me jump.

"Blimey, you're a big fella ain't ya?" I looked down to where the voice came from and saw a dwarf demon wearing a crumpled, wide pin striped suit of white and grey, making it look as though someone made the thing from old fashioned prison clothes. His face was painted into a crude sad face with high arches for eyebrows and a small black dot on the end of his nose. He was smoking a cigarette and wearing a bowler hat that had a dead rose attached to one side.

The Dwarf looked up at Sigurd and then shrugged his shoulders before walking around the other side of the striped box. It sounded like he was heaving himself up until his head came back into view.

"Payment in the hat, Sunny Jim." He said nodding his hat off his head and rolling it down his arm before catching it in his hand. I squealed as I saw his head. He had what looked like a massive bullet hole on the top of his bald skull and a spoon handle sticking out, at an angle.

"Ya looking at something, missy?" He said cocking his head to one side along with a hand on his hip. I almost gagged when I saw blood spill down his head in a little gush, thanks to the motion.

"No, she isn't. Now, how much Kobold?" Sigurd snapped making the little guy frown in a way that also made his lips scrunch to the side.

"Names Puck A.C.T.U.A.L.L.Y."

He said emphasising each letter slowly.

"Yeah, well tell someone who gives a flying fuck…*Puck*!" The dwarf huffed a cute little growl before giving Sigurd a sneer and shaking his hat.

"Price is a tenner, you big asshole, fifteen for bringing your own little Goth bitch in with ya!" At this, it was now Sigurd's turn to growl, only I had to say hands down he won on the intimidation front. The striped box shook slightly in reaction to Sigurd's outburst of anger. But before things could escalate, I fished out the fifteen quid and stepped up to put it in his hat.

"Well, at least it's cheap." I said in an overly enthusiastic tone.

"Yeah, just like your date." Puck said and Sigurd's rumbling growl got a level deeper. I just managed to grip his arm which was coming up to lash out at the suicidal dwarf.

"Sigurd please, let's just go deal with the reason we are here." I pleaded, before this guy lost his little head to a work related injury.

"Fine!" He snapped before relaxing his fist into a flat palm that he slapped down onto the box. Puck looked a little relieved and reached up to grab the spoon from his head. I couldn't help my gag reflex when I saw him slap a dollop of blood from the spoon onto the back of Sigurd's hand. I then watched as the blood turned into a stamp that was an upside-down triangle with a little V underneath it that the ends of the triangle curled across back on itself. I saw him then flex his large hand, after pulling it from the box.

"You're next, Goth Bitc…" He was stopped short when Sigurd's hand whipped out and cut the end of that word from his strangled breath.

"Beauty…I…mea…nt… beauty." He said with great difficulty.

"Aye, I thought you did." Sigurd said letting go, making the little guy cough.

"If you will…" The growl made him add a hasty "Please" and I stepped forward. I felt the big guy at my back and looked to the little guy in front of me, when I heard the soft words of encouragement whispered in my ear.

"Hand flat, palm down and don't make a noise as it burns."

"Uh…come again?" I said thinking this was one *Hell* of a bad idea!

"Don't worry Princess, it's more like a little tickle..." Puck leaned forward and whispered behind a little hand,

"Think of it as a loving caress by the Devil." He winked at me and I groaned whilst rolling my eyes.

"Yeah right!" I said as I rolled up my sleeve and slapped my hand down, just as Sigurd had done.

"That's the spirit, human!" He smiled showing a row of tiny pointed teeth that all had gaps in between. I tried not to grimace as he reached up once again for his spoon, but I don't think I accomplished it. Then I closed my eyes and repeated softly,

"There's no place like home, there's no place like home," making Puck chuckle.

"Oh, she's a corker this one!" He said and I opened my eyes just as the liquid touched my skin. The blood started to itch at first but then, as it changed shape, the burning started. I was about to move it away when Sigurd came to restrain me, keeping my palm firmly against the box.

"Give it time, *my* øjesten." He said sweetly and I let his scent roll over me as the burning started to subside. He eased his hold but instead of letting me go completely, he took my hand in his and led me away from Puck. I looked down at my slightly throbbing hand and saw that I now had the same mark that Sigurd did. It looked like a stamp you would have received at a nightclub.

"Welcome to The Devil's Ring ya bastards, you be sure to have fun now!" Puck shouted at us, as we walked through the curtained doorway. I looked back to see him grinning and snapping his teeth at me in what looked like pure Demonic glee.

"What…what was that?" I stammered out as I was practically being dragged along through the long curtain entrance, that didn't seem like it would ever end. Sigurd stopped swiftly and then raised my hand up for his inspection. His thumb made soothing little circles over it before answering me. I looked up at him and I could just imagine the vulnerability he must have seen in the depths of my eyes. I could safely say that, considering how I was feeling right now. I had no doubt I must have looked like a scared baby deer looking down the barrel of a shotgun, silently begging the hunter with my eyes.

"That is the Grimoirium Verum, or 'Grimoire of Truth'.

"The what?" I said while no doubt raising a sceptic eyebrow.

"It's also known at the Sigil of Lucifer." He said as though getting frustrated.

"Ok, so I am getting that it has something to do with the Devil, but what's it now doing on my hand?" At this he groaned and ran his free hand down his hooded head.

"Seal of Satan! Alright, it's the bloody Seal of Satan…you getting it now?" He snapped making me snatch my hand back to stare at the mark.

"So, let me get this straight, I have now signed myself up as some kind of Devil worshiper?" I snapped back. I swear I could hear his eyes rolling at my response.

"Not yet, no, but with your insane ideas about taking a little trip to his place of residence, then I wouldn't say you're far off…now come on and let's get this shit done, I'm hungry." Now it was my turn to roll my eyes as he walked on ahead.

"Why am I not surprised…three bacon butties, half my damn birthday cake and even swigging back the bloody milk jug with the tea service, didn't take the edge off!" I muttered whilst following him into the arched doorway at the end of the grubby material hallway.

"What can I say, gotta lotta meat on these old bones that like a little thing called substance." He said sarcastically before pounding a fist on his chest. I patted his arm and said,

"Sure you do, Caveman," making him growl. But right now that sound just added to the background of utter insane surroundings, dragging the only question from my gaping wide mouth,

"What the Fu…!" The sound of a foghorn sounded before my curse could be fully heard.

"Step right up my fudgling pretties and show the room your beautiful twin ditties!" A bellowing voice sounded from the centre of the cavernous space.

"He means breasts, doesn't he?" I said in a stunned voice, standing by his side in frozen wonder.

"God, I hope so…come on my little Goth snack." He said grabbing my hand to pull me further into the cosmic joke that was the room I was now standing in.

"Funny, Flintstone." I commented dryly.

We walked further into the circular room that looked as though it had been crudely carved from the solid rock and I shuddered to think of what was powerful enough to have accomplished such a mammoth task. The surface had then been whitewashed before different fixtures could be mounted. Like the entranceway, the place screamed out demonic fairground Carnival and had swathes of decaying material hung down in lines, creating some creepy version of a Big Top. The yellows were dirty, the oranges were ripped and frayed and the red were splattered in stains that not surprisingly looked to be blood. In the gaps between the hanging material there were upside down crosses, that no doubt also represented the Devil. But the most shocking was the person sized iron cages all stacked up in towers attached to different sections of the walls. These held a sickening array of different demons and…

"Chickens?" I questioned out loud making Sigurd lean down to whisper something,

"They are for the games, along with the fools that angered the Beast and are awaiting punishment." He nodded at the cages and I shuddered just thinking about what that punishment could entail.

The rest of the room was split into different sections but all focused around the large stage in the centre. It reminded me a bit like an abandoned theatre and all at once I was hit with the haunting memory that the dark shadows of Sigurd's mind had shown me. Was this why? Because he knew on some level that this was where my fate would bring us? I didn't have any of the answers and this was hardly the place to start questioning my large protector on the matter.

Seating was sectioned into three parts with large open spaces in between that were crowded with an array of demons like you would find in a nightclub. The fading burgundy material on the chairs was ripped and worn as if it had been installed decades ago and never bothered with since. The cobwebs and grime only added to my assessment, as when one was sat on, a little cloud of dust fanned up around the shoulders of a demon wearing a patchwork jacket. I felt sick when he turned his head to the side to speak to another Demon and I saw half his cheek was decayed, leaving a gaping grey hole where his jaw bone could be seen, like a gory window displaying his skeleton.

On the stage was who I imagined to be the Ringmaster, although not surprisingly, like none I had ever seen before. He stood in the centre alone, but his booming voice was the one that had shouted for the girls to step up. He was dressed in tight-fitting black trousers that tucked into knee-high boots of highl polished black leather that were buckled all the way up with copper spikes. His slim build was shown through the white shirt tucked into his waistband then finished off with a thick belt of blood-red silk tied tight and left hanging to his knees from the knot at the side. The ruffles around the neck of his shirt were framing the mass of red ruffles in the same crimson silk at his waist. This was all topped off with a black, red and white striped waistcoat, matching top hat that was double the regular size and black satin gloves that pulled up over the sleeves of his lavish shirt.

His costume, however, wasn't the big shocker, nor was the massive goggles that rested at the rim of his hat, making him look a bit like a Steampunk explorer. No, it was his face. The beaming white skin that was a startling canvas for the harsh black features that had you screaming 'evil'! Thin diagonal slashes formed wicked eyebrows that made him look constantly disapproving, ones that match his shadowed cheekbones. His thin black lips cut upwards in a sinister smile, that was a sarcastic contradiction to his disapproval, but his eyes added no clues to his feelings. They were two round orbs of cloudy white, stamped with a pair of black X's in the centre of shadowed lids. So, to say he was creeping me out, was a gross understatement!

He spun a long walking stick which looked like a deadly spike that had a metal demonic hand curled around the blade in a deathlike grip. The long claws spanned the distance around the spike twice and this was the end he tapped on the floor, before swinging it back up to tip his hat up as the girls stepped up to the stage. He waggled his arched eyebrows in a comical fashion and the crowd roared their approval also, at seeing half-naked demon girls.

The thing with demons that I was starting to realise, was that not all of them look completely demonic. Oh sure, there were enough elements to know I wasn't in Kansas anymore, but at least most had human figures and the girls were no exception.

The crowd was still split until the last girl had made her way through and up to the stage. The music started to play when the last girl of eight joined the others, who were now circling the Ringmaster. The song reminded me of something you'd find in a Burlesque show as each of the very different girls started to shake and offer up their goods for the Ringmaster's inspection.

"I thought you said this was a fight club?" I muttered sideways to Sigurd, who had stopped to scan the room. I just hoped it wasn't for a quick thrill at seeing so much skin.

"Oh, just wait lille øjesten, there will be blood, 'tis but the first act." I frowned and was left to do nothing but watch the show I'd never thought to see in all my ideas of 'The Devil's Ring'. I kind of had the whole fight club thing in my mind, being some dingy room big enough for betting crowds squashed tight against some rough version of a boxing ring; the kind lit by a single light bulb swaying by a dodgy looking wire. But no, no, I was now in Hell's version of a bloody circus with some fights and punishments thrown in. Yeah, this was going to be great for my stomach muscles I thought, as the first wave of sickening gag came from just looking at the crowd alone.

All the girls were so different in not only size and features but also in costume. There were tutus and bone covered jackets with curled tails that looked to be made from human skin. There were also hats and headdresses made up with everything from feathers and ribbons to the more gruesome bloody teeth and body parts. One girl wore her dark curls to the side, held there with a pinned brooch made from severed fingers, arranged in a flower shape. The painted pink nails matched her ruffled bolero jacket and sparkling bra.

Another was only wearing black underwear over a pair of fishnet tights and her back was pierced in a V shape with hooks. I curled my lip at the view of blood dripping down, as if it had just been done and the ribbon threaded through like the back of a corset did nothing to hide the grisly sight.

"Please don't tell me this is an appealing sight?" I whispered when I saw Sigurd had now started scanning the stage.

"Do I look like a boy scout to you?" Was his only answer and I grunted in response. I had to keep reminding myself that he was, after all, a demon and why would he not be attracted to his own kind?

As the music started to pick up and a voice sang out from over the speakers, this was the cue for the act to kick it up a notch. They all started dancing slowly in sync to the words as each one was introduced. Two walked up to the Ringmaster on either side and were introduced as twins and ran their hands seductively across his chest before thrusting a leg up each thigh and with him holding their backs flicked their upper bodies out to the side. Then he quickly slammed them back together so that they smashed their heads together and knocked them both unconscious on the floor. He simply then stepped over the two bodies and let the other girls drag them off the stage.

The roar of laughter drowned out the song for some moments while he dusted off his hands, as part of the act.

"Step right up as our Girls, Girls, Girls are going cheap, so just pay the man and pick one from the heap." He nodded to the two that were now dumped to the side.

"But the last one standing, however hideous or nice, will be, I'm happy to say, double the price! So come now, gentlemen that you are not…come strip these titties bare, heave them up, show them your man time, I'll throw them over there!" He sang out and nodded to two other girls who had started fighting. One was pulling the other's hair, making pins and pearls go flying, while the men rose from their seats to shout their approval. Then the Ringmaster danced side to side as the beat increased, to then swing his stick round and hit one of the girls who was bent over ready, giving her behind a deafening slap. Her head cracked back and the other girls dragged her off to add to the pile.

Some demons had stood up and were adding themselves to the queue, hoping to pay for an unconscious girl. As the show continued and eventually there was just one girl left, the song came to an end, just as the Ringmaster grabbed the waist of a short girl with a massive red tutu and breasts simply hidden by slashes of black tape, to manhandle. She squealed her delight as he grabbed a breast in his hand and kissed her until her lips bled. Then he pulled back swiftly to say,

"However, for these nights, this little bean can be my queen…" He then said to the crowd behind his hand,

"…let's hope she fights." And then hauled her up over his shoulder and carted her off the stage, with her giggling in delight.

"That's barbaric!" I said outraged, but Sigurd merely laughed next to me.

"Do the girls look like they are complaining?" He asked causing me to look towards the 'heap' of girls now all doe eyed and coming back around from their knocked out states. Each was getting sold off and all were looking far too pleased about it. One girl even whipped off her bra, then slapped it round her buyer's neck to drag him in for a bruising kiss.

I forced my eyes away from the sight, to take in the other horrors of the room. Whereas the seating was concentrated around the stage in a fan shape, the areas in between were where we seemed to be headed. The closer we got, the more it started to look like a type of market was also taking place.

"Come on øjesten, time to see if anyone here can tell us anything useful." He started walking past the rows of chairs, when I grabbed his arm to pull him back.

"Why can't we just ask for this Jared guy?" At this I was answered with a grunted laugh.

"Because, doing so might just end up getting us killed for the bother. Look, you're gonna have to just trust me on this øjesten, an Alpha Hellbeast isn't exactly your most welcoming of hosts, so just try and keep your head down and let me do all the talking, alright?" His voice did that 'Me man, you woman' thing again, so I decided to let it be and just nodded like a good little human pet. Hell, I am surprised he didn't just walk off, whistling and patting his thigh, saying 'come on, good doggie, does the little poochy want a treat?' I think he could hear my groan as I trailed behind him.

We walked past one group that looked to be waiting in line for a fortune teller as there was a little peacock coloured tent that held a small table. A big gypsy lady with a massive gut was covered in layers of jingling sequins and rich sunset colours wrapped around enough times to make a dress. She was drawing in the crowd with her large swaying hips and promises of fates told to those who wished to pay with another's pound of flesh.

"But that one there, I will do for free. Come here my pretty and let me taste the nectar of innocence." I quickened my pace when that offer was directed my way and the growing crowd laughed at my hasty retreat.

"Keep close to me." Sigurd growled low.

I braved a quick look back and was shocked to realise she wasn't the one that was the fortune reader at all. She merely accepted payment in a dripping sack and moved to one side to show a girl behind her. She was a small young girl that looked to be no more than fourteen and wore a straight, plain black dress over her tiny frame.

Sweet ringlets of black hung down in a middle parting and overall she would have been the most normal-looking person in the room that was if it hadn't been for the two Chinese coins in place of eyes, with a tiny white dot in the middle of the square-cut from each one. Then, of course, there was the blood-soaked hands and forearms that looked like she had dipped both her arms inside an open chest cavity. I saw one massive male bow deeply, before following her inside the tent, until the flap hid them from view.

I ended up walking into Sigurd's back as I hadn't realised he had stopped to talk to someone. I let out a whoosh as the solid back nearly knocked the wind from me.

"Careful." Sigurd cautioned, turning his hooded head down to see, no doubt, if I managed to stay on my feet. I couldn't really help it, I mean this place was just insane and had my curious mind doing backflips at the mental overload. If there had been a demonic version of Pandora, then this was like stepping into her box!

I pulled myself together and looked around Sigurd's colossal frame only to nearly lose my dinner once again.

"Oh, Jesus!" I said before I could stop myself.

"Oh, I doubt you will be seeing him around these parts, but hey, seeing as you missed the crucifixion, then we could have a reconstruction of the events, now we just need a pure soul, some nails, a cross and voila…but where would we find such a thing down here?" He asked tapping a dirty claw on the side of his cheek, before that cut up smile curled up enough to cover most of his face, showing me bloody row after row of teeth.

"Oh wait, I think I found one." The most frightening clown I had ever seen in my life finished with a sickening laugh and that tell-tale painted face that was anything but child friendly! His dirty white face paint was plastered on over burnt twisted skin, some pieces still hanging down flapping as he spoke. Red arches framed milky coloured eyes that just looked like someone had carved the holes with a fork.

Sigurd grabbed him suddenly by the overly large lapels of his joker suit of orange and blue. His silky shirt tore showing boiled skin underneath. I almost wished he hadn't bothered, seeing as it just added to the nauseating sight.

"Where is Marcus, Edwin?" Sigurd barked close to his face, one I didn't know how he could stand looking that closely at.

"Ah now, Marky boy…let me see." The clown chuckled sadistically before seeing something when looking up at Sigurd that quickly changed his features from amusement to sheer terror. I could just see the reflection in his murky eyes, as a black shadow started to form into what looked like a snake. Was that coming from under Sigurd's hood? I was just about to sneak a peek when the clown started to become very helpful. The shadow disappeared before I could see it for myself and the clown started to mumble out answers.

"He is calling forth the first fight." The clown nodded back to the stage area and Sigurd briefly glanced that way before turning his attention back on Mr Flappy Skin.

"Thanks for giving me a reason." Sigurd said, his voice getting deeper with every word.

"For what?" The clown laughed nervously.

"This!" Sigurd said before pulling his body closer to then knee him in the dangly man bits. The clown dropped to his knees and cupped his damaged balls with a high whistle. Sigurd turned away without another word. I, however, thought a few parting words were in order. I smiled sweetly and said,

"Not laughing now, Chuckles?" Then I gave him a little bow along with the one finger salute.

"øjesten!" Sigurd snapped, making me turn quickly to catch him back up. This wasn't exactly the type of place I wanted to be left alone in. I might have a little spunk in me, thanks to who I came here with, but take that protection away and I would be nothing but a quivering mess in the first hiding place I could find in this warped funfair of Hell.

We came to a stop, closer to the stage than I would have liked, but I had no option than to follow Sigurd's lead. I looked up when murmurs filled the room and I watched as a man emerged from the steps at the other side. He had a slim tall build that showed he wasn't lacking in lean muscle. He wore dark trousers with an old gun attached around one thigh. He also had a fringed scarf tied around his waist under a belt that held a sword to one side. His V shape torso was covered in a dark leather top that looked both worn and soft as it moulded to each contour. The neck was a separate panel that folded back at each corner showing a graceful neck.

The only way to describe his face was as a handsome jester. His pale face was painted with two slits of red that ran through startling blue eyes and down the length of his cheeks. They created horn shapes on his forehead that curled inwards and did the same by his chin. Another long straight arrow shape was the last painted piece that came from the centre of his bottom lip and all the way down the long column of his throat. But it wasn't his makeup that amazed me, but the presence in which he carried himself; the tilted chin that looked down on others, with high cheekbones and a sculptured jawline.

His piercing eyes took in everyone around him before he spoke and he arched one thin eyebrow, as though assessing the crowd. Then the faint music began and he shook his blazing red hair which was pulled back into sections, knotted and tied at each point with a little bell on the end. The sharp widow's peak pointed down his forehead and this combined with the red horn curls of makeup in the same colour was like a warning sign that shouted 'deadly'.

"Listen up my esteemed scumbags and assholes, I have great displeasure to welcome thee to pay witness to our first fight to the death. So, without further ado and for your perverted pleasure, raise your fisted hands and growl your greetings for SNOW WHITE AND THE *TEN* DWARFS!" He said shouting out the last part but still keeping his posh accented voice steady as a rock.

"Snow White?" I asked only to be shushed by Sigurd. The jester finished with a graceful spin on one foot and a regal bow to the other side of the room. I looked to where he aimed his bow to and saw the shadowed figures that had suddenly emerged from the parted crowd. Hushed murmurs added an extra baseline to the music already playing. The larger figure in the middle walked ahead of the rest and with him came a thick fog that rolled throughout the room with dramatic effect. I waited for these to be the obvious ones fighting, only to gasp when Sigurd leant down to whisper in my ear. But I couldn't hear his words over the loud announcement from the jester, which was no doubt the same as what Sigurd had confirmed,

"My Lord Cerberus."

The Beast had arrived.

CHAPTER TWENTY-SEVEN

FREAKING OUT ABOUT FIGHTING IN THE SHOW

"That's him?" I whispered as the hulking great figure emerged from the fog and shadows that seemed to follow his every step. I couldn't believe the massive deal that was making this man out to be the most hideous beast who controlled the Hell's gates.

"Really...Another biker?!" I said, this time not being able to keep my voice down.

"Quiet!" Sigurd snapped pulling me by the arm to stand behind him.

"What?" I couldn't understand the big deal. I mean, it just looked like the lead singer of a heavy rock band just walked in with his crew behind him. I peeked around Sigurd to get another look at the guy now taking a seat on a raised area which held a massive black throne. I screwed up my eyes trying to get a better look but the details on both throne and occupant were heavily in shadow.

"What did I say on keeping quiet and letting me handle this?" He said biting his fingers deeper into the top of my arm, just before the point of pain.

"Fine!" I snapped and yanked myself from his grasp, to fold my arms.

"But I hardly think what I said was life threatening!" I all but stamped my foot on the compacted earth that was the fairground floor. Sigurd just answered with a trademark growl and turned back to where he saw the jester was coming over. The stage area that had once held sadistically colourful entertainment now had been converted into a fight ring. Walls of metal poles entwined with twisted tension wire had shot up from the floor to encase the area and the jester simply grabbed the top wire and vaulted over effortlessly.

He now faced us and on seeing me, he cocked his head to one side, gracing us with a vicious smile, making his little bells jingle.

"Marcus." Sigurd nodded and the jester without taking his eyes from me, nodded back saying,

"Snake Eye." Then, before directing any more words at us, the sound of footsteps drew his attention back to the stage. I followed his gaze and saw that the space was now being filled by ten little guys all wearing the same thing. Dwarfs dressed in dark blue military uniforms with red piped jackets and matching metal buttons in V shapes down their breasts, all took their stations around the ring. Then I watched as a naked man in chains was brought forward by four guys dressed like freak show strongmen from the 1930's, who were all bald and had bulging muscles barely covered in bloody fur tunics. The pale man they dragged in towered over them and I couldn't decide if the strongmen were short or the pale man was overly tall.

As soon as they got him into the ring, the strongmen let go of the four chains that were wrapped around various parts of his body and made a run for it. Then the jester shouted over his shoulder,

"Light 'em boys!"

I saw someone near the wall nod and then slammed a massive throw switch down until the buzz of electric could be heard travelling along the tension wire around the ring. It was the same time as the large pale man chose to run at the fence, ready to jump it. Unfortunately, he was too late, as the power made its way around the ring and into his body. The shock kept him holding on for moments too long, before he was thrown backwards. He shuddered on the floor and then, curling his body one way and bow it back another, he started to change form. The sound of skin splitting and bone popping seemed to be the symphony people had been waiting for, because the crowd went wild. The man was a man no longer, as white fur folded outwards like petals of the flesh, opening up to the electric current that powered the change.

Meanwhile, the little army of guards started circling the beast escaping the confines of a man form, as if waiting for the transformation to finish. Soon, there was only a beast of white fur, claws attached to longer twisted limbs and elongated snout of furious snapping teeth. The dwarfs started to run around the ring faster than before and then an alarm sounded, being the cue needed for the crowd to start throwing down bets. Half-naked females, dressed like gothic showgirls in black and white stripes, all started to collect the bets in their top hats.

Then the heavy beat of pounding drums from a band which just emerged from behind the raised seating area and came into view. This became a heavy rock song as a background for screaming spectators and for a fight to the death…One that was just about to get bloody.

"I must confess Snake Eye, I did not expect to see you with a piece of forbidden candy. Which shop of damnation tempted you to stick your hand in the human cookie jar?" Marcus asked leaning a hip against a wooden post that held a black box which looked like a safe made from cooled lava. The girls were all coming back to dump their hats filled with bets into the door that was open, guarded no doubt, by Marcus.

"Of course, if you have had your sweet fill, then I would be only too happy to take the dark bit of fluff off your hands." Sigurd snarled and stood a little closer to me, in a clear sign that I was off limits. The jester's smile was pure evil as it widened across his face, the thin lines of makeup matching the fine arch of one eyebrow. He then winked at me, peeking out behind Sigurd and the snarl deepened to a growl.

He merely crossed his arms over his chest and then shrugged his shoulders as if he didn't care either way.

"So, if you're not here to share…which isn't very polite by the way… what is it you want exactly?" He said the last word directed at the long talons he was examining on one hand. The tips were dipped bloody over black nail varnish.

"I need to be granted a meeting with Cerberus." Sigurd stated with confidence oozing from every pore.

"That's Lord Cerberus to you!" He snapped, ending the remark with a creepy rake of his tongue between his teeth, making a hissing sound.

"Then in that case, from one Lord to another I demand my request be granted." Marcus started laughing at Sigurd's statement and pushed away from the post, after slamming the safe door closed and spinning the combination lock. He only came to a stop when he was looking up at Sigurd. Even with this being the case, the jester still must have been at least six feet tall.

"I'm sorry, but I wasn't aware you had claimed that title, My Lord Ouroboros…" He then took a step back and swept into a graceful, but mocking, bow before continuing,

"Forgive me for misplacing the red carpet in your honour, prey do tell me, how I could make up for such blatant show of ignorance."

"More like arrogance!" I commented, stepping from behind Sigurd, not being able to hold my tongue any longer.

"Ah, so it speaks." He said smiling this time, making me growl.

"Yeah and this bitch also punches, kicks and bites assholes like you, so prey tell me, do you like having your balls hanging where you can still play with them?" I asked stepping forward happily, making him take a step back. I thought the retreat was out of intimidation on my part, but I knew differently when I saw him bend over into a chorus of raucous laughter. It was an evil sound that grated on my nerves, like someone had stretched them out and was playing them like a violin.

Meanwhile, behind the amused jester Marcus, the fight was in full swing and the white creature had his claws fully extended. I don't know about Snow White and the Ten Dwarfs but snow beast and the axe wielding goblins seemed like a more accurate description. The ten soldiers were now, not only armed, but their faces had changed into a mass of boils, split skin and pus dripping holes.

They were running as one, trying to take the beast down by swinging at his legs, like miniature loggers going at a pair of tree trunks. The beast roared at the ceiling and then swiped out and down low, taking out at least six of the ten dwarfs still standing. They went down like pins at a bowling alley and when one started to crawl away in a desperate attempt to get from under the large feet, the beast took the opportunity to strike. He rolled his long tongue out over his dripping snout, all in anticipation for the crack of a spine that followed with one stamping foot on the little guy's back. His small limbs stopped moving and soon resembled nothing more than a child sized squashed bug.

The others soon found their feet and re-evaluated the white beast, who had started playing with their fallen companion's dead carcass. I had no clue how they were intending to bring down such a creature, but the jester's knowing voice soon drew my eyes from the brutal playground of the stage.

"I have no doubt you could my dear, but it will take more than spunk to get you what you seek. And you, 'My Lord' of the Ouroboros, well, you should know better, as I am sure you are more than aware the deep feelings *My Lord* Cerberus holds for the species of your pet. I suggest you both leave before he sees her and makes you take a bite out of her beautiful skin for his amusement." On hearing this, I decided it was a smart move by taking the few steps back behind my large growling protector.

"And you Marcus, should know better than to threaten any pet of *MINE!*" The deep demonic word wasn't only a threat to the man he was speaking with, as everyone that was close enough to reach out and touch me suddenly decided I was too much of a life risk. I didn't know what was worse; feeling like a bone being fought over by two dogs or being referred to as the damn dog!

I mean, don't get me wrong, I couldn't be more thrilled to know that instead of just saying 'ah to Hell with it, you take her, she is more trouble than she is worth', Sigurd was instead fighting my corner. But how I felt about being referred to as his pet was another thing and if he carried on doing so, then he was going to be cleaning up my shit in an entirely different way!

"Well then, I guess it's your funeral my old friend, as you

know the only way to be put in the same space as Lord Cerberus is to either be there for his entertainment or at his mercy, neither will bring you a good outcome, Snake Eye." At this Sigurd started laughing.

"By the Gods, has your mind become so old you have forgotten what happened the last time I was in that ring, for I recommend you dust it off before you feel the need to warn me of such things." Now it was the jester's turn to snarl his reply, losing that cool countenance and cocky visage.

"Yes and I am old enough to know better of times long past and times brutally changed. The sport of blood is not what it once was, thanks to the King, who no longer has his uses for it!" I gasped at the sound of Draven being mentioned and Sigurd pushed me completely behind him before Marcus could take notice of my response. After all, what would a little 'pet' like me know about someone as powerful as Draven, when someone like Jared Cerberus wouldn't see a mere human?

"Enough of this Marcus, just do what needs to be done to get me the meeting." At this he finally nodded in defeat and then muttered,

"It's your choice of a final resting place, my old friend," before turning his attention back round to the fight still taking place. I too couldn't help looking back at the bleak sight.

The music started to change into something heavier and more demonic as the show was obviously coming to the bloody end. A few more small corpses lay still, that had been battered and broken into a mere shell of the beings they were before. But six still remained and it looked to be all that was needed to bring down the beast. They decided the best attack was to form as one, all now standing on each other's shoulders to create the height needed.

So, as one swaying body of twenty four limbs, they worked together to pass up the biggest of the axes to the top dwarf. He then used it to swing back, making the rest wobble in a comical way, causing the crowd to break out in cheers of laughter. I was disgusted to say that, even when the force brought that axe back over his little head, to then crash into the face of the beast, it didn't stop the laughter. The beast howled in pain as the blade split his muzzle in two sections and the blood sprayed out over the front row, causing excited shrieks. I could only bury my face into Sigurd's back, to hide from the beast's last breaths on this plane. The crowd didn't follow my repulsed views as they erupted into a deafening applause, most even standing as the six dwarfs left standing all joined hands to take a bow.

"This is sick." I whispered into Sigurd's back.

"No pet, this is entertainment, Demon style!" Marcus was the one to answer me over his shoulder, just before the thrown switch was killing the power in time for the jester to once again take the stage. His lithe form bent over the wired fence like an Olympic high jumper, landing gracefully behind the six winners.

"A cheer now for destruction of 'Meh-The beast' brought down by the brothers Kobold!" The room again went crazy at the jester's praise and the dwarfs started to climb over the fence to then throw themselves into the crowd like they were the singers at a rock concert.

"What is the 'Meh…eh, something beast? And the Kobold, are those the little guys?" I asked not being able to help the bubbling of questions. I heard Sigurd's little groan before he turned to face me. This time, however, I could swear I saw the little flash of where his eyes would be in the shadows his hood created.

"The Kobold are a race of what you would think of as Goblins, although I can assure you, nothing like what your fantasy mythology dictates. They are more like demonic helpers that thrive from the leadership of others. And, as you have seen, are great little fighters in numbers." I shook my head wondering how much more of this night could I take, but when Sigurd carried on with answering my question, I discovered my limits,

"The Meh-The beast is also better known to your kind as a Yeti, but to us, a once faithful protector of the Kangchenjunga Himal Demon door that resides there in the Himalayas. He is a creature made by Jared Cerberus and was here today for his betrayal, or so I heard."

"This is his idea of punishment?!" I said outraged at the sheer brutality of it and feeling sorry for the soulless carcass now being dragged off stage. Sigurd merely shrugged his hefty weight, as if it didn't really matter. I walked a few steps to the stage and then whirled around when I saw the jester was now talking over the fence to someone making his way around the sides.

"What's he going to do with him next, make a rug outta him for his fireplace or just nail his ass to the bloody wall?" I snapped now facing Sigurd, only the grim line of his lips didn't look directly at me, but more like over my head and I soon knew why.

"Actually, I was considering mounting his fucking head on my wall, but now I am thinking of making room for another..." I felt a strong and insanely large hand circle the column of my neck, before I was yanked backwards into a hard chest. I felt lips at my neck and the next threat whispered along my skin, like a deadly sting.

"...and here we have such a pretty little head." He then snapped my head back with a brutal grip in my shoulder length hair before I looked up into the face of the Beast and now something told me my number was up!

"Let her go!" Sigurd ordered in a demonic command that made me flinch.

"Ah, so I have you to thank for bringing this little human snack to my attention. You know I don't usually like these weak, feeble creatures but I must confess, this one holds an appeal like I have never known. Wherever did you find her, Snake Eye?" He asked as his eyes never left my frightened ones. His fingers caressed my neck and did the same at the back of my head, but I was at a loss to know why. It was soothing down my fear, preventing it from reaching fever pitch.

"I will not speak of her until we are far from prying eyes, now release her." He took a step closer to me, the shadows beneath his hood starting to flow out and the soothing fingertips turned deadly in a heartbeat, once again putting my neck in a punishing hold. I cried out, making Sigurd stop and rethink his next move.

"You know what I could do with her with a mere flick of my wrist, so I suggest you keep your darkness in check."

"Don't hurt her!"

"Umm, now I am intrigued and must confess a strange urge myself to protect this body, rather than naturally peel the pale skin from her tender flesh…so I have to wonder…" he suddenly flipped me round to face him and finished with a gentle bent finger running down the length of my cheek.

"…what are you, my little bisque doll?" I closed my eyes and tried not to look at his face, thinking that given the harsh voice that matched Sigurd in the deep and gravelly department, nothing good could come from looking the Beast in the eye. I bit on my bottom lip and shook my head, hoping he got that I wasn't going to answer him. His booming laughter came right before my body was suddenly turned upwards. He literally just threw me over his shoulder. I braved opening my eyes to find Sigurd being held back by about five massive guards, rage evident on his twisted features. The Beast that held me just laughed harder making me shake and then finally said,

"Give it up my friend and save that fury for the ring, as you will most certainly be needing it!"

"No! I will fight, but only if you give me back the girl!" Sigurd roared at his back and I saw from upside down the shadows start to come out like tentacles, reaching for its prey. I tried to reach out and grab one, when one amused Lord Cerberus spun back around. I hoisted myself up and scrambled on to one enormous shoulder to get a look at what was happening to my friend.

"Don't worry… I will keep her close by until your fight is up and I have a feeling that we are going to become fast friends, this kitten and I." And to prove his point, his palm connected with my fleshy cheek in a swift slap to my bottom. I yelped at the burn his hand left and flopped back down from being perched on his shoulder.

"Now, are you going calm yourself or do I have to hurt her to prove a point?"

"I will do as you ask, just don't hurt her Cerberus!" Sigurd's voice had taken its deep depths to pleading and it broke my heart at the sound.

"And I am sure your kitten will do the same and be good for

me, won't you now?" I received a little shake when I didn't answer, for the tears that formed and found a place to disappear on the ground. I nodded my upturned head and whispered a weak,

"Yes."

"Come now, you can do better than that." He gave me another shake, this time stronger than the last and I had to hold onto his leather jacket to stop myself from being whipped from side to side.

"Yes!" I shouted making him laugh once again.

"Of course you will, as will your protector. Have no fear my new pet, this night promises to be entertaining…very entertaining." He added as he made his way back through the now parted crowd to the throne he once sat upon…

New pet and all.

CHAPTER TWENTY-EIGHT

MOLTEN SILVER

I was quickly finding myself dreading being turned upright and would have been quite happy to spend the remainder of my days this way, if it meant I didn't have to face Jared Cerberus. Ok, so this was a lie, but it still didn't mean I was in any rush to be looking into the eyes of the very beast that guarded the gates of Hell!

I wanted to make a fuss by kicking and screaming all the way back to the raised sitting area, but I knew this wouldn't help me, or the situation I had forced Sigurd into. I also didn't think it would have made much difference to the solid strength of one arm wrapped around my legs, holding them immobile. I bounced with every step but his shoulders were so wide they were ample enough in size to accommodate my bent waist.

My big metal skull belt buckle dug into my belly and I had to hold in the moan of relief when we finally stopped moving. I had tried in vain at first to pull down the skirt I had felt riding up, but after a few more spanks and feeling like a naughty child, I decided to give up. I refused to scream out and kept my lip firmly between my teeth to keep from doing so. However, when I felt his teasing hand worm a few fingertips in the holes of my rose pattern tights to play along the skin on my thigh, I had squeaked out a protest and tried to get away. He had just laughed again, hoisted me further up his shoulder and gripped my legs tighter.

I braced myself when I was lowered down the length of him and it turned out to be my first good look at the Demon Lord. I saw at the back of his head, hair now longer than mine and all of it pulled back into a leather tie. It was thick, wiry and a strange dark charcoal colour. I closed my eyes just as I saw the flash of silver in his penetrating eyes that were sizing me up, the same as I was doing to him, the only difference was that he didn't chicken out from one look.

When I felt my feet touch the ground, I braved a glance to find him wearing a very, worn pair of boots of cracked leather, obviously weathered with age. They came up to his calf, but the laces were only tied halfway so they flopped back down, covering some of the heavy buckles. Tucked into these was ripped grey denim, slashed at the knees, showing a slice of tanned skin. One thing about the Lord that screamed out was that he clearly liked to dress comfortably.

It finally reached the point where I could no longer hide from those penetrating eyes, as I felt my chin being gripped between a finger and thumb. He forced my head up and on the way I saw the stretch of material that practically groaned at being expected to cover such muscle mass. He wore a plain black T-shirt, leather waistcoat which, along with his leather jacket, also looked worn to the point of looking like rock hard skin on some type of black reptile.

But then, I had nowhere else to look other than to take the beast into my sights and hoped I would be the same this time tomorrow…that is, with my throat still intact and my lungs still breathing.

The first thing I noted was the black wiry beard that was shaped and trimmed on each side, only to come down longer on his chin into a point. He had a strong bone structure and a wide nose that suited the hard lines of his face. He also had a full pair of lips framed with the darkness of his facial hair and slightly arched eyebrows, one of which had a thick scar running through it. The end of the scarred flesh hooked slightly to one side, stopping halfway down his chin and disappearing behind his ear.

But the most prominent feature and the one I had dreaded looking into, was a pair of startling silver-grey eyes that were ringed by a thin black that bled slightly into the white. The skin around his eyes was naturally dark, adding a forbidding backdrop to the intense stare I received. This, combined with the almond shape of his eyes and deeply tanned skin, gave him an exotic island look. It was as if he had acquired his great muscle mass from days of making village huts, lugging around tree trunks and wrestling live boars.

And at that moment, I would have loved nothing more than to say how hideous he looked, but like the rest of the big players in this supernatural world, he was of course jaw-dropping handsome. Hard, rough and rugged were aspects that created a frightening beauty that one can only ever find in a beast of nature and Jared Cerberus was the Underworld's equivalent of looking into the pale eyes of a rare white tiger.

As soon as my face was released, I looked away, unable to bear the weight it took to look at him straight on. I felt too vulnerable and wondered if this was due to what he was. Did everyone feel this way around him, with an unexplainable reason to fear being in the predator's sights?

"Now, there is a face of an angel hiding behind all this war paint." He said while his thumb roughly smudged a line of my black lipstick down my chin. I noticed he wore heavy silver rings on three fingers, which added to the biker image. One was a series of metal flames that covered half his middle finger. The other two were thick twisted symbols I couldn't recognise. On his other hand I saw only one big thumb ring that was a horned skull with the point coming past his nail into a deadly tip.

I pulled my face from his hold, noticing how coarse the skin on his large hands was. Scars and calluses marred long thick fingers that first fisted by my face, as if wanting to reach out again, but held back. Either that or he was about to punch me, but for some reason I didn't think that was going to be the case. Proving I wasn't about to get smacked around, he turned from me and snapped out an order to a girl sat further down from him.

"Take her and clean that shit off her face!" At his barked order, a short girl full of bountiful curves got up and bounced over to me. She had bright orange hair with it cut in a harsh straight line high on her forehead. This highlighted the peach coloured skin on her round face and made her painted sunset lips a bright focal point in the creepy room. She had a piercing on either side of her cheeks, like two metal dimples and one bright red bar piercing the bridge of her nose.

Her choppy cut hair was pulled back into a high ponytail and swayed with her wider hips as she walked closer to me, with a fuller figure lady swagger. She gave me a wink when Jared turned his back on us both and said in a sweet voice,

"Come on, sweetie," and took my hand in hers to lead me away. I followed and felt somewhat relieved at meeting the first kind person in this Hellhole. She pulled me along with a sunny smile and winked at the singer when we passed the band. One look at those guys and winking was the last thing on my mind. I wrinkled my nose to hide my reaction to all the cracked black lines that covered their pale skin. They reminded me of full sized gothic male dolls, which had been smashed and been put back together using too much black glue.

We got to three doors at the back of the room and the signs on them surprised a laugh out of me. The ladies' was a picture of Little Red Riding Hood squatting in the woods. The men's was a picture of a wolf dressed as grandma looking over his shoulder as he peed out of the window of a girly bedroom and the middle door brought me up short. It was an explicit picture of the wolf bending Red Riding Hood over and taking her from behind. Of course, before I needed to ask, I could hear sounds of rough sex coming from behind the closed door, which was obviously coming to an end.

The orange haired girl held open the ladies' door for me and laughed at the sight of my crimson blush. She was still giggling when the door closed and we approached the sinks.

"Ah, don't worry honey, there's only one big bad wolf you

need to worry about around here." She winked at me again and swiped her tongue over her top teeth.

"I'm Smidge by the way." She added turning to face away from the mirror and shaking my hand. I bit my bottom lip in preparation for the lie that was about to come from me.

"I'm Cathy." I said, using the nickname an old teacher had given me once, before I got the rest of the school in the habit of using my middle name. Although, if I had thought about it, I could have just said my name was Tricks, after what the Oracle had named me in her first letter.

"Well *Cathy*, we don't get many humans here, which begs the question, what did you do to one of my kind to get into this shit-hole?" She asked, walking over to grab a couple of paper towels from the dispenser. I watched her and then my eyes focused on the back of her neck. I didn't see it before, but now under the brighter lights the bathroom had to offer, it was fully on show. This girl's shoulders were covered in yellowish scales that shimmered as her muscles moved but this wasn't all. Instead of just the bones of her spine being more pronounced, they actually came up so close to the skin, it stretched over the points as though the skin would soon rip open if she moved too quickly. Each bone was triangular in shape, giving her exposed back a reptilian side.

She turned back around, and I knew she waited for my answer. The thing was though, this was the part of the lying process I never got around to ironing out. I mean, for starters, I had a big ass warrior dude who told me he would handle all the talking! So where did that leave the world's worst liar...? In this shithole, up its own shitcreek, without a freakin' paddle, that's where!

"It's...well...it's a long story." I said lamely hoping miss cute, scaly and sunny lips would let the matter drop. She nodded and then started wetting the paper before handing me the soggy wad. When I frowned she nodded to the 'shit' on my face as wolfy back there had called it. I started to wipe my face clean and actually started to feel better after clearing my pores and not just from the heavy makeup. This place had you feeling all kinds of dirty and I felt like I needed a whole station of firemen to hose me down, to feel clean again…although this picture had its own dirty thoughts. I giggled at the thought of where my head was at.

Smidge raised an eyebrow and smiled at me without comment.

"Well, Jared was right, there is an Angel under there." I blushed again at her compliment.

"Ok, so can I ask you a question?" I decided to brave a question to the only kind person I had encountered.

"Go for it." She said shifting around her black tube top that connected to a bright orange layered skirt that matched her hair perfectly.

"You're like the only nice person that I have come across in here and I was wondering, what brings *you* to this 'shithole'?" She burst out laughing and then reached up to pull her hair apart making her ponytail tighter.

"I am Jared's personal assistant." I couldn't help my mouth from dropping.

"Really!?"

"Yep, have been since the end of the seven-year war." Ok, so if my mouth was hanging before, now it was touching the floor!

"But that was like seventeen…something!" I said not remembering the exact date.

"Summer of 1763 to be precise, but Hell, who's counting when you don't look a day over twenty, right?" She said nudging me and my numb brain told me to nod so as not to be rude. All the while, of course, I am mentally adding up the years as we exited the bathroom. It took me the whole journey back to come up with a figure, as maths was most definitely not my strong point.

"You're at least 250 years old!" I shouted out without engaging a filter or even the good sense to know that we were no longer alone. Smidge giggled as my hands flew to my mouth in a hopeless attempt at taking it back.

"I see you have been getting acquainted with my new pet, Smidge." Her boss said dryly. I did what I do best in these embarrassing situations and that was make it sparklingly obvious with a torrent of blood rushing to my face and a tight grip on my bottom lip. His powerful eyes flashed molten silver at the site of my shame and then he was from his chair and in front of me in a heartbeat.

"Now, why does this beauty seem familiar to me?" He said cocking his head to one side and bending slightly, trying to see me better. He was tall, but not gargantuan like Sigurd. He seemed more like Vincent's height of 6' 2" but he definitely had more hefty bulk than the Angelic Draven brother.

"I…don't know…you." I stuttered out, looking down at my feet. This time it was his ringed thumb that raised my face to his, thanks to the painful point that dug under my chin. He didn't say a word as he took in every detail of my face, one that was burning under the excruciating assessment. He ran the silver horn of his ring down my cheek no doubt leaving a dented trail which, thankfully, didn't break the skin.

"Not yet you don't." He made those four words sound like the threat he no doubt intended. I made a little yelp as he wound an arm around me and pulled me roughly to him. He then leant down to my neck and used his free hand to rip away the clasps that held the material from exposing my skin to his exploring lips. The little jacket didn't stand a chance and now a large flap hung limp showing my hidden cleavage which, thanks to the neck of my top, showed far too much skin.

I felt his rumble vibrate through my chest, which was pressed tightly to his solid torso and came out in a breath from the lips he had at my neck. He took my scent in with a deep fill of his lungs and another noise that sounded close to a gravelly purr sent goosebumps along my skin.

"Please." I whispered helplessly against him.

"Please indeed. Don't worry my pet, I will keep my vow and not harm you, but I said nothing about not playing with you." He laughed at the shudder that wracked my body and I was glad he was still holding me up, as I felt as though my legs would have given out on me. I was scared shitless of what this body that held me captive could do to me, but more importantly, was that on a small level my own body was betraying my good sense to getaway. Being held this way by such a commanding force was swamping my mind with memories of what it used to be like. To feel this need and this closeness from another being not of this world…well, it was like someone had just plugged me in.

It was as if my body craved this supernatural touch from another and it was only the utterly ashamed feeling that also flooded my fragile system, that stopped me from climbing up his body like the damn pet he called me. I had to close my eyes tight when his hands reached up and held me by the neck gently. I knew he was taking in my responses and I felt the slow probing around the edges of my brain. He was trying to gain access to my mind and I was thankful that I still retained enough power to hold my shields in place.

Sigurd had said that my mental walls would not work in here which, considering the amount of Demonic faces I had seen, he had been right. So, when the fortress that surrounded my thoughts held against such a commanding presence like Jared was inflicting, I was surprised when it held him firmly on the boundaries, denying him his power.

"Now, that is interesting and starting to make sense." He said leaning down so the words were only heard by me. Then he surprised the Hell out of me by granting me a brush of his lips on my nose in a sweet kiss, before taking my hand in his. He pulled me from my mental anguish and on opening my eyes I saw that he was pulling me into a chair situated next to his.

"Now, time to enjoy the show, as I am sure you would like the time to collect the right thoughts, that you will be sharing with me soon enough." There was no escaping the demand in that statement, so I did as he suggested and kept silent until I no longer had a choice. After all, I had come here for a meeting with the only man who could get me into Hell, so what did I expect…that he would just take me there like a tourist with a paying ticket? Of course, there was no getting around what I would have to tell him, but then what? What would he do when he knew the truth…and more importantly, would I be regretting it once the real show began?

Anyone seeing me sat here, being offered a drink by a waitress dressed as an evil Tinkerbell wearing a beanie hat, would have thought I was in Jared's VIP as a treasured guest. I took everything that was offered, as I had a feeling, very shortly I would be needing the alcohol. I looked to my side seeing the man himself, the Lord of his domain sat back on the most disturbing looking throne I had ever seen.

It looked like burnt wood that had been carved into a design which could only be described as twisted souls trapped into the shape of a large chair. Arms out-stretched up the back as if trying to break out of Hell and reach Heaven. These limbs formed an arch with one singular hand holding a sword. The blade had hands trying to grasp it, until the highest point came above the others and could be seen clearly over Jared's head. The sides were also carved black wood, only the flames of a hellish abyss licked at the start of the bodies trying to escape it.

You could say that if there was ever going to be a chair made for Hell's gatekeeper, then this fit the man down to the very last grasping finger of a damned soul.

"Her name?" I shot a look at Jared, who was firing this question at the bubbly Smidge, whose name I still didn't get.

"She told me it was Cathy, but she lied and not very convincingly." She shot me a smirk and I tried to shrink down in my seat to make myself smaller.

"No, I expect not, I could smell her pure soul even with a field of Gorgon shit between us, no mistaking one the Gods themselves take an interest in." He turned to look at me and I was thankful, at that moment, I had to direct my attention from his questioning gaze to take my drink from a tray.

"Look at me, girl!" The order made me spill my drink over the rim, as I jumped. I did as I was told and met his eyes with a pair of frightened ones of my own. I waited for him to speak and when he didn't I inhaled a premature breath of relief, only to let it all out again in a whoosh, as I was plucked from my seat.

"What are you…?"

"Be silent!" I decided to do as I was told, considering I was now being set in his lap, surrounded by muscle. He put me sideways so that his arm held me behind my back. My booted legs hung like limp noodles over the side of the black carved Hell of his chair and when I tried to move, his free hand held me down by resting his weight on my lap.

"Now, time to watch the show." He nodded towards the stage where another act was stepping into the centre. The Ringmaster was now back, but his once smart costume was now somewhat lacking, thanks to the obvious fun he had found with the girl he carted off stage. He was now missing his shirt but his ruffled tie was still in place. His trousers were on but he hadn't bothered to do up the button and if the bulge was anything to go by, he was definitely ready for another round with the tutu girl. You could even see her waiting at the side of the stage for his return, wearing a now ripped tutu, only one breast covered in the strip of black tape, and the Steampunk goggles on top of her head, that had once been on the Ringmaster's now missing hat.

He swung his massive stick in the air around his head and brought it crashing down to create a loud boom, silencing the room.

"Now, now you scummy bastards, listen to my words, it is time for the next show to begin, so I suggest you watch out for the birds. It's time to smell the roses and three cheers for freak acts galore, when the acid trip hits and Russian doll man dies, be sure to tip at the door!" He swung around his spiked stick towards the edge of the stage and the room burst into applause as the acts made their way through.

The Ringmaster jumped down and landed in front of his claimed girl. He then ripped off the remaining black tape, exposing the girl's other breast, before whipping his scarf around her body to use it to pull her nipple to his eager mouth. She let out a squeal before he pushed her backwards out of sight, all the while still latched on to her breast.

"Now, that is one randy bastard!" Marcus said as he stepped up to the seating area shaking his head. He stopped short and scanned up my body, which had no other option than to be sprawled out across his master's lap, in a dominating display.

"I'm glad to see you finding pleasure in the company of our new spunky human, Cerberus." He commented with a sly smirk, making Smidge giggle. He winked down at her and then snapped a short,

"Up!" Smidge rolled her eyes, before getting up and giving Marcus her seat. She was just about to sulk off when the smirking jester grabbed her around the waist and hauled her to his lap, mimicking Jared.

"Hey!"

"I thought I would give it a try, after all it looks so comfortable." He nodded to me and then hummed as his hands started to roam over her shoulders and down her bare arms.

"And with your delicious curves Smidgy, it feels, so *fucking good!*"

"Jared!" She shouted in outrage and I think I was the only one who heard him groan beneath me.

"Marcus, stop scratching at her scales for fuck sake, before she bites you and I have to patch your ass up again!" Marcus' hands flew up and he shouted,

"Fine!" And let a struggling Smidge go, only to swear in pain as she stamped down a booted heel on his foot.

"Asshole!" She snapped, but before she could move away quickly enough the loud crack from her behind getting slapped even made me jump. She whirled around with a pointed finger and he started laughing like the joker he looked.

"Sorry Smidgy, I just couldn't help myself, that big beautiful bum of yours is too much temptation for one man to bear!"

"Grrr! Jared I swear to the Devil, he will die by my hands one of these days… I don't give a shit if he is your best friend!" Jared laughed and I was dumbstruck gobsmacked when she walked past him and smacked him upside the head, making him laugh harder.

"Jackasses! The both of you!" Was her parting line, as she stormed off into the back. I couldn't believe, after all I had heard about this guy and his famous fury, that he was acting this way. It was like a group of mates all hanging out together and laughing over beers.

"You know, one of these days, she is right and will tear you a new hole if you keep teasing her." Jared warned, turning his neck to shoot a warning look at his friend, one I had mistaken for his minion.

"That is a fight I look forward to J, you know that." He said laughing and swiping a bottle from the tray the waitress held out to him.

"Anyway, where is 'Conan the Black' tonight?" Marcus asked still full of humour.

"Laugh it up asswipe, but that is another of my council, who won't bother with tearing you a new hole, but will just go straight for that jolly fucking head of yours, if he catches you calling him that again." Jared warned, making his friend laugh harder.

"Like to see him try, besides, what's he got…a date or something?" I looked up just in time to see the evil grin that Jared stamped down into a serious face, before giving his friend an answer.

"Not sure, but I think Smidge wouldn't mind a bit of Conan action." At this Marcus choked back on his swallowed beer and shot from his seat.

"The fuck she does!" Now this was the face of a very different jester, lost and dead was all the easy going amusement that oozed from his every word. No, now a mixture of rage and hurt was left in the wake of his face splitting grin that had turned into a harsh line.

"I will ring her bloody neck!" He started to walk back and to, as though he didn't know where to begin.

"And him?" Jared asked over his shoulder, as if he wasn't taking his threats seriously.

"Fuck him in the eye my friend, fuck him in the eye!" He said before swigging back the remainder of his beer and then smashing it on the floor before storming away. Jared burst into raucous laughter, making me bounce up and down.

"That wasn't very nice." I said in a quiet voice, which quickly brought his laughter under control. He gave me a bad boy grin and then flicked me at the end of my nose.

"No, but it was damned entertaining… besides, my friend needs a push in the right direction every now and again."

"And if it gets someone dead?" I couldn't stop myself from pointing out the obvious.

"Concerned for my people… *Cathy?*" He laughed when a frown was my only response.

"Must be that pure soul of yours…" He pulled my body closer to his and lowered his head to whisper in my ear,

"So let me set your pretty little head and locked mind at ease…this is what will happen… he will storm into Smidge's quarters, thinking of catching the two in the act and make a fool out of himself in the process, when he demands to know who she is seeing. Smidge will find the whole thing hilarious and therefore have her revenge, thanking me in the aftermath."

"And if he sees this Conan guy along the way and gets his head ripped off?" I challenged.

"His name is Orthrus and although he does not see the appeal of having someone like Marcus as a friend, he would not kill him, hurt him yes, but not kill him."

"And you know this because he works for you?" I said feeling braver with my questions, but this was probably down to the soothing play of his fingers on my side, where his hand still rested.

"He works with me and no, I know this not because he is my council member, but because he is my brother…now, you are missing the show." He said shocking me with this bit of information. I instantly wondered that if Jared refused to help me, would his brother be able to?

I was shook out of my thoughts as Jared physically turned my head to face the show.

"You think too much." He hummed along my neck before laying a lingering kiss there. My whole body tensed in his hold after that kiss and only relaxed again when his lips left my neck.

"I thought… you… didn't like humans." I asked cautiously, hoping to remind him that by rights he should be finding me repulsive. His fingers crept up my torso and only stopped moving when they held the full length of my neck in one large hand. He placed his fingers at my pulse point and tapped twice.

"I don't, but you are something more."

"What do you mean? I…I am human." It didn't sound convincing, coming from my flustered whispers.

"I can feel you girl, and your words fool no one. I can scent it here…" He held my head out to the side and took another deep breath before continuing to prove the weakness in my denial.

"…I can taste it here…" He licked at my skin, making me shudder, then tapped once again on my pounding pulse.

"…I can feel it here… and…" His hold left my neck and pushed his flat palm down until it lay in-between my breasts, over my heart.

"…I can hear it in here." He then moved himself back to rest his arm over my lap, as he had proved his point.

"Now, watch the fucking show." My head shot back round to the stage, just to get away from the closeness he was creating by whispering into my neck. I found myself trying to calm the torrent of emotions that were crashing like waves into my battered senses. There was only one word that tamed the storm my mind was getting lost in.

Draven.

It worked. My heart ceased its pounding and I wiped my sweaty palms down my skirt. I knew Jared was taking in my every move, but I was thankful when he didn't comment. Instead, we both took his advice or more like demand, and watched the show. Although, if he thought that watching what was now happening on the stage would help me relax, then he was damn crazy!

The creepy fairground music started back up as demon clowns started to ride little bikes, which looked to be made from small animal bones, around the stage. I recognised the music to be 'It's a long way to Tipperary', only when it got halfway through, it changed from the high-pitched whistle into a rock version, when the band started to play. This happened simultaneously to when all the hellish clowns stopped and started to squirt water from their flowers, at the crowd. The screams that filled the room coming from the smoking front row quickly told me that it wasn't water at all, but… acid!

I had to turn away from the disgusting sight of skin melting into raw flesh and the only place I had to go was into Jared's chest. I felt his rumbling chuckle but felt somewhat comforted by the hand at the base of my skull that held me to him.

"Not to your sweet taste, my pet?" I ignored his question and held onto his jacket in a steely grip. His hand slid down to my back and he patted me gently before assuring me softly,

"They have gone now." I lifted my head and looked up into the palest silver eyes, which for the first time, had a beautiful softness to them. He winked at me and then nodded back to the stage. I mumbled a small,

"I hate clowns," as I turned back and I felt his laughter once again. The next act was coming out and I almost tried to find home in Jared's chest again, only he held me still before I could get there.

"Just wait, they won't scare you…see, they are not part of the act." He said pointing at the two macabre harlequin clowns, who were carrying out a small girl who looked like a living doll. Her head was bent over at an angle and they used her outstretched arms as a way to move her into position. They set her down gently and floated around her like ghosts, dancing upon the grave. Their muted faces were frozen in shocked expressions, thanks to the masks they wore.

One broke away from the feather like dance and made a silent request that the audience be silent. His gloved hands went to her back and started to turn a large key, like one you would find on a giant windup toy. It was situated just above her massive skirt that flared out and stood rigid as if she had something hidden under the fabric.

As soon as the winding was finished the girl's small limbs started to twitch as if coming alive. Then, the clowns ripped off their masks, to show the same faces underneath, only this time painted with their own blood that oozed from their sliced throats. Well, at least we knew now why they were silent, as the cuts were so deep they no longer could use their diced vocal chords.

Just as the girl was waking fully, they both made a quick dash off the stage. She spun around on one foot like a petite ballerina and when her face came up, I saw the cutest features; a head full of curls pinned back into two pigtails and large brown eyes shone under the oil lamps, dotted around the huge space. She looked like a living cartoon character. The girl started to dance around the room, to the sweet lullaby that was playing and the innocent sight was leading me into a false sense of security that I knew I should not be falling for. This was of course proven with her next few steps.

The spinning in the centre of the stage was getting impossibly fast and just at the right moment, she unsnapped the material from her skirt. A sea of red silk flared out and hid the gruesome part of this dancing doll for seconds, before it floated away like a cloud. Her lower body was covered in an oversized birdcage that she was stood in the middle of. It was filled with a least fifteen scruffy black birds that had all pecked away at the skin of her bare legs!

Once again, I was left feeling sick at the sight and it was only when I heard the hushed tones behind me that I knew I was struggling to get away from the horror.

"Calm yourself and watch what happens next." I shook my head over and over wishing he would just let me be, but when I felt his merciless grip on my chin, I knew he wouldn't let me go without watching it to the revolting end.

The girl was soon joined by the rest of the acts and a large muscular woman, dressed like the earlier strongmen from the first act, came to her aid. She knelt down and used her strength to bend the bars open, releasing a black swarm to come flying out. The birds moved as one like a fog clogging the air. However, they didn't get very far. Another one of the acts came out and the heavily pierced man removed the blades that were embedded under his skin and they whizzed through the air, all hitting a bird each. The power of each throw propelled the little black bodies backwards and they landed in the centre of a round bullseye that someone was wearing on their chest.

The crowd cheered and the girl kissed her hands, throwing her invisible kisses into the audience which obviously adored her and her act.

"See how her legs have already started to grow back the skin. She doesn't feel the pain like you would think." Jared told me and I had to say it did ease some of the tension that seeing such an act caused. After that, things got a little crazier, if that was even possible! The acts all performed as one, moving into the centre when the music hit a chorus. The fire eater first blew on the sides of the stage and let out a stream of orange creating a line of dancing girls made up of large flames. The next stream out of his mouth created a flaming ringmaster, complete with tailed jacket, top hat, stick and dickey bow.

Other acts came and went in a flourish of the unbelievable. Jugglers that used surgical tools instead of balls, gymnasts that used the bodies of their partners as swings and the most nauseating of all was the living Russian doll. A man came out that was at least seven feet tall. He first opened his jacket and then dug large nails into his own flesh to open his own chest cavity. He cracked back his rib cage, creaking like opening a rusty cabinet door.

"I'm going to be sick!" I shouted before scrambling to get up from his lap. Thankfully he let me and I flew into the direction of where the ladies' room was. I had to pass the stage and did the stupidest thing in this situation, I looked at its centre. There a smaller version of the man popped out of his chest and rolled to his feet with his blood covering his costume. Then he did exactly the same thing as his taller brother had by opening up his own chest to then let another smaller man come rolling out. That was when I ran faster and threw my whole body into the door. I threw up, thankfully making it to the bowl just in time.

By the time I had finished my stomach hurt, my throat felt like I had drunk acid and my mouth tasted of churned bile. As I made my way from the toilets, I saw two guards stationed either side of the door, dressed in black combat gear. They didn't speak and neither did I. Instead, I just followed them back to the amused Jared, who only lost his cocky smile when he saw how pale I must have looked. He rolled his eyes and mumbled something I didn't catch.

He motioned for the two guards to leave and walked over to me. He groaned out of what seemed like frustration, as he bent to pick me up.

"I can walk."

"You look close to passing out pet, so now is not the time to argue." He sat back down with me and placed me in-between his legs, this time facing forward. An arm came around my front and passed me a bottle of water, even going as far as opening the cap for me. I didn't speak. I just took what was offered and downed the water, taking away the taste that was left, thanks to my weak stomach.

His actions kept surprising me. I couldn't help but wonder what had happened in his mind to stop him viewing me as the enemy? When he had described how he could feel it, what exactly had he meant by that? In the silence of the room and the stillness behind me I knew I needed to take advantage of this moment and talk to Jared. I needed to get answers and in return give him some of my reasons. He needed to know that I had come here solely to seek him out. So with this cemented in my mind, I started to turn to face the only being that could help me get into Hell. But that turned out to be the exact moment that the time had come for my own little slice of Hell on earth.

"Time for the main event." Jared announced, making my stomach flip over. I turned my gaze back to the stage so slowly it was almost as if, in my subconscious, I was giving myself time to brace for the nightmare that was still to come. But no matter how long it took, it didn't change the outcome. Sigurd was now at centre stage, waiting for a fight that I had gotten him into. That thought weighed heavy on my mind… that was until Sigurd's next actions had my jaw dropping. For now Sigurd, my hooded knight and shadowed warrior, was stood there in all his glory.

All his bare glory that showed every inch of him, now no longer hidden, but more importantly and for the first time…

I could finally see his face.

CHAPTER TWENTY-NINE

BLACK BETTY

When the veil lifted in the form of Sigurd tossing his jacket aside, I couldn't take my eyes from him. It was like having a blindfold take your sight from you for days and then at once being ripped away having you blinking rapidly. Well, that is what I was doing right now, blinking as though the sight before me wasn't real. It wasn't from seeing the formidable display of muscle upon muscle that made up his tall body. It wasn't even that most of his colossal body was covered in thick black tattoos of snakes that circled his torso in diagonal lines. No, what had me blinking was all I didn't expect to see and that was the breath-taking beauty before me. His face was the very meaning of stunning masculinity.

Hair the colour of desert sand was a disarray of choppy waves that was longer on the top, lying in every direction as though hands had been roughly raking through it. High sculptured cheekbones came down into a square jaw that was speckled with tawny coloured stubble. A long straight nose gave him a vicious and predatory air as he turned his head up to the sound of his opponent coming into the ring. But the real beauty came from his incredible eyes.

They were like the light in burning amber and dark drizzled

honey mixing together in swirls. Only, one was unusually different than the other. Brighter one minute and then darker the next. Almost as if the iris was coming alive, swimming around and pulsating with anticipation for the battle to come.

At some point Sigurd must have been asked to get ready for the fight, because now he stood, cracking his neck to the side, wearing nothing but his leather trousers with every other inch of him on impressive display. I recognised the tattoos that consumed most of his body as the Ouroboros, which wasn't surprising considering he was the master of them. What was surprising was just how alive they appeared. They weren't just flat against his skin, but they had a real depth to them. The further up on his arm they went, the thicker and more intricate they became, each one looking as alive as the body they lived on.

"Now, this is a sight I have been looking forward to." I couldn't help it when I turned quickly and shot daggers at Jared. He was, after all, the very reason that this fight was taking place.

"Please, you don't have to do this! I will tell you anything you want to know but please…please, don't make him fight." I decided begging was going to be a much better way to go in helping my friend from the dangerous situation I had put him in.

"Now, that sweet pleading just answers one of my questions." He said laughing.

"What do you mean?"

"What I mean is simple…" He paused to hold onto my neck with one hand and turn my head with the other, until I was once again facing the stage.

"…if you really knew the Demon you keep as company, then you wouldn't at all fear this fight." He hummed in my ear.

"But what about the Demon he fights, should I underestimate him too?" I said in clipped tones, not being able to take my eyes from the stage even if I had wanted to, thanks to the hand that still held me positioned, ready for his 'entertainment'. I felt the deep chuckle at my back before I felt lips at my ear,

"Never underestimate your enemy, young one and furthermore…" This time both his hands came to rest on my shoulders and he tugged me back sharply in time for him to finish his frightening words,

"…never underestimate me!" The 'me' part was not only emphasised by the fingers that bit into my flesh, but also the dangerous growl that was all the warning I needed to trust in his threat. When he heard me swallow a plum sized lump in my throat he relaxed his punishing hold on me.

"Now, relax back and enjoy the show, I think you will find the outcome surprising." He said now back to his comforting tone that still held that undercurrent of dominating command and well, this combined with his arm that banded itself across my upper body to pull me back to him, I had little choice than to do as I was told. So, needless to say, I 'relaxed' into him.

"Oh good, I didn't miss this bastard's bloodshed." I heard Marcus say behind us and I turned my head as he flung himself back into his seat, legs thrown casually over the armrest. I sent him my fiercest scowl hoping in the next ten seconds I would develop the supernatural power of heated death rays from my eyes. Unfortunately, there was no such luck seeing as his lips didn't come melting off his evil clown face!

"Get your ass outta of my seat, pencil dick!" Smidge said coming to stop in front of him with her arms folded and her orange hair slightly glowing with her anger.

"Sit your big ass down Smidge and I'll prove just how wrong that statement is by drawing a moan from those succulent ripe lips of yours." He said making slow work of licking his lips after creating a few tiny sparks when sharpening his wicked looking nails against one another.

"Arrrhhh!" She shouted storming off to Jared's other side to take the empty seat there. Marcus laughed heartily when he heard her mumble,

"Frustrating fucker!"

"Now, now children, play nice." Jared commented dryly.

"Now where's the fun in that, J?" Marcus asked then shouting,

"Wench!" to get the attention of one of the waitresses, who rolled her eyes before handing him a bottle.

"Don't worry Jared, he couldn't find the right hole to put

that 'pencil' in, if the dipshit had DickNav!" At this I couldn't help the laugh that burst through my anxiety from the upcoming fight. Marcus slammed down his beer, sloshing foam over the neck and leaned forward towards me,

"Think that's funny, human or do you wanna see me test my statement on your skinny ass!?" This turned out to be the wrong thing to say as Jared had suddenly lost his patience. His arm tensed around me in a protective way and he let out a booming word that hurt my ears,

"ENOUGH!" At this the whole room stopped and lowered their heads at the sound of such rage and the air became thick with the pulsating energy of their master's wrath. I looked to Sigurd and saw him make a move in the ring that brought him closer to me. I knew he was about to do something stupid just to save me in this but because I knew something he didn't, I quickly shook my head at him. He thankfully ceased in his risky plans but you couldn't miss the proof he was less than happy at seeing me in the arms of Jared. The beautiful amber heat in his eyes started to get consumed with black smoke, leaving only one flaming ring that spun with his building anger.

I did the only thing I could think of and mouthed the words,

"I'm okay," which thankfully was enough to unclench his hammer-like fists.

"Now get on with your fucking job, Jester and leave this human to ME!" The beast snapped out at the end, making it clearer than ice who was in charge. His once friendly manner gone the instant my life seemed threatened. This was how I knew I had nothing to fear from the beast at my back. The only question now was…why?

"Of course, My Lord." And with these words from Marcus, it meant I regrettably didn't have long to ponder this as the jester took off back to the stage. He jumped gracefully over the wired sides that acted as crude boxing ring ropes, ones I knew, would soon be coursing with electricity, caging in the fighters with power created by mere mortal men. This irony wasn't lost on me considering it was the supernatural world that fought against each other, as us lowly humans couldn't do it for ourselves. Well, we certainly were good at lighting the way for their 'entertainment' weren't we? I thought on a huff.

"I will have your held tongues now my gits and bitches, for the real fun is about to begin." Marcus said as he took centre stage, arms open wide, like he was solely created to be there.

"For our first contender is not unknown, as you can all see the snakes that scar his skin. I give you the Master of the Ouroboros and with him his shadowed kin. For the power that he controls, it is a wonder we do not see him grin." This part got a few laughs from the crowd but surprisingly most seemed to just stare at Sigurd with nothing short of awe and admiration. But one thing was definitely coming through and that was the excitement for the upcoming fight.

"But now I invite you to view our next contender and give your heads a spin. The mountain that mounts the steps is none other than Deumus Drekavac, so please cause a thunderous din." At this the crowd went wild with shouting, fist pumping and feet stomping causing it to become a frightening background base for the snarling growls that were coming from the parted crowd. I looked up just in time to see an enormous form pushing back demons, sending rows sprawling to the floor before stepping up to the stage. He too jumped over the wires and his feet landed with a cracking thud that caused dust to rise in a small cloud around his bare feet.

"Oh shit!" I felt the words escape my lips and paid no attention to the response at my back. I couldn't. I was frozen in suspended horror at Sigurd's opponent. This guy made Sigurd look like a regular sized man and with him being 6'5" at least I thought this was an unbelievable feat. But it wasn't just his height, it was everything else, including the look that expressed only one emotion and that was clearly the intent to kill…no, not just the intent but more like the pure, raw…need. It was the rippling muscles that tensed, while waiting for the word 'go'. It was the saliva that dripped from behind the teeth that couldn't be contained in a closed mouth due to him panting like a rabid dog. But it was in his eyes, the eyes that wanted nothing more than to see the blood of his kill on his hands. Hell, he looked like he wanted to bathe in it!

This was when my heart started pounding.

"So, sit back and enjoy or cause a ruckus within. But whichever you do, place your bets, on the demon win!" At this, the same ladies fanned out amongst the crowd like before and started taking bets from the eager horde of demon spectators. This was obviously the cue for Sigurd to get ready and he did this by circling to stand directly opposite the one called Deumus Drekavac, whose drool was now coming down his chin in a long disgusting chain until it pooled on the dirt floor by his feet.

He stood at least three inches taller than Sigurd and instead of the massive broad shoulders and defined graceful ridges of muscle that tapered down into a slim waist, Sigurd's enemy was just an undefined mass of bulk. He was like an old crone beaten with the ugly stick in her youth, who had got it on with a bull sized swamp thing and here now stood their love child! But when I say ugly stick, I actually mean a Being so ugly that his parents could have mass produced their own ugly sticks, 'cause bloody Hell…this was one ugly ass dude, who was taking ugly asses to a whole new level!

His skin was wrinkled like he had spent a lifetime living in a stagnant pond which animals only used to take a shit in, not drink from! It was ghost grey and all his veins were shown through the thin layer of his translucent wet skin. If it wasn't for the size and obvious strength in the raging creature of Hell, then I would say he looked ill. His head was devoid of hair and that too was wrinkled. Most of which gravity pulled down on his forehead in flappy swags of loose grey skin.

His eyes were two piercing black dots in a mist of dirty white, that were set deep into his large head. Like Sigurd, his clothing only consisted of trousers, only his were made from some sort of animal hide. Most of his chest was bare, but I couldn't escape the sickening straps of leather that were sewn directly into his skin. Attached to these he had crude metal hoops and some thick chains that acted as some form of armour. This must have been covering a weak spot of his, as the skin underneath his ribcage was darker, with black veins spanning out as if poison had been injected there.

"Wh…who…is that?" I mumbled.

"That, my pale pet, is Deumus, the human soul gatherer of the Drekavac." His deep voice informed me and then paused to swallow heavily at his bottled beer.

"And who is the 'Dre…acvk?" I said knowing I hadn't said it right, but not really caring considering I already hated the guy.

"The Drek…avac is a race of demons that are said to be created by the souls of those not of sound mind…" He corrected, then leaned into me and his voice once again did that soft rumbling that left little bumps along my exposed neck, when he spoke the rest,

"…crazed, deranged, mentally unbalanced and certifiably psychotic." He pronounced each word with his lips at my ear and almost snapping out with his teeth, making me shrink further away. But with nowhere to go, I had no other choice than to sink myself closer into his hold. He seemed to like this, as I felt a growly purr behind me.

"He…he looks… insane." I forced myself to say.

"Oh I will confirm that, he most certainly is, but well, considering the level he has gained through his gluttony of consumption, then for the Drekavac, madness lies hand in hand with the power they take from others…this, for the most, is why they are immune to their demise… the stronger their opponent, the stronger they become… so as you can imagine, fighting them has its difficulties…drink." He finished by bringing his bottle round and holding it to my lips, lips he could see because his head rested above mine and was now cocked to the side, looking down at me. But hearing all I had about this dude made me snatch the bottle from his hand and down the whole thing! Jared laughed heartily behind me and when I came back up for air I passed the now empty bottle back and wiped the dripping beer from my lips using the back of my hand.

"We have to stop the fight!" I demanded and this was when Jared's amusement ended and his hold on me became less of the comforting variety and more of the restraining kind.

"Calm yourself моя бледная красота" ('my pale beauty' in Russian) His foreign words combined with his strength anchoring me to him, made me put a stop to my struggles.

Once I did this he took a deep breath and released it in a long sigh.

"I know you have no reason to trust in my words, for you do not know me, but trust in something else…I know about you and the future you may hold for me, so I would not harm you and although my explanation is vague, it will be understood soon. But first, I only ask for your faith in your friend."

"But…my friend, he…he is powerful and if what you said…"

"Power is indeed great, on both sides of that ring, but Hell's essence powering the muscle, flesh and bone of my world is nothing compared to the power of the mind, power which even a human can possess…" He raised his free hand, the one not still curled around my torso and shifted his long fingers through my hair, holding it all on one side back to speak his next words, words that finally comforted me,

"…and the insane are not often known for their intelligence." This was the first time one of their kind had actually said anything remotely positive about a human and I found myself surprised that it had come from someone who was known for his dislike of humans. I was starting to open myself up to the idea of understanding the beast at my back.

There was some deeper meaning in his words. Also the rough use of his voice that was heard like velvet pulled amongst the jagged rocks in an effort to comfort me. The unyielding strength of solid muscle that was a contradiction to the soft and gentle rubbing his thumbs were playing, creating circles on my ribs. But more than that was the trust he asked for and the trust I couldn't help but give, even when my friend faced unbelievable odds at his command.

These thoughts were dragged from me as the girls had collected all their bets and Marcus was securing them away in the black rock safe. This meant only one thing…

The fight was on.

Drums started to beat out something that sounded vaguely familiar, but all my attention was glued to the two that had started to circle each other, both getting ready for the first move. Then the guitar added to the beat just as the Drekavac made his first move. He ran straight for Sigurd, bent over slightly as if readying himself to tackle Sigurd to the ground. But my friend was definitely quicker by side stepping and then spinning from the oncoming truck that was not only ugly but looked crazed!

The motion propelled the demon into the electrical current coursing through the wire and gave him a wakeup call of all wakeup calls. Sigurd widened his stance and then, after looking amazingly bored for a few seconds, he gave the furious Drekavac a head nod, almost asking for him to come at him and try again. That's when my shock hit new limits as the band started to add lyrics to the song being played, just as Mr Ugly Ass ran at Sigurd and this time encountered his massive fist. I couldn't help but blurt out the obvious,

"Seriously…Black Betty!?"

"What, not a fan of Ram Jam?" Was Jared's only comment, referring to the song being played as a theme tune to match with the sleek moves Sigurd was planting on his fighting partner. After I didn't answer I received a whispered,

"Or would you have preferred Marcus' other choices?"

"Them being?" I whispered back,

"Kung Fu Fighting, Live And Let Die or Michael Jackson's Thriller?" I snorted and answered truthfully,

"Uhh…no."

"Black Betty it is and you will soon find out why when the shadows come out to play." He replied just as Sigurd dodged a hit and spun to get in two quick kidney jabs. The move caused the Drekavac to take a large step forward to right himself. There was nothing clean or precise about this fight. It wasn't like when I had seen Draven fight or even my other supernatural friends. No, this was no graceful dance, this was dirty raw, this was painfully gritty and this was downright disgustingly brutal.

Punch after punch got landed, on both sides and neither one even looked to be slowing down. Out of the two though, it was clear that Sigurd was the more skilful fighter. Like Jared had said, Sigurd used his brain more than the incensed Drekavac's uncoordinated moves that were based only on berserker strength, fuelled by frenzied rage. This wasn't to say that Sigurd didn't feel some of these hits and everyone he did I would flinch and press myself firmer into Jared, out of a pure reflex action.

One of these times was when I saw Sigurd was in for a punishing blow but I let out my held breath when I saw him grab his opponent's arm. He then spun and using the Drekavac's own weight against him, he threw the massive body flying once again into the electric fence. With these moves he reminded me of a wrestler. And seriously, I didn't know how many times one dude could get smoked and still walk steady after it. I mean, the guy's trousers even started to cook, making the room smell foul like burning hair and steaming animal skin.

The Drekavac flung his arms back and threw his head up to the rock ceiling above to let out a blood chilling roar. Then his head came down and he finally cottoned on that charging at his opponent wasn't getting him anywhere. So he changed his tactics, if you could even call them that. He began circling around the centre where Sigurd stood, and this made my friend look like he was losing his patience. This was proven when he lowered his forehead and growled,

"What are you waiting for pretty girl, an invitation?" The snarl he got back made him smile, one that made me shudder, it was that cold.

"Come get it then bitch, I got fucking things to do!" This was enough to get him to move. I knew what he was doing by provoking him. He wanted the Drekavac not to think. He wanted to keep him in that manic state to use to his advantage.

"Taunt the beast by pulling on its tail and as it snaps back, in doing so only reveals its jugular ready for the claws." Jared whispered in my ear. Then, before I could stop myself, I leant back and did some taunting myself,

"Tell me Jared, do you have a tail?" I was happy when this unwise comment got me raucous laughter at my back, instead of the neck breaking move it could have. His arms hugged me closer for a second, before replying with what sounded a lot like flirting,

"Do you wanna find out, little dove?" I laughed back and my smile widened further when I saw Sigurd's next move. Just as the Drekavac stupidly charged again, Sigurd held his own wrist and when his target's head came close enough, he slammed his elbow into the oncoming face. It made a sickening crunch, but Sigurd didn't give him any time to register the hit. No, because after quickly letting go of his wrist, he was powering the heel of his palm upwards. Fast as lightning and bone charring as the thunder, he forced the Drekavac's nose bone up and with nowhere else to go but penetrating through his brain. The howl of pain pierced through my ears like a dagger, straight down past my eardrum. The Drekavac was finally on his knees and I held my breath, thinking this had to be the killing blow…oh how wrong I was.

This…

Was just the beginning.

CHAPTER THIRTY

DARK UPGRADE

I was stupidly readying myself for the roar of applause at the sight of the Drekavac falling to his knees. I soon discovered though that I would be waiting a while for this, as in, it never came. The reasons for this became clear in the next few seconds when Sigurd started to walk backwards as if preparing himself.

"End of round one, pet." Jared informed me. I whipped my head round and looked to his startling silver eyes. As soon as they read my shock they turned soft and this was mirrored in the small smile he gave me.

"There are two rounds to fights like this and the first is to prove the strength of the vessel they command."

"And the second?" I asked, if only to confirm my fears. He simply nodded back to the stage and yep, it had already started to become very clear as to what the next round was.

The music changed to a faster and heavier song, giving the next round a more serious vibe. A booming base line reverberated around the room and started to build the frenzied crowd to fever pitch as their stamping feet fell in tune to the drums. I was quickly gathering that this was the round that people were really waiting to see and the music choice only added to this theory.

I felt the air change before I saw anything happen. It was

the same as when you knew the storm was coming. The thick wave of clouds bringing with them the proof of something so powerful, it could easily destroy us all. This was what it was like when I watched these two beings start to call forth that power.

It wasn't only my visual sense that took note, but all my senses; my hair standing up along my skin, readying itself for the mental chill, the smell of dust being unearthed by each pounding foot from the crowd, the tension I created in my own fingertips by fisting my skirt in a bruising grip. And it was completed by the coppery taste in my mouth from biting the inside of my cheek bloody. All were overriding any rational thoughts of trying to stay calm.

It started with the Drekavac.

He was still on his knees, only now he had brought one up along with his head. That's when the rumbling started through the floor. I jolted in Jared's arms only to have them squeeze me in a show of strength. The enormous Drekavac started to pound one fist on the ring's dirt floor, also in time with the drums and the rumbling got stronger, making me jump each time his hand connected to the ground.

Then I watched with my mouth open as what looked like charred tree roots burst from under him and started to latch onto his legs, firing out like giant sling shots. He shifted his torso around as if he was trying to break free. I didn't yet know if this was Sigurd's doing or just the start of his change. But whatever it was had clearly had enough of his attempts to break free. The chains that were attached to the straps sewn into his skin suddenly leapt towards the roots and effectively began restraining him to the floor, so the roots could take further hold.

This continued until hundreds of stiff and twisted black vines entwined themselves over the rest of him, until utterly consuming the bulky mass that was his body. By the end, he looked like a jagged burnt tree in the shape of a man. It was as if it created some sort of wooden armour before someone set him alight, until flesh became fused with cruel nature.

Of course, this now also made him resemble a human battering ram. I mean, the guy was huge before, but now he was just freakin' monstrous! The black roots had created a type of breastplate that flared up and out at the tops of his shoulders in spikes. His arms and legs were like solid trunks of black petrified wood that branched out at the feet and hands. But all this was nothing compared to the change made on his head.

Four separate roots had started by wrapping around his neck like some wrought iron noose with all ends coming together at the front. Then, like twisted rope soaked in crude oil, it came up the front of his face. It was about the thickness of my wrist, but smaller branches broke off the spiral and spread out, covering his entire face. This created thin slanted eyes as his only feature left showing and within their depths looked like burning hot coals. Once the branches reached the top of his head, all four pieces uncoiled and flared out into spiralled horns. Now he really looked like a battering ram, only this time of the animal variety!

"This isn't good." I whispered aloud my fears and gripped on to my necklace hidden under my clothes for comfort.

"He isn't a destined Lord for nothing pet…look." I felt the nod Sigurd's way and I tore my eyes from the living tree monster to see another monster in the making.

Once again, I was witness to the extensive tattoos on Sigurd's body as they all started to spin. Only, unlike last time in Afterlife's VIP, I was now seeing all of them that covered the vast space of muscled skin. The thicker snakes that slashed diagonally across his chest were the first to start moving and by the time the last one on his middle finger started joining in, the ones across his chest had picked up speed. The thickest of these looked like an Aztec design, where the one next to that was obviously of Asian ancestry, looking more like a dragon than a snake. Whatever their design though, they were all now very much alive and a part of him; creatures in their own right swimming against the current of flesh and bone.

Soon, they were all spinning in opposite directions so quickly they became a blur, one that melted into each other and left behind over half a black body. It was as if someone had grabbed his hand and just dipped him into a vat of black paint with only one shoulder, arm and his head remaining untouched. This didn't last for long.

The parts of him that had remained unblemished soon became sucked into the shadows that started to seep from his very pores and float around him like clouds of black ink in water. It was as though every beat of his heart was feeding the darkness that wanted to cover its master from head to toe.

The Drekavac snarled in a way that sounded as if claws were raking lines into tree bark and in response the shadows howled like the wind whistling, before slamming into your window in anger.

The now black covered Sigurd rolled his neck, as the shadows finally took the remainder of his body into its mist, including his face, so that the only constant feature that remained seen was a pair of blazing eyes. Even his desert sand coloured hair had become as black as the moonless night.

"That's a lot of power I can feel there, buddy." Sigurd said and even his voice had dropped into the fearsome demonic realm. The Drekavac didn't reply but just snarled some more. Sigurd circled closer and then tipped his head forward in a provoking manner.

"You fancy a lot more...? Then you come and get it, pretty girl!" Sigurd finished taunting the Drekavac, making him roar. Then the band started blasting their instruments into the height of the heavy rock song in perfect timing for the fight to begin. And boy, did it begin!

Every eye in the room looked on as the roaring Drekavac ripped his rooted limbs from the ground and charged at my shadowed knight. His four horns became his only weapon, ones pointing directly at Sigurd's chest and just before they hit their target his body disappeared, leaving a smoking shell of his shape behind. The Drekavac broke through the mist at the same time my chest released my held breath in a painful shudder.

"Looking for me, dipshit?" Sigurd said before connecting his blackened fist into the side of the Drekavac's head, after a jump in the air to gain momentum for the downward thrust. His knuckles burst through the splintering wood, causing charred shards to scatter to the floor. The Drekavac didn't take long to regain his balance after a clumsy step to the side and then he spun to grab hold of Sigurd in a bear hug. The problem with this was that one second his arms were closing in on a solid body and the next they were encasing fading black vapour.

I was starting to get a good sense as to where Sigurd's power lay, as it was indeed hard to hurt someone you couldn't first catch. Each reach and every lunge was met with nothing gained by the Drekavac, but the same could not be said for Sigurd. Whether it was his fist or his foot, each meant a direct hit that would once again take chunks from the wooden beast.

I was just letting my hope firmly ground itself deep within me, to a point it was re-forming more into a knowing defeat on the Drekavac's part. That was until I looked deeper. A depth that forced a hard reality to seep in and start acknowledging just what a Drekavac could really do and that was…bloody regenerate.

Every hit the Drekavac took, every piece now missing from its grotesque form, was just another that could be healed. More roots were silently called from the ground to slither up their brothers and find home amongst the new space made. This now begged the question from the opposing side, for even if you couldn't catch a shadow to hit, how could you kill when your shadowed hits meant nothing?

The Drekavac, who was now fully healed, had backed up for another charge and I once again tensed as if ready to take the impact for myself. Sigurd stood tall, waiting and looking impatient for something he was waiting to happen.

"You wanna dance now...? Then come on …come on… COME ON!" Sigurd bellowed out making four massive smoked serpents emerge from his back. The Drekavac's four horns twisted round to point more firmly readying himself for a killing blow. Then he let rip. He ran flat out towards Sigurd and I couldn't help but scream out when I saw Sigurd side step but not quickly enough. The horned head flicked out, catching my warrior which propelled him behind the Drekavac.

However, Sigurd's step didn't even falter and something unbelievable happened. Sigurd snapped his head back around and smiled at the beast.

"Now, it's really time to dance, bitch!" My mouth opened in shock and with Sigurd's next move, it stayed that way. He opened out his arms wide to his sides and his head went back, looking up to the ceiling. Then he said in the calmest voice one would not expect in this moment,

"Go play, boys." And at this soft command, the serpents behind him shot forward, striking their prey at a ferocious speed. Each of his pets opened their vapour jaws, just before they crushed down on each branched limb and then with the click of Sigurd's fingers they shot back, taking their pickings with them. The Drekavac travelled the distance across the ring, as if he had been blasted that way by a great cannon at his back. Just as it neared Sigurd, he then kicked out aiming his booted foot square in the Drekavac's chest.

Three sounds simultaneously echoed around every witness in the room. The howling of Sigurd's serpents in a conquering battle cry, the screaming agony of a Demon's defeat, and more importantly, the sounds of four wooden limbs being ripped away from the torso that held them all together. A torso that was also making its way flying backwards from the impact of Sigurd's kick…minus its legs and arms, of course. No, these were still in the possession of Sigurd's pets, pets that seem to be in no hurry to part with their new spoils of war.

Everyone in the room seemed to be frozen. I expected any moment to hear the wild shouts of obvious victory for my friend and held my breath waiting for them. But like before…

They never came.

And like before, they never came because I was the only one in the room who didn't know what was happening or what to expect from these two fighters.

"Why…why is no one clapping?" I whispered to the presence at my back and I felt his hold tense quickly before he answered me.

"Because it is yet to be finished." He whispered back and I felt a frustrated tear form. I didn't know how much more my heart could take of this!

"Klaar." ('Be Ready' in Dutch) Sigurd said turning his head slightly to the side as if talking to his pets. At this, the huge rows of teeth each retracted from the limbs they held tight and each thudded to the floor like forgotten logs. The torso, that had remained unmoving, started to suddenly vibrate. It danced around on the floor as though there was someone trapped inside, trying to break free. The horned head whipped back violently, snapping some of the bark around its neck. Then, the roots started to fuse with the ground and before a noise could be uttered, they fired forward like a poison travelling through the veins of the earth. They hit Sigurd suddenly and before he could react, it latched onto his foot like a shackle. His body went taut like some puppet master had just pulled his strings. It looked as though he was being electrocuted.

All four serpents' heads roared in anger, before they started to get sucked back into Sigurd's body. They each shrunk away to nothing and with them the black smoke that concealed most of his body. It was like a vacuum was sucking his powers back through his pores and straight down to his foot. The numerous tattoos of war paint started to melt from his skin and down to the twisted wood that kept him prisoner. It was literally drinking the demonic essence right out of him.

I tried to stand, but the arms from the man behind me held me down.

"NO!" I screamed again and fought to escape my captor.

"Calm down." Jared said firmly.

"No! LET ME GO! I need to help him!" I tried to fight my way free but nothing was getting me anywhere fast and time was not my friend. For it was only seconds before there was nothing more in front of me than a defeated man. His sandy hair fell forward as did his shaking frame. He landed on his knees as the last of his power left him.

"NO! SIGURD!" I screamed.

"Calm yourself, Chosen One!" Jared demanded and if I wasn't in the process of watching my friend fall at the hands of his enemy and quite possibly his death, then I would have cared more on hearing Jared call me the Chosen One.

The shaking of the torso started to jump and bounce around the small space it occupied. Then I screamed as the last of Sigurd's shadows were absorbed and it started to once again turn into a man's form. Arms and legs grew, only this time bigger, strong and harder than before. The creature rose from the floor onto his feet and cracked his new limbs around as though testing them out. It made a sickening noise, like popping knuckles only ten times the strength of the average sound.

Meanwhile, Sigurd was still on his knees and his pale skin looked stark without his stripes of ink. The new version of the Drekavac took a pounding step closer to my friend and a tear fell from my eyes with each punishing step.

"Please, my friend…please." I let out the plea on a whisper, but in that moment Sigurd's head snapped up and saw me, as if he had also heard me. Then, I couldn't believe it when I saw another cocky smile from him. Added to this was a cheeky wink, before he came to his feet. Thank God he wasn't through just yet and I needed to do the same and stay strong for him. So, I swallowed the frightened lump and nodded back to him, mouthing the words,

"Go get 'em." To this I received a small nod, as a gentleman would do, tipping their head to a lady-in-waiting, upon receiving a request.

"Idő áttörni, és gyere haza srácok." ('Time to break through and come on home lads' in Hungarian) Sigurd spoke in another language, words which became the trigger to a silent bomb. The monster, Drekavac, had no choice other than to stop his advance as the shadows started to leak from beneath the roots in bursts. It rose up in a thick fog and then started to form back into Sigurd's serpents.

The Drekavac suddenly started to claw at itself as though it was trying to tear away the roots himself. I leant forward and squinted my eyes to take in the truth. It wasn't the roots it was trying to free himself from, but the dozens of smoke serpents that were now writhing around his frame. Each one had a head and each head had rows and rows of lethal teeth and each deadly point was being embedded into the body they came from.

The movements reminded me of the flickering of an old movie being projected. The pulsating flutter as though something was growing inside him with not enough room to move about in.

"What's the matter Deumus Drekavac, don't you like my

essence…?" Sigurd asked and then, taking a step forward, bent slightly at the twisting form of his struggling opponent, he continued,

"…can't you just taste it? The darkness that comes from stealing someone's power, couldn't you just *DIE* drowning on it...? What's that…?" Sigurd put his hand to his ear in mock surprise.

"…You don't like it?" He said sarcastically, as the captured roar of pain behind a lipless face, thundered our ears.

"Ah, I see…they just don't *like you...!* Very well." He said stepping back and he turned to look directly at me.

"For you, my fated one." He said softly, before running both his hands back, pushing his hair from his face. The last remaining Ouroboros in his eye seeped from the light of amber and slithered in a black line down his cheek. It was the smallest one, so tiny it was barely seen, as it travelled the length of his neck, over his shoulder and right down his muscle clad arm. For once I felt it was Jared's body that was rigid at my back, as if readying himself for the end.

"Here it comes."

"Here what comes?" I asked in response to the tense comment made.

"The strongest Ouroboros of them all and one only mastered by its true Lord." He whispered back. Ok, so now this was the mother of all shocks!

"You mean that tiny little slithering thing?" I asked raising my voice and Jared's reaction was to quickly clamp a hand over my mouth.

"Be careful little girl, for we all know that the large may fall and the small may be mighty, nothing in our world is what it seems…even you." At this, I decided to let it go, considering he was more than just a little right, he was absolutely right!

By this time the little snake in question had made its way down to Sigurd's hand and rested on the inside of his upturned palm. There it spun like the others had and soon all it took was a mere flick of his wrist for the black mist to emerge. This time though, it didn't come in the form of a snake at all, but something far more terrifying. Four spiked tentacles circled out from within the centre, uncoiling like something from the dark depths of the ocean.

Meanwhile, the other Ouroboros were making it their mission to punish the body that attempted to command them and steal the power from their rightful master. They were biting into the body quicker than the parts could be regenerated. The huge breast plate rose and fell in an unhealthy rhythm, that screamed panic was definitely setting in for the Drekavac and the serpents shrieked out as if more than ready for his end.

Sigurd then took the last strong strides needed to reach the Drekavac which, amazingly, was still on his feet.

"It ends and with it your fucking soul-sucking buffet!" Sigurd shouted in anger and the tentacles took these last words as a sign to do what needed to be done. They lunged forward and each end grabbed hold of a horn on his head, entwining themselves so tightly you could hear the splintering of wood. Then one demonic roar released, that this time was a command by Sigurd, each tentacle pulled taut like metal rope.

Then came the pull.

It spun the Drekavac round and round, but with it tearing the four horns from one another. This caused the strongest roots to break apart and this unravelled down the beast's face, then down the length of his chest, leaving behind the first body of the Drekavac we all saw in the beginning. It all happened in seconds as one minute there was a black rooted creature pulsating with too much demonic power and now there was nothing but the sad form of a beaten Deumus Drekavac. Now, it was his turn to fall to his knees and all around him was the proof of his coming end. The broken roots lay around the floor like confetti made by a demonic wood chipper.

But there was one job left to be done and Sigurd took the last step to do precisely that. With one move, he had the Drekavac's head in his hands. One more move, a turn of his whole body into an action that not only placed one knee to the floor but broke the Drekavac's neck with a sickening crack. Then, a more violent twist severed his head from his body altogether and this time I didn't shelter my eyes from the horror.

I saw Sigurd take a deep breath from the end of the battle,

before he rose to then throw the severed head to one side like trash. He then stood over him, held his palm out to the remains and closed his eyes.

The tentacles were the first to retract back up his body and soon the power that had been stolen from him, if only for a short time, quickly started to find their way home. Dozens of serpents formed, coming from inside the dead shell of the Drekavac and they swam through the current of the air to re-join their master.

My eyes felt like they were going to pop right out of my head as I saw each serpent take back the form of inked skin right where it used to be. After the biggest Aztec one was back in place, the lifeless body started to disintegrate on the floor, after seconds of beating trembles that caused it to seem alive for one last moment. Then, something incredible happened. One last serpent, this one bigger than the rest, came out and shot through Sigurd's arm. I heard him cry out a deep guttural sound that gave you the feeling that whatever was happening to him, was hard for him to take.

His own skin started to quake and ripple, as something beneath the surface was breaking through, something that hadn't been there before. That's when a new tattoo started to emerge. Black ink seeped up, bubbling at first and then, when the area was covered in a new strip next to the Aztec Ouroboros, it started to calm. The rising ink sucked back into his pores and left behind a crude form of a snake eating its own tail, situated around his upper body on a slant just like the others. This one was a huge brush stroke that left lines in places as if there wasn't enough ink on the brush. Unlike the others, its head and body had no details other than an inkless dot for its eye and a single stroke for a tongue coming from its open mouth.

Sigurd's body shuddered as the last of his new tattoo took form, then he looked down at the eroding body and said,

"Thanks for the upgrade, asshole!" He turned from the sight and I couldn't stop the gasp as he then kicked the head into the crowd like a football.

Finally, this was when the crowd went bat shit crazy. They

erupted from their seats and drinks, food, money and some people got thrown up over their heads in excitement. Sigurd merely rolled his shoulders once, before nodding to a guy in the shadows. He snatched his jacket out of the air single-handedly, while not even looking at the guy and I never thought at that moment I had witnessed someone looking so friggin' cool!

"He won!" I stated and I heard the deep chuckle from my back.

"He didn't win." I frowned and whipped my head round to stare at him.

"Of course, he did…which fight were you watching?" I asked folding my arms across my chest in a huff.

"That wasn't a fight, pet." I pulled back and then shook my head a little, in confusion.

"What? Then what the Hell was it?" I snapped.

And this was when Jared delivered the final shock of my night so far…

"Simple…"

"…it was an execution."

CHAPTER THIRTY-ONE

CONVINCING CERBERUS

"What!?" I shouted out, thanks to the bombshell Jared just delivered. This time when I twisted, I found myself able to move off his lap, which was both a relief and strangely… not. However, this was something I didn't want to look too closely at, so I continued to stand.

"How much clearer can I make it for you? Deumus Drekavac has been my prisoner for a long time and considering there was only one being walking this plane who could destroy him, let's say he has been awaiting his execution for decades. So, if that man finally walks into my domain, then I am going to take advantage of that fact."

"And me?" This granted me a bad boy grin and a shrug of the shoulders before he said,

"A soft and welcome company for such a momentous occasion."

"Soft?" I don't know why I asked. I just did.

"I liked having you in my lap, love and you…" He leaned forward and whispered seductively,

"…are most definitely soft." I couldn't help it I blushed ten shades of red, transforming that bad boy grin into a full blown smirk. I looked away and noticed Sigurd talking with Marcus and taking a wad of bills from his hand. I looked back and asked,

"So, this wasn't just a fight and all that back there before, what was that?" I asked flinging my hand out, pointing to where Sigurd and I first stood when Jared approached us and was more than a little rude. Hell, he was downright badass scary!

"That, my pet, was simply insurance. I had to make my point to Snake Eye so that he would follow through with his end of the bargain." I frowned and emitted a little growl.

"So you used me?" I shouted, making him laugh.

"Calm yourself kitten, we all got what we wanted and did I hurt you? Did your valiant knight die saving your virtue from the Beast…? No! You live, he lives and you have been granted what you came here to do, which was seek me out…a win, win wouldn't you say?" I rolled my eyes because what could I say to that, he was right and considering our earlier circumstances, the outcome was what we wanted…or at least I hoped.

"Alright then, can you answer me something that I probably won't get from my friend?" His eyes got soft before nodding once.

"What was that in there?" I asked looking over my shoulder to where the 'execution' took place.

"You will have to elaborate on that question, love."

"What I mean is how did you know he would win…? I mean…I…thought…" I shook my head trying to find the right words, but thankfully Jared decided to help me out.

"You thought when his power was taken, that was his end?" Now it was my turn to simply nod.

"Oh sweetheart, you really don't know anything about your friend, do you." It wasn't a question, so therefore I didn't answer.

"Alright little dove, let me enlighten you whilst your friend is still busy. He is Master of the Ouroboros, this much you know?" Jared asked at the same time as raising his arm to flick a few fingers in order to get the attention of the waitress. A pretty brunette dwarf came over in a shy manner and handed Jared a beer, gaining herself a wink. She blushed scarlet and bit her lip.

Well, I was happy to see I wasn't the only one with this annoying habit!

"This much I know." I confirmed, watching him take a long pull from the bottle labelled 'London Pride'.

"What you don't know is that he is the only one of our kind with this ability."

"Why?" I asked.

"Because long ago the fates threw him a question and instead of death, he chose…"

"Life?" I butted in, just because, well I couldn't help myself sometimes.

"No pet, he chose revenge."

"But I don't understand…how…?" I started to ask but he started shaking his head.

"This is a man's own story and I am not that man, but what I will tell you is this…" He leant forward again to lean a forearm on his knee.

"…that friend of yours is powerful enough to become a King in his own right, but it is a right he refuses to take. I know not the reasons for this… perhaps they are similar to my own." He said this last part more to himself than to me and before I could let my mouth run off without its filter he continued,

"But I do know about the extreme power that is there and his for the taking. So, in cases like the show he just put on, that is all it was pet, a show. Never could he have been defeated, simply because no being alive could control the Ouroboros and for the Drekavac to try was its own death sentence." Realisation was starting to seep in. Jesus, my protector was not just your everyday supernatural Joe! He was mega badass and with a royal title for the taking, one he didn't want. I wondered why that was and more importantly, why had I never heard Draven speak about this guy?

"So when that…uh…Dre…Drekvk…uh…tree dude took his power, he couldn't control it so Sigurd took it back?" After Jared finished laughing at my bad attempt at saying the guy's name and coming up with my new nickname for him, he answered me.

"Yes love, that and more."

"More?"

"The power gained from defeating others of similar power emerges as Ouroboros on his skin and as you no doubt saw for yourself, he now has new ink added to his brothers." He was referring, of course, to the new strip of black across his chiselled torso.

"And the one in his eye? What about that one, 'cause I noticed it was the only one that didn't leave him when that…uh…"

"Tree Dude?" Jared finished, smirking once again.

"Yeah him, so why couldn't he suck that one from him?"

"Upon Hell's gates woman, you do ask a lot of questions!" He commented making me defend myself the only way I knew how in this situation. I folded my arms across my chest and made a piss poor show of defending myself!

"Alright pet, but for future reference, pouting at me like that only makes you cute and adorable not pissed off and challenging, like you're going for!" At this my frown deepened which only added laughter to his amusement.

"He can't ever lose that Ouroboros because it was his first and is fused to his very soul…or so I hear. This is the root of all his power and no one could ever take that away from him, hence why this wasn't a fight at all. He knew what would happen and he counted on it. He waited until the right time, like the skilled warrior he is and used his own power against him. Like I said, no other could have defeated Tree Dude but the Master of Ouroboros, which is why I used you." The way he finished and said 'You' was on a guttural level that shouted danger, but being me, I ignored it.

"And how did you know exactly that was going to work?"

"Because Snake Eye has never had a weakness before and it was clear to see an opportunity was being handed to me on a platter." He said mockingly, making my anger rise.

"A platter!?"

"A very pretty platter… now you've wiped all that shit off your face at least." Ok, so this comment started to bump that anger up a few notches to furious!

"Why you…you…!" Ok, so granted, it wasn't the best come back of all time.

"Watch it love, I like it when my pets have bite, but try and remember the reason you are here." Jared said smoothly leaning back, looking casual.

"And why is that?" I snapped losing my patience. I saw the quick flash of hot silver glow in his eyes as he took in my attitude and he leaned forward slowly. He rested one elbow on his knee and held his chin with his fist. This pose was nothing short of deadly and it made me take a step back. My action made him smile and only gleaming fangs could be seen.

"It's nice to see you do have some self-preservation after all." He said, his smile growing. Then his eyes shifted behind me and I felt the presence of Sigurd, before I needed Jared's reactions to confirm it. It was hard to describe but I guess the only way would be that it was like he was connected to my blood. I could literally feel it singing, having him near once again. He grabbed my shoulder gently and turned me to face him. I was met for the first time with a close up of his tattoos and I couldn't help what I did next. I raised one hand, without looking him in the eye and ran a single fingertip over his new mark. I felt his slight tremble as though he had not been touched by a woman in a long time.

"Lille øjesten." He said as his fist raised my chin to meet his gaze. Then he bowed his head and asked seriously,

"Are you well?" I bit my bottom lip and gave him a small nod to indicate my yes. He relaxed his bunched muscles, which could be seen easily, as he hadn't yet changed from the fight. He then cupped the apple of my cheek and pulled me to his chest as if this eased some of his tension further.

"How touching." Jared commented before finishing the rest of his London Pride in one swig. My cheek was still plastered to Sigurd's rumbling chest when he growled low at Jared's remark. Of course, Jared ignored this entirely by slamming his empty bottle down on the arm of his throne and stood.

"Right, let's get this shit over with! The time has come for you to explain yourselves, so you'd better follow me…there are those in my realm that you don't want overhearing what the

Chosen One has to say." Jared stated as though I had bloody gone up to him and introduced myself…my real self that is!

"You knew?" I shouted pulling away from Sigurd's chest.

"Cathy…really?" That was all it took to get a groan of frustration from Sigurd.

"What? How was I supposed to know he knew who I was…? I'm in disguise, remember?" I said back at my frowning protector.

"Catherine Keiran Williams, next time you come to see the King of Hell's beasts just introduce yourself as Keira and leave the Goth shit at home...it doesn't suit you." Mr royal Jared Cerberus himself said, as if talking to a child. So, I did the only thing one could do in this situation…I folded my arms, gave him the mother of all pouts and resisted the urge to stamp my foot in frustration.

"Point made, my Liege." I sneered, only little good it did as he just threw his head back and laughed heartily. I rolled my eyes behind Jared's back as he started to leave and went to take a step forward to follow, when a hand stopped me.

"I think from now on it will be wise of me not to let you from my side." Sigurd said bending his large frame to whisper in my ear.

"I'm still alive, aren't I?" I said turning my head to him. He looked me up and down in a slow assessment and one side of his lips crept up in a knowing smile.

"Very much so…" He started and then tilted my head back further to finish seductively in my ear,

"So much so, that you are no doubt taunting a beast with this very clear fact…one who usually plays with his food." Sigurd's warning came through loud and clear and to a point where I shuddered against his hold.

"Yep, I see that took hold." He added before snapping a,

"Let's go." And off we went. Or more accurately, off he went, and I just got dragged along for the ride. I turned my head and took one last look at the stage, glad to see it turning smaller behind me. However, after seeing a Gorgon Leech being led into the centre in chains and then being freed to gorge itself on as many chickens it could in 30 seconds was a sight I could have done without. Well, that just taught me when walking away from bad memories to leave them well alone!

The walkthrough to wherever Jared expected us to follow was a weird one and to use the word 'weird' in my life meant a shed load more than your everyday, average use of the word. Weird in my world actually meant "Oh shit", "Bloody Hell" and "Jesus H Christ" all rolled into one!

It started by walking through a simple stone tunnel that was only wide enough to fit two people side by side. This part, not so high on the weirdometer, but when we came to a house front door at the end, then things started to creep their way up that meter. It was black painted high gloss with a shining brass number 3 in the centre panel. Jared had waited for us to get closer before opening the door, which added to the weird vibe as he didn't use a doorknob. No, instead he simply traced his fingertip over the number three and we all heard the echoing of many locks sliding open. He then pushed on the door and we continued to follow him to destination unknown.

This was when things got 'spooky weird'. We walked into what seemed to be a dilapidated house, complete with at least 50 years of cobwebs and dust covering every surface. The simple hallway opened up to show a staircase on the right-hand side and other closed doors on the left. There was also a heavy wooden sideboard up against the staircase that held a very old typewriter, covered in a thick layer of dust. Strangely, there was only one key that wasn't hidden under all the grime and that was the number 3. There were also broken bits of crockery and a glass vase that held what looked like dried weeds hanging limply to one side.

"What is this place?" I whispered to Sigurd but when I looked sideways to him all I got was a warning shake of his head. I decided not to push it and opted for silence. I waited until Jared and his entourage preceded us up the stairs. I then received an encouraging nudge from behind telling me to take the steps to up and beyond, so I did as I was silently told. Even the bloody steps had seen better days, with its once rich red carpet runner worn down to the wood on each lip of the edge.

I followed the voices up as I had dawdled long enough to

have lost sight of them. I was at the top of the staircase when I screamed out as a hand shot from around the corner and latched onto me.

"Methinks someone could benefit from a vodka chased chill pill." Marcus said from behind Smidge, who had scared the crap out of me in an attempt at showing me the way.

"I'm fine." I said in a shaking voice, which made him laugh. Of course, thanks to Smidge's quick actions, I soon had to stifle my own laugh as she elbowed Marcus in the gut.

"Will you two cut it out and get them in here!" Jared bellowed from some other room, but it was loud enough to rattle the glass in some of the pictures that were lucky enough to still have it. I wondered how you even did that and doubted my human lungs had the power to produce the same depth to vibrate a whole room. Still, it was one Hell of a way to get someone's attention that was for sure.

"Bitch." Marcus sneered.

"Dickhead." Smidge counteracted with a smile on her face.

"After you, big butt." It was my turn to scowl up at Marcus for that comment, but Smidge just laughed louder this time saying,

"I know you love it, dumbass!"

I was surprised when she pulled me past and I heard his response,

"I'd fucking worship it, if you'd let me." He said under his breath.

Smidge pulled me down the hall and around a corner at the end where we came up to a pair of double doors that were open. Then we stepped inside and weird left the building, being swiftly replaced by oh my God!

The room was an open plan study/sitting area that was so richly furnished I had to blink a few times just to take it all in. I looked to my left as I walked in and saw a large square sunk into the floor with three steps down. The area was big enough to sit at least twenty people comfortably, if the massive plum and gold coloured cushions were to go by. In the centre of this was a coffee table of the likes I had never seen. It was once the base of an enormous tree that had been sliced so close to the ground, it flared out before its roots had disappeared under the earth. It was a highly polished piece of wood that gleamed under the hanging gold lantern that was the size of a birdcage.

Further on from that, I could just see a black felted snooker table with coloured crystal balls scattered from a game left unfinished. The whole room was dark wood panelling up to waist height with thick cream wallpaper that had an elegant light gold swirl, most of which was covered by expensive looking oil paintings.

However, the whole room was dominated by a massive black lacquered desk that could have doubled up as a bed. It looked to have been made from one single piece of wood that had an elaborate war carving all along the front panel and this too gleamed under the many spotlights that were a part of the fancy moulded ceiling.

"Sit!" The order rang through the open space like a damning bell screaming high treason. I didn't know why it was, but the way Jared treated me now that Sigurd was back was far different than the comforting, playful guy at my back when watching the ring.

"Well, you wanted this meeting and your friend went to great lengths to get it for you, as you saw… I think it is time for confessions, Keira." It was the second time he had called me Keira and the shivers it shot through me didn't lessen. I looked back at Sigurd and he nodded, making Jared growl.

"I am allowing him in on this meeting to appease your tension, do not push it, pet." I took his warning as possessive, because every word was dripping in it.

"Alright, you want the reason I needed to speak to you, here goes…I need to get into Hell." At this, all conversation stopped. Marcus had been talking to, who I assumed was another member of Jared's council and Smidge had been speaking to someone on the phone. Now all eyes were on me and the phone was no longer by Smidge's ear. I guess I just dropped a show stopper with that one!

"Come again, little dove?" Jared asked as though I had been speaking Klingon.

"I want you to show me a way into Hell." I stated, this time slower and hopefully less thick on the Northern twang. He had been leaning forward to hear my answer and now he got the repeated, longer version he let out a sigh and deflated back.

"I see."

"You do?" I asked hopefully.

"I do, it is clear to me now that you are unfortunately deranged and in need of the medical profession.... Snake Eye, what were you thinking, taking on such a damaged bird?" At this I shot out of my chair facing his and took an offended step back.

"I am not deranged!" Jared simply snorted a huff and I felt Sigurd walk up behind me and place a calming hand on my shoulder.

"The girl speaks the truth and as hard as it is to be believed, she is right of mind." This must have been the wrong thing to say as Jared let his meaty fist come crashing down on his desk, one thankfully enough to be solidly made to withstand a beating.

"Enough! Marcus, show out our guests, they have suddenly outstayed their welcome!" He snapped looking, for the first time, disgusted with me.

"No wait! You can't! We need your help!" I shouted out quickly as Marcus was cutting the distance between us.

"Come on Keira, I told you it couldn't be done." Sigurd said as he started to try to lead me away.

"It can be done! If it can't, then why did the Oracle send me here? Why did she send me to him?" I said looking up at my friend but pointing at Jared. Marcus came to us and was just about to take my other arm to aid in leading me away, when Jared's hand flew up in a halting motion.

"Wait!" All three of us turned to Jared's stony face.

"The Oracle sent you?"

"Yes, she did." I said, firmly crossing my now released arms across my chest.

"You swear by this?" Jeez what did this guy want, a pinkie promise?

"Yes..." I leaned forward and finished with a definite,

"...I do." Jared relaxed back in his huge wing-backed chair and steepled his fingers.

"Alright Keira, I will play…for now. Sit back down and explain things to me." I did as I was told, mentally thanking my lucky stars to have this second chance.

"Ok, so you know who I am…right?"

"I do." I nodded and swallowed, ready for the hard part.

"And if you know who I am, then you know what I was to Dom… Dominic Draven?" God, even saying his name out loud was hard. A muscle in his jaw twitched but he only nodded back, obviously not saying what he really wanted to say.

"So you know where he is?" Now this question got me a frown.

"I do not." Now this shocked me. I would have thought every big player would have heard where Draven was.

"Keira." I heard Sigurd warn me from behind but it was already too late, the words were forming and bursting free before I could stop them and think about that warning.

"He's in Hell!" At this, Jared shot a hard look over my shoulder at Sigurd and I turned just in time to catch a brief head shake back. Now what was all that about?

"And the Oracle told you this?" I nodded and said,

"She told me that I would only find Draven once I had been to Hell, so I know he is there." Jared's eyebrows slashed together over his eyes in a deep frown. It was as if he didn't believe what I was saying and this was confirmed when he asked,

"But you don't *know* that he is there?"

"I do."

"But how…?" I interrupted him and spoke about something I hadn't yet told anyone, not even the Oracle.

"I know he is because I saw him getting dragged back there with my own eyes." At this I heard the inhaled breath of shock from a few people, including Sigurd at my back.

"Explain!" Jared commanded.

"He came to me in my room, not long after I found out he had died… he said…he said I needed to watch, to see him being taken back so that I understood. I think he meant to give me a clue, to let me know where he was, as it wasn't light I saw taking him, but…black hands dragging him back, burning him…then I saw…" I choked back a sob as I brought one of the most painful memories back to life.

"What Keira…what did you see?" Jared asked, softly this time and I looked up at molten silver through a watery haze of unshed tears. I looked down and let them slide free, hitting the desk I didn't even realise I was holding onto, in dainty droplets. When I heard him prompt me by saying my name on a whisper, my head rose slowly and I said the words that pained me,

"Fire..." Then I fell forward and Jared lunged over the desk to catch as I whispered on my last breath, before darkness over-took me…

"My Draven in the Flames."

CHAPTER THIRTY-TWO

BLACK SAND

I woke up and blinked away my blurry vision, only to focus on a pair of light green eyes. I frowned and blinked harder. It couldn't be… it just couldn't…could it? I kept my eyes open for longer this time and took in the rest of him; smooth shaved head, at least a few weeks' worth of stubble on a strong jaw, flat nose and a full pair of lips that were pulled together, looking worried.

"Did I break down again?" I asked in a groggy voice and was met with the soft rumbling of a laugh.

"No Red, you didn't break down again but shit sugar, you had me worried for a minute. How's your head darlin'?" I tried to sit up and felt hands come to my aid.

"Eddie?" I asked and felt a palm cup my cheek as I came upright.

"Yeah babe, that's me, your ET…hey, you ok…? I mean, it was only a little bang on the table when you tripped but honey, you are looking a bit pale…how're you feeling?" I squeezed my eyes closed and tried to shake some sense into my head.

"Wh…what's happening?"

"Well, Libs and the gang will be here in about ten minutes to help set up in the back and I lit the grill like you told me, but next time I think you should wait until people are around before attempting decorating on your own, babe." Eddie the mechanic said with light humour, whilst feeling for a bump in my hairline.

"I'm confused." I confessed making him laugh.

"That's what birthdays do to ya, babe."

"Birthday?" I asked as I started to take in my surroundings.

"Jeez, you really did a number to that pretty noggin I love so much. Yeah babe, your birthday…remember, bbq, streamers. Hell, I know you already peeked at your cake I ordered for you…just like every damn year…like you spend every bloody day in December trying to find your presents…if it wasn't so damned adorable then I would try and rein you in, but with Libby coming, what's the point." He said after moving away and whilst trying to pin up a banner I had obviously been doing before I fell.

Ok, so now I had fallen into some warped parallel dimension, where I lived here with Eddie the mechanic. I looked around and saw I was sat on a worn and obviously second-hand couch that was no doubt kept because it was one of the comfiest seats ever. The room was bright and decorated with dozens of my artwork, some I recognised and others yet to be painted by my hand. Pictures of family and friends covered the shelves amongst books, but the most featured in the frames were of me and Eddie. Ones by a lake laughing at the camera, another with a cabin in the background and Eddie situated behind my back, arms wrapped lovingly around me and then there was the biggest one. This one was on a large canvas hung over the fireplace and my mouth literally dropped open at the sight of us both stood under a flowered altar on our wedding day, in black and white.

Then I did a slow look down and caught sight of two things at once. One was a plain gold band and the other was a small but elegant diamond engagement ring situated next to it. One thought penetrated…

Holy shit!

My mind started going a million spins a minute, trying to piece together what this all meant? I must be dreaming, but God, it felt so real! I knew one thing for sure and that was I hoped insanity was grounds for divorce. I didn't know why but looking at Eddie as he started pinning balloons up either side of the banner he'd just hung for my birthday, I felt guilty even thinking the word divorce and I didn't even know the guy!

"Edison Tucker." I said his full name in a kind of trance, trying it out, as if saying it would break the spell.

"Oh shit, here we go." He turned around giving me a sheepish look and then said,

"But of course, I know by now that this is the best part about Christmas… even though I will remind you, I had to store your presents last year at the garage with my damn tools and even then you found them! Seriously, what is it with you, do the Williams sisters have inbuilt present radar?" He was laughing after his placating start to explaining and I gathered quickly that by me saying his full name was code for he was in trouble. I also noticed he knew my real last name. Well, I mean, this wasn't surprising considering I did marry the guy. Wait, what was I saying?!

I didn't marry him!

"You sure you're ok babe, only you're real quiet?" I brought my attention back to Eddie and saw he was now kneeling next to me and running his fingers through my hair, which I will mention was back to being long and blonde again.

"I'm not usually?" I asked stupidly, to which he burst out laughing again.

"Uh…that would be a no, babe."

"Ah." Was all I could think to say.

"That being the reason I am always asking you, do all English girls look as cute as you do when they never shut up?" I frowned and smacked him on the arm saying,

"Hey!"

"And there's my girl, welcome back honey." He gave me a beaming smile and kissed me on the cheek before standing.

"Oh well, peacetime over, we are now officially being invaded. Here comes Libby and crew…get the door babe, I'm hiding on the deck until Ella finds me…think I am gonna be a wolf this time." He said to himself as he walked out through a set of patio doors. Meanwhile, I stood dumbstruck in the capital city of twilight zone, only coming out of my numb state by the pounding on the door.

"Come on Kaz, I've got my hot potato salad balancing on my arm!" My sister's voice shouted through the door.

"Oh shit, tell me she didn't cook?!" Eddie said from around the side of the patio. I found myself speaking before I realised this crazy new universe I lived in had sucked me in.

"God, I hope not." I heard Eddie laughing again as I opened the door to a heavily pregnant Libby in a maternity summer dress. Then, whizzing past her legs in a red blur of curls, a five-year-old I assumed was Ella flew through the house shouting,

"Ready or not, I will find you, bear!" Making Libby shout,

"Ella!" And she skidded to a halt, turned and said,

"Oh yeah, Happy Birthday Aunty Kazzy cakes." I turned a stunned head to Libby and blurted,

"That's your little girl?" She sighed and said,

"I know what you mean, so much of Frank's side in her… the other day she asked me for her next birthday party if she could have a baseball theme, I nearly wept!" I snorted a laugh out.

"Can I go find Uncle Eddie now?"

"Go, be wild, run with nature and all that jazz… just be sure you come back a little girl who still likes hugging her momma!" Libby said in a funny accent and laughing, making Ella giggle. She smacked a kiss on her hand and threw it our way. Libby and I both caught it, as we used to do the same thing when we are kids. It came to me on sheer instinct and I wondered why I hadn't yet broken down into a fit of hysteria.

"Oh, by the way, he's not a bear anymore, he's a wolf." I told Ella before she went off running in search of my twilight zone husband.

"Cool! I love wolves, they're my favourite!" She shouted excitedly and was soon out of sight. About five seconds later I heard a big over exaggerated roar, a fit of girly giggles and knew she had found her wolf. Then something weird happened…well even weirder than this at any rate. Deep in the back of my mind I heard a real roar, only this one was so far from fake, it wasn't anything but terrifying and not in the least bit playful. My startled gaze shot to Libby, but she was in the kitchen grabbing some fizzy drink from the fridge and didn't look at all freaked out like me. Well, I mean why not, after all it was obvious she wasn't the one living in a different world and hearing monster's cries of anger in her head.

Nope just me!

"Hey, there's the birthday girl! Mrs Tucker herself, where do you want the beers and half the grocery store Libby bought…? 'Cause she is pregnant and does in fact need to eat everything in sight and going with her to the store is my new living nightmare." Frank said unloading some bags to his other hand after passing me the beers.

"I heard that!" Libby shouted and Frank winked and whispered on a smirk,

"Sure you did…sorry dear!" He walked into the kitchen and I was just wondering whether I should give Frank the real low down on living your nightmares, when I noticed something. I was just about to close the door, as this other reality was anchoring me to the scary mundane, when I saw a person standing on the other side of the street. I opened the door further and took an extra few steps out of the door to get a better look.

Could it be? No, this…he…could it? I dropped the beers and my unconscious steps led me all the way to the bottom of the driveway. From here, I didn't have to question it anymore, as I knew where my other life had taken me and the man standing there staring at me was proof of my real destiny.

"Draven?" I said his name and felt a gust of wind blow around my body in answer. I didn't even realise it until now that I too was wearing a summer dress, until instinct told me to hold down the skirt. But to be brutally honest, I couldn't give two worlds about pulling a Marilyn Monroe right at this minute because there, in the light of day, was my only living dream...

My only life's choice.

My only life's destiny.

My only.

"Is it really you?" I whispered and I just knew at that

moment the wind took with it my question and travelled to the other side.

"Keira."

"Keira!" My name came from two very different men, two totally different lives and was heard by two loving but very different Keira's. Which one did I want to be? Which life did I want to live? Which man did I love more? The easiest answer lit up my soul so bright it could have shadowed the sun's rays!

I turned to Eddie and with a single tear rolling down my cheek, I bit my lip to keep in the sob and mouthed the words,

"I'm sorry ET."

I let more tears go when I saw the pain twist bitterly in his face and turned away from what represented that life, to look towards the one I wanted like my next breath.

Then I ran for it.

I crossed the road and made it to the other side, the side of supernatural beings and prophecies. The side of Heaven and Hell at war, of flirty Vampire Kings that hold little Northern blondes to ransom, of Angels that kiss me goodbye like I'm an elixir of life and with funny Imps and beautiful Demons named Sophia, that call me sister. Sides of the Viking protectors, Biker shadow Knights and cute little chocolate skinned Oracles that wear tutus. But even all this lay in the background to the man in front of me now…

The only side there was for me.

The Draven side.

And so I ran and didn't stop until I threw myself into the arms of the only man in the world.

"Draven." I let out on a breathy whisper as his arms circled me. He held me close and pulled me up until my feet were off the ground so he could bury his face in my neck.

"Home," he said into my hair and I couldn't hold it back any longer. I burst into happy tears so strong he had to hold my trembling body. I heard him keep saying the same word over and over on my skin,

"Home… Home… Home."

"Yes." I whispered back and then moved my head back because I wanted to look at…no, I needed to look at him!

"You didn't wait for me…why Keira…why?" He said and the last word came out so anguished, it felt like being struck.

"I'm here Draven, I waited…I swear!" I looked into his eyes and when they looked over my head, I saw he was referring to the life on the other side. His dark eyes erupted into purple flames and then he turned his furious gaze down on me.

"Draven…I…"

"You carried on…I died and you carried on…you don't belong in my world and because of that I can't keep you." Hearing this now turned that simple strike into a killing blow!

"Draven, NO! Don't say these things! You have to know, I waited…Oh God I waited so long, I never gave up…I will never give up, do you hear me?!" I grabbed his face with both my hands and made him look at me.

"You don't believe me?!" I asked on a caught breath that didn't want to come out. Tears were now streaming down my face and felt like they would never stop.

"Draven, please!"

"No Keira, I understand now…I understand why this had to happen but I needed to see it for myself first, before I could let you go." I cried out as my pain doubled. My sobs were only allowing me a few words to come through.

"No…N…No! Don't…don't sa…say that!"

"It is the truth and what must be done, I'm sorry my Keira…my love, there is no other way, I see that now." He said sadly as though breaking and I knew he meant his words as seriously as he saw his duty to his people and I knew this because he let me go. He released me from his hold and it looked as painful as it felt.

"NO!" I panicked and wiped away my tears and snotty nose. I knew this was my last chance and I couldn't make him see by crying. He started to turn away from me and I grabbed him by the jacket he wore.

"Draven, no! Now listen to me! I have not done this to you, that life…" I motioned back behind me at the house I wanted no part of.

"…that is not what I chose! I am somewhere else right now and I am doing everything, and I mean every…*damn*…thing to find you! I won't stop…Jesus Christ, I won't ever stop…do you hear me! I will find you and when I do, I am NEVER letting you go! Do you hear me!?" I shouted as even more tears fell around me, but his face didn't change. He looked away from me and I stammered out,

"Dra…Draven…look at me."

"I'm sorry Keira, I truly am, but it was never meant to be." And then he tried to walk away, but I held on.

"Draven…Draven Please! I…love you." But no matter how I begged or how the declaration of love was bleeding from my heart, his eyes remained determined. He gave me one last look, touched a fingertip to my cheek and then turned away from me for the last time. I watch in utter slow agony as the material of his jacket slipped through my grasp. I was left to watch as his back became smaller and smaller the further away the road took him and when nothing was left, I crumpled to my knees on a tortured cry, that sounded as though it was ripped from my very soul!

I was so torn apart, that I barely even registered when the world around me started to blow away like everything was made from black sand…

Draven's black sand.

"Keira…Keira!" I heard my name being called and my hope soared. I lifted my head to see the last of the road disappearing but no Draven in sight. I was just looking back down when a hand came out of nowhere.

"Come with me Keira, I'll keep you safe." I looked up and saw Jared staring down at me, waiting for my hand.

"Can you hear me?!" I heard shouting in the distance, but where from I couldn't tell as that distance could no longer be seen.

"Who is that?" I asked in a croaky voice, just as the sun came from behind the clouds, turning Jared into a looming shadow stood above me.

"He can't help you Keira, only I can help you now."

"What do you mean...? I still…I can still get Draven back?" The shadow bent on one knee and said,

"Well now, that depends on what you are willing to give me in return?"

"What do you want from me?" I asked thinking there wasn't anything I wasn't willing to give.

"You may think that now Keira, but would you really give another life for his?" I jolted back surprised.

"How did you…?"

"Hear your thoughts? In this place I can do many things."

"And what is this place?" I asked looking up and taking in the nothing blank canvas that was my new world. He got closer to me and swept my loose hair back from my shoulder in a soothing gesture.

"This place is your projection, Keira. A place you feel safe enough to deal with your life's choices."

"I don't understand."

"We're in your mind, Keira." He whispered and just as my eyes widened, my body felt weightless. It was as though I was quickly sucked back into the now and I bolted upwards trying to catch onto something to slow my speeding flight backwards.

"Thank fuck for that! Keira…Keira can you hear me…? Answer me by the Gods be damned!"

"Shadow Knight?" I mumbled blinking quickly, trying once again to clear the blur. I was suddenly pulled into a tight embrace and I heard Sigurd's deep chuckle by my ear.

"Yes, lille øjesten, I am here." He sounded like a man who had just been put through the rough end of being helpless. I held onto him and kept taking deep breaths to try and hold back the tears that were desperate to break free. It was that 'crying for your mum syndrome'; you are utterly fine coping until,

A. You see your mum or

B. Someone asks if you're alright.

Both times bravery and pride go take a parachute jump out the window. That was what being safely in Sigurd's arms was like right now. All that had happened and not just with the dream, it was all trying to unload onto his shoulders to share the weight. Thankfully though, the other company in the room brought me under control before I could fall to pieces.

"Just a little bit longer." Sigurd whispered into the top of my hair as though he had heard every one of my thoughts. I nodded because I didn't have it in me to deny the truth of the matter. He let me go and held my face with both hands spanning the length of my head before letting me go completely. He lowered his head and caught my eyes, to which I nodded silently, communicating that I was ok. He nodded back and then released me.

"What happened?" I asked the room but it was Jared who answered me.

"I will explain but first…everyone out!" I saw Sigurd tense and the muscle ticking by his jaw told me he was grinding his teeth.

"That was not our agreement, Cerberus." He ground out.

"Things evolve, Snake Eye." He replied coolly and I wondered what I had missed when falling down the rabbit hole.

"Not today they don't." Sigurd said crossing his arms over his chest and I noticed he was now back to wearing his usual gear of black, black and dark grey. Even the hood was back but this time at least he didn't try and hide his face from me.

"You want me to help the girl, then we play by my rules. Now, I won't ask again." He stood strong, carrying out his order with just one look at the room, which was enough to get people moving.

"I will not leave her!" Sigurd however, was clearly not getting the hint, so I felt it necessary to intervene.

"Are you going to help me?"

"Keira." I ignored Sigurd's warning and waited for Jared to answer me.

"If it is in my power and our terms are met."

"And will you swear not to hurt me?" At this he didn't hesitate,

"I give you my vow that no harm will come to you while under my care, and as you know Snake Eye, a vow of mine is not given lightly." I bit my lip and looked towards Sigurd who was outright giving Jared the death glare. Therefore, I got up from the sofa I had been placed in and walked up to my protector. I put my hand on his forearm and waited for him to look down at me.

"Let me do this."

"No." He snapped, going back to glare at Jared. I gave his arm a squeeze to draw back his attention and said,

"I need to do this Sigurd, so I will ask you again, as a friend…please let me do this and I promise you…I promise that if he breaks his vow then I will…"

"…Then I will break him!" He interrupted me on a snarl at Jared. This prompted a laugh and Sigurd showed his fangs on a growl.

"Sigurd, please." My word, it really was my day for begging!

"Fine!" He snapped and turned from me, clearly anything but fine with this new arrangement. He stopped by the door the others had left through and said without looking at me,

"I will be close." And then he left, slamming the door until the frame shook.

"Okay…so now what?" I asked trying to break the tension. Jared gave me a coy smile and then motioned with an outstretched arm to the sunken seating area.

"Now we simply talk."

"Talk?" I repeated in question as I walked down the three steps to the unusual seating arrangement.

"I believe you are acquainted with the term." He teased and I relaxed at seeing the earlier Jared come back. His mood when we were alone was so different it was hard to keep up with him.

"Ha, ha, yes as a Northerner I am known to practise the art." I said making him smile and also thinking painfully back to Eddie's comment that was of a similar nature.

"Sooo…what are we going to be talking about?" I asked extending the 'so' for comical value, which again made him smile. Although, thanks to his answer, my own smile was swiftly swept away and was left gaping wide open in confusion. So I asked a dumb sounding,

"Come again?"

"You want a way into Hell, then that's what I will need." I shook my head as though this was just his idea of a cruel joke.

"Umm…could you just say what it is you'll be needing, as I

don't think I heard correctly last time?" This got me another smile before he confirmed the sick feeling I had in the pit of my stomach was in fact warranted,

"A human heart..."

Yep, that's what I heard.

CHAPTER THIRTY-THREE

AFFAIRS OF THE HEART

"Ok, so you know you're gonna have to explain that to me because I am telling you now, I am not killing some poor bugger for a beast's appetiser!" I said getting back up, making him do the same.

"Keira, sit back down and listen." He held out his hand and led me to sit beside him.

"I'm listening." I informed him in a haughty tone.

"I am not going to ask you to commit murder, I doubt you have it in you for starters....that is unless you have before unknowingly driven another to commit suicide due to your endless questioning?" My reaction to his tease was to elbow him in the side, which is what I did before I even thought about who I was really doing it too! He let out a muffled laugh that was both shocked and amused (the last one I sent a thank you up to God for!)

"Can you really blame me, human remember?" I received a shrug of the shoulders and a sly grin, but no words.

"Right, so I think this would be a good time to explain about the heart thing." I said bracing myself.

"Before we get to the fun stuff, let's first get our agreement concreted, shall we?" As I was sat next to him I decided to get cosy, so I turned to my side to face Jared and pulled one bent leg up to rest on the couch.

"Alright, what do you want from me, Jared Cerberus?" He mimicked my position turning to me, but instead he rested a bent leg on the other and bent his elbow at the back of the cushions.

"What I want isn't something physical, but what I need is nothing more than I gave to you."

"A headache then?" I couldn't help running my smart mouth, but I was happy to see he had the patience for it. I did get an eye roll though so I nudged him saying,

"Sorry, I promise to behave."

"Now I know that's not true." He winked at me and I joined him in the eye rolling.

"Ok, so you need…"

"A vow, Keira." This had me frowning before I asked in a wary tone,

"What type of vow are we talking about here?"

"A simple one really…I merely need you to vow that, when the time comes, you will back me in an endeavour that others will not."

"That's a bit vague, Jared." I commented wryly.

"Besides, I don't know what having me backing you would accomplish for your…um…cause." I added making him smirk before saying,

"Oh trust me, when the time comes your help will be paramount to my success, of this I have no doubt."

"Will anyone get hurt?" This was the most important question I had to ask before giving him anything. I would absolutely not hurt anyone to get what I wanted, no matter how much Draven meant to me!

"Not through your acceptance no, as for the rest… well, I am no Oracle but I will give you this…" He got slightly closer and said softly,

"The person it will mostly concern would never be hurt at my hands…*never* Keira." He said the word 'never' with such sincerity that I would have been a fool not to trust his words. I had no idea what future he spoke of but I knew that the world I was living in was all about chance and this was one of life's games that I wanted desperately to win. So, I made my decision in about five seconds from when he last spoke. I held out my hand for him to shake and said,

"I'm in! I, Catherine Keiran Williams, vow to back you when the time comes that you need it." He gave me a knowing smile, placed his hand in mine and in turn gave me his own vow,

"And in return, I, Jared Cerberus, King of all immortal Hellhounds and guardian of the Underworld gates from the River Styx, do vow to help you any way I can to get you through those very gates." He nodded his head to me respectfully and I found myself doing the same. Then we sealed the deal and shook on it.

"Right, well, considering we are on the subject of helping me bust in the joint, let's talk tactics. How exactly are we gonna get me in...? 'Cause you know I am not fond of the committing an horrendous crime and then topping myself plan." I added this last part for good measure, although now thinking back, I probably should have made that clear before my vow. I mean, his way of helping might be to just point me in the right direction to some Hell worthy deed and then hand me the knife to finish myself off with! Would he at least draw me a map for when I get there…or maybe there was Hell's version of a Holiday Rep to point me to the right bus.

"Now, I bet that's a scary place to be." He said laughing.

"What… where?" I asked shaking myself from my runaway thoughts.

"Inside that head of yours, if you could just see your adorable and very expressive face right now, you would know what I mean." I shot him a 'not impressed' look that got me a deeper laugh. Well, glad I could entertain his big Royal Ass! I thought on a scowl.

"As fun as this is to witness, I think it's time I put your overactive imagination to rest. When I said Keira, that I needed a human heart to get you in, I wasn't joking or being metaphorical."

"But…" He lifted a hand to silence me and said,

"I think it's time you heard my story, pet." Now this was something to shut me up! I was practically gagging to hear this story that I unconsciously brought my other leg up to cross them on the couch. He smiled at my action and relaxed back.

"Now, where to begin?" He dragged a hand down half his face and caught his shapely beard between his thumb and fingers pulling it down in what I gathered was a thinking habit.

"It was 1763 when I was brought into your world and I think you know by now what I was doing before this." I nodded, too scared to say a word that would prolong my wait in hearing his story.

"My rebirth was instigated by a man call Sir Francis Dashwood. This fool was the founder of the Hellfire Club and held his ridiculous cult meetings in the Hellfire Caves of West Wycombe." It became very clear with the venom he injected into his words, that he did not like the man he spoke of or this club, so to take his mind off his anger momentarily I said,

"West Wycombe…that's not far from here."

"You're right, but forgive me, where are my manners?" He said getting up as if needing some sort of distraction.

"Drink?"

"Please." Considering the story I had coming to me, I thought a drink was a bloody good idea! He walked over to one of the wooden panels and pressed against it. The whole panel then slid down into the floor and a stainless steel bar emerged behind it.

"Cool." I said in such a geeky way, even I winced after saying it. I think if I could have gotten away with slapping my hand to my forehead and saying 'Durr' I would have done, just to make myself feel better. However, he turned his head to me and gave me a knowing grin that said he was clearly entertained by my goofy behaviour.

He then shifted his immense shoulders and shrugged out of his worn leather jacket that was fitted biker style. I bit my lip at the sight of his bulging biceps under the long sleeves of his black t-shirt. He threw his jacket over the back of a dainty embroidered chair and the contrast was almost funny. He pulled his sleeves up his forearms and I got sight of some kickass tribal tattoos on one arm. The other wrist was covered in leather bands with what looked like crude hammered metal attached. I watched him turn his back to me and thought everything about him screamed badass! It wasn't just his black leather waistcoat that sat snugly to every sleek line of his muscular back, his worn biker boots half tied up his ankle or his heavy silver rings of flames and claws. It also wasn't his ripped jeans or tied back hair. It was just him. The way he moved like he owned everything in his world and didn't give a shit what the rest of that world thought, as long as they played by his rules.

He confirmed this when he didn't ask me what I wanted but I was thankful to see him grab a chilled bottle of white wine. He also brought a bottle of red under his arm and two black stemmed glasses. After putting the two glasses down he lifted both bottles to me and I nodded to the white. We were both silent as he poured the drinks. He handed me mine and then settled back with his red. He swirled it round as if trying to pluck the rest of his story from his memory bank and I couldn't help but think that this action looked totally out of character. I mean, here I was describing another big scary biker dude (In a completely different way to Sigurd) and he was drinking the wine like a connoisseur!

"So, where was I?"

"You were about to tell me about the Hellfire Club, Sir Francis Dashwood, how they brought you here, The caves, the need for a human heart and how you plan on getting me into Hell without…" I made a slitting my throat action and he threw his head back to release a throaty roar of laughter, then said,

"I think we'll have to order take out, as something tells me this is gonna take a while." I had to agree and also suddenly had the biggest craving for some crispy noodles with seafood.

Now, all I had to do was hope they delivered to a King Hell Beast's Devil's Ring!

I didn't think after hearing and seeing all that I had in one single night I would have been able to sleep, but damn, I must have been out like someone with narcolepsy! I knew this because after Jared had finished his story he excused himself to speak with Sigurd and the next thing I felt was being lifted into a pair of arms. I remember looking up into a hidden face and knew Sigurd was back to taking care of me. I couldn't help the deep sense of safety I felt being held close and therefore gripped onto his T-shirt tight, snuggled closer and rested a cheek on his chest before passing out again.

I woke when the light of day started to penetrate my hotel room. I rubbed the sleep from my eyes and stopped mid yawn when I noticed the dark figure of a man asleep in a chair. Sigurd had stayed in my room with me and I felt a lump form in my throat. Just the sight of him with his arms folded, hood pulled over his eyes and his legs outstretched in a lounged position, I felt my chest compress. I knew why he had done this and the answer was in the look of relief he gave me when I awoke from my nightmare in Jared's office. There were other rooms in the suite but instead, he spent the night in a chair close to my bed because he was worried about me!

This made me feel like crying. Here I was, on this ridiculous quest to save the man I loved and the family I thought loved me, which I built around that man, were nowhere to be seen. No, only one man stood by my side now and I knew already without him, I would have been kidnapped, possibly even dead twice. I didn't care that I was some mission for him. That I was some contract given to him by whom I had no clue. All these things meant nothing to me because looking at that man sleeping in the chair by my bedside, so that I wouldn't have a bad dream, was not only doing this for honour and duty. He really cared. And that, right there, was why I got up, grabbed the comforter on the end of the bed and lay it over him. I then leant down, kissed his cheek and whispered,

"Thank you, my Shadow Knight." And then I left to shower in one of the other bathrooms so as not to wake him.

Once in the shower I thought back to Jared's incredible story. My love for history wasn't lost on him considering I bombarded him with questions. What surprised me was how patient he was with me but what surprised me the most was how brutally painful his story was and how deeply it touched me.

In 1763, the human, Jared Weller, was a blacksmith in West

Wycombe. He was a quiet but hard working man and lived alone. He made it sound as if he was a recluse and didn't like being around people much. The reasons for this he didn't explain, but I could tell there was something more to this due to his tensed jaw, hard eyes and the flash of pain I saw in their depths. However, I didn't think it wise to push this as we were far from bosom buddy status.

Anyway back in 1763 rumours of Sir Francis Dashwood's after dark exploits weren't completely unheard of, but not exactly widespread knowledge either. Therefore, when Jared Weller was approached about a job by Dashwood's steward, Paul Whitehead, he simply agreed. Of course, he had no idea of the real reason he was picked for the 'job' and that was because he was the best candidate for what the Hellfire Club had in mind. This was for two reasons. The first being that he was a known recluse and therefore nothing was much done for a man who went missing, who had no family connections or even friends to care. But it was the second that was the most interesting and also… frightening.

It was discovered upon looking for the right person for their 'job' that the meaning of the name Jared is "he who descended" in Hebrew history. This, to them, meant no one else even came close to aiding them in their attempt to not only enter the Underworld but to steal a piece of it. As for this, they needed a human sacrifice and poor blacksmith Jared was to be the one.

Of course, the story didn't end with Jared's life. No, something they didn't count on was that Jared was the only living host who was both strong enough and royally connected, to contain a rather important being. Although, admittedly he had no clue to his supernatural bloodline at the time and this was the reason he simply didn't just die when they cut out his heart. See, not only did Jared mean "he who descended" but it also meant something much more.

In the Book of Enoch it is explained that Jared also meant "he who shall rule" because of his family connections that, unsurprisingly, were not of this world. This made him the perfect host in which to merge with the Hellbeast that the club mistakenly released in their moronic attempt to gain entry to

Hell. Just to mention at this point, I was not including myself in this stupidity as I actually had good, solid, valid reasons for my quest, not because I was some jumped up, spoilt rich man who didn't know what else to do with his money and wanted to impress his friends!

No guessing that I didn't exactly like the sound of this Dashwood guy after Jared's story and I didn't try to hide the fact. This I could tell when Jared's molten eyes turned soft, that he liked my bitch rant that erupted upon hearing what was done to him. Anyway, as the story continued I found I was glad these actions at least brought about the end to the stupid club!

This didn't surprise me as, until this point, it was just about a load of rich guys playing dress up and convincing themselves they had dark powers by worshipping Hades (who Jared told me was known better as the Devil or Lucifer). What they didn't know was that the Devil couldn't have given two donkey shits about what these guys thought (Jared's actual words) but he was then not too pleased when they stole his Alpha guard dog Cerberus. This part was a complete accident, as they didn't realise fully that the man Paul Whitehead chose, was the only one who would automatically absorb Cerberus, acting as his host. Therefore Jared and Cerberus merged into man and Beast combined.

I couldn't help but ask the question, why he couldn't just go home? The answer came as this,

"Once bound to a host, you need one of royal blood to send you back and considering I was royal blood, there was no going back." This made some sense until he started to explain about why he needed a heart to get me back in through 'his' gate.

After Jared Cerberus had been reborn, his first job was to close the gate and in the same way it had been opened, he needed a heart to bind to it to keep it locked. It didn't take him a second before he knew exactly which heart to choose...one belonging to Paul Whitehead. I had gasped a bit at the thought of him ripping the steward's heart out, which made him laugh before explaining further.

"I didn't kill him Keira, although when I first woke, I will admit it was an appealing thought." I released the breath I had been holding and he smiled. Then he explained how he bound Whitehead's heart (whilst it was still beating) and the Hellfire Club was no more. I think after royally fucking up their first ritual they had learnt their lesson (Again Jared's words, not mine).

But that still wasn't the end of it. It was decided, or more like demanded on Jared's part, that when Paul Whitehead died, which he did in 1774, that his heart then belonged to Jared. It was then placed in an urn at the Mausoleum that was situated on top of the hill where the caves were chiselled a quarter of a mile into. For reasons Jared didn't explain, all parties involved thought it best to keep the heart close to the caves and this worked well enough for years until in 1829, the heart was stolen by an Australian sailor.

This, believed by Jared, was down to a man named Admiral Sir James Stirling who was captain of the HMS Success at the time. He was in London at the end of 1828 with the Foreign Office trying to gain support for a settlement in the vicinity of the Swan River, Australia. He then departed right after receiving the heart from one of his lackeys on the 6 February 1829.

I naturally asked the question why…as in, a lot! But this was something he admitted he didn't have all the answers to. He did know, however, that all people involved were under the influence of his kind. The worst news came after this story was finished and that was that even to this day he still didn't know where the heart of Paul Whitehead remained. This was going to be a big problem for me, considering I needed that bloody heart!

He explained, after another rant of mine that consisted mostly of my lack of luck in life, that without the heart there was no way he could open the gate. This sucked the big one, which brought me back to now and why I was washing my hair like a woman possessed.

So there you have it, why man and beast became one and how the first werewolf was born…or kind of anyway, as I still wasn't sure what beast Jared turned into! I did know, however, I was totally screwed! We made a deal that he would help me, but what the ruggedly handsome bastard missed out when we were taking our vows, was that he couldn't actually help me, not unless I was the one who magically found the heart.

Which was when I came to the conclusion, after I had finished punishing my abused scalp, that it was in fact exactly what I had to do. I just hoped that a trip to Australia wasn't on the cards, as it was a Hell of a long way to go and not really what I had in mind when planning my trip down under… although I'm sure it could be hot as Hell all the same!

I got out of the shower, dried, dressed and was rubbing a towel in my hair when I walked into the suite's sitting room. Sigurd was now up and looked like he too had showered. I was surprised to see him without his jacket and his sandy hair now wet and slightly darker waves curling back from his hands. He looked so beautiful with the sun from the window lighting up his perfect features. Those high cheekbones, those ochre coloured eyes that matched the tawny stubble that dusted his jaw. I saw the darker ring of his Ouroboros pulse when his gaze turned to me. He gave me a head jerk and said,

"You alright, øjesten?" I gave him a small smile and walked to him. I don't know why but I gave his hair a little ruffle and said,

"I am, but you must be ready to consume a whole cow by now, it's at least noon." I joked making him release one of those, 'I'm not really angry but still a badass' growl at me that I laughed at.

"Don't worry big guy, I'll call room service." I looked back and smirked when I saw he was trying not to smile but when the edge of his lip curled up, both of us knew he was on a losing battle. I flopped down on the yellow couch and picked up the hotel menu. Then my eyes went sideways to note he was still watching me and I decided I wasn't satisfied with just a hidden smile, so I said,

"So, should I just order you a steak in every cut they do, or do you just eat it raw from the bone…? You look like a bloody steak kinda guy." The look I got made me laugh out loud and then I was fully satisfied when I saw him crack and start laughing along with me. And just like that, all the tension from the previous night was lost and added to the frightening past vault in my head. Worryingly it was getting quite full in there and I was only 23…oops no, now 24!

"Gimme that, you cocky little shit." He said, trying to go for stern only failing, this by the crinkles around his eyes giving away his enjoyment my banter brought him.

"Hey! Enough of the little shit, big guy or I can easily find you a new nickname, one less flattering to your physique." I said after throwing the menu at him on the 'Hey' part of that.

I ordered room service and while we were waiting I explained all that Jared had told me to Sigurd. I felt bad doing this but knew I had no choice than to share because I was seriously at a loss on what to do next. Sigurd didn't look at all surprised at my story and I put this down to being his age, he must have heard something about the King of the Hellbeasts. I mean, for a big player in his world like Sigurd I doubted when someone like Alpha Cerberus goes missing, it is simply swept under the Demonic carpet.

I sat back waiting for some genius idea but when the silence grew to lip biting proportions I snapped.

"So? What do we do now?" His head snapped up and he said,

"Fucked if I know!" I took that as a resounding he didn't know.

I deflated back to the sofa just as room service knocked. I got up to get it saying sarcastically,

"No, no, please don't get up…I'll get it." He laughed at my grumbling and I groaned angrily when he said,

"Then get to it, little woman." Ok, so I gave him that one, it was a good come back and if his laughter was anything to go by then he knew it also. I opened the door wide for the guy to wheel in the trolley that as predicted, was filled mostly with meat. I then looked around the room trying to locate my bag.

"Umm, just one sec." I said to the guy, trying to find my bag that would lead to my purse, which would then lead to this guy getting a tip. I looked to Sigurd and mouthed 'bag?' who nodded to a single chair by the window and there it was. I looked back to the fidgeting bellhop, who looked uncomfortable with my strange antics. I soon knew why when it was obvious he couldn't see Sigurd and saw me mouthing words to inanimate objects. Oh well, bigger tip it is.

I scrambled in my bag for a second, when I felt the Ouroboros book and that's when it hit me and also when I had to triple the tip, for I shouted out,

"Son of a bitch!"

CHAPTER THIRTY-FOUR

ASKING THE OBVIOUS

After I had sufficiently freaked out the poor room service guy and it had cost me a few notes, I turned back to Sigurd and jumped up and down with the book clutched to my chest. Needless to say, this was after the door closed. I didn't know if I was surprised or not that Sigurd was more interested in the food trolley than the sight of his book. Either way it was obvious the steaks were a good choice. I sighed and joined him when my stomach started to complain about its neglect.

"What's with all these rules anyway?" I said after swallowing a milk chocolate, Earl Grey and raspberry macaroon, yes that's right, I said Earl Grey in a macaroon! Gotta love some afternoon tea action in London!

Sigurd raised his head to see me cross-legged at the coffee table having just devoured most of the goodies on the three tier cake stand. I had the open Ouroboros book next to me and the looks I kept receiving from Sigurd, told me he was worried I would get clotted cream or posh egg salad on his precious pages. I had to grin every time.

"Well, considering you are the first to be blood bonded to me and the first human's blood tasted by its pages, then I have no clue, as I have not yet read them." I gave him my deepest frown and then skidded the book across the floor to where he sat.

"There you go buddy boy, knock yourself out!" I said with attitude and stuffed down the remainder of a scone piled high with a cream and jam tower.

"I think I prefer big guy, if you don't mind." I almost choked on a swallow when he added a wink. Of course, he knew he had won around when the only come back was a lame,

"Whatever."

"Ok, so it's obvious that given the first rule, the only way to break this bond is to kill me, which I would prefer was a last resort...if you don't mind." I gave him a mocking smile as my answer.

"And the other?"

"To kill you."

"Ah!" I said nodding a frightening understanding in a comical way. Because let's face it, anything other than humour right now and I would end up a sticky mess on this expensive floor in a pool of my own misery.

"So blood buddy, does this mean you will be joining us for Christmas dinner this year or what?" Again my coping mechanism came through in the form of sarcasm.

"I am thinking no." I couldn't help but laugh.

"Jeez, mum is gonna be so disappointed not to have my very own blood brother over for the festivities this year." A little corner of a smile emerged, and he said,

"I'll send a card" This made me laugh out loud.

"So, the rest is basically saying that it isn't a great idea for another to read the book or try and destroy the book. I also wouldn't advise using it to start a book club, considering anything that kills its readers isn't ever gonna make the bestseller list."

"Ain't that the truth?" I agreed.

"And the last rule?" I asked referring to the cryptic words of 'Communication of the bound cannot converse in a parallel time but speaking what needs to be said will find a time unparalleled'. This time Sigurd ran both hands through his hair and scratched the back of his head before answering.

"I am only assuming that this means that the Oracle has found a way to communicate through the book to you…and I take it from that spark in your eyes, that this has happened before.

"Yeah, right after she gave me the book a message appeared…well I say message in the loosest sense of the word considering it was like a cracking a Dan Brown novel!"

"A what?" He asked me with clear confusion written all over his face.

"Seriously?" I asked and he shrugged his shoulders before I muttered,

"Forget about it. Ok, so this is what we do know…We need a heart from a dead asshole that was stolen and could quite possibly be in bum fuggle nowhere of some Australian outback being eaten by coyotes as we speak, although, eww for them right?" He held up a hand and said,

"Ok…what now?"

"What, I didn't leave that part out of Jared's story did I?"

"What the fuck is 'bum fuggle nowhere' Keira?" I couldn't help it, I burst out laughing again.

"I don't like saying the F word unless it's completely warranted, so that's what fuggle means…look can we get back to my rant?" You could tell he was really trying to hold in his laughter and I was even impressed when he restrained himself and just motioned me to continue, with a hand gesture.

"Ok, so even if when we ask the book where it is and we catch a break when it gives the answer clear as day, then what…? I mean I still have to get Jared to fulfil his side of the bargain, break into the Hellfire Caves and then somehow break out my boyfriend…I don't know about you, but this seems like a lot of breaking of things."

"Yeah like a shit load of rules, that's what. Shouldn't kids at your age be getting drunk off your ass at parties and shit?" I gave him a disgusted and insulted look and said,

"Really…kids my age?"

"My mistake oh old and wise one, please remind me, exactly how many wars have you lived through again?" He asked crossing his arms over his chest and waited for my answer.

"Alright smart ass, let's just get on with the problem at hand should we." His look said it all…

He had won another bloody round!

The rest of the day continued with me and Sigurd bickering like we were actually related. It was as if the more time we spent together the stronger the bond became. We would start finishing each other's sentences and pretty soon all it would take was a single look and we knew what the other was thinking. But it was strange and not at all in a brotherly way, as there was no ignoring the unique pull that was heating up between us. For example, at one point in the day I got up to sit next to him, just because something in me needed the closeness. It was only after he started playing with my fingers that rested near his own, that I realised he needed that connection just as I did.

The other weird factor in all this was that it didn't seem to be a solely sexual urge, which helped in controlling myself around him. It was almost like our bodies' cells were communicating to each other and needed the contact to increase the intensity. This was the one thing we both avoided mentioning and I was glad. More than glad in fact, as I think my skin would have bubbled from my cheeks if this conversation ever arose. I mean here I was looking for death defying ways to spring my soul mate from a slammer in Hell and I was acting like a damn cat needing to be stroked!

Shameful, Keira Williams!

Thankfully 5:36 rolled around quickly enough and I sat staring at the clock on both my phone and the grandfather clock which displayed the same time right down to the last minute. Well, you could never be too careful and Sigurd obviously found this highly amusing as he didn't refrain from taking the piss out of me whenever he could. The last time he got shushed, as I only had one minute to go.

Then it came. I looked down at the closed book and took a deep breath to ask the only question that mattered right now.

"Mighty book of the Ouroboros…" I started all official sounding before Sigurd interrupted me,

"Jesus Keira, let's just get on with this shit…Book tell us

where the damn heart is!?" My mouth dropped on a gasp as disbelief set in.

"You did not just do that!" I said turning slowly as anger filtered through my bloodstream, taking root of my actions and when he shrugged his shoulders and said,

"What?" I let rip. I launched myself at him…literally. I saw his eyes widen quickly just before I landed on him and extracted an 'oomph' sound before I slapped at his arms over and over again.

"What the Hell?" He shouted but his questioning was being drowned out by my rage.

"WHY!? Why did you do that? You idiot!" He quickly grabbed my attacking arms and restrained me, pinning my upper body to his chest.

"Calm down!"

"Sod your calm down! Why? That was our one shot today and you ruined it! You…you…" I accused looking him straight in his eyes, one burning with a snake ring that started to move at the sight of my anger.

"Keira…"

"You just don't care! How could you do this to me?!" I was so lost in my devastation that I was missing what he was trying to tell me. He growled loudly and then gave my pinned arms a shake.

"Keira, look!"

"I just can't believe it, why you…!"

"Christ øjesten, just look for fuck sake!" My scowl turned into a drop dead plasma death stare before I turned my head to look at the failure of knowledge that I was certain I would find in a closed book. Of course, I didn't expect to see the book open and filled with new crimson words staining the pages. I also didn't handle his reaction to my 'overreaction' in the best possible way either. I turned my head back to see all the amber in his eyes being replaced by a dark storm and a glowing snake. Man, even his snake looked pissed with me!

So I did the only thing I could think of doing to defuse the situation. I gave him a nervous smile and mumbled a sheepish,

"Uh…my bad?" His eyes flashed darker and his lips

remained in a straight line of disproval. So, I tried a different approach, this one named bullshit. I leaned forward, gave him a kiss on the cheek and patted his back saying,

"Just kidding big guy, I knew you wouldn't let me down… good job partner." I tried to extract myself from his lap after he let loose another deep and throaty growl. However, when his fingertips bit into my arms before shifting down to hold my spread thighs in place, I decided the only course of action was to let him have his moment and bit my lip. Oh and I added a little whispered sorry in there for good measure. Luckily, this one clinched it for me as the darkness left his eyes and his hands became less demanding and more soothing.

"Do not let distrust taint the bond we have again, Keira… do you understand?" He demanded and I could only give him a small nod in return, now feeling a bit ashamed. He held me a little bit longer and his assessing gaze must have found my shame, for he then rested his forehead to mine.

"My silly blood mate." He said in a soft voice that only held a hint of the scolding I deserved.

"I'm sorry." I whispered again and he nodded once before letting me go.

"I know you are øjesten. Now go and get the answers you seek before you drive me insane." I gave him a little sideways smile and jumped from his lap to do just that. When I saw the words of hope I had so desperately needed right now, I had to close my eyes briefly in a silent prayer of thanks. That was until of course I opened them again and actually read those words!

Nine keystones sit at the Entrance
As guardians to the river Palace,
At a time after housing Royals
To become an Admirals place for Malice.

"Oh, you have got to be shittin' me!" Sigurd groaned, slapped his palms to his knees and then sat up to lean forward at the sound of my outburst.

"Christ, what now?" He asked when I let my head fall forward on the coffee table where I was sat with my legs folded under. I banged my forehead against the open book in hopes that a good smack to the brain might help in decoding this cryptic nonsense.

"Maybe you're right, maybe I should just be getting stupid drunk with all the other kids, 'cause I am telling you right now, this party is no fun!"

"Well, before we break out the cheap cider or beer that tastes of piss, let's take a look, shall we?" He leant across and whipped the book from under my head like a magician with a tablecloth, making my forehead slap the top.

"Uh…oww!" Not surprising, I didn't get much of a reaction to my rough treatment. However, this was soon forgotten when I thought I heard angels singing in the form of Sigurd saying,

"I know where this is."

"You do?" I shouted and jumped to my feet to plant myself in the seat next to him.

"I do. There is only one building that had nine keystones which referred to the principle rivers in England at its entrance. One that was built to be a palace to then be used by the Navy Board."

"And that is?" I asked gripping onto his forearm in anticipation.

"Somerset House." He replied to my question in a way that he must have been sure of my knowing it. It was confirmed that I didn't quickly after when I frowned and repeated,

"And that is?" This was when he released a trademark groan of frustration, something I was quickly getting used to considering I seemed to spend most of my time around Sigurd, annoying the crap out of him.

"Never mind, I will explain on the way."

"You mean we're going now?" I asked not even trying to mask my excitement.

"Grab your coat lille øjesten, it's time for a walk into the past." I did as I was told and was at the door waiting, trying to hook one arm in my sleeve and pull the doorknob with the other.

"You ready for this?"

"Do donkeys eat cherries?" He raised one eyebrow at me and I quickly said,

"Forget I asked…so ready for what exactly?" I asked as we stepped through the door.

"Breaking the rules." He stated as though what we were about to do was an everyday occurrence in his world. Well, for all I knew, my new found blood brother was a vigilante, criminal mastermind for the Underworld's underworld. So, of course, I gave him the only answer there was for me to give,

"Hell Yeah!"

CHAPTER THIRTY-FIVE

TRAPPED IN SHADOW PRISON

I was pleasantly surprised to find this Somerset House was a quick walk away from the Savoy hotel. Well, that was until Sigurd reminded me that the Oracle was the one who planned most of this, so I gathered it made sense setting her own personal sucker…I mean Chosen One…up in a place that was walking distance to all these places. It made me wonder if she didn't just do a search on Google… ideal places to stay for the tourist attractions Hell's Ring/ Cheshire Cheese and one Heart of Paul Whitehead… in other words one Somerset House!

"She really did have everything planned, didn't she?" I asked out loud as Sigurd manoeuvred amongst angry pedestrians like a policeman would handle a suspect.

"She sure did." He replied dryly, keeping his hood up as if shying away from the crowd. I looked up at him and then looked around at the mass of people that all walked past us like they weren't seeing a massive 6' 5" guy all dressed in black who kind of gave off Grim Reaper vibes. This was when I realised it wasn't the crowd he was shielding himself from, but the late day sun. I took a wild stab in the dark and gathered he wasn't a big sun lounger kinda guy. Well I guess that cut out the need to get up at stupid 'o clock and reserve a place by the pool with a towel when on your holidays!

"We're here." His gravelly voice brought me out of my daft thoughts, and I stared up at three colossal open archways that were the centre of nine Corinthian columns. My head went all the way back and I counted the nine keystones that all held a stern Godly face frozen in stone. I was actually impressed that from that small paragraph of cryptic nonsense he knew exactly where to go.

I was just taking in the splendour that was the entrance to Somerset House, when I was roughly pulled through the middle arch around a group of Japanese tourists snapping pictures. As cliché as it sounded, I couldn't say I blamed them as the place was simply stunning. It opened up into a large square, one big enough that I was sure it could be used for professional football, and that literally took my breath away. It was fronted with a large bronze statue that looked Greek in design with an obviously important man dressed in a toga. At his side stood a lion and the other side, the bow of an ornate ship. On the platform beneath him lay a large, muscled God spilling liquid from a rounded urn.

It was beautiful and as we walked closer I tried to pull Sigurd towards its information plaque. However, he was having none of this and steered me around it, giving me a view of Somerset House's vast courtyard.

"Hey, I wanted to read that!" I complained, which granted me an un-amused grunt before he stated,

"You're not here on a school trip, princess."

"Really? 'Cause you know I thought you would have made an excellent History teacher." I commented sarcastically.

"You think?" I actually coughed on my own surprise.

"Uh no, Mr grabby, draggy Magee." This time he growled down at me.

"Don't make me push your little ass into the fountains." He threatened and I jumped when the centre of the courtyard erupted into bursts of water in tall spurts. There must have been at least fifty of them and they all danced along in sync at different lengths. It was as though they flowed along to an unheard water song.

We continued walking towards the main building ahead and the smell of coffee and baked goods came from the numerous plates sat in front of customers enjoying a late daybreak. It was as if we had stepped into a French main street. People took pictures of the stunning architecture and a group of young girls were all daring each other to run in between the lines of water.

I looked around all the buildings that formed a square which could have been seen from space it was that huge! (Ok, so maybe a slight exaggeration but you catch my drift… it was damn big!)

"We are never gonna find it in this place." I said feeling my shoulders slump with defeat. I even felt the tears of frustration start to seep up from the worry I had on lockdown.

"Hey." Sigurd said softly before turning me to face him. He gripped my chin between his thumb and forefinger to lift my gaze to his. I saw the snake ring glow under the shadow of his big hood and his other hand rose to run the back of his knuckles down my cheek. His open palm came to rest on the side of my neck and he tugged me to his chest as the first tear fell. I felt his head lower and his lips first kissed the top of my head. Then he whispered tenderly,

"We will find the heart my øjesten, this I will promise you now." I nodded at his soft words of comfort and his fingers tensed at the column of my neck briefly. He let me go and I leant back to look up at him.

"But how?" I questioned in a small voice.

"Give me the book." I did as he asked and dug into my bag which was strapped across my chest. I located the book, slapped it into his waiting hand and said,

"Do your thing, big guy." This delivered me a wink I could barely see and a cocky smile that showed the hint of fang. Briefly it made me wonder what it was with Demons and fangs, but I didn't think now was the time for inappropriate questions.

Sigurd's large hand held the back of the book easily in one hand, whilst the other was placed over the raised leather snake on the top.

"Ojentaa Ouroboros." ('Reach out' in Finnish)

I watched as the tiny shadows under his hand crept out cautiously under the light of day before flowing like silk under water into the heart of the book. Sigurd shuddered and my reaction became the domino effect doing the same. We both ended up taking a step back at the same time but for different reasons, as his was to prevent what had already started happening…mine was to get away from it.

But I was too late.

I closed my eyes, not because I wanted to but because I had no choice in the matter. After a few seconds the darkness behind my closed lids released its hold, but soon I wished for that darkness back. My vision cleared into my truest nightmare, so that I couldn't stop the scream that tore from my soul. I looked around my basement prison and for a second thought I was back with Morgan. But no, this was so much worse, if that was even possible. See, it wasn't that experience that I feared the most, although that may be surprising considering what he put me through. Ever since I was seven and transformed into a human with extra abilities of supernatural sight I had the very real fear of one day being committed. The terror of living the rest of my days in a mental asylum was a haunting prospect and it was more than enough to keep my mouth shut on anything I ever saw.

But now…

The room was just like one I had seen before, a small square that held nothing more than a slither of a metal bed and walls void of any feeling. Well, at least it wasn't padded, I thought without humour. I looked to the heavy iron door, thinking that the frame length locks were massive overkill. What did they think I was going to do…hulk out?

I got up from the cobbled floor and blinked a few times at the unexpected. Wasn't it usual for places like this to be all stainless steel and cold tiles smelling of disinfectant? If anything this place had a damp stone and mossy smell. I brushed the dirt from my jeans and stood wrapping my arms around my belly for comfort.

"Hello?" I whispered as a way to test the waters. I heard

muffled footsteps from behind the door and the window behind me let through a slither of moonlight, enough for me to see the small square in the centre of the heavily bolted door anyway. It held three bars and was just above my head in height. I tensed my fingers into a fist and then released them as I decided I needed to see where I was. It looked like the same prison I had seen in Draven's temple, holding a very different female prisoner.

I slowly approached the door and my heart thundered in my chest as though I was walking through a haunted house waiting for a ghostly figure to walk past me. I reached out with stretched fingertips to feel the condensation dripping down the dark metal. When nothing happened and no sounds could be heard, I braved getting closer. I took another step until I could take no more and I lifted up to my tiptoes. It wasn't enough to see so I gripped onto the bars and held still. Each movement I made had to end in pause, making sure that the result was still silence.

My grip tightened and I started to lift myself up whilst at the same time putting my feet to the door in order to push myself higher. Thankfully, the rubber on my trainers was enough to stop my toes from sliding down, keeping my grip in place. I looked through the bars and scanned the room beyond. What I found chilled me beyond the bone. I found the back of my own face staring back at me.

My long hair still remained but was matted and dirty. Mascara created black tears of panic as I stared down at arms covered in blood. I was wearing a wedding dress torn at the shoulder and a tear sliced in the bodice.

"DON'T HURT HIM!" I screamed in the middle of the room as I spun without reason. My grip turned painful on the bars as some other part of me just knew that I was staring into the future.

"Oh God." I whispered but that was when the other me had finally found her focus. Her head snapped around and then she was gone. I took in a premature breath of relief that was short lived.

"AH!" I screamed out as my own terror filled eyes appeared right in front of the door's window. I let go and fell backwards on my backside with a painful thud that would definitely be painted an unappealing shade of blue in the foreseeable future. I shook my head and in an angry swipe at being so weak with the fresh pain, I ran the back of my hand across my face so as not to get dirt in my eyes.

"What do you want?!" I shouted feeling betrayed by my own self. The other me looked both sad and evil at the same time. My blackened eyes still streamed with tears but this time they looked angry.

"You killed the one I love!" She shouted back and I flinched at the verbal slap.

"I…I…"

"You…you…KILLED OUR LOVE!" The vision of me screamed out the end in a demonic voice that was a fleeting memory in the back of my mind. That voice…I knew that voice…who…?

As I tried to get my mind back in time down a road of demonic discovery, the other me had clearly had enough. She uncurled her bloody fingers and dropped behind the door, no longer in sight. I got up gingerly and ran back to my place at the door.

"Wait!" I shouted and lifted myself up once more but by the time I got there she was gone. The room beyond was empty and as I no longer had a mirror image to fixate on, I could take in the rest of the room. It was soon confirmed that this was indeed the room I'd walked into all that time ago in the Temple. But when I looked behind me I saw the window and wondered how. The Temple was situated deep under Afterlife but there the moon shone, just peeking out behind the clouds.

This was the thought that brought on the change. The room started to spin and some aspects of my cell started to morph into another room. I felt a speck of something land on my cheek and I raised my hands to smudge the ash that rested there. I rubbed my fingertips together and examined the black mark that formed from my actions. This was when I looked up to see dirt raining down from the ceiling and the walls started to move back. They then wrapped around forming a circular space with the stones shrinking into smaller blocks.

The floor was soon covered in not just soot but also leaves and dirty trodden straw. The window arched and elongated into a wider slit in the tower room the space had transformed into. Even the door ahead of me folded in on itself and just as I took a step to escape, iron bars, the thickness of my wrist, shot up from the ground like the fountains at Somerset House. What was left was half the room on my side in a semicircle, barricaded by a wall of bars.

"What the…?" That message was left unfinished as I spun around to see my own form once again, slumped over a bed of straw sobbing. I knew this was a different time, as my hair was as I saw it in the mirror this morning, short and black. I decided to slowly approach and just before my reaching hand found her bare shoulder, she turned abruptly, scaring me. It took a startled moment for me to realise that the Keira in the future wasn't staring at me but past me. I felt a chill creep over me as I took in her frightened gaze and readied myself for what I would soon see.

I took in a shuddered breath and looked around at the bars, not knowing what I would see in this nightmare realm. It seemed both mine and my future self both had the same urges as a double scream pierced the night. I stumbled back enough to hit the far wall before I fell due to my unsteady legs. The sight before me terrified me enough to take the strength from muscle and sanity from mind.

Gorgon Leeches filled the space beyond the bars, alongside other creatures of Hell I hadn't seen before. The tall flaky skin bodies flanked the Leeches and each one carried a weapon in the sickest of ways. Each blade or spear had the ends stuck firmly in their own flesh with darkened ash being the only sign of affliction. Each one had their eyes rolled back into their head and the one coming closer had his weapon of a steel bar rammed through his cheeks, keeping them locked painfully tight together. It caused his lips to form an elongated O making its entire face lengthen in a nauseating stretch.

The closer they came to the bars the more my panicked mind told me to do something.

"NO! SIGURD HELP US!" I was the only one shouting

the plea of hope as only I seemed to know this vision for what it was…an after effect from Sigurd's dark bond with my soul. I had to believe that! There could be no other logical reason for what we were seeing. At my desperate cry for help the walls started to vibrate, but I knew not a single stone moved under the helpless hold I had on the wall. It was just like when your vision blurs when you shake your head violently. It started to knock my equilibrium off course as the room continued its visual assault on my senses, but one important thing managed to penetrate through the fog.

A figure started to step through as the minions parted and the other me growled out her obvious hatred. I couldn't see the man clearly but what I could see was my reaction to him. My mirror image shot from the floor. I stood back and watched as she faced the man who came closer. At this point the room moved in such a rapid way, that my head pounded trying to keep up with their movements. I could feel that Sigurd was desperately trying to get me out of here and the only thing hanging onto this madness was me. It was a crazy need that kept me rooted to the spot, but somewhere in my subconscious I knew what it was doing and I was about to find out why.

"Ah, my disgusting parasite, how nice to see you again." I could just make out my fists clenching at my sides at the sound of his voice and I looked down momentarily to see my own doing the same. It was clear my captured self was in one mind about what she would like to be doing to the man stood in front of her. I couldn't recognise him thanks to the blurred edges Sigurd's efforts were creating, but even the sound of his voice was sending revulsion to pebble my skin. The future's Keira took a step forward and the room stepped it up a few notches on vibrations, making it next to impossible to see anything other than us two. But it was one name spoken that finally brought down the walls to this nightmare,

"Gastian!"

As soon as the name passed her lips the room cracked and light poured through the walls. It was blinding bright and I raised my arm across my eyes to protect myself. It was only when I felt a soft touch from a big hand trying to pry my arm away that I felt comforted for the first time.

"It's alright now Keira, you're back with me." Sigurd's warm breath travelled my neck and I quickly felt a strong presence at my back. He pulled my arm down and I braved opening my eyes. He was holding me from behind with his arms crossed over my torso. It took me a moment to gather my bearings and when I did I realised that Sigurd must have carried me to somewhere more private for me to finish my blood bound freak out. We were in a less busy part of the courtyard, hidden either side by the many floors of Somerset house.

"I'm back." I whispered as though waking from a deep sleep.

"I've got you, sweet øjesten." Sigurd rumbled softly behind me and pulled me in tighter. I don't think I was mistaken when hearing the relief in his voice and I relaxed further into him as a result. We both needed it, plain and simple.

We stayed this way for the silent minutes it took for both our heart rates to slow. Then I ruined the peace when a thought took precedence over what I had just been through.

"The book?" I both felt and heard the deep sigh he released before he let me go. He took a step back and then turned me to face him slowly. His actions had me bracing for the worst.

"What is it…no answer…or maybe she was just engaged?" I said hoping that injecting a bit of humour would dull the disappointment I was almost sure was coming. So much so, I was surprised when he grinned and then said,

"She left you a message…Tricks?" I couldn't help my reaction when I launched up into his arms giving him no choice than to catch me. He laughed at me and I turned my head to kiss his cheek.

"Thank you, my friend." I whispered through the material of his hood where his ear would be. His hold tightened for a second then he lowered me until my feet found the cobbled floor again.

"Are you alright?" He asked me and I nodded, knowing he was referring to the darkness his powers took me to. I turned to move, giving space to our intimate moment but his hand struck out and pulled me back to him. He lowered his hidden forehead to mine and declared severely,

"He will not take you, Keira…I will not let him take you from me." I shuddered under the strength of his vow and found I could only nod slightly. The grip he had on the whole side of my neck loosened after he had reined in his strong emotions and I was able to keep the space between us to a few steps.

The more time we spent with each other meant the more dangerous the territory we trod on. I decided to clear my throat as a way of bringing us back to the task at hand.

"Please tell me the message she left wasn't level impossible on the Oracle's version of puzzle cracking?" Sigurd grunted before saying,

"Take a look for yourself." This was said in a way that held no doubt, that yes, it was going to give me a headache. Sigurd pulled the book from behind his jacket as though he had kept it tucked in the waistline of his dark, belted jeans. I was about to take it and then hesitated a moment as I remembered what had happened not long ago, thanks to that book.

"It's alright Keira, that won't happen this time." I looked up at him with wide eyes and the guilt I found in his own gaze made me feel bad for him. I didn't say anything but as I took the book from him I gave his hand a reassuring squeeze. I opened it up, finding the right page straight away as it was the only one with any words written.

To my dear Tricks,
I hope you enjoyed your fun faired Trip,
Cause now it's time for hearts to be found,
And for you to bite your Lip.

The beats maybe long gone,
For life in the Deadhouse,
Now is the time to grab a King,
And play the happy Spouse.

Number 26 is facing you Ahead,
And a door with no number is not a coal Shed,

So take a deep breath and greet the Dead,
To find the still heart of one Paul Whitehead.

To your left is a name you know well,
But the date 33 won't get you into Hell,
So move away and look for another,
One that speaks fondly of the Queen Mother.

Skull and crossbones isn't down to a wooden leg,
For he was a doctor, so no need to beg,
For he doesn't hold the organ that you seek,
It's not even on this side, so go take a peek.

So leave the doctor alone
And look around the space,
For once you find the ½ topped cross,
You need to look under the pace.

Look to a number 7 set in pale stone,
The one you seek will rightfully sit upon the 7th throne,
Your lovely name you will no doubt find,
And an old withered heart lays waiting behind.

After reading the cryptic message aloud, it was as though I could feel the hope draining away with every word spoken. How on earth were we going to find anything that referred to these clues in a place this big?! I was just about to ask this out loud when I saw a group of people all following someone with a clip-board, across the courtyard coming closer towards us near the big bronze statue. That's when it hit me and I looked up to Sigurd to say,

"Honey, we are going on a tour!"

CHAPTER THIRTY-SIX

GEEK MAN WALKING

After walking into the main building and bursting into a fit of childish giggles thanks to the name above the door, we received our tickets for the last tour of the day. We had some time to kill and after seeing the last guy I watched Sigurd take care of, I was glad that wasn't meant in the literal sense! We decided to grab a coffee (tea for me of course) and sit down to wait. This I thought was the perfect opportunity to ask Sigurd about my dark dream.

"Ok, so I gotta ask…what is it with this dude Gastian and what exactly is his beef with me?"

"I don't know." He stated simply, after devouring the last bites of my cake slice he bought me…this, I had to add, was after finishing two slices bought for himself!

"Jesus, what is it with you and food…?" I leant forward and whispered,

"Ok pick one, you are A, going to be spending the next ten years in a remote colony in Antarctica, B, all the food you eat is going out of fashion tomorrow, with all bakers, butchers and chefs deciding to a career change or C, there is going to be a world Famine that I don't yet know about?" He growled with his mouth full and then I could hear the angry swallow that followed. I couldn't help but smirk.

"Your turn, A, I can use your bones as a toothpick, B, I could wash down my cake with a pint of your blood or C, I can bend you over my knee, render your ass a rosy red and use your back as a place to rest my plate…pick one." It was my turn to growl and it was his turn to smirk.

"Time to go, buttercup." He said mockingly, whilst grabbing my upper arm and hauling me up from the seat.

"But wait, you never told me about Gastian."

"Can't tell you what I don't know, sweetheart…now come on or we will miss all the excitement." The word excitement was most definitely a sarcastic overstatement for him as I knew he was dreading it…this was because in the last 45 minutes he had told me so at least 45 times!

I let him lead me over into the main entrance and only when I saw his reflection in the door's window did I pull back, gasping at what I saw.

"What the Hell!?" I shouted making an older couple stare at me disapprovingly.

"What?" Sigurd hissed, allowing me to pull him back before we walked inside. Having a firm hold of his jacket, I pulled him further out of the way of people passing us to get inside and tried to drag his head down by the hood so that he could hear my panicked whisper.

"Why do you look like that?!" I asked through gritted teeth.

"Keira, please try making sense…I don't know…" I didn't let him finish as I pointed over the sheer drop from the floors below and over the balcony that spanned the area either side of the main entrance. He started to look down when I shook his hood and said,

"Not there…there." I pointed across to the window that was directly ahead of us at the reflection standing next to me…one that definitely wasn't Sigurd!

"Ah."

"Yeah, 'ah' is right buddy boy, explain…now!" I looked back at him and saw a naughty smile start to form. I scowled at his obvious amusement at my freak out.

"What? So I don't want people seeing the real me, what's the big deal?"

"What's the big deal?! Are you serious? We are supposed to be acting as a married couple, like the book's message said!" I said all this while doing a tennis fan impression watching a game. I could barely tear my eyes from the reflection which others were clearly seeing as him.

"Yes well, I don't know if you noticed at all, but someone looking like me does tend to cause unwanted attention." I rolled my eyes and said,

"So yeah alright, you're unbelievably handsome and rugged and have the body of a God, with your tall frame and muscles on top of muscles but that doesn't mean you should go all big headed about it!" My outburst brought about the first time I had seen one of his kind actually bite his lip, but unlike me, it wasn't done out of shame. He pulled me closer to him until I had to reach up on tiptoes so as not to end up dangling by my arm a foot from the ground.

"I meant that people find me scary and intimidating øjesten, not someone that people want to sign up for the cover of a magazine. You wanted to come here and get what you're looking for. Well, to do that we not only need human interaction, but also their help…somehow I don't think they would have been as accommodating with someone that fits my description, do you?" Ok, so he had a point, but did he really have to rub it in? I mean my blush had already turned nuclear. He released me until my feet were once again flat on the floor and for long moments we just stared at each other like we were both fighting a greater urge. I shook those thoughts from my mind and slapped a great big warning sticker on that metaphorical case file.

"Ok, so I am getting that, but really…I mean… come on, you had to marry me to that guy!" I said pointing for the last time to his lying reflection. I referred to the 5ft guy who wore thick rimmed square glasses that reminded me of my granddad, a cream shirt with brown dickey bow and a pale blue V neck knitted vest on top. Brown cords and sandals over white socks finished the nerdy reflection. But this wasn't the worst part, oh no, I think the crème de la crème was the side parted comb over that was slicked down with only what can be described as car oil!

"So, I take it you're not into the geek look?" He asked bringing my stunned gaze back to the real him. Needless to say the sight was much more appealing!

"Umm, I don't think that counts as just plain old geeky…I mean my friend Pip is married to a geek and he is hot! Besides, I think it is safe to say that you look like you are trying hard to bring Granddad fashion into…well…fashion."

"You know of Adam's Imp?" His abrupt subject change had me pulling my head back and frowning.

"Her name is Pip and yeah, we are good mates, why?" I said not being able to rein in the attitude thanks to my protectiveness over my friend.

"It figures." He commented wryly as he turned from me about to make his way back to the main entrance. I reached out, grabbed his arm and snapped,

"And what is that supposed to mean?!"

"I know Pip and the trouble she gets in, so to assume you and her are friends in no stretch of the imagination considering trouble will inevitably find friendship with trouble. Now come on or we will miss this fucking tour!" He pulled me with him into the building and I made a noise in the back of my throat that was half growl and half moan. It was only when we were waiting with the rest of the tourists that I whispered,

"If you look harmless then I suggest curbing the language to match, we don't want people to think I'm married to an aggressive wife beater." Of course, this idea was a joke as one look at Sigurd's portrayal of my husband and it was outright laughable. But instead of commenting he leaned down, or thanks to his new height not at all and gave me a kiss on the cheek, finishing it with a,

"Yes dear."

We waited for the people ahead of us to move aside before handing over our tickets to the tour guide. She handed us a gold and white sticker each and I slapped Sigurd's to his chest with more vigour than was needed.

"There you go, honey boo." I said loud enough to draw

some strange looks. He took mine from the lady and returned the favour by placing it above one breast and making a show of patting it down unnecessarily. He was still doing it, only this time making it more than obvious he was using the opportunity to fondle my breast, drawing some even stranger looks. I batted his hand away and snapped through gritted teeth,

"It's fine!" He laughed once and then winked at a guy behind me saying,

"I had to be sure, sugar plum bum." I rolled my eyes when I heard the guy cough to hide a laugh and waited until everyone had moved so we were left at the back before elbowing Sigurd in the stomach. I got an umff sound and smiled when everyone turned around to face us.

"That's it love, cough it up." I said making a show of patting his back. After some more funny looks everyone turned back to the front to hear what the guide was saying. She introduced herself as Rachael and before starting the tour asked us all to refrain from using our mobile phones. Then, after explaining the details of our tour, we followed her outside to our first point of interest.

After all of the group had gathered round I couldn't help but notice people kept their distance from us. I put this down to some deeper human instinct of survival considering Sigurd's true nature. It was as though no matter how convincing his geeky disguise was, the truth was in the shadows lurking in wait. You could see it in his stance, as though ready to pounce and strike down any threat that might arise. People were smart to be wary and as a result we were given a wide berth in the circle.

The guide had taken us outside near the fountains and started the tour with the building's history. I soon found myself engrossed in hearing how Somerset house started life as a Tudor palace built by Edward Seymour, Duke of Somerset and virtual ruler at the time. This was because as Lord Protector of England, in the minority of his nephew, Edward VI, who was the son of the lady obsessed Henry VIII who seemed to collect wives the way others do tea sets! I don't think by the growly noise that came from Sigurd that he was a big fan either! Of course, it was a no brainer the reason why everyone took a step back and gave us an even greater space.

I hooked Sigurd's arm with my own and pulled him closer to the back of the group.

"Ok, down boy and less of scaring the human population if you can help it because see that meathead there…" I nodded to the guy who looked like he bench pressed his girlfriend every morning before breakfast.

"Even that guy is wary of you right now and given the way you look, that is doing nothing for his street cred."

"And why should I give a shit?" Sigurd rumbled and I looked into the opposite window to check his disguise was still in place. I had to squash down my surprise when I saw his fingers rise to push up a pair of thick rimmed glasses that weren't actually there. I shook my head trying to dislodge the weirdness this day kept throwing at me and tried a different tactic.

"Because we are trying to fit in, hubby dearest and I would like to end this day with a scabby, old heart of some asshole in my hand not you getting your geeky ass thrown out of here for being an asshole… capiche?" I whispered making him burst out laughing.

"Seriously…did you just say Capiche?"

"What? I can say Capiche." I frowned up at him when I saw his humour grow at my expense. Then his lips rose further up one side and he placated me with a head pat, saying,

"Alright Don, how about I whack the meathead with my heavy before my shakedown with our tour guide for ten large whilst you go on the lam?" I rolled my eyes at his chuckle as we took our place back with the group.

"Funny, but you forgot swimming with the fishes in that sentence."

"Ok, now we really need to work on your mobster 'cause they don't actually say that outside of a movie set and whilst we're at it, do me a favour and never say Capiche again." I scoffed at that and said a lame,

"Whatever."

"Too damn cute." I whipped my head up at his muttered comment, but he ignored me and when I tried to speak he just shushed me, nodding back to what the tour guide was saying. I huffed with my arms folded.

The tour continued around the courtyard until we had heard about what part of history influenced the architecture of the buildings and their enrichments, which clearly had a strong ancient Greek feel. You could tell that Sigurd found this completely boring and to a point where I wouldn't have been surprised if I would soon have to drag him along like an unruly child. I tried to see it from his point of view and wondered if I too had lived through these times would I have also found it tiresome? Every now and again I would catch his reflection in the many windows, rolling his eyes at something the guide said and wondered if what we knew of history was as accurate as we presumed? Well, if Sigurd's reactions were anything to go by then I was thinking not.

It was only at the point in the tour that got to the Navy side that we started to really take notice. According to Jared's story, Paul Whitehead's heart had been stolen from an Australian Sailor and this place held it within its walls, somewhere that one possessed Admiral Sir James Stirling had hidden it. I could almost feel the cells inside my body buzzing with the excitement of the adventure that had been thrust upon me. The thrill of the chase sent my mind into overdrive and I could almost taste the lips of my lost lover coming closer to lips eagerly waiting.

Soon…I just knew it.

Standing outside the Navy Office, which was situated next to the main entrance with a name that still made me snigger when reading it, I listened with interest as our guide spoke about the Navy's involvement with Somerset house. Then I heard a big yawn next to me and I wasn't the only one that shot daggers at Sigurd for his obvious show of boredom.

"What, she wore me out last night, alright." My mouth dropped as I processed what he just said. I heard a few laugh (mainly the men in the group) and some gasp clearly outraged (mainly the women). Meanwhile, the guide got everyone to move on from both the Navy and my shame. I turned and smacked Sigurd on the arm making him chuckle.

"Well, technically you did." He said behind me as I stormed

ahead fuming. I gritted my teeth as I heard his full-blown laughter following me.

"I don't remember being in that ring last night!" I gritted out as I tried to catch up with the group which I could see disappearing down the hallway.

"What can I say… taking care of you wears me out, lille øjesten."

"Then you're obviously getting old…maybe it is time to think about retiring to Florida after all." I had to smile when I heard the trademark growl replace sniggering laughter.

"Over my cold dead host!" He said in my ear before stamping large boots ahead of me, grabbing my hand at the last second to drag me along. I couldn't hold in the satisfaction that I had won another round.

"If you could all just look up the staircase and then back down again, you will notice the distinct difference between the floors above to the floors below. This was one of the ways that level of importance was clearly stated as the higher class worked on the top levels whilst the lower class obviously worked down below. You can see with the elaborate mouldings decorating the top floors and beautiful hand railings that compared to the plain lower levels, this distinction stands out clearly." We walked through just as the guide was starting her talk on this section but nothing in what she said was going to be of any help to what we were looking for. So far it just showed us an endless amount of doors and floors that we might have to look through. It was almost like showing us an aerial view of the garden maze and then dumping us dead centre to find our own way out.

The rest of the tour walked us through the outside balcony that looked over a main road and then the river that once had come right up to the building itself. From what I took in from the guide, the water went right underneath where we stood so that boats could pull into a big archway to let passengers disembark. It was cool to see how it would have been back then, but I had to admit that when she took us back inside and that wasn't the end of the tour, I was relieved.

We followed once again as she started to take us across to the other side of the building and down a spiral staircase that got more unrefined the further down we went. This was to the point that the steps became mottled with dimples in the stone resembling a grey leopard print.

"What is that?" I whispered as Sigurd kept firm hold of me as we descended the steep staircase.

"That is thanks to the metal in the boots of the workers." I looked down past where my own feet were heading and stared at the evidence of that extreme level of hard work that had ingrained itself into the very building itself. Once we reached the bottom floor it made me a bit dizzy looking up in the centre space all the way to the top. I couldn't help but back into Sigurd and felt better when his hands held onto my hips to keep me steady.

Like every place we stopped the lady started with stories of the past but by this time I had started to get frustrated that we would never get this done. So once again I listened to words that didn't help us in getting any closer to the damned heart!

"Patience øjesten, I know we are getting closer…not long now, my sweetheart." He brushed my short hair from my neck as I relaxed back into him. God, I hoped he was right! I didn't know how much more excitement I could let build, knowing that if this tour didn't produce the right clues then that hefty weight of hope would come crashing down.

Finally, we were on the move again and this time it took us to a more promising setting. After going around the corner and into a room that opened up, branching off to four different ways, I was glad to see it took us outside. Now, here was the real grit of Somerset house. Leaving behind the finery of the upper class we walked straight into the belly of the beast. Stepping through a time to where the real backbone of England's workers would find a hard life of dirt and sweat.

This was where all the coal sheds were housed, along a cobbled narrow street that hadn't really changed in over 200 years. I looked up and you could see all the levels to where we had first been stood outside the main entrance. You could even still hear the laughter of the children running through the fountains in that grand courtyard. A zigzag of staircases ran this way and that until it reached that level and I could easily see a way to break in if need be.

Ok, so now my thoughts were scaring me as I knew once you started analysing how easy a place was to break in, that meant only one thing…I had spent way too much time around badass Demons! What was next on my list, a trip to get myself some camouflage gear, black face paint and some night vision goggles?!

"Wait!" I said a bit too loud making the guide stop and give me one of those 'are you serious' looks. I bit my lip and said a quiet,

"Sorry, please…um…carry on."

We waited for the others to go ahead of us and I vaguely listened to our guide explain about the terrible work conditions and point out the shoots the coal came down inside the coal sheds that lined the walkway.

"Keira, what is it?" Sigurd asked once we were far enough away from everyone else.

"The book, I need to see the book again, I think I remember something in the Oracle's riddle." I flipped back the large flap on my bag and pulled out the book.

"Aha! See there, the number 26, we're on the right track… woohoo!" I said once finding the right bit in verse three and pointing to the same number on the black door in front of us.

'Number 26 is facing you Ahead,
And a door with no number is not a coal Shed,
So, take a deep breath and greet the Dead,
To find the still heart of one Paul Whitehead'

I couldn't help but jump up and down like happy fool, all the while slapping Sigurd on the arm like he should join me. Of course, he didn't but it was nice that I got a smile for my obvious enthusiasm.

"So, where to next?" I asked reading through the riddle again. Sigurd looked down over my shoulder and re-read the verses himself and it only took a second for him to say,

"This way." Then, grabbing the crook of my arm, he led me

down the open passageway to catch up with the rest of the group. We continued to pass the black doors of the coal sheds which all had flimsy looking locks on them that would be one simple kick away from opening for someone like Sigurd. See...! There it was again, with the breaking and entry thoughts. What happened to the days where my main thought process was about course work or which gloves to wear with what outfit?! Well, that one was easy to answer and began with a capital D…

Draven.

Even thinking the name had me both aching inside and walking faster to get to this bloody heart! Ok, so I doubted there would be any blood after all this time, which brought on the next morbid question in my mind…what would a 240-year-old heart look like?

"You still with me, øjesten?" Sigurd's question brought me out of my daft thoughts and back into the now. I nodded and started to concentrate on the numbers on the doors. I only pulled my arm from his hold when I got to the first door without a number. It was unlike all the other doors which had been made from panelled wood, but this one was smooth glossy black.

"This must be it." I said going up to run my hand over the door as if trying to judge what lay behind.

"No, it isn't." Sigurd's voice burst my bubble and I quickly found my hand no longer touching the door. Instead it was firmly encased in a much larger hand and being pulled in the opposite direction again.

"But it had no number and the book said…"

"That is number 17, look…the next door says 16." He pointed to the door as we passed.

"So…it still didn't have a number on the door, so that means…" Once again, he cut me off.

"That means it didn't have a number on the door, but it is still a coal shed and according to the crazy shit the Oracle told us, that's not what we're looking for." Ok, so he had a point there!

He continued on pulling me and it was only when we were by door number 12 and I nearly tripped over a drain on the floor that he slowed down. However, this wasn't because I had to practically run to keep up with his long legs, nearly falling over myself to do so, but because we had caught up with the group. They were all filing into a space where a set of double doors had been opened up. I looked to see the numbers on the doors and even though ten didn't have a number, the other side of the double doors was numbered 9. Which meant that one of the doors we walked through now, actually was the door with no number, just like the riddle said.

"Please gather round." The guide said and I let Sigurd pull me further inside past the others so that we were closer to the back. The feeling of the dark behind me was unnerving for one reason only and that was because I could almost taste the humming power emanating from Sigurd who stood at my back. I looked behind me and gasped as I saw the shadowed serpents seeping out from behind his back as though they had finally been allowed to break free from the confines of their flesh and bone cage.

"What are you doing?" I whispered in desperate tones.

"Ssshh and relax, soon no one will see us anymore, my øjesten." I swallowed the worried lump down and scanned the room for anyone who was looking at us even more strangely than usual. I was just about to do as suggested and relax when our guide spoke up,

"Welcome everyone…

To the Deadhouse."

CHAPTER THIRTY-SEVEN

THE DEADHOUSE

The Deadhouse wasn't what I expected it to look like, although what exactly I was expecting I didn't know. But one thing was for sure and that was I definitely wasn't expecting a horror movie boiler room. The small bricks that made up the walls were painted thick white which had long ago turned a dirty colour thanks to the damp streaks running down the walls from the overhead pipes. I couldn't tell how far the room went on as the darkness we stood in prevented it, but it was only wide enough to fit a car and not much else either side.

One thing I was certain and that was it definitely didn't lack the creep factor! As I had been pulled past the group I did have chance to notice the small recesses that held plaques either side of the walls making four in total. The only light in the room came from the open doors and a metal gate which obviously added to the security. This was left sticking out, causing looming shadows to branch out on the pale floor.

I felt Sigurd's arms surround me and then I tried not to scream out as his shadowed serpents did the same. It was a strange sensation, somewhere between a light touch from a cold hand and a damp mist travelling over your skin. My senses reacted by leaving a trail of tiny bumps over my body as they slithered around my torso. I jumped in Sigurd's hold when one of the heads reared back and hissed at me.

"Calm lille øjesten, they won't hurt you... Légy jó a háziállatok, nem ijedt a kis drágám" ('Be good my pets, don't frighten our little darling' In Hungarian) Upon hearing the foreign words spoken by their master, they pulled back and made little crooning noises that sounded very similar to a purr.

"Won't someone see us?" I whispered, rising to my tiptoes and turning my head to the side so my cheek rested on his chest. His two misted snake buddies shook their head at the same time he whispered his answer as a negative.

"The reason we are in the Deadhouse is to see these five tombstones you can see on the walls. Charles I's wife Henrietta Maria of France was a devout Catholic and when coming to this country she didn't come alone. In fact, she brought her whole entourage with her and, needing a place to practice their religion, Charles let her build a chapel in the grounds, which used to be situated in the Northwest wing. The chapel was designed by a man called Inigo Jones and when the new building of Somerset House was commissioned to be rebuilt in 1774, one Sir William Chambers had the chapel demolished. But for reasons unknown, other than his admiration for Inigo Jones he had five of the tombstones found kept and stored here." I listened to the guide explain the strange events that led up to the very room we were now stood in and wondered why these tombstones. One thing was certain and that was I couldn't wait to get a good look at them!

She continued to talk briefly about each one, but I quickly found myself distracted by the feel of bands of muscle pulling me deeper into the dark obscurity, one consumed by the shadows he ruled there.

"What are you...?"

"Silence now and trust me, sweet øjesten. It is time to let my Ouroboros hide us from view." I decided it was wise not to argue and this turned out to be right when the group started to move on to the next stop on the tour. I let out the breath I had been holding until the guide shut both the gate and double doors, locking them behind her. I was about to call out when Sigurd's hand clamped over my mouth.

"That would be foolish, honey." He spoke directly into my ear and it became the only sound over my pounding heart in the solid darkness. He gave me a moment to let my panic go and only when he felt my pulse slow did he release his control.

"You alright now?" He asked me softly and I nodded as he still gripped my chin in a loose hold.

"Good girl, now let's get to work." He let his hand drop from my face and took my own hand in a gentle grip.

"But how, I can't see a thing?" I asked hoping he was about to whip out a torch or maybe a mobile phone app that flashed Morse code.

"That's where I come in handy." He assured me.

We stopped moving and I felt his hands on my shoulders turn me slightly. I heard the whoosh of material moving back and then the small glow where his eyes would be. One came through like a silver light, where the other was a flame torched snake that circled his eye.

"I gather this means you can see in the dark?"

"And the stuffed animal prize goes to cutie here… now you look at the book and I will read out the tombstones to you." I smiled in the dark at his funny response and then pointed out the obvious.

"That's great and all, but I forgot to buy my set of night vision goggles…although they are now on the list…"

"Not going to be a problem. Get out the book." I did as I was told and only when I felt his hand over the cover did I quickly move a step back. The last thing I wanted was a trip down nightmare lane again! He didn't say anything but his actions made me shriek out. His slithering guard dogs snaked around me to hold me still and when I felt my elbow bang against something hard sticking out of the wall I knew it was for my own good.

"Ok, ok, I get the picture…down boys." I spoke to the shadows and another hissing purr was my answer as they released me, trusting that I would stay put this time. My attention was soon caught by the glowing red letters from the Oracle that now burned brightly on the page. This combined with the smouldering light from Sigurd's eyes was enough for me to at least see my hand in front of my face.

"Now what?"

"Read the fourth verse" I took the book into my hands now feeling the slight heat it gave off.

"To your left is a name you know well, But the date 33 won't get you into Hell, So move away and look for another, One that speaks fondly of the Queen Mother'...what's that supposed to mean?" He didn't answer me straight away but I felt myself being moved to the right side of the room.

"The other one you were stood in front of had the date 1633, so let's try this one...next verse"

"Ok, let's see... *'Skull and crossbones isn't down to a wooden leg,*

For he was a doctor, so no need to beg, for he doesn't hold the organ that you seek, it's not even on this side, so go take a peek'...ok so what do you see?"

"Well this guy was obviously the doctor so let's go back to the other side and see the only other one there." I again felt myself being shifted around until we must have been opposite the one he spoke of. We stood in silence for a minute and then after Sigurd exhaled loudly he said,

"Next one, Keira."

"Oh right, sorry...umm...ok it says, *'So leave the doctor alone And look around the space, for once you find the ½ topped cross, you need to look under the pace'*...pace no wait do you think she meant place?" I said re-reading that part again.

"No, the one we're facing has a cross above it, the date 1691/2 and the words *'requiesc in pace'* at the bottom...what's the last one?"

"The date 169 and a half...well that's weird... I wonder what that's about?"

"Focus, Keira." Sigurd said trying no doubt for patience.

"Ok, ok, my bad... last verse is *'Look to a number 7 set in pale stone, the one you seek will rightfully sit upon the 7th throne, your lovely name you will no doubt find, and...'*"

"And?" He prompted.

"And an old withered heart lies waiting behind...Sigurd this is the

one! Can you see it?" I said feeling my own heart soar that we had finally come this close. I waited for an answer from Sigurd but after too long of waiting I felt out for him in the dark and tugged on his arm.

"What is it…? Sigurd speak to me."

"This life for Immortality, the 7th of May 1674…" His voice sounded strange, as if talking to himself and caught in the unbelievable.

"So this is it?"

"Keira it has your name…*Queen Catherine and talks of the third sonne, the Queen mother and…"*

"So what, that just means we found the right one, just like the verse said." I didn't understand where this strange reaction was coming from. He almost sounded too far away as though trying to figure out something that wasn't there for everyone to see.

I was about to ask him to explain himself further, but his sudden actions stopped me. His fist shot out and hammered straight through the tombstone ahead of me, making me jump out of the way. The sound of crumbling stone raining down on the floor echoed along the walls. I could also hear his hand moving around in the hole he'd just brutally made.

"Come here." Before I could move to the order, his shadowy friends once again found it fun to play with the Human and moved me over in front of him. I could swear the little devils were trying to tickle me!

"Now, I am going to put your hand in there and I want you to grab it." Sigurd instructed, making me wrinkle up my nose.

"No, no, you can go for it…in fact, I insist."

"Keira." My name came out as a warning.

"But it's gross." Ok, so my argument wasn't a mature one.

"I'm sure you will be fine and I think we can safely say it won't bite…besides no demon can touch it remember, so unless you think our guide is up to doing extra occupational duties, then I suggest you get it over with." I groaned at the thought and before I could back out and shy away from my duties as Supernatural ambassador, I held my breath, put on my best disgusted face and shoved my hand right into where Sigurd had left a gaping hole.

"I've got it." I said quietly when finding more than just air with my probing fingers.

"Good work øjesten, now pull it out and put it straight into your bag…that's it." He instructed as I pulled the material wrapped package from inside its resting place. Once it was firmly in my bag, I breathed out a sigh of relief.

"Oh, thank God." In return, the feeling of a massive weight lifted and floated away with the week's turbulent events. We had the heart and now nothing could stop me from getting to Draven…

Nothing.

Once Sigurd had assured me he would see to the evidence of our thievery and busted us out of the Deadhouse, he relocked it and we silently found the quickest exit. For the most part he remained silent, if only for the brief muttering to himself. This was after we were back on the stone walkway heading away from the coal sheds, when he asked to see the book one last time. Then without any explanation he repeated two lines in the last verse to himself and I couldn't help the shiver that washed over me.

'The one you seek will rightfully sit upon the 7th throne,
Your lovely name you will no doubt find'

After this he didn't elaborate and for some reason I couldn't bring myself to ask. In fact, it was only when we were back up near the fountains did we finally speak to each other.

"What was that?"

"I have to go." We both spoke at the same time but I was the only one to reply and shouted,

"What?" In response to his abrupt need to leave.

"I'm sorry but I have to see someone." I couldn't believe what I was hearing.

"You're leaving me?" I asked in a small voice, trying not to get upset at the idea of going this alone again. He must have heard the waver in my voice as my emotions got the better of me. He took a deep breath, stepped closer to me and raised his hand to cup my cheek.

"Lille øjesten." He used a thumb to wipe away the single tear that escaped, one I wasn't even aware had grown and slipped away from me.

"I will come back for you little one, but you must make me a promise." I nodded, not trusting words right now, words that would no doubt bring on more useless tears, feeding the feeling of hopelessness.

"I want you to take the heart, go straight to the hotel and stay there until I return…can you do that for me?" He sounded so deep and soft. Listening to the way each word drizzled goosebumps along my skin, there was no way I could have denied him anything.

"I can do that but tell me…"

"I can't tell you why Keira, not yet. I will just have to ask you to trust me again…you will do that for me…yes?" I bit my bottom lip, looked away for a second and then after taking a shaky breath, said what he wanted to hear and what I knew to be true.

"Yes Sigurd, I can do that for you." His released a breath and let his hand slip round to grip my neck. He pulled me into his embrace and held me to him for silent minutes which gave me the secure strength needed to face being alone once again. I had become so dependant these last few days on my shadowed knight that I felt a little hollow at the thought of walking away from him. Vulnerable would be new word choice of the day and I wanted to cry like a little lost girl at the prospect.

I mean, what if he didn't come back? What then? No, I couldn't think like that! I had trusted him this far, with my very life in fact, so I needed to man up and just keep on trusting him! So with that in mind, I hugged him tighter before letting him go.

"You'll be back." I said in way of confirmation. He smiled down at me and said a gentle,

"Yes sweetheart, I will be back for you." I let those words float over me like a comforting blanket I wanted to hold onto, until I watched his large hooded form walk away from me. I then looked up to the clear sky, took a deep breath and after looking over my shoulder to see the main entrance of Somerset House one last time, I walked away giggling.

"Goodbye, Seaman's Hall."

The rest of the day was spent with me staring at the gauze wrapped package of Paul Whitehead's heart, sat on the suite's coffee table. Was it strange to be shocked that it was in fact heart shaped? I don't know what exactly I expected to find, definitely not in a nicely wrapped Tiffany's box that's for sure but really…just a bit of mummified wrapping was all it took to gift someone with your heart. I wondered if Sir Francis Dashwood just sat it on his coffee table that day and stared at it.

One thing was for sure and that was how quickly the day went by just watching something old do a whole load of nothing in the sitting room! My gaze wandered to the massive windows that showed London in all its lit up glory and I couldn't help but ask out loud,

"Where are you my friend?"

I must have had a brief thought about going to bed before crashing out on the sofa because, when I opened my eyes to the blinding morning sun, I quickly realised I had fallen asleep. I blinked back the grogginess to find the heart come into focus, still there on the table.

"So, what's on the menu today life?" I asked the empty room after I stretched out my arms and yawned. My stomach was the only one that answered me when it started to rumble. I decided it could wait until I'd had a shower at least, but by the sounds of things it disagreed.

"Tough luck belly, the only thing you're gonna get right now is soap." I got up and started walking to the bathroom when I stopped and looked back at my new friend sat waiting on the table.

"Euw…I can't believe I am gonna do this." I said rolling my eyes at myself and what I was about to do. This was how I ended up having a shower with a 240-year-old heart sat next to the bathroom sink. I just hoped the condensation didn't effect it and make it soggy, that was the very last thing I needed right now and I doubt I could have called room service and ask them if they have an airing cupboard I could dry it out in!

I got out from the shower, wrapped a towel around myself and looked down at the heart whilst I brushed my wet hair.

"So was it good for you?" I smiled to myself, winked at it and said,

"Of course, it was."

I laughed thinking that I was taking the whole new friend thing to extremes and could only hope that I would cry when it was time for us to part, like when Tom Hanks had to say goodbye to his volleyball Wilson. Ok, so maybe this was finally confirmation that I was losing the plot! Thankfully the sound of the suite's phone ringing didn't allow me to look too closely into the new side effects of being alone. I picked up the heart, weirdly no longer feeling the 'yuck' factor, and raced for the phone.

"Hello."

"Hello Miss Williams, I wanted to inform you that someone came in with a letter for you, would you like me to bring it to you personally?" It was the Hotel's concierge and in my over excitement I screeched back,

"Shit yeah!" I heard him cough back his shock on the other side.

"Umm, sorry I mean, yes please, that would be smashing." I winced as that didn't sound any better than swearing. Well, if he didn't think me a freak before, then that fake posh accent I was insanely going for would do it! At least he thought I was rich, so I had that going for me at least.

"Uh…yes Miss, of course, it will be with you shortly." I put down the phone thinking 'poor bastard having to deal with me', but then just ended up laughing while changing into some jeans and thinking about it again. So much for trying to be shy little Keira girl that faded into the background…I think that flight took off quite a while ago and took that plain pipe dream with it!

I heard the knocking and was soon about to open the door

thinking just how much my life had really changed, along with it my personality. I couldn't be sure if it was for the better or not, but one thing I was certain of and that was my inner strength had definitely quadrupled! Everything I had been through since that life shattering day when I no longer had Draven to lean on. I had lost my soul's protector and become the saviour in our combined life story. Even thinking about it made me bite my lip and start worrying about simply fucking the whole thing up!

The swearing in my mind just emphasised the importance of the task I still had waiting for me. All those questions that I had kept at bay until now just seemed to burst from the flood gates. So what, I have the heart but what if it means nothing? What if Jared can't keep his word and get me into Hell or more importantly what if he could…then what…bust in there, guns blazing, demanding my boyfriend back. Christ alive, but I didn't even know who I would be aiming that damn gun at because, of course, I still didn't know who had him!

Ok, so while I was about to answer the door, wasn't really the time for a meltdown, but answer me…whenever was?

"Miss Williams?" I heard from behind the closed door that I realised I was still standing behind with my grip on the handle.

"Yes, sorry I'm coming." I said in the steadiest voice I could muster. I closed my eyes tight and held in the frustrated tears that I refused to set free. No more being weak, if anything it was the time to grow an even thicker skin and get on with it, saying to Hell with Hell!

It wouldn't beat me and if it did, then I would just die trying, knowing that there are far worst things to die for than dying for love. And this little northern English girl was willing to get into that blazing underground death club, kicking and screaming if need be! So, with that firmly in my badass mode mind, I opened the door to my next adventure, ready to ride the very waves of the River Styx right to Hell's front door and this time…

Hell will know the damned.

CHAPTER THIRTY-EIGHT

HATEFUL HELLFIRE

I started to push my way through the crowd of tourists all on their way to various parts of London, cramming into the tube stations. I learned pretty quickly that when on the escalators to stand to the right so that the 'real' Londoners could run for their connections around the city. This was after a rather rude 'Get to the pissin' right, love', that I took a huffed sidestep to let the impatient cockney pass.

After opening the door to my suite, I raced to get ready to do as the latest letter instructed. Which brings me to now and feeling like a small clueless fish in a massive pond of irate barracudas. Well, at least I figured out that by getting myself an oyster card topped up with a twenty would cut down on time with the ticket barriers, which was what I gripped in my hand now like I would need it at every turn. I may have been born English but the capital city still intimidated the Hell outta me!

After checking out the Hellfire Club on Google, which thankfully was only in West Wycombe and was about a 30-minute train journey from here, I booked the first ticket I could. Now I was on my way to catch the Bakerloo line from Embankment station to Marylebone …sounds easy right, well that was until I noticed I was being followed!

It started on the same escalator that I had my first lesson in ways to piss off London businessmen. I don't know what it was that made me turn around, maybe it was the extreme vertigo I felt by looking down the steep descent into the underground, but whatever it was it made me spot the guy. Not that it was hard given what he looked like. Of course, the empty steps around him were setting off alarm bells.

The guy was a tall black man and built like a friggin Mack truck! He wore a combat jacket with a hoodie zip up underneath and in this heat it was massive overkill for the sunny summer day. The only part of his wardrobe I would give him for the weather was the aviator shades he had hiding his eyes. His hair was thick black dreads that he wore knotted at the base of his skull and the cords in his neck bulged as he saw me staring.

I turned away from him quickly, feeling more than a little intimidated by his size and decided I needed to make my move. I counted to three in my head and sidestepped to the left to move down the remaining steps with haste. I heard the commotion behind me of a woman outraged at being roughly moved aside. This meant I didn't need to look behind me to know that the chase had begun…however I still did and yep, this guy was now in pursuit mode alright. Thankfully I had size on my side as I quickly reached the bottom and weaved in and out of people.

My heart raced in sync to the rumbling on the tracks as a carriage came into view ahead. If I could just make it before he got there, then I could lose him. It was the one time I was thankful for the squeeze of people all trying to get on and one glance behind me confirmed that his size wasn't helping him.

The doors whooshed open and people fought to get off as others tried to do the opposite. I gripped my bag strap, put my head down and forged ahead in a tiny gap that I could see as one girl went one way and a man in a suit went the other. I crammed my way through them both and arched my back around another guy with headphones just in time to step into the one space left before the doors slid home.

A sea of disappointed faces became a blur in the background of one angry black fist that pounded on the door's glass just as we began to move. With his strained face staring down at me for the mere second it took to leave, was enough to catch the flash of molten silver over his shades. They clouded with red ink that spread out over high cheekbones like poison and he snarled his frustration at me like a jungle predator.

I could only take a breath again once we were zooming along the tunnels of the underground, leaving the mad demon behind. I looked up to see my white knuckle hold on the railing and knew it wasn't just thanks to the bumpy ride. I think it took every stop to Marylebone for me to finally calm my frazzled nerves. The walk through the station to find the right platform was a fast paced trek with a continuous look over my shoulder just in case. This turned out to be a wise choice as just as I rounded a corner I saw Mr scary big dude come storming around from the escalators, luckily not yet spotting me.

He must have caught the next tube barely minutes after my own to get here this fast. I quickly made it to the line of people waiting to buy tickets and thanked my lucky knickers when a spot opened up at one of the machines. After breaking the buying ticket record I grabbed my printed ticket to High Wycombe and ran for the barriers just as he spotted me. I looked to the guy at the end of the row of machines and thought to save time by asking him which platform I needed.

It was easy to see the panic in me and I was grateful he understood my need to hurry. I was just heading for my platform when I saw my stalker was quick on my tail. However, instead of going through the motions he just threw himself over the barriers with one hand. Then unlike my approach, he simply grabbed the same guy I had spoken with and I could just make out him raise his hand to my height before I disappeared down the stairs.

I nearly wept when I saw my train was already waiting there and I got on the first carriage so that I remained out of view just in case. The train wasn't very full at this time so it made walking through to the front of the train easy. This, of course, was until I looked out of the window and saw that he was back. I quickly sank down in between the seats and when I looked up I saw I was acting crazy in front another passenger. She looked about seventeen and was wearing a Shinedown T-shirt, so I said the first thing that came to mind,

"Great band." Her eyes widened at my comment, but I didn't let her say a word before I asked,

"Could you do me a favour and tell me when that massive black dude is gone?" I nodded to the window and she turned her stunned gaze away from me.

"He…he just went past." I gave her a smile and said,

"Thanks," before I got up and walked back up the train to where I started. I kept careful watch behind me and noticed one of the rail staff outside ready to whistle the train on. I was about to choose a seat thinking I had gotten away with it, when I leant over to see my stalker was back and getting on the bloody train!

"Shit." I said before getting back to the aisle and moving to one of the doors. I opened it quickly and stepped back onto the platform just before the train was about to leave.

"It's leaving right now, honey." I smiled at the guy in uniform and said,

"Don't worry, I will catch the next one." I couldn't help but smile when I saw it pulling away just as the black guy noticed he was leaving without me. I blew him a kiss and gave him a little wave. It wasn't hard to see him take his anger out on one of the chairs and shout the word, 'Fuck'. I was still chuckling to myself twenty minutes later when I was finally on the train heading towards High Wycombe.

Well, that was another demonic escapade I had dodged… maybe I should consider writing a 'how to' book when all of this was over. Again, I laughed to myself. Once I let the humour of my situation go, I reached in my bag and decided to re-read the letter I'd received that morning.

I smiled at the name at the bottom, knowing my friend hadn't left me for long. It was from Sigurd and although a little brief, I didn't hesitate to jump to his instructions. He told me to get myself on a train to High Wycombe and meet him outside the gates of the Hellfire Caves tonight. So, I decided to get there early and case out the joint… Sigurd would most likely cringe at my corny Mobster talk but I didn't care!

So just like that I had a new plan and was off once again,

only this time I had escaped a possible threat all by myself…go me! I had looked up the Hellfire Caves website to find it was a tourist attraction and that for a small fee of 5 pounds you could go inside and check it out, which is exactly what I planned to do.

I decided whilst I had some time to kill, I might as well get in my weekly phone call to Jack, Libby and my mum. I told Jack I was following a lead (feeling the role of a secret agent with a grin) I then told my mother and sister the same thing, which regretfully was mostly lies, being that I was having fun with Jack and RJ…ok, so it was *all* lies but what could I really say? I'm having a blast getting nearly kidnapped and I just got in my exercise of the day by running from a potential killer...? Erm no, I didn't think so.

So one train journey, one taxi ride and just under two hours later, I was now stood outside the Hellfire Caves looking up at the stone archway that was the entrance of the caves. Strangely it resembled a long forgotten Gothic church, with its tall flint facade and vaulted window divided by two slender stone columns. High flint walls also arched upwards surrounding the entrance to encompass a large open courtyard. But it was the eerie red glow coming from inside the caves that was no doubt added for theatrical purposes. If you asked me though it was just plain creepy!

At least I hadn't first shown up here late at night with no one around and if I checked it out now I would be ahead of the game. Plus, seeing it for the first time at night would have probably made me pee my pants and I wasn't ashamed to admit it.

I walked past the gates warning you of private property and felt a chill rack my body enough for my steps to falter. It felt like whatever was here from histories long dead didn't want me here. But then across the courtyard was the sight of happy families just coming from the caves, with laughing children trying to spook each other. Didn't they feel it?

I made myself walk closer and noticed a couple to my right sat down enjoying ice cream on one of the picnic tables. Large umbrellas were up shading a small group eating plates of chips and one of the cave's staff members came from a door on the left carrying a tray of cakes.

The closer I got, the less sinister the whole place looked, but I still couldn't shake the disturbing feeling that had tuned into my very consciousness. I tried to focus on the happy scene in front of me but this was quickly lost as pain crashed through my head as if I had been zapped.

"ACHH!" I gripped my head and fell down to one knee as the agony overwhelmed me. My eyes slammed shut and I pulled on my hair just for something to hold on to. I kind of hoped inflicting a different kind of pain on myself would bring me home. I don't know how long I stayed this way, but when I finally braved opening my eyes what I saw was the impossible.

Twelve men in robes all stood in the courtyard with five on each side of the caves entrance, all holding a flaming torch. The two remaining men then dragged a shouting man between them who looked like he had been beaten into submission. Long hair hung down over his face as he gave up the fight, looking down onto the ground. His feet were rendered useless as the men that held him wouldn't let him use them to walk. You could see the blood dripping from the raw flesh that had been exposed due to the gravel he was roughly dragged over.

The moon was full and high in the sky directly above the courtyard, but this time it was void of all tourist embellishments. In fact, it looked as though no one even knew about this place, or if they did they knew to keep well away or suffer the same pitiful fate as this man.

"Please! Let me go…Why do this? Why? What have I done to deserve such treatment?!" The man pleaded as the blazing lit entrance came closer, looking more and more like the entrance to Hell itself! I heard the sobbing and for a moment thought it was coming from the man about to face his doom. It was only when my hand covered my mouth to prevent a scream, that I felt the tears and knew I was the one sobbing. It was slow torture being made to be a part of this and shamefully I was almost glad when they finally got him to the entrance. I couldn't bear the pain of it any longer and the hate for those men filled my mouth like the metallic taste of blood.

Then something insane happened. A booming crack of lightning hit the clear sky coming from nowhere. I screamed in my fright and turned from the sky to see them struggling to get the man inside the tunnel. He twisted his body and lashed out with his hands to grip the sides of stone in a desperate attempt at saving his life. But this wasn't the reason I cried out. The reason was that the man's face came into view thanks to the flaming torches that hung either side of the doorway. I couldn't believe it!

"Jared!" I screamed out his name just as he looked up, found my face and said loud enough to carry along the flint walls to where I stood,

"Promises Keira…I want my promise… child."

I jumped as history blew away like a weathered building under a hundred-year-old storm. In its place was the sunny present and I stood in the centre of it with everyone watching me. Normally I would feel the need to explain myself or offer an excuse, but after what I just witnessed, I just couldn't bring myself to pretend.

Seeing the strong Alpha I knew as Jared Cerberus to then the poor tortured soul of simple blacksmith Jared Weller, I felt like my own heart had been crushed. I wanted to reach into my bag and crush Paul Whitehead's heart into dust for being the cause of so much pain!

What was done to him was cruel dark murder and I felt sick knowing that these men, thinking themselves above the law, used him for hellish gain. Well, I was glad when he came back as Jared Cerberus and put an end to their sadistic club!

"Can I help you?" It took some effort to focus on the person who asked me the question thanks to my building anger.

"Sorry?"

"Can I help you with anything?" A slim attractive girl stood in front of me waiting for a response. She had short black hair and was wearing a black polo shirt with the Hellfire Caves logo over one small breast.

"Umm…sorry, I guess I'm not with it today." I said quietly, thinking what I really wanted to say was, 'more like not with it this year'… Man that vision had really shaken me up.

"I just wanted to check out the caves whilst I'm here." She gave me a small smile and said,

"Come on, I'll get you a ticket."

I stood by the entrance for what seemed like the longest time. It was like facing the door to a haunted house and knowing what you needed was inside, but you feared what you would see. I don't know how many times I convinced myself to just wait for Sigurd to show up but each time I felt as though I needed to prove something to myself. I mean, if I wasn't strong enough to walk in there on my own in the light of day, then how would I fair crossing over into Hell itself? After all, it was just a few caves…right? Well standing staring at it right now I wasn't so sure.

I don't know how many people I saw coming and going but each one was laughing or smiling as though they had just stepped off a fairground ride. What would they really be like if they had any clue to the reality of what went on down there…? What if they had seen what I had? Would there be screams of terror? Would anyone weep desperate tears like I had done? These are the questions I would never have any answers to but one thing remained…

The caves didn't want me in them.

This was something that the whole place seemed to scream out at me like a pulsating threat, almost as if the very heart in my bag had started to beat along with its dark secrets. It was only once I took that first step through its warning gates did the pressure of the unwelcome start to ease. I walked into the red glow of the past and each side was filled with plaques of information of members of the Hellfire Club.

My lip curled as I came to the man responsible, one Sir Francis Dashwood. I stared into the face that seemed so respectable, one even holding a bible. I read the words below and my fingers curled into a fist before placing my hand over his face because I just couldn't stand to see it any longer.

"You did this." I snarled the words and pushed away from

his picture like I was pushing the man himself. I ignored the words of history for the first time in my life, as I knew it would only be setting a foolish man in good light, when it should have been sticky with darkness, just like the tunnel I was about to step into.

I looked to the fake flame lights that were attached to either side of the opening and it quickly transported me back to the vision of Jared's first life ending. The way the flickering light caught the distraught note of death in his features.

The complete realisation the end was coming was written in his eyes the way one sees the storm brewing. And they flashed silver, as though the beast knew his host was near. Well now I was the one that was near and with only my knowledge as power, I looked back at the entrance one last time to see the naive world looked a million miles away…and it was…it truly was.

As soon as I started to make my way into the first tunnel the first thing I noticed was how cold it suddenly became. The gravel under my feet crunched making it impossible to hear much beyond without stopping. I was thankful at least for the low lighting that didn't plunge you into complete darkness. It wasn't that far to the first part of the cave that branched off to the left after a creepy mannequin stood in a recess that represented the steward's cave, or at least so the plaque that was on the wall told me.

Considering I didn't fancy wigging myself out any more than I already was, I didn't give it more than a glance before continuing on. The next stretch was now considerably darker than the first part and it started to decline deeper underground. The next plaque I came to caused me to hug my centre as I read the title,

'Ghosts in the Cave'

The first name was none other than 'Paul Whitehead'. Now, that was one ghost that would regret showing up around me, unless he fancied getting his pale ass kicked and getting a piece of my mind while cupping his pasty white balls! Ghost or no ghost, I just didn't care, the heartless bastard was gonna get what was coming to him!

I decided not to read on anymore but just continue on only to find the nasty bugger had his own bloody cave. Here it explained about leaving his heart to Dashwood in a marble urn that was still there behind a gated door. They had dressed some poor dummy up to mimic Paul Whitehead that stood next to the resting place of where his heart should be. I felt some sick revenge twist my gut knowing that I had that very heart in my bag right now and I wanted to mock him with the fact. My actions happened without thought as I dug in my bag and grabbed the heart in a bruising hold. In fact, I was surprised that when I lifted it out it still remained in one piece.

"Here it is Whitehead…this is all that is left of you." I whispered holding it closer to the place the man used to spend his time and the raw power I felt buzzing along my veins was one that could easily become addictive. It was only when I heard someone approaching that it pulled me from my dark game and I quickly hid it from view.

I decided to let the people pass me, so I waited before I carried on, deeper down until coming to a junction. It was lighter on the right, so I chose that way for obvious reasons. This whole part went round in a circle so I didn't think I would miss much by choosing the easier route. When both sides came together it started to decline further still and I wondered just how deep underground you were when at the end.

Another plaque I looked at in disgust, as it named off the members of the Hellfire Club in 1762. I shook my head without reading the names as at this point, I didn't think it a good idea to increase the negative vibes I was projecting already…not in a place that had them in abundance.

The next part of the cave got considerably steeper and because of this I was putting the sudden drop of temperature down to that fact. I pulled my hood over my head to keep the chill from my neck and pulled my fingerless gloves further over my hands as I took cautious steps forward. One more step and it had me feeling as if I'd just walked through a different time once more. It was as if I'd just missed a step where there weren't any and I fell forward having to catch myself on the wall before I hit the floor.

My hand slipped on the damp stone but thankfully I had already saved myself from sacking it. Although when I pushed my hair back, I saw the white chalk that now covered my palm from the light. It was only when I spun around that I realised why the light was placed there in the first place. Large Roman numerals were carved into the stone of 'XXII' which thanks to the plaque underneath told me it meant 22.

"What's this?" I whispered out loud frowning but read on.

TAKE TWENTY STEPS

'Remnants of 18th century poems referring to a secret passage in the caves'

Take twenty steps and rest awhile,
Then take a pick and find the stile,
Where once I did my love beguile,
'Twas twenty-two in Dashwood's time,
Perhaps to hide this cell divine,
Where lay my love in peace sublime.

When Churchill turned against the club in the Wikes quarrel, he wrote a poem with lines in it that seemed to give the same hint:

Under the Temple lay a cave,
Made by some guilty, coward slave,
Whose actions fear'd rebuke, a maze,
Of intricate and winding ways,
Not to be found without a clue,
One passage only known to few,
In paths direct led to a cell,
Where Fraud in secret lov'd to dwell,
With all her tools and slaves about her,

Nor fear'd lest honesty should rout her.

When I finished reading, I was in shock. It was like something the Oracle would have written. But here it was, clear white writing on a black background with the light shining against it. There was no mistaking that this was something important and following my gut, I just knew this was the very spot that would aid me in getting into Hell. Well if it wasn't, then I would go as far as saying I would eat my own foot! Ok, so I wouldn't, but you get the level of passion I felt right now. This was it…

This was the gateway to Draven.

CHAPTER THIRTY-NINE

IT'S DARK IN HELL

The rest of the cave was as expected…dark, cold and depressing for me. Maybe if I hadn't had such an intimate connection then I would have enjoyed the history that only hinted at the sordid. But as it stood, I knew exactly what had gone on here and sordid wasn't a strong enough word for it!

I thought at one point I would throw up as I made my way from the Banqueting hall to the Inner Temple. The nauseating feeling that just washed over me was like being drowned in a negative sea of emotions. You could almost taste it in the frigid air the further away from the outside world I ventured. At one part you had to cross a small bridge to get to a large room they called the Inner Temple, where they had brightly dressed mannequins drinking around a table. This actually made me laugh out loud.

Did they really believe that a man would go as far as to dig over half a mile into the countryside and some three hundred feet down just for a bit of fun? Just for a quirky place to host parties? Well, I knew the truth and it was a damn sight darker than the smiling faces of the dummies that were putting on an unconvincing show of playing normal.

The River Styx was said to be what you crossed to get into

the Temple but these days it was little more than a small pool of water, although according to the plaque by the bridge it was said to be much deeper years ago and the only way across it was by boat. Now, knowing my mythological history and what I had read up on since being thrust into the world of the supernatural, I knew what this meant.

The River Styx was what separated the real world from the Hades ruled version of the Afterlife. Although Hell in the Christian sense was only where 'Bad people' were sent, in the Underworld mythology states there are different sections. The Elysium fields for the good, the Asphodel meadows for the indifferent or ordinary, and the Tartarus for the evil. However according to Roman beliefs Avernus is for the good and Inferno for the evil.

I also found it fascinating that one story my gran had told me when I was younger was about Achilles. According to the mighty legend that was Achilles, he was supposedly dipped into the river in his childhood. It was believed that the River Styx also had miraculous powers and could make someone invulnerable and immortal, so when he was lowered into the water he gained this same power to carry on throughout his life. However, when being lowered by his mother the only part that wasn't touched by the water was his heel, by which she held him. This was the reasoning behind his one and only weak spot known of course as the Achilles' heel.

Mine, no doubt, would be named Draven.

So, more importantly, getting back to the River Styx and the reasons in which I believed it would play a part in my next mission. The ferryman Charon was believed to have transported the souls of the newly dead across this river into the Underworld. In ancient times some believed that placing a coin in the mouth of the deceased would help pay the toll for the ferry. This is why I think coins were found in the caves themselves. I think Dashwood believed that by paying the ferryman across this part in the caves was the same as paying to get into the Underworld.

There was a plaque in the Banqueting Hall to explain that one of the first visitors of the caves when they first re-opened found a lump of chalk and embedded within was a series of coins. Not only is it odd in itself to find this, but what was stranger still was that they were scratched on in Greek characters. These characters read 'Francis' and 'HHHH' on the reverse. Discoverers of the coins believed this could denote to 'Hell' in being the Banqueting Hall and the church above representing 'Heaven'. However, I had my own theory.

I believed that Dashwood had these coins made for his twelve Apostles. His 'brothers' that were the only ones allowed to cross the river and enter the inner Temple, paying the 'Ferryman' with his own coins. This thought automatically made me think of my own coin which had never left my pocket. Did that have something to do with what was coming next? Was I to use that to pay my own way into Hell?

All these questions plagued me as I spent the rest of the day sat on one of the picnic benches picking at a club sandwich. I explained to the staff that I was meeting someone but didn't know when they would show, so that after ordering my fourth cup of tea, they didn't think me as much of a weirdo. I also got up and walked up the massive hill to the Dashwood Mausoleum that stood next to the Church of St Lawrence. It was closed off from the public but was open enough to see inside and had you only imagining what must have, gone on there.

Another mystery was the strange golden ball that sat on top of the tower of the Church, which was out of place for somewhere like West Wycombe. Again, the place was conjuring up more questions than answers.

It was actually surprising how fast the day went by and soon I noticed that they were telling the few other people around that they were closing at 5:30. I picked up my plate and mug to take into the coffee shop which, I noticed, also sold a few souvenirs. I put my empties down on the counter to look at the shelves. I found mostly corny skulls, witches cauldrons and your usual magnets, oversized pencils, rubbers and leather bookmarks, all imprinted with the Hellfire Caves logo. Then I picked up the essentials.

A chocolate skull, a cake bar, and tin of toffee, a book on the caves and a wind-up torch that also had the Hellfire Caves logo on it.

"A few gifts for the family?" The same girl that had helped me earlier asked as she came from the kitchen.

"Uh…yeah, why not?" She frowned at me for my weird answer and I decided to act somewhat normal for a change.

"They have a sweet tooth...hey, I don't suppose I could get a bottle of water off you as well…? You know, for the trip home." She smiled at me as she rang my items through the till.

"Sure thing, I gather your friend didn't show in the end?" She inquired politely.

"He's more of what you would call a night owl, so I didn't hold much faith that he would." I said not completely lying.

"That's a shame he missed out." I couldn't help but let loose a nervous giggle.

"Umm yeah…I guess, but I am sure he will get another chance soon." Like in a few hours just after you guys high tail it outta here! Of course, I didn't add this, but did manage to get in another nervous giggle for good measure.

"Well, I'd better be off, but thanks for your help and have a good evening." I said and she smiled once more replying,

"Yeah, you too." I turned and muttered,

"Doubtful, where I'm going."

After hooking the plastic bag handle around my wrist, I walked outside the gates as the last person to leave then I waited. On the other side of the flint walls was a small grass verge where I sat and when I looked around it gave me a good view to see what was happening with the staff. It didn't take long, as I gathered all that needed doing was a quick walk through the caves to make sure no one was still down there, before they could start to lock up.

I saw the girl walk into what must have been a control room as the lights went off just inside the entrance. Then I saw my opportunity, as she must have heard a phone ringing because she left the gates open to go and answer it. I waited until she went out of sight and then made a mad dash for that entrance. I jumped over the ticket barrier, thinking I didn't do it with as much flair as that black dude had, as I nearly fell forward. I righted myself and ran for the darkness of the caves so that when she came back, she wouldn't see me.

After about five minutes she returned still chatting on her mobile phone, telling someone she would be home soon and did they need her to pick anything up. I was just glad she was distracted as she locked the gate and didn't look too closely, or she would have seen me hugging the damp wall like an over-enthusiastic rock climber.

"Do we have any garlic to make the sauce?" Was the last thing I heard her say before it became silent. I waited for longer than was necessary before coming to the entrance which thankfully was still light due to the summer sky. The main gates were now locked but I knew this wasn't going to be a problem for Sigurd when he finally turned up.

The letter didn't say a time but I knew it would be dark so I had some hours to kill and I was damn certain I would be spending them right here in the light, not in the creepy caves that were now pitch black. So, I plonked myself down, put my back to the wall and bit into my chocolate skull.

I didn't know what time it was but it was now dark, my mobile phone was dead and I felt a bit sick from pigging out on chocolate, cake and toffee. But in my defence, that was all that was available to me at the time, so a dinner of sugar was what I got. The water was long gone and I had powered up the torch as much as my hands could do without giving into cramp. It was one of those dynamo ones that needed to be squeezed about a gazillion times before giving off enough light to last about three minutes but it was all I had.

So, for the last hour at least I was fed, powered and ready to go…just not down there… alone and in the dark with a load of pissed off ghosts that had heard me slagging them off most of the day! But as the minutes ticked by and still no Sigurd I was getting restless. What if I needed to be down there waiting? Although, even thinking it made me laugh at how stupid it sounded. I mean, why would he want that and if so, why not write it in his letter?

No, I was safer waiting up here, where at least there was a security light that hadn't plunged me into darkness. Oh, and there was also a fullish moon that aided in lighting the courtyard. It seemed to reflect off the flint and give it a silvery glow that I had been staring at for longer than was healthy. I had already tried the control room door to find it locked up tight. Now wouldn't that have been handy.

Long ago I had read the book and to my disgust, the plaques about Dashwood and other members that plastered the entranceway. I mean, I was that bored right now I could find joy reading a takeaway menu! In fact, I was just in the process of reading how many calories were in the brownie cake bar when I heard the rumble of an engine.

I got up and dusted myself off to walk to the gate, when I saw there was more than one motorbike coming closer to the main gates. My eyes widened as reality sank in and I crouched low so that they wouldn't see me. I scrambled to the ticket barrier and used that as cover to see what was happening.

I saw one of them flip the kickstand and dismount the bike. He walked over to the gates and with a swift kick in the middle they thrashed back, admitting the rest of the bikers into the courtyard. Well, unless Sigurd was in a 'Hellraiser' biker gang he forgot to mention, I knew I was in deep shit.

I looked to the tunnel that was my only means of escape and then back at the first guy who was pulling off his helmet. I swore out ten types of screwed in my head as I saw who it was. The same black mountain of a man, who had chased me around London's underground, had now found me and from the look of the scowl etched on his face, I didn't think he had forgiven me for giving him the slip.

I had two really bad choices ahead of me and only one of them meant not getting immediately kidnapped or worse, being the furthest place from Hell I could get…which depending on how the Gods looked at letting me in at the Pearly Gates… Well, there are all the new 'break-ins' to consider! Ok, humour kept me from crying like a helpless little girl right now, but it didn't help with putting the bad decision into plan. So with that in mind, I took in a steady breath just as I heard the big dude's threatening declaration,

"If she's here, we will find her." That's when I whispered,

"Oh Hell, no." And in the words of a good old western, I got the Hell outta Dodge! I picked my timing right as they all

turned to watch a larger bike roll in, one with its rider having silver flames on his helmet before I took my shot. I stayed as low as possible while still moving and managed to grab the strap of my bag before running for the tunnel. I ran into the dark abyss, feeling along the walls for support until I was far enough away to fumble with getting the torch out of my bag.

In my panic I dropped it on the floor before I had chance to click it on. I dropped to my knees feeling the gravel floor digging in through my jeans and frantically felt around for the little plastic torch that would save my life in this Hellhole. I felt it not far from my own boot and tried to get my shaking hands to co-operate long enough to click the bloody thing on!

The small beam of light was like seeing the sunrise after a lifetime of obscurity. I spun it one way and couldn't contain the scream when I saw a dummy dressed up like a steward stood behind a caged door. I fell back into the plastered wall in shock and had to get a grip for a few wasted seconds in order to brave going further.

"It's just a dummy Keira, get a grip girl…don't freak out now." I whispered in the dark feeling slightly comforted by the sound of a voice, even if it was my own. I didn't wait around to see if the guys outside had heard me. I just lifted my bag strap over my head and gripped the torch in a death grip.

"Be brave…be brave…be brave." I repeated as I continued on and took the most frightening steps I ever had before in my life. The echoed crunch of each step beneath my feet made it impossible to tell if anyone was behind me without stopping and that was just something I wasn't willing to do. It wouldn't take them long to guess that I had braved hiding in the caves, so I needed to use what little time I had ahead of them and hide somewhere.

My little torch offered me a small amount of comfort but only enough that it stopped me from walking into any walls. Anything other than that and I was on my own. It just wasn't powerful enough to penetrate this level of darkness. I had never encountered anything so frightening before. It was almost thick enough to reach out and touch. With each foot further the harder it became to breathe at a normal rate. The temperature was so cold, I could no longer put down my shaking to just the intense fear.

The last time I remembered being this cold was when being pushed into the frozen lake by Layla and being convinced I was going to die. Well, right now I was not far from the same feeling. I didn't actually know what was still making my legs move further on, but I didn't think I was that far from crumbling to the floor and praying for this nightmare to end.

It felt like the heavy blackness that surrounded me was weighing me down and a brick wall at my back was preventing me from escaping. I felt trapped in my own fear and I needed to calm myself down if only so that my breathless panting wouldn't give away my position. I tried to take deeper breaths… in…out…in…out they came and went but no matter what I tried telling myself, my heart wouldn't cease its hammering against my chest cavity.

I had to stop for a second, I had to just try and control this dread. I leant against the wall with the flashlight shaking in front of me, so I used both hands in an attempt to gain some control. That's when I realised I was silently sobbing and the tears I left behind were like an invisible trail of bread crumbs.

"Control…breathe and control breathe Keira…darkness can't hurt you…remember back…Why are we afraid of the darkness when the light shows us more of the land of nightmares?" I let this mantra sink in and used it to ease my deep-set fear, twisting it into something else. The grip on reality started to seep back in and I convinced myself that the danger wasn't down here but back up there and it…well… it was coming for me!

So, I decided to use the darkness as a tool, a means of hiding like a friend that would shield me against the real threat. I needed to trust the shadows like I trusted that Sigurd would come. He would save me, I just knew it but until then I needed to be strong. I needed to let go of the fear.

I wiped away my tears, gritted my teeth and my breathing became that of determination. I lifted my head and with a steadier hand, aimed my way to take firmer steps into what I now considered was my escape. And so I moved. Strong and sure onwards I went until I found one of the plaques on the wall. This time when I saw another dummy I didn't freak out other than let my breathing hitch at the unexpected. This was Franklin's cave and if I remembered correctly not far from the Banqueting Hall. This was going to be my aim, as I knew exactly where I was going to hide.

As I stopped at the junction I started to hear other people in the cave and knew it wouldn't be much longer before they were upon me. I picked the right tunnel and moved as fast as I could, all the time resisting the impulse to look behind me with the flashlight. I knew that would be another way to give them my position if they were close enough behind me, so I put a lock-down on that urge. I was just coming around to where the left side would have brought me and that's when disaster struck. The light from my torch started to flicker as the power started to diminish.

"Shit!" I whispered and started to work the dynamo to gain more power but the noise it made was too loud. I knew it wasn't far now so decided to continue on quicker. The dim light flickered off mid-step making me inhale sharply. I had to pump it a few times to get it back and I shrieked out when the light lit up two figures of small children right in front of me. I only just managed to keep hold of my bladder let alone the torch!

My mind quickly started to process what it was seeing and I remembered back to earlier. This was the children's cave and the small mannequins I saw now demonstrated how some children would find their way down here to play…which sounded just plain bonkers to me.

I moved on from this disturbing display pretty quickly, hating anything creepy that included kids, but in my haste I didn't see what was in front of me. I went straight into the wall ahead and let my hand save me from knocking myself out. I looked up to see something in the wall that didn't make sense… A face? I moved back and raised the flickering torch only to freak myself out again enough to scream. Right in front of me was some weird skull shaped head that had been carved into the stone. It looked like someone had created the eerie picture by using their fingertips to gouge into wet clay. The stark white face of chalk dripped with condensation almost like it was crying for my distress. Green moss grew around the top and framed its shocked features. Why would anyone make this?

I whipped my head around as I heard once more the distant voices coming from the passages behind me and wondered how long I had. Needless to say I did this thinking whilst on the move. I aimed what little light I did have and saw straight ahead of me was an opening, so I ran. I held on to my bag to stop it beating around my body with the movement and made it into the massive open space that was the Banqueting Hall. It was the largest space in the caves and it was easy to see this was the main hosting area for Dashwood and his friends.

I didn't really care about that now, as my thoughts were more along the line of, 'I hoped I had made the right decision to hide here'. I scanned the area just as my light started to completely give out on me but at least managed to find one of the deep alcoves before it did. Soon the dark wall at my back surrounded my entire body in a black cage of terror.

I felt around the rock until I was sure of the ledge I was about to hoist myself up onto and lifted my bag over before using my puny upper body strength to lift the rest of me up. I scrambled forward until I felt the bars on the door that kept me from going any further.

"Damn it!" I said in a frustrated whisper. I wrapped my fist around the metal and gave it a shake that echoed in the empty space. I cringed at the sound and knew I couldn't get away with doing that again. It didn't help that the ceilings in this room were about thirty foot high, giving every movement a boost in sound. I shifted my weight and sat with my back to the bars, with my legs tucked up tight to my chest.

Well, this was it. I could do no more and didn't have time or the light to find another spot to hide in. I had remembered the alcoves but forgotten about the bars preventing you from getting inside them. All the men needed was a decent torch and I would be done for. Ok, so a gun was now going on my new list of must haves…because those night vision goggles would have come in pretty handy right about now!

Waiting was another form of torture. Being sat in the dead

silence with despair as my only friend was not an experience I would ever like to relive any time soon. There was nothing worse than waiting for the unknown to find you scared out of your ever loving mind and unable to fight for your life. What could I do against Demons the size of wrestlers on steroids? Well, one thing I would be doing and that was throwing this piece of shit torch at them…fingers crossed I took out an eye!

When I first saw the light coming from beyond the passageway I had to slam my hands over my mouth so as not to scream. I even had to bite down on to my bottom lip to prevent the trembling. I knew this was it and what other choices did I have…? I was out of time and luck was no longer my friend.

"In here." A voice travelled to me and I tried to stay as still as the air in this room. I focused on my breathing but it was difficult when my lungs felt like they couldn't get enough air to circulate around my body and to my pounding heart. I finally got my first glimpse of who was after me as a black figure had to almost bend double to get through the opening. I was lucky in the sense that they were only armed with the small flare of light from the lighter he held.

I didn't want to get my hopes up but I knew that thing wouldn't be giving him much to go by. As he stretched up to his full height he lifted it up closer to his face and I saw the single flame reflected in the mirrored lenses he still wore covering his eyes. My stalker walked further into the room to allow the others at his back to also enter. Three big guys spread out as each took a space in the room that was on either side of the archway.

"Give it up girl, we know you're in here." The black guy stated in a firm authoritative tone, which told me he was the one in charge. Which begged the question…who the Hell was this guy?!

"She's here, I can hear her little heart pounding…we won't hurt you girl." I wanted to shout out, 'yeah right' but decided to bite my fingers instead. I heard him release a breath through his nostrils in frustration before he started moving around the room.

"The light isn't for our benefit." He told me as he made his way around. The sound of the gravel under his booted feet danced along my tightly strung nerves until I want to shout out not to come any closer.

"It's for yours pet, so you know where we are…it's for your fear..." He stopped and the small flame let me see enough of his face to witness him sniff the air like an animal sniffing out its prey.

"…The fear I can smell and…" He licked his lips before snarling the word,

"…Taste." He then smiled, flashing a fang that grew in length from his gums and down his chin. He stopped and waited, as though trying to judge something and then when obviously coming to a decision, he did something that nearly made my heart stop beating.

"It was your choice, pet…" His grin grew and he turned his head to the lighter he held and finished his sentence,

"Now it's mine."

Then…

He blew out the light.

CHAPTER FOURTY

TWENTY TWO STEPS FOR THE BROTHERHOOD

Now with the only light long gone and four men in the room with me in their sights, my chances plummeted just as my fear skyrocketed. I could hear the crunch, crunch, crunch of each footstep getting closer and I wondered if everyone else could hear the deafening chorus of my heart beating out like death's drum.

The irrational part of my brain wanted to close my eyes tight and repeat 'there's no place like home, there's no place like home'. Thankfully though I didn't give in to the compulsion and remained as still and silent as I could.

"Be sensible now, girl." His gruff voice surprised a sharp breath from me at how close it sounded. I reached down by my side until I felt the gravel there and so, so slowly grabbed a fistful of the tiny stones as my only means of a weapon. I knew it was a wasted effort, but I just didn't have it in me not to try and fight, even if it meant my death. These bastards wouldn't take me with ease!

One, two, three more crunching sounds, the last one being the loudest so far told me where he was in the room. My hold on the stones tightened until it hurt but it was a pain I welcomed. If anything, it brought me comfort to know that these little pebbles could hurt someone.

Then suddenly he was there! I screamed out as the lighter lit his face right in front of me and if that was his way to elevate my fear, then he couldn't have been more wrong! But the one thing it did at least do was give me a target. I turned my scream of fright into one of outrage and threw my handful of small projectiles in his face, watching with satisfaction as one cracked the lens of his shades. He took a few startled steps back and I took my chance. I jumped from the ledge, leaving my bag and in exchange reaching for the zippo lighter that still had flame. Then I legged it for the opposite exit into the next set of caves.

"RAAAHHH!" The roar echoed round the walls and I almost expected them to shift with the force and come crashing down on us all. I panted out my panic and kept running with one single flame to guide my way. I soon found myself torn between my haste and the light that wasn't taking kindly to my speed. It kept threatening to go out and at one point it hit its limit. I stopped, frozen in the dark and through my shaking hands, fumbled to try and re-ignite it.

"Come on! Come… on!" I shouted at it through gritted teeth until I got it the on the third try. The tight space of the tunnel reflected with an orange glow but was only enough light to show me a foot in front of me. However, I kept running. I could hear the shouting of angry voices coming at my back but knew I couldn't stop now. All ideas of them not hurting me after what I had done were long gone.

I quickly came to a junction and didn't think about the decision as I took the right, pushing away from the rock I bumped into. It hurt but my mantra then turned away from being afraid of the dark and more towards…

"It's just bruises Keira, it's not a severed head, which is what you will get if you don't get the fuck outta here!" I no longer cared if they could hear me anymore as there was only one place I could go and one place for them to follow. My mind started to work like a damn steam engine as I thought back to today. Where else could I hide, what else did I see?

"Wait…the river!" That was it! I remembered the river that bent round out of sight. The water was shallow enough to walk through and surely they wouldn't think to look there…would they? Well, there was only one way to find out. I bumped along the tunnel, propelling myself off the sides whenever I would get too close.

"God, where is it!?" I asked frustrated with not knowing what was around the corner and desperate to see the next section that would bring me out by the Inner Temple.

I finally came to the point where both ends met and when I rounded the corner a high-pitched scream exploded out into the caves! It actually took a second to figure out it came from me as a shadowy figure came at me. A ghost looked as though it came straight from the rock wall and came charging right at me. I tried to turn and I covered my head with my arms in a protective manner out of reflex.

"O…oh…GGG…od please…" I stammered through my arms knowing soon my legs would give way and I would no longer be able to move. All the things I had seen in my life and never once had I seen what I considered to be a ghost. It just proved that the things we fear the most in life was the unknown.

"Calm." A gentle voice spoke as it neared and I screamed again when I felt it touch me.

"NO!"

"Look at me…Keira, *see me.*" I knew that voice! That rough voice that had whispered in my ear, that had told me his secrets and of his first life passed.

"Jared?" I said as I felt my arms being gently lifted off my head.

"Is it really you?" I asked in a small voice that was on the verge of hopeful tears.

"Yes, pet." On hearing his answer, even before I saw his face to confirm the fact, I threw my arms around his neck and clung to him, thinking of the impossible act of ever having to let go. I felt his hand hold the back of my head to his shoulder and then realised we were both on the floor. When did I fall…when did he catch me? He was on his knees holding me to him with one hand at my head and the other ran up and down my back as I sobbed into his jacket.

"Ssshh now pet, I have you safe." He crooned softly into my hair.

"Yyyou…you'd better not be a bloody ghost." I stammered out after letting my emotional outburst run its course. I felt the rumbling in his chest as he laughed.

"I can assure you I'm not."

"Thank God." I muttered and he laughed again.

"Although I don't think we can thank any God on that account, now come, up you get." He said gripping the top of my arms, raising me to my feet. I wobbled a bit and he held me steady until he was satisfied. This was when my situation sank in enough to be useful.

"Jared, you have to listen to me, there…there are men out there, they…well, they chased me down here and there's this one guy, a massive guy that followed me earlier today and now he has more men and…and…" My head was going back and to, through this jumbled tale, as if expecting them to jump out at us around the corner.

"Keira, stop." When I didn't look at him I felt his fingers and thumb grab my chin. With my face still turned down I saw the small flame from the lighter I must have dropped in my shock. It was just enough light to show me his serious face after he held me still for a minute, before raising my head up to look at him. His silver eyes flashed in the dim light as he assessed me and only when my breathing had calmed did he speak.

"There is no threat, Keira." I knew he spoke the truth and was about to brave asking him what he had done to them, but decided I had enough horror for one day and didn't think adding a word by word description on a mini massacre would be wise…Not unless he had a fancy for watching consuming chocolate in reverse!

When he held out his hand, I decided to trust him and gave him my hand in return. He leant down and retrieved the lighter, flicking it closed and plunging us into darkness.

"What are you…?"

"I can see well enough for the two of us, so trust me. Keep hold of my hand and put your other hand on the back of my jacket. Take slow steps and you will be fine." I did as I was told, taking the back of his jacket in a tight grip making him chuckle.

We walked a few steps and after I stumbled into the back of him a few times he huffed out his frustration.

"Let's try something else." This was the only warning I got before he turned to face me abruptly and lifted me by the waist up his front. I gasped and quickly found a hold on his shoulders to keep steady.

"Wrap your arms around my neck." I did as I was told as I dangled a foot above the floor.

"Now wrap your legs around my waist and lock your feet at my back." I coughed before saying a confused,

"Sorry… what now?"

"Just do it, pet." I bit my lip in the dark at the intimate position this new hold put us in and could feel my cheeks burn, even in the icy temperature. When I complied with his gentle command, he leant his head down, brushing my neck with his nose, inhaling deeply. Then his lips skimmed up the column of chilled skin resting just by my cheek. This was so his praise could be heard clearly, making my heart skip a beat.

"Good girl, now hold on tight, I am going to be moving fast." I did as I was told making him smile against the side of my face before he took off. Thankfully, the strong hold he had on my upper body prevented me from being too jostled when he broke out into a mad run through the pitch-black tunnels. I tucked my head by his neck as the feeling of dizziness washed over me from travelling fast in a small space, I couldn't see but only feel.

It took no time at all to make it back up the tunnels and when he stopped, I felt kind of woozy from the speed.

"You can let go now, pet." I heard what he said but for some reason it took some time for me to follow through with the suggestion. I felt him chuckle before reaching behind his back to first unlock my legs before doing the same with my hold on his neck. I was surprised he didn't actually need to pry my fingers back, I held on that tight. He held me as I slid down his length and like before didn't release me until he was certain I wasn't going to drop as the sack of jelly I felt like.

It took me a moment to figure out where we were. I couldn't help but squint at the little light that was coming from somewhere in the room and I had to blink a few times to regain focus. Although, as soon as I did this, I immediately wished I hadn't, for there, leaning against the same ledge I had hidden in, was my big scary stalker!

It took me all of about ten seconds to realise none of the men were a threat to Jared, especially the black dude who was stood casually with his arms folded over his vast chiselled chest encased in leather. I wrenched from Jared's hold and backed away from him. His eyes narrowed at the sight of my retreat and a growl rolled up from his chest.

"Keira!" He said my name in warning but I shook my head.

"You…you're…with them." It wasn't a question but I still hoped for denial as an answer. It was when I didn't get it that I made my move. I spun quickly and made a foolish dash for the way out of the Banqueting Hall. It was quickly proven to be foolish when steel bands wrapped around me from behind and pulled me flush with a solid chest against my back. I started to squirm around in hopes of getting free when his growling stopped, and it started to sound vicious.

"STOP!" He roared hurting my ears. Of course, I did as I was told. I could feel his heavy breathing as his chest heaved, making each muscle tense from his rippled abs to defined pecs that pressed into me from behind…Oh yeah, I stopped moving alright!

Once he got his temper under control, I felt his hold ease so I could at least breathe without working at it.

"Testy little thing, isn't she?" I looked to the black guy who just looked a bit bored with the whole display of disobedience. Jared just growled at him and then whipped me around to face him. His silver eyes flashed in his obvious anger and I swallowed a frightened lump at seeing it directed at me.

"Don't. Do. That. Again." Each controlled word looked ripped from a pit of fury and all I could do was nod silently.

"So, what next?" Jared's burning gaze still tried to burrow a hole in my head when the question asked finally tore his wrath away.

"Everyone out, NOW!" Jared ordered in a booming voice

that vibrated through the cavernous space of the banqueting hall. The black guy slapped his hands on his thighs and said,

"You heard him boys, fun's over when the rabbit's caught." I frowned at being referred to as furry animal on a hunt but no matter how brave I was frowning, I still sank back against Jared when he stepped closer. He grinned down at me and then leaned into me to make sure he was heard,

"Some advice for next time, girl…" He looked over his broken shades and his eyes blazed the same colour as Jared's, only his had black rings around them.

"…don't run from the beast…it excites us, ain't that right bro?" I sucked in a hiss of surprise. His brother!

"Orth don't be a dick! Now go wait outside until this shit is done." His brother laughed a deep gravelly sound that was drowned out by the slap he delivered on Jared's back, one that despite the obvious power didn't make Jared move a muscle.

His brother's stride to the exit was surprisingly stealth like considering his immense bulk. He bent to duck his head through the opening and then, as if remembering something, he turned back.

"Oh and J, you owe me a pair of fucking shades, man!" Jared's response was to flip him the bird, making them both grunt. Meanwhile, watching the brotherly banter was making me shake my head like I had just stepped into an alternative universe. As soon as he was out of sight I pushed from Jared's hold once again, only this time it was to face him, not run from him. His brother might be a dick, but I wasn't one to turn down good advice!

"He's your brother! My scary stalker dude is you brother?!" I almost screeched with the force of emotion behind that question.

"I thought that would have been obvious." I couldn't help what I blurted out,

"But he's black!" Jared thought this was hilarious and actually doubled over to rest his hands on his knees he laughed with that much power.

"Wow is he, I never noticed…Shit, just what is my mamma

gonna say?" He laughed again at his own mocking question, making me put my hands on my hips.

"Have you finished?" He laughed again and then held up one hand saying,

"Just another minute…ok…ok, I think I'm good, Sherlock."

"Ha ha, very funny… you know what I meant Jared, it's not like you guys look like twins!" I snapped losing my patience.

"That was my brother Orthrus and yes, as you so accurately discovered, he is in fact a black man." I rolled my hand around at the wrist as if to prompt him,

"And?"

"And…Keira, his host is black, didn't have a mother remember…well at least not in the sense that you would understand anyway." I shook my head as I tried to make sense of all this.

"So, you guys were brothers in…" I looked down so he would know where I meant without me saying it. He gave me a cocky smile and said

"You mean…in Hell, Keira?" Behind his hand in a dramatic whisper, that once again had me rolling my eyes as he took the piss out of me.

"And now he's here…working for you?"

"Working *with me*, pet. Now should we continue with why we're here or would you like to know our favourite colour and how we like our steak?"

"I can imagine, given your true nature, the answer to those questions is the same." I said walking past him to go back over to the ledge where I had left my bag in my attempt to run.

"What black and well-toned…but of course I mean…well done?" He said cocking an eyebrow and then motioning to his tight black leather gear that moulded to his very toned body. I couldn't help the smirk break out when my back was to him. I lifted the strap over my head and walked back up to him. I patted him on the chest and said,

"Try red and bloody, come on fatty, time to get me into Hell." He burst out laughing, after getting over the initial shock of me calling him 'fatty' as though I was the first one in his entire existence. Well, just looking at him I knew that was a true statement considering there wasn't one ounce of fat on the guy…but still, it was fun teasing him for a change.

"You're lucky I find you cute, pet" I smiled at him over my shoulder,

"Oh yeah, why's that?"

"Cause you really don't wanna know how I like my meat or…" He stalked right up to me with his eyes scanning my body as he came closer until he was right by my ear,

"…what I do with it."

Ok, so this comment left me panting for a very different reason since being down here!

It was a lot easier getting around the caves now that I had Jared with me, as all I needed to do was follow him. It was also a lot more helpful seeing as he had a lantern with him that one of the men must have brought down with them. This, as Jared had demonstrated, was for my benefit only. Well, I can't say I wasn't grateful for it as if there was one thing, I was utterly sick of and that was the darkness.

I followed Jared back up the caves until we came closer to the beginning and I couldn't say I was surprised when I saw the plaque we were now stood in front of.

"Twenty-Two." I said looking up at the Roman Numerals etched in stone.

"Twenty-Two." Jared repeated. I was about to ask what it meant when Jared passed me the lantern to hold.

"Oh, ok." I muttered before I watched him reach out and trace his fingertip along the carved 'XXII'. At this point I had to almost bite my lip so as not to ask him what he was doing. As soon as his fingertip left the last numeral line, I shuddered as a chill passed through my body like someone just blasted us with air con on full.

"Okay, so…what now?" I asked hugging myself, letting the handle from the lantern dangle from my side.

"Just wait." Right after he said this something started to happen. The poem beneath the Roman numerals started to blur and the white words started to evaporate like acid had been poured over them. It was only when the last of the poem had been destroyed that something else appeared. The whole plaque started to become weathered and old in seconds. The plastic cracked at the edges and it bubbled in places like it had been exposed to extreme heat from the rock behind.

Then the new words appeared.

Dripping red lacquer seeped from the Roman numerals and dripped down in lines that connected together to form letters.

"The blood of the innocent souls taken here will open the door to where they rest." Ok, so it wasn't red paint…no, no, of course it was blood. Always with bloody letters! What was wrong with these guys, hadn't they ever heard of a marker pen?

"Oh lovely." I said not bothering to mask my sarcasm, which prized me with a frown from Jared. He was just about to speak, when he must have caught on that something was wrong. He turned his full attention back to the plaque that had new words forming. Now, instead of reading the original poem, it had twisted parts of it into something opposite and I don't know why but Jared looked utterly pissed!

Wait twenty steps and forget the mile,
Pick up where you left off and smile,
For one long lost love is now on trial,
So taking twenty two is not your time,
Now open the cell and leave the climb,
And wait for love lay in peace and prime.

"What the fuck?!" He shouted at the plaque after using his upper body as an aggressive cage with his fists on either side on the rock.

"I'm gonna take a wild stab in the dark here and say that wasn't supposed to happen?" If I had been smart I would have taken Jared's tensed body for a cue for quiet time, but seeing as I was going to Hell tonight, I think that killed the whole smart thing for me. He snarled at the plaque and pushed away from it with such force he made two fist shaped marks in the stone… yep definitely not smart, Keira!

"Come on." He snapped moving away from the plaque in anger.

"Wait, where are we going now, can we still get in?" He seemed to be counting his steps but stopped to face me abruptly.

"Don't worry pet, I have too much riding on that promise of yours to let you leave here tonight without visiting sweet home Underworld."

"Umm…isn't it sweet home Alabama?" I asked his back as he continued. He looked over his shoulder and said,

"Not tonight, sweetheart." I couldn't help the nervous laugh that escaped on hearing him answer in a Southern American accent…I thought shamefully, it might have even done funny things to my naughty parts!

He still looked like he was concentrating on his steps and after no more than half a minute he stopped. He turned to the wall and started to feel around for something on the rock. I lifted the light at the same time saying,

"Do you want me to…?" His sharp gaze sliced to me and I was faced with glowing eyes like liquid silver.

"Guess not." I answered myself and he went right back to work…whatever that work was exactly. He looked to the other side muttering to himself in another language, one I couldn't make out. He then looked up briefly and must have decided something because he started to shrug out of his biker jacket. He passed it to me and said a short,

"Hold this."

I did as I was told and watched as he leapt straight up and grabbed hold of something on the ceiling I couldn't see, so I made the mistake of raising the lantern. I screamed for like the millionth time tonight and dropped his jacket to scrabble back at the sight of freaky skeletons hanging there with their arms crossed.

"That's an expensive jacket, pet." I looked down and without taking my eyes from the skeletons that I quickly realised weren't real, I picked back up his jacket.

"Good girl, now stand back." He said and quickly I forgot about the stupid plastic scare props in sight of beautiful muscle. Jared was hanging on a metal grating stuck to the ceiling by one arm, making the t-shirt he wore ride up, exposing the edge of a tight six pack. I swallowed hard as I also took in the bulging bicep that strained the material around the top of his arm.

The whole length was covered in an intricate pattern of some kind of tribal tattoo, the likes of which I had never seen before. It was like ink cogs in a machine joined with puzzle pieces that were forged together in swirls of some lost tribe. What little I could see in this low light was incredible and I just wanted to get him under a sunny day to trace each line gently with my fingertips. There was something about it that just pulled you in, like the pieces were actually moving.

His other arm went up and started to wrench down the creepy dummies to drop on the floor like actual dead bodies. That's when I noticed the unusual bands of metal and leather that covered his other wrist and halfway up his forearm. Combined with his roguish charm, rough good looks, tattoos and biker style, this guy was one of the most kick ass guys I had ever met...! Ok, so given he was a Hell Beast King, this wasn't a surprising revelation, but he was still a good Supernatural being to have at your back.

Another body dropped and it snapped me out of my tingly girly bits…I mean shit, I was only human and everyone can appreciate the candy wrapper without biting into the bar! And the only bar I would be biting into had a capital D on the front.

"Ah, here you are you little bastard" I heard Jared say as he pulled on something I couldn't see. He used his whole body weight as he dropped to the floor pulling what looked like wire set into the ceiling above. The force of his fall caused a chain reaction as part of the tunnel started to crumble in a small line as the wire was pulled taut. He then wrapped the excess wire around in his fist a few times before using those big muscles to yank it one last time.

I turned to see a large chunk of the rock come away revealing an older looking wall behind it. It was as if the other stuff had just been plastered on to cover what was beneath. Jared let the wire go and started pulling bigger chunks off until there was about a metre square exposed.

In the centre of the wall was another one of those skulls I had seen earlier, the one that looked to have been made by fingers gouged into wet clay. This one was slightly more realistic looking and was rougher, whereas the other one had been smooth, like chalk.

This one was a dark grey and speckled with black droplets that made me wonder what made those marks. There were also four claw marks that went down the length of the face like an animal had gone at it. I couldn't help but look at the only animal in the room and raised my eyebrow in question. He looked sideways at me and just shrugged his shoulders, not confirming my silent assumption…though not denying it either.

"You ready for this, pet?"

"Not really." I said truthfully.

"Good answer." He replied and then went ahead and opened the doorway or more like…

A Gateway to Hell.

CHAPTER FOURTY-ONE

THE SILVER LINING IN CELLS

It turned out that just opening a door to Hell wasn't as easy as just turning a handle or knocking three times. But really…living the life I did, could I just expect something easy for once? Well, it would be a nice change that's for sure, but when Jared raised a hand to his mouth, I knew that a simple secret knock was just a pipedream.

"Oww." I hissed as I saw his fangs grow before he slashed the top of all his fingertips across one of them. Blood oozed from the torn skin and he fisted his hand a few times to get more blood pumping to the surface. Without a sound of pain or even discomfort from having nearly taken off the top of his fingers, he slapped his hand over the skull that was a perfect fit in his large palm. He ran his bloody fingertips down the four claw marks and then placed two of his fingers in the eye holes.

"פתוח, אני מלך הדם הזה" ('Open, I am this blood King' in Hebrew) He spoke the foreign words perfectly and I was just about to ask what they meant when he spoke another word,

"Neshamah." This time I couldn't help but ask,

"What does that mean?" Just as I sounded the question, I flinched as the skull disappeared into the stone and the sound of rock grinding against rock filled the passageway. I took a step back when Jared's arm straightened out to his side across my torso and moved me behind him. I looked around his bulky size to see bigger pieces of wall crumbling away like wet sand. It was like when the sea destroys the sandcastle and drags it back to become part of the shore. There was no longer any hard stone but now, in its place, was an opening the size of a small man.

"It can mean many things, but Neshamah in Hebrew means mainly the call of the soul… 'The Lord God formed man of the dust of the ground, and breathed into his nostrils the breath of life; and man became a living soul'… That's a bit of Genesis 2:7 for you." He said shocking me enough to gape at him. He bent his frame to fit through the space and when I didn't automatically follow he stuck his head back around the space and said,

"You coming or what?" I shook out the part where I had just heard a Hell's beast giving me a religious sermon and cleared my throat to say,

"Uh…yeah, I'm right with ya."

"So Hebrew?" I asked as we stepped into yet another tunnel.

"Hebrew has 22 letters in its alphabet and, considering Dashwood's entrance was 22 steps away from my own entrance, I decided it was apt when choosing the right containment words, sealing it back up is much simpler though."

"Ok, so you will need to explain a few things here, 'cause my head is going a million miles." He looked at me over his shoulder and said,

"Shocking," in a sarcastic tone.

"Oh come on, give me a break, I find all this fascinating."

"You need a hobby, pet."

"Yeah, so I have been told but you know, in between solving cryptic messages, trying not to be taken hostage, visiting freaky ass fight clubs, finding deadhouses, and being chased around in some bloody caves all night, in the hopes of getting into Hell to save my boyfriend, has kind of not given me much time for water sports, so if you don't mind just answering some of my question that would be swell." I added after counting all these points off on my fingers and not pausing to take a breath.

"Tell me all that was in a lifetime?"

"Uh…Try a few weeks, now is it so much to ask to appease my curiosity?"

"Jesus, you really are dangerous to be around." I gave him my 'ha, ha, so funny' fake smile, when he stopped to face me.

"Fine, here's how the story goes, Dashwood and his jumped up rich boy clan was made up of…

"The 12 apostles, I know."

"You know?" He said clearly shocked.

"Yeah, I mean…well, there's dummies and a plaque and everything."

"Dummies?" Now he looked very confused.

"Near the Inner Temple is the plaque explaining about Dashwood's apostles and dummies dressed up having a jolly old time in the Temple…and I gather from your face this is new to you?"

"Uh yeah, I don't exactly come back here for a vacation spot or just for shits and giggles…I hate this fucking place for a reason." I exhaled a large sigh, 'cause let's face it, what do you say to that?!

"Shit, they really have all that stuff as public knowledge?" I nodded but then added,

"They kind of put a softer spin on the 'Devil worshipping club' but yeah, it's all there, although I very much doubt all they did in the Temple was get dressed up, get rip roaring drunk and discover what was under a girl's skirt."

"Yeah, no shit." We kept on walking when I decided to remind him that he hadn't actually finished what he was going to say, so naturally I helped him out by say,

"Sooo…Dashwood's jumped up rich boy clan…?"

"The entrance we came through was different back in Dashwood's time. It was masked by a fake stone wall where, if you knew where to look, an open doorway could easily be found behind. When I first came back to this world I found my own exit from a cell they kept me in, only now it seems powers above my own have taken back control of it." He looked less than happy about that and even in the lantern's low light, I could still see his eyebrows knitted together in an angry scowl.

"Why is that do you think?"

"I don't know, but I can guarantee you one thing, pet…I won't stop until I find out." Given the determination in his voice I had little doubt in that promise.

"So, you didn't know what the poem meant?" He gave me a look that made me feel like I was acting like a dog with a bone. I couldn't say I blamed him.

"That would be a firm no, now end of conversation."

"But…" He whipped his head around and all he had to do was give me that warning look, shake his head and silently mouth the word 'NO' at me. I finally got the hint.

We walked in silence around all the twisted tunnels that, if believable, were a lot creepier than the original caves. This I put down to two things. The first being not only the lack of life but the lack of any evidence there ever was any. At least in the other caves there was always something to remind you that you lived in the modern world. Wires, light fittings, maps, plaques and even exit signs could be seen, but in here…there was nothing but cold hard stone.

Although I guess that wasn't strictly true, which brought on my second point. There definitely wasn't any lack of pain and suffering down here. That same cold hard stone was scarred with evidence that whatever went on down here couldn't be further from a tourist attraction. Claw marks ran metres in length at different angles and old dark spots of something I didn't want to think about were sprayed in various areas.

"You?" I asked in a small voice that didn't have one ounce of humour. He saw me looking at the marks and just before I reached out to trace one of the deeper claw marks, he snatched my hand, pulling it away.

"Let's just say you wouldn't want to see me angry." This was his only explanation as he pulled me further down into the unknown.

After we had turned this way and that, right and left into so many junctions, I knew that without a map to this place it would have been near impossible to find your way out. I didn't know how Jared knew it so well, and could only assume he had spent way too much time down here to know it from memory the way he did. This thought brought on a fresh wave of anger at what he had been through.

Instead of voicing my opinions, I followed silently as Jared navigated us around what looked like a stone version of a garden maze and the movie 'Labyrinth' came to mind.

"I swear if David Bowie pops out now singing about babes with power, I am so outta here." I said needing to break the tension of being in such a horrible place. Jared stopped dead but didn't turn around to face me. I was about to ask but he just shook his head and grunted his amusement rather than laughed.

"You are nuts, anyone ever tell you that?" I let a cheeky smile form.

"I'm nuts?"

"That's what I'm saying." This time I grunted.

"Yeah well, I'm not the one with a freak show circus for a fight club." This time he did laugh.

"What can I say, the revenue in breaking Demon flesh is good" I rolled my eyes and muttered,

"And you think I'm nuts."

We went round yet another corner just before the banter could continue, because soon I was faced with something that looked like it belonged in the Tower of London! A large open dome that looked to be the same size as the banqueting hall was the space we walked into now but with a very distinct difference. Whereas the banqueting hall had little alcoves, which according to the plaques, had been where lustful men could enjoy a masked woman of their choosing this had something more horrific!

The sight of all those tall, iron bars turned this large cave into a makeshift prison, using the bare rock as an impenetrable means of escape. On the walls that there weren't doors of rusted iron, there were things that were considered far worse than a cell. Hanging manacles dangled from chains, some with strained links no doubt from years of abusive use. There were also metal contraptions that hung on hooks as if waiting to be taken down once again for their only means in torture. These looked like they were meant to hold a person in a contorted ball or others in the reverse. Large iron holes for a head bent forward and then in the opposite direction, smaller holes at the end of iron branches that came out to hold the limbs behind their back.

It looked sick!

I made sure when walking to keep in the middle and after being silent for so long I think Jared must have wondered what was wrong with me. He looked behind him and with one look at my face, his eyes softened with what I gathered was sympathy.

"Come here, little pet." He held his hand out for me to take and I practically ran to him, needing his comfort right now. As soon as his fingers could curl around mine he yanked me to him, making me fall into his embrace.

"I didn't think… I'm sorry, pet." Confused at his words I pulled back as much as he would allow and looked up at him with wide eyes.

"About what?"

"This…" He spread his arms out to motion to the room before continuing,

"…all of it, everything you see is nothing to me. It never was…not where I come from, but looking in your eyes, the portal and viewing glass into your very soul and seeing there just how pure that soul really is…well, that is not a thing that even one such as I would want to see tarnished by the pain and suffering that went on in this room or what truly lies waiting for you." He turned his head to one of the largest cell doors that was partially hidden.

"Jared, look at me." When he did I couldn't help but raise my hand to his cheek, feeling the heat there even through the material of my glove.

"I passed Go and continued playing the game a long time ago when I could have just called it quits…I didn't. I stayed and even through all the horrors of your world, I still knew I had made the right choice. I don't know what exactly happened to Jared Weller to turn him from the world, but I think I get the impression you know what it's like to deal with loss and for loss to hold the power it does, you also have to have known love." At this he closed his eyes as if my words were actually causing his heart to hurt and he was working through the pain. I swallowed down my sadness for his discomfort and whispered words of love in this dreadful place,

"That's why I think you also know that what I do now is something I must and given the chance…something you yourself would do too, to stay in the game, because I promise you this Jared, the only thing that will get me off that board is going to be nothing short of death!" I vowed this with so much passion I felt a few tears fall, sealing that promise with raw emotion. He opened his eyes, flashed me his own silver emotion and nodded his head once.

"Then all I can do is keep you safe in the game, the best I can." I smiled up at him and said,

"That would be appreciated."

"Then in that case, let me show you the evidence of something happy that did happen in this shithole." At this I crinkled my nose, thinking that that surely would be impossible, and I told him as much,

"Happy? What could possibly have been happy down here?"

"My escape." He said giving me an evil smirk and I could have sworn I saw his pupils elongate, turning briefly into thin slits from that of an animal. Then he winked at me, grabbed my hand and led me to the last cell hidden in the dark.

The rusted door to this one looked to be double the size of the others. It had a massive contraption that looked to be the lock and the closer I got, the thicker the bars looked. I couldn't help but look at Jared and then stupidly wonder what he looked like in beast form. However, the sound of Jared effortlessly kicking the door open and busting the lock like it had been made of tinfoil, made me shudder those thoughts away. I quickly decided I had no great urge to witness Jared as a beast, considering the man himself was scary enough!

He held the dented door back and said gallantly,

"After you, pet" I bit my lip and walked into Jared Cerberus' first home in this human plane. Although, judging by the massive hole in the wall that a raging bull could fit through, I would say it wasn't his home for long!

"Ah yes, it didn't take me long to realise I preferred something a little more upmarket…more space, maybe somewhere with a view, oh and let's not forget more than a dirt hole to shit in." He said laughing at the disgusted face I pulled. I knew why he joked about this and it was for my benefit only. He was putting a cloak of humour over a disturbing part of history so that I wouldn't see the true horror of what lay beneath.

I looked from the crumbling mess that looked as if an engine powered piece of construction machinery had just ploughed through…or maybe a small tank would be a better description for the destruction left. Whichever fit better was irrelevant as I started to really take in the rest of the space. It was dark, damp and cold stone that looked like any other cave you could imagine…that was apart from one major difference.

"What is this?" I asked referring to all the symbols that decorated every available space on both the stone and the tiny marks that looked scorched into the thick bars of the door.

"Ah, well after Dashwood had these cells built and started to move onto the more serious side of Devil worship, he began by looking to history for some answers. Most of which were utter horse shit, just like these useless symbols that he thought could keep a demon contained." I silently took in each different symbol before asking,

"How?"

"He heard of a story back in the 1760's that in the French village of Gevaudan the people there were trying to deal with villagers being savagely attacked by some kind of animal. It was actually where fucking Werewolves came about, all thanks to some big ass rabid dog that went on a rampage attacking folk." He said sounding half pissed and half amused.

"So it wasn't anything like that?"

"Oh honey, there was no one like me before this shit happened." He yet again gave me another wink as he boasted and I couldn't help but smile even through my rolling eyes.

"But the poor mutt was said to be hurt by silver and so that stupid ass myth was born, hence those symbols that are Alchemical symbols for the metal" He nodded to where my hand was touching one that looked like two triangles attached. There were about 12 in total and ranged from moon shapes to tridents, duel cups and smaller circles attached to a larger one. I even snorted a laugh at the one that looked like a horned stick figure stood on top of a hill.

"So, they didn't work?" I looked back to the wall and saw the painted symbols on some of the fallen lumps of stone, so knew my answer before he said it.

"You wouldn't be asking me that if you saw what it means to be a Cerberus."

"I can imagine you're right about that."

"Of course, they weren't expecting me to show up." He said cracking his knuckles in a manly show of dominance he had every right to.

"So what were they expecting?"

"Truthfully?" I nodded at him and he shrugged his shoulders before saying,

"Fuck knows…a handshake with the Devil, a pat on the back by one of his Presidents…who really knows but the dead, but one thing I will say, given the cells, the useless symbols and abducting poor bastards like me, my guess is he simply wanted to sacrifice a human in order to give a demon a host he could use…maybe even control…whatever it was though died with my rebirth, as did the club."

"Well, I can't say I am sorry about that." I said leaving the destruction alone and walking over to where he stood. I hoped this was enough of a hint for us to get going. He raised an eyebrow before whispering a cocky,

"What's wrong pet, had enough of me already...? Are we that eager to jump to a hotter playing field?" My answer was to shrug my own shoulders at him, knowing that I had no great urge to see Hell up close and personal but was still buzzing at the prospect of seeing Draven again.

"Then give me your heart, pet." At this request the organ in question started to beat a lot quicker. He must have noted my reaction because he started laughing at me.

"Don't panic sugar, I don't mean it in the literal sense or that I want any declarations of love, just the heart you have in your bag." I bit my lip as a blush rose with his gentle teasing.

"But I…I thought you couldn't touch it?" This time he

grabbed my shoulders and guided me over to a darker corner where something lumpy sat under a dirty cover. He turned me and walked me closer to it and I screamed bloody murder when he suddenly grabbed the cover and yanked it hard enough to come off in one whoosh.

"You jerk!" I shouted moving back with nowhere to go but closer into his hold.

"Calm down pet, I think you can see he won't hurt anyone." I was seething mad with the man at my back for forcing me to see the only other one in the room with us.

"He's…he's…"

"I can assure you Keira, he's quite dead." He referred, of course, to the heavily decomposed corpse that sat in the corner on a low wooden stool as if he just needed a rest. Well, he was most certainly getting a good rest alright, nothing more relaxing than death!

The skeleton figure sat there patiently, still dressed in his 18th century finery, with a long jacket embellished with buttons down the length and large cuffs. Even his embroidered thigh length waistcoat and knee-high boots could be seen under years of filth. But more than any of this, I had to say the main feature had to be the ripped open chest cavity, where even the rib bones had been broken back like the lid to an old toolbox.

"I just thought that it would be better done swiftly…what is it they say, rip the band aid quickly for less pain."

"Plaster…so why is Captain McRib down here anyway?" Jared burst out laughing at my nickname for him and then sobered enough to ask,

"Plaster?"

"Band aid…It's called a plaster where I'm from, so answer the question, who is he?"

"That handsome fellow is none other than Paul Whitehead of course. Now all you need to do to make him dance is give him back his heart and it will open the gateway." This time I dropped the smart-ass comments and snapped round to say,

"Oh, sod that for a bag of chips! There is not a cat in Hell's chance I am going anywhere near Mr chatty pants over there!"

Ok, so I didn't exactly drop all of the smart-ass comments but I couldn't have been more serious with them!

"Assuming I understood you in all that northern charm, if you don't, then I am afraid the tour is over and there will be no more passing Go and collecting 200 for you, so…" He leant down, as most supernatural men had to do around me and whispered,

"…Game over."

"Ok, Fine! I get it…jeez you want me to do gross stuff but I swear I am drawing the line if you ask me to give him a makeover!" I said stomping my foot in frustration. He again just laughed at me. I decided not to bite and fuel his humour anymore but just get on with it. I did the easy bit first, considering I had begun to get to know Mr Whitehead's heart on a sharing shower basis. I reached in my bag and grabbed my new friend.

Then came the hard part.

I walked closer to what used to be the living, breathing and breaking the law, Paul Whitehead and couldn't help but take pause before getting too close.

"I must say, as amusing as this is, I would ask for you to get on with it before time catches up with you and you end up looking like his sister." I shot Jared daggers making his grin grow a notch. I refrained from the comeback I really wanted to say and opted for a grumbled swear word. Then I got back to the gruesome task at hand…or should I say at heart?

I held the wrapped package in one shaky hand and closed my eyes as I stepped closer to my target. I couldn't tell you how happy I was at least, that he was that far decomposed so as not to have any rotting fleshy bits or the smell that goes with death. Thinking along these lines gave me another new mantra and I started to whisper,

"Just a large stick man…it's just sticks, not bone, just sticks…"

"Keira!" Jared said my name like he was losing patience and I snapped out,

"I'm doing it, alright!" Then I used my anger and frustration to open my eyes and ram it home with one strong thrust.

Then I jumped back like a little girl, jumping up and down like trying to get rid of a spider.

"Eww! Eww, eeewwww!" I shook my head, pulled a face like I just licked in between cheesy toes and continued to jump up and down in a circle like this would somehow drive out the last two minutes of my memory!

"Good girl, now if you could just control the girly shit, then that would be nice." I decided to take a page out of his brother's book and flip him my middle finger as my reply. This was quickly ignored by both of us when stick man Paul Whitehead started to move! I screeched out an unattractive sound and hid behind Jared's back to watch.

The once very still corpse now raised his head as a series of shudders started to vibrate his old bones, starting from his chest. It was like his heart had actually started to beat again after all this time. Then in a blink, his arm shot out, causing me to yelp at Jared's back when Whitehead's bony hand slapped the rock behind him. I raised the lantern Jared had given me back to hold and watched in morbid fascination as I made out the blood that oozed from the organ and started to wrap around his bones like a red ribbon. It only went one way and travelled along his arm, leaving the rest of his body untouched.

Then Paul Whitehead's fingers, complete with long fingernails, tightened on the stone, causing his nails to clash with it. The lantern in my hold started to shake as I saw what he was doing and noticed, just as the blood reached the tips of his fingers, he drew his nails down the grooves left there by Jared's claws. Blood reached the thin crevices and filled the gaps in the rock like little dried riverbeds flooding for the first time in years.

"Shit!" I shouted as the whole cave started to shake. I dropped the lantern and held on to Jared's back with both hands, grabbing fistfuls of leather. I was about to shout over the noise, but then all senses became transfixed as moisture started to bead on the walls like condensation from an intense change of temperature. Heavy droplets fell just from one space above, like heavy rain that was concentrated just by the wall. Soon it formed a puddle and then started to boil.

"Wh…what's hap…?" I never got to finish the question as

the rumbling increased and Jared started to take steps back, pushing me along with him. I didn't know how the cave was still standing and thought for sure any minute we would be buried under an entire hill full of rock!

I managed to keep my gaze riveted to the spot where everything seemed to be happening, when a piece of the wall came away. It was about the size of a few bricks and an intense orange glow could be seen shining behind it. It looked like sunrise and as if attracted like a bug to light, I started to step around Jared to get closer. He turned quickly and held me still and to his chest.

"You don't want to do that just yet." And just as he promised, the orange glow showed its true form, as burning hot lava started to flow over the small gap.

"Oh God!" It started to spew out in a more powerful gush and in doing so, broke away more of the rock until it resembled a glowing molten waterfall. It hit the puddle with a hiss as steam automatically rose before it evaporated the water. Once it hit the cave's floor, it started to turn into a wave of smooth black rock that built up in layers as more lava fell. I didn't know what we were still doing here as surely it would soon consume the cell's space and us along with it.

"Do you trust me, Keira?" Jared asked in the calmest voice and my panicked gaze told him I didn't know if I could. He turned his head to look briefly at its progress before turning back to me and on a shocked breath he lifted me into his arms. Then he turned and for a relieved second I thought he was getting us out of there, but this turned out to be the opposite. He started to stride straight for the pouring lava and for once, I was too stunned to scream.

Then something amazing started to happen. The closer he got to the floor's flowing lava the quicker it turned into ageing grey dust and started to float away as though it never should have been there. By this time the scorching waterfall was now the size of a door, having melted the remaining rock away.

I gripped onto his shoulders and started making little panicked noises by the side of his face. His hold told me he wouldn't be letting me go any time soon and coupled with what we faced, I wasn't sure if this was a good thing or bad! One step, two steps and I hoped not our last step breathing as we approached the opening. Then, as if by a sensor, the lava started to part at the top and began to only to flow at the sides, still making the space large enough to fit through.

Then came our very last step as we walked through the overflowing magma, straight into another world…

Jared's Underworld.

CHAPTER FOURTY-TWO

SAY HI TO THE DEVIL WHEN YOU GET THERE

"You have got to be kiddin me!" I uttered after minutes of stunned silence with my mouth hanging open in unattractive shock.

"Not what you expected?" I turned to look at him and he laughed at the dumbfounded way I shook my head.

"Then enjoy it for the time you have here." He said and I happily did as he suggested. After the fiery entrance getting here I would have thought the theme continued, but I couldn't have been more wrong if I had tried.

We had walked straight from inside the mountain at our backs and onto sun bleached decking that ran on for miles in each direction. Then surrounding every square inch of us was nothing else but water like an enormous lake, rather than the raging river I would have expected. The water was so deathly still it didn't even lap against the mountain we stood next to.

The decked walkway was constructed above the water next to the rock, with stilted poles running along in intervals, until they went out of sight on either side. I then faced forward and saw a long dock that reached out over the pearlescent water as though it floated, so as not to disturb its harmony.

It was one of the most tranquil sights I had ever seen and I instantly felt a sense of peace flow over my soul, inducing a warm calm of the likes I had never felt before. It seemed to somehow reflect back from the turquoise surface, like a gentle blanket of morning mist rising up, giving it an ethereal feel.

"What is this place?"

"Keira, you don't have to whisper." He said smiling.

"I feel like I have to, this place…it's…it's so…"

"Serene?" He added helping me.

"Flat." He laughed out loud at my description.

"Well it is, I mean just look at that water, it doesn't even move…what type of water doesn't move?"

"The type that has no weather to guide it." I looked up to the sky after he said this and took in the infinite space of white. There were no fluffy clouds, no blinding sun, and no vast ocean of blue…just… still… white.

"I don't understand this place." I said looking back to Jared, who gave me a sympathetic look.

"The easiest way to understand it is if you think of it as a waiting room at a train station. There is a ticket office you walk up to but only they know your destination. They give you the right platform and you get on the train waiting there, after that…well…only the life you've lived determines that."

"And if you don't believe in any of this?" I asked looking back out on to the still topaz water.

"Then my guess is that none of this happens."

"Your guess?" His answer surprised me enough to ask.

"Keira, try to understand, this is all I know…I am a part of this world just as much as you are, so it matters not what we believe because we are already a part of its very makeup, it's DNA, both of us, we are not solely of your world." I frowned at his explanation.

"I'm human, Jared."

"As was I, but I always had something else inside me, a light or darkness that called out to this place, to one of its masters… why do you think you were chosen… Electus." I cringed at hearing the name I had first heard come from Draven's lips. Ever since the day that Draven no longer was of this life, I had come to hate it! Hearing it again felt like being struck with a backhander across the face and from the looks of Jared, he saw it there.

"Keira." He said softly and I turned from him as he reached out to cup my cheek.

"Don't!" I warned stepping away, putting some distance between us.

"Believe it or not pet, I had difficulties coming to terms with what hand my fate dealt me, but unlike you I had those choices taken from me…both times." When he said this last bit in an emotional whisper I turned back to him.

"Both?"

"That love you spoke of, the reasons that brought you here… that part of my history was also out of my control and no matter the amount of power gained that night, it could never bring me back what I lost." I let the bitter attitude I felt evaporate on hearing his pain. It was amazing to look at this creature of Hell, locked in the body of once a simple man, and see the common ground we walked on. To realise how similar we were was strangely heart-warming to me and I couldn't help my reactions to it. I threw my body into his and hugged him until it took my breath away.

Silent minutes passed us by, but no words were needed in our own private moment. And even stood on the edge of this hellish quest, it was one of the most beautiful moments I had ever known and for that, I couldn't have been more thankful. Not only for his friendship but for his complete understanding. It turned out to be all I needed to see me ready for this upcoming trial I had facing me.

"Thank you, my friend." I whispered into his chest and I felt the gentle kiss placed on my hair at the top of my head. We both released each other, and I sighed, knowing that my time was up. His look told me his understanding of the same thing.

"So…do I have to give this ferryman a call like I would a taxi or what?" This got me another handsome smile framed by that trimmed black wiry beard of his. Even the scar along his face didn't seem that frightening to me anymore.

"That won't be necessary." He said tapping me under the chin and then taking my hand to lead me.

"Come on, I'll show you." He started to take me down the dock which didn't even creak once at our combined heavy weight. This was something else I noticed, as other than Jared and myself, not one sound was heard coming from this place. In such an open space like this that was beyond eerie.

Once we got to the end of the dock and I looked out over the water, the colour changed as the mist got thicker and it suddenly became harder to see where the water ended and the sky began. After a few moments of Jared not giving anything away, I was about to speak, when I saw a shadow in the distance getting closer. This had to be the ferryman and suddenly it dawned on me what I was really about to do.

The closer the small boat got, the more the fog lifted and soon all of the water was shining bright and vibrant as if the sun had just popped back up. I looked up, almost convinced I would see it there but there was nothing but vast empty white space.

"Any last words of wisdom?" I asked watching the boat getting bigger.

"Here, take this." I looked down to see a coin in his hand with a three headed dog engraved in the silver.

"Why?"

"Because it will let the ferryman know where to take you. There's a friend of mine who might be able to help you find what you are looking for, or at the very least will be able to give you some answers…here, take it." He tried to pass it to me but I shook my head and reached into my jeans pocket. His eyes widened in surprise when he saw what I held in my hand.

"That's alright, I have my own." After the initial shock his eyes turned hard and he scowled down at my hand as if what I held was a blasphemy.

"Keira, where did you get this?" His voice was serious and hard, making me shiver. When I didn't answer he growled out my name in warning making me take a step backwards. He grabbed my forearm to both stop me from going too close to the edge and so he could lift up my hand to examine the coin.

"Fuck! Keira, you can't use this!" The sound of his fresh anger was startling and for a moment I couldn't react until he tried to take the coin from me. I closed my fist as tight as it would go without causing pain and wrenched my arm from his grasp.

"Why not?!" I shouted back.

"Because I know where and to whom it will take you and trust me when I say you do not want to go there. Now Keira…" He said in warning that was ringing in my head like an alarm I had no choice but to ignore. I took another step back as he made to reach out for my arm again.

"Stay back! Jared you know why I have to do this, I have no choice…I was given this coin for a reason!" His furious gaze turned into one of soulful worry.

"Look pet, I don't know who gave you that coin but it is dangerous…that place, Christ even I wouldn't want to go there! That level of Hell is not for you to see, let alone go and spend time there! Please honey, please…now just listen…" I bit my lip as I felt frightened tears rise, but I had to remain strong. So I silently shook my head at him and prayed for him to stop scaring me.

"I'm sorry, Jared." I said in an emotional whisper and turned away just as the boat was nearing the end of the dock. When I didn't hear anything but heavy breathing from behind me, I thought he had given up. Then I was roughly spun round and in an attempt to save the coin as he reached for it, a soundless 'No' was my only reaction when the coin flew from my grasp. I watched in slow motion as my only chance gathered more distance from my outstretched hand. In that precious moment time stood still and I couldn't breathe. How could I have come this far only to fail now?

How?

Just before my reaction to losing the coin could settle in my gut like poison, a hand flashed out of nowhere and plucked the coin from the air before it could fall into the water.

"Well now, wasn't that lucky." A chirpy voice said. I looked to the bearer of the voice and what I saw made me do a double take. A guy, who couldn't have been much older than me, was stood at the end of a thin boat, dressed in a striped black and white sweater, with a pair of black board shorts and to top off my shock, a boater hat worn to the side. I didn't know what I expected but whatever it was, then this guy was the furthest from it by a long shot!

"Keira, don't." Jared was close to pleading and his pained expression nearly undid me. I looked back to the ferryman who had started whistling a happy tune, whilst flipping my coin in between his fingers at a blurring speed. He looked like someone who was trying not to be a part of this uncomfortable position by pretending it wasn't happening. He caught me looking and said,

"Hey kids, don't mind me, you guys look like you're heavy into something." I was utterly speechless at hearing this guy talk, he was just so…well, so…normal! Jared growled low and my head shot back to him to see he was giving the ferryman a fierce scowl that looked like he wanted to rip out this guy's jugular.

"You're really not gonna listen to me?" I didn't know what to say so instead I just shook my head, giving him a sad look. His features turned to granite as he nodded once, taking my answer as absolute. Then he flipped his own coin at the ferryman and without looking the guy caught it.

"That's for the return trip. Make fucking sure she has her ass back on that boat or you have my permission to put her ass down on that boat by any means…understood?" He gave Jared a salute and quite possibly the cheekiest smile I had ever seen. He then took a step onto the dock and used one of the posts at the end to pull his boat closer, which I now recognised as a fancy black gondola. He held out his hand for me to take and just as I was about to, Jared snarled and grabbed me, spinning me so quickly it took me a minute to process what was happening. But before I could, Jared crashed his lips to mine and kissed me so quick it left me blindsided.

"If you don't come back, so help me pet, I will tan that hide when I find you!" My eyes opened wide at both the kiss and the threat, but before I could say a word Jared handed me over to the happy boatman. I was promptly sat down on one of the comfy black leather seats as I was spun underarm like a bewildered dance partner and received a wink, at the same time he tipped his hat and ran his fingers along the rim.

"And Charon…" The intimidating voice of Jared turned both our heads.

"In one piece, you got me?!" The dangerous smile he gave Jared gave me chills but in a typical happy go lucky manner, he replied,

"Not gonna be a problem Cerberus man, there are others where she is going that want the very same thing." I didn't understand this secret exchange going on between these two but I didn't miss Jared's response.

"That's what I am afraid of." Then before explaining it more he turned his back the same time the Ferryman pushed us from the side. I felt a pinch in my heart as I saw Jared walk away from me and I couldn't help wonder two things…was I doing the right thing and the other…?

What was that kiss all about?

"That's some pretty hard thinking you got going on, does it hurt?" I didn't realise I had my eyes shut tight as my thoughts were running riot. I opened them to see a friendly face tilted to the side smiling at me.

"Sorry, it's just been one of those days, you know." I said thinking about the new level of strange my life had jumped to.

"Oh, I know all about those days in this place, but the question is, what is a nice girl like you doing in a place like this? You don't look too dead to me…just saying." He said whilst picking up a long black pole from the water side of the boat.

"Umm…thanks."

"You're… umm… welcome." He winked again. I couldn't help but stare and smile at his unexpected teasing.

"Do I have something in my teeth?" He asked, rubbing his tongue over them to see for himself. I shook my head and offered an explanation for my rude gawking.

"Sorry to stare and all, but you're not exactly what I expected."

"What, roguishly handsome, a fine specimen of a being maybe, or just such a dashing representative of this very Underworld?" He asked grinning wide. I laughed, relaxing back into the seat. He was certainly a lively character for such a morbid job and he was cute. He reminded me of one of those guys who never wanted to grow up and loved life to its fullest. Whether that could be said for someone that did what he did I couldn't say but he fit the type. The ones who like to party hard, play harder and didn't give two shits what anyone thought about their life's philosophy and who could really blame them if they were happy.

But then there was this guy who had that same easy going nature all those things embodied that just oozed from him. It was in his messy brown hairstyle trying to be contained under his bent hat, his growing bushy beard that wasn't as neat as Jared's, but somehow still suited him. His eyes were soft and smiley with a hint of mischief ready to pounce out at the next opportunity. And then, there was his smile that made his eyes light up from somewhere deep and the lines there that said he did it often.

Oh yes, this guy made me relax alright, if anything he made me want to laugh out loud just for the fun of it. Definitely opposite to what he did in this place. It felt wrong for someone with so much life and soul to deal with so much death. Or was that the reason for it? To bring ease to those who had passed? That would make more sense than say, someone who looked like death.

"Hey, what's that?" I pointed to what now came into view. With the mist completely lifted it now gave me a clear sight of all the other docks that stuck out of the endless decked walkway. I couldn't even count them all there was so many. I could see other figures, tiny from as far out as we had quickly become.

"Oh them, don't worry they won't have to wait long." I frowned at what he could mean. Then I realised we weren't the only boat on the water.

"Oh God…they're dead and they're waiting to be picked up aren't they?" I asked quickly losing that relaxed state of mind his presence had put me in.

"As great as I am, I am still only one being, my pretty obol giver."

"Obol?" He gave me that cheeky grin of his again and replied,

"It means coin."

"Oh…and those…" I cleared my throat not knowing what to call all those unfortunate souls that, unlike me, would not be making the return journey.

"Those… well now, only their Charon will know the destination, once he has touched their soul."

"But wait, you didn't touch mine and I thought your name was Charon?" At this he burst out laughing and pushed the boat along after bending over to give a full belly laugh.

"Questions, questions, it's one of the things I do love about my job and usually this is the point where I become all serious and say in a masterful tone, 'Thou shall know when the Gods see fit". He said this last part in a booming Godly voice that made me jump and rocked the boat.

"And see, isn't it great! I get that same reaction every time! But for you I will answer your questions, as I doubt you will be coming back here for a while." He continued to push us along and I could see even more of the never-ending line of docks, to a point where I had to hold myself to stop from shaking. I mean I knew I was not naive to the ways of the world, for there must be death to grant life, I knew of the balance but to see it here, in front of my very eyes was…

Heart-breaking.

"Answer one, I did not need to touch you to read your soul as you had one of these." He said flashing the coin around in between his knuckles once again until it disappeared.

"And number two, there are many Charons, in fact as many that are needed…I am simply a small means to a larger end… but what a means! Don't you think?" He said wagging his eyebrows at me.

"Well, I for one definitely think you're a nice surprise." On hearing my comment he took off his hat and bowed, making a big floppy mess of loose curls escape. Then he pushed it all back with one hand and replaced his hat.

"Would you like to hear something once written about us?" I nodded making him beam at me.

"There Charon stands, who rules the dreary coast -
A sordid God: down from his hairy chin

A length of beard descends, uncombed, unclean;
His eyes, like hollow furnaces on fire;
A girdle, foul with grease, binds his obscene attire"

Once he finished, I pulled a distasteful face at him and said,

"That's wasn't very flattering for you or very accurate." At this his excitement grew, making him shout out,

"I know, right! The only thing I can think of is that he must have got one of us on a bad day." I burst out laughing at the thought.

As the journey continued onward I let my mind wander to all that had happened and what was still happening. Jared's face still haunted me when he saw my coin. Where was it I was going to exactly and should I have accepted his offer of help? No, I couldn't. So far I had followed all the rules from the Oracle and it hadn't steered me wrong yet. I just had to keep my faith in her and continue. I mean, what choice did I have now? But I must say my main concern had switched to not where I was going but more like to whom.

Jared's own words wouldn't leave my mind, playing over and over... *'Because I know where and to who it will take you and trust me when I say you do not want to go there'.* I shivered at the thought.

"It does start to get colder the closer we get to the gates." I looked up at Charon, who simply nodded ahead. I shifted in my seat and looked at what he meant. A gasp escaped me as I saw the most incredible sight. There, coming closer to us, was a structure so great, it didn't seem it could possibly be real. It made me wonder how long I had been sat there lost in my own thoughts.

Along the full length of the water until out of sight were the most colossal columns that were at least 200 ft high. They were sparkling white but with no sun to reflect off them, I didn't know how it was conceivable. The columns made up the start to a wall of tunnels big enough that the Lady Liberty could have walked under them with ease. Each archway over the opening reached up in a spear that pierced the sky for another 100 ft at least. I couldn't even count how many there were, but I could see some with small boats entering the dark tunnels.

"What are they?" I uttered in breathless fascination.

"Those are the destinations." I had to tear my eyes from the sight to gauge his expression.

"What do you mean?"

"Ah, now this is the part where people always get testy…let me ask you are you a deeply religious person?" His question threw me and I didn't know any other way to answer but truthfully.

"Umm, sort of…I don't know exactly what is beyond life, although this is giving me a pretty good idea alright." I laughed and then had to continue,

"Living with the supernatural, I now know about Gods, Angels and Demons, Heaven and Hell, but even being allowed to live with that knowledge, it doesn't seem to make me any more knowledgeable than the next person."

"Then I can answer you, for you will not bite my head off with your faith." He said winking at this last bit.

"The truth of the matter lies as such, if you believe in this place then it lives, it is that simple. You find many a crumbled passageway lies in ruins at the bottom of these waters from the death of a faith." My mouth dropped open in disbelief.

"So, what you're saying is that each one of those tunnels is a gateway into the end that they believe in, with the Gods that they worship?" Even as I asked for confirmation, I knew the truth. I remembered back to all that time ago on Draven's balcony. I remembered the day I finally found out what he was, and the words he used…*"Everyone sees things through different eyes and it is as simple as yes and no. It always has been. Religion means something different to everybody. Every race of life, throughout time has viewed God differently but they have all had something in common…they all believed. That is the difference."*

So that was the only difference. People had to believe in order to come here and find their own end.

"But wait, in that case what happens to those who don't believe?" At this he just shrugged his shoulders and said,

"Sorry, not in my pay grade to know but I will say this…" He leant closer to whisper,

"…I don't hear much about reincarnation, so what I don't

hear means it doesn't happen down here and what doesn't happen down here…could very well happen up there." He looked up and I followed his gaze staring into nothing but endless white.

"You mean Heaven?" I asked causing him to turn serious.

"No my obol giver, I mean up in your world."

I couldn't say much after that because my mind was like a spinning top in the hands of a small child. Naïve and innocent watching the colours of life blur with such speed, well that's what was happening to me right now. All those myths, all those stories now holding some sense of truth… All the world's fighting and killing in the name of a faith that people tried to control when there never was any.

Two men at war when both of their beliefs existed. And all for what…to come here at the end of days and see the mistakes they made. To see all this and know that glory was not ever to be found on earth but right here and right now. Glory in belief, whatever it maybe is true only if it is true to you.

Your very own personal Heaven or your very own personal Hell. That is what awaits us if we believe and if not, then maybe what Charon says is true as well. If there is no belief then maybe nothing happens but the simple reuse of our soul. Not for Demon, not for Angel but for plain old humankind.

Souls recycled.

"Look there, for that boat holds someone set out for The Elysium fields."

"That's the place for good…so like a Heaven?" I asked as the penny finally dropped. You didn't rise up to Heaven, but first you came here to let the fates decide what type of life you once lived.

"A lot of gateways if it isn't." I nodded my understanding.

"So where is it then that we are heading, if there is more than one version of Hell?" This was when for the first time Charon lost his easy-going smile, replacing it with one full of menace and sinister venom.

"Let's see shall we?" He said once again producing the coin I had given him for this crossing. We came to some sort of deeper section of the water as it had changed to a darker colour as far as I could see. For the first time down here, I actually began to let the fear seep in enough to root and take hold.

"Make a wish." He said and I didn't know if he was joking or not, however I still wished and said one name in my mind. Then he flipped the coin up and over the boat into the darker depths.

His eyes clouded over and his lids flickered for quick seconds before snapping open and looking to one of the tunnels to his right. I followed his sights and saw it was one of the darkest tunnels, with the waters not looking as calm as the rest.

"Your answer… off to one of the nine circles we must go."

"Nine circles…as in Dante's Inferno nine circles?!" His answer came like a spider crawling up my spine under my skin…

"And you were such a nice girl."

CHAPTER FOURTY-THREE

A DRAVEN AT HOME IN HELL

Charon pushed us off what seemed like a dip or small ledge in the water as, all at once, everything about this journey started to change. The water that was once still and tranquil quickly turned into an angry entity that made the boat rock. I held on just as he shouted over the roar of water,

"HOLD ON!" I gripped the edge of the boat with one hand and the bottom of my seat with the other. I also tried to use my legs as leverage, anchoring me down. I bravely turned my head to see the churning water ahead that twisted and gushed up into waves of white foam. It battered against the rocks that could now be seen rising up from the water. I didn't know how this small gondola could survive, along with us in it.

"AHHH!" My scream got swallowed up by the sound of water smashing into the sides of the tunnel we were about to enter into and amazingly Charon remained standing as he manoeuvred us out of danger. The front of the boat would dip down in between two rocks that were causing a clash of power with the water and then the back would fall, landing with a splash through the spray. I looked up to see the last of the white sky disappearing overhead as we entered the belly of the beast.

My grip on the boat became painful, but it was drowned out

by the heady mixture of adrenaline flooding my senses and life-threatening fear. I felt drunk on it and it wasn't only the extreme motions of the boat that were making me feel sick and dizzy. I just wanted it to be over! Why had I come here? How could I have possibly thought that I could have survived this? I wanted to shout STOP! I wanted to put an end to it all and call it quits just like any other scared witless fool would do, but then something happened.

"Draven." I uttered his name as a prayer. It was all I had to hold onto. But then, unbelievably, I saw that some of the rocks had started descending back under the water. Was it a sign, was it my faith? I had to try, so this time I shouted louder,

"Draven!" Making even more of the rocks disappear. It was really working! He must be here! He must be able to hear me somehow! Then, just as the worst of the rapids could be seen ahead, I swallowed the last of my fear. I gripped the sides now with determination and found my footing to follow through with what I thought was the best chance at living, or I would not be making it past this part without my body intact. I got up on shaky feet, steadied myself enough to make it to the front of the boat and held onto the wooden frame that curled towards me.

"WHAT ARE YOU DOING?!" Charon screamed from behind me and I answered,

"WHAT I HAVE TO!" Then I rose up with all my strength and shouted with everything I had left in me,

"DRAVEN, HEAR ME! I'M COMING FOR YOU!" And just like that, the rest of the rocks and dangerous boulders that would have made our journey nearly impossible, all erupted bursting into tiny versions of what they once were. I screamed, placing my arms over my head as the debris rained down over us and sank down to the floor of the boat.

It was only when we again entered calm waters did I raise my head and look round.

"Well, it looks like he heard you." Charon said after jumping down from his perch at the back of the boat. He produced a heavy lantern from underneath some plastic covering and lit it just as the last of the opening's light could be seen as a small white space in the distance. He then hooked it onto a fancy iron holder that curled at the top. It swung with the motion of the boat and the light from its windows danced along the tunnel's walls in a pretty display.

"Is it usually like that?"

"No, only when life tries to cross over…death however, it welcomes." I nodded thinking as much.

I was about to ask him if he knew who Draven was when his new appearance stopped me. Unlike before when his clothes had been clean and smart they were now ripped and thread-bare. The white stripes looked as though long ago they had turned so dirty it was hard to distinguish them anymore. His hat now looked as if it had been dumped in black ash where it had once been cream. But it wasn't just his clothes that had taken a turn for the darker. It was also his features which looked haggard and older. His beard was longer, scruffy to the point he looked homeless but the most change was in his eyes that no longer reflected cheekiness and humour.

Now they looked like the eyes of a man who had given up.

I decided that it would be a good idea to put a lockdown on my questions for now as he wasn't looking as friendly as he once was. So I sat back on my seat and waited for my destination to reveal itself, just holding onto hope that it would be into Draven's arms.

Time went on and, as it always does on a journey where you don't know the way, it was taking a small forever. The tunnel didn't change much and inside my mind I was going out of my head with worry. I didn't think I would have any bloody lips left for Draven to kiss by the time we got there!

Thankfully, not long after that we came to our first entrance. A tunnel that was cut right out of the rock was covered in lush green moss and was in the shape of a keyhole, thick enough just for a single boat not much wider than this one. Then, when I looked to see the rest of our tunnel, there were entrances the full length down on each side but all were different. The next was a grander entrance with tall pillars made up of hundreds of naked bodies all tightly entwined.

I looked away feeling awkward on seeing such a sordid display as they seemed so real, I wouldn't have been surprised if the tunnel started to fill with the sounds of rapturous moans. I looked further on and could only make out the next two tunnels, one of which had a crude statue of a grotesque, large creature gorging on fistfuls of flesh from something dead at his feet. The other was a startling contrast to this dark and dreary place as it shimmered from every point. It was large Roman columns that looked to be made from solid gold and reflected that same shimmer on the water, making that too look as if it was liquid gold.

Then, whilst my eyes strained against trying to see the other ones further on, I hadn't seen us turn before everything was snatched from view. I didn't even know which one we were now travelling down. I was thankful though, that this one was bigger than the first one I had seen, as that looked as though it would barely fit us. No, this one, although not as large as the tunnel we just came from, was a big enough size to not feel trapped in or claustrophobic. In fact, our little gondola seemed quite small and dainty for such a turbulent journey. Which made me ask, despite my earlier reasoning to stay quiet,

"I am surprised you guys don't upgrade to speed boats after doing rides like this on a daily basis." Instead of the friendly laughter or smile I expected, he almost looked like he was trying to hold back from taking a bite out of me. Eyes that once lit up with welcoming discussion and an easy going manner, now looked almost cruel and irritated. So much so, I was surprised he answered me, even though his tone demonstrated that he found the chore distasteful.

"There is no modern technology in this place." And that was all I got, so I firmly decided this time not to speak unless utterly necessary. I made a point of turning my body away from him and facing the front as we continued further on down into the unknown.

After a while, I was almost at a point where I feared I would start seeing things that weren't there. I don't know what the cut-off point would be for staring down a tunnel without seeing anything new for hours and not go crazy, but I had already felt I had hit my limit. My Charon still hadn't said a word to me and the last time I had looked at him, there had been a few more lines added to his gaunt face. Hell, it looked like the guy had aged about a year for every minute down here!

The even stranger thing was it wasn't just his face but also his clothes. They were getting to the point of falling from his body they were so tired and worn. It was such an upsetting thing to witness and now I could add trying not to look at him as well as speaking to him. Oh, it was Hell alright and we weren't even there yet!

We started to approach something in the distance but it was hard to make out with only the aid of a single lantern. I had to wait until we were closer to it and only then did the light hit the features of such an imposing statue. Three large heads had been carved straight into the rock and were big enough that they covered every inch of the opening we were now heading for.

The one in the middle was that of a man or God, opening his mouth wide, providing the new entrance. He had curling hair that dipped under the water and his expression said one thing…enter if you dare! The one on the left of this was a bull's head, with the horns disappearing into the roof of the tunnel as though he had just reared up and pierced them into the rock. The one of the right also had horns but looked more like a demonic Ram, with them curling up and round, coming to a deadly point. Both creatures either side also blew out flames from snarling nostrils which reached out like grappling fingers along the tunnel's walls.

Well, whoever lived here, they most definitely got the intimidating welcome down…forget belly of the beast, I was travelling straight into the mouth of Hell alright!

I looked up to see his teeth hanging down as though any minute they would clamp shut on us and that would be the end of that. The tunnel we travelled down now was smaller but looked more like a corridor in some ancient palace. Gone was the harsh rock, being replaced with heavily decorated walls of terracotta statues that seemed to be built into the structure. It reminded me of some kind of temple, only taking one look at what the statues were doing, my guess would be the type of worshipping they did was only that of the body.

There were too many figures to count as they all entwined

into one great massive orgy. Legs and arms were spread out in the most unusual ways, all to display their willing secrets to the world and the parts that fit them. Every single one of them had hold of the other, whether it be in their mouths or being mounted like rutting animals and every single one had a smile.

I wanted to be disgusted at the sight but found I would be condemning myself a liar of the worst kind, as the evidence was pure and simple…I was getting turned on. I didn't know what it was, but it didn't look like it was just about sex and any hole to fill or be filled. The reason for this was the closer you looked, the stronger actual love shone through. I knew that twenty different people could look at this the way one would with art and see something different. After all, that was the beauty in the creative world we lived in. Everything was personal.

Every book, song or painted picture was something different to us all. And it wasn't just exclusively to the 'Arts' but to anything…buildings, places and even people. That's what made the world beautiful! So could the same be said down here? Even in this sexually framed passage? Because what I saw wasn't just sex, but it was the way the women were also held. It was the way some gazed into the eyes of their lovers, the gentle hold on the heads as pleasure was delivered and the kiss given in praise to others. I know not many would agree but I couldn't help but see the beauty in this too.

However, that beauty was soon over and opening up into a dark open space with gigantic pillars that made me think we must be underneath a castle. Our little boat floated on by one and it was the same width as the black bricks that made up the circular structure. It was incomprehensible to think that if these pillars were this size then what was the size of the building they held up?

Well, I was about to find out as we went through an open archway at the end of this massive underground room. I sucked in an amazed breath as my head went up and up and up, taking in the imposing black castle that rose above us as though it had just this second, risen from the depths of a volcano. I had never seen black rocks cut into blocks and used to build Hell's version of a Fairytale castle.

That was the only way to describe this place. Turrets the size of skyscrapers were everywhere. It was like a city full of them had all gathered and joined together. They weren't just round but they were actually carved into giant soldiers and were all connected by sweeping passageways that looked like the bent over form of a woman. This wasn't just a castle on an epic scale, but it was also an art sculpture of mass proportions. From this angle I could just see that it was sexual slaves being held captive by heavily armoured soldiers. You could see the battlements on top of the helmets they wore that reached out to an angry grey sky of swirling clouds.

It surrounded us in a U shape so there looked to be no escape from this evil place. I continued stretching out my neck to keep it in sight, when it finally got to me as the whole place started to disappear when we entered another underground tunnel. This time there was no holding back on speech.

"What…is this place?" I asked in a voice that didn't sound like my own. I looked to Charon for answers and jumped in my seat. He now looked like a man possessed by something raging inside of him. He was actually looking at me as if he wanted to attack, only I couldn't tell you if it was for my blood or my body. His eyes had started to burn into me and all the skin around them looked scorched. Flames shone from deep within and I could see he looked to be fighting some consuming thoughts that made him crush part of his pole in two hands. I didn't move. I couldn't. It was like being in the sights of something deadly, whether it be a lion or a man, holding a gun to your head.

Adrenaline once again played with my body and I was transported back to another place, another moment in a dark time. I sat waiting just like now. Waiting for a sign, a noise or one movement that told me what to do. I sat there waiting with a blade to my veins and death in my hands. Now death was in someone else's hands and I had suddenly tired of waiting. Just like that day I had held my fate and now I would do the same.

My life was mine and even here, in what some souls knew as their last resting place, where resting consisted of torture and cruelty, my life was still my own. And I chose to take it and use it to live.

"You can't have me, Charon." I stated calmly rising from my seat to face this new demon head on. He wasn't what I thought or was it just this place? Was that what being here did to us? He hissed at me and brought his pole further out of the water as if ready to use in a different way. I held my ground only wishing I too had a weapon. Then a commanding voice cut through our showdown and for a moment my heart stopped beating.

"She is right Charon, you cannot have what belongs to another." Tears instantly appeared as I let that voice soak over me in a desperate need for safety. The only voice I could ever give my entire being to and the same voice I had not heard in my world for what felt like an entire lifetime…

"Draven."

CHAPTER FOURTY-FOUR

LONG LOST LUST

"Well now, I certainly can count myself as a Draven." I watched as a figure emerged from the steps to our right. I hadn't noticed during my altercation with Charon, but we had drifted to a very grand underground docking area that looked like steps leading up to a Temple. But the rest of the details were lost to me.

Draven was walking down the steps, flanked either side by two guards who were so heavily armoured that I couldn't make out much about them, other than they resembled a Gothic version of a Roman soldier.

"Draven…is…is that really you?" I felt the tears fall down my cheeks as my heart sped up with the very idea. Then the man in question came closer until he stood where the room's flaming torches lit up his features…features just like Draven's, only…

It wasn't quite him.

"No! I don't know…is this…what is this!?" I stammered finding my heart couldn't take another blow like this one. This man standing in front of me could be his brother or even the man himself if he ever aged…but wait, it couldn't be!

"I'm sorry my dear, please let me introduce myself. I am Asmodeus, one of the Seven Princes of Hell and formally known as the first hierarchy President of Lust but to you my dear, I am simply to be known as Dominic Draven's father." This was when my legs crumbled beneath me and thankfully, I fell slumped to the seat behind me. Ok, so now I knew I couldn't take another blow like this one! Draven's father! I screamed it in my head but thankfully only spoke it quietly to the room,

"Draven's father?"

"Charon, I think you have reached your limit being here, why don't you give us a moment alone." The older version of Draven had every ounce the amount of authority coating his every word, just like I remembered in his son.

Charon went to reach out to me, when a thundering demonic roar stopped him. I don't know whether it was the sound that rocked the boat or Charon trying to get as far away from me as possible.

"Raka!" ('Fool' in Aramaic) Draven's father ground out what sounded like an insult as Charon scrabbled backwards. Because of the sheer power in this man, I couldn't help but hold myself frozen as Draven's father stepped up to the boat. With one hand he dragged my end of the boat right up to him. Then, in a far softer tone than he granted Charon, said gently,

"Tlīthā qūm, come now." ('Young one stand' in Aramaic) I nervously raised my head to look up at him and for a moment I was captivated by the beauty I found there. When I didn't rise, he offered me his hand, nodding down to it, almost like he was engaging a frightened doe. I bit my lip and took his offering, making his eyes flash a powerful red for a small time.

He gave me only a whisper of his strength as he lifted me from the boat with such ease, wrapping an arm around my waist in order to raise me high enough to get me onto the platform. It was whilst being this close to him that I could see more than just Draven in him.

There was also Sophia, as he too had her black curls which brushed the top of his shoulders, although he did have touches of silver along the sides. He also had harsher lines on his handsome face that spoke years of knowledge. The only one that was hardly there to see was Vincent, but he still had the high cheekbones and long straight nose that his other son had. But mainly and more painfully, it was mostly my Draven that I saw in him.

He lowered me and I realised it was also Draven's height I now looked up at.

"Draven?" I said his name without being able to help myself. It felt like I was in a dream and in that dream I was transported into Draven's future. Would he ever age like this?

"I fear my appearance is playing tricks with your fragile mind, little one." I couldn't help it. I sucked in my bottom lip and tried not to cry. It felt like being lost as a child and finally finding an adult to guide you. He raised a hand, cupped my cheek and took away one side of the wet trails that had soaked my skin.

"They said you were beautiful." I didn't know who he meant but right now I couldn't care as the only thing that mattered to me wasn't who thought I looked beautiful, but it was the beauty that owned my heart.

"Please…oh please, can you take me to him." I pleaded, trying to hold back from just falling to my knees and outright begging. I would no doubt be saving that for later.

"Where the rewards in selfless acts lie, I will never understand." I didn't know what he was saying or why, but nor did I care.

"Please." This was one moment I would never be above begging. He released a sigh and regarded me with regret.

"I am sorry, love of my kin, but what you seek isn't here and hasn't been for some time." I shook my head not even letting his words penetrate. He was wrong!

"N…n…nnno! He has… to be, I know he is! Please…oh please…I can't…not again, please just take me to him, I will give you anything, my life, my soul…my…my…" I started with a stutter, then a rush of desperate words only to end up sobbing, but just managed to push out the last of my promised bargain,

"…my…everything…" Tears came thick and fast, making it impossible to see his reaction to me crumbling at his feet. There I found myself in a ball of misery as I let every second of faith, I held onto evaporate into what it was…the dust of an age old lie. God, would this emotional pain never end?! No! I needed the physical to bring me back, so I pounded the sides of my fists on the floor, drowning in a pit of agony that I felt so deep inside of me I couldn't see any way to rip it out!

I felt myself being picked up and cradled to a hard chest which, for a moment, I let myself pretend was Draven's.

"Ethpthaḥ!" ('To open' In Aramaic) I didn't take much in but briefly heard what sounded like a pair of massive doors opening. I didn't look. I was scared what looking up at him would do to me, so I held on. I didn't know what he was wearing, I didn't know where he took me and I didn't know if he was taking me up on my exchange for life. And I no longer cared! I couldn't, I just didn't have anything left in me. All I had been through, all those times that I put my life on the line, to come here and find what…?

Nothing…just… nothing.

Draven wasn't here and I had failed! I had lost everything all over again. Coming all this way just to learn this reality was like someone had just dumped dry ice in my belly and it was seeping into my very soul!

"How could this happen?" I mumbled into his chest, crying the last of it out. I felt myself being lowered before I received an answer, even though I didn't really expect one.

"You thought any blood of mine would be brought back here against his will?" I raised my head and had to wipe my blurry eyes on my sleeve, along with… I hated to say it, a runny nose. I then looked up to find him kneeling by my side.

"Wh…what do you… mmmean?" I asked sounding like I had a cold and trying not to cry at the end, as my breathing hitched.

"My poor young one, I think you have been steered into greater depths before you learned how to swim." I rubbed my nose again and said in a quiet voice,

"I can swim." He started laughing and it was a lovely warm sound that once again reminded me of my Draven. His finger traced one escaping tear and he unexpectedly brought it to my lips. When I didn't do anything but freeze, he smiled at me and nodded to his fingertip. So, I did what I thought he wanted and kissed the end of it.

"Nothing as beautiful as you should lose a part of herself… even something as fragile as a single tear, a tear that should never have been given permission to fall." I nodded and rubbed the rest of them away receiving a wink for my efforts.

"Right, now tell me of your tale and how it led you to my home, my sweet child." He got up and sat down next to me. Surprising a squeak out of me, he picked up my legs and laid them across his own.

"What are you doing?"

"Making us comfortable." He said with a mischievous glint in his dark eyes.

"Umm…isn't this a bit weird, I mean, I am kind of dating your son." I reminded him just as he removed my boots and started rubbing my feet.

"First of all, knowing my son and the blood that runs dominant in his veins, then you are not simply 'dating' him as you put it, you solely belong to him, owned by him…"

"No I…"

"Eh, eh…I haven't finished." He said holding up a finger, gently admonishing me. He also went back to rubbing my feet after first peeling back my socks and I just prayed that my feet didn't smell! And how did he make that simple act seem like he was peeling something a lot more concealing away? Wait, what was I thinking…? This was just plain old weird but also, oh so heavenly. I mean, jeez the man had skills alright!

"And secondly in reference to this…" He nodded down to my bare feet that were currently being dominated by his large hands.

"Just find yourself lucky that's all I am doing and you don't find yourself flat on you back, screaming for days under my ministrations, sweet girl." When he saw my mouth drop, he gave me a pure, down to the bone, badass grin and leaned closer to my mouth to snap at it with his teeth, making me snap my own mouth…shut tight, that was. He burst out laughing and said,

"I am the Devil's Prince of Lust, after all."

I gulped and licked my dry lips causing him to watch the action as though he would lean over at any minute and do the same thing. I decided there was only one way I could think of to take both our minds from the sexual fog that his presence emitted.

"I don't suppose there is any chance in Hell of a cuppa tea is there?" The grin he gave me painfully reminded me of Draven whenever he thought I was being cute and for the long minutes of being stared at, I didn't think he would grant my odd request. But the next thing I knew I was soon staring down at my own Homer mug full of the perfectly brewed tea being held out to me like a gift from…uh…well not the Gods but… The *Prince of Lust*. Now that was a weird sentence even for me!

I looked up from my own personal nectar to say thank you when he said,

"Where there is tea, there is hope."

I had to smile.

Whilst I was telling him the story from the beginning, I also had time to take in my surroundings. The room we sat in was a very long gallery type room that was completely made from the thick black blocks. It had at least ten pillars running in the centre the full length until I couldn't make out what was at the end. The pillars were made from a light grey stone that looked like solid ash. They arched up to the ceiling and the moulding interlaced with numerous other arches making up the intercut pattern above.

As dark as the stone was, it wasn't lacking character or light showing off that character to its fullest. The light came from the most unusual lamps. Thick bicep arms of red tinged brass came out of the heavy rocked wall, with their shackled hands holding flaming orbs.

But it wasn't just from the walls, as long slender female arms also provided light. They came out of the top of the pillars like tiered chandeliers but each was holding a light bulb upside down. The tops of each held a single flame and the oil could be seen in the glass at the bottom. Each one of these was shackled at the wrist and chains hung heavy in between, joining all the arms together.

It was pretty cool in a strange way, but the rest of the room had me blushing. Along the walls were various sized alcoves, each housing a sculpture of a sexual nature. Now if there had been just two people having sex with each other then I could just act like I was seeing something like this in a museum. But oh no, not for the President of lust!

Of the ones closest to us, there was one of a large apple four times the size of a football. In its centre was a woman's vagina with the snake's body coming from its core. It was coiled around the apple and its head rested just by the stalk, looking down at its own body emerging. I think most would gather this represented Eve in the most unforgiving light.

The one straight ahead looked like a large gold ball, but when you gave it more than a quick glance you could see it was something more. It was a contorted body with the face of a demon. A large penis stood tall and erect for him as he was having a jolly good time giving himself oral sex. As crude as this was it wasn't the worst part, as its bull sized balls were also in some sort of vice! Now that made me blush.

The ones further away in the next set of alcoves consisted of an overly muscled sea God holding across him a writhing mermaid. His trident, held tightly to her front, was trapping her breasts in between the three spears. The helpless mermaid had her head arched back in rapture as her tail had been pulled down enough to reveal a painfully large penis mid thrust, in between the glimpse of human legs. This one was made from old bronze, the type that turned green in places from the copper oxide.

The very last one I could make out was of two figures that were some sort of half animal doing it standing up, whilst other creatures licked at their moving sexes from either side. It was made from pot and one of the heads was half crumbled away from what I gathered was old age.

I wish I could say that was it, but the largest sex symbol in the room was actually the one we were sat on. It was the longest sofa I had ever seen, being at least three times as big as a regular three seater. The cushions felt like cashmere and were the same ash grey colour as the pillars. They were thick and one of the softest seats I had ever graced my bum the task of sitting on.

But this wasn't its most defining feature. No, it was the frame upon which all that comfort was placed on top of. Two larger than life naked women, that looked dipped in slick black oil, lay on their backs. Their heads were what were used as the feet of the sofa and their arched backs meant the sides consisted of high thrust out breasts and the arms bent so that fingers could tug on their own nipples. The legs met in the middle and lay over each other with their sexes scissored together.

It was a work of art really, but I wasn't sure I wanted to be sat atop of two naked women, getting my feet rubbed by Draven's dad, Mr Lusty! Of course, my wants weren't up for discussion and so here I was. I had just finished telling him everything, as once again the floodgates opened and I found there was no holding back. He had a strange calming presence about him that I imagined granted him with the skills for a different type of torture. After all, why inflict pain when pleasure worked just as well…for all parties involved.

Apart from taking in our naked surroundings, I also had chance to take in the man who controlled it all. He sat back with such ease but commanded his space in an effortless way. When I was finally allowed to move my legs, choosing to pull them underneath me and to the side he gave me a knowing smile that had me blushing. Of course, the blushing could also account for when he started brushing the backs of his fingers along one of the chair's breasts.

Now, I will say that seeing someone who looked like Draven, even an older version, wasn't the easiest thing for my raging libido but when he did things like that…well, now that had me close to panting! Another thing that really wasn't helping was what he was wearing. It looked to be a type of black toga made from some kind of hide, but I couldn't tell what. It fit tighter than a simple loose piece of material draped over one shoulder, so that you could see the sheer size of muscle he was packing. I wasn't sure whether he was bigger than Draven or they were just the same size and I had forgotten how big Draven really was. I just knew that, thanks to the design of the toga, it showcased his enormous arms off to their fullest.

He had one arm covered completely in a skin tight layer underneath his toga but I didn't know what material it was. It was like a soft black suede moulding to every curve and at first I thought he was wearing a single glove on this hand but when I looked closely I saw it was part of the sleeve. The arm that was left bare had thick leather straps crisscrossed over part of his bicep coming from his shoulder. His forearm also had a plate of brushed metal which covered the length of one side, growing wider near his elbow to fit. This was edged with small spikes that looked deadly enough in a fight. It was held on with straining buckles pulled tight around the muscle and in the centre was the same symbol I had seen on the back of my coin. It looked as if it had been burnt onto the metal with a branding iron.

"Well now, that was quite a story, my young one." All I could do was nod my acknowledgement. After all, I had said all there was to say and now I was at a loss.

"So, was Draven ever here?" I asked the question that had been eating away at me.

"My dear, understand this, if my son were ever to grace us with his presence in this realm, then he would not do so wrapped in the chains of others. He would live like the King he is and being as he is so much more in your world."

"What do you mean?"

"My lovely, he is a God amongst mere men." He said with pride shining through each word.

"And as I and his mother had intended it to be, including his brother and sister also. But it is the unique mix in my son that has never happened before, that rivals that of any God. He is just yet to discover it." I shook my head not fully understanding.

"What do you mean…has he…I mean how? Can he really have even more power?"

"You know nothing of the prophecy I take it?" He asked raising an eyebrow.

"I just know I am supposed to have something to do with it." At my answer he laughed.

"One does not know true power until it has been taken from them and one does not know true love until that also has been taken from them…mix the two concepts together and you will then find that there lies your true power."

"I don't understand." Now instead of laughing at me he simply gave me a small, knowing smile.

"You will…one day you will understand that your role in the prophecy wasn't a role at all but simply a choice made from love, like this journey you bravely chose to walk down…one day I promise you, you will know your own worth, as my son does." I looked down at my lap and tried to hold in the emotions his kind words brought to the surface.

"Can I ask you another question?" He lowered his head into a deep nod at my request.

"How is it you look like him?"

"Is it playing on your mind, child?" He asked finding the humour in my question. He didn't wait for the answer he knew.

"I have many forms, but this I thought necessary for your comfort, besides, my son is easy on the eyes is he not?" Again he was finding this all quite amusing and I must say his easy tone was helping my strangled nerves.

"Oh yeah!" I said on a sigh making him laugh.

"So what am I to do now?" I said after the humorous moment had passed.

"Well, I cannot tell you where my son is, only where he is not. But my advice…" I turned to face him and nodded when he didn't continue.

"Find someone who does." Well that was easier said than done when even the bloody Oracle thought that he was down here!

"Could he be…you know, in the other place?" I looked up out of habit.

"Ah, now that I definitely can't say. I know this might shock you given where my particular talents lie, but me and my dear Sarah are not really on speaking terms."

"Sarah?" I asked, not hearing the name being mentioned before.

"My wife, although she is somewhat difficult in her acknowledgement on that fact. The Hebrew name Sarah indicates a woman of high rank and is translated as 'princess' which is why I named her as such. She will always be *my Sarah.*" He said looking thoughtful down the long room until I followed his gaze.

There, in the middle of the room on a higher platform, was a sculpture of a single female and although I was too far away to make out any of her features, it was more the lack of what I could see was more profound. She was the only statue in the room that wasn't of a sexual nature.

I knew from his look alone that this was his Sarah and Draven's mother.

"Women are like flowers you know." I tore my eyes from the pale marble woman back to Asmodeus. He was once again touching the breast like he was using that as an example, taking in her smooth curves like a connoisseur.

"Us bees search out the one we want, whether it be the biggest, the boldest in colour, the dangerous ones full of thorns, petals so soft it could bring the strength behind our wings to fail…All of you, standing there waiting for the day we come to find you, our perfect flower waiting in the storms of life, holding on for us, being strong for us…" He snapped his piercing gaze back to me and suddenly the intensity of it had me squirming. His grip tightened on the breast before he finished,

"But some fail. Some lose themselves in the waiting. They wither up in the strongest winds and give up holding on. So, they let that wind take them, leaving nothing left for us bees to find…" He reached out and had my hands locked in his before I could blink.

"Don't let the wind take you, my son's Chosen… hold on until he finds his way and if you do, then I can promise you it will be worth facing the storm my world throws in your path." I nodded my understanding and gave him all I had left to give…

"I will always hold on."

It was a promise.

CHAPTER FOURTY-FIVE

BEHIND ENEMY LINES

After leaving the second Circle of Hell and saying goodbye to its President, the journey back was a lot easier than it had been coming here. First of all Charon, although still scary for the most part, must have had his warnings because he remained silent until we broke free of the tunnels. When this happened not only did he turn to smile at me once more, but he had also transformed back into his former happy self…clean clothes and all.

He even apologised for his behaviour and told me that it sometimes happens to Charons when they are not naturally comfortable in the place where the souls take them. This was one of those times. I told him there were no hard feelings and shrugged it off. I mean, what was I supposed to do, hold a grudge, throw a hissy fit and tell him I wouldn't ever be back? I didn't believe in any of those things. Anyway, the trip back gave me the time needed to sort through my head.

On first hearing Draven wasn't there, I had wanted to give up the fight. Hell, I think for a moment I did. But then after hearing what Draven's dad had to say about not giving up and holding on, I knew I could never just give up on Draven like that. And I wouldn't.

So, what was next? Draven's dad had walked me through a

small section of his castle (which was seriously cool) and as I turned to say my farewells I was roughly pulled into his embrace and licked…I kid you not…actually licked up my neck to my ear, where he whispered,

"Good journey, my sweet, sweet young one and…" He released me and placed something cold in my hand before saying,

"…until the next time we should ever need to meet." I looked down to see he had placed another coin in my hand ready to use should I ever need him again. I gave him big eyes of surprise and then said something that made him burst out laughing,

"Thanks, Draven's dad."

Well, after saying goodbye to Asmodeus the way no 'could one day be' daughter-in-law should ever do, I felt better than when I had first arrived. I mean, it was always nice to know that someone, who one day could become your in-law, actually liked you. Besides, it couldn't be a bad thing to have someone that powerful in Hell at your back, could it? I thought this as I palmed the coin in my hand before placing it back safely in my pocket. I had carried it with me for so long now it felt right being back there.

So, bringing me back to the now and a place where Jared waited, pacing along the same decking I had not long ago left. I used these last few moments to consider what to do next? I had already used what I had learned to gather there was something bigger at play here for everyone else to believe Draven was in Hell. So where was he really? The only answer I could come up with was so simple it was practically staring me in the face.

Thinking back to everything that had happened, it suddenly felt so obvious now, I felt like smacking myself. The attempts of my kidnapping, no one knowing where Draven was or having any concrete answers for any of my questions. The reality of it was that no one really knew!

But I think I did.

Could it be that Draven wasn't dead after all and just being kept prisoner by some kind of power he needed love's help to overcome. Was that what his father had implied when talking about Draven's restrained power within? Was I now a target simply because I was trying to find Draven, because thinking back, it had all started when I received my first letter from the Oracle. So did that mean that Draven's jailor could be this Gastian person?

Well, Draven's dad was right about one thing and that was I needed to be asking the right people and right now there was only one person I could think of who could help me.

"Lucius, I hope your ass is still in Germany." I muttered to myself before looking up to catch the look of relief on Jared's face. He stopped pacing and stormed to the end of the dock with a determined stride. I was about to take the offered hand from Charon when Jared snarled inches from his face.

"Well, alright then." Charon said pulling back comically. I had to say I felt a bit sorry for the guy now, after the day of being shouted at and turned into a nasty Lust Demon. Jared didn't bother holding out his hand for me to take…no, no, instead he just took me. He was still giving a warning glare to Charon as he lifted me clean out of the boat and popped me down by his side. Then, without another word, he took my hand and pulled me abruptly back towards the mountain.

"Um…thanks Charon." I said waving behind me, wondering what had gotten into Jared.

"No worries…I would say laters but you know…not what people wanna hear, so…" He just nodded his head as he gave me a salute in place of a wave.

"Hey, where's the fire?" I asked trying to get Jared to communicate with me using actual words instead of growly pissed animal noises.

"The fire? Seriously, you wanna play this bullshit with me?!" He snapped at me and I pulled from him, holding up my hands in surrender.

"What is your problem?" Ok, so this was totally the wrong thing to ask a beast on the edge. His eyes turned into black slits in a pool of hot silver, oh and of course he snarled at me.

"My problem?!" Even his voice had changed, crossing those fine lines between, man, beast and Demon.

"My fucking problem started when you decided it would be

good for a laugh to go off to a circle in Hell and right up to the fucking doorstep of the one who runs that shit! Do you have…" He cut his arm through the air in his anger before carrying on,

"…have, any fucking clue how dangerous that was…? DO YOU?" He roared this last part out at me and I could briefly see his fangs grow and his jaw elongate. Then I decided to do something stupid. I pushed him.

"How dare you! What right do you have to go ape shit at me for anyway? What do you care!? What would it have mattered to you if…oh wait…now I get it…you weren't worried about me, oh no...!" Oh, now he backed away. I stepped closer and poked him in the chest as I carried on delivering the truth of the matter,

"You were worried about your precious vow and what would have happened if I wasn't around to keep my side of the bargain!" I swear I saw him flinch and I felt some satisfaction in that, given the reasons why he seemed to be so worried about me or more like, what I could do for him!

"Well, what did you expect Pet, me here gushing over a piece of pretty ass?!" I gritted my teeth at his come back and then let rip. Before he saw what was coming, I slapped him shouting,

"You jerk!" And then stormed off in my anger, only I had no idea to where, seeing as I was in the Underworld! But at that minute I just didn't care, I was fuming angry!

"And where do you think you're going?" The words grumbled out of him as he wrapped both his arms around me from behind.

"Let me go!" I screamed but he just held on tighter.

"NO!" After that shout I decided to let my anger come off the boil and simmer. He must have decided to do the same because we just stayed like this and panted until our breathing calmed. Then he released a big sigh.

"Look, I…well damn it, I was worried about you *alright!*"

"You mean the bargain, don't you?" I reminded him bitterly then heard him try for patience in the form of another sigh.

"It should be just about that but it… wasn't. I was worried

about what would happen to you and what I could have done to get you back safely."

"You would have come for me?" I asked a bit dumbfounded.

"Yes." On that one word my breath caught before I asked,

"But why?"

"I don't know why and that's why I am so angry. It's like as soon as I met you something deeply ingrained inside of me was connected to you. As if someone flipped a switch that said I must protect you, even against my own kind and even with my own life." On hearing his declaration, I relaxed back into him, all fight flying right out of me.

"Maybe it's just the vow." I said looking for the simplest answer.

"Fuck the vow! All I know is these feelings are opening a big fucking hole, one I closed and buried a long time ago and nothing scares me in this world other than one thing and that is seeing that hole open up again…hear me now pet, I don't let anyone in…ever!" I bit my lip and nodded, not trusting myself to say anything right now.

"Now do me a favour… take my hand, follow me from here and forget this damn day, leaving it where it belongs."

"And where is that?" I asked on a whisper. He released me and we both turned but even now with his back to me I didn't miss what he said next,

"…Dead and buried."

We soon found ourselves back in the caves and making our way back through the complicated maze of bare rock. And for once, I was silent. I was still trying process all I had learnt but mostly trying to make sense of Jared's words. I didn't quite know what was going on with him but I knew being around me was messing with his head. I didn't want that. I didn't want to be anyone's painful reminder of a past long buried. But most importantly, where did that leave us now?

These thoughts plagued me and when I lost my footing and fell into his back, I felt him tense.

"Sorry." I muttered feeling embarrassed where once I wouldn't have.

"What are you planning, Keira?" I frowned at the unexpected question at first, not understanding where it had come from.

"What do you…?"

"Well, knowing what I've come to learn about you, I know that by me putting your ass on a plane home is going to be a wasted effort in keeping you safe... so I will ask again, what are you planning?" He asked turning to me, having stopped not far from the top, back near the Roman numerals '22'.

"I need to get to Germany." I stated firmly.

"And what's in Germany?"

"Lucius." At this I could see him raise an eyebrow.

"Please tell me you're joking." I crossed my arms over my chest and gave him my best 'I got attitude' look.

"And why would I be?" My answer got me an eye roll and him throwing his arms up dramatically.

"Jesus girl! What is it with you… you got the fucking yellow pages of badass Demons on speed dial?! Is there even one powerful killing machine out there you don't know!? Jesus! But of course…the fucking Vampire King!" His irate voice seemed to bounce from the damp stone surrounding us, making it even colder down here.

"It's not like that…you don't …" He wouldn't let me finish.

"Oh no? So let's see shall we, let's recap…" He stormed back to me coming so close I had to look up. Then he began counting on his fingers,

"First off, you come into my club with a bodyguard, who if he ever lets his iron control snap, could have torn through every fucking Demon there and is a King in his own right… then second comes me, another King who you fearlessly asked for help getting into Hell…right am I getting through yet…no, then let me continue…" He stepped again further into me making me back up with his intensity.

"…So, once in Hell comes the third guy, a God damn President in the circles that aids in ruling Hell itself! I mean do you have even the tiniest concept of how powerful someone like that is...? I judge from your wide kitten eyes that's a no!"

"Jared…" I reached out to him to get him to stop, but instead he grabbed my wrist and then twisted it painlessly behind my back. Once trapped, he then took the last steps pushing me back into the wall behind.

"Then I find my little pet wants to take a trip off to see the fourth guy, a fucking Vampire King, who is known throughout my world as being one ruthless bastard and that's coming from 'it takes one to know one', darling."

"But…" Again, he wouldn't let me speak. Instead he raised a finger to my lips to silence me before he continued his rant, which granted was making me out to be mentally incapable of making my own suicidal decisions.

"But then to top it all off and the very last slice of your crazy mind, is who you belong to. A being who is more powerful than all of the above and I am not ashamed to admit to it. The very one who commands us all, apart from you it seems, considering you can't just listen to him and fucking MOVE ON!" This was when it felt like he had slapped me! He knew…he knew!

"You know?!" He shook his head as if surprised that I was focusing on this part of what he had just said.

"I…" This was when I showed him a piece of that crazy!

"You knew! All this time you knew what I was trying to do, yet answer me this Jared, why is it you didn't seem very shocked that I came back to the dock without the one person I went there to save…? Answer me, why is that exactly?!" At this he let me go on a growl and walked away showing me his back.

"You knew he wasn't there…all this time and you still let me go to Hell and back and all for what…so you could get your fucking Vow from me! Oh, you were right about one thing, you're a ruthless bastard alright! So where is he then, do you know who has him?!" I was so near to screaming at him instead of shouting, but this was breaking my bloody heart! I felt betrayed, so utterly betrayed.

"You have this all wrong, pet."

"Don't call me that!" He held up his hands as he tried using a softer tone, saying,

"Alright Keira, but you have to listen to me, it isn't like that. I knew, yes, that you wouldn't be coming back with the King in tow, but I thought you would at least find some answers, *that's* why I wanted to give you my coin. But then when I saw what you really had planned, where you were really trying to get to, then that's when I tried to stop you." I had nothing to say to his confession other than to hear it all out. He took a moment and when I didn't speak he rubbed one hand at the back of his neck in frustration. It was surprisingly a very human thing to do.

"I don't know where the King is, Keira and I don't know anyone who does. When you came into my club, I felt something… I wasn't lying about that back there…I knew I needed to do this for you and what it would mean for me in return one day. It didn't take me long to figure out who you were, but by then it was too late. The King's rules had already been broken and I had to follow what the damn fates had set into place." This news made me react. I lost sight of my hurt long enough to ask,

"What do you mean by the fates?" His reaction to this worried me because his gaze lowered as though he couldn't look me in the eyes any longer.

"Jared?" He closed his eyes briefly, inhaled a deep breath and finally looked at me to deliver his last emotional bomb.

"The Oracle, Keira, she told me you would come and what would happen when you did." I sucked in my own sharp breath and took a stunned step back, using the wall to stop me from crumbling.

"She…she told you to make a Vow and that I too would make one in return…didn't she…DIDN'T SHE!?" I screamed this last part when he didn't answer me. He took in my anger and nodded.

"All this time I have been played."

"No, I don't think that's what this is." He tried to reason with me, but I was too far from the surface to claw out of my pit of betrayal that these people had plunged me into.

"Then what would you call it Jared, because from the very beginning I have been placed around this damn chessboard like a defenceless pawn, all for what, to give the big players a chance at something I couldn't see before, but now I see…now I see what this is!" I walked to push past him in this narrow tunnel but he grabbed my forearm to stop me.

"Then what is this, Keira?" He asked gently looking down at me with sad eyes of concern.

"This is your fate, Jared, this is everyone's fate at the expense of my own happy one."

"That's not true and you know it. Look Keira, I am not going to pretend that I know what will happen with you and the King, but I do know that I was meant to meet you, I was meant to feel this way about you and for what, so that I could get you into Hell for no real reason…?" I shrugged my shoulders, feeling deflated and hurt but then he shouted,

"Bullshit! Don't you see, everything that happens now is for a reason, but it's just a reason we can't see yet. Don't stop believing Keira, don't give up…*hold on Keira.*" Those words had me in a vice called faith and hope. They were the same words from Draven's father and now they had come back to me when I needed them the most.

"I know you feel betrayed, little pet, but I did all that was asked of me, I was told not to tell you what I knew and this I did on blind faith in the Oracle's words. Knowledge, pet, is a weapon sometimes best left until the last possible moment." I let myself absorb his words of wisdom and hated that he was right. If I had known any of this, would I still have gone through with it all? That I couldn't answer, but it still made me understand the why.

"Fine, but what about Sigurd, is he working with the Oracle as well? Is that who sent him to me and if that's true then…wait a minute." I said suddenly realising something that I had not thought of until now…something that chilled me to the core.

"Keira, what is it?"

"Where is Sigurd?" Jared shook his head and said,

"I'm not following…should he be here?" My eyes widened and panic seized me.

"He wrote me a note, but with everything that just went on I had forgotten…he… he was supposed to meet me, he is the reason I came here tonight."

"Give me the note." Jared ordered, now stepping back into his masterful role. I fished around in my bag, knowing that every second I took, the more frustrated Jared was getting with me.

"Here it is." I said passing it to him. He picked up the lantern he had dropped in our argument and held it over the note. It was a few tense moments before he said,

"Time to go," in a harsh voice. He stuffed the note in his back pocket and grabbed my hand to pull me quickly through the last of the tunnel.

"What is it…? Jared, just tell me!" I pleaded when he wouldn't answer me. Then he stopped abruptly, making me walk into his back again. He looked as though he was trying to figure out how to word his next statement. Then he turned to me with the lantern raised, which put his serious expression in the spotlight. Then he told me the startling truth.

"I got a visit from your Ouroboros master last night. He told me he had to leave the country… someone he worked for in Italy who needed to hear all that had happened. But before he left, we made a blood pact to seal my word in looking out for you in his place."

"What!?" I couldn't believe what I was hearing! He left me…he really left me?

"Keira, listen to me now. This is the reason I had my brother follow you and when he found out you were coming here, I assembled my men and came for you. I knew you had the heart and thought you had taken it upon yourself to try and get into Hell alone."

"So, Sigurd didn't tell you to meet me here?" Which was what I originally thought had happened.

"No, in fact he asked me to do the opposite, to wait and stall you if you became insistent, a task I found I could not withhold due to my own vow to you." I was fast trying to make sense of all this, but then the most important question had to be asked.

"So if Sigurd didn't write the note, then who did?" At this his face hardened as if ready to lose that barely contained fury he wanted to unleash with his next breath.

"Let's go." He didn't answer me but I had a feeling he had an idea.

We made it up the last tunnel with haste and emerged from the entrance to find that the darkness could not hide what faced us. Jared's brother and his men were all stood spaced out in a line which secured the entryway. I was quickly pulled behind Jared's protective frame as we approached his brother.

"Nice of you to join us J, wouldn't have wanted you to miss your welcome party." Orthrus said sarcastically then cracked his knuckles in the face of our danger.

"Wouldn't have missed it for all of Hell, brother." Jared replied dryly, looking from side to side, as if taking in each individual threat. Although, now looking at the small army of mutated demons that had us trapped in a corner, there looked to be too many threats to count.

"How many?" Jared asked one of the men at his brother's side.

"Twenty five here, but there could be more."

"That's five each boys, anyone that gets six picks a loser to buy around…plus looking at these ugly bastards I'm thinking a lap dance too." All heads nodded in agreement and I snorted my disbelief on hearing Jared's brother making a bet at a time like this.

"You have got to be joking?" I whispered at him from behind Jared's back.

"Do I look like a fucking Jester, little girl? This shit is ugly, and I will need a drink and a sweet piece of ass after a night of ugly…you volunteering, sweetie?" He asked winking at me.

"Knock it off, Orth!" Jared snapped without taking his eyes from the sea of uglies that Orthrus had named them…and rightly so, I thought shuddering.

"Speaking of Jesters, where is our buddy Marcus?"

"I sent him a text, so fingers crossed doing what he does best and coming up the rear." I bit my lip as that was quite funny.

"Play nice, brother" Jared said trying also not to laugh.

"Never gonna happen, *Brother!* So what's the plan here J, 'cause I gotta tell ya, we have been staring at these fuckers for a while now and I am getting bored of the zombie dumb ass show."

"No one has voiced their demands?" Jared asked, but before his brother could answer him, another voice took that liberty.

"Oh now, I wouldn't say that." I looked to see the army part to let through a man wearing a suit, one who I couldn't see properly thanks to the shadows that hid him.

"Oh yeah, I forgot about this asshole." Orthrus said as if he hardly mattered.

"Enough! Hand over the girl and I will consider letting you live, mongrels." Orthrus whistled low and said,

"Oh Hell no, did he just say that, Bro?"

"You know Orth, I think he did." Jared said in a voice that screamed so close to the edge of ferocity, I felt it buzzing through his back.

"Oh shit man, now you've gone and done it, do you not have any idea who my brother is, you dumb fuck!?" Orthrus taunted making his men snarl at the wave of demons getting ready to attack.

"I don't care what breed of dog he is, NOW GIVE ME THE GIRL!" He roared.

"You heard him brother, go give him your girls." Jared said to Orthrus smiling.

"With pleasure." He replied kissing his fists, before walking ahead of the rest.

"What is he doing?" I whispered into Jared's back.

"Just wait and see, pet."

"Very well… my Death soldiers, tear these dogs apart!"

And just like that, a swarm of mutated men were released from their verbal control and attacked…

A war at the Hellfire had begun.

CHAPTER FOURTY-SIX

BRING THE RAGE

Orthrus opened his arms wide in the centre of the courtyard and just as the first wave of demons came at him, something started to happen. The earth beneath him started to split but there was no rumble or evidence of the earth quaking other than the sight of it.

"What is he…?" I started to ask when the sight of something emerging from the hole in the ground had me stopping. The tear in the earth spanned the length of his legs and some sort of creature started to pull itself up, grabbing a foot first. Orthrus shuddered and then it all happened in a matter of seconds. The congealed black sand used his body to drag itself from the pit of what I could only imagine was Hell itself. It started to cover his legs first, wrapping itself around him then turning to thick liquid and seeping into his clothes. As it moved up his body with such speed, it then revealed something darker in place of the body that once was Orthrus.

I gasped as I got my first sight of the beast he was becoming. A pair of animal feet like no other stood holding the weight of the transformation taking place. They had four massive claws of thick bone that curled into the ground like spikes. His skin was black but looked like cooling molten rock that cracked, showing the glow of hot power beneath the surface. A larger back claw knifed out at the heel and I saw it pound into the ground before Orthrus fell forward as the last of his other self overtook him. He raised his upper body and roared into the night as the liquid sand disappeared into his open mouth, as if trying to drown him in his own demon form.

What was left was a living, breathing nightmare of a demonic beast the size of a bull. All his body looked to be made from cooling lava as if he had merged with the volcano's eruption instead of dying from it. But the sight of his hissing, cracking skin was nothing compared to his head…or should I say 'heads', as he had two of them. They looked different and if I could compare them to anything, I would say it was like a Rottweiler on steroids one side and a rabid German Shepherd on the other, only these two were bigger, meaner, demonic and more deadly!

The demon horde that came after him looked like an army of men once upon a time, but now they were nothing more than empty shells that only had death on their minds. There were no loved ones to fight for, there were no thoughts of country and honour and there was no fighting for protection. There was only death in their eyes and that death was their only need.

And Orthrus was in their sights. But from the looks of things that was just fine with him, as the first demon that got close enough found its head in a vice of jaws from two killers. In one second, it was raising its arm in attack and the next it was missing its head.

It was as this small army came closer, that I realised I had seen them before, and I gasped in my hands as that memory resurfaced. It had been the last time Sigurd's darkness had transported me into the land of nightmares…only now it was starting to look more like into the land of things to come. The time in my prison when those creatures had come closer was like a replay in reality as they once again made their way towards me.

They each had their own weapons of choice embedded somewhere in their bodies and their tall flaky forms were disfigured because of the fact. Dark ash corroded the area, like the next one coming closer to Orthrus. This one had an axe cutting into the side of his neck, making his head favour his unaffected shoulder. The blackened skin around the metal licked out along the peeling skin and made half of his dead face look charred and burnt.

Just as before, he got within distance of Orthrus' snapping fangs that dripped with saliva, the demon reached up and pulled the axe from its fleshy holder. Then with more strength than I would have counted on, he swung it at Jared's brother's heads. It nicked one pointed ear as he didn't move quickly enough, but that looked to be his last mistake. As his beast of a body twisted away, in the next move he was snaking back and ripping the arm that held the weapon, clean off.

As another came running at him, so he threw the arm out of his way, making the axe skid across the floor towards us.

"I think it's time to join the fun, boys." Jared said nodding each side at his men. They smiled as though he had just given them Christmas off and then they fell to the ground ready for their own change. I couldn't help but grip onto Jared's back as the earth split once more, only this time in three places. The one on our left, where Orthrus had been standing, changed the quickest. Only this time instead of black sand to cover him, it was thousands of tiny thin roots of grey snakes that slithered up from the hole.

In no time at all there was now a snarling beast that looked more like a giant wolf with spikes along its spine, although there was no soft fur to speak of. It stretched out as if readying for the fight and it sounded like tension wire being pulled tight.

By the time I looked to my right, the other two had already transformed. One looked a lot sleeker than the others and this wasn't just down to a more panther like body. No, this one wasn't like the others at all, as it was covered in a shiny thick red oil that was the colour of dark blood. I just hoped he didn't feel like shaking his fur because I didn't fancy a bloody shower!

The very last one was a similar size to Orthrus, who was the biggest one of the pack. His pale skin was pulled painfully taut over jagged bones that looked like they had inverted outwards. His own ribcage had fanned out and sharp bone became a weapon on his back, should anyone try and attempt to take him down. Even his skull had been morphed into flat horns that looked as if they could be used as a battering ram. And from the sight of him with his head lowered ready, I didn't think I was wrong.

They all looked towards Jared, their master and on his nod they all leapt into action. Each one of them mid leap landed on a demon and started tearing into him. Jared then turned to me and said,

"I need to get you safe." I looked behind us back to the caves.

"No, that's what he wants, that's why he surrounds us here, to try and force us back. He wants me to lose you in the caves so he…"

"JARED, LOOK OUT!" I screamed just as one of the creatures slipped passed the chaos and came barrelling towards us. He was covered in hammered metal plates that had been fused to his skin and his head looked like it was half machine. The terminator came to mind just as he crashed into Jared, who had positioned himself in front of me.

Jared, even in his human form, was still an unstoppable force. He flipped his body upright and grabbed the demon. He quickly did the same as me and zeroed in on the weak spot on his back as this was an area without plated armour. Then he delivered a series of kidney punches that came so quickly it was impossible to count them. The demon fell to his knees but not from pain. He used this motion as an escape from Jared's pounding fists.

I saw another demon look towards us and decide to get in on the action. But with Jared still focused on destroying the plated one, he didn't see what I was seeing. I backed up and a pair of white eyes locked on to me. I knew I had to do something and running off screaming like a little girl was going to be as practical as a chocolate gun, with candy bullets. I looked desperately around the space for any type of weapon and came across a severed arm with its hand still clutching an axe.

It couldn't have just been an axe…oh no, not me, it had to come with an arm! I thought as I ran to it. I looked up to see the demon coming closer, but he was slower than the rest, as he was dragging his foot behind him. I thought at first that he was already injured but then saw the glint from the moon shining from the leg length blade attached to his hip bone. Well, he might not be quick but he sure was packing!

I looked down at the arm and noticed with disgust that its fingers were still twitching around the axe's handle.

"Typical." I said and then stamped my foot down on its wrist hoping this would release his grip. I then quickly reached down and snatched the axe before its hand could fist around the wood again. I picked it up, feeling its hefty weight, wishing I had some more of Draven's mojo left in me. I looked up just in time to see the demon reach out and try to grab me. So, on a scream, I swung the axe round with all my puny strength. The demon reared back as I missed him but the momentum twisted my body more than I planned for and took me a few feet away from him.

I righted myself and dragged the axe back with me to be closer to Jared who looked to be finishing with the plated guy. He had just jumped up and delivered a downward punch to the top of the demon's head, where now a fist sized dent had caved in part of his face.

"Uh…Jared…could use a… little help over here." I said backing up further. Jared looked up from the guy on the floor to find me being stalked. He swiftly stomped down on the guy's spine, breaking his back in a sickening crunch of bones shattering. I used every shred of my strength to raise the axe up, hoping to use the weight to drive it down when needed. I jumped as I felt the axe being taken from me and I looked up to find Jared smiling down at me.

"You're just full of surprises, pet." Then he winked at me like we were on a date.

"And you're crazy." I said on a laugh. He nodded as though what I just said was obvious and then he proved that statement true. He cracked his neck and swung the axe to rest over his shoulder like some demonic woodcutter. The muscles bunched under leather and he strolled up to the demon who was still dragging his weapon behind him. It was looking quite helpless until it lashed out with its weapon infused leg with blinding speed. Jared jumped up enough to miss the propelled blade that spun the demon round. Jared then smiled before swinging the axe like a mad man. Parts soon started to be chopped off left, right and centre, so I looked away from the grotesque butchering.

My eyes quickly caught a flash of something by my feet and I screamed again as it was the plated demon that had crawled my way. He grabbed my foot in a painful hold with metal bent fingers and I stamped down on his shoulder to get him to release me.

"Oh. Just. Die!" I said each word with another stomp of my foot, but it was as if he couldn't even feel it.

"DIE! You stupid tin can!" I shouted and then shrieked when I saw an axe blade take off most of the demon's head.

"Tin can…really, that's the best you could do?" Jared asked with his eyes aglow with dangerous excitement. I kicked out of the dead demon's hold and said,

"I thought it would be degrading, but next time I will try 'little dick' and see if that helps." Jared burst out laughing as he pulled me to his chest and gave me a swift kiss. Then I was let go in breathless wonder, to see him back in serious killer mode.

"I need to get you safe." Then he looked around to assess the situation. There were piles of dead demons, most of which were missing vital parts of their bodies. I think if there had been lots of blood and gore I would have thrown up long ago. Thankfully though, this wasn't the case, as it was more like black dust and bits of burnt paper that came from the broken bodies. They were like man-shaped, skin sacked dirt.

His beasts were making short work of killing and I saw two trying to hold onto the one covered in oil but they couldn't grasp him for his slick body. He gripped one by the leg and rolled quickly, ripping the demon's limb away from the rest of its body. Then I saw the other two playing tug of war with one demon that had a mace for a head. He was trying to ram his face full of spikes into the bellies of the beasts that had him, but then he literally split in half from his crotch up to his chest. They left him with half his ribcage sticking out. Ok, so now I felt a bit ill!

"Yo J, can I crash this party of yours or what?" The voice came from above us and we saw Marcus stood in between the empty flint window frames, taking in the scene of carnage with a smile.

"About fucking time Marcus, get your ass down here." I felt the whoosh of air and then there he was standing next to me.

"Hey spunky, you causing trouble again?" He asked me, making Jared growl and Marcus grin.

"So what's the plan here J, you want me to do some roasting?" Jared raised an eyebrow at the thought, and I had no idea what he meant but from the sounds of it, I didn't want to!

"When I give the signal I want you to get Keira out of here. Transport her to the Mausoleum and wait for me there." Marcus crossed his arms and pouted before saying,

"Now that doesn't sound very exciting J, surely you're not going to make me miss out on all of the fun." Jared rolled his eyes and then stood back and raised his arm out at the fighting,

"Be my guest, Marcus." The evil smile that raised his sinister jester features made me shudder.

"Don't mind if I do, My Lord." He bowed gracefully and then straightened in one fluid motion. He was dressed like a modern-day pirate. With his long dark red leather jacket that had black metal buttons down its length and large cuffs folded back. With this he'd added a pair of skin tight jeans in light grey and a Beatles T-shirt with a loose thin scarf draped round multiple times.

Marcus stepped further into the centre and just as two demons came running at him from both sides he pulled a long thin blade from the holder hanging low by his thigh, hidden by his long jacket. He raised that blade to his lips, kissed it and ran it slowly through one closed hand. The blade came out the other side engulfed in red flames.

Just as the demons attacked, Marcus sidestepped one way and arched his blade up, cutting up the torso of one demon and then one step back had him slicing down into the next. Both fell to the floor in less than three seconds and only two steps.

"Man, he's good." I said looking on in awe. Jared just scoffed,

"Damn show off."

Jared's comment had me wondering why he hadn't yet changed himself. Was it to protect me better?

"I see dickhead showed up." Orthrus said now back in his human form, slick with sweat from his full body workout. Tight black muscles were still tensed and at the ready under his wet shirt. He looked like a tank ready to roll over someone.

"You gotta give it to him Bro, he's certainly got finesse." Jared commented at the sight of Marcus slicing apart his foe in a blaze of strokes.

"I don't gotta give him shit, unless it's mine to eat." Orthrus replied, rolling his shoulders. Jared laughed at his brother and smacked him on the back in some sacred brotherly code for love and respect.

All of Jared's men fell back to the line as all the demons in the courtyard had been forced to rest…and with no chance at getting back up again.

"So, what now, 'cause I gotta say, that seemed a bit too easy." Marcus said coming back last. He ran his hand over his blade and the flames died down to nothing before he sheathed it. However, a moment after that statement, another line of demons came from around the sides and collected together in front of us.

I turned to see Orthrus smack Marcus upside the head making the little bells in his red hair jingle.

"You just had to say it didn't you?" Orthrus scolded at Marcus.

"Just for you I did sugar lips, anyway quit your Conan belly a'rumblin, you know you live for this shit." Marcus counteracted.

"I also live for pounding on cocky little jester runts such as yourself."

"Cut it off you two and save it for the damn horde!" Jared snarled at them both and when his back was turned Orthrus rubbed his middle finger down his face and Marcus blew him a kiss in return.

"You have one more chance Cerberus, hand over the girl

and walk away." The suited man's voice rang out as a clear threat to my life and Jared started laughing.

"Well, at least the asshole knows who we are now." Orthrus said smiling.

"What's wrong Gastian, running out of death dealers and think you're pretty voice will scare me?" This got him a reaction as the mysterious Gastian bellowed a demonic rumble.

"Now that's what you call a comeback, pet." He said running a finger down my cheek with his lips twitching for a smile. I rolled my eyes at him and he broke out into a full laugh when I said,

"Men!"

"Bring the rage, my Brothers…bring the rage!" Jared shouted making his beasts snarl and snap their jaws with excitement.

"Alright bitches, you heard the man." Orthrus said nodding to his men to spread out as the next set of demons came closer. One of the largest ones didn't seem to be carrying a weapon so he moved quicker than the rest. Just as I was wondering what he was planning on using against these guys, he opened his mouth so wide, he dislocated his own jaw. Then he started to regurgitate something and soon the start of a thick chain could be seen coming up. I heaved a few times in the sight of him puking up metal, never being very good watching someone else being sick.

I was at least pleased to know I wasn't the only one that thought this was gross…but then it got worse. He bent over at the waist just as the chain was long enough to curl along the floor and then we all noticed another bit coming out from…oh God!..the other end!

"Oh Hell no… That is just sick…man that is wrong!" Orthrus said along with Marcus saying stuff along the same lines. Then Orthrus stepped up to Marcus, slapped him on the back and said,

"This dude's all yours, my man." The look Marcus shot Orthrus was enough to have me slap my hand to my mouth to try and squash down the laughter. Orthrus saw my attempt and gave me a friendly head nod that said he appreciated I was on his side.

"The Hell it is! You're the bastard that can lick his own balls, you go at him!" Orthrus dropped his amused face and growled.

"For that, both of you are gonna deal with him, now go." Jared ordered, turning serious all of a sudden.

"Fine, come on pencil dick, let's go kill this metal sucking fu…" I didn't hear the rest of his comment as Jared grabbed me and pulled me close.

"What's wrong?"

"I don't know, but it feels different this time, like he is waiting for something bigger to come. Promise me that when I give the word, you will go to Marcus, he will get you out of here somewhere safe, then I will come find you…understand?" I bit my lip at the thought of any of these guys getting hurt but didn't say anything, I just nodded.

"Good girl" He let me go and just before he turned back to the fight I grabbed his forearm.

"Jared…just play it safe…yeah?" He gave me that handsome grin of his and said,

"You worried about me, little pet?"

"I've got a vow to keep, remember?" I said smiling up at him. He gave me a quick kiss on the cheek and whispered,

"That you do, darling." Then we both took in the scene. The demon with the chains still had them dangling from both ends of his body but now had enough to swing around as weapons in each hand. I saw that neither beast particularly wanted to get within touching distance of the chains and I found this to be a bit funny, considering why. Here were all these mighty Hell beasts, and some of the most frightening creatures I had ever seen and they were worried about touching something as gross as where those chains had been…well minus the heinous situation we faced…that part was something I couldn't find humour in.

In the end though, they had no choice as Orthrus grabbed one bit of the chain in one head's mouth and the other bit in his second set of jaws. Then he jumped, twisting his body and in the process managing to loop the chain around the demon's neck. Then with both mouthfuls of metal he nodded to Marcus.

The same evil grin sparked something devious in his eyes as he produced a ball of flames in his hand. Then he dodged his way past a lunging demon and grasped the chain closest to the demon's mouth. This caused the metal to glow poker hot and that heat travelled along each link, not only on the outside but on the inside of his body also.

"Now!" Marcus shouted to Orthrus and the two-headed beast started to pull down on the ends of the chain just as that heat made its way around the demon's neck. One more pull like a pair of dogs with a bone and the massive demon's head singed right off his body. The rest of the demon, minus his head, fell to the ground just as the scorching chain burnt the rest of his body from the inside out.

"My Lord!" Marcus's shout shocked my head round in time to see a demon, whose torso was riddled with throwing knives, coming at us. Then, before I could shout out Jared's name, he had me wrapped in his arms and turned so that his back was to the demon. I felt his body vibrate before he jolted as though being struck over and over again. I heard him groan but more in discomfort than pain.

"Are you alright?" I whispered up at him, muffled in the warm cocoon his arms held me in.

"Peachy." He replied dryly, before looking over his shoulder. He must have seen the threat was over so he released me. I gasped as he turned around presenting a back that was full of embedded knives. But unbelievably this wasn't the reason for my reaction. It was less what was in his back and more what his back had become.

Instead of the back of a leather jacket moulded to a muscular back, now the leather had been shredded by the triangular shaped raised points that covered his back like scales. Only instead of them resembling the skin from a lizard, they looked more like a mixture of something Jurassic and hardened clumps of cemented fur.

Each one was ridged on top like a shell and the further down his back they went, the larger they were. They started off black closer to the skin and got lighter, being grey in the middle until the ends shone like metal tips.

Then he shook and the scales rippled, fanning out until all the blades dislodged and tinkled to the cobbled stone. It was incredible and I couldn't help myself from reaching out and trying to touch him. Just before my shaky fingers made contact, I found my wrist shackled and I looked up to see Marcus looking stern.

"I wouldn't do that if I were you." His warning was enough for me to take a step back, taking that threat seriously. Jared then took large angry strides to the demon who was about to discover the wrath of unleashed Hell's beast's fury. He lashed out and grabbed the demon by his neck, brought his face an inch from his and said,

"I liked that jacket." Then he twisted his wrist and snapped the demon's neck like it had been attached to his body with a toothpick.

"RRRRAAAAHHHH!" An ear shattering roar erupted, causing everyone to stop and look to the cause. Just near the entrance four of the demons were walking in what looked like a chained giant and struggling to do just that.

"Time to go." Marcus said, but before he could grab me, a demon caught him from behind, momentarily taking him off guard. This gave me enough time to watch Jared drop the demon like trash and step up into the middle of the courtyard. Along the way he casually kicked another dead demon out of his way and then nodded to Orthrus. His brother's heads both nodded back and then his eyes found mine.

Orthrus then let go of his other side and his beast peeled away, sliding from his body, once again looking like black sand. Once he was again in his human form, he slowly turned, looking for Marcus and rolled his eyes when he found him fighting off one of the demons. I saw him mouth the word 'asshole' before he started to fight his way over to us.

Meanwhile, my gaze turned back to Jared just in time to see two things happen simultaneously. The first had me suck in a frightened breath as the demons all let go of the chained giant at the same time, falling back to get away quick enough. The second had my mouth dropping as Jared shrugged off what remained of his ruined jacket. Then just as the giant man was about to reach him and I mean the very last second,

Jared changed.

His body rippled and unlike the others that had received their beasts through the ground, Jared was his own beast. His clothes tore, and then his skin split like a knife cutting through thick rubber until his host was no more. In its place was a beautifully terrifying creature to behold. He was by far the biggest out of his fellow beasts but he managed to look more graceful. He was a similar shape to a large cat, like a lion or a tiger rather than a wolf or large dog. The way he moved was so precise and calculating rather than brute strength attacking.

He had tall legs with massive clawed paws the same as his brother's beast had. However, his claws were longer and curled like polished talons. All of his body was covered in the same scales that I had seen on his back, only they were smaller and more tightly knitted together on his legs, giving the appearance of being smooth to touch. However, the ones near his back and around his neck were more pronounced. Kind of like a deadly mane as they looked sharp at the tips as if being dipped in silver.

But it was the lethal beauty in his face that really got to me. The adrenaline pounding through my veins for the upcoming fight had my pulse rate rocketing and he turned his face to me as though he could hear it.

A low forehead that connected to a thick muzzle and a wide nose at the end that was flat. Lines flared out from his nose that I imagined became more prominent when angry and snarling, which he didn't do when looking at me. His eyes were slanted and almond shaped which had lines running from the corners to his ears that gave him a cunning grace. They were the only thing left on him that remained like Jared, being piercing silver, only now with his black pupils in slits.

He was now all Cerberus and he was going in for the kill. The new demon was at least eight feet high and was huge. Not so much with defined muscles but more like just body mass as everything seemed to be overly large. His chest looked as though a stood up barrel had been sliced down the centre and then strapped together. His arms were longer than they should have been, which gave him a demonic primate vibe, made worse when he started swinging them around in an attempt to get to Cerberus.

The sheer speed in which Cerberus moved was incredibly fast and it was hard to keep up with his movements, unless he slowed to a calculating prowl. I could now understand where all the myths came from, because when Cerberus moved his head, there looked to be at least three of him due to the blurring speed.

I then focused back on the demon and it was his head that was the most distinct difference, when comparing him to a human male. Although most of his features remained the same, nose, eyes, ears and head shape, it was his mouth and his forehead that held the most differences.

Around his mouth there were no lips, just all open jaw with teeth that although the same shape as ours, were about ten times bigger. The fangs however hung down and locked with the bottoms ones, which were the same size as those of a jungle cat. This gave the appearance that his jaw was far too big for his face. Then there were the holes in his forehead that looked like someone had ripped out a central horn that was meant to still be there.

A pair of deep-set eyes gave the illusion that he might not have any, if it wasn't for the reflection from the moon that shone in them when he raised his head to roar at Cerberus.

And then he charged. Only this time Cerberus had obviously had enough of watching for his enemy's weaknesses. He let the raging giant run at him and at the last minute he used the flint wall of the courtyard to jump from, landing behind him. But this wasn't the only thing he counted on as the giant not being able to stop his momentum, went crashing into the stone head first.

"Show's over." Marcus said from behind me and just as things started to fade I saw Cerberus lunge for his back and deliver the killing blow to his neck.

"Wait!" My plea was lost somewhere in that courtyard, one we were no longer in. After a brief touch of darkness, I found we were now in some sort of mausoleum. It didn't take long, thanks to the moonlight shining down on pale stone, to realise I had seen this place before. Earlier that day in fact, I had walked up the hill behind the Hellfire Caves and looked through its locked gates.

It was a large open space of green grass and tall flint walls with no roof. It was an enormous hexagonal building with each side having a large arch flanked by Tuscan columns, as well as smaller arches, and rectangular openings. Most, I gathered, were designed to hold memorial slabs, busts or urns. All along the top in the corners of each bend were three vases of stone with the one in the middle being larger than the others. It was a beautiful structure, but right now I was a bit lost in what was happening below.

"Why did you do that?" I asked turning to Marcus.

"Orders spunky… just following orders. So you might as well get comfort…" His word ended abruptly on a shocked expression and a wheezing noise. I looked into his wide eyes amongst all the makeup he still wore and then when his gaze lowered, I followed it only to find an iron rod sticking out of his chest.

"Wh…at the… fuck!" He spluttered with blood not only seeping from his wound but now also his mouth. I was frozen in utter shock at what I was seeing. One second I was talking to the cocky face that spent most of his time fooling around and then next he was stood in front of me losing blood and looking far too close to death.

"Marcus!" I uttered his name and then something snapped me into action.

"I am going to get help!" I said taking a step back, about to turn when he just spluttered out one word…

"Run!"

CHAPTER FOURTY-SEVEN

PRISONER OF PROMISES

"RUN!" He bellowed at me when I didn't move.

"I'm not running." He groaned either in pain or frustration, I couldn't tell.

"I'm not leaving you to die…but I need to get…" I didn't end up finishing that sentence as Marcus screamed out in agony and I watched the steel rod in his chest start to move downwards, forcing him to his knees.

Then I screamed.

There was a demon stood right behind him holding the end of the rod, controlling Marcus like a diabolic Puppet Master. But more disturbing still, was that I had seen this demon before, only back in my nightmare he had that rod painfully set in between his cheeks. Now, there was just gaping holes either side where it had been, leaving his face misshapen even more than before.

"NO!" I screamed and without putting much thought behind my angry actions, I flew at him. I had no weapons other than my rage that blinded my fear. I pushed against his chest making him let go of the rod and Marcus. But, more unbelievable than him flying back through the air and landing on the wall of the mausoleum, was the damage I caused. He fell down like a repulsive broken doll and I looked at the damage one push of mine had caused. The whole of his chest cavity had caved in from my tingling hands and I was in such disbelief that I had to look down to see for myself, half expecting to see a weapon.

There was nothing.

"Get out of here! Run girl!" Marcus shouted at me, but instead of climbing the gates, I was running back to him. I skidded on the wet grass and fell in front of him. His head was slumped and a strange wheezing sound came with his breathing.

"Hold on, I will get Jared and he will…"

"You sho…d…should have run… gir…ly." He forced out in pain and then raised his head to look not at me, but the person I could now feel behind me. Before I could turn my head, I was seized from behind and stabbed in the neck with a needle. The world started to fade into a colourless fog, just as I heard words at my neck, from a voice…

I remembered,

"He's right you know…you should have run from me."

Then everything went black.

I woke up with a start to feel ice cold water being dunked over me. I shot up, coughing and spluttering, only to hear garish laughter echoing in the darkness.

"There, she's awake, now go n' tell the master so he can quit his belly achin'." I heard the heavy sound of a metal door bang shut then the grating noise of a lock sliding home.

I rubbed the water from my eyes and felt groggy, like waking after being on some heavy drugs…unfortunately it was from past experience that I knew this. This thought had me wrapped up in a moment of panic as I jolted from was must have been a bed. I fell in a heap on the floor with a painful thud and I scrabbled my way to a corner.

"It's not Morgan…it's not Morgan…it's not Morgan." I whispered over and over again. I pushed away that broken part of me until it was locked away in pieces, lost in a vault. Finally, I looked up from where I had huddled my knees to my chest and saw the moon's beam, coming through the bars on the window.

It lit up the space enough to semi recognise where I was. This prison was the same tower room from my nightmare. It may have started different in Sigurd's shadows but it had twisted into what I sat in now. So, it hadn't been a nightmare at all…it was my future!

I jumped up at this and ran over to the arched window and looked out to…nothing. We were too far up to see the ground in shadows so I would have to wait until the morning light. I turned back to the room and took in the small blocks that built up the circular room. Old iron pieces that once held candles stuck out of the rock, like battered arms hanging limp. The floor was covered in dirt and old straw. There was a small cot at the far end that looked to be made from crates and a battered mattress only a few inches thick.

I felt my lips start to quiver, not just from being cold and wet. The slow build of tears started to rise, threatening at any moment to fall, mixing with my cold damp skin. I didn't want to cry, I knew it wouldn't help but seeing Marcus slumped over like that…please…don't be dead. I held on to the idea that Jared had found him in time, but this didn't help with my emotional overload. I glanced at the wall of bars that was the only way I would be getting out of here, knowing that it wouldn't be tonight. So, I did the only thing I could do at that moment, whether it helped or not,

I cried myself to sleep holding onto my necklace.

I don't know how long I slept for, but I knew exhaustion made it a dreamless night. However, it was when I opened my eyes that I remembered I was already living through a nightmare. The sun shone through the window shedding more light on my dire situation. I gingerly got up, feeling the pain in my back from a hard night on this board for a bed. I was thankful at least that the grogginess had gone from whatever drugs they had injected me with.

I rubbed my neck where the needle had penetrated and thought out loud,

"Hell, its last year all over again." This was when I jerked to the sound of a door being opened in the distance. I remained still, half hoping no one would come and half hoping that they would so I would know what was going on. Another door pushed open and from the sounds of it, this one was much larger as it ground against the stone floor. Then came the sound of someone trying to whistle a tune, which no doubt produced more spit than actual sound!

A tall lanky string of shit waltzed in, swinging a bunch of metal keys round on a ring, looking smug.

"I see you've dried from your shower last night…consider that the start to your prison initiation process." The man who spoke was no questions asked ugly because the answers would consist of A: being dropped on his head repeatedly or B: mother and father were already mutants!

His eyes bulged, like one bum burp and out they would come flying. His lips were nearly non-existent they were so thin and what was there was cracked skin and some weird white snotty stuff collected in the corners. His nose was more like a beak that bent off to one side at the end. Jeez, even the guy's eyebrows looked like a pair of slugs had worked their way across to join in the middle and die!

Ok, I think you are getting that this guy was ten different types of ugly all wrapped into one bone thin package!

"I hope the next initiation step is the chance to kick your ass!" I said, my anger flaring. I heard a snigger from behind one of the pillars and the guy in front turned and snapped,

"Shut it, you dumb shit!" At this the snigger died.

"You think you're funny bitch, yeah? Well just wait and see what's coming to you, then you won't be so quick to disrespect me!"

"And you called him the dumb shit." I said sarcastically, knowing that whatever happened to me in this cell, the last thing on that bloody list would be to respect this guy...! Now, the guy hiding who laughed might be worth my time.

"What did you say to me!?" He boomed…or as much as he could with that nasally voice of his.

"Wow, deaf and dumb…really, what are the chances?" I said again, this time leaning against the wall like I had not a care in the world…when deep down I was praying to make it out of here in one piece.

"That's it now bitch, you will be sorry." He now looked enraged and if possible his eyes bulged further. He held out his hand behind him and snapped,

"Food!" To which a small guy appeared from behind the pillar just long enough to hand him a wooden bowl. I didn't really get a good look at the guy other than to see he was about five foot in height.

"This is your breakfast, enjoy it like the bitch you are." He said before he threw its contents at me, making it splat mainly on the floor and wall behind me. I closed my eyes as he started laughing at me and decided what he wanted was to see me get upset. So I opened my eyes, ran a finger along the slop on my cheek and then licked my fingers to taste the lumpy porridge.

"Thanks for that, from the taste of this shit, you just did me a favour." Then I grinned at him because to see his face turn beetroot red in frustration was a funny thing to behold. He looked ready to blow but before he did, he threw the empty bowl to the floor making it bounce and then stormed off swearing.

"Thhhat wasnhh't a good idea missth." The stuttering that came from behind the pillar sounded gentle, not threatening. I scooped the rest of the porridge off my face and top and shook it off onto the floor.

"What can I say, I am just a glutton for punishment… besides, that demon's toothpick doesn't scare me." Not after all I had seen in my short life!

"He doesth me." I gave his general direction a small smile and said,

"What's your name?" I asked hoping, in spite of the low chances, that I could make a friend here, one who might help me.

"Perthcy."

"Well Percy, I'm Keira and I would love to know what I am doing here?" I said getting up and walking closer to the bars, hoping to lure him out of the shadows.

"You don'th know?"

"Not really, but I am guessing it's because of a man called Gastian." At the sound of me saying his name, a hissing noise came from behind the stone.

"He isth no man." I wanted to say 'no shit' after seeing what guests he brought to the party last night but decided to give the little guy a break on the sarcasm.

"So, who is he or more importantly what does he want with me?"

"I don'th know but he doesn'th like you very mucth." He said like this was news to me. Again, I squashed down the sarcastic remarks and stretched my head to try and see the other rooms from my cell.

"Percy, do you know where I am or do you know if anyone else is kept here?" I asked, suddenly thinking that maybe somewhere in this rotting shell, Draven could also be held prisoner.

"I am not thsurpossed to talk to you about thhat." As soon as I heard the slightly panicked edge to his stutter, I knew I had lost him by going too far with my questions.

"Okay but do me a favour…don't listen to what that idiot says to you."

"Why are you being thso niceth to me?" I shrugged my shoulders and then answered honestly,

"I don't like bullies and besides, you laughed when I threatened to kick his ass, so in my book that counts for something."

"Don'th be niceth to me, I don'th dethserve it." He said in a sad voice that had me feeling sorry for the guy. It was obvious he was only doing what he was told in this situation and in the supernatural world of the fittest, I was afraid my new friend must have come low down on that scale.

"Well, you haven't hurt me and you have not bullied me, so that is a big plus in my situation."

"PERCY, GET YOUR ASS IN HERE NOW!" I cringed at the sound of my new best friend being a dick once again and bellowing for my 'actual' new friend.

"I have to go, but don'th make him mad again, I don'th wanth him to hurt you."

"I can't promise that my new friend, as I have a feeling it might just become a favourite pastime for me." I heard a burst of cute giggles before another yell had him leaving without a word or giving me my first real glimpse of the guy.

Now that I was alone, I let my mind begin the process of self-preservation and trying to find a way out of here! I didn't know where I was, so trying to reach out for help was not a doable idea at the moment. I had looked out of the window and saw that not only were we in the middle of some nowhere field, but that I was at least six storeys up, which translated to suicide if I had the inclination to see if I could fly.

The next step was to see if there was any weak spots in the bars but that took all of about five seconds and a swear word to realise that was a big fat no go! Then came the walls, running my hands along them to see if there was any crumbling but without my very own Jared in beasty form, I wasn't getting anywhere with that either. So, after a frustrating few hours, I slumped down on my rickety bed and tried to stare a hole in the wall.

In the end I got so bored I started to peel away the porridge that had hardened worryingly into something that resembled cement and plaster. I was now glad that ugly stick man had thrown it at me instead of demanding I eat every morsel like some creepier version of the witch in Hansel and Gretel.

I was halfway through a really big peeling bit, that shamefully was exciting me (And yes, this was an indication of the deterioration of my mental state) When I heard the doors opening again. I was secretly hoping for it to be just Percy with maybe a McDonald's bag in hand. Of course, when I saw the sleazy walking pencil, I knew one could only hope.

"Hey Bitch, miss me?"

"You know I would say 'like a hole in the head' but I met a guy last night with an actual hole in his head. I reckon he would take that over five minutes of looking at your butt ugly face...! So no, I really didn't." Again, I had to smile as I saw him go a blotchy fuchsia colour, reminding me of someone allergic to fruit being dipped in a vat of the stuff.

"Laugh it up you stupid slut, I am the one who brings you food and once again…oops!" He said tipping the plate and I watched something fall that could have been a sandwich but I couldn't be sure. Then he stamped on it, giving me what he must have classed as his best 'badass' smile. I felt like introducing him to a few of my male friends where he would receive a crash course on the very meaning of Bad Ass!

"Wow, you know it actually looks more edible now, why don't you take the first bite."

"Oh, you think you're so clever, well let's just see what that smart mouth comes up with when you are begging me for food and water!" I heard a stuttering as Percy must have been back and trying to find the right thing to say in this situation.

"Yyyyou know you can'th do thhhat, Dimme."

"Shut your trap! I can do what I damn well want, this is my prison, you stupid little shit!" Meanwhile I had burst out laughing.

"What's so funny, Bitch!?"

"You name is Dimme?" I said unable to hold back on the perfect timing for revenge.

"Yeah so what?!"

"As in Dim…? What's your last name, Witted?!" He growled at me and it was about as intimidating as being faced with a featherless baby bird pecking at me. I say baby bird, 'cause that was the ugliest baby anything I could think of.

"Have fun losing weight, 'cause I won't be back here until I hear you beg me for food!" I clapped my hands and stated,

"Oh, thank you Lord, some good news today after all! I would take death overseeing your bony ass again and as for begging…I would rather eat my own clothes first!"

"Don't be so sure, Bitch!" He snarled and then stormed out.

"Oh dear…my, my, masther isth not going to be pleasthed." Percy stammered worryingly.

"Don't worry about it, just be sure to let him know when I am close to death and then ask him if you're allowed to bring me a cheeseburger." I said only half joking.

"How isth it you're not worried?"

"Because believe it or not, I have been in stickier situations than this and going without food is just like a stay at a diet camp, not my idea of torture…although I wish I could stop thinking about burgers." I heard him giggle and I winked over at where I thought he was hiding.

"I won'th leth him stharve you." I gave him a grateful smile but said,

"Look Percy, I don't want you getting into any trouble because of me."

"I will come in the nighth, he won'th know, I promiseth you to be back." I nodded my head, as much as my bravado act might be convincing, I didn't know how long I could hold out on the food front.

"Thank you." He made a nervous giggle again and I bet if I could see him he would be blushing.

"I bether go before he shouths at me." I nodded and gave him a little wave.

That night I woke to my name being whispered in the dark, to find a piece of bread, a chunk of cheese, an apple and a tin cup of water just outside my cell.

My new friend had kept his promise and now it was my turn to keep mine…

To Draven.

CHAPTER FOURTY-EIGHT

THE BLOOD THAT WON'T BURN

It had been nine days since that first day, or at least that is what Percy had told me when I got confused. It was strange how all days seemed to mingle into one long blur. Even with the light from the window, I still found myself muddled as to which time of day it was as my sleeping pattern had changed.

It started when the dreams came.

There was an enormous sandstone wall that ran the full length around a sandstone city. People were dressed from a history long gone and I stood in what seemed to be a market-place. Handmade stalls were everywhere, in no particular pattern. They sold bowls full of spices, herbs and dried leaves piled high into pyramids. Others sold, fruits, vegetables, furs, baskets, and pottery painted in pretty colours in all shapes and sizes.

The dreams always started the same. I am stood amongst the hustle and bustle of the place, looking round in wonder, trying to make sense of this old world. I am in the middle of the largest space between stalls as if it's the main path, when I hear the great thundering of hooves. I look up to see men on horse-back racing their way straight to me and that's when I realise I am stood in a road leading straight to the massive palace behind me.

Everyone else around me has moved out of their way, but I am frozen. I cannot move one muscle other than what it takes for my body to produce a single tear. For there, coming right at me, leading the army of men is…

Draven.

He looks so strong and powerful on the back of his midnight black horse. He is armoured as if ready for battle and his fierce expression tells me his sword and shield aren't his only weapons. I let the slight breeze take away his name whispered on a breath and from his sharp gaze it looks as though he heard me.

It's in these sweet moments that last only a few beats of my heart, that a sense of peace envelopes me and I welcome every last morsel of it…before a different Hell rips it from me.

The world turns dark just as he forces his horse into greater speed right at me. I know it will kill me and just as he gets closer enough to see the purple in his eyes, I fall to the ground to protect myself. Only he doesn't hit me. No, he goes straight through me and when I finally brave opening my eyes, I find him galloping away from me with a great army behind him.

That is when my dream turns so dark, I scream out for him to come back to me. But he doesn't hear my plea for all he can hear is the cries for battle as he races headfirst into a wall of armed demons and an Underworld unleashed for War.

So, because of this dream, I no longer wanted to find comfort in sleep and when I couldn't hold it at bay any longer I'd wake screaming much to the glee of my captor Dimme. Sometimes I'd wake feeling like I was drowning in the blood of the battle, my dead friends around me like broken ragdolls. But then I would realise like the first night, I was just being woken to an icy bucket being thrown through the bars.

I would grit my teeth and come up with a witty comment much to the displeasure of the sadistic string bean that was my tormentor. This was actually one of the things that managed to keep me sane, as I would spend my solitude thinking up new insults that would make my day purely for unmaking his.

I wasn't a cruel person, I like to think far from it, but that demon deserved far worse than my harsh words. I would talk to Percy when I could and he would tell me of the beatings he would receive at Dimme's hands. I still hadn't seen his face but his stuttering voice brought me so much comfort in this nightmare, he was like my light in the darkness.

He told me that a long time ago his Possession officer was forced into a blood pact with Dimme, over some debt and as a means to pay him he handed over possession of the new Demon he was training to accept his host at the time. That demon was none other than my poor friend Percy. Now until Dimme would release him into the world to face it alone, he was stuck doing his will for the rest of his miserable days.

The hardest part of all this was knowing the real reason Percy kept himself hidden, was from shame at what had been done to his face. I wanted to ask but the deeper stuttering had me worried if I pushed too much, I would upset him. I knew however, with every bone in my body that Dimme was the reason. Percy was a good demon stuck being slave to one he loathed for being so evil.

The worst part to all this, in those nine days, wasn't the hunger or the intense thirst. It wasn't the stench that I lived in or the fact that I had become part of that stench by not being allowed to wash. Hell, it wasn't even having a bucket for a toilet and shamefully not having any privacy sometimes. No, it was in that nine days the amount of times that I saw him hit Percy and trying not to react to it every damn time! I knew that if I made even the slightest flinch that looked as if I cared, then I would be condemning Percy to even more pain as Dimme would have found my weakest spot of all.

Throughout this I would only cry at night, sometimes to the sound of Percy's soothing words, but all he would hear from me was the word 'Sorry'. I wanted to find the hidden strength in me so badly, that I felt like my head would explode from trying so hard. I not only wanted it to lead to a way out of here, but also to aid in my new mission…I wanted to save Percy.

I needed to save Percy.

I had to!

My heart bled for him and that was why a bitter and twisted

side grew in me. I felt good whenever I delivered an insult that would cause a reaction from Dimme. I wanted to hurt him, to humiliate him in front of those he considered weaker than him. I wanted to show up the bullies for what they really were…weak and scared!

"Only the weak and scared would prey on those they truly feared, for if a smaller man was ever to rise and take a stand against the bigger then that would be their end…that was their real fear and they warped it into a power they thought would keep them powerful…but they were wrong and one day I will prove this to you my friend." I told Percy one night.

"I hope that one day you will." His voice had not stuttered at all this time and I knew right then that in anger it never would.

"There is a warrior in you my friend and hope for us yet." I whispered once I heard the doors lock up for the last time that night.

Which leads me to now and nine days into my un-judged sentence.

"Good morning, Skeletor." I said as Dimme walked up to my cell like he did every morning. He grinned at me, so I don't think he got the He-man reference…pity, it took me half of yesterday to come up with that one! Of course, it wasn't lost on me the irony of my 'bony' jokes considering I was being half starved to death. I didn't like to think of it as Karma for my nasty behaviour, but just plain old payback. What he didn't know was that if he really wanted to torture me right now all he would have to do is bring me a mirror and that would do the trick, I thought on a laugh.

"Something funny, you disgusting Bitch?" Eh…kettle black much!

"I was just thinking, you know if you swallowed a meatball you would look pregnant." I laughed harder at his thunderous face and didn't even flinch this time when he threw water at me… After all, I needed the wash!

The only thing I was lucky for was that he thought I must have some supernatural mojo at work in helping me not starve to death, as he never once suspected Percy was the cause. This either made him 'supernaturally thick' or it was just so unbelievable what my friend would do for me that it wasn't conceivable enough to consider. I liked to think a mixture of the both.

"Soon you won't have the strength to laugh!" I had heard this last comeback for a few days now and it was more annoyingly repetitive than threatening.

"Yeah, so you've said…again and again… Say, do you know when that's gonna happen? Do you? 'Cause you make me want to rip my ears off and choke you with them every time I hear that line." Yep and there was his trademark blotchy face…score million to Keira and a big fat zero for Mr Puniverse...!

Ooh, that was a good one and was so getting used tomorrow!

"You know, I was going to wait until later to do this, but I think any time to watch you cry is as good as any." I frowned at this new change of events, normally he just stormed out looking ready to implode.

"Pass me the bag you scarred little turd." Don't flinch, don't flinch, I said over and over hoping this wasn't one of those days that he hit him. Instead I slowly released a held breath when I saw him take something from Percy's out-stretched hand, only to suck it back in again when I saw what it was.

"That doesn't belong to you." I said in a voice that I didn't recognise belonging to me. It was one that didn't threaten violence but more like promised it.

"That's where you're wrong. See, my master said I could just burn it if I chose, but I don't think he realised what it was you had hidden inside." He said in that snotty nasally voice that grated against my skin. He held my bag that was now torn on one side of the strap, like it had just been yanked from me.

"You will be sorry." I warned as he reached inside and pulled out the Ouroboros blood bound book.

"Oh I don't think so, let's just take a peek and see what secrets I can report back to my master, shall we?" I felt the tingling in my fingertips and thought this might be one of those times my anger could transform into a useful weapon.

Then I calmed slightly when I realised I didn't need to panic about anything, which was proven when I heard his high pitched yell of pain. He had tried to open the book, only the snake on the front had lashed out and bitten him. He clutched his pale hand to his chest and I saw the black venom from the bite start to travel along his veins.

"I did warn you." I said not even bothering to cover sounding smug as I crossed my arms over my chest.

"Shut up, Bitch! Percy, hand me that torch!" He snapped and that was when I lost all my cool demeanour.

"NO!" I shouted at him, coming to the bars to get closer in hopeful aid to stop what I knew he was about to do. He kept his beady eyes to me and smirked as he took the torch from the shaking hand of Percy.

"It really does mean so much to you, don't it?" He asked making me hate him even more. I felt my eyes turn into hard slits as I let the true rage fill me to the point where my hands grew hot against the metal bars.

"Then watch it burn, Bitch!" He said raising the torch to the book and watching the flames engulf its pages. I watched the snake on the front hiss and writhe around the page in the face of danger.

"NO!" This time I screamed, and it was Dimme's turn to laugh. He dropped the square of black charred pages as the flames curled the edges into ashy flakes, ready for a mere hint of a whisper in order to fly away.

"No!" I said, falling to my knees. I had to save it, I couldn't lose that bond, not when it was one of the very things I was counting on getting me out of here. I knew that Sigurd would somehow find me…he would tell Jared and maybe even Lucius…They would come for me…they had to!

With this in mind, I decided my promise mattered more to me than my own flesh, so even though it was still burning, I quickly reached out my hand through the bars and snatched it back to me to hold it to my chest. I felt the heat of it but instead of pain, I felt light. I inhaled sharply as I felt part of myself being absorbed into the book. As though it was looking for something in me and once it found it, it homed in and drew from its strength.

"NO! That's not supposed to happen!" I heard Dimme

scream out in anger and even with my eyes closed, I smiled to myself at the sound, for I knew without looking that the book was whole once again. But even better, it was now in my arms and the only way it was leaving them was being pried from my cold dead body!

I looked up at him but what he saw in my eyes had him backing up, stumbling over the fresh bucket he brought.

"No! It's…it's not possible! You're human!" He spluttered out in shock and I had no idea what it was in me he was seeing, but I knew fear when I saw it. And the next sight of him running from the room was confirmation of this.

"Ke…ira?" Percy's voice was unsteady, also seeming a little frightened of me.

"It's alright, Percy." I said blinking a few times wondering if what Dimme had seen was still there.

"Your eyeths, they…changed." I didn't really have much to say to that as I couldn't explain it myself. I looked down at the leather-bound book in my hands and noticed that not only was it without a mark from what happened…so was I. Surely I should have been burnt?

"You can come out my friend." I said getting up to sit on the cot, feeling as if all the energy had suddenly been zapped out of me. I had asked this of him many times before, but never once had he come from the safety of the shadows he knew…

Until now.

A little man walked out, who I realised was smaller than what I'd originally thought, being closer to four feet than five. He had on him a dark brown cloak, like a monk's habit and the hood was concealing all of his face.

"You don't have to hide from me." I said pushing up my sleeves and holding both of my arms out for him to see my scars. I saw him raise his head and I just caught sight of the burn marks on his chin.

"I…I don'th wanth to fffrighten you." I smiled at that and said,

"I have seen many things, many terrifying things that most would class as monsters, but those monsters were all my enemies. You're not my enemy…are you, Percy?" He shook his head making the low hood sway.

"Then I have nothing to fear in your face." I saw his little shoulders slump in defeat as my words rang true. Then he raised his hands enough for me to see them wrapped in thin white gauze and guide his hood back from his face. I knew that what I was about to see would be heart-breaking, but I didn't want to react. So, I prepared myself the best I could.

What shocked me the most wasn't the face of burnt flesh, but it was the face behind the scarred mask. No amount of puckered skin and twisted scarring tissue could keep the beauty beneath it from beaming out at me. I slipped from the bed and walking on my knees, I approached him slowly. He seemed to want to back away and I raised my hand in a show of peace.

"Please, let me." I said softly and I didn't move again until he nodded. I looked at his face now nothing could be hidden and no amount of fire could take away a pair of beautiful eyes that were frantically looking around as if waiting for a harsh hand. I felt like crying for him but knew that wasn't what he needed. So instead of pity, I gave him what I thought he needed…a kind touch.

I reached out and he froze in fear but I would soon give him nothing to fear…not ever again if I could help it. My hand slipped through the bars and I quickly cupped his cheek before he could pull back from me.

"I think you're beautiful Percy, make no mistake about that, for your pure soul shines through and no amount of hateful words or harsh punishments will ever make that beauty die… ever." I looked deep into his sea green eyes and saw the tears start to form, making them look like an enchanted lake, that I could only hope was filled with trust. I watched one lone tear fall down the uneven path of his cheek and I caught it, wiping it away with my thumb.

"You will never be alone again, for I will take you with me, Percy." Then we both cried our own silent sobs, mine brought on when he trusted me enough to take my other hand in his smaller one.

"Thhank you, my Fffriend." He said smiling at me for the

first time. All I could do was nod and clasp his hand tighter in mine.

That night came the next Quarter Moon and with it something new. I was stood looking up at it through the window when I heard the usual doors grating along the stone as they were being pushed open. I was not in the mood for any more of Dimme's twisted pastimes as the day's events had drained me. The emotional rollercoaster from nearly losing the book, to the heart-breaking reveal of Percy and then to a day full of asking the book questions it refused to answer.

No secret messages filled me with hope, not one new word seeped into its pages and now it looked as though I had something new to contend with. I ran over to the bed and placed the book I still held on to under the thin mattress. I was on my knees rearranging the straw I had piled on top for extra warmth when footsteps stopped behind me.

Then something disturbing crept over me like spiders covering every inch of my skin, all running over each other to find their own place next to my flesh.

Then came the pain.

It was as if they had all bit down at once. I lowered my head and couldn't help the cry that broke free. I wanted to be strong but the pain was unimaginable. I just wanted it to end and it had only been seconds. It took me back in time to two different points. The first was that night so long ago in the bathroom at Draven's. Sammael was the cause back then but he was long gone and sent back to the Hell from which he'd escaped. So the question was…who was my tormentor now?

This brought on the second part of my journey into the past, only back then it had been into the future. Sigurd had shown this to me and I had been in this very room with my other self-trying to get back. Well, there was no getting back there now, that time had gone and with it my protector. There were no arms of comfort ready to pull me from this place and hold me close. There was only me and what little power I had.

'Concentrate, Keira.' I told myself. That's when it happened. I felt the same tingling at my wrist and looked down to see one of the stones in my bracelet was glowing. I then looked up to the Quarter Moon and felt a sense of relief wash over me like a wave crashing up the cliffs of my mind. 'Control it' the wind whispered over the water and suddenly there I was. I was stood on a cliff face using my inner strength to push the waves back until the water became calm once more. And as those waves started flowing in the other direction, an impossible one back out to sea, it took with it my pain.

I took away my pain.

Now I could move. Now there were no biting spiders or fooling my mind into believing anything I didn't myself control. I twisted my head and looked up to see outside of my prison, a room full of demons…and I didn't even flinch.

Gorgan leeches with their faces full of teeth and cracking limbs all clicked their jaws, sounding out like giant crickets. In between them were more of the death army that had fought that night. Only unlike the dream, the one in front of the rest was no longer the creature with a steel bar locking his cheeks together. Because I sent him back, killing his already death host. Which made me wonder for the hundredth time…was Marcus still with his host?

As in the dream, the demons all parted to let through the one responsible for all of this. I stood and faced him with no fear left, only undiluted anger at what he had done to me.

"Ah, my disgusting parasite, how nice to see you again." The same vile words passed his lips but this time it was different because now they were from lips I finally recognised…

"You!"

CHAPTER FOURTY-NINE

TWO DOWN, TWO TO GO

I couldn't believe it! After all this time of wondering who it was that was after me and now I was faced with this guy!

"This is not happening!" I said thinking back all that time ago to that cold night following a cruel punishment.

"Oh believe me you vile creature, this is happening and it just so happens to be my revenge." At this my fingers curled into fist.

"I saved your life!" I screamed at him, but he just threw his head back and laughed at me. Then he straightened as if someone flicked his crazy switch,

"You ruined my LIFE!" He screamed back at me, giving me a flash of his demon side. I shook my head trying to piece this all together, but I was in too much of a shock.

"It was you all this time…I should have let Draven kill you!" I said gritting my teeth at the end through my anger and not only at the man responsible, but also at myself for being weak in Draven's world.

I remembered it so well now. I was in Afterlife VIP when I bumped into a suited man… *"How dare you touch me, you vile human bitch! Someone should teach you manners you disgusting parasite…GO and fuck off!"* His words had been as such when he pushed me from him. Draven had seen and in his rage split his council's table in two. That night I begged Draven to save this demon's life after he had made the man in front of me now, beg my forgiveness in a broken mess. I had run from Draven, run from the horror and realisation of it all. Run from a world he commanded and ruled over with his iron will. And now I was here and I couldn't run anymore…

But I knew what he wanted.

"You took Draven… you took me and now what…? You want to see us both beg!?" I said looking back at him with new eyes. He started laughing again.

"You really are a stupid bitch, aren't you?" I didn't respond as he continued laughing at me.

"Oh, this is so much better than watching you beg like the human dog you are! No, I don't have your precious King! You really think if I had that type of power over him, I would be wasting my time with you!"

"Then why?" I asked making him laugh even harder. Then I lost it, I grabbed hold of the bars and screamed,

"TELL ME WHY?!" The laughing stopped and I heard Dimme suck in a frightened breath before whispering…

"There, I told you master…she has the essence of…"

"YES! I can see that you fool! You don't scare me!" He snapped back at me and again I felt the same power making my fingertips tingle.

"You want to know why but the why is so simple. That night you ruined me, everything I worked for, my riches, my power, my position…all of it gone just because you couldn't walk in a fucking straight line!" This time it was my turn to laugh.

"And now look who the stupid one is…this is all because you couldn't keep your temper in check because someone fucking bumped into you…are you that senseless? If you had taken a second to think why a human would have been there in the first place it might have saved your ass…but don't go blaming me for your own foolish actions!" This comeback had now turned this smug bastard into an angry bastard instead, but I didn't care!

"You vile creatures don't deserve to walk among us! But don't worry I will be getting my revenge."

"So, leaving me here to rot is your big 'master' plan?" I said mocking him.

"No, that is just for my pleasure before I regain what was taken from me. I care little what happens to the likes of you and with the King now out of the way…well, it was almost too easy."

"You're forgetting one massive flaw in this plan, Draven is not here you prick…so how do you suppose your revenge will work if he doesn't even know you have me!?" This time he didn't laugh but raised one side of his mouth in a knowing smirk.

"Your 'Draven' can't give a shit about you where he is and I care little about pointless, but more importantly, penniless revenge." I let go of the bars trying to make sense of it all. What did he mean…where Draven was?

"Then what…?" I didn't finish as he stepped up to the bars himself and said,

"It is simple, I am going to sell you to the highest bidder, make back my money, regain my power and not give you one more single thought…I will however be most pleased if whoever buys you is a cruel bastard, but one can only hope." At this I screamed and lunged for him. I didn't end up doing as much damage as I would have liked but he was now sporting three bloody scratch marks down his face. He wailed out like a banshee, clutching his injured face in his hands and said,

"You will regret this!" But that was the last I heard as Gastian and his minions all vanished from the room, leaving me with my thoughts.

That night something in me changed and I knew it was all down to the Quarter Moon and the bracelet of stones. How did I know this? Well, after Gastian and his demon posse left me, the book woke up and told me so.

On the first Quarter Moon, the Blue moonstone stone will light the path for a protector to find his balance. Blood will bind together these souls and aid them both when travelling towards the prophecy. Clarity of mind and inner vision will flow clearly, building trust for future altered states of awareness.

Life lessons will be learned through each other's fates, entwining destinies into one goal…
Life must be conquered.

This I knew referred back to my birthday and when Sigurd had saved me. But why was the book only telling me this now… was it because up until this point I had not asked or even taken much notice of my bracelet? Well, now I was taking notice and found that for the first time, two of the stones instead of being a milky grey colour, were different than before. The first one that must have changed was now a stunning deep sky blue that had such a depth to it, the stone almost looked alive.

I touched it and felt its energy buzzing through me, as if somehow keeping me balanced. Then I turned around the black cord they were all attached to and found the next stone. This time it had been changed into a pure white stone that had a pearlescent sheen across the top of its smooth surface. I looked down at the book and asked it,

"And the second Quarter Moon?

On this second Quarter Moon, the white moonstone encourages the wave of calm in these fraught seas. It carries with it the energy needed from this moon, as the height of this power you will gain through strength of mind and will. It will aid in stimulating psychic perception and vision in this world and that of the dream realm you hold the key to. Learn from past lessons and this moon will magnify one's emotions into a powerful weapon of imprisonment of the mind.
Train yourself to do this and you will find Nightmares cannot hurt what they cannot control.

Now I knew what I had to do and why the Oracle had given me this bracelet. She must have foreseen my journey and knew I would need its guidance. But if that was the case, then why hadn't anyone come to rescue me or even before any of this, why had she not warned me about the kidnapping so that I might have prevented it?

There were just too many questions like this and more than enough for me to go a little insane. I asked the book over and over but other than these two passages it would tell me no more. Not even on the other stones, so that I might have a small idea on what was left to come.

I remember her saying that it was only on the Last Quarter Moon that I would find Draven and this thought had me in tears. Was I really to go through so much more before I would finally find him and even more importantly would I be strong enough by then to fight for him?!

"Yes! I must." I said aloud wiping away useless tears. I looked up from my helpless huddle and saw the Quarter Moon in the centre of my window. It was like a beacon of hope and from that moment on I knew what I needed to do with this time…

Make myself stronger.

Eleven days went by and if it hadn't been for Percy, I knew I would have been dead. The only food that I had still only came to me at night but the effects of it could be seen in my protruding ribcage and collar bone. I had lost an alarming amount of weight in the almost three weeks I had been here. However, in all that time not once had an attempt been made to rescue me.

It was as though not one person knew where I was and even through the book no one had contacted me. I used to hold it to my heart at night and with all my mental strength, try and get a message out there. I would sometimes feel something, like words trying to get through, but then when I looked down the words would already be fading. It was both so exhausting and soul destroying that after six days of this I gave up.

I might have given up the idea of anyone contacting me but I still held on to hope that someone would still rescue me. I had no choice, as the alternative of being sold was far too scary to face. So instead, I used my time wisely like the book had suggested I do and that night it turned out to be a definite blessing. See, when Gastian said that I would regret my attack on him, he hadn't been wrong as I discovered what powers he still held.

Percy had tried to caution me but I had been too wrapped up in what the book had said about the moonstones to concentrate on his warnings. That night, after Percy had left me my food, when I quickly started to devour it, it turned out that it left me just as quickly when I had to throw it all back up violently.

As with the spiders, Gastian had piled my room full of delicious looking food after I finished my meal that had me salivating again. I forgot myself and started to pick up hot meat pies that once you bit into them would be filled with blood coming from the heart inside. I would drop the pie and grab a jug full of lush cool water only to find urine as it hit the back of my throat burning.

I then looked around the floor and suddenly every single bit of food was infected. From the rotting fruit to the maggots inside crusty bread or black flies writhing around on top of roast meat. Then came the large brown rats living inside large cakes and the disgusting human body parts made to look like normal food.

I retched into my bucket over and over until nothing was left but the bile I continued to bring up in spit. This was all made worse when I could still see it covering the floor of my cell, even hear the rats munching away on whatever their mouths feasted on. Then I would just end up heaving all over again.

I wanted to start screaming, begging for someone to come and get me out of there! I even gripped onto the bars, ready to shout out but then I stopped myself as I cried into my hands. I opened my eyes to see the white Moonstone with its wire moon shape holding it to the cord and knew what I needed to do. So I did what I had done countless times before, only this time I would work and work until I passed out if need be, but I would do it so much that pushing these nightmares back became second nature to me.

So for eleven days that's precisely what I did. I trained my mind into a weapon against weapons. A shield to those who wished to use their powers of mind control against me, so that when the next night came and with it a new nightmare, I was ready for it. So for five days I fought off everything Gastian threw at me until one day they just stopped completely. I didn't know if this was down to him giving up or that my mind had become so powerful he just couldn't get through anymore. Whichever it was, this imprisonment had given me two things…

One was power and the other was Percy.

When it came to my little friend, I still didn't know his story and I decided not to push for it as I knew he would tell me in time. I also found our limited time we had to talk was the highlight of my day as he would ask me questions about my life. He seemed fascinated by hearing me talk about Draven, as he had heard a lot about the King but never met him. I think it really hit home about Draven's true position in Percy's world when he seemed star struck just listening to me talk about him. Almost like me popping round to a neighbour's house and telling them I was off out to have a pint with Johnny Depp dressed as Jack Sparrow!

But our time, as I said, was limited mostly to the nights when it was safer for Percy to spend time unbeknown to Dimme aka, Skin'diana Bones. So when he walked in now alone in the light of day I was instantly worried.

"Percy, what's wrong?"

"I don'th have mucth thime but wanthed you to know hhe's coming for you." His words were panicked and even more slurred than usual in his agitated state.

"Who, Gastian?" He nodded looking around and then pulled out a ring of keys ready to get me out.

"Whoa, what are you doing?"

"I am setthing you ffree." I knew this was my one chance here but something didn't feel right and I knew in my gut what it was.

"No Percy, don't." He stopped and looked up at me, no longer trying to hide his face.

"Why noth?"

"Because there is no way to do this without them knowing it was you and without knowing we can get out of here together safely, I won't risk you getting caught and punished." I didn't care if this was my one shot at freedom at the expense of a friend's life I wasn't willing to risk it!

He started to fiddle with the key and try again to open the door until I put my hand on his to stop him.

"Percy no! Please, don't do this…there has to be another way."

"There isn'th time, thhey come for you now." He said, his hand starting to shake.

"Then let them take me and I will try and get away at this auction thing, but I refuse to do it now…do you trust me, Percy?"

"Yesth" He nodded and I pulled the key from the lock and handed it back to him through the bars. I then fished in my pockets until I found Draven's father's coin, as it was one of the things not yet taken from me.

"Here take this, it is something precious to me and I want you to keep safe until I see you again and Percy…" I paused as I placed the coin in his hand to then keep hold of it when I said,

"If you let me do this my way I promise you… *I promise you my friend*… I will find a way for us both to come out of this safely." He looked ready to cry but shook his head anyway for another yes and then ran from the room before I saw the first of his tears fall.

"Oh, Percy." I said aloud. I now knew the lengths that Percy would go to free me and when someone risked their life for yours, that friendship was immeasurable!

It wasn't long before they came for me and with Dimme being my main tormentor in all this, it was no surprise that he was front row with a beaming smile slapped on his face! Of course, it was Gastian who was leading the demonic mob and he too was looking especially pleased with himself.

"So, it's the big payday today then?" I asked picking dirt from my nails trying to look uninterested, when deep down inside I was just hoping when the time came that I wouldn't start screaming like a little girl who wants her mamma!

"It is indeed parasite, so it's time to get you presentable, as I am not sure I will even get ten pounds for you in that state, although if it were left up to me I would gladly keep you in this cesspit where you belong." I schooled my anger at his words and said on a laugh instead,

"Well, I am facing a room full of shit for brains!" At this Dimme reclaimed his trademark angry blotches and Gastian sneered at me, making my work here complete.

"Get in there and hold her down!" Gastian ordered as he pulled out a syringe and started to draw liquid from a small glass bottle. The cell finally opened and the demon horde filed in making me shoot from the bed and back into a corner.

"NO!" I screamed as they all lunged for me at once. I tried to escape them but it was no use, as all I could do was squirm around in their flaky hands.

"GET OFF ME!" I screamed as their already bruising hold tightened painfully.

"Hold her down!" I tried to twist but it was no use as my face was slammed down to the floor, so my cheek rested against the dirty stone. My arms were held back at a painful angle and I could no longer move without fear of breaking something. So all I could do was wait for the stab of the needle and the drugs to override my system, rendering me unconscious.

And for once…

I welcomed it.

CHAPTER FIFTY

THE AUCTION

The next time I opened my eyes it was to the sight of red darkness. It took me a moment to bring my senses back under my control and realise what I was faced with. I started by blinking my eyes but even that felt weird at first. My lashes kept tickling on something that was around my face but it wasn't a blindfold. I managed to push away enough of the grogginess to focus on the dark red blur in front of me and in doing so, I saw thin black bars in front of some sort of red material that was only letting in a small amount of light.

"Where am I now?" I whispered to myself. I was just managing to come through the rest of the effects of the drugs that seemed a lot heavier than last time. It made wonder if they had to give me a few shots in the time it took them to get me here…wherever here was exactly?

I tried to sit up and when it felt like my brain was going to dribble out of my nose, I raised my hands to my head to find them shackled together in a pair of ornate silver cuffs that fit snug to my wrists.

"What the…?" I said following the thick chain attached to them all the way up to the top of the strange cell I seemed to be in. The chain wasn't pulled taut at the moment but hung loose around the floor which I was sat on. High above me was something I couldn't really make much sense of. It seemed like a swinging metal bench like you would find hanging from a tree in a garden. That was all I could make out from down here, but it led me to follow the thin metal bars that went up into what looked like a cage in the shape of a Japanese pagoda. In fact, it kind of started to look like…

"It can't be…a birdcage?" As soon as I said it the more I really saw that it did, in fact, look like a giant birdcage with a swing hanging in the middle of it.

"This does not look good." I said as I saw the chain attached to the very top of the domed roof which had another smaller roof in the centre, exactly like those old antique birdcages you find people using for quirky ornaments. And for God's sake, my own mother had one with a plant growing from it in her conservatory! Well, if I ever got out of here alive, then that thing would be finding itself in the skip!

When I finished examining my unusual surroundings, someone must have turned up the lights as I could now make out more and discovered what part I was to play in the birdcage and yep, you guessed it... I was the damn bird!

I can't say I was displeased to wake and find I no longer smelled like I had washed in a compost heap with a rotted fish for a sponge and left to dry like a wet dog. Although, now being clean did feel beyond good but did beg the question as to who had cleaned me? This gave me chills and it wasn't just down to my bare arms, which I kept hugged around my belly.

I had been put into a massive dress all made entirely from feathers. It had a swan white corseted top that laced at the front, leaving too much cleavage on view for my liking. The feathers reached up to a high point over each breast and then fitted tight down the waist to join the skirt. There was a wide white satin sash that hung around the waist and tied in a floppy bow behind my back. But it was the skirt that was truly incredible and also ridiculously huge!

The top layer to the skirt was made from long black feathers all hanging downwards in a graceful way and finished on a curve around the sides, then fell longer at the back. Then came the underskirt which was a mass of layer upon layer of large white ostrich feathers that fluffed out all around me and went way beyond my feet when I finally stood up. It was as stunning as it was crazy being dressed as a giant bird, but I had to admit that I was happy I didn't have some over the top showgirl feather headdress, straight out of Vegas, to go with it!

No, instead my hair had been styled and swept back in a side parting and then pinned under, creating volume to the back with what little hair I now had. Over this was a single white ostrich feather held in place like a headband with what felt like jewels attached to one side.

I couldn't see my hair, only feel it to know this was the style and it was the same with the mask that had been also pinned under my hairline to stay in place. I felt around my eyes and knew this was the reason for the weird sensation on my face when I had first woken up. My lashes would brush the top of the eye holes in the mask, telling me I also had makeup on my lashes to make them longer. I could feel the feathers along the mask that was a perfect moulded shape for my face and when I looked down at my nose, I saw the feathers were black. Simple, but elegant, ballet shoes in white were added to the costume and their ribbons were tied around my ankles keeping them firmly in place.

After I had finished looking around at my new crazy situation, it didn't take me long to discover what was happening as I heard the sounds of crowded footsteps all beneath me. It sounded as if someone had just opened the door and people of the masses were now all flooding in. I wanted to move but I was too afraid to, so that no one was aware that I was now awake.

I still couldn't see anything other than the red glow from the light behind the material, but the noise of people was getting louder by the second. Did they know I was in here? For some reason, I didn't think if I started screaming blue murder that people would come running to my aid.

So here I was, dressed like I was playing a part in Swan Lake, now about to go up for a sick human auction! I waited for the sound of the crowd to calm down as I knew they must have now taken their seats, considering I could no longer hear chair legs being moved along the floor. It's amazing what your other senses can pick up when you can no longer rely on your eyes and you concentrate enough. For example, I could smell dust and old metal. There was also a chill in the air and that, combined with the echoing sound of people chatting, told me that I was most likely in a large open space, high above the ground. But I was only left to speculate as the Auction was about to begin.

"Good evening to you all on this fine night. I would like to welcome you to this year's collective auction." A round of applause sounded and also some thudding of feet where others were obviously getting more excited.

"As you will see in your catalogues handed to you at the door, we have a wide range of rare pieces on offer with also a surprise last minute addition to our collection. Which I think you will all agree is a most treasured find indeed and one held in the utmost secretive of circles." This part brought on a lot of 'Mmms' and 'Ahhhs' as I could imagine they were all looking up at the covered cage I sat chained to.

"Right, then let us begin." I heard more shuffling and then,

"Starting with lot 23, here as you can see held up on my left is the rarest of all the Pokémon cards. This particular one was never released in English and only four are said to exist in the world. I have a starting bid on the table of 15,000 dollars, do I hear 16,000?" I could barely believe my ears and actually coughed out my shock on hearing I was being sold in the same auction as a bloody Pokémon card! Ok, so getting my whole priorities mixed up I couldn't help but think… 'I'd better get a higher bid for me than a stupid piece of card!'

I listened to the auctioneer reeling off figures and upped the price until it finally sold for $25,000.

"Next is lot 19 the iPhone 4S Elite Gold. This darling phone is made by Stuart Hughes and is designed with 500 internally flawless diamonds that total over 100 carats. The Apple logo itself has over 50 diamonds. And if that is not enough for you, then the navigation button has a 7.4 carat single-cut internally flawless natural pink diamond, which as you all know is extremely rare. But alas, that is not all, as it also comes with the chest which is made from solid platinum with original pieces of bones from the T-Rex…shall I start the bid at say 9 million."

"What!" I couldn't help myself from shouting…were these people crazy?! Luckily, I don't think people were too concerned with me as the noise of the bidding was underway. This ridiculously expensive phone reached 11.5 million and sounded as though it went to someone who could only grunt…well for that price, I hoped the guy got free calls for life included!

"The next lot is number 2 in your catalogues and goes by the name Chupacabra. This goat sucker has come all the way from Puerto Rico and in his previous owner's own words, he's glad to be rid of the 'nasty little bastard'. A diet of animal blood is all that is needed to keep this demon in good health. I know there has been some interest in this lot, but as the owner was adamant to get rid of him there has been no price set, so we will start the bid at as little as 10 dollars, do I hear 15?" I could hear the snarling and gathered the 'nasty little bastard' was being shown to the crowd as the bidding for him commenced.

I had to say that right now I could relate to that goat sucker as I knew what it was like to be caged, soon to be put on display and sold. In the end the creature only sold for 85 dollars and I knew its buyer was an enthusiastic woman, as I could hear her gleefully shouting out as the last price was accepted.

"Next, we have lot 14 and in keeping with the pet part of the auction we have for sale this rare Red Tibetan Mastiff. It is considered in the human world as the most expensive dog, but as we all know in our world this is not the case, as a Hellhound at the last auction raised a mighty 30 million. However, we still have a starting bid on this fine animal, whose owner has named him Eugene and has thrown in the diamond encrusted dog collar. Let's start the bidding at the vendor's lowest asking price of 1 million, do I hear 1.5 million?" I listened to this lot get up to 2.5 million and then the auctioneer said,

"Come on people, this is a great lot and not one I want to go for so little. Please remember this breed has its direct ancestry leading all the way to Apedemak, who for those of you lacking in our history was a lion-headed warrior God, worshipped in Nubia by Meroitic people. Also, the Maahes has been linked, who was of course an ancient Egyptian lion-headed God of war." After this little history lesson the price reached 4 million within a few minutes and poor Eugene had a new owner who spoke in what sounded like Chinese.

It went on like this for what seemed like a long time and things auctioned ranged from The Sultan's Golden Cake that was decorated with gold leaf, that went for $1500, to one of the lost Fabergé eggs from the fall of the Russian Royal Family in 1917 that sold for a cool 10 million dollars.

But in total they must have got through about 40 lots, which also included two dinosaur fossils "locked in mortal combat" according to the auctioneer that went for 8 million dollars. Now, this would have been something I would like to have seen but really, if I was honest with myself, I would have been fascinated to have seen all that was sold.

They had a whole section of five lots dedicated to antique weapons from a pair of pistols, that were once owned by President George Washington during America's War of Independence and then there was some Emperor dude's gold dagger, who built the Taj Mahal! I have to say though, that one of my favourites had to be the 1954 Superman Lunch Box that sold to a deep voiced man who won with his bid of 14, 500 dollars. But with each time the hammer struck down again and again ringing out like a death drum, it only brought me closer to my doomed fate of being sold.

"Now, time for the last item from the catalogue with lot number 35. This beauty was made for Lamborghini's 50th anniversary and is called The Veneno and as most of you here know this is Spanish for 'poison' and rightly so. With its V12 it thunders out a 750 horsepower which will bring you to 60 in 2.8 seconds. As you can see from the write up it also reaches speeds of a daring 220 mph. So, for all you speed junkie Angels and Demons out there, then this lot is for you. So let's start this off at the company's own buying price, but please do remember that there are only three of these hardtops made, so that will reflect on the bidding. Who will bid me to start off with 4 million?" I started to listen for the bidding but then got distracted by the sound of a chain moving.

I looked down to see the chain attached to my restraints had started to snake on the floor before lifting. I watched in horror as it kept going until pulling my bound hands up with it. I stood to give it even more slack, but this ended up just giving me a few more seconds before it started to lift my whole body off the cage floor. I cried out as the pain lashed through my shoulders from being held up by just my wrists. The metal from the cuffs started to cut into my skin and I held onto the chain to relieve some of the pressure.

I looked up as I twisted round like a giant fish on a hook and saw that the swinging perch was coming closer. Then the pulling of the chain stopped, and I hung limp for a painful second before swinging my body towards the seat. I then held on tighter to the chain and on a yelp brought my legs up enough to hook them over the metal swing. I shimmied my butt up until I was sat on it and tried to keep myself steady but it was difficult. I ended up battling to keep myself from falling back or forward but with my arms pulled above my head and with the perch moving under me, it felt like I was partaking in a circus act… and not doing a very good job at that!

Then I heard the hammer go down on the price of 6.5 million for the Lamborghini and I braced myself for what was coming next.

"Right, ladies and gentlemen, now it is time for the mysterious lot you have all been waiting for and our crown jewel of the night. Stewards, if you please." The auctioneer said and then suddenly, in a great whoosh, the red curtain was pulled back from my cage and great gasps filled the enormous space. Tears filled my eyes as I looked down on the sea of people and took in the sheer size of the auction with utter disbelief.

I couldn't comprehend how so many faces looked up at me now and not one single one of them looked at me with horror of what was being done to me. If anything, it was sick fascination and wonder that shone back in their eyes. I looked from them in disgust and focused on the vast room they held the auction in.

It looked to be a late-Gothic style building with a central glass dome that had part of its roof covered in metal squares. The great hall must have been at least 50 meters long and just as wide, with rows and rows of highly decorated pillars. There were galleries on all four sides and the upper one that I was closest to must have had at least 30 of these ornate pillars alone. Arches filled every space along the room's full circumference and in the middle on the second floor were two stone plinths that jutted out with one either side as a mirror image. They looked fit for a king and the ideal place to stand and wave at his loyal subjects below. It was a truly stunning piece of architecture and one I would have no doubt admired more if it was not for my dire circumstances.

My cage was hanging in the centre, directly behind the raised platform the auctioneer stood on next to a podium. This angle gave me a clear view of all the people taking part in the auction, sat on row after row of red velvet chairs which had been laid out in arches like in a theatre. But it wasn't just the hundreds of people sat down, but also every available standing space was taken up adding hundreds more. All had paddles with numbers on ready for their bids to be written down and assigned to their winning lots. I couldn't help but look round wondering which number I would soon belong to?

I looked down to see the auctioneer nod to someone on the side out of view. I was then a bit happier at least when the chain lowered enough for me to grab onto the sides of the swing so that my shoulders no longer felt like they would pop off. I felt the lasting ache when they lowered and I tried to roll my arms to relieve the remaining tension, whilst still gripping on for dear life.

"I now present to you our last lot of the night and by far the most prestigious we have ever sold in our many years holding this auction." The auctioneer actually took a moment to take off his small round glasses and rub his face as though he couldn't quite believe what he was about to say. He nodded to the crowd, replaced his glasses and gripped each side of the podium to lean forward.

"I give you all…The King's Electus!" He raised his arm up to me and the whole room gasped in utter shock and then erupted into a deafening roar of applause once more. My hands gripped the sides of my perch in frustration and when looking around the room I saw Gastian stood on the sidelines looking smug.

"Yes, yes, please everyone, calm yourselves." He waited for the room to hush down their tasteless excitement before explaining 'the goods' in further detail.

"As you can all be in no doubt about the seriousness of this last lot or the ramifications behind taking part in this bid, I will stress that you all made a vow upon entering into this auction and what has taken place here tonight is to remain under secrecy within the realms of that vow." Even as he said this some people actually stood up and walked out after nodding their respects to the auctioneer. Good, I thought, knowing that at least six people remained faithful to Draven…although, out of hundreds didn't look like good odds.

"You can understand then that the valuing of this lot has taken some great thought, as it is seemingly priceless, but like nearly all of my vendors, they are here to make some money, so without further ado, I will begin." I was very tempted to shout out a string of obscenities when I heard the guy call me a 'lot' for the umpteenth time but decided to hold my tongue in case my punishment was being held up by my wrists again.

"This lot is not numbered but named 'The Chosen' and personal details of the girl will be given along with purchase. As you can see she is a fine female specimen and although rumours of her status of her not being the Chosen One that are running worldwide, we are happy to confirm these rumours are not true. Found in her personal effects was the book of Ouroboros, given to her from the very Oracle herself, one to which she is blood bound. This is also included in the sale and one does not have to worry about the Master of the Ouroboros channelling through the book to find her, as the vendor has already had a warlock take care of this problem, which will reflect on the price, as I'm sure you can understand." On hearing this important piece of information, I at least now knew why no one could have contacted me throughout my imprisonment. Gastian had obviously heard from the snivelling Dimme about the book and gone to great lengths to prevent anyone from communicating with me.

There were nods and most started discussing amongst themselves, whilst looking up at me every now and again. I finally knew what it felt like for all those poor zoo animals being gawked at all day!

"I must also caution before the auction starts, that anyone who bids does so under their own risk of life as rules state clearly that no supernatural contact is to be made with this particular human and as we all stand here now, we are in fact in breach of that ruling. Anyone not willing to take those risks may leave like the others with our well wishes and hope to see you back here again next year." Once again I was pleased to see this time ten more people stood up and left.

"Very well, now that all formalities are out of the way, let us start. This is a lot for the elite, so we will begin with an elite starting price, do I hear 10 million?" Now I was the one to gasp…really, 10 million?! I have to say, even though I knew I was letting go of some mental marbles for even thinking it, I couldn't help but be a little flattered at the price set. I think if these feathers had been really attached, they would have puffed upon hearing that.

"10 million, do I have 15?" The auctioneer was soon having to go up in the tens instead of the fives and soon after that by the twenties! I was dumbfounded by the ludicrous prices being shouted and when it got up as far as 350 million, I nearly fell from my perch! What in the Hell did these people think they were going to get for that price…me crapping gold and sneezing diamonds?!

It had finally started to slow down and I noticed it was now down to three bidders and none looked like the friendly captive type. I was just about to start coming up with escape plans in my head, when a booming voice cut through the auction and vibrated the walls with the sheer strength of it.

"One Billion!" Was the next price shouted from a shadow in the back and the Auctioneer looked to Gastian and when he nodded, he brought down his hammer, sealing my fate when he shouted…

"The Electus is Sold!"

CHAPTER FIFTY-ONE

WORTH EVERY PENNY

At the sound of my sale, I felt like an arm had just been pushed down my throat and forced my heart into my stomach! Was I really just going to be going from one sorry prison and on to the next and what would my next captor be like? Well, one thing was a given, I doubted it would come with my very own Percy!

"If you please Sir, can you show us your paddle number?" The auctioneer asked loudly trying to reach the back of the room. I held my breath as I saw a shadow walk in between the crowd and soon it was going to be my very first view of my buyer. I think, like everyone, we were expecting the buyer to just come to the edge of the gallery's balcony and hold up a number, but he didn't do this.

Oh no, not for this man! People started to fill the room with murmurs that seemed to travel straight from those who quickly got out of his way, as though this man was someone very important. The hum of noise washed along the crowd in a wave of gossip and I soon found out why. The mystery man simply stepped up on top of the stone banister and grabbed hold of the centre pillar, situated in between the six arches that faced me on the second level. This was done with such grace and masterful flair, I knew what I was seeing had to be true.

I released a stuttered breath as the reality hit me dead centre in the chest and a sob was wrenched from deep within my fragile soul. For the first time in three weeks of brutal imprisonment, I now felt my heart soar and my hope regain strength. I felt the tears fall from beneath the mask and I didn't care one damn bit that a hall full of people could see it. I only had emotions for the man now stood at the pillar staring right at me, with that bad boy smile I had once grown to know so well. Then I whispered his name and prayed to the Gods that created him that this dream wouldn't shatter.

"Lucius." He must have heard me because he nodded slowly and then winked at me before dropping to the floor below. I was left breathing heavy and trying in vain to hold back the flood of emotions that threatened to take over my senses. Was it possible…? Had I been saved?

Following the sight of Lucius, everyone quickly bowed down in their chairs and all around the hall was an echoed sound of those stood, falling to their knees. The auctioneer took in the sight of Lucius striding down the centre aisle straight to the podium. He fell to his knees also and lowered his head until he found the floor.

"My Lord." He uttered in quivering fear.

The sight of Lucius wearing a pair charcoal suit trousers, matching waistcoat and a light grey shirt unbuttoned at the neck, which was also casually rolled around his thick forearms, was a sight to behold for anyone. His dress shoes clicking on the stone floor made for a powerful beat as he ate the distance to the shaking auctioneer.

When Lucius made it to him, he looked down with disdain and motioned without words for him to rise with a simple bend of all his fingers from the hand still held relaxed at his side. He did what he was told and rose to face my buyer.

"The Electus is yours My Lord and I have been assured you will not be disappointed."

"No, I imagine not." Lucius said letting me hear the hidden meaning in his smug gaze up at the cage. I finally let myself smile back knowing from now on everything would be ok and he would take care of me. I was not alone any longer.

I saw him look back at the crowd and nod to some woman with a massive hat, one that looked like a flying saucer had landed on her head. He nodded to my cage and whoever she was, she jumped up and bowed to him over enthusiastically, making him roll his eyes.

"You have something for me to sign?" Lucius snapped at the auctioneer and he nodded anxiously before running off to get what I assumed was my paperwork. Now I really felt like a prized cow being sold! Meanwhile the woman with the massive hat had disappeared into the crowd and the auctioneer seemed to be arguing with Gastian over the other side of the podium. Well, I knew one thing, the second I got down from this bloody cage I was going to be having words with my kidnapper and letting my fists do the talking…oh, who was I kidding, I would just ask Lucius to do that for me!

"Hey Toots, how's it hangin?"

"PIP!" I shouted as I saw that the woman wearing the big hat was in fact Pip! She was stood on one of the middle plinths on the second level and she dramatically whipped her hat off, letting all her green and blue hair fall down. She wore it in a mass of voluminous tight curls resembling a green afro with a blue halo from the tips.

I couldn't help but grin until my jaw hurt when I saw her and took in what she was wearing. It was some kind of poncho dress made from long hair that reached from her shoulders down to mid-thigh. It was sectioned in different colours and looked like she was wearing part of a rainbow! With this she'd added a belt that looked as if a pair of monster hands were holding her waist. She completed the look with a pair of knee high striped socks with high heeled blue wellington boots that had little red and yellow cars all over them.

"Tootie Cake." She said beaming at me. Then she threw her hat into the crowd below, bowed to them all as they cheered like this was all part of the show. Then she launched herself at my cage, landing on the sides like a little monkey! She climbed up the bars until she was level with me on my perch making her hair poncho sway in a mesmerizing display of colours. Well, if I was the captured black and white bird then she was definitely the wild free parrot in this picture!

"I have to say, I'm not digging the new crib Toots, but the new look is bitchin'...! Although…you do kinda need your roots doing" I laughed at her and shook my head whilst thanking all the Gods combined for her!

"Sorry honey, I would have tidied up and done a touch up if I'd known you were coming." I said making a joke back, but also thinking my blonde roots were that last of my worries!

"Nah, I see you've been tied up" She nodded to my bound hands and we both giggled.

"Sometime tonight, Mrs Ambrogetti!" Lucius shouted up, making Pip roll her eyes.

"He's taken to calling me that when I don't move my itty bitty heinie quick enough…he's no fun these days but now you're back, the fun has already begun!"

"Glad I could help." I said grinning like an idiot. Then she winked at me and carried on climbing to the top. Once at the cage's roof she must have done something with the mechanism because the whole cage started to lower to the ground. I gripped on tightly to my swing as it started swaying with the movement, so I was glad when the bottom of the cage finally found the floor. It hit the stone with an echoed thud and then Pip shouted from above,

"Hold on tight Tootsy chick…TIMBER!" she shouted as she released the chain that was attached to my wrists until it came crashing down to the floor, no longer holding me prisoner in this cage. I felt the pull on my wrists from the momentum, but thanks to Pip's warning I had a good hold and was ready for it.

I watched Lucius take no time at all to get to the cage's door and rip it from its hinges. He ducked his head to come inside and looked up at me.

"Jump down now, my little bird, I will catch you." I bit my lip thinking there was a flaw in this plan.

"I…um…" His arms were open ready and he started to get that impatient look as I hesitated.

"I didn't come all this way to drop you, sweetheart…now

jump!" He added firmly at the end. I took a few deep breaths and suddenly wished I had been given wings when being dressed like this and being forced to take my first flight alone. I let go of the swing and closed my eyes as I scooted to the edge to then drop down into Lucius' waiting arms. I released an 'umff' sound as his arms caught me and didn't open them again until I heard Lucius say softly,

"My little Keira girl."

I looked up to see Lucius and couldn't help the fresh tear that fell at finally seeing my friend again. Just as I couldn't help my reactions that followed as I threw my arms up and around his neck to hold on as tight as I could. I heard him chuckle which shook me as I hugged him. He wrapped his arms around me and whispered,

"I take it you missed me, Pet?" I shuddered at hearing him call me the same name that Jared did and this reminded me of all the questions I would need to bombard Lucius with…but right now was our time and I was not going to ruin it with my runaway mouth.

"I missed you, so, so much Lucius!" I said back making him squeeze me tighter before letting me go and raising my bound hands from his neck. He rang a finger along my cheek and then under my mask to capture the tears he knew where there.

"I love to see you cry for me, Keira." I bit my lip at the hidden meaning in that statement and could only nod.

"It's good to see you're still shy." I looked up at him and let loose a little growl making him throw his head back and roar with laughter.

"Come on, let's get this done." He said taking my hands and snapping first the large chain that now hung down on the floor and then forcing the cuffs apart so I could finally move my arms to my sides. He found one of my hands and took it in his to pull me from the cage. I pulled back a little and said,

"Thanks for catching me, Lucius." This time I got the bad boy Lucius when he looked down grinning and said playfully,

"I only wanted to look up your skirt, Keira." Then he winked at me, making me laugh. Pip then came up behind me and whispered in my ear,

"He's telling the truth you know, I could have lowered your little birdy seat but he wanted a chance at your knickers." I turned to face my friend and as soon Lucius let me go, I threw myself at her.

"I missed you Winifred Pipper Ambrogetti!" She shushed me and then whispered,

"Less of the Winifred Toots, you trying to piss on my street cred?" I laughed at her and then said,

"What street cred?" She gave me an evil glare that was just too damn cute and then pulled back my mask and let it snap back. We both fell into giggles.

We both turned and separated when we heard the auctioneer coming back. He had with him some paperwork and it was actually bringing it home to me that Lucius had amazingly paid 1 billion dollars for me!

"If you would just sign here and here, My Lord."

"Turn around." He ordered and the flustered auctioneer turned quickly and presented his back for Lucius to use.

"Wait!" I shouted stepping up to him to try and stop this madness.

"Lucius, you don't have to do this, this is one *billion* dollars we're talking about here! He's doesn't own me…no one does!" I said after pointing to Gastian, who stayed a safe distance away, the coward!

"I am afraid that's where you're wrong love, once a lot has been put into the auction, then it is no longer the vendor who owns you, but the auction house. There is no leaving this room for you without them receiving my vow to pay, as you are bound to them until my signature releases you." Lucius told me softly giving me a small smile.

"Here you go, My Lord." The auctioneer who was still waiting tried to hand him a long feathered quill over his shoulder. But instead of taking it he flashed me a wider grin and then I jumped as he put his hand up my skirt and plucked one of the feathers from my dress.

"I think I prefer this one." He said winking at me, then turned back around and bit into his hand.

"What are you…?!" I started to say but then stopped as he

dipped the end of the feather into his escaping blood and then turned back round to sign the document without a moment's hesitation.

"Cool, huh?" Pip said behind me and I shot her a gross look over my shoulder making her laugh. As soon as he lifted the makeshift quill from the pages, having signed twice, I felt something heavy lift from me. It was as if there was some kind of spell that had kept me rooted to this place that I hadn't been aware of until now.

"The funds are being transferred as we speak."

"Very good My Lord, it was a pleasure doing business with you as always." The auctioneer said bowing and then rose to nod to some men dressed like Edwardian gentlemen complete with top hats. I quickly understood this silent order as they went to stand behind Gastian and grabbed him.

"UNHAND ME!" He shouted as they half dragged him forward.

"What is the meaning of this!?" He demanded as he was brought in front of Lucius and the auctioneer.

"I am sorry my dear fellow, but I must adhere to the commands of those above me." The auctioneer said and then Lucius leant forward, and I was happy to see Gastian flinch with fear.

"And your side of the commission was just too much to give up." Lucius informed him making Gastian's eyes bulge as realisation struck.

"You can't do this!" He shouted making Lucius' lips curl back on a snarl.

"Do you have anything you would like to add to this, my Keira girl?" Lucius asked me without taking his eyes off him. I went to step around him and his arm went ridged in my path. The look I gave Lucius must have been answer enough for what he was thinking because he let me pass him. I stood in front of Gastian and let my hate for what this man had put me through in the last three weeks build and build until I felt the familiar tingle in my fingertips.

"What, Bitch?!" I heard the growl behind me from Lucius but it was quickly muffled by the groans of pain from Gastian.

My answer to his question had been simple…I punched him hard enough to crack his head back and with it his nose, as now blood gushed from the break.

"BOO YA, SISTER!" Pip cheered and I faced back round to see her jumping up and down like a madwoman, along with cheers from the audience, who I was shocked to see were on my side.

"He's all yours, Luc." I said flexing my hurting knuckles but knowing the pain was soothed in the sight of my little revenge.

"Time to get paid, Gastian." Lucius said and in reply he screamed out,

"GIVE ME MY MONEY!" Then in the quickest move I have seen yet, Lucius was behind him with his head locked in his arms. He didn't even have time to struggle as Lucius simply snapped his neck and killed him in one effortless move. He let his body drop and said,

"Consider yourself paid."

The crowd cheered again as if this was a bonus part of the evening and everyone stood up clapping until Lucius growled out his displeasure, putting a quick stop to the commotion. My mouth was hanging open and Pip jumped past me and stomped on his dead body saying,

"Yeah asshole, no one messes with my friend Toots!" Then in true Pip fashion stuck her tongue out at him.

"You can deliver the Veneno to my home in Munich, now give me her things." Lucius ordered, snapping the auctioneer's attention from the dead host lying on his floor. Meanwhile, I was trying to remember what the name meant, being sure I'd heard it sometime during the auction, but what was it?

"Of course My Lord and the delivery will be on the house." At this Lucius gave him a sarcastic smile and said,

"How generous of you, spending over a billion and getting the goods delivered." Pip laughed and then said,

"Yeah I know right, they could have at least thrown in a piece of that Sultan's Golden Cake for free but nope, nada, not even a free pen!" She made a 'humpf' sound and turned flicking her hair, hitting the auctioneer's chest with cute curls. She walked over to me and hooked her arm in mine saying,

"Come on Toots, this party sucks cat balls and then blows them into the wind!" I looked over my shoulder to see my broken bag being passed to Lucius along with the Ouroboros book. I let Pip guide me past the gossiping crowd and we walked under one of the many arches.

"Pip, what's a Veneno?" She burst out laughing and informed me through the giggles,

"It's Lucius' new baby, I just knew he wouldn't be able to resist the Lambo."

"What!?" She laughed again and said,

"Oh Toots, how I missed your funny ways." My funny ways…this coming from Mrs Funny pants herself! But it was easy to admit that I had missed her so much and being away from everyone in my past life with Draven, had been getting harder by the day. Now though, it finally felt like I had found as least one half of that family, but would I be so lucky in finding the other?

We walked through the old building and as soon as we made it outside, a Limo was waiting for us. I looked around the small street before being quickly hustled inside the car by Pip. I was still wrestling with all my feathers when I asked,

"Where's Lucius?"

"Missing me already, Keira girl?" Lucius said as he folded himself into the car and took the seat next to me. Pip fluffed up her hair and said,

"Nah, she missed me way more, she might have cried for you Mighty Master Maximillion, but I got the bigger hug." I had to laugh at his nickname.

"Oh, you find that funny now do you?" Lucius said turning in his seat as the car started to pull away. He rested one bent leg on the other and ran a hand along the back of the seat to play with the feathers at my back.

"Nope, absolutely not."

"I see your lying skills are still as shit as ever." He said looking as though he was trying to hold back a grin.

"So where are we? And how did you find me and what happened to…?"

"Oh here we go…" He said to himself looking up at the roof of the car.

"Alright my Keira, we are going to play a game."

"OOOH I love games!" Pip said bouncing in her seat and then she clapped her hands and said,

"Does it smell like cheese, but doesn't come from an animal…oh wait but Adam is mostly like an animal…I mean he does this growly thing when I go down on…"

"LALALALA" I sang out like old times.

"I don't even want to venture a guess this time, squeak." Lucius said dryly.

"I thought it was a guessing game and that you meant Adam's toes…don't you think it's weird how his left foot smells worse than the right one."

"Really?" I couldn't help it, I had to ask.

"I know right, total freak but I love em freaky!" She said before she slid off the seat to sit cross legged in front of a sleek counter to raid the minibar.

"Alright, now that my second in command's feet are out of the conversation, *where they belong…"* He said this last part as a stern message to Pip, who just waved a hand behind her, whilst her other one was pulling out a bottle of champagne.

"…let's get back to my game, it's called the 'I will only ask one question at a time' game." Pip snorted as she popped the cork.

"That's pretty shit for a game's name Luc, can't you call it something…'Question Flash Time' or 'Flash my answer, bitch' or, or, or 'Flashin' my Bitch up'…you know, something catchy like that?" I tried to keep a straight face when Lucius groaned and let his head fall back like he was asking for patience from the powers above.

"And why again does it have to have the word 'Flash' in it 'cause you know the last one really didn't make sense." I added thinking this was quite possibly one of the strangest conversations I had ever had and not one I would have put high on the probability list when just being saved from being bought…or is it just plain bought, as technically Lucius had just bought me… and oh God, did this mean he owned me?!

"See Squeak, this is what your mouth does to people, it makes their faces look that confused." Lucius said to Pip after looking at me, but she just gave him the finger and said,

"Hey Toot's! Whose side are you on anyway? You can never over use the word Flash and it fits in with so many different scenarios."

"Yes, like if you don't stop talking I will gag you in a flash." Lucius said this time making her growl at him, which was one of the cutest things!

"Fine! But I am so not playing your stupid game now!" She said pouting.

"Good 'cause you're disqualified. Now, where were we?" Lucius said turning back to me and I had to hold in my smile when I saw Pip push her nose up, making faces behind him.

"Do me a favour here sweetheart, try and concentrate on my voice and not on Miss Piggy over there…who *won't* be disciplined by her husband if she carries on." This got her to behave and act semi normal…well, as semi normal as Pip could do anyway. And if I knew Pip the way I did, this was one threat she would not be pushing as she just loved to be disciplined by her husband… more so than Christmas apparently.

"So what were we talking about?" I asked feeling totally lost in the craziness that Pip starred in.

"Ask your 'one' question at a time, love?" He said looking exasperated and like he was sick of dealing with children.

"You bought me!?" I don't know why but all earlier questions left me but this one. It was as if the realisation of how much he'd spent was seeping in and I was left feeling very emotionally vulnerable because of it.

"And?" Lucius said as if this was as everyday as reading the newspaper or better still, like sucking blood for a Vampire!

"And you paid one *Billion* dollars for me! I mean, that's just ridiculous…do you even know what you could do with money like that…? All the people you could help, the islands you could buy? And as for paying you back…" At this he burst out laughing and then slid closer to me.

He pushed back some of the hair that had come loose on my neck then gently peeled back my mask. He pushed it down until it hung around my neck and then he gripped my chin between his thumb and finger to turn me to look at him. My heart was pounding, and his grin told me he could hear every beat. He leaned in as though he was going to kiss me and in an impossibly slow move his lips changed direction and reached my ear. There he took it into his mouth and gently bit on the lobe playfully before he let it go with a pop.

Then I heard some of the most profound words I had ever heard in my life…

"Worth every single penny."

CHAPTER FIFTY-TWO

RIPPING OFF LOOSE ENDS

The whole car journey must have taken all of fifteen minutes and all I had learnt in that time was that we were in Antwerp, Belgium. Well, this wasn't strictly true, I did also see Pip sulk about not being involved with Lucius' 'One at a time question game' but to be fair there was only so much you could learn in the five minutes I had left after their mini squabble.

So, this was what I had learned. It turns out that the Auction I featured in was run by a secret society called Lega Nera, which is Italian for the 'Black League'. But when I started to ask more about this mysterious 'Black League', Lucius just raised an eyebrow at me and then tapped my nose twice in gentle chastisement for breaking his 'one question at a time' rule.

I must have wrinkled my nose because Lucius did it back to me before touching his nose to mine and Pip started laughing at me.

"Still doing that Tootie wrinkler?" Pip asked me after she had downed her third glass of champagne. I shot her my best 'whatever' face making her giggle.

After this Lucius continued to tell me that due to the Lega Nera's illegal status it held its auctions in different places all over the world. So, given its high secrecy, the vendors are only given a weeks' notice in which country it is to be held and a few days until the actual venue's address is released to the supernatural world's rich list. No guessing needed to whom I knew was on that list!

This year the Lega Nera's auction was held in Handelsbeurs or better known to those like me that can't speak Flemish, it was Antwerp's old Stock Exchange building. According to Pip, who got quite excited at this point in our conversation, it was actually a reconstruction of the original building of 1531 which was burnt down as a result of the first fire in 1583. Then, after being rebuilt back to the original plans, came the second fire much later in 1858. By this time the old plans were no longer used, and was once again rebuilt, only this time in a late-Gothic Brabant style.

At first, I couldn't understand why this would be something to get Pip excited about until she explained that the fire in 1858 was down to the first time the Society's auction was held there. The story was that a performing elephant that was being sold went 'ape shit' (Pip's words) and went charging through the crowd, knocking oil lamps as she went. Her name was Martha and Pip had actually bid to buy her. This was much to Adam's extreme displeasure, so much so he outbid her with a plan to give her away to a zoo. That was of course until she had to be put down, due to her 'wig out' so that the humans wouldn't discover what had been going on under their very Belgian noses!

I asked about the first time the fire happened and she said,

"Bugger if I know, I only cared about Martha." I found I could only smile at her endearing statement for a brief love affair with a 15,000 lb elephant, which brought us to now.

We were just pulling up outside Lucius' private jet at Antwerp International Airport. As soon as I saw the sleek plane waiting on the tarmac it instantly plunged me back to that very first night when meeting Team Lucius.

Pip had been dressed in the tiniest pair of shorts and a Thundercats T-shirt with the sleeves cut off, despite the cold weather. I even remembered her kick ass, black spiked cowboy boots that looked deadly! Even back then when she was part of the crew that kidnapped me, I still thought she was one of the coolest chicks I had ever laid my eyes on, and ever since that night, that thought had only zoomed right up to epic on the cool scale!

Even now, when the car stopped and I watched as Pip decided to give up using the glass and instead just downed the rest of the champagne from the bottle. She caught me looking and with an expression that wondered how anyone could get through a bottle that big within fifteen minutes she said,

"What?! It comes with the Limo rental." I couldn't help but laugh when she shrugged her shoulders and then reached into the cooler and grabbed the remaining two bottles. I saw Lucius shake his head, smiling as he opened the door. He reached in and took my hand in his to help me from the car, making me realise I still had on my shackles which now had a broken piece of chain on the insides. I stepped out and one look at the plane had me wondering if they had tools onboard, 'cause I didn't fancy making these 'bracelets' a permanent Keira addition!

"I will get them off you once we take off." Lucius said pulling me from my DIY thoughts.

"How did you know?" At my question he nodded to my face and stated,

"Expressive eyes," making me blush and in turn making him laugh.

"Oh, but that right there offers so many possibilities." He said nodding to my burning cheeks and at this flirty comment my blush went nuclear!

"PIPPER!" Adam shouted from the open plane door. It only needed one look to see that he was not the composed Adam that I was used to. His shirt was untucked on one side and his hair looked like he had spent six hours raking his fingers through it, making his usual smart appearance look unkempt. Well, given the panicked shout out to his wife, it was easy to gather who he had been worried about.

Pip stuck her head out of the car and when she saw Adam her whole entire soul lit up. She bounced from the limo and forgetting all about her bounty she threw the bottles of champagne behind her and ran at him. He jumped down all the steps in one move and then caught her as she jumped into his arms. This was all in seconds and to the sound of glass smashing on the tarmac. A spray of bubbles and pale liquid flew up and it was like adding a firework to their pure love reuniting.

I couldn't help the goofy smile that erupted at watching Pip cover his face in little kisses making his usual black rimmed, square glasses go askew. But he quite obviously couldn't care less as he held on to her with one strong arm under her rear, so he could use the other hand to check that she was all in one piece.

"Did you miss me, pumkee?" Pip asked him before sucking in her pink lip ring, looking cute twisting a curl around her finger. You couldn't miss the growl he gave her but the whispered,

"Fuck yeah," was easy to read on his lips. I laughed when I heard Lucius groan next to me as we walked up to them both.

"Get a grip man, it's only been a few hours." He told Adam but I don't think a man like Adam really gave a shit what anyone thought when it came to his wife…not even his Vampire sire Lucius.

"Thank you for taking care of her in my place My Lord, but I will not be doing that again." Oh, bless him but he looked like he had been trying not to pull his hair out for all that time.

"You know why you couldn't come, my second, not after what happened in 1858." I looked to Pip but she just mouthed,

"I will tell you later." It didn't take much but if I was to venture a guess it would have something to do with an elephant named Martha…although I never thought I would be associating a sentence like that with anyone I knew, let alone someone like Adam!

After feeling every inch of his wife (which from the meowing coming from her, she didn't mind one bit) only then did he let himself take in the rest of the world, which mainly included me.

"Keira." I smiled at him as he tried to straighten his glasses, even with Pip trying to bite the frames.

"Hey Adam." I said blushing and his grin was the only warning I got before he hooked an arm over my shoulder and pulled me into his free side for a hug, still holding onto his wife with his other arm.

"Good to see you again, little bird." Pip laughed when I groaned at the mention of 'Little bird'.

"First chance I get I am getting out of this damn dress!" I complained making them all laugh… well, all except Lucius who chose that moment to lean into my ear and say,

"That can be arranged quickly enough." Then I felt his hands at my hips and he gripped the feathers there enough to get the message across. I swallowed hard and thankfully Pip was the one to save me. She jumped down from Adam and grabbed my hand to pull me inside the plane, saying,

"I like birdy Toots, so no tearing it off her yet…Hey Tootie pie have you ever seen Sesame Street, 'cause you know big bird was always my favourite!"

"Ha, ha Pip." I said as I followed her inside the plane.

It took me a moment to realise this was the exact same plane that had taken me all the way to Germany the first time and I nearly laughed out loud at how different the circumstances were now. If anyone had told me all that time ago that I would be back on here, now thrilled to be with Lucius once again, then I would have not only called them nuts, I would have thrown a book of 'How to perform a Lobotomy' at their head!

Adam entered the plane next and asked the stewardess to tell the captain that we were ready to take off in five minutes. I let Pip drag me over to the middle of the plane. She plonked herself down in a seating area that was two cream leather sofa's facing each other with a high polished table in between. Now we sat facing each other I heard Lucius enter the plane asking about take-off. I looked over my shoulder and saw Lucius not only had my bag with him, but also he passed something on to Adam.

"Catch, Birdy Tweet!" Pip shouted bringing my attention back round to find her throwing something at me. I caught the black shopping bag that had some gothic shop name on it I had never heard of. I gave her a 'what is it look' and she flicked her pointy nails to the bag and I had to giggle to myself when I saw how they were painted this time. It started as a story with a cute bunny chewing on some grass and then came a toxic waste can spilling on the same grass on the next finger. By the end of her nails it showed the cute bunny turn in to a Frankenstein demon bunny with blood dripping from a set of fangs. My only thought was what on earth the poor manicurists thought when Pip told her what she had in mind this week!?

I quit staring at her nails and opened the bag, taking out the sparkly tissue paper first. I lifted up a black T-shirt that had a skull and crossbones on the front that said in bloody writing underneath,

'I Party like a Pirate, so let me Play with your Captain'. I lowered the material to find her cheeky face nodding.

"Oh ARRRR it's GRRReat isn't it, me matey?" I closed my eyes, bit my lip to stop from laughing and shook my head at hearing her corny pirate voice. I took a deep breath about to tell her that big bird was looking more appealing when she repeated excitingly,

"There's more…look in the bag, look in the bag!" I don't know what else I expected… maybe a hat, a plastic hook or Christ, I wouldn't be surprised if a live Parrot flew out squawking 'Pieces of eight, Pieces of eight' wearing a wooden leg! What I wasn't expecting was a pair of red and black striped bloomers that had white embroidered words on the rear that said, 'Spank me here to raise morale.'

"There's a bedroom you can change in back there." I raised my eyebrows and scratched my head before saying,

"Eh…Yeah, no I can't wear this, honey." On hearing this she pushed out her lips to pout and looked down at the floor. I was just letting her cute sulking face get to me enough to say fine, when she smiled and pulled out another bag from underneath the seat.

"I know, that's why I got you this stuff as well, you big pansy!" She grinned, passing me the bag and I got up to go change. I walked past her and patted her on head saying,

"My good little Imp." Her little growl made me chuckle. I walked to the back of the plane and heard Lucius shout behind me,

"Two minutes, Keira Girl." I smiled a secret smile at hearing his usual nickname for me and I didn't want to admit it did funny fluttering things to my stomach. I just held up my arm over my head and gave him a thumbs up to indicate I heard him then I ran for the room.

It was amazing what they could fit into the space allocated for a bedroom, as I dropped my bags onto the king-sized bed. But not really having the time to nose around, which was what I really wanted to do, I decided to get on with it. I started to feel around my bodice for some sort of opening, a zip, clips, buttons, lock and key…but nothing! How on earth did they get me in this bloody thing in the first place…pour me into it, shoot me from a cannon… make the bloody thing around me when I was conked out?!

"Oh for God's sake, get off you stupid… stupid… stupid thing!" I said in frustration as I tried to get it from the skirt and pull it over my head.

"Can I be of assistance, my dear?" Lucius said scaring me enough to fall backwards, landing on my bum.

"Oww!" I mumbled with my head under my skirt and a face full of feathers.

"Shut up, this isn't funny." I said still hidden under the feathered layers, to Lucius who was making no attempt to hide his laughter.

"Oh, but I must disagree, from where I am stood I can assure you it is a very amusing sight." I huffed and wrestled the feathers back from my face, blowing at some of the small loose ones that were trying to fall down my forehead.

"So what would you like me to tell the Captain the reason behind the delay is exactly…dress attack?"

"You're loving this, aren't you?" I said frowning up at him casually stood leaning on the door frame.

"Yes. Now tell me what are you trying to do?" He said trying not to laugh again.

"What does it look like I am trying to do, make a damn nest and lay an egg? I am trying to get this damn monstrosity off me, of course!" I snapped making him hold his lips in his mouth to stop from laughing further.

"Oh just forget it Mr Not At All Bloody Helpful!" I started

to try and twist again when I heard him sigh and walk away from the door frame.

"Come on little chick, let's get you out of this dangerous dress." He bent, grabbed both my hands and hauled me up to my feet. Once there he let me go and with me still facing him, he grabbed the back of my dress.

"Can't call this a chore." He said giving me a hot look before the sound of my dress being ripped in two was thankfully louder than that of my pounding heart. I felt the air hit my body as he pulled it away from me and I quickly gripped onto the front to keep myself hidden.

"I…I uh…think I got it from here." I said biting my lip at the sudden intimate setting and not missing out on the lustful looks that were making Lucius' eyes burn hot.

"Are you sure, I would hate to leave only to have you need me to rescue you again?" I smirked at his playfulness and said,

"I think I will brave it." He shrugged his shoulders and then replied,

"Pity," before he turned around to leave. Once again, he informed me,

'No more than two minutes Keira girl, or I will come back to aid you… wanted or not." This threat got me moving my ass! As soon as the door closed, I tore through the new things Pip had given me, flinging knickers and a bra out of the new bag, mentally thanking Pip for remembering the essentials.

I was soon dressed in a long light grey skirt that was made from T-shirt material which hung low on the hips thanks to losing far too much weight. I found a long sleeved maroon coloured top but decided to make Pip smile, so I added layers with the short sleeved pirate top over it. I also found a pair of orange Dr Seuss All Stars that laced up the high tops with thick black ribbon. Well, at least they matched the bright orange and black striped knee high socks she had added to the pile. The last thing I put on was a black zip up hoodie that had a sweet Goth scroll pattern around the wide bell sleeves in raised light grey and the same design continued around the long hood that hung the whole way down my back.

I knew I was running past my two minute mark when I

heard the engines power up and heard Lucius threatening to come and get me.

"I'm coming! Just a second." I was in the middle of pulling pins out of my hair like a madwoman, when I squealed out as I was spun quickly and found my stomach connecting with a hard shoulder. I was hoisted up in a fireman's lift and put my arm around Lucius' front, trying to hold on to the chiselled chest I could feel underneath his shirt and fitted waistcoat. He carried me back to the main seating area, holding onto my legs with one arm. Then he bent, dumping me in the seat opposite Pip and Adam. He knelt down and buckled me in with the seatbelt before taking the seat next to me, all without one single word.

"I said I was coming." I grumbled, making Pip giggle into Adam's neck, which she was currently snacking on…well, ok not really but close enough!

"And I said two minutes… you were five, so in future consider what you have learnt in that it takes all of three minutes for my patience to run out." He said not looking at me but out of the window as we started up the runway. I didn't have any comeback to this other than to pull a mocking 'telling off' face behind his back.

"Keira, it's a dark night and I am looking out of a window that reflects, you do the math." Inside I let loose a 'GRRR' in frustration but all that came out was a whispered,

"No one likes a smarty pants."

Once we were up in the air Lucius turned to me and unbuckled my seatbelt and it was only then I noticed that I was the only one on this flight that obviously needed to wear one. Well, considering the rest of them would be just fine and dandy if the plane did decided to pull a Buddy Holly on us…poor guy and great music.

"So, my dear wife, did you buy me anything nice at the auction?" Adam asked Pip before plucking her from her seat and onto his lap, not being content with her just sat next to him. She started sucking in her lip ring and looked from side to side as if stalling.

"Well, my little Winnie?" He said playing with one hand and running his fingers along his name tattooed on her knuckles. It was only now I noticed that she wore a massive ring underneath his name that said 'Loves me' in a pop art font.

"Uh…well I…see this is what happened…I uh…no."

"No?" He mocked playfully leaning back to look at her.

"Uh huh."

"Well, it's lucky one of us didn't forget." He said trying to hold back the grin until he produced what Lucius must have given him before take-off. He pulled it from the side of his chair and handed her one 1954 Superman Lunch Box sold in Auction for 14,500 dollars! Her reaction was priceless as her eyes turned into wide green pools of surprise.

She turned to look over her shoulder at Lucius and said,

"You sneaky peek-a-boo bastard!" He shrugged like it was nothing and Pip went back to attacking Adam with raspberry blows in between sloppy kisses. You could tell his reserved control on his wife's crazy thank you actions was nothing but a mask for someone who was clearly loving every minute of his wife's attentions.

"Permission, My Lordy, to take this man in the back and ride him like I'm at a rodeo?" Pip asked staring in Adam's eyes as though she had just fallen in love with him all over again. Lucius raised an eyebrow as Adam moved his head to the side to look at his Lord. Lucius just rolled his eyes and said,

"Is it wise to rile the beast this high up?"

"Oh don't sweat it boss man, I got it covered and do this thing with my inner muscles that just gets him to calm right down…see Toots, if you twist this…"

"LALALALA" I said hold my hands over my ears.

"Come on handsome, let's go play beauty and the geek." She said pulling off his glasses and putting them on herself, intending on playing the geek. He snapped his teeth at her nose making her giggle before picking her up like she weighed nothing at all and she swung her new lunch box around her index finger.

"Now don'tcha kids come running if you hear him scream now, yah hear?" She said pushing Adam's glasses up her nose and then making a V with her fingers to point first to her own eyes then to us two like she would be watching.

"Are we ready, my lady?"

"Up and onward, my dear husband." She said, pointing to the back of the plane over his shoulder, in a posh English accent which was actually pretty good. They started walking off and I stood up calling her name. Adam turned so she could see me as he was still carrying her. I unzipped my hoodie, so she could see my pirate T-shirt and I said,

"Have fun with your captain!" And I winked at her, making her salute me and blow me a kiss for wearing her chosen outfit.

"Oh and my second."

"Yes, My Lord?" Adam asked just as Pip was squirming trying to take off her belt in his hold.

"Mrs Ambrogetti was very disobedient tonight, punishment will be needed." Adam's eyes flashed his demon side before he lowered into a bow, making Pip forget the belt and grip on.

"It will be done, My Lord." Pip let out an excited squeal and then over Adam's shoulder she shouted,

"You the man, Luc!" Then her husband carried her out of sight.

"You know you just made her night, right?" I said the obvious, but he chose not to answer. No, instead he nodded to his lap and ordered,

"Come here!"

"You know, I think I'm good here." I replied but why I bothered I didn't know. I mean this was Lucius we were talking about! I didn't know whether he knew the rules on personal space or whether he just chose not to care for them, either way I was plucked out of my seat and placed in between his legs. Lucky for me the seats were big enough to accommodate the both of us without me having to actually sit on him.

"Let's get this off you, shall we?" He said raising my shackled hands in his. I was then left with my mouth gaping open at the sight of his thumb nails growing into deadly shards and then start glowing poker hot. They reminded me of tiny swords still being made in the fire. With the way he held my hands, with his arms surrounding me, all he needed to do was swipe each point down the centre of the metal cuffs until they broke away under the intense heat. I was surprised it didn't burn me, but before I could ask I felt the same points gently start making little circles on my open palms.

"I was worried about you, my little doll." He said letting his words skim along the skin on my neck and he chuckled when he felt me shudder. I didn't know what to say, so for once stayed silent. I also stayed deadly still in sight of those dangerous thumbs still playing with my hands. It was only when I saw the wicked nails start to descend back into his normal looking thumbnails that I finally relaxed back into him.

I then watched his hands leave mine and start travelling up the length of my arms. They followed the slow path right up to my shoulders then up my neck until his hands cupped my head, where he then started the delicate task of removing the rest of the pins from my hair. I was amazed at such a gentle touch coming from such a big man, as he made quick work of freeing my hair from the updo some unknown person had put it in.

"I thought it was a wig in order to disguise you." He said softly, making me realise how different I must look from the last time he saw me.

"It is a disguise, just a real one done by me." I informed him trying in vain to keep my voice steady. He decided not to make a comment and I didn't know whether it was due to the waver in my voice that told him I didn't want to talk about it, or just that he had nothing to say…either way I was thankful.

Once all the metal grips had been discarded to the floor he ran his fingers up and under and I couldn't help but groan as he massaged my scalp with his large hands.

"I am glad you are safe in my care again, my little Keira girl." He said in husky tones that sent shivers down my body straight to my damn toes. I couldn't say I didn't agree with him on that, but then with that single thought, I bolted upright and shot out of his hold and stood panting. What the Hell was I doing enjoying his touch and basking in the safety I now felt, when others who had kept me safe were still out there! Did they know what had happened? Did Sigurd know where I was? Did Jared get to Marcus in time? Hell, did Jared even get out of there safely? And what about Percy...? I had to find him and save him from a life of misery with Dimme!

Jesus what was wrong with me?

"Keira, sit down and take a breath."

"I can't! Shit, shit, shit!" I said freaking out as everything hit me all at once. It was as though once I saw my rescue as a reality, I had been somewhere in between 'I still can't believe this is real and I am not in that crap hole prison' and 'I am so deliriously happy I have not been sold to an abusive Demon overlord that wants to use me as a human footstool'! When really, I should have been freaking out about this before I even got on this plane!

"Calm yourself and talk to me…now!" He added the ordered 'now' when I didn't listen to him, but with that quick change from gentle coaxing to commanding Lord, it had me sitting before I even thought about it. Now that I was sat facing him, he released a sigh before leaning forward resting his arms on the table in front of us.

"Now ask your questions, Keira." I bit my lip and said quietly,

"No games?"

"No games, but I will advise you to take breaths in between." He commented giving me a knowing smile.

"Do you know where Sigurd is or Jared Cerberus…? Did he get to Marcus in time? Did he beat back Gastian's army at the Hellfire Caves?" I knew I was supposed to take it easy on the questions but I found that once one came, others rushed out to follow.

"My, my we have been making new friends haven't we, my little dove?" He said leaning back in surprise.

"Wait a minute…you didn't know any of this?" I asked letting my shock be known.

"What, that you now obviously know the Shadow King on first name basis? Gone on a date to the Hellfire Caves with The King of the Hellbeasts? Or the fact that you have been caught in the middle of a war with Gastian's demons of the damned…? Oh, before getting kidnapped of course…Fuck me Keira, did you put out a damned ad asking for trouble?" He snapped this last part at me as his anger got the better of his usual cool facade.

"Yes, yes I did, didn't you read it last year when my second kidnapping happened?" I asked him sarcastically, snapping right back. He took a deep breath and I did the same.

"Right, let's start this again and start it from the beginning…what the Hell has been happening to make you turn this insane?" I scowled at him and then snapped,

"Draven died on me, that's what!" At this not so shocking revelation, I was more than a little surprised to find Lucius trying to hide his bewilderment.

"But…you knew that…right?" I asked slowly wondering what in my world was going on!

"Right, Lucius?" I said again when he didn't answer me.

"Yes… that's what I know." He said and this was the point that I knew with utter certainty…

Lucius was lying.

CHAPTER FIFTY-THREE

MY BRAVE CONTACTS

The rest of the short plane journey was spent having the difficult conversation where I had to tell Lucius every single thing that had happened to me. Starting back with the day Leivic turned up delivering me with the killer blow, to the Oracle giving me back hope, that started my mission and then of course, finishing with where I was now.

His reactions were a mix of disbelief, concern and controlled anger. Every now and again he would swear under his breath, which I would purposely ignore or he would speak in other languages, giving me no option other than to ignore. Either way, it was pretty obvious he was less than happy about what I had been through, which then brought on our first argument, starting with him saying,

"Why the fuck didn't you contact me!?"

"Are you shitting me right now?! Contact you? You and every other supernatural that I knew were the ones who disappeared!" He looked about to say something, but I wasn't quite finished with my tantrum.

"No Lucius, don't even bother 'cause I have heard this record before and I didn't like it the first time!"

"Keira, calm down and explain without the smart mouth!" He had the balls to say, which totally got my back up even more.

"Ok, let me spell it out for you, using small words so my smart mouth doesn't upset you…You. Abandoned. Me!" I said not being able to help my building anger at every single person Draven had brought in my life and then ripped away! I knew I wasn't being fair to Lucius, because he did in fact save my ass, but at that moment I lost every 'right action' to the shadows of every 'wrong action' that was done to me since that day.

Draven was never meant to die! We weren't supposed to go through all that with Morgan, Sammael, Lucius, Layla and then some wacked up 'horned God wannabe' like Malphas, then for him to just leave me! That was not how the story was supposed to end. He was my soul mate, the better part of me and lastly, my love's saviour… but now, well… now I was expected to be his saviour and I wasn't even strong enough not to cry at the injustice of what he himself did to me!

I didn't understand any of it. Did he not think that by having everyone I loved around me, that this would have not made me stronger? Was that why? Did I have to know my own Hell on earth before facing his?

I didn't realise that I asked this last question out loud because I found at some point I was on the floor sobbing in Lucius' arms and he was answering me tenderly,

"I don't know love, I just don't know what he was thinking… no one does."

After this embarrassing little breakdown of mine and an apology from me, Lucius sat me down and explained all he knew…or all he was willing to tell, as it still seemed as if he held something vital back.

He told me that Draven's decision to put his plan into action should anything happen to him was final, no matter what those closest to him tried to say on the matter…Lucius included. No one knew what happened in his search for the Oracle, but once he found her it all changed for me that day. He started planning for something only he knew was coming, which was either his death or his capture but that was something no one seemed to know.

However, only one thing was ringing clear, Draven simply used this new rule as a way of keeping me safe from his world or what he knew would happen if I tried to rescue him. And considering all that had happened so far, I was starting to understand why. Which begged the question, what would have happened if I had just let it be? Would I have moved on to Eddie at some point in my life? Was that my ultimate choice, normality in the human world or the dangerous path I now walked down?

Well, one thing was for certain, there was no going back now, so what did it matter? What's done is done and I would stop at nothing in getting back to Draven, even if I ended up dead while getting there! Just one more sight of Draven and I just knew my soul would finally find its peace…

Whatever may come to pass.

The next thing I learnt from Lucius was that he had no clue what part Sigurd and Jared had been playing in my life since he had received his orders to leave me alone. That was of course, until he heard I was in trouble, from none other than…

Jack.

Lucius had given me a quizzical look when I shouted out his name and nearly ended up crying again at the strength and bravery of my very human friend. I had told him before leaving that if I didn't get in contact then to get in touch with Lucius, no matter what it took.

"Yes and what it took was about fifty messages left until someone took him seriously enough to pass me the damn phone! Of course, one mention of not only your name but also the one you gave him for me and of course the plans you had to find Draven was enough for me to take him seriously." Lucius had told me, cracking his knuckle one handed, expressing his agitation at this memory.

So, thanks to the persistence of a good friend, Jack had played the biggest part in saving my bacon from being sold at the meat market. I knew the first chance I got, I would have to call Jack and when saying as much to Lucius he told me how he had first reassured the 'boy' that he received 'fake' word from me to say I would be in touch shortly. What on earth I was going to tell him because of this I didn't yet know, but Lucius told me he had no other choice as Jack was adamant he would travel all the way here and see I was alright for himself if need be. Oh yeah, a phone call was on my 'to do first list' alright!

It was only on the drive on the way to Lucius' nightclub 'Transfusion' that I thought to ask the question,

"Ok, so if it was Jack that originally got you looking for me, who was it that pointed you to the Auction?"

"A contact on the inside of Gastian's plans came forward just in time and being of course on the Lega Nera guest list, I was informed where it would be held as I always receive an invitation." I rolled my eyes at his snobbery and said a muffled,

"Course you do."

"So, who was your contact?" I asked after he didn't explain any further.

"I forget his name but he was rewarded and sent on his way." Lucius sent Pip a strange look that said, 'Isn't that right?' making her quickly pipe up with,

"Oh right, yeah we sent him off all happy and shit."

"O…kay." I said unconvinced, wondering what the heck was going on. I was about to dive in headfirst and ask outright, when one look at Pip told me not to bother. After all, I knew I could just get it out of her later as Pip was easy to crack for information.

"Ok, so there is another matter I need to discuss with you." I said turning to face Lucius, who, as always, was sat next to me in the back of another Limo.

"Like?"

"Well a few things actually, but first there is someone I need to find." I watched him take a deep breath and sigh, letting me know with that reaction he thought I meant Draven…and yeah, of course I wanted his help in that, but first there was the promise I had made that I had to see through.

"It's not what you think, Luc."

"No?"

"No, it's not. I need to find out where they kept me before the auction." His reaction was not one I thought it would be which would be shock. No, instead I got a slight smirk and as he rubbed a hand over his mouth he asked,

"Really? And your reasons for this would be…?" I sucked in

one side of my bottom lip and held it there thinking of how to put this correctly.

"I'm not expecting anyone to understand, but there is someone there I need to help…someone who helped me when he didn't have to and someone that…well, someone I have come to care about, very…very much…he saved my life, Lucius." On hearing my voice thick with emotion he dropped his smug attitude and gave me a caring smile.

"I will help you find this person, Keira."

"You promise?" I had to hear it.

"I do." He said nodding his head once in what looked like respect for my unexpected request. Then he turned to Adam and said,

"You know what to do, get it done." Adam nodded in the same way Lucius had done and said his usual,

"Yes, My Lord." Then he got out his smartphone and was soon talking to someone in what sounded like German. I tore my gaze from Adam's phone call and noticed, as I turned back Lucius, Pip now looked even more excited than usual, bouncing on her hands which she held under her bottom.

"I also need to find some way of contacting Sigurd, as the book we are bound to has had some sort of spell put on it." Ok, so now this was starting to sound like something straight from Harry Potter!

"So I heard. I happen to know someone who has dealings with 'Snake eye'. I will get word to him and yes, before you ask, I will also get word to Cerberus as well, as I know you are anxious about your new eclectic group of friends." He said sounding both amused and annoyed.

After hearing this I started to let myself relax, knowing that soon everyone would know I was in safe hands and hopefully I would be hearing the same thing about them. I let my tensed shoulders slump back into the comfy seat and I saw Lucius watch me from the corner of his eye.

"Why don't you rest, you have had a long night and must be tired?" Lucius advised and I shook my head.

"I can't, I have too many things I need to do when we get there."

"Everything will still be waiting for you to 'deal' with, but you need to rest also…so close your eyes and rest for a while." Just the sound of his voice was making my eyelids all of sudden feel heavy. It was like he was hypnotizing me with that soft lull added to every word.

"Maybe I could just close my eyes for ten minutes, just the time it takes us to get there…you will wake me when we get there, won't you?" For some reason my saying this and giving in, made him look as if he had just won some epic battle.

"Of course." Although the way he said this wasn't inspiring much confidence in me but by this point I was suddenly so tired it's all I could think about.

So I gave in and slept and my last conscious feeling was when Lucius plucked me from the seat and cradled me to his chest.

I woke up to the sound of a rumbling noise, but as soon as I became aware of it the noise stopped. I gingerly opened my eyes feeling the effects of more than a ten-minute sleep. I almost growled out his name knowing that he didn't wake me, but then stopped when I took in the new sights. The first of which was one I had seen before and I watched my own reflection mouth the word 'Shit'.

I stared up at the ceiling full of mirrors encased in black lacquered frames of all different designs, shapes and sizes. It was like a gothic montage all showing the same thing, that of me lying in an enormous black sleigh bed under rich crimson coloured sheets. Oh yeah, I remembered this alright, only the last time was after Pip had bitten me. I quickly turned my head from side to side to expose my neck, checking just in case I had been caught again, only this time by someone with bigger teeth than my little Imp!

After that panic was squashed a new one quickly arose after looking more closely in the mirror and seeing Lucius' naked body next to me. My hands flew to my mouth to keep in the little scream that nearly came out. Once I had my reactions under control, my hands curled into loose fists I held at my mouth not knowing what to do. I looked up at my own worried face and then decided to brave a look to my left.

Lucius was lying on his side, facing me with his eyes closed. His long lashes fanned out along the almond shapes casting shadows on the tops of his cheeks. There was just enough light coming from a lamp that someone had left on, to properly let me drink in my fill of this vulnerable side to Lucius I had never seen before.

He had an ethereal beauty that made me want to reach out and run my fingertips along his pale skin. His lips were a perfect balance of not being too full and not too thin and I had to bite my own so as not to giggle. I don't know why but like this he looked younger and although always considered handsome, right now I would have gone more with cute. I think it was because he was void of a devilish grin that promised dark pleasures and predator eyes that could make the strongest of beings squirm.

But now I was seeing him without any masks of authority or reactions to carnal thoughts. Now, he was just a sleeping man of masculine beauty drifting along in his dream world that looked like he had found peace there. It made me wonder what Lucius' dreams were about. What did a being as powerful as Lucius find when he closed his eyes?

After I took the minutes being captivated by this side of Lucius, I started to let my eyes drift down. After all I was only human…had I used that excuse once or twice before? Well, whatever worked to keep my guilt at bay long enough to take in the sights. I almost forgot that what happened to Lucius that day at the Temple had changed him forever. Well looking at him now I was definitely reminded.

His upper body was twisted facing me with one arm bent being used as a pillow for his head, making his muscles bunch and the other was lay over his wide chest. Like this I could see that sexy curved line men got from having muscular shoulders that then formed into wide and a lengthy bicep. Whereas before, Lucius had a slimmer build of muscle to Draven's body, now that was no longer the case, thanks to receiving the same powers from both Heaven and Hell.

But it wasn't just his bulk up that marked these changes. It was the lighter streaks of gold in his sandy coloured hair that had innocently fallen over one side of his face. It was the deeper tone to his voice, giving him a slightly deeper authoritative edge than before. Hell, it was even that his fingers looked stronger, which were currently curled in the sheets in an iron grip. I wondered why and what had changed in his dreams to give him reason to hold on?

I didn't have to wait long for my answer as his voice interrupted my silent appraisal.

"Enjoying yourself?" I jumped at his question and seemed frozen to the spot. Not that I had ever been caught stealing before as you would actually have to steal in the first place, but if I had, then this was what I imagined getting caught would feel like. Or did stealing the heart count…? Because technically I was just returning it to its rightful owner. Ok, ok, so getting back on course, maybe by looking at someone when they slept was like stealing?

"Uh…I…I wasn't looking." It wasn't my best line by a long shot and one cheeky grin told me he knew this. I watched him push all his hair back with one hand and I couldn't help but bite my lip at the sight.

"No? So, you just woke up on your side facing me and for the last ten minutes have been staring into a space I just so happen to fill?"

"Er…yeah?"

"I will take your lame 'Yeah' and raise you a 'Bullshit'."

"Alright fine, I was looking! Happy now?" I said losing my patience and he laughed at my outburst. I watched him turn onto his back and stretch out his arms behind his head.

"Well come on sugar don't be shy, you sit right here and get a closer look." He said patting his covered groin, making me growl at him.

"Not funny."

"Do I look like I just want to be tickled?" He said turning back round to his original position, giving me that bad boy 'I wanna play' look.

"Do you want to explain to me what I am doing in your bed?" I demanded in my best pissed off voice.

"Snoring." He replied smirking.

"What! I don't snore!" He leant toward me and then whispered,

"Yeah honey, you do." This was when I smacked him on the arm and quickly realised that it wasn't very effective when all I felt was solid flesh. This just angered me more.

"I. DO. NOT!" I said leaning in myself meeting him in the middle. We were now both only inches apart and where he was grinning, I was scowling.

"Don't worry, it will be our little secret." He whispered and then kissed me quickly on the end of my nose.

"I think I liked you more when you were a scary, controlling, badass Vamp kidnapper." I said folding my arms across my chest and only now just realising I was wearing one of his bloody shirts! I opened my arms back up and looked down under the sheets to see apart from a pair of knee-high socks, it was also all I was wearing!

"You have all of five seconds to explain, Lucius or I swear to God no supernatural power on earth will stop your balls from hurting." I threatened holding the bridge of my nose in a non-effective way of gaining patience.

"Well, seeing as we have very different ideas on what you could do to my balls, I will explain, Miss Killjoy. You fell asleep and I carried you up here, where I took off my shirt to give to Pip to dress you in. By the time I returned you were snoring your little orange socks off and I fell asleep laughing at you… happy now?" I smacked him again and said,

"I don't snore!" He laughed again and said,

"Yes Keira…you do." I rolled my eyes and then muttered,

"Whatever," knowing I was not going to win this game of his.

"So why didn't you wake me up like you said you would do?"

"Because you were exhausted and even I am not enough of a bastard to wake someone when they have endured all that you have." At this my anger softened enough to make me say a small,

"Thanks."

"Besides, I knew eventually the snoring would wake you." I groaned in frustration before I started to say,

"I do not…" And then that sentence trickled off because I suddenly remembered the rumbling noise that woke me up, only as soon as I became aware of it, it had stopped.

"Oh God!" I said slapping my hands over my mouth for the second time that morning.

"Ah, there it is." I shot him daggers and said,

"Shut up!" Only making him laugh harder, which managed to jiggle the mattress. Then Lucius did a very human thing and stretched out his arms and yawned. I was so taken back that I didn't realise I was staring at him until he said,

"What?"

"Uh, you yawn?" Wow I really didn't wake up as the brightest bulb this morning, did I?

"And?" He replied before rolling to grab his mobile phone from the bedside table.

"I just…never heard it before." Stupid Keira, stupid Keira!

"You have never heard me cum before either, would you like to?"

"Eww you're a pig!" I said slapping his chest for the third time, only this time he grabbed my wrist, reminding me of being in last night's shackles.

"Try to hit me again and I will have no other choice but to restrain you." He promised with a dark purr to his voice that screamed pure sin. I followed his heated eyes as they moved up to focus on the swags of chains attached to the twisted metal bar above us. It ran along the top curve at the head of Lucius' incredible black sleigh bed. My eyes widened as I remembered from last time the black leather manacles attached to the middle of those chains.

"I'll…" I had to clear my voice before pushing the rest of that statement out,

"…be good." Lucius let go of my wrist and said,

"Pity," before he flipped the covers back and I watched him get out of bed, completely butt naked. My mouth dropped open like a damn goldfish at the sight of all that pale flesh that curved into too many muscles to count. His back looked strong enough to carry boulders on and his thighs big enough to run with them. I didn't know if I had closed my eyes by this point and the perfect backside I was still seeing had just been imprinted onto my retinas or if I just couldn't close my eyes because of the perfection. Either one there it was, Lucius' naked body and it was a thing of pure lustful beauty!

"You're staring, little doll." He said, his voice full of mischievous mirth and clearly loving catching me practically drooling at him. I snapped my eyes shut, still seeing his perfect butt and mumbled something that I hoped sounded like an apology. I turned around to face the other way and bolted upright in the bed to swing my legs on the floor.

His bed was so huge that my feet didn't even touch the thick gothic looking rug that I was making sure I kept looking at. I followed every grey line of the giant fleur de lis that was made from a series of delicate swirls and curled branches. It was a beautiful rug and at that moment keeping my mind from the beautiful body behind me. Only once the rug no longer held an appeal I switched to take in my knee high socks, counting the stripes of black against orange…or was it orange against black…?

"Ah!" I jumped when I felt Lucius' hand on my shoulder and heard him chuckling softly.

"Found anything interesting down there?"

"Pip left my socks on." I said because A: I was stupid and B: anything was better than blurting out 'you're a beautiful man'. I felt his head come closer until I felt his chin rest at my shoulder. He looked down at my feet and said,

"And how very adorable they look." This time I just blushed instead of speaking, thinking this was the wisest choice. My breath caught when I felt him move his chin back and one hand came up to my neck to brush my hair away to the other side. He held it there as it was now short enough to come back on its own and I quickly found it hard to breathe when his fingers suddenly made a fist in my hair.

"You look good in my shirt." Lucius hummed along my neck as his free hand came up to play with the collar. Although he was only skimming his fingertips along where the two sides of his open shirt met the first fastened button, it felt like his touch continued all the way down to the junction of my legs. It was such a confusing mix of sensations. On one side I had his commanding hand gripping my hair, roughly tipping my head to the side so he could get better access and then the other was caressing me so softly it was almost like a lover whispering endearments.

"Lucius." I released his name on a gasp as he let loose the first button so his fingertips could just reach the top of my breasts. I think I must have started panting at this point or close to it because he stilled after he heard the plea in his name, neither of us knowing if it was to stop or keep going. Later I would find myself thanking the Heavens that he saw it as a sign to stop, because feeling a man's touch again was like soothing the wound before tearing it open again.

I had to give him credit for making light of the situation when he just kissed my neck and said,

"I think it best if you get dressed into something other than my shirt, pet…" Well I did think this was making light of it until he added,

"…before I take you whispering my name as a sign to rip it from your very biteable skin." Then he sucked in some of that skin and held it with his teeth, only to then smile around his mouthful when I sucked in a shuddered breath. Then as quickly as it started he let me go and I felt the bed move as he got off the other side.

"Get dressed love, I have a surprise waiting for you." He said being back to his usual playful manner.

"Uh, what time is it?" I croaked out like I was trying to form words around the squash ball I had unknowingly swallowed.

"It's getting on for ten." He said and I looked round to see he was adding a long-sleeved t-shirt to the stonewash jeans he already had on.

"Oh, that's not too bad then." I said watching as he pulled each sleeve up his forearms. It was a rust coloured material that was a V neck only because it had been torn that way, along with the frayed edges around the waist and arms. It was tight around his torso, showing the lines of his pecs and only just hiding the six pack I had seen earlier…oh and of course it looked delicious on him, damn it!

"Not too bad?" He inquired.

"Yeah, means I didn't sleep that late." At this he laughed shaking his head to himself as though he found this to be another funny Keira moment.

"Keira, its ten at night, you slept through the day."

"What?!" I shouted jumping from the bed to face him. It was only when he gave me that predatory gaze looking me up and down, did I pull down on his shirt, making sure it covered everything north of my knees.

"Guess I was right, you must have been tired… and now you must be hungry." He added after my belly made itself known on an embarrassing rumble.

"You get ready and I will see to getting you some much needed food." He said going back to being gentle caring Lucius. He walked to the door that I knew led into the rest of his apartment but as he opened the door he stopped to look back.

"Keira girl."

"Yeah?" I said waiting for what was coming next,

"I thought the snoring was cute."

I heard him chuckling at my embarrassed groan as he closed the door.

As soon as I knew I was alone I ran to use the bathroom I remembered from last time, only now I was in a rush I barely took in the black and red theme that continued from Lucius' ostentatious bedroom. However, I did give the monstrous black clawed tub a wishful glance thinking how long it had been since I had last soaked my body.

Not having the time, I had to be content with having a quick wash hoping there would be chance later to give this luscious bathroom the time it truly deserved. After brushing my teeth and trying to brush through my hair at the same time, I gave up with the knotted nest and spat out the heavenly toothpaste that I would have kissed rats for only days ago.

After visiting the posh toilet, I quickly made short work of getting dressed back in the clothes I had barely worn last night and thanks to Pip I found them folded up on a lavish cherry red Chesterfield couch.

I then ran out of Lucius' bedroom door to be hit with the heavenly sight of two things, one made my stomach growl in anticipation and the other made me scream out with pure joy…

"Percy!"

CHAPTER FIFTY-FOUR

BARGIN WITH BLOOD, NOT YOUR BODY

"Keira!" Percy shouted back as I ran at him. We joined together and tears ran down both our cheeks as the emotions soared. I pushed back his hood and put my hands either side of his scarred face to pull him to me to kiss his forehead. He looked up at me, bit down on his own lip as it quivered right before he wrapped his arms around me.

I heard Pip's squeals of delight in the background at seeing our reunion. I just couldn't help the tears. I felt, in this moment, so relieved seeing him here and safe, having worried that once I left, Dimme would end up torturing him beyond anything he could come back from. The bond we had forged together during that time was one that would never leave me, no matter what.

And just to put it in perspective, anyone that ended up taking punishments after sneaking out to get me tampons and then being the poor soul who had to dispose of them is someone who not only goes beyond the duties of friendship, but is someone worth risking my life for.

"How?" I asked after we had both had our moment to calm down.

"Ith wasth all your mas…ss…masthers idea." He said stuttering even more and I knew this was down to being emotional.

"Umm Master… you know, I think I like that." Lucius said making a joke of what Percy said. I turned to him and found him leaning against the bar area casually, as if this was all an everyday occurrence. Pip and Adam were also there and sat watching all this play out. She gave me a little wave and then said,

"I dressed him." I turned back to Percy who was no longer wearing a scruffy brown monk's habit. Pip had quickly brought him to the now and with a vengeance.

"You made him a punk!?" I said stating the obvious.

"Hell yeah I did, doesn't he look cute?" She said jumping off the sofa and coming to pat him on the head. He beamed up at her with one of the biggest grins I had ever seen on him and I had to laugh as it was clear he had found his new mentor. He looked so different than the worried and downtrodden friend I had met back in that horrible place and I couldn't stop smiling as I took in the new Percy.

In just a few days Pip had transformed him into a smaller version of Ruto! He was now wearing a pair of ripped, black skinny jeans, a faded KISS t-shirt and a thin knitted top that hung open at the sides, showing multiple belts with spikes. The only thing that remained the same was that he wore the floppy hood up, but this time not completely covering his face. He even had on a beanie hat underneath which had grey skulls along the rim as if it had been stamped.

"Ok, someone's gotta fill me in here." I said looking back to Lucius. He pushed away from the bar and came to take my hand. He then led to me to one of the other couches and sat me down ready to explain.

"Your little friend over there risked the wrath of his master as he stole his money and travelled all the way here from Switzerland to come to tell me about his kidnapped friend being sold at auction." My gaze shot to Percy and I asked in shock,

"You did that?"

"I wasth going to pay ith back." He said looking sheepish, but I couldn't give a flying monkey's turd about the money as it was him I was worried about.

"Percy, why did you do that? You could have been caught or

killed or that stringy piece of piss could have found out and… and…" I felt Lucius' hand grip my thigh and I realised I was panicking.

"I…I am fffine thhhough…th'see. Bethsides I have thsomething of yourths" He said softly pulling my coin out of his pocket and handing it me.

"Keira, it will be fine, he is safe now." Lucius told me quietly but at that precise moment Ruto walked into the apartment and announced,

"Luc, there is someone here calling himself Dimme, although dumb shit is my preferred choice." I tensed at hearing the name and Lucius loosened his grip so that he could soothingly stroke my leg.

"Ssshh, breathe little bird." He whispered in my ear. I flashed Percy a panicked look that matched the one I found staring back.

"Tell him to wait." Ruto nodded respectfully at Lucius' order and turned to leave.

"Oh and Ruto…"

"Yes, My Lord?"

"Stay at his back." Upon hearing this, Ruto's lips split into a murderous grin that promised the sight of blood before the night was over. Again he just nodded and then this time swiftly left the room.

"What are you going to do?" I asked Lucius nervously pulling one sleeve down past my fingers and then twisting it over and over again. Lucius looked down at my actions and then chuckled before taking my hands in his.

"Trust me, my Keira girl, to do what needs to be done." I didn't know if this was supposed to comfort me or just make me panic more but either way I found myself being pulled from my seat and walked out of the door. I looked behind me to see Percy following with his hand being held in Pip's swinging one. She looked absolutely gleeful and winked at me when she caught me looking. How could she be so happy? Did she know what was coming?

We all walked from Lucius' apartment back into the VIP of Transfusion and somewhere I had not been for what seemed like a lifetime. It was like déjà vu all over again for me, only this time instead of being led by Pip, I was being led by Lucius himself. So this time when Lucius starting walking to the back of his sex themed VIP, I knew I would once again find myself in the private part of the club. This had been the same room that I had been reunited back with Draven after Lucius had taken me. Of course, it was also the same room I had gone a little nuttso, having destroyed most of it in my rage thinking Draven had cheated on me.

We walked through the double doors and I felt my breath hitch as I struggled to hold in the frustrated tears. I soon found myself being hit with the ghosts of that memory so strong it was as though I could reach out and touch the Draven there from the past. What wouldn't I give right now to have that single moment back? At least back then I knew Draven existed in the world and was trying to find me but now…well, the uncertainty in what I was doing was almost soul crushing.

The room was as I remembered it before I had run from it in a broken mess caused by my anger. It was a single open plan room about half the size of the VIP at Afterlife. The décor was modern and cold, with its stark white leather seating and its blue backlighting. The only other features in the room were black flooring, stainless steel tabletops and glass, glass and more glass. The one thing I did notice was that all the flat screens that displayed different aspects of Transfusion had been replaced but were now switched off.

"I thought it best considering what happened last time." Lucius said when he must have noticed me staring at the screens. He didn't sound the least bit angry at what my actions must have cost him, but considering the guy just spent a cool one billion dollars on me, I doubt a few TV's and some new plastering was that much of big deal.

I let him lead me over to the same seating area as before and that pinch in my chest got tighter. He sat down in the middle which had a higher back than the rest of the U shaped couch and he pulled me down with him. I was about to argue the fact that I had once again been placed in front of him, but then I thought better of it. I mean what was the point, when did I ever win against these men? If it wasn't Lucius, then it was Sigurd bossing me around or Jared sitting me on his lap stroking me like his damn 'Pet'. There only seemed to be two types of supernatural men in my world and that was those who wanted to dominate me and those who wanted to kill me…oh and then there was Percy who, thank the Lord, was neither of those things!

The leather gave way to our combined weights and Lucius leant back getting relaxed and comfortable as if what was about to happen was nothing more than tonight's entertainment. Me, well I was a nervous wreck not knowing what was coming.

Lucius nodded to the wrestler sized doormen we had passed and on cue they opened the doors once more to let Dimme in, who was closely followed by Ruto at his back. I heard Lucius snort his amusement at the sight of Dimme who looked a bit like a thin limp willy with legs.

His slimy gaze flew to me as I was dead centre, but when his scowl turned threatening Lucius wasn't amused any longer.

"If you don't want to make this any worse than it already is, then I would strongly suggest eyes on my Master." Ruto said from behind him, making him jump.

"I have done nothing wrong!" He snapped haughtily, doing himself no favours.

"No? Then let me enlighten you, you dumb fuck! See, what I have here in my lap, well this stunning creature is mine and well, you not only aided in keeping her from me, but you also tried to FUCKING STARVE HER TO DEATH!" Lucius quickly lost all of his cool and roared this last part at him coming straight from the depths of his more dominant demon side. It was so loud I thought we would have a reconstruction, or more like deconstruction, of when I trashed the room. The fixtures rattled and I heard a few pieces of the glass around us crack. In my automatic reflexes, I had covered my ears with my hands and soon I had Lucius grip my wrists to pull them gradually from my head.

"Sorry my pet…" He apologised sweetly being now a complete contrast to how he was only seconds ago, and I had to say, given how scary Lucius can be, I was glad I was receiving the nice end.

"So Dim what do you suggest I do with you?" Lucius asked regaining his calm eerie voice that really screamed, 'Danger! Stand back or better yet, RUN FOR YOUR LIFE!'

"I…he…it wasn't my fault My Lord…I was only following my…my master." Dimme had lost all his bravado now and was a hair's breadth away from grovelling on his bony knees.

"Yes, well your master died at my hands last night and is no doubt getting his skin peeled from his flesh as we speak…I have many friends in low places you see." He said smirking as he looked down to Hell, in his reference to his 'friends' and I couldn't hold back the sly little grin at seeing Dimme swallow down a hard lump of fear.

"So, the question remains, do I send you down to wait in line for the same punishment or simply deliver it here myself?" I had to hand it to Lucius at this point, he was utterly terrifying without even trying at it. So much so in fact I was half expecting to see Dimme pee his pants any minute now.

The hand that Lucius had been using to play with my hair suddenly gripped me tighter and pulled until my head went back to look up at him. It didn't hurt, but it spoke volumes to the room as to who, at that moment in time, I belonged to. I remembered as much from my last time in Lucius' domain. So I went along with it as I knew what he did was only for my own good.

"What do you think, little doll?" Upon Lucius asking me this question as to Dimme's fate, he must have panicked because one second he was saying,

"But my Lor…" And then was cut off abruptly by Ruto who had produced a large blade from somewhere on his body and was quickly holding it to Dimme's throat.

"He didn't order you to speak." Ruto informed him in the lethal composed voice that sometimes gave me the creeps coming from such a young-looking person.

"But of course, my innocent little Keira couldn't possibly choose someone else's fate, so perhaps one of your own will speak up for you…Percy, come here." Lucius motioned for

Percy to come forward after releasing my hair and I watched him step closer after Pip encouraged him to do so. The level of shock on Dimme's face made his jaw drop and consequently Ruto's blade nicked him on the neck.

"Yessth my… Master." He managed to correct some of his stutter on the word 'master' out of respect and I gave him a smile to cheer him on.

"You came here against your possession officer's knowledge because your actions against him would have seen you punished, correct?"

"Yessth My Lord" He said now with a bit more bite to his words. I didn't know where this was going but having my trust in Lucius, I knew it wasn't looking good for Dimme.

"And what punishment would he have given you, Percy?" I gave Lucius a quick glance to see him staring at Dimme with such severity there was no doubt what he had in mind.

I looked back to Percy to see him square off his shoulders and raise his head up before he whipped his hood back and stood there proud in all his beautiful but painful glory. He answered with one word so profound that it not only chilled me to the core but forced a single tear to run down my cheek as a silent show of support.

"Fire!" He said in an entirely different voice that did not sound as though it came from my Percy. No, this voice came from a warrior… from a fighter and more importantly the strongest of them all…

A survivor.

"Then so be it…Adam." I watched him first kiss his wife on her nose before he detangled himself from Pip, who was hanging around his neck like a baby koala. Adam then walked over next to Percy and put his hand on his shoulder to show him he agreed that Percy was one of them now.

"Yes, My Lord?"

"Why don't you introduce him to Abaddon." Lucius instructed and my head shot around to see he was serious. I was about to scream 'are you out of your friggin mind!' but he just mouthed the single word 'trust' to me and I decided I had no other option. Lucius nodded back to the scene now unfolding and thanks to my shudder, Lucius wrapped an arm around my middle and pulled me tighter into the comfort of his hold and then whispered,

"Don't look away Keira, your little friend needs to draw his strength from you…so be strong for him, as I know you can." I did as I was told, nodding to Percy when I saw guilt flash there.

Then it really began.

"With pleasure." Adam rumbled, letting the first touches of his deeply contained other self merely skim the surface. I actually didn't know what was more frightening to witness, the monster that was known as Abaddon, who was every last thing Hell signified? Or was it the geeky accountant who first pushed up his glasses before placing a single tip of his index finger on Dimme's arm. Of course, the second sounded a lot less threatening, that was until it released pure Hell inside his body and literally started to cook Dimme from the inside out.

It looked as though it started with his very soul and licked outwards to make blistering skin. Ruto released his hold over him when he knew it was no longer necessary. Dimme wasn't going anywhere with his host that was soon becoming a charred version of his former self. His skin popped and crackled like a cooking pig, making me gag. The extreme heat was coming from the fire that you could see raging under the flesh and his face had become a grotesque jack 'o lantern as you could see the brief glow behind his eyes and in his open mouth before the flames erupted from both.

Any minute I was expecting him to just burst open like a skin balloon trying to contain the fire but this didn't happen. Adam gently ran the same fingertip down his blackened arm and then, as if he had been made of paper, pieces of his remains started to turn to white ash and float to the floor like dainty snowflakes.

And that was the end of my short term jailor and Percy's long term tormentor. I really tried to be the better person and find some tiny part of me that felt sorry that it had happened this way, but one look at the horrific abuse he put my friend through, I just couldn't do it. I did however get up from Lucius' lap, walk over to my unmoving friend and put my arms around him to pour every ounce of comfort I had in me to give.

"I promised I would make it right, but in the end Percy, you did it! You were the one brave enough to save me and in doing so, you saved yourself…I am…so, so…proud of …you." I said this last part through the tears that fell from raw emotions that had ripped me wide open for all to see. It felt like I couldn't remember a time where I didn't cry anymore, whether it was through sadness, fear, pain, humiliation, anger, extreme happiness or utter relief. My tears stood as evidence to the gaping hole Draven had put there and it only seemed to fill in times like this. Times where the friends I had gained before or the new friends that had been placed on my journey's path came to find me. Whatever the time, whatever the place and whatever the trials put in place, no matter the heartache I faced, there they all were …ready to save me.

But I not only felt saved, more importantly I felt blessed and I didn't need the Gods for that, because all I needed was what I always had…

My friends.

After all that had happened there was only one thing left and that was for Percy to declare his loyalty to Lucius. He did so with such fierce determination it was humbling to witness. He knelt at Lucius' feet and sliced into his palm to offer his new master his own blood to bind his faithful service. However, it wasn't just the honour I saw in Percy's eyes that was so surprising to me, but it was that same honour I saw in Lucius' that shocked me the most. He truly looked pleased to be gaining such a person into his fold and there I was, nearly crying all over again because of it!

"Do you Percy, declare your soul into my ownership, sealed with your very blood, branding you as one of my own?" Lucius had asked him and Percy, even with his own tears pouring down his puckered skin, decided to use them to prove the sincerity of his commitment to his new Lord. After cutting into his skin, he captured the salty drops from his chin that mixed with his blood. Lucius seeing this nodded sincerely, accepting Percy's deep sign of respect for what it was, nothing short of a life sacrifice. Percy was telling Lucius this way that if ever the chance arose, he would lay down his life to save him.

"I do, with all that I am." He said this with not once shred of a stutter it made me realise why. Percy was a Herculean Hero trapped inside a body that had never been given the chance to bloom. He had never in his life until now been shown his true worth, not until Lucius had asked him to make this vow. After all, this wasn't something he had to do. He could have just made Percy leave and go on his merry way into a world he didn't even know. But he didn't do that. No, what he did do was go above and beyond what anyone of us ever expected him to do.

"Then Percy, I hereby decree that not only are you now one among us, but I have decided to position you inside my very council and swear to you my protection until the day comes that you no longer want to exist in this world." At these words I wasn't the only one expressing my shock.

"I…I…My Lord, I…" Percy was having a hard time understanding what this meant but Lucius looking slightly amused, just leant closer to him and said,

"Just accept it, lad." Percy beamed up at him as though he was looking into the very eyes of his own personal God and then nodded quickly saying,

"I won't let you down, Sir." Again I was amazed that when talking to Lucius his voice was completely different. Like the man inside him desperate to get out was allowed that freedom when in the presence of his master.

"You already haven't." Lucius replied and then looked at me making it very clear what he meant by that statement. A deep blush rose in response to such a heated look, that I had to look away first. Only when I could no longer feel Lucius' hungry gaze on me I looked back to see him dip a finger in the small pool of blood that had gathered in Percy's palm before lifting it to his lips to suck it clean. I watched as he shuddered after closing his eyes and only seconds went by before they flicked open again. First they were the blood red I was used to seeing on Lucius whenever his emotions ran high, but now since his change there were also added swirls of yellow ochre swimming in the centres.

"Right, now that business is out of the way, now for something personal." Lucius stated getting up and motioning for Percy to do the same. I looked back and made eye contact with him, giving my friend the thumbs up, receiving a shy smile back.

I was still looking at him silently laughing when I felt Lucius touch my arm, startling me.

"Come Keira, dine with me." With the intense way he was still looking at me, it felt more like he was asking me out on a date and not willing to take no for an answer. I couldn't find anything witty or smart mouthed to say, as my defence mechanism refused to kick in, so instead I just found myself nodding. He led me away, back to his apartment and just when Pip was about to follow, Adam grabbed hold of her and shook his head telling her no. I wondered what it was about as the look from Adam's face said that he knew what Lucius was planning. Now that made me nervous!

Lucius didn't speak all the way, nor did he look back at me. I mean why would he, it's not as if he had to keep checking to see if I followed considering it felt like he wasn't letting go of my hand any time soon. He opened the door and let me in first with his outstretched arm until he had to eventually let go.

"Leave!" At first I thought he was talking to me and was about to snap 'make up your damn mind', when I saw a half-naked waitress with a shaved head and several facial piercings who I recognised from last time. She had been replacing the food that must have gone cold from earlier, with another covered tray. One look from Lucius in his masterful mode told her to leave the trolley and cut and run.

Once the door closed the air suddenly felt thick with what needed to be said. I just opened my mouth to say what was on my mind when Lucius spoke.

"Sit down and eat before you fade into nothing." I looked down at myself suddenly feeling self-conscious and hugged my once fleshy belly. He gave me a raised eyebrow that said don't challenge me and snapped,

"Eat!" I let my stomach answer him as it chose once again the perfect timing to groan. I did as I was told, which was quite possibly the easiest command I had yielded to, considering I was starving. I walked to the dining table the food was all set out on, which was set separated back from the room in its own raised alcove. I stepped up to the first covered plate and when I revealed its hidden treasure, I groaned out loud at the sight.

"My new council member told me how you had a cheese-burger craving for three weeks." I turned to find him stood closer than before and the smile I gave him softened his gaze. We both took our seats and before I had even scooted my chair all the way in, I had the greasy goodness in my hands and taking my first mouthful from the Heavens.

"Oh God!" I moaned round my mouthful. I even think my eyes must have rolled back up in my head because Lucius started chuckling at me.

"That good?" He asked and I nodded like a mad woman around my next mouthful, not giving any care that I was acting like a pig.

"You have no idea and if you told me it was made from the ass-end of a rat right now I would still eat it like it's going out of fashion." At this he burst out laughing again and I couldn't help but smile around my next bite. He was so handsome when he smiled like that and it was hard to take my eyes from the sight.

"You not hungry?" I asked when I noticed he wasn't touching any of the covered plates.

"Not for food." This was when the heated gaze came back full force. I swallowed the food as though I was trying to swallow his words and they too didn't want to go down.

"Keira, I have a proposition for you to consider."

"Okay…what are you proposing exactly?" I asked feeling that prickling sensation at the back of my neck when you know something is coming and it is screaming danger.

"I will take you to Draven."

"You will! Oh my God Lucius, that is just…I mean, oh God this can't be… wait…so does that mean you know where he is?!" I shouted now ignoring the back of my neck altogether. I didn't care what he wanted from me, if it was going to get me to Draven then I would do anything!

"I think I just might but…"

"But what…what do you want in return?" I asked only to wish afterwards I hadn't been so eager to know, as what he said next made my burger slip from my hands and the food I had already consumed turn to lead.

Just two words…

"One night."

CHAPTER FIFTY-FIVE

SEEING THE MOON LIGHT

To say it took me a while to process those two words was an understatement. Upon reflection, then maybe my initial reaction to it was a little over the top. I still remember his face of delighted amusement as I jumped from my seat so quickly it knocked the chair back. At this point I couldn't even find the words as the shock was still seeping its way into the part of my brain that begged the question…did I just hear that right?

I had just placed my open hands to the table and lowered my head, shaking it slowly as if this would help the understanding process. Needless to say it didn't and when Lucius stepped closer and placed his hand on mine, I acted like I had been stung. I whipped my hand from his and backed away from him as though I was facing my most dangerous challenge yet…

Temptation.

"Keira…" Lucius purred and I retreated further, nearly falling backwards as I didn't account for the step the raised dining room was set on. Thankfully I righted myself in time and just as his hand came out to grab me I turned and ran from him. I knew he could have caught me, so I was more than glad when he didn't try. It was obvious that the pure horror on my face was enough to tell him I needed time alone. And time alone was what I received as I ran to his room and then through into the bathroom where I barricaded myself in, with not only the lock on the door but also throwing a cabinet across the frame for good measure.

And this was where I remained for the rest of the night.

Knocks came and went from so many different people, they all mingled into one. At some point of my solitude I realised this was a strange reaction from me but the underlying reasons were there, as if they had been cut out of me. A shameful reaction to go with the shameful truth…damn temptations of the worst kind! I hated myself for giving it even a single thought of possibility.

I should have shouted and screamed at Lucius for even thinking of such a thing, but I found myself so petrified of giving in to a moment's weakness, I just had to run. I wanted so badly to be this girl who had faced all these death-defying trials and come out on top, come out of it all with the one man I loved. But no one ever said in these trials would be the lure of a man I had grown to have secret feelings for, if only a very small percentage of what I felt for Draven.

So, with this heart-breaking revelation came my breakdown. Because it wasn't just Lucius, and the truth of the matter was what I felt for Lucius was the same as what I felt for them all. Vincent and his forbidden kiss. Sigurd and his blood binding bond that fused a small part of his soul with mine. Jared with the bargain we made and the conflicting possessiveness he felt towards me. And then there was Lucius and the last words he had said to me that day…

"That power won't ever love me back and she was right, power was only ever gained in loving her."

And so I cried and sobbed and held onto my chest like the hole Draven had left was freezing around the edges. I knew how easy it would have been to say yes, but how hard it would be to live with that answer given. I couldn't do it, no matter what it promised me in the end.

So this was it, this was what all I had gone through came

down to. The biggest test of them all and I didn't even know if I was making the right decision. Was this really what fate had in store for me? A man I considered a friend, who I always knew wanted so much more than the only thing I could offer him. But now what? Did he really think that he could use this opportunity as a tool to show me how he cared or was this just another game played from an added opponent?

I felt as though I didn't know anything anymore. Only it felt more than that, it felt as if I was running towards Draven, but without even realising I was on damn treadmill that would always keep me back. I felt that no matter what I did I could never run fast enough!

I don't know when it happened but at some point I must have exhausted myself because I felt my body being lifted. I knew Lucius had hit his limit on letting me wallow in my misery and in the back of my mind I could only hope this was enough of a sign to take back his deal. I was lowered into his bed, wrapped in his arms and fell back to sleep, hoping that the next day would be a day that answers weren't needed from questions not asked.

Of course, this was not the day I woke up to, or should I say night as living with Vampires my nights had become my days. I was at least thankful that this time I woke alone. I rubbed my sore eyes from hours of pitiful sobbing and sniffed trying to unblock my nose thanks to wasted energy on breathing through the panic.

I was hit by so many emotions, but I had to say the top two were shame and anger. Both were directed at myself but only one was aimed at Lucius and it was obvious which one. So, whilst I was letting this one overrule over every other one, I took my opportunity to put it to good use. I whipped the covers back and stormed into the sitting room to let rip.

I found Lucius having some sort of meeting with every one of his council and I barely registered the newcomers, Liessa and her husband Caspian, before I screamed,

"HOW DARE YOU!" I stood there panting with my fists clenched by my sides, wanting so much to put them to good use. Every head turned to face me, including Percy who was the newest council member. But I cared nothing for the mortified looks I received as I only had vengeful eyes for Lucius.

"My Keira girl, good to see you…"

"Cut the shit Lucius! You and me need words!" I snapped cutting off his bullshit condescending tone. He sighed and then said softly,

"As you wish." He rose from his seat to face me.

"How could you do this to me? How could you use me like that?" He frowned at my take on his proposition and I circled around the couch to come closer to him. Meanwhile the others all looked around in shock at my freak out.

"Use you?" He asked as though he couldn't believe he was even asking me this question.

"Then what would you call it?!"

"I…" He found himself stumbling for the right way to answer.

"You! You are using my pain for your gain!" I was losing it as my voice rose to just below a scream. I was shaking with the force of it, knowing that he was using this situation to get his rocks off from a one night stand, which might leave him smiling but leave me broken from guilt for the rest of my life!

"What? No, You…I…" It was the first time I was watching Lucius struggle for words and I realised that all the surprised looks weren't from witnessing my outburst but from Lucius' inability to handle it. We both stopped to look at everyone and then both shouted together,

"GET OUT!"

"GET OUT!"

Within seconds the room once again only belonged to us as it had done last night. Only instead of the flight option I opted for then, now I was there to fight. We stood facing each other, both breathing heavy and both trying to hold something back.

"I need to explain." He finally said in a sharp voice that sounded close to the edge.

"Damn straight!" I said poking at the beast that barely held back a growl.

"The offer I made you last night was…"

"Ridiculous." I cut in this time making him growl.

"Watch it, little girl." He warned but I stood my ground.

"Or what Lucius, 'cause you know you can't force the issue, that's not part of the deal!" I snapped being malicious.

"And what do you mean by that exactly?" Oh, he wanted a bitch, then he was gonna get a bitch!

"Well, let's call this what it is and cut the bullshit, the only reason you want me is for some fucked up way of getting back at Draven. But for that you need me willing or what would be the point…?" At this point he really did hit the roof! He roared, losing all his iron control and burst into his demon self. I took a single step back but other than that, I held my ground.

I knew it was a low blow, but it wasn't one I could have taken back even if I wanted to, which right at that moment I didn't. This was for the pure plain fact that this was the only reasoning I could have as if it was for anything more, like the fact the bastard cared, then he would never have asked this of me. No one with half a brain would ask someone they had feelings for to do something that would rip them to shreds later on!

Or at least that is what I thought before seeing Lucius change. His gleaming white horns stood proud at his back and with them the angel's wings that went from white to yellow, then rust to blood-red in the centre of his back. He was like the rising phoenix and as he rolled his shoulders I could see the flash of gold that tipped his impressive horns.

"You should be running, little girl." He said this in his demonic voice that cut into me as if the claws that grew from his fingers were gouging grooves in my bones. I swallowed down my fear and stood my ground in the face of a demon about to blow.

"I am not afraid of you!" I said and was impressed that I did so without the waver in my voice.

"Then you are even more foolish than I thought minutes ago." He snarled as he started to advance slowly on me.

"What, when I spoke the truth?"

"A truth you clutch at so desperately to shadow the real reasons behind what is really going on here." I shook my head but my eyes must have shown him the insecurities of what lay beneath.

"NO!" I screamed but with my outburst came his own as he flipped one of the large couches back as though it was pumped up with air. However, when it went crashing against the far wall and smashing a big hole there, it looked as though that air had been replaced by iron bricks. I jumped but not only at the sounds of destruction but also the speed in which he reached me.

His hands took possession of the top of my arms in a bruising hold and I twisted to try and escape.

"No…no…Lucius…pl…" I pleaded but he lowered his head to mine and whispered over my lips,

"Please." Then I screamed as he wrapped his arms around me, lifted until my feet no longer touched the ground and ran at the closed window. I turned my head to watch and his name came strangled from my throat as the window exploded outwards. Then he launched us both through it with a twist of his body. I found myself being held to his front with my back to the coming ground and I screamed in sight of my death.

Glass scattered the ground like deadly snow but thankfully there was no one there underneath to receive the brunt of his actions. I closed my eyes and buried my head in his chest having to trust in him not to kill me.

"Please." There it was, the word whispered again in prayer hoping to break through the damage I had done. I felt his legs hook around mine as the weight of them was pulling me away from him. Now I was trapped to the length of him and I was soon glad of this when I felt his wings start to move. He pulled us both upright, so I opened my eyes again to see us flying off into the night.

I didn't know where he was taking us, but just as long as it wasn't at greater heights, so he could do more damage in dropping me, was fine by me. Thankfully, his strong grip on me told me he wasn't letting me go anywhere and even through our argument I still found comfort being held in his arms.

He didn't say a word or even steal a look down at me the whole time. It gave me the chance to study the harsh lines of his chiselled face, which at this minute was clearly set in annoyance. Normally his smirking lips were the indication of a playful character set in a granite body but now they were gone and in their place a grim line of resolve.

Only when it became too painful to look at the evidence of what I had done, did I turn away from him. I looked out to the night and saw the orange glow of Munich's massive city hall coming closer. I bit down on my bottom lip hoping the bite of pain would help control the raging current of my emotions. I didn't want to hurt Lucius and I knew my words would cut deep but what other option did I have? I wanted to push him away… so, so far away that this bargain would have been the last thing on his mind. What had I really expected? For him to throw Draven's whereabouts at me like an insult? Did I really think that was going to happen?

My internal questioning stopped as I saw him fly us closer to the rising clock tower. I briefly saw the dark shape of an angelic figure mounted at the very top of the spire we were circling.

"What are we…?" I braved to ask but stopped when his wings suddenly folded inwards making us drop quickly. I let out a little cry as we fell past the bells and then some windows before I felt a thud vibrate through Lucius as his feet hit something.

"Open your eyes, Keira." Lucius commanded softly and with this I felt him lower me down until my own feet touched the floor. I forced my eyes open and looked up to see Lucius watching me. His features were half shadowed but his eyes blazed with emotions he barely kept unleashed. I could no longer stand it and I raised my hand to caress his cheek. I was only a hairsbreadth away when his hand snatched out to grab my wrist to prevent my touch. I couldn't deny that it hurt but not in the physical sense.

"Don't!" One warning was issued by the depth of his hurt. I was about to speak, not really knowing what I would yet say when quickly I was spun away from him. At first I thought it was because he could no longer stand the sight of me, but then I took in the sight in front of me and gasped.

"I brought you here for a reason." He spoke so gently and if there had been any other sound I would have missed it. But looking out to the beauty before me, I could understand why his voice lowered to such a tender tone. Right in front of us was all of Munich lit up around us and although we were in the thick of the city, up here we couldn't have been more alone.

"This… is your place?" I forced the words out, barely making it past a whisper.

"Yes." He answered honestly, and I quickly felt like crying again. He had brought me here to his special place and the reasons made me start to shake.

"You know why?" He asked me and at the same time started to rub his hands up and down my arms. I could only nod. What else could I do as I could barely speak for fear of what I would say? A man like Lucius didn't bring you here to tell you of his revenge plots for a night of sex with his ex-friend's girlfriend. A man like Lucius didn't bring you here to boast about his plans of seduction, just because he could. No.

A man like Lucius brought you up here for one thing…

A confession.

"Keira I…"

"Please Lucius…don't do this." I begged, my voice close to breaking.

"I have to, my little Keira girl and I will not ask for your forgiveness." I felt his hands come to rest on my shoulders and he held them there for the longest seconds before finally bringing them to circle my neck. I sucked in a quick breath as I felt him lower his lips to my ear. Suddenly the whole world no longer mattered as I felt, heard and absorbed every word he was about to say,

"I bargained not for one night of your body but for the chance of a lifetime to own your soul." A single tear fell and the hands I had gripping onto the bars slowly let go. I took a needed breath and then let my emotions for this man take over every last thought. I turned in his hold and crushed my lips to his.

In his shock he was frozen, no doubt in the questions begging this to be a dreamless reality. Only when his senses told him so did he react, taking all of me and giving me back everything that was him. His lips took possession in such a way that left me blinded by the intensity of it all. His tongue tasted every last bit of me until it was branding this moment to both our minds' memory, never to be replaced by another time. This was ours and only ours belonging to no one else in the world, that could touch us up in this fairytale tower.

I had kissed Lucius before but this time it was different. There was no blinding sun, no feeling of revenge or guilt or bittersweet in knowing what we were doing was wrong. It was just…

Us.

The passion grew to a burning fever that left us clawing at each other's clothes in hopes of getting skin to skin. I felt my clothes tear and one hand tore the material away from my body as though it was a poison being stripped from my flesh. He pushed me up against the bars that prevented the public from trying anything stupid, like trying to fly without wings and with that thought I could understand the pull. This right here felt like falling under, knowing that if I hit the ground that one last feeling of being free was worth a lifetime of being scared of the heights faced.

So I held on to Lucius and I fell.

Our bodies were so close to entwining in the most sensual way two people ever could. I felt his hands touching my now naked body anywhere he could get and in a frenzied way mine did the same to his suddenly bare skin. It was like we were both lost and with nothing out there to find us we were unstoppable. Spiralling down into the point of no return as all it would now take was for one first thrust and Lucius would be inside me, with nowhere else to go but to finish what he started.

Then something happened…

Something found us.

Behind the clouds in the night sky came a light which I saw reflected back at me in Lucius' open eyes. He was looking right at it so what we saw, we saw together. I felt a tingling in my wrist and felt the power there mirrored by the Quarter Moon I saw in Lucius' eyes. We let go of each other at the same time and Lucius took a step back where I couldn't.

The spell was broken.

We both were motionless bodies painted naked in the Quarter moon's light, with only our heavy breathing penetrating the stillness. We were panting at each other as though the very Gods had caught us creating a new sin. And that's when we felt it. Being together that way was something that could have destroyed the very fabric of time, pulling at its seams until there was nothing left but the remains of what was once beautiful. It was the chance of something bigger for both of us and one second later it would have been ripped from us with nothing but one perfect moment to speak of. But what was one perfect moment in the sight of hundreds, thousands…millions of lifetimes all each with their very own perfect memories just waiting to be lived through.

This was what we both nearly just lost and each of us now knew it. Not just for me with Draven but even Lucius had his own chance at the happy forever after that was coming to him. All he had to do was wait.

And now he knew it wasn't me he had to wait for…

It was his soul mate.

CHAPTER FIFTY-SIX

BROKEN TIME

I would have liked to say the next two weeks went past in a blur of time but that would have been a big fat lie. In fact, so much of a lie that I wouldn't have been surprised if one of the Gods had struck me down with a bolt of lightning for speaking such bullshit!

But there was little I could do about it so I just had to suck it up and wait. However, it wasn't as if nothing had happened in this time. In fact, lots of things had happened, just not in the whole 'getting me closer to Draven' side of things. I think the greatest change was between Lucius and myself. After that fated night where we nearly crossed that invisible line, things had become…different.

Oh don't get me wrong, he was still the same flirty badass he always had been, but it was the intensity that had calmed and been replaced by a playful friendship. It was as though that night he saw something in the very Cosmos that answered an unspoken question. When I saw that moon, I saw my life with Draven slipping away for good, but when Lucius saw that moon, he saw a life that he would never even have a taste of if we had made that last unforgiving step.

Now we had come to a mutual understanding and thankfully, he agreed to help me to find Draven, as he cryptically stated once that it was now in his best interests as well as mine. I tried to ask him what he meant by this, but other than a knowing smirk he didn't answer me. So that is where he spent most of his time, in his lavish office doing what I could imagine was time spent searching for clues as to who had Draven and where they were keeping him.

Which left me in the hands of one naughty little Imp. But I wasn't left completely clueless, for one, I found out from spending many days with Pip about the whole Martha elephant incident… all after getting my roots done of course.

This day was spent like most of my others, sat in her crazy apartment being bug eyed from the moment I stepped foot in her domain up until I left to go back to Lucius'. No wonder he told me he never went in there as it always left even his supernatural self with a colossal headache!

It was what could only be described as what you could imagine if an amusement park's funhouse and a wacky comic bookstore had a love child… this would have been Pip's apartment.

There was everything from curtains made from hundreds of 80's piano ties, Eiffel tower seats, a sofa made to look like a hamburger, with tomato, cheese and lettuce cushions and an actual old caravan painted bright pink, with lime green stripes parked in her living room. We even had tea in there one afternoon, and I must admit it took me back to last year sat in a winter wonderland, under a tree, drinking from strange cups.

However, this year was unbelievably, even stranger when I found myself sitting down inside the caravan whose interior was covered in lush green grass. It still had in it the bench seats and table in between but all that and more was growing and I wondered if she had to trim it often. I had to laugh as at the centre of the table was a bunch of daisies growing there instead of being in a vase.

The tea set was another thing entirely. In keeping with the woodland theme the set consisted of a ceramic flower and toadstool set. The tea pot, being the odd part out, was in three tiers, starting with the biggest at the bottom made to look like a crazy multi coloured townhouse. The front door was stamped with the word 'Liquid Bliss' and held the brewing tea. The second 'floor' was a window stamped 'Milky Piss' and the last one was the smallest teapot with a tiny clock tower stamped 'Sugary Kiss'.

They all had a spout and when poured depending on the level you held it at, first came the tea, then the milk and lastly the sweetener. Thankfully for me, Pip held her finger over the end of the sugar so that I wouldn't get any. You would have thought by this description alone that this would have been the weirdest parts but no, this honour went to the two pet teacup pigs she had sat in giant striped and spotted cups with us.

"Adam wanted to call them Belly and Scratch." She informed me as she petted them lovingly.

"Aww is that because they love having their bellies scratched?" I'd asked innocently as she handed one of them over to me. I cradled the cutest little bundle in my arms just as she shook her head and then covered his big ears with her hands. She nodded for me to do the same to the girl I held. Only when they could no longer hear us did she whisper,

"No, it's because Adam loves Pork Belly and I love Pork Scratchings." On hearing this I just closed my eyes and shook my head trying not to laugh.

"So, what did you name them instead?"

"Oh, well this little dude is 'Over' and his girlfriend over there is 'Left'" Now at this I did burst out laughing.

"You named your pet pigs, Left and Over!" I said between the snorting I couldn't help.

"Yeah and if you carry on sounding like them I will start calling you 'There'". I couldn't help it, at this we both burst into a fit of more giggles!

After we had calmed and were drinking our tea, still with 'Left', 'Over' on our laps and me being called 'There' for the rest of the afternoon by Pip, she started to tell me the story of what happened with Martha the Elephant.

The story began with Pip bidding on Martha and Adam bidding against her with the intention of donating her to a zoo, as sanctuaries in this time period we're unheard of. Pip obviously wanted to keep her as a pet but no surprises there. However, as the bidding went on, some of the men carrying through a large suspended gong from China tripped and as the gong hit the floor it scared the Elephant.

Pip, being Pip, charged after Martha in an attempt to calm her down (although offering her a Fry's chocolate bar wasn't ever going to lead her on the road to success). The elephant charged at her making Adam lose control over Abaddon. He erupted into his other self and in doing so, not only killed the elephant accidentally but also set the building on fire. Hence, why Adam was now banned from all Lega Nera events. I had to say that I felt for him after hearing this story and found out that to make it up to Pip he bought her an Aldabra giant tortoise that she named Duncan, which she later changed to Michelangelo after her favourite Teenage Mutant Ninja Turtles character.

Unbelievably, I met 'Mikey' who was 174 years old and had not a fondness for pizza but for doughnuts… with jam of course. But with Mikey also came a rat called Splinter, a pet hedgehog called Shredder and a yellow canary called April. Going into Pip's home was a bit like a petting zoo, only instead of the usual enclosures you would expect to find, these creatures were living it up in utter luxury. April lived in a miniature New York apartment, complete with kitchen decorated in bird poop. The rat lived in a mock Japanese style sewer and had been taught to walk a rope ladder on command. It was without a doubt crazy, but crazy beautiful as it was obvious she absolutely adored her pets.

The rest of my days spent with Pip brought about a magical madness that can only be described as like being friends with someone related to Willy Wonka. Her living room was cut into two different sections. The first was obviously Adam's and looked like an old English library/office. Dark wood panels matched the dark wooden floors and the deep red leather in the furniture. A massive oak desk carved into eagle's legs that had big brass claws which pierced the floorboards. Old books and classical paintings from the renaissance period added to the feel of the place. It felt more like this space belonged to a professor of some kind, not the right hand to a Vampire King.

But now Pip's side of their home was what made me drag my gaping mouth around the place. There was everything from shelves of old cartoon action toys, every colour of Carebear, lamps made from her 'own' chest x-ray, doors covered with Barbies glued to them (all wearing evening dresses) to a giant black swan that used to be a lake boat now converted into a fluffy seating area.

The swan (who I was told was called Fanny) sat in the centre of the room inside a large ornate gothic pool. There was a little bridge that you could walk over to get into the 'swan sofa'. Once in there, Pip would flick a switch and what I first thought was yellowish water started to pour from the swans open mouth. Then I saw her grab a glass from a little cupboard under the seat and fill it up to take a swig of what she informed me was actually white wine. Needless to mention, that when I re-crossed the bridge I could no longer do so in a straight line.

But putting aside the tables that looked like pints of dripping blood and the fang shaped fairy lights that covered the entire ceiling of her bathroom or even the bar area set up like a freaky mad scientist's lab, complete with cocktails in beakers, vials and test tubes, I still found myself with plenty to talk about and always someone to listen.

In fact, it was at the end of my two weeks waiting and whilst I was watching Pip painting her nails we discovered something important. See, while all this time was going by, I was left to do nothing whilst Lucius tried to track down Draven's whereabouts. This was the most frustrating part of my journey so far and even more so than being captured and held in that disgusting tower. At least then I was being held against my will and had no other choice in the matter but now, as I watched Pip draw little miniature ice cream cones, I was close to tearing my hair out!

I had brought along with me my Ouroboros book in the hopes that my shadowed knight would once again try and contact me. Or even the Oracle, who after all this time had still not sent me one word. In fact, the only person I had heard from briefly through Lucius was that Jared knew I was safe and in turn I knew he and all his men…including Marcus, were all fine. I did, however, get the impression that Jared had tried to see me, but Lucius wasn't allowing it. I tried to talk to him about it one day only to get shut down with 'He knew best'.

So here I sat, on one of Pip's outrageous day beds that was a big round iron nest, complete with egg shaped cushions and long foam brown twigs. If anything, by the end of this journey, I would be surprised if the urge to go out and buy a damn bird would ever leave me!

But then it hit me as I was playing with my bracelet absent-mindedly that the next quarter moon had passed by two weeks ago and I had forgotten to ask the book what it meant. I ended up scaring Pip into giving herself a wonky cone as I squawked something in my excitement at finally having something to do.

"Hey, I just messed up mint choc chip!" She complained with a cute whiney pout. I leant over, kissed her nose and said,

"You'll get over it!" Then I quickly opened up my book and looked around for the time.

"Is there a clock in this madhouse?" She gave me a smile that screamed evil genius and tapped her lip ring before she said,

"I will give you a clue." I rolled my eyes and said a warning,

"Pip!"

"No, no, it will be fun, trust me, I am a Jedi master and a member of the Browncoats." She said proudly sitting up and propping an egg behind her…although thankfully not a real egg given the amount of punching she did to get it into shape!

"Eh…Browncoats?" I asked knowing like any conversation with Pip, we were getting off course quicker than a rally car.

"Oh, My Bejesus and Kentucky fucking chicken! Tell me you have watched Firefly before?!" She had her hands over her ears as if waiting for my answer was going to physically hurt her.

"Umm…that would be a no." I winced as I said it, knowing now the girl was going to put me through I don't know how many hours of Firefly chatter and more than likely doing so whilst watching the entire show. She closed her eyes, put her pointed nails to her forehead like she had a migraine and shook her head for my shame.

"Er…Pip, can we try to focus here?" I asked after she still wasn't moving.

"Fine! But only if you promise me one thing." I had a bad feeling about this.

"Go on."

"Firefly marathon after your little book wig out." I rolled my eyes and said,

"Pip, if it will get me the damn time, then I will even go out there and buy myself a damn Brown coat!" I said shaking the book in hopes of showing my urgency. Note to self…next time Pip says something weird, just don't ask and pretend to know what she is talking about!

"Oh don't worry about that, I have plenty…did you know that when they cancelled the show, loads of people set up a charity and they…?"

"Pip, can we possibly leave out the Browncoats for now and focus on my little 'wig out?'" I asked making quotation marks around what she liked to call my dilemmas.

"Oh right…ok, so this is your clue…" I groaned out loud and stuffed my head in another one of the egg pillows I had on my lap.

"You can play them in the round or play them in the air, but these little suckers aren't going anywhere, for they tell me the time when I listen to their rhyme but thank the rock, God they don't chime."

She finished off her cryptic poem with a massive grin and then it fell away just as quickly when 'We will Rock you' by Queen blasted from the far wall.

"Ah shit!" She moaned as I turned my head to find a massive wall display that was actually a wall sized clock. It had twelve records all fixed in a circle and two mounted guitars in the middle that acted as the arms of the clock. It was pretty damn awesome and it also showed me it was two o'clock in the afternoon. I had to giggle as I recalled her riddle.

"That was pretty good." I told her which soon had her smiling again.

"What time does the book wakey wakey eggs and all that jazz?" Pip asked nodding at my leather bound friend.

"5:36." On hearing this she bounced up and down on her egg.

"Coolioso, then we have three hours and thirty…ummer lingy thingy ding dongs…" She turned back round to count and finished,

"Thirty four and half minutes to introduce you to the delicious Captain Malcolm "Mal" Reynolds…let me just go and get my coats and guns." And with that she jumped from the nest, nails long forgotten and this Captain 'Mal' in the forefront of her mad mind.

So there I was, hours later, sat in Pip's theatre room in a huge armchair that was made from thousands of teddy bears glued together in the shape of a giant teddy bear. Pip was sat next to me coiled in a giant stuffed toy snake whose tail acted as a footrest and we were both wearing long brown jackets and had replica guns from the show in our laps. To say in the beginning I felt like a colossal idiot was an understatement, but then I could only be thankful I wasn't watching Star Wars in a Chewbacca outfit …! Oh yeah and I was now officially addicted to Firefly.

Now, as I got into watching space cowboys adventures set in the year 2517, I was shocked to find Pip's Mickey Mouse alarm going off. She clicked her wristwatch off and paused the episode.

"Time to do your thing." I nodded and handed my gun over to one of the bigger bears on the armrest to take care of whilst I opened the book. I asked it to tell me about the third Quarter moon and when the next one was, which the Oracle said would lead me to Draven.

This was my answer:

On this third Quarter Moon, the Yellow Moonstone gives great insight into things yet to come. It supports the heart and stimulates the mind when making great decisions that will change the foundation to ones future. It aids those difficult choices, bringing out the best in people and increasing loving energies needed in Divine situations where the mind is sometimes overruled by lust. Worlds maybe divided and time may seem against you but what is time to a clock with no hands.

The next Quarter Moon breaches your skies tomorrow evening after long Goodbyes.

I jumped up out of my seat after I read the last line and stood there panting as if I could barely breathe.

"What is it…what did it say, Toots?" Pip asked with a quiver to her voice that was full of concern. I turned back round to face her and simply said,

"That I will see Draven again." Her large green eyes widened with excitement and strangely a bit of worry I didn't understand.

"When?" I bit my lip at her question and felt a single tear fall before I said…

"Tomorrow night."

CHAPTER FIFTY-SEVEN

LAKESIDE PLANS

After quickly re-reading the book's words again and again, I jumped from my seat, ready to storm the castle which was Lucius' city home in search of the only man who could help me. Problem was I found I had to wait until nightfall when he woke up. This was quite possibly one of the most frustrating moments of my life and Pip could do little to get me to stay calm. She must have stopped me half a dozen times from running into his room and jumping on his bed like an over excited kid at Christmas.

It was times like this that I was thankful to Pip for re-arranging her sleep patterns for me so that I didn't become a complete night owl or a bored to tears daylight walker. She told me that this was no big deal as she was an Imp and therefore needed little sleep. Her exact words were along the lines of 'More chance for mischief'.

In fact the very reason we spent so much time in her apartment was because Adam would get restless if he didn't feel her close by. I did, however, have to put a limit on helping her chain him to their bed (which turned out to be a giant round cage shaped like a castle turret), as that went far beyond the realms of friendship…plus he kinda scared the shit out of me!

So, some hours later and with most of my nails long gone, I was soon barging into Lucius' stylish office that had a strong influence of art deco. Even the espresso cup he drank from was made in sharp lines and bold colours. He was also on the phone and didn't look impressed at my intrusion.

"Ich werde Sie zurückrufen" ('I will have to call you back' in German) He cancelled his call and raised one eyebrow at me in question.

"And to what do I owe this pleasure little Keira…brown-coat?" I flushed as I looked down at myself and I had indeed forgotten I was still wearing Pip's Firefly outfit. Well, at least I didn't still have the gun so Lucius would think I planned on robbing him…but fat chance at that, although, I was now wondering if I could get him to tell me Draven's whereabouts at gunpoint?

The sound of Lucius laughing brought me from my semi-violent thoughts.

"Keira, tell me you didn't barge in here just to look cute and confused because as amusing as that is…" I cut him off by slamming the book down and sliding it across to him so that it faced the right way for him to read. He looked down and I could see his stunning grey eyes work as he read each word.

"I think we have re-established our new relationship, my dear." I groaned in frustration and said,

"Not that, the last line." He released a big sigh and then leant back in his chair.

"And what of it Keira, it's just another Quarter Moon?"

"It's not just another Quarter Moon, Lucius…don't you see that…look." I held out my arm and my bracelet, which now had a beautiful Yellow moonstone to match the others, gleamed under the spotlights.

"There is only one stone left." Lucius crossed his arms across his chest.

"And?"

"And, it means that on the last Quarter Moon I will be reunited with Draven!" I said not being able to help getting animated throwing my arms up, hoping this time he would take me more seriously.

"Keira…" And there it was. That same way he would say my name every time I would get impatient at how long it was taking or how I wished he'd let me do something, go somewhere, ask someone…just anything other than sit around wasting my time when I could be getting closer to finding him.

"No Luc! I am not going to wait any longer, I can't do it…I need to find him."

"Just give it some more time, Keira." He tried now with the soothing voice and the next stage after this tactic would be enveloping me in his arms and telling me everything would be alright before sending me on my not so merry way.

Well, not this time.

"But that's just it, there is no more time! The Oracle told me I would see Draven again on the last Quarter Moon, the fourth stone would change and that is tomorrow!" On hearing this he finally started to look as though it was sinking in.

"And the Oracle…she definitely said this…those exact words, think about it carefully, little doll?" I put both my hands on his desk, leant forward and said in clear certain words,

"Yes Lucius, I swear by the Gods that is what she said." He looked at me for a moment, as if trying to pry the very truth from the exact time that had long passed. It didn't take long before he found it and after another big sigh he nodded.

"Very well, I cannot intervene any longer…forgive me." He said this last part looking up at the Heavens.

"Lucius?" I asked not understanding…well, that was until he opened a drawer in his desk and pulled out a small piece of folded parchment paper. He handed it to me and when I opened it I couldn't help the gasp that came from me.

"Is this what I think it is?" I asked but he didn't answer me. Instead he picked up his phone and after a few seconds said,

"Adam, have the jet refuelled and ready to leave." After a few seconds more he then added,

"Italy." He put the phone down and faced the rage that was building from inside me.

"You knew!?" I shouted like a whistling teapot too long on the boil.

"Try to understand, this was for your own good, Pet." Ok,

now sod the teapot I was now going for a steam train off the rails!

"YOU KNEW!" I screamed now wishing I had the super-human powers of strength so that I could flip his desk out of the way so I could strangle him.

"I knew." He said those two little innocent words which I never expected would be the ones to light the fuse that made me blow. I was surprised that it didn't come in the form of violence or even me screaming about how I would make it my mission to murder him in his sleep. No, instead I just leant further into the desk and said with as much venom as I could muster,

"Fuck your jet and fuck you!" And then I turned and stormed out of that office with the address Lucius had given me firmly in my grip. My plan worked for about five feet until I felt Lucius' arms band around me, restraining me to his chest. I didn't struggle. I no longer had the heart for it.

"Listen to me very carefully, little dove, because you don't know what you are about to walk into by going to that address." He said all this leaning down to my ear and I couldn't help but take note of the seriousness in his tone. I remained frozen in his arms but this didn't hide the hurt and anger I still felt as I panted as though my lungs were too furious to work properly.

"And what exactly am I walking into?" I asked through gritted teeth.

"A world of hurt." I couldn't help but shudder in reply.

"That's the right reaction to have."

"Are you going to stop me?" I asked tensing my body as I awaited his answer.

"No, because it is not in the fates any longer, but I can at least warn you and have you know, I did what I felt I had to do in order to protect you…I…I only wanted you safe, my little Keira girl." At the sound of the emotional hitch in his voice my body couldn't help but soften in his hold. As soon as he felt this he turned me quickly and crushed my body to his in a fierce hug.

"I'm sorry Keira, for whatever might happen next, but I want you to know, you will always be welcome with me and my people…" He pulled me back by the arms so I could look up at his face before he whispered,

"I will always protect you."

And this turned out to be our goodbye.

Lucius, being a man of his word, protected me all the way to a hotel in Milan and even provided me with a driver to take me to the address when the time came. I knew I had a lot to think about and even more so after the cryptic way Lucius tried to warn me about something he wasn't allowed to say. So now I didn't know where the danger lay. Was it with the people that had him or what would happen to me if I got caught? I asked Lucius if he could help me rescue him but he just shook his head and said that in this matter, if I couldn't set him free, then no one could.

The flight hadn't taken long but it was long enough to drive me insane with questions I had no answers to. I found I couldn't stay still as the adrenalin, from so many heightened emotions coursing around my body, was making what felt like my very soul vibrate.

It had been hard saying goodbye to everyone but seeing how well Percy was coming on under the careful instructions of Adam and Pip, it was lovely to finally see him happy. And boy was he taking his new role seriously. He even had Hakan teaching him some fighting moves and Ruto teaching him to use weapons. During my stay, Pip and I would often spend our nights watching them and cheering on Percy whenever he got it right. Pip even went to the extreme of dressing up like a gothic cheerleader, which caused Adam no end of embarrassment when he would find a tent in his pants. It was moments like this that his helpful wife would drag him away giggling and spell out ADAM in her new cheers.

When it came to saying goodbye to Pip she started sobbing like a baby, which was hard to take seriously when the person crying was wearing a pair of knitted square glasses without the lenses but with lickable candy canes as the arms. In the end Adam had to pick her up and carry her away from me or the plane would never have left without an extra passenger. All the while I would hear him whisper,

"You know you can't go love, she must do this alone." Which just made my own tears fall even harder.

My goodbye with Lucius had been just as emotional for me, but no words were needed after his last promise. He had simply kissed me on the forehead and called for Adam to come and take me where I needed to go. I had little in the way of luggage, thanks to my kidnapping, as I had been rescued with nothing but the feathers on my back. However, thanks to Pip I was not taking this trip naked and had with me a small cabin bag with everything in it that I needed.

Which brought me to now and hanging up the few items I had to wear, which thankfully were more my taste than Pip's. I was just placing the few toiletries I had in the spacious bathroom's counter when I looked up to see a tired looking Keira staring back at me. I could barely believe it was actually me, not really taking in my new appearance until now. So much time had passed since the beginning of this trip, yet thanks to everything that had happened, it felt like only yesterday that I was getting on that first flight leaving the States behind.

And now my quest had brought me to Italy, which hopefully would end up being my last destination in finding Draven. I didn't want to think about what I would do if I got to this address and found my search had to continue further. No, I couldn't think that way, not after everything I had been through to get to this point. I had to remain strong, just a little while longer, if not for me then for Draven's sake.

With all of this going on around in my head, I thought it would have been impossible for me to find sleep, but as soon as my head hit the pillow I found for the first time today the questions finally stopped.

The next day I woke late in the afternoon with only one thing on my mind…Draven. I couldn't wait to see him again, but before I let my excitement rule my head I needed a game plan. I had tried looking up the Villa at Lake Como to see if there was any information on it but it was as though it didn't even exist. I was just glad that when I handed the driver the piece of paper, he seemed to know where it was.

The drive wasn't that long, just over an hour, but given the amount of time I had now been separated from Draven, then even an extra hour felt like an extra month! The summer heat felt thick, like a storm was coming and I wiped my sweaty palms down the dark denim of my jeans. I had decided to wear black clothes, despite the weather, as I wanted to go as undetected as possible if I was going to pull off any kind of rescue mission.

I was just glad that I had the foresight to buy a baseball cap from one of the shops by the hotel I'd stayed in. As we were travelling I gathered up all my hair and tied what I could back with an elastic band I found at the bottom of Pip's bag she'd given me and put the cap on, pulling my hair through the back. I looked down at myself and thought I just looked like a tourist. I had wanted to wear a pair of my gloves but knew this would be too obvious in this weather and for the first part of my mission, I wanted to blend in.

I was wearing a black vest that had on it a faded grey rose, (one of Pip's), jeans and a pair of heavy duty boots in case I found myself in a situation that required running or kicking. My bag contained the Ouroboros book, a small first aid kit just in case, a map of the area, a Spiderman wallet with some Euros (a gift from Pip) with a credit card (provided by Lucius), a new passport, a new smartphone (complete with everyone's numbers) and a few miniature bottles of spirits, including tequila (also a gift from Pip).

So, with my decent sized bag acting as an unusual survival kit hanging around my torso on its long strap, I got out of the car to look around the area we had just pulled up to. I had asked the driver not to get too close to the actual house so that I wouldn't be seen by anyone. From the start it was pretty obvious the type of place it was going to be from the amount of private estates we passed on our way. The multimillion-euro homes could only just be seen through their gates, amongst their beautifully designed gardens and almost all of them exclusive, which translated into, 'hard to break in!'

I got out my map, which the driver had circled for me and walked along the winding road which I could see was taking me closer to the lake. It must have been the last house along the road, which also happened to be the biggest, if the view in front of me was anything to go by.

The whole property was surrounded by a high stone wall that was sectioned by Roman style columns, each mounted at the top with Goddess figures. From what I could see, as I passed by the guarded gates, the Villa itself was made from large sandstone blocks with parts rendered and painted in a pale terracotta colour. As I walked as slowly as I could without looking too obvious, I noticed there were at least three different buildings all surrounding the main mansion but all were situated on different levels. The one closest to the lake was the hardest one to see as it was blocked by all the trees, but from what I could see it looked as if most of that building was covered in ivy, reminding me of Afterlife.

I heard someone clear their throat and jumped. The security guard by the gate nodded for me to carry on and I laughed nervously holding up my map.

"Sorry, I think I'm lost." I said thinking how stupid, as the guy probably couldn't understand a word I said, but then he surprised me by not only speaking English but also having an American accent.

"There won't be anything you're looking for beyond this point as its all private property…where are you looking for?" He motioned for me to come over and I gulped down my panic. He looked like he was going to look at my map which, considering the place he guarded was circled, I didn't think it one of my best ideas to let him see it.

"Oh…uh…that's alright, you know I think I will figure it out." I said just as I heard a car coming down the road. As it slowly got closer I decided to use the new powers I was forced to learn and threw up every mental barrier I could, just in case whoever was in that car was not of the human world.

I watched the guard quickly get back to his post and the gates started to open to let in the blacked-out Bentley saloon car that was coming our way. I quickly pulled down my cap and turned just as it swung round to enter, making the big flashy tyres crunch on the gravel of the long driveway. I started to walk away from the car not knowing who was inside but willing my head to keep down the driving urge to look.

I had the greatest need to pull down on sleeves I wasn't wearing or start tugging on gloves I had bravely left behind. So instead, I held on to my map and pulled out my phone taking pictures of the countryside, trying to pull off the whole tourist gig. It was only when I heard the roaring of bikes coming along the same road, that I nearly dropped both phone and map. I looked back at the car that was disappearing out of sight and noticed no one was looking so, instead of hoping the whole tourist thing still worked, I stepped into the wooded area and hid.

I crouched down low and as I heard them coming, I could only pray no one could see me. I really wanted to look but knew I couldn't chance it, just as I couldn't do with the Bentley. In my head though the possibilities seemed vast and the list of bikers I now knew was growing. There was Vincent, Sigurd and now Jared's lot of beasts…who was next I had no clue but the most important question remained, were any of those riders someone I knew?

By the time I had memorised a good enough lay of the land, I had a firm idea in my mind of where would be best to sneak in. I could only hope they didn't have motion sensors, cameras everywhere but most of all, nasty growling attack dogs, Mr Burns' style!

I decided it wasn't so much the getting in part that would be the hardest, although I wasn't expecting the red carpet welcome, it would really be the getting out that would be the tricky bit. I had spent the rest of the day checking out the surrounding area and found there was a small gap that led straight through the woods down to the lake. It was from this bit that you could climb down to the water and swim round to the lakeside of the property, which just so happened to have a stone wall that could be easily jumped over.

So, the plan was to use a tree to climb close to the main wall to get in and depending on what state Draven had been left in, to get to the lake and jump in, then using the darkness as a good cover to escape. The best part of this plan was that the closest property to where the woods led to the lake looked to be locked up tight and without occupants. This meant my driver could wait down the private road and wait for us without being seen, or more importantly asked to leave.

I was lucky in the sense that Lucius must have told my driver to do as I said with no questions asked, because it surprised me when I didn't receive any weird reactions to my odd directions.

Which brought me back to now and under the cover of night I zipped up the black hooded sweater shirt I had brought with me, as now the weather had turned a little wild. The angry clouds and clammy heat of the day told me there was going to be a summer storm tonight and I wanted to be ready for it. I hooked my thumbs into the thumb holes of the Goth style top and pulled the big baggy hood over my head to conceal myself further. I told the driver to park by the empty Villa and wait for me no matter what.

He nodded to me in way of acceptance as I'd learnt early on he didn't really say much. This was just fine by me considering I had plenty to occupy my mind without having to explain myself at every crazy decision I made. I watched him back out of sight and leave me at the same spot he had done earlier that day when I was playing spy mode Keira.

"Well, here goes." I said quietly to myself and started to walk down the road until the start of the property came into view. After my stakeout hidden by the bushes, I'd noted how often the guards walked by and knew that anywhere near the gated entrance wasn't going to be any way I could get in. The only parts of the property they didn't seemed too bothered about were the lakeside walls, which couldn't be accessed by anything but a boat. This they had covered by mounted cameras I'd seen when I climbed a tree to get a better look. This was also what gave me the idea in the first place as there was one particular tree that overhung the wall, making it the easiest place to gain access.

So that was where I was now headed, into the woods using

my mobile phone screen as a small torch so I wouldn't break my leg. I walked in a U shape which brought me closer to the lake and the side not as well monitored. I found my spot with only one small slip up where I had to backtrack and was soon looking at my first hard task.

I took a deep breath and rubbed my hands together as I looked up at the tree I needed to climb. I just reached up for the first branch and then screamed when the first bolt of lightning lit the sky, followed quickly by the booming thunder. Thankfully, the noise hid my fright and I held my hands to my chest as a mental crutch to help slow my erratic breathing. I thought as if what I was about to do wasn't nerve racking enough!

I let myself have a few minutes to rebuild my courage and then I went for it. I jumped up, cursing my short height when it took me three attempts to grab hold of the branch. Once I did it I then used my legs, walking up the trunk to get to the next branch. I was surprised as I made short work of climbing up to the wall's height and found myself actually grinning when I could swing my leg over the other side.

Once there, I reached out to grab hold of the next tree that was a little more difficult to climb due to its lack of branches. My foot slipped just as I reached out but thankfully I caught hold just before I could fall, which ended up just scraping my palm on the rough bark. I hissed at the sting but kept going, not preventing the quiet sigh of relief when my feet finally touched the grass.

I looked back up at the wall, just glad I didn't have to go back that way as I knew I would've been completely screwed! I rubbed my hands down my jeans and looked around to make sure I was out of sight and that's when I noticed all the weird stuff.

All the statues that were dotted around the landscaped garden were destroyed. It looked as if it was something that had been done recently and definitely not through age. But on further inspection I also noticed that they weren't the only evidence of someone's rage. All the lights that should have been illuminating not just the garden art, but also for security reasons were also smashed. Of course, not that I was complaining, as this certainly made things easier for me and even more so when I walked around one corner to find broken pieces of what used to be the cameras.

This had to make me wonder who did this and if it was in some way to benefit me…did Lucius get word to someone on the inside? Either way, this type of destruction was obviously seen as the norm considering they hadn't yet been fixed. Either that or the people who held Draven didn't fear for his possible escape. Which begged the question…was I enough to make it possible?

Well, I was soon to find out as I neared the house. I kept in the shadows and tried not to jump whenever the sky lit up with lightning, hoping it wouldn't give me away in case any guards veered off their normal route and saw me acting like a cat burglar. I walked further round, staying close to the walls of the house, until I could see the lake as it spread out in front of me. It was a startlingly beautiful sight as it produced the biggest natural mirror, reflecting the impressive storm above it. The show it put on was nothing short of masterful and dangerously magnificent, which went hand in hand with what I was about to do.

I continued to stick to the wall as I moved further down the gardens, until I could see the last building that was right on the lake's front. It was in a U shape and had a raised walkway all around its ground floor, and it too was decorated with broken statues. One Goddess' head looked as though it had been punched through with an iron fist. If anything, it just added to the creepy vibe the storm produced for my fearful mission.

The building was set into levels and looked half built down into the rocks below, the same ones I had seen when forming my getaway plans. I also found the front of it had a number of balconies and knew when I saw them from the rocks I climbed, that this would be my way in. The old ivy that clawed its way up the side of most of the building would act as a natural ladder similar to the one I had used once before back at Afterlife.

Well, at least this one wasn't as high up so that had to be a bonus. I was lucky that there were just enough lights from the windows above that I could see but not be seen. I made sure my bag strap was secure and started to pull at the thick ivy to make sure it would hold. When I was happy, I looked up to the first balcony and just hoped the door was left unlocked. I climbed up to stand on the top of the balustrades that went around a patio area which meant I was already a third of the way there. Then I took a deep breath, grabbed a hold and started to pull myself up.

Thankfully it didn't take me too long and I soon found myself reaching out to grip the edge of the stone wall that wrapped around the large balcony above. I had a sudden thought of 'Again with bloody balconies!' when a noise had me freezing on the spot. I heard a woman's voice but it got cut off when the thunder came quickly after the flash. I looked to see if there was some room for me to stand next to the glass doors so that I could remain hidden but was surprised to see one of them was slightly open.

I decided I couldn't stay here all night hanging on like a stunned monkey, so as quietly as I could, I climbed over the ledge. I made sure my swinging bag didn't make a noise and I held it back as I stepped a little closer to the glass doors. It looked as if the last person who closed them hadn't done it properly, as the gap was just enough to hear voices through.

The light coming from the room was low and flickering as though it came from a candle. Footsteps tapping on hard wooden floors walked by the door for a second and I held my breath, thinking I was about to get caught. That's when I heard the female voice again, only this time, I recognised it.

"I am here, as ever, to serve you, My Lord." My hand flew to my mouth as I heard Aurora ask the question, but it became a true task of sheer willpower I didn't realise I possessed, when I heard who answered her,

"You know what I want from you, as I do every night Aurora, so close the door and approach my bed to do your promised duty to your King." I sucked in a painful breath and tears clouded my sight, as for the first time, since the beginning of May, I heard the only voice I had longed for. The only voice I had awakened from sleep and cried out in my despair for. The only voice I would have bled for and the only voice I nearly died for.

Would have died for…

Draven's voice.

CHAPTER FIFTY-EIGHT

SHATTERED HEARTS AND CHASING STORMS

I felt the first of my tears fall just as the first of the storm's rain fell from the sky. It was as if it knew my pain and shared in my devastation. I had to be wrong in what I heard. That couldn't be my Draven asking his ex-girlfriend into his bed…it just couldn't be…it was…impossible.

But I had to be sure.

So, I gathered up the last of my strength and I did the unthinkable, only to catch the unthinkable.

I took those very last steps in my quest to find the only man I'd ever loved and faced my window of truth. So now here I stood, directly in front of my dead boyfriend, watching as his ex-lover started to straddle her radiant body over his bare one, which was lay waiting. He raised his arms above his head and held them against a rock wall that acted as a massive headboard to an oversized bed.

Aurora was wearing a shimmering nightgown that was not only see-through but also split up both her legs which she now had bent on either side of Draven. I felt like a wide-eyed doe caught watching the truck coming closer and the longer I waited the more I knew it would end me…but like that innocent doe, I couldn't look away from the killing blow.

"Are you ready, My Lord?" She asked sweetly, making it

even more difficult for me to breathe. Then, when it finally got too much to bear I closed my eyes to try and clear my vision through the tears that just wouldn't stop flowing. When I opened them again, I looked at Draven's face and saw his determination set in hard lines of this woman's master. He closed his own eyes for a moment and then said through gritted teeth as though he was trying to hold something back,

"Do it!" I saw the smile from Aurora that Draven didn't and then felt sick as I let the pain start to drown me. I was hypnotized to watch as Aurora leant further over him and whisper some sweet endearment I couldn't hear just over his closed lips. She then reached out to grip onto his arms and started to stretch out on the length of his body before pulling his arms up and holding them securely to the rock. I continued to torture myself as I watched as the energy started to build up under her hands, causing Draven's own skin to start to glow with power.

That's when it all hit me. That conversation we'd had so long ago about Draven having to hold back when being intimate with me. Was this what this was? Was this Draven getting what he obviously needed, something he could never get with me? I sucked back a sob as I finally got it. Draven wasn't dead, he…he…

He was just dead to me!

I watched the last I could before breaking beyond a point of not being able to get my shattered heart out of there. It was just as Draven's back arched in a deep moan as Aurora raked her nails down his forearms that lit up under his veins. It looked like pure carnal pleasure and this caused more than just my heart to crack further but it also completely destroyed my mental barriers.

This happened at the same time the lightning forked the sky, the rain battered down at my body and the thunder echoed my cry, screaming into the night. The glass doors blew inwards with the force of the gale behind me and shattered, mirroring my own soul that Draven had ripped out of me.

Aurora's head whipped around and I saw her whisper my name as she stared right at me. That's when the Draven storm really hit as his head snapped up and now I had his purple eyes burning into mine. Then he roared, bellowing out like I had never heard Draven's demon erupt before. Aurora fell backwards with the force of it and landed on the floor by the foot of the bed.

I thought he would jump up but he seemed to be trapped by his arms that I could now see fused to the rock. He snarled at me and I took a step back which finally released me from this nightmare. I took another making him snarl louder this time.

"Don't you dare run!" His Demon warned in a frightening growl that made me shake in a fear I had never felt once before from Draven. So I did the only thing I could do…

I ran.

I turned and jumped the edge, grabbing the ivy letting it scrape down my hands as I tried to drop down from the balcony as quickly as I could. I heard Draven going crazy with rage and my feet hit the grass followed by my knees as I fell upon hearing Draven's demand,

"RELEASE ME… NOW!" I knew from this I had one chance to get out of here and I was going to take it if it was the last thing I was still able to do! I forced myself up and ran while Draven was obviously still trying to free himself. I didn't know what kind of sex games they had been about to play, but right now I was just thankful Draven couldn't get his hands on me!

I ran down the bank, getting closer to the lake and turned when I got to the path that would lead me to where I needed to be. I heard masses of glass smashing all at once from behind me. I heard screams and didn't release they were mine until the roaring stopped.

"KEIRA!" Draven thundered out my name, making the storm mirror his rage with light and sound…but still I ran. The rain poured down soaking my hair, slapping it to my face as I looked behind me to see Draven emerge onto the balcony. He was looking for me and I quickly threw up a mental force so strong I knew no one would ever be able to break it down, not even Draven.

"KEIRA! COME BACK!" He screamed again making part of the balcony around him crumble as though from an earthquake…but I kept running. Even when I saw his wings erupt as his full Demon side burst forth, drowning the man I once loved in Hell's power.

Tears had now mixed with rain and travelled down my face in a never ending current, all fuelled by the greatest hurt one could ever imagine. But it was this raw pain I used to make myself go on…I forced myself to move, to get as far away from this loathsome place which had brought me nothing but the truth I unearthed…

The truth of Draven's deceit.

"GET THEM NOW!" This was the last order I heard being followed by the thunder as the night now truly took on a murderous element. I tried not to look back just before I jumped down to the next level, but when I saw Draven drop down from the destroyed balcony, I knew my time had run out. I landed, thankfully this time on my feet and ignored the pain that shot up through my legs from the impact.

I saw the place I was trying to find and ran to the side of the wall. From here I couldn't see much, but just as that thought entered my mind, something unbelievable happened. I first saw it being reflected back at me from the water's surface. It wavered with the movement of the water and I bit down on my lip to hold in the growing need to cry out. The last Quarter Moon had come out from behind the clouds, beaming through the raging storm that couldn't seem to touch it.

I looked up and nodded, knowing that this was the very last time it would help me, but just not in the way I would have thought or hoped…It no longer lit the way on my journey in getting to Draven but now in my only means of getting away from him.

So, with that heart wrenching help, I looked down at the rocks behind the wall that led into the lapping water. I dropped my bag over the side so it landed without getting wet and then I pulled myself up and did the same. I let myself fall just as I heard the search party coming my way. I didn't know if Draven had seen me, so I needed to move and get my ass in the water. I picked up my bag and scrambled over the rocks until I came to the area I had seen that would be perfect for hiding. I threw my bag into the bushes and then lowered myself into the water sucking in a sharp breath as the cold penetrated my clothes through to my skin.

I started treading water but all the while holding onto the jagged rocks that kept me from view. At this point I could just see the shadows of people on the water, thanks to the freaky glow of moonlight and with the added wingspan it was easy to spot which one Draven was. They weren't that far away as I could still hear them, so I remained as still as I could so as not to disturb the water, giving away my whereabouts.

"You're sure you saw her come this way?" I felt my body shudder as I could now add another to my list of people who had betrayed me. Vincent's voice was easy to detect as he asked his brother this question and soon Sophia's could be heard, making me want to bite my fist from crying out.

"She must have turned back when she realised there was no escape for her here." Draven's hard voice cut through me deeper than the cold water that felt as if it was seeping past my skin and into my bones.

"Can you feel her?" Sophia asked and for a moment there was silence but it was hard to ignore that strong pull of power that was Draven trying to find me. I closed my eyes and gripped onto the rock in a painful hold that kept me grounded enough to keep him from my mind.

"No and she is nowhere near powerful enough to evade my reach."

"Are you sure, she could be in the water or what if she fell?" Vincent was clearly worried and out of them all thinking closer to the truth, but his idea was thankfully cut off by Draven's arrogance.

"NO...!" He snapped.

"...I would have felt her."

"But you know after this time the bond has..." Vincent was silenced by first the growl and then the warning,

"I suggest you don't say another word, Brother!" Draven's demon warned, sounding too far on the edge that no wonder nothing more was said.

"My Lord, there has been no signs of her yet, but a guard at the gate remembered seeing a girl late this afternoon, just before you arrived back." This time it sounded like Zagan speaking, but again Draven shouted him down just as he did with his brother.

"It wasn't her."

"But My Lord, he described her as…"

"IT WASN'T HER!" He roared and in doing so I heard a big splash which sounded like one of the statues had just crumbled off its plinth and into the water.

"Now go and FIND HER!" Draven commanded which then just left two shadows remaining.

"It wasn't her, Vincent… I still would have felt her nearby, I know this." Draven sounded determined to believe this and I shook my head at how little the great and mighty King really knew!

"I hope you're right brother…I really do." I watched as one shadow left and knew Draven still remained when I heard a breaking voice speak to himself,

"As do I, Brother…*where are you, Keira?*"

The trek back up the rocks and into the woods took so much longer than I thought it would, even when I stupidly, stupidly, stupidly imagined I might have an injured Draven in tow. I can definitely say the hardest part was getting out of the water. After I watched Draven's shadow walk away from me, I bawled so hard I actually went under the water a few times. It was only when I was snorting out lake water that I knew I needed to pull myself together.

So, by using the last of my strength, I managed to get my soggy ass out of the water, collect my bag and drag myself over the rocks until I found the small gap of wooded area that would take me to the empty Villa. By the time I got there it felt as though I had aged by another ten years. I was a shivering mess in wet clothes and a broken heart. I tried not to think about what was actually happening to my life or I don't think I would have made it two steps. So, I took things one priority at a time which was 'Getting the Hell out of there!'

When I saw the car, I couldn't help the sob of relief and the closer I got the weaker I felt. The driver must have seen me coming and opened both his door, got out and opened mine in the blink of an eye. I shouldn't have been surprised that he was of the supernatural variety, as what did I really expect, working for Lucius? Well, in this case, I could be nothing but grateful if it got me in the car quicker. I just got to him and that's when my legs decided to give out. My nameless driver who had barely said two words to me, caught me before I crashed to the floor and picked me up.

At this point I didn't even realise I was crying as hard as I was, until I found myself curled up on the back seat of the luxury car, with a blanket around me. I don't know how long I remained like this obviously in such a state of shock that I could only just find enough energy to keep breathing.

I could vaguely hear the driver speaking with someone and I gathered it would have been his boss. This was enough to get me to sit upright and take note of where we were. It looked as if he had been instructed to take me back to the hotel in Milan, which was just fine with me. Given the way I felt right now, I didn't know if once in a bed I would ever make my way out of it again.

I felt stripped bare and left out in the wilderness, cut wide open and bleeding ready for the wolves to finish me off. Draven had filled my life with deceit and spun a lie so great, that I had believed it enough to go to Hell and back just to save him. But as the dark world passed us by and with it more time for realisation to set in, I was starting to understand the very depth that I had been played…

By everyone.

This caused even more raw tears to flow, but this time these were created by anger. Lucius had known Draven was still alive which is why I got that warning…and Pip, all those funny looks of sadness when she would see how I asked for help in finding Draven. All those tears shed in her arms when the waiting got too much to bear.

She had known.

Then there was Vincent. The day I cut my hair off and left it for a man I had just found in bed with another woman, after trying to convince me he was dead! I just didn't get it, why go to all that trouble if all he wanted to do was reconnect with his Ex.

It didn't make sense and even more so given his reaction to me running. Why even try and find me if he didn't want me anymore?

There was a side of me that wanted to shout 'turn the car around' and demand answers but the torn and shredded pieces of me just couldn't do it. The agony was all too fresh and I needed to sort my head out before ever facing that man again. It was as if all the questions I had before had now been buried by a thousand others and through the pain one word kept on getting dragged to the top of the pile…

Why?

So many whys.

Why the Oracle lied to me and sent me on this merry quest of death, beasts, Hell and prisons? Had Sigurd known, had Jared known, Christ even looking back at it even Gastian had tried to warn me! But I had been a blind fool that couldn't let go of the man I thought loved me with every fibre in his body, mind and soul…just like I did…

Just like I had done.

I pulled my wet clothes away from my body and then gave up trying to peel them from my chilled skin. What did I care at this point if I got sick with flu? I was too far gone in my misery to give a shit anymore and didn't think it was possible for anything else to make me feel worse than I already did. Ok, so I know this wasn't completely true, but I just couldn't help giving in to self-pity, not after this killer blow.

I was so far fallen into my Draven induced pit of torment, that I only just realised we were back in the city and making our way to the hotel. The rain still pelted down the windows, blurring my world, but doing nothing for my excruciating memory of Draven there underneath his old lover. Or was she ever an old lover…was it possible I had been played from the very start?

NO! I just couldn't think of it that way…he couldn't have done that to me, but then if he could do something as painful and destroying as playing dead, then who knew what else the man was capable of?!

I decided to try and conquer these fears before I would soon be able to add crazy to the array of raging emotions playing my body to a painful tune. I just couldn't wait to get back into my hotel room, take a hot bath and never leave in the hopes of thawing not only my cold body, but also the icy layer that was frosting over my heart.

My driver didn't pull in front of the hotel, but instead turned down a side alley. He stopped the car and just as I was about to ask what he was doing, he opened my door and a hand reached in to help me out. I grabbed my bag and scooted over to take the hand given. I unfolded my sorry state from the car and noticed a side door that was open, so that light was flooding the industrial sized rubbish bins.

I turned to look at my driver but he just nodded back to the door and when I saw a member of the kitchen staff carrying out a large black sack, I knew what this was. He had driven me around the back entrance so that I wouldn't have to be seen by the rest of the hotel's guests. I looked down at my soaked clothes and feeling the raw skin around my nose and soreness blinking caused me, I could more than imagine what I looked like.

"Thanks." I sniffed out the small word of gratitude and then started my walk of shame through the kitchen, thankful it was only the very few that would witness it. I was surprised I even managed to hold my head up high, but then a voice stopped me.

"He will find you, you know." My driver's voice was enough to push a single tear up and down my cheek, falling in the path of many others before it. I didn't look back at him when I replied, but instead looked down at my hands.

"I know."

Once inside the hotel room, as soon as I managed to slam shut the door, I lost the very last of my strength. I slid down the door and cried until I lost my voice. I cried until my tears ran dry and I cried until it hurt to breathe. My body shook with violent tremors until I curled myself up on the floor in a foetal position and held my knees tight to my burning chest.

I don't remember how long I stayed like this, but I must have fallen asleep from exhaustion at some point because it was long enough for me to dream. I would like to have said it was a re-load of tonight's events, where I found Draven in bed alone.

Where I ran to him and instead of Aurora's body he waited for, it was mine instead. I dreamt of his shock that quickly turned to immense joy, instead of the undiluted rage I had received.

But my life was not a dream.

My life was back as it had always been.

Full of living nightmares.

I got up feeling like I was just dragging around an empty carcass with every step I made. I wondered if this was what a soulless vessel felt like, before being taken over by a new host. I thought on this for a while as I ran my bath, going through the motions just to survive. I knew I needed to get out of my damp clothes which must have dried marginally while I found misery a comfortable position on the floor.

So, I got out of my clothes and stepped into the hot bath that made my skin itch. Skin I felt like I wanted to crawl out of it instead of wash clean.

Once again, I didn't know how long I sat in the tub holding myself, hoping that by hugging my legs this might somehow help in keeping me together. I remembered back to the day that Draven lied the first time to me and how that had felt. Seeing another woman walk up to Draven and act like she was his fiancée was bad enough but this…

This might just end up in killing me.

I got out of the bath and wiped away the steam from the mirror to reveal the evidence of what was left, once Draven had torn me apart. It was when staring at myself that I made the decision. I could let this man destroy what was left, which granted right now didn't feel that much, or I could fight. I could fight for what I did have in life and that was the only thing a person needed… A family who loved you. Friends that cared enough to go against what they believed in, in order to protect you. A child that would grow up calling you Aunty Kazzy and could learn from your trusting mistakes. This was the only thing that mattered to me now and this was what I needed to fight for!

I held my hand over my image, looked down at the sink and vowed,

"I can do this…you can do this Keira…you have to…to… *survive once more.*" I couldn't help this last vow breaking on a sob.

After this profound moment of clarity, that came surprisingly quick, I picked myself from the pity shelf and got ready for my next plan. I first got changed into another pair of jeans and a long sleeved t-shirt that was worn navy, with faded white handprints done in the shape of a butterfly. I also put back on my long gloves, getting back the lost security that I no longer felt from my so call supernatural family. That family had all lied to me, so now it was time to stop playing in this dangerous game and get back to the only family who mattered.

I rang the airport and found that the next flight back to the states was in about four hours and after giving them some card details, booked myself on it. I then packed what little I had, dried my hair and left the hotel room, one that I hoped never to remember. I was just making my way to the lifts, when I heard Vincent's voice from around the corner.

"I will go in first Sophia, as I fear she will not yet be up to the happy reunion you are hoping for."

"But…" Sophia started to argue, but Vincent's stern voice cut her down.

"No! I could barely convince Dom to wait by the entrance. I do not have the patience to do so with another stubborn sibling." I looked around desperately, hoping to see my next escape when I saw the clear exit sign above a door. I ran the few feet and opened the door hoping not to make too much noise. I dropped my suitcase knowing that I didn't need any of it and it would only aid in slowing me down.

Then I flew down the stairs, hoping Vincent would be busy thinking I'd silently refused to open the door. I felt a slight twinge of guilt which I quickly squashed down to being irrational. After all, the deceit from his side had been far greater and what else could I have done? I didn't want to be in the same damn country as Draven, let alone the same room! No, I had no other option than to run…again.

I made it all the way down the stairs before hearing anyone else entering the stairwell, thankful I hadn't been on the top floor. I remembered from earlier that night the way back into the alleyway and at this time in the morning, I could only hope there was very little staff around. As I made my way through to the restaurant, thanking the architect that he'd designed the place so that I wouldn't have to go into the Hotel's lobby, I found the swinging doors into the kitchen.

One guy mopping the floor started talking to me in Italian which I gathered meant I was in the wrong place.

"You have no idea, matey." I said making him frown with lack of understanding. I tried to think of the best way to get him to show me the right door leading to the alleyway, when it came to me while looking down at his mop.

"I…sick…you know, bluah." I made a sick noise and then decided to step it up a notch with the acting. I held my hands to my mouth and pretended I was out of time. His eyes widened and he quickly ushered me to the back, where he flung open the back exit…after all, no one liked mopping up vomit.

I ran outside, turned and shut the door rudely, hoping the guy would just think me as a shy puker. Looking down the alley was a gamble that paid off, as there was no one in sight. Now, all I needed to do was make it to the airport and I was scot free. So, holding my mental barriers in place like a spiritual Fort Knox, I made my way to the street, at the same time I saw all the Dravens emerge from the hotel. Luckily though, I'd had the foresight to just peek my head around the side and then back out of sight when I saw them.

Draven was once again looking for his lost human pet, but all I could think was how…

The tables had quickly turned.

CHAPTER FIFTY-NINE

WORST KIND OF WALKING ALONE

"I spoke to the front desk and they said they have not seen her come back to the hotel since leaving in the afternoon." I heard Vincent relay the information back to who I knew was Draven, given the snarl of anger.

"Find me the driver and bring him to me now!" Draven snapped out his orders and I suddenly both thanked my driver for the idea to bring me around the back, but also felt sorry for him once Draven had caught up with him.

"Sophia, phone!" Draven demanded and I could just imagine how he looked, standing there holding out his hand waiting impatiently for Sophia to do as he wished.

"Lucius… you told me she would be here and *she isn't fucking here!"* On hearing Lucius' name becoming even tighter entwined in the web of deception, I took another stab to the heart.

"I want to speak to your driver and be warned Lucius, I will tear the bastard apart if he has harmed her!" I shuddered at the violent promise in Draven's voice.

"He never brought her back to the hotel you said she would be at, so think clearly old friend, as your punishments are mounting every minute she is kept from me!" I couldn't believe what I was hearing! All this coming from the man who had done everything in his power to break away from me… And now what? Was this a slice of immense guilt that was driving him to find me? A sudden thunderclap above his head of conscious clarity at the things he had done to me?

"I don't have time to indulge you in your excuses or your feeble reasons, you were given an order and you disobeyed it along with your council! Now force my hand at leniency for you and your kind by fucking finding her!" Draven roared this last part and must have thrown the phone to the ground as I could see the small parts dance across the alleyway's entrance from where I hid.

"Maybe you should have listened to what he had to say." Vincent tried for reason.

"He had his orders and disobeyed them, as did you! I want her found Vincent and only then will I find the truth, when I force her answers… now go and tell the men to tear the city apart if need be, but just find her!"

"Very well, My Lord." Vincent said calmly, knowing there was no use trying to talk sense into a man whose rage fuelled him right now. There was a time, not that long ago, when I used to be the only one to tame the beast in him, but those days were long gone…so far that they were already becoming dust in the desert of a lost mind.

"Sophia, have someone monitoring all transport, make taxis a high priority." Vincent said as his way of parting, because after this I never heard his voice again, nor did I hear any other sound but that of a car speeding away. After they were no longer a threat, I lifted the hood of a sweater that Pip had packed for me which thankfully, was black. She had wanted to pack one that was bright green and had fleece yellow spikes that made you look like a dinosaur. Not a great choice for acting stealthily around a busy city, even if most of that city was still in bed, given the early hour.

At least it was still raining, which would be reason enough to not look suspicious, but I had to be careful. It was still dark which was on my side, but I didn't know how long I would have before the sun started to come up. Of course, the major problem I had now was how on earth was I going to get to Milano Malpensa Airport without the help of a taxi?!

Well, I knew one thing and that was I couldn't just wait around here for him to figure out I had in fact come back to the hotel. Sooner or later they would talk to one of the staff members who remembered seeing me or worse…find my poor fated driver. So, the only thing left to do was to walk and try to find some sort of transport that would get me there without being detected.

This didn't sound quite as simple when hearing the way Draven had wanted 'his people' to tear apart the city to find me, but I had reason to feel confident if you considered that I had twice now been right under his nose and still I went by undetected. This made me realise just how powerful my blocks had become and all thanks to a short time in a hellish prison trying to evade an evil captor…

It was a Hell of a year even for my standards that was for sure!

I soon realised the area of Milan that I had been staying in was in the heart of the beautiful city, but the further I walked, the more I became lost in the guts of the city. I started wandering down streets and then into run-down industrial districts, where the tightly knit neighbourhoods became less attractive than those in the city's centre. Whereas before I was coming across stunning architecture and pale marble sculptures, matching the settings in which they sat, now those were long gone, replaced by what looked like the makings of a dangerous place.

So here I was, walking alone with not a clue where I was going and not having even one person I could call that I trusted to help me. And the further I walked, the more it seemed I was leaving the regal part of the city behind me. I had been asking myself if I was doing the right thing by running from Draven, or was it just considered cowardly? Well, whatever the answer, the truth of the matter remained…

For the first time since meeting Draven, I could honestly say, in my heart of hearts, I no longer wanted to see him, so damn the Oracle and damn the prophecy she spoke of! I had been played, simple as that and there was not one possibility that I would stand around and let it happen again, so if that meant running, then that was what I was prepared to do.

By the time I had sorted out about ten per cent of the shit rattling around in my head, I realised I had walked into the rougher side of a bad neighbourhood, if the graffiti and burnt out cars were anything to go by. I looked around for the direction I'd come from, but thanks to being so deep in my personal downfall, I couldn't even tell where that was. I had just walked for what could have been hours with no direction in mind, just one that took me further from Draven.

Well, now that had cost me as I saw a few homeless people asleep in doorways trying no doubt to keep out of the rain that had now begun to trickle instead of pour. In fact, I looked to be the only shmuck walking around in it. But I couldn't give one damn shit about what people thought of me. I did however hope that the dodgy looking group all stood round a running car didn't take much notice.

I saw about three guys stood there smoking what I quickly smelled was weed and one guy inside the car who was lighting something that looked like a crack pipe. Music I didn't recognise blared from the speakers and I looked around to notice there was no one else in sight. The car was parked next to what looked like an abandoned warehouse and I could only hope they were more interested in the bottles of spirits they were swigging back than what I was doing.

I knew I had two options, one was to turn around and run, which would no doubt end up drawing their attention. Then there was my other option, which was to just walk past as quickly as possible, in the hope they wouldn't take any notice of me. The deciding factor turned out to be two taxis that I saw not that far away. Just down the road they had both parked up and were chatting, smoking and obviously having a break.

I knew Sophia was going to be monitoring the taxis, but at this point I really didn't care, just so long as it got me out of this part of the city! So this was where I made my millionth mistake in life.

As soon as I started walking past, one of them must have spotted me because they began shouting things in Italian. I just ignored them and tried to walk even faster, ready to wave to the taxi drivers if they would just look up.

"Dove vai, vieni a giocare con noi" ('Where are you going, come play with us' In Italian)

I heard their shouts getting closer, so I decided to make a run for it. The taxi drivers weren't that far away now and if I made enough of a racket then surely they would look up…That was until I felt a hand clamp over my mouth.

I began struggling as soon as I felt it but could do nothing to stop them as my body was being dragged backwards. This could not be happening! I tried to contain my panic and think about how I was going to get out of this, but right now the only thought swamping my rational mind was utter disbelief that this was actually happening to me…again! I watched with horror in my eyes as the taxi drivers went from my sight and not once did they even look up.

"Portala qui e cerchiamo di avere qualche divertimento" ('Bring her here and let us have some fun' in Italian) I could hear the others getting excited behind me and the sound of the last one getting out of the car as the door slammed shut. Then I was pushed away by the one who had his hand held over my mouth, using the back of my head to do so. I fell forward on a failed step but managed to right myself before I went down. I quickly spun round to face my attackers to find them advancing.

"Vieni qui e succhiare il cazzo!" ('Come here and suck my cock!' in Italian) I didn't know what the one on the left was saying but considering he had grabbed the front of his pants I could only guess.

"Fuck you!" I shouted knowing the F word was universal when said in anger.

"Look we found English Bitch, Mi capita di andare per primo." (mean's 'I get to go first') Another one said first in broken English then something I couldn't understand in Italian. I started backing up as they all started to come closer and the scrawny one on the left finished the dregs of his liquor bottle before throwing it to smash on the ground. This was when I ran, which was looking to be the theme of the night.

I felt one of them grab me from behind, this time by the hair and I screamed out at the pain inflicted to my scalp. I let my natural reactions take over and turned in his hold biting through the hurt. I then grabbed his shoulders to me and kneed him as hard as I could in the groin. He screamed out and dropped to the floor cupping his injured package. Well, that was one down but as the other three ran for me, I doubted I was strong enough to put the rest down, no matter what Draven had taught me in his training room.

I was left backing up again as they approached, knowing out running them was no longer a good plan. Now it was the scrawny one's turn to try it on, only he wasn't going to make the same mistake as his friend on the floor groaning. He motioned for the other two to get me from the sides and for once I just wished it was like it was in the movies. You know, when the main dude is surrounded and staring at ridiculous odds of surviving. But of course, the dude is also a master at every martial art known to man! Of course, it always helps when each of the bad guys just comes at him one at a time, like they had collected a bloody ticket at the meat counter…I mean why don't they just all jump the guy all at once?

Well, I wasn't the main combat ninja dude, and this wasn't a movie, which translated into, I was in big shit as all three of them went for me all at once. The flight mode kicked in and I tried to get away only to be roughly pulled and pushed, grabbed and slapped to where they wanted me. Hands holding me everywhere bit into my flesh and dragged me back over to the car where the rock music created the perfect base for the horror that I knew was about to happen.

I heard the bark of an order in Italian, just before I was spun and slammed into the side of the car. Pain rippled up my back as the unforgiving metal hit me and I looked up in time to see the one I had kneed was now back on his feet. He stormed over to where the others had me pinned to the car by my arms. I kicked out and watched as he avoided the kick only to see his fist coming at me full force before it connected with the side of my face.

"English Bitch!" He roared at me, hitting me again, only this time I felt my lip burst and my mouth quickly filled with the metallic taste of blood. The throbbing exploded across my cheek, making me feel sick as my brain felt rattled inside my skull. I tried not to give in to the feeling and soon panic over-rode any other sensory action, as I saw the guy motion to his friends again.

I watched horrified as he started to unzip his jeans, freeing his excited erection. This was when I went crazy, bucking and kicking so much it was a mission for his friends to hold me still. He tried to step up to me but I screamed and spat the blood from my mouth in his face, doing anything in my power to keep him from me. He hit me again, but this did nothing in stopping the rage that was building up in me. If only I could free the power I had somewhere hidden deep down in me as I had done before. But there was no tingling of fingertips or supernatural aid that came to help me.

I was all alone in this.

In the end my soon to be rapist must have thought it too risky to get his kicks this way. I was grabbed roughly by the hair once more and with the help from the others together, they managed to get me to the front of the car. I was pushed over it and this time only held there by one guy as he stepped up behind me. My hips dug into the car and I decided my only chance was to become still, as though I had accepted my fate.

"Now you want my cock, yes?" He said grinding his erection into my behind. I felt him reach round to undo my jeans and as he did this he leant his chest over my back to whisper in my ear.

"I give you my cock, Bitch." He snarled and just as his hand dipped down to touch me in my open jeans, I made my move.

"Yeah…well this Bitch gives great head!" I said as I slammed my head back as hard as I could just at the right moment, feeling his nose crack on the back of my head. In his shock and agony at having his nose broken he let me go. I wasted no time in bolting up and running away from the car.

I must have made it all of five feet when I felt myself being tackled to the ground. I felt the body on top of me try to turn me and just before I let him I grabbed a fistful of gravel. As soon as he got me round I threw the stony handful in his face and took his surprise to twist his body off mine. I scrambled up and delivered two kicks to his ribcage before turning to face the other two that had left their bleeding friend to get me. Their lustful faces were now a thing of the past as only revenge entered their minds when they saw me.

"COME ON YOU BASTARDS!" I yelled out knowing the only thing left for me was to fight till the bitter end. I saw that the one with the broken nose had clearly had enough of me as he had slumped down by the car. The other one cradled his ribs and a nasty scratch across his forehead running into his eye. Looking at him I think I could also count him out of the fight, which just left these two who had been the ones to hold me down at the car.

I kept backing up so as to prolong the time they got to me, hoping for a plan to formulate but when I saw one of them produce a small blade from their jacket, I knew I was screwed! I tried not to let him see the panic on my face but from his smile I had failed. I retreated so far that I knew I would soon feel the warehouse wall at my back but with that dirty looking knife coming closer I was all out of options…or was I?

Just as they both ran at me, I gave it my last shot at survival. I not only dropped all my mental barriers but I pushed on them so hard I hoped it would have the opposite effect of keeping Draven out.

"DRAVEN!!!!!" I screamed out at the heavens, smashing my walls and feeling the pulse of power that I released along with it. That's when I felt the first slice of the blade that cut along my belly as the guy had slashed out at me before fully reaching me. My hand went to the hurt but then right back up again blocking the first hit. I even repeated what I had been taught by Draven, saying 'High Parry' in my mind. The other guy tried once again with his knife but this time in a stab motion, telling me this wasn't just an attack on an innocent woman anymore, this had now quickly switched to murder.

I was thankful for my quick reactions as I dodged the

damaging blow and the momentum of his actions took him forward into the side of the warehouse. Meanwhile, I foolishly took my eyes off the other guy and felt a stomach punch that hit closer to the side. It hurt but at least didn't hit its mark in winding me. I was then pushed until I landed side on into the warehouse wall putting me at a dead end I couldn't afford to be in.

Before I had a second to get out of it they were both on me and the fight ended with the blade held under my neck. I knew this was it, as one wrong move from me and it was all over. The guy smiled at me and I could smell the stale taste of whisky he had been drinking all night. His eyes were red rimmed and erratic as the drugs coursed through his veins, pumping him full of falsehoods that told him he was doing the right thing.

"Dead Bitch!" He said and I knew this was it. I sent out that last of the love left inside of me that wasn't broken, as a silent message to those I cared for and simply waited for the pain to come.

"Che cosa è stato?" ('What was that?") I heard the guy next to me say something I couldn't understand and looked to see something rumbling over our heads. The early pre-dawn was thundering as I saw the darker shadow descending at a speed only I had witnessed before, giving way to the landing of a demon I would know anywhere.

"Oh, you are all so dead." I informed him just before the screaming erupted, this time though, it didn't come from me. The guy next to me, who had been aiding his friend in holding me to the wall, found his body ripped from the spot in a blur of shadows. My eyes weren't powerful enough to see the actions clear enough, but all I knew was that one minute he was next to me and then he was on the ground with a broken neck. I almost gagged as I saw his head facing the wrong way, staring at me with dead eyes, that put a whole new meaning to the saying 'eyes in the back of your head'.

The two I had left injured on the floor were screaming at the sight of what true murder looked like. The guy who still had me pinned by the throat looked around frantically and just before the pressure became deadly, the blade crumbled into metal dust. I looked past the face of pure terror and right into one that truly created it.

Draven stood behind my attacker with not a single ounce of Angel in sight. It looked as if he had shot right out of Hell itself with the flames still engulfing his body. Eyes swimming red like the blood he would soon find covering his hands, burned into mine. I couldn't believe this was to be our first moment together after all this time. This was to be the first face of Draven I was to see as we reunited once again. As heartbreaking as seeing him for the first time in Aurora's arms was, I couldn't tell which was more so…now or then.

"Draven." I whispered his name like a prayer that had come true. This was when he snarled, and his hand shot out around the guy's neck. My eyes quickly left Draven's demon form and found my attacker's eyes that were now bulging from the pressure. They haemorrhaged, turning frightened white into blood red making me once again want to be sick.

Draven moved his arm out to the side taking the body he held with it so that soon the guy was dangling by his neck in Draven's grasp. He tried pointlessly to claw at his hand, but it was no use. This move left Draven and me face to face without anything between us. I saw the flicker of emotion, one other than rage, flash across his face and for a single moment the eyes that were staring back at me went purple.

I was too frightened to move, as it was like looking in the eyes of a rampant beast you knew could erupt into killer at any moment…and I was right. His gaze dipped down to do a scan of my body and I quickly knew what he would find. A bruised cheek and a bloody lip was one thing but a bloody slash across my stomach and jeans that were still undone from my rape attempt was another.

His eyes took in my state and within seconds knew what it all meant and so did I. These men were not leaving this world without being punished. Draven's eyes told me as much when they exploded back into his demon side and he roared his head back, bellowing his fury with his wings bursting backwards.

"Which one?" His demon asked me, making me shake with a fear deeper than one I'd known. I had seen Draven's demon

many times before but never like this... never before so out of control that the very flames around him hummed and vibrated with power. It even looked as though he was growing. Like Hell's trapped energy inside him couldn't be contained to the body it had been given.

"Draven I..."

"WHICH ONE?" He thundered back at me cutting me off. I knew I had no choice, as these men's actions had already condemned themselves to death, but the one I nodded at now would no doubt receive whatever horrors he could conjure up in his nightmares...that and more.

So I did the only thing I could do, which was nod at the guy with the broken nose who was trying to get in the car to make his getaway. Draven looked behind to see for himself, all the while still holding his arm out straight with a human dangling from it. He nodded and then the engine suddenly blew up, knocking the guy back just as he opened the driver's door.

Draven seemed satisfied enough that he wasn't going anywhere for now, so looked back at me one last time. Then he gave me my last order speaking the only word needed,

"Go!" I didn't need to be told twice as I held on to the bag at my side and ran out of there as fast as my frightened legs could carry me. Draven had looked truly possessed by the Devil himself and his version of payback wasn't one I wanted to stick around and lay witness to. So I did as I was told and got the Hell out of there!

I ended up running and running until my lungs were close to giving up...but still I ran. I ran until everything in me burned and demanded things of my body it just wasn't willing to give anymore. I just wanted to stop, crumble into a helpless heap to allow the shock to sink in, letting the shakes that wanted to be released rack my body. But I couldn't. I was a survivor and survivors didn't quit. They didn't just sit down and say die. So I kept running until my body gave up before my mind did.

I didn't know how far I had come but bent over panting trying to kill the stitch that cut into my side along with the actual slash I had there. I soon found I could no longer stand either as first my knee landed, quickly followed by the other.

So there I sat, knelt on one of Italy's cobbled streets, lost, alone, hurt and head hanging down, staring at the wet stone, praying for the last of the storm that mirrored my life.

And what did praying to the Gods give me…

A taxi.

CHAPTER SIXTY

A WORLD OF HURT

As the taxi pulled up I sent up a whispered thank you to whoever had heard my silent prayers. A middle-aged man got out and came to me, speaking first in Italian, words I couldn't understand.

"I'm alright." I said as he started to help me up.

"English sì?" I nodded to him and let him help me into the back of the car as my legs didn't yet feel like they were strong enough to support me.

"Stupidi giovani prendere farmaci!" ('Stupid young people taking drugs') He got me in the back muttering something in Italian.

"Ospedale?"

"Uh…?" I dumbly responded as I didn't understand the word.

"Hospital, sì?" He asked just as he flipped up the sun visor giving me a quick glimpse of a family photo he had stashed there.

"Oh…no, no not hospital, airport… Milano Malpensa Airport." He frowned but then lifted his shoulders in a shrug before pulling away. I was just thankful that this early in the morning a taxi happened to come across me and hoped I could take this as a sign for no more incidents in getting me home. I knew the likelihood of me catching that flight was slim to none, but at least I would be there where I could wait. Hell, I would bloody live there for a whole week if it would eventually mean me getting a flight home!

I let my head fall back on to the headrest and closed my eyes for a few seconds as the night's events tried to creep their way in. I then snapped my eyes open as I refused to let them. I couldn't allow myself to think back to what had almost happened, both if I had not decided to fight or if I had not called out for Draven and he had answered that call.

I could only imagine that I would have just ended up another dumped body joining the mile-long list of other victims killed for being stupid enough for walking anywhere in the world alone. It being Italy had nothing to do with it, as every country in the world had its dark side of beauty that was invisibly labelled 'no woman's land'.

"Are you alright?" I heard the driver ask and I looked from the window where I had subconsciously been watching the world whiz by but not taking any of it in. The guy had a strong Italian accent but his English was better than I first thought.

"Yeah…I'm fine." I said this as if the words were glue, thick and sticky lies that didn't want to be said. I saw him motion in his mirror to my face and said,

"Are you sure, you really look like you need a hospital?" On hearing that very word I closed my eyes and sighed.

"Look, I don't want to seem rude and mean this in the nicest way possible…but please… just drive…alright?" I didn't want the guy to think I was mean or anything, but I couldn't have this guy taking me to the hospital or worse, the police. I was happy when I saw him just nod and look back at the road.

"So if not a hospital, where to?" He asked again making me frown. Hadn't he heard me the first time?

"Eh…like I said before, just the airport will be fine…thank you." I said leaning forward closer to the circle of holes through the Plexiglas so that he could hear me properly. He nodded to show he heard and once again I settled back against the worn black leather. You could see in the distance the sun had just begun to rise as the guy took the motorway out of the main part of the city.

He was a kind looking man who had laughter lines around the eyes and a streaking of grey peppered in jet black hair near his ears. He was what I would class as typically Italian with sun-kissed skin, dark soft eyes and a face that spoke of a world of knowledge. I just bet that nice looking family of his was back at home, all tucked up in bed like they should be.

God only knew what he thought of me, dressed like a lost little Goth, half beaten and found half collapsed by the side of the road…I was just thankful the guy had given up trying to convince me to go to the hospital, but it did beg the question, why didn't he then insist I go to the cops? Maybe he just didn't want to be caught up with my drama any more than he needed to be. Get me from A to B and we would both be happy.

I lifted my bag up and plonked it down next to me, thinking it might be a good idea to do some first aid. I rummaged through my bag, noticing that the looks from the driver were a mixture of concern and frustration. I decided to ignore it as I lifted up my top, hissing as the blood stuck to the raw sliced skin. Thankfully it looked much worse than it was, as now the bleeding had stopped. I knew the cut hadn't been that deep but bloody Hell it was enough to sting like a vinegar and salt shower to a thousand paper cuts!

I jumped slightly when the light above me turned on so that I could see it better and I nodded my thanks to the driver, wondering how he'd done that?

Still looking down, I dug my hand in my bag until I felt one of the little bottles of spirits, feeling for the one with the little red hat. Once that beauty was in my hand I pulled it out and flipped off the hat, unscrewed it and broke the seal.

"Is that wise?" The driver asked me, obviously keeping a close eye on me.

"Probably not." I replied before downing my first swig of tequila. I felt the burn of liquid and welcomed it, unlike what I was about to do next. I then poured some across my stomach washing the slice, making the dried blood run down in little bloody rivulets.

"Arrrh!" I cried at the bite of pain and tried to shut out the tears that sprang to my eyes. I took a few deep breaths and did it once more just to be sure I had cleaned it well enough. After all I remembered seeing that dirty blade and Hell only knew what he had done with it before me!

Once I thought I had been through enough self-inflicting torture, I opened up the first aid bag that was no bigger than both my hands put together.

"Bloody Hell, Pip." I moaned as the first thing I saw was a bag of jellybeans sat on top. Everything had been labelled and the first one read *'For the pain of missing a colourful friend'*. Alright that was the very last time I was putting Pip in charge of the important stuff!

I moved these to one side and found a lipstick saying, *'For when you're ready to kiss again'* and also a hand warmer in the shape of cupid that heated when something inside is clicked. This one said, *'To warm a damaged heart'* and this was when I realised what Pip had done. This wasn't a kit to help heal the body, but to heal the mind…she had known.

The next items helped slightly more as I found a packet of Aspirin labelled *'for the heartbroken hangover'*, which I swallowed down chased by the tequila, much to the disapproval I saw in the driver. I looked through the rest of the items, finding a business card advertising a gay club with the ladies night circled in red marker. The other side held the note *'Just in case the Royal bastard made you wanna play for the other team…they would be lucky to have you hot stuff ;o)'*

The driver shot me a look when I laughed.

"Oh Pip." I whispered before continuing on, finding the last piece to be a chocolate heart lollypop that she had obviously made herself as the icing simply said, *'To help in forgiving me'*. I bit down on my lip to hold in my emotions and nodded to myself when I knew what needed to be done.

I first pulled off one of my gloves and used it to clean around the wounded area the best I could and then folded it to cover the cut, in case it started weeping again. Then I felt inside my bag for my phone. I scrolled through the contacts, knowing the very first person I needed to speak to. She answered on first ring, but I didn't allow her to say anything other than,

"Toots?"

"I forgive you." I said and then hung up knowing she would know that's all I had to say right now. She didn't call back as I didn't expect she would, so I scrolled to the next name on my list.

"Jack." I said his name on a whisper, feeling the tears form.

"Keira?!" He asked half in disbelief, half in hope.

"Yeah, it's me." I said trying not to break down. I also tried to ignore the funny looks I was getting from the driver, so turned my body sideways in the seat to face the side window.

"Kaz, where have you been?!" Jack sounded worried and I wondered why he asked this question. See, after I had gone missing and Jack had got Lucius on the case, they had decided the best course of action was crowd control. Or in this case, 'family and friends control' as the last thing they needed was the police being dragged into the disappearance of one Keira Johnson/ Williams…again!

So to keep this from happening, Pip had made the rounds and rang not only Jack and RJ but also my mum and sister, pretending to be me, exact voice over and everything. So other than thinking I was going through a weird spell, the next time I actually spoke to them they were none the wiser. So I had to remind myself this was only the second time I was calling Jack, having no clue what Pip had said to him as me, but just praying she had kept the crazy flirting to a minimum.

"Why?" I asked confused by his question, as it was only a few days before that I had rung him from Pip's apartment.

"Because I have had your ex-boyfriend half crazed on the phone demanding from me if I had heard from you or know where you are."

"And what did you tell him?" I asked already knowing the answer to this one.

"I told him about the last time I heard from you and that you were in Germany staying with the friends you had there…I also…" I almost groaned knowing this was the start of how Draven knew about the hotel I was staying at.

"It's alright Jack, you can tell me." I encouraged knowing the damage was already done.

"Well, when he asked if I knew what you were doing there, I kind of let it slip that you were there looking for him." And yep there it was, the final catalyst in contacting Lucius, no doubt to demand answers.

"It's fine Jack, I found him so there's no need to worry." I heard him exhale a big sigh before asking,

"How did it go?" Now it was my turn to sigh. Then I answered truthfully,

"It was Hell on earth." Strangely I heard both Jack and the driver curse at the same time, but only one of them I could understand. I looked up to see him quickly flip the bird at another driver, so I put it down to a 'Co winky dink' which was Pip's way of explaining a coincidence.

"That bad huh?"

"You have no idea."

"So what now?" He asked making me look to the rising sun and lift up my wrist to check out what colour the very last stone had turned. I was amazed to see it had now become a beautiful rainbow moonstone and I couldn't help but wonder what this one had meant. I looked back at the orange glow that was the clear signs to another day and I said the only thing on my mind,

"Now, I come home."

"You ready for that?" He asked and this was where I really hit him with the lies Draven had now warped into a truth.

"Jack honestly...? Remember what you said to me, about how some things are better left?" I asked him knowing he would.

"Yeah Keira, I do…so this means…?"

"So…The relationship I had with Dominic Draven is now well and truly *dead* …so yeah I would say I was more than ready for that." I had to wipe the single tear that fell on saying such painful words. The car swerved into the next lane and started speeding past the other cars, making me wonder was this guy all of a sudden desperate to get rid of me. I was close to telling him to slow it down but considering the small amount of traffic around, I decided if he got me there sooner it wouldn't be a bad thing.

"Well I can't say that I'm not glad, the guy was no good for you and I said that from the start."

"I know you did Jack and if I could go back in time and take your advice I would, just to kill the pain I feel now but I can't." I think I made my point enough with that confession so that would be the last comment I would get like that one.

"Point made." I nodded and ran a hand through my hair, gripping a fistful near the base for a second. The frustration I felt was more with myself than it was with Jack.

"Thanks Jack, you're a true friend, you know that right?"

"Yeah Keira, right back at ya." I gave him a half smile he couldn't see and then said,

"I gotta go."

"Alright but ring me whenever you manage to get a flight. I'm cool with picking you up when you need it, just give me a call…alright honey?" I put my head back and closed my eyes before saying,

"Yeah, will do Jack, see ya soon." And then I hung up, knowing any longer and I would have cried.

I was quickly feeling the last of my reserved energy being zapped out of me and all I wanted to do now was curl up and fall into a deep dreamless sleep. I turned my head and rested it on the back seat to watch the countryside whizzing past me, when something suddenly clicked…

We were not only heading far from the city but also in the wrong direction. And it was as we passed one sign that said Como on it that it finally clicked into place. All those little reactions to the things that had been said, all those things I myself had said. I turned back round to face the driver and couldn't help myself when I asked,

"Do you have a family back in the city?" For a minute the 'Driver' looked surprised by my question and then looked around before saying a sharp,

"No." I wanted to laugh out loud for the first time in a day.

"Right" I said knowing there was no end to this man's lies.

"Did you steal this car then?" I asked making him do a double take at me in the mirror. Before he could answer I said,

"Pull down the visor." He did as I asked and when he saw the man's family staring back at him he knew I had caught him in the lie.

"So I don't suppose this is the part where you pull over the car and let me go…is it?" I asked looking back out of the window, knowing the answer when I heard the locks click.

"No, that part is long gone." I sucked in my bottom lip and nodded my frustration, to hold back the yelling that I felt soon in coming.

"That's what I thought. So what now, you take me back to that fortress by the lake and force your answers from me?" I asked, injecting a bite of vindictiveness into the part at the end, so that he would know I heard him when he said this to Vincent. I saw him grip the steering wheel in a crushing hold, only to fix the damage again…if only the damage done to me was that fixable.

"I would suggest silence right now, Keira." He warned and my anger wound up even tighter, getting ready to strike.

"And I would suggest if you want that fucking silence then you pull over and let me out of this fucking car, but I doubt that is going to happen now is it?" I snapped back adding to the very few times I had actually said the F word in front of Draven.

"Careful, Keira."

"Careful, Dominic." I mimicked back, knowing how much he hated to hear his first name coming from me in anger. When I heard his growl, I knew I had gotten to him.

"Well, I gather we have enough time for confessions Draven, so here's an idea, you first!" I said after a time and yet another sign for Lake Como.

"Not now, Keira." This made me snap and my reactions couldn't be helped as I leant forward and punched the plastic divider between us and shouted,

"No NOW, Draven!" At this his head snapped around and he growled at me.

"Do that again and you will regret it."

"I regret many things when it comes to you Draven, but

right now, not one of them is showing you how fucking angry I am!" I said trying my best to inflict even the tiniest amount of pain he had done to me.

"I know you are hurt…"

"You think?" I snapped, interrupting him, knowing how much he hated this as well if the look I received was anything to go by.

"So therefore, I will take that into account for the things you say." On hearing this I became furious!

"I couldn't give a shit about how you take what I say Draven, but if I could choose, it would to be taken very seriously as I never took you for a disbelieving fool!" Oh this hit its mark alright but instead of reacting to his rage I was almost stunned by it. I mean why did he even care what I said to him? So without responding to him swearing in another language, saying God knows what about me in the process I just sat back in the seat and stared out of the window silently.

I mean what else could I do, or what else was I left to go on? It wasn't like Draven was giving me any answers or excuses or anything for that matter. No, instead I was getting a big fat nothing with shit loads of heartbreak on the side!

Once I gathered Draven had regained his control through a series of deep breaths and muttered words in whatever language sounded good at the time, he had calmed enough to ask,

"Are you in any pain?" I rolled my eyes through my growing misery and said,

"None you should be concerned about."

"And the parts that shouldn't concern me…what of them?" He asked and I quickly made him regret it.

"The nonphysical pain...? Well, that I am drowning in." I added looking back to the window once more, finding his own look of pain too much to bear. He had no right to it, no right at all given what he had put me through!

The rest of the drive neither of us spoke and I was thankful for it given that whatever he said was going to either put me in tears or have me lashing out in a fit of rage. I could see us coming closer to the same place I had foolishly found yesterday, that was barely even a nightmare away. I knew I only had one last chance to do what I wanted to do that was before I had discovered Draven was the one driving, taking over the poor guy's vessel and using it as a tool to play puppet master.

I reached for my phone and scrolled to one last number, making Draven growl when he heard who answered the phone.

"Keira girl, are you alright, are you hurt?" Lucius asked me, sounding truly worried.

"I'm alright, Draven found me." I heard his sigh of relief and it was one I wanted to be angry with but found I couldn't.

"He wouldn't allow me to contact you."

"I thought as much." I replied quietly.

"And now?" He asked obviously referring to Draven and the fact that he had not yet destroyed my phone in protest.

"Well, now I gather he has learnt that adding to my pissed off hurt state wouldn't be the best of ideas right now." I said looking at Draven's glowing purple ring in another man's eyes.

"I can imagine not. So the question remains, what can I do for you, Pet? Because if it is to ask me to aid you in getting away from Draven, then I am afraid that would have to be a no." I had to smile a little at the sound of Lucius being diplomatic.

"It's not that Luc, but I did want to ask you something."

"Go ahead my little…" He trailed off knowing that calling me my nickname right now was probably not the best of ideas with the level of shit he was already in with Draven.

"I just wanted to confirm what I think I already know." I took a deep breath and then asked,

"Did you know before you saved me…did you always know he was alive?" I saw Draven flinch and I closed my eyes readying myself for the ache to come.

"Yes, I did." I swallowed down the hard lump of rock-solid reality and said,

"Then I want to thank you and tell you that you were right in the last thing you said to me when I left." I heard Lucius sigh before saying,

"Alright Keira girl, I understand."

"Goodbye, Lucius." I said and then hung up just as Draven was pulling the taxi up to gates that were opening for us. He turned his head and looked straight at me to softly ask,

"I have to know, what was the last thing he said to you?"

"He told me of the only thing I would find here." I said finding it painful looking at the purple I saw there.

"And that was?" I looked away from him and said in a voice that held no more emotion, but just proved how much there really was hidden there…

"A world of hurt."

CHAPTER SIXTY-ONE

LEVELS OF BETRAYAL

Draven pulled the taxi through the open gates and I watched as they closed behind us, knowing I had come right back to where it all started. Till then I had been set firm on a mission to find and free the man I loved...but now that mission was over. In fact, with my first sight of Draven it was enough to tell me that mission had never even really started. I was like a soldier still fighting a war long ago lost and not knowing how to let go of failure.

The car stopped and I watched as the driver suddenly slumped forward and then off to the side, where he remained passed out. I looked out of the side window that now faced the main house and a figure emerged from the front steps. Draven was flanked first by his council and then some of the guards from Afterlife, some of whom I was used to seeing daily. The whole sight had me sucking in a tight breath in an attempt at holding on to my anger in place of the pain that wanted to consume me. But no matter how strong I pretended to be, tears still found their way past my barriers. They trickled down even as he reached the door and pulled it open.

"Come on, Keira," said a voice that wasn't making it any easier to bear. At least before when talking with Draven, he had been in the body of a sweet family man, just doing his job. But like this…Draven's powerful presence, his towering frame and his commanding voice, no matter how softly spoken, still caused me such a depth of agony that I just couldn't do it!

"Keira, get out of the car." It wasn't said harshly and not even with a hint of frustration, but there was something there… an underlining current lacing his words and it was only when I figured out what it was did the anger return full force.

It was pity.

I hated pity.

I loathed pity.

But coming from Draven it became so much more than something I loathed. It became a trigger. One single shot fired straight to my heart leaving nothing left for Draven to hold onto…ever again.

I nodded to myself, knowing deep within my soul this was the end and all that was left was saying so, but to do that I first had to face my Demons, Angels and every other bastard left pulling my strings. Because this was it, I was finally done.

I wiped my tears away angrily and got myself out of the car, ignoring Draven's reaching hand. I stood refusing to look at him but still seeing my other life for the first time in months. The very ones who had all stood up at once and left me, all because their Master commanded it. And now here I was, where none of them expected me to be. Stood outside the fortress doors after infiltrating the lies and staring them all in the eye as though we had not once been side by side.

Because now I was no longer part of the family Draven had knotted me into, but I was back to being the outsider looking in. The one who had once dreamed of belonging in Draven's world…well now I knew of the pain that lay waiting there, like a poisonous snake waiting to strike when your guards were down.

There was a piece of it in every person here and as I walked past, head held high with not an ounce of fear in my eyes, I knew what they knew. What their eyes told me, what my eyes told them. But more importantly, what their Master's told us all from the very beginning, I just didn't want to see it. This wasn't the end because for me…

There was never a beginning.

I felt the air around me start to change and I knew this was down to the Master at my back. Most of his council lowered their heads in submission, but it was only Sophia and Vincent who weren't affected.

"Keira I..." Vincent started to reach out to me but I side-stepped out of his touch and turned my head away, not being able to bring myself to even look at him right now. I knew that what was happening wasn't his fault, just as it hadn't been anyone else's fault who cared for me. But right now the wound was just too raw to find comfort in those that helped inflict it, no matter what their orders had been.

I felt the pain radiating from him like an ice cold fog rising from the stone steps I walked upon. I looked straight ahead when I saw I had passed him and his sister. But I not only saw the entrance looming in front of me, but also Vincent turning away in anger from the rest of the group, thanks to the reflection in glass provided by the double doors. I must have paused for a moment as I knew that walking through those doors was the very last place I wanted to go. That's when I felt it.

Draven's hand touched the small of my back to motion me on, but for me that one single touch, the first real one in so long, felt like his mark branding into my flesh. I shrieked out like I had in fact been burned and jumped out of his reach, still feeling the tingles that hummed along my veins, lighting the way for fresh pain to penetrate my heart.

"Don't touch me!" I screamed it at him, facing him for the first time and really taking in his face. The harsh lines told me just how deeply my words had cut him, but I didn't care! He had no right to that hurt, no right at all. He had caused all of this and damn him if I didn't want him to feel sliced open because of it, because God and the Devil only knew how much I really did need it right now!

"Very well, Keira." He said softly as he must have known how truly on the edge I really was. I could no longer stand looking in those eyes, eyes I had once been mesmerised by, happy in the knowledge that I could freely get lost in their depths. I looked to see all the shocked faces my outburst had caused and for a moment I knew what I was seeing...

The prophecy was now lost in their eyes.

"Inside." Draven's one word wrenched me from all those faces that looked to have been depending on me for something I would never know.

I turned away, gladly complying if it meant getting away from them all. Zagan who had helped control my Hell's army now looked lost, consoling someone I once considered to be a sister. Celina looked in surprised sympathy stood next to Takeshi, whose disappointment couldn't be hidden under soulful eyes. The only one not here condemning me was Ragnar and I found I was glad for it as I think this would have been the last of the torture I could endure before I broke, confessing sins I never knew I had committed.

So, I turned away from them all, not in a dignified walk, head held high as it once was but now I ran. I let everything go and ran from the faces that would forever haunt me. Those judging faces that spoke of my failure in a way I couldn't explain.

This was Draven's decision not mine. He had left me, not the other way around! I should have stayed and argued this point but instead I let the coward in me rule my emotions and my actions. I heard Draven behind me shouting my name but it meant nothing. I just ran, not taking in any of my surroundings as doors and corridors all merged into one.

I didn't know where I was going, but for some reason my journey led me to only one door. It was at the end and stood directly in front of me like a beacon to Pandora's Box. It was the one you knew you shouldn't open. The one you knew you should be running from not towards, but it couldn't be helped. It was there in front of me and I knew that all I would find behind it was the very last piece to Draven's lies…but still I reached out for the handle and opened the door.

"You!" Aurora looked up in surprise at the venomous word I spat out. She was sat amongst the broken room looking like a broken doll herself. It had been the same room I had first found Draven in and the only thing left in one piece looked to be the enormous bed with the strange rock wall headboard. I looked to the smashed glass doors that now led out to a crumbling

balcony and saw a flash of my earlier self looking in. The agony I saw there was like no other and the word devastation didn't even begin to touch the surface of it.

I looked back to Aurora, who had risen from the floor and I witnessed her make her second mistake. She sniffed and wiped the tears away from her pale cheeks and asked,

"Keira, why did you have to come back…what have you done?" This was when the bad stuff started to happen. It began with the tingling in my fingers, as a rage so profound started to seep up from the darkest place within me so that I couldn't have controlled it if I had tried. I had no clue as to how it really happened, but one minute I was stood there taking in the destruction of the room and then I was adding to it.

Every broken piece of furniture started to rise from the floor in slow motion. Fragments of Draven's anger held prisoner under the spell of my own fury, but it wasn't just pieces of wood and glass that I commanded…it was also Heaven's unlikely Angel.

Aurora's frightened face was held frozen as was her body which my anger held in place. She too was suspended in a time only I controlled. Her tense limbs were powerless to stop me and I knew with only one thought I could have torn them from her body like a bully would to a spider.

Something in my head was screaming at me to stop, that this wasn't right…this wasn't me! But then the feeling of my heart being ripped from my body and used to paint this picture was what kept everything locked into the space I commanded. I felt the power hum through me like a current so strong I had to control the urge to not let it shake my body to pieces.

"Keira!" Draven shouting my name entered somewhere in the shadowed corners of my mind, but this influence that had me by the fist wouldn't let him in. It would only watch as the reason for all my pain was held as my captive and ready to be destroyed if only I would give into the need for revenge…but then that word didn't sit right with the parts of my brain screaming to stop.

"Keira, listen to me… try to hear my voice." I let myself be lulled into the bliss that was someone I loved.

"Draven?" I said his name and watched as everything I controlled dropped by a few inches. I heard him exhale as though finally getting through to me.

"That's it, listen to my voice now… this isn't you, Keira… you wouldn't harm anyone, so let her go." On hearing him trying to save her, that determined part that wanted to hate lifted everything a little higher making Aurora scream.

"No! Keira you have to try and hear me when I say that is not the reason I am trying to stop you from doing this. What you saw with me and her wasn't as it seemed! Please Keira, I stop you now only because once you cross this line there is no going back…don't you see, this is a test!" I heard everything Draven was saying and I felt the tears flowing freely down my face as I wanted so much to believe him but how could I.

Then I asked the only thing I knew would stop the madness that raged inside me like the rivers of Hell.

"D…ddo yyou…do you… love her?" My broken words finally made it through and only when I received his answer did I let the world fall and free them all from my pain.

"No!" Draven said in such a way there was no possible way it was a lie, not even after everything he had done…this one word I would have laid my life down for and trusted in it to a point where I would have traded in every beat my heart had left.

He didn't love her…which meant what he had done to me wasn't all so that he could be with her. The realisation crippled me with both relief and confusion. Aurora screamed as she dropped to the unforgiving floor, along with everything else in the room, but when she started to say something, Draven just snarled one word at her,

"Go!" and then he caught me as I too crumpled to the floor.

"It's alright my love, I have you now…I've got you again." His voice felt like tasting a pill I was addicted to. So long I had been without it and now I had no choice than to let it sweep over me like a warm blanket, only hoping it wouldn't smother me to death.

"Let me in." Draven asked as he held me in his arms, pulling me closer to him and breathing me in like I too was his own curing drug. We were like two addicts who had been reunited with their poison, knowing how dangerous they were to each other but as with all drugs of choice…

It was only the aftermath that ate away at your soul.

"I can't, not again." I said sobbing in his arms knowing I couldn't hold on to the feeling of his loving protection around me as it wasn't real. It was all lies that no matter what words said or no matter what time lived through, one could never erase.

"Try… just try and let go of your walls, Keira and I promise you with every vow in Heaven and Hell there is, I will keep you safe, nothing will hurt you here." He said holding me tighter to him and I sucked in one last sob as his words alone did just as much damage as his action had.

"You can't promise me that." I said turning in order to get closer to him, as I never wanted this moment to end, even if it was under these circumstances I just needed to hold on a little longer. Grip on a little tighter.

"Why can't I?" He asked me, his words brushing the top of my forehead. I shuddered in his arms as his touch took away the last of my energy to fight.

"Because you can't protect me from yourself." This was the last thing I had the strength to say as he tore down the last of my feeble remains of the barriers I had holding him at bay. I felt his presence there take hold, flowing through me and just before the darkness he clouded my mind with overtook me, I heard his last words whispered in my ear, that I knew were words he didn't really intend for me to hear,

"That's what I have been doing all this time, my love."

I woke up feeling groggy and it took me a moment to look back and understand why I was now waking in a room I had never seen before. Although, I must admit this was becoming a bad habit of mine. In the last four months just how many rooms I didn't know had there been? How many different countries had I woken up in and how many views from an unknown bed had I seen?

And all for what, just to find myself alone in the very last bed of my journey, before going home empty handed. This was when it all came thundering back to me making me groan in pain.

"Here, take these, it should help." Vincent's soft voice startled me as he threw an aspirin bottle at me, landing on the big bed. I looked to the door to find him standing there, arms folded as if he had readied himself for my rejection. I sat up hissing at the pain on my stomach from the cut and also the thumping in my head from being punched…as in a lot! I popped the pill cap with one hand and grabbed the unopened bottle of water with the other. After the pills were where they needed to be, I put both down and nodded to the Angel in the doorway.

"You can come in Vincent, I promise not to be a bitch this time." I said shaking the sleepy fog from my head and rubbing my eyes, drawing a new hiss when I touched the bruise there.

"I guess being the Angel in this picture I should feel remorse on my brother's side for killing them, but one look at what they did, and I can only find myself sorry I had not been there to help him." I snorted a humourless laugh thinking back to the horrors that early morning held.

"Yeah well get in line, if I had found a weapon Draven would have found them in pieces." I said not knowing if this was strictly true but it sounded good at the time.

"From what he told me you didn't do too badly without one… what is it with you and breaking noses anyway?" He asked smiling as he came closer to sit on the bed facing me.

"Well, Hilary was a bitch and deserved it at the time, as for the other guy…I didn't really care for his idea of making friends." On hearing this Vincent's anger flashed through white, clouding the beautiful crystal blue that usually looked back at me. In sight of his growing rage I placed a hand over his tensed fist and said,

"Hey, I'm fine…Draven got to me in time so let's not go there… alright?" He looked down at my hand on top of his and before I could speak another word of comfort, he had me in his arms, holding me to him like he never wanted to let go.

"I'm so sorry, Keira." He whispered over my head as he pulled me to the crook of his neck. I felt the emotions rise up but

remembering all of yesterday, I found I no longer wanted to cry. I had nothing left in me and that was the truth. No more uncontrollable rage. No more tears from an ever flowing well of pain. And no more hate for those around me who had acted like puppets in a brutal play at the expense of my heart. I was left numb.

"What's done is done Vincent, there is no taking it back, there is only living on past it." I said and after another moment he pulled back to look at me. He looked to be evaluating if what I said was truly what I meant, as I gathered anything said ruled by emotions was never a good place to start when looking for that new beginning.

"You think you can?" he asked me, withholding nothing.

"If Draven can, why can't I?" I replied with another question.

"Is that what you think, that Dom has been 'living past it'? No one lied to you when they said he was no longer living, Keira." I shook my head in confusion at what he meant.

"I don't..."

"Dom has been in Hell, Keira, just not the one you think."

"I...what do you..."

"That's quite enough, Brother." Draven's voice interrupted my questioning what he meant and for a moment Vincent's eyes closed as if in discomfort. Then, without a word in parting to me, he stood and walked over to Draven who had been watching our exchange from the doorway. At the sight of him I felt my heart pinch before beating that little bit quicker. I didn't know what it was in life that did this to us, but as soon as your soul connects on that level with another, it is then forevermore interlocked to it like no other soul on the planet.

I had seen this man in every way possible... naked, vulnerable, angry and cold, protective, fearful, loving, devoted and hopeful. And every other hundreds of emotions out there and still it was as though I was seeing him for the first time, after being forced without his perfection in my life for too long.

Vincent walked up to him and said,

"You're still not going to tell her, are you?" Draven didn't answer him but just shook his head in a small motion to indicate what Vincent already knew. This didn't shock me considering Draven hadn't given me any answers so far, not even in the sight of both my anger and my heart wrenching grief. But what did shock me was what Vincent said next and shocking me even more was Draven's reply to it.

"Then you don't deserve her."

"No, I don't." Draven said as simply as if he had been told this by the very Gods themselves. I didn't think my heart could break anymore but upon hearing this I know it did. Was this what his leaving me was about? Had I just heard my reasons voiced for the first time?

"How do you feel?" I had been so deep in my shock that I hadn't noticed Vincent had now left and for the first time it was just Draven and I, alone and as we truly were.

"Confused." I said as all physical pain was now a thing of the past, overshadowed by the biggest question of all…why?

"That's not surprising." He said and like his brother before him he wouldn't come any closer until I said something.

"If you fear for my nails scratching out your eyes, I think you're safe, although I wouldn't let me loose in your kitchen just yet…too many pointy ends." I said dryly, trying to kill the tension being in his presence was bound to bring. He didn't laugh but I at least noticed a light spark brought to his eyes.

"I will have to remember that." He replied stepping further into the room. I was expecting him to approach the bed like Vincent had done and I braced for it, knowing what being so close to him would do to me, but in the end, I needn't have worried. Instead of coming too close, he moved a chair with his mind until it was over a metre away from the bed. I had to say it hurt that he didn't want to be close to me, but then I really couldn't expect anything else could I…? I had to keep reminding myself that this wasn't a reunion, this was an ending.

"I think you and I are overdue a chat, don't you?" He said after a moment of silence had let me take in my surroundings. The room was a pretty girly room that screamed chintzy, but tastefully so. It was actually such a feminine room it was difficult to see Draven being comfortable in it.

The walls were whitewashed stone and on the only flat wall

that must have been the divider to an ensuite bathroom, there was a blue and white china pattern painted, one that you would normally have found on an old Chinese plate. I looked down at the bed I was in and saw there was a folded comforter at the end in the same design which also matched the cushions both on the bed and on the cute wing backed chairs. I could at least be glad I was no longer in the same room I had found Aurora in.

This thought brought on one of deep shame at my actions and Draven must have seen it written across my face.

"How is Aurora?" I felt disgusted with myself for asking but couldn't help it.

"I hear she's fine." He stated like he cared little on the matter and I couldn't hold back the feeling of great relief I felt when I heard that he hadn't seen her for himself.

"What happened?" I asked him, looking down at my hands that were fiddling with the sheet still covering half of me.

"You don't know?" He asked in a surprised voice that had me really looking at him more than my usual aching glance. He was wearing a pair of light denim jeans and a charcoal shaded long sleeve t-shirt moulded to the hard lines of his ever impressive upper body…it was a painful sight to someone who, up until now, had been so used to touching such perfection.

"I…well since you…you know…" He nodded knowing what I was trying to say without words.

"I started to feel stuff happen when I get angry only…it never really seems to happen when I want it to…like when those guys…"

"I would advise you not finish that sentence." His voice had turned hard and I saw the flash of purple lurking there around his beautifully angry eyes.

"Did you…?" He knew I was trying to ask about what happened to them all, but he cut me down with a harsh,

"They got what they deserved and more! I will not have them mentioned again, do I make myself clear?" I frowned at him and then when I saw his hands ball into fists, I decided to simply snap out,

"Crystal!" and have done with it. He nodded once and after

he must have thought the silence was long enough for me to calm, he said,

"Why don't you continue by telling me when it happened the first time." I thought back to the first time as he suggested and was surprised to find when the first time was.

"I was on the balcony in Germany, it was just after Lucius had taken me. I was so angry, that it just kind of happened." I said wondering at the fact that I might have lost my mind, considering here I was having this relatively calm conversation with a man I had thought dead for months.

"What happened?" Draven asked leaning forward to rest a bent arm on his knee. His hand spread out over the lower half of his face that was dark with thick stubble, making the muscle in his arm bulge and I forgot just how huge the man really was.

"I threw a shot glass across the lake at the mountain opposite and it not only hit it, but it caused some damage."

"Why didn't you tell me this before?" He asked almost accusingly, which made me snap,

"Oh what, do you mean before you left me to go and find an Oracle that didn't need saving or after that, when you then decided not to come home and just play dead instead!?" I was at least thankful for the flash of pain I saw, no matter how brief it was.

"I understand…" I held up my hand to stop him and said,

"Unless you do fancy that eye scratching after all, then I would definitely not say that you understand anything when it comes to my feelings." I said this in a way that spoke volumes to how hard I was trying not to lose it.

"If you think this has been in anyway easy for me Keira, then you are decidedly mistaken." His eyes bore into mine as if he was trying to will me to see something in that sentence he couldn't say…but instead of giving him that hope, I hit him where I hoped it hurt the most.

"Oh really, well let's put this to the test then Draven, how would you have felt that day if it had been Libby turning up at your door and telling you *I* was the one who was dead!?" I saw the agony that thought brought him when it wasn't red that circled his eyes…or Hell, it wasn't even purple…no, it was all

Heaven's blue light, an emotion I hardly ever saw on Draven…I knew I had gotten through.

"That's what I thought, so don't you dare say that you understand what you have put me through, Draven…never again, you get me?" I said swinging my legs around and leaning forward to make him understand exactly what I was saying.

"Alright Keira, I think you've made your point."

"Agreed." I said, getting up from the bed, making Draven lean back in his chair.

"Where are you going?" He said as though I was about to bolt out the door any minute.

"To the bathroom, unless you want to come with me to carry on with this delightful conversation whilst I pee?" He gave me pointed look that said I was acting like a child without actually saying the words. I just shrugged and then said,

"Your loss." And stormed off to the bathroom, knowing relieving my bladder came second to needing to put some space between us. I didn't know what was harder, us fighting with anger, standing in the aftermath of a battlefield filled with the evidence of our heartbroken fuelled power all around us…or this. Simple, calm and even reasonable to a degree that could be called civil. Either way it hurt just looking at what was no longer mine. The man I could no longer touch like I once had or the love I made no attempt to hide, as I had to do now. Because love was a weakness in this war and my heart couldn't afford to lose again.

After using the toilet and peeing like I had needed to for days, I came out of the room asking how long I had been asleep for, when a commotion stopped me dead.

"You can't keep me from her! Where is she…? I care not for your kingdom and I swear you this, I will tear everything apart to find her! Keira...! KEIRA!" I walked in just as Draven stepped in front of me as though to protect me. But the man looking for me was not one I would ever need protecting from, no matter what Draven thought he knew. I tried to side step only to see one mountain trying to stop another as Ragnar struggled to hold back the man trying to enter.

"Sigurd? Is that really you?"

"It's me Lille øjesten…now let me through old man!" He said, calming his rage enough to speak softly to me.

I cried out at the sight, shouting,

"No, let him through! Please…I need him!" Draven's head snapped round to face me and the jealous temper flaring there in his eyes was easy to spot, considering I'd had great experience with it not that long ago. Ragnar looked back to Draven, then to me and my heart melted at the sight of two men who had protected me with their very lives, time and time again.

But it was only when seeing these two stood side by side did the penny finally drop and my hands flew to my mouth in shock. I could barely believe it until the words came out and I saw the reaction to my assumption, which turned out to be a deeper level of betrayal…

"Ragnar's your father!"

CHAPTER SIXTY-TWO

BAD BLOOD

For a moment everyone seemed to be in a state of shock and it was obvious from different reasons for each of us. Draven looked as though he couldn't believe I even knew who Sigurd was, let alone that I was trying to get around him to get to the man.

"You told her!?" Ragnar bellowed the question at his son and Sigurd rolled his eyes before answering his father.

"I think it's obvious enough she figured it out without my help, old man." He remarked dryly making Ragnar look even more pissed, which was a clear sign when his potted skin turned a deeper shade of red.

"Ok, can someone please tell me what's going on here?!" I said before the father/son bickering stepped up another notch.

"I second that...Ragnar, what is the meaning of this?" I turned to Draven who now had his arms folded, looking even more pissed than Ragnar did. Well, at least I wasn't the only who had no clue what the Hell was going on...which in this year seemed to be a first!

I sidestepped Draven given he now had his arms folded, but this turned out to be a mistake. Before I had even made one step to Sigurd he had wrapped his arms around me and picked me up, turning on one foot so that I was once again behind him.

"I think not…now stay." I frowned up at him and then snapped,

"Stay? What am I now, a damn dog?" He growled down at me proving what I already knew about who was the dog in this picture…well he was the one who had hurt me after all, I think calling the man a dog was pretty fitting!

"Well said, øjesten." Sigurd said getting in on the action, which just aided in getting Draven more outraged.

"I suggest you control your child, Ragnar as I will only grant so much patience your family's way." Draven threatened without looking away from my eyes, which I think were matched evenly on the pissed off scale.

"Child! Ha! Yeah, well this child was the one saving your woman's ass when you were taking this little vacation, so maybe you should add some fucking respect along with that patience, buddy!" Sigurd had clearly had enough and the tick in Draven's jaw told me he had some time ago.

"You will hold your tongue, boy and know your place in sight of the King!" Ragnar almost roared at his son but Sigurd didn't look in the slightest concerned. He just turned his hooded head and snarled,

"He isn't my fucking King, Elder!" At this Draven lost all control and spun from me. He had Sigurd by the throat and in turn Sigurd did the same. They were quickly locked in this stronghold, both changing into their demons in a show of dominance. Draven's veins flooded with pulsating purple and Sigurd unleashed his shadowed serpents that slithered in the air around by his shoulders.

The two provoked men were similar in height, with Sigurd being only an inch or so taller. Their bulky bodies were both tight with muscle giving in to the anger they displayed and seeing them opposite each other you could also see their height wasn't the only similarity. Both of them were huge and both of them were acting like animals!

"Oh for Christ's sake...! Stop it now!" I said rushing to try and split them up, but it was as if I wasn't even here.

"You need to leave, son." Ragnar said trying to get him to back down.

"The Hell I do! I have protected her and it looks like my job hasn't finished yet!" Sigurd said making Draven react by bringing Sigurd's face closer to his, to roar in his face,

"She doesn't belong to you!"

"And she no longer belongs to you as you foolishly gave up that right when you relinquished your protection!" He argued back.

"She was safer without our kind being involved! Why do you think I ordered for no contact allowed and for it to be punishable by death!" Draven said this last part facing Ragnar.

"My Lord, you wouldn't listen, but she was still in danger." Ragnar tried but Draven shouted in denial,

"NO, *she wasn't!"*

"Why don't you tell him just how much, old man? You were with me that day." I frowned taking this all in, feeling sick to my stomach at how much of my life was kept hidden from me.

"Explain!" Draven snarled without looking at Ragnar.

"I know what you ordered, My Lord, but I owe the girl a life debt and in the ways of my people I could not just walk away leaving her unprotected."

"She was in no danger." Draven was adamant in this but it was about time the guy got slapped with his own damn saying.

"Assumption is the mother through which mistakes are born" I whispered making him glare at me through his anger, but before any of us got to say anything more Ragnar continued,

"At first, I just sent my son there to make sure, but then the killings started in the mountains."

"What killings!?" This time it was Sigurd who answered, only he looked like he took greater pleasure in it than his father had,

"From the remains of what was left of the bodies, I would assume demon but there was something else." Draven finally released Sigurd and I was thankful when Sigurd did the same.

"Tell me!" Draven looked as though he couldn't believe this was happening but the leader in him continued to demand from those around him what he needed to know.

"It looked like both Angel and Demon were working together, but from the scorch marks I found near the bodies, I would say the Demon had been summoned and was without a host." I thought back to that day when Jack had first told me about the attacks on the hikers found.

I had remembered feeling the same weak feeling of nausea I did now, when hearing how they had needed too many body bags for just a few bodies. But this was the first I was hearing about it being supernatural, although at the time, given that Sigurd had dropped some evidence of his own, that being an Oreo cookie packet I had given him, I had thought he had been involved. Well, I guess I had been right in a way, but it would have been nice coming from the man himself!

"And how do you know it had anything to do with Keira and wasn't just some random attack?" Even I knew with this question Draven was clutching at straws because let's face it, if something supernatural is going down and I am anywhere within a fifty-mile radius, then it's a given it would have something to do with me! I was starting to wonder if the whole of the supernatural race didn't consider me as a bad penny.

"Really...? This is Keira we are talking about, Hell just her name should mean trouble!"

"Hey!" I said even though I was just thinking along the same lines not moments before.

"Sorry kid, but you know it's true." He said smiling down at me making me roll my eyes and bump my hip into his leg. Draven took in our exchange with a frown and his flashing eyes told me not to do that again for fear of Sigurd finding his throat ripped out.

"Whatever" I said for both their sakes.

"Anyway, I got there before the humans were all over the scene and found a picture of Keira that had no doubt fallen from the killer. It had obviously been taken by someone in her class and considering your sister isn't the one sat next to her, I would say it was after your disappearing act." Oh shit, and it was going so well! Sigurd looked smug when Draven took a step toward him in anger, but I quickly intervened by placing my hands on Draven's chest that felt like I was pushing against a rolling boulder.

"Draven, please." I pleaded looking up at him trying to drill holes into Sigurd.

"No Keira, I would be happier if you let him." Sigurd said pulling his hood back giving us all a chance to see the serpent in his eyes start glowing.

"Knock it off big guy and quit being a big ass! He might have left me unprotected but so did you! I seem to remember you saying you would come back for me!" I challenged in an unbelievable turn of events…was I really kind of sticking up for Draven?!

"And I seemed to remember you promising me you would keep your little ass in that hotel room until I did come back for you!" He growled back.

"You do not speak to the Chosen One like that, boy!" Ragnar almost roared and we both shouted back,

"I'm not the Chosen One!"

"She's a pain in the ass!" Only one of those statements was said in earnest but Draven looked ready to blow at both of them.

"Enough!" He ordered shutting us all up.

"I will have the matter investigated but as far as I am concerned you are no longer required in your services, the girl will be protected from here on…Ragnar, release your son of his duties." Once again, we both spoke out our annoyances at the same time.

"The Girl?!"

"The Hell I will!"

Draven ignored us both and nodded at Ragnar to continue, but as soon as he put his hand on his son's shoulder he shrugged it off aggressively.

"No Viðara, it is not possible, you know the bond won't allow it." Sigurd said making Ragnar's hand drop as if he had just remembered what his son said was true.

"I think everyone needs to just take a minute here." I said trying to diffuse the situation that I knew was about to erupt again any minute. Besides I didn't think Draven was going to take the fact that Sigurd and I were still blood bound as a happy, happy, joy moment!

"What bond?" This time it was his demon asking and I replaced a hand to Draven's chest feeling the power there pulsing beneath my cold fingers. Wait…why was I suddenly feeling so cold? And my head felt like it wouldn't stop moving… was it moving, or was it just my vision turning funny?

"I feel a bit strange here." I whispered but no one heard me or rather they chose to ignore me in sight of their hatred for each other.

"blóð auðit innan minn Ouroboros bók!" ('Blood fated within my Ouroboros book' in Old Norse) I didn't know what Sigurd had said to him but it was enough for Draven to go ballistic!

"YOU LIE!" He roared and once again they were at each other's throats! Only this time Draven had Sigurd up against the wall and pieces of the stone crumbled from the impact. There now looked to be a Sigurd shaped indent that would forever be decorating Draven's Italian home, as the stone dust rained to the floor.

"Stop it!" I screamed as Draven was using his forearm against Sigurd's neck, holding him there with what looked like little strain. Sigurd in response, wasn't helping when he started smiling. The snake started to spin and I knew this was not a good sign as things were about to go from bad to destroyer worse in seconds.

"Do something!" I shouted at Ragnar who was simply standing there with his arms crossed like a disappointed parent watching two boys fighting.

"If you think what I say is not the truth, then you should call upon your fates for you know they cannot lie, as who do you think it was that bound us!" Draven thundered a deeper roar than before at the ceiling making pieces of it crack with the force. I had covered my ears as the woozy feeling started to increase, making me feel like my head was going to fall right off. The pain in my stomach started to cramp and I desperately wanted to end this bickering and just lie back down, but first it looked like I was going to have set a few things straight.

"Draven it's true, he's not lying the Oracle…the Oracle." I couldn't finish but Draven had heard all he needed to erupt once more. Sigurd pushed back and when I saw the tattoos on his hand start to spin I knew what that meant. I ran at them both…well more like fell into them and tried to pry them apart with what little strength I had.

"I SAID STOP IT!" I screamed at them both but then something strange happened. My heart felt like it was going to explode out of my chest and I couldn't take air into my lungs quick enough. I felt the dizziness and nausea hit me like I was once again being punched in the face. Then I started to fall.

"Keira?"

"øjesten?" Both Draven and Sigurd said my name which sounded slurred and stretched. My head was spinning or was it just my brain? I couldn't tell, but soon the world was horizontal and my head fell back. I opened my eyes to see Ragnar holding me, but his red face was blurred.

"Hey you." I said up at him but I didn't receive a smile back for the one I gave him.

"What's wrong with her!?" Sigurd asked just as it started to feel like someone had turned up the AC to the igloo setting. I felt myself being transferred to Draven's arms before he said,

"She's burning up." Were they crazy, I was freezing!

"Keira, can you hear me?" Draven asked, all anger now replaced with concern.

"Cooold…sooo…so…cccold." I tried to say but now my teeth were chattering.

"She has a fever, I need to bring her temperature down now!" I felt myself being carried somewhere but it was only when I heard the sound of water being run that I gathered it was the bathroom.

"Everyone out! Ragnar inform my brother and bring him to me… now go!" Draven sounded barely in control as shakes started to jar my body in his hold.

"Come on Keira, keep with me, sweetheart."

"Drra…ven…wha…happ…" I couldn't finish the sentence properly, but he answered me all the same.

"I don't know. How long have you felt like this?" I shook my head and said weakly,

"Dunno"

"You have been asleep for nearly two days, that is more than enough time for an infection to develop…were you ill before you found me…? Keira, try and focus…Keira!" He roughly jerked my body to get me to respond and did it again when I felt my head falling back on his arm.

"Keira!" My head snapped back up and I opened my eyes to find my vision still fuzzy.

"No…ill." I said hoping this was enough for him as I wasn't up to speaking much.

"Dom?"

"In here!" Draven shouted back to his brother who was in the other room.

"What has happened to her?!" Vincent's disbelief was warranted considering I seemed fine not an hour ago.

"I don't know but she is burning up with fever and is finding it difficult to stay coherent…" Draven started to recall but then erupted,

"Get him out of here!" Draven's roar made me moan from the increased pounding it created in my head.

"Just let me see her, I think I know what it is." Sigurd said and from the sounds of it all cockiness was gone, replaced only by the desperate need to help.

"No!"

"Dom let him help if he can, come in Sigurd." Vincent said sternly.

"I have been feeling strange for few days and thought it might be connected to Keira." Sigurd said and I felt an extra pair of hands on my body, this time feeling around my temple.

"Explain." Vincent asked despite the rumbling growl of Draven's displeasure.

"Our connection, it feels…wrong somehow."

"Connection?" Vincent asked, only this time it was Draven who answered grimly,

"They are blood bound."

"But how, when?!" Well if you could get Vincent to shout then you knew it was really an 'oh shit' moment, I thought giggling in the fog.

"I think we can add delirious to the list of symptoms," Sigurd said dryly and I just managed to raise my middle finger at him before shouting,

"Si…ck!" Being thankful that Draven turned me in his arms so that I could vomit into what I think was the sink.

"And another one." Sigurd said making Draven snarl,

"That's not helping, Viking!"

"Did she have a bag with her when you found her?" Sigurd asked forgetting Draven's comment.

"Yeah, why?" Vincent asked as Draven was busy whispering encouraging endearments in my ear, whilst smoothing back my hair.

"The book," was all Sigurd had to say to get Vincent shouting,

"Sophia her things, where are they?"

"Sop…hia?" I said trying to lift my head to look.

"Ssshh now, take deep breaths…that's it, can you drink?" I couldn't see but I felt the rim of a glass being held against my bottom lip. I gulped in a mouthful only to spit it back out to rid myself of the horrible taste. The next few were drank down eagerly to kill the burn.

"Here…here it is…oh Keira." Sophia said as she must have joined the party. Thankfully the Dravens liked big bathrooms otherwise this would have been a bit of a squeeze given how big these men were!

"Hey." I said not wanting to be any ruder than I had been with her.

"vándr blóð!" Sigurd cursed and I opened my eyes to see him holding my book…only I didn't know whether it was my blurred vision or the fever, but now the snake on the front looked black and infected with thin veins of ink coming from its body. It looked…

"Poisoned?" Sophia asked but Draven dismissed it the same time Sigurd did as they both said,

"Bad Blood."

"Bad Blood."

"You mean…blood poisoning… as in Sepsis?" No one

answered Vincent, but I quickly felt my top being raised up to expose my stomach. From the reactions of those around me I would say they all hit the jackpot, when everyone sucked a sharp breath.

"What the fuck! How did that happen?!"

"You said you saw her clean the wound?" Vincent said ignoring Sigurd's outburst.

"I did but the infection must have already taken hold as I was searching for her." Draven said as though this was all his fault, which if you wanted to find a place to start then I guess it kinda was, but it wasn't like it was Draven who had slashed at me with a dirty knife.

"She needs healing." Sophia said the obvious, but when the room went silent, I gathered this wasn't as easy as that.

"Dom?" She prompted but again there was no response to what she said, only a commanded,

"Sophia, I need you to test the water, first we need to get her temperature down…everyone else out!" Draven ordered the rest to leave and only when I heard the door close did I start to feel large hands pulling sweat dampened clothes from my body. I had to say that when I envisioned this part of our reunion all those weeks ago, this would not have played a part of the fantasy.

"It's fine, place her in and I will take care of her." Sophia ordered just as Draven was removing the last of my underwear. I felt Draven lower me and I sucked in a stuttering breath at the feel of the tepid water.

"By the Gods, look at her, she has lost so much weight, Dom." Sophia sounded so hurt by the sight of me that I felt out for her hand to squeeze it.

"I know." Whereas Draven sounded like he had just discovered what real pain felt like.

"Draven." I said his name trying to give him comfort but by his reaction he must have thought I needed it because he knelt down to me and placing a slow kiss on my forehead he said,

"I will be right outside, you are not alone…not anymore." I felt the weight of those words stay with me and comfort me like all my past torment was now over…that was until Sophia asked the question,

"Are you going to heal her?" But it was Draven's answer that made my blood run cold and it had nothing to do with the fever that now raged through my body…

"You know I can't"

CHAPTER SIXTY-THREE

ONE LAST TIME

After hearing those last words from Draven, I think it was safe to say I was lost. What did he mean 'he couldn't'? I had tried to speak to Sophia after he left but she just hushed me and told me to conserve my strength, so I decided to give up. So, with very little in options I found it easier just to give in to Sophia's care.

She washed me gently with a velvety washcloth, taking care around the infected area of skin that had been cut. The one thing we both did was try to pretend we weren't listening to the argument that was going on in the next room. Although I can imagine Sophia was getting it a lot clearer than my foggy mind was…oh and of course supernatural hearing had to help.

The occasional word like 'Hospital' and 'Healing' and 'Time' was heard but if I had to choose one that would make it on the 'word of the day calendar' that one would have to go to the F word, which mainly came from my Viking warrior Sigurd, (I'd had a last minute name change from Shadowed knight protector) although that could be put down to my fever.

Speaking of which my symptoms hadn't gotten any better by the time Draven stormed back into the bathroom to get me back out of the tub. It was obvious from one thunderous look that the argument was continuing and so far without much success.

"Wait for us outside, Sophia." Draven said gently receiving a sisterly pat on the arm as she went past, closing the door behind her. I tried to sit up and I don't know why, but the first thing I wanted to do was cover my nakedness. Foolish, given the amount of times this man had seen me naked. But I guess after both Sophia's and his reaction to my new look, I felt a bit ashamed at not being able to take better care of myself.

"You don't need to do that, sweetheart, I would never be capable of forgetting even an inch of you." He said softly, surprising me with how tender he sounded. I didn't know what to say to that and was at least glad I could blame it on my illness.

"Let's get you out and dried…alright?" I nodded, not being able to look at him fully for fear of what I would find. This meant that when he finally did touch me I jumped making him whisper,

"Easy now."

I let him get me up and out of the bath which was the easy part. The harder part came when I tried to stay on my own legs whilst he dried me off. In the end he sat me down and ran the towel over my body, no doubt creating even more heat than when he first got me in the bath to cool my temperature down. I felt the lump in my throat the entire time his hands were on me and there was no way I could look at him. I just kept my head to the side and let him finish, both hating and thanking the fact that he was so professional about it. There was nothing sexual in the way he touched me, but it wasn't by any means not affecting the emotional side of me.

He would stop a few times when his hands could feel the bones in my ribcage and then the same again by my collar and hip bones. It was at this point I couldn't stand it any longer.

"I'm…sorry." I said feeling a tear creeping out from under my closed lid.

"Hey." He said as he caught the tear and wiped it from running down my cheek. He gripped my chin and turned my head to look at him to say,

"I never want you to say that word to me again…okay?" I nodded feeling foolish and hating what we had between us. It was like a line we were no longer allowed to cross, both of us holding ourselves back, but not knowing which way to turn either.

"Draven I…" I was about to ask what happened now, not referring to my new health problem, when I started coughing. This was when the moment ended and Draven got back into action. He started to dress me in a pair of light cotton pyjama bottoms with matching top that I knew Sophia had supplied. The trousers were red and dark blue tartan and the top a navy blue vest that was soft on my burning skin.

I couldn't keep up, one minute I was freezing, the next it was like my blood was boiling beneath my skin and all the while it felt like my head wasn't attached properly! But if I was honest, I would have much sooner dealt with the pain than give up this precious time in Draven's arms. And as sad as that was to admit, even after everything he had done to me, the simple fact was that I wasn't strong enough to help myself.

So here I was, as much clinging on to the dream as I was clinging on to the man himself and wouldn't allow myself to think about what would happen to me once he let me go again…and how would I survive it the next time?

Draven carried me back through to the room and lay me gently on the bed like the lover I remembered. Everyone else was still in attendance and I waited to see what they had to say. I felt too weak to even sit up but when the decision was made clear by Draven, I knew I still had some fight in me.

"Alright, Vincent I want the helicopter fuelled and ready to leave, Sophia I want you to notify the hospital and tell them who…"

"No!" I shouted interrupting him before he could finish that sentence.

"Keira." He said my name as if he was about admonish a small child. I struggled to pull myself up but just ended up having Draven stop me by placing his hands on my shoulders and applying the little pressure needed to get me falling back. So, I kept shaking my head over and over until the nausea came back, but again Draven just placed his hands on either side of my head to cease my actions.

"Keira stop it…you need to listen to me, I know you're frightened but I will be with you…"

"No…no, no, no, no, no, no, no." I repeated over and over until he ended up trying to calm me with his hands smoothing up and down my arms, whispering 'Ssshh' and 'It will be alright'.

"I told you she wouldn't go for it." Vincent said and Sophia quickly agreed with him.

"We spoke of this! She is going to a hospital and that is the end of it!" Draven snapped but I just grabbed at his hand trying to get him to feel the desperation in me. It wasn't just a small fear of hospitals but something deeper inside me. It was as though the thought of going there was wrong…like fate would be depending on this point in time and I couldn't let it go.

"Heal me…please." I whispered trying to grip his fingers harder but not quite making it.

"We will, just hold on and we…"

"Look there is no time! Can't you see that?" Sigurd shouted, hearing enough of my pleading. It was quite obvious from Draven's low growl rumbling from his chest that he didn't agree.

"Oh, for fuck sake just move out of my way and let me do it!" Sigurd said coming closer and this was when Draven reacted. He was up from the bed in one of my frantic heartbeats and stood guarding me like the Gods themselves couldn't get to me.

"I said No!"

"And why not?" I could just see around Draven enough to make out that Sigurd had come to stand toe to toe with him and we were once again back to where we started.

"Don't… fight" I said weakly.

"Because I don't want your shadows touching her and I think you know what I am talking about." Draven said sternly but surprised me when this time he kept his fury under control. I waited for Sigurd to retaliate but it never came.

"Come on my niðr, you have done all you can." Ragnar said

coming up to lay a hand on his son's shoulder and I had to say my heart bled for him. It was a tense moment before I heard Sigurd admit defeat in the form of a released sigh.

"I will be here lille øjesten, should you need me." He said looking down at me round Draven's unmoveable frame, his frown not one meant for me.

"Th…anks big… guy." I said coughing in between.

"Sophia call them, make sure they know who they're dealing with." Draven said again making me grab at his arm, but only getting a fistful of his sleeve.

"You can't!" I said looking up at him with tears in my eyes.

"I'm sorry, but I have no choice." I let the tears fall and shook my head, knowing deep down in my soul this was so utterly wrong.

"Go, all of you." Draven ordered and I heard people all filing out of the door.

"Please…I am…*begging you…heal me."* I said when I thought we were alone.

"Keira I…"

"I will do it." Vincent said and I released a held breath, along with a whispered 'thank you', sent to the Heavens for this man.

"No, you…you can't!" Draven said placing a hand on his brother's chest to stop him from coming any closer.

"And why not?" Vincent asked sounding different.

"You know why." Draven snapped making Vincent lean forward and respond in a scary quiet voice,

"I think you gave up that right, Dominic, when you walked away and left the rest of us to pick up the pieces of a broken hearted girl we both love." I sucked in a laboured breath when I heard the first words of love being spoken aloud. Vincent loved me...? He must have meant as a sister…but then I remembered that kiss and it was hard to think of it like that anymore. I didn't know how to feel about this new piece of information, but the light that sparked in my heart couldn't be ignored.

Draven took a step back in shock and his hand dropped from his chest like it didn't belong there.

"It is not the time for this Vincent, so as your brother, not as your King, I will ask you to stand down and let me do what is best for her." Draven sounded calmer than I would have expected at a time like this and if I was to guess, I would say Vincent's confession had not come as so much of a shock as I would have thought it should have.

"And why don't you, for once in your *fucking existence*, ask her what she wants?!" Vincent snarled and it was only the second time I had ever heard him lose it.

"This isn't your fight brother, so I beg of you… don't make me act on force." Draven was now gearing himself up as he shifted his body, waiting for Vincent to make the next call.

"That fight is long overdue, now get out of my way or give her what she needs and the only *'Gods be damned thing'* she has asked of you!" Vincent's voice had changed at the end and instead of sounding like a demon's fury it sounded like a God's!

"Please…don't do this…I…can't let…come in between… you." I cried and then hated what I had to do for this to stop the madness that was ripping these two apart and me right along with it!

"I will go…take me."

"Keira?" Vincent said my name in question to my whispered ramblings.

"Hospital." I felt Draven kneel by my side and take one of my clammy hands in his.

"You would go to hospital just to stop this fight with my own brother?" Draven's voice sounded thick with emotion and I could only nod, knowing what I was giving up for two brothers I loved…

The connection to Draven I craved.

The connection I had come this far to find.

The connection I had nearly given my life for…

But one I wasn't prepared to ruin theirs for.

"Very well Keira, I will do as you ask…now leave us Vincent so that I can heal the woman we love." He said standing and I cried out on a broken sob from such relief I could barely breathe.

"You are making the right choice."

"By the Gods I hope so…for all our sakes." Draven said clasping the hand his brother placed on his shoulder to show the strength in his support. Then he watched him leave before turning back to look down at me and the sadness I found there brought on more tears.

"Why are you crying, Keira?" He whispered softly, leaning over me and smoothing back the hair from my damp forehead.

"Be…because I'm…sor…sor…rry." I said breaking down even more.

"Hey, come on now, didn't I tell you you're not allowed to say that word again?" I nodded and I felt him wipe under my eyes, taking the tears away with his thumbs. He gave me the time I needed to get myself to calm down until there were no more tears. I opened my eyes to find him sat next to me on the bed, playing with some strands of my hair in his fingers, taking in the shorter length, seeing the black instead of the gold that once was there.

"You did this?"

"Yeah."

"Why?" He asked with his dark eyes flashing from my hair to my eyes.

"I guess… I thought it would help…looking different… finding you." His eyes ringed purple at my broken admission.

"So, you did this for me?" I couldn't voice my answer this time, not unless he wanted me in tears again. I gave him a small nod which he mirrored back.

"You don't like it?" I was taken back by the question but answered him,

"Not really, I don't think I make a very cool Goth." I said making him smile for the first time, even if it was slightly held back.

"I must confess I miss the sight of my golden Goddess… but Keira, the beauty you possess starts from in here…" He placed two fingers at my heart and then continued,

"…and flows out to here." To then run the back of his knuckles down my cheek. I blushed at his tender words and hoped it was hidden under the fever that plagued my system.

"Let's begin, shall we?" He said and I started to bite my lip in worry as I knew before we started what I really needed to ask him.

"I…um, well…"

"Just ask, sweetheart." He said looking down at me as he ran his thumb from my chin, to the hollow of my throat, leaving sparks like lighting a match with the sensation. He smiled when I swallowed heavily under his touch and only stilled his actions when I didn't continue.

"What will happen when…?"

"When I heal you?" He finished off for me and I nodded, hoping he would find the real meaning in that question.

"Ah, I see." He must have seen it in my face, what I was really asking. He took a deep breath and then said,

"You know what will happen, Keira, which is why you need to be sure this is what you want?" This was when it finally hit home. The reason why Draven didn't want to heal me. It was because we would end up crossing that line neither of us had the bravery to talk about. I found the realisation of it hurt too much to look at him, knowing he didn't want me that way anymore, but was willing to do so just to save me. It was the cruellest of remedies for both of us, but for very different reasons.

"Look at me." He didn't force me but just waited patiently for me to obey and when the strength of his gaze got too much to bear, I finally looked back at him, the reason for my shame written openly across my face.

"If you think I don't want this then you're wrong." He told me firmly, looking down at my body so that there was no mistaking what he meant.

"Then why…?"

"Let me explain something to you…" He said interrupting me. He sat up straighter and took one of my hands in his to play with my fingers as he spoke, which managed to take away some of my sickly symptoms. Did just his touch help start the healing?

"Why do you think the stories speak of Adam and Eve being placed to live in a Paradise on earth, when really he filled that paradise with temptations of sin?" I smirked before offering my view.

"Because the part of that story they left out was that God was just a big kid playing with an ant farm and the tree of knowledge was really a snickers bar?" I said feeling my heart soar when this time I got a full Draven smile. And other than seeing my niece being born, it was quite possibly one of the most beautiful sights I had seen in this year so far.

"I missed your humour." Draven told my hands before he raised the one he was still playing with to place a kiss on my palm. The sensation shot straight to the centre of me, making me shudder.

"Free will, Keira. It's what the story is really about. Every human has the chance to make the right choice or in this case, the wrong one…but either way they both have something in common."

"Which is?"

"No matter what path people take, it will affect someone, whether it be immediate or further down the road. Eve was tempted by the apple and Adam tempted by Eve's offering. They both knew it was wrong, but free will gave them that choice and they each took it despite the consequences."

"What are you trying to tell me here, Draven?" I asked frowning at what he was getting at.

"That when the right temptation is around, the wrong choices are most likely to win, no matter who it hurts down the road." He said this looking like a man at confession but still I had to ask,

"And what is the right temptation for you, Draven?" I whispered knowing what his answer would be but needing to hear it voiced all the same.

"Temptations of my heart." I felt a single tear roll down my heated cheek on hearing that Draven still loved me. So this was the reason I didn't yet have the right details. He hadn't wanted to heal me because he knew what it would do to us both after the act.

Which meant only one thing…

We would soon have to part ways.

"It's time for my sin, Keira." He suddenly said looking up at me with his own heat, only his was one burning straight up from his controlled level of lust. I swallowed down a hard lump of doubt and before I was just about to voice the new feelings I had on 'our sin', he was touching me. As soon as those large hands spanned either side of my stomach and started moving my top up, I had lost all thoughts of right choices.

I watched as the material bunched up and up until it left my stomach bare and left the reason this moment was happening on display. The cut was red and swollen with a clear path fanning outwards to where the damage had travelled. The infection had spread and we both knew that if left untreated it would start to attack my organs, if it wasn't already.

"You ready?" I put my head back, closed my eyes tight and nodded knowing that the first feeling to wave over me would be pain. I felt Draven move above me and when his hand held my side securely, I knew its only purpose would be to hold me down. I didn't think you could hear the sound of skin being sliced open, but I seemed to know when Draven tore into his palm ready for the healing, as I flinched.

"You have to breathe, Keira." Draven said thoughtfully making me let go of the breath I was holding like it was my last. Only when I did this did he touch me or I should say…Ignited me!

The second his bloody hand came into contact with my wound the room filled with a blinding light and the power of that single joining tried to lift my whole body from the bed. I cried out at the intensity of it as I felt the essence of him flow into me for the first time in months. It was as though my blood had been craving his and as soon as it found it again it latched on to it, not ever wanting to let it go again.

Fire and ice duelled within the confines of my body, turning the network of veins and arteries into a playing field. I felt that part of Draven was travelling around inside me, taking the parts of me it wanted and giving me what I needed to bind me back to Draven. It even found its way to my scalp and the tingling continued like the wind was blowing in my hair.

This wasn't like the usual healing I had received from

Draven before. The only way to describe it was like being given the chance to relive through our first joining, only speeding forward to our very last. It was like every time we made love. Every time Draven left a piece of himself behind and taking something in return. It was like all those times had combined into one single moment.

This one perfect moment.

My blood was humming beneath my skin and I opened my eyes to see myself glowing. It was as if my veins had been replaced by fibre optic lights, as you could literally see his own power being transferred into me. And my body was lapping it up like cream coated morphine. Then came the need.

That sexual need so great I felt my body would set itself alight if it didn't seek release. I looked up to see Draven above me with the same intensity I felt, staring back at me. My hand went to his that was still fuelling me, filling me to the brim with the essence of him.

"Dra…Draven…have…to…to…stop." I panted knowing any longer and I would come undone beneath him, losing the thread of myself as he pulled and pulled me deeper.

"No!" He growled and the hand that held me down moved to pin my wrist to the bed. The liquid purple in his eyes swam around the iris like it would soon spin out of control and I knew when it did, it would ignite his body in the same supreme energy. I used my other hand to grip at the one he used, knowing he couldn't restrain me without first moving it. Or so I thought.

He leant down to my neck and without a second of warning he bit down into my flesh and started sucking the blood from me in desperate gulps in order to complete the connection. I came screaming his name and instead of clawing at his arm, I was now doing so by his neck. I felt the vibrations of his groan and of my release simultaneously thumping through me. But it wasn't enough and soon I was clawing at his back, trying to get to his skin.

"Draven…I need…I need…" He released my neck and with my blood still staining his lips he said over me,

"I know what you need." Then he licked the last of me from

his lips in a slow sensual swipe, before crushing them to mine in a bruising kiss. As I opened up to him it felt as though my soul was reaching out to him and I couldn't have been happier when he answered it. He took the kiss to a place I'd never known before, as I tasted my life's blood on his tongue, making something so dark and sinister right to Heaven's gates. He tasted every inch of me as if I was a new discovery that needed the time taken to do it right.

I felt his body above me shaking from the strain it seemed to take in holding himself back enough not to just pound into me and one move from me would be all it took…so I took it! I snaked my free hand down in between our bodies and grabbed hold of his straining erection in a strong grip. He broke the kiss to snarl down at me like a wild animal being taunted by its keeper and I smiled back at him, not feeling the fear that maybe I should have.

"That feels like you want me." I said biting my lip, causing him to watch my action like I was stripping myself bare for him. Then he did something so out of character I was left with my mouth gaping. He did the same thing as I did, snaking his hand down and dipping his hand under my pants, bringing two fingers through the valley to gather the moisture there. He then brought his dripping fingers back up and staring me right in the eyes, he sucked both fingers into his mouth. It was slow, it was bad and Holy Mother of God, it was sexy!

"That tastes like you want me." He then said making me moan and arch my back, pressing myself into him. Thankfully, he took the hint when I heard the sound of my pants being torn away and I looked up to see him align himself with me. His hands came up to my neckline and he gripped the material with both hands. With a sudden jerk to my upper body he tore the material down the middle, freeing my breasts for his feast.

After pulling the useless top from under me, throwing it to the ground in a bunched fist, he then cupped both my breasts making them fill his powerful hands. He groaned at the sight before bending his head to suck at each nipple in turn, turning this part of me into a meal. My heart hammered and I had to grip his shoulders just to hold onto something solid. I could feel the length of him branding my belly, it near pulsating with the wait it had to endure, moisture seeping from the end making me want to weep with the wait as well.

I moaned and writhed under him as he kissed, sucked, nipped and even painfully bit at the two points that felt like instruments played in a master's hands. All of which felt like he was making love to them, worshipping them as if they each had their own separate wants and needs.

"Draven, please!" I begged after feeling this for so long I thought I might lose my mind.

"Say it again." He demanded still with lips around my beautifully abused flesh.

"Draven, please." I felt him smile around me before letting me go with each nipple receiving a last flick of his expert tongue.

"Now, time to make you scream it." His demon was the one to add the heat at the end of this promise and I shuddered beneath him. I felt him move down the bed, running his hands down my body in the slow torturous way only the man you want knows how. He raked his nails down my sides and I cried out at the blissful trails it left behind.

"A feast for the fucking Gods!" He swore and it too managed to add to the heat he built inside me. Then his hands spread out on my inner thighs and before I could say a word of protest his hands applied the pressure needed to pry my legs apart, pinning me wide open for his pleasure. His head lowered and at the first touch of his tongue tasting me, I screamed. And I screamed. And I screamed some more. And Draven was right, after he had made me come and then come again, he had me begging the only way he wanted me to…screaming it.

"DRAVEN PLEASE!"

I gripped his hair, feeling the silken strands through my fingers before I pulled at him, desperate in something I didn't have the brainpower to fully comprehend. Did I want him to carry on, did I want him to stop or would I die if he did?!

"That's my girl." He said rising up above me and bringing my legs up over his arms, open and ready for the finale of the show. I tried to tear at his clothes, needing to feel his skin against mine but his eyes flashed a darker purple, before he said,

"No, Keira." I frowned not understanding why he didn't want to show me his upper body, to complete his nakedness. I must have closed my eyes as I tried to figure it out because Draven's voice was at me once more, commanding things of me in way that heated my insides.

"Now show me those eyes, I want to see your soul light up as it reunites with mine." I opened them, trying to keep them more than half lidded but after the orgasms he had given me it was hard to find the strength. He leant down to nip at my nose and said,

"Oh my poor girl, don't worry, I wouldn't ask too much from you my love, just give me what I want to make your Master happy." I opened my eyes a little wider and nearly sobbed the question,

"What do you want of me, Draven?" The smile I received was all demon as he quickly plunged himself into me to the hilt, growling out and as I screamed in the perfect pitch to what he wanted, when he told me my answer,

"I want to devour every reaction from you, as I consume what will always be mine!"

And then he began to consume me, taking me whole as though he had become a man obsessed with only one action, only one goal and my God it felt painfully perfect in every way!

He moved inside of me and all that was left for me to do was hold on and give him what he wanted. Every scream, every pant, every breathless word that came from my lips he ate up with his dark gaze, like it was feeding his very soul. He took it all in… my abused bitten lips, my little panicked cries every time he hit that spot inside of me and hands that had to curl around the metal headboard like I was holding on from fear of falling from this dangerous ride. I felt completely studied and every time my face showed a different reaction he would groan and moan, turning him on to impossible levels.

But it was when his hands moved down to each grab a handful of the soft flesh of my cheeks, using them to apply more pressure and gain more power for each drive into me, that I felt utterly owned and possessed, closing my eyes and shaking my head as I felt the building of another shattering orgasm I didn't know I would survive.

"Not yet, I forbid it!" He ordered and then the feeling would retreat back in on itself making me cry out in protest.

"No!"

"Yes Keira, I command it!" His thrusts became slower but remained just as hard as he powered himself into me, almost making me wonder if this was another of his ways in getting his essence into me because it felt like soul branding!

But every time he hit that same spot, I would arch and tense just to get closer, like chasing the storm I knew would crash into me and take me whole. But Draven was waiting for what he always waited for…my lover liked to come with the sound of me begging.

"Please." I whispered as it built up again and again just to be ripped away from me before I could complete the union.

"No!" I cried again.

"Not good enough little love, I want to hear it, I want the world to hear it and I want the *fucking Gods to HEAR IT!"* He roared the last part at me as his body erupted into its demon form in preparation for we both knew what was coming.

I let the tight coil of my insides and the pressure in my mind, ready itself for the release of endorphins I had started praying for. The need was indescribable and as he let it build one last time I just knew the amount of pleasure would be too much to handle this time. My muscles screamed through the movements he demanded of them but knowing the outcome, I knew they would never give up until they had no other choice too.

I was crying now and Draven leant down to taste those tears causing the shaking of my fingertips down to my very toes as the last of the tension built.

"That's it, get ready for it, I want my girl screaming my name." The heat that speared across my forehead was the first tell-tale sign what was coming and it beat any fever I might have known before.

"Open your eyes for me and give it to me NOW!" He bellowed and I gave him what we both wanted more than our next breaths.

"DRAVEN PLEASSSSEEEEE LET ME COME UUUH-

HHHHH!" I screamed and screamed over and over, my body jacked knifed up as an orgasm so intense exploded within me, I saw a blinding light fill the room. Draven held onto me upright as he thundered his own release seconds later and his head strained up to the Heavens. The sound that came from him was nothing forged from the realms above…oh no. The glass in the windows shattered outwards and the stone walls cracked with the force of Draven's earth shattering eruption.

The utter euphoria that came flooding through every molecule in my body was working in tandem with my shuddering body as my climax continued. It was as if it would never end unless death found me and I had to say, if this was it, then I would die screaming in utter heavenly bliss. It was torture and it was pain, but my God it was beautiful, even more so than it should ever have allowed to have been.

I felt the bands of his steel arms loosen their bruising hold and it was sickening, but I relished in the thought of there being the marks on my body as evidence to our lovemaking. It was as much beautiful as it was brutal and it was the most erotic and magical experience of my life. So no matter what came next, even if he were to throw me from this very room and banish me for all eternity from seeing him again, I still would not have been able to find it in me to regret one single second of it!

But I still released a sigh of relief when he didn't do either of these things. No, instead he gently lowered me back to the bed and placed a sweet kiss to my forehead before pulling back to look at me. His eyes had taken on a lighter shade, one that I knew made his Angel side more pronounced.

"Are you alright?" I smiled up at him with what I knew was a sappy grin making him run his thumb over my happy lips.

"You were magnificent and I am sorry I lost so much control in sight of such perfection." He looked torn and I couldn't stop myself from raising my own hand to his face.

"Hey, don't do that." His eyes widened at my words but he didn't argue with them, he just shifted his body down next to mine for what might be the last time. He pulled me tight into his embrace, wrapping himself around me and fitting me in the shelter of his bigger body.

"Sleep now sweetheart and don't think about tomorrow." I did as Draven asked but couldn't help doing so with tears running down my face, dripping on to the still covered arm he used as my pillow.

And all because of the last words he said to me,

"You're my apple, Keira."

CHAPTER SIXTY-FOUR

WHEN THE APPLE FALLS

I woke up feeling as if someone had replaced me in the night with a healthier version of myself. It felt as though I had drunk straight from the Holy Grail! I sat up and couldn't help but lift the covers to see the changes I could feel there. For starters, the slice in my belly was no longer there, with not even a scar to tell me where it had been. I poked my stomach and found myself laughing out loud at the added weight I found there.

"You could have asked me." I muttered on another laugh as I felt my hipbones that were nowhere near as bony as they had been yesterday. It looked as if Draven had a few extra ideas when it came to healing me last night. Even my breasts had a little more plumpness to them, one that I had lost before, thanks to my forced diet in camp Hell!

"Men…it figures." I said lifting them up and testing the weight, which was right back to what they had been. I had tried to put back my weight on when staying with Lucius, but through stress never really managed it other than a few added pounds. Well, now thanks to Draven he'd kind of took the fun right out of trying to put on weight, killing my new plan of stuffing myself silly with chocolate and cakes when I got home.

I soon found out, however, that my new weight was the least

of the changes made, as I felt silky strands tickling my waist, something I hadn't felt in so long. I cried out loud when I pulled handfuls of long blonde locks forward feeling it pull on my scalp, confirming enough that it was back!

"Oh Draven." I whispered into my hair as I brought it to my face to take it all in. I thought back to our conversation before the healing began and found myself smiling when I remembered him asking if I liked my new hair. Then I blushed as thoughts of the actual 'healing' were taking place and I'd felt the tingling in my scalp, knowing this was when it was happening.

After looking at myself naked taking it all in, I decided it was better to be dressed in case anyone had the thought to pop by. I looked around hoping to find Draven's forgotten T-shirt somewhere when I remembered something important from last night. Draven had refused to take it off…so why was that?

The sound of voices not far away brought me out of my wonderings enough to find a white robe. I quickly put it on and ran to the bathroom to use the facilities. Washing away the evidence of what happened between me and Draven last night quickly brought a deep blush to my cheeks, one that lasted till I was back in the room and running back into the bed when I heard someone coming. I jumped in and covered my lower half up just so there was no chance they would get an eyeful.

Well, if I still wasn't blushing from the bathroom then I was when Draven walked through the door. The very sight of him had me biting my lip, which just managed to bring on thoughts of what he had been biting last night.

He was wearing a pair of worn stonewash jeans that were no doubt designer as they fit him like they were made using a mould of his perfect behind. With this he had on a plain black t-shirt that managed to show some of what I missed last night in the lines of his muscle. And I couldn't help but notice he had his arms covered again with a light grey suit jacket. Now I thought about it, the more curious I got, wishing the light had been better the night I had first seen him, where as painful as the fact was, there was no getting away from the memory that he had been naked beneath Aurora.

"You're awake." Draven stated the obvious, which only happened rarely and I knew the reason behind it was because he was nervous…a feeling Draven wasn't used to having.

"Yeah." I didn't think it was possible for things to be awkward between us after sex, but here it was. If anything, when it came to me and Draven, it was the making love part that was the only thing we seemed to get right. He looked as if he didn't know whether to approach me or not.

"You can sit down you know…I'm not going to jump on you or anything." I wanted to snap it out, but in the end, it sounded more like a joke, so when he gave me a small smile, I let him think his actions weren't hurting me.

"You wound my pride…I must be losing my touch." He joked back sitting down on the edge of the bed.

"You're much too cocky for that to ever happen, I would just put it down to a bad day." He gave me a sad look and then when he turned back to focus on his shoes he muttered to himself,

"Yeah, bad day." I was about to ask him what he meant but he suddenly turned to me and asked,

"Are you sore?" This time I laughed and said,

"Well, I may be walking like I lost my donkey for a little while, but I think you got that I had a good time." This made him burst out laughing and it filled me with pure joy to hear the sound. So much in fact, I had to hold in the tears that threatened to spill.

It was so painful how much I loved this man and even after everything he'd put me through, I would be the biggest sinner of all if I tried to say any differently. But that was my problem wasn't it? Because I still couldn't have this man, no matter what had happened in this broken room or in this iron bed. Now that line we crossed was back between us and no matter what happened from this point onwards, we would never be able to get it to disappear again.

"Oh and thanks for the upgrade, I told you I wasn't rocking the Goth look." I said needing to hear his laughter or see his smile for just that little bit longer. He picked a loose wave that was resting on top of the covers where I was sat forward and started to wrap it around his thick finger.

"I cannot lie and say it isn't nice to see you like this again, Keira, but it is also…" His voice sounded thick, like the words were stuck and I had to prompt him to carry on.

"Also?" His eyes looked up from my hair in his hands and he shocked a breath out of me when he replied,

"Painful." When he looked away, letting my hair fall from his fingers and looking angry with himself, I reached out to grab his arm and pull him back to me.

"Draven, don't…" But my words were cut off when I managed to pull the sleeve of his jacket up a bit, giving me a glimpse of what he was trying to hide. I gasped at the brief sight of all those thin scarred lines that made up some sort of pattern I couldn't see. It looked fresh, red and raw, as though it had been done over and over again, never given the chance to fully heal.

He roughly pulled back down on his sleeve and stood from the bed to get from my reach.

"What the Hell is that?! What have you done to yourself?" I demanded, feeling my head spin at the sight of him hurt. Draven who never so much as received a scratch was now hiding away his body and the secrets it held.

"That is no longer your concern." His words were like a sucker punch in the chest.

"How dare you! If that is the case, then how is it that my own wellbeing and care is any of yours!?" On hearing my angry comeback, he turned suddenly and barked,

"Your life will always concern me!" I couldn't help it, at this I laughed, only there was nothing amusing about it. I whipped the covers off, quickly thanking I had on my robe and stood opposite him ready for the challenge.

"Oh yeah, then where were you exactly when I nearly got eaten by a Pishachas Demon? Or the time I broke into Afterlife and had bloody commandos shooting at me…? I mean, like really shooting at me for fuck sake…! Or when I got jumped by two guys and poisoned down an alleyway after trying to get into Devil's Ring? Uh? Come on Draven WHERE *WERE YOU?* Oh and let's not forget my little trip down to actual Hell, where I had a nice little chat with your Dad...!" I was so lost in my rant by this point, I actually started walking him backwards, poking him in the chest with each point I made, not paying attention to his shock or his building rage.

"…Who, by the way, doesn't think I'm such a bad catch for you and couldn't understand what you were thinking...! Although back then I hadn't really understood what he was talking about, but hey guess what, now don't I feel like the biggest idiot ever! So come on…tell me, what was so important to you that you thought leaving me alone in your world would be such a swell idea, because I have to say, when I was then involved in a battle between Hellbeasts and death dealers just before being kidnapped and left to starve in a tower, then I could really have done with you around. Oh yeah, I bet just one look at you storming the castle and coming to find your old buddy Gastian would have worked a treat!" At this point I was too far gone to stop and take note of Draven changing into his demon form as he took in all I had to tell him…his famous temper growing to monumental proportions…but I was already past the point of no return, no matter the storm that was coming.

"But you know what, you must have been far too busy knocking hip bones with little miss 'all leg and no backbone, Aurora to come to my aid… no, no you just left that up to everyone else around me who had the guts to do it themselves…! For fuck sake Draven, even Jack did his part and he is a human, but what am I saying…? I mean nothing to you but a few letters saying goodbye, one last romp in the sack and enough money to buy me off your back…is that what you thought it would take…money? You have no fucking clue who you're dealing with and the funny part of all this is, that if you'd had the balls to just tell me the truth, that you didn't want me anymore, then I would have LEFT YOU ALONE!" I couldn't contain the scream or the red mist that had taken over my thought process.

"But no! I fought, I fought, Draven, with everything I had in me and when all that was gone, I somehow managed to find even more! And you know why I did all this…? ALL BECAUSE I LOVED YOU!" By the end of this I was panting and so was Draven. But then I took in the reality of the situation and quickly realised I had gone way, way too far in all that I had told him.

His demon was breathing down at me and when it finally spoke, I nearly shook with fright and all he had asked was,

"Have... You… Finished?" I fearfully nodded and that's when the world around us…

Exploded.

It once again seemed I was to be the cause of yet another destroyed room in Draven's Italian Villa. I watched the room literally explode outwards like a bomb had just been detonated. My head whipped round in slow motion as the blast went outwards coming from the released wrath that was Draven.

I screamed at what I was seeing but then found myself quickly engulfed in flames that didn't burn me. I jumped nearly out of my skin as not only a pair of arms wrapped around me but also a pair of blazing wings. I looked back up in desperate panic, searching for Draven's face in the madness of his actions. Only the Draven I knew was so far gone it was amazing the two men were still the same entity.

"Draven, please don't do this." I tried to bring him back but the eyes burning into me, scorching my soul with the mistakes I'd made weren't coming back any time soon.

"I didn't want this!" His demon confessed and his hold on me tightened, crushing me to him, which barely allowed me to breathe.

"Please, stop it!"

"There is no way to stop this… there was no way to stop me other than tying me to the very gates of Tartarus when the nights came." He sounded like something was overtaking him, ripping the words from the Angel his Demon was trying to bury.

"I don't…Draven I don't understand." I said and the single tear I saw fall down his cheek evaporated before it could make any distance. He looked in pure agony and no matter what I had wanted Draven to feel before… it was never this…never this.

"I had to set you free of all this and it was the only way I was allowed to." He nodded down to indicate himself in his demon form as he referred to what part of himself he was setting me free of.

"No…you couldn't…how could you do that…why? For God's sake Draven tell me why?" I begged him to tell me, to just put me out of my misery and let me understand why he put me through it all.

"I was shown the life you could have but I needed the hurt to keep you away, I needed to use your pain…the pain I inflicted to keep you from me… why Keira…? Why couldn't you have just stayed away…? Why did you have to…?" I felt the tears again and again streaming down my face as I looked up at the man I loved, burning inside and out all for one reason, one reason I had to know,

"Why did…did I have to what Draven?" I cried out, only seeing him now through a watery mask that could hide nothing in what happened next. He placed his forehead to mine and added the last nail hammered in closing up my heart…

"Damn your love for me!"

And in damning the love I had for him, he had just killed it with only five words said. Just five words and the very last piece of me he owned was no more. He had finally accomplished what he had set out to do…

He'd killed our love.

Suddenly the world around us calmed and I didn't know if it was down to me or down to his realisation. Either one, Draven turned back to his human form and we were left standing in the destruction of what our souls breaking apart had created. The link we had forged back last night had just shattered and I felt it leak out of me as though someone had just cut the power. We were one no more and now I knew why he had done what he had done. Everything had become so clear I couldn't breathe from it.

It was simple really, as he had told me once. The everlasting memory of love brought forth from death had the power to change the world. But just as that love could change it for the better, living with the knowledge of it not returned, could no doubt change it for the worst. A sacrifice is all it takes for a leader to be reborn, but one truth dragged back through the lies left in its wake and it could all come crashing down like the sands of time it took to put it there.

And it had come crashing down into dust at our feet.

Sacrifice gone, prophecy over.

Chosen One no more.

I stumbled away from him and when he tried to catch me I screamed,

"No!" I managed to catch myself so I only half fell to the floor, but the pain was excruciating enough for me to want to stay there.

"Keira I…"

"No! For the love of God don't say another word! Not unless you finally want to kill me!?" I said making him wince as though I had struck him. He looked close to saying something but with one glimpse at the pain he'd inflicted, he must have thought better of it. I got up and looked where to put my bare feet in the mess that scattered the floor as I was certain I would find the pieces of my heart down there amongst the wreckage.

"You know you could have saved me of all this, if you…if you had only said those very words to me instead of…. Good-bye." I couldn't stop the tears, Hell it felt like they would never stop! If I thought I knew pain before then I was wrong. That couldn't even touch on what I felt now and how I was still standing I didn't know.

But I was.

And not only was I still standing, but I stood tall and strong as I turned to him, knowing this was the last time. The apple had fallen and I, like Eve, had been cast out, only this time there would be no Adam to follow in my damned footsteps back to a harsher reality. Because Adam was the traitor to my heart and had been ever since that first day he ever spoke of his love for me.

Because love wasn't supposed to be damned or cast aside like it no longer mattered. Love wasn't supposed to be so easily turned into something you loathed to find staring back at you. But one look at Draven told me all I needed to know…

This was the end.

Only now it was my turn to finish it.

I walked up to what was still left of the door and with a strength that no longer surprised me, I ripped the hanging panel from its bent hinges, casting it behind me. Then I turned to face the picture of a broken man stood in the mess he'd created. He needed to know one last thing.

"I want you to do me a favour, Dominic, any time you try and convince yourself you did all this for me…" I swallowed my tears back just a little longer and said,

"…just remember it wasn't only the *'damned'* love I had for you that brought me to find you…" I saw him frowning as if readying himself for a truth that would change everything to him but nothing to me…not now.

"…it was the Oracle." And with that I reached up to find the necklace he gave me and snapped it off, knowing that now that connection was dead, there was no reason left for me to wear it.

So I left it, letting it fall from my hands and leaving it where it now belonged, in the rubble, right along with the…

Broken pieces of my heart.

CHAPTER SIXTY-FIVE

OUR DEMONS SPEAK AT LAST

I would have liked to have continued the story, saying this wasn't the end and walking out of that room was followed by Draven running after me, sweeping me up in his arms and begging for forgiveness…but, that didn't happen.

What did happen was me walking away from that room to the sound of roaring pain drowning out the rest of the world. Draven's cry was a hard thing to hold on to as my last memory of him, but he gave me no other choice.

I held on to my now bare neck, feeling as if a piece of me had been taken by the wind with no luck of ever finding it again. I felt like a walking, wandering dead girl, just hanging around waiting for one last hug from a loved one. I needed to get out of here and that's when I started to run. I had no clue where I was going, but only stopped when I looked behind me and ran straight into a massive body.

"Keira?" I looked up and up, to find a Viking looking down at me.

"Ragnar!" My shouting his name was the only warning he got before I threw myself into him and cried as my world ended.

I didn't remember much about what happened next but if I was to try and think back, it would start with Ragnar picking me up and cradling me in his massive arms like a small weeping child. The next thing I knew was finding myself in a different room and being handed a bag with some clothes in it.

"From Sophia." Ragnar said before pushing me gently in the direction of a bathroom. This was where I was now and looking at myself for the first time since Draven had destroyed me for the second time. It was like being transported back in time, as I found the reflection of a girl with soulless empty eyes of grey blue and long limp hair that had once known the touch of an Angel's love. And what was I now?

I suddenly punched the glass until it cracked, needing to see myself the way I felt.

"Now you are just you, Keira." I said to the pieces of the girl in the mirror that finally reflected back what Draven had done. Then I did the only thing I could do…

I left my Hell behind.

When walking from the house in clothes I had barely looked at when putting them on, I found Ragnar following me.

"You're leaving?" I turned to look back at my friend to see concern and frustration mingle as one.

"I want you to give him something from me." I said not answering his question but giving him his answer all the same. I had the idea after I had changed and Ragnar had given me back my bag that still had in it my passport, purse, cards, everything it had before, including the Ouroboros book. So, looking down at the book and its empty pages, I thought about all the people who had gone against Draven and helped me through this wasted journey.

This had me quickly realising the danger of Draven's wrath I might have brought to people's doors, which I had to prevent and I knew just how to do it. So, in a turnaround of events taken place, I wasn't the only one now leaving Draven instead of him leaving me, but I was also the one writing a letter.

I was just amazed that the book let me rip a page from its spine to use for my letter. But that might have had something to do with the faded snake on the front. I ran the tip of my finger around where the serpent used to be raised, only now it just looked like a burnt part of leather with the shape of the missing snake. I couldn't help feeling a little sad looking down, knowing this was not only the end of my journey, but also so many connections I'd made along the way.

Which was why I spent the time in writing Draven that letter, one only made more powerful by what it was written upon. I pulled the letter from my bag, which I would have left with the man at the gate had Ragnar not followed me out.

"Give him this." I said and then passed him the folded piece of thick paper that contained my very last wish from Draven.

"You won't say goodbye to the others?" He asked taking it and then folding his arms over his chest. I looked back up at the house to see Vincent stood by the window with Sophia by his side, one arm around her shoulders in comfort.

"No, there is no need, not unless Draven refuses the last thing I ask of him." I nodded back up at Vincent when he gestured the same motion down at me.

"I don't think that will happen." Ragnar said and I managed to give him a small smile before agreeing,

"Neither do I."

"So, I guess this is it, but before I go…can I ask you a question?" He nodded and I took a deep breath before asking,

"That day I saw Sigurd standing watching my house, the day he wasn't alone…it was you with him, wasn't it?"

"Yes." It was a simple answer, one that only managed to bring on greater confusion.

"But why?"

"Why?" He repeated and when I nodded, he lost some of his tough man stance and dragged a hand over the lower part of his face before nodding to a stone bench, one that was curved around a landscaped flower bed that mimicked the shape. I followed him and sat down next to him, making our size difference near comical.

"It is not well known but a Viking can only hope their death will mirror their life. To die in battle to those who fight, to die in childbirth to those who cherish bringing life to the world…but when a life is saved then it must be offered back in return." I shook my head and said,

"But what does that have to do with me?"

"When I lost myself to the Demon within me, you risked your life to bring me back. For me to have died how I did not live my life would have only meant greater shame on my family name…just like the first time." I felt the weight of his meaning after he'd told me when he was my bodyguard how his wife and daughter had died, only for his own death to be thrown into a pit of snakes…which only just made me wonder, did that have something to do with why his son held the snake as a mark?

"Lodbrok is my proud name and you risked your life to keep it so. I owed you a life debt and seeing that my niðr Sigurd owed me one, I passed his debt onto you." His chestnut coloured eyes looked down at me with beaming pride and I knew it wasn't just for his son, but for me also.

"niðr?"

"It means 'son' in my native tongue, old Norse."

"And let me guess, Viðara means father?" He smiled and nodded. I felt like smacking myself on the head as I remembered when Sigurd had been in my hotel room, on the phone to Ragnar calling him that, and I hadn't had a clue!

"So that life debt…it's been paid off now…right?" I asked making Ragnar chuckle, which sounded like it first came up through sandpaper.

"I would say my niðr did well in his duties, given what he had to work with." He said full of humour and I nudged him, or at least tried to and said,

"Hey, I'm not that difficult!" At this he raised a disbelieving eyebrow, which made me give in,

"Alright…so I can be a little stubborn." Making him once again chuckle.

"Speaking of your niðr, can you give him this for me?" I pulled out the book and was about to pass it to him when he looked over my head and said,

"Why not do so for yourself?" I followed his gaze to see Sigurd pushing his bike around the corner, which was where the garages must have been.

"I will." I said standing, making him do the same.

"I will see you again…right?" I said feeling the lump in my throat form at the thought of not seeing my Viking Guardian again.

"Oh, I have no doubt about that, lille øjesten." He said leaning his massive bulk down enough to grip my head gently in his giant paws and tilting my head up enough so he could kiss my forehead. Then, before I got chance to ask him what that meant, he left me with yet another tear falling down my cheek.

I turned around to where Sigurd was lifting a long leg over his bike and I found myself running to him, just to stop him before he went roaring off.

"You leaving for good?" I asked him, making his hooded head look up from the front of his bike. He leant back and did a slow inspection of the old Keira.

"Well, well, look who's back." He said whistling and I was surprised I had a smile for him, not because it was Sigurd but surprised that I had one for anyone right now. It was as though something was giving me the strength needed just to get home.

"What can I say, I have hung up my superhero Goth cape for the foreseeable future." He looked up at the Heavens and said,

"Oh thank you God of Chaos for reining in one of your children!"

"Ha, ha!" I said hitting him on the arm.

"So, I gather from your heartwarming meeting with the old man that you're leaving too?"

"You saw us?"

"I didn't want to impose on the gooey moment." I rolled my eyes and he purposely pulled his hood back to show me him doing the same, making me laugh. It was strange, but just being around him and his father was helping with the pain I knew was ready in the wings, waiting for its chance to strike.

"You're not by any chance going to an airport are you?"

"To get you back where you belong, I will give you a ride to any damn airport you want, darling." I couldn't help but agree with him. I really needed to get back to where I belonged and it was no longer with any of the people I had left in the building behind me.

"Thanks, big guy."

"Hop on little pain in my ass." He said winking at me with his snake eye, making it spin a little as if excited. He handed me a helmet, letting me figure out the clasp as he kicked the bike into life. This time I was no longer scared of the ride to come, but I had to put that down to the ride that had brought me to this point.

And after that one, I didn't think there was anything left for me to be afraid of anymore. So, with one last look behind me as we pulled away, because I knew with a certainty I was right, there was nothing left to fear because…

All my nightmares had already come true.

Draven

As I watched the other part of my soul being taken from me, I felt the wood of the window's frame give under my hands as I crushed it into splinters. I wanted to tear the room apart until there was nothing left for me to stand in…fuck that, I wanted to tear this whole Gods be damned house down to the very foundations until I finally felt enough pain physically to spare me a moment of the bitter agony that was tearing me apart!

I wrenched my tortured gaze from the window before my rage hit levels that would equal an 8.5 on the Richter scale or before I did what every molecule in my host wanted to do. My hands cracked into fists at just the thought of pleasure gained from ripping that Viking's hands from his body, just so he could never touch her again.

Watching her leave made the brandings on my skin itch and burn just like it did every night I fought to stay away from her. They had been fighting the bindings and invisible chains I had forged to Tartarus, ever since her arrival, like a Legion of Zagan's army. Sometimes I welcomed the irritation, giving me something other to focus on than the world of things that reminded me of my Goddess. But right now, they only aided in proving once again why I had no other choice but to give her up.

I thought on all the things she had told me of what she went through to 'save me' and I knew with the last words she said to me that I had been played by the fucking Fates! The lies told to both of us were mounting, but with her life still hanging in the balance, I couldn't risk acting on my doubts…no matter how much it destroyed me not to.

No! First I needed to look into all that had transpired in the time she had been without my protection. Why had I listened when I knew in my gut that leaving her with nothing but her human fate to guide her was not enough?

When I think about what could have happened…what did happen, reasons why I wanted to annihilate those involved, reminding my people of the very reasons they feared me! I wanted to prove my Hell's heritage by making them beg me to let them claw their way into the inner ring of the seventh circle of my home in Hell! But this just brought on thoughts about my own father, who would not be out of reach in his castle from finding my wrath at his gates. Maybe I should take Sophia with me this time, she always did love to play Devil's advocate.

When I heard all Keira had to say, I was stunned by the sheer level of love the girl could have for me. I didn't think it was possible for the strength of her love to match my very own and my pride was overflowing for the power she possessed. Of course, it was also overridden by the murdering desire that raged through my host like a hurricane needing to destroy everything in its path, but the girl in front of me.

Keeper of my heart and soul.

And what had I been forced to do…damn that keeper and love she displayed with her very life. But what choice did I have? After all I had been forced to do to her, she still looked up at me as though I was her whole world, when in reality I had ripped her fucking world apart, leaving her left with nothing more than the pieces twice trampled on. No wonder she tore the necklace I gave her from her neck as if it was burning her flesh wearing it any longer, and by the Gods had it killed me to watch.

I crossed over the vast space that was my personal suite on the grounds, after having to first fix the damage I inflicted to the adjoining room that Keira had stayed in. I couldn't let her see the level of my obsession that looked more like a shrine to the girl. I'd had every picture I could get hold of printed onto large canvases that covered all of one wall. Some of which were just enlarged pieces of her that I needed to see on a daily basis. One of her at home, baking in her sister's kitchen, sweet mixture on her face, reminding me painfully of teasing her about licking it off when her sister wasn't looking. I still remember seeing the blush that never ceased to get me battling my host for control of an erection that wanted to remain in her presence. The damn thing was like a homing missile where she was concerned!

There was another one of her taken at Christmas, when she sat in a pair of those adorable pyjamas, trying on a woollen knitted hat someone had given her, that would have been a preferable size for my chief of security, Ragnar. She had pulled it down her face until her little nose was peeking through and although it was the only one where most of her face was hidden, the smile she had graced the camera, made my heartache every time I looked at it.

I would sometimes find myself just staring at this wall for hours, trying to piece together enough to hold onto the details as I remained locked to Tartarus, my prison of choice. I would have Palladio blasting through the speakers as I geared myself up for another night in my personal Hell, the very one Keira had been trying to free me from.

But having Keira back, just having that sweetness there in my life for what would be considered a fleeting moment of time in the endless years of my existence, had been ambrosia coated agony. It had been all that was needed to keep me going and yet never enough to get me through. Seeing her body laid out beneath me once more, writhing in the pleasures only she had the right to ask of me, was my Heaven's paradise. I hadn't lied when I spoke of her being my apple's sin. The very reason I would choose madness over logic, just for one taste of that honeyed core that is my Keira.

Even one more time, giving in and healing her had been my breaking point. When she had begged me I had nearly wept like the adolescent I was never given that chance to be. But when she put all that fear aside just to bring peace back to two arguing brothers, I could no longer deny her for what she asked, no matter the sweet pain she would bring me in reclaiming her soul.

As soon as I bit into her and the first drop of her life had coated my tongue, I had to close my eyes against the emotion that was ripping its way out of me. For someone who kept such a tight control over their human side, it was astounding to me that one small girl could shred me to pieces as if I were nothing more than a paper man.

To her hear beg for me, beg for things only I knew I could give her was a cruel bliss that rendered me solely in her control. Not that she knew any of this. Not that she knew all the supernatural effort it took in holding myself back, holding off just to drag a few more of those breathy moans from her. A few more moments to see her straining body as I took and took, her never knowing just how much she gave and gave back in return.

My beautiful girl.

I had to tear my gaze from her pictures. The memories still so fresh in my mind, that the Demon in me pounded inside my host to go and reclaim her…again and again. So, with an angry scowl for being so weak, I turned back to my room. One that I would not taint by being the place that took me back to Hell each night. I would not let another soul into this space, let alone the female hands it took each time to send me back to Tartarus.

To know how Keira had first found me, just before Aurora sent me back to the abyss, was just another cruelty I had inflicted upon her. If she only knew the real depth of disdain I had for the Angel in her given task, she would have curled her lip in disgust for what I had to endure, not for what she had seen.

Aurora meant nothing to me other than a torturer's means to an end. And if it wasn't for her Heavenly connections to those who controlled Tartarus, then she would be the very last being I would have ordered to help. The fact that she would insist every night dressing like a harem girl only made the process more infuriating to bear.

I couldn't help the growl that rumbled up from a beast of anger, one that had lived inside me for so long now it was getting harder to find the man within. But turning to what Keira's fair hands had created for me had me calming.

The only other colour in my space, other than my beautiful girl, was from the beautiful paintings that she had given to me. One of which I headed to now. This one painting was one she always wanted me to get rid of as it reminded her of foolish times. It was one she painted whilst under the influence of alcohol, which was testament alone in how much my little vixen could consume.

By the Gods, I had seen warriors consume less and not be able to put two coherent sentences together, let alone fight, but my little love could not only hold her poison but paint an exquisite masterpiece after this fact.

By the memory of Zeus, I would even find myself getting hard at the thought, yet the woman had little idea at just how weak she made me! Me…the King of all my kind, strong enough to bring even some Gods to their knees and this little innocent lamb could click her fingers and have me dance naked at her feet for her amusement…And Holy Hell wouldn't I just get off on it!

But this was what my days had become. Mental ramblings over a girl I obsessed over every minute the day passed and every extended one in Tartarus through the nights. Which made the picture I touched now even more significant to our forced parting.

It was of a pulsating heart, one not painted like that of the organ. It was suspended in a dark forest as though locked there. It glowed through the dangerous night, despite its looming surroundings and the way she had added depth to the simple shape brought it out on the canvas.

But this wasn't the part that felt like it mirrored my own, that beat desperately to get back to its true owner. It was the huge, jagged lightning bolt that came from above and struck the heart's core, splitting it in two. And seeing that the bolt came from above where the fates resided and played their games of chance with little regard for which of the strings they pulled and were attached to whom, I would say it was more than a little fitting.

I remember Keira telling me the large side was my heart as I was the stronger one in the relationship. I had given her a look at the time she couldn't read, but I refused to say where that look was really born from. It only proved what little she really knew when it came to my love for her, but one thing was certain, now there was no taking back the chance to ever prove it.

On closing my eyes for a moment to try and not think about the level of hurt I had to act on just to get her to leave, but it helped little. I opened my eyes the same time as I opened the picture door that hid the safe behind. I put in Keira's birthday as the combination along with my thumbprint in the middle console. The door clicked open and in it I placed her necklace along with the other treasures that lay there, all from my girl.

My most prized possession, other than Keira, was the collection of diaries she had given me of her life before the one I knew. I had read every word written and had them branded to my memory so that I didn't miss a thing.

Everything from the day she didn't get picked on the school team for netball, to the times she saw Demons and Angels in her day to day life. It was amazing, even at such a young age, the strength she displayed and the courage she not only possessed but conveyed onto others around her. She was a creature to be worshipped, admired and adored just for being her. And in every way she was my Chosen One, my Electus, but other than to risk her life, which I was never going to be prepared to do, I had no choice than to let her live a life without me in it.

The thought always turned me murderous.

I heard my brother coming but seeing that I allowed no one into this room that I considered for my eyes only, he waited by the door, knowing I would come out when ready. I slammed the safe door shut hearing the beep but keeping my anger in check long enough to be careful in closing the hinged painting.

I was across the room taking no care in travelling at a human's pace as I wanted to get this meeting over with as soon as I could, having enough time to come back here before starting my nightly sentence. It was the only comfort I had and as little as it did to soothe back the pain, it was something.

This time between my brother and I had been building since the day I announced my plans to leave Keira. The fight went on for hours until even our hosts had long since given up. As always no one won the fight, but when Vincent had crossed the line by declaring his love for my Keira, a fact I knew long ago, I had almost gone too far with a blade at my brother's neck.

Since that day we refused to talk about the reasons why. Only parts of it Vincent actually knew, but what he didn't was about to come to light today. Something else in my life I had to look forward to, I thought with a sarcasm I normally couldn't abide.

"Vincent." I said trying my best not to sound as aggressive as I almost always did. The only one these days who didn't get this venomous side of me was my little sister, although she could more than hold her own.

"I have something for you." I knew he did as Ragnar would have no doubt opted to avoid me at all costs at this moment. I knew he had disobeyed me, but how could I punish the demon that passed on a life debt just to continue to protect my human, where I had failed. If anything, I owed my chief of security my very life in return!

"I know, follow me to the roof." I said needing the air before my time in Tartarus. Hell, who was I kidding, I only wanted to see if I could catch her scent on the wind one last time. The fact that I hadn't been able to scent her or feel a connection just proved how damn arrogant I had become. When she had whispered my very words back to me about presumption, I knew then and there her powers had grown incredibly strong and in such a short time, even without the proper guidance.

I didn't look behind me to see Vincent following, as I knew my brother would have followed me into Tartarus every night, if

I would only let him. I walked to the nearest balcony and without much thought put into the action, I jumped first to the railing and off it straight up until coming to the rooftop garden Sophia had insisted on. I landed, using a little too much force needed, which ended up with me fixing the cracked Italian stone my feet had destroyed.

Vincent's more graceful landing was something that made me want to growl, but I managed to control it by grinding my teeth instead.

"You know what this is?" Vincent asked as he handed the small piece of paper over. I knew what it was and how much control she must be able to wield over the book of Ouroboros to tear from its bindings. My girl was becoming more impressive by the day. What I didn't know was what it contained, although given how well I knew Keira's heart, I could easily guess.

Draven,

This is not a letter of goodbye or sweet sentiments like the lies you wrote to me. I think everything that needed to be said (or more like heard on my part) was completely understood.

So I am writing to you now to ask but two things of you, in hopes you feel enough guilt to grant them to me.

All the people involved in helping me mainly did so for risk of their life to save my own. Therefore I can only hope you will keep this in mind so as to prevent any punishment you feel the need to inflict.

Try to remember your actions are the sole reason behind what I did and without first the lies, then the truth would have lived without danger. I hate to point the blame here but it's hard not to when I am given no reasons behind your actions other than cryptic sentences that you know will drive me crazy! But you and your kind were always good at that one, so I guess I should not be surprised.

But this is not all I ask. In choosing to be with you I therefore gained a family and as much as you don't like it, I ask for you not to keep them from me, or me from them. I love them all and just because of us breaking up, I do not need you breaking my heart further by taking them away from me… again. Please, this is all I ask of you and if it's begging you want to hear then consider this letter just that.

Well that's it I guess, nothing more to say between us than a painful hope

that the decisions you made bring you a happiness, for I know they will not for me.
But I guess you already knew that.
Take care of my family
Keira.

No being on earth or beyond had the power to stop the roar that erupted out of me as I fell to my knees and cursed the fates. I felt Vincent near me which offered me a fraction of comfort, but it was not enough…it would never be enough!

"Why brother…just tell me why?" He asked of me and this time I broke. I could feel the tears falling with no way to stop them. The pain that each one represented was immeasurable! My heart was fucking breaking and one girl held all the pieces and what had I done…

Broke her.

"Dom, please just say the words…" Vincent begged me and I wanted to bitterly laugh at the irony her words had meant, that were now reminded by my own kin. He wanted to know the level of misery I lived in then so be it. I would tell him and then he would finally know what I would eventually become if I stayed with the girl I loved.

"If I stay, then the fates say I will…" I broke on a sob I was not proud of but knew couldn't be stopped as the words of realisation were finally heard for the first time…

"You will what brother…*you will what?!*" Vincent's desperate plea to know would also break him, as how could it not? But no matter now as my mouth opened to say the words…

"I will kill her."

EPILOGUE

KEIRA, IN EVERYONE'S EYE, THERE'S AN APPLE

The flight back to Portland from New York was, thankfully, a quiet one. Most people on the plane were asleep and I wish I was ready to join them. You could almost tell what people were doing on this flight, whether it was for business, or coming back from seeing family and vice versa. Either way I doubted anyone could guess the same for me.

At the airport back in Milan I had the emotional task of saying goodbye to Sigurd, really not knowing this time if I would see him again. I pulled the book from my bag and passed it to him, which felt as if he was also taking a piece of me on his next journey, wherever that may lead him.

"I think there might be one more thing for you to see, øjesten." He said holding the book out and as he placed one hand over the injured snake, I saw under his hood the serpent in his eye start to spin and glow. I waited until I watched a shadowed tattoo appear under the cuff of his jacket. It snaked around his hand and onto the book so that when he moved his hand the Ouroboros was back.

He gave me back the book and my hands shook as I opened its pages.

The fourth Quarter Moon - The Rainbow moonstone. To aid

those that feel alone, lost or Vulnerable. It helps those that need emotional healing and acts like a prism, diffusing the energy throughout the aura. It provides deep psychic protection and senses emotional trauma. This stone is aligned with the Goddess needed in your aid if the fates feel it is permitted to act justly so. But to gain their help, you must first act justly so.

"And now…? What of the bracelet now?" I asked out loud hoping the book was in the giving mood.

The New Moon - The Grey Moonstone represents new potential to the Goddess, which is needed as an offering. This stone will aid in the new gifts handed to the one chosen by the Electus. Useful in all unseen realms but more so to the shadowed lands, ruled by the Ouroboros King. In doing so you will find him his future and with it whosoever carries the mysteries and powers of the new moon, where all things that exist in his world are hers to potentially foresee. Choose wisely and be granted favour with the fates you seek.

So, in a nutshell, I had to pass on the bracelet when the time came to the right girl. One I would unknowingly be condemning her life to this unseen world in which I lived. But the part about Sigurd meeting this girl added a massive weight to an already pair of weighty shoulders. And how would I know who the right girl was?

I almost threw the book back at Sigurd who had not seen what had been foretold to come. The words in fact were already bleeding from the page but wait…they were reforming something else.

"I think this is your reply just coming in." Sigurd said dryly just as the single line holding my answer started to become legible. It simply said,

Consider Your Terms
My Undying Promise
To You
Draven

After this, my last goodbye of the day was given as a silent embrace and a single tear falling, telling him all he needed to know.

Mine from him however was a lesson to be learned. I was just about to cross the road to hear him call my given nickname one more time. I turned to look back at my shadowed knight sat atop his steel steed to hear him say,

"Lille øjesten means 'Little Apple', it's what my father always called you…the only other person he called that was my sister. It means…The apple of her father's eye, she who is greatly loved…I just thought you should know the level of our love, Keira." And then, without another word, he fired up his bike and left me stood silently sobbing as the tears couldn't be helped.

Suddenly, being someone's apple was no longer a bad thing.

"Are you alright?" A young girl I sat next to asked me. She could be no more than about fifteen, but the depth of knowledge behind those chocolate eyes was startling. She was thin and looked to be still in the awkward growing stage, having no breasts or no hips to speak of. She wore big baggy clothes like she was unsure of herself and wanted to keep her slight frame under the protection of a rock band hoodie and baggy trousers.

But the beauty in her face was remarkable and angelic in an innocent kind of way. Oh, she was going to be a real beauty alright and just wait till my world got their first look at her! Large eyes, satiny dark hair and naturally red lips…she was stunning.

"Uh…yeah…actually no." I answered honestly.

"I didn't think so." She said and before she continued, she looked to the woman sound asleep next to her.

"This time next year things will be different you know." She informed me as if she knew this with absolute certainty.

"But when the time comes, I wouldn't lift up your skirts and walk up those steps if I were you." I frowned and then said,

"Who are you?" In a whisper.

"I'm sorry, I don't mean to freak you out or anything…it's just, sometimes I can't help it you know…" She looked over her shoulder at the woman asleep again and when she was satisfied said,

"…it's why I have been passed around so much…makes me wonder if this next family will want me or for how long."

"You're an orphan?" I knew I guessed right when I saw her wince.

"Yep, that's me, I'm without a family and everyone else is without a clue." She looked sideways at me and then said,

"Sorry." I couldn't help but give her a small laugh.

"Oh, trust me on this one honey, when I say I know how you feel, I know how you feel…I may not be an orphan, but trust me I know what it's like to be something that people would never understand." The look she gave me was priceless, one of pure shock and if I wasn't mistaken, also fear.

"You're different too?" The girl looked as if she was close to sitting on my lap.

"Yeah, since I was seven, although I don't think it's the same thing you have…you're clairvoyant right?" She nodded and kept looking around as if she would soon be found out.

"It's okay, I know how people can judge you and distrust you, but that will all change…one day you won't have to hide who you are from everyone."

"How can you say that?" She shook her head and then added,

"No, that would never happen." I nudged her shoulder and said,

"Have faith, I know these things, one day there will come a guy hidden in a hooded form. You will be scared at first…I know I was." I said on a laugh, looking out of the window I was sat next to.

"He's pretty big but handsome all the same and man, if you have a thing for tattoos, then you will love this guy. But the main thing is, he will help you when the time comes and he will guide you when you ask him to…the only thing to do now is hold on to who you are, no matter what they…" I nodded to all the rest of the 'normal' people on the plane,

"…all think of you. There is only one you, there will only ever be one you and remember, the only thing that matters is being true to just you." And this was the point where I pulled the bracelet off my wrist for the first time since my birthday and re-attached it to the wrist of a girl that I knew in my very bones was one day going to go through her own journey and when that time came…

I wanted her to be ready.

"By the way, I'm Keira." I said after she examined the bracelet as though she had been waiting for it all her life. I smiled as I witnessed the tingles that I knew travelled up her arm, just like mine had.

"I'm Leora." She whispered, still not being able to take her eyes from the stones and I sent up a little prayer to the Goddess,

'Please, take care of this one'.

The flight hadn't been long but I was thankful it gave me enough time to meet my own 'chosen one'. We both chatted away until I heard we would be landing soon and I had needed a pee for a while. I got up and went to the part of the plane that was curtained off, noticing the toilets as I had boarded. Someone was in there, so I waited feeling a strange sense that I knew who was behind the doors.

I looked back down the aisle to see that Leora looked as if she was trying to tell me something but her counsel worker had woken up and was trying to get her to put on her seatbelt.

"Miss, the plane will be landing shortly, please take your seat." I looked to the hostess and said,

"But I just need the…" And that's when there was a flush and the sound of the door unlocking. We both turned to see the man exit and I could swear you could hear the hostess swoon.

"I'm sure you can let her, as I am sure you will be quick, won't you now miss…" The smoothest French accent flowed from the lips of a gorgeous man that looked as if he'd stepped off the screen for an aftershave ad.

"Uh…" I struggled and the hostess ran a finger down the hanging clipboard and said,

"Catherine Williams, 27C."

"Yeah, what she said." I replied dumbly, making him chuckle.

"Well, as I was saying, I am sure Miss Williams can be quick now, can't you?" I nodded like a dumb blonde and only when he went to slide past me, did I do the same. The brief contact was enough to tell me there was something strangely alluring about this guy.

When I had the fastest pee on Keira record I opened up the door to find the hostess waiting, tapping her foot impatiently.

"You don't have time to get to your seat, so please sit in one of the empties." I looked around and saw my mystery guy was sat waiting for me with his arm extended at the back of the unoccupied seat next to him. He patted the top and said,

"I would be honoured, Catherine." The way he said my name was like a promise for things to come.

"Eh…yeah, sure, why not?" I said taking the seat.

"Please, allow me." He said taking me by surprise when he started to buckle my seatbelt for me. I lifted my hands out of the way and he looked up from bending over me slightly to give me a smirk and a wink.

"I'm Alex…" He extended his hand after straightening and as soon as I placed my hand in his he continued,

"Alexander Cain."

Just then a shudder laced through my body as though someone was trying to tell me something and that something was simple…

This guy wasn't all he seemed.

To Be Continued…

ABOUT THE AUTHOR

Stephanie Hudson has dreamed of being a writer ever since her obsession with reading books at an early age. What first became a quest to overcome the boundaries set against her in the form of dyslexia has turned into a life's dream. She first started writing in the form of poetry and soon found a taste for horror and romance. Afterlife is her first book in the series of twelve, with the story of Keira and Draven becoming ever more complicated in a world that sets them miles apart.

When not writing, Stephanie enjoys spending time with her loving family and friends, chatting for hours with her biggest fan, her sister Cathy who is utterly obsessed with one gorgeous Dominic Draven. And of course, spending as much time with her supportive partner and personal muse, Blake who is there for her no matter what.

Author's words.

My love and devotion is to all my wonderful fans that keep me going into the wee hours of the night but foremost to my wonderful daughter Ava...who yes, is named after a cool, kick-ass, Demonic bird and my sons, Jack, who is a little hero and Baby Halen, who yes, keeps me up at night but it's okay because he is named after a Guitar legend!

Keep updated with all new release news & more on my website

www.afterlifesaga.com

Never miss out, sign up to the

mailing list at the website.

Also, please feel free to join myself and other Dravenites on my Facebook group
Afterlife Saga Official Fan
Interact with me and other fans. Can't wait to see you there!

facebook.com/AfterlifeSaga
twitter.com/afterlifesaga
instagram.com/theafterlifesaga

ACKNOWLEDGEMENTS

To my Dravenites,

As always you guys are the first I wish to thank and feel blessed that you are all still taking this amazing journey with me as you have done with Keira in The Quarter Moon. It has been an emotional rollercoaster writing this book, but I know I could not have done it without all the love, support and understanding each and every one of you.

My next thanks go to the people who not only believe in me but make it their mission to push me to into believing in myself. As much hard work as I have put into this book there are also others behind the scenes that do so as well, so that you all can enjoy this story the way I always hoped.

To my Mum who devotes her time to seeing that each and every one of you never discovers just how bad (and sometimes funny) my spelling really is. As let's face it, no one really wants to read about Draven's Demon battling with his 'Angle' side :o)

We all Love you for it Mum!

Also to my sister who gives Afterlife books beautiful life with every front cover she designs, so complaints why we never get Draven naked on the front cover go to…only joking…we love you too! You make Afterlife shine and now thanks to you hundreds of people are saying,

"We Crave the Drave"

To all of my family and friends for not only following me down this mad road but also making it the craziest trip of a lifetime!

I would also like to mention Claire Boyle my wonderful PA, who without a doubt, keeps me sane and constantly smiling through all the chaos which is my life ;) And a loving mention goes to Lisa Jane for always giving me a giggle and scaring me to death with all her count down pictures lol ;)

And last but not least, to the man that I consider my soul mate. The man who taught me about real love and makes me not only want to be a better person but makes me feel I am too. The amount of support you have given me since we met has been incredible and the greatest feeling was finding out you wanted to spend the rest of your life with me when you asked me to marry you.

All my love to my dear husband and my own personal Draven… Mr Blake Hudson.

My thanks also go to the staff at The Cheshire Cheese Pub London, Somerset House London, The Savoy Hotel London and the Hellfire Caves at West Wycombe for all their help with my research.

My interpretation of the events and characters held in the Hellfire club are totally fictional for the purposes of the story and in no way portray the historical background of the club.

The historical events are recorded as follows…

> *'In its heyday, the Hell-Fire Club had certainly indulged in mock religious ceremonies at the annual election of the Abbot for the ensuing year and also at the initiation of new members. But the main purpose of the Club was, as Wilkes aptly put it, that 'a set of worthy, jolly fellows, happy disciples of Venus and Bacchus, got occasionally together to celebrate woman in wine and to give more zest to the festive meeting, they plucked every luxurious idea from the ancients and enriched their own modern pleasures with the tradition of classic luxury.'*

I would also recommend a visit to any of the above as these

are some of the England's hidden treasures and I can only hope with my writing to have done them justice.

I hope you have all enjoyed this part of the story and look forward to my next instalment as much as I am looking forward to writing it. So, until next time, much love and as always…

Happy Reading ;o)

ALSO BY STEPHANIE HUDSON

Afterlife Saga

A Brooding King, A Girl running from her past. What happens when the two collide?

Book 1 - Afterlife

Book 2 - The Two Kings

Book 3 - The Triple Goddess

Book 4 - The Quarter Moon

Book 5 - The Pentagram Child /Part 1

Book 6 - The Pentagram Child /Part 2

Book 7 - The Cult of the Hexad

Book 8 - Sacrifice of the Septimus /Part 1

Book 9 - Sacrifice of the Septimus /Part 2

Book 10 -Blood of the Infinity War

Book 11 -Happy Ever Afterlife /Part 1

Book 12 -Happy Ever Afterlife / Part 2

Transfusion Saga

What happens when an ordinary human girl comes face to face with the cruel Vampire King who dismissed her seven years ago?

Transfusion - Book 1

Venom of God - Book 2

Blood of Kings - Book 3

Rise of Ashes - Book 4

Map of Sorrows - Book 5

Tree of Souls - Book 6

Kingdoms of Hell – Book 7

Eyes of Crimson - Book 8

Roots of Rage - Book 9

Afterlife Chronicles: (Young Adult Series)

The Glass Dagger – Book 1

The Hells Ring – Book 2

Stephanie Hudson and Blake Hudson

The Devil in Me

OTHER WORKS FROM HUDSON INDIE INK

Paranormal Romance/Urban Fantasy

Sloane Murphy

Xen Randell

C. L. Monaghan

Sci-fi/Fantasy

Brandon Ellis

Devin Hanson

Crime/Action

Blake Hudson

Mike Gomes

Contemporary Romance

Gemma Weir

Elodie Colt

Ann B. Harrison

Lightning Source UK Ltd.
Milton Keynes UK
UKHW010627110322
399921UK00001B/148